ORAL
AND
MAXILLOFACIAL
TRAUMA

ORAL AND MAXILLOFACIAL TRAUMA

Edited by

RAYMOND J. FONSECA, DMD

Dean, University of Pennsylvania School of Dental Medicine,
Philadelphia, Pennsylvania

ROBERT V. WALKER, DDS, FACD

Professor,
Division of Oral and Maxillofacial Surgery,
University of Texas Southwestern Medical Center,
Dallas, Texas

Volume 1

1991

W.B. SAUNDERS COMPANY
Harcourt Brace Jovanovich, Inc.

Philadelphia, London, Toronto, Montreal, Sydney, Tokyo

W.B. SAUNDERS COMPANY
Harcourt Brace Jovanovich, Inc.

The Curtis Center
Independence Square West
Philadelphia, PA 19106

Library of Congress Cataloging-in-Publication Data

Oral and maxillofacial trauma / edited by Raymond J. Fonseca, Robert V. Walker.
    p.   cm.
  ISBN 0-7216-2568-1 (set).—ISBN 0-7216-2566-5 (v. 1).—ISBN 0-7216-2567-3 (v. 2)
  1. Face—Wounds and injuries. 2. Mouth—Wounds and injuries. 3. Maxilla—Wounds and injuries. I. Fonseca, Raymond J. II. Walker, Robert V.
  [DNLM: 1. Maxillofacial Injuries. 2. Wounds and Injuries—therapy. WU 610 0628]
RD523.067   1991
616.5′2044—dc20
DNLM/DLC   90-8193

Acquisition Editor: Darlene Pedersen

Editor: John Dyson

Developmental Editor: David Kilmer

Manuscript Editor: Bonnie Boehme

Designer: Lorraine B. Kilmer

Production Manager: Frank Polizzano

Illustration Coordinator: Joan Sinclair

Indexer: Angela Holt

Set ISBN 0-7216-2568-1
Vol. 1 ISBN 0-7216-2566-5
Vol. 2 ISBN 0-7216-2567-3

ORAL AND MAXILLOFACIAL TRAUMA

Printed in the United States of America.

Last digit is the print number: 9   8   7   6   5   4   3   2   1

To Marilyn, Tiffany and Gabe —
the inspirations in my life.

R. J. Fonseca

To Emily —
who has endured a lot and allowed
great things to happen.

R. V. Walker

CONTRIBUTORS

ISAM AL-QURAINY, M.B., CH.B., M.C.Ophth., D.O.

Research Fellow, Tennent Institute of Ophthalmology, University of Glasgow, Glasgow, Scotland.

Ophthalmic Consequences of Maxillofacial Injuries

ROBERT H. BARTLETT, M.D.

Professor of Surgery, University of Michigan Medical School; Attending Staff, University of Michigan Medical Center, Ann Arbor, Michigan

The Metabolic Response to Trauma

ROBERT A. BAYS, D.D.S.

Associate Professor and Chairman and Graduate Program Director, Department of Oral and Maxillofacial Surgery, Emory University School of Postgraduate Dentistry; Chief of Oral and Maxillofacial Surgery at Emory University Hospital, Crawford W. Long Hospital, Grady Memorial Hospital, and Henrietta Egleston Hospital for Children; Consultant, Atlanta Veterans Administration Center and Scottish Rite Hospital, Atlanta, Georgia

Pathophysiology and Management of Gunshot Wounds to the Face

JAMES E. BERTZ, D.D.S., M.D.

Clinical Professor of Oral/Maxillofacial Surgery, Northwestern University; Attending Staff, Scottsdale Memorial Hospital—North and South, Humana Hospital, and Good Samaritan Hospital, Phoenix, Arizona

Management of Soft Tissue Injuries

GEORGE E. BONN, D.D.S.

Attending Staff, Veterans Administration Medical Center, and Associate Staff, Long Beach Memorial Medical Center, Long Beach, California

Shock

ROBERT BRUCE, D.D.S., M.S.

Clinical Professor of Oral and Maxillofacial Surgery, University of Michigan School of Dentistry; Attending Staff, E.L. Bixby Hospital, Ann Arbor, Michigan

Mandibular Fractures

MICHAEL N. BUCCI, M.D.

Attending Neurosurgeon, Anderson Memorial Hospital, Anderson, South Carolina

Neurologic Evaluation and Management

ROBERT M. BUMSTED, M.D.

Professor and Vice Chairman, Otolaryngology-Head and Neck Surgery, University of Chicago; Attending Staff, University of Chicago Hospitals, Chicago, Good Samaritan Hospital, Downer's Grove, and Ingalls Memorial Hospital, Harvey, Illinois

Nasal Fractures

RICHARD E. BURNEY, M.D., F.A.C.S.

Associate Professor of Surgery, University of Michigan Medical School; Attending Surgeon, Trauma Service and Chief, Division of Emergency Services, University of Michigan Hospitals, Ann Arbor, Michigan

Abdominal Evaluation and Management

ROBERT L. CAMPBELL, D.D.S.

Professor of Oral and Maxillofacial Surgery and Professor of Anesthesiology, Medical College of Virginia; Attending Staff, Medical College of Virginia, Richmond, Virginia

Anesthetic Management of Maxillofacial Trauma

MICHAEL CHANCELLOR, M.D.

College of Physicians and Surgeons of Columbia University, New York, New York

Urologic Injuries

DAVID W. COOK, M.D.

Chief Surgical Resident, Oregon Health Sciences University, Portland, Oregon

Emergency and Intensive Care of the Trauma Patient

CHRISTOPHER L. DAVIS, D.D.S., M.D.

Clinical Instructor, Department of Oral and Maxillofacial Surgery, University of Southern California, Los Angeles; Attending Physician, Memorial Hospital Medical Center of Long Beach and Downey Community Hospital, Los Angeles, California

Shock

GORDON N. DUTTON, M.D., F.R.C.S.

Consultant Senior Lecturer in Ophthalmology, Tennent Institute of Ophthalmology, University of Glasgow, Glasgow, Scotland

Ophthalmic Consequences of Maxillofacial Injuries

EDWARD ELLIS III, D.D.S., M.S.

Associate Professor, Division of Oral and Maxillofacial Surgery, University of Texas Southwestern Medical School; Attending Staff, Parkland Memorial Hospital, Dallas, Texas

Fractures of the Zygomatic Complex and Arch

STEPHEN E. FEINBERG, D.D.S., M.S., Ph.D.

Associate Professor and Chairman, Department of Oral Medicine/Oral Pathology and Oral and Maxillofacial Surgery, University of Michigan School of Dentistry and University Hospital, Ann Arbor, Michigan

Healing of Traumatic Injuries

RAYMOND J. FONSECA, D.M.D.

Dean, University of Pennsylvania School of Dental Medicine; Attending Staff, Hospital of the University of Pennsylvania and Children's Hospital of Philadelphia, Philadelphia, Pennsylvania

Mandibular Fractures; Management of Soft Tissue Injuries

DAVID E. FROST, D.D.S., M.S.

Clinical Assistant Professor for Research, Department of Oral and Maxillofacial Surgery; Part-time Faculty, University of North Carolina at Chapel Hill; Attending Staff, Durham County General Hospital, Durham, North Carolina

Applied Surgical Anatomy of the Head and Neck

BEAT HAMMER, M.D., D.D.S.

Clinic for Maxillofacial, Plastic and Reconstructive Surgery, Department of Surgery, University Clinic of Basel, Basel, Switzerland

Rigid Fixation of Facial Fractures

JOHN F. HELFRICK, D.D.S., M.S.

Professor and Chairman, Department of Oral and Maxillofacial Surgery, University of Texas Health Science Center, Houston, Texas

Early Assessment and Treatment Planning of the Maxillofacial Trauma Patient

JULIAN T. HOFF, M.D.

Professor, Department of Surgery, and Section Head, Neurosurgery, University of Michigan Medical School; Attending Staff, University of Michigan Hospitals, Ann Arbor, Michigan

Neurologic Evaluation and Management

HENRY T. HOFFMAN, M.D.

Assistant Adjunct Professor, Division of Otolaryngology, University of California, San Diego, San Diego, California

Traumatic Injuries to the Frontal Sinus

RICHARD E. JONES, M.D.

Associate Professor of Orthopedics, University of Texas Southwestern Medical School; Chief of Orthopedic Surgery, Veterans Administration Hospital, Dallas, Texas

Initial Assessment and Management of the Polytrauma Patient with Orthopedic Injuries

NESTOR D. KARAS, D.D.S.

Resident in Oral and Maxillofacial Surgery, Division of Oral and Maxillofacial Surgery, University of Texas Southwestern Medical Center, Parkland Memorial Hospital, Dallas, Texas

Radiographic Evaluation of Facial Injuries

BARRY D. KENDELL, D.M.D., M.S.

Part-time Clinical Assistant Professor, Faculty of Oral and Maxillofacial Surgery, University of North Carolina School of Dentistry at Chapel Hill; Attending Surgical Staff, Durham County General Hospital, Durham, North Carolina

Applied Surgical Anatomy of the Head and Neck; Management of Facial Fractures in the Growing Patient

JOHN N. KENT, B.A., D.D.S., F.A.C.D., F.I.C.D.

Boyd Professor and Head, Department of Oral and Maxillofacial Surgery, Louisiana State University Medical Center School of Dentistry; Chief of Oral and Maxillofacial Surgery, Charity Hospital; Chairman of EENT, Hotel Dieu Hospital; Consultant, Ochsner, Children's, Doctors, Veterans Administration, East Jefferson Hospitals, New Orleans, Louisiana,

Biomaterials for Cranial, Facial, Mandibular and TMJ Reconstruction

MARVIN M. KIRSH, M.D.

Professor of Surgery, Section of Thoracic Surgery, University of Michigan Medical School; Attending Staff, University of Michigan Medical Center, Ann Arbor, Michigan

Management of Nonpenetrating Chest Trauma

CHARLES J. KRAUSE, M.D.

Professor and Chairman of Otolaryngology Head and Neck Surgery, University of Michigan Medical School, Professor and Chairman, Department of Otolaryngology, Head and Neck Surgery, University of Michigan Medical Center, Ann Arbor, Michigan

Traumatic Injuries to the Frontal Sinus

TIMOTHY F. KRESOWIK, M.D.

Assistant Professor of Surgery, University of Iowa College of Medicine; Attending Surgeon, University of Iowa Hospitals and Clinics, Iowa City, Iowa

Nutritional Considerations Following Trauma

PETER E. LARSEN, D.D.S.

Assistant Professor, Department of Oral and Maxillofacial Surgery, Ohio State University College of Dentistry; Attending Staff, Ohio State University Hospital and Columbus Children's Hospital, Columbus, Ohio

Healing of Traumatic Injuries

DENIS C. LEE, B.S., M.C.

Professor of Art and Professor of Postgraduate Medicine, Director, Graduate Program; Medical and Biological Illustration, University of Michigan Medical School; Assistant Professor of Plastic Surgery and Director of Medical Sculpture, University of Michigan Hospitals, Ann Arbor, Michigan

Maxillofacial Prosthetics for the Trauma Patient

DANIEL LEW, D.D.S.

Associate Professor and Chief, Oral and Maxillofacial Surgery, Louisiana State University Medical Center School of Dentistry; Attending Staff, Louisiana State University Medical Center, Veterans Administration Medical Center, Shriners Hospital, and Doctors' Hospital, Shreveport, Louisiana

Diagnosis and Treatment of Midface Injuries

STUART E. LIEBLICH, D.M.D.

Assistant Professor, Oral and Maxillofacial Surgery, University of Connecticut School of Dental Medicine; Attending Staff, Hartford Hospital and Newington Children's Hospital, Avon, Connecticut

Infection in the Patient with Maxillofacial Trauma

KENNETH A. MacAFEE II, D.M.D.

Assistant Professor and Clinic Director, Department of Oral and Maxillofacial Surgery, University of Pennsylvania School of Dental Medicine; Clinical Instructor and Lecturer, University of Pennsylvania Oral and Maxillofacial Surgery; Residency Training Program, Staff Surgeon, University of Pennsylvania Medical Center, Philadelphia, Pennsylvania

Burns of the Head and Neck

ROBERT E. MARX, D.D.S.

Associate Professor of Surgery and Director of Graduate Training and Research, University of Miami School of Medicine, Jackson Memorial Medical Center; Director, Center for Maxillofacial Reconstruction at Jackson Memorial Medical Center, Doctors Hospital of Coral Gables, Miami Veterans Administration Medical Center, Miami, Florida

Reconstruction of Avulsive Maxillofacial Injuries

JAMES R. MAULT, M.D.

Department of Surgery, Duke University Medical Center, Durham, North Carolina

The Metabolic Response to Trauma

BARBARA B. MAXSON, D.D.S., M.S.

Assistant Professor of Dentistry, University of Michigan School of Medicine; Staff Prosthodontist, University of Michigan Hospitals, Ann Arbor, Michigan

Maxillofacial Prosthetics for the Trauma Patient

KATHLEEN HOGAN MAYO, D.D.S.

Clinical Associate Professor, University of Michigan School of Dentistry, Ann Arbor; Attending Staff, St. Joseph's Hospital, Pontiac, Michigan

Burns of the Head and Neck

EDWARD J. McGUIRE, M.D.

Chairman, Section of Urology, Department of Surgery, University of Michigan Medical School, Ann Arbor, Michigan

Urologic Injuries

DALE J. MISIEK, B.A., D.M.D.

Associate Professor of Oral and Maxillofacial Surgery, Louisiana State University Medical Center School of Dentistry, New Orleans; Director of Residency Training, Oral and Dental Surgery, Charity Hospital; Active Staff, Hotel Dieu Hospital, New Orleans, East Jefferson General Hospital, Metairie; Courtesy or Consultant Staff, Eye, Ear, Nose and Throat Hospital, Tulane Medical Center, Veterans Administration Medical Center, Touro Infirmary, Southern Baptist Hospital, Mercy Hospital, Children's Hospital, New Orleans; Doctors' Hospital, East Jefferson General Hospital, Metairie; St. Jude Medical Center, Kenner, Our Lady of the Lake Regional Medical Center, Baton Rouge, Louisiana

Biomaterials for Cranial, Facial, Mandibular, and TMJ Reconstruction

THOMAS E. OSBORNE, D.D.S.

Assistant Professor of Oral and Maxillofacial Surgery, Emory University School of Postgraduate Dentistry; Assistant Chief of Oral and Maxillofacial Surgery, Grady Memorial Hospital; Attending Staff, Crawford W. Long Hospital and Henrietta Egleston Hospital for Children; Consultant, Atlanta Veterans Administration Hospital, Atlanta, Georgia

Pathophysiology and Management of Gunshot Wounds to the Face

JAMES K. PITCOCK, M.D.

Assistant Professor of Surgery, Otolaryngology-Head and Neck Surgery, University of California, Irvine; Director; Head and Neck Surgical Oncology, University of California, Irvine Medical Center and Long Beach Veterans Administration Medical Center, Orange, California

Nasal Fractures

MICHAEL P. POWERS, D.D.S., M.S.

Assistant Professor, Department of Oral and Maxillofacial Surgery, and Assistant Professor, Department of Surgery, Case Western Reserve University School of Medicine; Attending Staff, University Hospitals of Cleveland; Active Staff, Meridian Euclid Hospital, Euclid, Lakewood Hospital, Lakewood, and Consultant, Veterans Administration Medical Center of Cleveland, Cleveland, Ohio

Diagnosis and Management of Dentoalveolar Injuries; Management of Soft Tissue Injuries

JOACHIM PREIN, M.D., D.D.S.

Head, Clinic for Maxillofacial, Plastic and Reconstructive Surgery, Department of Surgery, University Clinic of Basel, Basel, Switzerland

Rigid Fixation of Facial Fractures

JEFFREY L. RAJCHEL, D.D.S., M.S.

Attending Staff, St. Joseph's Hospital and Memorial Mission Hospital, Asheville, North Carolina

Emergency Airway Management in the Traumatized Patient

JURGEN REUTHER, M.D., D.M.D.

Professor and Head, Department of Oral and Maxillofacial Surgery, University of Würzberg, Würzberg, Federal Republic of Germany

Rigid Fixation of Facial Fractures

WILFRIED SCHILLI, M.D., D.M.D.

Professor and Head, Department of Oral and Maxillofacial Surgery, University of Freiburg, Freiburg, Federal Republic of Germany

Rigid Fixation of Facial Fractures

RICHARD F. SCOTT, D.D.S., M.S.

Assistant Professor, Department of Oral and Maxillofacial Surgery, University of Michigan School of Dentistry, Ann Arbor, Michigan

Oral and Maxillofacial Trauma in the Geriatric Patient

J. ROBERT SCULLY, D.D.S., M.S.

Attending Staff, St. Joseph's Hospital and Memorial Mission Hospital, Asheville, North Carolina

Emergency Airway Management in the Traumatized Patient

STEEN SINDET-PEDERSEN, D.D.S.

Staff Member, Department of Oral and Maxillofacial Surgery, Aarhus University Hospital, Aarhus, Denmark

Rigid Fixation of Facial Fractures

DOUGLAS P. SINN, D.D.S.

Professor and Chairman, Division of Oral and Maxillofacial Surgery, University of Texas Southwestern Medical Center; Director, Division of Oral and Maxillofacial Surgery, Parkland Hospital, St. Paul Hospital, University Medical Center, and Children's Medical Center, Dallas, Texas

Radiographic Evaluation of Facial Injuries; Diagnosis and Treatment of Midface Fractures

MARK R. STEVENS, D.D.S.

Assistant Professor of Surgery, Division of Oral and Maxillofacial Surgery, University of Miami School of Medicine, Jackson Memorial Medical Center; Director, Center for Dento-facial Deformities and Director, Center for Temporomandibular Joint Disorders, Jackson Memorial Medical Center, Doctors' Hospital of Coral Gables, Miami Veterans Administration Medical Center, Miami, Florida

Reconstruction of Avulsive Maxillofacial Injuries

RICHARD G. TOPAZIAN, D.D.S.

Professor and Chairman, Department of Oral and Maxillofacial Surgery, University of Connecticut School of Dental Medicine; Professor of Surgery, University of Connecticut School of Medicine; Clinical Chief, Department of Dentistry, University of Connecticut John N. Dempsey Hospital, Farmington, Connecticut

Infection in the Patient with Maxillofacial Trauma

DONALD D. TRUNKEY, M.D.

Professor and Chairman, Department of Surgery, Oregon Health Sciences University, Portland, Oregon

Emergency and Intensive Care of the Trauma Patient

TIMOTHY A. TURVEY, D.D.S.

Professor, Department of Oral and Maxillofacial Surgery, University of North Carolina School of Dentistry; Attending Staff, University of North Carolina Hospitals, Chapel Hill, North Carolina

Management of Facial Fractures in the Growing Patient

L. GEORGE UPTON, D.D.S., M.S.

Professor and Interim Chairman, Department of Oral Medicine, Pathology and Surgery, University of Michigan School of Dentistry and Associate Professor, University of Michigan Medical School; Attending Staff, University of Michigan Hospitals; Co-director, University of Michigan Cleft Palate Team, Ann Arbor, Michigan

Management of Injuries to the Temporomandibular Joint Region

ROBERT G. VIERE, M.D.

Spine Fellow, Case Western Reserve University School of Medicine; Spinal Cord Injury Fellow, Cleveland Wade Park Veterans Hospital, Cleveland, Ohio

Initial Assessment and Management of the Polytrauma Patient with Orthopedic Injuries

GEORGE A. ZARB, B.CH.D (MALTA); M.S., D.D.S. (MICH.); M.S. (OHIO), FRCD(O), DR. ODONT (H.C.)

Professor and Chairman of Prosthodontics, Faculty of Dentistry, University of Toronto; Consultant, Hospital for Sick Children and New Mount Sinai Hospital, Toronto, Ontario, Canada

Maxillofacial Prosthetics for the Trauma Patient

DEBORAH L. ZEITLER, D.D.S., M.S.

Associate Professor and Director of Graduate Studies, University of Iowa; Attending Staff, University of Iowa Hospital and Clinic, Veterans Administration Medical Center, City of Iowa, Iowa City, Iowa

Burns of the Head and Neck

ACKNOWLEDGMENTS

Oral and Maxillofacial Trauma represents the culmination of four years of a labor of love. Our gratitude to the numerous expert contributors cannot be expressed completely in words. These persons provided us with comprehensive authoritative treatises in their respective areas. This book exemplifies the interdependence of man and the higher level of achievement that can be reached through cooperative efforts.

We would also like to extend our thanks and appreciation to all the residents we have worked with, many of whom are contributors to this text. They have provided the intellectual stimulation, inspiration, and friendship without which this book would not have been written. We would also like to thank Bonnie Andrews and Natalie Giuliano for their assistance in the preparation of this manuscript.

Personal thanks are also due to the editors and staff of the W.B. Saunders Company for their constant support and patient collaboration.

PREFACE

Approximately four years ago the seed of a thought was planted. At that time we envisioned a text that would represent the most definitive reference source for the practitioner treating the oral and maxillofacial injured patient. It was first our desire, and then ultimately our goal, to assemble a multiauthored text on the subject, bringing together the authorities in the field of oral and maxillofacial trauma. As might be anticipated, this original seed grew into a flower beyond our expectations.

Oral and Maxillofacial Trauma is an amitious endeavor consisting of four sections and 33 chapters. We have divided the book into four sections on the basis of the four distinct areas presented.

Section One covers the basic principles in the management of the trauma patient. Included in this section are chapters discussing the metabolic response to trauma, the healing of traumatic injuries, nutritional considerations following trauma, and the pathophysiology and management of shock.

Section Two is divided into seven chapters that deal with the recognition and management of concomitant injuries in the patient with maxillofacial trauma. Each chapter in this section could be the subject of an entire text; therefore, we have attempted to present the subject matter with emphasis on diagnosis and initial management of these injuries. We were fortunate to recruit some of the most widely respected experts in their fields to contribute chapters in this section.

Section Three begins with one of the most comprehensive and well-illustrated chapters in existence on applied surgical anatomy of the head and neck that is not in an atlas. The remainder of the chapters in this section discuss oral and maxillofacial injuries. Each chapter represents the diagnosis and management of a specific anatomic structure, area, or tissue.

Section Four deals with special considerations in the area of maxillofacial injuries. Chapters discussing the management of geriatric and pediatric patients are presented. The pathophysiology and management of gunshot wounds, burns, and infections are discussed in separate chapters. Treatment of patients with extensive facial injuries requiring secondary reconstruction, use of alloplastic materials, and prosthetic rehabilitation are presented comprehensively. An excellent discussion of anesthetic management of the traumatized patient is also presented. Finally, a detailed multiauthored chapter on rigid fixation of facial fractures is presented.

Our goal was to assemble a comprehensive text that would encompass as broad a perspective as possible within two volumes. We apologize for the areas that we inadvertently missed or did not cover as thoroughly as our readers would have liked. Nevertheless, we are extremely proud of *Oral and Maxillofacial Trauma* and offer it as the most comprehensive text on the subject.

RAYMOND J. FONSECA
ROBERT V. WALKER

CONTENTS

II SYSTEMATIC EVALUATION OF THE TRAUMATIZED PATIENT

VOLUME 2

IV SPECIAL CONSIDERATIONS IN THE MANAGEMENT OF TRAUMATIC INJURIES

I

BASIC PRINCIPLES in the MANAGEMENT of TRAUMATIC INJURIES

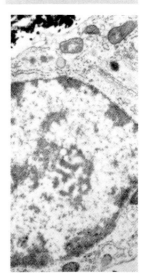

CHAPTER 1

THE METABOLIC RESPONSE TO TRAUMA

JAMES R. MAULT, M.D., and
ROBERT H. BARTLETT, M.D.

OVERVIEW

Traumatic injury produces dramatic alterations in normal physiology and metabolism that are manifested through systemic neuroendocrine responses as well as inflammatory mediators. Initial responses are directed at maintaining adequate oxygen delivery and energy substrates to sustain vital organs and salvage damaged tissues. With the release of catecholamines and vasoactive hormones, cardiac output is increased and extravascular fluids are mobilized to maintain blood volume while respiratory and renal functions adjust to maintain acid-base status. Metabolically, the normal state of energy and protein biochemistry is disrupted by autonomic stimulation and release or suppression of various endocrine hormones that cause an increase in energy expenditure and alter substrate requirements. As a result, plasma levels of glucose, fatty acids, and amino acids are increased through glycogenolysis, lipolysis, gluconeogenesis, and endogenous protein breakdown to supply the new metabolic demands and altered catabolic priorities. Research in recent years has shown that inflammatory mediators released from the site of injury also play a significant role in the metabolic changes of trauma. These mediators, released from activated immune cells and from cells specifically damaged by the injury, cause tissue edema and vasoconstriction locally but act systemically to cause fever and alter protein and lipid metabolism.

Although the cardiopulmonary responses in trauma and shock have been studied for decades, with numerous pharmacologic and technologic interventions readily available, insights into the metabolic responses to injury have only recently been gained. Contemporary investigations have shown that the resulting hypermetabolism, substrate imbalance, and nitrogen wasting described previously have a direct influence on the morbidity and mortality of trauma victims. This chapter describes the mechanisms and consequences of the metabolic response to traumatic injury, as well as the current approach to managing these effects.

HISTORICAL PERSPECTIVE

Although trauma has been a major source of morbidity and mortality to humans since the beginning of time, little was known about the body's response to an acute injury until the late eighteenth century. One of the earliest observations was made in 1794 by John Hunter, an English surgeon and biologist, who noted that the body's responses to injury were protective in nature and beneficial to the host.[1] However, many of these observations were often misinterpreted and led to clinical practices such as blood letting and leaching during this era.

A better understanding of the physiologic response to trauma began with the work of a clinical chemist in Glasgow, Scotland, named David Cuthbertson. By performing careful measurements of urinary solutes, Cuthbertson noted enhanced losses of nitrogen and potassium in injured patients.[2] He also measured energy expenditure by indirect calorimetry and described an increase in oxygen consumption that accompanied the increased protein catabolism in injured patients. With these measurements, he was the first to describe the "post-traumatic fever" by documenting an increase in body temperature in the absence of infection.[3]

By far the most significant contribution to the modern understanding of metabolism in the injured patient came from Francis D. Moore, Moseley Professor of Surgery and Chairman of the Department of Surgery at The Brigham and Women's Hospital in Boston. In the course of more than 30 years of a remarkable career, Dr. Moore performed sophisticated measurements of metabolism at the bedside and established an intensive care unit in which tabulations of fluid, electrolyte, energy, and protein balances were meticulously maintained. His specific contributions to the field are numerous and include the surgical management of fluid and electrolyte balance and descriptions of the metabolic responses to anesthesia, starvation, trauma, and burns and during convalescence. His text *Metabolic Care of the Surgical Patient* remains the classic reference in the management of critically ill patients.[4]

With the establishment of formal critical care units and highly specific assay techniques beginning in the late 1960s, a more detailed understanding of the metabolic response to trauma has been achieved. In recent years, identification of the precise hormones and inflammatory mediators responsible for these changes has provided the first opportunities to block or reverse their deleterious effects. One of the contemporary pioneers in this field is Douglas Wilmore (again from The Brigham and Women's Hospital in Boston), whose book *Metabolic Management of the Critically Ill* is an outstanding resource for anyone involved with the care of these patients.[5]

NEUROENDOCRINE RESPONSES

As described earlier, after trauma the patient experiences a significant disruption in normal metabolism that includes an increased metabolic rate, accelerated net protein breakdown, and alterations in carbohydrate and lipid biochemistry. These changes have been well studied and follow a predictable time course that can be separated into two distinct phases (Fig. 1–1).[2] The *ebb phase* is the brief period immediately following injury during which sympathetic discharge and rapid mobilization of fluid and glucose are required to maintain adequate delivery of oxygen and energy substrate to vital organs in the face of hypovolemia and shock. This phase lasts approximately 12 to 24 hours, depending on the degree of trauma and the interval between injury and the institution of resuscitative measures. Survival 24 hours after trauma progresses into the more prolonged *flow phase,* which is characterized by hypermetabolism and negative nitrogen balance. This stage typically lasts 2 to 3 weeks. The sequelae of these phases are produced by differing neurologic and hormonal control mechanisms that are described in detail further on.

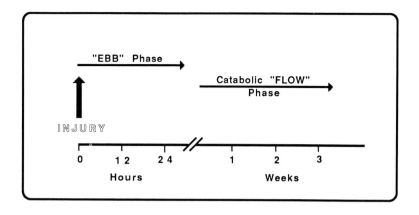

FIGURE 1-1. The ebb and flow phases of metabolism after trauma. The ebb phase occurs immediately after injury and is most significant for sympathoadrenal discharge. The flow phase follows with sustained hypermetabolism and protein wasting, thus described as the catabolic phase.

Acute Ebb Phase Metabolism

The physiologic events that develop immediately after trauma are both dramatic and complex. The first response is discharge of the sympathoadrenal axis, generating high plasma concentrations of epinephrine, norepinephrine, vasopressin, and dopamine in a magnitude commensurate with the degree of injury.[6] The hemodynamic consequences of these responses are vasoconstriction, preservation of blood volume, and increases in heart rate, blood pressure, and respirations (all of which are directed at maximizing oxygen delivery to the brain).

Metabolically, this sympathetic discharge produces an acute hyperglycemia that is maintained for approximately 24 hours via several pathways. In muscle and liver, glycogen stores are rapidly broken down, and circulating lactate is converted to glucose via gluconeogenesis. Epinephrine has additional effects on plasma glucose, since it inhibits glucose uptake by tissues, stimulates glucagon secretion, and suppresses the release of insulin from the pancreas. Finally, sympathetic stimulation of the adipose tissue results in lipolysis, producing nonesterified fatty acids and glycerol, which are converted into glucose by the liver.[7]

Concomitant with the sympathetic response after injury, the hypothalamic-pituitary axis is also activated.[8] Upon stress, the pituitary releases adrenocorticotropic hormone (ACTH), which acts on the adrenal cortex to secrete glucocorticoid hormones, such as cortisol and aldosterone. Other hypothalamus-derived hormones—prolactin and growth hormone—are also elevated immediately after trauma, but their roles in the ebb phase response are minor. These mechanisms and their target organs and responses are illustrated in Figure 1-2.

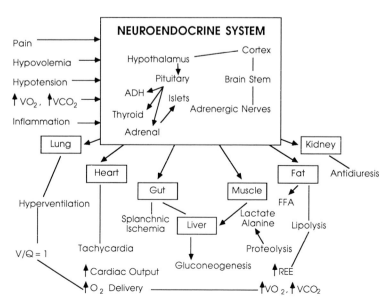

FIGURE 1-2. The neuroendocrine response to trauma.

Catabolic (Flow) Phase Metabolism

With survival longer than 24 hours after trauma, the hemodynamic status is usually stabilized, and the metabolic priorities shift into the flow, or catabolic, phase. During this period, which typically lasts 2 to 3 weeks after injury, the resting metabolic rate is persistently elevated, muscle mass undergoes significant proteolysis, and total body nitrogen balance becomes negative. Many of these sequelae are attributed to the counter-regulatory hormones glucagon, cortisol, and epinephrine. This concept is supported by Bessey and colleagues,[9] who produced hypermetabolism, negative nitrogen balance, glucose intolerance, and insulin resistance in nine normal volunteers after continuous infusion of cortisol, glucagon, and epinephrine. However, in severely injured patients, the plasma levels of these hormones are typically normal at 7 to 10 days after injury, when maximal nitrogen loss typically occurs.[10] Clearly, other factors—such as the suppression of somatomedin and growth hormone or the release of inflammatory mediators—contribute to the hypercatabolism of the flow phase.

INFLAMMATORY MEDIATORS

Although the neuroendocrine responses to trauma have been observed and studied for more than a century, it is only in the past decade that research has identified the wound itself as the origin of substances responsible for many of the metabolic changes common to injury. The *wound* is the site (or sites) of tissue damage that produces an inflammatory reaction, including disruption of cell membranes, activation of complement and white cells, and release of inflammatory products that cause thrombosis, vasoconstriction, and tissue edema. However, several of these compounds are released into the vascular space, are distributed systemically, and produce significant metabolic changes. The most notable of these mediators are the lymphokines and arachidonic acid metabolites, the natures of which are described in the following sections.

Lymphokines

Lymphokines are polypeptides produced by lymphocytes as well as other cells in response to injury, inflammation, or infection. They are generated throughout the body and can act locally as paracrines or, if produced in sufficient amounts, can be distributed through the vascular space and act systemically. Several lymphokines have been isolated and are named *interleukins,* with a number assignment representing a distinct amino acid sequence that elicits a specific set of effects.[11] Although a significant proportion of lymphokines exert their effects only on immune functions, interleukin-1, interleukin-2, and tumor necrosis factor are known to cause profound changes in systemic metabolism.

INTERLEUKIN-1

Interleukin-1 is produced by several types of cells, including T and B lymphocytes, natural killer cells, skin keratinocytes, brain astrocytes, microglia, epithelial cells, mesangial cells, and vascular tissues.[12] It is released by these cells in response to inflammation and injury, as well as exposure to antigens or toxins. Within a few hours of injury, interleukin-1 can be detected in the circulation, initiating multiple biologic effects. Its known immunologic properties include activation of resting T lymphocytes and macrophages, induction of hematopoietic growth factors, and chemotaxis of neutrophils. In addition, interleukin-1 stimulates the synthesis of other lymphokines, collagen, and collagenases. Metabolically, the consequences of the effects of interleukin-1 are numerous and will be described individually.

Fever. It is interesting that the study of lymphokines, interleukin-1 in particular, began during efforts to elucidate the mechanism of fever in humans. The first studies, which date back more than 30 years, recognized that while the thermoregulatory center of the body was located in the hypothalamus of the brain, most fever-producing diseases were in locations distant from the central nervous system. Therefore, it was postulated, some type of soluble factor must be introduced into the circulation at the peripheral site to cause fever. The existence of this factor, which was named "pyrexin" and "endogenous pyrogen," was confirmed by the production of fever in a noninfected animal from an injection of the plasma of an infected, febrile animal.[13,14] As more detailed studies were performed, it was discovered that pyrexin, now recognized as interleukin-1, is just one of several factors produced by lymphocytes.

Recent studies have further delineated the mechanism of fever. In the 1970s, another group of factors known as prostaglandins was determined to cause a fever in the same manner as for interleukin-1.[15] It is now known that interleukin-1 induces the synthesis of these prostaglandins in the hypothalamus, which in turn raise the thermoneutral setpoint of the hypothalamus and cause fever.[16] This finding is further supported by the fact that antipyretics such as aspirin and ibuprofen block the production of prostaglandins and that no fever is produced when one of these agents is administered prior to interleukin-1 injection.[17]

Anabolism and Catabolism. Accelerated liberation of amino acids from muscle and their uptake for protein synthesis by the liver and other visceral organs are characteristic of trauma. In a notable series of investigations, Clowes and coworkers[18] showed that when plasma from patients with sepsis or trauma was added to incubated normal human muscle tissue obtained at biopsy, proteolysis was increased 190 per cent above control values. Further study has identified a split product of interleukin-1 named proteolysis-inducing factor as the agent responsible for this phenomenon. At the same time, this factor has been shown to induce hepatic protein synthesis, often using the amino acids it liberates from muscle.[19] However, many of the effects of interleukin-1 have also been shown to occur with the endocrine hormones commonly secreted in trauma, so that the mediators and exact mechanism of altered protein turnover in trauma remain to be defined.[20]

INTERLEUKIN-2

Interleukin-2 is another of the polypeptide cytokines produced by activated T lymphocytes in response to injury or infection. Although most descriptions of interleukin-2 attribute its effects to modulation of immune function,[21] recent evidence suggests that it may also contribute to the acute phase response. Administration of interleukin-2 has been shown to cause fever, tachycardia, "flulike" symptoms, and induction of neurohormonal responses. In addition, these effects are blocked when the cyclooxygenase inhibitor ibuprofen is administered prior to interleukin-2 injection,[22] suggesting that the mechanism producing the effects of interleukin-2 is manifested through the release of prostaglandins.

TUMOR NECROSIS FACTOR

Many of the metabolic effects of interleukin-1 are produced by another lymphokine known as cachectin or tumor necrosis factor (TNF).[23] Interleukin-1 and TNF share similar actions in the acute phase response and have been shown to act synergistically in a variety of circumstances, such as tumor necrosis, hypotension, and inflammatory reactions.[12] However, in contrast to interleukin-1, TNF has no direct effect on lymphocyte activation. In addition, the pyrogenic response of TNF occurs only peripherally, not centrally, as with interleukin-1.[24] A property unique to TNF as a lymphokine is its effects on adipose tissue in which lipogenic enzymes are inhibited and triglycerides are mobilized.[25] Many of these effects may be manifested via prostaglandin synthesis and have been selectively inhibited by cyclooxygenase inhibitors.[26]

Products of Arachidonic Acid Metabolism

Substances derived from arachidonic acid initiate, amplify, and modulate the inflammatory response. Arachidonic acid, chemically referred to as eicosatetraenoic acid, is a 20-carbon unsaturated fatty acid that exists as a phospholipid component of mammalian cell membranes. It is released into the cellular cytoplasm through the activation of membrane phospholipase in response to trauma, contact with lymphokines, or direct exposure to lysosomal enzymes or oxygen-free radicals.[27] Although arachidonic acid has no biologic activity of its own, cytosolic enzymes convert it into metabolites known as prostaglandins and leukotrienes (Fig. 1–3). These end products are then released from the cell into the interstitium and vascular space as they are produced. The combination of prostaglandins and leukotrienes created from arachidonic acid metabolism varies according to cell type. The sources and metabolic effects of individual prostaglandins and leukotrienes are described as follows.

PROSTAGLANDINS

In the presence of the enzyme cyclooxygenase, arachidonic acid is converted into the prostaglandin endoperoxides, which, according to cell type, are converted into specific prostaglandin end products, such as thromboxane, prostaglandin E_2 (PGE_2), or prostacyclin (Fig. 1–3). Thromboxane, which is produced by platelets and macrophages, is a potent vasoconstrictor of small and large vessels as well as a powerful platelet aggregating factor.[28] These primary actions of thromboxane have been shown to act in combination to impair blood flow to organs, thus causing ischemia that can lead to shock.[29] It is interesting that prostacyclin, which is produced by endothelial cells, has the opposite effects of thromboxane. It causes vasodilatation and prevents platelet aggregation.[27]

The arachidonic acid derivative that has the most significant metabolic effect is PGE_2. It is produced in macrophages and neutrophils, as well as other specialized cells, in response to the lymphokine interleukin-1.[16] PGE_2 has several local inflammatory effects that cause edema (through microvascular dilatation and increased perme-

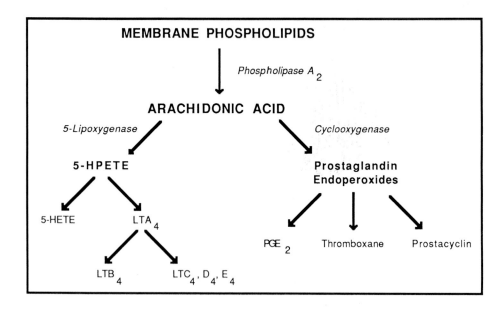

FIGURE 1–3. Arachidonic acid metabolism. In response to direct injury or activated white cells, arachidonic acid is produced from membrane phospholipids. The prostaglandins (PG) and leukotrienes (LT) are produced in the presence of the enzymes cyclooxygenase and lipoxygenase, respectively.

ability) and suppression of neutrophil degranulation. However, PGE_2 also has a strong influence on systemic metabolism. Over the past decade, investigations have demonstrated that the presence of circulating interleukin-1 induces the production of PGE_2 in the hypothalamus, and that PGE_2 production in the hypothalamus is a direct cause of fever.[17] In addition, interleukin-1 also stimulates the production of PGE_2 in skeletal muscle, which results in lysosomal proteolysis and muscle protein breakdown.[18,30] Thus, it appears that the fever, hypermetabolism, and increased protein and calorie requirements associated with trauma are due, in part, to the production of prostaglandins.

LEUKOTRIENES

An alternate outcome of arachidonic acid metabolism is the production of leukotrienes via the enzyme lipoxygenase (Fig. 1–3). Leukotrienes influence multiple pathophysiologic processes, such as immune cell chemotaxis, edema, inflammation, asthma, and shock, and have potent actions on several organ systems.[31] The cardiovascular effects of leukotrienes are significant and consist of coronary vasoconstriction, depression of myocardial contractility, vasodilatation of the pulmonary vasculature, and constriction of systemic microvasculature, which, in combination, lead to ischemia and shock. With these demonstrated effects, the central role of leukotrienes in the promotion of anaphylaxis is well accepted.[32] It is interesting that the clinical efficacy of steroids in preventing anaphylaxis may be due to their inhibition of phospholipase synthesis, which, therefore, precludes the promotion of leukotrienes.[33]

CLINICAL IMPLICATIONS

The management of metabolic changes that occur with trauma directly influences survival and subsequent recovery. Clearly, the hypermetabolism and protein wasting associated with injury can, if not properly supported, lead to impaired immune function, multiple organ failure, and sepsis.[34] The early introduction of aggressive nutritional support provides substrates for acute phase protein synthesis, sustains immune response and energy needs, and ameliorates protein catabolism. Morbidity as determined by length of stay in the hospital and mortality have been reduced with the performance of nutritional assessment and the institution of parenteral nutrition.[35-38] However, although these methods diminish the consequences of the metabolic changes that take place, glucose intolerance and skeletal muscle proteolysis persist in these patients.[39,40] A further understanding of the alterations in substrate utilization and the identification of agents that block or reverse these changes are necessary.

Management of Hypermetabolism and Altered Substrate Requirements

The previous sections have described a multitude of neuroendocrine and inflammatory mediators that contribute to the metabolic derangements of trauma. However, clinical decisions must be based on the net effect of these combined influences. The following sections describe the changes in energy and protein metabolism relevant to the management of these patients.

ENERGY METABOLISM

Cuthbertson was the first to document the increase in metabolic rate that follows trauma.[41] Many others have confirmed that oxygen consumption rises as much as 100 per cent above normal after injury and that this elevation in resting energy expenditure (REE) persists throughout the catabolic, or flow, phase.[36,42,43] The physiologic basis of this hypermetabolism is multifactorial, with exacerbation of caloric requirements by resetting of hypothalamic control, recycling of substrates, and heat loss via the wound and its healing requirements.[44-46]

In the clinical setting, the energy requirements of patients who have experienced trauma vary greatly according to severity of illness, operative procedures, infection, and burn size. Calculations of caloric requirements in these patients using the standard formulas[47] result in gross errors when compared with actual measurements.[48] Several investigators have shown significant morbidity and mortality associated with underfeeding[36] and overfeeding,[49,50] and therefore, actual measurement of energy requirements is recommended for these patients. Finally, the mixture of nonprotein energy substrates (i.e., the carbohydrate to lipid ratio) for administration appears to be of little significance if the total caloric intake is adjusted to match measured requirements.[51]

PROTEIN METABOLISM

A major feature of flow phase catabolism is the breakdown of muscle protein to provide amino acids that can be deaminated for gluconeogenesis or taken up directly by the liver for synthesis of acute phase proteins. Most authors agree that these changes in both amino acid turnover and protein synthesis are caused by circulating inflammatory mediators, such as interleukin and prostaglandins, as well as by the catabolic hormones cortisol, epinephrine, and glucagon. In addition, one investigator has shown that extended bed rest in normal individuals results in a negative nitrogen balance due not to atrophy but rather to decreased protein synthesis.[52]

The clinical management of protein requirements should include measurement of nitrogen balance and administration of protein or amino acids to match losses. In addition, evidence suggests that specialized amino acid requirements exist during the catabolic phase and that administration of solutions with high concentrations of branched-chain amino acids enhances nitrogen balance.[53,54] However, despite these measures, positive nitrogen balance is difficult to achieve in severely injured patients. One answer to this problem may be the use of recombinant human growth hormone, which, it has recently been found, causes nitrogen balance to become positive and promotes anabolism in surgical patients with hypocaloric feedings.[55-57]

Pharmacologic Intervention

Research into the development of therapeutic agents to assist in the management of critically ill patients has produced some exciting prospects. For instance, blockade of prostaglandin production from arachidonic acid has been shown to be effective in averting some of the metabolic events associated with injury. Aspirin and the non-steroid and anti-interleukin agents ibuprofen, indomethacin, and dipyridamole bind to cyclooxygenase and eliminate its biologic activity. Clinical use of these agents has prevented an increase in oxygen consumption and hypermetabolism in patients who have suffered trauma.[26,58] It is interesting that muscle proteolysis persists in the presence of these agents, despite normothermia.

The sympathetically mediated metabolic responses to trauma may also be attenuated by specific pharmacologic agents. Alpha-adrenergic blockade, using phentolamine, decreases protein catabolism in surgical patients receiving parenteral nutrition, while beta-adrenergic blockade, using propranolol, decreases glucose turnover and improves glucose tolerance.[59] The use of these agents in the clinical setting, however, may be limited by the hemodynamic status of the patient.

1. Hunter JA: A Treatise on the Blood Inflammation and Gunshot Wounds. London, 1794.
2. Cuthbertson D: The disturbance of metabolism produced by bony and nonbony injury, with notes on certain abnormal conditions of bone. Biochem J 24:1244–1263, 1930.
3. Cuthbertson D: Post-shock metabolic response. Lancet 1:433–437, 1942.
4. Moore F: Metabolic Care of the Surgical Patient. Philadelphia, WB Saunders Company, 1959.
5. Wilmore D: The Metabolic Management of the Critically Ill. New York, Plenum Medical Book Company, 1977.
6. Davies C, Newman R, Molyneux S, Graham-Smith D: The relationship between plasma catecholamines and severity of injury in man. J Trauma 24:99–105, 1984.
7. Barton R: Neuroendocrine mobilization of body fuels after injury. Br Med Bull 41:218–225, 1985.
8. Buckingham J: Hypothalamo-pituitary responses to trauma. Br Med Bull 41:203–211, 1985.
9. Bessey P, Watters J, Aoki T, Wilmore D: Combined hormonal infusion simulates the metabolic response to injury. Ann Surg 200:264–281, 1984.
10. Stoner H: Metabolism after trauma and sepsis. Circ Shock 19:75–87, 1986.
11. Dinarello C, Mier J: Lymphokines. N Engl J Med 317:940–945, 1987.
12. Dinarello C: Interleukin-1: Amino acid sequences, multiple biological activities and comparison with tumor necrosis factor (cachectin). Year Immunol 2:68–89, 1986.
13. Atkins E, Wood W: Studies on the pathogenesis of fever. I. The presence of transferrable pyrogen in the blood stream following insertion of the typhoid vaccine. J Exp Med 101:519–526, 1955.
14. Atkins E, Wood W: Studies on the pathogenesis of fever. II. Identification of an endogenous pyrogen in the blood stream following insertion of typhoid vaccine. J Exp Med 102:499–516, 1955.
15. Stitt J: Prostaglandin E₁ fever induced in rabbits. J Physiol (Lond) 232:163–179, 1973.
16. Dinarello C, Bernheim H: Ability of human leukocytic pyrogen to stimulate brain prostaglandin synthesis in vitro. J Neurochem 37:702–708, 1981.
17. Dinarello C: Molecular basis of fever in humans. Am J Med 72:799–819, 1982.
18. Clowes G, George B, Villee C, Saravis C: Muscle proteolysis induced by a circulating peptide in patients with sepsis or trauma. N Engl J Med 308:545–552, 1983.
19. Clowes G, Hirsch E, George B, et al: Survival from sepsis: The significance of altered protein metabolism regulated by proteolysis inducing factor, the circulating cleavage product of interleukin-1. Ann Surg 202:446–458, 1985.
20. Watters J, Bessey P, Dinarello C, et al: Both inflammatory and endocrine mediators stimulate host responses to sepsis. Arch Surg 121:179–190, 1986.
21. Robb R: Interleukin-2: The molecule and its functions. Immunol Today 7:203–209, 1984.
22. Michie H, Eberlein T, Spriggs D, et al: Interleukin-2 initiates metabolic responses associated with critical illness in humans. Ann Surg 208:493–503, 1988.
23. Beutler B, Cerami A: Cachectin and tumor necrosis factor as two sides of the same biological coin. Nature 320:584–588, 1986.
24. Morimoto A, Sakata Y, Watanabe T, Murakami N: Characteristics of fever and acute-phase response induced in rabbits by IL-1 and TNF. Am J Physiol 256:R35–41, 1989.
25. Torti F, Diekmann B, Beutler B, et al: A macrophage factor inhibits adipocyte gene expression: An in vitro model for cachexia. Science 229:867–869, 1985.
26. Evans D, Jacobs D, Revhaug A, Wilmore D: The effects of tumor necrosis factor and their selective inhibition by ibuprofen. Ann Surg 209:312–321, 1989.
27. Kuehl F, Egan R: Prostaglandins, arachidonic acid, and inflammation. Science 210:978–984, 1980.
28. Hamburg M, Svensson J, Samuelsson B: Thromboxanes: A new group of biologically active compounds derived from prostaglandin endoperoxides. Proc Natl Acad Sci USA 72:2992–2998, 1975.
29. Lefer A: Role of the prostaglandin-thromboxane system in vascular homeostasis during shock. Circ Shock 6:297–303, 1979.
30. Baracos V, Rodemann H, Dinarello C, Goldberg A: Stimulation of muscle protein degradation and prostaglandin E₂ release by leukocytic pyrogen (interleukin-1): A mechanism for the increased degradation of muscle proteins during fever. N Engl J Med 308:553–558, 1983.
31. Feuerstein G, Hallenbeck J: Leukotrienes in health and disease. FASEB J 1:186–192, 1987.
32. Samuelsson B: Leukotrienes: Mediators of immediate hypersensitivity reactions and inflammation. Science 220:568–575, 1983.
33. Naray F, Rosenkranz B, Rolich J, Fejes ST: Glucocorticoid effect on arachidonic acid metabolism in vivo. J Steroid Biochem 30:155–159, 1988.
34. Cerra F: Hypermetabolism, organ failure, and metabolic support. Surgery 101:1–14, 1987.
35. Abel R, Beck V, Abbott W, et al: Improved survival from acute renal failure after treatment with intravenous essential L-amino acids and glucose. Results of a prospective double-blind study. N Engl J Med 288:695–699, 1973.
36. Bartlett R, Dechert R, Mault J, et al: Measurement of metabolism in multiple organ failure. Surgery 92:771–779, 1982.
37. Abbott WC, Echenique MM, Bistrian BR, et al: Nutritional care of the trauma patient. Surg Gynecol Obstet 157:585–597, 1983.
38. Robinson G, Goldstein M, Levine G: Impact of nutritional status on DRG length of stay. JPEN J Parenter Enteral Nutr 11:49–51, 1987.
39. Warnold I, Eden E, Lundholm K: The inefficiency of total parenteral nutrition to stimulate protein synthesis in moderately malnourished patients. Ann Surg 208:143–149, 1988.
40. Shaw J, Wolfe R: An integrated analysis of glucose, fat and protein metabolism in severely traumatized patients. Ann Surg 209:63–72, 1989.

41. Cuthbertson D: Observations on the disturbance of metabolism produced by injury to the limbs. Q J Med 1:233–246, 1932.
42. Bartlett R, Dechert R, Mault J, Clark S: Metabolic studies in chest trauma. J Thorac Cardiovasc Surg 87:503–508, 1984.
43. Long C, Schaffel N, Geiger J, et al: Metabolic response to injury and illness. Estimation of energy and protein needs from indirect calorimetry and nitrogen balance. JPEN J Parenter Enteral Nutr 3:452–456, 1979.
44. Little R: Heat production after injury. Br Med Bull 41:226–231, 1985.
45. Wolfe RR, Herndon DN, Jahoor F, et al: Effect of severe burn injury on substrate cycling by glucose and fatty acids. N Engl J Med 317:403–408, 1987.
46. Wilmore D: The wound as an organ. *In* Little RA, Frayn KN (ed): The Scientific Basis for the Care of the Critically Ill. Manchester, England, Manchester University Press, 1986.
47. Harris J, Benedict F: A Biometric Study of Basal Metabolism in Man. Carnegie Institute Publication No. 279, Washington, DC, 1919.
48. Foster G, Knox L, Dempsey D, Mullen J: Caloric requirements in total parenteral nutrition. J Am Coll Nutr 6:231–253, 1987.
49. Askanazi J, Rosenbaum S, Hyman A, et al: Respiratory changes induced by the large glucose loads of total parenteral nutrition. JAMA 234:1444–1447, 1980.
50. Lowry S, Brennan M: Abnormal liver function during parenteral nutrition. Relation to infusion excess. J Surg Res 26:300–307, 1979.
51. Shaw J, Holdaway C: Protein-sparing effect of substrate infusion in surgical patients is governed by the clinical state, and not by the individual substrate infused. JPEN J Parenter Enteral Nutr 12:433–440, 1988.
52. Shangraw RE, Stuart CA, Prince MJ, et al: Insulin responsiveness of protein metabolism in vivo following bedrest in humans. Am J Physiol 255:E548–E558, 1988.
53. Cerra FB, Mazuski JE, Chute E, et al: Branched chain metabolic support. A prospective, randomized, double-blind trial in surgical stress. Ann Surg 199:286–291, 1984.
54. Cerra F, Blackburn G, Hirsch J, et al: The effect of stress level, amino acid formula, and nitrogen dose on nitrogen retention in traumatic and septic stress. Ann Surg 205:282–287, 1987.
55. Manson J, Wilmore D: Positive nitrogen balance with human growth hormone and hypocaloric intravenous feeding. Surgery 100:188–197, 1986.
56. Ziegler T, Young L, Manson J, Wilmore D: Metabolic effects of recombinant human growth hormone in patients receiving parenteral nutrition. Ann Surg 208:6–16, 1988.
57. Manson J, Smith R, Wilmore D: Growth hormone stimulates protein synthesis during hypocaloric parenteral nutrition. Role of hormonal-substrate environment. Ann Surg 208:136–142, 1988.
58. Shaw JH, Wolfe RR: Metabolic intervention in surgical patients. An assessment of the effect of somatostatin, ranitidine, naloxone, diclofenac, dipyridamole, or salbutamol infusion on energy and protein kinetics in surgical patients using stable and unstable radioisotopes. Ann Surg 207:274–282, 1988.
59. Shaw J, Holdaway C, Humberstone D: Metabolic intervention in surgical patients: The effect of alpha or beta blockade on glucose and protein metabolism in surgical patients receiving total parenteral nutrition. Surgery 103:520–525, 1988.

CHAPTER 2

HEALING OF TRAUMATIC INJURIES

STEPHEN E. FEINBERG, D.D.S., M.S., Ph.D.,
and PETER E. LARSEN, D.D.S.

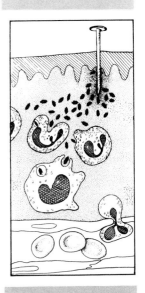

A clear understanding of wound healing is vital to a rational approach to the practice of repairing oral and maxillofacial injuries. This chapter reviews the major biologic processes of tissue repair of the integument, bone, cartilage, and peripheral nerve. Some attempt is also made to discuss factors that may affect the normal process of wound repair in traumatic injuries.

SOFT TISSUE

There are three phases of repair in soft tissue wounds (Table 2–1). In the first phase (inflammatory), there is an immediate vascular response that results in inflammation of the wound. There is a cellular infiltrate that initially consists of polymorphonuclear leukocytes, followed within 24 hours by monocytes, which become the dominant cell by the fifth day. The mononuclear macrophages are actively engaged in phagocytosis. Formation of new blood vessels at the edges of the wound is also noted in association with the mobilization of cells, resulting in the synthesis of granulation tissue.

The second phase of wound repair (proliferative) is established by the fourth or fifth day. Macrophages are still predominant, but with time there is an increasing number of fibroblasts. The fibroblasts are active in the synthesis of extracellular collagen and proteoglycans. The fibroblasts in the wound are closely followed by the endothelial buds of capillaries. When the second phase of repair is established, the wound is filled with vascular granulation tissue containing new capillaries, fibroblasts, macrophages, and mast cells. There is also noted at the end of this phase of repair an intrinsic increase in the mechanical strength of the wound.

The third phase (maturation) is characterized by extensive remodeling with a further increase in wound strength, which is the result of a decrease in the numbers of fibroblasts and macrophages concurrent with a decrease in vascularity. This situation creates a dense and relatively avascular scar of collagen fibers. With time there is a certain degree of remodeling of the collagen. An overview of the process of soft tissue healing is shown in the schematic diagram in Figure 2–1.[1]

TABLE 2-1. PHASES OF REPAIR IN SOFT TISSUE WOUNDS

I.	Inflammation	Vascular response
		Cellular infiltrate
		Polymorphonuclear leukocytes
		Macrophages
		Neovascularization
		Synthesis of granulation tissue
II.	Proliferation	Cellular proliferation
		Macrophages
		Fibroblasts
		Collagen synthesis
		Endothelial cell proliferation
		Mature formation of granulation tissue
		Increase in mechanical strength
III.	Maturation	Collagen remodeling
		Increase in wound strength
		Decrease in vascularity
		Macrophages
		Fibroblasts
		Formation of scar tissue

There are three types of wound healing: (1) primary intention, (2) delayed primary closure, and (3) secondary intention.

1. Primary Intention.   Healing by primary intention occurs when full-thickness wound edges are approximated shortly after the primary wound has been created. Epithelialization and contraction have little to do with the healing of primarily closed wounds, even though minimal epithelialization occurs within 24 hours[2] and seals the wound from bacterial contamination. Furthermore, epithelium does not provide strength to the closed wound.

2. Delayed Primary Closure.   Closure of grossly contaminated wounds should be delayed, to allow host inflammatory and immune responses to control contamination. Most significant is that delayed primary closure does not delay the development of wound strength.[3,4] Delayed primary closure decreases the morbidity from wound infection, while the development of wound strength remains unchanged.

3. Secondary Intention.   This form of healing is by natural biologic processes without surgical intervention, and it usually occurs in large wounds associated with soft tissue loss or avulsion. Although epithelialization and collagen deposition are involved, contraction is the most important phenomenon in the spontaneous closure of large open wounds. Unless contraction occurs and brings dermal structures together, the granulating surface is covered only by a layer of epithelial cells that are useless in providing coverage with strength and integrity.

Phase I: Inflammatory Response

Acute Inflammation

The physical response to injury, regardless of its type or source, begins with inflammation. It has become quite clear in recent years that the inflammatory response follows any type of injury and is considered a vital part of the repair process. If no inflammation is present, there will be no repair of tissue.

The tissue destruction and hemorrhage caused by trauma produce an opening through which factors from the external environment (bacteria or foreign debris) can gain entrance to the wound and eventually the host. Inflammation resulting from trauma may initially appear to differ from that resulting from bacterial infection or from physical agents such as heat, cold, and radiant energy. In actuality, the basic

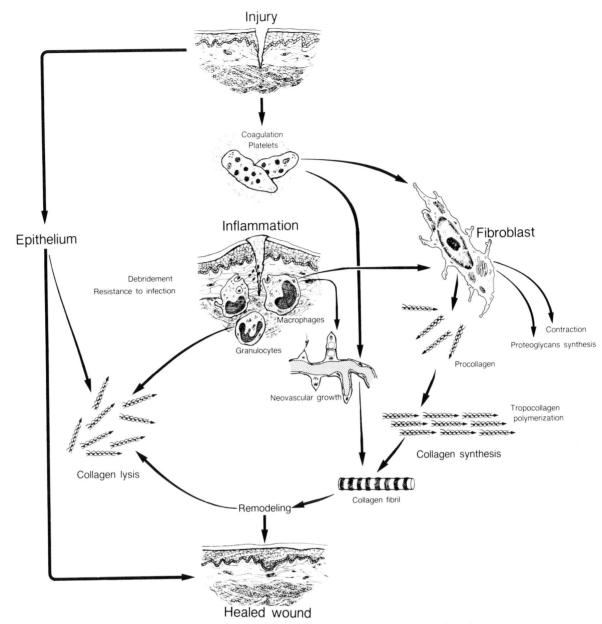

FIGURE 2–1. Overview of the process of soft tissue healing. (Modified from Hunt TK, Van Winkle W: Fundamentals of wound management in surgery. *In* Wound Healing: Normal Repair. South Plainfield, NJ, Chirurgecom, Inc., 1976.)

inflammatory response is the same regardless of the inciting factor. However, in most trauma cases, there is physical interruption of blood vessels, with immediate hemorrhage, and more or less extensive cell destruction at the exact site of injury, and, in many instances, a path to the external environment is created, permitting body fluids such as blood to drain. In addition, bacteria and other foreign substances may now be able to gain access to the wound. The response of the body to injury regardless of its nature is basically the same, and the most significant element of that response is seen in blood vessels.

VASCULAR REACTION

The vascular changes seen in an inflammatory response are distinct from the mechanism of hemostasis, which is accompanied by retraction of transected vessels and deposition of fibrin with formation of a blood clot in the wound. In the inflammatory response, immediately following injury there occurs a transient constriction of the local vessels lasting 5 to 10 minutes. At the same time, the vessel walls become lined with leukocytes that have become sticky and adherent to endothelium of the small vessels (20 to 30 μm in diameter); erythrocytes and platelets may also adhere to the vessel wall. The vasoconstriction is followed by active vasodilatation of all local small blood vessels and by increased blood flow.

Coincident with vasodilatation, increased permeability occurs at the level of the small venules. Increased vascular permeability appears to be the result of changes in the vessel wall, most likely induced by the local release of histamine. The endothelial cells swell and round up, creating separations between themselves and at the same time exposing the underlying basement membrane. Plasma, containing electrolytes and macromolecules, leaks through the gaps formed between the endothelial cells and enters into the site of injury.

CELLULAR MOVEMENT

Once leukocytes become adherent to the vessel wall, they migrate through by an active process of diapedesis. This process is accomplished by the leukocytes forcing their way through the basement membrane to the extravascular space. There is an indication that the defect in the vascular wall may be real and of a temporary nature. This theory is based on observations that a second cell will often follow the initial leukocyte through the gap and that erythrocytes will move passively into the extravascular spaces through the same channels.[5]

Once the leukocytes penetrate the vessel wall, there is a positive but somewhat random motion that allows the cells to concentrate at the site of injury. The predominant cell form at the injured site is the polymorphonuclear leukocyte (Fig. 2–2). These cells are short-lived when compared with the mononuclear cells, so that in an older or chronic inflammatory response the latter will predominate. The most important cell in the healing process of the wound is the macrophage.[6]

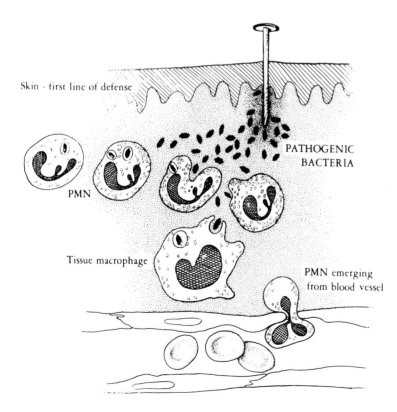

Skin - first line of defense

PATHOGENIC BACTERIA

PMN

Tissue macrophage

PMN emerging from blood vessel

FIGURE 2–2. Schematic representation of phagocytosis by polymorphonuclear leukocytes (PMNs) (neutrophils) and tissue macrophages following penetration of the skin and introduction of pathogenic bacteria into deeper tissues. The PMNs are more efficient in phagocytosis than are the macrophages. Note that the PMNs are mobilized into tissues from blood vessels during the inflammatory process. (From Bellanti JA: Immunology. 3rd ed. Philadelphia, WB Saunders Company, 1985, p 276; with permission.)

The inflammatory exudate is composed of escaped fluid from local vessels, migrating leukocytes, and nonviable tissue at the site of injury. As the polymorphonuclear cells die and are lysed, the exudate assumes the character of pus. During the acute inflammatory process, cells accumulate in specific areas called "cell aggregation centers."

The major factors determining whether an area of inflammation will produce enough pus to constitute an abscess are (1) the extent of injury to normal tissue, (2) the extent of the cellular reaction, and (3) the extent to which polymorphonuclear cells accumulate and die. The second and third factors are, in turn, determined by the state of the local circulation and, in particular, lymphatic drainage, since these vessels are more fragile than the vascular system.[7]

Sequence of Wound Repair

Immediately after wounding, the process of coagulation begins. This process involves both the humoral aspects of coagulation and the cellular response. The principal cellular response concerns the interaction of the platelets with thrombin and collagen. The platelets mechanically adhere to one another to control hemorrhage and provide components and initiators of the intrinsic process of coagulation.

Once the coagulation process is complete, the various types of cells appear in the wound in an orderly and reproducible sequence. The earliest cells to appear in the wound are the polymorphonuclear leukocytes (neutrophils) and the blood monocytes. On entering the wound, the latter become the principal macrophages responsible for debriding the wound. Neutrophils appear within a few hours, remain in large numbers for another day or two, and then rapidly decline in number if there is no concomitant infection. Monocytes enter the wounds and rapidly modulate into macrophages, reaching their maximal numbers 24 hours later. A significant number of macrophages persist even in primarily closed wounds for at least several weeks and longer in open or dead-space wounds.

Fibroblasts and capillaries appear in the wound slightly later than leukocytes. In linear incisions, the fibroblasts begin to appear within 1 day and become maximal in number within 1 week to 10 days; capillaries follow in a similar time course. The fibroblasts are responsible for the formation of connective tissue components—specifically, collagen and the glycosaminoglycans—and later for the formation of elastic fibers.

During the process of resolution and remodeling to form the final scar, the highly cellular granulation tissue becomes transformed into a relatively acellular mass, and a majority of the fibroblasts and capillaries disappear. The hallmark of granulation tissue is the marked proliferative response of the fibroblasts that is accompanied by the formation of new capillaries and by the synthesis and secretion of large amounts of connective tissue matrix components.

Chemical Mediators in Wound Healing

The acute inflammatory response can be considered from the standpoint of mediators involved in triggering this reaction. The mediators can be grouped into two categories: vasopermeability factors and chemotactic factors.

VASOPERMEABILITY MEDIATORS

All of these mediators, irrespective of their structure, cause contraction of smooth muscle from one or another source. They all seem to act on actin microfilaments within endothelial and periendothelial cells, inducing a reversible opening of junctions between the endothelial cells. The cells contract, and consequently, the opening of the junction permits a passage of plasma solutes across the vascular barrier.

Vasoactive Amines

Histamine.   Histamine enhances the permeability of arterioles, capillaries, and venules to albumin, then globulin, and finally fibrinogen.[8,9] The venules are the first to be affected, and within a brief period, the normal permeability of the venules returns, concurrent with leakage of proteins through the capillaries. Histamine increases the permeability of these vascular structures by inducing contraction of the endothelial cells and exposing the underlying basement membrane of the endothelium.[10,11]

Histamine is synthesized locally and is released from preformed, stored sources. Raising the tissue levels of histamine results in the dilatation of precapillary sphincters of the terminal arteriolar bed. All known types of tissue injury can cause the de novo synthesis of histamine.

5-Hydroxytryptamine (serotonin).   Serotonin is a more effective chemical than histamine in increasing capillary permeability.[12] Outside the central nervous system, serotonin is formed from the amino acid tryptophan, mainly in enterochromaffin cells of the gastrointestinal wall. An overflow of serotonin from these cells into the blood is removed actively by the liver and by endothelial cells, particularly in the lung. Serotonin escaping from hepatic and pulmonary endothelial cells is taken up by the blood platelets and mast cells for subsequent release during tissue injury.

The precise role of serotonin in the tissue injury response is controversial. Serotonin may cause contraction of arterial and venous smooth muscle and arteriolar dilatation, the net hemodynamic effect of the amine being determined by the balance between vasoconstriction and vasodilatation of these structures. Serotonin appears to increase the permeability of blood vessels by inducing numerous endothelial openings or gaps in a manner analogous to that of histamine.[10,11]

Peptides

Kinins (bradykinin, leukokinins).   Kallikreins, derived from the Greek word for pancreas, *kallikreas,* are enzymes that convert a precursor protein into biologically active polypeptides, the kinins.[13,14] One such kinin, bradykinin, is a potent local tissue hormone, which mediates the four cardinal signs of inflammation: redness (rubor), swelling (tumor), pain (dolor), and heat (calor).

Cationic peptides.   These peptides are derived from lysosomal granules of neutrophils.

Acidic Lipids (Prostaglandins)

The membrane enzyme phospholipase A_2 is activated by aggregations of blood platelets on the vascular endothelium to release arachidonic acid into the extracellular spaces.[15] The arachidonic acid is enzymatically oxygenated to form the precursor endoperoxides of the prostaglandins (PGs) and the lipoxygenase-mediated products, the hydroxyl acids. The endoperoxides, PGG_2 and PGH_2, are highly reactive short-lived and chemically unstable compounds, which are promptly converted to the biologically more active thromboxane A_2, PGD_2, PGE_2, $PGF_{2\alpha}$, and prostacyclin (PGI_2). The synthesis of prostaglandins, as well as the type of prostaglandins formed in a given tissue, is influenced by products of tissue injury, concentrations of glutathione and norepinephrine, and ions such as copper and zinc, which accumulate in the area.

Neurotransmitters (Norepinephrine, Epinephrine, and Acetylcholine)

The walls of arteries and arterioles contain adrenergic and cholinergic nerve fibers. In some tissues, the sympathetic adrenergic nerve fibers may even extend down to the capillary level. Tissue injury will stimulate the release of neurotransmitters, as evidenced by increases in the concentrations of norepinephrine in effluent blood and lymph during the initial few moments and of acetylcholine accompanied by elevated levels of cholinesterase activity somewhat later.

Mild tissue injury releases norepinephrine into the arterial wall and causes irregularities in the endothelial folds and the appearance of edematous, clear vacuoles in the endothelial cells. These endothelial cell changes enhance platelet and leukocyte adherence onto the vascular surface.

CHEMOTACTIC MEDIATORS

Chemotactic mediators are substances that promote directed migration of cells. The migration is unidirectional and occurs in response to a diffusing concentration gradient of a chemical attractant. The movement is always in the direction of the increasing concentration of the chemotactic factor. These chemotactic factors are responsible for the recruitment of leukocytes to the site of tissue injury. The most important leukocyte in the acutely injured patient, and the first one to the site of injury, is the neutrophil. The particulars known about the cellular mechanism (or mechanisms) of chemotaxis are as follows[16]:

1. Specific receptors exist on the surface of the chemoattracted cell. The chemotactic factors bind rapidly and reversibly to these receptors. Once the mediator binds to the receptor, it is hydrolyzed by enzymes on the cell surface.

2. Cell movement is associated with ionic fluxes that are established across the cell membrane. Ca^{2+} ion movement represents the most important cationic flux that results in a transient hyperpolarization of the cell membrane.

3. Enzyme activation, on and within the cell membrane, can occur simultaneously and result in the production of hydrogen peroxide and superoxide anions.

4. Changes in the protein profile on the surface of the cell can be seen with the addition of a neoprotein in conjunction with the deletion of other surface proteins.

5. A subcortical condensation of microfilaments, important in the locomotion apparatus of the cell, is visible along the leading edge of the cell.

Chemotactic factors can be regulated by hydrolysis through the action of lysosomal neutral proteases or through specific inhibitors of each of the individual mediators. Chemotactic factors can be generated through several mechanisms and pathways, as discussed in the following sections.

Complement System. The complement system consists of a group of inactive proteins that play a central role in the inflammatory response. One of the activated factors, C5a, has the capability of splitting off its C-terminal arginyl residue by a serum carboxypeptidase to form C5a-des-arg, which is a potent chemotactic factor for attracting neutrophils to the site of injury.[17,18] It is known that nonspecific tissue injury, such as surgical or mechanical trauma, can result in the release of neutral proteases that can cleave C5 into chemotactic peptides[19,20] (Tables 2–2 and 2–3).

Immune System. The immune system consists of a cell-mediated segment using T lymphocytes and a humoral segment mediated by B lymphocytes. The T lymphocytes, when stimulated, produce a variety of factors called lymphokines. One of these factors, leukocyte-derived chemotactic factor (LDCF), is a specific chemoattractant for macrophages.[21,22] Transfer factor, a dialyzable extract of lymphocytes chemotactic for neutrophils, is preformed in the lymphocytes prior to antigenic stimulus and is thus not considered a lymphokine.[23,24] Transfer factor is a separate factor from the activated split products of the complement system.

The B lymphocytes, when activated, differentiate into plasma cells and secrete immunoglobulins. The immunoglobulins, when combined with antigens, trigger the activation of the complement system, resulting in the production of chemoattractants, such as C5a-des-arg.[25]

Phagocytic System. The phagocytic system is composed of abundant cells that contain numerous granules within their cytoplasm. During the process of phagocyto-

TABLE 2-2.   ACTIVATORS OF COMPLEMENT SYSTEM

I.	Classic pathway	Immunoglobulins
		IgG (human subclasses 1, 2, and 3)
		IgM
		Nonimmunoglobulin activators
		Bacterial lipopolysaccharide (lipid A portion)
		C-reactive protein bound to pneumococci
		Retroviruses
		Heart mitochondrial membranes
		Polyanions (e.g., polynucleotides)
		Urate crystals
II.	Alternative pathway	Polysaccharides (e.g., insulin)
		Yeast cell walls (zymosan)
		Bacterial cell wall components (lipopolysaccharide, peptidoglycan)
		Influenza and other viruses
		Schistosoma and other parasites
		Cryptococci and other fungi
		Certain tumor cells
		Cobra venom factor
		Nephritic factor (autoantibody that stabilizes C3b, Bb)
		X-ray contrast media
		Dialysis membranes

From Bellanti JA: Immunology. 3rd ed. Philadelphia, WB Saunders Company, 1985, pp 108–110; with permission.

TABLE 2-3.   BIOLOGICAL EFFECTS OF COMPLEMENT ACTIVATION PRODUCTS

SUBSTANCE	BIOLOGICAL ACTIVITY
C3a	Smooth muscle contraction
	Increase of vascular permeability
	Degranulation of mast cells and basophils with release of histamine
	Degranulation of eosinophils
	Aggregation of platelets
C3b	Opsonization of particles and solubilization of immune complexes with subsequent facilitation of phagocytosis
C3e	Release of neutrophils from bone marrow resulting in leukocytosis
C4a	Smooth muscle contraction
	Increase of vascular permeability
C5a	Smooth muscle contraction
	Increase of vascular permeability
	Degranulation of mast cells and basophils with release of histamine
	Degranulation of eosinophils
	Aggregation of platelets
	Chemotaxis of basophils, eosinophils, neutrophils, and monocytes
	Release of hydrolytic enzymes from neutrophils
C5a-des-arg	Chemotaxis of neutrophils
	Release of hydrolytic enzymes from neutrophils
Bb	Inhibition of migration and induction of spreading of monocytes and macrophages

From Bellanti JA: Immunology. 3rd ed. Philadelphia, WB Saunders Company, 1985, p 110; with permission.

sis, the contents of the granules are released into the environment. The contents of the granules of neutrophils can generate chemotactic factors by activation of the complement system.[26,27] Sulfhydryl proteases, released by neutrophil degranulation, are capable of modifying the structure of immunoglobulin G (IgG) to a new conformation with chemotactic properties, called leucogresin.[28] Leucogresin has been found in high concentrations in wounds with accumulations of neutrophils.

Cells Involved in Wound Repair

BLOOD PLATELETS

Blood platelets are non-nucleated fragments of bone marrow–derived megakaryocytes that circulate in the peripheral blood for 9 to 11 days.[29] Their cytoplasm contains glycogen and several types of dense granules that, when released, are involved in the early events associated with tissue injury. When platelets come into contact with the connective tissue of the subendothelium of a traumatized vessel, they adhere to the exposed collagen. The collagen-induced adherent platelets degranulate and release adenosine diphosphate (ADP),[30] 5-hydroxytryptamine or serotonin,[31,32] prostaglandins,[33] and thromboxane A_2.[34] On release these substances initiate binding of other platelets to the initial layer of adherent platelets to form aggregates. The aggregated platelets secrete part of their granular contents and, together with fibrin, form a mass of material that creates a hemostatic plug.

Platelets degranulate during the formation of the hemostatic plug and release constituents that increase vascular permeability (serotonin, kinins, and prostaglandins) and contribute to the inflammatory response accompanying tissue injury. In addition, mitogenic activity has been localized to the platelet alpha granules.[35–37] Since platelets contain only a rudimentary protein synthetic apparatus,[38] they are a storage vehicle for active mitogens that are released upon exposure to such agents as thrombin, collagen, and ADP (Fig. 2–3). The mitogenic activity is seen with the release of platelet-derived growth factor (PDGF).[39,40] It has been postulated that PDGF can be released in relatively large quantities during the early stages of wound healing because of its chemotactic properties for both leukocytes and fibroblasts and its mitogenic properties to enhance cell proliferation.[41]

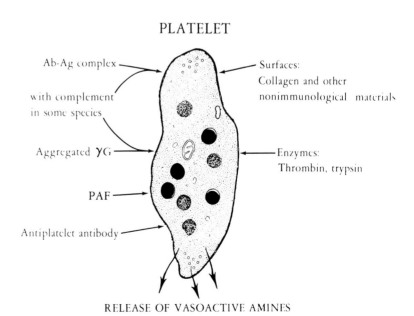

PLATELET

Ab-Ag complex
with complement
in some species

Surfaces:
Collagen and other
nonimmunological materials

Aggregated γG

Enzymes:
Thrombin, trypsin

PAF

Antiplatelet antibody

RELEASE OF VASOACTIVE AMINES

FIGURE 2–3. Some stimuli that can induce release of vasoactive amines from platelets. (From Bellanti JA: Immunology. 3rd ed. Philadelphia, WB Saunders Company, 1985, p 253; with permission.)

POLYMORPHONUCLEAR LEUKOCYTES (NEUTROPHILS)

It is now believed that the main function of the neutrophil in the early phases of wound repair is autolysis and release of its intracellular contents, in contrast to the widely held concept of phagocytosis.[42]

The neutrophils migrate into the tissue spaces by first sticking to the vascular endothelium, followed by migration or diapedesis through the endothelial cells.[43] Once they reach the site of injury, they release the contents of their cytoplasmic granules (Fig. 2–4). There are two types of granules found in the neutrophil, primary or azurophilic and secondary or specific. Primary granules are larger than secondary granules, but both are forms of lysosomes, membrane-bound structures containing digestive enzymes capable of degrading tissue macromolecules at an acid pH. The primary granules contain enzymes, such as collagenase, elastase, cathepsin, and cationic proteins, which are attracted to mast cells.[44] Cathepsin G and elastase may convert kininogens to kinins and activate complement (Table 2–4).

The presence of neutrophils is not an essential prerequisite for wound repair. Studies in neutropenic animals following the administration of antineutrophil serum have shown that mononuclear macrophages appear in the wound in normal numbers and that the proliferative phase of wound repair is unaffected.[45]

MACROPHAGES

The mononuclear phagocytes that are involved in the response to an injury arise from precursor cells in the bone marrow and circulate in the blood. These cells exit from the blood, undergo structural and functional alterations, and evolve as tissue macrophages or histiocytes.[46–48] In the first few days after injury, the neutrophil predominates; however, by about the fifth day, macrophages predominate, and they remain until the reparative sequence is done.

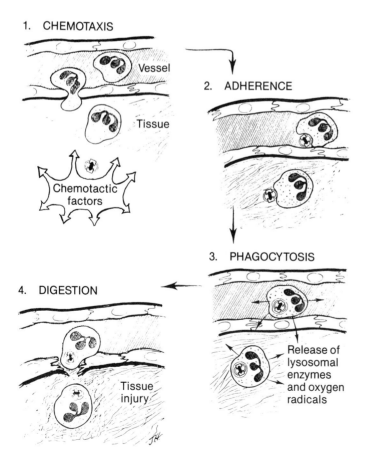

FIGURE 2–4. Sequence of reactions leading to tissue injury associated with PMN influx. Note that in addition to chemotaxis, adherence, phagocytosis, and the digestion process, which normally result in particle inactivation, there may also be the release of neutrophilic constituents (lysosomal enzymes) that result in tissue injury. (From Bellanti JA: Immunology. 3rd ed. Philadelphia, WB Saunders Company, 1985, p 255; with permission.)

TABLE 2-4.   INJURIOUS CONSTITUENTS OF NEUTROPHILS

CONSTITUENT	ACTIVITY
Collagenase, elastase, and cathepsin A	Hydrolysis of basement membranes, internal elastic laminae, cartilage and other connective tissue; generation of C5 fragments, angiotensin II
Basic proteins (3)	Increased vascular permeability
Basic protein (1)	Activation of mast cells, release of vasoactive amines
Leukotrienes C_4 and D_4	Increased vascular permeability, contraction of smooth muscle
Kininogenase	Hydrolysis of kininogen with release of vasoactive kinin
Procoagulant activity	Generation of fibrin, activation of platelets
Platelet activation factor (PAF)	Activation of platelets, increased vascular permeability, contraction of smooth muscles, activation of neutrophils
Leukotriene B_4	Attraction of leukocytes
Lysosomal enzymes	Digestion of tissue constituents
Oxygen radicals	Damage to cells

From Bellanti JA: Immunology. 3rd ed. Philadelphia, WB Saunders Company, 1985, p 258; with permission.

Primary repair is seen to occur uninhibited when major reductions in the numbers of circulating and tissue polymorphonuclear cells and lymphocytes are accomplished. In contrast, when the macrophage is eliminated from the healing wound by either systemic hydrocortisone or antimacrophage serum, there is an impairment in both wound debridement and migration of fibroblasts into the wound.[49]

The regulatory role of macrophages seems to be closely linked to their stage of differentiation or activation or both. It thus appears that the metabolic, growth regulatory, and secretory properties of macrophages vary, depending on whether they are at rest, as resident inflammatory cells, or in an activated state.

Macrophages can be activated by products of activated lymphocytes (lymphokines),[50] immune complexes,[51] and the complement cleavage product C3b.[51] Activation results in a series of responses that are important in the process of wound repair (Fig. 2-5). It has been suggested that macrophages may determine the rate of ingrowth of new vascular endothelium in the healing wound. The growing buds of endothelium are preceded by the migration of macrophages into the wound, implying that activated macrophages produce an angiogenesis factor that stimulates the migration and proliferation of endothelial cells.[52]

When macrophages migrate into the wound through the surrounding tissue and blood vessels, they ingest debris and their biochemical activity is enhanced. This improved activity is accomplished by the release of hydrolytic enzymes into the extracellular spaces. Neutral proteases, such as collagenase, elastase, and cathepsin B and D, catalyze the conversion of plasminogen to plasmin, which in turn lyses fibrin into the fibrin degradation products, which may also function as directional factors in wound healing.[53-59]

There is evidence that macrophages can release a polypeptide, interleukin-1, that can function as a mitogenic messenger for lymphocytes.[60] In addition, others have noted that macrophages can influence fibroblast proliferation.[61-63] Thus, available data strongly suggest that macrophages are key cells in the inflammatory response as well as in the repair process of tissue injury (Table 2-5).

MAST CELLS

The mast cell is considered the sentinel cell because of its strategic location at the portals of entry of noxious substances into the body and because of its prominence at body interfaces subject to traumatic injury, such as skin and mucous membranes. Mast cells are distinguished by their large osmophilic-dense cytoplasmic granules and are derived from migrating basophils. The only tissues that are free of mast cells are

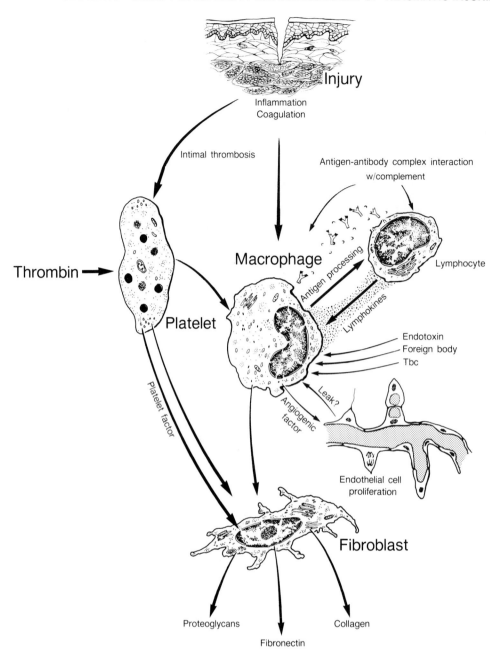

Figure 2–5. Cell interactions that lead to wound healing. The macrophage plays a central role that involves its activation by lymphokines, release of angiogenic factor, and collaborative roles with platelets, lymphocytes, and fibroblasts.

TABLE 2–5. MACROPHAGE PRODUCTS WITH POTENTIAL AS CHEMICAL MESSENGERS OF INFLAMMATION AND WOUND REPAIR

1. Neutral proteases
    Plasminogen activator
    Collagenase
    Elastase
	6. Reactive metabolites of oxygen
	    Free radicals (O_2^-, OH^+)

2. Acid hydrolases
    Protease
    Lipases
	7. Bioactive lipids
	    Arachidonate metabolites
	    Platelet activating factor

3. Complement components C1–C5	8. Factors chemotactic for polymorphonuclear leukocytes

4. Enzyme inhibitors
    Plasmin
    Alpha-macroglobulin
	9. Factors regulating protein synthesis
	10. Factors promoting replication of:
	    Lymphocytes
	    Fibroblasts
	    Microvasculature

5. Binding proteins Fibronectin	11. Antimitogenic factors for lymphocytes

From Boucek RJ: Factors affecting wound healing. Otolaryngol Clin North Am 17:243, 1984; with permission.

MAST CELL

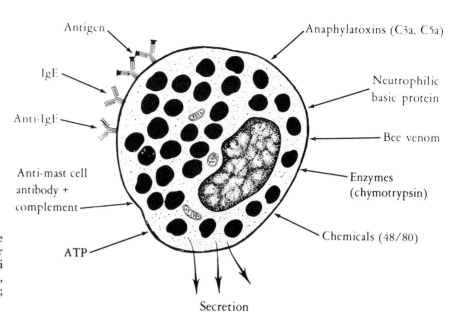

FIGURE 2–6. Stimuli that can induce release of vasoactive amines and other material from mast cells. (From Bellanti JA: Immunology. 3rd ed. Philadelphia, WB Saunders Company, 1985, p 250; with permission.)

compact bone, cartilage, and the kidneys. The specific immunoglobulin E (IgE) recognition units of the mast cell, its sensitivity to other activating agents, its perivenular location, and the qualitative and quantitative aspects of its mediators support the mast cell's role as an initiator of host defense to injury (Fig. 2–6).

The mast cell plays a prominent role in the inflammatory response by virtue of its array of chemical mediators (Table 2–6). It contains stored or preformed and unstored mediators. The preformed mediators are available for release at the time of perturbation of the cell. The unstored mediators require cellular activation to initiate generation or uncovering of their activity. After the release of these mediators, a humoral phase is begun that manifests itself as asthma, rhinitis, urticaria, or anaphylaxis. During the humoral phase, mediators such as histamine and slow-reacting substance of anaphylaxis (SRS-A) allow for the entrance of water, electrolytes, and plasma protein into the microenvironment. The immunoreactive proteins, such as complement and immunoglobulin, contained in this infiltrate may then amplify the response. The maintenance of a patent channel for this influx is accomplished by the anticoagulant activity of heparin and by the proteolytic activity of chymase.[64]

LYMPHOCYTES

Lymphocytes, thymus (T) and bursa (B), are attracted to the site of injury by the by-products of activation of complement. Lymphocytes contain a number of enzymes

TABLE 2–6.   CHEMICAL MEDIATORS DERIVED FROM THE MAST CELL

PREFORMED	UNSTORED
Histamine	Slow-reacting substance of anaphylaxis (SRS-A)
Heparin	
Eosinophil chemotactic factor of anaphylaxis (ECF-A)	Platelet activating factors (PAFs)
Neutrophil chemotactic factor (NCF)	Lipid chemotactic factor (LCF)
Chymase	
N-acetyl-beta-glucosaminidase	

From Yurt RW: Role of the mast cell in trauma. *In* Dineen P, Hildrick-Smith G (eds): The Surgical Wound. Philadelphia, Lea and Febiger, 1981, pp 37–62; with permission.

TABLE 2-7. PRODUCTS OF ACTIVATED LYMPHOCYTES (LYMPHOKINES)

I.	Mediators affecting macrophages	(a)	Migration inhibitor factor (MIF)
		(b)	Macrophage activating factor (MAF)
		(c)	Macrophage aggregation factor (? same as MIF)
		(d)	Factor causing disappearance of macrophage from periosteum (? same as MIF)
		(e)	Chemotactic factor for macrophages
		(f)	Antigen-dependent MIF
II.	Mediators affecting neutrophil leukocytes	(a)	Chemotactic factor
		(b)	Leukocyte inhibitor factor (LIF)
III.	Mediators affecting lymphocytes	(a)	Mitogenic factors (interleukin-2)
		(b)	Antibody enhancing factors
		(c)	Antibody suppressing factors
		(d)	Chemotactic factor
IV.	Mediators affecting eosinophils	(a)	Chemotactic factor (requires antigen-antibody complexes)
		(b)	Migration stimulation factor
V.	Mediators affecting basophils (mast cells)	(a)	Chemotactic augmentation factor
		(b)	Histamine releasing factor
		(c)	Interleukin-3
VI.	Other cells	(a)	Cytotoxic factors—lymphotoxin
		(b)	Growth inhibitory factors
			(1) clonal inhibitory factor
			(2) proliferation inhibitory factor
		(c)	Osteoclast activating factor (OAF)
VII.	Immunoglobulin binding factor		
VIII.	Procoagulant activity		
IX.	Skin reactive factor		
X.	Interferon		
XI.	Immunoglobulin		

From Bellanti JA: Immunology. 3rd ed. Philadelphia, WB Saunders Company, 1985, p 182; with permission.

whose products serve as mitogenic chemical messengers in the repair process. Lymphocytes are responsible for other local polypeptide messengers, the lymphokines (Table 2-7). The lymphokines have the capability to suppress hypersensitivity reactions by activating the arachidonic acid metabolism of macrophages, the products of which inhibit the further production and activities of lymphokines.[48,65]

Several studies have revealed that T lymphocyte participation in wound healing is a finely tuned mechanism dependent on the existing balance between T lymphocyte subpopulations. It has been shown that T lymphocytes can secrete lymphokines that are capable of regulating fibroblast growth and activity.[63] In contrast, T lymphocytes have also been demonstrated to be capable of inhibiting fibroblast migration and protein synthesis via soluble mediators.[66] Immunosuppression of T helper function has been shown to impair wound healing,[67] while inhibition of trauma-induced suppressor T lymphocyte generation was found to increase wound maturation.[68] In addition, recombinant human interleukin-2 has been found to enhance wound healing.[69] Total depletion of the T lymphocyte population with an anti-Thy 1.2 monoclonal antibody results in a significant impairment of wound healing, as assessed by breaking strengths of fresh scars and the hydroxyproline content.[70]

Phase II: Proliferation

Epithelialization

Epithelialization of an injury on any surface of the body begins within hours. Before such epithelial regrowth can occur, it requires a foundation of vital cells upon which the epithelial margins may advance. It is thus essential that the exudate and necrotic debris first be removed, and then whatever subepithelial defect exists can become filled in with granulation tissue. Three separate but overlapping phases of epithelial activity have been shown to exist: migration, proliferation, and differentiation.

Migration and proliferation of the epithelial cells are seen within 24 to 48 hours after injury at the wound margins. There is a tumbling or "leapfrogging" of basal cells as they migrate into the wound. These migrating cells are larger and have a more flattened appearance than the basal cells of unwounded epidermis. The process of sliding or rolling over one another seems to be governed by several factors: Contractile cytoplasmic fibrils similar to those present in myofibroblasts are thought to be important in epidermal cell motility,[71] and the intercellular junctions (desmosomes) and cell-substrate junctions (hemidesmosomes) also determine the movement of these cells.[72-74]

There is also an intimate relationship between the migrating epidermis and the continual production of collagen (AB_2) by these cells.[75] It has been shown by several investigators that collagen is an important factor in the early stages of wound repair involving epithelial cell migration. The presence of type IV collagen[76,77] has been found to be critical to the preferential attachment of epithelial cells in culture. In addition, others have demonstrated selective adherence of the epithelial basal cells to a collagen substrate,[78] as well as the effects of collagen on cell adherence,[79,80] cell differentiation,[81] and protein synthesis.[82]

Although the migration of epithelial cells is random, they are guided by the orientation of the substrate ("contact guidance") and by communication with other epithelial cells ("contact inhibition"). If an epithelial cell encounters another epithelial cell, its direction of movement is changed until it encounters another like cell. Continued migration of the epithelial cell appears to be inhibited when the cell is finally in contact on all sides with other epithelial cells. This contact inhibition is seen only with other epithelial cell–like cells and not cells from a different germ layer.

Concurrently with the migration of cells from the wound margins, fixed basal cells adjacent to the wound edge and in the transected skin appendages begin rapid mitosis and replace the migrated cells. As resurfacing of the wound is accomplished, the migrated cells themselves commence mitosis and thicken the new epithelial layer. When coverage of the wound surface beneath the scab is completed, the scab sloughs off and the new cells on the surface of the epidermis begin to keratinize.

The involvement of epithelial cells in the healing process is not limited to the re-establishment of tissue integrity. These cells are associated with two more phenomena: (1) They produce, either alone or as a result of interacting with mesenchyme, collagenase, which is the collagen-degrading enzyme[83-85] that initiates the clearance of collagen, regulates its amount, and also plays a role in epithelial movement[86]; and (2) epithelial cells produce a non–species-specific mitogen (growth factor) that enhances epithelialization and keratinization following systemic administration (subcutaneous) or topical application.[87,88]

Fibroblasts

The origin of wound fibroblasts and the pathway by which these cells arrive at the site of injury have been controversial. At present, it is thought that several different types of cells of mesenchymal origin are capable of differentiating into fibroblasts under appropriate conditions. The fibroblasts migrate along strands of fibrin deposited in the wound during initial clotting. At the wound site, the fibroblast population both migrates and increases by proliferation. The release of a macrophage-dependent factor that is associated with fibroblast proliferation has been shown to exist by several investigators.[61] In comparing the occurrence of fibroblast proliferation and migration, it is evident that migration precedes proliferation, thus indicating that cell division is not necessarily directly associated with cell migration.[89] Fibroblasts have been shown to have chemotactic attraction to types I, II, and III collagen and collagen-derived peptides, with binding of these peptides directly to the fibroblasts,[90,91] thus indicating the importance of collagen to fibroblast migration.

Fibroblasts produce a variety of substances essential to wound repair. Initially, they manufacture glycoproteins and mucopolysaccharides (glycosaminoglycans), components of connective tissue. Later the fibroblasts manufacture collagen. As the amount of collagen increases at the wound site, the glycoprotein and mucopolysaccharide content decreases.

Finally, the conversion of fibroblasts into contractile cells, myofibroblasts, by structural, compositional, immunologic, and functional changes, contributes substantially to the contraction and ultimate closure of the healing wound.[92-95]

Collagen

There are a number of distinct collagens in the body.[96] Each protein is a triple-helical macromolecule located in the extracellular space. However, the various types of collagen are chemically and immunologically distinct proteins and are products of different genes.

1. Type I collagen is the most abundant protein in the body. The fibers formed by type I collagen are large and often grouped in bundles like a rope or cable. Type I collagen provides the major structural support to tissues. The production of type I collagen is very closely associated with fibroblasts.

2. Type II collagen is located almost exclusively in hyaline cartilage and is formed by chondrocytes.

3. Type III collagen is frequently absent from bones and is synthesized by fibroblasts and smooth muscle cells. Type III collagen has sometimes been called reticulum fibers and has been shown to be a major constituent of blood vessels and several internal organs, such as the spleen and intestine.

4. Type IV collagens are found mostly in the basement membrane. Basement membrane collagens do not form fibrils, and thus their matrix appears amorphous. The basement membrane contains several distinct components that most likely interact to create this matrix.

5. Finally, type V collagen has been found in a variety of tissues, including placenta and blood vessels, and is histologically associated with smooth muscle cells (Table 2–8).

TABLE 2–8. DIFFERENT TYPES OF COLLAGENS

TYPE	TISSUE DISTRIBUTION	CELLS	CHEMICAL CHARACTERISTICS
I	Bone, tendon, skin, dentin, ligament, fascia, arteries, and uterus	Fibroblast	Hybrid composed of two kinds of chains; low content of hydroxylysine and glycosylated hydroxylysine
II	Hyaline cartilage	Chondrocytes	Relatively high content of hydroxylysine and glycosylated hydroxylysine
III	Skin, arteries, and uterus	Fibroblasts Smooth muscle	High content of hydroxyproline and low hydroxylysine; contains interchain disulfide bonds
IV	Basement membranes	Epithelial cells	High content of hydroxyproline and glycosylated hydroxylysine; may contain large globular regions
A chain, B chain	Basement membranes	Uncertain	Similar to $[\text{alpha(IV)}]_3$ but may contain larger globular domains

From Prockop DJ: Collagen biochemistry and the design of agents to inhibit excessive accumulation of collagen during wound repair. *In* Dineen P, Hildrick-Smith G (eds): The Surgical Wound. Philadelphia, Lea and Febiger, 1981, p 97; with permission.

New collagen can be found in healing wounds as early as the second day. The peak rate of synthesis in a primary healing wound appears to occur about the fifth to seventh day. The early collagen is highly disorganized and exists as a gel. The collagen synthesized in the surface of the wound that is "granulating in" by secondary intention also exists as a gel.

During the healing process, there is a fine balance between collagen synthesis (deposition) and lysis (degradation). Collagen degradation is mediated by the enzyme collagenase, which is secreted by numerous cells, such as macrophages and epithelial cells. In the normal unwounded dermis, collagen synthesis and degradation occur in equilibrium. After wounding, however, the rates of both collagen synthesis and degradation rise and fall in an ordered, sequential fashion,[83,97,98] so that enough collagen is synthesized, cross-linked, deposited, and removed to provide wound strength and integrity without excessive scarring.

Ground Substance

The ground substance is composed mainly of proteoglycans and fibronectin. The connective tissue proteoglycans were known several years ago as acid mucopolysaccharides, while during the 1960s they were referred to as glycosaminoglycans. At present, the protein polysaccharide complexes are referred to as proteoglycans because they are predominantly carbohydrate in nature. The main glycosaminoglycans found in tissue are hyaluronic acid, chondroitin-4-sulfate, chondroitin-6-sulfate, dermatan sulfate, keratan sulfate, and heparin and heparan sulfate[99] (Table 2–9).

It is generally accepted that synthesis of proteoglycans does not occur until significant amounts of collagen have been laid down,[100,101] since fibroblasts are responsible for their synthesis. It is thought that proteoglycans are responsible for the stabilization of extracellular collagen fibrils and the maturation of collagen.[100,102–104] The stabilization and maturation of collagen allow combination with fibronectin in the processes of cell-to-cell and cell-matrix adhesion.[105] Investigators have shown that hyaluronic acid is present initially in high concentrations but decreases after the fifth day, whereas the concentrations of chondroitin-4-sulfate and dermatan sulfate increase after the fifth day.[7]

TABLE 2–9.   GLYCOSAMINOGLYCAN COMPOSITION

	REPEATING DISACCHARIDE	LOCATION
Hyaluronic acid	Glucuronic acid (beta 1-3) glucosamine	Embryonic tissues, synovial fluid, vitreous humor, umbilical cord, cartilage, early healing tissue (inflammatory phases)
Chondroitin-4-sulfate, chondroitin-6-sulfate	Glucuronic acid (beta 1-3) galactosamine-4-SO$_4$	Cartilage, skin, cornea, blood vessel wall, nucleus pulposus, later healing (associated with collagen synthesis)
Dermatan sulfate	Iduronic acid (beta 1-3) galactosamine-4-SO$_4$[a]	Skin, blood vessels, heart valves, umbilical cord, scar
Keratan sulfate	Galactose (beta 1-4) glucosamine-6-SO$_4$	Cornea, cartilage, nucleus pulposus
Heparin, heparan sulfate	Glucuronic acid-2-SO$_4$ (1-4) (1-4) glucosamine-2-SO$_4$ and -6-SO$_4$[b]	Many tissues in mast cells (heparin), universal cell surface component (heparan sulfate)

[a] Also contains glucuronic acid; some of the iduronates are 2-sulfated.
[b] Much variation in degree of sulfation; contains alpha- and beta-links and some iduronate.
From Bentley JP: Proteoglycans of the connective tissue ground substance. In Hunt TK (ed): Wound Healing and Wound Infection: Theory and Surgical Practice. New York, Appleton-Century-Crofts, 1980, p 47; with permission.

It has been shown that enhancement of cell attachment by collagen takes place via a mediator in the ground substance, fibronectin.[106] Fibronectin is a large glycoprotein containing two similar or identical polypeptide chains that are linked by disulfide bonds at one end of the molecule. The interaction of fibronectin with collagen is highly specific and occurs at a single region of the collagen molecule.[107] The interaction of fibronectin with collagen and cells most likely also involves the glycosaminoglycans, heparan sulfate, and hyaluronic acid, because of their documented ability to enhance binding of fibronectin to collagen.[108-111]

It is thought that fibronectin might participate in wound repair because of its ability to bind to fibrinogen and its presence in the fibrin clot as a result of this binding.[112] In the initial response to a wound, fibronectin could join collagen and fibrin in the damaged area because it binds to both of these macromolecules.[113]

Other vital roles for fibronectin in wound repair may occur in the earlier stages. The aggregation of platelets requires fibronectin to interact with collagen,[114,115] and fibronectin is required for optimal phagocytic activity by macrophages.[112,116] In addition, fibronectin has been shown to play an important role in the migration of fibroblasts along a collagen substrate and to have chemotactic properties for fibroblasts.[111,117,118]

Thus, it appears that fibronectin at the site of injury could independently, or in conjunction with collagen, have multiple functions in repair. These functions include promoting platelet aggregation, stabilizing the fibrin clot, attracting new cells for repair, promoting adherence of cells in the tissue, and stimulating cells to produce a matrix used in repair.[111,119]

Tensile Strength

It is during this phase of collagen deposition that the tensile strength of the wound increases the most rapidly. Tensile strength is defined as the load per cross-sectional area that can be supported by the wound.[120] Tensile strength increases at a rate proportional to the rate of collagen synthesis. As a sufficient quantity of collagen is produced, the number of fibroblasts in the wound diminishes. The disappearance of fibroblasts marks the end of phase II of wound repair and the beginning of the maturation phase of wound healing.

Phase III: Wound Maturation

The scar that is formed in phase II of wound repair is an enlarged, dense structure of collagen. The collagen fibers are randomly oriented and highly soluble, resulting in a fragile tissue union. During the maturation phase of wound healing, pronounced changes in the form, bulk, and strength of the scar occur. Microscopically, the architecture of the collagen fibers changes from a random to a more organized pattern. The strength of the wound continues to increase despite the disappearance of fibroblasts from the wound and the resulting reduction in production of collagen. The magnitude of the loss of the size of the collagenous mass depends on several factors, such as the presence of the original noxious agents, the effect of physical factors (tension, pressure), the oxygen supply to the wound, and the patient's age.[121] Remodeling is a spontaneous process that will continue to occur for years after the initial tissue injury. Collagen turnover plays an intricate role in the remodeling process, in which there is an interplay between collagen deposition and degradation. If the rate of breakdown exceeds that of production, the scar becomes softer and less bulky. If, on the other hand, the rate of production exceeds that of breakdown, a keloid or hypertrophic scar may result. The progressive strengthening of the wound and the progressive insolubility of collagen appear to be results of both intramolecular cross-linking of the chains of the tropocollagen molecule and intermolecular cross-linking between collagen fibrils, filaments, and fibers. The resulting scar is usually never as strong as the tissue it replaces.

Once the scar matures, the collagen polymerizes and the scar increases in density as a result of a decrease in fluid and volume. This process results in tissue shrinkage and compromise on tissue function and corresponds to the phenomenon of wound contracture, which takes place in the later stages of wound healing.[121] Contracture is quite different from what occurs early on in wound repair, wound contraction. Wound contraction is the movement of full-thickness skin toward the center of the skin defect. It is an active process by which a wound shrinks by drawing in surrounding skin. Contraction of wound margins toward the center of the defect appears to be an active process that is secondary to fibroblastic movement into the wound bed. The cells responsible for wound contraction have been shown to contain within their cytoplasm a contractile protein similar to that found in smooth muscle and have been appropriately referred to as "myofibroblasts."[122,123] Evidence seems to indicate that these contractile myofibroblasts are derived from tissue fibroblasts rather than smooth muscle cells.[124]

BONE

Bone is a unique structure with several specific functions. It is the major reservoir of calcium in the body and serves to support the human frame.[125] It also acts as an anchor for the origin and insertion of the surrounding musculature and protects vital soft tissue structures. The skeleton plays an important role in locomotion. In spite of its vital role in providing body support and strength, it is light, constituting only one tenth of body weight. Bone is extremely strong, with a breaking strength comparable to medium steel, and yet it has flexible and elastic structure. Bone may be bent or twisted and will still return to its former shape following removal of the deforming force, provided the force has not exceeded the limits of elasticity. Although it is able to resist axial stresses, bone is limited in its ability to resist rotational forces.[126] Bone and the liver are the only organs capable of undergoing spontaneous regeneration with restoration of lost structure.

Bone Structure

Bones are divided into two major structural types: tubular and flat. Tubular bone functions to provide normal weight bearing and locomotion. Flat bone, such as the skull, serves to protect vital soft tissue structures. Anatomically, tubular bones consist of the diaphysis (the central portion) and the epiphysis (ends of the bone), or the secondary ossification center. At the junction of the diaphysis and epiphysis is a major growth area, the epiphyseal plate. This is the area in which normal longitudinal growth occurs. Flat bone has no epiphyseal plate.

Bone is surrounded by a fibrous sheet called the periosteum. This sheet is subdivided into an outer fibrous layer and an inner layer called the cambium, which is a source of new bone cells. The periosteum appears to have its greatest osteogenic potential in children. This potential may be important in fracture healing, since nonunion is rare in children.

The inner portion of bone, the marrow cavity, is lined with a fibrous sheet called the endosteum. The haversian system, or osteon, is the functioning unit in mature bone and is composed of a central haversian canal surrounded by concentric layers of bone. The surrounding lamellae have lacunae, each containing an osteocyte with a cytoplasmic process extending through canaliculi to communicate with the haversian vessels or other canaliculi. The size of the osteon is limited by the fact that the haversian canal supplies nutrition, and bone cells in general cannot survive farther than 0.1 mm away from a capillary.[127]

Bone Formation

Bone is generated by two separate mechanisms: endochondral and membranous bone formation. Endochondral bone formation occurs at the epiphyseal plates in long bones and the condylar head of the mandible and accounts for growth in length. It requires the laying down of a preformed cartilage model. The cartilage is gradually resorbed and replaced by bone. This sequence of events also occurs in the healing of bone fractures. Growth in width occurs by appositional bone formation.

Membranous bone formation does not involve a cartilaginous stage. Mesenchymal cells differentiate into osteoblasts, which lay down osteoid, which is then mineralized to form bone. This type of bone formation occurs in the calvarium, most facial bones, the clavicle, the mandible, and subperiosteal bone. The type of bone formation has a direct bearing on the repair of a particular bone; that is, the skull heals by fibrous union and not with new bone formation.

Bone Composition

Typical lamellar bone composition is approximately 8 per cent water and 92 per cent solid material. The solid material is divided into 21 percent organic phase and 71 per cent inorganic phase.

Organic Constituents

The organic material, or matrix, supplies form to bone and supporting structure for the deposition and crystallization of inorganic salts. The matrix is more than 90 per cent collagen, with the remainder being proteoglycans. Bone collagen is type I and consists of two $alpha_1$ chains and one $alpha_3$ chain. This type of collagen is similar to that found in skin and tendon.[96] One sees a persistence of type II collagen (cartilage) into the later stages of bony union in the normal healing of fractures. This observation adds credence to the thought that normal fracture healing takes place by endochondral bone formation within the callus. If compression plating is employed in the fixation of fractures, minimal callus forms and primarily type I collagen is seen.

Inorganic Constituents

The principal inorganic salt is crystalline hydroxyapatite, $Ca_{10}(PO_4)_6(OH)_2$. The mineral crystals are extremely small, being 25 to 75 nm in diameter and approximately 200 nm long. This feature provides a very large surface-to-volume ratio. There is a shell of water surrounding the surface crystals (hydration shell), and ions may move freely between the hydration shell and the crystalline surface. It has been shown that bone crystals align in a specific pattern within the collagen.[128] The long axis of the crystal is parallel to the longitudinal axis of the fiber, in a band pattern within the collagen fibril. This arrangement occurs within the "hole" zone of the collagen fiber, which increases the surface area of the fiber. As a result, the skeleton of a 150-pound man contains enough hydroxyapatite to cover approximately 100 acres.

Cellular Components

There are three principal bone cells identified during formation and remodeling. They are the osteoblast, osteocyte, and osteoclast.

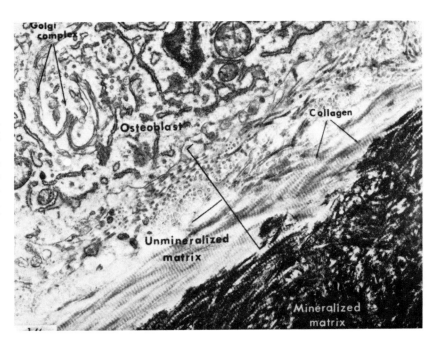

FIGURE 2-7. Osteoblast engaged in synthesis. The cytoplasm is indicative of a cell actively involved in the export of proteins. An elaborate Golgi complex and rough endoplasmic reticulum are evident. The unmineralized front containing collagen fibrils is adjacent to the mineralized matrix, which is the site of release of the internally produced matrix.

OSTEOBLASTS

Osteoblasts are the cells that are responsible for bone matrix synthesis and are evident during growth, remodeling, and repair processes.[129-131] They may be derived from the cells of the inner surface of the periosteum, the cambium layer, or from differentiation of osteoprogenitor cells in the adjacent mesenchymal tissue.[132-134] Osteoblasts do not have the capability to divide and function; they can only form bone. They range in size from 15 to 20 μm and, when active, have the characteristic features, microscopically, of cells actively involved in protein synthesis: rough endoplasmic reticulum and prominent Golgi apparatus[132] (Fig. 2-7).

OSTEOCYTES

Osteocytes, presumably derived from osteoblasts, are found buried deep within mineralized bone matrix and are connected with one another and with osteoblasts on the bone surface by extensive projections or canaliculi.[130] Osteocytes are flat and oval on cross section and range from 20 to 60 μm in their longest dimension. These cells are thought to play an active process in the nutrition of bone by transfer of oxygen and metabolites (calcium), via their extensive canalicular system, to the blood (Fig. 2-8A and B).

OSTEOCLASTS

Osteoclasts are a heterogeneous group of multinuclear cells (2 to 100 nuclei) with common properties.[135-137] They are generally larger than the other bone cells, ranging in diameter from 20 to 100 μm. Osteoclasts are found where bone is resorbed and are laden with lysosomal enzymes, such as acid phosphatase and cathepsin.[138,139] When these cells are in contact with the bone surface, their membranes form numerous processes (ruffled borders) that appear to penetrate the bone surface (Fig. 2-9). The role of osteoclasts in the resorptive processes has been demonstrated both by in vitro studies[135,136,140] and in investigations of bone diseases such as osteopetrosis, in which osteoclast function is abnormal.[141] Osteoclasts are thought to be derived from one of three possible origins: (1) from an osteoprogenitor stem cell differentiating into osteocytes, osteoblasts, and osteoclasts; (2) from the mononuclear phagocyte system; and (3) from an unidentified circulating mononuclear cell (the preosteoclast).[135,137,139,142-144]

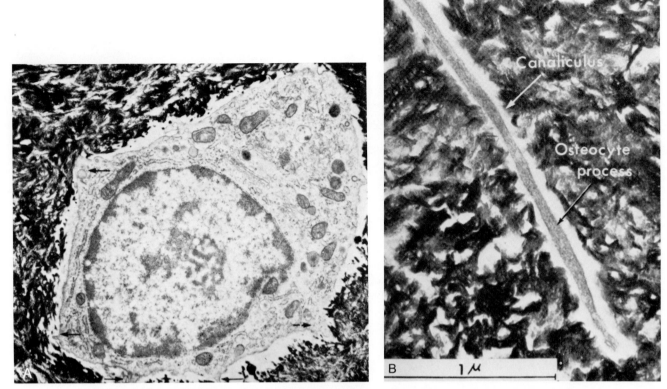

FIGURE 2–8. *A,* Photomicrograph of an osteocyte with its cytoplasmic processes visible on the periphery *(arrows). B,* Longitudinal section of cytoplasmic process of osteocyte in *A.* It is through this extensive canalicular system that osteocytes are able to transfer oxygen and metabolites (i.e., calcium) from blood to nourish the surrounding bone.

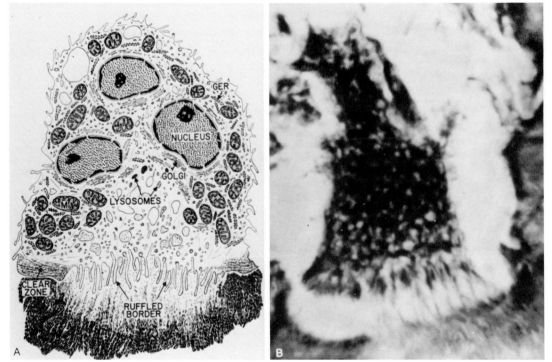

FIGURE 2–9. *A,* Pictorial representation of an osteoclast. Osteoclasts are relatively large multinucleated cells. Their cytoplasm is laden with lysosomal enzymes, a well-developed Golgi process, mitochondria (M), and rough endoplasmic reticulum (GER). The active process of bone resorption occurs at the convoluted membrane of the osteoclast (ruffled border). *B,* Photomicrograph of an osteoclast with a prominent ruffled border.

Biophysical Properties

The osseous structures of the face and cranium consist of a dense outer portion of compact bone, the cortex, and a meshlike inner portion of cancellous (trabecular) bone, the medulla. The cortex provides most of the strength and rigidity to bone, but the underlying cancellous bone is arranged along the lines of stress. Cortical bone is stiffer than cancellous bone; it can withstand greater stress but less strain before failure. Stress can be defined as the load per unit area that develops on a plane surface within a structure in response to an externally applied load. Strain is defined as the deformation that is seen at a point in the structure under load.[145]

Stress can be applied in several ways: tension (stretching), compression (shortening), torsion (twisting), shear (sliding), or bending (compression and tension)[146] (Fig. 2–10). The contraction of muscles attached to the loaded bone alters the distribution of stress placed on the bone. The result is a decrease in or elimination of the tensile stress by production of counter-compressive strength from the muscle contraction.[145] When bone fractures under a traumatic blow, the fracture is seen to occur on the surface that is under the most tension.[146]

The energy storage capacity of bone varies with the speed at which it is loaded. The higher the speed of loading, that is, the greater the force of the traumatic blow, the more energy the bone stores prior to fracture. The speed of loading is clinically significant because it influences both the pattern of fracture and the amount of soft tissue damage. When a bone fractures, the stored energy is released. At a low loading speed, the energy can be dissipated through the formation of a single fracture line, resulting in little displacement of the soft tissue and remaining intact bone. At a high loading speed, the energy does not dissipate rapidly enough through a single break; thus, it is more likely to cause a comminuted fracture with extensive soft tissue damage[145] (Fig. 2–11).

Fracture Healing

When sufficient traumatic injury is generated so that the inherent strength of bone is overcome, a fracture occurs. Unlike other tissues, which often respond to injury by the formation of a scar, bone has the capacity to heal itself through actual regeneration. This physical property is necessary, as it allows the injured bony struc-

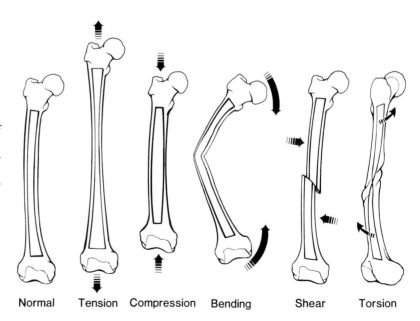

FIGURE 2–10. Schematic representation of various loading models (stress) seen on bone. (Modified from Nordin M, Frankel VH: Biomechanics of Whole Bone and Bone Tissue. Philadelphia, Lea and Febiger, 1980, pp 15–60.)

Normal   Tension   Compression   Bending   Shear   Torsion

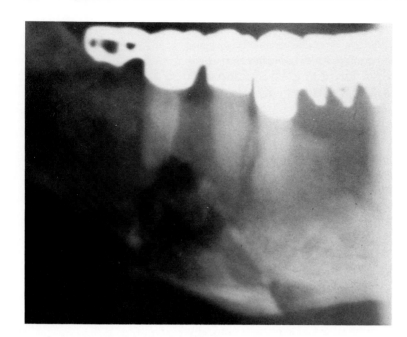

FIGURE 2–11. Radiograph of a comminuted mandibular body fracture that resulted from a high loading force. The force was dissipated at the point of impact, resulting in the comminution. This patient suffered no other mandibular fractures.

ture to regain its preinjury strength and function. Repair is, in many ways, only a continuation of the physiologic process of remodeling and functional adaptation.

Sequence of Fracture Healing

In general, fracture results in a well-defined progression of tissue responses that are designed to remove tissue debris, to re-establish vascular supply, and to produce a new skeletal matrix. The timing and the specific histology of the processes that occur to accomplish healing are dependent on the location of the injured bone as well as on local and systemic factors.

Like soft tissue, bone can heal by primary or secondary intention. Spontaneous bone healing without surgical intervention and healing that occurs after semirigid fixation progress by secondary intention. Healing by primary intention occurs only when the following conditions are met: excellent anatomic reduction, no or minimal mobility, and good vascular supply at the fracture site.

Although similar terminology is also applied to soft tissue wounds, an analogy between the two should be avoided. In soft tissue injury, healing by secondary intention involves the filling of a gap by granulation tissue, with subsequent replacement by a scar, which is less functional. Secondary bone healing is so termed because initially an intermediate fibrous tissue is formed within the fracture gap and is only subsequently replaced by bone, as opposed to primary bone healing, in which no intermediate fibrous tissue is formed. However, unlike the scar formed by secondary intention healing in soft tissue wounds, bones that have healed by secondary intention continue on through adaptation and remodeling toward a form and function similar to what was present prior to injury. Figure 2–12 is an overview representation of the different aspects of primary and secondary bone repair that will be discussed in the following sections.

SECONDARY BONE REPAIR

Fractures undergoing spontaneous healing, as well as those treated by a majority of the currently used treatment modalities, undergo secondary bone healing. Secondary bone healing involves a well-defined sequence of steps: (1) initial stage, (2) cartilaginous callus, (3) bony callus, and (4) remodeling. During the initial stage, hematoma formation occurs, concurrent with an inflammatory response, which brings new vascularity and mesenchymal cells that differentiate to form a fibrocartilaginous callus. This fibrocartilage then ossifies to form the bony callus, which subsequently undergoes remodeling and functional adaptation in much the same way as the preinjured bone.

Initial Reaction.   The disruption of blood vessels and subsequent decrease in blood supply, accompanied by the generation of heat from the energy necessary to induce fractures, lead to hypoxia and cellular death at the fracture site.[147] This situation produces necrosis at the bone ends of the fracture for a variable distance.[148] This aseptic necrosis leads to inflammation and edema. The inflammatory response induces the release of numerous vasoactive angiogenic pyrogens, which produce vasodilatation within a few hours of injury.[149]

Hemorrhage from the dilated, damaged vessels of the endosteum, periosteum, and haversian system leads to hematoma formation.[150] A great deal of emphasis has been placed on the importance of the hematoma in healing. The clot is invaded by a variety of blood-borne elements, which could contribute to healing. However, experimental fracture healing has not been impaired when the clot is removed by aspiration.[151] In addition to granulation tissue within the hematoma, there may exist fragments of bone and muscle. The small, nonvital muscle will undergo autolysis within 5 to 10 days, while pedicled, vascularized muscle undergoes fibrosis and does not interfere with healing unless it is found between the ends of the fractured bone.[150] Small bone fragments may undergo surface deposition of bone by migrating periosteal cells, while associated devitalized marrow undergoes fatty degeneration.

Somewhat overlapping this inflammatory hematoma formation is the initiation of cellular proliferation. Within 8 to 12 hours, DNA synthesis and proliferation by the cells of the cambium layer of periosteum begin.[152] This process initially involves the periosteum of the entire injured bone but decreases over a few days to remain only in the area of the fracture. The basic work of Urist[153] and others[154] has established that these cells are pluripotential and give rise to osteoblasts, fibroblasts, and cells with chondrogenic potential.

As these cells start to proliferate, capillary ingrowth begins. The fibroblasts formed during the proliferative stage migrate into the wound and begin to lay down collagen. This combination of collagen and a rich capillary network forms granulation tissue. In this stage, a low oxygen tension as well as a low pH is noted in the early granulation tissue.[155] It is thought that these conditions of lower pH and tissue oxygen tension trigger a response within the hematoma toward the formation of hyaline cartilage.[150,156,157]

In addition to decreased oxygen tension and decreased pH, it is thought that the movement that occurs when bone fragment are not immobilized with rigid internal fixation causes continued compression and tension at the site of the fracture and also directs cells toward the formation of cartilage.

Cartilaginous Callus (Soft Callus) Formation (Fig. 2–12A).   Callus formation begins externally as well as internally. Externally, nodules of cartilage are separated by fibrous septa.[151] As the blood vessels within the septa increase, the tendency toward hypoxemia is reversed, and two changes occur simultaneously: (1) Further calcification of the cartilage takes place, trapping chondroblasts and converting them to chondrocytes; and (2) osteoblasts increase in number, and osteoclasts become apparent for the first time.[151]

While this external callus is forming, an internal callus between the bone ends also forms. This area has a better blood supply and therefore less necrosis. No intermediate fibrocartilage is formed; instead, osteoblasts from the endosteum form an internal bony callus directly.[158,159]

When bone begins to heal after fracture, a cuff or callus forms around the fracture site to stabilize the involved area. The callus significantly increases the area of

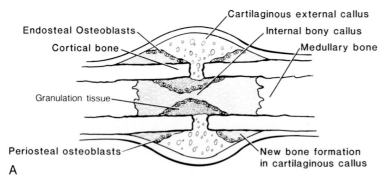

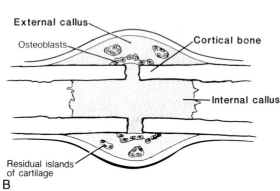

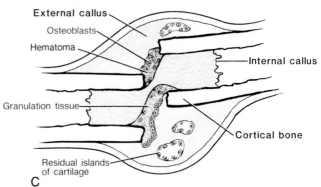

FIGURE 2–12. *A,* Late cartilaginous callus stage. The internal bony callus has bridged the defect with direct bone formation by endosteal osteoblasts. Peripherally, the cartilaginous callus has formed and is undergoing ossification. *B,* Bony callus stage. The internal bony callus is complete. Ossification of the cartilaginous callus has left small islands of residual cartilage. *C,* Bony callus stage. Fracture with significant displacement illustrating adaptation of the callus.

inertia, thereby increasing the strength and stiffness of the bone, especially resistance against bending and torsion, during the healing period.[126]

Hard Callus (Bony Callus) Formation (Fig. 2–12*B* and *C*). In a fashion similar to the endochondral formation of bone that occurs during growth and development, the cartilaginous callus undergoes calcification into woven bone. The spaces within the cartilaginous callus allow for further vascular ingrowth, which brings with it a change in the environment. This increase in oxygen tension, aided by the transportation of nutrients to the site via the above-mentioned vasculature, is conducive to the formation of osteoblasts. Ham and Harris[160] believed that these osteoblasts pre-existed at the fracture site and that there was some stimulus to cause them to begin activity. McLean and Urist[161] believed that the cells were derived from connective tissue precursors. Probably both factors contribute somewhat,[162] as abundant osteoblasts are present within the endosteum, while numerous precursors are available within the tissue surrounding the wound. It is well known that these precursor cells can be induced into bone-forming cells both in vivo and in vitro.[163]

The osteoblasts deposit osteoid on the spicules of calcified cartilage, and the osteoid then undergoes a calcification process, forming bone. The process begins peripherally and has been shown by Lane[164] to progress as a homogeneous calcification of the cartilaginous callus (Fig. 2–12*A*).

Initially, the bone that is formed is randomly arranged (woven bone) and then undergoes organization and change to lamellar bone during the final stage of healing, which is the remodeling stage.

Remodeling. The newly formed woven bone, which is somewhat random in organization, undergoes remodeling into the more familiar pattern of lamellar bone. This is a slow process that progresses in accordance with Wolff's law, which states that a change in the functional state of bone causes structural or architectural changes in the tissue through bioelectric field production.

As osteoclasts participate in remodeling by resorption of bone, factors are released that help to drive and direct the remodeling process further. Bone morphogenetic protein (BMP), a collagenase-resistant glycoprotein isolated by Urist,[165] is one of these factors. BMP acts as a mitogenic and transforming growth factor, inducing differentiation of mesenchymal cells toward bone formation.[150]

The preceding overview applies to fractures for which fixation is such that movement can occur at the fracture site. Two other situations exist. The first of these is that of linear fractures of flat bones of the skull as well as some facial bones. In this case, there is, at best, limited movement, and the surrounding tissue is very vascular. Periosteal osteoprogenitor cells differentiate into osteoblasts, and bone is laid down directly without a cartilaginous phase.[150,151] The second condition is that which exists when rigid internal fixation is used, so that the effective strain that normally induces callus formation is negated and nearly perfect anatomic reduction is achieved. In this instance, healing occurs primarily.

PRIMARY BONE HEALING

Primary bone healing occurs when enough rigidity and anatomic reduction exist to preclude the need for mechanical stability afforded by a callus.

Primary healing probably occurs in cancellous bone even without this rigid mechanical stabilization if there is no gross mobility (W.J.W. Sharrard, personal observation, 1984). Osteogenic cells and capillaries proliferate in the medullary bone on both sides of the fracture, forming new bone along the fracture site.

In cortical bone, union without callus formation was reported as early as 1949,[166,167] when it was observed that radiographs of long bone fractures that had been plated failed to show callus formation. Schenk and Willenegger[168] were the first to observe the histologic features of primary bone healing.

The healing that occurs in cortical bone fractures in which rigid fixation has been accomplished occurs in two different ways: (1) gap healing and (2) contact healing. Some authors have classified contact healing as primary bone healing and have placed gap healing in a separate category.[158,169] Others consider both gap and contact healing to be variations of primary bone healing.[127] For the purpose of this discussion, they will both be considered variations of primary healing, as they share a requirement for rigid fixation and produce a healed fracture without intermediate cartilaginous callus formation.

Gap Healing. Even with rigid fixation by means of a device that produces a stable relationship between the fracture ends under the deforming forces produced by muscle pull and function, a perfect anatomic reduction seldom exists. In some areas of the fracture, small gaps occur between the bone segments, and within a few days after fracture, gap healing begins at these points[127] (Fig. 2–13). Blood vessels from the periosteum, endosteum, or haversian canals invade the gaps, bringing mesenchymal osteoblastic precursors. Bone is deposited directly on the surfaces of the fracture fragments without resorption and without intermediate cartilage formation. If the gaps are less than 0.3 mm, lamellar bone forms directly.[127] Gaps from 0.3 mm up to a critical value, 0.5 to 1.0 mm, fill with woven bone, and lamellar bone is subsequently laid down within the trabecular spaces.[170]

FIGURE 2–13.   Gap healing has occurred opposite to the compression plate, with direct bone deposition between the cortical ends. Contact healing is taking place within the cortical bone in the area of compression. The osteoclastic cutting cones have produced cores into which osteoblasts lay down new bone (*inset*).

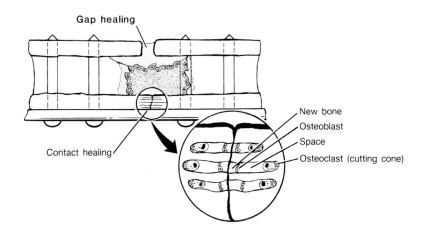

The formation of lamellar bone occurs over 6 weeks. At the end of this time, the lamellar bundles are oriented at right angles to the longitudinal axis of the remaining bone.[158] Fractures repaired by gap healing have been shown to be considerably stronger than similar fractures healed by secondary repair in the same time, despite the often large quantity of periosteal bone present within the bony callus of secondarily healing bone.[158]

Over several months, remodeling then leads to a change in the direction of the bundles to reorient them along the long axis of the repaired bone.[158] This reorientation is coincidental temporally with a return to full strength of the injured bone.

Contact Healing.   In areas in which contact is achieved, the interfragmentary gap is essentially zero. As vascular and cellular ingrowth cannot proceed as it does in fractures in which a gap exists, a special process of bone formation occurs. This has been termed "contact healing."

Contact healing occurs through the formation of a bone metabolizing unit (BMU),[171] a bone remodeling unit (BRU),[172] or a bone repair unit (BRU),[173] all synonyms for the newly forming (or regenerating) osteon. Histologically, the BRU (BMU) is an advancing group of osteoclasts followed by vessels and cells, which differentiate into osteoblasts and form new bone.

Osteoclasts begin to cut away cores on either side of the fracture, progressing toward the fracture site, through necrotic bone and into the opposing bone end (Fig. 2–13). The osteoclastic cutting cone proceeds at a rate of 50 to 80 μm/day.[174] The resultant core, which is 200 μm in diameter, provides a pathway for vessel ingrowth and osteoblastic proliferation, with formation of new bone. This process has been likened to a "pegging together" of the fracture ends by newly formed bone. The osteon forms at a rate of 1 to 2 μm/day.[151] This lag between resorption and osteon ingrowth produces a transient porosity in the compact bone visible radiographically up to 3 months after fracture in humans,[127] with complete reconstruction of the cortex requiring up to 6 months.[127] During this period, the fixation device must maintain the stability of the fractured segments.

In summary, primary healing in cortical bone occurs in two different ways: gap healing and contact healing. Gap healing begins almost immediately in areas where a space of up to 1 mm exists between the fractured ends. Gaps are filled by appositional bone formation, with the pattern dependent on the dimension of the space being filled. Remodeling then restores the normal preinjury architecture, with formation of longitudinally oriented lamellar bone with viable haversian systems. In areas of contact healing, consolidation is achieved through haversian remodeling alone. Osteoclasts produce pathways between fracture fragments, which are then bridged by newly formed regenerating osteons. In both of these cases, but particularly in that of contact healing, haversian remodeling must occur prior to achieving adequate bone strength. The existence of an initial lag phase and the inherent slower growth of the osteon, when compared with the speed of bone resorption by the osteoclasts, make it necessary for the fixation mechanism to provide stability for a longer period than in other forms of healing.

Factors Affecting Bone Healing

The regulation of bone repair is a complex process that requires interplay between hormones and systemic and local growth factors. The proliferative response of osteoprogenitor cells in the periosteum, endosteum, and marrow, as well as the production of the cartilaginous-fibrocartilaginous matrices and fibro-osseous callus, can be conceptualized as the result of cell-cell interactions (inflammatory reaction— hematoma and callus formation stages) and cell-matrix interactions (remodeling phase).[150]

Inflammatory Reaction — Hematoma Stage (0 to 5 Days After Fracture)

The inflammatory reaction involves polymorphonuclear leukocytes, lymphocytes, migrating macrophages, and monocytes that fuse to form resident macrophages in the hematoma. Rifas and others have isolated a macrophage-derived growth factor (MDGF) that is mitogenic for rat osteoblast-like cells and chondrocytes.[175] The hematoma also contains platelets, which produce platelet-derived growth factor (PDGF), which is mitogenic for fibroblasts.[176] PDGF release from human platelets is stimulated by the arachidonic acid precursor for prostaglandins.[177]

Callus Formation Stage (4 to 40 Days After Fracture)

Periosteal and endosteal mesenchymal cells begin to differentiate and form the fibrocartilaginous callus. The chondroblasts produce a cartilage growth factor (CGF-1).[178,180] There is additional evidence that after a critical cell density is reached, a second chondrogenic growth factor (CGF-2) is produced and is in turn important in the production of the cartilage-specific type II collagen and hyaluronic acid.[180] It has been shown that the production of hyaluronic acid at this point in bone healing may be instrumental in terminating the intense phase of cell proliferation.[181] The osteoprogenitor cells, which differentiate to form osteoblasts (endosteum and marrow), can also produce one or more mitogenic growth factors. Three autologous bone growth factors (BGFs) have been successfully isolated from rat calvarial osteoblast cultures.[182–185]

Bone growth factors are seen to be most important at the stages of intramembranous and endochondral ossification. Other factors implicated in mitogenesis and tissue differentiation are involved in the earlier stages of resorption of the hematoma and in the degradation of devitalized skeletal tissues.[150] Macrophages, fibroblasts, and osteoblasts can produce the enzyme collagenase, which can degrade the fibrin and collagen of the hematoma.[186–188] The macrophages and osteoclasts can act to remove or resorb devitalized bone at the fracture site. Monocytes can interact directly with T lymphocytes to produce a lymphokine, osteoclast-activating factor (OAF), which stimulates the development of the osteoclast's resorptive ultrastructure and its specialized function.[189,190]

Remodeling Phase (25 to 50 Days After Fracture)

The remodeling phase requires cell-matrix interactions, in contrast to the previous stages, which involve cellular mechanisms to remove devitalized bone until the fracture is healed.

Resorption liberates a collagenase-resistant glycoprotein moiety, BMP, that has been well described by Urist.[165,191,192] BMP is believed to be responsible for the osteoconductive properties of demineralized bone matrix. When implanted subcutaneously in experimental animals, BMP or BMP-enriched substrates cause a mitotic invasion of cells that eventually form bone in extraskeletal tissues. The proposed steps involved in this process are chemotaxis of progenitor cells and proliferation of mesenchymal cells and their differentiation into chondrocytes, followed by calcification of the cartilage matrix, vascular invasion, and bone differentiation.

There are numerous other polypeptide growth factors that play an intricate role in the repair of bone fractures (Table 2–10).[150] With the advent of the understanding of cell-cell and cell-matrix interactions, one can now begin to differentiate between the two arguments in the orthopedic literature concerning the healing of bone — namely, creeping substitution versus osteoconduction.

The term *creeping substitution* is a histologic definition. It refers to the observed ingrowth of new vessels, to the subsequent appearance of the first resorptive osteo-

I.	Vascular ingrowth	Plasma fibronectin 　Anchors cells in the ground substance 　Required for collagen formation Endothelial cell–derived growth factor 　Mitogen
II.	Callus formation	Platelet-derived growth factor 　Mitogenic: Fibroblasts, bone cells 　Activates monocytes 　Promotes bone resorption Epidermal cell growth factor 　Mitogen: Cartilage, bone 　Inhibits type I bone collagen synthesis Fibroblast growth factor 　Mitogen: fibroblasts, chondrocytes Insulin-like growth factor 　Chondrocyte proliferation 　Chondrocyte proteoglycan synthesis Nerve growth factor 　Mitogen
III.	Bone formation/ remodeling phase	Epidermal growth factor 　Promotes bone resorption Fibroblast growth factor 　Promotes bone resorption in high doses Insulin 　Synergistic effect with bone growth factors Interleukins (monocyte products) 　IL-1: Fibroblast proliferation 　　　Collagenase production 　　　Prostaglandin production 　IL-2: T-cell growth factor 　　　Stimulation of bone resorption by 　　　　osteoclastic activation factor (OAF) 　　　　production

From Simmons DJ: Fracture healing perspectives. Clin Orthop Rel Res 200:100, 1985; with permission.

clasts, and to the generation of osteoblasts from perivascular connective tissue cells. The presence of serum and autocrine mitogenic factors and the effects of tissue-specific differentiating factors, that is, CGF-1 and CGF-2, at each of the different histologic stages of fracture healing are all elements of the process known as creeping substitution.

Osteoconduction, in contrast, defines the mechanism that effects cellular *transformations* and thus is considered a process that is separate from creeping substitution even while it contains some elements in common. In this process, osteoconduction is accomplished by the diffusion of BMP glycoprotein from resorbing (demineralized) bone matrix, effecting the initial proliferation and differentiation of mesenchymal cells to chondroblasts.[193,194]

Nonunion of Fractures

Nonunion is a result of an impairment or delay in the natural healing process of bone. It implies a failure of the fracture hematoma to become transformed into an osteogenic matrix, so that it is ultimately converted into nonosteogenic fibrous tissue. Nonunion is considered a terminal condition of failed osteogenesis, which is identified by mobility of the bone ends in all planes after an interval of time (10 weeks) when injuries of a similar nature under comparable conditions would have resulted clinically in stabilization of the fragments, radiographic evidence of a progressive decrease in the radiolucency at the fracture site, and the presence of histologically identifiable osteogenic tissue.[195]

Nonunion is a result of one or several of the following etiologic factors that can initiate or propagate a delay in or lack of osseous union.

Inadequate Reduction

Inadequate reduction can result in marked distraction of the fractured margins of the bone. This distraction may result from excessive traction from insertion of muscles onto the fractures and displaced bone or may be secondary to interposition of soft tissue between the bone ends. It is thought that soft tissue interposition may block the formation of a fracture hematoma, preventing bridging between the bone ends.[196] In situations involving an excessive amount of distraction, the fracture hematoma may not be able to "bridge the gap," or the defect may persist because of soft tissue interposition.

Inadequate Fixation

Inadequate fixation can result in excessive motion at the fracture site, producing delayed union or nonunion. Motion can lead to the formation of an external callus and secondary bone healing rather than the primary type of healing seen with rigid fixation; if the motion is excessive, it may cause a disruption of the fragile capillaries that migrate into the fracture hematoma, resulting in a delay in or lack of maturation of the hematoma.

In contrast, fracture healing is enhanced by compressive forces, as seen with the use of rigid compression plates (discussed previously and in Chapter 33). Others have shown that limited, but not excessive, movement at the fracture site may also be beneficial. Goodship and Kenwright[197] observed stimulation of osteogenesis in intact bones exposed to intermittent deforming forces. Motion at the fracture ends, to some degree, is definitely advantageous from the standpoint of stimulation of the stabilizing callus. The callus tissue response is felt to be a function of bioelectric potentials that are generated within the bone and stimulate osteoblastic production and activity.[151]

Infection

An acute or chronic osteomyelitis at the fracture site can lead to delayed union or nonunion of the separated bone margins. The infection causes an alteration of the local pH at the fracture site, secondary to entering bacteria or to lysosomal enzymes from invading polymorphonuclear cells resulting from the host's inflammatory response or to both. The decrease in local pH, coupled with excessive mobility during the early phases of osteogenesis, influences the piezoelectric aspect of bone formation, in turn affecting the orientation of the fibroblasts migrating across the fracture line.[195] The investing sheath derived from the external layer of the periosteum and contiguous soft tissues no longer advances to act as a supporting scaffold and turns inward at the fracture line to form a fibroblastic barrier preventing bony union.

Vascularity

A decrease in local tissue vascularity may occur secondary to trauma, disease, or age. This decrease in vascularity results in a reduction of the oxygen tension at the site of fracture, which leads to differential survival of fibroblasts over more specialized cells, producing a fibrous union or nonunion. Bradley[198,199] has shown, histologically and radiographically, that with advancing years the blood supply to the mandible changes from a centrifugal to a centripetal force because of atherosclerotic changes that occur in the inferior alveolar artery. The principal source of blood supply to the mandible is then derived from periosteal vessels—thus the importance of avoiding excessive periosteal stripping in atrophic mandibles in the elderly.

Systemic Factors

Systemic factors that may predispose a fracture to nonunion include the following: deficiencies of vitamins C and D, with their respective effects on the collagen metabolism and mineralization process of bone; anemia, with its effect on tissue oxygenation; chronic ingestion of steroids, producing osteoporotic changes; aging, resulting not only in a compromise in vascularity but also in osteoporosis; and diabetes, with associated changes in vascularity.

Electrical Stimulation of Fracture Healing

Bone is a structurally dynamic tissue. It modulates its shape in response to changes in load and can heal itself spontaneously. Bone is also electrically dynamic. Steady voltages have been reported along intact and damaged bone, and short-lived voltages have been measured in response to loading.[200-202]

When bone is stressed with a bending force, the tension side of the bone develops an electropositive charge, whereas the compressed side becomes electronegative, causing a piezoelectric effect.[203] It has been shown that bone is primarily formed at the electronegative, concave, or compressed area of the developing callus. If active electrodes are inserted through the bony cortex, new bone is seen to form around the cathode and bone resorption takes place around the anode.[204]

It is thought that small electric currents provide a "trigger stimulus" or threshold that initiates a sequence of cellular events. These events involve the dedifferentiation or proliferation of uncommitted (stem) cells and their subsequent differentiation into an osteogenic cell line. This concept is supported by observations that direct currents (1) stimulate DNA synthesis in chick cartilage cells and in the calvaria of rat embryos, (2) increase the ultrastructural features of bone cells associated with collagen formation, (3) alter the morphologies of the cells at the light microscopic level, and (4) increase the accumulation of alkaline phosphatase on osteogenic cell surfaces. These effects are specific to bone cells, with evidence that fibroblasts and splenic lymphocytes do not respond.[205-207]

It is believed that living bone drives an electric current through itself and into sites of damage. Such *fracture currents* consist of two components: an intense, decaying current dependent on bone deformation and a stable, persistent current driven by a cellular battery. The latter is carried mainly by chloride ions. In polarity and magnitude, endogenous fracture currents closely resemble clinically applied currents that are successful in treating chronic nonunion in fractured bones, which suggests that the defect in biologic nonunions may reside in the electrophysiology of repair.[208]

CARTILAGE

Articulating joints are the functional connections between different bones of the skeleton. In synovial, or freely moving, joints, the articulating bone ends are covered with a dense white layer of connective tissue that is 1 to 5 mm thick—articular cartilage. Physiologically, articular cartilage is considered an isolated tissue in the sense that it is devoid of blood and lymphatic channels as well as free nerve endings. In addition, the cellular density of articular cartilage is less than that of most other tissues.

The main functions of articular cartilage are (1) to spread the loads applied to the joint so that they are transmitted over a large area to decrease contact stresses and (2) to allow relative movement of the opposing surfaces with minimal friction and wear.[209]

Articular cartilage is composed of a solid matrix that accounts for 20 to 40 per cent of its wet tissue weight, of which 60 per cent is collagen fibers, approximately 38 per cent is interfibrillar proteoglycan gel (which has a high affinity for water), and about 2 per cent is cells or chondrocytes.[210]

Articular cartilage has a limited capacity for repair and regeneration, and if the stresses to which it has been subjected are large, total failure can occur quite quickly. It is believed that progression of this failure is related to (1) the magnitude of the stresses experienced, (2) the total number of stress peaks experienced, and (3) the intrinsic molecular and microscopic structure of the collagen-proteoglycan matrix.[209]

The normal response of any tissue to trauma, as we have seen previously in this chapter, has three phases: necrosis, inflammation, and repair.[211] Cartilage undergoes the same phase of necrosis as seen in other tissues. The cells at the site of injury die, and the matrix is disrupted to varying degrees, depending on the extent of trauma. Less cell death is seen because of the insensitivity of chondrocytes to hypoxia. The entire second phase, inflammation, is absent, since it is mediated by the vascular system. No clot can form, since there is no release of blood from ruptured vessels. The absence of an inflammatory response or vascular phase, needed to recruit blood vessels and undifferentiated cells, limits severely the reparative phase in response to trauma. However, if the damage to the cartilage extends through the basal layers and into the subchondral bone, where vascularity exists, then all three phases of repair become possible.

Superficial Injury

Lacerative or superficial injuries in articular cartilage that do not penetrate below the calcified zone evoke only a short-lived metabolic and enzymatic response, which fails to provide sufficient numbers of cells or matrix to repair even minimal defects. In addition, these lesions remain unchanged for at least 2 years and do not progress either to chondromalacia or to an osteoarthritic type of degenerative process.[211–216]

Penetrating Injury

The response to a lesion of articular cartilage that extends deep to the tidemark between cartilage and osseous tissues is completely different and represents a situation that is seen clinically. Injury to the vascular subchondral bone elicits a repair response that is more characteristic of other vascularized tissues.[212,217,218] The defect in the articular cartilage fills with blood, which becomes organized into a fibrin clot that is invaded by capillaries to form granulation tissue. Bone that forms more deeply does extend toward the surface but does not pass beyond the old margin between calcified and osseous end plate. Mitchell and Shepard[219] demonstrated that early in the course of repair the defect of primary fibrous tissue is converted to a hyaline-like chondroid tissue with a higher concentration of proteoglycans. At 12 months after injury, the tissue appears more fibrous than cartilaginous, and the surface layers and cells are more typical of fibrocartilage than of hyaline cartilage. Convery and others[220] have shown that the nature of the repair is partly dependent on the size of the defect, those less than 3 mm showing complete repair but those greater than 9 mm never showing complete repair. In defects that are not too large, the cartilaginous material fills the defect and restores the surface continuity but may undergo degeneration, leading to a localized, nonprogressive focus of osteoarthritis.

Of clinical importance is the work of Salter and others.[221,222] They showed that subchondral bone defects made in the distal end of the rabbit femur healed more rapidly, with tissue more closely approximating hyaline cartilage than fibrocartilage, when they were subjected to continuous passive motion.

Blunt Impact

Only a few studies have attempted to analyze the results of either single or multiple closed impacts on articular cartilage.[223,224] It was shown that loading or impactive injuries exceeding a critical threshold cause injury not only to the chondrocytes but also to the underlying bone, resulting in subchondral thickening of the bone that progresses rapidly to an osteoarthritic lesion. This lesion may be reversible if the extent and magnitude of the injury are not extreme.

THE RESPONSE OF PERIPHERAL NERVE TO INJURY

Because of its highly specialized cellular function, the nerve cell lacks the ability to regenerate or differentiate. Once a nerve cell dies, it can never be replaced. However, in peripheral nerves, depending on the proximity of injury to the cell body, regeneration of the nerve fiber can occur. Although the ultimate goal in the management of the traumatic nerve injury is return of function, this is accomplished by obtaining the immediate goal of establishing an optimal environment to encourage this regeneration. Understanding the biologic processes involved in nerve injury and regeneration aids the surgeon in the creation of such an environment.

Nerve Structure

The nerve fiber is an extension of the nerve cell membrane and cytoplasm. Local injury not only involves damage to the tissue in close proximity to the insult but also produces changes some distance away in the nerve cell body. Complete understanding of these local and distant changes requires a review of the normal structure and physiology of the nerve.

Each nerve cell body contains a nucleus, which is usually centrally located within the nerve cell body. The cytoplasm that surrounds the nucleus is called the perikaryon, while that which fills the axonal extension is termed axoplasm. Golgi vesicles, while not present in the axon, are common in the cell body; mitochondria are present in the axons as well as within the cell body. Characteristic inclusion bodies known as Nissl bodies or chromophil substance are found within the nerve cell body and represent endoplasmic reticulum and associated ribosomes. Strands of fine fibrillar material extending from the cytoplasm of the nerve body into the axoplasm, known as neurofibrils, are involved in axoplasmic flow.[225]

As the axonal processes leave the central nervous system, they are bundled together to form nerves (Fig. 2–14). The peripheral nerve consists of numerous axonal extensions, which at this level may also be called fibers. In myelinated nerves, each individual axonal extension is insulated by a myelin sheath, which is, in essence, a Schwann cell. The junction of two Schwann cells leaves an area devoid of myelin in which the cytoplasmic membrane of the nerve cell is in close proximity to the extracellular environment, termed a node of Ranvier. These nodes play a role in saltatory

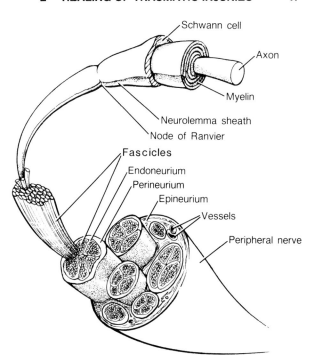

FIGURE 2–14. Structure of a myelinated peripheral nerve.

conduction and are also important in the degeneration and regeneration of the nerve after injury. In unmyelinated nerves, Schwann cells are still present, but they ensheathe several axons in intervals along the fiber.

Groups of fibers are surrounded by fibroblasts, capillaries, and collagen fibers and constitute the endoneurium. Bundles of these fibers and the associated endoneurium are encased by perineurium, a lamellar structure of epithelial-type cells. This bundle of fibers is termed a fascicle. The perineurium serves as a diffusion barrier and is remarkably resistant to mechanical trauma as well, especially stretching.[226] Within the nerve, fasciculi do not run as continuous, discrete entities but form a complex plexus by repeated divergence and fusion. In one area, multiple fascicles may exist, while in another, only one or a few fascicles are present. The fascicular pattern seldom remains constant along the nerve, which is of clinical significance during the repair of avulsive lesions.[227] The epineurium, consisting of a loose network of collagen fibers, fibroblasts, elastic fibers, and blood vessels, encases each of the fascicles (interfascicular epineurium), as well as surrounding the perimeter of the composite nerve (external epineurium).

Nerve Injury

Trauma may consist of simple compression, stretching, or transection of the nerve. Any of these may lead to disruption of neurotransmission. Sunderland[228] has outlined a classification system that divides neurotrauma into five degrees of injury (Fig. 2–15). The first degree of injury involves no loss of axonal continuity, while second- to fifth-degree injuries consist of an increasing extent of axonal disruption and injury to supporting structures. The biologic response is slightly different from one degree of injury to another, and each will be discussed separately.

In first-degree injury, or neurapraxia,[229] axonal conduction is interrupted, while axonal continuity is maintained. Although conduction is blocked, axonal transport continues proximodistally and distoproximally. The changes seen in first-degree injuries are most often associated with compression and ischemia. When compression is applied in the form of edema secondary to nerve injury, venous outflow obstruction occurs, followed by decreased arterial supply. This interruption of intraneural blood flow has been shown to accompany axonal destruction and degeneration.[230] As the

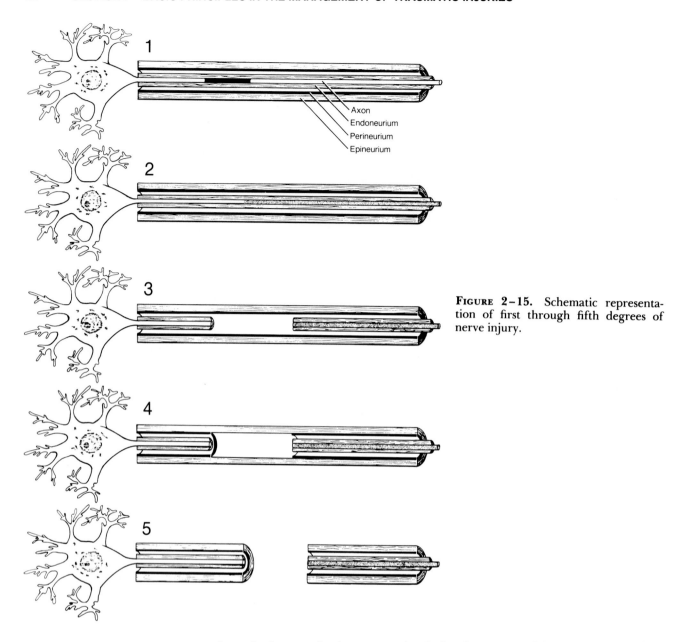

FIGURE 2–15. Schematic representation of first through fifth degrees of nerve injury.

axonal continuity remains intact, prognosis for the return of function is excellent, although some authors believe that some permanent histologic alteration is inevitable.[231]

Second- to fifth-degree injuries involve varying amounts of damage to the supporting structures. On the cellular level, all have in common the disruption of axonal continuity, which is followed by two stages: degeneration and regeneration (Fig. 2–16). It is common to talk about these as if one followed the other, but they actually occur almost simultaneously.[232]

The processes that occur during the degenerative phase are remarkably different proximal and distal to the site of injury. Wallerian degeneration occurs in the distal axon and extends proximally to the first node of Ranvier. The remainder of the proximal axon undergoes relatively little change, while the nerve cell body initially begins processes to enhance cell survival.

Interruption of the retrograde phase of axoplasmic flow may be the signal for central changes in the nerve cell body, which begin within 6 hours after axonal transection.[233] The Nissl granules disintegrate and disperse within the cytoplasm (chromolysis). The nucleus is displaced to the periphery, and alterations in the neural filaments occur. A transition from production of neurotransmitter substance to protein synthesis commences. If the division is not so proximal as to cause excessive cytoplasmic loss and overcome the nerve cell body's ability to survive, it will take the cell 2 to 3 weeks to make this transition, at which time the protein synthesis can contribute to the process of axonal regeneration. If the cell is unable to survive, perineural microglial cells assume a phagocytic role.

While these changes occur in the nerve cell body, wallerian degeneration begins within 24 hours in the distal axon, extending one to two nodes into the proximal axon as well. The rate of degeneration depends on the presence and thickness of the myelin sheath, with unmyelinated fibers degenerating most rapidly.

Earlier investigators thought that wallerian degeneration occurred simultaneously throughout the entire distal axon, but it is now known that degeneration begins at the site of injury and spreads along the axon (Fig. 2–16).[234]

Within 24 hours of injury, neurofibrils within the distal axon disappear. The axoplasm increases in optical density and begins to clump. This process leaves large,

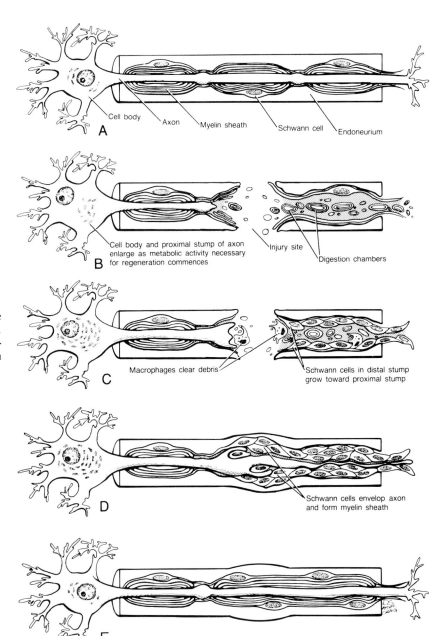

FIGURE 2–16. Stages of peripheral nerve healing. *A*, Normal nerve cell and axon. *B*, Early wallerian degeneration. *C*, Phagocytosis and Schwann cell proliferation. *D*, Axon growth. *E*, Repaired nerve fiber.

vacant spaces within the myelin sheath or, in the case of unmyelinated nerves, within the enveloping Schwann cell membrane. Soon after, the myelin sheath begins to degenerate. The characteristic layered appearance becomes homogeneous and granular and forms rings around the clumps of axoplasm. These digestion chambers, as they have been called, consist of layered myelin rings with luminal centers. These are well developed by 72 hours after injury.[235]

Macrophages of neural and extraneural origin are mobilized to phagocytize debris along the degenerating axon. Schwann cells, which proliferate early and persist until late repair, contribute somewhat to this activity; however, their primary role is to guide regeneration. These newly formed Schwann cells form dense cellular cords known as *bands of Büngner* along the former axon. Initiation of Schwann cell mitosis is thought to be triggered by a chemical mediator released as a result of axonal and myelin degeneration.[236]

If the nerve cell survives and the nerve cell body is able to make the necessary conversion from production of neurotransmitter substance to protein synthesis, the process of regeneration begins. Proteins synthesized in the nerve cell body are transmitted toward the site of injury, where they are needed for the regeneration process.[237]

The most distal extent of the proximal axon not having undergone degeneration begins to sprout multiple unmyelinated branches within 48 hours of injury. These unmyelinated fibers are surrounded by a basal membrane and are called a *regenerating unit.*[238] These new sprouts are basically extensions of cytoplasm with specialized tips, termed growth cones. These tips are mobile and constantly explore the environment as they advance.[237]

Originally, it was thought that axon sprouts made their way into old endoneurial cylinders rendered empty by wallerian degeneration. It is now known that these axons push distally as a result of measurable increased axoplasmic pressure and that they are guided by a natural affinity for the Schwann cell's surface in a phenomenon known as homotropism.[235] There is evidence that nerve growth factor–like proteins induce this tropic phenomenon,[239] and it is at the level of the growth cone that this interaction occurs. Rather than entering old empty cylinders, the progressing axons actively invade and displace Schwann cells, forming a new pathway. As the axons grow, myelogenesis is stimulated, and the nerve becomes remyelinated (if it was a myelinated nerve originally).[236]

This active growth of axons distally may be opposed by several factors. Should excessive Schwann cell proliferation occur, the sprouting axon may be unable to penetrate the cellular pathway. Although an intact tubular system is not necessary to guide the regenerating nerve, if tubules collapse, they may actually obstruct the progress of a regenerating axon. Finally, excessive production of scar tissue may block the regenerative progress of the axon.

If the axon can overcome these obstructions, it will continue to grow distally and reinnervate the motor end plate or peripheral sensory receptor, whichever is appropriate. During this reinnervation process, terminal branching occurs. This is a process whereby regenerating axons reinnervate a greater number of end plate or sensory receptors than in the original axon. Terminal branching is a compensatory mechanism to overcome the loss due to nerve cell body degeneration and aberrant axonal regeneration.[240]

This process of degeneration and regeneration is common to second- through fifth-degree nerve injury. Associated structural alterations also occur and account for differences in healing between these different injuries as well as the variable prognosis.[231]

In second-degree injury (axonotmesis), axonal degeneration occurs, but the endoneurium remains intact. The degenerative process occurs as described, with simultaneous distal regeneration. As no damage to supportive structure occurs, regeneration often progresses unimpeded, and the prognosis for return of function is good.

In third-degree injury, endoneurial tubular continuity is disrupted. The perineurium and epineurium remain intact. In addition to degeneration, which occurs as previously described, endoneurial disruption also causes damage to the intrafascicular vascular network, leading to hemorrhage, edema, and ischemia. Axons may incorrectly enter the wrong endoneurial sheath, resulting in misdirection of end organ reinnervation. Although the Schwann cells do influence and attract axonal regeneration, they are not capable of selectively attracting the regenerating proximal axon that originally occupied that pathway. This endoneurial damage also predisposes to increased collagen formation at the wound site, which in itself blocks the reinnervation process and leads to significant residual functional abnormalities with these types of injuries.

Fourth-degree injuries involve trauma that also affects the perineurium. The regenerating axon not only may enter the incorrect tubule within its own fascicle but also may enter a tubule within an adjacent fascicle. A large amount of structural damage and multiple possible pathways for regenerating axons lead to poor reinnervation and neuroma formation as well.

Fifth-degree injuries (neurotmesis) result when there is disruption of the extraneural epineurium. The largest amount of scar formation, aberrant axonal regeneration, and neuroma formation occurs in this type of injury. This factor accounts for the high degree of deficit seen in injuries of this type.

Clinical Application

The surgeon is most concerned with the process of regeneration, as, at present, little can be done to alter the degenerative aspects of nerve injury.

In general, management of the injured nerve requires creation of an optimal environment for reinnervation. This goal is accomplished by maintaining close coaptation of the transected nerve ends, achieving a tension-free interface, and minimizing scar formation. These conditions may occur spontaneously in the injured nerve but often require timely surgical intervention. A complete review of the philosophy of nerve repair is beyond the scope of this discussion, as, even with all that is known, much controversy exists regarding treatment modalities and timing of repair.

REFERENCES

1. Hunt TK, Van Winkle W: Fundamentals of wound management in surgery. *In* Wound Healing: Normal repair. South Plainfield, NJ, Chirurgecom Inc., 1976.
2. Madden JW: Wound healing. *In* Sabiston D (ed): Textbook of Surgery. Philadelphia, WB Saunders Company, 1971, pp 271–294.
3. Hugo NE, Epstein L, Cone A, et al: The effect of primary wounding on the tensile strength of secondary wounds. Surg Gynecol Obstet 131:516, 1970.
4. Madden JW, Peacock EE Jr: Studies of the biology of collagen during wound healing. I. Rate of collagen synthesis and deposition in cutaneous wounds of the rat. Surgery 64:288, 1968.
5. Shoshan S: Wound healing. Int Rev Connect Tis Res 9:1, 1981.
6. Irvin TT: The healing wound. *In* Bucknall TE, Ellis H (eds): Wound Healing for Surgeons. London, Bailliere Tindal, 1984, pp 3–28.
7. Peacock EE Jr, Van Winkle W Jr: Wound Repair. 2nd ed. Philadelphia, WB Saunders Company, 1976, p 669.
8. Johsonwint B, Gross J: Regulation of connective collagenase production derived from epithelial cells of multiple sources. J Cell Biol 1:A158, 1981.
9. Sepp H, Grotendorst G, Sepp S, et al: Platelet-derived growth factor is chemotactic for fibroblasts. J Cell Biol 92:584, 1982.
10. Clementi F, Palade GE: Intestinal capillaries. II. Structural effects of EDTA and histamine. J Cell Biol 42:706, 1969.
11. Majno G, Gilmore V, Leventhal M: On the mechanism of vascular leakage caused by histamine-type mediators. Circ Res 21:833, 1967.
12. Parratt JR, West GB: Release of 5-hydroxytryptamine and histamine from tissues of the rat. J Physiol 137:179, 1957.
13. Edery H, Lewis GP: Kinin-forming activity and histamine in lymph after tissue injury. J Physiol 169:568, 1963.
14. Rocha e Silva M, Baraldo WT, Rosenfeld G: Bradykinin, a hypotensive and smooth muscle stimulating factor released from plasma globulin by snake venoms and by trypsin. Circ Res 25:520, 1969.
15. Weissman G: Prostaglandins in acute inflam-

mation. *In* Current Concepts. Kalamazoo, MI, Scope Publication, The Upjohn Company, 1980.

16. Ward PA: The acute inflammatory response and the role of complement. *In* Dineen P, Hildrick-Smith G (eds): The Surgical Wound. Philadelphia, Lea and Febiger, 1981, pp 19–25.

17. Fernandez HN, et al: Chemotactic response to human $C3_a$ and $C5_a$ leukotaxis in vitro and under stimulated in vitro conditions. J Immunol 120:109, 1978.

18. Fernandez HN, Hugli TE: Primary structural analysis of the polypeptide portion of human $C5_a$ anaphylatoxin. J Biol Chem 253:6955, 1978.

19. Hill JH, Ward PA: C3 leukotactic factors produced by a tissue protease. J Exp Med 130:505, 1969.

20. Hill JH, Ward PA: The logistic role of C5 leukotactic fragments in myocardial infarcts of rats. J Exp Med 133:885, 1971.

21. Ward PA, Renold HG, David JR: Leukotactic factor produced by sensitized lymphocytes. Science 163:1079, 1969.

22. Altman LC, Snyderman R, Openheim JJ, et al: A human mononuclear leukocyte chemotactic factor: Characterization specificity and kinetics of production by homologous leukocytes. J Immunol 110:801, 1973.

23. Gallin JI, Kirkpatrick CH: Chemotactic activity in dialyzable transfer factor. Proc Natl Acad Sci USA 71:498, 1974.

24. Altman LC: Chemotactic lymphokines: A review. *In* Gallin JI, Quie PG (eds): Leukocyte Chemotaxis. New York, Raven Press, 1978.

25. Frank MM: Complement. Kalamazoo, MI, Scope Publication, The Upjohn Company, 1975.

26. Borel JF, Keller HV, Sorkin E: Chemotaxis. XI. Effect on neutrophils of lysosomal and other subcellular fractions from leukocytes. Int Arch Allergy Appl Immunol 35:194, 1969.

27. Ward PA, Hill JH: C5 chemotactic fragments produced by an enzyme in lysosomal granules of neutrophils. J Immunol 104:535, 1970.

28. Hayashi H: Intracellular neutral SH-dependent proteases associated with inflammatory reactions. Int Rev Cytol 40:101, 1975.

29. Harker LA, Finch CA: Thrombokinetics in man. J Clin Invest 48:963, 1969.

30. Hovig T: Release of a platelet-aggregating substance (adenosine diphosphate) from rabbit blood platelets induced by saline "extract" of tendon. Thromb Diath Haemorrh 9:264, 1963.

31. Baumgartner HR, Born GVR: Effects of 5-hydroxytryptamine on platelet aggregation. Nature 218:137, 1968.

32. Packham MA, Guccione MA, Greenberg JP, et al: Release of ^{14}C-serotonin during initial platelet changes induced by thrombin, collagen, or A23187. Blood 50:915, 1977.

33. Hamberg M, Svensson J, Wakabayashi T, et al: Isolation and structure of two prostaglandin endoperoxides that cause platelet aggregation. Proc Natl Acad Sci USA 71:345, 1974.

34. Hamberg M, Svensson J, Samuelsson B: Thromboxanes: A new group of biologically active compounds derived from prostaglandin endoperoxides. Proc Natl Acad Sci USA 72:2994, 1975.

35. Witte LD, Kaplan KL, Nossel HL, et al: Studies of the release from human platelets of the growth factor for cultured human arterial smooth muscle cells. Circ Res 42:402, 1978.

36. Kaplan DR, Chao FC, Stiles CD, et al: Platelet alpha-granules contain a growth factor for fibroblasts. Blood 53:1043, 1979.

37. Gerrard JM, Phillips DR, Rao GHR, et al: Biochemical studies of two patients with gray platelet syndrome. J Clin Invest 66:102, 1980.

38. Warshaw AL, Laster L, Shulman NR: Protein synthesis by human platelets. J Biol Chem 242:2094, 1967.

39. Ross R, Glomset J, Kariya B, et al: A platelet-dependent serum factor that stimulated the proliferation of arterial smooth muscle cells in vitro. Proc Natl Acad Sci USA 71:1207, 1974.

40. Rutherford RB, Ross R: Platelet factors stimulate fibroblasts and smooth muscle cells quiescent in plasma serum to proliferate. J Cell Biol 69:196, 1976.

41. Ross R, Raines EW, Bowen-Pope DF: The biology of platelet-derived growth factor. Cell 46:155, 1986.

42. Ross R, Odland G: Human wound repair: Inflammatory cells, epithelial-mesenchymal interrelations and fibrogenesis. J Cell Biol 39:152, 1968.

43. Janoff A, Schaefer S, Sherer J, et al: Mediators of inflammation in leukocyte lysosomes. II. Mechanism of action of lysosomal cationic protein upon vascular permeability in the rat. J Exp Med 122:841, 1965.

44. Sherer J, Janoff A: Observation on mast cell rupturing agents in different species. Lab Invest 18:196, 1968.

45. Ross R: Inflammation and formation of granulation tissue. *In* Lepow IH, Ward PA (eds): Mechanisms and Control. New York, Academic Press, 1972, p 29.

46. Dannenberg AM Jr: Macrophages in inflammation and infection. N Engl J Med 293:489, 1975.

47. Nathan CF, Murray HW, Cohn ZA: The macrophage as an effector cell. N Engl J Med 303:622, 1980.

48. Unanue ER: The macrophage as a regulator of lymphocyte function. Hosp Pract 14:61, 1979.

49. Leibovich SJ, Ross R: The role of macrophage in wound repair: A study with hydrocortisone and antimacrophage serum. Am J Pathol 78:71, 1975.

50. Ruco LP, Meltzer MS: Macrophage activation for tumor cytotoxicity induction of tumoricidal macrophages by supernatants of PPD-stimulated bacillus Calmette-Guerin immune spleen cultures. J Immunol 119:889, 1977.

51. Allison AC, Ferluga J, Prydy H, Schorlemmer HU: The role of macrophage activation in chronic inflammation. Agents Actions 8:27, 1978.

52. Polverini PJ, Cotran RS, Gimbrone MA Jr: Activated macrophages induce vascular proliferation. Nature 269:804, 1977.

53. Wahl LM, Wahl SM, Mergenhagen SE, et al: Collagenase production by endotoxin-activated macrophages. Proc Natl Acad Sci USA 71:3598, 1974.

54. Wahl LM, Wahl SM, Mergenhagen SE, et al: Collagenase production by lymphokine-activated macrophages. Science 187:261, 1975.

55. Wahl LM: Prostaglandin regulation of macrophage collagenase production. Proc Natl Acad Sci USA 74:4955, 1977.

56. Werb Z, Gordon S: Elastase secretion by stimulated macrophages. J Exp Med 142:361, 1975.

57. Werb Z, Gordon S: Secretion of a specific collagenase by stimulated macrophages. J Exp Med 142:346, 1975.

58. Morland B, Kaplan G: Macrophage activation in vivo and in vitro. Exp Cell Res 108:279, 1977.

59. Morland B, Morland J: Selective induction of lysosomal enzyme activities in mouse peritoneal macrophages. J Reticuloendothelial Soc 23:469, 1978.

60. Boucek RJ: Factors affecting wound healing. Otolaryngol Clin North Am 17:243, 1984.

61. Leibovich S, Ross R: A macrophage-dependent factor that stimulates the proliferation of fibroblasts in vitro. Am J Pathol 84:501, 1976.

62. Leibovich SJ: Production of macrophage-dependent fibroblast-stimulation activity (M-FSA) by murine macrophages. Exp Cell Res 113:47, 1978.

63. Wahl SM, Malone DG, Wilder RL: Spontaneous production of fibroblast-activating factors by synovial inflammatory cells. J Exp Med 161:210, 1985.

64. Lagunoff D, Benditt EP: Proteolytic enzymes of mast cells. Ann NY Acad Sci 103:185, 1963.

65. David JR: Lymphocytic factors in cellular hypersensitivity. Hosp Pract 6:79, 1971.

66. Rola-Pleszczynski J, Lieu H, Hamel J: Stimulated human lymphocytes produce a soluble factor which inhibits fibroblast migration. Cell Immunol 74:104, 1982.

67. Fishel R, Barbul A, Wasserkrug HL, et al: Cyclosporin A impairs wound healing in rats. J Surg Res 34:572, 1983.

68. Barbul A, Sisto D, Rettura G, et al: Thymic inhibition of wound healing: Abrogation by adult thymectomy. J Surg Res 32:338, 1982.

69. Barbul A, Knud-Hansen J, Wasserkrug HL, et al: Interleukin 2 enhances wound healing in rats. J Surg Res 40:315, 1986.

70. Peterson JM, Barbul A, Breslin RJ, et al: Significance of T-lymphocytes in wound healing. Surgery 102:300, 1987.

71. Gabbiani G, Chaponnier C, Huttner I: Cytoplasmic filaments and gap junctions in epithelial cells and myofibroblasts during wound healing. J Cell Biol 76:561, 1978.

72. Krawczyk WS: A pattern of epidermal cell migration during wound healing. J Cell Biol 49:247, 1971.

73. Gabbiani G, Ryan GB: Development of a contractile apparatus in epithelial cells during epidermal and liver regeneration. J Submicrosc Cytol 6:143, 1974.

74. Krawczyk WS: Heavy meromyosin binding microfilaments in epidermal cells during wound healing. Arch Dermatol Res 258:63, 1978.

75. Stenn KS, Madri JA, Roll FJ: Migrating epidermis produces AB$_2$ collagen and requires continual collagen synthesis for movement. Nature 227:229, 1979.

76. Kleinman HK, Murray JC, McGoodwin EB, et al: Localization of the binding site for cell attachment in the alpha (1) chain of collagen. J Biol Chem 253:5642, 1978.

77. Murray JC, Stingl G, Kleinman HK, et al: Epidermal cells adhere preferentially to Type IV (basement membrane) collagen. J Cell Biol 80:197, 1979.

78. Stanley JR, Foidart JM, Murray JC: The epidermal cell which selectively adheres to a collagen substrate is the basal cell. J Invest Dermatol 74:54, 1980.

79. Karasek MA, Charlton ME: Growth of postembryonic skin epithelial cells on collagen gels. J Invest Dermatol 56:205, 1971.

80. Liotta LA, Vembu D, Kleinman HK, et al: Collagen required for proliferation of cultured connective tissue cells but not their transformed counterparts. Nature (Lond) 272:622, 1978.

81. Reddi AH: Collagen and cell differentiation. In Ramachandran GN, Reddi AH (eds): Biochemistry of Collagen. New York, Plenum Press, 1976, p 449.

82. Emerson JT, Pitelka DR: Maintenance and induction of morphological differentiation in dissociated mammary epithelium on floating collagen membranes. In Vitro 13:316, 1977.

83. Grillo HC, Gross J: Collagenolytic activity during mammalian wound repair. Dev Biol 15:300, 1967.

84. Grillo HC, McLennan JE, Wolfort FG: Activities and properties of collagenase from wound healing in mammals. In Dunphy JE, Van Winkle W (eds): Repair and Regeneration. New York, McGraw-Hill Book Company, 1969, p 185.

85. Donoff RB, McLennan JE, Grillo HC: Preparation and properties of collagenases from epithelium and mesenchyme of healing mammalian wounds. Biochim Biophys Acta 227:639, 1971.

86. Gross J: Aspects of the animal collagenases. In Ramachandran GN, Reddi AH (eds): Biochemistry of Collagen. New York, Plenum Press, 1976, p 275.

87. Starkey RH, Cohen S, Orth DN: Epidermal growth factor: Identification of a new hormone in human urine. Science 189:800, 1975.

88. Franklin JD, Lynch JB: Effects of topical applications of epidermal growth factor on wound healing: Experimental study on rabbit ears. Plast Reconstr Surg 64:766, 1979.

89. Stewart RJ, Duley JA, Allardyce RA: The migration of fibroblasts in an in vitro wound. Br J Exp Pathol 60:582, 1979.

90. Postlethwaite AE, Seyer JM, Kang AH: Chemotactic attraction of human fibroblasts to Type I, II and III collagens and collagen-derived peptides. Proc Natl Acad Sci USA 75:871, 1978.

91. Chiang TM, Postlethwaite AE, Beachey EH, et al: Binding of chemotactic collagen-derived peptides to fibroblasts: The relationship to fibroblast chemotaxis. J Clin Invest 62:916, 1978.

92. Gabbiani G, Hirschel BJ, Ryan GB, et al: Granulation tissue as a contractile organ: A study of structure and function. J Exp Med 135:719, 1972.

93. Ryan GB, Cliff WJ, Gabbiani G, et al: Myofibroblasts in human granulation tissue. Hum Pathol 5:55, 1974.

94. Guber S, Rudolph R: The myofibroblast. Surg Gynecol Obstet 146:641, 1978.

95. Gabbiani G: Reparative processes in mammalian wound healing: The role of contractile phenomena. Int Rev Cytol 48:187, 1979.

96. Prockop DJ, Kivirikko KI, Tuderman L, et al: The biosynthesis of collagen and its disorders. N Engl J Med 301:13, 1979.

97. Cohen IK, Moore CD, Diegelmann RF: Onset and localization of collagen synthesis in open rat wounds. Proc Soc Exp Biol Med 160:458, 1979.

98. Enquist IF, Adamson RJ: Collagen synthesis and lysis in healing wounds. Minn Med 48:1965, 1965.

99. Bentley JP: Proteoglycans of the connective tissue ground substance. *In* Hunt TK (ed): Wound Healing and Wound Infection: Theory and Surgical Practice. New York, Appleton-Century-Crofts, 1980, p 45.

100. Jackson DS, Flickinger DB, Dunphy JE: Biochemical studies of connective tissue repair. Ann NY Acad Sci 86:943, 1960.

101. Bently JP: Rate of chondroitin sulphate formation in wound healing. Ann Surg 165:186, 1967.

102. Highberger JH, Ross J, Schmitt FO: The interaction of mucoprotein with soluble collagen: An electron microscope study. Proc Natl Acad Sci USA 37:286, 1951.

103. Watts GT, Baddeley RM, Wellings R: Wound collagen: Effect of depolymerizing agent on wound granulation tissue. Nature 201:636, 1964.

104. Jackson DS: Biosynthesis of collagen fibers. Clin Sci 38:7, 1970.

105. Culp LA, Murray BA, Rollins BJ: Fibronectin and proteoglycans as determinants of cell-substratum adhesion. J Supramolecular Struct 11:401, 1979.

106. Ruoslahti E, Vaheri A, Kuusela P, Linder E: Fibroblast surface antigen: A new serum protein. Biochim Biophys Acta 322:352, 1973.

107. Kleinman HK: Connective tissue structure: Cell binding to collagen. J Invest Dermatol 71:9, 1978.

108. Jilek F, Hormann H: Fibronectin (cold insoluble globulin). VI. Influence of heparin and hyaluronic acid on the binding of native collagen. Z Physiol Chem 360:597, 1979.

109. Ruoslahti E, Engvall E: Complexing of fibronectin glycosaminoglycans and collagen. Biochim Biophys Acta 631:350, 1980.

110. Yamada KM, Hahn LE, Olden K: Characterization of fibronectin interactions with glycosaminoglycans and identification of active fragment. J Biochem 255:6055, 1980.

111. Clark RAF: Potential roles of fibronectin in cutaneous wound repair. Arch Dermatol 124:201, 1988.

112. Vaheri A, Ruoslahti E, Mosher DF: Fibroblast surface protein. Ann NY Acad Sci 312:1, 1978.

113. Mosher DF, Schad PE, Kleinman HK: Crosslinking of fibronectin to collagen by blood coagulating factor XIII[a]. J Clin Invest 64:781, 1979.

114. Bensusan HB, Koh TL, Henry KG, et al: Evidence that fibronectin is the collagen receptor on platelet membrane. Proc Natl Acad Sci USA 75:5864, 1978.

115. Santoro SA, Cunningham LW: Fibronectin and the multiple interaction model for platelet collagen adhesion. Proc Natl Acad Sci USA 76:2644, 1979.

116. Hopper KE, Adelmann BC, Gentner G, Gay S: Recognition by guinea-pig peritoneal exudate cells of conformationally different states of the collagen. Immunology 30:249, 1976.

117. Ali IV, Hynes RO: Effects of LETS glycoprotein on cell motility. Cell 14:439, 1978.

118. Gauss-Muller V, Kleinman HK, Martin GR, Schiffman E: Role of attachment factors in attractants in fibroblast chemotaxis. J Lab Clin Med 96:1071, 1980.

119. Foidart JM, Berman JJ, Paglia L, et al: Synthesis of fibronectin, laminin and several collagens by a liver-derived epithelial line. Lab Invest 42:525, 1980.

120. Black MM, Van Noort R: Wound strength. *In* Bucknall TE, Ellis H (eds): Wound Healing for Surgeons. London, Bailliere Tindal, 1984, pp 29–41.

121. Chvapil M, Koopmann CF: Scar formation: Physiology and pathologic states. Otolaryngol Clin North Am 17:265, 1984.

122. Gabbiani G, Ryan GB, Majino G: Presence of modified fibroblasts in granulation tissue and their possible role in wound contraction. Experientia 27:549, 1971.

123. Hirschel BJ, Gabbiani G, Ryan GB, et al: Fibroblasts of granulation tissue: Immunofluorescent staining with antismooth muscle serum. Proc Soc Exp Biol Med 138:455, 1971.

124. Gabbiani G, Majino G, Ryan GB: Evidence for motile and contractile fibroblasts. *In* Kulonen E, Pikkarainen J (eds): Biology of Fibroblast. London, Academic Press, 1973, pp 139–154.

125. Boskey AL, Posner AS: Bone structure, composition and mineralization. Orthop Clin North Am 15:597, 1984.

126. Nordin M, Frankel VH: Biomechanics of Whole Bone and Bone Tissue. Philadelphia, Lea and Febiger, 1980, pp 15–60.

127. Schenk RK: Histophysiology of bone remodeling and bone repair. *In* Lin OCC, Chao EVS (eds): Perspectives on Biomaterials. Amsterdam, Elsevier Science Publishers, 1986, pp 75–94.

128. Glimcher MJ: Handbook of Physiology: Endocrinology. Vol 7. Baltimore, The Williams and Wilkins Company, 1976, pp 25–116.

129. Escarot-Charrier B, Glorieux FH, vander-Rest M, et al: Osteoblasts isolated from mouse calvaria initiate matrix mineralization in culture. J Cell Biol 96:639, 1983.

130. Owen M: Histogenesis of bone cells. Calcif Tissue Res 25:205, 1978.

131. Rodan GA, Martin TJ: Role of osteoblasts in hormone control of bone resorption—a hypothesis. Calcif Tissue Int 32:439, 1981.

132. Ham AW, Cormack DH: Histophysiology of Cartilage, Bones and Joints. Philadelphia, JB Lippincott, 1979.

133. Owen M: The origin of bone cells. Int Rev Cytol 28:213, 1970.

134. Young RW: Nucleic acids, protein synthesis and bone. Clin Orthop Rel Res 26:147, 1963.

135. Marks SC Jr: The origin of osteoclasts: Evidence, clinical implications and investigative challenges of an extraskeletal source. J Oral Pathol 12:226, 1983.

136. Osdoby P, Martini MC, Caplan AI: Isolated osteoclasts and their presumed progenitor cells, the monocyte, in culture. J Exp Zool 224:331, 1982.

137. Horton MA, Rimmer EF, Moore A, et al: On the origin of the osteoclast: The cell surface phenotype of rodent osteoclasts. Calcif Tissue Int 37:45–50, 1985.

138. Addison WC: Enzyme histochemical properties of kitten osteoclasts in bone imprint preparations. Histochem J 10:645, 1978.

139. Kaye M: When is it an osteoclast? J Clin Pathol 37:398, 1984.

140. Kahn AM, Simmons DM, Krukowski M: Osteoclast precursor cells are present in the blood of preossification chick embryos. Dev Biol 84:230, 1981.

141. Marks SC, Walker DG: The hematogenous origin of osteoclasts: Experimental evidence from osteopetrotic (microphthalmic) mice treated with spleen cells from beige mouse donors. Am J Anat 161:10, 1981.

142. Bonnucci E: New knowledge on the origin, function and fate of osteoclasts. Clin Orthop Rel Res 158:252, 1981.

143. Underwood JCE: Editorial: From where comes the osteoclast? J Pathol 144:225, 1984.

144. Horton MA, Rimmer EF, Lewis D, et al: Cell surface characterization of the human osteoclast: Phenotypic relationship to other bone marrow–derived cell types. J Pathol 144:281, 1984.

145. Frankel VH, Nordin M: Basic Biomechanics of the Skeletal System. Philadelphia, Lea and Febiger, 1980.

146. Huelke DF, Harger JH: Maxillofacial injuries: Their nature and mechanisms of production. J Oral Surg 27:451, 1969.

147. Ham AW: A histological study of the early phase of bone repair. J Bone Joint Surg 9:825, 1930.

148. Heppenstall RB: Fracture healing. In Heppenstall RB: Fracture Treatment and Healing. Philadelphia, WB Saunders Company, 1980.

149. Rhinelander FW, Phillips RS, Steer WM, Beer JC: Microangiography in bone healing. II. Displaced closed fractures. J Bone Joint Surg 50A:643, 1968.

150. Simmons DJ: Fracture healing perspectives. Clin Orthop Rel Res 200:100, 1985.

151. Simmons DJ: Fracture healing. In Urist MR (ed): Fundamental and Clinical Bone Physiology. Philadelphia, JB Lippincott, 1980, pp 283–330.

152. Tonna EA, Cronkite EP: The cellular response to fracture studied with tritiated thymidine. J Bone Joint Surg 43A:352, 1961.

153. Urist MR: Induction and differentiation of cartilage and bone cells. In Schjeide OA, DeVellis J (eds): Cell Differentiation. New York, Van Nostrand Reinhold, 1970, p 504.

154. Kernek CB, Wray JB: Cellular proliferation in the formation of fracture callus in the rat tibia. Clin Orthop Rel Res 91:197, 1973.

155. Manoli A II: Structure and physiology of bone. In Mathog RH (ed): Maxillofacial Trauma. Baltimore, The Williams and Wilkins Company, 1984, pp 39–58.

156. Girgis FG, Pritchard JJ: Experimental production of cartilage during the repair of fractures of the skull vault in rats. J Bone Joint Surg 40B:274, 1958.

157. Brighton CT, Krebs AG: Oxygen tension of healing fractures in the rabbit. J Bone Joint Surg 54A:323, 1972.

158. Reitzik M: Cortex-to-cortex healing after mandibular osteotomy. J Oral Maxillofac Surg 41:658, 1983.

159. Bryant WM: Wound healing. Clin Symp 29:3, 1977.

160. Ham AW, Harris WR: Repair and transplantation. In Bourne GH (ed): Biochemistry and Physiology of Bone. Vol I. New York, Academic Press, 1971, pp 338–399.

161. McLean FC, Urist MR: Bone: Fundamentals of the Physiology of Skeletal Tissue. 3rd ed. Chicago, University of Chicago Press, 1968.

162. McKibbin B: The biology of fracture healing in long bones. J Bone Joint Surg 60B:150, 1978.

163. Chalmers J, Gray DH, Rush J: Observations on the induction of bone in soft tissue. J Bone Joint Surg 57B:36, 1975.

164. Lane JM: Biochemistry of fracture healing. In Resources for Basic Science Educator. Monterey, CA, American Academy of Orthopaedic Surgeons, 1978.

165. Urist MR, Sat K, Brownell AG, et al: Human bone morphogenetic protein (hBMP). Proc Soc Exp Biol Med 173:194, 1983.

166. Danis R: Théorie et Pratique de l'Osteosynthèse. Paris, Libraires de L'Académie de Medicine, 1949.

167. Danis R: Théorie et Pratique de l'Osteosynthèse. Paris, Masson et Cie, 1949.

168. Schenk RK, Willenegger H: Morphological findings in primary fracture healing. Symp Biol Hung 7:75, 1967.

169. Hutzschenreuter P, Steinemann S, Perren SM, et al: Some effects of rigidity of internal fixation on the healing pattern of osteotomies. Injury 1:77, 1969.

170. Johner R: Zur Knochenheilung in Abhängigkeit von der Defektgrosse. Helv Chir Acta 39:409, 1972.

171. Frost HM: Bone Dynamics in Osteoporosis and Osteomalacia. Springfield, IL, Charles C Thomas, 1966.

172. Rasmussen H, Bordier P, Kurokawa K, et al: Hormonal control of skeletal and mineral homeostasis. Am J Med 56:751–758, 1974.

173. Schenk R: Die Histologie der primären Knochenheilung im lichte neuer Konzeptionen über den Knochenumbau. Unfallheilkunde 81:219, 1978.

174. Schenk R, Willenegger H: Fluoreszenmikroskopische Untersuchungen zur Heilung von Schaftfrakturen nach stabiler Osteosynthese an hund. In Richelle LJ, Dallemagne MJ (eds): Calcified Tissue. Liège, Belgium, University of Liège Press, 1965, p 125.

175. Rifas L, Shen V, Mitchell K, et al: Macrophage-derived growth factor for osteoblast-like cells and chondrocytes. Proc Natl Acad Sci USA 81:4558, 1984.

176. Scheving LA, Yeh YC, Tsai TH, et al: Circadian phase–dependent stimulatory effects of epidermal growth factor on deoxyribonucleic acid synthesis in the duodenum, jejunum, ileum, caecum, colon, and rectum of the adult male mouse. Endocrinology 106:1498, 1980.

177. Linder BL, Chernoff A, Kaplan KL: Release of platelet-derived growth factor from human platelets by arachidonic acid. Proc Natl Acad Sci USA 76:4107, 1979.

178. Azizkham JC, Klagsbrun M: Chondrocytes

contain a growth factor that is localized in the nucleus and is associated with chromatin. Proc Natl Acad Sci USA 77:2762, 1980.

179. Klagsbrun M, Smith S: Purification of a cartilage derived growth factor. J Biol Chem 225:10895, 1980.

180. Shen V, Rifas L, Kohler G, et al: Fetal rat chondrocytes sequentially elaborate separate growth and differentiation-promoting peptides during their development in vitro. Endocrinology 116: 920, 1985.

181. Lash JW, Vasan NS: Glycosaminoglycans of cartilage. *In* Hall BK (ed): Cartilage, Structure, Function and Biochemistry. Vol 1. New York, Academic Press, 1983, p 215.

182. Canalis E, Peck WA, Raisz LG: Stimulation of DNA and collagen synthesis by autologous growth factor in cultured fetal rat calvaria. Science 210:1021, 1980.

183. Peck WA, Rifas L: Regulation of osteoblast activity and the osteoblast-osteocyte transformation. *In* Massry S, Letteri J, Ritz ER (eds): Regulation of Phosphate and Mineral Metabolism. New York, Plenum Press, 1982, p 393.

184. Drivdahl RH, Howard GA, Baylink DJ: Extracts of bone contain a potent regulator of bone formation. Biochim Biophys Acta 714:26, 1982.

185. Wergedal JE, Baylink DJ: Characterization of cells isolated and cultured from human bone. Proc Soc Exp Biol Med 176:27, 1984.

186. Heath JK, Meikle MC, Atkinson SJ, et al: A factor synthesized by rabbit periosteal fibroblasts stimulates bone resorption and collagenase production by connective tissue cells in vitro. Biochim Biophys Acta 800:301, 1984.

187. Heath JK, Atkinson SJ, Meikle MC, et al: Mouse osteoblasts synthesize collagenase in response to bone resorbing agents. Biochim Biophys Acta 802:151, 1984.

188. Sakamoto S, Sakamoto M: Isolation and characterization of collagenase synthesized by mouse bone cells in culture. Biomed Res 5:39, 1984.

189. Horton JE, Raisz LG, Simmons HA, et al: Bone resorbing activity in supernatant fluid from cultured human peripheral blood leukocytes. Science 177:793, 1972.

190. Raisz LG, Luben RA, Mundy GR, et al: Effect of osteoclast activating factor from human leukocytes on bone metabolism. J Clin Invest 56:408, 1975.

191. Urist MR, Lietze A, Muzutani H, et al: A bovine low molecular weight bone morphogenetic protein. Clin Orthop Rel Res 162:219, 1982.

192. Urist MR, Delange RJ, Finerman GAM: Bone cell differentiation and growth factors. Science 220:680, 1983.

193. Huggins CB, Urist MR: Dentin matrix transformation: Rapid induction of alkaline phosphatase and cartilage. Science 167:897, 1969.

194. Nogami H, Urist MR: Explants, transplants and implants of a cartilage and bone morphogenetic matrix. Clin Orthop Rel Res 103:235, 1974.

195. Rowe N: Nonunion of the mandible. *In* Mathog RH (ed): Maxillofacial Trauma. Baltimore, The Williams and Wilkins Company, 1984, pp 177–185.

196. Altner PC, Grana L, Gordon M: An experi-

mental study on the significance of muscle tissue interposition on fracture healing. Clin Orthop Rel Res 111:269, 1975.

197. Goodship AE, Kenwright J: The influence of induced micromovement upon the healing of experimental tibial fractures. J Bone Joint Surg 67B:650, 1985.

198. Bradley JC: Age changes in the vascular supply of the mandible. Br Dent J 132:142, 1972.

199. Bradley JC: A radiological investigation into the age changes of the inferior dental artery. Br J Oral Surg 13:82, 1975.

200. Friedenberg ZG, Kohanim M: The effect of direct current on bone. Surg Gynecol Obstet 127:97, 1968.

201. Friedenberg AB, Roberts PG, Didizian NH, et al: Stimulation of fracture healing by direct current in the rabbit fibula. J Bone Joint Surg 53A:1400, 1971.

202. Friedenberg ZB, Zemsky LM, Pollis RP, et al: The response of non-traumatized bone to direct current. J Bone Joint Surg 56A:1023, 1974.

203. Bassett CAL, Mitchell SN, Gaston SR: Treatment of ununited tibial diaphyseal fracture with pulsing electromagnetic fields. J Bone Joint Surg 63A:511, 1981.

204. Richez J, Chamay A, Bieler L: Bone changes due to pulses of direct electric microcurrent. Virchows Arch [A] 357:11, 1972.

205. Bourret LA, Rodan GA: The role of calcium in the inhibition of cAMP accumulation in epiphyseal cartilage exposed to physiological pressure. J Cell Physiol 88:358, 1976.

206. Rodan GA, Bourret LA, Harvey A, et al: 3′, 5′ Cyclic AMP and 3′,5′ cyclic GMP: Mediators of the mechanical effects on bone remodeling. Science 189:467, 1975.

207. Rodan GA, Bourret LA, Norton IA: DNA synthesis in cartilage cells is stimulated by oscillating electric fields. Science 199:690, 1978.

208. Borgens RB: Endogenous ionic currents traverse intact and damaged bone. Science 225:478, 1984.

209. Mow VC, Roth V, Armstrong CG: Biomechanics of joint cartilage. *In* Frankel VH, Nordin M (eds): Basic Biomechanics of the Skeletal System. Philadelphia, Lea and Febiger, 1980, pp 61–86.

210. Mow VC, Lai WM: Mechanics of animal joints. Annu Rev Fluid Mech 11:247, 1979.

211. Mankin HJ: The response of articular cartilage to mechanical injury. J Bone Joint Surg 64A:460, 1982.

212. Campbell JC: The healing of cartilage defects. Clin Orthop Rel Res 64:45, 1969.

213. DePalma AF, McKeever CD, Subin SK: Process of repair of articular cartilage demonstrated by histology and autoradiography with tritiated thymidine. Clin Orthop Rel Res 48:229, 1966.

214. Fuller JA, Ghadially FN: Ultrastructural observations on surgically produced partial-thickness defects in articular cartilage. Clin Orthop Rel Res 86:193, 1972.

215. Ghadially FN, Thomas I, Oryschak AF, et al: Long term results of superficial defects in articular cartilage. A scanning electron microscope study. J Pathol 121:213, 1977.

216. Meachim G: The effects of scarification on articular cartilage of the rabbit. J Bone Joint Surg 45B:150, 1963.

217. Calandruccio RA, Gilmer WS: Proliferation, regeneration and repair of articular cartilage of immature animals. J Bone Joint Surg 44A:431, 1962.
218. Meachim G, Roberts C: Repair of the joint surface from subarticular tissue in the rabbit knee. J Anat 109:317, 1971.
219. Mitchell N, Shepard N: Healing of articular cartilage in intra-articular fractures in rabbits. J Bone Joint Surg 62A:230, 1980.
220. Convery FR, Akeson WH, Keown GH: The repair of large osteochondral defects: An experimental study in horses. Clin Orthop 82:253, 1972.
221. Salter RB, Field P: The effects of continuous compression on living articular cartilage. An experimental investigation. J Bone Joint Surg 42A:31, 1960.
222. Salter RB, Simmonds DF, Malcolm BW, et al: The biological effect of continuous passive motion on the healing of full-thickness defect in articular cartilage. J Bone Joint Surg 62A:1232, 1980.
223. Radin EL, Ehrlich MG, Chernack R: Effect of repetitive impulsive loading on the knee joint of rabbits. Clin Orthop Rel Res 131:288, 1978.
224. Repo RJ, Finlay JB: Survival of articular cartilage after controlled impact. J Bone Joint Surg 59A:1068, 1977.
225. Davidson PF: Microtubules and neurofilaments. Possible implications in axoplasmic transport. Adv Biochem Psychopharmacol 2:889, 1970.
226. Lundborg G: Intraneural microcirculation. Orthop Clin North Am 19:1, 1988.
227. Kline DM: Diagnostic determinants for management of peripheral nerve lesions. In Rand RW (ed): Microneurosurgery. 3rd ed. St Louis, CV Mosby, 1985.
228. Sunderland S: Nerves and Nerve Injuries. 2nd ed. Edinburgh, Churchill-Livingstone, 1978.
229. Seddon J: Three types of nerve injury. Brain 66:237, 1943.
230. Lundborg G, Myers R, Powell H: Nerve compression injury and increase in endoneurial fluid pressure: A miniature compartment syndrome. J Neurol Neurosurg Psychiatry 46:1119, 1983.
231. Horn KL, Crumley RL: The physiology of nerve injury and repair. Otolaryngol Clin North Am 27:321, 1984.
232. Liu HM: Schwann cell properties. II. The identity of phagocytes in the degeneration of nerve. Am J Pathol 75:395, 1974.
233. VanBeek A, Kleiner HE: Peripheral nerve injuries and repair. In Rand RW (ed): Microneurosurgery. 3rd ed. St Louis, CV Mosby, 1985.
234. Lubinska L: Early course of Wallerian degeneration in myelinated fibers of the rat phrenic nerve. Am J Pathol 75:395, 1974.
235. Ketchum LD: Peripheral nerve repair. In Hunt TK (ed): Fundamentals of Wound Management. New York, Appleton-Century-Crofts, 1979.
236. Spencer PS: Neuronal regulation of myelinating cell function. Soc Neurosci Symp 4:275, 1979.
237. Schwartz M: Molecular and cellular aspects of nerve regeneration. CRC Crit Rev Biochem 22:89, 1987.
238. Morris JH, Hudson AR, Weddell G: A study of degeneration and regeneration in the divided rat sciatic nerve based on electron microscopy. Z Zellforsch Mikroskop Anat 124:76, 1972.
239. Levi-Montalcini R: The nerve growth factor 35 years later. Science 237:1154, 1987.
240. Fisher TR: Nerves. In Bucknall TE, Ellis H (eds): Wound Healing for Surgeons. London, Bailliere Tindal, 1984.

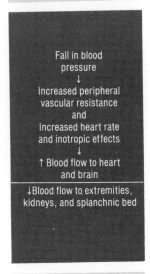

CHAPTER 3

Fall in blood
pressure
↓
Increased peripheral
vascular resistance
and
Increased heart rate
and inotropic effects
↓
↑ Blood flow to heart
and brain
↓Blood flow to extremities,
kidneys, and splanchnic bed

SHOCK

GEORGE E. BONN, D.D.S., and
CHRISTOPHER L. DAVIS, D.D.S., M.D.

Treatment of the traumatized patient requires that the physician be knowledgeable in both diagnosing and treating shock. Shock may be defined as ". . . an acute, generalized, inadequate perfusion of critical organs that, if continued, will produce serious pathophysiologic consequences."[1] Hemodynamic, endocrine, and metabolic alterations result and produce the clinical signs of shock, that is, arterial hypotension; rapid, thready pulse; decreased urine output; thirst; increased respiratory rate; vasoconstriction; acidosis; and central nervous system dysfunction. The major underlying event is a shift from aerobic to anaerobic metabolism.

Prompt identification and elimination of the underlying cause of shock will usually reverse the chain of events resulting from cellular dysfunction. Delay in treatment may result in permanent cellular and organ damage and may lead to irreversible shock and death.

CLASSIFICATION

Shock occurs whenever cardiac output is insufficient to create enough flow and pressure in the vascular bed to perfuse vital organs and cells.[2] This situation may result from many different factors, which fit broadly into four categories — oligemic, cardiogenic, obstructive, and distributive[1] (Table 3–1).

Oligemic Shock

Oligemic (hypovolemic) shock, which may be defined as a reduction in the amount of fluid pumped through the vascular bed, is the most common type of shock in the victim of maxillofacial trauma and is thus listed first. It is important to understand, however, that all forms of shock may be encountered following trauma.

Oligemic shock may be divided into hemorrhagic and nonhemorrhagic shock. In hemorrhagic shock, blood loss may be either from external sources, such as lacerations, or from internal sources, such as gastrointestinal bleeding (e.g., ulcer), femoral

TABLE 3-1. CAUSES OF SHOCK

Oligemic	Hemorrhagic loss of intravascular fluid Nonhemorrhagic loss of fluid (burns, peritonitis, crush injuries, surgical wounds, pleural effusions, ascites, vomiting, diarrhea, hyperglycemia, diabetes insipidus, excessive diuretic use and other dehydration, adrenocortical insufficiency, pancreatitis)
Cardiogenic	Myopathies (myocardial infarction, congestive cardiomyopathy, acute viral myocarditis, cardiac amyloidosis) Dysrhythmias and arrhythmias Mechanical factors (mitral regurgitation or stenosis, acute aortic regurgitation or stenosis, ventricular septal defects, idiopathic hypertrophic subaortic stenosis, cardiac tumors, such as atrial myxoma)
Obstructive	Constrictive pericarditis, cardiac tamponade, tension pneumothorax, pulmonary embolism, pulmonary hypertension, coarctation of the aorta
Distributive	Sepsis, neurogenic factors, endocrinopathies (e.g., adrenal insufficiency, hypothyroidism, hypoglyglycemia), anaphylaxis, microcirculatory dysfunction (e.g., polycythemia vera, fat emboli, sickle cell anemia), drug overdose, metabolic acidosis

fractures, crush injuries, or ruptured internal organs (such as the liver and spleen). Acute blood loss of up to 15 per cent of the circulating blood volume is usually associated with minimal hemodynamic change. A 15 to 25 per cent loss of blood volume may not cause hemodynamic change as long as the loss is not rapid, but the metabolic changes associated with shock may be initiated. Rapid loss of 30 per cent or more of the blood volume will cause shock if the loss is venous in nature, and a less than 30 per cent loss of the arterial blood volume will also cause shock.

Nonhemorrhagic shock is that which is found with a massive shift of fluid from the intravascular compartment into the extravascular compartment. This decrease in plasma may be associated with burns, peritonitis, crush injuries, pancreatitis, surgical wounds, pleural effusions, and ascites.

Nonhemorrhagic oligemic shock may also be due to water loss, such as that occurring with protracted vomiting or diarrhea, hyperglycemia, diabetes insipidus, excessive diuretic use, salt-wasting nephritis, and adrenocortical failure.

Cardiogenic Shock

Falling into the category of cardiogenic shock are any forms of shock resulting from intrinsic cardiac disorders.[2] The most common cause of cardiogenic shock is left ventricular failure secondary to acute myocardial infarction. Ten to 15 per cent of patients with myocardial infarctions who reach an acute care medical facility will be in cardiogenic shock.[1] The characteristics of cardiogenic shock associated with left ventricular failure are (1) decreased cardiac output, (2) decreased systemic arterial pressure, and (3) increased pulmonary venous pressure.

Right ventricular infarction can also precipitate cardiogenic shock, although in this setting the systemic venous pressure will be elevated and the pulmonary venous pressure may be within a normal range.

Another source of cardiogenic shock that should be investigated is cardiac dysrhythmias. Any dysrhythmia that renders the pump inefficient may result in cardiogenic shock.

Less common causes of cardiogenic shock include mitral regurgitation; acute aortic regurgitation or stenosis; acute viral myocarditis; cardiac amyloidosis; hypertrophic cardiomyopathy; left ventricular inflow obstruction, such as rheumatic mitral stenosis, atrial myxoma, or left atrial thrombus; and intracardiac shunts, such as ventricular septal defects.

Obstructive Shock

Obstructive shock can be caused by any factor extrinsic to the heart that reduces adequate left or right ventricular filling and thus does not allow adequate cardiac output. Causes may include diseases of the pericardium, such as constrictive pericarditis, or cardiac tamponade with pericardial effusion. Tension pneumothorax or any shifts in the mediastinum may also cause obstructive shock. Some conditions produce decreased left ventricular filling along with right ventricular failure, such as pulmonary embolism, primary pulmonary hypertension, or the Eisenmenger syndrome (pulmonary hypertension associated with congenital communication between the left- and right-sided circulation). Such entities as tumors obstructing flow into the heart are rare but may also be added to the list of causes of obstructive shock.

Distributive Shock

Distributive shock is the "pooling" of blood within the vascular system that results from an abnormal distribution of fluid secondary to changes in regional vascular resistance. This type of shock may be considered either neurogenic or vasogenic. Arterial hypotension may occur in spite of markedly increased cardiac output owing to a profound decrease in peripheral vascular resistance. This form of shock has been referred to as "warm shock," since cutaneous vasodilatation may occur.

One of the most common causes of distributive shock, massive sepsis, is usually heralded by the onset of a hard, shaking chill, elevated temperature, mental obtundation, tachycardia, and tachypnea. Cardiac output is frequently elevated but may be reduced. It commonly occurs in older individuals or obstetric patients or in those who have recently undergone urologic manipulation. Although nonbacterial organisms can cause septic shock, the most common organisms associated with septic shock are gram-negative enteric bacilli, staphylococci (e.g., toxic shock syndrome), *Streptococcus pneumoniae, Neisseria meningitidis, Neisseria gonorrhoeae,* and clostridia.

The characteristics of septic shock include arterial hypotension, decreased peripheral resistance with sequestration of blood in venous pools, normal central venous pressure, normal blood volume, and renal ischemia. This response is thought to be due to bacterial cell wall endotoxins consisting of macromolecular lipopolysaccharide complexes. The endotoxins produce hepatic and splenic venoconstriction and release of vasodilating substances, including histamine and prostaglandins, thus decreasing total peripheral resistance.

Another cause of distributive shock, often found with traumatic spinal cord injuries, is neurogenic shock. This peripheral pooling resulting from loss of the neurologic vasoconstrictor potential is also commonly seen with spinal anesthesia.

Distributive shock also occurs in endocrinopathies such as adrenal insufficiency, hypothyroidism, and hypoglycemia. Other causes include anaphylaxis and microcirculatory dysfunction, as found with hyperviscosity syndromes, emboli, sickle cell anemia, and polycythemia vera.

CLINICAL MANIFESTATIONS OF SHOCK

With a few exceptions (e.g., adrenocortical insufficiency), most signs and symptoms of shock result from low peripheral blood flow and increased adrenal sympathetic activity (Table 3–2). Patients will appear anxious and restless in the early stages of shock, becoming apathetic and exhausted later because of decreased cerebral perfusion. If measures to reduce shock are not taken, these symptoms may progress to coma. The skin is typically cool and pale and blanches easily, with poor capillary refill. In septic distributive shock, the skin may actually be warm and clammy owing to peripheral vasodilatation. In neurogenic or anaphylactic distributive shock, the skin is frequently cool and clammy.

TABLE 3-2.   POSSIBLE CLINICAL MANIFESTATIONS OF SHOCK

1. Restlessness later progressing to apathy and exhaustion
2. Rapid, thready pulse
3. Cool, pale skin (may be warm with septic shock)
4. Poor capillary refill
5. Low blood pressure
6. Thirst
7. Increased respiratory rate and depth
8. Dyspnea with shock of cardiopulmonary etiology
9. Nausea and vomiting
10. Decreased urine output
11. Coma (in later stages)

The patient's pulse will typically be rapid and thready owing to a compensatory attempt to increase cardiac output in the face of decreased available volume of circulating fluid. In some forms of distributive shock associated with high cardiac output, the pulse may actually feel stronger than normal.

Thirst is a common finding, most likely resulting from increased adrenal secretion associated with trauma. The physician must be wary of possible water intoxication, though, if the patient is allowed to drink water in the presence of shock-induced renal impairment.

There will usually be an increase in the respiratory rate and depth to compensate for either metabolic acidosis or primary ventilatory disturbances, as in pulmonary edema from left ventricular failure. In addition, with left-sided congestive heart failure, one will typically see other classic signs, such as dyspnea, hypoxemia, and an S_3 gallop.

Low peripheral venous pressure accompanying shock may make intravenous line access difficult. This condition, however, will not usually be present in cardiogenic shock.

Nausea and vomiting are common in hypovolemic shock, as is a marked decrease in body core temperature. However, in septic shock the patient's temperature may exceed 104 to 105°F.

Urine output will almost invariably be decreased as a compensatory effort and as a result of renal ischemia. In an attempt to retain sodium and fluid, urinary levels of sodium will be decreased to less than 10 mEq/L unless acute tubular necrosis has occurred, in which case this compensatory mechanism is lost.

In most forms of shock, hemodynamic measurements will reveal decreases in systolic and mean arterial pressures, cardiac output, central venous pressure, cardiac index, pulse pressure, and pulmonary artery wedge pressure and increases in peripheral vascular resistance. Nearly opposite hemodynamic findings may be seen in some forms of shock, such as septic and occasionally neurogenic shock. Mixed findings may be found in cardiogenic and obstructive shock. These measurements are discussed in more detail later in this chapter.

PATHOPHYSIOLOGIC CHANGES IN SHOCK

Shock can be described in terms of its hemodynamic, endocrine, metabolic, and cellular consequences.

Hemodynamic Changes

Blood pressure is dependent on cardiac output and peripheral vascular resistance. When cardiac output falls, as in cardiogenic, oligemic, or obstructive shock, blood pressure will remain stable as long as a compensatory increase in the peripheral vascular resistance occurs.

Decreased blood pressure usually triggers an increased sympathetic action. Baroreceptors in the atria and carotid and aortic arteries detect the decrease in blood pressure and send impulses to the hypothalamus and vasomotor center in the medulla, which in turn send out sympathetic impulses with release of catecholamines to cause increased inotropic and chronotropic effects on the heart as well as peripheral vasoconstriction and selective vasodilatation (Fig. 3–1).

The combination of alpha- and beta-adrenergic effects will result in different effects on different organs. These effects generally follow a sequence that would seem logical in an all-out effort to save the organism. For example, the heart may receive 25 per cent of the cardiac output, as opposed to its normal 5 to 8 per cent. Similarly, the brain may receive up to 80 per cent instead of its usual 15 to 20 per cent of the cardiac output. This increased flow to the brain happens at the expense of blood flow to other organs less important to immediate survival, such as the kidney, splanchnic bed, skin, and muscle. Indeed, the kidney can suffer greatly.

The kidney, under normothermic conditions, can tolerate periods of ischemia up to a potential maximum of 90 minutes. The immediate physiologic response to most forms of shock is oliguria. With increasing periods of ischemia, however, parenchymal changes will occur that may result in high-output renal failure with moderate glomerular damage and may eventually result in true cortical necrosis with acute anuric renal failure.

Alpha-adrenergic arteriolar vasoconstriction also produces a form of autotransfusion by lowering the hydrostatic pressure in the capillaries and allowing colloid osmotic pressure of the plasma to draw greater than normal volumes of fluid back into the vascular space from the interstitial space.

In addition to the sympathetically mediated vasoconstriction, the renin-angiotensin-aldosterone "axis" will be initiated by low renal blood flow, causing even more arterial vasoconstriction.

Again, in response to baroreceptor stimulation, the pulse will usually be elevated in an effort to increase cardiac output in the face of decreased blood pressure. The amount of fluid either lost or sequestered, the amount of venous return to the heart, the functional status of the ventricles, and the presence or absence of obstructive factors involving the heart will determine the success of this compensatory phenomenon.

Studies have shown that even large volume losses in healthy adults (1000 ml) do not increase the pulse significantly if the patient is in a supine or prone position. This observation and the fact that the pulse may be elevated owing to fear, anxiety, and pain make the pulse a poor monitor in the acute phase of shock. The pulse is better used as an adjunctive monitor over the long term to help measure treatment results after resuscitation maneuvers have been instituted and extraneous factors like fear and pain have been eliminated.

Cardiac output generally decreases progressively in oligemic, obstructive, and cardiogenic shock, in spite of the body's compensatory mechanisms, unless therapeu-

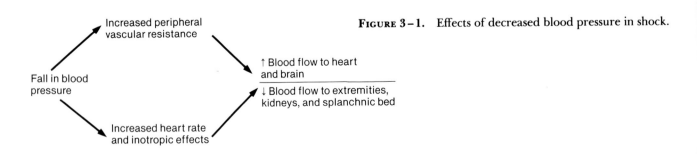

FIGURE 3–1. Effects of decreased blood pressure in shock.

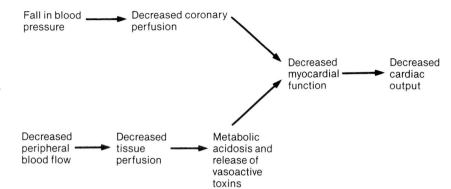

FIGURE 3–2. Causes of decreased cardiac output in shock.

tic intervention is initiated (Fig. 3–2). In septic or neurogenic shock, cardiac output may at first be elevated to compensate for decreased systemic vascular resistance to maintain adequate blood pressure. In later stages, however, the cardiac output will also falter.

Hemoglobin and hematocrit measures are highly unreliable during shock. On the one hand, there may be hemodilution as a result of the vasoconstriction caused by catecholamine release, leading to a decreased hydrostatic pressure at the capillary level and allowing extravascular interstitial fluid to enter the blood stream. On the other hand, later in the course of shock, arteriolar sphincters, once contracted by alpha-adrenergic activity, begin to relax. Meanwhile, the venous sphincters remain contracted, creating elevated hydrostatic pressure in the capillaries with extravasation of plasma into the interstitial fluid. This shift of fluid from an intravascular to an extravascular position is further compounded by damage to capillary endothelium from ischemia. The result is hemoconcentration and, in late stages, sludge formation. Finally, massive loss of plasma, as is found in nonhemorrhagic oligemic shock, will also be associated with an artificially high hematocrit.[3,4]

Endocrine Changes

Endocrine changes cause alterations in ion concentrations, hemodynamics, and utilization of energy substrates (Table 3–3).[3] Decreased blood flow to the hypothalamus results in secretion of adrenocorticotropic hormone (ACTH) from the anterior pituitary. This secretion of ACTH stimulates secretion of cortisol from the adrenal cortex, which has well-known salt-retaining, inotropic, and catabolic effects. Aldosterone produced during shock causes retention of sodium and thus also fluid reten-

TABLE 3–3. ENDOCRINOLOGIC EFFECTS OF SHOCK

1.	Increased secretion of ACTH	Increased cortisol levels with inotropic and catabolic effects (see Nos. 4, 5, and 6)
2.	Increased secretion of ADH	Increased water reabsorption and decreased urine output
3.	Stimulation of the renin-angiotensin system	Increased aldosterone levels with retention of sodium and decreased urine output
4.*	Increased serum glucose	—
5.*	Increased urea levels	Increased urine nitrogen content
6.*	Increased levels of free fatty acids	Acidosis

* In spite of the body's attempt to produce energy from these substrates, less effective means of energy production from these substrates are operational during shock.

tion. In exchange for the sodium, potassium is released by the kidney. If the kidneys fail as shock progresses, high serum potassium levels will result.

Insulin and glucagon levels are also elevated in response to shock, thus increasing the serum levels of glucose, urea from protein degradation, and free fatty acids from fat metabolism. Increased urinary excretion of nitrogen from protein degradation (negative nitrogen balance) is an indicator of the severity of shock as long as the kidneys are functioning well. Increased glucose and free fatty acid production causes metabolic effects that will be discussed in a later section.

Antidiuretic hormone (ADH) is also released during shock with any hypotension, hypovolemia, or lowered serum osmolality. ADH causes greater water reabsorption from the distal convoluted tubules and collecting ducts of the kidney in an attempt to increase intravascular volume.

During shock, however, the decreased blood flow to the kidney can greatly reduce the glomerular filtration rate. This, combined with the effects of aldosterone and ADH on the kidney, can greatly decrease urine output and eliminate the exit route of potassium, urea, and other metabolic degradation products created during shock. To make matters worse, the kidney also produces renin during shock that will be converted to angiotensin and aldosterone, as mentioned above, causing added renal vasoconstriction, which further limits urine output.

Metabolic Changes

The metabolic response to shock is to convert protein, carbohydrates, and fat into energy. Elevated insulin and glucagon levels are associated with a rise in the levels of serum glucose, urea, and free fatty acids. There is also an increase in glycogenolysis in the liver, resulting in an increase in the glucose pool with elevation of blood glucose. Degradation of proteins in gluconeogenesis produces free amino acids and increases the urine output of protein, zinc, potassium, phosphate, and sulfur. Catecholamine release with shock initiates lipolysis, producing free fatty acids and glycerol.

The tricarboxylic acid cycle, or the Krebs cycle, is the usual means by which these breakdown products can be converted to adenosine triphosphate (ATP), water, and carbon dioxide under normal aerobic conditions. The carbon dioxide can be expelled via the lungs. However, in shock, with its low-flow state and hypoxic conditions, metabolism changes from aerobic to anaerobic pathways. During anaerobic conditions, carbohydrates are converted to pyruvate and then to lactate. Proteins and fats are also converted to organic acids, and as the concentration of these substances rises in the body, the patient will experience acidosis (Table 3–4).

The more acid that is produced in this manner, the more depleted the natural buffers in the blood become, and the body becomes unable to turn the acid into carbon dioxide. Respiratory compensation for metabolic acidosis fails, and the condition progressively worsens. The ability to recover from shock is, among other factors, greatly dependent on the severity of the acidosis present.

TABLE 3–4. METABOLIC EFFECTS OF SHOCK

1. Metabolic acidosis
2. Hyperventilation in an attempt to offset metabolic acidosis
3. Respiratory alkalosis
4. Sodium and water retention
5. Increased excretion of potassium, nitrogen, zinc, phosphorus, and sulfur (useful indices of the magnitude of injury)

Cellular Changes

During shock, the electrical activity of the cell and its ion transport system becomes disrupted. The sodium and potassium adenosine triphosphatase (ATPase) pump activity fails. Potassium leaks out of the cell, and sodium builds up within. Along with the sodium comes fluid.[4] The damaged cells swell at the expense of the extracellular fluid. This situation, plus the presence of acidosis due to ischemia, causes intracellular disruption, including lysosomal breakdown.[5] Lysosomes release a number of powerful enzymes, especially proteases that directly damage cells and capillary basement membranes. Nuclear chromatin begins to clump, the endoplasmic reticulum dilates as the cell becomes edematous, and ribosomes detach from the walls of the endoplasmic reticulum and scatter, resulting in disrupted protein synthesis. The cell membrane becomes increasingly unstable, and cell death ensues.

IRREVERSIBLE SHOCK

A patient who fails to respond to the replacement of blood loss and resuscitative measures is said to be in irreversible shock. Although the clinical symptoms of irreversible shock are striking, the cause of the unremitting deterioration of the circulation is not completely agreed upon. A frequent cause of irreversible shock is infection with gram-negative bacteria with their endotoxins. However, irreversibility may result with any type of shock, and there seems to be a common denominator that runs through all irreversible shock, regardless of the initial etiology: a disturbance within the peripheral circulation. Many still argue that the heart may play a more significant role in the genesis of irreversible shock. Others have shown, however, that the heart is better able to resist the deleterious effects of hypoxia than the peripheral circulation and that the heart actually depends on the peripheral circulation for proper function.[6]

In oligemic shock, there is, as mentioned before, a great outpouring of epinephrine, leading to intense vasoconstriction of precapillary arteriolar sphincters as well as postcapillary venular sphincters. This situation results in ischemic anoxia of the involved peripheral tissues in an all-out effort to keep the heart and brain functioning for survival. This phase of shock is easily reversible by prompt administration of blood or other suitable substances to restore normal circulatory dynamics.

If shock is prolonged and resuscitation efforts are delayed, the condition of ischemic anoxia changes to congested, stagnant anoxia. The sequence of events that leads to this condition is presumably as follows. As a result of the low-flow state in the peripheral capillaries during vasoconstriction, metabolic wastes accumulate, leading to acidosis, which renders the arteriolar sphincters less sensitive to catecholamines. More and more epinephrine is secreted, but as shock progresses, arteriolar sphincters are not able to maintain tone, despite heroic attempts by the body to secrete these vasoconstrictors. For an unexplained reason, venular sphincters continue to maintain tone. The end result is that blood has difficulty in leaving these stagnant capillary beds. Thereafter, hydrostatic pressure begins to increase above the serum oncotic pressure, and fluid leaves the capillaries, moving into the interstitial space in large volume.

As this process of stagnation continues, ischemia may become so severe that the capillaries begin to slough and rupture, allowing whole blood to escape into the interstitium. This process further reduces the blood volume and venous return to the heart, and irreversible shock is at hand. Eventually, cardiac output and coronary blood flow decrease to the point at which arrest or fibrillation occurs. It is easy to understand from this why, by this time, adding more whole blood or other substitute to the system has little sustained beneficial effect. It, too, ends up in the stagnant peripheral pools. Emphasis, then, should be placed on the early diagnosis of shock, with appropriate therapy being rendered prior to the point of irreversibility.

THERAPY

General Principles of Therapy[5]

1. The best treatment for shock is prevention. If shock cannot be prevented, one should concentrate on limiting its depth and duration.

2. A diagnosis should be sought concerning the underlying cause of the shock, and then measures should be instituted to treat the underlying cause. For example, if the shock is secondary to cardiac arrhythmia, the arrhythmia should be treated appropriately. If the cause is cardiac tamponade, cardiac paracentesis is indicated. If the underlying problem is sepsis, an underlying site of infection should be sought. The causative organism should be isolated and treated with appropriate antibiotics. This principle applies to all forms of shock.

3. The patient's condition and the severity of shock should be measured at regular intervals. Parameters may change rapidly, and occasional, dispersed measurements may direct therapy in the wrong direction. Subjective impressions of the patient's condition are also deceptive.

4. Frequent monitoring, especially of ventilation, acid-base balance, and fluids and electrolytes, is indispensable for rational decision making. The discussion of these and other important parameters of monitoring will follow.

5. Excessive oscillations in therapy should be avoided. The temptation to restore derangements to neutrality with undue rapidity should be resisted, for this may be dangerous, especially in the treatment of chronic acid-base or electrolyte disturbances.

6. Practitioners should discourage themselves from treating only numbers. Practitioners should be guided by objective measurements whenever possible, but they should not allow themselves to be deceived by laboratory data that contradict clinical judgment. Repeat measurements under such circumstances may be appropriate before or during institution of therapy.

General and specific therapy for trauma (e.g., Advanced Trauma Life Support) is discussed in Chapter 5. This chapter remains directed at the treatment of shock.

Monitoring

Close monitoring of various parameters in the patient with shock will allow rational decision making for treatment. Of course, the amount, frequency, and type of monitoring will vary, depending on factors too numerable to mention in this text. Obviously, the patient's blood pressure and level of consciousness are two of the first things measured when a patient presents with shock. If possible, an arterial line should be started to have a continuous measure of the arterial blood pressure. This line will also allow easy access for blood gas, electrolyte, and hematocrit and hemoglobin determinations, which will be necessary as treatment progresses. The pulse will also show trends as shock develops and as treatment is rendered. Soon after it is recognized that a patient may be developing shock, baseline hemoglobin and hematocrit values should be obtained. They will most likely be inaccurate because of the hemodilution or hemoconcentration that occurs at various stages of shock, but, once again, a trend may be followed during treatment. Other laboratory studies to be obtained as a baseline and then monitored periodically include serum electrolytes, blood urea nitrogen (BUN), creatine, and liver function tests, including coagulation studies. Blood should also be sent for typing and cross-matching immediately, when appropriate. Changes in renal and hepatic functions can affect these parameters as shock progresses. A Foley catheter should be inserted immediately to monitor urinary output and the progress of fluid-electrolyte management. Urinalysis and urinary electrolytes and osmolarity may be important parameters to follow during therapy.

If there is a question about the underlying etiology of a patient's shock condition, if heart failure is thought to be involved, or if there is no immediate response to fluid therapy, a central venous catheter should be inserted to measure central venous pressure (right atrial pressure). If the central venous pressure is low, as well as the cardiac output and arterial blood pressure, one is usually dealing with oligemic (hypovolemic) or possibly neurogenic factors. With a fluid challenge, the cardiac output and arterial blood pressure should rise. The central venous pressure may remain low or normal in a patient with a healthy myocardium until a point is reached at which nearly adequate fluid resuscitation has been accomplished. If fluid loss continues, such as occurs with bleeding or burns, for example, there may be no rise at all in the central venous pressure or blood pressure after a fluid challenge. If the central venous pressure rises but the blood pressure does not, this may be indicative of cardiogenic or obstructive shock.

There are, of course, limitations to a central venous pressure measurement. First of all, it cannot be regarded as a gauge of cardiac performance, since it does not truly measure left ventricular function. The central venous pressure also does not necessarily reflect blood volume because it is affected not only by blood volume but also by the tone of the venous capacitance bed and the ability of the right ventricle to accommodate increased intravascular volume. It is possible to have an elevated central venous pressure in the face of decreased blood volume, if associated with cardiopulmonary problems. Conversely, a low central venous pressure may be seen in septic shock or other distributive shock with an increased blood volume.

The actual central venous pressure measurement is less important than the direction in which it moves in response to a fluid load. This factor is especially true in septic or cardiogenic shock, in which the central venous pressure may be deceptively high and more fluid may actually be needed, in spite of the elevated central venous pressure. If the patient clinically appears to be hypovolemic, fluid should still be given cautiously while close monitoring of the central venous pressure trend and pulmonary function is performed.

There are also the hazards of improperly placing the tip of the catheter, thus rendering erroneous central venous pressure measurements. The placement of the central venous catheter should always be checked radiographically. In addition, there is the possibility of infection originating from a central venous catheter, especially if the catheter is placed under emergency conditions without attention to aseptic technique or if the catheter is left in place for prolonged periods. Other complications include pneumothorax, hemothorax, myocardial perforation, embolization of sheared tips, air embolism, damage to the brachial plexus, and injury to the brachial artery, depending upon the site of venipuncture. In spite of these problems, the central venous pressure can be indispensable in the treatment of many cases of shock.

Another very helpful monitor is the Swan-Ganz catheter. This catheter allows the measurement of pulmonary artery pressure and pulmonary capillary wedge pressure—an indirect measurement of pulmonary venous pressure and left atrial and left ventricular end-diastolic (filling) pressures—and permits computation of cardiac output through dye dilution or thermodilution techniques. Pulmonary wedge pressure may be a useful parameter in cases in which the central venous pressure seems abnormally high, if myocardial infarction or other cardiopulmonary abnormality is suspected, if shock seems refractory for some reason, and in cases of shock involving an elderly person, in whom even small changes made in hemodynamics may have a profound effect. Pulmonary wedge pressure is also useful in cases of septic shock or respiratory failure, when the central venous pressure may be high but the patient clinically appears to need fluids.

Use of Swan-Ganz catheters may produce complications, including many of those seen with central venous catheters. They may also cause rupture of the chordae tendineae, cardiac arrhythmias, pulmonary infarction, and formation of clots at the tip of the catheter. Again, however, these catheters are indispensable in indicated cases.

Fluids

Together with adequate oxygenation of ventilation, the central key to managing most cases of shock, particularly oligemic shock, is the early, aggressive, and rational administration of fluids.

The volume of the intravascular space is extremely variable and is influenced by many vasomotor and chemical factors. The capacitance of the vascular bed may be increased or decreased in response to differing circumstances and in different types of shock. Consequently, the amount of fluid required in different patients will vary.

The American College of Surgeons Committee on Trauma has classified hemorrhagic shock into four classes based on the amount of blood lost. They have made recommendations on appropriate fluid resuscitation based on these four categories[7] (Table 3–5).

CLASS I

Class I includes patients who have had an acute blood loss of up to 15 per cent of their total circulating blood volume. In this group, the pulse and respiratory rates will increase, but usually only minimally, and the arterial blood pressure is ordinarily normal. Blanching of the nail capillary bed by pressure may increase owing to greater vasoconstriction. Orthostatic hypotension is usually not present. Examples of situations involving hemorrhage of this magnitude include blood donation, pronounced epistaxis, most minor fractures, some surgical procedures, and minor injuries to solid intra-abdominal organs. Hemorrhage of this degree is treated by replacing lost blood volume with crystalloid solutions in a ratio of 3 ml of crystalloid solution to every 1 ml of blood lost. It is, in most instances, unnecessary to administer blood products to patients in this class. Of course, the patient's plasma volume and hemoglobin and hematocrit before the event might dictate otherwise.

CLASS II

Class II patients have lost approximately 20 to 25 per cent of their circulating blood volume. They have symptoms of tachycardia, tachypnea, and hypotension. There will usually be a drop in cardiac output, an increase in peripheral vascular resistance, and narrowing of the pulse pressure. Orthostatic hypotension is also present, but there is usually no diminution in urinary output. Examples of hemor-

TABLE 3–5.   CLASSIFICATION OF HEMORRHAGIC SHOCK BY AMERICAN COLLEGE OF SURGEONS COMMITTEE ON TRAUMA

Class I	Acute blood loss of ≤15% of total blood volume Pulse and respirations usually increased Blood pressure may not be significantly affected
Class II	Acute blood loss of 20–25% of total blood volume Increased pulse and respirations Decreased blood pressure Usually no decrease in urine output
Class III	Blood loss of 30–40% total blood volume Increased pulse and respirations Decreased blood pressure Decreased urine output
Class IV	40–50% loss of total blood volume Lack of vital signs Decreased urine output Obtunded mental status

rhage of this magnitude would include some surgeries, fractures of pelvic and long bones, contained vascular injuries, and trauma to the liver and spleen. Treatment in this class is with crystalloid solution, again in a ratio of 3 ml of crystalloid solution to 1 ml of blood lost. Blood products are usually not necessary as long as bleeding has stopped. However, long bone fractures and hepatic or splenic lacerations can continue to bleed for some time, and transfusions may be indicated in anticipation of further blood loss or surgery to repair injuries.

CLASS III

Patients in Class III have lost 30 to 40 per cent of their circulating blood volume. All previously mentioned symptoms of oligemic shock occur, as well as a decrease in urine volume. Examples of injuries causing this magnitude of bleeding include splenic or hepatic rupture, vascular and thoracic injuries, and multiple trauma with fractures. Resuscitation begins with crystalloid solutions in the usual 3 : 1 ratio but also includes transfusion of whole blood or red blood cell concentrates.

CLASS IV

Class IV patients will have lost 40 to 50 per cent or more of their circulating blood volume. All signs and symptoms of shock described in Classes I through III are present, and the patient usually "lacks vital signs" and is obtunded. Injuries that cause hemorrhage of this magnitude include uncontrolled vascular and thoracic injuries; severe injuries to the liver, spleen, and kidney; and multiple trauma. Management consists of obtaining as extensive a history as possible and performing a physical examination directed at the initial treatment of life-threatening injuries. Respiratory distress or cardiac dysrhythmias are immediately assessed and treated. Vital signs are obtained, and adequacy of ventilation is assured, using an endotracheal tube if necessary. Bleeding is controlled by compression. Vascular access is obtained, preferably using two 16-gauge or larger intravenous lines. While venous access is being secured, blood is taken for typing and cross-matching donor blood. Baseline laboratory tests and blood gas values are obtained, and a Foley catheter is placed in the bladder. Fluid challenge is begun with crystalloid solutions, the amount depending to some degree on the amount of fluid lost and being lost, but roughly consists of giving fluid at a rate of 200 ml over a 10-minute period. Vital signs are again assessed as well as the central venous pressure, pulmonary capillary wedge pressure, and cardiac output, if indicated. Appropriate adjustments in fluid administration are then made, with observation of the patient's actual condition. Frequently, continuous fluid administration is required to maintain a urine output of 50 ml/hr for an adult.

As fluid therapy proceeds, blood products are prepared to supplement crystalloid solutions for resuscitation. If indicated, non–cross-matched type-specific blood can be used to sustain life. Incompatibilities resulting from lack of cross-matching are usually minor, and type-specific blood can usually be obtained in several minutes, as opposed to 45 minutes for cross-matched blood.

If a patient has received 10 units of blood or more within a 3-hour period, platelets should be administered because of the scarcity of them in preserved donor blood.

During convalescence, patients should be monitored for anemia secondary to excess extracellular fluid re-entering the intravascular compartment, as well as possible continued blood loss.

Solutions Available for Treatment of Shock

Regardless of the cause of shock, the main treatment objectives are restoration of adequate oxygenation of cells and organs and restoration of circulatory adequacy.

The ideal fluid for attaining these objectives would restore extracellular fluid volume, exchange oxygen for metabolic waste at the cellular level, replace the same substances lost in shock, and be free of adverse effects. A fluid that serves all these functions does not exist, but many substances are available that embody at least some of these characteristics. Rational fluid resuscitation utilizes available products that have the properties most appropriate to the individual situation.

While awaiting whole blood or packed red blood cells for the treatment of hemorrhagic shock, colloid or crystalloid solutions may be used to resuscitate patients, but some controversy exists over which are better. Some argue that colloids remain in the intravascular space longer, thus avoiding pulmonary edema. Most studies show that crystalloids work just as well in expanding the intravascular volume and are less expensive, do not need compatibility testing, do not transmit infectious disease, and replace essential ions.

Of the different types of crystalloids, lactated Ringer's solution is most appropriate for resuscitative treatment. It has isotonic quantities of anions and cations, and its lactate is converted to bicarbonate as long as the liver is functioning well.

Dextrose in water solutions are usually inappropriate for resuscitation because they replace lost body fluids with free water without ions. Dextrose in water with electrolytes may be useful in cases involving hypoglycemia, as, for example, in some cases of septic shock; but in most cases of shock, there is plenty of blood glucose because of gluconeogenesis and glycogenolysis.

Normal saline solutions may be used, but they lack other ions and may result in excessive sodium load.

Lactated Ringer's solution does have one major disadvantage: Transfused blood will coagulate if it is run through an intravenous line containing lactated Ringer's solution. The calcium in lactated Ringer's solution negates the anticoagulant effect of citrate in stored blood. Normal saline should be flushed through the line before any stored blood is administered.

When the degree of hemorrhage associated with shock requires blood transfusion, the most appropriate product to administer is whole blood or packed red blood cells. There are many potential complications associated with administering stored blood, including transfusion reactions, disseminated intravascular coagulation, and transmission of infectious disease, to mention just a few. Blood should obviously not be withheld on this basis, however, in the trauma patient who needs it.

When large transfusions are administered, several factors should be kept in mind about stored blood. The longer blood has been stored, the less 2,3-diphosphoglycerate (2,3-DPG) it contains and thus the higher affinity the hemoglobin will have for oxygen. This characteristic decreases the blood's ability to release oxygen to peripheral tissues. In spite of this, no proven advantage of fresh blood over blood that has been stored for longer periods has been demonstrated in resuscitating victims of shock.

In addition, platelets and clotting factors V and VIII become very scarce in stored blood after several days. The most common coagulation problem with massive transfusion is dilutional thrombocytopenia. If more than 10 units of blood have been transfused in 3 hours or less, platelet transfusion should be considered. Rarely is there a transfusion-induced coagulopathy associated with low levels of factors V and VIII, but if coagulation values become prolonged and bleeding continues, one should consider administration of fresh frozen plasma.

Citrate intoxication can also occur as a result of massive transfusion with blood containing citrate preservatives. Hypocalcemia results from the binding of ionized calcium by citrate, leading to hypotension, narrowed pulse pressure, and elevated left ventricular end-diastolic, pulmonary artery, and central venous pressures. The electrocardiogram will show prolonged QT intervals. In this condition, calcium chloride can be given cautiously, avoiding hypercalcemia. Most patients can withstand an infusion of one unit of blood every 5 minutes without requiring supplemental calcium.

Finally, the potassium concentration in stored blood increases to as much as 35 mEq/L by 21 days of shelf life. Significant hyperkalemia seldom occurs unless transfusion rates exceed 100 to 150 ml/min. If it does occur, its most immediate treatment is the administration of insulin and glucose, although less emergent and safer methods are available if time permits.

Correction of Acid-Base Disturbances

The lung and kidneys are inextricably related to acid-base relationships. The arterial pH should be maintained between 7.35 and 7.50 in patients who are in shock. Improving systemic perfusion and oxygenation will usually increase aerobic metabolism and help prevent acid-base discrepancies. The type, purity, and degree of acid-base derangement are determined by study of the arterial pH, P_{CO_2}, and bicarbonate.

METABOLIC ACIDOSIS

Metabolic acidosis persisting after fluid administration and use of inotropic agents is corrected with sodium bicarbonate after the calculation of base deficit. Bicarbonate deficiency should be corrected relatively slowly to avoid an overcorrection toward alkalosis. About half of the amount of bicarbonate needed by calculation should be given over the first hour or two. Arterial P_{CO_2}, pH, and bicarbonate should be remeasured and alterations in treatment made. If severe iatrogenic alkalosis ensues, cardiac arrhythmias or ventilatory depression may result. Bicarbonate should not be added blindly to solutions given to patients in shock with the assumption that the patients are in an acidotic state. With restoration of cellular and organ functions, metabolic alkalosis may subsequently develop and should be considered during later monitoring.

RESPIRATORY ALKALOSIS

This derangement can usually be corrected by adding dead space to the patient's ventilatory system or by decreasing ventilation by lowering the respiratory rate when appropriate. Sedation may also be required, but very judiciously so as not to interfere with the evaluation of mental status when necessary. Tidal volume should not be decreased unless the P_{CO_2} falls below 25 mm Hg in spite of all other efforts.

METABOLIC ALKALOSIS

Noniatrogenic metabolic alkalosis is very uncommon in patients who are in shock. In some cases, it can be attributed to one of several causes, such as hypokalemia from excessive diuresis or steroids, conversion of lactate and citrate to bicarbonate from intravenous fluids and transfused blood, excessive removal of gastric secretions through a nasogastric tube, or repeated administration of antacids to combat the gastric acidity associated with stress gastric bleeding. In other patients, no attributable cause can be found, but sepsis may at times cause alkalosis via alterations in cell metabolism. Treatment consists of giving 10 to 20 mEq or more of potassium chloride per hour until the serum potassium level is 4.5 to 5.0 mEq/L and giving enough saline to raise the serum chloride level to 100 to 110 mEq/L. If alkalosis persists, acetazolamide (Diamox) may be required. Diamox is a carbonic anhydrase inhibitor that reduces the hydration of carbon dioxide. As with metabolic acidosis, if exogenous corrective measures have been instituted, one must be alert to possible autocorrection or overcorrection during recovery.

RESPIRATORY ACIDOSIS

This derangement suggests that the patient has inadequate ventilation caused by pulmonary problems, central nervous system depression, or compensation for a moderate-to-severe metabolic alkalosis. Such patients may need endotracheal intubation and ventilatory assistance.

Sympathomimetic and Sympatholytic Agents

Sympathomimetic agents and sympatholytic agents are neither the only nor the most important approach to the treatment of shock. A detailed description of all the various drugs and their indications, contraindications, and physiologic effects in each type of shock is beyond the scope of this book. Although some authors have questioned the rationale of ever using these agents, most believe that they are important elements in an overall plan of treatment designed to deal with the cause of shock, the pathophysiologic derangements particular to each patient, and the secondary effects produced by each agent that may interfere with response to therapy.[7,8] The choice of an agent is often a compromise, depending on the individual situation and the varying effects of the drugs available for treatment. The ultimate aim is the restoration of blood flow and adequate tissue perfusion. This objective may require the use of a combination of different drugs.

Steroids

Much controversy also surrounds the use of corticosteroids for the treatment of shock. There exists ample literature both to support and to discourage steroid use. Steroids seem to have their most positive results in the treatment of septic shock, for which studies have shown them to have a remarkable effect on reducing mortality rates.[9]

To support the use of steroids, some authors claim they are finding patients who have no overt adrenal insufficiency until they sustain an acute severe injury or develop sepsis, at which point they are unable to increase their plasma cortisol levels appropriately. This homeostatic failure is termed relative adrenal insufficiency. These authors recommend treatment with at least 200 to 300 mg of hydrocortisone given intravenously every 4 to 6 hours. They also claim that massive doses of steroids may increase the stability of lysosomes and cellular membranes and may improve cardiovascular function by raising the cardiac output and decreasing peripheral vascular resistance.[5]

To summarize, whether or not there is increased survival of patients in shock as a result of steroid administration and in which circumstances steroids work best are still under investigation.

Antibiotics

Antibiotic therapy directed at the specific organism involved is a cardinal rule that should be implemented immediately in cases of septic shock. Along with blood cultures, a Gram stain of fluid from the involved area of infection should be taken; in addition, cultures should be taken for aerobic and anaerobic organism growth and sensitivity testing. If the causative organism is unknown at first, initial treatment should include drugs that provide coverage of both gram-negative and gram-positive organisms — for example, oxacillin or nafcillin and gentamicin.[1] (*Note:* With advances in new antimicrobials, those recommended for such "shotgun" coverage are likely to change constantly.)

Antibiotic prophylaxis during other types of shock is advocated by some authors who state that because of the decreased function of the reticuloendothelial system and possible loss of integrity of the intestinal wall due to ischemia, bacteremia and sepsis may arise.[5] There is no hard evidence that this measure is efficacious.

COMMON PITFALLS IN THE TREATMENT OF SHOCK

Walt and Wilson[5] have developed a checklist used in their intensive care units that they systematically review whenever a patient fails to respond satisfactorily to therapy. They list the most common pitfalls as follows:

1. Unappreciated continuing fluid or blood loss
2. Inadequate fluid replacement
3. Inadequate ventilation and hypoxia
4. Unrecognized pneumothorax
5. Pulmonary emboli
6. Cardiac tamponade
7. Inadequately treated or unrecognized sepsis
8. Acid-base and electrolyte disturbances
9. Adrenal insufficiency
10. Hypothermia markedly impairing cardiovascular function

As can be seen by such a checklist, treating the wrong diagnosis or failing to search for more than one cause of shock in an individual patient would be the most likely scenario.

CONCLUSION

The main considerations in the management of shock are early diagnosis of the underlying cause; aggressive treatment of all physiologic derangements; and evaluation of therapy with serial objective studies, using trends, not individual numbers, upon which to base subsequent treatment.

REFERENCES

1. De Sanctis RW, Zusman RM: Scientific American, Nov 1982.
2. Shires GT: Care of the Trauma Patient. New York, McGraw-Hill Book Company, 1966.
3. Committee on Trauma, American College of Surgeons, Walt AJ (ed): Early Care of the Injured Patient. Philadelphia, WB Saunders Company, 1982.
4. Zweifach BW, Froneck A: The interplay of central and peripheral factors in irreversible hemorrhagic shock. Prog Cardiovasc Dis 18(2):147–180, 1975.
5. Walt AJ, Wilson RF: The treatment of shock. Adv Surg 9:1–39, 1975.
6. Lillehei RC, Longerbeam JK, Bloch JH, Manax WG: The nature of irreversible shock: Experimental and clinical observations. Ann Surg 160:682–710, 1964.
7. Tarazi RC: Sympathomimetic agents in the treatment of shock. Ann Intern Med 81:364–371, 1974.
8. Abboud FM: The sympathetic nervous system and alpha-adrenergic blocking agents in shock. Med Clin North Am 52:1049–1060, 1968.
9. Schumer W: Steroids in the treatment of clinical septic shock. Ann Surg 184:333–341, 1976.

CHAPTER 4

Enteral feeding regimen
An isosmolar concentration (300 mOsm or less) is used first.
A continuous infusion is started at 50 ml/hr.
The volume of infusion should be advanced 25 ml every 12 to 24 hours.
When at the desired volume, the concentration should be increased incrementally.

NUTRITIONAL CONSIDERATIONS FOLLOWING TRAUMA

TIMOTHY F. KRESOWIK, M.D.

The detrimental effects of malnutrition following an operation or trauma were recognized many years ago. Surgeons have been at the forefront of nutritional research and were instrumental in the development of current techniques of total parenteral alimentation. Although the importance of nutrition is unquestionable, the optimal route of administration, the type and quantity of substrate administered, and the timing of instituting nutritional support are less clear. When advances in parenteral alimentation made it possible to provide full nutritional support to essentially any patient, many surgeons adopted the following philosophy: "If a little is good, more must be better." All methods of nutritional support have complications. In addition, hazards associated with overfeeding have been recognized. To use this modality safely and cost effectively, one must carefully weigh the risks and benefits of nutritional support for each individual.

CONSEQUENCES OF MALNUTRITION

Most of the initial human studies of malnutrition were performed by health care workers in underdeveloped countries. Two forms of malnutrition were described: marasmus and kwashiorkor. Marasmus results from a diet deficient in both protein and calories. Kwashiorkor develops from dietary protein deficiency when caloric intake is maintained. Marasmus is easily recognized because of the accompanying severe wasting, while kwashiorkor may be more subtle owing to the continued maintenance of body mass. Because of the protein depletion that accompanies kwashiorkor, the extracellular fluid space is expanded and peripheral edema and ascites develop.

Adults or children with marasmus or kwashiorkor demonstrate a decreased resistance to infection. Various components of the inflammatory and immune responses are depressed in malnourished individuals.[1-3] Decreases in lymphoid organ mass and circulating lymphocytes develop, with a greater reduction of T lymphocytes than B lymphocytes. The in vitro proliferative response of lymphocytes to various mitogens is decreased. The delayed hypersensitivity reaction is often absent in severe malnutrition. Even though blood immunoglobulin levels are maintained, antibody responses are often reduced. This reduction may be due to a deficiency of helper T cells rather than a defect in the immunoglobulin-producing B lymphocytes. Lowered complement protein levels accompany severe malnutrition. The absolute numbers of polymorphonuclear neutrophils (PMNs) are not usually decreased in malnutrition, but their function may be impaired. The major functional defect appears to be in intracellular microorganism killing. It is obvious that many aspects of host defense capabilities are affected by malnutrition and can account for the observed increased susceptibility to infection.

Over the past 50 years, numerous studies have demonstrated increased mortality, increased rates of infection, and delayed wound healing in malnourished surgical patients.[4] In studies done in the surgical intensive care unit at the University of Michigan, we noted that even relatively brief periods of starvation (less than 1 week) were associated with increased mortality rates.[5,6] Of importance is the fact that the deleterious effects of malnutrition can be reversed with nutritional therapy.[7,8] Recovery of some aspects of host defenses and a reduction in postoperative or post-trauma morbidity and mortality can occur with as little as 1 week of intensive nutritional support.[9] Nutritional therapy is an important adjunct in the treatment of the critically injured patient.

NUTRITIONAL ASSESSMENT

Because of the deleterious effects of malnutrition on the recovery of patients from surgical or traumatic insults, efforts have been directed at defining objective criteria of malnutrition so that patients at the highest risk can be identified and appropriately treated. One of the earliest recognized and still commonly used parameters of the nutritional state is the serum albumin level. Low serum albumin levels were found to correlate with both the degree of protein malnutrition and an increased morbidity and mortality following surgical procedures.[4] Typically, serum albumin levels greater than 3.5 mg/dl are considered to be normal and levels less than 2.5 mg/dl to represent a severe degree of protein malnutrition.[10] Increased morbidity and mortality in surgical patients are associated with serum albumin levels less than 3 mg/dl. Albumin has a half-life of 20 days and therefore is not sensitive to recent periods of protein deficiency. Other serum proteins with shorter half-lives, such as transferrin, prealbumin, and retinol-binding protein, have been proposed as more sensitive indicators of visceral protein depletion.[11] In practice, however, all the measures of visceral protein have significant limitations in the critically ill trauma patient. Stress, blood loss, and fluid replacement have major effects on serum protein levels. It is easy to find well-nourished patients who have measured serum albumin levels of less than 3 mg/dl in the postresuscitation period. In the recovery phase, fluid shifts have a much more dramatic effect on serum protein levels than does nutritional therapy. Although visceral protein measurements may have utility in defining the degree of malnutrition, and thus the risk of complications, if obtained prior to any surgical or traumatic insult, they have limited value in the care of the trauma patient.

Attempts have been made to define nutritional status by measurements of body mass. Body weight is the most obvious measure of body mass, and optimal body weights for a given height and frame size have been determined from insurance statistics. Although a pre-event history of significant weight loss may be helpful in assessing an individual's nutritional state, absolute levels of body weight have little value in evaluating the patient who has experienced trauma. Total body weight obviously reflects all the various components of body mass, including adipose tissue and fluid. Post-trauma or postsurgical changes in body weight most often reflect fluid gains or losses rather than changes in the other components of body mass. Other methods used to assess body mass, such as midarm circumference and triceps skinfold thickness, are limited by difficulties in obtaining reproducible measurements and are affected by the diffuse tissue edema that often occurs in the severely injured patient.

The association of malnutrition with compromise of host defenses has led to attempts at defining the nutritional state by using indicators of host defense capability. As noted previously, lymphocytes, especially the T lymphocytes, are decreased in malnutrition. The total lymphocyte count can easily be determined from a white blood cell count and differential, with a total lymphocyte count greater than 1800 considered to be normal and a level of less than 900 to indicate severe malnutrition.[10] The delayed hypersensitivity response can be tested by using several common antigens, such as mumps, *Candida albicans,* purified protein derivative (PPD), streptokinase-streptodornase, and/or *Trichophyton.* The induration that develops after intradermal administration of these antigens is qualitatively or quantitatively assessed. Although both the total lymphocyte count and the delayed hypersensitivity response correlate with nutritional status and can be predictive of increased complications and mortality, they have limited usefulness in the trauma patient. In the setting of severe stress, the associated hormonal changes, especially the elevated cortisol level, may lead to a decreased lymphocyte count and impaired delayed hypersensitivity response. Blood transfusions and general anesthesia may also depress these indicators of host defense capability.[12,13]

It is obvious that these measures for nutritional assessment have limited value in trauma patients. All of the objective indicators that have demonstrated value in assessing patients who are in a steady state have significant limitations in acute trauma. A clinical impression based on the history and physical examination may be the most valuable indicator. General clinical evaluation has been shown to have a high correlation with abnormalities in virtually all of the discussed objective measures.[14] When pre-existing malnutrition is suspected on the basis of clinical assessment in a severely injured trauma patient, early vigorous nutritional support should be instituted in an attempt to reduce the risk of any increased morbidity and mortality.

METABOLIC RESPONSE TO STARVATION AND TRAUMA

The two major nutritional requirements are an energy source and a protein source. Carbohydrate, fat, or protein can be used as an energy source. Protein or, more accurately, amino acids are required to maintain the body's myriad of amino acid–based components, such as enzymes, immunoglobulins, transport proteins, and structural and contractile elements. In addition to these two basic nutritional requirements, vitamins, minerals, trace elements, and certain essential fatty acids must also be supplied. To design an optimal program of nutritional support for the trauma patient, one must also have an understanding of the adaptive response to starvation and the normal metabolic response to trauma.

The body can use endogenous stored carbohydrate, protein, or fat as fuel (Table 4–1). Carbohydrate is stored as glycogen in the liver and in skeletal muscle; however, the total amount of glycogen stored can supply less than 1000 kcal in the average 75-kg man. In contrast, there is approximately 15 kg of fat, which could supply 140,000 kcal. There is on the order of 13 kg of protein, but one half of this amount is inert structural protein and is unavailable as a fuel source.[15] Even though the protein that is available (primarily skeletal muscle) could be metabolized and theoretically yield 24,000 kcal, no protein is stored to be used as a fuel source. All the protein in the body is serving a function, and thus any use of endogenous protein as a fuel source must be considered detrimental.

During a 24-hour fast in an unstressed state, a normal man would require approximately 1800 kcal. This caloric requirement would come from metabolizing approximately 75 g of protein and 160 g of fat. Certain tissues are glucose dependent, and when glycogen stores are gone, glucose is synthesized in the liver from

TABLE 4-1. CALORIC RESERVES IN NORMAL HUMANS

Source	Amount (kg)	Kilocalories
Glycogen (liver and muscle)	0.225	900
Fat	15.0	140,000
Protein	6.0	24,000

Modified from Cahill GF: Starvation in man. N Engl J Med 282:668–675, 1970.

amino acids. The tissues that are dependent on glucose include brain and nervous tissue, red and white blood cells, bone marrow, and the renal medulla. The brain differs from the other glycolytic tissues in completely metabolizing glucose to carbon dioxide and water. In the other tissues, glucose is metabolized to lactate and pyruvate, which circulate back to the liver and kidney and can be converted back to glucose. This process is known as the Cori cycle. The energy for this glucose synthesis comes from the oxidation of fat. So, in effect, the majority of the protein that is broken down provides glucose for the brain. In addition, skeletal muscle can use amino acids directly as a fuel source.[15]

Most tissues in the body are able to metabolize fatty acids or acetoacetate and beta-hydroxybutyrate, which are products of partial fat metabolism in the liver. Acetoacetate and beta-hydroxybutyrate are known as ketone bodies. In a prolonged fast, the brain is able to adapt partially to using ketone bodies rather than glucose as its fuel source. This adaptation allows for protein sparing in the fasted state. With adaptation, after several weeks of unstressed starvation, the amount of glucose required can decrease to approximately 15 g/day.[16]

Unfortunately, this response to unstressed starvation is not what happens in the severely injured trauma patient. Many of the adaptation responses do not take place because the hormonal milieu is different from that found in starvation and mediators released by the inflammatory response alter many metabolic processes. The severely injured patient, especially if multisystem organ failure develops, is hypermetabolic and may have very high rates of protein catabolism. The protein breakdown is much higher than what would be required to produce glucose during simple starvation.

NUTRITIONAL REQUIREMENTS

In defining energy requirements, various terms are used. The basal metabolic rate (BMR) is the amount of energy required to fuel the metabolic processes necessary for maintenance of cell integrity in the postabsorbtive state.[17] The resting energy expenditure (REE) is the sum of the BMR and energy expended to metabolize food. The BMR can be estimated using various formulae. One of the most commonly used formulae is that of Harris and Benedict.[18]

$$BMR \text{ (males)} = 66.42 + 13.75 \times wt \text{ (kg)} + 5.00 \times ht \text{ (cm)} - 6.78 \times age \text{ (yr)}$$

$$BMR \text{ (females)} = 655.10 + 9.65 \times wt \text{ (kg)} + 1.85 \times ht \text{ (cm)} - 4.68 \times age \text{ (yr)}$$

The energy unit used for nutritional purposes is the kilocalorie (kcal). Estimates of the BMR may not be appropriate for the trauma patient. The formulae do not take into account the hypermetabolism associated with trauma or sepsis. Although various factors can be used to adjust the predicted energy expenditure, there is a very large variability among patients.

Techniques are available that allow measurement of the REE. Indirect calorimetry refers to calculation of the REE based on a measurement of oxygen consumption.

In a patient who has a pulmonary artery thermodilution catheter in place, oxygen consumption may be determined by obtaining the cardiac output, mixed venous oxygen content, and arterial oxygen content. The reverse Fick equation establishes the relationship between these parameters.

Oxygen consumption
= (arterial O_2 content − mixed venous O_2 content) × cardiac output

Obtaining oxygen consumption data in this way is prone to inaccuracy because each of the three measured variables has error in measurement, resulting in an even larger error when they are combined to obtain the oxygen consumption. Oxygen consumption can also be measured directly using various techniques. At the University of Michigan Medical Center, oxygen consumption is measured via a volumetric method.[5] This method involves placing a patient on a closed circuit breathing system of 100 per cent oxygen and determining the amount of oxygen that is consumed by the patient through measurement of volume loss in the system. This method has proved to be accurate in all patients, including those on mechanical ventilators. The relationship between REE and measured oxygen consumption is shown in the following formula:

REE (kcal/24 hr)
= oxygen consumption (L/min) × 5 kcal/L × 60 min/hr × 24 hr/day

Actual measurement of the REE allows more precise tailoring of the energy component of the patient's nutritional support.

The other major component in designing a patient's nutritional support regimen is protein. Although protein can be utilized as an energy source, it is primarily supplied to provide the amino acid building blocks for the patient's own proteins. Therefore, only the carbohydrate and fat content of the diet should be used to calculate the number of calories required to meet the patient's energy needs. The protein requirement is calculated separately. The average protein requirement in the unstressed patient is on the order of 0.8 to 1.0 g/kg of ideal body weight. As is true for energy needs, protein requirements in the stressed patient with trauma or sepsis are higher. Some have recommended supplying as much as 2 to 3 g of protein per kilogram of body weight per day in critically ill patients.[19] It is difficult to predict the exact protein requirements of a given patient. Estimation of the patient's rate of protein breakdown can be determined by monitoring the urine urea nitrogen (UUN) excretion. There is a small amount of nonurea urinary nitrogen, and some nitrogen is lost in normal stool and skin desquamation; but UUN represents the majority of nitrogen loss. By measuring the urea in a 24-hour urine collection and adding a factor for the additional losses, a patient's nitrogen excretion and thus the rate of protein breakdown can be estimated. In practice, adding a constant factor of about 3 g to the UUN determination acceptably estimates nonurea losses. Nitrogen balance for a given patient can be determined by subtracting the nitrogen excretion from the nitrogen intake. Approximately 6.25 g of protein corresponds to 1 g of nitrogen.[10] Nitrogen balance is thus determined by the following formula:

Nitrogen balance (g) = protein intake (g)/6.25 − [UUN (g) + 3]

The goal should be to achieve a positive nitrogen balance on the order of 4 to 5 g. The amount of protein provided can thus be tailored to a given patient's needs. However, it should be noted that in patients with large open wounds the loss of serum proteins directly through the wound may represent a significant nitrogen loss and make determination of total body nitrogen loss on the basis of urine urea invalid.

Nutritional support has to include certain essential minerals and vitamins in addition to protein and energy sources. Multivitamin preparations that contain quantities of most essential vitamins at or above recommended levels are available in both enteral and parenteral forms. Although most water-soluble vitamins can be given in quantities far exceeding the required amounts without harm, the fat-soluble vitamins A, D, E, and K have toxic side effects when given in excess. Most patients on a balanced oral diet or on a defined oral formula diet do not require vitamin supplementation; however, more specific attention must be paid to these needs in a patient on total parenteral nutrition. In addition to standard vitamin preparations, trace elements such as zinc, copper, manganese, chromium, and selenium must be supplied. Standard trace element formulae for intravenous use are available. The diet must also contain enough fat to prevent essential fatty acid deficiency.

ENTERAL NUTRITION

The ideal route of administration of nutritional support is the gastrointestinal tract. Every effort should be made to utilize this route. Obviously, a patient with severe orofacial trauma or one who requires ventilatory support cannot eat normally. These situations, however, do not preclude enteral nutrition, which is preferred because it avoids some specific complications of parenteral alimentation. There are clear differences in the hormonal responses to enteral versus parenteral nutrition.[20] Enteral nutrition does not have the high incidence of liver and gallbladder dysfunction associated with parenteral nutrition. The liver and gallbladder dysfunction have, at least in part, been attributed to the lack of the normal enteral hormonal responses.[21] With total parenteral nutrition, there also appears to be atrophy of the intestinal mucosa.[22,23] It has been postulated that intestinal colonization and loss of the mucosal barrier may contribute to sepsis and multisystem organ failure in the critically ill patient.[19] Enteral nutrition appears to preserve more effectively the integrity of the intestinal mucosa.[24] Enteral nutrition is, in most cases, much less expensive than any form of parenteral feeding.

Enteral nutrition is not without complications. Obviously, the gut must be functional. A paralytic ileus often accompanies multisystem organ failure or sepsis, and constant interruptions of enteral feeding because of intolerance can result in progressive malnutrition. In an unconscious patient or a patient with impaired upper airway protective reflexes, aspiration is always a constant danger and a potentially fatal complication. Significant fluid and electrolyte imbalances can also occur with enteral nutrition. Although enteral feeding is, in most cases, safer than parenteral feeding, careful monitoring of fluid balance and serum electrolytes is still required.

In patients who are unable to eat or drink normally, enteral nutritional products can be given via several routes, including nasogastric or nasoenteric tubes, gastrostomy tubes, and feeding jejunostomies. Many soft, mercury-weighted feeding tubes are commercially available. These tubes often come with self-lubricating external surfaces and stylets for ease of placement. The weighted end is designed to facilitate passage through the pylorus via normal gastric motility; however, placement distal to the pylorus often requires fluoroscopic or endoscopic assistance. There are differences between the administration of enteral diets into the stomach and administration into the small bowel. On the one hand, the stomach tolerates bolus feedings and high-osmolarity products, whereas bolus administration or high-osmolarity feedings given directly into the small bowel will result in rapid fluid shifts and dumping-type symptoms. On the other hand, small bowel feeding decreases the risk of aspiration. Studies have shown that the ileus following laparotomy primarily involves the stomach and colon.[25,26] Small bowel motility and absorptive capacity are often retained. Therefore, the direct feeding into the small bowel of products that are essentially completely absorbed—that is, elemental diets—can be initiated immediately after laparotomy.[27,28] This feature permits early institution of enteral nutritional support even in those multiply injured patients who require laparotomy. Placement of a feeding jejunostomy tube should be considered at the time of initial laparotomy in severely injured patients who are likely to have a prolonged period without normal oral intake. Feeding jejunostomies can be placed rapidly, have a low incidence of complications, and often markedly simplify nutritional support.

Liquid enteral products have differences in substrate makeup, caloric density, and osmolarity. An important consideration in the critically ill patient or patient in the postoperative period is the presence of lactose in some products. Adult lactase deficiency is prevalent in many population groups and may occur on a temporary basis in critically ill patients or those in the postoperative period. Therefore, lactose-based products should not be given to these patients to avoid complications of lactose malabsorption (diarrhea, bloating). Different amounts of protein for a given caloric density are available and allow tailoring of a patient's nutritional regimen to their predicted or measured requirements. The severely injured trauma patient may benefit from the high-nitrogen formulae. The caloric density of the formulae generally varies between 1 and 2 kcal/ml. The higher density formulae allow the administration of less volume, which may be important in fluid-overloaded patients; however, the higher caloric density is associated with a higher osmolarity. The higher the osmolarity, generally the less well tolerated is the formula in terms of diarrhea and bloating. Osmolarity is also important when considering the so-called elemental diets. Elemental formulae are composed largely of oligosaccharides as a carbohydrate source and amino acids as a protein source. These compounds can be absorbed directly without requiring digestion, which may allow earlier postoperative administration and greater tolerance in some critically ill patients. However, by virtue of their composition, these formulae have a very high osmolarity. It is important to distinguish between patients who do not tolerate tube feedings because of impaired digestion and patients who do not tolerate the high osmolar load.

Many of the problems associated with tube feeding can be avoided by cautious initiation of therapy (Fig. 4–1). Continuous drip feedings are generally better tolerated and are mandatory for administration into the small intestine. The initial administration should begin with an isosmolar concentration; thus, whether or not a given formula needs to be diluted depends on its osmolarity. Isosmolar formulae (300 mOsm/ml) are available and can be started at full strength, but some of the elemental formulae approach 900 mOsm and therefore must be diluted to one-third strength or less at first. The initial drip should be begun around 50 ml/hr and increased at increments of 25 ml/hr every 12 to 24 hours. Once the volume per hour is reached that will fulfill caloric requirements at the full strength of the formula, the concentration can be gradually increased in those formulae that were initially diluted. The rate of advancement may need to be slowed if bloating or diarrhea develops. When tube feedings are begun, intermittent gastric aspiration should be performed. If the patient develops high gastric volumes (i.e., > 200 to 300 ml), the rate of administration should be slowed to avoid potential aspiration. Diarrhea can often be controlled by adding a pectin-based (e.g., kaolin-pectin [Kaopectate]) or motility-suppressive agent (e.g., diphenoxylate hydrochloride with atropine [Lomotil] or loperamide hydrochloride [Imodium]) to the tube feeding. Patients with low serum albumin levels seem to tolerate tube feedings very poorly.[29] Supplemental albumin may be beneficial in improving tolerance to tube feeding.

An isosmolar concentration (300 mOsm or less) is used first.

A continuous infusion is started at 50 ml/hr.

The volume of infusion should be advanced 25 ml every 12 to 24 hours.

When at the desired volume, the concentration should be increased incrementally.

FIGURE 4–1.   Enteral feeding regimen.

PARENTERAL NUTRITION

In the patient who is not a candidate for enteral nutrition, complete nutritional needs can be met via the parenteral route. Parenteral nutritional support can be given via central or peripheral venous access. Administration of parenteral support via the peripheral route is limited by the high osmolarity of the solutions. High-osmolar solutions are not tolerated by peripheral veins, frequently resulting in phlebitis. Less concentrated (usually 10 per cent dextrose or less) solutions, and thus those of lower caloric density, must be used for peripheral as opposed to central venous administration. In a hypermetabolic patient, large volumes of solution would have to be given to meet caloric and protein needs. The incidence of phlebitis can be lessened by concomitant administration of lipids.[30] The lipid solutions tend to decrease the overall osmolarity of the solution and should be given just proximal to the infusion site via a Y-connector to the line containing the dextrose and amino acid solution. Peripheral venous alimentation may be useful in those patients who have no pre-existing malnutrition and are likely to require support only for relatively short periods. In patients at high risk because of their pre-existing nutritional state or hypermetabolism, central venous administration is a better alternative.

Central venous administration of alimentation solutions is usually into the superior vena cava, with access obtained via the subclavian or internal jugular route. The incidence of pneumothorax occurring as a complication of attempted percutaneous central venous access is lower when the internal jugular vein route is chosen. However, the internal jugular route does have some disadvantages when the line is needed for alimentation. The placement of the line in the neck is associated with more movement, and it is difficult to keep a dressing intact, which may increase the incidence of line sepsis. A properly placed subclavian venous line can be cared for quite easily. If at all possible, any line that is used for alimentation purposes should be dedicated to that function alone. Administration of parenteral alimentation solutions via multilumen catheters or through catheters used for other infusions is associated with a higher incidence of line sepsis.[31,32] The tip of the catheter should be in the superior vena cava because of the greater flow present. The greater flow lessens the risk of thrombosis secondary to the high osmolarity of the solutions. Even though the tolerance of high-osmolar solutions is much better via the central route than peripherally, the incidence of thrombosis remains significant. Studies of the incidence of catheter-associated upper extremity thrombosis have indicated that the rate may be as high as 25 to 35 per cent.[33] There is a significant incidence of morbidity, including pulmonary embolism, from upper extremity thromboses. The addition of heparin to the alimentation solution may decrease the incidence of this complication.[34] The other major complications of central venous line placement include pneumothorax and inadvertent arterial puncture and venous perforation, resulting in extravasation of fluid or bleeding. To reduce the incidence of complications, placement of these catheters should be done only under direct supervision by an experienced person.

The caloric source for parenteral alimentation is usually glucose or lipid emulsions (Table 4–2). The caloric value of glucose is 3.4 kcal/g. Typical glucose concentrations in solutions for parenteral alimentation range between 10 and 35 per cent. This concentration range corresponds to a caloric density of between 340 and 1200 kcal/L of solution. A 10 per cent dextrose solution used for peripheral venous administration would supply 340 kcal/L as glucose. The most commonly used concentration for central venous administration is 25 per cent, corresponding to 850 kcal/L. The caloric value of fat is approximately 9 kcal/g. A 500-ml bottle of 10 per cent lipid emulsion corresponds to 550 kcal because of the 100-kcal contribution of glycerol and egg phosphatide to the caloric value. Lipid emulsions are also available in a concentration of 20 per cent (500 ml = 1000 kcal). Lipid can be safely given to most patients in amounts up to 3 to 4 g/kg/day and supplying as much as 60 per cent of the patient's caloric needs.[10]

Calories supplied by lipid or dextrose appear to be of equal value in meeting

TABLE 4–2.   CALORIC VALUE OF PARENTERAL
FUEL SOURCE

SOURCE	CONCENTRATION/ VOLUME	KILOCALORIES
Dextrose (3.4 kcal/g)	10%/1 L	340
	25%/1 L	850
Lipid (9 kcal/g)	10%/500 ml	550*
	20%/500 ml	1000*

*One hundred kilocalories from glycerol and egg phosphatide.

patient's energy needs.[35–37] The hepatic dysfunction that can accompany parenteral nutrition was initially attributed to lipid administration because fatty infiltration of the liver was a common histologic finding in patients on parenteral feeding. It now appears that the fatty infiltration and hepatic dysfunction may be secondary to excess glucose calories rather than lipid administration.[38] Excess calories given as glucose are converted to fat in the liver. In addition, when excess glucose is converted to fat, there is an increased production of carbon dioxide. The ratio of carbon dioxide produced to oxygen consumed is expressed as the respiratory quotient (RQ):

$$RQ = \text{carbon dioxide molecules produced/oxygen molecules consumed}$$

The RQ differs for the various substrates, with a value of approximately 1.0 for carbohydrate and a value of 0.7 for fat. However, when excess carbohydrate is converted to fat, the RQ is 8.0. This factor may be important in patients with diminished ventilatory capacity and thus ability to excrete carbon dioxide.[39] The excess carbon dioxide production may make weaning the patient from the ventilator difficult because of carbon dioxide retention. Decreasing the caloric load or supplying more of the calories as lipid will reduce the amount of carbon dioxide produced. The RQ can be determined after measuring oxygen consumption and carbon dioxide production. The nutritional support regimen can be modified based on the information provided by the RQ about substrate utilization. A low RQ (<1.0) implies fat utilization, which can be either endogenous stores or administered lipids. A high RQ (>1.0) indicates that carbohydrate is being converted to fat, suggesting that overfeeding is taking place.

Lipid emulsions have an advantage in their low osmolarity, and thus nonirritating character, which decreases the incidence of phlebitis. The high caloric density allows lower total volumes of alimentation solution for a given number of calories. At least 1 or 2 500-ml bottles per week of 10 per cent lipid emulsion should be given to the patient on total parenteral alimentation to prevent fatty acid deficiency. However, because of the advantages of lipid over glucose, higher amounts (i.e., 30 to 50 per cent of nonprotein calories) can be recommended. If lipemic serum develops in a patient, the amount of lipid may have to be decreased.

The amino acid content of parenteral alimentation solutions typically varies between 2.5 and 5.0 per cent. The amino acids contribute significantly to the osmolarity of the solution, and peripheral formulae usually contain the lower concentrations. When used as a caloric source, amino acids provide 4 kcal/g. However, nonprotein calories should be used to meet the patient's energy needs so that the amino acids can be used to support the patient's protein synthesis. The standard amino acid formula used in parenteral alimentation is generally a mixed amino acid formula that contains essential and nonessential amino acids. Special amino acid solutions, such as formulae containing almost exclusively essential amino acids (those that the body cannot synthesize de novo or from other amino acids) and formulae high in branched-chain amino acids (leucine, isoleucine, and valine), are also available.

The essential amino acid formulae were proposed as being ideal for patients in renal failure. This concept is in keeping with the usual practice of restricting nitrogen intake in those patients in chronic renal failure. However, the extrapolation of this practice to the treatment of critically ill patients with acute renal failure must be done with caution. Acute renal failure in a trauma patient usually occurs when the patient has suffered severe injury. These patients are highly catabolic and thus require large amounts of protein to stay in positive nitrogen balance. Restricting amino acid intake in these patients leads to large protein deficits and could possibly contribute to the high morbidity and mortality seen in surgical patients in whom acute renal failure develops. In this setting, it seems more prudent to treat the patient in acute renal failure as one would treat any other critically ill patient. Adequate amounts of amino acids should be administered to meet their total protein requirements. Although this practice may result in acceleration of their uremia, the uremia can be controlled by frequent dialysis or hemofiltration. No advantage of essential amino acid formulae over mixed amino acid formulae has been demonstrated for patients in acute renal failure.[40]

Other types of specialized amino acid formulae are those containing higher concentrations of the branched-chain amino acids. These formulae generally contain between 25 and 50 per cent of the total number of amino acids as leucine, isoleucine, or valine. The basis for these formulae rests on studies that indicate that branched-chain amino acids are preferentially metabolized in the stressed patient. In skeletal muscle, these amino acids are taken up and either metabolized completely as a caloric source or used in protein synthesis. Branched-chain amino acids are also said to promote hepatic protein synthesis possibly because of a regulatory effect.[41,42] However, clinical studies to date have shown conflicting results regarding the benefit of these formulae. Some studies have shown improved overall nitrogen retention when compared with mixed amino acid formulae with equal amounts of nitrogen and total calories.[43,44] However, other studies have shown no benefit on overall nitrogen retention and thus protein synthesis.[41,42] Branched-chain amino acid formulae have also been proposed as being beneficial for those patients in hepatic failure.[45,46] Patients with hepatic failure and encephalopathy have higher ratios of aromatic to branched-chain amino acids in their blood than do normal subjects. It has been postulated that the high concentration of aromatic amino acids may play a role in encephalopathy. However, some studies have not demonstrated a reduced incidence of encephalopathy with the use of branched-chain formulae.[47,48] It must be concluded that, although branched-chain amino acid formulae have a theoretical advantage over standard formulations, clinical studies to date do not document this benefit.

As is true for enteral alimentation, parenteral feeding is usually instituted gradually over a 2- to 3-day period. This practice allows time for adaptation to the high glucose load. Urine and blood sugar levels should be monitored carefully while instituting parenteral feeding. If the patient becomes persistently hyperglycemic, insulin can be added to the solution. Because of some loss of insulin to the coating of the bottle and tubing, insulin is begun at a concentration of 20 units/L. The amount can be increased gradually until the patient's blood glucose level is controlled. A patient who has had stable blood glucose values while on a regimen of intravenous feedings and who suddenly becomes hyperglycemic should be examined carefully for a source of sepsis. Sudden glucose intolerance may be an early sign of developing sepsis.

Decisions about the number of calories and amount of protein given to an individual patient may be made empirically at first. The caloric needs can be based on the Harris-Benedict formula, or a rough approximation of 35 kcal/kg can be used. For example, the caloric needs of a 70-kg individual would be estimated at 2500 kcal. If 2 L of a standard 25 per cent dextrose, 4.25 per cent mixed amino acid solution were administered, this would supply approximately 1700 nonprotein kcal and 85 g of amino acids. The amino acid intake would therefore be at just over 1 g/kg. Concomitant administration of either two 500-ml bottles of 10 per cent lipid or one bottle of 20 per cent lipid would supply an additional 1000 kcal, just exceeding the

TABLE 4-3. COMPARISON OF PARENTERAL
FEEDING REGIMENS

REGIMEN	NONPROTEIN KILOCALORIES	PROTEIN (G)
2 L 25% dextrose/4.25% a.a. 500 ml 20% lipid	2700	85.0 g
3 L 20% dextrose/4.25% a.a. 500 ml 20% lipid	3000	127.5 g
4 L 15% dextrose/4.25% a.a. 500 ml 20% lipid	3000	170.0 g

patient's calculated requirement (Table 4-3). The lipid portion of the caloric intake would be 37 per cent of the nonprotein calories. The patient's actual caloric expenditure could then be measured using indirect calorimetry, and protein catabolism could be approximated by collecting the patient's 24-hour urine to determine UUN excretion. If the patient was found to be hypermetabolic, with an energy expenditure closer to 3000 kcal, or to have increased nitrogen excretion, the regimen could be modified. For example, 3 L of a 20 per cent dextrose or 4 L of a 15 per cent dextrose solution would each supply approximately 2000 kcal of glucose. The respective amino acid intake for the three- or four-bottle regimen of 4.25 per cent amino acid solution would be 127.5 g and 170 g. Administration of 1000 kcal as lipid would result in meeting the patient's caloric needs of 3000 kcal, and 30 per cent of the patient's kilocalories would still be administered as fat. This specific approach to a nutritional regimen may not be necessary in all patients. It is useful in the critically ill patient, who will require nutritional support for a long period, to ensure that the patient's protein and energy needs are met, at the same time avoiding the complications of overfeeding (e.g., liver dysfunction, carbon dioxide retention).

Other additives to parenteral alimentation solutions include various electrolytes, vitamin solutions, trace elements, and heparin (Table 4-4). Heparin is typically added at a concentration of 1 unit/ml to reduce the incidence of venous thrombosis at the site of administration. Standard multivitamin and trace element preparations are available. Most vitamin preparations do not include vitamin K as a standard additive because vitamin K will antagonize the action of warfarin-type oral anticoagulants. In most patients, 5 to 10 mg of vitamin K per week will meet requirements. This can be

TABLE 4-4. UNIVERSITY OF MICHIGAN STANDARD FORMULA
FOR CENTRAL VENOUS PARENTERAL ALIMENTATION[10]

Amino acids (4.25%)	42.5 g
Dextrose (25%)	250.0 g
Calcium	4.5 mEq
Magnesium	5.0 mEq
Potassium	40.0 mEq
Sodium	35.0 mEq
Acetate*	74.5 mEq
Chloride	52.5 mEq
Phosphorus	12.0 mM
Heparin	1000 units
Multivitamins (one bottle/day)	2 ml
Trace elements (one bottle/day)	1 ml
Vitamin K (once/week)	5 mg
Volume: 1050 ml	
Osmolarity: 1825 mOsm	

* Forty-five milliequivalents is from amino acids.

TABLE 4–5.   ELECTROLYTE REQUIREMENTS FOR PARENTERAL ALIMENTATION[10]

Calcium	10–15 mEq/day
Magnesium	8–24 mEq/day
Potassium	90–240 mEq/day
Sodium	60–150 mEq/day
Acetate	80–120 mEq/day
Chloride	60–150 mEq/day
Phosphorus	30–50 mM/day

given parenterally on a daily or weekly basis. Typical electrolyte requirements are listed in Table 4–5. Special attention should be paid to potassium and phosphorus when parenteral feeding is begun. As a patient becomes anabolic, especially with glucose as a caloric source, rapid intracellular shifts of potassium and phosphorus can occur, with resultant hypokalemia or hypophosphatemia or both. The serum concentrations of all of the added electrolytes should be monitored on a regular basis.

A patient's acid-base status may be altered by the alimentation solution. The original amino acid formulations used amino acid chloride salts, which resulted in a high incidence of metabolic acidosis. All of the commonly used amino acid solutions have now converted to acetate salts. A typical liter of solution for central venous alimentation with 4.25 per cent amino acids would contain 45 mEq of acetate from the amino acid component. Metabolic acidosis is now a very rare complication of parenteral feeding, but metabolic alkalosis may occur. This condition is common in patients who have other sources of acid or chloride loss, such as high nasogastric outputs. These patients are already prone to metabolic alkalosis, and the alkalosis may be exacerbated by acetate in the alimentation solution. When a severe metabolic alkalosis develops, all added acetate above the amino acid contribution should be discontinued. Hydrochloric acid can be added directly to the solution in concentrations up to 50 mEq/L, if necessary, to correct a severe alkalosis.[49]

Catheter sepsis is a significant concern in patients receiving parenteral nutrition. In the otherwise stable patient who develops signs of sepsis, the catheter is sometimes obviously the source of the infection and should be removed. The problem is much more complex in the critically ill trauma patient, who often has multiple reasons for signs of sepsis. Central venous access is often a problem in these patients, and the risks of removing catheters at the first signs of sepsis and doing new central venous punctures may outweigh the benefits. Multiple strategies have evolved for the diagnosis and treatment of possible catheter sepsis. One area of controversy is the practice of changing catheters over a guide wire in a case of suspected catheter sepsis. Some have objected to this technique because of the belief that catheter infections originate at the skin entrance site, suggesting that the entire catheter tract is contaminated and that changing a catheter over a guide wire would traverse the contaminated tract. However, others have suggested that the skin entrance site is not the only and possibly not even the most common cause of infectious seeding of the catheter.[50] Contamination at the catheter hub during tubing changes or bacteremic seeding or both may be a significant factor. There is evidence that supports the practice of changing the catheter over a guide wire for the purpose of diagnosis and possibly treatment in suspected catheter sepsis.[51] The advantage of this approach is that it eliminates the considerable risks of another central venous percutaneous puncture in this group of patients. This approach is especially valid when the catheter is found not to be infected and therefore would have been changed needlessly. Various techniques for determining whether the catheter is indeed the source of apparent sepsis have been described. One technique compares semiquantitative cultures of blood that has been drawn through the catheter with cultures of peripheral blood.[52] It has also been suggested that Gram stains of the catheter will allow visualization of microorganisms on the catheter.[53] The catheter tip can be rolled across an agar plate to obtain cultures. In cases in which these techniques do not document catheter tip infection, the change of the catheter over a guide wire is probably adequate. In situations in which the catheter tip is implicated as a septic focus, the insertion site should probably be changed if the patient has continued signs of sepsis.

Another potential source of sepsis in the patient receiving parenteral nutrition is acalculous cholecystitis. This complication can obviously occur in the absence of parenteral nutrition and may in fact represent the lack of enteral feeding rather than the use of parenteral feeding. Acute acalculous cholecystitis may occur because of gallbladder ischemia, which develops as a result of a relatively low-flow state in combination with gallbladder distention. In many patients who are receiving total parenteral nutrition, gallbladders become distended because of a lack of gallbladder stimulation. Stasis and distention of the gallbladder may result in nonvisualization of the gallbladder on such tests as a radioisotope biliary excretion scan. These scans, which have a high accuracy for diagnosing acute cholecystitis when nonvisualization of the gallbladder occurs in the nonfasted patient, have a very high false-positive rate in the fasted or parenterally nourished patient.[54] This factor makes the diagnosis difficult. In alert and responsive patients, the clinical examination can be very helpful in determining focal tenderness over the gallbladder. In the unresponsive patient, the ultrasonographic appearance of the gallbladder may be helpful. A thickened gallbladder wall is more suggestive of cholecystitis than is simple distention. At times, the diagnosis cannot be excluded, and exploration with cholecystectomy is required without a definitive preoperative diagnosis. Prevention of this complication is important. If at all possible, the patient should receive at least part of the nutritional regimen enterally. Administering some oral fat may help to stimulate the gallbladder and prevent overdistention. Daily intravenous administration of cholecystokinin has also been suggested and has been shown to be beneficial in an experimental model.[55]

It is clear that although nutritional therapy is very important, it is not without risk. Determining which patients will benefit from aggressive nutritional support is not always easy. In the critically ill patient at high risk for multiple organ failure, early, aggressive nutritional support may indeed reduce morbidity and mortality. It is important to consider a plan for the patient's nutritional support at the beginning of the hospital stay. This plan should include enteral feeding if at all possible. The amount of time that a given patient can tolerate the lack of significant nutritional support is variable. On the one hand, the previously well-nourished patient may tolerate a moderate period of starvation with no ill effects. On the other hand, the patient with pre-existing malnutrition may be adversely affected by even brief periods of inadequate nutritional support. With a solid foundation in nutritional concepts and with proper monitoring of the patient, most serious complications related to nutritional support can be avoided. It is probably better to err on the side of instituting nutritional support in some patients who would have tolerated a period of starvation rather than be forced to overcome problems related to iatrogenic malnutrition.

REFERENCES

1. Chandra RK: Nutrition, immunity, and infection: Present knowledge and future directions. Lancet 1:688–691, 1983.
2. Kahan BD: Nutrition and host defense mechanisms. Surg Clin North Am 61:557–570, 1981.
3. Gross RL, Newberne PM: Role of nutrition in immunologic function. Physiol Rev 60:188–301, 1980.
4. Mullen JL: Consequences of malnutrition in

the surgical patient. Surg Clin North Am 61:465–487, 1981.
5. Bartlett RH, Dechert RE, Mault JR, et al: Measurement of metabolism in multiple organ failure. Surgery 92:771–779, 1982.
6. Kresowik TF, Dechert RE, Mault JR, et al: Does nutritional support affect survival in critically ill patients? Surg Forum 35:108–110, 1984.
7. Koster F, Gaffar A, Jackson TM: Recovery of

cellular immune competence during treatment of protein-calorie malnutrition. Am J Clin Nutr 34:887–891, 1981.

8. Law DK, Dudrick SJ, Abdou NI: Immunocompetence of patients with protein-calorie malnutrition: The effects of nutritional repletion. Ann Intern Med 79:545–550, 1973.

9. Mullen JL, Buzby GP, Matthews DC, et al: Reduction of operative morbidity and mortality by combined preoperative and postoperative nutritional support. Ann Surg 192:604–613, 1980.

10. The University of Michigan Medical Center Parenteral and Enteral Nutrition Manual. 4th ed. Ann Arbor, MI, University of Michigan, 1986.

11. Grant JP, Custer PB, Thunlow J: Current techniques of nutritional assessment. Surg Clin North Am 61:437–464, 1981.

12. Howard RJ, Simmons RL: Acquired immunologic deficiencies after trauma and surgical procedures. Surg Gynecol Obstet 139:771–782, 1974.

13. George CD, Morello PJ: Immunologic effects of blood transfusion upon renal transplantation, tumor operations, and bacterial infections. Am J Surg 152:329–337, 1986.

14. Baker JP, Detsky AS, Wesson DE, et al: Nutritional assessment: A comparison of clinical judgement and objective measurements. N Engl J Med 306:969–972, 1982.

15. Cahill GF: Starvation in man. N Engl J Med 282:668–675, 1970.

16. Meguid MM, Collier MD, Howard LJ: Uncomplicated and stressed starvation. Surg Clin North Am 61:529–544, 1981.

17. Elwyn DH, Kinney JM, Askanazi J: Energy expenditure in surgical patients. Surg Clin North Am 61:545–556, 1981.

18. Harris JA, Benedict FG: Biometric Studies of Basal Metabolism in Man. Washington, DC, Carnegie Institute of Washington, Publication 279, 1919.

19. Cerra FB: Hypermetabolism, organ failure, and metabolic support. Surgery 101:1–13, 1987.

20. Gimmon ZV, Murphy RF, Chen MH, et al: The effect of parenteral and enteral nutrition on portal and systemic immunoreactivities of gastrin, glucagon and vasoactive intestinal polypeptide (VIP). Ann Surg 196:571–574, 1982.

21. Petersen SR, Sheldon GF: Acute acalculous cholecystitis: A complication of hyperalimentation. Am J Surg 138:814–817, 1979.

22. Rombeau JL, Barot LR: Enteral nutritional therapy. Surg Clin North Am 61:605–620, 1981.

23. Heymsfield SB, Bethel RA, Ansley JD, et al: Enteral hyperalimentation: An alternative to central venous hyperalimentation. Ann Intern Med 90:63–71, 1979.

24. Alverdy J, Chi HS, Sheldon GF: The effect of parenteral nutrition on gastrointestinal immunity: The importance of enteral stimulation. Ann Surg 202:681–684, 1985.

25. Nachlas MM, Younis MT, Roda CP, et al: Gastrointestinal motility studies as a guide to postoperative management. Ann Surg 175:510–522, 1972.

26. Condon RE, Cowles VE, Schulte WJ, et al: Resolution of postoperative ileus in humans. Ann Surg 203:574–581, 1986.

27. Hoover HC, Ryan JA, Anderson EJ, et al: Nutritional benefits of immediate postoperative jejunal feeding of an elemental diet. Am J Surg 139:153–159, 1980.

28. Page CP, Carlton PK, Andnassy RJ, et al: Safe, cost-effective postoperative nutrition: Defined formula diet via needle-catheter jejunostomy. Am J Surg 138:939–945, 1979.

29. Kaminski MV: Enteral hyperalimentation. Surg Gynecol Obstet 143:12–16, 1976.

30. Fujiwara T, Kawarasaki H, Fonkalsrud EW: Reduction of postinfusion venous endothelial injury with intralipid. Surg Gynecol Obstet 158:57–64, 1984.

31. Pemberton LB, Lyman B, Lander V, et al: Sepsis from triple- vs single-lumen catheters during total parenteral nutrition in surgical or critically ill patients. Arch Surg 121:591–594, 1986.

32. Wolfe BM, Ryder MA, Nishikawa RA, et al: Complications of parenteral nutrition. Am J Surg 152:93–98, 1986.

33. Horattas MC, Wright DJ, Fenton AH, et al: Changing concepts of deep venous thrombosis of the upper extremity — report of a series and review of the literature. Surgery 104:561–567, 1988.

34. Brismar B, Hardstedt C, Jacobson S, et al: Reduction of catheter-associated thrombosis in parenteral nutrition by intravenous heparin therapy. Arch Surg 117:1196–1199, 1982.

35. Nordenstrom J, Carpentier YA, Askanazi J, et al: Metabolic utilization of intravenous fat emulsion during total parenteral nutrition. Ann Surg 196:221–231, 1982.

36. Nordenstrom J, Askanazi J, Elwyn DH, et al: Nitrogen balance during total parenteral nutrition: Glucose vs. fat. Ann Surg 197:27–33, 1983.

37. Gazzaniga AB, Bartlett RH, Shobe JB: Nitrogen balance in patients receiving either fat or carbohydrate for total intravenous nutrition. Ann Surg 182:163–167, 1975.

38. Sax HC, Talamini MA, Brackett K, et al: Hepatic steatosis in total parenteral nutrition: Failure of fatty infiltration to correlate with abnormal serum hepatic enzyme levels. Surgery 100:697–704, 1986.

39. Askanazi J, Rosenbaum SH, Hyman AI, et al: Respiratory changes induced by the large glucose loads of total parenteral nutrition. JAMA 243:1444–1447, 1980.

40. Feinstein EI, Blumenkrantz MJ, Healy M, et al: Clinical and metabolic responses to parenteral nutrition in acute renal failure: A controlled double-blind study. Medicine 60:124–137, 1981.

41. Sax HC, Talamini MA, Fischer JE: Clinical use of branched-chain amino acids in liver disease, sepsis, trauma and burns. Arch Surg 121:358–366, 1986.

42. Bower RH, Muggia-Sullam M, Vallgren S, et al: Branched chain amino acid–enriched solutions in the septic patient: A randomized, prospective trial. Ann Surg 203:13–20, 1986.

43. Cerra FB, Mazuski JE, Chute E, et al: Branched chain metabolic support: A prospective, randomized, double-blind trial in surgical stress. Ann Surg 199:286–290, 1984.

44. Cerra FB, Blackburn G, Hirsch J, et al: The effect of stress level, amino acid formula, and nitrogen dose on nitrogen retention in traumatic and septic stress. Ann Surg 205:282–287, 1987.

45. Cerra FB, McMillen M, Angelico R, et al: Cir-

rhosis, encephalopathy, and improved results with metabolic support. Surgery 94:612–618, 1983.

46. Freund H, Dienstag J, Lehrich J, et al: Infusion of branched-chain enriched amino acid solution in patients with hepatic encephalopathy. Ann Surg 196:209–220, 1982.

47. Kanematsu T, Koyanagi N, Matsumata T, et al: Lack of preventive effect of branched-chain amino acid solution on postoperative hepatic encephalopathy in patients with cirrhosis: A randomized, prospective trial. Surgery 104:482–488, 1988.

48. Millikan WJ, Henderson JM, Warren WD, et al: Total parenteral nutrition with F080 in cirrhotics with subclinical encephalopathy. Ann Surg 197:294–303, 1983.

49. Mirtallo JM, Rogers KR, Johnson JA, et al: Stability of amino acids and the availability of acid in total parenteral nutrition solutions containing hydrochloric acid. Am J Hosp Pharm 28:1729–1731, 1981.

50. Sitges-Serra A, Linares J, Garau J: Catheter sepsis: The clue is the hub. Surgery 97:355–357, 1985.

51. Bozzetti F, Terno G, Bonfanti G, et al: Prevention and treatment of central venous catheter sepsis by exchange via a guidewire: A prospective controlled trial. Ann Surg 198:48–52, 1983.

52. Vanhuynegem L, Parmentier P, Potvliege C: In situ bacteriologic diagnosis of total parenteral nutrition catheter infection. Surgery 103:174–177, 1988.

53. Cooper GL, Hopkins CC: Rapid diagnosis of intravascular catheter associated infection by direct Gram staining of catheter segments. N Engl J Med 312:1142–1147, 1985.

54. Warner BW, Hamilton FN, Silberstein EB, et al: The value of hepatobiliary scans in fasted patients receiving total parenteral nutrition. Surgery 102:595–601, 1987.

55. Doty JE, Pitt HA, Porter-Fink V, et al: Cholecystokinin prophylaxis of parenteral nutrition–induced gallbladder disease. Ann Surg 201:76–80, 1985.

II

SYSTEMATIC
EVALUATION
of the
TRAUMATIZED
PATIENT

CHAPTER 5

EMERGENCY AND INTENSIVE CARE OF THE TRAUMA PATIENT

DAVID COOK, M.D.,
and DONALD TRUNKEY, M.D.

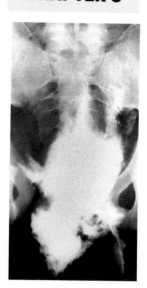

INTRODUCTION AND EPIDEMIOLOGY

Trauma is the most serious and yet the most preventable health care problem in this country. It is the leading cause of death and disability among Americans between ages 1 and 34 — greater than all other causes combined.[1] More than 150,000 lives are lost each year in the United States as a direct result of injuries, and it is estimated that for each death at least two or three permanent disabilities occur (Fig. 5–1). The death rate secondary to injury has climbed exponentially in all age groups and now accounts for 80 per cent of all deaths among teenagers and young adults.[2] Urban violence has also increased exponentially. Because young, productive citizens are primarily affected, the losses are staggering. In 1985, approximately 112 million work days were lost secondary to injury, and the cost resulting from lost wages, medical expenses, insurance, property damage, and indirect work loss exceeded 107.3 billion dollars. More than 20 million hospital days each year are accounted for by injured patients, far exceeding those needed for patients with heart problems and cancer.[3] Potential years of life lost secondary to injury also far exceed those lost because of heart disease, cancer, and stroke. Whereas death rates from heart disease and stroke have fallen over the past decade, the death rate from injury has risen by about 1 per cent per year.[4]

Deaths secondary to trauma have a trimodal distribution that can be characterized as immediate, early, or late[4] (Fig. 5–2). Those categorized as immediate occur within seconds or minutes of injury and are invariably the result of lacerations of the heart, major blood vessels, brain, brainstem, or spinal cord. These immediate deaths represent approximately 50 per cent of all deaths from trauma. Even with optimal conditions, salvage of these patients is minimal. The few who are saved are those in large cities, where rapid transport to a trauma center is available. Because of the extent of injury in these patients, it is doubtful that improved surgical care could result in decreased death rates. The major emphasis, therefore, should be placed on prevention.

Early deaths are those that occur within 2 to 3 hours of injury. Approximately 30 per cent of deaths due to injury fall into this category. These deaths primarily result from hemorrhage and brain injury, such as subdural or epidural hematomas, hemo-

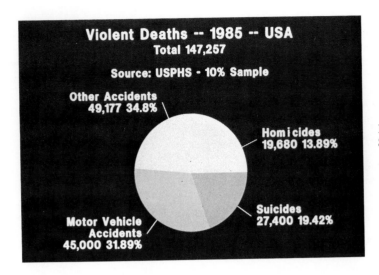

FIGURE 5–1. Causes of violent deaths in the United States in 1985.

pneumothorax, liver or spleen lacerations, femoral fractures, or multiple lesser injuries leading to significant blood loss. The vast majority of these injuries are treatable by current surgical and medical techniques. In these cases, the interval between injury and definitive care is critical in reducing death and disability.

The third peak, comprising late deaths, accounts for approximately 20 per cent of deaths due to injury. These deaths occur days or weeks after injury, and nearly 80 per cent of cases result from infection, sepsis, and multiple organ system failure. The exact causes of multiple organ failure have not been fully elucidated, although several risk factors that might lead to infection and sepsis have been identified, including head injury, shock, peritoneal contamination, and malnutrition. Mortality rates are high and directly related to the number of organ systems involved.

Although it is unlikely that improved care or biologic research can reduce the number of immediate deaths, timely, definitive surgical and postoperative care is imperative in decreasing both early and late deaths. The management of the trauma patient remains the responsibility of the surgeon caring for that patient. The surgeon's role begins with the admission of the patient and involves supervision of all treatment and associated personnel through discharge and subsequent follow-up.

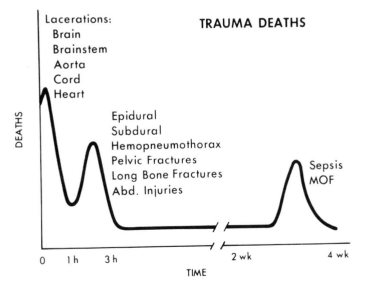

FIGURE 5–2. Trimodal distribution of deaths secondary to trauma.

TABLE 5-1. PHASES OF TRAUMA CARE

Prehospital	Airway protection Control of external hemorrhage Fracture stabilization Spine stabilization Rapid transport
Primary assessment and resuscitation	ABCs (Airway, Breathing, Circulation) Volume resuscitation Monitoring
Secondary survey and diagnosis	Comprehensive physical examination Chest radiograph Laboratory tests and other radiographic evaluation Continued monitoring and resuscitation
Definitive care	Surgery Nonoperative management Nutritional support
Rehabilitation	

The importance of the surgeon's central role has been documented in several U.S. studies.[5,6] These studies have demonstrated that the most important factors in reducing preventable trauma-related deaths in the hospital are prompt surgical response and organized surgical care. Furthermore, subsequent studies have found that regionalization of trauma care and training of the participating medical personnel in current methods of trauma care lead to significant reductions in trauma-related deaths in the hospital.[7,8] Trauma management, therefore, should be a practical, well-organized system of caring for the injured patient.

Care of the trauma patient can be separated into several phases: prehospital, primary assessment and resuscitation, secondary survey and diagnosis, definitive care, and rehabilitation (Table 5-1). Although not exact, these are useful in the development of appropriate care of the trauma patient.

PREHOSPITAL CARE

Safe removal and rapid transport to the nearest medical facility able to manage the trauma patient appropriately are the two primary goals of the prehospital phase. Minimizing in-field interventions, such as starting intravenous lines, placing dressings, or applying pneumatic antishock garments, is important in expediting definitive care when transport times are less than 20 minutes. Although perhaps useful with longer transport times, the delay and any risk involved in these maneuvers may outweigh their benefits. Delivery of the patient to a facility that can provide immediate definitive surgical care to the trauma patient, rather than delivery to the closest medical center, has also been demonstrated to decrease unnecessary deaths and disability.[9]

The vast majority of deaths in the prehospital period are a result of direct cerebral and high spinal cord injuries, exsanguination, and respiratory compromise secondary to airway obstruction or ventilatory disruption. Not all patients are salvageable, but to reduce death and disability, there must be rapid, effective treatment and the shortest possible interval to definitive surgical care.

Patients who die in the field with massive head injuries resulting in early apnea or herniation are not salvageable. The patient with a lesser degree of injury who is salvageable will not usually develop significant intracranial pressure or mass lesions for 30 to 60 minutes. However, these patients may lose consciousness and fail to protect their airway, resulting in cerebral hypoxia. A lifesaving measure that may be provided by the paramedic in these instances is endotracheal intubation, which provides both ventilation and airway protection. The patient may then be hyperventilated en route to definitive neurosurgical care. Mannitol should be given in the field only under protocol or medical control. Spinal protection is an essential maneuver and can be accomplished quickly in patients requiring it.

Exsanguination is second to central nervous system injury as the most common cause of prehospital death. With the exception of controlling external sources of bleeding by direct pressure, field interventions are controversial. The major cause of exsanguination is internal bleeding, which is controlled only with surgical intervention. Pneumatic antishock garments and the establishment of intravenous lines may have potential benefits, but these must be weighed against risks, including delay of definitive surgical care. In general, intravenous fluid administration should be reserved for transport times greater than 30 minutes or for those patients bleeding in excess of 50 ml/min. The use of hypertonic solutions may, however, prove useful in certain circumstances. The pneumatic antishock garment may provide partial tamponade of bleeding sites in the lower extremities or stabilize fractures, but there is no evidence that overall survival is improved when it is used in an urban setting.

A common cause of internal bleeding in the trauma patient is the long bone fracture, particularly when it involves the femur. The gold standard for prehospital care of a fractured femur is a traction splint, which not only controls hemorrhage but also prevents further neurovascular damage.

The third cause of death in the field is acute respiratory problems, including airway obstruction and ventilatory compromise. Endotracheal intubation is an effective treatment for the majority of patients with these problems, can be taught effectively, and can be mastered by paramedics. The esophageal obturator airway is not an effective alternative, as it does not provide sufficient airway protection and the incidence of inadequate ventilation is high.

Although dependent on the locale and the status of the patient, prehospital care should provide airway protection, including endotracheal intubation, if indicated; spine stabilization; fracture stabilization; and rapid transport.

PRIMARY ASSESSMENT AND RESUSCITATION

Although the vast majority of trauma patients who are brought to an emergency room do not have life-threatening injuries, some 5 to 10 per cent do. These patients must be rapidly and effectively assessed and treated. The treating physician must have a well-organized plan that allows for identification of urgent problems as a first priority and subsequently enables him or her to perform a comprehensive evaluation. The goals of emergency trauma care are the rapid restoration of respiration and perfusion to acceptable levels.

One of the first decisions to be made concerns the patient's relative stability. A rapid primary assessment should take no longer than a few seconds and allows the physician to determine whether the patient is dead or dying, unstable or stable. The patient's respiratory status, circulatory status, and level of consciousness must be quickly assessed.

For the patient who is unstable, dead, or dying, resuscitative steps must be taken immediately. Airway problems are the most urgent, and left untreated, they will be the most rapidly fatal. Occasionally, injuries resulting in airway obstruction or ventilatory insufficiency are not completely obvious. These might include lung or chest wall injuries, which can severely impair ventilation. The signs of respiratory embarrassment, however, are usually clear—stridor, cyanosis, anxiety, use of accessory muscles of respiration, intercostal retraction, and tachypnea with a respiratory rate of more than 25 per minute (Table 5–2).

The oropharynx should be cleared with a tonsil sucker or the examiner's fingers, if the patient is unconscious. The examiner should pass two fingers through the glottic area to remove any foreign material. This maneuver should not, however, be

TABLE 5–2. SIGNS OF RESPIRATORY EMBARRASSMENT

Stridor
Cyanosis
Anxiety
Tachypnea rate >25/min
Intercostal retraction
Use of accessory muscles

attempted in the conscious patient, as it may further exacerbate distress. The back of the tongue should then be brought forward by displacing the angles of the jaw anteriorly or, in the patient with massive maxillofacial injuries, by pulling the tongue forward with a towel clip or the examiner's fingers. The oral airway or, at times, the nasal airway can then be inserted to help keep the tongue forward. With a well-fitting face mask, several breaths of 100 per cent oxygen should then be given. If bag and mask placement is not possible because of facial fractures, high-flow oxygen via the nasal or facial route should be started. If ventilation has not been established with the preceding measures, one should immediately proceed to intubation through the mouth or nose. In the vast majority of instances, intubation — either oral or nasal — is successful (Fig. 5–3). However, in the occasional patient with massive maxillofacial injury, bleeding, foreign body, or other distortion of the anatomy, an airway must be secured by emergency tracheostomy (Fig. 5–4). Access to the trachea may be attained quickly through the cricothyroid membrane. A transverse incision over the membrane is made, and the membrane is incised transversely. A curved clamp on the handle of the scalpel may then be inserted to enlarge the tracheal opening, allowing insertion of a No. 5 or No. 6 cuffed endotracheal tube. In the emergency setting, this method is preferred to the classic tracheostomy, as it is easier and much faster. Concerns with vocal cord dysfunction and tracheal stenosis following cricothyroidotomy have been shown to be insignificant, and the single contraindication is blunt laryngeal injury.

Endotracheal intubation and tracheostomy usually require neck extension; however, in the unconscious patient, the status of the cervical spine is often unknown. In these instances, the examiner must quickly assess which is of greatest threat to the patient, although the airway must, in the life-threatening situation, have priority. Axis traction can be applied while the airway is secured, but other methods of cervical spine stabilization should not interfere with these procedures. Once the airway is established, the examiner should assess ventilation. A rapid pulmonary examination

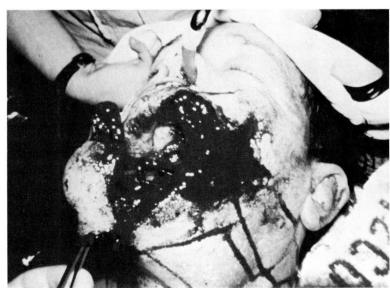

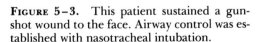

FIGURE 5–3. This patient sustained a gunshot wound to the face. Airway control was established with nasotracheal intubation.

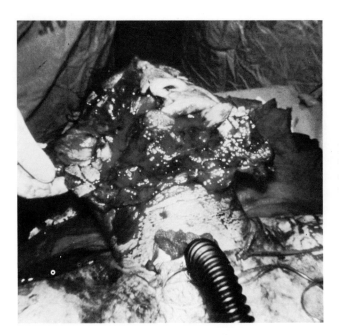

Figure 5–4.   This patient has a self-inflicted shotgun wound to the face. In contrast to the patient in Figure 5–3, orotracheal or nasotracheal intubation was impossible, necessitating tracheostomy in the emergency room.

can detect paradoxical chest wall movement, splinting, crepitus, and pain on palpation, suggesting rib fractures. Auscultation is also performed but may be of limited value in the emergency situation, as differences in breath sounds may be impossible to hear. Treatment of ventilatory problems can be initiated while this rapid assessment is being completed. Open pneumothoraces are closed with occlusal dressings. Flail segments of the chest wall are stabilized, and chest tubes are inserted to evacuate hemothoraces or pneumothoraces. The patient who has been intubated, yet remains in respiratory distress, should have chest tubes placed prior to further evaluation. Bilateral tubes should be used if there are no lateralizing signs or if the placement of a tube on the side of obvious injury affords no relief of respiratory distress.

In the majority of instances, external bleeding has been controlled by paramedics on the way to the emergency room. If not, it should be controlled simultaneously with establishment of an airway and ventilation. Simple pressure applied directly to the bleeding site will almost always achieve control until definitive treatment can be given. Traction splints should be placed for femoral fractures if this has not been done in the prehospital setting. With the exception of traumatic amputations, tourniquets are not indicated. Probing of wounds and blind clamping are also not indicated, as they may jeopardize the chance for primary vascular repair and can lead to permanent nerve injury.

The next priority in the dying or unstable patient, after control of airway and bleeding problems, is to assess the cardiovascular status. One of the first things to do in the trauma room is to feel the patient's extremities. Then, as one is assessing the patient's airway, the neck veins may be observed. If the patient is cool and pale or the capillary filling is delayed longer than 2 seconds, shock is assumed to be present until proved otherwise. If the neck veins are flat, one can assume that shock is secondary to hypovolemia until determined otherwise. However, if the neck veins are distended, five conditions must be ruled out immediately (Table 5–3). These include tension pneumothorax, pericardial tamponade, air embolism, myocardial contusion, and myocardial infarction.

The increasing intrathoracic pressure and mediastinal shift associated with a tension pneumothorax impede venous return (Fig. 5–5). Ventilatory function is similarly compromised, as one lung is collapsed and the other is compressed. Patients with a full-blown tension pneumothorax will be in shock and respiratory distress and

TABLE 5-3. ETIOLOGY OF DISTENDED NECK VEINS
Tension pneumothorax
Pericardial tamponade
Air embolism
Myocardial contusion
Myocardial infarction

may have distended neck veins, tracheal deviation, ipsilateral hyper-resonance, and diminished breath sounds on the involved side (Table 5–4). Not all patients manifest these signs, however. The patient might be obese, and identification of distended neck veins, for example, might be impossible. More often, the patient may have associated hypovolemia, with flat neck veins. Noise in the trauma room also makes auscultation and percussion difficult. Because a tension pneumothorax can be rapidly fatal and the diagnosis can be difficult to make, the examining physician must often treat presumptively by inserting a 16-gauge needle in the second intercostal space of the involved side, this to be followed by tube thoracostomy.

The second life-threatening emergency is pericardial tamponade. A high index of suspicion is necessary to diagnose and treat this disorder in a timely fashion. When a patient is in shock, has distended neck veins, and has no evidence of tension pneumothorax, tamponade must be considered. Pericardiocentesis may be a lifesaving procedure. This is accomplished by inserting an 18-gauge spinal needle in the subxiphoid area at a 45-degree angle and advancing slowly while aiming at the left midclavicular area. As an adjunct, the V lead of the electrocardiograph can be monitored during the procedure. Removal of as little as 10 ml of blood may dramatically reverse hypotension.

Often this procedure will be unsuccessful in removing clotted blood. If this is the case or if tamponade induces cardiac arrest, immediate emergency thoracotomy should be done on the left side unless tamponade is a result of penetrating trauma. In this case, thoracotomy should be done on the side of injury. An incision is made one interspace below the nipple, beginning at the sternum and carried laterally as far as possible. To facilitate exposure, costochondral cartilages are incised. The pericardium is then opened along the anterior surface in a caudal to cephalad direction to avoid the phrenic nerve. Clots are evacuated, and any holes are quickly occluded. Open heart massage may also be initiated, and defibrillation may be attempted. If resuscitation is successful, the heart is repaired in the operating room.

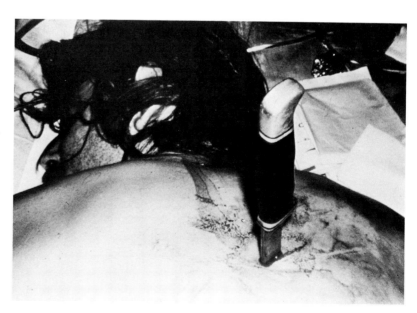

FIGURE 5–5. Penetrating wounds of the chest are *always* suspect for producing tension pneumothorax, which is the easiest life-threatening emergency to treat in the emergency room.

TABLE 5-4.   SIGNS OF TENSION PNEUMOTHORAX

Shock and respiratory distress
Distended neck veins
Tracheal deviation
Ipsilateral hyper-resonance
Diminished breath sounds

Blunt or penetrating chest injury may lead to air embolism. Although not commonly diagnosed, it occurs in approximately 4 to 5 per cent of all major thoracic trauma. Air embolism is most often associated with penetrating injuries, such as stab or gunshot wounds, but may also occur after blunt chest trauma in which case the embolism is caused by lung lacerations secondary to fractured ribs.

The pathophysiology of air embolism is a bronchopulmonary venous fistula. Those patients who are breathing spontaneously will have a pressure differential from the pulmonary vein to the bronchus, so that hemoptysis may be a presenting sign. However, if the patient has Valsalva-type respirations, grunts, or is intubated with positive pressure, the pressure differential is reversed, causing systemic air embolism. These patients present with any combination of three findings.

1. Focal or lateralizing neurologic findings in the absence of obvious head injury

2. Sudden cardiovascular collapse after intubation and positive-pressure ventilation

3. Froth obtained with aspiration of arterial blood for blood gas determinations (Table 5-5)

The neurologic changes are a result of air in the cerebral circulation and can be confirmed by finding air in the retinal vessels on funduscopic examination. Cardiovascular collapse is secondary to air in the coronary circulation, which may be identified after thoracotomy. Up to two thirds of patients will have signs or symptoms of air embolism upon, or shortly after, presentation to the emergency room. The remaining third will manifest symptoms in the first 24 hours, although, on occasion, symptoms may occur as late as 5 days after injury.

The treatment of air embolism is immediate thoracotomy, preferably in the operating room. Many of these patients are dead or dying, however, and will have had an emergency room thoracotomy. Often, it is obvious which thorax is involved, and the thoracotomy is performed on the ipsilateral side. On occasion, the diagnosis has not been made, and the thoracotomy is done simply in an attempt to resuscitate the patient. In these circumstances, a left anterior thoracotomy is preferred. If the left side of the chest is opened and air is found in the coronary vessels, with no obvious lung injury present, the sternum is transected, the right side of the chest is opened, and the hilum of the right lung is clamped. In any case, the primary objective is to clamp the hilum of the involved lung quickly, thereby reducing the inoculum of air to the left atrium.

TABLE 5-5.   PRESENTING SIGNS OF AIR EMBOLISM

Hemoptysis
Focal or lateralizing neurologic findings in the absence of
  obvious head injury
Sudden cardiovascular collapse after intubation and positive-
  pressure ventilation
Froth with aspiration of arterial blood

Once the hilum is clamped, other resuscitative measures may be carried out. If air is identified in the coronary vessels, 1 ml of $\frac{1}{1000}$ epinephrine can be given intravenously or down the endotracheal tube to increase systemic pressure and drive air out of the microcirculation. Holding the ascending aorta with the thumb and index finger for one or two strokes will help to evacuate air from the coronary vessels. It is also prudent to vent the left ventricle or aortic arch with a needle to remove as much residual air as possible once the hilum has been clamped. Definitive treatment consists of oversewing the lacerations of the lung and, in some instances, performing lobectomy or, rarely, pneumonectomy if there has been extensive injury.

Myocardial contusion is usually the result of blunt chest trauma, occurring in as many as 60 per cent of cases. Although the great majority of patients are not symptomatic, serious dysrhythmias can result, usually within the first hour.

The diagnosis of myocardial contusion is difficult. Any patient struck in the anterior chest, especially those sustaining sternal contusions or fractures, should be suspected of having myocardial contusion. The physician must be especially suspicious in cases involving children, as the high compliance of the child's thorax may permit significant cardiac injury without the usual fractures. A history that the patient was extricated from behind the steering column should also arouse suspicion. Pain is usually present but is invariably due to chest wall trauma and not to the myocardial contusion.

The electrocardiogram may show an injury pattern but is frequently not specific. Nuclear scans and myocardial enzyme levels also do not correlate well with the development of clinical symptoms. Two-dimensional echocardiography, however, is useful in assessing the presence of myocardial contusion.

Any patient with chest wall trauma and suspected myocardial contusion should be monitored for 24 hours, especially if there has been evidence of dysrhythmia. Treatment consists of managing the dysrhythmia if it develops. Signs and symptoms of myocardial failure are treated like those of cardiogenic shock secondary to infarction. Lidocaine or other antiarrhythmics and inotropic support are given as needed. Monitoring should continue until there has been a 24-hour period without significant dysrhythmia.

Late complications of myocardial contusion include aneurysm formation, cardiac rupture, and, rarely, permanent conduction defects.

The last condition that one must consider is cardiogenic shock occurring as a result of myocardial infarction. The infarction may have preceded injury or may result from blood loss, excessive catecholamines, or hypoxia. The treatment is similar to that for myocardial contusion.

In the majority of cases, the patient's unstable status, or shock, will be secondary to hypovolemia. One must rapidly assess the degree of shock and gain access to the circulation. The number of intravenous lines and the volume of resuscitative fluid will depend on the patient and the degree of injury. If a patient has sustained injury 2 hours previously and is in mild shock, a 16-gauge or larger catheter placed percutaneously in an upper extremity may suffice. However, for patients in moderate or severe shock, two or more large-bore catheters are imperative. The number depends on the clinical severity of the shock. Access can be quickly gained by cutdown. The safest and quickest cutdown is on the saphenous vein over the medial malleolus. In the upper extremity, the basilic vein may be cut down in the antecubital space, allowing one to pass a catheter centrally if needed. The catheters used for cutdown should be 14 gauge or larger in the adult. Short catheters should be used for the saphenous vein at the ankle to maximize flow. A No. 5 or No. 8 French pediatric feeding tube provides the needed large bore and may be employed as a central venous monitoring line when used for the antecubital cutdown. Cut-off intravenous extension tubing is also an acceptable large-bore line. Catheters should not be placed in injured extremities. Percutaneous femoral vein catheters also allow rapid access to the circulation without major complications. These are not preferred sites under usual circumstances but may be best if the physician is uncomfortable with cutdown. It should be emphasized that sufficient intravenous access must be gained prior to proceeding to operative therapy, as once drapes are in place, rapid access is difficult.

Some advocate central percutaneous subclavian or jugular puncture for line placement in the trauma patient. We, however, discourage this, as risks are magnified in the emergency situation. It can be not only difficult and time consuming but also dangerous to attempt placement in the restless, combative, hypovolemic patient. Central veins are flat in the hypovolemic patient, and attempts at cannulation carry at least a 15 per cent complication rate. A critically injured patient may not tolerate further embarrassment caused by iatrogenic pneumothorax. Furthermore, the central venous catheters are long and narrow, limiting flow rates.

Once the first intravenous line is established, blood should be drawn for type and cross-match, hematocrit, and white blood cell count. Part of the specimen should also be saved for further studies when indicated, including electrolytes, blood urea nitrogen (BUN), creatinine, amylase, glucose, and toxicology.

Resuscitation is initiated with a balanced salt solution, such as lactated Ringer's solution, as this helps to alleviate metabolic acidosis, decrease blood viscosity, enhance perfusion of microvasculature, and replenish interstitial fluid losses. Two liters of balanced salt solution can be given to the hypovolemic patient as rapidly as possible. Colloid solutions may also be used effectively in resuscitation; however, they offer no distinct advantage and add significant cost. Less fluid volume may be required, but these are not better than crystalloid solutions. Protein colloid solutions increase tissue oncotic pressure, which delays fluid reabsorption. In addition, an increase in late pulmonary complications has been associated with colloid resuscitation.[10]

Nonprotein colloid solutions, such as hetastarch, have been investigated, and although their use requires less total fluid volume, they have not been shown to be superior to balanced salt solutions. Hypertonic saline solutions have also been investigated in the resuscitation of burn and trauma victims. The exogenous infusion of excess sodium ions leads to endogenous infusion of free water into the extracellular space. The result is that less total fluid is required for resuscitation. Acid-base disturbances and hypernatremia may develop in these patients, however, limiting the amount of solution infused. Whether these small volumes of fluid represent an advantage in resuscitation remains to be seen.[11]

Whole blood or packed red blood cells constitute the second component of intravascular resuscitation, as adequate oxygen-carrying capacity must be assured. The amount of blood administered is governed by the clinical situation. We feel that type-specific whole blood offers several advantages in the emergency situation. Type-specific whole blood has a lower viscosity than packed red blood cells, which tend to sludge, and therefore can be administered more rapidly through intravenous lines. It is also quicker to obtain than cross-matched blood and is well tolerated by most patients, carrying only a small risk of transfusion reaction. Low-titer O-negative blood may be used if type-specific blood is not available, but it may occasionally cause difficulty with typing and cross-matching for subsequent transfusions.

Autotransfusion also provides compatible blood with minimal delay. In the most favorable situation, blood can be drained from hemothoraces into a container with citrate anticoagulant and infused. Blood from the abdominal cavity may also be used, but one must be certain that it is not contaminated, which is often not possible initially when blood is needed most. Large amounts of autologous blood may precipitate coagulopathy; thus, the amount one can transfuse is also limited. Ideally, in the severely traumatized patient, the hematocrit should be maintained at or near 30 per cent, a compromise between desired levels of viscosity and oxygen-carrying capacity. Some patients, however, will require the maintenance of higher hematocrits (i.e., 35 to 40 per cent) owing to cardiac dysfunction.

Resuscitation should continue as needed and is modified by the patient's response. The return of blood pressure and perfusion indicates restoration of intravascular volume. Continued instability or lack of response signals inadequate resuscitation or uncontrolled hemorrhage or both. If 3 L of balanced salt solution has been infused and the patient remains in shock, control of hemorrhage should become part of the resuscitation. External bleeding sources can easily be controlled by direct pressure, but if none are evident, the patient should be taken to the operating room immediately. In these instances, further efforts to stabilize the patient without controlling the hemorrhage will be unsuccessful. Definitive surgical care must be given before any other workup is performed.

If the patient's response to the initial infusion of balanced salt solution reflects improved perfusion, blood pressure, urine output, and mental status, one can proceed with deliberate diagnostic evaluation. It must be remembered, however, that a life-threatening situation can develop at any time during the treatment of the trauma patient. Previously discussed problems that can develop quickly include pneumothorax, massive hemorrhage, pericardial tamponade, cardiac dysrhythmias, airway obstruction, and uncal herniation. These must be dealt with immediately, postponing further workup, to avoid unnecessary death.

Once the airway and ventilation are established, bleeding is controlled, and resuscitation of the cardiovascular system is under way, the initial resuscitation should be evaluated. A brief neurologic examination is performed, physiologic parameters are evaluated, and a Foley catheter is placed in the urinary bladder.

The neurologic examination actually begins with the initial contact with the patient, the examiner observing the level of consciousness and movement. Subsequent neurologic examination should take no more than 20 seconds, being done only to establish baselines, not to make a definitive diagnosis. Besides observing the level of consciousness and checking the extremities for movement, spontaneous or in response to command or pain, the examiner checks the pupils for size and reactivity.

Trauma to the brain can cause a number of alterations in mental status, ranging from coma, confusion, or combativeness to delusions or euphoria. In addition, these altered states may be produced by hypoxia, hypovolemia, or inebriation. The primary priority in treating these patients with altered states of consciousness must be to recognize and treat hypoxemia and shock if present. The second priority is to recognize and treat brain damage. One should never ascribe an altered state of consciousness to inebriation or brain injury until hypoxemia and shock have been dealt with or ruled out. It is also important to mention here that hypotension rarely occurs as a result of central nervous system injury. Instead, one must assume that there is another source of blood loss, the only exception being spinal cord injury and paraplegia. Further neurologic evaluation, including the definition of lateralizing signs, can be performed once resuscitation has been achieved. Repeated assessments of the patient's neurologic status should be done at 15- to 30-minute intervals.

Assessment of resuscitation is based on the quantitative improvement of physiologic parameters. Pulse and blood pressure are the most readily available and are generally reliable. A low blood pressure or a rapid pulse indicates moderate or severe shock and should alert the physician to take further resuscitative measures. Pulse pressure, peripheral perfusion, and urinary output are also useful. Skin perfusion is probably the most sensitive physical sign in assessing resuscitation of the patient in shock. Poor perfusion in most instances indicates shock, although those patients who are frightened or who have suffered cold exposure may have cold, pale skin and may be normovolemic. Warm, well-perfused skin indicates adequate cardiovascular resuscitation except in patients who are inebriated, in those who have lost neurologic control of their systemic circulation, or in those who have carbon monoxide poisoning. An adequate urine flow also usually indicates adequate resuscitation, although it is an unreliable sign in inebriated patients, diabetic patients, or patients who have been given contrast agents or mannitol. More invasive methods of monitoring may be used but should be discouraged in these settings. These techniques, such as central venous pressure monitoring or Swan-Ganz catheterization, rarely provide information that is not obvious to a skilled examiner.

SECONDARY SURVEY AND DIAGNOSIS

Approximately 15 per cent of trauma patients presenting to the emergency room fail to stabilize after initial resuscitative efforts, making immediate operative intervention to control hemorrhage or evacuate mass lesions in the cranial vault imperative. The remaining 85 per cent of trauma victims will arrive in a stable condition or will stabilize after resuscitation, allowing the physician to complete a rapid, comprehensive, head-to-toe examination. This secondary assessment must be done systematically to avoid overlooking injuries and to guide further evaluation and treatment. An injury may go unrecognized for hours and lead to unnecessary disability or death. Particular attention should be given to a complete neurologic and orthopedic examination, as these injuries can be severely disabling.

Histories are kept brief during the initial phases of evaluation, but some information must be obtained. The medical history should include allergies, medications, medical illnesses, and prior surgery. If the patient cannot communicate, often this information can be gleaned from family members or friends and perhaps from personal effects identifying medical problems. The circumstances of the accident and the magnitude of the forces involved should be learned from either the patient or the rescue team. The patient's condition, when first seen by medical personnel and during transport, should also be ascertained. For example, the report of a collapsed steering wheel coupled with that of a patient who was not wearing a seat belt while driving alerts the physician to consider certain thoracic injuries, even though chest trauma may be ambiguous.

PHYSICAL EXAMINATION

In general, the physician must inspect and palpate the entire body, noting penetrating wounds and contusions, identifying areas of pain and tenderness to palpation, and looking for asymmetry or distortion. This examination is most easily accomplished by working from head to toe. During the course of this evaluation, the examiner will encounter injuries that mandate immediate therapy and others that may require further detailed assessment.

Head and Neck

Maxillofacial injuries may pose two life-threatening problems: airway obstruction and hemorrhage. The nose and throat must be examined for adequacy of the airway. Blood from the nose or a retropharyngeal hematoma should be a warning of potential airway obstruction. Complex facial injuries will often require cricothyroidotomy or tracheostomy. Brisk bleeding from the scalp or face with loss of greater than 100 ml/min can be controlled by closing lacerations with an interlocking monofilament suture. This closing of lacerations can be done rapidly and redone later with more attention to plastic technique. Nasopharyngeal or pharyngeal bleeding may require intubation to prevent aspiration, although nasopharyngeal bleeding can often be slowed. A No. 20 French Foley catheter with a 30-ml balloon is inserted through one nostril into the nasopharynx, and the balloon is inflated. When traction is applied, the balloon will lodge in the nasopharynx and tamponade the bleeding.

Clear fluid draining from the nose should alert one to the possibility of a cerebrospinal fluid leak, which is pathognomonic for basilar skull fracture. This fluid may be assumed to be cerebrospinal fluid if the glucose concentration is equal to the blood glucose concentration or if, when dropped on a gauze sponge, it forms a "double halo."

Once brisk bleeding is controlled, the face and scalp are palpated and inspected for hematomas, lacerations, and any deformities. Palpation of the facial prominences will detect most major facial fractures. The orbital rims, zygomatic arches, mandible, and nose should be palpated. The maxilla should be examined for unstable fractures by grasping the upper incisors and attempting to rock the maxilla back and forth. Inspection may reveal a Battle's sign or raccoon eyes with injuries more than 24 hours old, again suggesting basilar skull fracture.

The eyes are thoroughly checked for extraocular movements. The inability to gaze upward suggests an orbital blow-out fracture, while dysconjugate gaze indicates neurologic damage. Pupils are checked for size and reactivity, and the fundi are inspected. Injury to the eye is assessed, and clues to the presence of intracranial pathology are gained. Binocular vision and visual acuity should also be assessed.

The ears are examined for blood in the external canals and blood behind the tympanic membranes. Whereas blood in the ear canal is suggestive of a basilar skull fracture, blood behind the tympanic membrane is virtually pathognomonic. Hearing is also roughly evaluated at this time.

As in the primary survey, neck veins are evaluated. Distended neck veins suggest a cardiac cause of shock, and flat veins suggest hypovolemia. Swelling indicates bleeding into one of the fascial planes and should alert the physician to possible airway obstruction. An expanding hematoma will distort laryngeal anatomy, making intubation extremely difficult. These patients should therefore be intubated early. The neck is palpated for tracheal deviation, suggesting tension pneumothorax, and for cervical spine tenderness. Subcutaneous emphysema indicates a rupture somewhere in the tracheobronchial tree or, less likely, somewhere in the esophagus. The patient with suspected neck injury should be maintained in an axial orientation until cervical spine films are obtained.

Chest

Careful visual inspection and palpation of the entire chest cage are performed during the secondary assessment. Each rib, the sternum, spinous processes, and clavicles should be palpated, as this will reveal fractures even when radiographs are normal. Poor chest wall movement on one side may indicate a collapsed lung or splinting secondary to pain. Paradoxical motion may be present, indicating a flail segment. Frequently, however, the trauma patient's inspiratory effort is light, making paradoxical motion difficult to detect. Chest wall abrasions and ecchymoses alert the physician to search for damage to underlying organs in the chest or abdomen. Percussion of both sides of the chest may help one to make a diagnosis of pneumothorax or hemothorax but is otherwise not helpful. Both hemithoraces should also be auscultated again to assist in diagnosing pneumothoraces. Muffled heart tones suggest pericardial tamponade.

Abdomen and Lower Chest

The lower chest and abdomen are considered a single unit in the trauma patient. Some of the most commonly injured organs (e.g., spleen and liver) lie in part under the lower ribs. Penetrating injuries of the lower chest can easily damage many intra-abdominal organs. The abdomen may, therefore, be a notorious diagnostic trap. In fact, up to 40 per cent of patients with significant hemoperitoneum have no clinical manifestations. In most instances, intraperitoneal hemorrhage manifests as unexplained hypotension, a falling hematocrit, and a rising white blood cell count, as well as occurring with signs or symptoms of associated injuries, such as rib or pelvic fractures.

Inspection is again most important, as ecchymoses and abrasions suggest underlying organ damage. The location of penetrating injuries should be noted, although further characteristics should be tempered, as they may be in error. Knife wounds can be gently explored, but the examiner must remember that the patient's muscles were in a different position at the time of injury and may now cover a penetrating tract. Gunshot wounds should be described but not labeled as entrance or exit wounds. The contour of the abdomen and movement of the abdominal musculature are also observed. Abdominal distention may indicate intra-abdominal gas or bleeding but should never be used as the sole sign of internal blood loss. In a typical 70-kg man, a 1-cm increase in abdominal radius would represent as much as 3 L of blood loss. Palpation of the abdomen can detect hematomas in the abdominal wall. Involuntary guarding may indicate irritation of the parietal peritoneum. Percussion of the abdomen can be useful in detecting gastric distention, which should be immediately treated with a nasogastric tube. Peritoneal irritation can also be confirmed. Dullness to percussion suggests intra-abdominal fluid such as blood. Auscultation offers little information, as the absence of bowel sounds often simply represents an ileus in response to other injuries. Bowel sounds may be present even after rupture of a viscus.

A rectal examination is often performed as part of the primary assessment prior to passage of a Foley catheter; the examiner notes the location and size of the prostate, sphincter tones, and the presence of blood in the rectal vault. If not included in the primary assessment, it should be done in the secondary examination, along with evaluation of the perineum and genitalia. The perineum should be inspected for lacerations and hematomas, the urethral meatus for blood, and the scrotum or labia for hematomas—often indicating retroperitoneal hematoma. The vagina can be palpated for lacerations, foregoing a speculum examination at this time.

Vascular System

The four extremities, groins, and neck are palpated and inspected. Adequacy of perfusion, temperature, and pulses are noted. Poor perfusion of all extremities suggests shock, while poor perfusion of one with good perfusion of the others indicates arterial injury. Expanding or large hematomas also suggest arterial injury. The area around any penetrating injury should be auscultated for the continuous to-fro bruit of an arteriovenous fistula. Blood pressures should be obtained in both arms to assess the subclavian arteries.

Musculoskeletal System

In addition to noting deformities and hematomas, the examiner should inspect the skin overlying the musculoskeletal system for lacerations, abrasions, and ecchymoses. Limbs that are grossly distorted should be gently realigned. Palpation can elicit tenderness or instability, indicating fractures or muscle, tendon, or ligament injury. The large bones are palpated first, followed by the pelvis, clavicles, and smaller bones of the extremities. Those patients with major fractures will usually arrive with splints in place. Unsplinted fractures should be splinted as soon after initial resuscitation as possible. Splinting such fractures not only reduces pain but also decreases further blood loss, tissue damage, and damage to adjacent neurovascular structures. Realignment of dislocations or fractures that have compromised the blood supply of the extremities may re-establish flow. Open fractures should be cultured and then covered with sterile dressings. If the patient is stable, appropriate radiographs may then be obtained.

NEUROLOGIC RE-EVALUATION

The secondary assessment of neurologic function expands upon the first. Mental status is described using the categories of the Glasgow Coma Scale. The eyes are characterized as opening spontaneously, to speech, to pain, or not at all. Verbal response is described as oriented, confused, inappropriate, incomprehensible, or none.

Cranial nerve information can be extrapolated from examinations of the ears, eyes, nose, and throat, but careful attention is necessary when examining vision, pupil size and reactivity, and extraocular movements. Motor function is also part of the Glasgow Coma Scale: spontaneous purposeful movement, purposeful movement to voice, purposeful movement to pain, withdrawal from pain, abnormal flexion, abnormal extension, and no response. A cursory sensory examination and evaluation of deep tendon reflexes should be done with suspected spinal cord injury or when injury to neurovascular structures in an extremity is suspected.

As in the primary assessment, the purpose here is to establish baselines to assist in later evaluation. However, if deterioration in neurologic function occurs, a more thorough evaluation, including a computerized tomographic (CT) scan of the head must be performed. This secondary assessment is also important in the recognition of the signs and symptoms of increasing intracranial pressure so that treatment may be initiated.

DIAGNOSTIC TESTING

Once the patient has been thoroughly examined, further diagnostic testing can be done and plans made for continued care. Frequent reassessment is crucial in this phase of management, however, as the sequelae of serious injury may be delayed. Reassessment, which causes no delay in ongoing evaluation, allows for the early detection of deterioration.

The risks and benefits of each test must be carefully weighed. In addition to accuracy and reliability, it is important to consider the time involved in obtaining results of a test and how the results will affect management of the patient.

BLOOD AND URINE TESTS

All patients subjected to major trauma should have blood and urine tests done. These tests can be performed quickly and with minimal risk, but surgery should not be delayed if the results are not immediately available. A hematocrit should be done with the first sample. Although a single determination is often misleading, being dependent on fluid resuscitation, serial determinations are particularly useful in following patients with occult hemorrhage.

Serial white blood cell counts should be obtained and, again, are more useful than a single determination. The appearance of a left shift or neutrophilia may reflect an inflammatory response, indicating intraperitoneal pathology. Blood glucose concentrations should also be obtained in the trauma victim.

Whereas hyperglycemia can be detected on urinalysis, hypoglycemia cannot. Hypoglycemia may be the result of an insulin reaction, which, left unnoticed, would be extremely deleterious. Serum amylase levels may be of some value but should not be relied upon. Levels greater than 300 Somogyi units/dl suggest pancreatic injury, especially if serial determinations are evaluated. However, significant pancreatic injury may be presented with normal levels, and in addition, levels may be elevated with injury to other organs. Blood should be obtained for typing and cross-matching.

Tests that might be considered but not routinely done include serum electrolytes, BUN, creatinine, liver function tests, and coagulation studies. Arterial blood gas determinations can also be useful, as oxygenation (Po_2), ventilation (Pco_2), and resuscitation (pH) are assessed.

Urine should be sent for microscopic examination to determine the presence or absence of red blood cells. Reagent strips may also be used to detect protein, glucose, ketones, bilirubin, and occult blood and to measure pH. Myoglobinuria is detected in this fashion, which is important in patients with severe crush injuries or burns involving muscle. Urine can also be checked for drugs and toxic substances.

RADIOGRAPHY

Every trauma patient should have a chest radiograph early in the course of resuscitation. Information learned can be lifesaving (Fig. 5–6A and B). With the exception of the patient who has had an emergency room thoracotomy, no patient should proceed to surgery without a chest film. A portable film is adequate. A patient in hypovolemic or cardiogenic shock without an obvious source of extracavitary blood loss must have (1) bleeding into the chest or abdomen; (2) cardiogenic shock due to myocardial failure, pericardial tamponade, or a tension pneumothorax; or (3) a ruptured hemidiaphragm with displacement of abdominal viscera into the chest. The chest film can direct the surgeon to the appropriate body cavity, saving time in the long run.

A number of other abnormalities may be detected on the chest film that might be difficult to identify on physical examination. Hemothorax or pneumothorax can easily be missed on the physical examination in the trauma room but will be obvious on the chest radiograph. An infiltrate indicating pulmonary contusion may be seen within 1 hour of injury, and mediastinal air can be identified, suggesting tracheobronchial disruption. Fractures of the posterior portion of the first or second rib, apical capping, displacement of the mainstem bronchi, and deviation of the nasogastric tube, along with a widened mediastinum or obscured aortic knob, are signs of aortic or intrathoracic great vessel injury. An abnormal position of a nasogastric tube

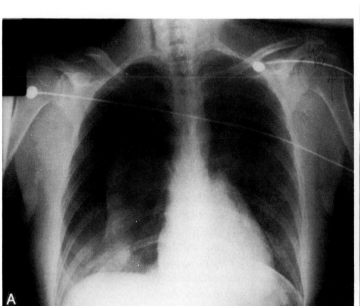
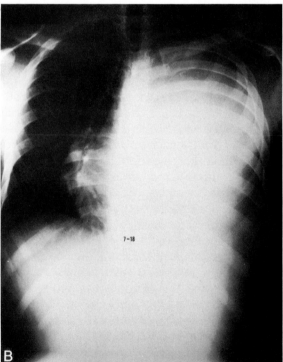

FIGURE 5–6. A and B, The chest radiograph is the single most important test in the resuscitation of the trauma patient. A shows a patient with pneumothorax that was not suspected on physical examination. B shows a massive hemothorax and is the obvious source of shock in this patient. A patient with shock, a normal chest radiograph, and no long bone fractures should lead the surgeon to suspect the abdomen as the source of hypovolemia.

may indicate rupture of the left hemidiaphragm with abdominal viscera in the chest. Certain conditions, however, may not be detected on the chest radiograph. Rib fractures are often not demonstrated even with views showing rib detail, and usually no abnormality is seen with acute pericardial tamponade.

All hemodynamically stable patients with major craniofacial trauma or with physical signs or symptoms of cervical spine injury should have radiographs of the cervical spine. A lateral view including the seventh cervical vertebra is the most important. This view will demonstrate misalignment in most patients with an unstable spine. The seventh vertebra is important to visualize, as it is involved in many fractures. The anterior or posterior borders of the spinal canal may be out of line, the atlas or odontoid may be displaced, or the vertebral bodies may be fractured. The findings on the lateral view might then indicate the need for a full series, including odontoid, oblique, anteroposterior, and flexion-extension views.

A plain film of the abdomen has little place in the management of the trauma patient. However, if the patient with multiple injuries remains stable and if time permits, some information may be gained. Fractured vertebrae or transverse processes indicate that significant force was involved in the injury. The psoas shadow may be obliterated, suggesting retroperitoneal bleeding, and air around the duodenum indicates retroperitoneal rupture of the duodenum.

More important are the intravenous pyelogram, excretory urogram, cystogram, and urethrogram. An intravenous pyelogram should be obtained in any stable patient with hematuria, defined as greater than 100 red blood cells per high-power field in an unspun specimen, or, even in the absence of hematuria, in a stable patient with severe blunt trauma or penetrating injury near a kidney or ureter. Contrast (100 ml) is administered intravenously early during the course of resuscitation. The first film will then give most of the information that is needed.

A cystogram should be obtained in those patients with hematuria or significant pelvic or lower abdominal trauma. An anteroposterior view and either an oblique or a lateral view of the bladder are taken after instilling 150 ml of contrast into the bladder via a Foley catheter. The oblique and lateral views are important, as many ruptures of the bladder are posterior and would be missed with an anteroposterior view only.

A urethrogram should be obtained in any patient with a suspected urethral tear, manifested by blood at the meatus, or in any male patient with severe pelvic trauma. Similarly, if there is difficulty passing a Foley catheter, a urethrogram should be done. The urethrogram is done by gently injecting 30 ml of contrast through the meatus.

Computed tomographic scanning has dramatically changed the evaluation of the trauma patient (Fig. 5–7). Previously inaccessible areas of the body, such as the pelvis, head, and abdomen, can be imaged in three dimensions. Fractures of the spine, pelvis, and facial bones can also be evaluated more thoroughly.

Computerized tomography of the head should be obtained in any hemodynamically stable patient with a suspected depressed skull fracture or severe neurologic deficit. It should also be done in any patient who is even moderately stable and whose neurologic status is worsening. CT need not be done in every obtunded, inebriated patient as long as no other neurologic deficit is present, unless obtundation persists for more than a few hours. CT is also considered definitive for the diagnosis of depressed skull fractures, epidural hematomas, subdural hematomas, intracerebral hematomas, and cerebral edema.

A CT scan of the abdomen can help evaluate hemodynamically stable patients who have been subjected to blunt trauma to the lower chest or abdomen. This scan is especially valuable in those patients with equivocal indications for laparotomy or those with spinal cord damage or obtundation. Both intraperitoneal and retroperitoneal bleeding can be detected and quantified to some degree, and the damaged organ is often identified. The CT scan is also accurate in assessing the organs damaged by blunt trauma—liver, spleen, kidneys, and pancreas (Figs. 5–8 and 5–9). Retroduodenal air or edema, indicating duodenal rupture, or free intraperitoneal air can also be detected.

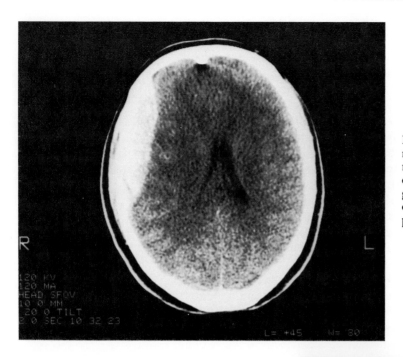

FIGURE 5–7. This patient presented with no neurologic signs and suddenly experienced a deterioration in condition, with confusion and obtundation. The right pupil became dilated. Emergency computerized tomography (CT) shows an epidural hematoma on the side of the dilated pupil.

FIGURE 5–8. This patient was in a high-speed motor vehicle accident and arrived in the emergency room in shock. After resuscitation, a CT scan of the abdomen was obtained and shows rupture of the spleen *(arrows)* and intraperitoneal blood. At operation, the spleen was so severely damaged it could not be salvaged.

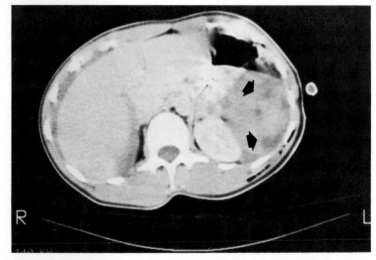

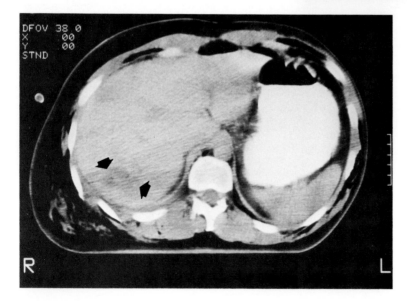

FIGURE 5–9. This man was involved in a motor vehicle accident. He had chest rib fractures on the right side and minimal abdominal tenderness. CT shows a liver laceration with minimal intraperitoneal blood *(arrows).* The patient did not have an operation.

Diagnostic peritoneal lavage is a commonly used means of detecting intra-abdominal injury and the need for laparotomy in both blunt and penetrating trauma. The indications for peritoneal lavage are the same as those for a CT scan of the abdomen: equivocal findings on abdominal examination or neurologic abnormalities that preclude adequate abdominal examination. Peritoneal lavage is quite accurate in detecting intraperitoneal blood but is less reliable in detecting gut perforation or retroperitoneal injury, making CT the preferred diagnostic modality in most instances. However, excellent results, especially in blunt trauma, and low rates of complication can be achieved using the open technique of peritoneal lavage.

To perform lavage, the bladder is first emptied by passing a Foley catheter. The skin below the umbilicus is infiltrated with local anesthetic, and an approximately 2-cm longitudinal incision is made through the skin and down to the fascia (linea alba). The fascia is grasped, retracted anteriorly, and incised with a No. 11 blade or punctured with the catheter trachea. With careful hand control, the catheter is then inserted into the peritoneal cavity. Approximately 1 L of saline is instilled into the peritoneal cavity, allowed to equilibrate, and drained off. If more than 500 ml is recovered, the lavage is considered technically adequate. A red blood cell count greater than 50,000/mm^3 or a white blood cell count greater than 500/mm^3 suggests injury to the abdominal viscera. Incisions or scars indicating prior surgery or injury should be avoided. One can use a supraumbilical incision or can place the incision in an upper quadrant instead.

Arteriography, although carrying some risk to the patient, is the definitive test to evaluate arterial injury. A thoracic aortogram should be obtained in any hemodynamically stable patient who has a suspected disruption of the thoracic aorta or great vessels. Suspicion should be raised if a patient has decreased blood pressure in the left arm or wide mediastinum or obliteration of the aortic knob on the chest radiograph (Fig. 5–10A and B).

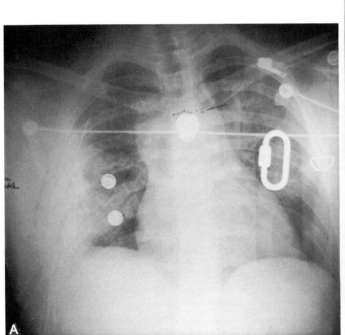
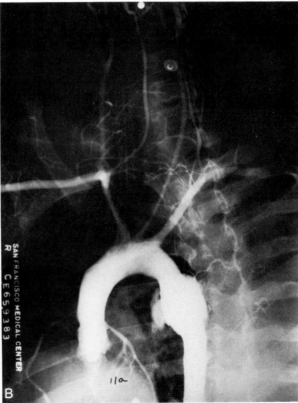

FIGURE 5–10.   A and B, The initial chest radiograph (A) in this patient shows a widened mediastinum. After the patient was resuscitated, an emergency arteriogram was performed and confirmed the diagnosis of a contained rupture of the aorta (B).

Selective arteriograms may be used in the stable patient to evaluate suspected arterial injuries in the neck and extremities. This practice is especially important if a penetrating injury is near an artery or if the patient has a hematoma, bruit, decreased distal pulse, diminished peripheral perfusion, or compromised neurologic function associated with the penetrating injury. Severe blunt trauma to the knee should also arouse suspicion of arterial injury.

If arteriograms are not obtained when there is suspicion that a large artery has been injured (i.e., carotid, brachial, femoral, and popliteal arteries), the vessels should be explored. In certain circumstances, arteriography may be preferable to exploration. For example, those stable patients with penetrating injuries to the base or upper one third of the neck should have arteriography, as the vessels are difficult to expose and arteriography can help in planning the operation. This is in contrast to the middle third of the neck, where the vessels can easily be exposed and no time should be lost on arteriography. In general, with injuries to the middle third of the neck or extremities, exploration is preferred (1) if the patient is unstable, (2) if the hematoma is expanding, or (3) if the extremity distal to the injury is ischemic. Arteriography with embolization is another therapeutic option. For example, severe pelvic fractures with significant hemorrhage may be difficult to control by external fixation or pressure, making embolization necessary.

Other diagnostic procedures occasionally useful in the evaluation of the trauma patient include echocardiography, endoscopy, and contrast studies of the gastrointestinal tract. Echocardiography can be useful in sorting out a pericardial tamponade in a stable patient and in evaluating cardiac contusion (two-dimensional echocardiography). Endoscopy, using either rigid or fiberoptic instruments, allows one to assess organ structures that are often difficult to assess by other means, including the larynx, trachea, esophagus, and rectum. In addition to endoscopy, radiographic studies with contrast may be necessary to detect injuries in these areas, as these tests do not provide identical information (Fig. 5–11A and B).

The physician must use sound clinical judgment in selecting any diagnostic test when evaluating the trauma patient. Unnecessary studies may delay treatment that is already indicated, thus increasing morbidity and mortality.

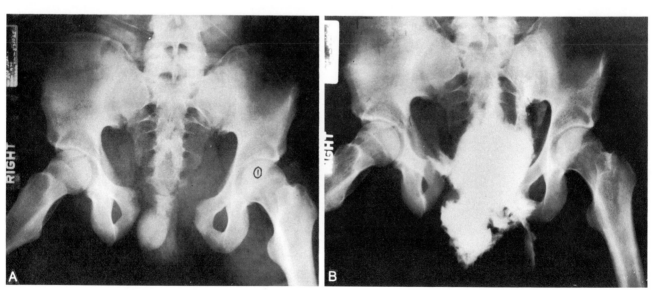

Figure 5–11. *A* and *B*, These radiographs show a severe pelvic fracture. The incidence of associated genitourinary injury approximates 30 per cent in patients with this fracture; the genitourinary injury is confirmed by the urethrogram.

OPERATIVE PRIORITIES

The determinants of priorities are severity of injury and hemodynamic stability, with the overriding concerns being to minimize mortality and maintain a functional human being. Although approximately 80 to 85 per cent of injuries are not life threatening or permanently disabling, 15 to 20 per cent are and demand prompt, definitive surgical care. This care may begin within minutes of the first evaluation or may be delayed up to a week after injury.

The goal of care is to return the patient to preinjury health as soon as possible. Basic surgical principles are applied in accomplishing this goal, including hemostasis, maintenance of perfusion, restoration of integrity, debridement of devitalized tissue, and prevention of infection. Hemostasis should be achieved rapidly and maintained to avert hypotension, with care taken to avoid devascularizing tissue. Blood flow should be re-established quickly, depending on the importance of the involved tissue and the degree of other injuries. Restoration of integrity may be delayed, as in peripheral nerve repairs, or accomplished immediately, as in repair of small bowel or stomach injuries. Nonviable tissue should be debrided often, requiring several operative examinations to determine if further resection is necessary. Prevention of infection involves not only the use of perioperative antibiotics in contaminated cases but also application of the above principles.

Priorities subsequent to the initial emergency room assessment and resuscitation are essentially determined by whether the patient's condition is unstable, both hemodynamically and neurologically, or whether his or her condition can be stabilized. In the unstable patient, resuscitation in the emergency room should be limited to 15 minutes, and no diagnostic studies, except CT scan in the head-injured patient and chest film, are necessary. Other studies and evaluations must await completion of surgery. However, the patient who arrives hemodynamically stable or whose condition stabilizes shortly after arrival may be deliberately evaluated. Value judgments must often be exercised in these instances when considering therapeutic planning. For example, the hemodynamically unstable patient with a widened mediastinum on chest film should undergo exploratory laparotomy prior to aortogram.

Upon arriving in the operating room, the trauma patient must be prepared and draped over a large area so that the surgeon can gain access to any body cavity expeditiously. This sterile field should include the anterior portion and both lateral portions of the torso, extending from the neck and clavicles cephalad to the groins caudad and from table top to table top laterally. This preparation can be accomplished quickly and should be done prior to the induction of anesthesia so that if deterioration occurs, immediate thoracotomy or laparotomy can be done. The head may be prepared for craniotomy concurrently.

The midline incision is preferred, as this allows rapid access to the wide exposure of the abdomen and can be extended up the sternum as a sternum-splitting incision or into the right or left side of the chest. A trap door incision can similarly be fashioned by extending the incision along the clavicle, removing the medial portion of the clavicle, and then extending into the third or fourth intercostal space. This incision allows access to posterior mediastinal structures, such as the left subclavian artery.

When the presence or site of intra-abdominal injury is uncertain, one should start with an upper midline incision from the xiphoid to just above the umbilicus, as most complicated problems lie in the upper abdomen. If intra-abdominal injury is encountered and appears to be major, the incision should be quickly extended to the pubis.

The patient should be eviscerated so that each quadrant can be rapidly inspected and packs placed temporarily to absorb free blood. Each quadrant of the abdomen and the mesentery is inspected rapidly (within 1 to 2 minutes) so that the major source of hemorrhage can be identified first. The application of packs controls bleeding from many arterial injuries. If bleeding can be controlled by the placement of packs or by direct pressure, volume should be restored prior to further dissection. A directly exposed vascular injury may lead to sudden decompression and cardiac arrest in a previously hypovolemic patient.

Bright red blood in the abdomen indicates an arterial injury. In the upper abdomen, this may indicate injury to the visceral portion of the aorta or one of its major upper abdominal branches. Proximal control, including opening the left side of the chest if the hematoma extends to the diaphragm, must therefore be achieved. If free from hematoma, the aorta may be controlled at the crura of the diaphragm after dividing the gastrohepatic ligament.

Minor sources of hemorrhage should not distract one when major hemorrhage is ongoing, especially venous bleeding. Venous bleeding is often not as obvious or dramatic as arterial bleeding owing to the low pressure involved. By placing packs, almost all venous bleeding can be controlled and volume restored. Hepatic vein or intrahepatic vena caval injuries may result in massive hemorrhage, evident with downward retraction of the dome of the liver. Although direct compression of the liver parenchyma and direct ligation or repair of the veins may be carried out, an intracaval shunt may be necessary to control bleeding.

Once hemorrhage has been controlled with packs or clamps, attempts should be made to control fecal soilage prior to definitive surgery. Obvious holes are temporarily closed with running suture or with Babcock clamps.

After neurologic and torso injuries have been treated, one must decide whether or not to proceed with treating associated maxillofacial or orthopedic injuries. If the patient is hypothermic or hemodynamically unstable, fractures should be documented and splinted and the patient taken to the intensive care unit for further resuscitation. A planned return to the operating room is made within 24 hours, at which time orthopedic and maxillofacial injuries are treated and a secondary exploratory laparotomy for abdominal toilet is carried out. If, however, the patient's condition is stable after neurosurgical and torso injury treatment, orthopedic or maxillofacial injuries should be treated while the patient is under the same anesthetic.

INTENSIVE CARE PRIORITIES

The primary purpose of the trauma intensive care unit is to treat and support organ system dysfunction as it arises. Most often these complications are the result of the injury itself or sepsis but may also be caused by pre-existing medical conditions or therapy given to the patient. The primary goal, then, must be prevention of complications. To accomplish this, one may categorize priorities as follows: (1) unified direction of care, (2) mobilization of the patient, (3) removal of all tubes as soon as possible, (4) nutrition, and (5) rehabilitation (Table 5–6).

Optimally, the care of the trauma patient is under the guidance and direction of a single individual, that being the first person who evaluated the patient and directed emergency and operative care. Continuity of care is then assured. This individual should also provide support services and direct the many consultants necessary in managing the patient.

Mobilization and pulmonary toilet are critical in managing the acutely injured patient. These practices minimize atelectasis and decrease the incidence of pneumonia. The incidence of pulmonary emboli can also be reduced with early mobilization.

TABLE 5–6.   INTENSIVE CARE PRIORITIES

Unified direction of care
Mobilization
Removal of tubes
Nutritional support
Rehabilitation

Anabolism is restored, organ failure is minimized, and rehabilitation is enhanced with early mobilization.

All tubes and lines placed in the emergency room, with the exception of the endotracheal tube, should be removed within 24 hours of injury. Frequently, these are placed under less than sterile conditions in the emergency setting and can serve only as a source of sepsis. They should be viewed as a wick between the patient and the environment.

Nutritional support should be started early, preferably within 48 hours of injury, in those patients likely to have a prolonged catabolic phase or in those unable to feed themselves. Outcome following therapy for major trauma is largely influenced by the individual's overall nutritional status. Trauma patients have significantly increased caloric and protein requirements. Failure to provide these needs may precipitate complications. Protein malnutrition results in muscle wasting, delayed wound healing, impaired immune function, abnormal red blood cell function, prolonged ventilatory dependence, and delayed bone callus formation.

Essentially, two methods of nutritional support are available: hyperalimentation and enteral feeding. Although enteral feeding is the safest, cheapest, and most effective means of providing nutritional support, it may not always be possible in the severely injured patient. Total parenteral nutrition via a central vein must then be relied upon for replacement of nitrogen losses and ongoing maintenance requirements. Optimally, a feeding jejunostomy or feeding tube is placed during the initial surgery. The goal, using either method, is to establish a positive nitrogen balance with a minimum of complications. This goal requires frequent assessment of the patient's overall status, including physical examination and laboratory evaluation. A standard "cookbook" approach cannot be used successfully in these patients.

Acute rehabilitation is the final priority. This rehabilitation should be initiated as soon as possible after injury and might include things as simple as skin protection and passive motion of joints in the unconscious patient. Active physical therapy by nurses or physical therapists should be started early in the intensive care unit and continued through the hospital stay. The psychologic aspect of major trauma, although difficult to quantitate, is also a major problem in the postinjury period and must be recognized. Emotional support for and by the family is essential, and professional psychologists or psychiatrists should be utilized as needed.

REFERENCES

1. Fischer RP, Miles DL: The demographics of trauma in 1985. J Trauma 27:1233–1236, 1987.
2. Baker SP: Injuries: The neglected epidemic. Stone lecture 1985. American Trauma Society Meeting. J Trauma 27:343–348, 1987.
3. Health Insurance Association of America Source Book of Health Insurance Data, Washington, DC, Public Relations Division of Health Insurance Assoc of America, 1986–87.
4. Trunkey DD: Trauma. Sci Am 249:28, 1983.
5. West JG, Trunkey DD: System of trauma care: A study of two counties. Arch Surg 114:455–463, 1979.
6. West JG, Cales RH, Gazzanga AB: Impact of regionalization: The Orange County experience. Arch Surg 18:740–744, 1983.
7. Trunkey DD: Toward optimal trauma care. Bull ACS, October 1984, pp 2–6.
8. Shackford SR, Mackersie RL, Hoyt DB, et al: Impact of a trauma system on outcome of severely injured patients. Arch Surg 122:323–327, 1987.
9. Border JR, Lewis FR, Aprahamian C, et al: Panel: Prehospital trauma care—stabilize or scoop and run. J Trauma 23:708–711, 1983.
10. Virgilio BW, Rice CL, Smith DE, et al: Crystalloid vs colloid resuscitation: Is one better? Surgery 85:129–139, 1979.
11. Moss GS, Gould SA: Plasma expanders: An update. Am J Surg 155:425–434, 1988.

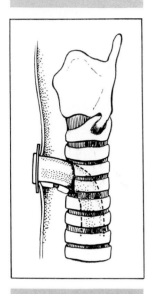

EMERGENCY AIRWAY MANAGEMENT IN THE TRAUMATIZED PATIENT

JEFFREY L. RAJCHEL, D.D.S., M.S.,
and J. ROBERT SCULLY, D.D.S., M.S.

The most sophisticated of techniques in treating facial trauma can be quite meaningless if attention is not first directed to the victim's airway. Injuries to the head and maxillofacial areas can easily jeopardize the patient's ability to maintain respiration. Because of this life-threatening reality, the primary concern of anyone providing emergency care for trauma victims must be to establish and maintain a patent airway and to provide adequate ventilation.

Paracelsus, in the sixteenth century, was the first known to provide emergency ventilation, using a common fireside bellows to induce air into the lungs of apparently dead persons, and adaptations of this method were used throughout Europe for more than 300 years.[1] Although resuscitation and surgical techniques have been improved and modified, the list of priorities when managing the traumatized patient with multiple injuries has remained essentially unchanged. The mnemonic advocated by the American College of Surgeons in Advanced Trauma Life Support (ATLS) is as follows: (A) airway maintenance with cervical spine control, (B) breathing, (C) circulation with hemorrhage control, (D) discerning the neurologic status of the patient, and (E) exposing or undressing the patient to facilitate complete physical evaluation.[2] This chapter considers (A) and (B).

Since early deaths after trauma are frequently due to the failure to recognize subtle or obvious indicators of airway obstruction, any consideration of acute respiratory failure requires recognition of signs and symptoms. Patients may demonstrate stridor (a high-pitched, noisy respiration), intercostal retraction, tracheal tug, hoarseness, or labored breathing. Pallor, tachycardia, and an increase in blood pressure are early signs of hypoxia and hypercapnea.[3] These findings may be accompanied by confusion, agitation, unconsciousness, or cyanosis (cyanosis becomes recognizable when the arterial saturation is 80 per cent or less in a healthy adult).[4] In patients with obvious respiratory distress, examination should include the following:

1. Attention to mandibular mobility
2. The size and mobility of the tongue
3. The state and fragility of dentition
4. The amount and viscosity of secretions
5. The presence of hemorrhage or masses in the oral cavity and pharynx

Thorough auscultation and percussion of the lung fields are performed to rule out pneumothorax and hemothorax.

SYSTEMIC APPROACH TO AIRWAY MANAGEMENT

Although the surgeon must always be flexible in regard to the presentation of a patient's injuries, a logical sequence of actions should be pursued to establish and maintain a patent airway (Table 6–1).

1. **Recognize airway obstruction.**

Those conditions associated with airway obstruction in the acutely injured and stabilized trauma victim must be recognized. When signs and symptoms of concern have been presented, the clinical examination should include the following procedures:

- *Look* to see if the patient is using accessory musculature to aid in respiration. Observe closely for any evidence of dyspnea.
- *Listen* for abnormal sounds. Croupy respirations with marked inspiratory crow are characteristic of upper airway obstruction.
- *Feel* for symmetric movement of air on inspiration and expiration.[2]

2. **Clear the airway.**

The oral cavity should be investigated and cleared of any foreign bodies, which may be potential sources of aspiration and airway obstruction. Even minimally equipped emergency rooms will have some instrumentation for this task. At the least, gloved digital manipulation could be a lifesaving maneuver. Hemorrhage, blood clots, and secretions should be suctioned with a rigid suction device, and, if possible, the oropharynx should be directly visualized with a laryngoscope.

3. **Reposition the patient.**

On occasion, an alert patient with facial trauma will position himself or herself to minimize the respiratory effort. If this positioning does not violate medical and surgical considerations for concomitant injuries, he or she should be allowed to maintain this posture until definitive treatment modalities can be initiated. It is best to allow the patient to maintain an existing airway through self-posturing than to jeopardize the airway by forcing him or her to assume another position.

If the patient is supine, with decreased consciousness, obstruction from the tongue or from injured and unsupported soft tissue prolapsing into the hypopharynx can be corrected by manipulation of the mandible in a chin lift or jaw thrust maneuver.[2] In the chin lift, the fingers of one hand grasp the anteroinferior border of the mandible, and the thumb is placed on the lingual surfaces of the lower incisors or alveolar ridge. The chin is then gently lifted. Care is taken not to hyperextend the neck if a cervical spine injury is suspected. The jaw thrust maneuver is accomplished by grasping the angles of the mandible and elevating the jaw anteriorly. The thumbs can be used to retract the lips. Both procedures can effectively displace the tongue away from the posterior pharyngeal wall. It is generally appropriate to attempt jaw

TABLE 6–1. SYSTEMATIC APPROACH TO AIRWAY MANAGEMENT

1. Recognize airway obstruction
2. Clear the airway
3. Reposition the patient
4. Utilize artificial airways
5. Perform endotracheal intubation
6. Cricothyroidotomy
7. Tracheostomy under optimal conditions

repositioning prior to placement of any artificial airway. The patient's head and neck should never be hyperextended or hyperflexed to establish or maintain the airway if the cervical spine has not been cleared.

4. **Utilize an artificial airway if a patent airway cannot be maintained.**

ESOPHAGEAL OBTURATOR AIRWAY (EOA)

Although the EOA is generally not utilized in emergency room care, the surgeon may encounter a patient in whom an EOA has been inserted in the field (Fig. 6–1).

The esophageal obturator is a blind tube that is inserted into the esophagus. An inflatable cuff is located just above the end. Holes located near the upper end allow air to pass into the pharynx. The use of this device can cause vomiting in responsive patients, and therefore, its use should be limited to the unconscious patient.

If the patient regains consciousness and tracheal intubation is unnecessary, the EOA is removed by placing the patient on his or her side, deflating the cuff, and withdrawing the tube in a slow, deliberate manner. Suction equipment should be available during this procedure. However, the EOA should not be removed in the unconscious patient prior to placement of an endotracheal tube. Since regurgitation of stomach contents can be expected, it is important to have the cuff inflated on the endotracheal tube and good suction available before deflating the esophageal airway cuff and subsequently removing the EOA.[5]

The use of this airway is controversial. Evidence suggests that carbon dioxide retention and inadequate ventilation volumes occur in some patients.[6] Possible complications include false passage into the trachea and laceration or rupture of the esophagus.[7-11]

ORAL AND NASOPHARYNGEAL AIRWAYS

Both of these airways are designed to displace the tongue anteriorly off the posterior pharyngeal wall, allowing the patient to breathe through or around them. The oral airway is more efficient but should be used only in the unconscious patient because of stimulation of the gag reflex and possible vomiting. Care must be taken to advance the tongue prior to its placement. The oral airway must not push the tongue posteriorly and block, rather than clear, the airway.

The nasopharyngeal airway is inserted into one nostril and is advanced along the

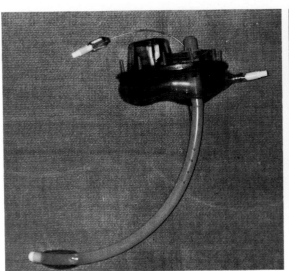
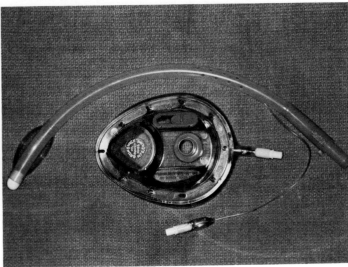

FIGURE 6–1. Esophageal obturator airways.

nasal floor and into the posterior pharynx behind the tongue. It is well tolerated by the conscious patient, since placement does not stimulate the soft palate. The tube should be lubricated and not forced (forcing may occur with obstruction of the nasal cavity or with use of too large an airway) to avoid nasal hemorrhage.

It is important to realize that both of these devices are temporary adjuncts to establishing and maintaining an airway and should not be considered definitive airway management. The nasopharyngeal airway can be blocked with clots or secretions, and both airways are easily dislodged in the unattended patient.

5. **Perform endotracheal intubation.**

The level of consciousness and the status of the cervical spine will determine which technique is chosen.

6. **Perform a cricothyroidotomy.**

If the upper airway obstruction is complete and intubation impossible, a cricothyroidotomy is recommended in an emergency situation.

7. **Perform a tracheostomy.**

When indicated, and if the procedure can be performed under optimal conditions, a tracheostomy should be done.

ENDOTRACHEAL INTUBATION

Probably the most consistently reliable and time-proven method of securing a patent airway in the trauma patient with a compromised airway is endotracheal intubation. If any of the preliminary techniques in the systematic approach mentioned previously are unsuccessful or contraindicated or leave the trauma team with any doubt of their future security, the operator should immediately intubate the trachea via the oral or nasal route. Intubation requires a minimal amount of the victim's precious time when performed by a skilled operator, and the tube can be secured while the patient's other injuries are addressed.

Indications for Tracheal Intubation

Indications include the following:

1. When airway patency is threatened and noninvasive modalities are unsuccessful

2. When a patient is in extremis and time urgency demands the quickest, surest means of securing a patent airway

3. When complete control of the airway is needed for tracheal suction or pulmonary toilet

4. When the airway needs to be protected from aspiration of blood or gastric contents

5. When there is a need for controlled positive-pressure ventilation.

6. If there is a probability of a future tracheostomy or cricothyroidotomy.

Contraindications to Tracheal Intubation

Contraindications are rare but may include the following:

1. Confirmed or suspected cervical spine injury is a relative contraindication to oral intubation, since this could require movement of the cervical spine and subsequent trauma to the cervical cord. The most dangerous movement is flexion.[12]

2. The presence of cerebrospinal fluid rhinorrhea or fracture of the anterior cranial fossa is a relative contraindication to the nasal route, since use of the nasal route could predispose the patient to meningitis secondary to contamination from nasopharyngeal organisms.

3.   The presence of a retropharyngeal swelling noted on a lateral cervical spine film is a strong contraindication to endotracheal intubation because of possible rupture and aspiration.

4.   A fractured larynx may make endotracheal intubation impossible.

Various designs of endotracheal tubes are available, but all have several features in common. The tube is open at both ends, with a standard 15-mm adapter for connection with a bag-valve attachment or anesthesia connectors. The tracheal end has an inflatable cuff for sealing the airway (except in the smaller pediatric sizes) and allows for positive-pressure ventilation and protection of the airway from aspiration. The integrity of the cuff should be checked prior to insertion.

The laryngoscope is used to visualize the glottis and is available in two basic types: those with straight blades and those with curved blades (Fig. 6–2). Both have a

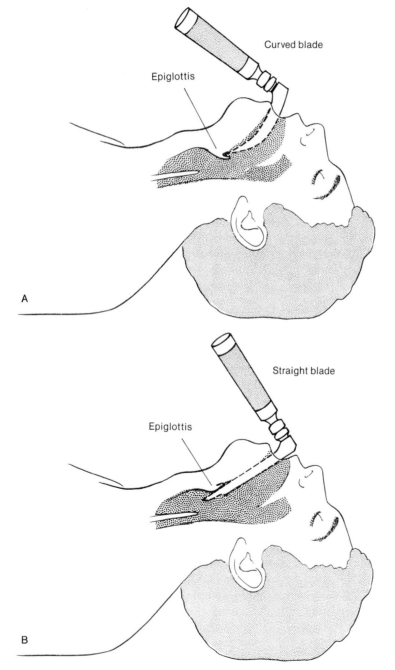

FIGURE 6–2. Proper position of the tip of the curved *(A)* and straight *(B)* blades.

TABLE 6-2. ENDOTRACHEAL TUBE SIZES*

	DIAMETER (MM)		MILLIMETERS (MM)
	Interior	*Exterior*	*Minimum Length*
Preterm	2.5	4.0	10
	3.0	4.5	11
Term	3.5	5.0	12
6 mo	4.0	5.5	13
1 yr	4.5	6.0	14
	5.0	6.5	15
2 yr	5.0	6.5	15
4 yr	5.5	7.0	16
6 yr	6.0	8.0	18
8 yr	6.5	8.5	20
10 yr	7.0	9.0	21
12 yr	7.5	9.5	22
14 yr	8.0	10.0	23
Adults	8.5	11.5	
	9.0	12.0	
	10.0	13.0	

*This information has been compiled from various sources and is intended as an approximate guide only. The "minimum length" column indicates the shortest length of an oral endotracheal tube required for intubation.

battery-operated fiberoptic light source on the blade. The tip of the straight blade is placed under the epiglottis during intubation. The tip of the curved blade is placed into the vallecular space between the base of the tongue and the epiglottis.

Some experts feel the curved blade minimizes the incidence of retching, since the tip contacts the superior (or pharyngeal) surface of the epiglottis, which is innervated by the glossopharyngeal nerve (cranial nerve IX), rather than stimulating the inferior (or tracheal) surface of the epiglottis, which is innervated by the vagus nerve (cranial nerve X).[13] This finding has not been shown conclusively in clinical studies, and moreover, the final determinant of success in using either technique is the specific training and skill of the operator.

There are many guidelines or "rules of thumb" for selecting tube size, and none are without exceptions. Table 6-2 shows an accepted guide for selecting the tube diameter and minimum length based on the patient's age.

Direct Laryngoscopy

A direct laryngoscopy technique can be performed during intubation only if a cervical spine injury has been ruled out radiographically. To achieve direct visualization of the trachea, there are three axes that need to be aligned with respect to one another: those of the mouth, the pharynx, and the trachea (Fig. 6–3). This alignment requires the neck to be flexed forward and the head extended backward, putting the patient into the "sniffing position."[14] The laryngoscope blade is then inserted into the mouth, following the natural contour of the pharynx, and upward traction is exerted along the long axis of the laryngoscope handle. The position of the tip of the blade is dependent on whether the straight or curved blade is used.

The procedure for oral endotracheal intubation via direct laryngoscopy is as follows. Once the operator has assured that adequate ventilation and oxygenation are in progress, he or she inserts the blade into the right side of the patient's mouth, displacing the tongue to the left. The epiglottis and vocal cords are visually examined and then the endotracheal tube is gently inserted into the trachea without applying pressure to the teeth. Gentle external pressure at the level of the thyroid cartilage (the Sellick maneuver) can sometimes aid the operator in visualizing the cords and can

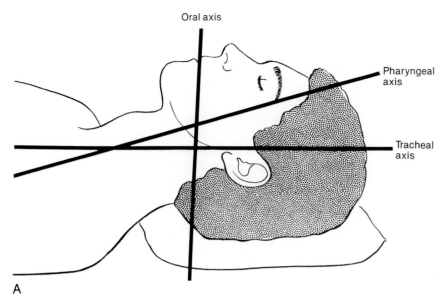

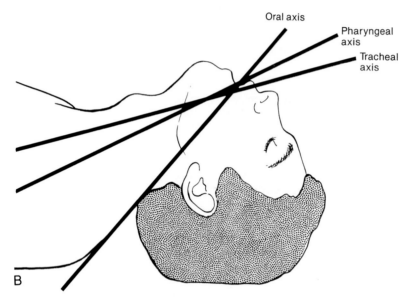

FIGURE 6–3. *A* and *B*, Two examples showing how extending the head allows the three axes to be nearly aligned to one another.

facilitate passage of the tube into the trachea. The operator inflates the cuff with enough air to provide an adequate seal. The correct placement of the tube is checked by mouth-to-tube or bag-valve–to–tube ventilation while observing lung expansion. The operator auscultates the chest and abdomen to verify bilaterally symmetric breath sounds. Finally, the tube is stabilized.[15]

The entire intubation procedure should be accomplished within seconds, or in the same length of time required to hold the breath before exhaling. If the intubation cannot be successfully completed, attempts should be discontinued and the patient should be ventilated before trying again. Ideally, the exact position of the endotracheal tube should be verified by chest film.

Difficult intubations are often anticipated by preoperative assessment of the patient. If there is any doubt concerning the operator's ability to secure the airway, spontaneous respiration should not be abolished prior to intubation. In such cases, an intubation technique in the awake patient is indicated.

Blind Endotracheal Intubation

Blind endotracheal intubation is the method of choice in the presence of cervical spine injuries (or if they are suspected), when the oral route is not available or impossible, and when intact protective reflexes are essential until the airway is secured. This technique requires greater technical expertise and gentle sensitivity on the part of the operator. It is an invaluable modality to have available whenever one manages patients with maxillofacial trauma.

If a cervical spine fracture is suspected, the cervical collar is left in place to help immobilize the neck. Once adequate ventilation and oxygenation are in progress, the nasal passage is sprayed with an anesthetic and vasoconstrictor; 4 per cent cocaine is very effective. The tube end is lubricated with a local anesthetic jelly, and the tube is inserted into one nostril while an assistant maintains manual cervical spine immobilization. The tube is slowly and firmly guided along the nasal floor. Every effort should be made to avoid nasal hemorrhage. Once the tube has entered the pharynx, the operator listens to the flow emanating from the tube end. The tube is carefully advanced until the sound of air is maximal. This sound of air suggests that the location of the tip is at the opening of the trachea. (It may be necessary to rotate the tube manually to maintain the tip in the midline.) While continuing to listen, the operator determines the moment of inhalation and advances the tube.[15]

If the intubation is unsuccessful, the procedure is repeated and pressure is applied to the thyroid cartilage (the Sellick maneuver). It is most important to ventilate and oxygenate the patient intermittently. Once the tube has entered the trachea, tube placement is verified and stabilized externally.

Another method that could facilitate intubation in the awake patient is use of a stylet and digital manipulation. The stylet is placed into the tube so that it is approximately 0.5 to 1.0 inch shy of the tube end to avoid soft tissue trauma during the procedure. The distal end of the tube is bent to a nearly 90-degree angle and is inserted into the nostril. It is then gently and firmly guided into the pharynx. The intubation technique may then proceed as discussed previously, or if tolerated, the operator can insert two fingers into the hypopharynx, guiding the tube and gently lifting the epiglottis. Once the tube has passed through the vocal cords, the operator continues to advance the tube with gentle pressure as the stylet is withdrawn.

Alternative Methods of Intubation

There are times when oral or nasal tracheal intubation is difficult to achieve even with the techniques just described. Several alternative methods have been developed for use in these situations. The most widely used and dependable techniques are fiberoptic laryngoscopy and retrograde transcricoid intubation.

FIBEROPTIC LARYNGOSCOPY

The use of the fiberoptic laryngoscope has been well documented as an alternative to blind nasal intubation. The laryngoscope acts as an introducer and allows direct visualization of the larynx. The distal 5 cm can be maneuvered with the aid of a proximal nob. Neck movement is not required. The newer fiberoptic laryngoscopes are equipped with built-in suction devices.[16]

RETROGRADE TRANSCRICOID INTUBATION

The retrograde transcricoid intubation technique (Fig. 6–4) was introduced in the early 1960s to facilitate intubation in patients with deformities of the mouth.[17,18] For this maneuver, a standard endotracheal tube of appropriate size, a through-the-needle catheter or flexible-tip guide wire, and a needle (16- to 18-gauge intracath-

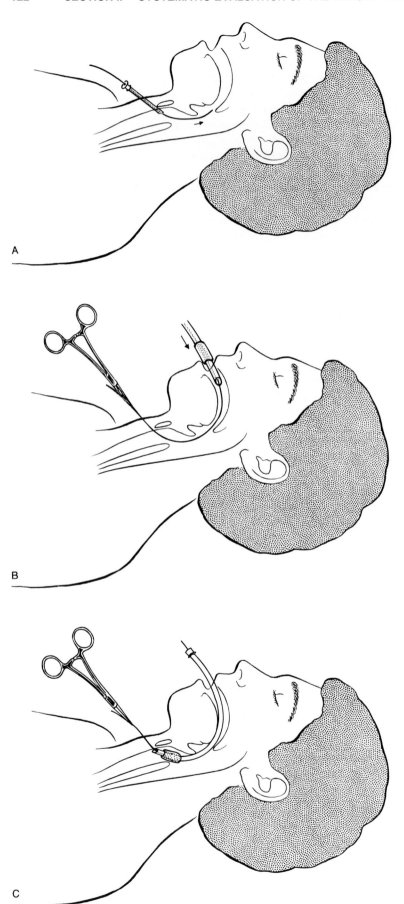

FIGURE 6–4. *A,* Guided retrograde transcricoid intubation. Plastic catheter is fed through the needle and into the pharynx. *B,* Endotracheal tube is passed down the catheter guide. *C,* Endotracheal tube is passed into the trachea.

eter) and syringe are obtained. The length of catheter or wire must be sufficient to facilitate the working distance; generally, 70 cm is adequate.[19]

Following skin preparation and with allowance for sterile technique, the inferior aspect of the cricothyroid membrane is punctured with a needle to avoid the cricothyroid arteries. Aspiration of air confirms the proper placement. The needle and its bevel are then turned cephalad, and the syringe is removed. The catheter or wire is fed through the needle into the pharynx. If advancement is impeded below the vocal cords, gentle manipulation can be achieved by either rotating the needle or moving it around the fulcrum of its site of insertion. When the catheter passes into the pharynx, it may be guided out through the mouth with forceps or digital manipulation while being fed in from below. Alternatively, if nasal intubation is intended, after preparing the nose with a topically applied vasoconstrictor, a suction catheter is passed through the nose and into the pharynx, and that, too, is withdrawn through the mouth. The suction catheter and guide wire are joined with tape, and the guide wire is then led back through the mouth and out through the nose by the suction catheter.[20]

The needle is then withdrawn from the trachea, and small hemostats are utilized to secure both ends of the guide wire. The oral or nasal tube is advanced over the upper end of the through-the-needle catheter or guide wire protruding from either the mouth or the nose. (Reports have suggested that the guide be fed through the side hole of the endotracheal tube into the lumen and then out the proximal end. This method potentially allows an extra 1 cm of tube to be placed below the vocal cords prior to guide removal.[21]) The tube is then advanced over the guide and into the pharynx and from there to the opening of the larynx. When the tube is in the correct position, the catheter or guide wire should be cut at the skin of the neck, and the upper half is withdrawn through the tube to prevent unnecessary contamination of the trachea.

Extubation

Assuming the victim has been successfully resuscitated and stabilized, he or she will need to be extubated. Oxygen, succinylcholine, suction, and equipment for reintubation should be immediately available. To avoid aspiration, the pharynx should be suctioned free of any secretions prior to deflation of the cuff and extubation of the trachea. The tube is removed during expiration. Pressure on the reservoir bag just prior to tube removal helps ensure that the lungs will be inflated and the initial gas flow will be outward. This pressure can also facilitate a cough and the expulsion of any aspirated material. Laryngospasms and vomiting are the most serious and immediate hazards.[22]

Complications

There is a relatively low incidence of complications from endotracheal intubation, and even these can be minimized by skillful technique and an understanding of their causes. They may be categorized as occurring (1) during direct laryngoscopy and endotracheal intubation, (2) while the tube is in place, and (3) after extubation, either immediately or in a delayed manner.[22,23]

Complications during direct laryngoscopy and endotracheal intubation include the following:

1. Esophageal intubation
2. Intubation of the right mainstem bronchus
3. Inability to intubate
4. Induction of vomiting
5. Dislocation of the mandible
6. Fracture of the epiglottis

7. Airway hemorrhage secondary to trauma
8. Avulsion of the vocal cords (usually from a stylet)
9. Dental trauma
10. Hypertension, tachycardia, bradycardia, or dysrhythmias
11. Dislocation of the cervical spine during hyperextension or hyperflexion
12. Conversion of a cervical spine injury without neurologic deficit to a cervical spine injury with deficit

Complications while the endotracheal tube is in place include the following:

1. Obstruction
2. Accidental extubation
3. Rupture or leakage of the cuff, resulting in possible aspiration
4. Tracheal mucosa injury or ischemia
5. Infection

Complications following extubation include the following:

1. Laryngospasm
2. Aspiration
3. Pharyngitis, laryngitis, and tracheitis
4. Infection
5. Laryngeal or subglottic edema
6. Laryngeal ulceration with or without granulation tissue formation
7. Tracheal stenosis
8. Vocal cord paralysis

TRACHEOSTOMY

The tracheostomy is one of the oldest operations in medical history. The earliest known references to this surgical procedure are found in the Rig-Veda, a sacred Hindu book, published circa 2000 BC, and in Egyptian manuscripts dated 3500 years ago.[24,25] As early as AD 200, Antyllus described that

> . . . wherefore bending the patient's head backward, so as to bring the windpipe better into view, we are to make a transverse incision between two of the rings, so that it may not be the cartilage which is divided, but the membrane connecting the cartilages.[2,4]

Reports continued to appear in the literature; however, it was not until the early 1600s that tracheostomy was considered an acceptable procedure for upper airway obstruction. (Lorenz Heister introduced the term tracheotomy in 1718, and Negus suggested the term tracheostomy in 1938. Prior to this, the operation was commonly called a laryngotomy or bronchotomy.[24])

Credit for surgical refinement and systematic study is often given to Chevalier Jackson. He defined factors leading to complications of the tracheostomy, such as high incisions, using improper cannulae, and poor postoperative care.[26]

Clinical situations that require a tracheostomy have met with recent controversy as clinical data on alternative procedures become available. Indications include the following:

1. Upper airway obstruction caused by trauma, soft tissue swelling, fractures, infection, hemorrhage, or foreign bodies
2. Facilitation of tracheobronchial toilet
3. Anticipated prolonged mechanical ventilation
4. Facilitation of management of concomitant problems, such as cervical spine injuries or oncologic resections in the head and neck.[4,27]

The relief of upper airway obstruction is the only indication listed that potentially requires a tracheostomy to be performed on an emergency basis. It has been reported that the rate of complications with emergency tracheostomy is two to five times greater than with an elective operation.[28] This greater rate is usually due to haste; inadequate lighting, equipment, or assistance; and uncooperativeness on the part of the patient. This procedure should be done under optimal conditions, preferably in the operating room.

Upper airway obstruction is now a less common reason to perform an emergency tracheostomy than once believed. Ventilation can usually be restored by endotracheal intubation. Even difficult cases can be assisted by a fiberoptic laryngoscope, retrograde techniques, or a bronchoscope. If upper airway obstruction is complete and intubation impossible, emergency airway management requires surgical or needle cricothyroidotomy.

Anatomic and Surgical Considerations

The surface anatomic landmarks of the anterior midline of the neck should be palpated before initiating surgery (Fig. 6–5). Superiorly, the thyroid cartilage is the first prominence, followed by the less prominent cricoid cartilage. The tracheal rings are more difficult to palpate as one proceeds inferiorly because the trachea is more posterior as it descends into the chest. At the level of the suprasternal notch, the trachea lies 1.0 to 1.5 cm deeper than at the level of the cricoid cartilage. (The normal adult trachea is 9 to 10 mm in diameter and approximately 9.5 to 12.2 cm in length, with about half located in the neck.)[23]

The skin incision is marked with the patient's head in a normal position, and then positioning is completed with slight hyperextension of the head and neck. Noncompliance with this technique (marking the patient while he or she is in the extended position or extreme hyperextension) can result in a disparity between the skin incision and the tracheal opening. This disparity could establish undesirable tension, with possible tracheal and esophageal damage, vascular erosion, or tube displacement.

Following the infiltration of local anesthetic, a transverse incision approximately 3 to 5 cm in length is made through skin and subcutaneous tissue about 2 cm below

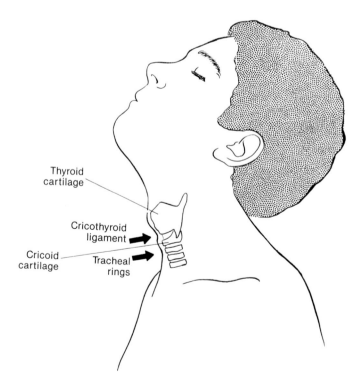

FIGURE 6–5. Surface anatomic landmarks of the midline of the neck.

Thyroid cartilage

Cricothyroid ligament

Cricoid cartilage

Tracheal rings

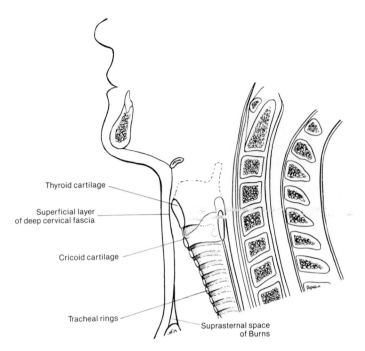

Thyroid cartilage

Superficial layer
of deep cervical fascia

Cricoid cartilage

Tracheal rings

Suprasternal space
of Burns

FIGURE 6–6. Internal anatomy of the midline of the neck.

the cricoid cartilage. (The horizontal incision is generally advocated for its improved cosmetic result. Those who favor the vertical incision stress the importance of maintaining a midline dissection and the potential for increased anatomic damage when changing directions during the surgery.) This incision, which corresponds to the second or third tracheal rings, may vary in length, depending on the size of the patient and the thickness of anterior neck structures. The investing or superficial layer of deep cervical fascia is identified and vertically dissected. It should be recalled that this fascial layer splits into two layers just above the sternum; one attaches to the anterior and one to the posterior surface of the sternum. The small space between the two layers is filled with loose connective tissue and is called the suprasternal space of Burns (Fig. 6–6). The lower ends of the anterior jugular veins and their transverse connecting branch, the jugular venous arc, also lie in this space.[29] (On occasion, the two jugular veins are replaced by a midline median jugular vein.)

Posterior to the superficial layer of the deep cervical fascia and the space of Burns is the infrahyoid fascia, which overlies the infrahyoid muscles. These vertical muscle fibers have not been found to cross the midline, and therefore, the surgeon should find and bluntly dissect through the "white line," or linea alba.

The pretracheal fascia and isthmus of the thyroid gland now become visible. It should be a rule to pass through this pretracheal fascia by blunt dissection to avoid vascular injury and significant hemorrhage. The inferior thyroid veins, which usually empty into the left brachiocephalic vein, the inferior thyroid artery, which originates in most instances from the thyrocervical trunk, and the thyroid ima artery are all found in this plane of dissection. The incidence of occurrence of the thyroid ima artery varies widely from 1.5 per cent to 12.2 per cent. It usually arises from the largest branch of the aortic arch, the brachiocephalic trunk (innominate artery), but can also originate from the right common carotid artery or directly from the aortic arch.[13,29]

The brachiocephalic artery and left common carotid artery are also contained in this same layer but are infrequently endangered during surgery in the adult. This is not true in children, since the great vessels and the apex of the lungs are situated more superiorly.

After careful longitudinal dissection of the pretracheal fascia, the thyroid isthmus is either retracted superiorly or divided between clamps, and the two severed portions are oversewn. When this reflection of the gland is completed, the surgeon should be able to visualize the tracheal rings. Dissection should be sufficient to identify the cricoid cartilage and the first four tracheal rings.

The actual technique for entering the trachea varies among surgeons, though two axioms should be observed:

1.   The cricoid cartilage and first tracheal ring must not be cut or injured.
2.   No attempt should be made to incise below the level of the fourth tracheal ring (Fig. 6–7).

Failure to comply with these concepts could easily result in subglottic stenosis of the larynx, tracheal damage, or vascular erosion. This leaves the second, third, and fourth rings as the ideal site for the tracheal window.[4]

A number of incisional designs for opening the trachea have been advocated. These include a single midline longitudinal incision; a cruciate incision; and a T, U, or inverted U incision. Experimental and clinical data demonstrate no greater incidence of postoperative complications related to the type of tracheal incision.[27] Of far greater importance are such factors as the location of the incision, duration of cannulation, tracheostomy tube selection, and postoperative care.[23]

Once the tracheal incision is completed, the lumen is evaluated, and a tracheostomy tube is selected that occupies two thirds to three fourths of the tracheal diameter. The surgeon should carefully check the position of the tube to avoid false passage into the mediastinum. In addition, the tube is evaluated for proper fit to ensure no undue pressure when the neck plate is flush against the neck.

It is important not to close the wound tightly and in layers, or surgically induced emphysema may result. One or two sutures through the skin and subcutaneous tissue are sufficient. A square gauze is cut to fit around the cannula and under the neck plate before the cloth tape is securely tied. Finally, the chest is auscultated bilaterally to ensure symmetric breath sounds.

Complications

The clinical effectiveness of the tracheostomy was very poor for many centuries. In the thirteenth century, it was described as "semi-slaughter" and "the scandal of surgery." It was reported that only 28 successful procedures were performed prior to 1825.[31] The tracheostomy has certainly undergone refinement with the passage of time. Improvements in anesthesia, instrumentations and lighting, tracheostomy tubes, and surgical training have all contributed to the emergence of the tracheostomy as one of the more frequent operations in patients who are in critical condition.

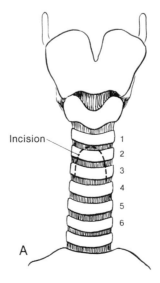
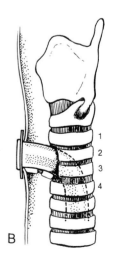

FIGURE 6–7.   Tracheostomy. *A,* Extent of tracheal incision. *B,* Attachment of tracheal flap to skin.

And yet, significant complications do occur. The recent literature contains numerous studies on the incidence of tracheostomy complications; they range from 6 per cent to 48 per cent.[31] In two of these surveys with a large sample size (Rogers with 688 cases and Chew and Cantrell with 1928 cases), the overall complication rates were 9.6 per cent and 15.8 per cent, respectively.[32,33]

Tracheostomy complications can be divided into two broad categories: (1) perioperative and (2) postoperative. Perioperative complications include the following:

1. Hemorrhage
2. Hypoxia (false passage, obstruction, tube displacement)
3. Pneumothorax
4. Interstitial emphysema (pneumomediastinum, subcutaneous emphysema)
5. Tracheoesophageal fistula
6. Damage to the recurrent laryngeal nerves

Reports of perioperative tracheostomy complications demonstrate an overall morbidity of 0 per cent to 51 per cent. A recent prospective study revealed an overall complication rate of 6 per cent; the most common perioperative difficulty encountered was hemorrhage control.[31]

Postoperative complications include the following:

1. Hemorrhage
2. Infection
3. Hypoxia (obstruction, tube displacement)
4. Aspiration
5. Tracheal stenosis
6. Tracheal ulcers and erosions
7. Unsatisfactory cosmetic result

In a discussion of late complications, one study commented as follows:

> . . . the single most important factor determining the incidence and severity of complication was the length of time the tracheostomy tube was in place. The morbidity was 65 per cent after the tracheostomy tube had been present more than 30 days.

From 0 to 7 days, the morbidity was approximately 20 per cent; from 7 to 14 days, 40 per cent; and from 14 to 30 days, 50 per cent.[34]

HEMORRHAGE

Hemorrhage can be troublesome during the surgical procedure but is minimized when the dissection is limited to the midline and the main vessels are properly identified and ligated before division. The thyroid gland can be a significant source of hemorrhage if not properly clamped and oversewn. Although intraoperative mortality has been reported from this complication, it is apparently rare. Studies demonstrate that the need to control bleeding in the perioperative period with transfusion ranges from 0 per cent to 5 per cent.

Delayed hemorrhage can be devastating, with exsanguination in minutes. It is of interest that these patients will often present a self-limiting signal episode prior to the catastrophic event.[35] Any evidence of late hemorrhage from a tracheostomy should prompt immediate consultation with a thoracic surgeon. This complication is usually caused by erosion of a major vessel and can occur any time from days to weeks following the surgery, most commonly between the first and second postoperative weeks. It is believed that excessive pressure at the cuff or distal end of the cannula leads to erosion of the wall of the trachea and major vessel. This erosion can result from improper tube selection or skin and tracheal incisions that are not coincident and produce tube rotation. Significant local sepsis, together with a marked inflammatory response, can also be a contributing factor leading to possible life-threatening hemorrhage. Although other vessels have been reported, the innominate artery is most commonly cited in postoperative hemorrhage from a major vessel after a tracheostomy.[23]

If significant bleeding does occur, it is recommended that the tracheostomy tube be removed and a cuffed endotracheal tube be replaced. The cuff is then inflated to help tamponade the vessel until surgical control can be obtained.[35]

INFECTION

One large study found infection (3.3 per cent of the number of cases reviewed) second in frequency to hemorrhage as a complication of tracheostomy.[33] A tracheostomy alters the protective defense mechanism to infection, since it is virtually impossible to keep the surgical site free from bacterial flora indigenous to the nasopharynx. Cultures taken from the cannula confirm that the lower trachea contains a bacterial flora similar to that of the nasopharynx in approximately 72 hours.[35] The surgical site is particularly susceptible to infection from improper aseptic technique as well as contaminated suction equipment and ventilators. The most commonly isolated organisms include *Pseudomonas aeruginosa, Staphylococcus aureus,* hemolytic streptococci, and monilia.[33,34]

TRACHEAL STENOSIS

The incidence of tracheal stenosis following tracheostomy ranges as high as 98 per cent, whereas, functionally, symptomatic stenosis varies from 8 per cent to 20 per cent.[36] The normal adult trachea, which is about 9 to 10 mm in diameter, can be compromised by 25 per cent to 50 per cent without clinical evidence of disability.[37] Easily detectable stridor at rest is produced when the tracheal diameter is reduced to 5 mm or less.

The pathogenesis of postintubation stenosis has been well studied both clinically and experimentally. The primary lesion most commonly occurs at the level of the tracheal stoma or cuff and results from pressure in excess of the mucosal capillary perfusion pressure (about 30 torr).[36] Therefore, it is generally believed that cuff pressure should not exceed 20 torr.[38] This information helps to explain why the widely practiced technique of hourly deflation of the tracheostomy cuff could fail to protect the trachea from injury.

It has been shown, however, that careful inflation of the cuff to allow an audible leak during inspiration significantly eliminates tracheal injury. The cuff is first inflated to a no leak position and then air volume is withdrawn until an audible leak occurs with each inspiration.[35]

DAMAGE TO THE RECURRENT LARYNGEAL NERVE

The recurrent laryngeal nerve arises from the vagus nerve and innervates all the muscles of the larynx except the cricothyroid muscle (which is innervated by the superior laryngeal nerve). They are classically described as coursing superiorly in the neck in the groove or angle between the esophagus and trachea. Clinically, they may run considerably farther laterally than this, and the right nerve is especially likely to do so. It has been noted in cadaver dissections that the right recurrent laryngeal nerve may be a centimeter lateral to the trachea.[13]

Care must be taken to maintain a midline dissection and not wander posteriorly or laterally. Paralysis of one recurrent laryngeal nerve may be asymptomatic. However, it may cause some dyspnea upon exertion or hoarseness. Bilateral paralysis may produce immediate and profound dyspnea, which would require permanent tracheal cannulation.[13]

PNEUMOTHORAX

The incidence of pneumothorax secondary to tracheostomy in adult studies ranges from 0.1 per cent to 5 per cent.[31] This complication is generally considered more common in children, since the pleural domes are more superior in the neck and therefore more prone to direct injury during surgery.[35] In addition, the connective tissues of the neck are looser in children and potentially allow increased air tracing, leading to pneumomediastinum and rupture of the pleura.[33] One study of tracheostomy in children (46 cases) reported an incidence of pneumothorax of 17 per cent.[39] Two much larger studies in children and infants cited an incidence more compatible with adult statistics (Oliver, 5.8 per cent; Hawkins, 5.2 per cent intraoperative, 3.3 per cent postoperative).[40,41] It is a good policy for all patients undergoing tracheostomies to have a chest radiograph following the procedures, especially children.

Mortality with Tracheostomy

Since a tracheostomy is generally performed on critically ill or severely traumatized patients, statistical data on deaths directly due to this procedure are difficult to determine. Therefore, reports on the incidence of tracheostomy mortality should be viewed with caution. These rates range from 2.4 per cent to 10.0 per cent in children and infants, whereas deaths in adults vary from 1.1 per cent to 8.9 per cent.[32,40,42,43] The most common fatal complications in order of frequency are consistent from study to study. They are (1) hemorrhage, (2) displaced tube, (3) infection, (4) obstruction, (5) aspiration, and (6) tracheal erosion with resultant stenosis or fistula.[32,43]

Postoperative Care

Obstruction is a common complication and frequently occurs from plugging of the tube with crusting of blood, mucus, or mucous plugs. Thick secretions can result from bypassing the upper airway and its natural humidification. Tracheostomy and cricothyroidotomy care include the use of well-humidified air at all times and aspirations of the tracheobronchial tree whenever necessary, using sterile technique.

One recommended "trach care" routine is to hyperventilate with 100 per cent oxygen for 2 to 3 minutes prior to suctioning, instill up to 5 ml of sterile normal saline, and suction deeply but not too overzealously. (Full suction should not exceed 2 to 3 seconds, and intermittent suction is the maneuver of choice. The catheter should be repassed as long as significant amounts of secretions are obtained.) Cough and deep breathing should be promoted, and if the patient is capable, he or she should be ambulated. This regimen is performed every hour for the first 48 hours, every 2 hours on the third and fourth postoperative days, and every 4 hours thereafter. The inner cannula is cleansed three times each day, and the dressing is changed two or three times daily. The tube should be changed each week. The patient's condition will dictate variations in treatment.

CRICOTHYROIDOTOMY

The cricothyroidotomy, which has also been known as a coniotomy, interthyroid laryngotomy, and superior or high tracheotomy, was first described by the French surgeon and anatomist Vicq d'Azyr in 1805 and later described in detail and recommended by Tandler in 1916.[44] As a result of Chevalier Jackson's classic paper in 1921,[45] the use of this procedure was generally abandoned and received no serious challenge for more than 50 years. In 1976, Brantigan and Grow presented a favorable report of 655 patients with cricothyroidotomy.[46] Since that time, numerous reports have appeared in the literature, both in defense and in condemnation of this technique.

The potential indications for cricothyroidotomy are similar to those for tracheostomy.[47] Additional advantages include the following[46]:

1. In emergency situations, the cricothyroidotomy can be performed more rapidly, generally in less than 2 minutes.

2. Extensive knowledge of neck anatomy is nonessential. The procedure can be performed safely and efficiently by nonsurgeons, with minimal instrumentation. There is enhanced safety and ease of technique in patients with suspected cervical spine injury, cervical kyphosis, or obesity.

3. The rate of operative complications is low and generally not influenced by the urgency of the procedure.

4. The airway entrance in a cricothyroidotomy can be isolated from the operative site in certain procedures, such as radical neck dissection.

5. There is potential improved cosmesis of the resultant scar. The incision is shorter and corresponds favorably to a skin crease at the neck-throat angle.

The cricothyroidotomy is currently contraindicated in the following cases[47,48]:

1. In children and adolescents
2. In the presence of laryngeal injury, inflammation, or infection
3. When an endotracheal tube has been in place more than 7 days
4. In patients with respiratory difficulties after previous endotracheal intubation

Anatomic and Surgical Considerations

The cricothyroid space is located by first palpating the thyroid cartilage (Fig. 6–8). The cricothyroid ligament or membrane is approximately 2 to 3 cm inferior to the thyroid notch and denoted as a slight concavity between the thyroid and cricoid cartilages. The cricothyroid space is approximately 9 to 10 mm vertically, and the horizontal distance averages 30 mm. The vocal cords lie 1.5 to 2.0 cm superior to the cricothyroid ligament.[47,48]

The cricoid cartilage is the only component of the larynx and trachea that extends completely around the air passage. This cartilage is shaped essentially like a signet ring and rigidly separates the esophagus. This feature effectively reduces the possibility of tracheoesophageal fistula.

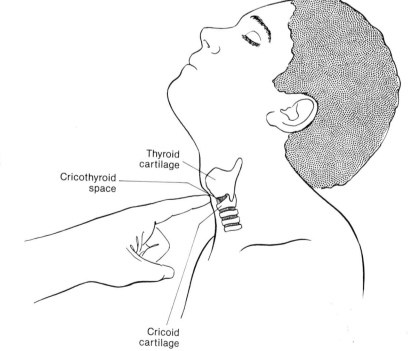

FIGURE 6–8. Identification of cricothyroid space by palpation with index finger.

Thyroid cartilage

Cricothyroid space

Cricoid cartilage

The procedure is performed with the patient under local or general anesthesia and with the head and neck in a hyperextended position. Extreme hyperextension is unnecessary and contraindicated if a cervical spine injury is suspected. Once the anatomic landmarks have been identified, a transverse incision approximately 2 cm long is made just superior to the cricoid cartilage. This is done to avoid the cricothyroid branch of the superior thyroid artery, which runs transversely across the membrane at its superior extent.[29] This incision is made through skin and subcutaneous tissue.

The cricothyroid ligament, which is covered by the superficial layer of the deep cervical fascia, is then identified. It is also referred to as conus elasticus and is composed of the median cricothyroid ligament anteriorly and the thyroepiglottic ligament laterally.[49] This lateral portion of the conus is covered by the cricothyroid muscle. The opening into the trachea is made with a short, stabbing transverse incision and then enlarged bluntly. (The cricothyroidotomy is completed by dissection through the skin, the subcutaneous tissue, the superficial layer of the deep cervical fascia, the cricothyroid muscles and ligament, and the mucous membrane of the larynx.[13,29]) An appropriately sized tracheostomy tube (6 to 8 mm) is inserted under direct vision. (If a tracheostomy tube is unavailable in an emergency situation, an endotracheal tube may be placed initially.) The skin is not sutured, and the tapes of the tracheostomy tube are tied in the usual fashion.

Complications

Many complications associated with the tracheostomy either have not occurred or are reported with much less frequency following a cricothyroidotomy. These include (1) significant hemorrhage, (2) pneumothorax, (3) tracheoesophageal fistula, (4) damage to the recurrent laryngeal nerve, and (5) death.

Perioperative complications of the cricothyroidotomy are hemorrhage and improper placement. Postoperative complications include voice changes, infection, and stenosis. Brantigan and Grow reported an overall complication rate of 6.1 per cent.[46] Others have found an incidence ranging from 0 per cent to 28 per cent.[48,50]

HEMORRHAGE

To date, there have been no reports of major vascular hemorrhage following a cricothyroidotomy, probably because of the lack of significant structures overlying the cricothyroid ligament and the more superior position of the tracheostomy tube. Reported bleeding was controlled in each case with suture ligation or packing. Minor bleeding ranged from 0 per cent to 2.7 per cent in the studies evaluated.[50,51] The occurrence of this complication could be reduced by avoiding a technique in which a skin incision and an immediate membrane puncture are used.

IMPROPER PLACEMENT

Presurgical positioning of the patient and palpation of anatomic landmarks are crucial. The trachea should be visualized, and the tube should be placed under direct vision. This placement of the tube is facilitated by an average soft tissue thickness of approximately 10 mm for a cricothyroidotomy compared with 20 mm for a standard tracheostomy (Fig. 6–9).[47]

The rate of occurrence of this complication is indirectly proportional to the experience of the surgeon. One study noted that

> . . . in two patients, the tracheostomy tube was originally placed above the thyroid cartilage by an inexperienced member of the surgical staff requiring replacement at the appropriate site.[51]

Reports of improper placement range from 0 per cent to 1.3 per cent.[51,52]

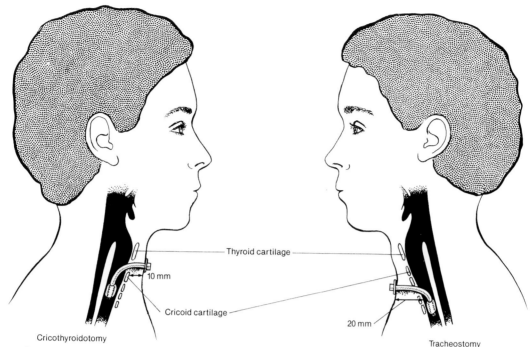

FIGURE 6–9. The average soft tissue thickness to pass through for a cricothyroidotomy is 10 mm, whereas that for a tracheostomy is 20 mm.

VOICE CHANGES

Subjective voice changes of hoarseness, loss of volume, and deeper pitch have been reported in from 0 per cent to 27.6 per cent of cases.[53] A composite evaluation of 11 studies completed in the past 10 years demonstrates that this is the most common complication associated with cricothyroidotomy.[47] In most patients, these changes were transient, but secondary surgery to remove granulation tissue posterior or inferior to the cords may be necessary.

INFECTION

In a manner similar to the tracheostomy, a cricothyroidotomy alters the normal bacterial flora of the trachea. Significant infections occur in 1 to 2 per cent of tracheostomies, although rates as high as 20 per cent have been reported.[28,34] Clinical experience with cricothyroidotomy, however, demonstrates that infections are rare. Brantigan and Grow found that infections occurred in only 3 of 655 patients (0.46 per cent).[46]

STENOSIS

Although other complications occur more frequently, the incidence, as well as potential severity, of laryngeal stenosis ". . . remains the overriding consideration in determining whether or not the use of a cricothyroidotomy is justified."[51] Brantigan and Grow reported stenosis in eight patients (1.2 per cent), five of whom required tracheal resection. In a recent study, which was a follow-up of their original work, the incidence of subglottic stenosis was 2.6 per cent.[48] A composite evaluation of 11 studies demonstrated an incidence of 1.5 per cent.[47] These results compare favorably with reports of symptomatic stenosis following a tracheostomy, in which an incidence of 18 to 20 per cent has been cited.[37,54]

Strictures that occur after a tracheostomy commonly occur at the level of the stoma or cuff, whereas stenosis following a cricothyroidotomy is generally found at the cuff or just inferior to the vocal cords. Treatment of stenosis has included oral steroids, dilations and endoscopic removal of granulation tissue, tracheal resection, the use of a hollow prosthesis, and division of the cricoid cartilage.

Even though symptomatic stenosis is rather infrequent and has been successfully treated in the majority of reported cases, concern for recurrent stricture and possible permanent cannulation is justified. Reported recommendations for the prevention of tracheal stenosis after a tracheostomy or cricothyroidotomy include the following:

1. Avoid removal of tracheal cartilage.
2. Carefully insert a tube of proper diameter (two-thirds to three-fourths the lumen diameter) to prevent pressure necrosis and mucosal erosion.
3. Inflate the cuff with only enough pressure to allow the ventilator to work.
4. Deflate the cuff for 5 to 10 minutes every hour.
5. Replace the cuffed tube with a noncuffed tube when the ventilator is discontinued.
6. Avoid a tracheal window in patients endotracheally intubated 7 days or longer.
7. Avoid a tracheal window in patients with laryngeal infection or tumor.
8. Utilize a large-volume, low-pressure cuff.

Mortality with Cricothyroidotomy

Mortality directly relating to the cricothyroidotomy is rare, even in emergency situations. A survey of the literature revealed only four cases. The causes of death included (1) asystole during a routine tube change,[46] (2) loss of airway during the surgical procedure,[55] (3) inability to reinsert the tube "following the unfortunate removal,"[51] and (4) a plugged cricothyroidotomy tube.[56]

PROLONGED ARTIFICIAL AIRWAYS

Critically ill patients who require prolonged artificial airways can be managed with endotracheal intubation, tracheostomy, or cricothyroidotomy. Controversy exists concerning the use of a prolonged single technique and timing the conversion from one technique to another. Some studies suggest that complications from a tracheostomy are more frequent and severe than those from prolonged endotracheal intubation. Over the years, this observation has apparently led to an increase in the duration of intubation in patients of all ages. Neonates are often intubated for 6 weeks or more,[57] while children 3 years and younger may be intubated 2 to 3 weeks before a tracheostomy is performed.[58] Reports of endotracheal intubation for more than 50 days with minor complications[59] have led to recommendations for adults that ". . . oral and nasal intubation is probably the method of choice when an artificial airway is required for less than three weeks."[36]

Those who advocate tracheostomy claim the following:

1. It permits more efficient removal of secretions, thereby decreasing possible contamination and occlusion from mucous plugs.
2. It improves the comfort of the patient.
3. It has a decreased incidence of accidental extubation.
4. It allows greater latitude in techniques of gradual decannulation.

Opponents counter these advantages by citing studies that demonstrate the incidence of secondary bacterial invasion of the lungs as eight times more common after a tracheostomy than after prolonged intubation.[60] In addition, a tracheostomy has a mortality that ranges from 3 to 15 per cent,[61,62] whereas the overall mortality following prolonged endotracheal intubation is less than 1 per cent.[61]

Unfortunately, prolonged endotracheal intubation is not risk free. A recent prospective study reported that after 11 days of endotracheal intubation there was a 12 per cent incidence of laryngotracheal stenosis. This stenosis was often shown to be extensive, beginning at the vocal cords and extending the length of the endotracheal tube. Patients whose endotracheal intubation was then converted to a tracheostomy had a higher incidence of tracheal stenosis. This finding suggests that long-term endotracheal intubation increases the risk of tracheal injury if a subsequent tracheostomy is performed.

> The preponderance of data on laryngeal and supraglottic complications of endotracheal intubation suggests that these complications are more common with intubation periods of more than seven to ten days.[31]

There is also the consideration of oral versus nasal intubation in long-term airway maintenance. One study has compared laryngeal pathology following long-term oral and nasal endotracheal intubations. Tracheal injury associated with nasal intubations occurred half as often. This finding was possibly due to less tube distortion (thereby decreasing the incidence of pressure necrosis), increased tube immobilization, and smaller endotracheal tube size.[63,64]

Endotracheal intubation, tracheostomy, and cricothyroidotomy all present potential hazards for long-term airway management. Available data have shown increased risks associated with a tracheostomy or cricothyroidotomy when an endotracheal tube has been in place for more than 7 days prior to conversion. Therefore, patients requiring assisted ventilation for less than 7 days could be managed effectively with endotracheal intubation. After 7 days, the patient is re-evaluated. If extubation is likely before the fourteenth day, the tube is maintained with consideration of nasal intubation. If assisted ventilation is anticipated for extended periods, conversion to a tracheostomy or cricothyroidotomy should be considered. Which of the latter two methods is then chosen is still a matter for debate and should depend upon the standard of care for the given institution and the expertise and experience of the surgeon.

REFERENCES

1. JAMA 227:834, 1974.
2. Advanced Trauma Life Support Course for Physicians, 1983–1984. Chicago, IL, American College of Surgeons, pp 5–45.
3. Daughtry DC: Thoracic trauma. In Tracheostomy. Boston, Little, Brown and Company, 1980, pp 23–38.
4. Feldman SA, Crawley BE: Tracheostomy and Artificial Ventilation. 2nd ed. Baltimore, The Williams and Wilkins Company, 1972.
5. McIntyre KM, Lewis AJ: Textbook of Advanced Cardiac Life Support. 1983, pp 40–42.
6. Meislin HW: The esophageal obturator airway: A study of respiratory effectiveness. Ann Emerg Med 9:54–59, 1980.
7. Strate RG, Fischer RP: Mid-esophageal perforations by esophageal obturator airways. J Trauma 16:503–509, 1976.
8. Pilcher DB, DeMeules JE: Esophageal perforation following use of esophageal airway. Chest 69:377–380, 1976.
9. Carlson WJ, Hunter SE, Bonnabeau RC: Esophageal perforation with obturator airway. JAMA 241:1154–1155, 1979.
10. Harrison EE, Nord HJ, Beeman RW: Esophageal perforation following use of the esophageal obturator airway. Ann Emerg Med 9:37–41, 1980.
11. Yancey W, Wears R, Kamajian G, et al: Unrecognized tracheal intubation: A complication of the esophageal obturator airway. Ann Emerg Med 9:31–33, 1980.
12. Blaylock RL: Pathophysiology of head and spinal cord injuries. In Irby WB (ed): Current Advances in Oral Surgery. Vol II. St Louis, CV Mosby, 1977.
13. Hollinshead WH: Anatomy for Surgeons. Vol I. The Head and Neck. 3rd ed. Hagerstown, MD, Harper and Row, 1982.
14. McIntyre KM, Lewis AJ: Textbook of Advanced Cardiac Life Support. 1983, p 42.
15. Advanced Trauma Life Support Course for Physicians, 1983–1984. Chicago, IL, American College of Surgeons, pp 33–34.
16. Iverson KV, Sanders AB, Kaback K, et al: Difficult intubations: Aids and alternatives. American Family Practice 31:99–112, 1985.
17. Butler FS, Cirillo AA: Retrograde tracheal intubation. Anesth Analg Curr Res 39:333–338, 1960.
18. Waters DJ: Guided blind endotracheal intubation. Anaesthesia 18:158–162, 1963.
19. McNamara RM: Retrograde intubation of the trachea. Ann Emerg Med 16:680–682, 1987.
20. Brown AC: Special anesthetic techniques in head and neck surgery. Otolaryngol Clin North Am 14:587–614, 1981.
21. Bourke D, Levesque PR: Modification of retrograde guide for endotracheal intubation. Anesth Analg 53:1014–1015, 1974.

22. Stoelting RK: Endotracheal intubation. *In* Irby WB (ed): Facial Trauma and Concomitant Problems. 2nd ed. St Louis, CV Mosby, 1979.

23. Irby WB: Facial Trauma and Concomitant Problems. 2nd ed. St Louis, CV Mosby, 1979, pp 93–142.

24. Stock CR: What is past is prologue: A short history of the development of tracheostomy. ENT 66:60, 1987.

25. Alberti PW: Tracheotomy versus intubation: A 19th century controversy. Ann Otol Rhinol Laryngol 93:333–337, 1984.

26. Jackson C: High tracheotomy and other errors—the chief cause of chronic laryngeal stenosis. Surg Gynecol Obstet 32:392, 1923.

27. Heffner JE, Miller KS, Sahn SA, et al: Tracheostomy in the intensive care unit. Chest 90:269–274, 1986.

28. Skaggs JA: Tracheostomy: Management, mortality, complications. Ann Surg 35:393–396, 1969.

29. DuBrul EL: Sicher's Oral Anatomy. 7th ed. St Louis, CV Mosby, 1980, pp 519–526.

30. Borman J, Davidson J: A history of tracheostomy. Br J Anaesth 35:388, 1963.

31. Stock MC, Woodward CG, Shapiro BA, et al: Perioperative complications of elective tracheostomy in critically ill patients. Crit Care Med 14:861–863, 1986.

32. Rogers LA: Complications of tracheostomy. South Med J 62:1496, 1969.

33. Chew JY, Cantrell RW: Tracheostomy, complications and management. Arch Otolaryngol 96:538–545, 1972.

34. Mulder DS, Rubush JL: Complications of tracheostomy: Relationship to long term ventilatory assistance. J Trauma 9:389–401, 1969.

35. Walker DG: Complications of tracheostomy: Their prevention and treatment. J Oral Surg 31:480–482, 1973.

36. Berlauk JF: Prolonged endotracheal intubation vs. tracheostomy. Crit Care Med 14:742–745, 1986.

37. Andrews MJ, Pearson FC: Incidence and pathogenesis of tracheal injury following cuffed tube tracheostomy with assisted ventilation: Analysis of a two-year prospective study. Ann Surg 173:249–263, 1961.

38. Stauffer JL, Olson DE, Petty TL: Complications and consequences of endotracheal intubation and tracheotomy. A study of 150 critically ill adult patients. Am J Med 70:65–76, 1981.

39. Rabuzzi D: Intrathoracic complications following tracheostomy in children. Laryngoscope 81:939–946, 1971.

40. Oliver P: Tracheostomy in children. N Engl J Med 267:631–637, 1962.

41. Line WS, Hawkins DB, Kahlstrom EJ, et al: Tracheotomy in infants and young children: The changing perspective 1970–1985. Laryngoscope 96:510–515, 1986.

42. Louhimo I, Grahne B, Pasila M, et al: Acquired laryngotracheal stenosis in children. J Pediatr Surg 6:730–736, 1971.

43. Stemmer EA, Oliver C, Carey JP, et al: Fatal complications of tracheotomy. Am J Surg 131:288–290, 1976.

44. Dingman RO, Natvig P: Surgery of Facial Fractures. Philadelphia, WB Saunders Company, 1964, pp 97–110.

45. Jackson C: High tracheostomy and other errors—the chief causes of chronic laryngeal stenosis. Surg Gynecol Obstet 32:392, 1921.

46. Brantigan CO, Grow JB: Cricothyroidotomy: Elective use in respiratory problems requiring tracheotomy. J Thorac Cardiovasc Surg 71:72–81, 1976.

47. Feinberg SE, Peterson LJ: Use of cricothyroidostomy in oral and maxillofacial surgery. J Oral Maxillofac Surg 45:873–878, 1987.

48. Esses BA, Jafek BW: Cricothyroidotomy: A decade of experience in Denver. Ann Otol Rhinol Laryngol 96:519–524, 1987.

49. Pansky B: Review of Gross Anatomy. 5th ed. New York, Macmillan, 1984, pp 62–67.

50. Morain WD: Cricothyroidostomy in head and neck surgery. Plast Reconstr Surg 65:424–428, 1980.

51. Boyd AD, Romita M, Conlan A, et al: A clinical evaluation of cricothyroidotomy. Surg Gynecol Obstet 149:365–368, 1979.

52. O'Connor JV, Kuruganti R, Ergin A, et al: Cricothyroidotomy for prolonged ventilatory support after cardiac operations. Ann Thorac Surg 39:353–354, 1985.

53. Jakobsson J, Andersson C, Wiklund PE: Experience with elective coniotomy. Acta Chir Scand [Suppl] 520:101, 1984.

54. Dane TEB, King EG: A prospective study of complications after tracheostomy for assisted ventilation. Chest 67:398–404, 1975.

55. Sise MJ, Shacksord SR, Cruickshank JC, et al: Cricothyroidotomy for long term tracheal access. Ann Surg 200:13–17, 1984.

56. McDowell DE: Cricothyroidostomy for airway access. South Med J 75:282–284, 1982.

57. Hawkins DB: Hyaline membrane disease of the neonate. Prolonged intubation in management: Effects on the larynx. Laryngoscope 88:201–224, 1978.

58. Line WS, Hawkins DB, Kahlstrom EJ, et al: Tracheotomy in infants and young children: The changing perspective 1970–1985. Laryngoscope 96:510–515, 1986.

59. Via-Ruque E: Prolonged oro- or nasotracheal intubation. Crit Care Med 9:637, 1981.

60. El-Nagger M, Sadagopan S, Levine H, et al: Factors in making a choice between tracheostomy and prolonged translaryngeal intubation in acute respiratory failure: A prospective study. Anesth Analg 55:195, 1976.

61. McGovern FH, Fitz-Hugh GS, Edgemon LS: The hazards of endotracheal intubation. Ann Otol 80:556, 1971.

62. El-Kilany SM: Complications of tracheostomy. Ear Nose Throat J 59:123, 1980.

63. Whited RE: A prospective study of laryngotracheal sequelae in long-term intubation. Laryngoscope 94:367–377, 1984.

64. Dubick MN, Wright BD: Comparison of laryngeal pathology following long-term oral and nasal endotracheal intubations. Anesth Analg 57:663, 1978.

CHAPTER 7

NEUROLOGIC EVALUATION AND MANAGEMENT

MICHAEL N. BUCCI, M.D., and
JULIAN T. HOFF, M.D.

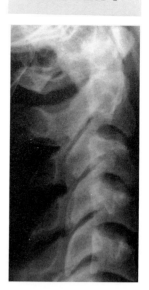

Trauma is the leading cause of death in the United States for persons aged 1 to 44 years and is the third leading cause of death overall. In more than 75 per cent of cases, head injury accounts for a significant portion of the morbidity. Physical and functional morbidity frequently follows brain injury, even in seemingly minor trauma.[1-10]

A precise approach is necessary in the evaluation of the head-injured patient. One should adhere to the rule of the "three S's":

Simple	To facilitate triage, the examination should be simple to perform.
Systematic	An accurate and reliable format will ensure that all organs are assessed and treatment is begun in a timely fashion.
Standardized	The examination should be easily recorded and standardized so that multiple examiners may perform and record the examination and note any neurologic changes.

Despite newer advanced imaging tools and techniques, the neurologic examination remains the most important factor in the rapid assessment of central nervous system (CNS) injury.

This chapter outlines in detail the neurologic examination, beginning with the initial management of trauma and concluding with the grading of injury severity. Separate sections address head injury and spinal cord injury and include methods of diagnosis and treatment.

INITIAL ASSESSMENT

Resuscitation — Initial Trauma Management

The prompt management of the traumatized patient is critical to optimize neurologic outcome. Initial assessment consists of adequate protection of the airway with intubation (if required) via the nasotracheal route. This intubation may be contraindicated with severe midface trauma, thereby requiring surgical cricothyroidotomy or tracheostomy.[11]

The cervical spine must be immobilized at the same time. It must be remembered that *major CNS trauma always includes cervical spine fracture until proved otherwise.* A hard cervical collar or the so-called "extrication" collar must be placed with manual in-line traction of the cervical spine. Paired sandbags can be used if a collar is temporarily unavailable.

Patients in an unstable condition who require ventilatory assistance are usually placed on a mechanical ventilator. This step also provides a means of treating elevated intracranial pressure (ICP).[12-14] Patients with adequate ventilation should have oxygen administration to ensure that CNS parenchyma has maximal support.[15,16]

Circulatory stabilization with intravenous crystalloid is best carried out using large-bore peripheral access. Central venous access should be reserved for patients requiring central venous pressure monitoring or for those patients with poor peripheral access.

History and Rapid Initial Examination

Once the initial stabilization is complete, a detailed history and complete physical examination are essential. If the patient is unable to give an accurate history, witnesses to the injury must be questioned.

Essentials of the history that must be ascertained through questioning include the following:

1. Was there a witnessed loss of consciousness following the injury? How long a period was involved?
2. Was there a lucid interval immediately after the injury and preceding a loss of consciousness?
3. Has there been a change or deterioration in the patient's mental status?
4. Did the patient have any seizures or syncopal events following the injury? Was there tonic deviation of the eyes toward one particular side?
5. Was there associated spinal column trauma? Did the patient complain of tenderness along the spine?

After the history is taken, a detailed general physical examination is essential. The examination should adhere to the "three S's." A rapid neurologic assessment can be made within 3 to 5 minutes, thereby facilitating definite diagnosis and treatment.

The following body systems should be examined initially.

Mental Status

Is the patient conscious or unconscious?

Respirations and Vital Signs

Is the patient breathing spontaneously, or is he or she being assisted? What is the pattern and type? Is the patient hypotensive, or are there signs of autonomic dysfunction?

Associated Trauma

Is there associated major or multiple trauma? Specific areas to check include the following ones.

SCALP

The scalp should be checked for lacerations and fractures.

PERIAURICULAR REGION

The examiner should check for Battle's sign, which is an area of ecchymosis behind the ear that can occur with basilar skull fractures, particularly in the middle fossa. The examiner should also check for hemotympanum, which is blood behind the tympanic membrane, giving a blue hue on examination. Cerebrospinal fluid (CSF) otorrhea can also occur as a result of basilar or mastoid skull fracture.

PERIORBITAL REGION

The examiner should check for "raccoon eye," which is an area of ecchymosis around the eye that can occur with basilar skull fractures, particularly those arising from the anterior cranial fossa.

FACE

The examiner must check for facial symmetry. Complete paresis or paralysis implies lower motor neuron trauma, usually at the ipsilateral stylomastoid foramen. Incomplete or lower facial palsy implies a contralateral upper motor neuron lesion, usually in either the cerebral hemisphere or the subcortical region.

CAROTID ARTERY

Soft tissue injury to the neck can manifest with areas of contusion or laceration, palpable thrill, or audible bruit. Most often, however, an injury in this region is silent. Carotid artery injury or dissection should be suspected when the patient presents with a hemiparesis and no other signs of localized intracranial disease.

Cervical Spine

One must assume that every head injury has an associated cervical spine injury until proved otherwise. The physician should view the radiographs personally to rule out a cervical spine fracture or fracture-dislocation. Patients with an unrestrained cervical spine must be immobilized in a carefully placed hard cervical collar until cervical spine radiographs can be obtained.

Ocular Function

PUPILS

Are they equal in size? Do they both react to light? The "swinging flashlight" tests both direct and consensual responses to light. It determines various disorders, such as the following.

Marcus Gunn Pupil. This is an afferent pupillary defect due to optic nerve damage. The involved eye constricts to light in the opposite eye (consensual) and dilates as the light is "swung" into the involved eye.

Traumatic Pupil. This occurs usually as a result of direct trauma to the globe with damage of the iris constrictor muscles. Often, this disorder is difficult to distinguish from a third nerve palsy.

Third Nerve Palsy. Various forms exist; however, the most common form occurs as a result of uncal or transtentorial herniation, usually from a laterally expanding mass that causes compression of the third nerve as it exits from the midbrain. On physical examination, one classically sees a unilaterally dilated pupil that does not respond to light (either directly or consensually) and appears laterally displaced owing to paresis of the medial rectus muscle. This lesion often produces contralateral hemiparesis because of simultaneous compression of the ipsilateral cerebral peduncle. If the lesion is large and causes rotation and compression of the contralateral cerebral peduncle, a false localizing sign may occur, namely, ipsilateral hemiparesis (so-called Kernohan's notch phenomenon).

EXTRAOCULAR MUSCLES

The patient should be checked for various palsies.

Lateral Gaze Palsy, Unilateral.   The abducens nerve, or cranial nerve VI, has the longest intracranial course and is frequently damaged by lesions that cause increased ICP or by direct trauma to the clivus region.

Paresis of Upward Gaze.   This condition most often occurs with tumors of the pineal region but also with acute hydrocephalus or hemorrhage, causing compression of the midbrain tectum. Parinaud's syndrome consists of paresis of the upward gaze. Lack of convergence and lack of light reflex are common manifestations of this syndrome.

OCULOVESTIBULAR AND OCULOCEPHALIC REFLEXES

Cold caloric testing has limited usefulness in the initial neurologic assessment. Similarly, testing for doll's eyes should *not* be performed in patients with suspected cervical spine injury.

CORNEAL REFLEXES

The corneal reflex should be checked using a cotton wisp, lightly stroking the surface of the globe. The afferent limb is a function of the first division of the trigeminal nerve, and the efferent limb is a function of cranial nerve VII. An absence of corneal reflexes usually implies pontine damage or dysfunction and is often associated with abnormal extensor posturing of the limbs.

Gag Reflex

The gag reflex is usually checked by inserting a tongue blade into the posterior pharynx and depressing toward the hypopharynx. The reflex arc is carried by cranial nerves IX and X and can be congenitally absent. However, in the setting of trauma, absence of this reflex is an ominous sign and implies caudal brainstem dysfunction.

Motor Examination

Tone, strength, and reflexes need to be assessed. Detailed sensory testing can be delayed until the formal examination; however, pin-prick sensation and proprioception need to be assessed in all limbs.

TONE AND STRENGTH ASSESSMENT

1.   Increased tone or paratonic resistance that is unilateral usually implies compression of the contralateral cerebral peduncle (or the ipsilateral peduncle in Kernohan's notch phenomenon).

2.   Flaccid tone implies either brainstem infarction or spinal cord transection.

3.   Hemiparesis can localize to the contralateral hemisphere, cervical spine (Brown-Séquard syndrome), or contralateral carotid artery.

TABLE 7-1. RAPID INITIAL ASSESSMENT OF THE NEUROLOGICALLY INJURED PATIENT

C R A N I A L	
C	Consciousness
R	Respirations and vital signs
A	Associated trauma
N	Neck
	1. Cervical spine injury
	2. Carotid injury
I	Eyes
	1. Pupils
	2. Extraocular muscles
	3. Corneal reflexes
	4. +/− Oculovestibular and oculocephalic responses
A	Airway
	1. Gag reflex
L	Limbs
	1. Motor examination
	2. Reflexes
	3. Sensation

DEEP TENDON REFLEXES

1. Hyper-reflexia usually occurs with compression lesions in the contralateral cerebral peduncle or internal capsule. Extensor plantar reflexes (the Babinski sign) are a concomitant finding.

2. Areflexia occurs in the setting of spinal shock after spinal cord trauma or transection. After a period of weeks, the initial flaccidity changes and becomes spastic hyper-reflexia.

A useful mnemonic for the rapid initial assessment of the neurologically injured patient is contained in Table 7-1.

DETAILED MANAGEMENT

Once the rapid neurologic assessment is complete, initial triage and management can begin. While this phase is progressing, the complete and detailed history and physical examination can be carried out.

The history should be obtained in a stepwise fashion, proceeding from the history of the present illness to the past medical history (including allergies and medications) to the pertinent social, family, and review-of-systems history. The current history is the key element, as most neurologic disorders can be accurately diagnosed on the basis of the history alone.

The detailed physical examination should include thorough inspection, palpation, and auscultation of all body systems. In particular, facial trauma should be carefully inspected, as this will often give clues to the nature of CNS trauma. For example, an elderly man who presents with signs of quadriparesis and contusions about the chin and forehead is likely to have sustained a "central cord" syndrome from a fall causing cervical spine hyperextension in a presumably osteoarthritic spine.[17]

In general, all organ systems should be examined and injuries treated. Hypotension is rarely, if ever, a result of head trauma, except in the terminal phase of brain herniation. Hypotension and a normal heart rate, on the other hand, are frequent concomitants of "spinal shock" following spinal cord transection.[18-20]

A detailed neurologic examination should then be performed. In a systematized fashion, the following points should be covered.

Mental Status

The overall state of alertness should be noted, as well as the patient's ability to state his or her name, the place, the time, and the date. Memory and the ability to do calculations should be tested, as frontal and temporal lesions can alter these. Right-left discrimination, reading, and writing should be assessed. Lesions of the left posterior cerebral artery distribution can cause alexia and a homonymous hemianopia without agraphia.

Cranial Nerves

CRANIAL NERVE I (OLFACTORY)

The sense of smell should be assessed, especially in patients with CSF rhinorrhea and possible cribriform plate fractures. Contrecoup frontal lobe contusions can also cause an alteration of smell function.

CRANIAL NERVE II (OPTIC)

The fundus should be directly visualized with an ophthalmoscope. Elevated ICP can cause papilledema or flame hemorrhages.

Pupillary size can reflect changes at various levels of CNS trauma. Midposition pupils that react reflect lower diencephalon and upper midbrain lesions, while small, nonreactive pupils often indicate primary pontine dysfunction.

Visual acuity should be checked with a near card. Visual fields should be assessed by gross confrontation. Homonymous hemianopia can occur with lesions of the temporal and parietal lobes (incongruous) and occipital lobes (congruous).

CRANIAL NERVES III, IV, AND VI (EXTRAOCULAR MUSCLES, OCULOMOTOR, TROCHLEAR, AND ABDUCENS)

The cardinal fields of gaze should be checked in each direction, including intorsion and extorsion.

The abducens nerve (cranial nerve VI) has a long intracranial course and is frequently damaged either by direct trauma or as a consequence of raised ICP. Examination reveals a paralyzed lateral rectus muscle and failure of ipsilateral abduction. Brainstem compression or dysfunction may manifest as dysconjugate gaze or bilateral gaze palsy caused by interruption of the medial longitudinal fasciculus (cranial nerves III and VI).

Increased ICP may cause midbrain compression, with resultant paresis of the upward gaze (Parinaud's syndrome). Light-near dissociation also occurs with this syndrome.

A traumatic mydriasis can sometimes cause a dilated and nonreactive pupil that does not respond to parasympathomimetics such as pilocarpine.

CRANIAL NERVE VII (FACIAL)

Facial asymmetry is looked for in both the upper and the lower halves of the face. Lower motor neuron paralysis occurs usually at the stylomastoid foramen secondary to blunt trauma or fracture, resulting in a complete facial palsy. The upper half of the face has bilateral hemispheric innervation. Therefore, an upper motor neuron lesion, such as an extradural hemorrhage, may cause a contralateral lower facial palsy, with sparing of the upper half of the face.

CRANIAL NERVE V (TRIGEMINAL)

Diminished pin-prick sensation can occur with either direct trauma or intracranial contusion. The corneal reflex involves afferent input through the trigeminal nerve and causes efferent output through the facial nerve. Commonly, pontine dysfunction causes an absence of corneal reflexes bilaterally.

CRANIAL NERVE VIII (VESTIBULOCOCHLEAR)

Unilateral deafness may occur following petrous ridge fracture. Rarely, a unilateral lesion involving the superior temporal gyrus may cause partial bilateral hearing loss.

CRANIAL NERVES IX AND X (GLOSSOPHARYNGEAL AND VAGAL)

The gag reflex is a lower brainstem reflex elicited by compression of the posterior pharynx by a tongue blade. Absence of the gag reflex is an ominous sign, indicating lower brainstem damage and impending neurologic demise. Unilateral lesions may cause ipsilateral pharyngeal weakness, resulting in contraction of the uvula away from the side of the lesion.

CRANIAL NERVE XI (SPINAL ACCESSORY)

Sternocleidomastoid and trapezius muscle strength should be checked bilaterally, although these muscles are rarely involved in CNS trauma.

CRANIAL NERVE XII (HYPOGLOSSAL)

Tongue protrusion should be midline, and damage to the hypoglossal nerve will produce ipsilateral weakness, with protrusion of the tongue toward the weak side. Infarctions involving the anterior spinal artery may cause ipsilateral tongue weakness and contralateral hemiplegia resulting from involvement of the ipsilateral medullary pyramid (inferior alternating hemiplegia).

Motor System

A complete examination of extremity musculature is carried out, with particular reference to tone and power.

Tone can be increased with direct pressure on the corticospinal tract anywhere along its path from the internal capsule (with extradural hematoma) to the spinal cord (with Brown-Séquard syndrome). Spinal shock secondary to spinal cord transection results in decreased tone (flaccidity).

The power of the individual muscle groups is measured on a scale from 1 to 5, as follows:

5 — Normal strength
4 — Weakness; resistance overcome
3 — Antigravity strength only; no resistance
2 — Movement without antigravity strength
1 — Flicker of motion only

The respective muscle groups are referenced in terms of fractions of five (i.e., four fifths, or strength is "four out of five").

Gait

When possible, assessment of the patient's gait provides important information regarding the extent of injury. Both station and gait should be examined, including casual, tandem, heel, and toe walking. Cerebellar dysfunction can result in ataxia of gait, with ipsilateral location.

Cerebellum

Finger-to-nose, heel-to-shin, and rapid, alternating tests again yield valuable information regarding coordination and fine motor movements. Hemispheric lesions usually lateralize ipsilaterally, while midline (vermian) lesions tend to manifest with bilateral dysfunction.

Sensory System

Pin prick, position, vibration, and light touch can localize lesions, particularly at the spinal cord level. Pain and temperature abnormalities localize to the lateral spinothalamic tract, while proprioception and vibration localize to the posterior columns.

Deep Tendon Reflexes

Pathologic reflexes (hyper-reflexia) will occur either unilaterally or bilaterally, depending on lesion localization. Compression of the ipsilateral cerebral peduncle by an expanding unilateral mass will produce contralateral hyper-reflexia with an extensor plantar reflex (the Babinski reflex). Central expansion or herniation will frequently produce bilateral hyper-reflexia. Spinal shock produces an absence of reflexes below the level of the lesion.

GRADING THE SEVERITY OF INJURY

Neurologic injury can be further characterized either anatomically or functionally.

Anatomic

Plum and Posner described coma anatomically, using respirations, pupils, eye movements, and motor examination to localize lesions and to describe further the rostrocaudal progression of brainstem herniation.[21]

Tests for oculocephalic (doll's eyes) and oculovestibular (cold caloric) responses can yield valuable information. Both tests assess the integrity of the brainstem. With an intact brainstem, the eyes should remain fixed straight ahead while the head is forcefully turned to one side or the other (doll's head maneuver). Injection of cold water into one ear causes conjugate movement of both eyes ipsilaterally with an intact brainstem (cold caloric testing).

Table 7–2 summarizes the rostrocaudal progression of coma secondary to central herniation. Cheyne-Stokes respiration is characterized by periods of hyperventilation separated by periods of apnea. In apneustic breathing, gasping, irregular respirations are separated by long periods of apnea.

TABLE 7–2. ROSTROCAUDAL PROGRESSION OF COMA SECONDARY TO CENTRAL HERNIATION

Stage	Breathing	Pupils	Eye Movements	Motor Status
1. Diencephalon	Cheyne-Stokes	Small, reactive	Normal cold calorics	Decorticate posturing
2. Midbrain–upper pons	Neurogenic hyperventilation	Midsize, midposition	Abnormal, dysconjugate	Decerebrate posturing
3. Lower pons–upper medulla	Apneustic	Fixed, midrange	No calorics	Flaccid
4. Medulla	Eupneic, ataxic	Large, fixed	No calorics	Flaccid

Decorticate posturing (abnormal flexion posturing) implies destruction of cortical input to the red nucleus of the midbrain (rubrospinal tract), resulting in flexion posturing in the limbs. Decerebrate posturing (abnormal extensor posturing) reflects the absence of cortical input further caudally, resulting in extensor posturing in the limbs (vestibulospinal tract).

Functional

Jennett and Teasdale, described the Glasgow Coma Scale in an attempt to characterize both the severity of injury and the possible outcome.[6,22-24] The scale uses three parameters: eye opening, best motor response, and best verbal response. Table 7–3 presents the scale and the points assigned to each category, with a sum total ranging between 3 and 15. In severe head injury, the scale usually reads between 0 and 8; in moderate head injury, between 9 and 12; and in mild head injury, between 13 and 15.

DIAGNOSTIC STUDIES IN HEAD INJURY

In the light of readily available computerized tomography (CT), the value of plain film skull roentgenograms is diminishing and is currently controversial.[25,26] At this writing, we still recommend routine skull roentgenograms after all significant trauma as long as taking these films does not delay a more important CT scan. All patients with major head trauma or neurologic deficit should have a CT scan (Fig. 7–1).

TABLE 7–3. GLASGOW COMA SCALE

Eye opening (E):
4 — Opens eyes spontaneously
3 — Opens eyes to voice
2 — Opens eyes to pain
1 — No eye opening

Best motor response (M):
6 — Obeys commands
5 — Localizes to pain
4 — Withdraws to pain
3 — Abnormal flexor response
2 — Abnormal extensor response
1 — No movement

Best verbal response (V):
5 — Appropriate and oriented
4 — Confused conversation
3 — Inappropriate words
2 — Incomprehensible sounds
1 — No sounds

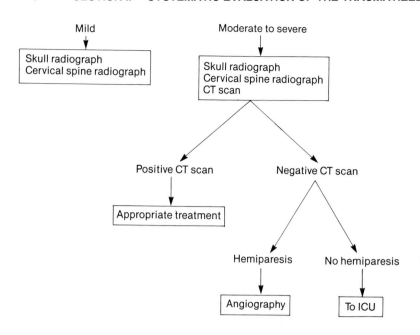

FIGURE 7–1. Radiologic studies after head injury. CT = computerized tomography; ICU = intensive care unit.

SPECIAL PROBLEMS IN HEAD INJURY

Scalp Injury

Scalp injury may cause serious hemorrhage. Bleeding can usually be controlled with a simple pressure dressing. Arterial bleeding can be readily controlled by firm finger pressure along the edges of the wound or by hemostats applied to the galea. All scalp wounds should be closed as soon as possible, unless they overlie a depressed fracture or a penetrating wound of the skull, which requires debridement in the operating room.

Management

SCALP LACERATIONS

A generous area should be shaved and washed. If the laceration is large, a gauze sponge in the wound will prevent debris from entering. The wound should be cleansed thoroughly with copious irrigations of saline. Foreign bodies that may lead to infection or leave unsightly tattoos must be removed. All devitalized tissue should be carefully debrided, taking care not to excise viable tissue.

The wound should be closed with multiple interrupted vertical mattress sutures of stainless steel wire or monofilament nylon, or the galea and skin are closed in separate layers. Meticulous technique is necessary.

SCALP AVULSIONS

Avulsions of the scalp usually include all layers of the scalp, sparing the pericranium. They are treated by experienced surgeons in complete operating room facilities. The area surrounding the wound is shaved and thoroughly irrigated. If the avulsion is small, the edges are sparingly trimmed. Primary closure can often be accomplished. If the denuded area is large, the wound may be covered with a single layer of fine mesh gauze. A large dressing is placed on the gauze, and a firm circumferential dressing is applied to exert even pressure over the area. Delayed closure can be performed several days later. Large scalp wounds can also be repaired by microsurgical techniques, including vascular anastomosis, provided the avulsed scalp has been preserved and surgery is undertaken soon after injury.

Skull Fracture

Classification

Skull fractures may be classified according to the following:

1. Whether the skin overlying the fracture is intact (closed) or disrupted (open, or compound).
2. Whether there is a single fracture line (linear), several fractures radiating from a central point (stellate), or fragmentation of bone (comminuted).
3. Whether the edges of the fracture line have been driven below the level of the surrounding bone (depressed) or not (nondepressed).

Management

Linear or stellate nondepressed open fractures can be treated by simple closure of the scalp after thorough cleansing. Open fractures with severe comminution of underlying bone are treated in the operating room, where proper debridement can be carried out. The dura is inspected to make certain that no laceration has been overlooked.

SIMPLE SKULL FRACTURES

Linear, stellate, or comminuted nondepressed fractures, although classified as *simple* fractures, are potentially serious if they cross major vascular channels in the skull, such as the groove of the middle meningeal artery or the major dural venous sinuses. If these vessels are torn, epidural or subdural hematomas may form. Patients with these fractures are kept under close observation until the examiner is certain that no such bleeding is occurring. A fracture that extends into the accessory nasal sinuses or the mastoid air cells is considered to be open because it is in communication with an external surface of the body.

DEPRESSED SKULL FRACTURES

Depressed fractures often require a surgical procedure to elevate the depressed bone. If no untoward neurologic signs exist and the fracture is closed, an operation may be delayed until a convenient time.

DEPRESSED OPEN SKULL FRACTURES

As soon as the patient's general condition permits, a depressed open skull fracture is elevated, debrided, and closed.[27] The scalp wound is not closed, and no attempt is made to remove any foreign body protruding from the wound until the patient is in the operating room and all preparations have been made for craniotomy.

BASAL SKULL FRACTURES

Basal skull fractures may cause rhinorrhea or otorrhea if the dura and arachnoid are torn; they may also cause bleeding from the nose or ears if skin or mucous membranes are lacerated. It is often difficult to tell if blood is mixed with CSF. Sometimes a CSF-blood mixture can be detected at the bedside by placing a drop of bloody discharge on a cleansing tissue; if CSF is present, a spreading yellowish-orange ring appears around the central red stain of blood. If a CSF leak exists, antibiotic prophylaxis may be used but is controversial.[27,28] The patient's head is elevated to 30 degrees, and fluid intake is restricted to 1200 ml/day. The patient is cautioned against blowing the nose, a maneuver that can contaminate the intracranial space. If a leak persists, spinal drainage may be effective to reduce ICP and seal the leak. Craniotomy is often required for leaks that continue for more than 2 weeks. Fewer than 5 per cent of patients with traumatic CSF leaks actually require surgical repair.

Head injury, with or without skull fracture, may cause tears in the vascular channels coursing through the meninges and can lead to serious intracranial hemorrhage.

Epidural Hematoma

Hemorrhage between the inner table of the skull and the dura mater most commonly arises from a tear of the middle meningeal artery caused by a skull fracture across the arterial groove in the temporal region. Arterial bleeding strips the dura from the undersurface of the bone and produces still more bleeding because the small bridging veins from the dura to the skull are torn. The hematoma rapidly increases in size and compresses the cerebral cortex. If sufficient hemispheric compression occurs, the medial portion of the temporal lobe (uncus and hippocampal gyrus) is forced into the tentorial notch; this causes pressure on the third cranial nerve and dilatation of the pupils on the same side. Hemispheric compression shifts the brainstem toward the opposite side of the tentorial notch. Compression of the cerebral peduncle on the side of the hematoma causes contralateral hemiparesis, which may progress to decerebrate posturing. The triad of *transtentorial herniation*, consisting of (1) coma, (2) fixed, dilated pupil, and (3) decerebration, is a classic clinical syndrome.[21,22,29]

An epidural hematoma may arise from torn venous channels in the bone at a point of fracture or from lacerated major dural venous sinuses. Because venous pressure is low, epidural venous hematomas usually form only when a depressed skull fracture has stripped the dura from the bone and left a space in which the hematoma can develop.

Clinical Presentation

Epidural hematoma classically follows a blow to the head that causes unconsciousness for a brief period.[30] After the patient regains consciousness, there may be a "lucid interval," during which there are no abnormal neurologic symptoms or signs. As the hematoma enlarges sufficiently to compress the cerebral hemisphere, there is gradual deterioration of consciousness that progresses to coma and death if the hematoma is not evacuated.

Although epidural hematoma is a curable lesion, mortality remains high because the gravity of the insult is not often recognized early. A patient may appear normal during the lucid interval and thus may be discharged. At home, the patient is assumed to be sleeping but, in fact, is unconscious because the hematoma has increased in size and compressed the brain.

Diagnostic Studies

Because misdiagnosis is a real danger, any patient with a history of a blow to the head leading to a period of unconsciousness should have a thorough examination, possibly including a CT scan or skull roentgenograms (Fig. 7–2).

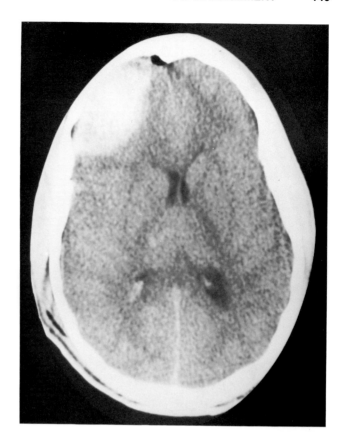

FIGURE 7–2. Acute epidural hematoma showing high-attenuation lesion in the right frontal lobe region. Note the lenslike nature of this lesion.

Management

If imaging studies reveal a fracture, the patient is hospitalized and the level of consciousness is checked at least hourly. If no fracture is demonstrated, the patient may be discharged, but a reliable person is instructed to awaken the patient frequently to be certain that he or she is arousable and not comatose. A follow-up examination the next day is prudent.

Impairment of the sensorium is the first indication that an operation may be urgently needed. If the operation is delayed until herniation occurs and brainstem hemorrhages develop, the patient is likely to remain comatose even though the hematoma is evacuated.

Subdural Hematoma

Subdural hematoma occurs most commonly when veins bridging from the cortex to the venous sinuses are torn or when an intracerebral hematoma extends into the subdural space.[31] The hematomas may be large, even though the bleeding is of venous (low pressure) origin.

Diagnosis and Management

ACUTE SUBDURAL HEMATOMA

Acute subdural hematoma is associated with severe head injury and arises from a combination of torn bridging veins and frank laceration of the cortex. The hematoma is usually discovered during CT scanning or angiography (Fig. 7–3). Evacuation of

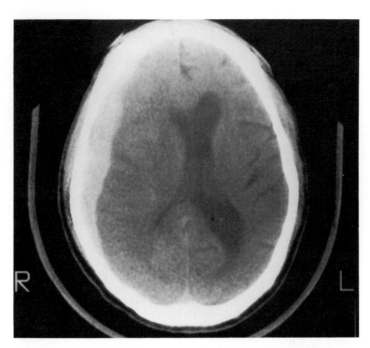

Figure 7–3. Acute panhemispheric right subdural hematoma with right-to-left shift. The lesion conforms to the shape of the cortical surface.

the clot may result in significant improvement, but often a major neurologic deficit remains because of the widespread cerebral contusion, laceration, or both.

SUBACUTE SUBDURAL HEMATOMA

The subacute lesion becomes apparent 3 to 10 days after injury and is associated with progressive lethargy, confusion, hemiparesis, or other hemispheric deficits. Removal of the hematoma usually produces striking improvement.

CHRONIC SUBDURAL HEMATOMA

A chronic subdural lesion arises from tears in bridging veins, often after a minor head injury. The hematoma is small initially; later it becomes encased in a fibrous membrane, liquefies, and gradually enlarges. The lesion is most common in infants and elderly patients.

The history is one of progressive mental change, with or without focal signs (e.g., progressive hemiplegia or aphasia). Papilledema may be present. These findings often suggest a diagnosis of brain tumor. The diagnosis is confirmed by angiography or CT scanning (Fig. 7–4). Treatment consists of drainage of the hematoma through burr holes. If the fluid reaccumulates, craniotomy may be necessary.

SUBDURAL HYGROMA

Subdural hygroma is a collection of clear or xanthochromic fluid in the subdural space. It probably forms through a tear in the arachnoid that allows CSF to escape into the subdural space, where it is trapped and cannot be absorbed. The resulting fluid mass causes the same symptoms as those seen with chronic subdural hematoma. The condition is treated by draining the fluid through burr holes.

Primary Brain Injury

The extent of brain damage is the primary determinant of treatment for patients with head trauma.[4,32–36] The prognosis is related to the type and degree of primary brain injury and to the nature of injuries to other parts of the body.[3,11,23,37–41]

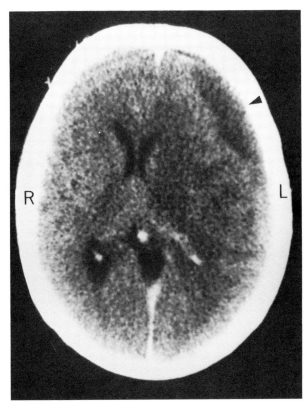

FIGURE 7–4. Left frontal chronic subdural hematoma with left-to-right shift. Note the low attenuation associated with this lesion.

Injury to the brain results from rapid deceleration, acceleration, or the shearing and rotational effects of a blow to the head. These mechanisms may produce *concussion,* a temporary loss of consciousness with no permanent organic brain damage; *contusion,* bruising of the brain; or *laceration,* frank disruption of brain substance. The types of primary brain injury can occur singly but more commonly are seen in combination.

Clinical Presentation

Contusion may be local, causing focal signs and symptoms (e.g., hemiparesis or aphasia), or it may be generalized, with widespread damage to the brain. Increased vascular permeability in contused brain tissue allows cerebral edema to develop.[42,43] Decreased respiratory exchange in severely injured patients leads to anoxia and hypercapnia; the resulting cerebral vasodilatation contributes still further to cerebral swelling.

Management

Contusions and lacerations of the brain usually cannot be treated surgically, but some neurosurgeons resect the most severely contused portions of the brain in selected cases. Intracerebral hematomas are usually associated with lacerations; if the hematoma is large, surgical evacuation is indicated.

SPINAL CORD INJURY

Diagnostic Studies

The hallmark of the initial radiologic assessment of the neurologically traumatized patient is the lateral cervical spine radiograph. This radiograph is usually obtained as a portable lateral radiograph while the patient is immobilized in a protective, rigid collar.

Obvious fractures and dislocations are identified, together with widening of the posterior spinous process interspace secondary to ligamentous disruption.

The following are fundamental points in the interpretation of cervical spine radiographs:

1.   The lateral film is considered *inadequate* if the C7–T1 region is poorly visualized. Although several authorities consider visualization to C7 as "adequate," fractures at C7–T1 are difficult to visualize in this region. Traction on the shoulders or a swimmer's view is often helpful in radiographically defining this region.

2.   Soft tissue swelling *anterior* to the vertebral bodies (C3) should not be greater than 5 mm. Extensive retropharyngeal hemorrhage secondary to fracture increases this width.

3.   The interspinous distance between all levels down to T1 should be checked. Ligamentous disruption will frequently widen the distance at the site of the disruption.

4.   It is best to check the vertebral body alignment using the posterior border of the vertebral body. Bone can be retropulsed posteriorly, causing anterior compression of the spinal cord even though the anterior borders are aligned.

5.   Fracture-dislocations that displace the superior vertebral body 25 per cent of its width over the inferior vertebral body are referred to as unilateral locked facets, while those measuring 50 per cent or greater are considered bilateral locked facets.

After the lateral radiograph is "cleared," the anteroposterior and open-mouth odontoid views are obtained while the patient remains immobilized. If all films are normal and the patient does not complain of significant neck pain, the collar can be safely removed, provided the neurologic examination does not localize to the cervical spine. If ligamentous disruption is suspected and the neurologic examination yields normal findings, careful flexion and extension views may be obtained with the physician present.

Cervical spine CT nicely demonstrates areas of abnormality on the plain radiographs (Fig. 7–5). Canal diameter, anterior and posterior elements, and soft tissue compromise (disc) can be readily visualized on high-resolution CT. Sagittal reconstruction can further delineate areas of fracture-dislocation. CT has virtually replaced the need for cervical myelography in this disorder.

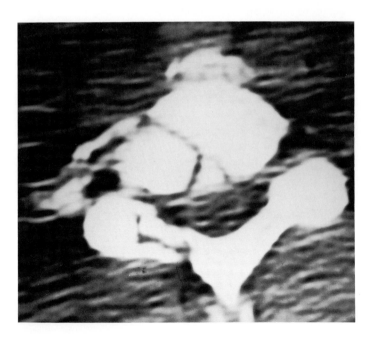

FIGURE 7–5. Cervical spine computerized tomographic (CT) scan showing fractures of both anterior and posterior elements of the cervical spine. There is minimal compromise of the spinal canal diameter.

Magnetic resonance (MR) imaging shows the cervical spine and spinal cord in sagittal and axial views very well. However, MR is currently limited by the long imaging times required for processing.

Diagnoses

Fractures

The following list summarizes many of the common fractures seen in cervical spine trauma.

JEFFERSON FRACTURE

The Jefferson fracture is a comminuted fracture of the ring of C1, infrequently associated with neurologic compromise because of the capacious spinal canal in this region.

HANGMAN'S FRACTURE

Hangman's fracture is a fracture through the pedicles and laminae of C2 that is commonly due to a hyperextension injury of the upper cervical spine.

ODONTOID FRACTURE

Three types of odontoid fracture have been described:

I — Fracture through the upper dens
II — Fracture through the waist of the dens
III — Fracture extending into the C2 body

FRACTURE-DISLOCATION

Fracture-dislocation most often involves the C5 – 6 region and is associated with varying degrees of disruption, ranging from pure ligamentous disruption to posterior element fracture to combined posterior and anterior element fracture. Unilateral and bilateral locked facets occur as a result of this mechanism of injury. The injury most commonly is caused by hyperflexion.

COMPRESSION FRACTURE

A compression fracture is a fracture caused by a vertical blow to the head or axial loading injury. Mild forms consist of a wedge compression fracture with a "teardrop" chip broken off the anterior lip of the vertebral body (see legend, Fig. 7 – 6). A severe form consists of a "burst" fracture, with the entire vertebral body crushed, usually with intraspinal bone fragments.

Soft Tissue Injuries

MUSCULOSKELETAL STRAIN

Hyperextension injuries of the cervical spine that are not associated with fracture or dislocation constitute a large portion of soft tissue injury. Flexion occurs with recoil; however, it is usually less forceful. Some authors have referred to this injury pattern as "whiplash injury."

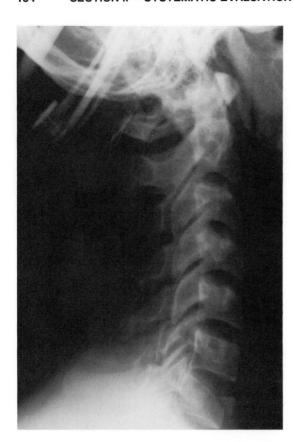

FIGURE 7–6. Cervical spine radiograph demonstrating a C7 compression fracture with an anterior "chip" or teardrop fracture.

CENTRAL CORD SYNDROME

This syndrome occurs in the setting of forceful hyperextension and backward thrusting of the neck, usually in an elderly patient with cervical spondylosis and stenosis. Paralysis occurs in this syndrome without vertebral injury. The upper extremities are usually weaker than the lower extremities owing to the somatotopic organization of the corticospinal tracts, with arm fibers medial and leg fibers lateral.

Management

Cervical spine fractures are usually best managed with the patient in skeletal traction, often with the use of halo traction and a Stryker frame, or a roto-kinetic bed.[44–47] Gardner-Wells tongs can also be applied effectively.

The halo ring is attached to the skull by a four-point screw system. Weight is applied to the ring to reduce the fracture and realign the spine. Approximately 5 pounds of traction is used for each level to the fracture-dislocation (e.g., a C5 fracture usually requires 25 pounds of traction).

Patients are usually kept immobilized for 7 to 10 days prior to definitive treatment. Failure to reduce the fracture adequately may require early operative intervention. After this period, patients are (1) placed into a halo vest orthosis, (2) selected for operative fusion, or (3) fused and immobilized in a halo vest.

The indications for surgical stabilization versus halo vest immobilization alone are less well defined.[44,45] Generally, unstable cervical spine fractures (i.e., complex fractures involving anterior and posterior elements, multiple levels, or fracture-dislocations) should undergo operative fusion and decompression.[44,45,48] Anterior vertebrectomy and fusion are indicated in burst fractures with anterior compression, while posterior fusion with wire and autogenous bone graft are best performed for posterior element disruption. Occasionally, both anterior and posterior procedures are required to decompress and stabilize the spine.

Upper cervical spine fractures are better immobilized with the halo vest orthosis than are lower cervical spine fractures.[45,49] Hangman and Jefferson fractures respond well to immobilization in a halo vest and seldom require operative intervention. Unstable C1–2 fracture-dislocations commonly require posterior cervical fusion and postoperative immobilization in either a hard collar or a halo vest.[50,51]

Soft tissue injuries are best treated with hard cervical collars for a brief period of relative immobilization, along with analgesics and muscle relaxants.[52,53]

Special Problems

Post-treatment instability can lead to nonunion, malunion, or increased neurologic deficit. Frequently, unstable lower cervical spine fractures managed without operative intervention result in instability, which usually requires operative intervention.

Similarly, in patients with ligamentous disruption alone who are managed in a halo vest, posterior interspinous instability frequently develops, requiring operative fusion. Most authorities agree that these injuries should be managed surgically, followed by immobilization.[44,45,47,48]

Prognosis

Sometimes the patient with an incomplete cord injury can walk again, provided early care is protective and rehabilitation is aggressive and well planned. However, patients with complete lesions rarely recover function below the lesion. Rehabilitation for these patients is directed toward self-care and vocational readjustment. Most persons with these handicaps can eventually achieve independence. Life expectancy is shortened slightly in paraplegic persons and significantly in quadriplegic persons. Long-term problems associated with skin care and recurrent urinary infections account for the shortened life expectancy.

REFERENCES

1. Barth JT, Macciocchi SN, Giordani B, et al: Neuropsychological sequelae of minor head injury. Neurosurgery 13:529–533, 1983.
2. Becker DP, Miller JC, Ward JD, et al: The outcome from severe head injury with early diagnosis and intensive management. J Neurosurg 47:491–502, 1977.
3. Davis RA, Cunningham PS: Prognostic factors in severe head injury. Surg Gynecol Obstet 159:597–604, 1984.
4. Gennarelli TA, Spielman GM, Langfitt TW, et al: Influence of the type of intracranial lesion on outcome from severe head injury: A multicenter study using a new classification system. J Neurosurg 56:26–32, 1982.
5. Grossman RG, Gildenbeg PL: Head Injury: Basic and Clinical Aspects. New York, Raven Press, 1982.
6. Jennett B, Bond M: Assessment of outcome after severe brain damage. A practical scale. Lancet 1:480–484, 1975.
7. Langfitt TW: Measuring the outcome from head injuries. J Neurosurg 48:673–678, 1978.
8. Marshall LF, Smith RW, Shapiro HM: The outcome with aggressive treatment in severe head injuries. Part I. The significance of intra-cranial pressure monitoring. J Neurosurg 50:20–25, 1979.
9. Marshall LF, Smith RW, Shapiro HM: The outcome with aggressive treatment in severe head injuries. Part II. Acute and chronic barbiturate administration in the management of head injury. J Neurosurg 50:26–30, 1979.
10. Young B: Sequelae of head injury. In Wilkins RH, Rengachary SS (eds): Neurosurgery. New York, McGraw-Hill Book Company, 1985, pp 1688–1693.
11. Bertz JE: Maxillofacial injuries. Ciba Clin Symp 33:3–10, 1981.
12. Langfitt TW, Gennarelli TA: Can the outcome from head injury be improved? J Neurosurg 56:19–25, 1982.
13. Miller JD, Becker DP, Ward JD, et al: Significance of intracranial hypertension in severe head injury. J Neurosurg 47:503–516, 1977.
14. Tinsdall GT, Patton JM, Dunion JJ, O'Brien MS: Monitoring of patients with head injuries. Clin Neurosurg 22:332–363, 1975.
15. Bucci MN, Decher RE, Arnoldi DK, et al: Elevated intracranial pressure associated with hypermetabolism in isolated head trauma. Acta Neurochir 93:133–136, 1988.
16. Bucci MN, Dechert R, Arnoldi D, et al: Meta-

bolic requirements in severe head trauma. Surg Forum 37:524–526, 1986.

17. Schneider RC, Cherry G, Pantek H: Syndrome of acute central cervical cord injury with special reference to the mechanisms involved in hyperextension injuries of the cervical spine. J Neurosurg 11:546–577, 1954.

18. Bennett G: History. *In* Howarth MB, Petrie JG (eds): Injuries of the Spine. Baltimore, The Williams and Wilkins Company, 1964, pp 1–59.

19. Tator CH: Early Management of Acute Spinal Cord Injury. New York, Raven Press, 1982.

20. Yashon D: Spinal Injury. New York, Appleton-Century-Crofts, 1978.

21. Plum F, Posner JB: The Diagnosis of Stupor and Coma. 3rd ed. Philadelphia, FA Davis, 1980.

22. Jennett B: Assessment of the severity of head injury. J Neurol Neurosurg Psychiatry 39:647–655, 1976.

23. Jennett B, Teasdale G: Aspects of coma after severe head injury. Lancet 1:878–881, 1977.

24. Teasdale G, Jennett B: Assessment of coma and impaired consciousness: A practical scale. Lancet 2:81–84, 1974.

25. Masters SJ: Evaluation of head trauma: Efficacy of skull films. Am J Neuroradiol 1:329–337, 1980.

26. Phillips LA: Emergency services utilization of skull radiography. Neurosurgery 4:580–582, 1979.

27. Hammon WM: Analysis of 2187 consecutive penetrating wounds to the brain from Vietnam. J Neurosurg 34:127–131, 1971.

28. Harsh GR III, Harsh GR IV: Penetrating wounds of the head. *In* Wilkins RH, Rengachary SS (eds): Neurosurgery. New York, McGraw-Hill Book Company, 1985, pp 1670–1678.

29. Davis RA, Davis L: Decerebrate rigidity in humans. Neurosurgery 10:635–642, 1982.

30. Bucci MN, Phillips TJ, McGillicuddy JE: Delayed epidural hemorrhage in hypotensive multiple trauma patients. Neurosurgery 19:65–68, 1986.

31. Bucci MN, Farhat SM: Metastatic adenocarcinoma of the prostate as a cause of subdural hematoma. J Urol 135:803–804, 1986.

32. Adams JH, Graham DI, Murray LS, Scott G: Diffuse axonal injury due to nonmissile head injury in humans: An analysis of 45 cases. Ann Neurol 12:557–563, 1982.

33. Gennarelli TA, Thibault LE: Biomechanics of head injury. *In* Wilkins RH, Rengachary SS (eds): Neurosurgery. New York, McGraw-Hill Book Company, 1985, pp 1531–1536.

34. Gennarelli TA, Thibault LE, Adams JH, et al: Diffuse axonal injury and traumatic coma in the primate. Ann Neurol 12:564–574, 1982.

35. Hardman JM: The pathology of traumatic brain injuries. Adv Neurol 22:15–50, 1979.

36. McCormick WF: Pathology of closed head injury. *In* Wilkins RH, Rengachary SS (eds): Neurosurgery. New York, McGraw-Hill Book Company, 1985, pp 1544–1570.

37. Annegers JF, Grabow JD, Groover RV, et al: Seizures after head trauma: A population study. Neurology 30:683–689, 1980.

38. Giannotta SL, Ahmadi J: Vascular lesions with head injury. *In* Wilkins RH, Rengachary SS (eds): Neurosurgery. New York, McGraw-Hill Book Company, 1985, pp 1678–1688.

39. Gurdjian ES: Impact Head Injury: Mechanistic, Clinical and Preventive Correlations. Springfield, IL, Charles C Thomas, 1975.

40. Miner ME: Delayed and recurrent intracranial hematomas and post-traumatic coagulopathies. *In* Wilkins RH, Rengachary SS (eds): Neurosurgery. New York, McGraw-Hill Book Company, 1985, pp 1666–1669.

41. Rimel RW, Giordani B, Barth JT, Jane JA: Moderate head injury: Completing the clinical spectrum of brain trauma. Neurosurgery 11:344–351, 1982.

42. Bucci MN, Hoff JT: Barbiturate therapy in neurosurgery: A reappraisal. Contemp Neurosurg 8:106, 1986.

43. Giannotta LS, Weiss MH, Apuzzo MLJ, Martin E: High dose glucocorticoids in the management of severe head injury. Neurosurgery 15:497–501, 1984.

44. Bohlman HH: Acute fractures and dislocations of the cervical spine. J Bone Joint Surg 61:1119–1142, 1979.

45. Bucci MN, Dauser RC, Maynard FA, Hoff JT: Early operative fusion versus halo-vest immobilization for post-traumatic instability of the cervical spine. Surg Forum 38:499–501, 1987.

46. Bucci MN, Dauser RC, Maynard FA, Hoff JT: Management of post-traumatic cervical spine instability: Operative fusion versus halo vest immobilization. Analysis of 49 cases. J Trauma 28:1000–1006, 1988.

47. Hardaker WT Jr: Halo immobilization of cervical spine injuries. *In* Wilkins RH, Rengachary SS (eds): Neurosurgery. New York, McGraw-Hill Book Company, 1985, pp 1723–1727.

48. Alexander E Jr, Davis CH, Forsythe HF: Reduction and fusion of fracture dislocation of the cervical spine. J Neurosurg 27:558–591, 1967.

49. Ewing CL, Thomas DJ, Sances A Jr, Larson SJ: Impact Injury of the Head and Spine. Springfield, IL, Charles C Thomas, 1983.

50. Alexander E Jr, Forsythe HF, Davis CH, Nashold BS: Dislocation of the atlas on the axis: The value of early fusion of C-1, C-2 and C-3. J Neurosurg 15:353–371, 1958.

51. Schneider RC: High cervical spine injuries. *In* Wilkins RH, Rengachary SS (eds): Neurosurgery. New York, McGraw-Hill Book Company, 1985, pp 1701–1708.

52. Berry H: Psychological aspects of whiplash injury. *In* Wilkins RH, Rengachary SS (eds): Neurosurgery. New York, McGraw-Hill Book Company, 1985, pp 1716–1719.

53. Schneider RC, Kennedy JC, Plant ML: Sports Injuries: Mechanisms, Prevention and Treatment. Baltimore, The Williams and Wilkins Company, 1985.

CHAPTER 8

MANAGEMENT OF NONPENETRATING CHEST TRAUMA

MARVIN M. KIRSH, M.D.

Pulmonary contusion

↓

Increased respiratory work

↓

→ Hypoxia and acidosis ←

↓

Decreased cardiac output

↓

Myocardial contusion

Chest injury is responsible for 25 per cent of the more than 150,000 deaths due to automobile accidents. In another 25 to 50 per cent of these deaths, thoracic injury or a complication thereof plays a major contributing role. Chest injury occurs, as well, in a high proportion of victims who survive their injury, as 50 per cent of automobile accident victims incur nonfatal chest trauma of some sort. Crush injuries and falls from a variety of causes often involve the chest. The most common injury following blunt chest trauma is rib fracture, usually with pulmonary contusion, in approximately 90 per cent of cases. Pneumothorax occurs in 30 per cent of cases of chest trauma, hemothorax in 20 per cent, heart and great vessel injury in 8 per cent, diaphragmatic disruption in 1 per cent, tracheobronchial disruption in 0.3 per cent, and esophageal disruption in 0.1 per cent. Major thoracic surgery is required in only 10 to 15 per cent of victims of blunt trauma. Twenty-five years ago, the mortality from isolated chest injuries approached 50 per cent. However, improvements in ambulance transport systems and in prehospital care not only have increased the number of potentially salvageable patients but also have lowered the mortality to less than 20 per cent as well. It is hoped that earlier recognition, better understanding of the pathophysiology, and improvements in management will even further reduce the number of deaths caused by thoracic injuries.

GENERAL PRINCIPLES OF MANAGEMENT

The condition on arrival in the emergency room of the person who has sustained blunt trauma to the chest varies greatly. Most patients are first seen while in critical condition with obvious chest injuries and require immediate treatment. It is also important to recognize that serious intrathoracic injury can occur without obvious external chest injuries or rib fractures. The semirigid chest wall of the elderly in the process of fracturing ribs absorbs energy that would otherwise be transmitted to the lung parenchyma and great vessels. However, the flexible chest wall of the young patient will transmit essentially all the kinetic energy to the thoracic contents. Thus, the absence of rib fractures does not rule out the possibility of life-threatening injuries. If the injury is not recognized early, death frequently results. The individuals caring for patients who are suffering from blunt chest trauma must not be deceived by an initially good condition and must always be alert for the likelihood of later clinical deterioration. Careful and frequent observation of any patient with blunt chest injury is as important as the initial evaluation.

Patients with severe thoracic injuries frequently sustain multiple extrathoracic injuries. The physician's attention must not be diverted from thoracic injuries by obvious extrathoracic injuries, such as abdominal, maxillofacial, or central nervous system (CNS) injuries. After any immediate life-threatening emergencies have been treated, the physician should undertake a careful history, if possible, and should methodically examine all systems in the injured patient. Knowledge of the patient's past medical history, allergies, and medications may influence subsequent therapy. Clues to the likely injuries may be gained from the knowledge of the circumstances under which the injuries occurred.

Arterial blood gas (ABG) determinations are a means of indirectly measuring and following the functional impairment caused by pulmonary injury. Often, the first sign of impending respiratory failure may be the marked hypoxia exhibited. Serial ABG determinations compared with baseline data obtained in room air may be useful in predicting trends in respiratory function. Using an F_{IO_2} of 0.21 permits consistent serial comparisons and gives a more accurate estimation of the severity of the respiratory impairment. Patients should be followed initially every 4 hours for 48 hours with ABG determinations to detect subtle changes that prompt modification of treatment.

RIB FRACTURES

Contributing factors to rib fractures appear to be related to the age of the patient and the anatomic locations. Fractures of the ribs are more common in adults than in children because the cartilage in children is more resilient and can absorb the impact without breaking. In contrast, the ribs of elderly persons are brittle and can be broken even by minor degrees of trauma. The ribs usually break at the point of impact or at the posterior angle, which structurally is the weakest point. The fifth through ninth ribs are the ones most commonly broken. The lower two ribs are mobile and yielding and therefore fracture least often. Because of the location, lower rib fractures are often associated with injuries to the liver, spleen, and kidney.

The number of ribs fractured and the degree of displacement of rib fragments and injury to the underlying lung are dependent on the force and direction of the impact and the area of its distribution. If the injuring force is applied over a wide area, especially in the anteroposterior projection, the ribs buckle outward and thus break in the midshaft position without injuring the pulmonary parenchyma. A direct injury tends to drive the rib fragments inward over a limited area and can cause lacerations of the pleura, pulmonary parenchyma, and intercostal vessels, producing pneumothorax, hemothorax, or both; pneumothorax or massive intrathoracic bleeding may be life threatening.

A delayed complication that is apt to occur in elderly patients or in patients with pre-existing chronic lung disease is pneumonia and possibly respiratory failure. Rib fractures are invariably accompanied by pain. To reduce the pain to tolerable levels, the patient both consciously and unconsciously restricts excursion of the chest wall by shallow breathing. Such shallow breathing results in the ventilation of fewer alveoli. The unaerated alveoli collapse, secretions accumulate, and atelectasis develops. Because coughing causes pain, the patient consciously reduces coughing and thus becomes less efficient in removing secretions. As a result, additional atelectasis develops, thereby setting up a vicious cycle, which, if uninterrupted, could lead to death. It is during the first few days after injury that the pain is most severe and the patient is at the greatest risk from respiratory complications. Although this sequence of events is unlikely to occur in young, healthy patients, it is imperative that rib fractures never be considered insignificant until proved so.

Almost all conscious and alert patients with rib fractures experience a pleuritic type of chest pain that is usually localized to the site of fracture. The pain is localized when one rib is fractured, but it may occur over a wide area when a number of ribs are fractured. The pain is aggravated by coughing, deep breathing, and motion. On physical examination, there is tenderness to palpation, and if displacement is present, bone crepitus may be felt.

The diagnosis is suggested by the history of trauma and the eliciting of pain on palpation and is confirmed by visualization of the fracture site on chest roentgenogram. Since anterior or lateral rib fractures may not be seen on a posteroanterior chest roentgenogram, it is best to obtain left anterior oblique and right anterior oblique views as well, so that all regions of the ribs may be visualized. In obese or thick-muscled patients, the Bucky technique may be necessary for adequate visualization. Serial chest roentgenograms should be obtained in all patients with rib fractures, since delayed pneumothorax or hemothorax may develop late after the initial injury because of trauma to the lung, parenchyma, or intercostal vessels by rib fragments.

When rib fractures are complicated by pneumothorax or hemothorax, these complications must be treated promptly, before treatment of the rib fractures. Treatment of rib fractures is dependent on the severity of the injury, the age of the patient, the presence of pre-existing lung disease, and the pain threshold of the patient. In the elderly patient, a rib fracture is a serious injury; these patients should be hospitalized regardless of the initial appearance. Similarly, patients with poor cardiovascular reserve or underlying chronic lung disease should be admitted, since the additional insult of the rib fracture may result in pulmonary or cardiac decompensation. In these elderly patients or in patients with pre-existing lung or cardiac disease, therapy should be instituted early and aggressively to prevent pulmonary complications. Narcotics should be given immediately to control pain and may be repeated as often as necessary. Large doses should be avoided because of the respiratory depressant effect. Intercostal nerve block that includes two nerves above and two below the fracture sites will relieve pain and permit the patient to ventilate and cough.

With adequate relief of pain, the patient can be made to cough and breathe deeply, and bronchial secretions can be effectively expelled, thereby minimizing the danger of developing atelectasis and pneumonia. Other helpful measures include intratracheal suctioning, ultrasonic nebulization by mist or by intermittent positive-pressure breathing (IPPV), and chest physical therapy. Since adhesive chest strapping decreases respiratory excursion bilaterally, it is indicated only in the simplest of injuries and in the healthiest of patients.

On occasion, patients with rib fractures have an associated small pleural effusion on the initial chest roentgenogram. A follow-up chest roentgenogram should be obtained within several days to ensure that a large effusion has not developed.

First Rib Fractures

The first rib, in its protected position low in the neck, is short, broad, flat, and relatively thick. Consequently, it requires an extremely violent force to be fractured. Major chest, abdominal, and cardiac injuries are infrequent, since the force needed to fracture the first rib is confined. However, *there is a high incidence of serious maxillofacial or neurologic injuries.* Injury to the subclavian artery and neck has been reported to occur in 5 to 15 per cent of patients with first rib fracture. The indications for arteriography in first rib fractures, whether isolated or not, should include patients with the following:

1. Absent or decreased upper extremity pulse
2. Evidence of brachial plexus injury
3. Marked displacement of fragments, especially if posterior

4. Altered serial chest roentgenograms (increased pleural cap or hemothorax)
5. Subclavian groove fracture (seen anteriorly)

There is no specific therapy for first rib fracture. The only significance of these fractures is to alert the physician to the possibility of associated intrathoracic and extrathoracic injuries, especially in the maxillofacial complex.

FRACTURED STERNUM

In this age of the steering wheel, fractures of the sternum are frequently seen. They occur most often in patients of more advanced age because in children and young adults the elasticity of the thoracic cage is such that the force of the impact can compress the sternum against the spinal column without breaking it. Nearly all the fractures occur in a transverse fashion, and most occur in the body of the sternum near its junction with the manubrium. Fractures of the xiphoid process rarely occur because of its protected position between the flare of the costal margins bilaterally. Severe trauma is usually necessary to produce a sternal fracture. The sternal fracture suggests that severe associated injuries might be present. Injuries associated with a fractured sternum include the following:

1. Flail chest
2. Pulmonary contusion
3. Ruptured bronchus
4. Hemothorax or pneumothorax
5. Hemopericardium
6. Lacerated pericardium
7. Myocardial contusion
8. Cardiac rupture
9. Ruptured thoracic aorta
10. Abdominal visceral injuries
11. Spinal injuries

The diagnosis is confirmed by visualization of the fracture site on only a lateral or an oblique chest roentgenogram. All patients with sternal fractures should be investigated for associated cardiac or other intrathoracic injuries. Surgical treatment of the sternal fracture should be delayed until evaluation and possible treatment of the associated injuries have been completed. Treatment of the sternal fractures is dependent on their severity, and in undisplaced fractures, treatment should be directed toward the relief of pain. Analgesics will usually suffice, but on occasion the injection of lidocaine or related compounds into and around the fracture site is needed for relief of pain. If pain cannot be relieved by these measures, operative stabilization should be performed. Open reduction and stabilization should be carried out on all patients with severely displaced fractures, especially those who also exhibit paradoxical motion. The mortality occurring with sternal fractures is directly attributable to the associated injuries and not to the fracture itself.

FLAIL CHEST

Flail chest usually results when there are multiple fractures in several ribs, with or without separation of the costochondral junction, or when rib fractures are associated with fracture of the sternum. As a result of the multiple fractures, the injured or damaged segment of the chest wall no longer maintains its continuity with the remainder of the chest wall and becomes flail. The flail portion of the chest wall is then subject to changes in intrathoracic pressure and begins to move independently of and in an opposite direction to the intact portion of the chest wall. The flail segment may occur in the lateral, anterior, or posterior portion of the chest. The lateral type of flail chest is the most frequent and is characterized by multiple fractures of two or more adjacent ribs in the anterolateral or posterolateral region of the chest. The anterior type of flail chest occurs when the ribs become separated at their costochondral junction, with or without an associated fracture of the sternum. The posterior type results when the ribs in the back of the chest are fractured; the unstable segment lies posteriorly. The paradoxical motion is usually slight because of the support supplied by the scapula and muscles in this region and because the excursion of the posterior rib is normally less than that of the anterior portion.

Because a great force is required to produce a crushing injury of the chest, associated intrathoracic and extrathoracic injuries are common. In Brewer's and Steiner's series,[3] extremity fractures occurred in 17 per cent of patients, abdominal injuries occurred in 21 per cent of patients, and neurologic injuries occurred in 21 per cent of patients. A similar incidence of associated injuries has been reported by other investigators. More important are the associated intrathoracic injuries: pulmonary contusion, pneumothorax, hemothorax, and hemopneumothorax. In Brewer's and Steiner's series of patients with crushing chest injuries,[3] pulmonary contusion, hemothorax, and pneumothorax occurred in 68, 49, and 33 per cent of patients, respectively. These associated injuries may make diagnosis and treatment more difficult and may increase the mortality as well.

Pathophysiology

The physiologic alterations that occur with flail chest result not only from the disruption in chest wall mechanics but also from the associated pulmonary injury as well. As a consequence of the chest wall injury, the bellows action of the muscles of the chest wall is reduced. During inspiration, the intact portion of the rib cage expands, drawing air into the lungs. However, the flail portion does not expand, since it is no longer in continuity with the normally expanded portion. Atmospheric pressure is exerted on the unstable segment, forcing it inward. This inward motion is enhanced by the gradient produced by the negative intrapleural pressure. A reverse relationship develops on expiration in that the intrathoracic pressure exceeds atmospheric pressure and the flail segment is pushed outward, while the remainder of the thorax contracts normally. Thus, the loss of the structural integrity of the thoracic cage does not permit sufficient negative intrapleural pressure dynamics, and in an attempt to overcome these abnormalities, respiratory work increases.

The associated pulmonary parenchymal injury produces additional physiologic derangements. As a result of the lung damage (contusion, atelectasis), there is a marked reduction in lung compliance, an increase in airway resistance, a decrease in pulmonary diffusion, and alterations in ventilation-perfusion ratios. These changes lead to an even further increase in respiratory work.

Diagnosis

Careful observation of the chest wall excursion will demonstrate the presence of paradoxical respiration. Excursions of the chest wall are best observed while standing by the patient's side. At times, paradoxical respiration can be demonstrated only by having the patient breathe deeply or cough.

In patients with the anterior type of crushing chest injury, the resultant breathing pattern is of the seesaw type; that is, when the chest wall sinks in, the abdominal wall goes up and vice versa. The paradoxical motion of the chest wall may not be seen initially, since the tissue swelling and chest wall hematoma may obscure its movement. In addition, paradoxical motion of the chest wall will not be seen if the patient does not breathe deeply enough to create an intrapleural atmospheric pressure gradient.

Paradoxical motion of the chest wall is most severe and leads to the worst physiologic consequences when multiple fractures occur anteriorly, especially with bilateral costochondral separations or fractures of the sternum. Posterior fractures produce less extensive paradoxical motion and rarely lead to serious physiologic consequences.

The chest roentgenogram is of limited value in establishing the presence of paradoxical respiration, but it is useful in demonstrating the presence of chest wall fractures, pulmonary contusion, atelectasis, hemothorax, or pneumothorax.

Arterial blood gas measurements are of value in estimating the severity of the patient's condition on admission, even in the absence of obvious symptoms. The measurements are also helpful in following the clinical course of the patient once therapy is instituted. As a general rule, most patients with flail chest will have a low Pa_{O_2} on admission (<80 mm Hg while breathing room air). A pH value in the range of 7.40 to 7.49 and a Pa_{CO_2} greater than 40 mm Hg indicate the presence of a more serious degree of hypoxia. Since hypoxia will stimulate compensatory hyperventilation, patients with serious degrees of hypoxia may have ABG values that show an alkalotic pH (7.50) and a low Pa_{CO_2} (<20 mm Hg) in addition to a low Pa_{O_2} (<60 mm Hg).

Treatment

The treatment of flail chest depends on the severity of the chest wall injury, the condition of the underlying lungs, and the degree of hypoxia. In patients with unilateral paradoxical motion, those with a small volume of chest wall paradox, mild-to-moderate pulmonary contusion, and a Pa_{O_2} greater than 60 mm Hg while breathing room air (or greater than 80 mm Hg while breathing supplemental oxygen), or with a tidal volume greater than 10 to 15 ml/kg of body weight, can be treated without mechanical ventilation. Instead, the treatment regimen is the same as that discussed for pulmonary contusion. Patients undergoing therapy in this manner should be observed carefully and followed with frequent measurements of ABG. If signs of ventilatory insufficiency develop, intubation with an endotracheal tube must be promptly carried out and mechanical support of ventilation instituted.

Patients who initially present with evidence of pulmonary insufficiency (a Pa_{O_2} less than 60 mm Hg while breathing room air or less than 75 mm Hg while breathing supplemental oxygen and a tidal volume less than 10 ml/kg), as well as severe bilateral paradoxical respiration, should be initially treated by endotracheal intubation and mechanical ventilatory support. Mechanical ventilation not only improves ventilation but also reduces the work of breathing, thereby relieving hypoxia and decreasing oxygen consumption and need.

The mortality from flail chest varies from 15 to 89 per cent in the literature. The mortality is directly related to the age of the patient, the severity of the injury, and the number of associated injuries. The mortality for patients under 30 years of age or for those whose sole injury is the flail chest is less than 3 per cent, whereas it approaches 40 per cent in those with head injuries and 50 to 60 per cent for those older than 60 years.

PNEUMOTHORAX

Pneumothorax is a common complication of nonpenetrating chest trauma. In the majority of patients the pneumothorax is unilateral, but in 10 to 15 per cent of cases, the pneumothorax may be bilateral. The majority are caused by automobile accidents, but pneumothorax may result from blast injuries, falls from heights, direct blows to the chest, and car-pedestrian collisions. When atmospheric air has direct access to the pleural cavities through the wound, the condition is a communicating pneumothorax, often called a "sucking" chest wound. When the integrity of the skin and chest wall remains intact and the atmospheric air has no direct access to the pleural cavity, the pneumothorax is termed noncommunicating or closed.

Closed or Noncommunicating Pneumothorax

Closed pneumothorax is most often caused by a fractured rib that is driven inward by the impact force and lacerates the lung. In general, this pneumothorax tends to be self-limiting because the resultant pulmonary collapse has a sealing effect. This is termed a *simple pneumothorax.*

However, at times the pulmonary collapse does not have a sealing effect. Air from the damaged lung is allowed to enter the pleural cavity. Since the air cannot escape from the pleural cavity, it tends to accumulate under pressure, producing a *tension pneumothorax.* Since the clinical presentation and management of simple pneumothorax and tension pneumothorax are dissimilar, these conditions will be discussed separately.

Simple Pneumothorax

Simple pneumothoraces are usually classified according to the volume of the hemithorax occupied by air and the degree of pulmonary collapse. A pneumothorax that occupies 15 per cent or less of the pleural cavity in association with minor degrees of collapse is classified as small, one that occupies between 15 and 60 per cent of the pleural cavity is classified as moderate, and one that occupies more than 60 per cent of the pleural cavity in association with almost complete collapse of the lung is classified as large. As a rule, only patients with moderate or large pneumothoraces are symptomatic. *However, it is important to remember that in some patients, especially those with pre-existing lung disease, a small pneumothorax may compromise pulmonary function sufficiently to cause symptoms.*

The most frequent symptoms in patients with moderate-to-severe pneumothorax are chest pain and shortness of breath. These symptoms occur about 50 per cent of the time. On physical examination, the breath sounds are distant or entirely absent over the involved hemithorax. At times, this finding may be difficult to interpret because pain and splinting prevent the patient from breathing deeply. Subcutaneous emphysema is present in about 25 per cent of the patients.

Diagnosis

The diagnosis of pneumothorax is suggested by the history and clinical findings and is confirmed by chest roentgenogram. A chest roentgenogram should be obtained at the earliest possible time to estimate the size of the pneumothorax, but it should not take precedence over initiation of emergency treatment.

Treatment

The treatment of closed pneumothorax is dependent on the volume of the pneumothorax, the degree of pulmonary collapse, the severity of the respiratory symptoms, the presence or absence of associated injuries, and the likelihood that a nonthoracic operation and general anesthesia may be necessary. Only those otherwise healthy patients whose pneumothorax is small, who are without respiratory symptoms, and in whom the likelihood of an operation is negligible can be treated without the insertion of a chest tube and by careful observation. Another chest roentgenogram should be obtained 6 to 8 hours after the patient's admission and daily thereafter until complete re-expansion of the lung has occurred. If the pneumothorax increases in size, a chest tube should be inserted. Generally, the lungs re-expand fully in 2 to 4 days and remain expanded.

The indications for closed-tube thoracostomy are as follows:

1. Pneumothorax of moderate to large size
2. Presence of respiratory symptoms, regardless of size of pneumothorax
3. Increase in size of pneumothorax that initially was treated conservatively
4. Recurrence of pneumothorax after initial chest tube was removed
5. Patient who requires ventilator support
6. Patient who is about to undergo general anesthesia
7. Associated hemothorax
8. Bilateral pneumothorax
9. Tension pneumothorax

Tension Pneumothorax

Patients with tension pneumothorax are acutely ill and in marked respiratory distress. They are restless, agitated, dyspneic, and at times cyanotic. On physical examination, the patients are hypotensive and have tachypnea and tachycardia. Breath sounds are absent over the involved hemithorax. *The cervical trachea is displaced toward the uninvolved side.*

The diagnosis is confirmed by chest roentgenogram, which demonstrates a large collection of air in the involved hemithorax, with a shift of the mediastinum toward the unaffected lung.

Tension pneumothorax is life threatening and demands immediate diagnosis and treatment. The treatment must strive to return the intrapleural pressures to atmospheric levels. If no other equipment is available, a large-bore (No. 15) needle can be inserted into the involved hemithorax through the second or third intercostal space to achieve partial decompression while preparations are made for closed-tube thoracostomy.

Open Pneumothorax

Open pneumothorax (sucking chest wound) that results from blunt chest trauma is associated with large defects in the chest wall. As a rule, the patients present with signs and symptoms of respiratory distress. During respiration, a sucking wound is often heard. Subcutaneous emphysema is often present and is usually extensive, spreading to involve both hemithoraces, the cervical region, the head, and the anterior abdominal wall.

Sucking wounds of the chest demand immediate surgical treatment. The patient should be intubated immediately and placed on a respirator, and the wound should be covered with sterile dressings. An intercostal chest tube should be inserted in an area removed from the injured area.

HEMOTHORAX

Like pneumothorax, hemothorax is a common sequela to blunt chest trauma and is usually unilateral. However, bilateral hemothoraces may occur in 10 to 20 per cent of victims of blunt chest trauma. The source of bleeding may be the lung, the heart, the great vessels and their branches, an intercostal artery or vein, the mediastinal veins, or the vessels of the diaphragm and chest wall. Bleeding from the lung may result if the broken end of a fractured rib is driven inward by the impact force and tears the lung. Compression injuries also can produce bleeding from the surface of the lung. Hemothorax may adversely affect the cardiovascular system. If the hemothorax is large, the hypovolemia will cause hypotension and decreased cardiac output. The decrease in cardiac output leads to the development of metabolic acidosis. The intrapleural accumulation of blood and air compresses the lung, thereby interfering with ventilation and causing hypoxia. If the intrapleural collection of blood is large, the mediastinum is shifted toward the uninvolved side and will cause compression of the uninvolved lung, further aggravating the ventilatory problems. The combination of hypovolemia and hypoxia is treacherous and is usually lethal unless corrected.

Diagnosis

If less than 400 ml of blood is lost, there may be little or no change in the patient's appearance and vital signs, and there may be no physical finding of intrapleural fluid present. With large losses (>1000 ml), the findings of internal hemorrhage are present—pallor, restlessness and anxious expression, tachycardia, and decreased or decreasing blood pressure. The patient may complain of dyspnea and a peculiar tightness in the chest. On chest roentgenogram, the pleural fluid is best visualized with the patient in the upright position.

Management

Although hemothoraces can be managed by repeated thoracentesis, they are best managed by the insertion of a large-bore (No. 32 or No. 36 Argyle) catheter. Tube thoracostomy allows constant monitoring of continued blood loss, as well as continued drainage for better re-expansion of the lung. The tube should be inserted through the fifth or sixth intercostal space in the midaxillary line, with the patient in the semi-upright position. Most patients with moderate hemothorax can be treated successfully with volume replacement and closed tube thoracostomy and will not need a thoracotomy. However, those patients with a massive hemothorax (>2000 ml) or those who continue to bleed should undergo an immediate operation for control of bleeding.

HEMOPNEUMOTHORAX

Patients with hemopneumothorax, as identified by air-fluid level on the chest roentgenogram, should have two chest tubes inserted: one through the fifth or sixth intercostal space at the midaxillary line and the other through the second or third intercostal space at the midclavicular line. Patients should be evaluated and treated as discussed in the sections on pneumothorax and hemothorax.

PULMONARY CONTUSION

Pulmonary contusion is defined as damage to the lung parenchyma that results in hemorrhage and edema without accompanying pulmonary laceration. It is a common finding in patients who have sustained blunt chest trauma. The incidence in victims of nonpenetrating chest trauma varies between 30 and 75 per cent. Although often mild and frequently masked by other more dramatic injuries, as well as being associated with multiple injuries, pulmonary contusion deserves special consideration in the management of *any* patient with blunt chest trauma because it is now well recognized that when undiagnosed and consequently untreated it is frequently progressive and may be fatal because of respiratory insufficiency. Pulmonary contusion has played a major role in 25 per cent of the deaths resulting from chest injuries sustained in automobile accidents.

Most of the victims of automobile accidents sustain the pulmonary contusion when their chest strikes the steering wheel. The precise pathogenesis of pulmonary injury in these patients is unknown, but most believe it is analogous to the mechanism thought to operate in a blast injury — a forceful high-pressure wave that compresses the thoracic cavity. The force is also transmitted to the lung by virtue of its continuity with the tissues of the chest wall. The increase in intrathoracic pressure compresses the lung by diminishing the size of the thorax and results in parenchymal hemorrhage and edema. When the force of compression is removed, decompression occurs and the distorted thorax springs back, creating an instant of negative intrathoracic pressure that leads to additional injury in the areas ruptured during compression.

Among the factors that influence the severity of the lesions produced are the amount of padding on the chest wall and the flexibility of the chest. Obese patients do not sustain as severe a pulmonary contusion as asthenic patients. If the ribs are sufficiently elastic, severe compression of the lung can occur without a break in the costal cage. Some of the most severe pulmonary contusions we have seen have occurred in patients who exhibited no rib fractures or discontinuity in the chest cage.

Pulmonary contusion is frequently associated with multiple injuries and is often subjected to incidental resuscitative measures, such as the administration of large volumes of fluid, that are directed at other injuries. The rapid administration of large volumes of noncolloidal fluid has been shown in both experimental and clinical studies to have an adverse effect on the already damaged lung.

The pathophysiology of untreated pulmonary contusion can be succinctly summarized in Figure 8–1.

Treatment

It should be emphasized that the keys to successful management of patients with pulmonary contusion are as follows:

1.   Early and vigorous therapy, as the first 24 hours of treatment are by far the most important

2.   Restoration and maintenance of oxygenation while avoiding resuscitative measures that might aggravate the pulmonary contusion

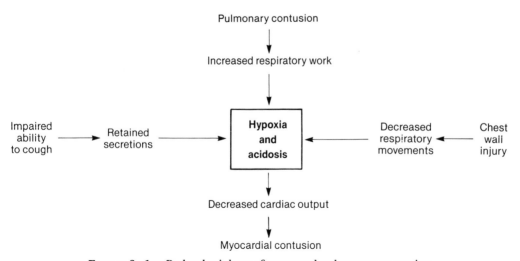

FIGURE 8–1.   Pathophysiology of untreated pulmonary contusion.

3. Good tracheobronchial care, including intratracheal suction and physical therapy

The following steps should be taken in the treatment of pulmonary contusion.

1. A percutaneous radial artery catheter should be inserted for frequent blood gas determination, and a Swan-Ganz catheter should be inserted to monitor filling pressures and cardiac output.

2. Crystalloid solution should be restricted to 1000 to 1500 ml during resuscitation and 50 ml/hr thereafter.

3. To decrease excess fluid within the lung, 40 mg of furosemide should be administered immediately and 20 mg every 6 to 12 hours until no longer needed.

4. Serum pressure is maintained by infusing albumin (25 g/L of fluid) at 50 ml/hr for 48 to 72 hours.

5. Since large doses of steroids have been shown to reduce the size of experimentally induced pulmonary contusion by lysosomal stabilization of the cell wall and by decreasing capillary permeability, methylprednisolone (30 mg/kg of body weight) should be administered immediately and in divided doses thereafter for 2 to 4 days.

6. A nasogastric tube should be inserted and connected with low suction.

7. Adequate relief of pain is obtained by the use of small, frequent doses of narcotics or intercostal nerve blocks.

8. Since the damaged lung is susceptible to infection, broad-spectrum antibiotics should be administered. Cultures of the sputum should be obtained periodically and antibiotics altered accordingly.

9. If the patient is not intubated, Pa_{O_2} is maintained above 60 mm Hg by administering oxygen by mask or nasal cannula. Sterile techniques must be employed during endotracheal suctioning. Ultrasonic nebulization by mist or IPPV with bronchodilators such as aminophylline should be used when there is evidence of bronchospasm.

10. Indications for ventilator support by means of an endotracheal tube are listed in Table 8–1. The lowest FI_{O_2} should be used to maintain Pa_{O_2} at 60 mm Hg. Positive end-expiratory pressure (PEEP) should be used if a Pa_{O_2} of at least 60 mm Hg on an FI_{O_2} of 0.6 cannot be maintained. The hematocrit should be kept between 40 and 45 per cent by transfusions of whole blood or packed red blood cells. Bank blood contains a reduced amount of 2,3-diphosphoglycerate; consequently, the ability of hemoglobin to release oxygen is decreased. Therefore, freshly drawn blood or packed red blood cells should be used to increase the oxygen-carrying capacity of blood.

11. The pH should be maintained between 7.35 and 7.45, since an alkaline pH may shift the oxygen dissociation curve to the left and reduce the ability of hemoglobin to release oxygen.

TABLE 8–1.   INDICATIONS FOR RESPIRATOR SUPPORT

FUNCTION	VALUE
Mechanics	
Respiratory rate (per min)	>35
Vital capacity (ml/kg body weight)	<15
FEV_1 (ml/kg body weight)	<10
Inspiratory force (cm H_2O)	<−25
Oxygenation	
Pa_{O_2} (mm Hg)	<60 (supplemented with O_2)
A-aDo_2 (mm Hg)	>450 (on 100% O_2)
Ventilation	
Pa_{CO_2} (mm Hg)	>55
Vd/V_T	>0.60

FEV_1 = forced expiratory volume in one second; Vd = volume dead air space; V_T = tidal volume.

12. A significant contribution to the demise of many severely injured patients today is inadequate nutritional support. In patients with major chest injury, the impairment of host defenses secondary to malnutrition, with subsequent sepsis and death, becomes a major concern. These patients often have associated injuries that limit mobilization, create increased metabolic demands, and compromise the mode of enteral alimentation. Combinations of alimentation utilizing peripheral, enteral, and central routes are all employed early to stop catabolism. Immediately after these patients are resuscitated, attention must be directed to providing nutritional support to avoid the complications of sepsis and multisystem failure.

The course of pulmonary contusion is determined by the severity of the initial injury. In patients with mild pulmonary contusion who do not require ventilatory support, the course of the illness is characterized by rapid resolution within 72 hours. In patients who require ventilatory support, there is gradual improvement, with the patient being able to be weaned from the ventilator by 12 to 14 days. In any patient with a pulmonary contusion in whom clinical improvement is delayed, one should suspect a superimposed complication, such as pneumonia, fat embolism, or pulmonary embolism. Despite optimal therapy, approximately 15 per cent of patients with pulmonary contusion die of progressive respiratory insufficiency.

CERVICAL TRACHEAL DISRUPTION

Cervical tracheal injuries are caused by direct trauma to the cervical area. The automobile passenger who sits beside the driver is especially prone to develop such an injury when the accident occurs. A woman with a long, supple neck suffers supraglottic injuries, whereas a man with a normal or short neck is often injured subglottically. These injuries are referred to as the padded dashboard syndrome. Rupture of the cervical trachea may occur without any external evidence of trauma. A variety of symptoms of cervical trachea disruption have been reported. They include subcutaneous emphysema, inspiratory stridor, hoarseness, hemoptysis, dyspnea, coughing, localized pain or tenderness, and even cyanosis. The most uniform early sign is subcutaneous emphysema that develops rapidly and spreads extensively over the anterior chest wall and anterior aspect of the neck. Pneumothorax is a common complication but is usually minimal and responds promptly to intercostal tube insertion.

Disruption of the cervical trachea must always be considered in any victim of blunt chest trauma and manifests respiratory distress in association with extensive cervical and anterior chest wall subcutaneous emphysema. If a ruptured cervical trachea is suspected, the correct initial emergency management is to perform a tracheostomy. As soon as the patient's airway is established and his or her condition stabilized, the tracheal disruption should be repaired. Associated injuries to the cervical spine, esophagus, and great vessels in the neck must be ruled out, especially if there is a cervical hematoma present. Prior to removal of the tracheostomy tube, the functional status of the vocal cords as well as the presence of a previously unrecognized laryngeal fracture should be determined.

RUPTURE OF THE AORTA

The patient with a suspected thoracic vascular injury should be *immediately* evaluated by a thoracic surgeon. That anyone survives traumatic rupture of the aorta is almost unbelievable. However, 10 to 20 per cent of persons who have sustained a traumatic rupture of the aorta reach the hospital alive because the aortic blood is contained temporarily by the adventitia or mediastinal pleura. Left untreated, this thin-walled false aneurysm follows an unpredictable course but usually ruptures within 3 weeks after the injury. To prevent this catastrophic outcome, it is imperative that the diagnosis be established quickly, so that appropriate therapy can be carried out.

Traumatic rupture of the thoracic aorta can be caused by one of the following mechanisms:

1. Horizontal deceleration with or without chest compression, such as occurs in motorcycle or automobile collisions
2. Marked compression of the chest, such as occurs when a person is run over by a car or kicked in the chest by an animal
3. Vertical deceleration, such as occurs when a person falls from a great height or is struck by a car
4. Crushing injuries that involve some flexion to the spine

The more frequent sites of rupture of the thoracic aorta are as follows:

1. The descending aorta just distal to the origin of the left subclavian artery (aortic isthmus).
2. The ascending aorta proximal to the origin of the innominate artery
3. The origin of the innominate artery from the aortic arch

Other sites of involvement include the distal descending aorta at the aortic hiatus in the diaphragm, the midportion of the descending aorta, and the left subclavian artery.

INJURIES OF THE DESCENDING THORACIC AORTA

The single most important factor in establishing the diagnosis of acute traumatic aortic rupture is maintenance of a high index of suspicion and a constant awareness of the likelihood of this lesion in anyone who has sustained an accident characterized by sudden deceleration, regardless of whether or not there is external evidence of chest injuries. One third of the patients will have no external evidence of thoracic injury at the time of the initial physical examination. Despite the severe nature of the injury, the clinical findings are usually deceptively meager. Those of importance are the acute onset of upper extremity hypertension, especially if coupled with evidence of massive blood loss; the presence of a harsh systolic murmur heard over the precordium or posterior intercapsular area; and a difference in blood pressure between the upper and lower extremities. These findings, either alone or in combination, will occur in one third of patients with aortic rupture.

Other clues seen during the physical examination that should prompt suspicion of thoracic vascular trauma include (1) steering wheel imprint on the chest; (2) palpable fracture of the sternum, scapula, or both; and (3) massive hemothorax.

Radiography of the chest is invaluable in arousing suspicion of aortic rupture. Radiographic features suggestive but not diagnostic of intrathoracic vascular injuries are listed in Table 8–2.

Traumatic rupture of the aorta may occur in patients with a normal chest roentgenogram. In addition, the location of the aortic rupture cannot be determined by the plain chest roentgenographic findings. The only definitive means for establishing the diagnosis of acute aortic rupture is aortography. It is the "gold standard" for evaluating thoracic vascular injuries. The use of computerized tomography (CT) and magnetic resonance imaging (MRI) is currently *not* recommended. Aortography should be performed on any patient who has sustained a high-speed deceleration injury or blunt trauma to the chest, whether or not there is external or radiographic evidence of thoracic wall injuries, clinical findings suggesting aortic rupture, and changes in the serial chest roentgenograms. The following list summarizes the indications for aortography in victims of blunt chest trauma.

1. History of deceleration injury

TABLE 8-2.   RADIOLOGIC CLUES SUGGESTIVE OF THORACIC VASCULAR INJURY

Widening (>8 cm) of the upper mediastinum
Loss of aortic knob contour
Left apical pleural hematoma cap
Fractured sternum and/or scapula
Fractured first and/or second rib
Hematoma of thoracic outlet
Massive left hemothorax
Depression of the left mainstem bronchus more than 140 degrees from the trachea
Calcium layering in the aortic knob (double shadow sign)
Loss of aortopulmonary window on lateral chest film
Anterior displacement of the trachea on lateral chest film
Fracture-dislocation of the thoracic spine on lateral chest film
Deviation of the trachea to the side opposite the mediastinal hematoma
Deviation of the nasogastric tube in the esophagus away from the midline
Obliteration of the aortopulmonary window on lateral chest film

2.   Any of the chest roentgenographic findings listed in Table 8-2
3.   Massive hemothorax
4.   Pulse deficits
5.   Upper extremity hypertension
6.   Systolic murmur
7.   Unexplained hypotension

Because lethal secondary rupture of the false aneurysm is likely, immediate surgical repair should be done as soon as the diagnosis is established and the site of rupture localized. Aortography should always precede thoracotomy unless contraindicated by rapid deterioration of the patient's condition. In patients with multiple injuries, a brief delay in establishing management priorities is advisable. The decision of whether to treat the major associated injuries (celiotomy) first or to repair the aortic rupture first must fit the circumstances. Initially in our experience, treatment of the coexisting abdominal injuries was carried out prior to thoracotomy in six patients, five of whom exsanguinated before thoracotomy could be performed. In addition, six other patients died because repair of the aortic rupture was delayed for various reasons. This experience, as well as the fact that the untreated aortic rupture follows such an unpredictable course, has led us to recommend that aside from rapidly progressing craniocerebral injuries, such as epidural hemorrhage, or massive intra-abdominal bleeding, traumatic rupture of the aorta deserves the highest priority and thus that its repair be carried out first.

When repair of the aortic rupture must be delayed because another operation is needed or because the condition of the patient (severe closed-head injury) makes thoracotomy inadvisable, patients should be managed like those with spontaneous aortic dissection. The systolic blood pressure should be maintained below 120 mm Hg with guanethidine and reserpine, in conjunction with propranolol. These drugs lower the blood pressure and decrease the force of contraction of the heart, which reduces the "shearing jet effect" of the pulse and decreases the possibility of aortic rupture.

INNOMINATE ARTERY INJURY

In cases in which the patient survives long enough for diagnosis and repair, avulsion of the innominate artery from the aortic arch is found to be second in frequency only to rupture of the aorta at the aortic isthmus. Associated injuries, such as rib fractures, flail chest, hemopneumothorax, fractured extremities, head injuries, facial fractures, and abdominal injuries, occur alone or in combination in more than 75 per cent of patients.

The diagnosis may be difficult, since there are no characteristic physical findings. Diminution of the radial or brachial pulse occurs in about 50 per cent of patients with innominate artery avulsion and may be the only clue to the diagnosis. Signs and symptoms of distal ischemia are uncommon and cannot be relied on to draw attention to the injury.

The chest roentgenographic findings are usually no different from those in descending aortic rupture. Aortography must be performed for the diagnosis to be established.

Because of the ever-present danger of sudden cataclysmic hemorrhage from secondary rupture of the pseudoaneurysm, the treatment is immediate surgical repair.

SUBCLAVIAN ARTERY INJURY

Although most subclavian artery ruptures result from deceleration types of injuries, an occasional rupture has occurred from impingement of a fractured first rib or clavicle on the vessel. Clinically, the cardinal sign is absence of a radial pulse in association with signs and symptoms of distal ischemia. However, this sign is present only in patients with associated thrombotic occlusion of the artery. In patients with partial lacerations and without thrombotic occlusion, the radial pulse will be palpable because of continuous flow through the injured vessel. The chest roentgenogram shows the presence of a widened superior mediastinum without obscuration of the aortic knob shadow. Accurate diagnosis of the injury requires aortography. Treatment of acute subclavian artery rupture is immediate surgical repair.

CLOSED INJURIES OF THE HEART

Cardiac involvement in nonpenetrating trauma probably occurs more often than realized. The incidence of cardiac injuries in postmortem examination and clinical series ranges from 10 to 75 per cent. This figure would indicate that there are 200,000 or more cardiac injuries yearly. The spectrum of cardiac injuries varies from rapidly fatal cardiac rupture to asymptomatic lesions that are detectable only by serial electrocardiograms. Acute heart lesions include contusion; transmural myocardial necrosis; and laceration or rupture of the pericardium, myocardium, cardiac chambers, and cardiac valves. The superficial location of the heart directly behind the sternum allows serious damage to be transmitted to the heart from an external blow. Cardiac injuries may also occur when a fragment of the fractured bony chest wall is driven into the heart.

The following list summarizes clues to cardiac injury.

1. Bruise on sternum
2. Fractured sternum
3. Cyanosis of upper half of body
4. Unexplained hypotension
5. Massive hemothorax
6. Pericardial tamponade
7. Atrial or ventricular arrhythmias
8. Electrocardiographic evidence of myocardial ischemia or infarction
9. New cardiac murmurs
10. Muffled heart tones

MYOCARDIAL CONTUSION

Because a myocardial contusion is almost always well tolerated and because the clinical signs are transient and difficult to recognize and may vary widely in severity or may occur without external evidence of chest injury, the exact incidence of myocardial contusion is difficult to determine. It is estimated to occur in 20 per cent of victims of blunt chest trauma. The most frequent cause of contusion by far is the steering wheel injury from sudden automobile deceleration. It has also been reported to occur from blows to the chest, falls from great heights, and upper abdominal trauma.

Diagnosis

Symptoms of cardiac contusion may be absent or masked by other severe injuries. The clinical and diagnostic features of myocardial contusion are similar to those of myocardial infarction. The most common symptom, occurring in 70 per cent of patients with myocardial contusion, is precordial pain. This pain is identical in location, intensity, character, and radiation with that of myocardial ischemia or infarction but usually cannot be relieved by coronary vasodilating agents. Although the majority of patients have associated chest wall injuries, the pain of myocardial contusion is generally distinguishable from the musculoskeletal pain. The precordial pain may be immediate in onset or delayed for hours or days following injury.

In the absence of complications such as pericardial tamponade, ventricular arrhythmias, or congestive heart failure, the physical findings are few, and the diagnosis of myocardial contusion is rarely obvious on physical examination. The most frequently encountered physical finding is tachycardia, especially in a patient with relatively insignificant injuries. An additional finding that would lead one to suspect the existence of myocardial contusion or other cardiac injury is the presence of a bruise of any size over the sternum.

The electrocardiogram is the most reliable method of establishing the diagnosis of myocardial contusion in patients with thoracic injuries, regardless of whether or not symptoms are present. The incidence of electrocardiographic evidence of cardiac injury after blunt chest trauma varies from 18 to 38 per cent. Although the electrocardiographic changes are frequently present at the time of the patient's arrival in the emergency room (or shortly thereafter), they may not appear until 24 to 72 hours later. Thus, serial electrocardiograms should always be made at 24-hour intervals. The most frequent electrocardiographic findings are ST segment and T wave changes similar to those observed in myocardial ischemia and infarction. These electrocardiographic changes are usually reversible, but they may be observed for as long as a month following injury.

Cardiac arrhythmias are another frequent electrocardiographic finding stemming from myocardial contusion. A great variety of arrhythmias and conduction disturbances have been reported. They include atrial fibrillation, atrial flutter, supraventricular tachycardia, ventricular tachycardia, ventricular fibrillation, asystole, right and left bundle branch block, sinoatrial block, and complete heart block.

Serum enzyme determinations (serum glutamic-oxaloacetic transaminase, lactic dehydrogenase, and creatine phosphokinase) are of no value in establishing the diagnosis of myocardial contusion because the levels are usually elevated as a result of the associated musculoskeletal injuries.

Radionuclide imaging with ^{99m}Tc-Sn polyphosphate and echocardiography have been found to be of little value in establishing the diagnosis of cardiac contusion and should not be performed routinely in patients with nonpenetrating chest trauma.

The diagnosis of myocardial contusion is made easily in young patients who have no past history of cardiac difficulties and who, after sustaining blunt trauma to the chest, have precordial pain, tachycardia, arrhythmias, and electrocardiographic changes characteristic of myocardial ischemia or infarction. In older patients, particularly if there is a history of pre-existing cardiac disease, the diagnosis of myocardial contusion may be more difficult, especially since myocardial contusion may aggravate the pre-existing disease.

Myocardial contusion should be strongly suspected in any patient with a reported or suspected history of nonpenetrating trauma to the chest in whom, within a short time, signs and symptoms of cardiac disability develop, accompanied by electrocardiographic abnormalities. It is the responsibility of the physician who evaluates such a patient to keep the possibility of myocardial contusion always in mind.

Treatment

The majority of patients with cardiac contusion have a good prognosis, and those who die usually do so because of other injuries. However, in approximately 20 per cent of patients with cardiac contusion a decrease in cardiac output may develop. Because of this, as well as the fact that the damaged area may serve as a focus of electrical instability, general anesthetics should be avoided whenever possible in the period immediately following injury. If an operation is deemed necessary, the risk must be assumed.

Monitoring of the central venous pressure or the pulmonary capillary wedge pressure with a Swan-Ganz catheter is of great value in these patients. Serial cardiac output determinations using thermodilution techniques are of inestimable value. The potential for these patients to develop arrhythmias dictates the need for continuous and careful electrocardiographic monitoring. Patients should receive a continuous infusion of lidocaine (2 to 3 mg/kg of body weight per hour) during the operation and for 48 to 72 hours postoperatively.

It is important to remember that hypotension in these patients may be due to pump failure and not necessarily to hypovolemia. However, procedures that are not urgent should be delayed until there is electrocardiographic evidence of complete healing or stabilization of the myocardial damage, which usually takes anywhere from 2 to 6 weeks.

PERICARDIAL TAMPONADE

Hemopericardium with acute tamponade is usually due to a severe cardiac injury, such as laceration of one of the coronary arteries; to extensive myocardial laceration; or to cardiac rupture. The tamponade temporarily causes a reduction or cessation of hemorrhage from the cardiac wound. Because an intact pericardium is an inelastic structure, there is a limit (150 to 200 ml) to the amount of blood that can accumulate rapidly before marked depression of cardiac function occurs. The primary compensatory mechanisms are as follows:

1. Peripheral vasoconstriction raises arterial blood pressure.
2. Tachycardia increases cardiac output in the presence of a reduced stroke volume by multiplying the number of strokes per minute.
3. Increased venous pressure supports cardiac filling by maintaining the venoatrial gradients and is itself the result of redistribution of the arterial blood into the venous system by vasoconstriction.

The compensatory mechanisms are initially effective in supporting the circulatory functions, but eventually they fail if the tamponade is unrelieved, leading to the death of the patient.

Diagnosis

Acute cardiac tamponade is difficult to recognize in patients with nonpenetrating chest injuries because of the coexisting thoracic, abdominal, or cerebral injuries.

The arterial hypotension, peripheral vasoconstriction, and tachycardia that are invariably present are often attributed to peripheral blood loss, and cardiac tamponade is overlooked.

Patients with cardiac tamponade are, as a rule, restless and agitated and complain of air hunger. The pulse pressure is narrow, and the pulse is barely palpable. A pulseless patient may be conscious with tamponade. Cyanosis of the upper half of the body is a frequent finding. The classic triad of cardiac tamponade consists of elevated central venous pressure, muffled heart tones, and paradoxical arterial pulse pressure. Although one or more of these may exist in patients with tamponade, the complete triad is rarely present, as cardiac tamponade can occur with normal heart tones. A finding that is highly suggestive of acute cardiac tamponade is the presence of distended and pulsating cervical veins when the patient is in an upright position. As a rule, the cardiac silhouette is not enlarged in acute tamponade, since the production of tamponade is dependent on the rapidity of its formation rather than on the amount of blood. Low voltage is characteristically present in the electrocardiogram.

The diagnosis of acute cardiac tamponade requires a high index of suspicion. It should be considered in every patient who has sustained blunt trauma to the chest, especially if the circulatory collapse is out of proportion to the severity of the wound and the amount of blood loss. It should also be considered in every patient who is first seen with or who develops an elevated central venous pressure (> 15 cm H_2O) or pulsating, distended neck veins when he or she is in the upright position. If the diagnosis is suspected, immediate pericardiocentesis should be performed, using the subxiphoid approach, with the patient in the upright position. Once the diagnosis of cardiac tamponade secondary to nonpenetrating trauma is established, the patient should undergo immediate thoracotomy, with control of the source of hemorrhage and complete decompression of the pericardium.

REFERENCES

1. Appelbaum A, Karp RB, Kirklin JW: Surgical treatment for closed thoracic aortic injuries. J Thorac Cardiovasc Surg 71:458, 1976.
2. Avery EE, Morch ET, Benson DW: Critically crushed chests: A new method of treatment with continuous mechanical hyperventilation to produce alkalotic apnea and internal pneumatic stabilization. J Thorac Surg 32:291, 1956.
3. Brewer L, Steiner L: The management of crushing injuries of the chest. Surg Clin North Am 48:1279, 1968.
4. Fulton R, Peter E: Physiologic effects of fluid therapy after pulmonary contusion. Am J Surg 126:773, 1973.
5. Franz J, Richardson JD, Grover FL, Trinkle JK: Effect of methylprednisolone sodium succinate on experimental pulmonary contusion. J Thorac Cardiovasc Surg 68:842, 1974.
6. Garzon A, Seltzer B, Karlson E: Pathophysiology of crushed chest injuries. Ann Surg 168:128, 1969.
7. Grover FL, Ellestad C, Arom K, et al: Diagnosis and management of major tracheobronchial injuries. Ann Thorac Surg 28:384, 1979.
8. Gundry SR, Wilton G, Burney R, et al: Double-blind assessment of mediastinal widening and its role in predicting aortic rupture in trauma patients. J Trauma 23:293, 1983.
9. Hankins JR, Shen B, McAslan T, et al: Management of flail chest: An analysis of 99 cases. Am Surg 45:176, 1979.
10. Kirsh MM, Sloan H (eds): Blunt Chest Trauma — General Principles of Management. Boston, Little, Brown, and Company, 1977.
11. Kirsh MM, Orringer MB, Behrendt DB, Sloan H: Management of tracheobronchial disruption secondary to nonpenetrating trauma. Ann Thorac Surg 22:93, 1976.
12. Kirsh MM, Behrendt DB, Orringer MB, et al: The treatment of acute traumatic rupture of the aorta — ten year experience. Ann Surg 184:308, 1976.
13. Moore BP: Operative stabilization of nonpenetrating chest injuries. J Thorac Cardiovasc Surg 70:619, 1975.
14. Orringer MB, Kirsh MM: Primary repair of acute traumatic aortic disruption. Ann Thorac Surg 35:672, 1983.
15. Phillips EH, Rogers WF, Gaspar MR: First rib fracture: Incidence of vascular injury and indications for angiography. Surgery 89:42, 1981.
16. Trinkle J, Furman RW, Hinshaw M, et al: Pulmonary contusion — pathogenesis and effect of various resuscitative measures. Ann Thorac Surg 16:568, 1973.
17. Trinkle JK, Richardson J, Franz JL, et al: Management of flail chest without mechanical ventilation. Ann Thorac Surg 19:355, 1975.
18. Wise A, Topuzlu C, Mills E, Page HG: The importance of serial blood gas determinations in blunt chest trauma. J Thorac Cardiovasc Surg 56:520, 1968.
19. Yee ES, Thomas AN, Goodman PC: Isolated first rib fracture: Clinical significance after blunt chest trauma. Ann Thorac Surg 32:278, 1981.
20. Zuckerman S: Experimental study of blunt injuries to the lung. Lancet 2:219, 1940.

CHAPTER 9

ABDOMINAL EVALUATION AND MANAGEMENT

RICHARD E. BURNEY, M.D., F.A.C.S.

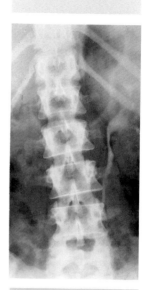

Although maxillofacial injury and abdominal injury are not generally thought to be associated, they coexist with sufficient frequency that a general knowledge of the mechanisms of abdominal injury, clinical findings, methods of diagnosis, and principles of management merit review. The purpose of this chapter is to highlight important aspects in each of these areas. No attempt is made to provide detailed information, as several recent comprehensive texts are available for those who are interested in pursuing this subject further.[1-3]

Unless the airway is compromised or exsanguinating hemorrhage from facial injury is present, the diagnosis and treatment of abdominal injury will ordinarily assume a higher priority in the management of the injured patient than will evaluation of maxillofacial injury. The surgeon called to assess maxillofacial injuries in a patient with multiple injuries should inform himself or herself about the mechanism of injury, the possibility of abdominal injury, and the status of the evaluation of this possibility before permitting others to proceed with a treatment plan that might involve lengthy radiographic or operative procedures that would remove the patient from frequent monitoring of vital signs or delay abdominal diagnostic procedures indicated on the basis of history or clinical findings.

MECHANISMS OF INJURY

Abdominal injury is of concern when the mechanism of injury involves the delivery of mechanical energy in any form to the torso of the body. The most common causes of such injury in the United States include motor vehicle accident, pedestrian-vehicle accident, motorcycle or bicycle accident, falls, shootings and firearm accidents, and assaults.[4] Specific information about the circumstances of the accident, the environment in which it occurred, and the speed or distance involved is important in determining the likelihood of significant injury. The larger the forces in play, or the greater the speed, the more likely it is that major injury has occurred. Concentration of force, as when the chest strikes a steering wheel or the abdomen a handle-bar, will also increase the probability of injury. When forces are concentrated on a specific area of the abdomen or flank, the underlying organs are those most at risk. When force is distributed widely, as in a fall or ejection from a moving vehicle, all organs are at risk. Conversely, the greater the surface over which energy is dissipated, or the longer the distance over which deceleration can occur, the less likely it is that injury will result.

Notwithstanding these general statements about causation of injury, the specific biomechanics of intra-abdominal injury have not been well characterized, and what information is available derives more from clinical description and anecdote than from scientific study. A recent book on the biomechanics of human trauma by leaders in the field, for example, does not contain a chapter on abdominal trauma, exemplifying the lack of basic scientific information in this area.[5]

Blunt Abdominal Injury

It is useful to consider blunt abdominal trauma in terms of injury to solid organs, to hollow viscera, and to supporting or surrounding structures.

SOLID ORGANS

The large solid organs of the abdominal cavity—the liver, spleen, and kidney—consist of soft vascular parenchyma surrounded, contained, and protected by a fibrous capsule of varying strength. Injury results from the direct application of forces that tear the capsule or disrupt the underlying parenchyma or both. Force may be transmitted as a direct blow or a shear stress. The liver is so large that it is at risk almost regardless of the direction of the force. The kidney is most susceptible to lateral or flank blows or falls. Parenchymal fracture may be simple and linear, or stellate and complex, depending upon the direction and force of the blow.

The immediate threat from solid organ injury is hemorrhage into adjacent cavities or tissues, leading to clinical hypotension or shock within minutes to hours after injury. This hemorrhage occurs more often from hepatic and splenic injury than renal. In the liver, hemorrhage results from the tearing of large hepatic veins; in the spleen, it results from the disruption of splenic sinuses. Parenchymal dysfunction may occur later, related as much to ischemia as to direct injury, but it is not usually life threatening if the initial hemorrhage is controlled and prolonged hypotension is avoided.

The pancreas is an exception to this pattern, because it is not as firmly encapsulated and lies in direct continuity with the duodenum. Injuries in this area result from direct compression of the pancreas against the lumbar spine. These can be isolated to the pancreas or can involve both pancreas and duodenum. Illness and complications associated with isolated pancreatic injury result from enzyme release more than from hemorrhage and vary with the extent of parenchymal damage and pancreatic ductal disruption, from minor inflammation to life-threatening pseudocyst or abscess when unrecognized and untreated. Injuries to the pancreatic head, duodenum, or both, can also be complex and life threatening, particularly if associated with duodenal perforation, because the combination of enzyme release, hemorrhage, and spillage of intestinal contents predisposes to shock, peritonitis, abscess, and fistula formation.

HOLLOW VISCERA

Bowel perforation as a result of blunt abdominal trauma is far less common than solid organ injury and occurs in perhaps 1 to 3 per cent of patients with serious abdominal injury. Duodenum, proximal jejunum, and distal ileum are the most common sites of traumatic intestinal perforation, followed by colon.[6] Perforation of esophagus and stomach occurs rarely. The exact mechanism is unknown, but direct compression of a portion of the bowel that is relatively fixed by a short mesentery against a solid support such as the lumbar spine, causing a blow-out, is the most commonly cited hypothesis. Significant hemorrhage is uncommon; isolated bowel injury can occur with almost no accompanying bleeding.

Bowel perforation leads to the spillage of intestinal contents and to peritonitis, which may not become clinically evident until 12 to 24 hours after surgery.[7] In animal models, the farther distal in the gastrointestinal tract the perforation occurs, the higher the bacterial content and the more rapidly peritonitis is likely to occur.

Perforation of the urinary bladder occurs either from direct force applied against a distended bladder or from the action of sharp fragments of adjacent fractured pubic rami. Extravasation of urine can be either intraperitoneal or extraperitoneal. If the urine is uninfected, there are few obvious consequences of this other than hematuria, at least initially.

SUPPORTING STRUCTURES

Supporting structures of the abdominal viscera include the diaphragm, the bowel mesentery and supporting vascular structures, and the retroperitoneal soft tissues.

Injury to the diaphragm requires tremendously high forces and almost always occurs in association with other serious injuries. Blunt lateral impact is more likely to cause diaphragmatic rupture than is frontal impact, although rupture can occur after either if the force is great enough (PA Kearney and associates, unpublished observations). Possible mechanisms of diaphragmatic rupture include deformation of the chest wall, stretching and tearing the diaphragm, and direct pressure of displaced viscera acting hydraulically, and these may be different for lateral and frontal impacts. The left side of the diaphragm is injured more frequently than the right for reasons that may relate both to the likelihood of impact on that side and to protection of the right side of the diaphragm by the liver (PA Kearney and associates, unpublished observations). Diaphragmatic rupture on the left can lead rapidly to respiratory distress as abdominal viscera translocate into the pleural space, compromising cardiorespiratory function.

Injury to other supporting structures results from direct application of force and leads to hemorrhage as the primary consequence. Retroperitoneal soft tissue injury, particularly in association with unstable pelvic fracture, can result in massive hemorrhage. Avulsion or laceration of the bowel mesentery, on the other hand, is a source of intraperitoneal hemorrhage that can be severe but is more frequently self-limited. Bowel ischemia can result but is rare unless the mesenteric injury is extensive, because of the normally rich mesenteric collateral blood supply.

Penetrating Trauma

Penetrating trauma occurring anywhere from the nipples to the groin or buttock creases can cause abdominal injury. The trajectory of missiles or knife blades is not always predictable, and one should never assume that such an injury, particularly a gunshot wound, has not caused intraperitoneal injury but should always seek direct evidence. The mechanism of damage is direct penetration of solid organs or perforation of arteries, veins, hollow viscera, or supporting structures. The primary concern is major vascular disruption leading to life-threatening hemorrhage or organ ischemia.[8] The secondary concern is gastrointestinal or urinary tract perforation leading to peritonitis. Penetrating trauma is more likely to cause injury to multiple organs than is blunt trauma. The extent of parenchymal disruption after gunshot trauma depends upon a variety of ballistic factors, including velocity, mass of the bullet, deformation, and a tendency to tumble in flight.

PHYSICAL EXAMINATION

The approach to the trauma patient advocated by the American College of Surgeons, Committee on Trauma, in their advanced trauma life support course is both practical and sound.[9] Initial assessment of the patient consists of a primary survey for life-threatening injuries that have compromised or are likely to compromise the airway, breathing, and/or circulation of the patient and that includes identification of major, potentially reversible neurologic injury. Resuscitation appropriate to the correction of these problems is begun immediately, including intubation of the airway, placement of chest tubes for hemothorax or pneumothorax, insertion of two peripheral intravenous lines 16 gauge or larger, infusion of balanced salt solution or blood if indicated, and so on, until initial stabilization is achieved. A secondary survey follows, in which a systematic, more careful evaluation of the patient is carried out from head to toe. The need for serial examinations is emphasized.

It is a truism, but worth repeating, that to be most useful, the physical examination of the abdomen in the traumatized patient must be carried out and interpreted in the context of the history of the injury and the complaints of the patient. This examination is intended to identify the possibility of abdominal injury when one has not been suspected or to confirm the possibility of injury when the history, complaint, or both suggest it. An initial or single examination, while helpful, is of limited value. It cannot, for example, be relied upon either to confirm or to rule out significant injury if the history of the accident or the complaint of the patient suggests one may be present. Definitive diagnosis will normally require more specific diagnostic procedures or a period of observation and monitoring or both.

Any patient who has sustained a concentration of force to the chest or abdomen and who complains of abdominal pain must be assumed to have an intra-abdominal injury and will require further diagnostic evaluations. A patient who, because of proper restraint use or the nature of the accident, is unlikely to have sustained concentrated abdominal forces, and who is alert and has no complaints referable to the abdomen, such as pain, pressure, shoulder pain, or nausea, may not need further diagnostic studies. Both complaint and abdominal examination are either unavailable or unreliable in patients with altered mentation resulting from closed-head injury or alcohol or drug use, and diagnostic work-up in such patients must proceed primarily on the basis of the history of injury.

Trauma patients present with such a variety of injuries and exhibit such marked variability in the symptoms and signs that specific statements about individual physical findings are rarely generalizable and general statements are frequently of little use. Nevertheless, a few observations about the physical examination will be offered.

Inspection of the patient at rest will sometimes provide a clue that there is abdominal injury. The patient with abdominal injury is frequently restless and uncomfortable in a nonspecific way, and the respiratory excursion is halting and shallow, not smooth and regular. Distention of the abdomen early after injury is often the result of distention of the stomach by swallowed air but can also be a reflection of underlying ileus, hemorrhage, or peritonitis.

The abdomen should be auscultated and percussed gently in all quadrants before being palpated. If bowel sounds are present, their character is usually recorded but is useful mainly for later comparison. Percussion may be more sensitive for eliciting signs of peritonitis than is palpation. Palpation will elicit pain from surrounding structures, such as bruised or broken ribs, or from overlying abdominal muscles, which frequently renders further examination more difficult to interpret. Tenderness on palpation is an important but nonspecific finding that must be followed up by more specific diagnostic testing.

The abdominal wall should be examined for evidence of restraint-induced linear contusion overlying the viscera. Proper lap and shoulder restraint placement will lead to visible contusion horizontally across the anterosuperior iliac spines and diagonally across the upper chest. The finding of a seat belt contusion across the midabdomen is evidence of improper lap belt placement, which may lead to perforation of the large or small bowel as a result of compression across the lumbar spine. In the presence of such a physical finding, the diagnosis of bowel perforation should be sought by peritoneal lavage or computerized tomography (CT), and the patient should be monitored carefully for signs of peritonitis.

The placement of a nasogastric tube and Foley catheter, while part of the normal resuscitation procedures, should also be considered part of the physical examination of the trauma patient. Decompression of the stomach will aid respiration, allow examination of the contents of the stomach, and prevent acute gastric dilatation. Return of fresh blood from the stomach or bladder can be an important clue that proximal gastrointestinal or urinary bladder perforation has occurred, and the tubes provide a conduit for the instillation of contrast material for subsequent radiographic examination. If there is evidence of urethral injury, blood at the urethral meatus, contusion at the base of the penis or scrotum, or bogginess in the region of the prostate, a urethrogram should precede the passage of a Foley catheter.

The physical examination of the traumatized patient is important, but the re-examination of the patient is more important. With the exception of the patient who presents in shock with massive hemoperitoneum, all significant abdominal injuries will evolve over a period of hours as further bleeding occurs or peritonitis develops. The most effective strategy in the diagnosis of abdominal injury is to pursue aggressively the *possibility* of abdominal injury using one or more diagnostic procedures, so that the diagnosis is either made or ruled out before obvious hypotension or clinical peritonitis develops.

PLAIN RADIOGRAPHS

A plain posteroanterior (PA) or anteroposterior (AP) chest radiograph should be routinely obtained in patients with abdominal trauma. This radiograph will show direct evidence of associated thoracic injury, such as rib fracture, widened mediastinum, or diaphragmatic rupture, and sometimes will reveal indirect evidence of intra-abdominal injury, such as pneumoperitoneum or displacement of the gastric outline by splenic hematoma as well.

Plain films of the abdomen and pelvis are of limited value for the diagnosis of organ injury and have given way to CT or other organ-specific diagnostic studies when the possibility of intra-abdominal injury is being vigorously pursued. Free air is an unusual finding early after injury, even in patients with bowel perforation, and bowel gas patterns are usually not diagnostic.[7] Plain films can be useful for identifying gross fractures of the pelvis and lumbar transverse processes but cannot be relied upon to identify nondisplaced or acetabular fractures.

LABORATORY EXAMINATION

A variety of hematologic and chemical tests on blood and urine should be routinely obtained in the patient with serious injury. The purpose of these is to screen for abnormalities that might be unsuspected in a critically ill patient, who cannot afford to have a coagulation defect or an electrolyte abnormality missed. These values also serve as baseline measurements for later comparison. A few routine laboratory examinations are especially pertinent to abdominal evaluation.

Urinalysis should always be performed. Although there are disagreements about the significance of a small number of red blood cells in the urine, there is no question that the presence of a substantial number (hundreds) of red blood cells or gross hematuria is a good indication of renal injury and should be followed by up a more specific study, such as intravenous pyelogram (IVP) or CT.[10]

The serum amylase level should be obtained in all patients with abdominal injury. It is used primarily as a screening test for pancreatic and pancreaticoduodenal injury and for proximal small bowel perforation. Although elevation of the amylase level is neither perfectly sensitive nor highly specific, such an elevation, particularly in the presence of abdominal pain, should prompt further investigation, such as soluble-contrast radiographic upper gastrointestinal examination or CT, with the aim of looking specifically for one or more of these injuries.[11,12]

Liver function tests that reflect cellular integrity, such as serum glutamic-oxaloacetic transaminase (SGOT) and lactic dehydrogenase (LDH), may be elevated early after hepatic contusion but not necessarily after laceration with little associated parenchymal damage. The serum bilirubin and alkaline phosphatase levels, which reflect ductal function, usually remain normal early after injury.[13]

Laboratory examinations, like the physical examination of the abdomen, are best used as screening devices, not necessarily to rule out injury but rather to confirm the possibility of injury and provide a basis for further inquiry. Again, the circumstances of the accident and the strength of the forces involved must be taken into account in interpreting the test results.

DIAGNOSTIC PROCEDURES IN ABDOMINAL TRAUMA

The confirmation of the location, extent, and nature of abdominal injury requires the application of aggressive diagnostic methods, procedures, and techniques. The physician treating a patient with blunt abdominal trauma must assume that there is an injury to one or more abdominal organs until he or she can be assured through evaluation and testing that this is not the case. Aggressive, rapid diagnosis of blunt abdominal trauma is the best way to ensure that serious occult injuries will not be missed. The decision to proceed with additional diagnostic procedures is made after the preliminary examinations outlined previously have been carried out and the findings considered.

Diagnostic methods have been devised that detect abnormalities in four types of organs: solid organs; hollow viscera; bones containing the abdominal viscera, particularly the pelvis; and major vascular structures. Diagnostic procedures, therefore, are directed at identifying, quantifying, and localizing the following: solid organ injury, gastrointestinal perforation, and hemorrhage, whether intraperitoneal or retroperitoneal.

The methods used most commonly and effectively are diagnostic peritoneal lavage; CT; angiography; exploratory celiotomy; simple radiographic contrast studies of the upper gastrointestinal tract, urethra, and bladder; nuclear scintigraphy; and ultrasonography. Each of these techniques has a particular anatomic location in which it is most effective and in which it is most likely to be applied with benefit. Diagnostic peritoneal lavage is most useful in the diagnosis of intra-abdominal injury. CT scan can be used effectively in the diagnosis of both intraperitoneal and retroperitoneal and pelvic injury. Angiography is used for detection of injury to the major blood vessels, particularly the aorta and iliofemoral vessels, but is also used to determine the site of specific hemorrhage, particularly in major injuries of the pelvis with associated disruption of large blood vessels in this region. Exploratory laparotomy is directed primarily at intraperitoneal injury but may also be used for retroperitoneal and pelvic injury. Contrast studies of the bladder, stomach, and duodenum are used specifically for the diagnosis of injury involving those organs. Radionuclide scintigraphy is mainly suited to the detection of injuries of the liver and spleen and tends to be limited to those organs but may also be used for visualization of the kidney. Ultrasonography may have a limited role in the diagnosis of hepatic and splenic injury but is more useful for monitoring changes in the liver, spleen, and kidney after injury.

Peritoneal Lavage

Peritoneal lavage is most useful in identifying significant hemorrhage in the patient who does not exhibit signs of peritoneal irritation and whose condition appears stable at the time of presentation, but who in fact has solid organ injury or hollow viscus perforation, which might not otherwise be discovered for many hours.

Peritoneal lavage is indicated in any patient who has a history of abdominal trauma and has either abdominal pain or abdominal tenderness or in a patient whom one suspects on clinical grounds to have sustained a significant intra-abdominal injury. Peritoneal lavage is also indicated in any patient with multiple injuries whose abdomen cannot be evaluated because of head trauma, drug ingestion, or alcohol overdose.[14,15] In addition, peritoneal lavage may be useful in patients in whom one is unable to do serial examinations of the abdomen, for example, because of an impending prolonged operative procedure. In this situation, it is important to rule out intraperitoneal injury before initiating prolonged anesthesia.

The objective of peritoneal lavage is to obtain fluid for analysis from the pelvic fossa by placing a catheter in that space and either aspirating the fluid or lavaging this space with additional fluid so that an aspirate of fluid that has mixed with the contents of the peritoneal cavity may be sampled.[16] Blood collects in the pelvic space because of the anatomic recess there. If the catheter is not directed into this space, a false-negative lavage may result. False-negative results may be obtained when adhesions from previous abdominal surgery prevent extravasated blood from reaching the pelvic fossa.

Peritoneal lavage is an invasive surgical procedure and should be treated like any other procedure in which the peritoneal cavity is violated, using appropriate sterile surgical precautions and technique. The procedure should be explained to an alert patient prior to beginning, because it is important to have some degree of cooperation by the patient to perform peritoneal lavage safely. In the presence of potentially life-threatening injuries, an operative permit need not be obtained prior to performing peritoneal lavage. It is important to empty the bladder with a Foley catheter to avert injury during insertion of the lavage catheter into the peritoneal cavity. The stomach should be evacuated with a nasogastric tube to prevent inadvertent injury.

The closed technique is the quickest and simplest method for performing peritoneal lavage.[17,18] Because it is performed blindly, it has a slightly higher incidence of complications, such as false passage of the catheter or failure of the catheter to enter the proper intraperitoneal pelvic space. It also has the highest frequency of false-positive lavages from injury of intraperitoneal organs at the time of catheter insertion. A catheter and trocar are inserted through the skin incision, approximately perpendicular to the skin. With a rotational motion, the trocar is pressed firmly against the fascia and twisted back and forth until it pops first through the fascia and then through the peritoneum and into the peritoneal cavity.

After the catheter has entered the peritoneal cavity, it is directed into the fossa of the pelvis. Peritoneal dialysis catheters have a gentle curvature identified by a black line to assist in this maneuver. The fluid contents of the pelvic fossa are aspirated. If there is no return of blood, fluid, or other material, 20 ml/kg of Ringer's lactate or saline is rapidly infused into the pelvis, up to a total of 1 L of fluid. After the pelvic cavity has been lavaged with the fluid, the plastic intravenous fluid bag is placed on the floor to allow the fluid in the pelvis to siphon back into it.

Insertion of a lavage catheter over a guide wire may reduce the incidence of catheter-related complications encountered in the closed technique. An 18-gauge needle is inserted into the peritoneal cavity through the small stab wound under conditions similar to those described previously. A guide wire is then passed into the peritoneal cavity, the needle is removed, and the catheter is inserted over the guide wire.[19]

In the semi-open technique,[16] a 2- to 3-cm infraumbilical skin incision is made, long enough that when the midline abdominal fat is separated, the fascia at midline can be identified. A small incision is then made in the fascia to facilitate easy insertion of the trocar. At the completion of the procedure, the skin is closed with sterile wound tapes.

In the open technique,[20,21] a 2- to 3-cm incision is made vertically in the midline fascia, which allows direct identification of the peritoneum and insertion of the catheter into the peritoneal cavity under direct vision. This technique is the safest and guarantees intraperitoneal placement of the lavage catheter but is also the most difficult and time consuming, because it requires closure of the abdominal wall fascia by direct suture.

There has been a general tendency for persons who do lavage frequently for major trauma to adopt the more tedious and difficult open technique because of its safety. It takes only about 10 minutes longer to use the open technique, if the proper lighting, equipment, and assistance are at hand.

INTERPRETATION

The evaluation of peritoneal lavage effluent can be done either by gross inspection or with the help of the clinical laboratory. Aspiration of 10 to 20 ml of gross, nonclotting blood is generally considered positive evidence of significant intraperitoneal hemorrhage and represents a positive peritoneal lavage. Aspiration of bile or gastrointestinal contents also represents positive evidence of visceral perforation and should lead to immediate laparotomy.

Most often, however, neither of these findings occurs, and lavage of the peritoneal cavity with fluid is carried out. In general, if 1 L has been infused, 500 to 700 ml of lavage fluid should be returned after peritoneal lavage. Failure to get an adequate return of lavage fluid may indicate that the catheter has not been placed in the pelvis and that the results of lavage are invalid.

The lavage effluent must then be examined for evidence of hemorrhage or perforation. Gross inspection of the fluid as it returns through the tubing may give a clue about whether the lavage is positive. One criterion for a positive result is the inability to read newsprint through the fluid as it returns through the catheter. Minimal microscopic analysis of lavage effluent fluid consists of a red blood cell count and a white blood cell count, which can be carried out rapidly by the clinical laboratory. We also obtain bilirubin, glutamic-oxaloacetic transaminase (GOT), and alkaline phosphatase[22] values on the lavage fluid and at times request a Gram stain of the fluid as well.

A red blood cell count of 100,000 mm^3 is generally considered a positive lavage.[15] Some investigators believe that a red blood cell count of 50,000 represents a positive lavage, and each institution should make a decision regarding what level of red blood cell return they will consider positive. A white blood cell count greater than 500 is also considered evidence of significant intraperitoneal injury.[23] If less than a liter of fluid is infused, the cell counts should be corrected to reflect this before being interpreted.

If the lavage is negative or equivocal and yet the possibility of severe intra-abdominal injury exists, the lavage catheter may be left in place, attached to the skin, and the lavage repeated 4 to 6 hours following admission.[24] This practice allows detection of the delayed intraperitoneal leukocytosis that occurs in occult bowel perforation. In some instances, it has also identified delayed bleeding from rupture of the liver or spleen, which was not apparent at the time of the patient's first presentation.[25]

Peritoneal lavage is neither foolproof nor 100 per cent accurate. If the results of peritoneal lavage are not consistent with a deteriorating clinical picture of hypotension, falling hematocrit, or progressive signs of peritonitis, these clinical findings should take precedence.

Computerized Tomography

Because it is noninvasive, CT is used with increasing frequency for the diagnosis of abdominal trauma.[26] It can be used as an alternative to peritoneal lavage to diagnose solid organ injury and gives three-dimensional pictures of the nature and extent of both intraperitoneal and retroperitoneal abnormalities. Although the CT scan may be more specific in regard to the organ injured, if the patient has signs of significant intra-abdominal injury and vital signs are not stable, peritoneal lavage is quicker and is almost certainly a more efficient technique for confirming intraperitoneal injury prior to emergency laparotomy.

The indications for CT in the patient with blunt trauma are history or evidence of abdominal trauma or signs of specific organ injury, such as hematuria, elevated amylase levels, or pelvic fracture, which may have associated retroperitoneal injury. If CT is to be done, it should be done before peritoneal lavage, because the findings of the CT will be altered by the presence of fluid and air in the abdomen that results from peritoneal lavage. Prior lavage does not invalidate CT, however, and CT can be obtained after lavage as long as the radiologist is aware that lavage has been done.[26a]

CT invariably requires removal of the patient from a place such as the emergency department or intensive care unit to the radiology unit, where critical care monitoring may be difficult. The preparation for CT must, therefore, take this into account. The airway, in particular, must be secure. Any patient who has respiratory distress should be intubated, and experienced personnel should accompany the patient to manage the airway. Suction and oxygen should be available. Large intravenous lines should be well established and secure prior to moving the patient to the CT suite. It is also useful to have in place a nasogastric tube and a Foley catheter.

A careful history should be obtained to ensure that the patient is not sensitive to the intravenous administration of iodine contrast agents. The protocol at the University of Michigan calls for instillation of 500 ml of a 3 per cent iodine contrast solution via nasogastric tube into the stomach 45 minutes prior to the initiation of CT. Additional contrast may be put in through the nasogastric tube at the time of CT as well. In addition, 100 ml of 50 to 60 per cent iodine contrast solution may be given intravenously during CT. If the liver and spleen are to be well visualized, it is best to use both intravenous and oral contrast.

The length of time needed to obtain a CT of the abdomen depends on the difficulty encountered in moving and monitoring the patient, the cuts that are to be taken, and the detail with which one wishes to visualize specific organs in the abdomen. If every organ in the abdomen is to be seen, the patient may spend 30 to 45 minutes on the CT table. If interest is limited to only the pelvis, or only the upper abdomen, the examination may be shorter.

CT interpretation requires an experienced radiologist who is familiar with CT examination for trauma. Details of CT abnormalities in blunt abdominal trauma have been well described by Federle.[27] Solid organ injury can be detected as a lack of homogeneity, a mottled appearance, or disruption of the outline. At times, a visible fracture can be seen, or there may be an alteration in attenuation after infusion of intravenous contrast.

Intra-abdominal or retroperitoneal hematoma can be seen as displacement of normal organs and as positive images of fluid or blood. In addition, there is no change in attenuation in a hematoma with the administration of intravenous contrast. Hematoma adjacent to a solid organ suggests laceration even when the laceration itself is not seen. Hollow viscus injury may be identified as extravasation of air or contrast, and vascular injury to an intra-abdominal organ may be seen as failure of that organ to enhance after administration of intravenous contrast.

The advantages of CT are that it is noninvasive and, if it and the special technicians and radiologists who perform it are readily available, relatively rapid. It is not limited by organ specificity; it will image all organs in the abdomen. It also gives good three-dimensional anatomic detail of many injuries. It is especially useful for retroperitoneal injury and the imaging of organs in the retroperitoneum, which are difficult to identify not only by peritoneal lavage but also at exploratory laparotomy.

There are also some disadvantages of CT. CT equipment may not be immediately available; neither may an experienced person to interpret the scan as well as experienced technicians to perform it. The patient must be cooperative and, to obtain good images, must lie still and be able to hold the breath for brief periods. Agitated patients may have to be sedated.

CT suites are usually located well away from the emergency department, and the patient must thus be transported some distance for the CT examination. This situation requires the transfer of emergency personnel and the movement of a critically injured patient to an area in which resuscitation may be difficult.

If intraluminal contrast agents are to be used to good advantage, there will be a delay between the time when the CT is requested and when it can be carried out. This delay may be as long as 30 to 45 minutes if contrast in the small bowel is required. Contrast agents that are used in CT may interfere with subsequent angiography. Finally, if peritoneal lavage has been performed, the fluid remaining in the abdomen as the result of peritoneal lavage may lead to a false-positive reading, as hematoma or as an abnormal fluid collection.

Exploratory Laparotomy

Exploratory laparotomy is still the definitive diagnostic and therapeutic maneuver for most life-threatening abdominal injuries. The primary indication for immediate exploratory laparotomy after blunt trauma is unexplained or refractory hypotension in which intra-abdominal bleeding is suspected and no other bleeding source can be identified. Any evidence on the basis of peritoneal lavage or CT of solid organ disruption with significant associated hemorrhage or hollow visceral injury should be confirmed in the operating room. Any patients with an unexplained fall in hematocrit, progressive peritonitis, or progressive abdominal distress over 6 to 12 hours should also be examined in the operating room.

Despite the increasing sophistication of noninvasive diagnostic methods and imaging techniques, exploratory laparotomy for blunt abdominal trauma remains important and useful. In a patient who has signs of peritonitis, hypotension with abdominal trauma, or the possibility of an intra-abdominal catastrophe secondary to trauma, the abdomen should be explored as the definitive diagnostic step. Although one always tries to avoid laparotomy in which no injury is found, performing a laparotomy that yields no findings is preferable to failing to explore the abdomen in a patient with life-threatening injury.

Simple Contrast Studies

Simple contrast studies are those in which contrast material is infused intravenously or instilled directly into a hollow visceral organ or infused intravenously to demonstrate renal parenchymal anatomy and function. They should be done promptly, on the basis for history and clinical suspicion, to rule in or out a rupture or perforation of the gastrointestinal or lower urinary tract. Studies such as these can be done in the emergency department with portable x-ray equipment or in a standard radiographic suite with fluoroscopy.

In the patient who has upper abdominal blunt injury and in whom one entertains the possibility of gastric or duodenal injury, an upper gastrointestinal series using water-soluble contrast can be done to detect gastric or duodenal perforation or pancreaticoduodenal hematoma. An elevated amylase level, abnormal retroperitoneal air shadows, and blood in the nasogastric aspirate are indications for gastroduo-denal contrast study. Intraluminal extravasation of contrast can be seen either intra-peritoneally or retroperitoneally, depending upon the location of the defect. Pylorospasm may cause delayed flow of contrast into an injured duodenum, and the study should not be considered complete until all aspects of the duodenum and proximal jejunum have filled with contrast. If the patient has other indications for CT, it may be best to perform the CT first, because of the problems with CT imaging artifact caused by the standard strength of gastrointestinal contrast materials.[27]

An alternative contrast material is air. Radiographs taken after insufflation of the stomach with 300 ml or more of air through a nasogastric tube can reveal free air under the diaphragm or retroperitoneal bubbling in the region of the duodenum after perforation.

Contrast can be instilled into the pancreatic duct through the flexible fiberoptic endoscope (endoscopic retrograde cholangiopancreatography). This practice pro-vides an alternative approach for identifying injury to the pancreatic duct when the head of the pancreas and duodenum are not injured but the mechanism of injury and other findings suggest possible pancreatic disruption.[19]

Any patient who presents with blood at the urethral meatus or in whom there is difficulty passing a urinary catheter after trauma, especially in association with pelvic fractures, should undergo retrograde urethrography and cystography. Other indica-tions for retrograde urethrography are gross hematuria and the appearance of only scant, bloody urine in the presence of apparently stable vital signs and adequate hydration. These are presenting signs of bladder rupture. The presence of a floating prostate on the digital rectal examination, which should be done prior to insertion of a urinary catheter in any trauma patient, similarly should lead one to suspect urethral injury and should be investigated with a retrograde urethrogram.

Intravenous pyelography has been the standard radiographic contrast study for evaluating the kidneys when there is gross or microscopic hematuria after truncal trauma, although it is being gradually replaced by CT as the latter becomes more available. The purpose of IVP is twofold: first, to demonstrate bilateral function of the kidneys and, second, to look for the integrity of each kidney or evidence of extravasation of contrast material, indicating fracture of the parenchyma or calyceal system. If the patient is to have CT, this will visualize the kidneys well, and IVP need not be done. Similarly, if the patient is having an angiogram, a flat plate of the abdomen after the angiography will frequently demonstrate the kidneys and ureters.

If neither of these procedures appears to be indicated, and there is hematuria, bilateral kidney function can be assessed rapidly by intravenous administration of 50 to 100 ml of contrast material, such as Renografin or Hypaque-50, followed by a plain radiograph of the abdomen 10 minutes later. This procedure may be done in the emergency service, in the operating room with portable radiographic equipment, or in a standard radiographic suite. Better visualization of the ureters can be obtained with IVP than with CT, but CT will ordinarily give better anatomic detail of the injury to the renal parenchyma. Failure to visualize all or part of a kidney on IVP suggests renovascular injury and is an indication for emergency angiography. Al-though views of the bladder can be obtained after IVP, they are not as reliable as a cystogram for identifying injury to the bladder.

Radionuclide Scintigraphy and Ultrasonography

Radionuclide scintigraphy in blunt trauma[28] is used for the detection of hepatic or splenic injuries, primarily in children, for whom many surgeons feel that peritoneal lavage is not appropriate. It may occasionally be useful in the adult patient with suspected liver or spleen injury after focal rather than generalized abdominal trauma, particularly if they present in a delayed fashion.

One advantage of radionuclide scanning is that, while noninvasive, it may provide a functional assessment of vascular integrity of the organ as it fills with radiolabeled contrast, giving an estimate of blood flow. The disadvantages are several[27,29]:

1.   Radionuclide scintigraphy cannot be repeated frequently because of retained activity.

2.   Its organ specificity limits its application to persons with focal as opposed to generalized trauma.

3.   It does not quantitate intraperitoneal bleeding.

4.   It gives a negative image of the injury, which means that the injury is demonstrated as the absence of activity.

5.   It has a 5 to 10 per cent occurrence of false-positive and false-negative examinations.

Radionuclide scintigraphy should be used only in stable patients because of the time required to complete the scan and because of the usual long distance between the scanning area and the emergency service. Studies in children report a high sensitivity and specificity in the detection of injuries to the liver and spleen, but in these studies presumptive injuries were not confirmed by direct observation at laparotomy in all cases.[28]

The performance of radionuclide scanning requires bulky, relatively immovable equipment. The settings on the collimators for this equipment are important, and skilled technicians need to be available to set up the machinery, as well as experienced radiographers to interpret the scans. These, as well as the necessary radionuclides, may not always be available on an emergency basis.

Ultrasonography can be used on an acute basis to detect injuries of the liver and spleen as well as to identify blood or fluid adjacent to these organs or in the pelvis.[30] It has not gained favor for initial evaluation because acute ileus can affect the quality of the image and because it has such a limited repertoire. Scintigraphy is considered superior to ultrasonography for the diagnosis of hepatic and splenic injury.[31] Ultrasonography may be useful for follow-up examinations of hepatic or splenic injury identified by other means and treated conservatively.[30]

MANAGEMENT OF PATIENTS WITH ABDOMINAL INJURIES

Patients with significant abdominal injury or those who are highly suspected of having possible major injury should be admitted to a trauma surgery service experienced in the management of these problems. Medical staff should be available to monitor the progress of the patient every few hours. Hemorrhagic shock or peritonitis from undetected injury can result in sepsis or the sudden cardiovascular collapse of the patient up to 36 hours or more after injury and can lead to death or a prolonged course of treatment for multiorgan failure. Even with the sophisticated diagnostic testing now available, surgical exploration of the abdomen remains the definitive management step for patients whose abdominal examination is abnormal and whose clinical course is not improving or is deteriorating. Management of the patient with abdominal injury must always be carried out with the option of emergency surgery immediately available.

The physical examination of the patient should be repeated roughly every 6 hours. Steady improvement is expected in the patient without serious intra-abdominal injury. Anything short of this should arouse suspicion. In carrying out repeat examinations, one should pay particular attention to new or continued feelings of pressure or pain in the abdomen, pelvis, or shoulders, which may have been poorly localized or discerned at first. Attention should be paid to the development of distention, tenderness, or ileus, which may reflect a progressive peritoneal inflammation.

Urine output should be monitored hourly. A fall in urine production is a reliable early sign of inadequate resuscitation or developing hemorrhagic or bacterial shock. Volume resuscitation, not use of diuretics, is the initial treatment of choice, followed by a search for the cause of hypovolemia. Fever and marked elevation of the white blood cell count are late signs of undetected intraperitoneal catastrophe.

Patients should be given nothing to eat by mouth until one is confident that no abdominal injury exists. Sudden or increased abdominal pain soon after early feeding will occur in the presence of pancreatic and bowel injury. Patients with large retroperitoneal hematomas, usually associated with pelvic fractures, will frequently develop severe and prolonged ileus and should not be fed until there is clear evidence of normal bowel function, which may not occur for several days to a week.

Whereas operation for hepatic or splenic injury was mandatory in the past, nonoperative management is practiced now with increasing frequency for both children and adults who are hemodynamically stable and do not require blood transfusion. This practice places an increased burden on those monitoring the course of the patient in the first few days after injury, during which persistent or recurrent hemorrhage may occur. Whether the need to operate can be predicted from noninvasive testing and whether early operation is more effective in splenic salvage remain controversial questions.[32-34]

When splenectomy has been carried out, immunization against pneumococcal organisms should be provided, as well as instructions regarding antimicrobial prophylaxis for any subsequent episodes of high fever or unexplained illness to prevent late deaths from overwhelming pneumococcal sepsis, which can occur after splenectomy.

Patients with severe abdominal as well as facial injuries, unable to eat normally, must be given adequate nutrition nevertheless. Caloric losses within the first few days after injury can be substantial, from 5000 to 10,000 Kcal, and enteral or parenteral feeding should be begun within 5 to 7 days, if not sooner, by nasogastric feeding tube, jejunostomy, or central venous hyperalimentation. Enteral feeding, when possible, is preferred.

CONCLUSION

The diagnosis of abdominal trauma must be initiated promptly to identify those patients with immediately life-threatening hemorrhage or injury. In stable patients, the continued evaluation requires time; attention to the details of the history and circumstances of the injury; thoughtful observation; careful, repeated examination of the patient; and the aggressive use of methods now available to make organ-specific diagnoses. The management of abdominal injury takes precedence over that of most other injuries during the first 48 to 72 hours after injury. After that, the total management of the patient with multiple injuries requires careful communication and coordination to ensure that complications such as delayed hemorrhage, ileus, starvation, and sepsis are avoided while other problems are attended to.

REFERENCES

1. Blaisdell FW, Trunkey DD (eds): Trauma Management. Volume I. Abdominal Trauma. New York, Thieme-Stratton, 1982.
2. Shires GT (ed): Care of the Trauma Patient. 2nd ed. New York, McGraw-Hill Book Company, 1979.
3. Zuidema GD, Rutherford RB, Ballinger WF (eds): The Management of Trauma. Philadelphia, WB Saunders Company, 1985.
4. Baker SP, O'Neill B, Karpf RS: The Injury Fact Book, Lexington, MA, Lexington Books, DC Heath and Company, 1984.
5. Nahum AM, Melvin J: The Biomechanics of Trauma. Norwalk, CT, Appleton-Century-Crofts, 1985.
6. Bergqvist D, Hedelin H, Karlsson G, et al: Intestinal trauma: Analysis of 101 cases. Acta Chir Scand 147:629–635, 1981.
7. Burney RE, Mueller GL, Coon WW, et al: Diagnosis of isolated small bowel injury fol-

lowing blunt abdominal trauma. Ann Emerg Med 12:71–74, 1983.

8. Collins PS, Golocovsky M, Salander JM, et al: Intra-abdominal vascular injury secondary to penetrating trauma. J Trauma 28 [Suppl]:S165–S170, 1988.

9. Committee on Trauma, American College of Surgeons: Advanced Trauma Life Support. Chicago, IL, American College of Surgeons, 1984.

10. McAninch JW, Federle MP: Evaluation of renal injuries with computerized tomography. J Urol 128:456–460, 1982.

11. Olson WR: The serum amylase in blunt abdominal trauma. J Trauma 13:200–204, 1973.

12. Bouwman DL, Weaver DW, Walt AJ: Serum amylase and its isoenzymes: A clarification of their implications in trauma. J Trauma 24:573–577, 1984.

13. Burney RE, Mueller GL, Mackenzie JR: Evaluation of experimental blunt and penetrating hepatobiliary trauma by sequential peritoneal lavage. Ann Emerg Med 12:279–284, 1983.

14. Olsen WR, Redman HC, Hildreth DH: Quantitative peritoneal lavage in blunt abdominal trauma. Arch Surg 104:536–543, 1972.

15. Perry JF, DeMeules JE, Root HD: Diagnostic peritoneal lavage in blunt abdominal trauma. Surg Gynecol Obstet 30:742–744, 1970.

16. Root HD, Hauser CW, McKinley CR, et al: Diagnostic peritoneal lavage. Surgery 57:633–637, 1965.

17. Olsen WR: Peritoneal lavage in blunt abdominal trauma. J Am Coll Emergency Physicians 2:271–275, 1973.

18. Sachatello CR, Bivins BR: A technique for peritoneal dialysis and diagnostic peritoneal lavage. Am J Surg 131:637–640, 1976.

19. Gomez GA, Alvarez R, Plasencia G, et al: Diagnostic peritoneal lavage in the management of blunt abdominal trauma: A reassessment. J Trauma 27:1–5, 1987.

20. Pachter HL, Hofstetter SR: Open and percutaneous paracentesis and lavage for abdominal trauma. Arch Surg 116:318–319, 1981.

21. Perry JF Jr: Blunt and penetrating abdominal injuries. *In* Current Problems in Surgery. Chicago, Year Book Medical Publishers, 1970.

22. Marx JA, Bar-Or D, Moore EE, et al: Utility of lavage alkaline phosphatase in detection of isolated small intestinal injury. Ann Emerg Med 14:10–14, 1985.

23. Vij D, Horan DP, Obeid FN, et al: The importance of the WBC count in peritoneal lavage. JAMA 249:636–638, 1983.

24. Mueller GL, Burney RE, Mackenzie JR: Leukocytosis in peritoneal lavage effluent after selected abdominal organ injury in an experimental model. Ann Emerg Med 11:343–347, 1982.

25. Alyono D, Perry JF Jr: Significance of repeating diagnostic peritoneal lavage. Surgery 91:656–659, 1982.

26. Trunkey D, Federle MP: Computed tomography in perspective. J Trauma 26:660–661, 1987.

26a. Kearney PA, Vahey T, Burney RE, et al: Computed tomography and magnetic peritoneal lavage: their combined role. Arch Surg 124:344–347, 1989.

27. Federle MP: Computed tomography of blunt abdominal trauma. Radiol Clin North Am 23:461–475, 1983.

28. Gilday DL, Alderson PO: Scintigraphic evaluation of liver and spleen and injury. Semin Nucl Med 4:357–370, 1974.

29. Uthoff LB, Wyffels PL, Adams CS, et al: A prospective study comparing nuclear scintigraphy and computerized tomography in the initial evaluation of the trauma patient. Ann Surg 198:611–616, 1983.

30. Froelich JW, Simeone JF, McKusici KA, et al: Radionuclide imaging and ultrasound in liver/spleen trauma: A prospective comparison. Radiology 145:457–461, 1982.

31. Kuligowska E, Mueller PR, Simeone JF, et al: Ultrasound in upper abdominal trauma. Semin Roentgenol 19:281–295, 1984.

32. Nallathambi MN, Ivatury RR, Wapnir I, et al: Nonoperative management versus early operation for blunt splenic trauma in adults. Surg Gynecol Obstet 166:252–258, 1988.

33. Powell RW, Green JG, Ochsner MG, et al: Peritoneal lavage in pediatric patients sustaining blunt abdominal trauma: A reappraisal. J Trauma 27:6–10, 1987.

34. Buntain WL, Gould HR, Maull KI: Predictability of splenic salvage by computed tomography. J Trauma 28:24–34, 1988.

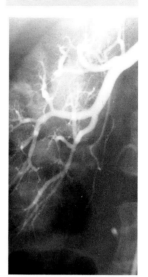

CHAPTER 10

UROLOGIC INJURIES

MICHAEL CHANCELLOR, M.D., and EDWARD J. MCGUIRE, M.D.

Urologic injuries occur with some frequency in association with violent trauma. In general, violent forces of sufficient severity to produce maxillofacial injury have the potential to produce injury to the genitourinary tract.

CLASSIFICATION OF INJURIES

Genitourinary trauma may be considered blunt or penetrating. With certain notable exceptions, penetrating injuries usually require operative intervention, while blunt trauma often does not.[1] Urologists divide traumatic injuries into those of the kidney, ureters, bladder, and urethra, since all require different diagnostic procedures and different treatment.

RENAL INJURIES

Blunt Renal Injuries

Blunt renal injuries are usually, but not invariably, associated with hematuria. Blunt renal trauma is more likely if there are accompanying rib fractures. Frequently, the diagnosis of rib fracture is easier to make on physical examination than by radiographic study, particularly if the fractures are nondisplaced, which is the most common situation. Blunt renal trauma is usually the result of a sudden deceleration injury, which can produce two unique types of renal injury: an intimal injury to the renal artery, with subsequent total renal ischemia; and avulsion of the ureter from the renal pelvis, an injury more common in children than adults. In addition, an abnormal kidney, such as an unrecognized ureteropelvic junction obstruction or a pelvic or horseshoe kidney, carries a risk of being severely injured with relatively trivial traumatic forces.

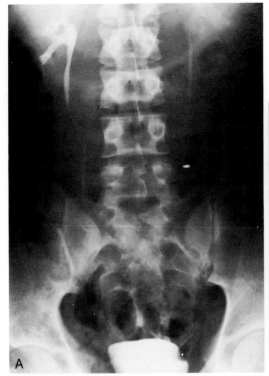

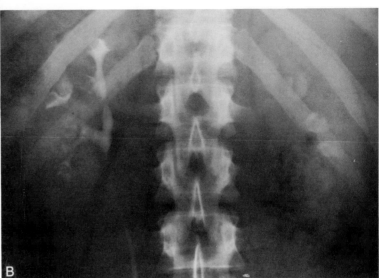

Figure 10–1. *A* and *B*, Intravenous pyelogram (IVP) showing decreased function of left kidney.

Blunt renal injury can be classified into three distinct types by findings on intravenous pyelography (IVP).

1. **Type I.** A type of renal injury associated with hematuria but not associated with *any* abnormality on intravenous urography. This kind of renal injury can be treated simply by observation.

2. **Type II.** A type of renal injury usually associated with hematuria, with an abnormality of the affected kidney on IVP examination. The injury can range from a minimal delay in excretion to renal disruption (Figs. 10–1 and 10–2).

3. **Type III.** A type III renal injury is associated with no function on an IVP. These findings suggest an arterial injury (Figs 10–3 and 10–4).

At present, most major trauma centers utilize computerized tomography (CT) scanning for abdominal injuries.[2] That study provides much more detailed information on the degree of renal injury and the extent of renal parenchymal damage. Nevertheless, most urologists are guided with respect to operative intervention by the clinical status of the patient rather than the radiographic findings, except in cases of nonfunction of the kidney, when immediate arteriography and exploration, in that order, are indicated.[3]

Although a major renal injury is a serious problem, deaths are much more frequently related to injuries to other organs. Of 100 blunt renal injuries, 65 per cent will be minor and the remaining 35 per cent major, involving renal shattering or vascular pedicle injuries. Major renal injuries have a close association with injuries to other body organs.

DIAGNOSIS

History and Physical Examination and Laboratory Studies. Any history of blunt abdominal, chest, flank, or back trauma should make the examiner aware of the possibility of renal injury. Since the diagnosis is almost exclusively radiographic, appropriate immediate studies should be obtained. These can be an intravenous

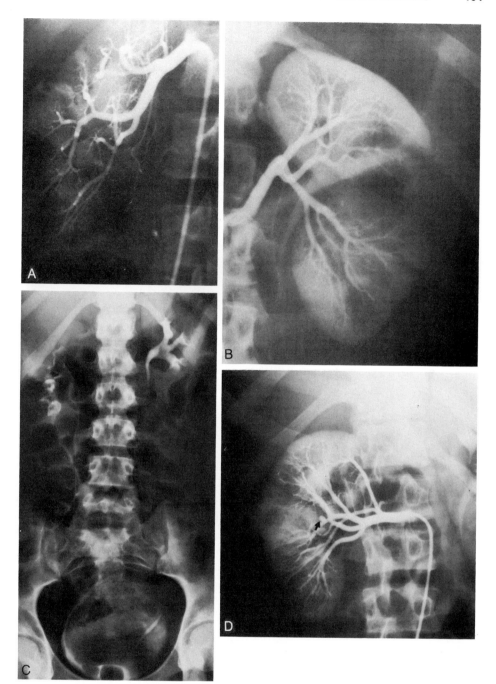

FIGURE 10–2. *A*, Selective renal arteriogram revealing a moderate renal laceration. *B*, Major renal laceration involving both parenchyma and collecting system. *C*, A 25-year-old man sustained a stab wound to the right flank. IVP illustrates the entire right collecting system and bladder filled with blood clot. *D*, Renal arteriogram of same patient revealed a complete laceration of a renal artery *(black arrow)*, which was found to be communicating with the collecting system.

urogram, if the patient's condition permits, a CT scan, or an aortogram. Ultrasonography can be used for screening but is often not precise enough for accurate diagnosis in this circumstance.

The physical examination may help to confirm the possibility of renal injury, particularly if there are signs of contusion or rib fracture, but a normal examination in no way precludes a serious renal injury.

The presence of hematuria is always significant, but a normal urinalysis does not in any way exclude renal or other urinary injury.

Radiographic Studies. The IVP remains the standard method of diagnosis, but the standard low-dose bolus injection technique is inadequate, and drip infusion pyelography, or a high-dose bolus injection, is less likely to result in underestimation of the degree of injury. If a significant abnormality is detected, some urologists

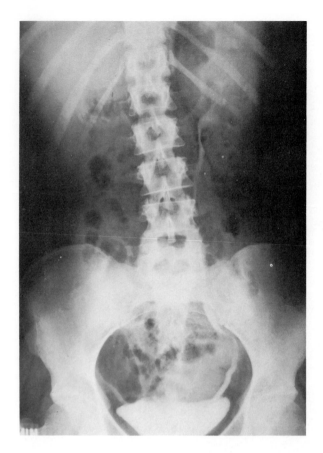

FIGURE 10–3. No function of the right side on IVP.

proceed with an immediate arteriogram, but others do so only if there is no renal function identified on the intravenous urogram and use arteriography in those instances in which it appears that the kidney may be shattered or that operative intervention is a very likely possibility.

CT scanning is gradually replacing both the IVP and the arteriogram. Some

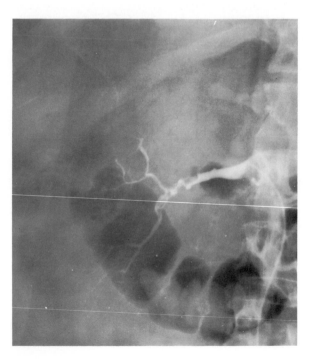

FIGURE 10–4. Selective renal arteriogram of the same patient with multiple thrombi in the renal artery secondary to an intimal tear.

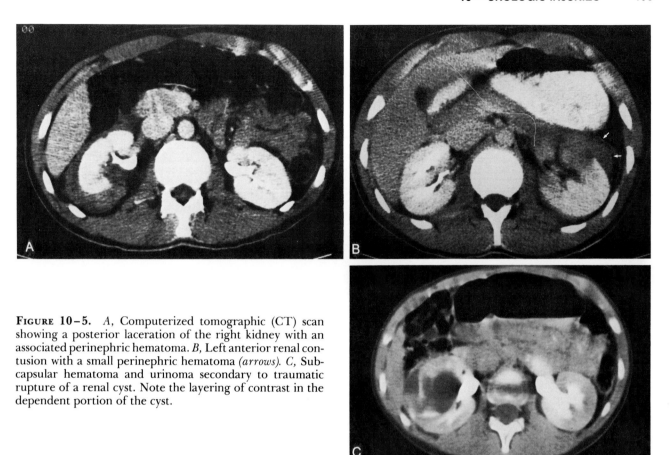

FIGURE 10–5. *A,* Computerized tomographic (CT) scan showing a posterior laceration of the right kidney with an associated perinephric hematoma. *B,* Left anterior renal contusion with a small perinephric hematoma *(arrows).* *C,* Subcapsular hematoma and urinoma secondary to traumatic rupture of a renal cyst. Note the layering of contrast in the dependent portion of the cyst.

authors feel that identification of the precise degree of renal injury and, thus, an accurate decision on the necessity for operative therapy can be made immediately rather than as the patient's clinical condition, under very close observation, dictates (Fig. 10–5).

In some circumstances, the patient's condition may preclude obtaining any of the previously mentioned studies, in which case a simple abdominal and chest film may be all that there is time for before immediate operation is undertaken. This situation gives rise to a problem wherein the urologist, called into the operating room for consultation, sees only a large unilateral or bilateral retroperitoneal hematoma. A rather classic problem then arises, since the urologist has no real idea of the nature and extent of the injury and whether or not there is a normal kidney on the contralateral side. Unfortunately, the urologist is unlikely to be able to determine this accurately simply by opening the retroperitoneal area or by palpation. Moreover, opening the retroperitoneal area incurs the risk of massive continuing hemorrhage. Even in this circumstance, it is frequently better to proceed with an on-the-table bolus single-shot intravenous urogram before further exploration is attempted. In unusual conditions, even that is not possible, and the urologist may have no choice but to proceed with exploration.

MANAGEMENT

Blunt renal trauma can be managed conservatively in approximately 65 to 75 per cent of cases. Operative rates vary from series to series, but nephrectomy is done in more than half of the patients who undergo operative therapy. Absolute indications for operation include nonfunction of the kidney on intravenous urogram, a shattered kidney, or continued bleeding with unstable vital signs.

Secondary hemorrhage and a Goldblatt kidney with hypertension are the major late complications of conservative therapy. Both are relatively rare. Abscess formation, usually associated with urinoma and related to extravasation, may follow either conservative or operative therapy.

Operative management is directed toward renal salvage, with debridement of devitalized tissue and repair of renal lacerations, or partial nephrectomy. The initial operative step is control of the renal pedicle outside Gerota's fascia before specific renal exploration is attempted. This maneuver involves access to the aorta and vena cava by mobilization of the small bowel on the right, and mobilization of the colon on the left, or an approach through the lesser sac on the left. An alternative method is balloon catheter placement in the renal artery at the time of arteriogram, which can be used for a temporary occlusion of the artery, as needed, during the procedure.

Penetrating Renal Injuries

Associated nonrenal injuries are very common in this group and constitute the underlying reason for operative exploration. In contrast to blunt trauma, for which up to 70 per cent of patients are managed conservatively and without operation, virtually all penetrating injuries ultimately come to exploration.[4]

Although recently some stab wounds have been treated expectantly, it is our practice to explore all penetrating injuries. Preoperative evaluation is identical with that outlined for blunt trauma except that the circumstances are different, and there are no rules for penetrating trauma except that the examiner must think of every structure that could conceivably be injured by a missile or a sharp instrument. It is said that the surgeon should have an idea, if possible, of the caliber and type of weapon used. However, in practice that is rarely possible, except in the case of hunting accidents, when the extent of the injury incurred by an individual shot with a high-velocity rifle is only too apparent, and in the case of war injuries, in which very high velocity small arms are commonly used. The surgical principles for dealing with penetrating trauma are well established, and the extent of the procedure is dictated by the amount of tissue damage. When the surgeon is in doubt, resection is the better course. Healthy bleeding margins should be present at the edges of all resected tissue, and painstaking, thorough exploration of every nook and cranny saves time, effort, and trouble later.

URETERAL INJURIES

Ureteral injuries are relatively rare, and except in children, in whom avulsion injuries occur wherein the ureter is torn from the renal pelvis, they are most commonly related to penetrating trauma (Fig. 10–6). Total ureteral disruption may not be associated with hematuria, and a high degree of suspicion is required during the initial evaluation of a patient with penetrating trauma to the abdomen or chest. Unrecognized ureteral injuries cause leakage of urine, abscess formation, urinoma formation, and disruption of primary repair of vascular structures or bowel and can result in very difficult secondary operative procedures. Appropriate radiographic studies, including high-dose infusion pyelography, retrograde pyelography, and CT scanning, should be obtained immediately if the ureter could conceivably be in the path of a missile or penetrating instrument of any kind (Fig. 10–7).

Treatment

Repair of ureteral injuries depends on the location of the lesion and on its extent. The ureter can be divided into thirds. The upper third and lower third are somewhat

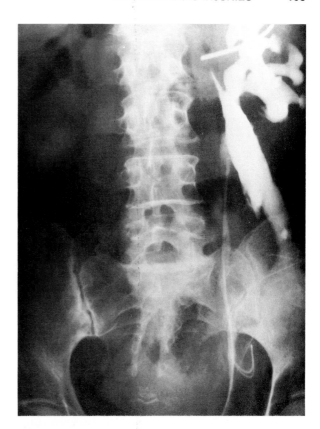

FIGURE 10–6. Retrograde pyelogram reveals a partial disruption of the ureteropelvic junction. Note the extravasation of contrast along the psoas muscle and the moderate hydronephrosis above the point of disruption.

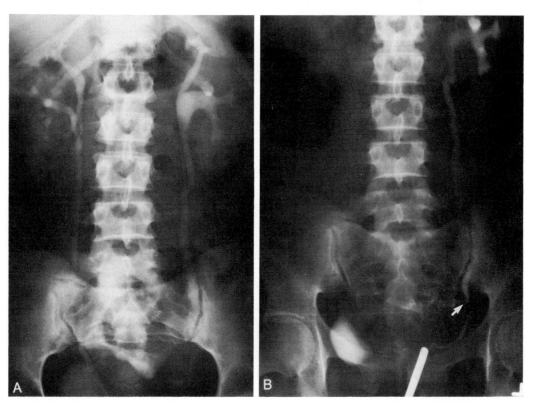

FIGURE 10–7. *A,* IVP of a 16-year-old girl who sustained a stab wound to the left lower abdomen. There is a slight fullness of the left collecting system, with possible extravasation of contrast from the distal left ureter. *B,* Retrograde injection confirms a partial laceration of the distal left ureter *(arrow).* The bladder is markedly displaced to the contralateral side secondary to a large pelvic hematoma and urinoma.

more amenable to operative repair. The middle third has a more tenuous blood supply, and it is, by virtue of its location, more difficult to deal with. In general, proximal ureteral injuries can be repaired by debridement and reanastomosis over a stent, and if the length of ureteral injury precludes direct repair, both the kidney and the distal ureter can be mobilized to permit an anastomosis without tension. Injuries to the distal third of the ureter can be directly repaired, the ureter can be reimplanted, or the bladder can be mobilized by a variety of methods to permit bridging of the gap between functional ureter and bladder. The middle segment of the ureter can be repaired directly, a transureterostomy can be performed, or a bowel interposition segment can be used. Finally, a renal autotransplantation can be performed and permits repair of almost total ureteral loss in that the renal pelvis can be anastomosed to a "neoureter" fashioned from a bladder flap.

BLADDER INJURIES

Blunt abdominal trauma in children can result in bladder rupture, and occasionally this occurs in adults, particularly when the bladder is full and an individual suffers trauma while wearing a seat belt. More commonly, bladder injuries are associated with pelvic bone fractures or disruption of the ring of the pelvis involving fracture of the ischium, as well as disruption and widening of the sacroiliac joints.

In the initial physical assessment, a search for signs of external trauma to the skin of the lower abdomen and pelvic area and manual side-to-side compression of the bony pelvis, which will elicit a painful response, suggest a traumatic bone injury. Although hematuria is often present, voided urine samples are usually not obtained in individuals with pelvic traumatic injuries because of the danger of extravasation of urine as a result of micturition. A routine pelvic film is taken as quickly as possible. If a pelvic fracture is present in male patients, a retrograde urethrogram should be obtained immediately to determine the integrity of the penile, bulbous, and prostatic urethra before passage of a urethral catheter into the bladder. Injuries to the urethra preclude safe catheterization. These should be identified or ruled out before the bladder is catheterized and drained (Fig. 10–8). Once the catheter is in place in the

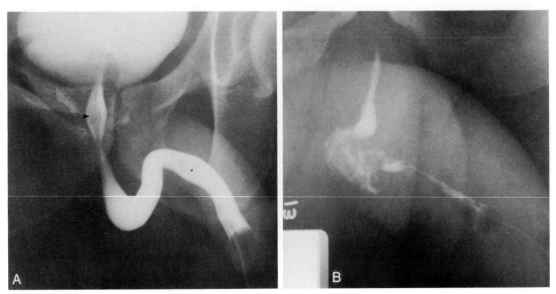

FIGURE 10–8. *A,* Normal retrograde urethrogram. Arrow indicates normal impression of the verumontanum. *B,* Retrograde urethrogram reveals extravasation from the bulbous urethra. The marked swelling of the penis is secondary to extravasation of blood and urine within the confines of Buck's fascia.

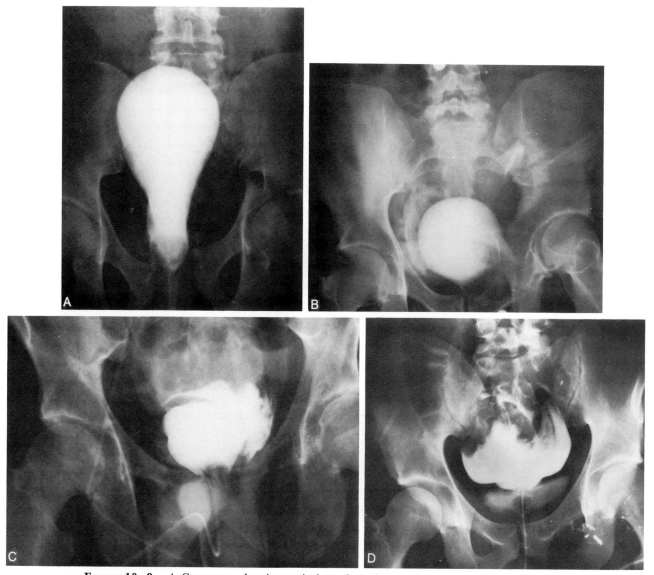

FIGURE 10-9. *A,* Cystogram showing typical teardrop-shaped bladder caused by compression of the bladder by massive pelvic bleeding. *B,* Extraperitoneal bladder disruption. Note the severe comminuted fracture of the pubic rami on the left side. Surgical exploration revealed that a bone fragment had lacerated the bladder. *C,* Another example of an extraperitoneal bladder rupture. *D,* Cystographic appearance of an intraperitoneal bladder rupture. Note the contrast material outlining both the peritoneal surfaces and the bowel interfaces.

bladder, a high-volume cystogram can be obtained, including films while the bladder is filling, filled, and empty, to check for extravasation, and the urine should be examined for the presence of blood (Fig. 10-9).

Treatment

Standard urologic practice for bladder injuries involves placement of a suprapubic tube and drainage of the perivesical space. If the injury is large, a direct repair is required. In some circumstances, particularly in cases of small lesions with only extraperitoneal extravasation, it can be permissible to use urethral catheter drainage only. That decision can be made only on a highly individual basis. Although the technique is satisfactory in some cases, it is not recommended for more serious bladder injuries, particularly those associated with intraperitoneal extravasation, or in individuals in whom there is little possibility of attaining mobility within 5 to 7 days of the injury.

URETHRAL INJURIES AND INJURIES TO THE EXTERNAL GENITALIA

The most significant urethral injuries occur in male subjects suffering pelvic trauma and bone fracture. The disruption of the urethra commonly involves the area that traverses the pelvic floor. In general, these patients present with severe lower abdominal and pelvic pain and distended bladder and frequently blood at the external urethral meatus. A gentle retrograde urethrogram should be performed. If there is extravasation, an immediate operation with placement of a suprapubic tube is indicated. If other injuries prevent immediate operation, a percutaneous suprapubic cystostomy can be placed as a temporizing measure.

Treatment

There is no uniformity of opinion regarding the best method of treating a ruptured membranous urethra. The sequelae of the injury are serious and difficult to deal with and include urethral stricture formation, impotence, and contamination of the injury site as well as potential contamination of pelvic bone fractures. Some urologists use only suprapubic tube drainage, feeling that direct repair often does more harm than good. Others attempt to repair the injured area with debridement and reanastomosis, and still others will attempt only antegrade passage of a catheter to splint the injury. In any event, all of these methods can result in either primary healing or stricture formation. In addition, impotence, ejaculatory incompetence, and the occasional loss of proximal urethral sphincter function and incontinence can occur.

Very occasionally, female patients present with urethral injuries that are most frequently associated with difficult childbirth but can result from other kinds of trauma.

INJURIES TO THE ANTERIOR URETHRA

Straddle injuries to the urethra occur when the urethra is forced against the bony pelvis by some firm object impacting against the perineum. Blood is commonly present at the urethral meatus, as are palpable swelling and tenderness, often associated with ecchymosis in the perineum and scrotum. Diagnosis depends on retrograde urethrography and can be supplemented by endoscopy. Frequently, simple catheter drainage is sufficient for treatment, but extensive or penetrating injuries must be explored, usually in combination with placement of a suprapubic tube for temporary urinary diversion.

TESTICULAR INJURIES AND TESTICULAR EMERGENCIES

Sudden testicular pain is a common emergency room complaint. A history of trauma should be elicited, and in cases of direct, forceful testicular injury, an effort should be made on the physical examination, and with the use of ultrasonography, to determine whether the tunica albuginea is intact. If there is frank testicular rupture, immediate exploration and repair are indicated.

A vague history of minor trauma is commonly elicited in patients who ultimately turn out to be suffering from testicular torsion, ureteral colic, or epididymitis, and such a history should be viewed as having little bearing on the problem until proved otherwise.

REFERENCES

1. Thompson IM: Expectant management of blunt renal trauma. Urol Clin North Am 54:29–32, 1977.
2. McClennan BC, Fair W: CT scanning in urology. Urol Clin North Am 6:343–374, 1979.
3. Peters PC, Bright TC: Blunt renal injuries. Urol Clin North Am 54:17–28, 1977.
4. Sagalowsky AZ, McConnell JD, Peters PC: Renal trauma requiring surgery. J Trauma 23:128, 1983.

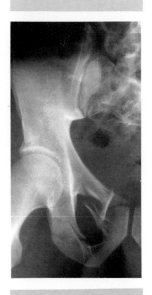

CHAPTER 11

INITIAL ASSESSMENT AND MANAGEMENT OF THE POLYTRAUMA PATIENT WITH ORTHOPEDIC INJURIES

ROBERT G. VIERE, M.D., and
RICHARD E. JONES, M.D.

The purpose of this chapter is to present a systematic approach to the management of musculoskeletal injuries in the polytrauma patient. Emphasis is placed on the early evaluation and treatment of these injuries, beginning at the scene of the accident and extending through early definitive care. It is important to remember that musculoskeletal injuries rarely occur in isolation, and associated injury to surrounding soft tissue must always be considered. The orthopedist must work with other specialists in a cooperative effort, first and foremost, to save the patient's life and, second, to provide the framework for maximal functional recovery. The treatment and sequelae of trauma can have both physical and psychologic effects on the victim. Although the saving of life is the prime objective in trauma care, it is important to maintain an aggressive posture with regard to the functional recovery of the individual trauma victim. There is not a distinct line between lifesaving maneuvers and the optimal care of musculoskeletal injuries. Too often in the past, the patient's musculoskeletal injuries were given low priority, and the delay in definitive treatment had negative impact on the patient's ultimate recovery. It has been shown in recent studies that early definitive care of musculoskeletal injuries can have a direct effect on mortality rates, as well as future morbidity.[1,2]

EARLY ASSESSMENT AND CARE

At the accident scene, the job of early assessment and care falls to the emergency medical technician (EMT). His job can be divided into three main categories.[3] The primary goal is to provide treatment for acute life-threatening conditions: inadequate ventilation, circulatory failure, or exsanguinating bleeding. The EMT must be able to establish an airway and administer ventilatory and cardiopulmonary resuscitation and support.

Second, the EMT must be able to dress wounds and to splint fractures appropriately for transport. Finally, the EMT must be skilled in the extrication of the victim, controlling the scene of injury, and emergency driving.

In this chapter, we limit ourselves to a specific discussion of musculoskeletal injuries, as other areas are covered elsewhere. The job of the EMT in the field can be broken down into three segments[4]:

1. Assessment
2. Protection from further injury
3. Transport

Assessment begins when approaching the scene by observation of the patient's position and surroundings. If the patient is conscious, he or she can communicate about painful areas or any significant neurologic deficits. In the unconscious patient, it is important to observe any spontaneous movements and preferential movement of one side of the body. It is important to examine the patient in a brief but systematic approach, looking for any obvious bleeding, wounds, or deformity. It is also important to note the presence and quantity of bleeding at the scene.

All injuries should be splinted at the scene. Movement of the patient from the vehicle or scene to the stretcher should be done using proper techniques for control of the head and body, to prevent further trauma in patients with possible spinal injury.[4] This proper technique generally means application of a Philadelphia collar and sandbags on either side of the head, with taping to a spine board, for the transport of patients with possible cervical spine injuries. In suspected thoracic and lumbar spine injuries, the patient should be securely strapped to a long spine board during transport.[3]

The management of open wounds at the scene should follow three general rules:

1. Control bleeding.
2. Prevent further contamination.
3. Immobilize the part and keep the patient calm and quiet.

Bleeding can generally be controlled by application of a pressure dressing. Pressure can be applied by hand, by pressure bandage, or by air splint. A tourniquet should be used only as a last resort. If the open wound is related to an associated fracture, appropriate splinting of the fracture is very important.

Splinting of Fractures

Fractures can be splinted with numerous types of improvised and conventional devices.[5] Several types of splints are available in modern ambulance systems, as follows.

FOAM-PADDED BASSWOOD OR HARD PLASTIC

These splints are, in practical terms, similar to improvised splints in that they are used to span a fracture by a rigid external device.

PREFABRICATED SPLINTS

These splints are made in the shape of upper and lower extremities and are designed as one size fits all. These splints do not offer optimal immobilization; therefore, they should be used only when other options are not available.

MALLEABLE SPLINTS

The Cramer wire splint and the structural aluminum malleable (SAM) splint fall into this category. These can be shaped and padded to fit the part. They are secured with bandages and work well for temporary immobilization.

THOMAS SPLINTS

The Thomas splint is used for immobilization of fractures of the femur. The leg is secured to the splint along its length with broad bandages and application of traction to the foot, by way of a padded hitch and Spanish windlass.[5]

INFLATABLE SPLINTS

These splints have gained widespread use in the immobilization of distal fractures, for which they can apply pressure over wounds, as well as immobilize. They do not work as well for proximal fractures, since they do not adequately extend above the fracture site and may give a feeling of false security that the fracture is splinted, when, in reality, it is not. These splints should also not be applied for long periods or at high pressure (greater than 30 mm Hg) owing to reduction of blood flow.[5] They need to be applied after the removal of clothing, since folds of clothing can cause skin problems.

Open fractures should be splinted in a manner similar to that of closed fractures, except for the addition of a pressure dressing. After the patient has been immobilized, he or she should be transported as expeditiously as possible.

EMERGENCY ROOM TREATMENT

Upon arrival in the emergency room, the patient should have a thorough evaluation by a team of physicians skilled in the care of the trauma patient.[6] After immediate life-threatening problems have been addressed, the patient should have a systematic examination of the musculoskeletal system. If patients are conscious and cooperative, they can help in this by their subjective reports of pain. Examination for tenderness, palpable step-off, or deformity of the spine should be done, along with a thorough neurologic examination if a spine fracture is suspected. The rest of the body should be examined, with observation for any lacerations, contusions, or deformity. Palpation of accessible body areas, including the shoulder, pelvis, long bones, hands, and feet, should be performed. Range of motion, both active and passive, of all joints should be assessed. Examination of all joints for any effusion or swelling that could suggest previously spontaneously reduced dislocation or ligamentous injury should also be performed. All dressings should be removed to evaluate open wounds. On the basis of the location and depth of these wounds, a directed examination to rule out any vascular, tendinous, or peripheral nerve injury should be done. Wounds should be copiously irrigated in the emergency room and redressed. Wounds that are clean with no deep injury can be sutured under sterile technique in the emergency room. Other wounds should be left open and covered with a dilute povidone-iodine (Betadine) – or saline-moistened gauze and sterile dressing for definitive care in the operating suite. All patients involved in a significant motor vehicle accident should have, at a minimum, a lateral cervical spine radiograph. If the patient is unconscious, or otherwise unable to cooperate with the examination, radiographs of the entire spine should be performed to rule out an occult injury. Other radiographs should be obtained on the basis of clinical suspicion. Open fractures present unique problems in themselves. Some general principles should be followed in their management.

Treatment of Open Fractures

The goal in the treatment of open fractures is to restore function to the limb and patient as fully as possible. To achieve this goal, the prevention of infection is of primary importance. Infection can lead to malunion, nonunion, and even secondary amputation. In open fractures, it is the size of the open wound and amount of devitalized tissue that are the primary determinants of prognosis.[5] The classification

TABLE 11–1

Grade I	An open fracture with a wound less than one centimeter long and clean
Grade II	An open fracture with a laceration more than one centimeter long without extensive soft tissue damage, flaps, or avulsions
Grade III	Either an open segmental fracture or an open fracture with extensive soft-tissue damage or a traumtic amputation

From Gustilo RB, Anderson JT: Prevention of infection in the treatment of 1,025 open fractures of long-bones. J Bone Joint Surg 58A:453–458, 1976; with permission.

of open fractures set forth by Gustilo and Anderson[7] allows for some prognostication and treatment guidelines in the care of the patient with an open fracture.

In the emergency room, all open wounds should be irrigated in a preliminary fashion to remove gross debris. Aerobic and anaerobic cultures should be taken prior to debridement. The wound should then be dressed with a dilute povidone-iodine (Betadine)– or saline-moistened gauze and compressive dressing. Extremities should be splinted to prevent further injury until definitive debridement is carried out in the operating room. Antibiotic coverage should be instituted promptly after cultures have been obtained. Originally, the antibiotic of choice was a first-generation cephalosporin.[7,8] Recent studies have shown a greater incidence of the isolation of gram-negative pathogens from wound cultures.[9] As a result, more recent recommendations suggest the use of a second-generation cephalosporin,[10] a first-generation cephalosporin with an aminoglycoside,[9] or a single third-generation cephalosporin.[9]

Open fractures can be categorized into three grades or types based on the extent of soft tissue injury (Table 11–1). Grade III injuries can be further broken down into three categories (Table 11–2).

Specific treatment of open fractures is dependent upon the location and specific fracture patterns, which will be discussed individually. However, there are some general principles of treatment that are applicable to all open fractures.[5,7,9,11] The most important aspect of open fracture care is the meticulous debridement of all debris and devitalized tissue. Other important principles include fracture stabilization, antibiotic therapy, repeat debridement at 24 to 48 hours, as warranted, and delayed primary or secondary closure of the wound at 5 to 7 days.[9]

Grade I open fractures can be treated by whatever method the fracture pattern dictates, since the infection rate is similar to that with closed fractures[11] (Fig. 11–1A to E).

The infection rate for grade II (Fig. 11–2A to C) open fractures is significant,[7,9,11] and the gains of early internal fixation must justify the increased risks. Acceptable infection rates have been found with closed intermedullary nonreamed nailing of open fractures,[12,13] which is a consideration.

In grade III open fractures (Fig. 11–3A to F), the infection rate can be very high.[7,9,11] Internal fixation should be used only when needed as a limb-saving proce-

TABLE 11–2

Grade IIIA	Adequate soft-tissue coverage of a fractured bone despite extensive soft-tissue laceration or flaps, or high-energy trauma irrespective of the size of the wound.
Grade IIIB	Extensive soft-tissue injury loss with periosteal stripping and bone exposure. This is usually associated with massive contamination.
Grade IIIC	Open fracture associated with arterial injury requiring repair.

From Gustilo RB, Mendoza RM, Williams BN: Problems in the management of Type III (severe) and open fractures: A new classification of Type III open fractures. J Trauma 24:742–745, 1984; © by Williams & Wilkins, 1984.

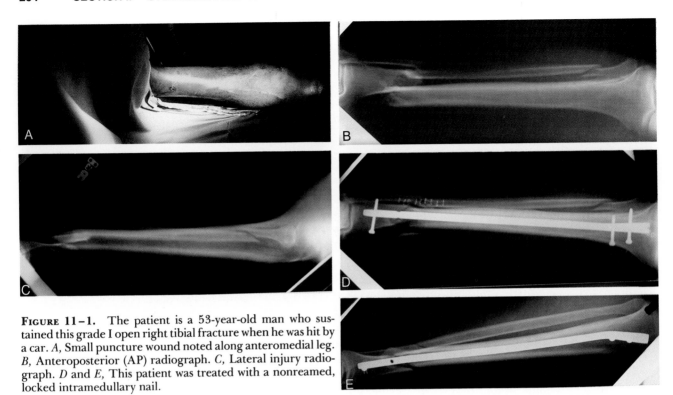

FIGURE 11–1. The patient is a 53-year-old man who sustained this grade I open right tibial fracture when he was hit by a car. *A*, Small puncture wound noted along anteromedial leg. *B*, Anteroposterior (AP) radiograph. *C*, Lateral injury radiograph. *D* and *E*, This patient was treated with a nonreamed, locked intramedullary nail.

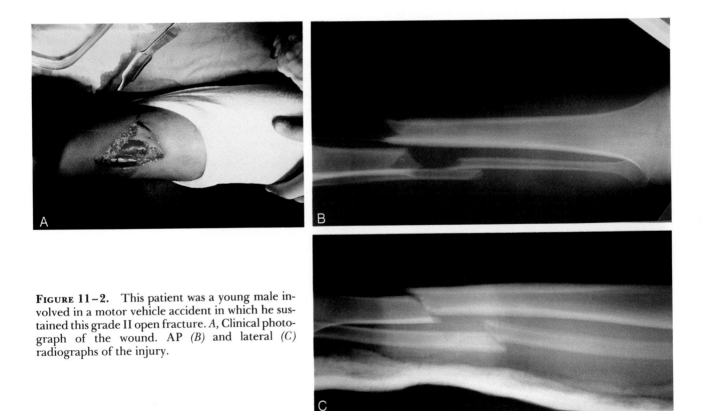

FIGURE 11–2. This patient was a young male involved in a motor vehicle accident in which he sustained this grade II open fracture. *A*, Clinical photograph of the wound. AP *(B)* and lateral *(C)* radiographs of the injury.

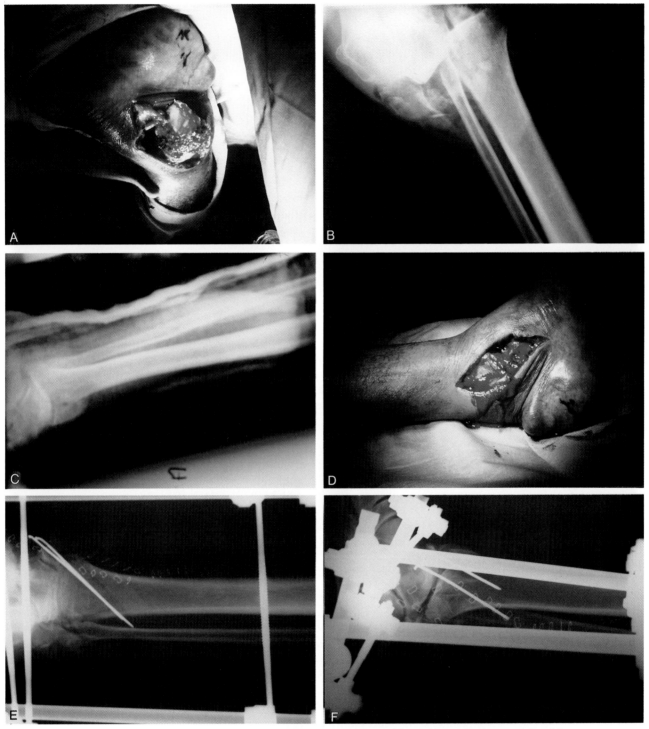

FIGURE 11–3.   The same patient from Figure 11–1 also sustained this grade III open left ankle fracture. *A,* Photograph prior to reduction shows significant periosteal stripping and loss of articular cartilage. AP *(B)* and lateral *(C)* radiographs of the injury. *D,* Photograph of the ankle after debridement, irrigation, and reduction. AP *(E)* and lateral *(F)* radiographs after stabilization with an external fixator placed across the ankle.

dure, for protection of an arterial repair that cannot be done by other means, or when preservation of joint function justifies the risk. In general, external fixation is the treatment of choice for initial stabilization.

Open intra-articular fractures present a unique challenge. The majority of open intra-articular fractures have type I wounds.[5] The low infection rate with type I injuries makes it possible to use immediate internal fixation after meticulous debridement. Because of the increased risk of infection in type II and type III open fractures, careful surgical judgment is necessary. In simple fracture patterns, minimal internal fixation can generally be placed with very little added injury to the soft tissues.[5] In severely comminuted open intra-articular fractures, the stabilization provided by internal fixation may actually be beneficial in soft tissue healing and infection prevention.[11]

The bone most commonly involved in grade III open injuries is the tibia.[9] This is because a relatively large portion of the bone is subcutaneous. Owing to the severity of grade IIIC injuries, the relatively poor functional results obtained, and the high rate of secondary amputation, it has been suggested that serious consideration be given to primary amputation in these injuries.[14]

Fractures involving the various anatomic areas of the body present unique concerns and, as such, will be discussed separately.

CERVICAL SPINE

As mentioned previously, great care should be taken in the transport of patients with suspected cervical spine injuries. A high index of suspicion can be the physician's greatest ally in the diagnosis of spinal injuries. Timely and accurate diagnosis can have serious implications for the patient's ultimate recovery. In many cases, the patient can direct the physician to an area of spinal trauma by subjective complaints and objective findings. There are, however, certain circumstances that should prompt a more directed clinical suspicion in the recognition of cervical spine injuries,[15] as follows:

1. The patient with external head trauma in whom bleeding from these wounds may distract from the cervical spine situation
2. The patient who may have sustained closed-head trauma, with an altered level of consciousness, that precludes complaints of pain
3. The patient who presents in a coma
4. The acutely intoxicated individual
5. The elderly patient who presents with a scalp laceration with associated hemiparesis
6. The victim of multiple injuries

These are just some examples of patients who should have, as a minimum, a lateral radiograph of the cervical spine. There is also the problem of the patient who requires endotracheal intubation in the setting of possible cervical spine injury. It has been recommended that they undergo nasal tracheal intubation, without axial traction and with the head and neck stabilized in the neutral position.[16] In the patient in whom an unstable cervical spine injury has been diagnosed and either further diagnostic evaluation or surgery is needed for other injuries, skeletal traction through a halo or skull tongs is the recommended method of immobilization until either definitive surgical stabilization or placement in a halo cast[17] or vest is performed.

Anteroposterior, lateral, and open-mouth odontoid views are recommended in the initial evaluation of the patient with suspected cervical spine injury. On the basis of these films and the clinical evaluation, further diagnostic procedures can be obtained. The CT scan, both with and without associated myelogram, can be very helpful for the patient in whom plain films do not give adequate diagnostic information. Thin-section tomography can also play a role in the diagnostic evaluation of cervical spine injuries.[18] The advent of the magnetic resonance scan has given us a new opportunity to view the neurologic elements and to get a much clearer picture of the relationship of the fracture and disc fragments to neural injury.

Injury to the cervical spine can fall into one of three broad categories:

1. Pure ligamentous injuries
2. Fractures without associated ligamentous injuries
3. Fracture-dislocation

Between each intervertebral segment there are at least three joints—the intervertebral disc and the paired posterior facet joints. Each of these joints must be accurately assessed in regard to normal flexion, extension, and excursion. It should also be remembered that in children normal variations can sometimes be misconstrued for injury due to epiphyseal variations, unique vertebral architecture, and incomplete ossification and hypermobility.[16] These variations need to be kept in mind during the evaluation of a child with a history of neck injury, pain, and stiffness.

We would like to discuss some specific injury patterns in the cervical spine that are most commonly encountered in clinical practice.

Fractures of the atlas (Jefferson's fracture) occur owing to axial load to the top of the head. The lateral masses of C1 are spread apart and, as such, do not cause encroachment of the neural canal. These fractures can generally be treated in a halo cast[17] for 6 to 8 weeks, followed by a cervical orthosis for an additional 6 to 8 weeks.[5]

Fractures of the odontoid process have been classified into three groups.[18] Type I consists of fractures of the top of the dens due to avulsion of the annular ligaments. Because this fracture is above the level of the restraining transverse ligaments, it is generally stable. These fractures routinely heal with simple immobilization in a collar. The type II fracture occurs at the junction of the dens with the vertebral body. These fractures can be very troublesome. A recent multicenter study by the Cervical Spine Research Society[1] noted that although the success rate was higher with posterior C1–2 fusion, there were also more complications. The patients at greatest risk for nonunion are those over the age of 40 who have significant displacement at the fracture site. Posterior displacement appears to be more worrisome than anterior displacement. In the young patient with a minimally displaced fracture, the halo vest is still the treatment of choice. Type III fractures are ones in which the fracture line extends down into the cancellous portion of the vertebral body. The halo vest is still the treatment of choice for this fracture as well, although surgery may be needed for the very unstable fracture.[1]

Fractures of the pedicles of the second cervical vertebrae have been classically called hangman's fractures. This fracture is generally caused by axial load with the head in the extended position. In the unstable fracture, the body of C2 will displace anteriorly. The treatment of choice for the minimally displaced fracture is simple immobilization in a halo vest. For the significantly unstable fracture, in which anterior displacement cannot be controlled by the halo, initial skeletal traction for 3 to 4 weeks prior to application of the halo may be necessary. This fracture is through bone at the level of the pedicles and will generally heal very readily if immobilized.

In the patient with a history of neck injury, progressive ligamentous damage can lead to advancing degrees of subluxation or dislocation. On the initial radiographs, there may be no evidence of abnormality or, perhaps, only slight widening of the posterior elements. The cervical muscle spasm may be splinting the neck. If flexion-extension lateral views do not show any instability, this patient should be placed in a cervical collar, with repeat flexion-extension views taken after the spasm has resolved. This time usually is 10 days to 2 weeks. The normal amount of motion between intervertebral segments was delineated by Panjabi and White.[19] Instability is defined as more than 3.5 mm of translation of any vertebral segment on another or more than 11 degrees of angulation between vertebral bodies. Further degrees of ligamentous injury may manifest as a facet dislocation. Unilateral facet dislocation most often occurs in the lower cervical spine. The extent of damage to the ligaments and discs is often less severe than with bilateral facet dislocations.[20] In the unilateral facet dislocation, there is approximately 25 per cent forward vertebral body subluxation.[5] In the anteroposterior radiograph projection, minor deviation of the spinous process may be noted, with a slight widening of the intervertebral disc space at the joint of Luschka. In the bilateral facet dislocation, a true lateral view can clearly delineate the pathology. There is a significant incidence of neurologic involvement in facet dislocations. In the unilateral facet dislocation, the most common injury is a nerve root lesion.[20] In the bilateral dislocation, there is a much higher incidence of complete transverse cord lesions.[20] The initial treatment, to obtain reduction, consists of application of traction through skull tongs positioned in slight flexion. If this method is not successful, operative reduction through a posterior approach is indicated. The possibility of increased postoperative neurologic deficit because of retropulsed disc fragments must always be considered, and subsequent anterior discectomy may be needed. It is wise to perform preoperative myelography or magnetic resonance imaging to delineate possible anterior disc fragments prior to posterior surgical reduction.

Vertebral body fractures are quite variable in their severity and clinical presentation. These may range from minor anterior body compression fractures to severely comminuted burst fractures with retropulsion of bone fragments in the canal. The treatment needed varies with the degree of fracture or the presence of neurologic deficit. A complete discussion of the various neurologic syndromes and pathologic injuries to the cervical spinal cord is beyond the scope of this chapter. Several excellent textbooks are available if further information is needed.

Another indication for early operative intervention is gunshot wounds to the cervical spine. This intervention is to prevent both cervical spinal cord fistulae[5] in patients with dural injuries and infection in patients who have sustained transpharyngeal gunshot wounds to the neck.[21]

THORACOLUMBAR SPINE

Anatomically, the thoracic spine is inherently more stable. This stability is due to the surrounding rib cage, which decreases available motion and helps to splint the spine. The parallel nature of the ribs does permit comparatively more free motion in rotation than in other planes. Neurologic injury above T10 is almost entirely cord injury, and as such, significant injuries to this area tend to be irreversible.

The lumbar spine, because of the anatomic features of the vertebrae and the large intervertebral discs, tends to allow more free motion between segments than does the thoracic spine. There is a wide area of flexion-extension but a much greater restriction on rotation because the orientation of the facet articular surfaces is much closer to the sagittal plane.

The thoracolumbar junction consists of a transitional area from the thoracic spine, with its surrounding rib cage, to progressively more lumbar-like vertebrae. Injuries in this area may involve the sacral segments of the spinal cord (clonus medullaris) or intradural nerve roots that make up the cauda equina. Recovery from injury to the clonus is dependent upon the initial severity of the injury.[22] However, cauda equina and nerve root injuries are much less predictable. Injuries below L1 do not involve the spinal cord and injure the cauda equina only.[22]

The three-column structural classification of thoracolumbar fractures by Denis[23] is the most commonly accepted method of determining stability in thoracic and lumbar fractures. In this classification, the spine is compartmentalized into anterior, middle, and posterior columns. Injury to any two columns signifies an unstable fracture pattern.

Spinal fractures can be either minor or major.[23] Minor injuries consist of fractures to the articular, transverse, or spinous processes, as well as isolated fractures of the pars intra-articularis. The major injuries can be broken down into four major types based on the mechanism of injury.[23] Each of the major injury types will be discussed briefly.

The first fracture pattern is the compression fracture. The compression fracture is produced by a failure of the anterior column in compression. These injuries can occur as anterior or lateral compression fractures. Compression fractures are seen without neurologic injury,[23] and these fractures are stable in the acute setting. In severe compression fractures (> 50 per cent anterior vertebral body height loss), there may be progressive kyphosis, dependent upon the status of the posterior column, the age of the patient, and bone quality.

The second fracture pattern is the burst fracture, which is due to failure of both the anterior and the middle columns in axial compression. These injuries can be subdivided based upon the exact configuration of the fracture pattern.[23] A significant number of these patients present with a neurologic deficit.[23] The burst fracture is most common in the thoracolumbar and high lumbar regions and has a high incidence of incomplete neurologic deficit.[5,22,23]

The third major pattern is the seat belt–type injury. This injury consists of failure of both the posterior and the middle columns under tension.[23] These injuries can be subdivided based upon the path through which the fracture line travels. It can occur at one level through bone or through ligaments alone. It can also occur at two levels, through ligaments and bone.[23] Seat belt–type injuries occur most commonly in the thoracolumbar junction. Patients with these injuries tend to have a low incidence of neurologic deficit on presentation. The mode of treatment is dependent on the type of injury, neurologic deficit, age, status, and desires of the patient.

The last major injury category is that of fracture-dislocations, which are the result of failure of all three columns under compression, tension, rotation, or shear.[23] These injuries can be subdivided based on the mechanism of failure into flexion-rotation, shear, and flexion-distraction injuries. There is a high incidence of neurologic deficit in these patients on presentation and their condition is extremely unstable, both mechanically and neurologically. Fracture-dislocations can be seen at any level of the thoracic or lumbar spine but occur most commonly in the midthoracic or thoracolumbar spine. These injuries require surgical stabilization. There is some controversy over the timing of surgical intervention. In the complete lesion, there is no need for acute surgery.[22,24,27] In the incomplete lesion, there is a theoretical benefit to doing acute decompression and stabilization as early as possible, although this has not been definitively proved.[22,23] It has been shown that laminectomy does not improve neurologic recovery[27] and may, in fact, worsen an incomplete neurologic deficit.[24] Early stabilization does decrease spinal deformity,[27] hospital stay,[25] and time to wheelchair ambulation.[26] There is some evidence that decompression either by restoration of anatomy with internal fixation or by anterior decompression, if anterior bone fragments continue to remain, can improve recovery in the incomplete lesion.[24,28,29] Some improvement in neurologic function can be seen with late anterior decompression after neurologic recovery has reached a plateau.[29]

Spinal cord injury in children has added significance over that in an adult. Loss of truncal muscle support leads to a high incidence of progressive spinal deformity in children.[30] The higher the level of neurologic injury and the younger the patient, the greater the risk of progressive deformity. This deformity may need to be addressed by spinal fusion and should always be kept in mind when caring for the child who has sustained a spinal cord injury.

PELVIS

In the patient who has sustained blunt trauma, a pelvic fracture may constitute a major source of blood loss, with resultant hypotension. The goal in the field is to transport these patients to a major trauma center where pelvic bleeding can be controlled or replaced as expeditiously as possible. A significant portion of the mortality related to pelvic fractures is due to retroperitoneal hemorrhage. The use of pneumatic antishock trousers has been touted as a means of limiting hypotension and stabilizing pelvic fractures in transport. Their use is controversial. The pneumatic antishock trousers have been shown in hemodynamic studies to control hypotension by increasing afterload.[31] The theoretical central shift of blood volume has not, to date, been seen to occur.[31] The trousers have been demonstrated to limit inspiration when the abdominal section is inflated,[32] and the time required for deflation may lead to problems of weaning the patient from the trousers. This factor is of significance especially when concurrent injuries to the lower extremities are hidden beneath the trousers. In the urban setting, with short transport time, there is no demonstrable beneficial effect on blood pressure index or mortality.[32]

In the emergency room, initial resuscitation and replacement of blood volume are essential. Patients with unstable pelvic fractures can lose a significant amount of blood in the retroperitoneal space.[33] A thorough history of the nature of the trauma, time of the last passed urine, and time and amount of the last food and drink can be beneficial. An empty viscus (e.g., gastrointestinal tract, bladder) is less likely to rupture.[5] Inspection of the perineum for lacerations, ecchymoses, or deformity is important.[5] The gross stability of the pelvis can be determined by compressing or distracting the wings of the ilium. A rectal examination should be performed to search for possible rectal laceration or a high-riding prostate, which indicates a ruptured urethra. During the complete evaluation of the patient, other areas of concurrent bleeding must not be overlooked. It has been noted that false-positive peritoneal lavage may occur with pelvic fractures.[34] A negative peritoneal lavage is highly reliable and should allow management with the assurance that no intraperitoneal injury exists.

Plain radiographs should be taken of the cervical spine, chest, pelvis, and other areas of suspected injury. Inlet and outlet tilt views should be obtained to determine the planes and amount of displacement in Malgaigne's fractures. If the patient had a full bladder at the time of injury or sustained bilateral pubic ramus fractures (straddle fractures), a urinary tract injury should be suspected.[22] A urethrogram should be obtained prior to catheterization in the male patient who presents with blood at the urethral meatus, high-riding prostate, hematuria, or inability to void.[22] Computerized tomographic (CT) scans have been found to be very helpful in assessing osseous pelvic injury in the patient with multiple trauma.[3] Although the majority of bleeding from pelvic fractures is venous and related to the fracture surfaces, for the uncommon arterial bleeder, arteriographic embolization may be helpful.

The treatment of pelvic fractures is dependent upon the presentation of the patient and the particular fracture pattern. Pelvic fractures can be broken down into minor and major fracture patterns.[22] The minor fractures consist of fractures of the individual bones without a break in the continuity of the pelvic ring. A minor fracture may also be a single break in the pelvic ring. The fractures are generally low-energy injuries and are stable. The major pelvic fractures are those that constitute a double break in the pelvic ring and can be classified into three patterns.[22] These are as follows:

1. Malgaigne's hemipelvis fracture-dislocations
2. Straddle fractures
3. Combined hemipelvis fractures

The Malgaigne fracture-dislocation can be divided into three groups.[35] Group I injury shows only anterior disruption of the pelvic ring (Fig. 11–4A) on plain radiographs, although slight anterior sacroiliac joint ligamentous tearing or occult sacral fractures are common (Fig. 11–4B). In group II injuries, in addition to the anterior injury, a complete tearing or avulsion of the anterior sacroiliac ligament, with sparing of the posterosuperior ligament complex, is present (Fig. 11–5A and B). Group III injuries consist of complete anterior and posterior disruption (Fig. 11–6A). The anterior disruption is through the symphysis pubis or pubic rami, and the posterior injury consists of complete tearing of the anterior and posterior sacroiliac ligaments (Fig. 11–6B), fracture through the posterior aspect of the ilium (Fig. 11–6C), or a

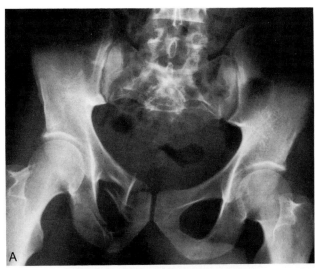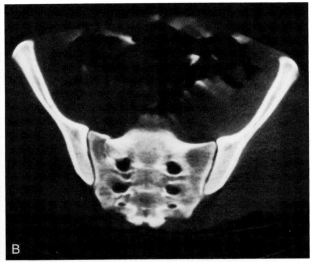

Figure 11-4. This patient was involved in a motor vehicle accident. *A,* AP radiograph of the pelvis reveals what appears to be unilateral fractures of the superior and inferior pubic rami. *B,* A computerized tomography (CT) scan of the posterior elements reveals an occult sacral fracture.

displaced sacral fracture.[26] Group I and II injuries are generally stable, while group III injuries are unstable.

The straddle fracture does not include an interruption of the normal weight transmission to the pelvis but deserves classification as a major fracture pattern because of its high rate of associated complications.

The combined hemipelvis fracture (Fig. 11-7) consists of combinations of the other major fracture patterns and minor fracture patterns.[35]

The minor fracture patterns are stable injuries and can be treated symptomatically. They should not alter the general treatment course. Group I and II major injuries are also stable and can be treated with mobilization and ambulation, as tolerated. Because the straddle fracture does not involve the main weight-bearing arch, care can be chiefly symptomatic. Generally, the patient's symptoms will modify the position they choose, and a comfortable position will be a good one for this patient's injury.[5] As the patient's pain subsides, he or she can begin with ambulation, as tolerated, without weight-bearing restrictions.

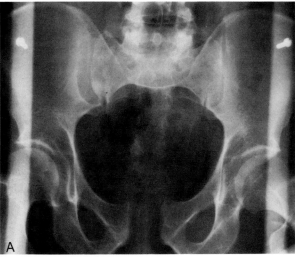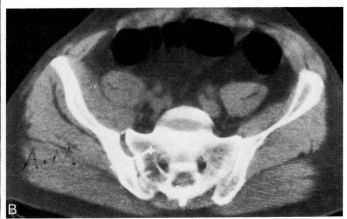

Figure 11-5. *A,* This patient sustained an anterior symphysis disruption. The right sacroiliac joint also looks abnormal. *B,* A CT scan of the patient in *A* reveals a disruption of the anterior sacroiliac ligaments.

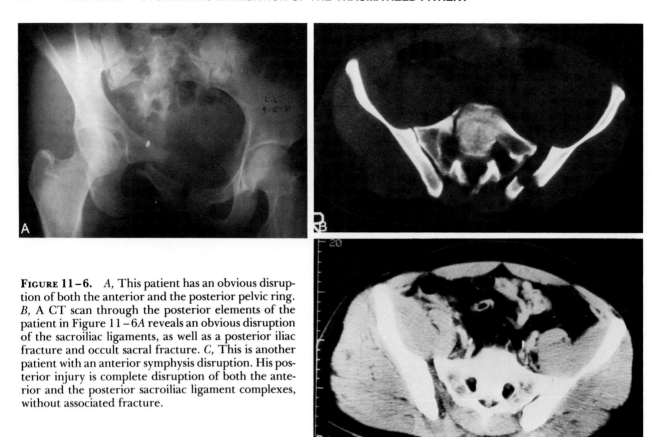

FIGURE 11–6. *A,* This patient has an obvious disruption of both the anterior and the posterior pelvic ring. *B,* A CT scan through the posterior elements of the patient in Figure 11–6*A* reveals an obvious disruption of the sacroiliac ligaments, as well as a posterior iliac fracture and occult sacral fracture. *C,* This is another patient with an anterior symphysis disruption. His posterior injury is complete disruption of both the anterior and the posterior sacroiliac ligament complexes, without associated fracture.

The treatment of unstable pelvic fractures is still controversial. Although bed rest, slings, traction, and posterior reduction with casting are still accepted methods of treatment, a more aggressive approach to unstable pelvic fractures is generally recommended today. Initial stabilization of unstable pelvic fractures with an anterior external fixation frame has been advocated by many authors.[22,33,36,37] This technique has gained wide popularity because application is easy and complication rates are low.

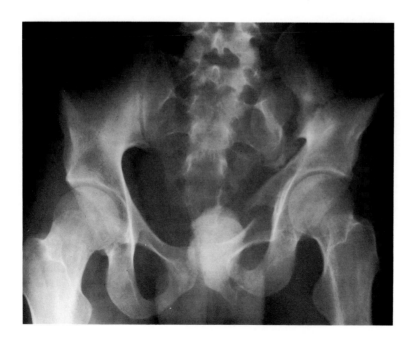

FIGURE 11–7. This patient has a complex pelvic fracture with anterior pubic ramus fractures and posterior sacroiliac disruption. Note also the fracture through the iliac wing.

It has been reported to decrease mortality[33] and is believed to decrease hemorrhage at the fracture site. To date, this latter contention has not been objectively shown.[33] The technique accepts fracture reduction, at least posteriorly, which is often far from anatomic,[35] but the reduction is usually better than that which can be obtained by other nonsurgical means.[22] Preliminary results reported by some authors have been encouraging, despite less than anatomic reduction.[37,38] The complications of this technique are related to pin tract and occasional urinary tract problems. Urethral injuries can occur with closing down anterior symphysis separations.[39] The benefits of the technique are that it allows for rapid immobilization of the fracture[23,26] and early mobilization of the patient. As with early fixation of long bone fractures, immobilization of pelvic fractures has been shown to decrease the incidence of adult respiratory distress syndrome.[40,41] The frame should be applied in such a way as to permit access to the abdomen, should surgical intervention be needed.

As more experience with open reduction and internal fixation of pelvic fractures is obtained, this method is rapidly becoming the treatment of choice for displaced fractures of the pelvis. In combination with anterior external fixation, internal fixation of posterior injuries has been shown to achieve good results.[40] The goal is immediate internal fixation; however, the risk of uncontrollable hemorrhage requires significant clinical experience in deciding which injuries can be approached on an immediate basis and which should have delayed internal fixation. A delay beyond 3 weeks may preclude obtaining an anatomic reduction because of the progress of the healing process.[40] Fractures of the acetabulum pose a unique challenge. The risks associated with pelvic fractures in general need to be addressed in addition to injury of a major weight-bearing joint. Accurate radiographic evaluation is important, and those projections previously described for pelvic fractures are helpful. CT scans can be highly beneficial in delineating anatomy. Skeletal traction has been advocated in the past, and if the superior weight-bearing dome of the acetabulum is intact, this may be adequate treatment. This traction requires at least 12 weeks of bed rest, which, for the majority of polytrauma patients, is unacceptable. The surgical approach to these fractures is dependent upon the particular fracture pattern. These fractures should be undertaken by a surgeon who not only has a thorough knowledge of the pertinent anatomy but also has significant surgical experience with these injuries. If the procedure of open reduction and internal fixation is feasible, it can have many benefits. This method allows for early mobilization of the patient and should decrease the risk of early post-traumatic arthritis. It also restores the osseous structure of the acetabulum, should late reconstruction be necessary.

LOWER EXTREMITY

Posterior dislocation of the hip, with or without associated posterior acetabular rim fractures, is most often incurred by impact of the flexed knee against the dashboard. Dislocation of the hip should be considered an orthopedic emergency. After resuscitation of the patient, examination, and radiographic documentation of the dislocation, a closed reduction should be attempted. An attempt at closed reduction in the emergency room with the patient under intravenous sedation is recommended. Otherwise, general anesthetic in the operating room is indicated. If reduction is successful, testing for stability of the hip is crucial. If there is an associated posterior rim fracture and the hip is unstable in flexion, open reduction and internal fixation of the rim fragment are indicated. After reduction, careful radiographic assessment for any retained fragments in the joint should be obtained. Irreducibility of the hip is rare in the patient who is adequately relaxed. If open reduction is necessary, it should be undertaken as expeditiously as possible because the risk of avascular necrosis is increased the longer the hip remains dislocated.

The treatment of fractures of the proximal femur is anatomic reduction with internal fixation. There are very few exceptions to this rule. The ipsilateral fracture of the hip and femur presents a unique technical challenge. In this injury, treatment of the hip should take precedence. The hip fracture in this pattern is usually a transcervical or basilar neck fracture.[22] No one method of treatment can be considered the standard for this injury.[22] The treatment of choice, when feasible, is intramedullary fixation of the shaft fracture with screw fixation of the femoral neck fracture. The surgeon's ability to fix this fracture pattern internally has been improved with the advent of new intramedullary nails that allow for screws into the femoral head through the nail. These devices can be used even in the ipsilateral intertrochanteric fracture and femoral shaft combination. The long-term results of this particular instrumentation are not yet available. The ability to obtain relatively rigid fixation in the patient with multiple trauma to allow for early immobilization has obvious benefits.

The treatment of choice of isolated femoral shaft fractures is intramedullary nailing. The use of an intramedullary nail, which can be locked both proximally and distally, has significantly increased the number of femoral fractures that can be treated in this manner. It has been shown that early intramedullary nailing of femoral fractures can have a positive effect on the incidence of adult respiratory distress syndrome.[2] Nailing of femoral fractures within 24 hours is recommended whenever feasible.

The so-called "floating knee injury," with fractures of the ipsilateral femur and tibia, poses a threat to life from blood loss and from fat and/or pulmonary embolism.[22] The occurrence of these two fractures alone indicates a multiply injured patient.[42] Associated injuries frequently occur to other organs and should be looked for and treated appropriately in patients with this injury pattern. There is a high incidence of open fractures with this injury pattern.[22] The treatment of the individual femoral and tibial fracture should be dictated by their unique circumstance. However, both fractures should be treated by a means that allows rigid fixation, not only for immobilization of the patient but also for early joint range of motion.

In the patient who has sustained lower extremity trauma, more obvious injuries may distract attention from knee dislocation. A knee dislocation is another orthopedic emergency. The position of the knee on the initial examination is not always indicative of the extent of injury. The immediate displacement due to a violent force may have been much greater with spontaneous repositioning of the joint. The immediate treatment consists of closed reduction, as soon as possible, to restore circulation and lessen the chance of nerve injury. Frequently, paramedical personnel are available at the site. If atraumatic reduction can be performed right away, it is desirable.[38] It is important that the person doing the reduction document the position of the leg and that this information accompany the patient to the hospital. Knee dislocations are classified by the relationship of the tibia to the femur. The five different types of knee dislocations are as follows:

1. Anterior
2. Posterior
3. Medial
4. Lateral
5. Rotary

Anterior dislocations are the most common and have the highest incidence of vascular injury. In a study by Jones and colleagues,[43] 45 per cent of 22 anterior dislocations had vascular compromise. Arteriography should be considered in all patients with presumed knee dislocations because of the high incidence of vascular injuries. If the patient presents with obvious vascular injury, an arteriogram should be performed only if it will not delay definitive surgical repair. A clinical examination may not detect arterial injury in these patients.[16] If vascular repair is needed, fasciectomy should be performed in the same setting. Repair of the ligamentous structure should not be done at this time. Occasionally, placement of pins across the joint or application of external fixation is needed if total stability of the knee is necessary. This is usually required only when a patellar tendon avulsion has occurred along with the other ligamentous damage.[38] Most knees can be immobilized adequately in the A position (approximately 15 to 30 degrees) with a hinged knee brace. The application of ice and strict elevation are also recommended. The small amount of motion available in the brace is desirable for evacuation of fluids.[38] Full ligamentous repair should be performed in 10 to 14 days and can be done without risk to the previous arterial repair.

Fractures of the tibia commonly occur in patients who have sustained significant trauma. The need to immobilize the patient precludes cast treatment in all but the most simple fractures. In the majority of fractures, a method of fixation that is stable and allows for early range of motion is beneficial. In the emergency room, initial management consists of alignment to the limb with careful assessment of neurovascular status. The limb should then be splinted to prevent further injury. Although the patient may have other injuries that require attention, it is imperative that close monitoring of the limb be performed to diagnose a compartment syndrome, should that develop. Compartment syndrome arises when the tissue pressure becomes greater than capillary perfusion pressure, with resultant tissue necrosis. In the conscious patient, the first sign is increasing pain out of proportion to the injury and pain with passive flexion or extension of the toes. When the patient is unable to respond to pain, the compartment pressures must be monitored by manometric or Wick catheter techniques.[44] In the patient who has sustained a crush injury to the limb, it is important to monitor not only for local compartment syndrome but also for systemic manifestations referred to as the "crush syndrome."[45] These include muscle necrosis with myoglobinuria or renal failure, shock, and the cardiac sequelae of hyperkalemia and acidosis.[45]

There are some unique fracture patterns that require special attention. The segmental tibial fracture is important because the intercalated segment has lost its medullary blood supply. For this reason, intramedullary nailing is the treatment of choice for these injuries. Plating of segmental fractures leads to further stripping of the periosteal blood supply and should be used only when excellent stability can be achieved and there is a contraindication to nailing.[38]

Some aspects of the care of open tibial fractures have been described previously. In grade I, II, and IIIA fractures, the wound can usually be closed by delayed primary closure or skin grafting. Grade IIIB injuries require a unique plan of action. External fixation is the stabilization method of choice. A staged reconstructive effort, as described by Byrd, is recommended.[41] This method entails repeat debridements until the wound is ready for either local muscle rotation or free flap coverage. Byrd recommends that coverage be obtained within the first week of injury. Treatment of other tibial fractures should be tailored to the individual patient's needs.

Fractures about the ankle generally constitute intra-articular fractures and should be treated with open reduction and internal fixation. Complex fractures of the distal tibial plafond or pilon fractures present a challenge to even the most skilled surgeon. These fractures have been broken down by Mast and Spiegel into three types[23] (Table 11–3). The type I fracture is essentially a malleolar fracture and can be treated by plate fixation of the fibula and screw fixation of the routinely large tibial fragments. The type II fracture also consists of large reconstructable fragments. A

TABLE 11–3

Type I	Malleolar fracture with posterocranial talar luxation due to large posterior plafond fragment
Type II	Spinal fracture of the tibia with extension into the plafond
Type III	Compressive fractures with pure impaction of the talus into the distal tibia with or without fibular fracture

From Meyers MH: The Multiple Injured Patient with Complex Fractures. Philadelphia, Lea and Febiger, 1984, p 294; with permission.

buttress plate is required to neutralize the comminuted area. Cancellous bone grafting should be performed when comminution is present. Type III fractures are more difficult, since severe comminution is present. The fibular fracture should be reduced and stabilized first. If the tibial articular fragments can be reconstructed, this should be done with application of a medial buttress plate, and cancellous bone grafting of the metaphyseal defect should be performed. When the fibula is highly comminuted and cannot be used to regain length and the tibia is also highly comminuted, screw fixation may be impossible.[22] In this setting, stabilization is best obtained by external fixation across the ankle. The timing of surgical intervention is very important. Ideally, this surgery should be performed in the first 12 hours, prior to significant swelling and edema. If this is not possible, then it is best to wait at least 7 to 10 days[22] to allow resolution of skin edema.

The foot is a complex interaction of various bones, joints, ligaments, and muscles that constitute the weight-bearing end organ of the lower extremity. Chronic painful conditions of the foot, the sequelae of trauma, can cause permanent, severe functional impairment. It is important that injuries to the foot be given the respect and attention they deserve. There are two injuries that demand particular attention.

The talus is one of the most important bones in the foot owing to its unique position between the leg and foot. The talus has multiple articulations. Fractures of the talus require anatomic reduction and stable internal fixation to prevent early post-traumatic arthritis. The high rate of avascular necrosis with displaced fractures of the talar neck requires early intervention in the hope of preventing this serious complication. Fractures and fracture-dislocations of the tarsometatarsal joints (Lisfranc's joints) also demand prompt attention. Delayed or inadequate treatment can lead to chronic intractable pain that precludes normal weight bearing. Treatment of these injuries consists of closed or open reduction with either a Kirschner wire or screw fixation. Compartment syndromes can occur in the severely traumatized foot and should not be overlooked.

UPPER EXTREMITY

The goal of treatment in upper extremity injuries in a multiply injured patient is early mobilization of the patient. Most injuries about the shoulder girdle are easily treated if the problem is well defined and correctly managed. Fractures of the clavicle can generally be treated symptomatically. Injury to the underlying vascular structures rarely occurs; however, a high index of suspicion must be maintained. The scapula is surrounded by heavy musculature, and fractures of this bone are well splinted by these muscles. Displaced fractures of the glenoid represent the one scapular injury that requires open reduction and internal fixation.

Shoulder dislocations are very common. Anterior dislocations constitute approximately 90 per cent of dislocations, and possible injury to the axillary artery and nerve must be considered. The hallmark in the diagnosis of shoulder dislocation is lack of rotation and a squaring-off of the shoulder profile. In the unconscious patient, the lack of external rotation may be the only evidence of posterior dislocation. Treatment consists of atraumatic reduction performed as expeditiously as possible. The position of splinting is dependent upon the direction of dislocation. The arm is splinted against the abdomen in anterior dislocations and in mild external rotation in posterior dislocations.

Proximal humeral fractures are classified according to the number of fracture fragments into two-, three-, and four-part fractures. Two-part fractures are through the surgical neck of the humerus and can be routinely treated with sling and swath immobilization after closed reduction. The treatment of three-part injuries is dependent upon the displacement of the lesser or greater tuberosity and whether the fragment causes impingement. As a general rule, displaced three-part fractures require open reduction and internal fixation. In the four-part fracture, the humeral head is by definition avascular because it has no retained soft tissue attachments. The recommendation for this injury is endoprosthetic replacement of the head with attachment of the tuberosities to the prosthesis.

The vast majority of humeral fractures will heal by closed means. This injury is very difficult to control unless the patient is upright. Because of its proximity to the humeral shaft, radial nerve palsy is not uncommon. In the patient with multiple trauma, the inability to have the patient sit upright may be an indication for operative fixation in a fracture that, were it an isolated injury, could easily be treated in a closed manner.

Fractures about the elbow are commonly intra-articular. The elbow is very sensitive to the development of heterotopic ossification, and for this reason, these injuries should be treated by anatomic reduction and fixation. Surgery delayed beyond 5 days after injury increases the incidence of heterotopic ossification.

Forearm fractures are very common injuries. Open fractures of the radius and ulna should be treated by the principles previously discussed. Because of the precise mechanics required for forearm pronation and supination, a fracture involving both bones in an adult is an absolute indication for open reduction and internal fixation. This injury can be controlled well by external splinting; therefore, definitive care can be delayed up to 2 or 3 weeks without seriously jeopardizing the final result. Careful monitoring for possible compartment syndrome is essential. The majority of distal radial and ulnar fractures can be treated by closed means. The severely comminuted distal radial fracture may best be treated by external fixation.

The hand is a highly integrated complex organ in which even slight deviations from normal can cause important functional deficits. In the severely injured hand, it is important to follow some general principles of management. These principles, as delineated by Sandzen,[22] are as follows:

1. Primary wound care
2. Salvage and protection of viable tissue and amputated parts
3. Restoration of skeletal anatomy
4. Conversion of an open contaminated wound to a closed clean area as soon as possible
5. Primary, delayed primary, or secondary reconstruction
6. Physiologic immobilization and mobilization

Primary wound care consists of meticulous wound cleansing and debridement. No viable tissue should be sacrificed because coverage of many vulnerable structures in the hand is imperative. Vessels, nerves, and tendons will desiccate if not kept moist. Skeletal anatomy should be restored by fixation of fractures. This is most easily accomplished with Kirschner wires.[46] The wound should be closed by whatever means are necessary. The use of skin grafts and cutaneous flaps, both local and distant, can be very beneficial in this regard. If the wound is clean, bone reconstruction with grafts or vascularized bone transfer can be done on a delayed primary basis within a few days of the injury. The use of irreconstructable parts destined for deletion can be helpful. Nerve repair or grafting should wait until the wound is clean, covered, and without evidence of infection. During the healing process, the hand should be immobilized in a position of function. Stable fixation of all fractures is desirable, so that mobilization of all joints is maximized.[46] Tendon reconstruction should be one of the last steps and should not be undertaken until full passive motion of the involved digits has been obtained. This discussion relates to the severely injured hand with multiple problems. Injuries to individual structures should be managed by methods that are outlined in standard hand texts.

CONCLUSION

In this chapter, we have tried to present an organized approach to some orthopedic injuries commonly found in the polytrauma patient. This review in no way constitutes a complete discussion on any one topic. The underlying theme of the entire discussion is that the patient should be mobilized to the upright position at the earliest possible time. At one time, the patient with multiple injuries had quite a discouraging prognosis. With aggressive management in the initial phase, these patients now have a much brighter prognosis, not only for surviving but also for full functional recovery.

REFERENCES

1. Clark CR, White AA: Fractures of the dens. J Bone Joint Surg 67A:1340–1348, 1985.
2. Johnson KD, Cadambi A, Seibert GB: Incidence of adult respiratory distress syndrome in patients with multiple musculoskeletal injuries: Effect of early operative stabilization of fractures. J Trauma 25:375–384, 1985.
3. Dunn EL, Berry PH, Connally JD: Computed tomography of the pelvis in patients with multiple injuries. J Trauma 23:378–383, 1983.
4. Emergency Care and Transportation of the Sick and Injured. 3rd ed. Chicago, Il, American Academy of Orthopaedic Surgeons, 1981.
5. Rockwood CA, Green DP: Fractures. Vols 1–3. Philadelphia, JB Lippincott, 1984.
6. Border JR, LaDuca J, Seidel R: Priorities in the management of the patient with polytrauma. Prog Surg 14:84–120, 1975.
7. Gustilo RB, Anderson JT: Prevention of infection in the treatment of 1,025 open fractures of long bones. J Bone Joint Surg 58A:453–458, 1976.
8. Patzakis MJ, Harvey JP, Ivler D: The role of antibiotics in the management of open fractures. J Bone Joint Surg 56A:532–541, 1974.
9. Gustilo RB, Mendoza RM, Williams BN: Problems in the management of Type III (severe) and open fractures: A new classification of Type III open fractures. J Trauma 24:742–746, 1984.
10. Antrum RM, Solomkin JS: A review of antibiotic prophylaxis for open fractures. Orthop Rev 16:81–89, 1987.
11. Chapman MW, Mahoney M: The role of early internal fixation in the management of open fractures. Clin Orthop Rel Res 138:120–131, 1979.
12. Hasenhuttl R: The treatment of unstable fractures of the tibia and fibula with flexible medullary wire. J Bone Joint Surg 63A:921–931, 1981.
13. Velazco A, Whitesides TE, Fleming LL: Open fractures of the tibia treated with Lottes nail. J Bone Joint Surg 65A:879–884, 1983.
14. Caudle RJ, Stern PJ: Severe open fractures of the tibia. J Bone Joint Surg 69A:801–807, 1987.
15. Bohlman HH: Complications and pitfalls in the treatment of acute cervical spinal cord injuries. *In* Tator CH (ed): Early Management of Acute Spinal Cord Injury. New York, Raven Press, 1982.
16. Bivins HG, Ford S, Bezmalinovic Z, et al: The effect of axial traction during orotracheal intubation of the trauma victim with an unstable cervical spine. Ann Emerg Med 17:25–29, 1988.
17. Nickel VL, Perry J, Garrett A, Heppenstal M: The halo — a spinal skeletal traction fixation device. J Bone Joint Surg 50A:1400–1409, 1968.
18. Anderson LD, D'Alonzo RT: Fractures of the odontoid process of the axis. J Bone Joint Surg 56A:1663–1674, 1974.
19. Panjabi MM, White AA: Basic biomechanics of the spine. Neurosurgery 7:76–93, 1980.
20. Braakman R, Vinken PJ: Unilateral facet interlocking in the lower cervical spine. J Bone Joint Surg 49B:249–257, 1967.
21. Jones RE, Bucholz RW, Schaefer SD, et al: Cervical osteomyelitis complicating transpharyngeal gunshot wounds to the neck. J Trauma 19:630–634, 1979.
22. Meyers MH: The Multiply Injured Patient with Complex Fractures. Philadelphia, Lea and Febiger, 1984.
23. Dahners LE, Jacobs RR, Jayaraman G, Cepulo AJ: A comparative study of external fixation devices for unstable pelvic fractures. J Trauma 24:876–881, 1984.
24. Bohlman HH, Freehafer A, Dejak J: The results of treatment of acute injuries of the upper thoracic spine with paralysis. J Bone Joint Surg 67A:360–379, 1985.
25. Dickson JH, Harrington PR, Erwin WD: Results of reduction stabilization of the severely fractured thoracic and lumbar spine. J Bone Joint Surg 60A:779–805, 1978.
26. Jacobs RR, Asher MA, Snider RK: Thoracic lumbar spinal injuries: A comparative study of recumbent and operative treatment in 100 patients. Spine 5:463–477, 1980.
27. Osebold WR, Weinstein SL, Sprague BL: Thoracic lumbar spine fractures — results of treatment. Spine 6:13–34, 1981.
28. Bradford DS, Akbarnia BA, Winter RB, Seljeskog EL: Surgical stabilization of fracture and fracture dislocations of the thoracic spine. Spine 2:185–196, 1977.
29. McAfee PC, Gohlman HH, Yuan HA: Anterior decompression of traumatic thoracolumbar fractures with incomplete neurological deficit using a retroperitoneal approach. J Bone Joint Surg 67A:89–104, 1985.
30. Lancourt JE, Dickson JH, Carter RE: Paralytic spinal deformity following traumatic spinal cord injury in children and adolescents. J Bone Joint Surg 63A:47–53, 1981.
31. Gaffney FA, Thal ER, Taylor WF, et al: Hemodynamic effects of medical anti-shock trousers (MAST garment). J Trauma 21:931–937, 1981.
32. Trunkey DD, Lewis RF: Current Therapy of Trauma — II. Philadelphia, BC Decker, 1986.
33. Gylling SF, Ward RE, Holcroft JW, et al: Immediate external fixation of unstable pelvic fractures. Am J Surg 150:721–724, 1985.
34. Hubbard SG, Bivins BA, Sachatello CR, Griffen WO: Diagnostic areas with peritoneal lavage in patients with pelvic fractures. Arch Surg 114:844–846, 1979.
35. Bucholz RW: The pathological anatomy of Malgaigne fracture dislocations of the pelvis. J Bone Joint Surg 63A:400–404, 1981.
36. Kellam JF, McMurtry RY, Paley D, Tile M: The unstable pelvic fracture — operative treatment. Orthop Clin North Am 18:25–41, 1987.

37. Slakis P, Karaharju EO: External fixation of unstable pelvic fractures. Clin Orthop Rel Res 151:73–80, 1980.

38. Montgomery JB: Dislocation of the knee. Orthop Clin North Am 18:149–156, 1987.

39. Cass AS, Behrens F, Comfort T, Matsura JK: Bladder problems in pelvic injury treated with external fixator and direct urethal drainage. J Trauma 23:50–53, 1983.

40. Browner BD, Cole JD, Graham JM, et al: Delayed posterior internal fixation of unstable pelvic fractures. J Trauma 27:998–1006, 1987.

41. Byrd HS, Spicer TE, Cierney G: Management of open tibial fractures. Plast Reconstr Surg 76:719–730, 1985.

42. Copes WS, Champion HR, Sacco WJ, et al: The injury severity score revisited. J Trauma 28:69–91, 1988.

43. Jones RE, Smith EC, Bone GE: Vascular and orthopaedic complications of knee dislocation. Surg Gynecol Obstet 149:554–558, 1979.

44. Mubarak SJ, et al: Acute compartment syndromes: Diagnosis and treatment with the aid of the wick catheter. J Bone Joint Surg 60A:1091–1095, 1978.

45. Mubarak SJ, Owen CA: Compartmental syndrome and its relation to the crush syndrome: A spectrum of disease. Clin Orthop Rel Res 113:81–89, 1975.

46. Green PP: Operative Hand Surgery. 1st ed. New York, Churchill-Livingstone, 1982.

III

MANAGEMENT of HEAD and NECK INJURIES

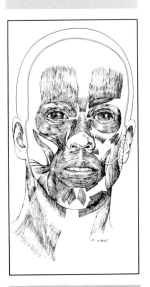

CHAPTER 12

APPLIED SURGICAL ANATOMY OF THE HEAD AND NECK

DAVID E. FROST, D.D.S., M.S., and
BARRY D. KENDELL, D.M.D., M.S.

Since traumatic injuries disrupt the anatomy, the surgeon who is to repair and replace these traumatized structures must have an in-depth knowledge of normal anatomy. In addition, the operator must consider possible variations of normal and other associated structures that may be in close relationship to the traumatized area. Although numerous texts have been written on basic anatomy,[1-11] it is thought that for completeness this textbook should include a review of major head and neck anatomy. Details on specific problems and treatment modalities are found in the appropriate chapters. It is our intent to discuss the general anatomy, its inherent relationships, and some of the technical problem areas that should be considered in the management of traumatic facial injuries.

SKIN LINES AND LINES OF LANGER

The natural skin lines and wrinkles are major factors in determining the final soft tissue aesthetic result for the patient with facial trauma. The character and aesthetics of a scar are affected by its relationship to the location and direction of normal skin lines.

The natural skin lines and wrinkle lines are different from the lines of Langer, which denote the collagen fiber direction within the dermis. Langer believed that the skin was less extensible in the direction of the lines of tension that cross them.[2,12] In the face, Langer's lines have been shown to run across natural creases and flexion lines, thus making scars generated by incisions and trauma along those lines more noticeable. It is, therefore, recommended that elective incisions be made in or parallel to the lines of facial expression or the natural skin lines where possible[13] (Fig. 12–1).

SCALP

The scalp is made up of five layers, three of which are closely bound together. These are the skin, dense connective tissue, and galea aponeurotica. Deep to this layer

FIGURE 12-1. Natural skin lines and wrinkle lines are recommended for elective incisions.

is the loose connective tissue and the periosteum or pericranial layer.[1,6,8] The scalp will bleed freely because the vessels are bound firmly in the dense connective tissue layer (Fig. 12-2). This firm union and the extensive blood supply make bleeding frequently excessive and often difficult to control rapidly with hemostats. Pressure will usually control the open bleeders, and the rapid application of Raney clips will control full-thickness lacerations or elective incisions. Because of the nature of the loose connective tissue layer, dissection of the scalp will be rather easy in this tissue plane. In a like manner, however, the effusion of fluid will spread rapidly in this plane, leading to a boglike edema.

The innervation of the scalp comes from the trigeminal nerve anteriorly and

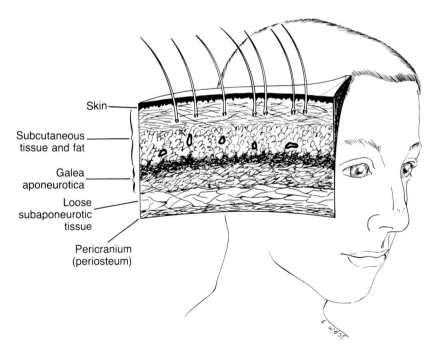

Skin

Subcutaneous tissue and fat

Galea aponeurotica

Loose subaponeurotic tissue

Pericranium (periosteum)

FIGURE 12-2. Layers of scalp.

laterally and from the cervical nerves (C2, C3) posteriorly.[1,4] If one keeps dissection within the loose connective tissue layer, these nerves are avoided. In the supraorbital region, the superior orbital branch of the trigeminal nerve passes through either a notch or a foramen to innervate this area of the scalp. The supratrochlear nerve is located slightly medially and innervates the upper lid and the medial area of the forehead.[14] Care should be taken when elevating flaps and managing lacerations in this area. As with most areas of the anatomy, when the skeleton makes angles or muscles insert, there is a more dense attachment of the skin and soft tissue. In the scalp, this is most notable in the glabella and supraorbital regions.

SKIN OF FACE

The skin of the face becomes specialized in the area of the eyelids, which are composed of two structural lamellae: the external lamellae formed by the orbicularis muscle and its overlying skin and the internal lamellae of the tarsal plate and conjunctiva.[15] The skin of the eyelid is extremely thin and delicate and contains small lacrimal, sweat, and sebaceous glands as well as fine hair follicles[16] (Fig. 12–3).

The skin of the nose is tightly attached to the lower lateral cartilages in the tip area. In other areas, the skin is less tightly adherent to the underlying infrastructure. The skin is thin in the nasal root and tip areas and thicker in the supratip region.[4]

OSTEOLOGY

The bones will be considered in the traditional facial thirds[3,5] (Fig. 12–4A and B).

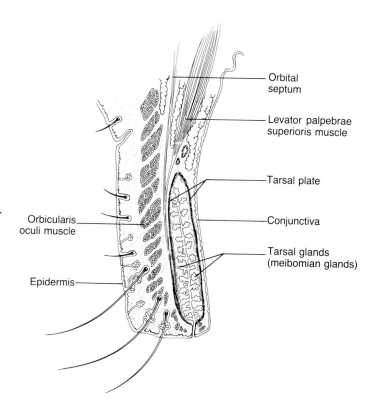

FIGURE 12–3. Cross-section of eyelid.

Orbital septum

Levator palpebrae superioris muscle

Tarsal plate

Conjunctiva

Tarsal glands (meibomian glands)

Orbicularis oculi muscle

Epidermis

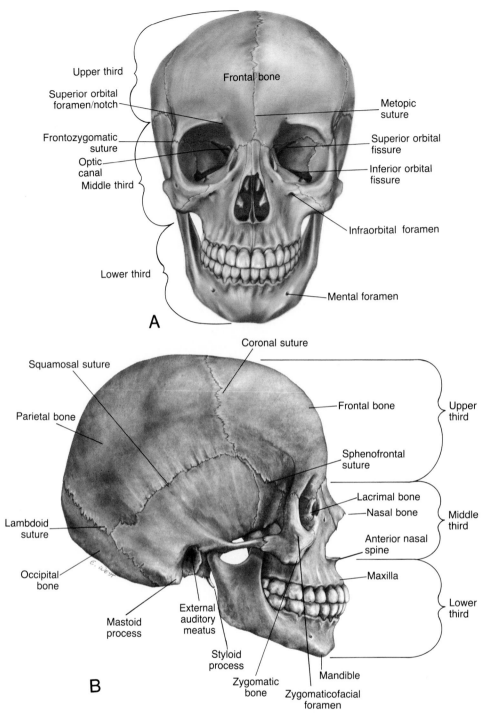

FIGURE 12–4. *A*, Frontal view of skull. *B*, Lateral view of skull. Facial thirds are noted.

MIDFACE

The maxilla, zygoma, lacrimal, nasal, palatine, inferior nasal concha, and vomer bones are collectively referred to as the middle third of the facial skeleton.[4,17,18] Although the sphenoid, frontal, and ethmoid bones are not classically facial skeleton bones, they are frequently traumatized in midfacial fractures and thus should be considered in the midfacial skeleton. The bones will be discussed separately, but their interconnections are of utmost importance because they tend to increase support to each other.

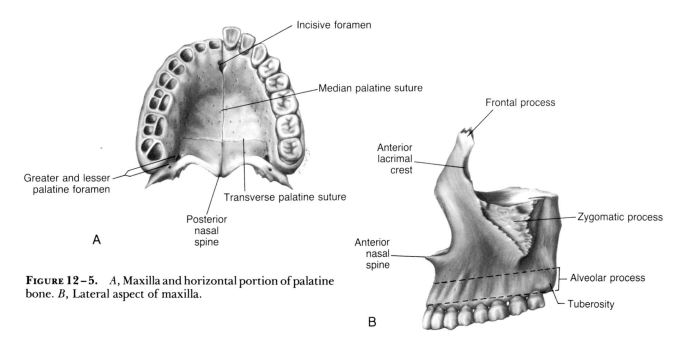

FIGURE 12–5. *A*, Maxilla and horizontal portion of palatine bone. *B*, Lateral aspect of maxilla.

Maxilla[1,2,4,6,8,10,19] (Figs. 12–5*A* and *B* and 12–6)

The maxilla is a paired bone of the upper jaw, fused to form one, and is the central focus of the middle third of the face. Each hemimaxilla contains a large pyramid-shaped body, the maxillary sinus (antrum of Highmore), and four prominent processes—the frontal, alveolar, zygomatic, and palatine.

The body of the maxilla is hollow and contains the maxillary sinus. The anterior wall of the sinus is the facial surface of the maxilla and is usually quite thin. The medial wall is the lateral nasal wall. The sinus opens superiorly and medially into the nasal cavity at the semilunar hiatus in the middle meatus. The superior wall or roof of the sinus is the orbital floor, and the floor of the sinus is the palatine and alveolar processes of the maxilla.

The frontal process arises from the anteromedial corner of the body and articulates with the frontal bone to form the medial orbital rim. The medial portion of the frontal process fuses with the nasal bone and may, therefore, be termed the nasofrontal process. Posteriorly, the process articulates with the lacrimal bone to form the anterior portion of the medial orbital wall. This area of articulation with the frontal bone, nasal bone, and lacrimal bone is prominent in the facial skeleton and is frequently fractured by blunt trauma.

FIGURE 12–6. Medial aspect of maxilla and palatine bones.

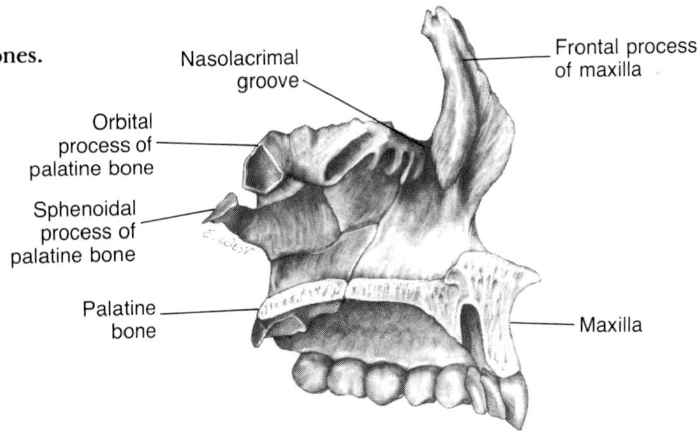

The inferiorly extending portion of the maxilla is the alveolar process, which contains the maxillary teeth. The teeth are key to the accurate management of many midfacial fractures. This process may be fractured from direct trauma and, therefore, may be functionally separate from other portions of the maxilla.

The horizontal process arising from the lower edge of the medial surface of the body is the palatine process. It joins the process of the other side and forms the major portion of the hard palate.

The zygomatic process of the maxilla arises from the anterolateral corner of the maxilla and articulates laterally with the zygoma. Together they form the inferior orbital rim and the greatest portion of the orbital floor. The infraorbital foramen is on the anterior surface of the zygomatic process of the maxilla.

Surgical Note: The classic Le Fort I fracture passes through the anterior wall of the maxilla, extending posteriorly to the pterygoid plates. It is important to remember that this is a paired bone and, even though it is fused in the midline, in adults it will behave like two separate bones when manipulated. It may often be separated along the midpalatal suture in the more extreme facial fractures.

Zygoma[1,2,4–6,11,15,20] (Figs. 12–4A and B and 12–7)

The zygoma (zygomatic, malar bone) is a paired bone that makes up the essence of the cheek prominence. This thick, strong, diamond-shaped bone forms the lateral and anterior projections to the midface and is composed of four processes. The frontal process forms the lateral orbital wall and articulates with the frontal bone at the frontozygomatic suture. It is this articulation that is either separated or rotated in isolated zygomatic fractures. The temporal process forms the zygomatic arch and articulates with the temporal bone. The maxillary process articulates with the maxilla to form the infraorbital rim and part of the floor of the orbit. Finally, the fourth process joins the maxilla on the lateral wall and forms the zygomatic eminence. This is an area of thickened bone that is usually available for fixation in the treatment of zygomaticomaxillary complex (ZMC) fractures. Along the crest of the zygoma on the inferior aspect is the insertion of the masseter muscle. The direction of force for this muscle is down and backward, and its contraction will contribute to displacement of

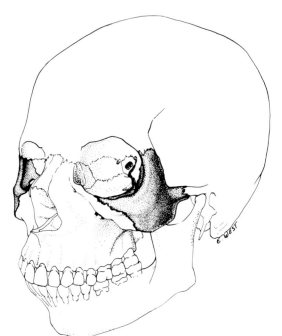

FIGURE 12–7.   Zygoma (malar) showing articulations.

the complex fracture of the zygoma and may precipitate redisplacement in the improperly fixated fracture.

The zygoma articulates with the sphenoid on the posterior aspect of the frontal process. This articulation is with the greater wing of the sphenoid and forms the lateral wall of the orbit.

The only foramina of the zygomatic bone are the zygomaticofacial foramen, which opens from the orbital surface of the bone and passes to the eminence, and the zygomaticotemporal foramen, which opens to the infratemporal fossa. The zygomaticofacial and zygomaticotemporal branches of the second division of the trigeminal nerve pass from within the orbit to the surface and give sensory innervation to the associated structures.

Surgical Note: The classic zygomaticomaxillary fracture (tripod, ZMC, and trimalar) involves this bone and its articulations. Details on the fracture and its management are found in Chapter 18. The options of surgical manipulation for reduction include the following.

TEMPORAL FOSSA APPROACH[14,20-23]

The Gillies approach is made via an incision in the hair-bearing area of the scalp approximately 2 cm above and 1 cm anterior to the ear. This incision is carried down to the level of the temporalis fascia. The only structure of anatomic significance is the superficial temporal artery. This vessel courses across the area of the incision and can be identified by palpation and thus avoided by the properly placed incision. If it is encountered, it can be ligated and cut without complications. The temporalis fascia runs to the arch of the zygoma. An incision would be made through this fascia to expose the muscle and develop a path for the passage of instruments for the manipulation of the zygoma. The main anatomic concern is being too superficial to the fascia, thus introducing the elevator lateral to the arch.

LATERAL BROW APPROACH[14,15,20,21,24]

The lateral brow incision is made to allow easy access to the frontozygomatic suture, as this area frequently requires open inspection, manipulation, and stabilization. Again, no major anatomic structures lie in close approximation. The incision is made full thickness to bone, and the periosteum is reflected to expose the fracture. Generally, some form of elevator is placed posteriorly in the infratemporal fossa to aid in elevation of the fracture. Care should be taken not to lever against the temporal bone and displace any nondiagnosed, nondisplaced skull fractures. The incision is generally placed in the hair of the brow. The usual rule of making an incision perpendicular to the skin margin can be altered in this area, since the incision should be made with the long axis of the hair follicle to avoid damaging the follicles, which could prevent the regrowth of hair. This hair should not be shaved for numerous reasons. The hair will grow back, but slowly, and it will be a different texture and may often be sparse. Probably the most significant problem is that of aligning the hair-bearing skin margins during suturing. If this is not done properly, there will be an unsightly step in the brow when the hair does regrow.

APPROACHES TO THE INFERIOR RIM[12,14,15,18,20,25]

The multiple surgical approaches to the inferior rim and articulation of the zygoma and maxilla are described in Chapter 18. These approaches give access to the inferior orbital rim, the orbital floor, the lacrimal duct area, and, in some cases, the medial and lateral orbital walls. There are few anatomic problems if care is used to identify the layers of the inferior lid, most specifically the orbicularis oculi, the orbital septum, and the inferior orbital rim. The approaches from the skin include the infraciliary incision and a lower incision through an existing skin crease. The infraciliary incision is aesthetically pleasing but may result in excessive and prolonged edema of the eyelid. The lateral extent of this incision, combined with the frequently needed lateral brow incision, compromises the lymphatic drainage of the lower lid. The skin is thin in this area, and the skin flap must be developed carefully. The incision through the orbicularis oculi is done longitudinally to expose the inferior orbital rim. The incision through the periosteum should be on the facial aspect of the bone but above the infraorbital nerve.

TRANSORAL APPROACH[15,17–19]

The floor of the orbit, as well as the infratemporal fossa, can be approached through a buccal mucosal incision in the posterior maxillary vestibule. The eminence of the zygoma becomes available for stabilization via this approach. The maxillary sinus can be entered, and the floor of the orbit, the inferior rim, and the eminence of the zygoma can be elevated from within. Posteriorly and superiorly, the infratemporal fossa can be entered, and the zygomatic arch and zygomatic body may be elevated. The buccal fat pad often interferes with visualization but is generally of no significant anatomic concern.

TRANSCONJUNCTIVAL APPROACH[5,14,21]

The final approach to the orbital floor is via the transconjunctival incision. Its only advantage is the avoidance of the slight facial scar from the infraciliary approaches. In the case of trauma, this is usually not a major factor. The incision is made through the conjunctivae at the lower border of the inferior tarsal plate, with the lower lid retracted inferiorly. The dissection can then be made either preseptally or retroseptally. The advantage of preseptal dissection is better control of the orbital fat. The approach to the orbital floor is otherwise the same, and there are no significant anatomic problems associated with these approaches.

Nasal Bones[1,2,4,6] (Figs. 12–4 and 12–8)

The nasal bones are rectangular and articulate with the frontal bone superiorly and with each other in the midline. At the superior articulation, they are relatively thick, but inferiorly they are much thinner, and it is in this area that most fractures occur. The nasal bones articulate posteriorly with the frontal process of the maxilla.

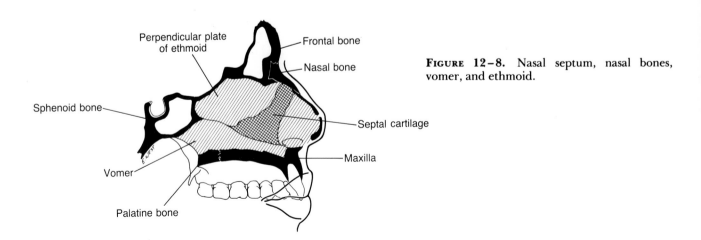

FIGURE 12–8. Nasal septum, nasal bones, vomer, and ethmoid.

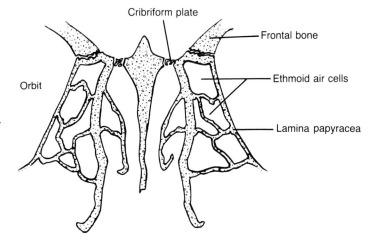

FIGURE 12-9. Frontal section of ethmoid bone.

Ethmoid Bone[1,2,4-6,11,19] (Fig. 12-9)

This unpaired bone is central to the facial structure, and it is an integral part of the nasal structure, both orbits, and the anterior cranial base. The perpendicular plate forms the superior and anterior portions of the nasal septum and attaches to the cribriform plate. It articulates with the vomer posteroinferiorly and with the sphenoid bone posterosuperiorly.

The cribriform plate articulates with the frontal bone anteriorly and laterally and with the sphenoid bone posteriorly. Hanging bilaterally from the cribriform plate are the superior and middle nasal conchae. The middle concha has the thin-walled ethmoid air cells, which extend lateral to it. The multiple septa that pass relatively perpendicular to the conchae extend laterally to the thin plate of bone that constitutes the majority of the medial orbital wall. This bone is the lamina orbitalis of the ethmoid. It is extremely thin—hence its name, the lamina papyracea.

Surgical Note[11,15,17]: The thin lamina orbitalis may be fractured in blunt orbital trauma. The anterior ethmoid artery is a point for ligation as it passes from the orbital to the nasal aspect of the ethmoid bone. As this artery is one of the terminal branches of the ophthalmic artery, a branch of the internal carotid artery, it is not affected by the usual measures to control facial bleeding and may require direct ligation via a medial canthal approach. The anterior ethmoid foramen is approximately 1.5 cm deep from the medial orbital rim. Rarely is any surgical manipulation of this bone necessary or possible.

Vomer[1,4,7] (Fig. 12-8)

The vomer is a plow-shaped bone that is located in the midline of the nasal fossa and forms the posterior portion of the nasal septum. It articulates with the palatine, maxillary, and ethmoid bones, and it rarely is of significant concern in the primary management of facial trauma.

Palatine Bones[1,2,4,5] (Figs. 12-5A, 12-6, and 12-10)

The paired palatine bones connect the maxilla with the sphenoid bone. This extremely irregularly shaped bone is composed of a major horizontal portion and the perpendicular plates. The horizontal plate articulates with the maxilla anteriorly and with the palatine bone of the opposite side in the midline to form the posterior aspect of the hard palate.

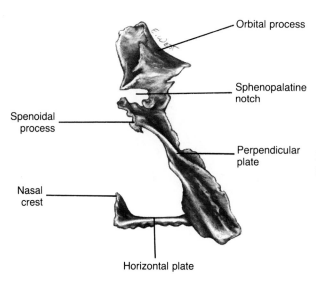

Orbital process

Sphenopalatine notch

Spenoidal process

Perpendicular plate

Nasal crest

Horizontal plate

**Posterior view,
right palatine bone**

FIGURE 12–10. Palatine bone. Note orbital surface and nasal and palatal aspects.

The vertical plate passes superiorly behind the maxilla and articulates posteriorly with the lateral pterygoid plate of the sphenoid. A ledge of the vertical plate terminates in a small contribution to the orbital floor at the posteromedial aspect. The sphenopalatine foramen is formed by the junction of the sphenoid and the palatine bones. This foramen attaches the posterior aspect of the nasal cavity with the pterygopalatine fossa.

Surgical Note[8,17]: Manipulation of the maxilla will generally accomplish adequate reduction of the palatine bones. It is important to remember the small contribution to the orbital floor, as extreme trauma to the maxilla and palate may cause some displacement or involvement of the orbital contents.

Inferior Nasal Concha[2]

This paired bone forms the bony support of the inferior turbinate bilaterally. It is only of surgical significance when it obstructs the inferior meatus and the nasal lacrimal duct.

Frontal Bone[1,4,14,26,27] (Figs. 12–4 and 12–11)

The frontal bone is a cranial bone that is unpaired and forms the anterior portion of the calvarium. The importance of this bone in facial trauma is its relationship to the anterior midfacial skeleton and the paranasal sinuses. The frontal bone articulates with the zygoma laterally and the maxilla and nasal bones medially. Inferiorly and deep in the middle of the face, it articulates with the ethmoid and lacrimal bones, and posteroinferiorly it articulates with the wings of the sphenoid bone. Posterolaterally, the frontal bone articulates with the parietal bones.

The frontal bone forms a great portion of the roof of the orbit, and laterally its thickened projections articulate with the zygoma at the frontozygomatic suture and form the lateral orbital walls. The thickening of the frontal bone in the anterior region forms the supraorbital ridges. These curved elevations connect the zygomatic portion of the frontal bone with the midportion and its articulation with the maxilla and the nasal bones. The supraorbital notch or foramen crosses this rim and transmits the frontal vessels and nerves.

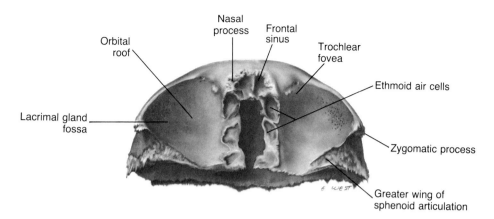

FIGURE 12–11. Frontal bone from inferior view. Note articulation with nasal and ethmoid bones.

The frontal sinus lies in the frontal bone in an area superior to the articulation with the nasal bones. About 4 per cent of the population do not have a frontal sinus. The sinus is not a simple chamber but rather is subdivided into compartments or recesses by incomplete bony partitions. There is usually an intrasinus septum that divides the left from the right. Drainage into the nose is by a well-formed duct, the nasofrontal duct. The duct itself is soft tissue and may follow a serpentine course to the anterior middle meatus of the nose, where it empties. The frontal sinuses are protected somewhat from injury by the supraorbital ridges. The anterior wall of the sinus is of low resistance, but the ridges are of high resistance.

Surgical Note: Multiple incisions and techniques of management for the frontal sinus exist. The major anatomic point of concern is the inner table, which, when fractured, will demand a neurosurgical evaluation. Other areas of concern are the supraorbital nerves, which can usually be saved with careful dissection and removal from the supraorbital foramen by the use of a small osteotome. The neurovascular bundle can then be retracted with the orbital contents.

Sphenoid Bone[1,2,4,6,19] (Fig. 12–12)

The sphenoid bone is a single midline bone situated at the base of the skull that creates the anteroinferior extent of the cranial base and the posterior transition from facial bones to cranial bones. This complex bone has many processes that have delicate articulations with the adjacent cranial and facial bones.

The sphenoid articulates with the temporal and occipital bones to form the cranial base, and anteriorly and superiorly it joins the parietal and frontal bones to complete the cranial complex. It meets the vomer and ethmoid in the midline anteriorly and meets the zygomas, palatine bones, and sometimes the tuberosity of the maxilla to complete its articulation with the facial skeleton.

The body of the sphenoid is hollow and forms two cavities separated by a thin bony septum. The hollow cavities are the sphenoid sinuses, and they drain into the sphenoethmoidal recess above and behind the superior nasal concha. Although air-fluid levels can be frequently noted on radiographs, surgical management in the trauma patient is rarely necessary.

LOWER FACE

Mandible[4,6,10,16,18,28–31] (Figs. 12–13 to 12–15)

Despite the fact that the mandible is the largest and strongest facial bone, by virtue of its position on the face and its prominence, it is very commonly fractured when maxillofacial trauma has been sustained. Mandibular fractures occur twice as

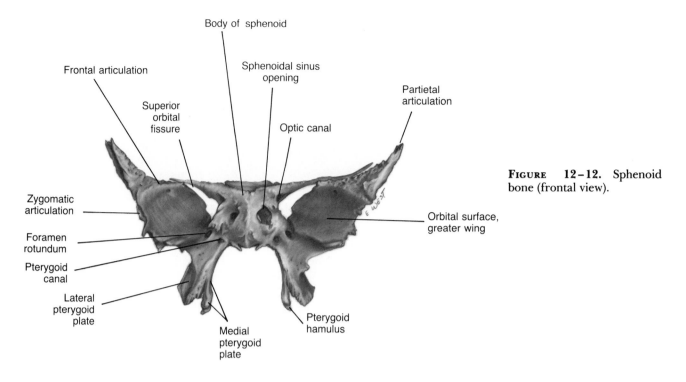

Anterior view, **sphenoid**

FIGURE 12–12. Sphenoid bone (frontal view).

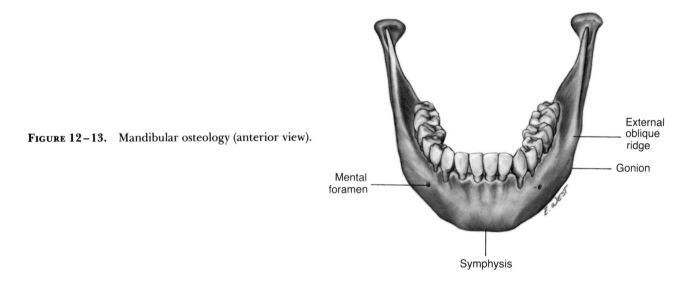

FIGURE 12–13. Mandibular osteology (anterior view).

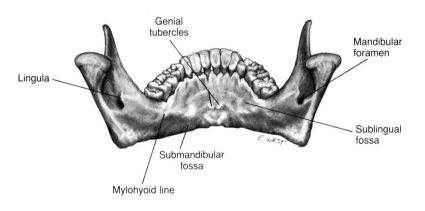

FIGURE 12–14. Mandibular osteology (lingual view).

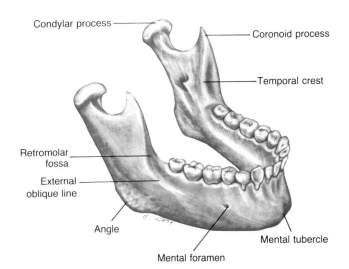

Figure 12–15. Mandibular osteology (oblique view).

often as midface fractures[29,32]; however, it has been shown in cadaver experiments that almost four times as much force is required to fracture the mandible versus the maxilla.[30] The osteology of the mandible, various muscle attachments and their influence, and the presence of developing or completed dentition all play a significant role in producing so-called inherent "weaknesses," and therefore fractures are seen more frequently in certain isolated areas.

The mandible is composed of the body and two rami, with their junction or angle forming the prominent gonion. The angle formed may vary between 110 and 140 degrees, with a mean of 125 degrees.[15] The angle decreases slightly during growth owing to changes in the condylar process, shape, and size. With aging, the angle becomes more obtuse.[30] The body is **U** shaped and has an external and internal cortical surface. The external cortical plate is thickest at the mental protuberance and in the region of the third molar. There is also a thickened triangular mental protuberance bounded laterally by the mental tubercles. The mental foramen is located on the external surface in the vicinity of the root apices of the first and second premolars. There are variations in the exact location of the foramen, as pointed out by Tebo and Telford.[33] The opening is directed backward and laterally and transmits the mental nerves and vessels.[18,34] The oblique line runs from just inferior to the mental foramen posteriorly and superiorly to the ascending ramus.

The internal cortical surface is elevated in the midline near the inferior border by the mental spine. Associated with this may be two pairs of discrete bone prominences, termed the genial tubercles. These represent the origin of the geniohyoid muscles (inferiorly) and the genioglossus muscles (superiorly). Running horizontally and slightly superiorly from front to back is an oblique ridge, the mylohyoid line, representing attachment of the mylohyoid muscle. Below this is found the shallow depression created by the submandibular gland, called the submandibular fossa. Superior to the mylohyoid line and located anteriorly is the sublingual fossa, where the sublingual gland is found in close approximation.

The ramus of the mandible, when viewed from the side, is a quadrilateral structure. The lateral surface may be rough and thickened in the region of the angle by the insertion of the masseter muscle. On the medial surface is the mandibular foramen, which leads downward and forward into the mandibular canal and which transmits the inferior alveolar nerve and vessels. The lingula is a medial bony projection to which is attached the sphenomandibular ligament. The mylohyoid groove extends from the lingula and runs anteriorly and inferiorly to the submandibular fossa. Below this is a roughened area created by insertion of the medial pterygoid muscle.

The mandibular notch is located on the superior edge of the ramus and is bounded anteriorly by the coronoid process and its temporalis attachments and posteriorly by the neck and head of the mandibular condyle. A detailed description of condylar head anatomy is found in the section on temporomandibular joint (TMJ) anatomy. Attached to the neck of the condyle anteriorly is the insertion of the lateral pterygoid muscle, and laterally is the attachment of the lateral ligament.

The body of the mandible supports the alveolus and dental structures. The body and alveolus have dense cortical outer and inner tables of bone, with central spongy or cancellous bone.

The strengths of the mandible are apparent when one examines the thick, round inferior border and the mental protuberance. The periodontal ligament and bone alveolus also combine with the trabecular pattern in the cancellous bone and are directed in a parallel fashion up the ramus to transmit pressures up to the condylar region.[35,36] The thickening on the inner aspect of the condylar neck or crest of the neck apparently acts like a main buttress of the mandible as it transmits pressure to the temporomandibular joint and the base of the skull.[29,32] The temporal crest runs from the coronoid process to the retromolar triangle distal to the terminal molar. The thickened posterior border of the mandible may act like an additional crest.[28,29]

Significant structural forces are created at the angle of the mandible owing to the cantilevered nature of its shape. The bone height at this angle is therefore critical in determining its strength as well as the presence of the perfectly aligned muscle sling created by the masseter and medial pterygoid muscles.[37] Thus aging, with its potential for bone and alveolar resorption, weakens this area.

Areas that exhibit weakness include the area lateral to the mental protuberance, the mental foramen, the mandibular angle, and the condylar neck.[29] If teeth are present, the socket is a weak zone, especially if teeth are impacted or unerupted. Even though one would think the child in the mixed dentition stage to be highly susceptible, the fact that the child's bones are so resilient and flexible offsets the disadvantage of the unerupted teeth.[30]

The Temporomandibular Joint[1,6,10,17,18,35,39–43] (Figs. 12–16 and 12–17)

The TMJ is a freely movable synovial joint located between the glenoid fossa of the temporal bone and the head of the mandibular condyle below. An articular disc (meniscus) divides the joint into two cavities. The articular surfaces of the joint and the condyle, as well as the central portion of the meniscus, are composed of collagen. This feature differentiates this joint from most other articulations because the surfaces are not covered by hyaline cartilage. Histologically, this avascular fibrous tissue may contain cartilage cells and, therefore, may be termed fibrocartilage.[10,17,18]

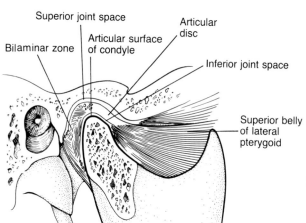

FIGURE 12–16.   Temporomandibular articulation (lateral view).

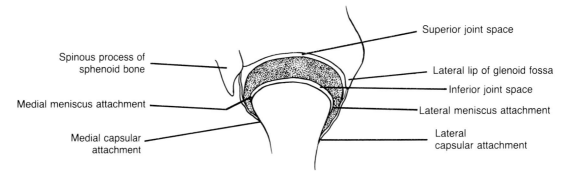

FIGURE 12–17. Temporomandibular articulation (anteroposterior view).

The condylar head is a semicylindroid process 15 to 20 mm long and 8 to 10 mm thick. The long axis of the condyle is related to the position of the ramus of the mandible and not the skeletal or frontal plane. The angle formed by the two condylar axes varies between 145 and 160 degrees. The articulating surface of the condylar head faces superiorly and forward, giving an appearance of the condylar neck being bent forward. When viewed anteriorly, the condylar head projects significantly medial to the inner surface of the ramus, but less so laterally.

The temporal bone provides the articulating surface to the skull. This bone is located anterior to the tympanic bone. The fossa is composed of a posterior slope and the convex part of the articular eminence. The squamotympanic suture forms the boundary between the tympanic bone and temporal squama. The posterior part of the fossa has a raised crest joining the articular tubercle and postglenoid process. The roof is relatively thin, separating the fossa from the middle cranial fossa. The anterior portion of the fossa or articular eminence is a broad horizontal ledge that is convex in the anteroposterior direction and concave in the transverse direction.

The articular disc is an oval, fibrous, biconcave structure that is thicker posteriorly. The disc continues posteriorly into a thick layer of loose connective tissue of varying vascularity. This tissue continues posteriorly to fuse with the posterior wall of the articular capsule.

The fibrous capsule surrounding the joint is thickest on the lateral surface and is considered a separate, distinct ligament, the temporomandibular ligament. It extends from the tubercle on the root of the zygoma to the lateral surface of the neck of the mandible behind and below the lateral pole of the condyle.

The articular capsule in general attaches from the temporal bone to the neck of the condyle. There is a loose attachment between the temporal bone and the meniscus, with considerable ability to move; however, the attachment from the meniscus to the condyle is much stiffer and is reinforced both medially and laterally. Other ligaments to consider in this region are the stylomandibular and sphenomandibular ligaments. The stylomandibular ligament originates from the styloid process and extends downward to the posterior border of the ramus of the mandible. The sphenomandibular ligament runs from the spine of the sphenoid and the squamotympanic fissure to the lingual on the medial aspect of the mandibular ramus. The maxillary artery, its middle meningeal and inferior alveolar branches, and the auriculotemporal and inferior alveolar nerves pass between this ligament and the mandible.

The meniscus, a fibrocartilaginous structure, histologically may show varying degrees and locations of cartilage cells.[1] The shape and size of the meniscus also vary. It is thinnest where it is in contact with the posterior slope of the articular tubercle. It has attachments anteriorly and medially, and it bends laterally with the capsule. The posterior attachment contains various nerves and blood vessels.

The nerve supply to the joint is principally from the auriculotemporal nerve, with some additional innervation via the masseteric nerve.

Mandibular Fracture Location

The mandible has various strengths and weaknesses, as previously discussed.[28,29,31,35-37,44] The common sites of mandibular fracture, therefore, are the mandibular condyle region, the mandibular angle region (especially in the presence of an impacted or semi-erupted third molar), the mental foramen or body region, the mandibular parasymphysis, and any component of the dental alveolus. In the very young and the aged patient with mandibular atrophy,[30] other factors, such as developing tooth buds in the child or a decrease in the cancellous/cortical ratio in the old, comes into play. Because of the **U** shape of the mandible, eccentric forces often create bilateral fractures—one at the site of injury and the other contralaterally. Nahum[36] has shown that forces in excess of 800 pounds are required to fracture the symphysis and both condylar necks. He has further demonstrated that the mandible is more sensitive to lateral impacts than to those from the frontal direction.

Anatomic Factors in Fracture Displacement

The direction of the causative blow, the direction of the line of fracture, and muscle pull will all influence the amount and direction of bone displacement.[4,6,18,30,33,36,42,45] Muscle forces acting in the anterior region of the mandible, including those inserting in the mental region on the inner surface, are those of the geniohyoid, genioglossus, digastric, and mylohyoid muscles. These will act to displace anterior segments inferiorly and posteriorly, with some possible medial component.[13,42]

In the posterior mandible, the muscles of mastication generally will cause upward and forward displacement. This observation is especially true in the pterygomasseteric sling region. The medial pterygoid will also create a medial component of pull. The temporalis muscle has two components of attachment and creates elevating forces as well as retraction forces. In a similar way, the lateral pterygoid has two attachments. The internal component is responsible for superior, anterior, and medial forces, while the external component pulls the condyle down, anteriorly, and medially. If the balance is disrupted owing to a fracture, displacement results.

The fracture angulation or direction in the mandibular angle and body region can vary. Depending upon its orientation, muscle influence may be enhanced or prevented from actively displacing the proximal segment (Fig. 12–18). If the fracture is horizontally in a downward and forward direction, this is termed favorable because of its locking effect at the fracture site. If the horizontal direction is downward and posterior, the active pull of the posterior elevator muscles, such as the temporalis, masseter, medial pterygoid, and lateral pterygoid, will displace the proximal segment superiorly. The vertical angulation of the fracture or bevel will inhibit the medial forces of the elevator group if the fracture direction is posterior and medial. This condition is termed vertically favorable. The opposite is true of the vertically unfavorable fracture traveling anteriorly and medially.

Other factors affecting the amount of displacement are the presence or absence of teeth in occlusion; muscle protection, such as in the pterygomasseteric sling region; and the exact relationship of the fracture positions to muscle insertion. This last factor is especially apparent in condylar neck injuries and their relation to the lateral pterygoid muscle insertion. If a fracture occurs above the insertion of this muscle on the neck of the condyle, little displacement occurs. If a lower level fracture occurs, displacement of the condyle will be medial and anterior owing to action of the lateral pterygoid muscle.

Surgical Note: Important to the treating surgeon are those fractures that may compromise the patient's airway. Whenever the fracture creates an unstable situation for the tongue, consideration needs to be given to immediate temporary stabilization, intubation, or other means of supporting the airway. Mandibular fractures that may

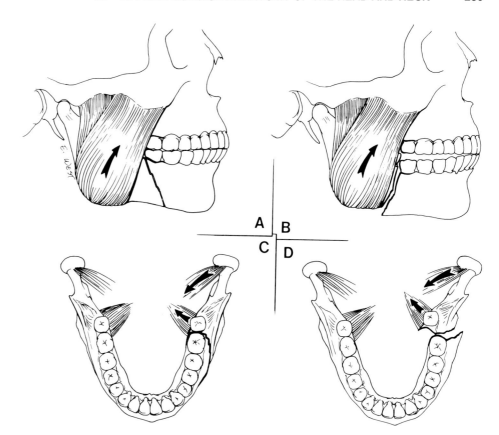

FIGURE 12–18. Mandibular angle fracture. *A*, Horizontally favorable. *B*, Horizontally unfavorable. *C*, Vertically favorable. *D*, Vertically unfavorable.

create airway problems include bilateral subcondylar fractures, bilateral parasymphysis fractures, and any maxillofacial trauma with massive edema or oral lacerations with subsequent bleeding.

Mandibular surgical approaches are as follows (Fig. 12–19): Extraoral approaches include the (1) Risdon, (2) condylar, and (3) symphysis; intraoral approaches are the (1) angle and (2) mental or parasymphysis.

EXTRAORAL SURGICAL APPROACHES

An absolute description of various surgical procedures is possible in an elective situation; however, when dealing with a trauma patient, each approach is designed

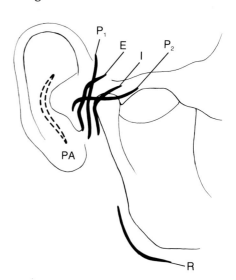

FIGURE 12–19. Surgical approaches to the posterior mandible and temporomandibular joint. P_1 and P_2 = preauricular approach; E = endaural approach; I = inverted "hockey stick" approach; R = Risdon approach; PA = postauricular approach.

taking into consideration the location of the injury, the extent of the injury, the method of stabilization to be used, possible coexisting soft tissue injuries, and potential anatomic factors.[16,28,31,32,35,37–42,45]

The basic principles of making soft tissue incisions in natural skin folds may be more difficult to apply in the presence of severe edema and lacerations. In dealing with mandibular trauma in this section, we will discuss the more common surgical approaches utilized for open reduction and exploration.

Preauricular and Condylar Approach

Several soft tissue incision designs have been described, including the inverted **L**, as described by Blair[39]; the **T**, as described by Wakely[38]; and the endaural approach advocated by Lempert.[46] Dingman and Moorman[1] slightly modified Lempert's approach and reported it in 1951. The facial nerve poses the most significant obstacle and potentially the most serious complications when damaged.

The endaural incision is started in the skin crease immediately adjacent to the anterior helix and is carried downward to the level of the tragus. The incision can then be placed in the gap between the spine of the helix and the tragus, which is filled with fibrous attachments for the lamina of the tragus. (While in the auditory meatus, the incision remains in contact with the bony tympanic plate.) This incision results in a better cosmetic appearance. It is important not to extend the incision or dissection inferiorly, since damage to the facial nerve as it exits the stylomastoid foramen may result. In the upper aspect of the incision, the superficial temporal vessels may be encountered as well as the auriculotemporal nerve. The nerve is retracted, and the vessels are retracted or ligated. The temporalis fascia is incised, and the muscle is undermined and reflected from the root of the zygomatic arch. The condyle is palpated with the help of manual movements of the body of the mandible. Depending on the extent of the dissection necessary at this point, the operator should be cognizant of the medial structures, including the maxillary artery, the middle meningeal artery, and the auriculotemporal nerve inferiorly, as well as the pterygoid plexus of veins lying anteromedially. It may be necessary in some instances also to do a Risdon approach as well when performing an open reduction in low fractures.

Risdon and Submandibular Approach (Fig. 12–20)

During the procedures to reduce and stabilize various mandibular angle fractures and, in some cases, low subcondylar fractures, some form of approach from the inferior mandible is required. Parameters used to establish an incision include the following:

1. The anteroposterior fracture location
2. The natural skin folds
3. Langer's skin lines
4. The position of the marginal mandibular branch of the facial nerve

For this reason, the incision is usually located approximately 2 cm or two finger breadths below the inferior border of the mandible. It is necessary to make an incision long enough to expose and identify anatomic structures such as the facial artery and vein as well as to achieve sufficient access to the fracture itself. After marking the skin, the head is extended and turned to one side. The incision may be cross-hatched to reapproximate soft tissues during final suturing in an anatomic manner without making a "dog-ear" at one end.

The initial incision is made through the skin and subcutaneous tissues, and any bleeding is controlled by electrocautery. The skin and subcutaneous tissue are then undermined adequately. At this point, the operator should visualize the well-demar-

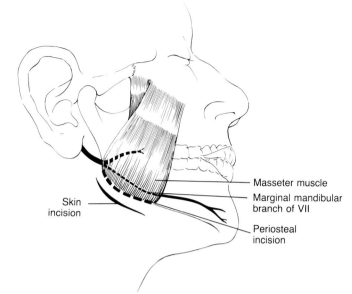

FIGURE 12-20. Risdon approach illustrating the relationship of the marginal mandibular branch of the facial nerve (VII) to the inferior border of the mandible and the periosteal incision (*dotted line*).

Skin incision

Masseter muscle

Marginal mandibular branch of VII

Periosteal incision

cated muscle lines of the platysma. The muscle may be carefully entered at one end of the incision by a mosquito hemostat and may be bluntly dissected from beneath toward the other end of the incision, keeping parallel to the inferior border of the mandible. The corner of the patient's mouth should be carefully observed during this procedure, as the marginal mandibular branch of the facial nerve travels just below the platysma muscle. The undermined muscle can be checked by carefully clamping portions, followed by complete sectioning by knife or scissors.

Next, the facial artery should be identified by palpation initially, then by blunt dissection if necessary. The marginal mandibular nerve should run directly over this artery. The artery is usually found anterior to the vein. If necessary, these structures can be isolated and ligated. The submandibular gland should be visible at this point. It may be necessary to separate the lower pole of the parotid gland from the submandibular gland. In other individuals, these structures may be separated by the stylomandibular ligament.

Palpation and isolation of the inferior border of the mandible will reveal the thickened pterygomasseteric sling. This can be sharply divided along with periosteum and can be elevated from the bony mandible until adequate visualization and mobilization of the mandible are achieved.

The Risdon modification of this incision involves a more posterior and vertical incision posteroinferior to the angle of the mandible. The advantage to this approach is that there is less likelihood of damage to the marginal mandibular branch of the facial nerve, yet good exposure is maintained for most procedures except angle fractures located more anteriorly.

INTRAORAL SURGICAL APPROACHES

Angle

Often when the presence of an impacted or partially impacted lower third molar in the line of fracture at the angle necessitates removal, an intraoral approach is reasonable for application of fixation either by wire osteosynthesis or with plates. Generally, the anatomic considerations in flap design are based on the position of the tooth (i.e., buccal, lingual, or erupted), the amount of bone displacement, and the type of fixation that will be used (e.g., rigid internal fixation may require more extensive incision). It may be necessary to strip some of the superficial tendon of the temporalis muscle off the ascending ramus. When dissection is carried down to the inferior border of the mandible, the operator must stay within the periosteal sheath to avoid damage to branches of the facial nerve as well as the facial artery and vein as they course around the mandible in the antegonial notch region.

Parasymphysis and Body

The intraoral approach to the parasymphysis and mental nerve region of the mandible affords the operator excellent visualization as well as the advantage of observing the occlusion at the same time as reduction and stabilization are performed. In addition, an extraoral scar can be avoided. Two types of incisions can be used: a vestibular or a gingival sulcus incision. In the parasymphysis and midline area, a vestibular incision should be placed far enough into the unattached mucosa to prevent postoperative gingival stripping by scar contracture. Care should also be taken to avoid the mental foramen region with the incision. Careful dissection of the mental nerve and, if necessary, nerve relocation can be carried out safely if access to the fracture is restricted. Stripping of the attachment of the various muscles of facial expression, such as the depressor anguli oris, the mentalis, and the platysma, does not seem to produce any deleterious effects on the postoperative result; however, release of these attachments does increase the changes of postoperative hematoma formation, and pressure dressings are recommended.

MUSCLES[4,6,16,18,31,36]

Muscles of Facial Expression (Fig. 12–21)

Although this group of muscles does not have a strong influence on the displacement of fractures, soft tissue damage found in major maxillofacial trauma as well as various surgical approaches necessary to repair deeper structures will invariably affect these muscles. If consideration is not given to their presence during repair and treatment planning, unsatisfactory aesthetic results will be encountered.

Muscles in this group all lie superficially and hence influence the skin.[18] They perform major activities, such as closing the eyelids as well as closing and opening the lips. All muscles in this group are innervated by the facial nerve. They can be categorized into the following areas:

1. The muscles of the scalp and auricle
2. The muscles around the orbit
3. The muscles of the nose
4. The muscles of the mouth
5. The platysma muscle extending down the neck

Anatomically, these muscles blend together at various points, and it is impossible to dissect or differentiate individual muscles at these spots. This is especially true near the corners of the mouth, where the modiolus is a convergence of six muscles. Included in this group is the buccinator muscle, which has no bone origin but instead arises from the pterygomandibular raphe and forms a continuous sheet with the orbicularis oris. The other muscles arise from bone attachments.

Muscles of Mastication[4,6,16,18,31,36] (Fig. 12–22A–C)

As discussed in prior sections, the muscles of mastication play a significant role in bone displacement following mandibular fracture. Their actions must also be consid-

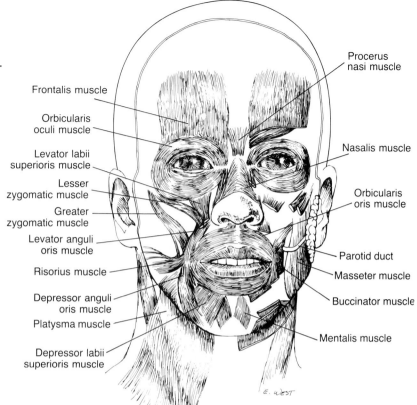

FIGURE 12–21. Muscles of facial expression.

Frontalis muscle

Orbicularis oculi muscle

Levator labii superioris muscle

Lesser zygomatic muscle

Greater zygomatic muscle

Levator anguli oris muscle

Risorius muscle

Depressor anguli oris muscle

Platysma muscle

Depressor labii superioris muscle

Procerus nasi muscle

Nasalis muscle

Orbicularis oris muscle

Parotid duct

Masseter muscle

Buccinator muscle

Mentalis muscle

ered during treatment planning, as the type and direction of placement of fixation devices may be influenced by future muscle pull.

All muscles of mastication are innervated by branches of the mandibular nerve, a division of the trigeminal nerve.

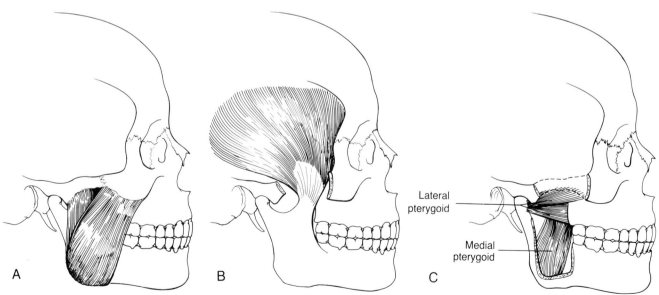

FIGURE 12–22.   Muscles of mastication.   *A*, Masseter muscle illustrating two heads. *B*, Temporalis muscle. *C*, Medial pterygoid muscle and lateral pterygoid muscle.

MASSETER MUSCLE

The masseter muscle is a large, rectangular, superficial muscle composed of superficial, middle, and deep portions (Fig. 12–22A). The superficial portion arises from the lower border of the zygoma, and the most anterior fibers arise from the zygomatic process of the maxilla. These fibers generally run downward and posteriorly. The middle part arises from the medial posterior third of the zygomatic arch, and the deep part arises from the medial surface of the zygomatic arch and from fascia over the temporalis muscle. These fibers are directed more vertically downward. All three portions are inserted together into the lateral surface of the mandible. The attachments extend to include the lower one third of the posterior border of the ramus and to the lower border as far anteriorly as the second molar. The masseter is innervated by the masseteric nerve, which reaches the deep surface of the muscle through the mandibular or coronoid notch. Blood supply is furnished by the masseteric artery, a branch of the internal maxillary artery.

The muscle acts like a powerful elevator. The deep fibers are also involved in mandibular retraction.

TEMPORALIS MUSCLE

The temporalis is a fan-shaped muscle lying in the temporal fossa (Fig. 12–22B). Its origin is from the floor of the fossa below the inferior temporal line. It also arises from the deep surface of the temporal fascia. The temporal muscle bundles converge toward the deep surface of the zygomatic arch and insert into the coronoid process medially at the apex and along its anterior border. The attachment extends down to the ramus of the mandible. There are some fibers of the posterior part that may radiate into the articular disc of the TMJ.[17]

The innervation to the temporalis muscle is via the deep temporal branches of the mandibular nerve. Blood supply is furnished by the middle and deep temporal arteries, branches of the superficial temporal artery and internal maxillary artery, respectively.

The action of the temporalis muscle is mainly elevation. There are some retracting capabilities of the posterior fibers.

MEDIAL PTERYGOID MUSCLE

The medial pterygoid muscle is found on the medial side of the mandibular ramus. (It is considered the counterpart of the masseter muscle; however, it is weaker overall.) It possesses two heads of origin (Fig. 12–22C). The larger, deep head arises from the medial surface of the lateral pterygoid plate and from the pyramidal process of the palatine bone. The superficial head arises from the pyramidal process of the palatine bone and from the tuberosity of the maxilla. The two heads unite, pass downward and backward, and insert into the medial surface of the mandible near the angle.

The innervation of the medial pterygoid muscle is via masseteric and buccal nerve branches of the mandibular nerve. A branch of the maxillary artery provides blood supply.

The medial pterygoid muscle acts mainly like a synergist of the masseter muscle during elevation of the mandible. It can also act along with the lateral pterygoid muscle to protrude the mandible.

LATERAL PTERYGOID MUSCLE

The lateral pterygoid muscle occupies the infratemporal fossa (Fig. 12–22C). It has two heads; the large inferior head arises from the lateral surface of the lateral pterygoid plate, while the upper head arises from the infratemporal surface and crest of the greater wing of the sphenoid bone. The muscle fibers are oriented posteriorly and converge and insert partly into the capsule of the TMJ, but mainly into the front of the mandibular condylar neck.

Innervation comes from the masseteric and buccal nerves, and blood supply is via a branch of the maxillary artery.

Suprahyoid Muscles

This group of muscles connects the hyoid bone with the skull (Fig. 12–23). Their basic function is elevation of the hyoid bone and depression of the mandible, depending on the activity of these muscles as well as coincident activity of the infrahyoid muscle group.

DIGASTRIC MUSCLE

The digastric consists of two bellies united by an intermediate tendon. The posterior belly arises from the mastoid notch of the temporal bone, from which the fibers are directed forward and downward. The anterior belly is shorter and attached to the lower border of the mandible at the digastric fossa close to the symphysis. Fibers from here are directed downward and posteriorly. A tendon between these two bellies is attached to the body and the greater horn of the hyoid bone by fibers of the cervical fascia, which form an aponeurosis. The tendon can slide in the formed loop.

Innervation to the posterior belly is by a branch of the facial nerve, and innervation to the anterior belly is by the mylohyoid branch of the inferior alveolar nerve.

The digastric pulls the chin backward and downward, which assists the lateral pterygoid to rotate the mandible into an open-mouth position.

MYLOHYOID MUSCLE

The mylohyoid is found above the anterior belly of the digastric, arising from the mylohyoid line on the internal surface of the mandible from the third molar region posteriorly almost to the symphysis anteriorly. The direction of the fibers is toward the midline, where they form a tendinous raphe. The posterior fibers do insert into the body of the hyoid bone. The mylohyoid, therefore, forms the floor of the oral

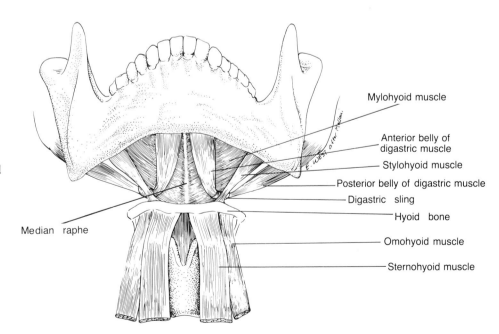

FIGURE 12–23. Suprahyoid muscles.

Median raphe

Mylohyoid muscle

Anterior belly of digastric muscle

Stylohyoid muscle

Posterior belly of digastric muscle

Digastric sling

Hyoid bone

Omohyoid muscle

Sternohyoid muscle

cavity. The diaphragm formed is thicker in the free posterior margin, which forms an important surgical landmark. The lingual nerve, the deep process of the submandibular gland, and the hypoglossal nerve pass deep to the posterior border.

Innervation is by the mylohyoid branch of the inferior alveolar nerve, and vascular supply is via the submental artery, a branch of the facial artery.

The principal muscle action of the mylohyoid is elevation of the tongue.

GENIOHYOID MUSCLE

The geniohyoid is situated above the mylohyoid and arises from the inferior genial tubercle behind the mandibular symphysis. It inserts into the front of the body of the hyoid bone. The muscles of the right and left contact and may fuse. The fibers proceed downward and slightly posteriorly to attach to the upper half of the hyoid bone.

Innervation is provided by the hypoglossal nerve, which consists of branches of the first and second cervical nerves. The action of the geniohyoid is to pull the hyoid bone up and forward or to pull the mandible down and posteriorly.

STYLOHYOID MUSCLE

The stylohyoid is a slender muscle arising from the lateral and inferior surfaces of the styloid process. Fibers insert into the hyoid bone at the junction between the body and greater horn. The tendon of the digastric commonly splits the stylohyoid near its insertion.

Innervation is provided by the facial nerve. The muscle functions like an elevator and retractor of the hyoid bone or like a stabilizer of the hyoid during various other muscle functions.

Infrahyoid Muscles

The infrahyoids are four straplike muscles that anchor the hyoid bone to the sternum, clavicle, and scapula (Fig. 12 – 24). Their function is either to depress the hyoid and larynx or to stabilize and fix the hyoid in position during contraction of the suprahyoid muscle group.

STERNOHYOID

The sternohyoid arises from the back of the manubrium and medial end of the clavicle. The muscle fibers run superiorly and converge but remain separated by the fascia termed the linea alba colli. The sternohyoid fibers attach to the inferior border of the hyoid.

OMOHYOID

The omohyoid consists of two bellies united by tendon. The muscle origin is the upper border of the scapula near the suprascapular notch. The inferior belly runs forward and upward under the sternomastoid to the tendinous attachment. The superior belly runs upward and inserts into the lower border of the hyoid bone. The intermediate tendon is attached to the manubrium and to the first costal cartilage by a facial sling.

STERNOTHYROID

The sternothyroid lies under the sternohyoid muscle, where it arises from the back of the manubrium and inserts into the thyroid cartilage.

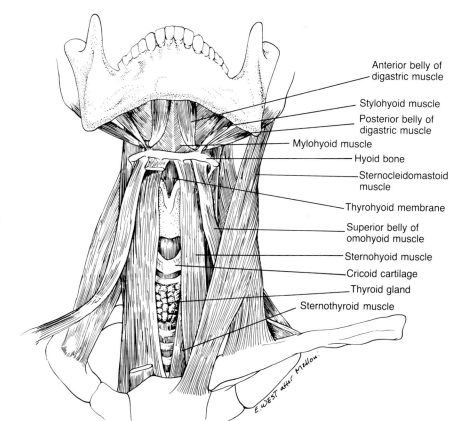

Anterior belly of digastric muscle

Stylohyoid muscle

Posterior belly of digastric muscle

Mylohyoid muscle

Hyoid bone

Sternocleidomastoid muscle

Thyrohyoid membrane

Superior belly of omohyoid muscle

Sternohyoid muscle

Cricoid cartilage

Thyroid gland

Sternothyroid muscle

FIGURE 12–24.   Infrahyoid muscles.

THYROHYOID

The thyrohyoid originates where the sternothyroid attaches at the oblique line of the thyroid cartilage and, therefore, may be considered an extension of this muscle. It inserts into the lateral part of the greater horn of the hyoid bone.

Innervation of the infrahyoid muscles is by the first, second, and third cervical nerves. The sternohyoid, omohyoid, and sternothyroid are supplied by the ansa cervicalis, whereas the thyrohyoid receives innervation from the hypoglossal nerve.

Soft Palate Musculature[2–4,6,10] (Fig. 12–25)

The soft palate and pharynx are functionally and anatomically related. Though rarely involved in minor traumatic episodes, they are frequently involved in gunshot wounds and more severe traffic accidents. Their anatomic description will be addressed here.

LEVATOR VELI PALATINI

Arising from the petrous portion of the temporal bone and the eustachian tube and extending medially and inferiorly to join its counterpart from the opposite side, this muscle functions to elevate the vertical posterior portion of the soft palate. It functions in harmony with the tensor veli palatini and pharyngeal constrictors to close the oral pharynx from the nasal pharynx.

Motor innervation is via the vagus nerve (cranial nerve X), and sensory innervation is from the pharyngeal plexus and cranial nerve IX.

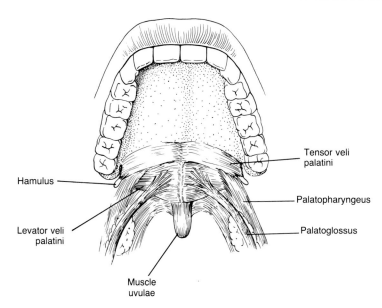

FIGURE 12–25.   Soft palate musculature.

TENSOR VELI PALATINI

Taking its origin from the base of the medial pterygoid plate, the spine of the sphenoid bone, and the eustachian tube, this muscle then courses vertically to the pterygoid hamulus, where it passes around and courses horizontally into the soft palate. The function is to raise or tense the soft palate and open the eustachian tube during swallowing.

Innervation is via the mandibular division of the trigeminal nerve (cranial nerve V).

MUSCULAR UVULAE

This small muscle arises from the posterior nasal spine and the aponeurosis of the palate. The muscle passes posteriorly and inserts on the mucous membrane of the uvula. The function is to shorten the uvula.

The nerve supply is from the vagus.

Pharyngeal Musculature[2-4,6,10] (Fig. 12–26)

SUPERIOR, MIDDLE, AND INFERIOR CONSTRICTORS

These muscles from superior to inferior make up the lateral and posterior walls of the pharynx and function in harmony to close or constrict the pharynx. Their origin, from superior to inferior, respectively, is the medial pterygoid plate; the pterygomandibular raphe, the upper border of the greater cornu of the hyoid; and the larynx. They all insert on the fibrous median raphe. The three are paired and overlap each other vertically.

The innervation is via the vagus by the pharyngeal plexus.

DILATORS AND ELEVATORS

Palatopharyngeus.   This is the posterior tonsillar pillar. It originates in the soft palate and passes vertically to insert on the posterior border of the thyroid cartilage. Innervation is via the pharyngeal plexus.

Salpingopharyngeus.   This is generally considered a part of the palatopharyngeus. It runs vertically from the auditory tube to blend with the palatopharyngeus. It is also innervated by the pharyngeal plexus.

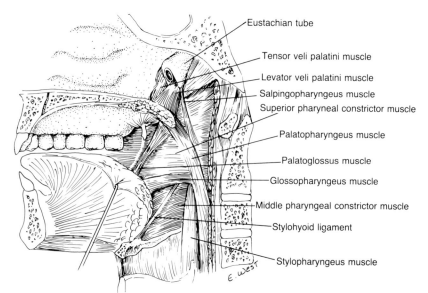

Eustachian tube
Tensor veli palatini muscle
Levator veli palatini muscle
Salpingopharyngeus muscle
Superior pharyneal constrictor muscle
Palatopharyngeus muscle
Palatoglossus muscle
Glossopharyngeus muscle
Middle pharyngeal constrictor muscle
Stylohyoid ligament
Stylopharyngeus muscle

FIGURE 12–26. Pharyngeal musculature.

Palatoglossus.   This muscle forms the anterior tonsillar pillar, arising from the anterior aponeurosis of the soft palate and inserting on the lateral side of the tongue, where it merges with the transverse fibers of the tongue. Innervation is from the pharyngeal plexus of nerves.

Stylopharyngeus.   Arising from the styloid process, this cylindrical muscle passes inferiorly between the superior and middle pharyngeal constrictors. As it passes behind the middle constrictor, it spreads and unites with its counterpart from the opposite side. The function is to dilate or widen the pharynx.

The stylopharyngeus is innervated by a branch of the glossopharyngeal nerve.

ARTERIAL BLOOD SUPPLY TO THE HEAD AND NECK[4,6,16,18]
(Fig. 12–27)

Generally speaking, the external carotid artery and its branches are responsible for the arterial blood supply to the facial region. Exceptions include those areas supplied by branches of the internal carotid artery to the upper face and portions of the nasal cavity.

The aortic arch is the origin of the common carotid artery on the left side, and the right common carotid artery is a branch of the brachiocephalic or innominate artery.

Surgical Note: When performing ligation of the external carotid, it is of surgical importance to be cognizant of the relationship of the external and internal carotid arteries at their origin. At this point, the internal carotid artery is posteromedial, and the external carotid artery is anterolateral. The level of this division is generally at the superior border of the thyroid cartilage.

The External Carotid Artery

During its earliest course, the external carotid artery is quite superficial, lying below the investing layer of deep cervical fascia, the platysma, the superficial fascia, and the skin. As it progresses superiorly, it runs through the submandibular triangle to the retromandibular fossa, through the substance of the parotid to the level of the mandibular neck. Here it gives off its branch, the superficial temporal artery, and continues deep to the condyle, turning medially and anteriorly as the internal maxillary artery (Fig. 12–27).

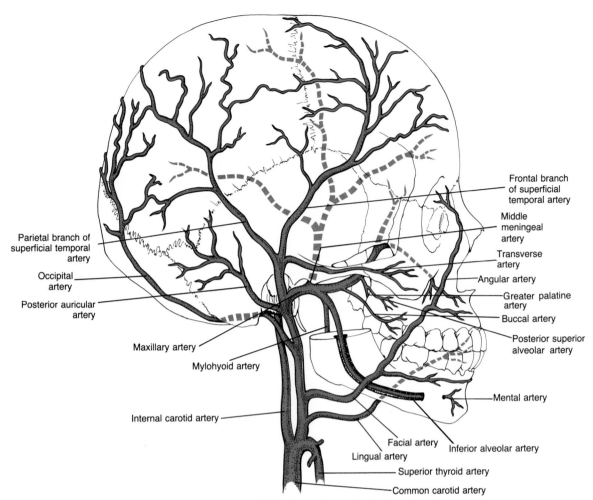

FIGURE 12–27. Arterial blood supply to the head and neck.

Branches of the External Carotid Artery

SUPERIOR THYROID ARTERY

The superior thyroid artery arises from either the common carotid or the front of the external carotid below the hyoid bone and under the sternocleidomastoid muscle. Its course is downward and forward, deep to the infrahyoid muscles to the apex of each lobe of the thyroid gland, where it divides into infrahyoids, superior laryngeal, cricothyroid, and glandular branches.

LINGUAL ARTERY

This branch arises from the front of the external carotid either as a common vessel with the facial artery or as a separate entity. It is at the level of the hyoid or above. Its course begins horizontally forward to the posterior border of the hyoglossus muscle, continuing forward deep to the hyoglossus along the upper border of the hyoid bone lying on the middle constrictor. It reaches superiorly a space between the genioglossus muscle and the inferior longitudinal muscle of the tongue. At this point, it turns horizontally and runs along the lower surface of the tongue in a tortuous fashion to the tip of the tongue. In severe facial trauma with penetrating wounds, ligation of the lingual artery may be necessary. Branches include the following.

Suprahyoid Artery. The suprahyoid runs along the upper border of the hyoid bone, sending branches to muscles attached to the bone and anastomosing with the opposite side.

Dorsales Linguae Artery. The dorsales linguae arises under the hyoglossus muscle and ascends to the dorsum of the tongue.

Sublingual Artery. The sublingual artery arises at the anterior border of the hyoglossus. From there it runs forward in the floor of the mouth medial to the sublingual gland, which it supplies, along with mucous membrane of the floor of the mouth and the mylohyoid muscle.

Deep Lingual Artery. This is actually the terminal continuation of the lingual artery in the substance of the tongue. It supplies the tongue and then forms an anastomosis with the opposite side, the arcus raninus.

FACIAL ARTERY

The facial artery arises from the front of the external carotid in common with the lingual artery (linguofacial trunk) or as a separate branch just below the posterior belly of the digastric muscle. It ascends in the carotid triangle and enters a groove on the posterior border of the submandibular gland. It turns downward and forward between the submandibular gland and the medial pterygoid muscle, where it then winds around the lower border of the mandible at a point in front of the anterior border of the masseter muscle. At this point, the facial artery is usually located anterior to the facial vein. The facial artery runs upward and forward on the face, ending as the angular artery at the medial angle of the eye by anastomosing with branches of the ophthalmic artery. Its general course is tortuous throughout the face, with considerable individual variations.

Surgical Note: Ligation of the facial artery and vein is often required during the open approach to the inferior mandible. The facial artery is generally considered to have cervical and facial divisions.

Cervical Division

1. *Ascending palatine branch.* Origin is close to the lateral pharyngeal wall and runs along the outer surface of the superior pharyngeal constrictor. It accompanies the levator veli palatini and supplies the soft palate, portions of the pharynx, and the tonsils.

2. *Tonsillar branch.* This is the main artery to the tonsil. It may arise from the anterior border of the masseter muscle. The facial artery runs upward as the ascending palatine as well.

3. *Glandular branch.* This supplies the submandibular gland.

4. *Submental branch.* This is the largest branch given off by the facial artery in the neck. Its course is forward on the mylohyoid, where it supplies muscles in the area; then it turns upward over the lower border of the mandible.

Facial Division

1. *Inferior labial artery.* This artery penetrates the orbicularis oris, supplying the skin, muscles, and mucous membrane of the lower lip. From here it anastomoses with the opposite side.

2. *Superior labial artery.* This is larger than the inferior branch. It has a course and distribution similar to the inferior labial artery although to the upper lip.

3. *Lateral nasal branch.* This branch supplies the ala and dorsum of the nose.

4. *Angular artery.* This is the termination of the facial artery. It anastomoses with the dorsal nasal and palpebral branches of the ophthalmic artery, thereby establishing a possible route of communication between the external and internal carotid arteries.

OCCIPITAL ARTERY

The occipital artery arises from the back of the external carotid artery at about the same level as the facial artery. Its origin can vary, however, in either direction.

Near its origin, the hypoglossal nerve winds around it. The artery runs through the carotid triangle backward and upward to the lower border of the posterior belly of the digastric and then crosses the internal carotid artery and internal jugular vein. Under the sternocleidomastoid muscle, it occupies the occipital groove on the temporal bone. Posterior to the sternocleidomastoid, it pierces the trapezius and divides into various scalp branches. Branches include a sternomastoid branch; a mastoid branch; a descending branch, which can be important because of anastomoses with the opposite side during external carotid ligation; meningeal branches; and occipital terminal branches.

POSTERIOR AURICULAR ARTERY

This artery arises from the back of the external carotid above the posterior belly of the digastric. It follows the stylohyoid muscle upward under cover of the parotid gland and terminates between the mastoid process and the auricle. Branches include stylomastoid, posterior tympanic auricular, and occipital.

ASCENDING PHARYNGEAL ARTERY

This small vessel is the only medial branch of the external carotid artery. It arises low just above the division above the common carotid artery and ascends between the internal carotid and the pharyngeal wall to the base of the skull. Branches are given off to the wall of the pharynx and adjacent muscles. Near the base of the skull, there is an anastomosis with the pterygoid artery of the maxillary artery.

SUPERFICIAL TEMPORAL ARTERY

This artery is the smaller terminal branch of the external carotid artery, with its origin in the parotid gland behind the neck of the mandible. It crosses the zygomatic arch and divides into frontal and parietal branches. The auriculotemporal nerve runs along posterior to the superficial temporal artery. Branches include the transverse facial artery, which arises in the parotid gland and runs forward across the masseter between the zygomatic arch above and the duct of the parotid below and is accompanied by zygomatic branches of the facial nerve. There it supplies the parotid gland and duct, the masseter, the skin, the auricle, and the joint capsule. The terminal branches divide above the zygomatic arch into the frontal and parietal branches. There are also deep branches during its course to the middle temporal artery.

Surgical Note: The identification and protection of the superficial temporal artery are important during open procedures involving the condyle. Incision and flap design is usually such that the artery is anterior to the approach and is reflected in the soft tissue flap.

MAXILLARY ARTERY

The maxillary artery is the larger of the terminal branches arising in the parotid gland behind the neck of the mandible. At this point, the maxillary artery turns at right angles to the superficial temporal branch, where it courses anteriorly and upward through the infratemporal fossa. There is a varying relation between the artery and the lateral pterygoid muscle.[14] In more than 50 per cent of persons, the artery is on the outer side of the muscle, passing between the mandible and the sphenomandibular ligament. In the remaining individuals, the artery is located medial to the lateral pterygoid muscle.

Branches of the maxillary artery are numerous and complicated (Fig. 12–28). In an attempt to group the branches for ease of understanding, they are divided into the following parts.

Mandibular Part of the Maxillary Artery. The first part runs forward be-

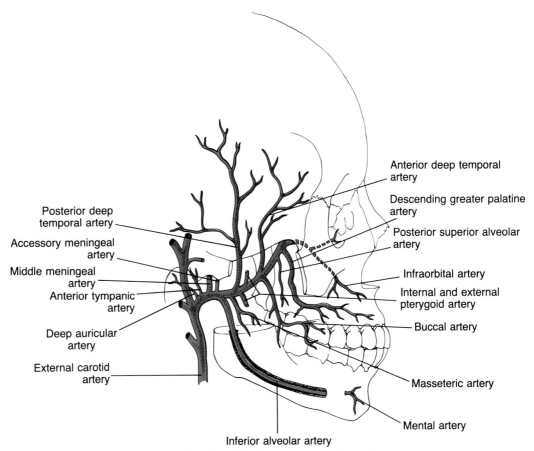

FIGURE 12-28. Maxillary artery and branches.

tween the neck of the mandible and the sphenomandibular ligament. Most of its branches accompany branches of the mandibular nerve.

Deep auricular artery. This artery ascends through the parotid gland to supply the meatus and tympanic membrane.

Anterior tympanic artery. This artery supplies the tympanic membrane.

Middle meningeal artery. Clinically, this is the most important branch of the maxillary artery. It runs upward between the sphenomandibular ligament and the lateral pterygoid muscle. It passes between the two roots of the auriculotemporal nerve and enters the cranium via the foramen spinosum, which is located in the sphenoid bone (Fig. 12-29). It then branches into a tympanic branch and splits into an anterior and a posterior branch.

Surgical Note: This artery, because of its medial location to the condyle, could be potentially damaged during open procedures in the condylar region or directly damaged by severe condylar displacement.

Inferior alveolar artery. This artery descends between the sphenomandibular ligament and the ramus of the mandible. The nerve lies anteriorly, and both enter the mandibular canal via the mandibular foramen. The branches of the artery include the lingual and mylohyoid prior to entering the canal and the dental, mental, and incisor branches after entering the canal. In the mandibular canal, the artery sends branches into the marrow spaces and the teeth via apical branches and periodontal branches, and the mental artery branches off and exits via the mental foramen to supply the soft tissues of the chin. The continuation terminal branch is the incisive, which continues its course within the mandible to anastomose with the incisive artery of the opposite side.

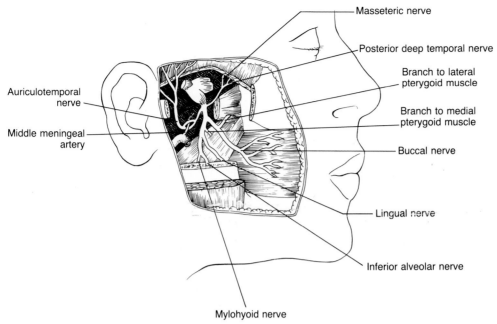

FIGURE 12–29.   Mandibular division of the trigeminal nerve.

Second Part of the Maxillary Artery.   The second portion of this artery comprises the following.

Anterior and posterior deep temporal arteries.   These arteries ascend between the temporalis muscle and the skull to supply the temporalis.

Masseteric artery.   This passes with the corresponding masseteric nerve behind the temporalis to pass through the coronoid notch and enters the deep surface of the masseter muscle. It also has branches supplying the joint capsule.

Pterygoid branches.   These branches supply the pterygoid muscles.

Buccal artery.   This artery accompanies the buccal nerve to the buccinator, which it supplies, including the skin and mucous membrane of the cheek.

Third Part of the Maxillary Artery.   This portion provides extensive branches and supplies the upper teeth, portions of the face and the orbit, the palate, and the nasal cavity.

Posterior superior alveolar artery.   This artery takes a tortuous course down in the infratemporal fossa and onto the posterior surface of the maxilla. Here small branches supply the gingiva and dental branches, entering canals to the molars and premolars, as well as the maxillary sinus lining.

Infraorbital artery.   This artery arises in the pterygopalatine fossa; it enters the orbit through the inferior orbital fissure and courses anteriorly in the infraorbital sulcus, then in the infraorbital canal, and finally through the infraorbital foramen with the corresponding nerve. Before leaving the canal, the anterior superior alveolar branch is given off. Branches are given off to various orbital muscles throughout its route through the orbit.

Descending palatine artery.   This artery is one of the terminal branches arising in the pterygopalatine fossa. After descending through the pterygopalatine canal, it gives off the greater palatine artery, which passes through the canal of the same name running forward in the roof of the mouth, thus supplying the hard palate. The lesser palatine branches pass via the lesser palatine canals to supply the soft palate.

Artery of the pterygoid canal.   This vessel frequently arises from the descending or greater palatine artery, which runs backward through the pterygoid canal with the corresponding nerve.

Sphenopalatine artery.   This is the last of the terminal branches. It enters the nasal cavity through the sphenopalatine foramen and gives off the posterior lateral nasal arteries to the conchae, meatuses, and paranasal sinuses. Its eventually terminates in the nasal septum and, as such, is important in epistaxis.

The Internal Carotid Artery[4,6]

The origin of the internal carotid artery is approximately at the level of the thyroid cartilage (see Fig. 12–27). It is at first behind and medial to the external carotid artery, but during its course it moves away from the external carotid and eventually is separated by the styloglossal and stylopharyngeal muscles. It enters the middle cranial fossa through the carotid canal and travels into the cavernous sinus and divides into anterior and middle cerebral arteries.

During its course through the neck, there are no branches. It is curved and can follow neck movements without stretching. The internal carotid is closely related to the internal jugular vein and the vagus nerve. The vein describes a half-spiral around the artery.

Major branches after leaving the cavernous sinus include the ophthalmic artery, which follows the optic nerve into the orbit. This branch supplies the eyeball, muscles, lacrimal gland, and eyelids. Other branches of note include the central artery of the retina, the posterior and anterior ethmoid branches to the nasal cavity, the medial and lateral palpebral branches, and the supraorbital branch. The final facial branch of the ophthalmic artery is the nasal branch.

VEINS OF THE HEAD AND NECK[4,6,16] (Fig. 12–30)

Venous drainage to the head and neck can be looked at from the standpoint of being superficial and deep in function. The superficial drainage is mainly via the external and anterior jugular veins, whereas most of the deep venous drainage is via the internal jugular vein. There is significant anastomosis between all veins, both intracranially and facially, as well as superficial and deep. The superficial veins empty into the internal jugular vein at a low point, and it in turn joins the subclavian vein to form the brachiocephalic or innominate vein behind the sternoclavicular articulation.

Consideration of the potential disruption of a vein with subsequent bleeding is always important in the trauma patient as well as a potential retrograde spread of infection in the postoperative phase.

Internal Jugular Vein

Beginning at the jugular foramen, the vein is located posteromedial to the internal carotid artery. During its descent, the vein is closely related not only to the internal carotid artery but also to the vagus nerve. Various deep structures drain into the internal jugular vein. Those that are germaine to this subject include the common facial vein, which drains the superficial and deep parts of the face, and the lingual and sublingual veins.

Common Facial Vein

The area of drainage of this vein corresponds more or less to the distribution of the facial, maxillary, and superficial temporal arteries. It originates from the joining of the facial and retromandibular veins near the angle of the mandible. The common facial vein empties into the internal jugular vein at about the level of the hyoid bone.

Surgical Note: The common facial vein is often violated in instances of traumatic

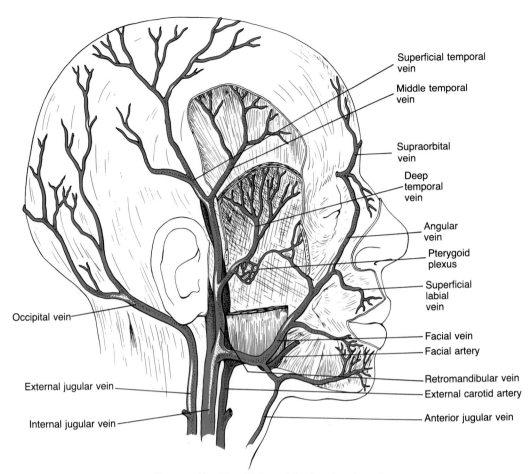

Superficial temporal vein

Middle temporal vein

Supraorbital vein

Deep temporal vein

Angular vein

Pterygoid plexus

Superficial labial vein

Facial vein

Facial artery

Retromandibular vein

External carotid artery

Anterior jugular vein

Occipital vein

External jugular vein

Internal jugular vein

FIGURE 12–30.   Veins of the head and neck.

hemorrhage or iatrogenic hemorrhage during various approaches to the maxilla, zygoma, condyle ramus, or body of the mandible. Ligation, pressure, and hemostatic cautery are all useful in controlling venous bleeding in these areas.

Anterior Facial Vein

The frontal vein, which drains the anterior scalp region, empties into the angular vein at about the bridge of the nose, where the angular vein continues downward toward the cheek. Near the commissure, the facial vein descends along with the facial artery, where it crosses the inferior border of the mandible close to the anterior edge of the masseter muscle attachment. The vein is normally posterior to the artery at this location.

Surgical Note: The vein is normally identified, ligated, and cut during submandibular approaches to the mandible.

Retromandibular Vein

At approximately the level of the neck of the mandible, the retromandibular vein is created by the junction of the superficial temporal and maxillary veins. The vein is located within the substance of the parotid gland, where it descends to leave the gland at its lower pole. Initially, the vein and the external carotid artery are closely related, but as it descends into the face, the vein and artery diverge. In the preauricular region, the superficial temporal artery is often closely related to two veins, the superficial temporal vein and the more anteriorly located middle temporal vein. Surrounding the maxillary artery in the infratemporal fossa is the pterygoid plexus of veins. The pterygoid plexus empties into the retromandibular vein below the level of the neck of the mandible medially.

Surgical Note: Many of the deep veins of the face drain into this plexus, and this is an area for potentially significant bleeding during mobilization of Le Fort–type maxillary fractures, which separate at or through the pterygoid plates. Because this is essentially a blind area during the treatment of most fractures, pressure and local measures are the only methods of hemostasis available.

External Jugular Vein

The posterior auricular and occipital veins join below the ear to form the superficial external jugular vein. From this point, the vein descends across the sternocleidomastoid muscle and eventually drains into the internal jugular vein.

Anterior Jugular Vein

Significant variability in the position and presence or absence of one or both sides is found. This vein is located anteriorly, or even as a single midline vein, coursing inferiorly around the anterior aspect of the sternocleidomastoid muscle to empty into the internal jugular vein.

NEUROLOGIC ANATOMY[4,6,16,18,31,32,34,46]

Surgical Note: The most frequent injuries to nerves of the head and neck subsequent to major maxillofacial trauma involve the superficially positioned facial nerve or those cranial nerves found within bony canals that are fractured, such as the inferior alveolar nerve, the infraorbital nerve, and the optic nerve. The surgeon must also be cognizant of neuroanatomy when designing soft tissue flaps or applying any form of stabilizing appliance. Discussion is limited to the trigeminal, facial, and hypoglossal nerves in this chapter.

Trigeminal Nerve

The trigeminal nerve is composed of both sensory and motor fibers. The sensory distribution essentially covers the entire anterior head and face, while the motor division innervates the muscles of mastication. The trigeminal nerve arises from the ventral surface of the cerebral pons. The semilunar or gasserian ganglion, which is the sensory root ganglion, is found in Meckel's cavity near the foramen lacerum. From this location arise the three sensory divisions of the trigeminal nerve. The motor portion eventually joins the mandibular division in its course. The first division of the trigeminal nerve is the ophthalmic nerve, which enters the orbit through the medial part of the superior orbital fissure. The second division is the maxillary nerve, which exits the foramen rotundum and goes into the pterygopalatine space. The mandibular nerve, or third division, leaves the foramen ovale and continues into the infratemporal fossa.

Figure 12–31 shows the normal cutaneous innervation of the three divisions of the trigeminal nerve. The mandibular angle region is variably innervated by branches of the two upper cervical nerves.

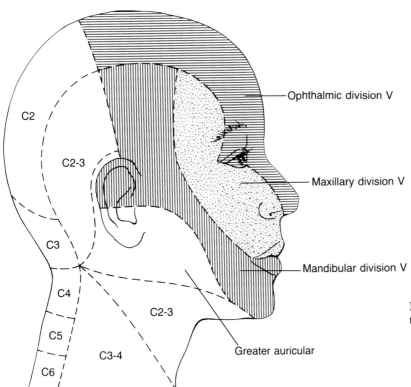

Ophthalmic division V

Maxillary division V

Mandibular division V

Greater auricular

FIGURE 12–31. Cutaneous sensory distribution of the trigeminal nerve.

OPHTHALMIC NERVE (Fig. 12–32)

In the orbit, the ophthalmic nerve divides into three branches. The nasociliary nerve travels along the medial orbital roof, where it branches into the nasal cavity. The frontal nerve proceeds anteriorly to the skin of the forehead, and the lacrimal nerve courses along the lateral orbital roof to the lacrimal gland and the skin at the corner of the eye.

MAXILLARY NERVE (Figs. 12–32 to 12–34)

After exiting the skull through the foramen rotundum, the maxillary nerve enters the pterygopalatine fossa, where it splits into three major branches.

Pterygopalatine Nerve.   Shortly after leaving the main trunk of the maxillary nerve, the pterygopalatine nerve seems to enter the pterygopalatine ganglion, but instead the fibers are only closely adherent and continue. Near the ganglion, the superior posterior nasal branches enter the sphenopalatine foramen into the nasal cavity, where they supply the middle nasal concha. Lateral branches supply the upper and middle conchae, while medial branches supply the septum, and terminal branches enter the nasopalatine or incisive foramen to innervate incisor teeth, gingiva, and palatal tissue.

The major portion of the pterygopalatine nerve continues through the pterygopalatine canal. While in the canal, some small branches enter the nasal cavity and supply the inferior nasal concha, along with the middle and inferior nasal meatuses. Further in the canal, a branch enters the greater palatine foramen and sends branches anteriorly in the palate. Another branch passes through the lesser palatine foramen and supplies the tonsillar and soft palatine tissues.

Infraorbital Nerve.   This nerve courses from the infratemporal fossa through the inferior orbital fissure and into the orbit, where it runs in the infraorbital groove, which transforms into the infraorbital canal, and then exits through the infraorbital foramen to supply superficial structures of the face. Branches of the infraorbital

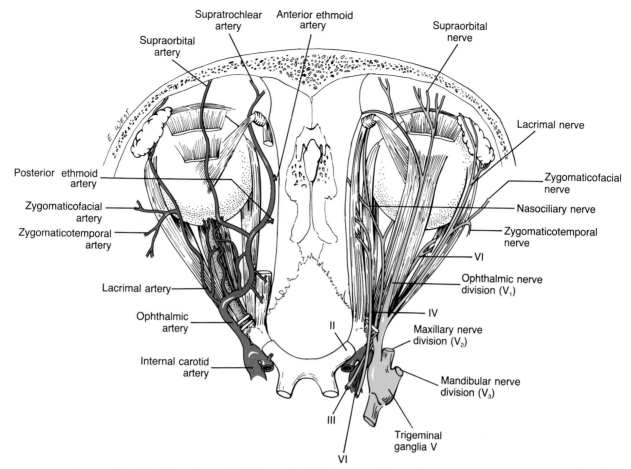

FIGURE 12–32. Superior orbital view. *Right,* Nerves and musculature. *Left,* Cutaway showing arterial supply.

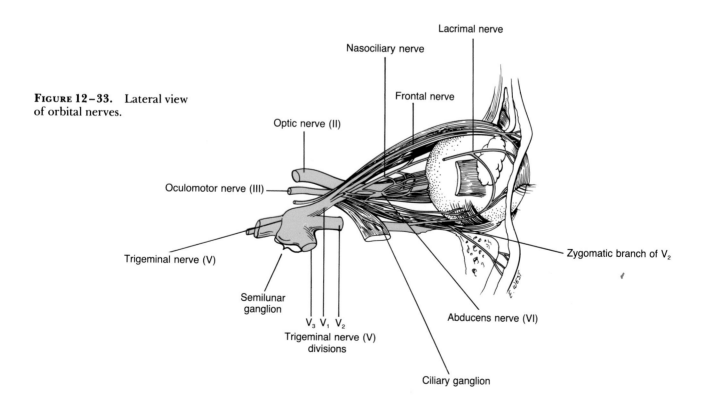

FIGURE 12–33. Lateral view of orbital nerves.

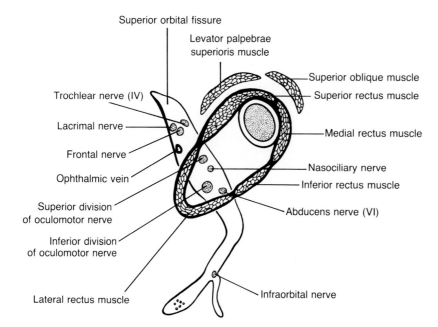

FIGURE 12–34. Orbital apex, superior orbital fissure, and relations of contents. Right orbit.

nerve include the posterior superior alveolar nerve, which leaves in the infratemporal fossa. From here it divides and sends branches through the posterior maxillary wall and into the maxillary sinus. The middle superior alveolar nerve leaves the infraorbital nerve while in the groove, where it enters the superior aspect of the maxillary sinus. The anterior superior alveolar nerve leaves while the infraorbital nerve is in the canal, which sends branches to the maxillary sinus and nose. Sensory distribution is provided to maxillary teeth, alveolar bone, periodontal ligaments, and gingiva.

Zygomatic Nerve. In some instances, this nerve may be a branch of the infraorbital nerve. Its course is lateral through the orbit, where it sends a branch up to the lacrimal nerve, which consists of postganglionic parasympathetic fibers from the pterygopalatine ganglion. The zygomatic nerve then continues on through the zygomatico-orbital foramen and into the zygomatic bone. Here a branch, the zygomaticofacial nerve, exits the bone and supplies the skin over the cheek, while the zygomaticotemporal nerve exits into the temporal fossa, where it supplies the skin of the temple region.

MANDIBULAR NERVE (Fig. 12–29)

The mandibular nerve contains both sensory and motor nerve fibers and exits the skull through the foramen ovale and into the infratemporal fossa. The motor branches to the muscles of mastication are given off as the masseteric nerve, posterior and anterior temporal nerves, medial pterygoid nerve, and lateral pterygoid nerve.

Buccal Nerve. The course of the buccal nerve starts next to the greater wing of the sphenoid and then runs on the medial surface of the lateral pterygoid, where it then passes between its two heads. It sends motor fibers to the lateral pterygoid and temporalis muscles. The buccal nerve then follows the anterior edge of the temporalis muscle and perforates the buccinator muscle. The sensory distribution of the buccal nerve includes the buccal gingiva in the posterior mandible, cheek, and a portion of the mucous membrane of the upper and lower lips.

Lingual Nerve. During its initial course, the lingual nerve is found in close proximity to the inferior alveolar nerve. Later it separates and is found anteromedially in relationship to this nerve. The lingual nerve descends between the medial and lateral pterygoid muscles, and at the inferior border of the lateral pterygoid muscle, the chorda tympani fibers connect. As the lingual nerve passes beyond the lateral pterygoid muscle, it proceeds laterally along the lateral surface of the medial pterygoid muscle, and then it turns sharply anteriorly on the superior surface of the mylohyoid muscle. In the floor of the mouth, the course of the lingual nerve is very close to the oral mucous membrane, especially posteriorly in the area of the superior pole of the submandibular gland. As it moves anteriorly, the nerve runs medially and proceeds below the submandibular or Wharton's duct and ends by sending fibers into the tongue substance. The lingual nerve provides sensory distribution to the gingiva and mucous membrane of the mandibular lingual and mucous membranes of the floor of the mouth, as well as the lower and upper surfaces of the body of the tongue back to the circumvallate papillae. The lingual nerve carries terminal taste fibers to the anterior two thirds of the tongue. The origin of these fibers is from the facial nerve and is relayed to the lingual nerve via the chorda tympani nerve. The regional anatomy of the floor of the mouth will be discussed further on.

Inferior Alveolar Nerve. As discussed in its initial course the inferior alveolar nerve has a close relationship to the lingual nerve. After separating approximately 5 mm below the cranial base, the inferior alveolar nerve is between the lateral and medial pterygoid muscles. The inferior alveolar nerve passes around the lower border of the lateral pterygoid muscle and then proceeds to the medial aspect of the ramus of the mandible to enter the mandibular foramen. It has been shown that in approximately 34 per cent of mandibles the neurovascular bundle divides soon after the beginning of the inferior alveolar canal.[44] Other studies have not shown quite as high an incidence, varying from 0.96 per cent to 8 per cent.[34] The superoinferior course of the nerve in the mandible is such that it descends to the lowest point near the first molar and then rises again. In a lateromedial position, the canal and bundle are closest to the lateral cortical plate in the third molar area, but the nerve remains fairly constant in its relationship to the medial cortical plate throughout its course[34] (Fig. 12–35). The mylohyoid nerve branches off the inferior alveolar nerve prior to entering the canal. This nerve runs downward and anteriorly in the mylohyoid

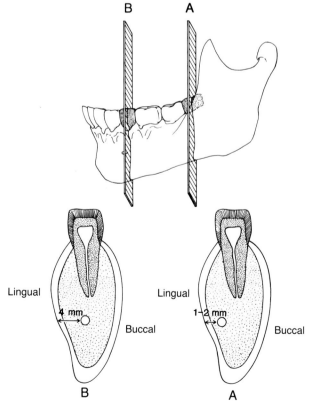

FIGURE 12–35. Position of the inferior alveolar canal as it travels anteriorly in the mandible.

groove, and then it provides branches to the mylohyoid muscle and to the anterior belly of the digastric muscle, as well as sensory fibers to the chin area.

Exiting the mental foramen, the inferior alveolar nerve divides into three terminal mental nerves, which supply sensation to the chin, lower lip, and mucous membrane of the lower lip.

Auriculotemporal Nerve.   The auriculotemporal nerve divides from the mandibular nerve immediately below the cranial base and divides to encircle the middle meningeal artery. After reuniting, it courses downward and posteriorly, crossing the neck of the mandibular condyle. It enters the substance of the parotid gland and divides into two branches, one of which turns upward anterior to the outer ear, closely related to the superficial temporal artery crossing the zygomatic arch. Its position is important to consider in an open approach to the preauricular region. Terminal branches supply the outer ear, the external auditory meatus, the capsule of the mandibular joint, and areas of the parotid gland. Other terminal branches supply the skin in the greater posterior temple region.

Facial Nerve

The motor fibers of the facial nerve provide innervation to the muscles of facial expression as well as to the occipital and auricular muscles and to the platysma, posterior belly of the digastric, and stylohyoid muscle. In addition, it supplies fibers for deep sensitivity of the face and for taste to the anterior two thirds of the tongue and palate. The facial nerve also transmits preganglionic visceral efferent fibers to the lacrimal gland, the sublingual and submandibular glands, and other minor glands.

The facial nerve, after leaving the brain, enters the inner auditory meatus. The nerve bends sharply at the tympanic cavity and travels posteriorly above the oval window and then continues in the posterior wall of the tympanic cavity. The facial nerve then leaves the canal and exits through the stylomastoid foramen.

Surgical Note: Damage to the facial nerve is possible in severe maxillofacial injuries with basilar skull fractures anywhere in the area of the course of the nerve and would result in ipsilateral paralysis of the muscles of facial expression.

Of concern to the surgeon is the close proximity of the main trunk of the facial nerve, where it exits the stylomastoid foramen and the mandibular condyle. After exiting the foramen, which is situated posterolateral to the styloid process, the nerve enters the substance of the parotid gland, where it divides into its upper and lower divisions just posterior to the mandible. From this point, the two branches curve around the posterior mandible, where they form a plexus between the parotid gland and the masseter muscle. The terminal branches of the facial nerve then spread in a fanlike fashion as five separate nerves (Fig. 12–36). These branches are the temporal, zygomatic, buccal, mandibular, and cervical branches. There are often variations in the pattern of distribution.[16]

TEMPORAL BRANCH

This terminal branch exits the parotid gland anterior to the superficial temporal artery. Muscles supplied include the auricular muscles, the frontal muscle, the superior portion of the orbicularis oculi, and the corrugator muscle to the eyebrows.

Surgical Note: During an open approach to the TMJ, violation of the nerve is possible. Quite often, temporary weakness is appreciated by the fact that the patient cannot squeeze the ipsilateral eye together or wrinkle the forehead. This inability is usually caused by retractor trauma or soft tissue edema and, if so, should resolve over the first week.

ZYGOMATIC BRANCH

The course of this nerve is anterosuperior, crossing the zygomatic bone. Innervation is to the orbicularis oculi muscle.

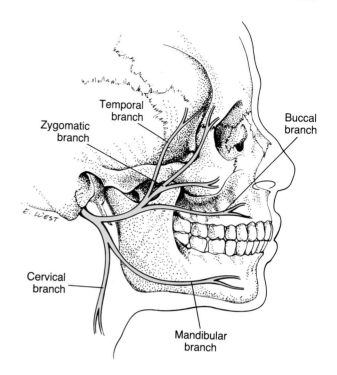

FIGURE 12–36. Distribution of the facial nerve. The exact configuration can vary significantly, and this illustration is only an example.

Surgical Note: Inadvertent damage may occur during open reduction of the zygomatic arch or use of a Byrd screw or zygomatic hook during closed approaches.

BUCCAL BRANCH

Running almost horizontally, this nerve will often divide into a separate branch above and below the parotid duct as it runs anteriorly.

Surgical Note: Injury is possible in association with soft tissue trauma to the cheek region.

MANDIBULAR BRANCH (Fig. 12–37)

Branches of this nerve run anteriorly parallel to the inferior border of the mandible. In some cases, the course of this nerve is above the inferior border, but often it is found below.

Surgical Note: The marginal mandibular branch is an important structure encountered at the inferior border of the mandible just beneath the platysma muscle fibers during an open approach to the mandibular angle and body area. For this reason, an initial incision made approximately 1.0 to 1.5 cm below the inferior border should avoid direct exposure or trauma. The terminal innervation of this nerve is to the ipsilateral muscles of the lower lip and to the mentalis muscle.

CERVICAL BRANCH

This inferior branch exits the parotid gland above its inferior pole and runs downward underneath the platysma muscle, which it innervates.

Hypoglossal Nerve

After exiting the brain, the hypoglossal nerve passes through the hypoglossal canal and winds around the vagus nerve inferiorly, to which it is bound with some

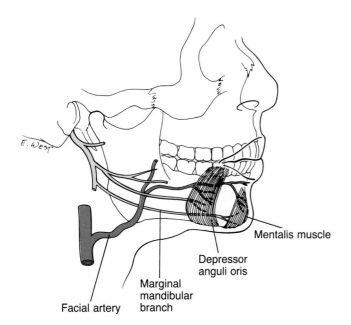

FIGURE 12–37. The marginal mandibular branch of the facial nerve and its relationship to the facial artery.

Mentalis muscle

Depressor anguli oris

Marginal mandibular branch

Facial artery

connective tissue. The nerve then courses inferiorly across the medial aspect of the stylohyoid and digastric muscles. It then curves slightly upward across the internal and external carotid arteries as well as the occipital and lingual arteries on their lateral side (Fig. 12–38). Continuing forward along with the sublingual vein, the nerve follows the lateral surface of the hyoglossus muscle. At the posterior extent of the mylohyoid muscle, the nerve runs along the superomedial surface to split into several fibers into the substance of the tongue in a fanlike fashion. The hypoglossal nerve is responsible for motor innervation to all the muscles of the tongue. The nerve, however, contributes fibers to the ansa cervicalis which descends along the internal carotid artery and joins branches of the second and third cervical nerves to contribute to the hypoglossal ansa. From the loop, branches are sent to the omohyoid, sternothyroid, and sternohyoid muscles.

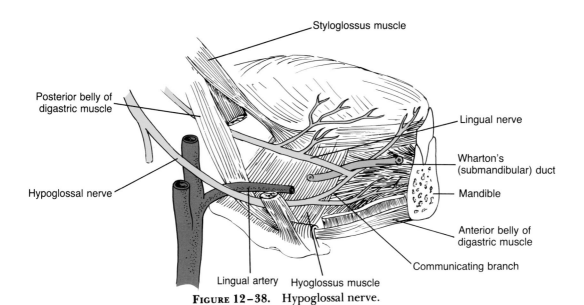

Styloglossus muscle

Posterior belly of digastric muscle

Hypoglossal nerve

Lingual nerve

Wharton's (submandibular) duct

Mandible

Anterior belly of digastric muscle

Communicating branch

Lingual artery   Hyoglossus muscle

FIGURE 12–38. Hypoglossal nerve.

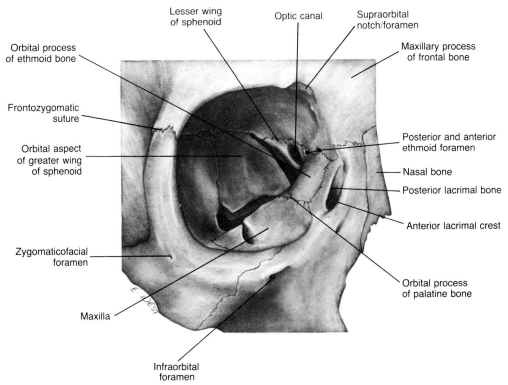

FIGURE 12–39. Orbital osteology.

REGIONAL ANATOMY

Orbital Anatomy[1,4,11,15,17,47] (Figs. 12–32 to 12–34 and 12–39 to 12–42)

The configuration of the bony structure of the orbit is that of a pyramid with its base facing anteriorly, with each orbit having an intrabony volume of approximately 35 cc. Each bony orbit is composed of seven bones (Fig. 12–39), as follows:

1. Frontal
2. Zygoma
3. Maxilla
4. Lacrimal
5. Ethmoid
6. Sphenoid
7. Palatine

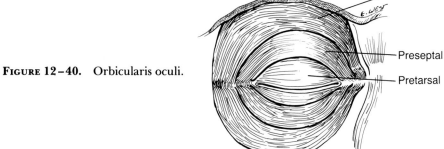

FIGURE 12–40. Orbicularis oculi.

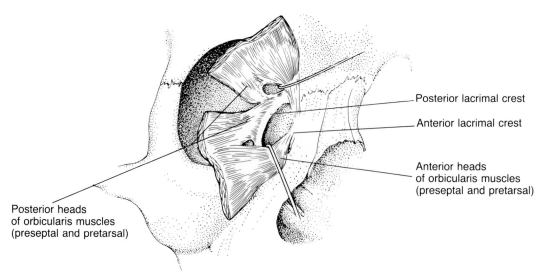

FIGURE 12–41.   Medial palpebral ligament.

The medial walls (lamina papyracea of ethmoid, lacrimal, and palatine bones) are nearly parallel to the sagittal plane. The medial wall is the thinnest wall of the orbit, but it derives some increased strength by the trabeculization of the ethmoid air cells. The lateral walls (zygoma, sphenoid, and frontal) diverge from the apex at approximately 45 degrees. The lateral orbital rim is formed by the zygoma and is posterior to the medial, superior, and lateral orbital rims. The floor of the orbit (maxilla) is the roof of the maxillary sinus and is relatively thin and anatomically weakened by the passage of the infraorbital nerve. The roof of the orbit is formed mainly by the frontal bone and partly by the sphenoid bone. The trochlea, which transmits the tendon of the superior oblique muscle, is a special periosteal attachment in the area of the junction of the medial wall and the roof of the orbit approximately 4 mm posterior to

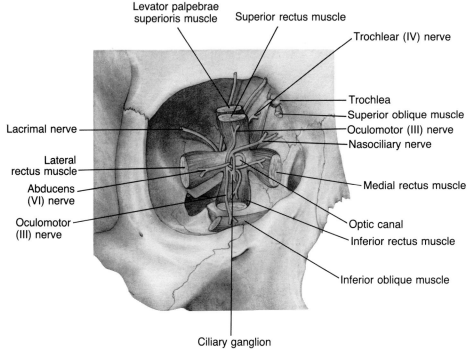

FIGURE 12–42.   Frontal view of orbital musculature and nerve relations.

the orbital rim, and its integrity must be maintained during medial orbital exploration. If it is disrupted, it must be securely reattached. The roof of the orbit continues forward to form the superior orbital rim. The superior orbital rim has either a notch or a canal for the supraorbital and supratrochlear neurovascular bundles. As with the trochlea, the frontal orbital rim and its integrity must be maintained during medial orbital exploration, and if it is disrupted, it must be securely reattached. The roof of the orbit continues forward to form the superior orbital rim. The superior orbital rim has either a notch or a canal for the supraorbital and supratrochlear neurovascular bundles. The frontal bone articulates laterally with the zygoma at the frontozygomatic suture. The orbital rims are extremely strong and provide protection for the globe.

Consideration must be given to the position of the infraorbital nerve and the terminal branches of the trigeminal nerve (cranial nerve V_2) during any dissection of the inferior rim or orbital floor. The infraorbital nerve supplies sensation to the skin of the face in this region and the conjunctiva of the lower lid. The anterior superior alveolar nerve descends as a terminal branch either in or along the maxilla. This nerve supplies the sensation to the anterior maxillary teeth and the gingivae. The associated small arteries that run with these nerves are generally not of surgical concern and are rarely identified. Although their sacrifice is not problematic, every attempt should be made to maintain or decompress the sensory nerves in this area.

The orbital soft tissue is separated from the orbicularis oculi and extraorbital soft tissue by the orbital septum. This septum constitutes a diaphragm at the entrance to the orbit that functionally separates the tissue spaces of the lid from those of the orbit. It essentially is a continuation of the periosteum of the orbit (periorbita) and the periosteum of the outer surface of the adjacent facial bones. From here it extends into the upper and lower lids. The septum fuses with the connective tissue anterior to the superior and inferior tarsus. Medially, it passes posterior to the posterior lacrimal crest, thus eliminating the lacrimal sac from the orbit proper.

Orbital Muscles[1,4,6,11,47]

ORBICULARIS OCULI (Fig. 12–40)

This muscle is composed of a palpebral division, which further divides into preseptal and pretarsal subdivisions, and an orbital division. The palpebral division arises from the medial palpebral ligament and inserts into the lateral palpebral raphe. A portion closest to the medial margin of the lid arises from the posterior lacrimal crest and is known as the pars lacrimalis or muscle of Horner. The larger portion of the medial palpebral ligament arises from the anterior lacrimal crest. The lateral palpebral raphe is attached to the osseous protuberance on the inner aspect of the lateral orbital rim of the zygoma (Whitnall's orbital tubercle) and passes medially to the lateral commissure of the eyelid, where it divides into two slips. The muscle is innervated by temporal and zygomatic branches of the facial nerve (cranial nerve VII) at the lateral and inferior raphe. Paralysis prevents tight closure of the eye and can predispose to ectropion and epiphora.

Surgical Note: The medial palpebral ligament gives anatomic support to the lacrimal sac and is involved in the emptying of the sac. Its position dictates the shape of this area (Fig. 12–41). Every attempt to correct a traumatic displacement should be made, and in a similar fashion, care should be taken to avoid displacing this ligament in the reduction of fractures and the management of soft tissue trauma.

LEVATOR PALPEBRAE SUPERIORIS

This muscle of the upper lid is a direct antagonist to the orbicularis oculi, raises the upper lid, and exposes the globe. It arises deep in the orbit from the lesser wing of the sphenoid. It passes above the superior rectus as a thin, flat muscle and becomes broad as it ends anteriorly in an aponeurosis, which splits into three lamellae. Innervation is by the oculomotor nerve (cranial nerve III) as it enters the orbit through the superior orbital fissure (Fig. 12–34).

RECTI MUSCLES

The recti muscles arise from a fibrous ring that surrounds the superior, inferior, and medial aspects of the optic foramen (Fig. 12–34). The ring continues as a tendinous band over the inferior and medial aspects of the superior orbital fissure. This fibrous ring in its lower division (tendon of Zinn) gives rise to the inferior rectus, part of the medial rectus, and the inferior head of the lateral rectus. The upper division of this fibrous band (superior tendon of Lockwood) gives rise to the superior rectus, the remainder of the medial rectus, and the superior head of the lateral rectus. Each rectus muscle then passes anteriorly in the orbit in the position implied by its name and inserts as a tendinous area of the sclera anterior to the equator of the globe and approximately 6 mm behind the margin of the cornea.

All but the lateral rectus are innervated on their deep surface by the oculomotor nerve (Fig. 12–32). The lateral rectus is innervated by the abducens nerve (cranial nerve VI). These muscles form a cone that gives some protection to the optic nerve (cranial nerve II), which passes anteriorly within their confines (Fig. 12–42). Between the two heads of the lateral rectus, the two divisions of the oculomotor nerve, the nasociliary nerve, the abducens nerve, and the ophthalmic vein enter the muscular cone. The optic canal, which lies within the confines of the origin of these muscles, transmits the optic nerve and the ophthalmic artery (Fig. 12–34).

SUPERIOR OBLIQUE MUSCLE

This muscle takes its origin immediately above the optic foramen, superior and medial to the superior rectus muscle. It passes anteriorly and ends in a tendon that passes through a fibrocartilaginous ring attached at the trochlear fovea of the frontal bone. The tendon bends posteriorly at this ring and passes beneath the superior rectus to insert into the sclera posterior to the equator of the globe on the laterosuperior aspect (Fig. 12–32). This muscle is innervated by the trochlear nerve (cranial nerve IV), which enters the orbit through the superior orbital fissure and passes above the other orbital nerves and enters the muscle from the inferior aspect.

INFERIOR OBLIQUE MUSCLE

The inferior oblique muscle is a thin muscle that arises from the orbital surface of the maxilla lateral to the lacrimal groove. It passes laterally on the bony side of the inferior rectus and then inserts into the sclera posterior to the equator of the globe and between the superior and lateral rectus muscles. Innervation is supplied by the oculomotor nerve.

Medial Palpebral Ligament

MEDIAL CANTHAL LIGAMENT[4,6,7,11,13,15,47]

This ligament attaches the tarsal plates to the medial wall of the orbit and aids in the attachment of the orbicularis oculi musculature to the medial orbit. It gives structure and configuration to the palpebral configuration (Fig. 12–41). Traumatic disruption will lead to pooling of lacrimal flow in the medial palpebral area.

The medial canthal ligament attaches to the anterior lacrimal crest of the maxilla and the posterior lacrimal crest of the lacrimal bone. Between these slips of muscle runs the lacrimal sac. The orbicularis oculi muscle, which arguably contributes a portion of its musculature to the prominent posterior slip of the ligament, is referred to as the pars lacrimalis or Horner's muscle. The position of this muscle aids in the efficient collection of tears by creating a positive and negative pressure change on opening and closing the eyelids. This pressure change ensures the flow of tears through the lacrimal sac.

Proper replacement of the traumatically displaced medial canthal ligament is essential to restore proper function to this area. Options for the management of the ligament are discussed in detail in Chapter 19.

Orbital Blood Supply [6,7,11,17] (Fig. 12–32)

The ophthalmic artery is the branch of the internal carotid artery that supplies the orbit. This vessel enters the orbit through the optic canal with the optic nerve. It initially passes inferior and lateral to the optic nerve. The first branch is the central retinal artery. From the inferior lateral position, it passes over the optic nerve toward the medial orbital wall. As the ophthalmic artery passes around the optic nerve, it gives off branches to the lacrimal gland and long posterior ciliary branches to the lateral aspect of the globe. As the lacrimal artery passes anteriorly along the superior aspect of the lateral rectus muscle, it supplies muscular branches and terminates in the lateral palpebral artery and zygomatic branches. The lateral palpebral branches supply the lateral eyelids, and the zygomatic branch passes through the zygomatico-temporal foramen to reach the temporal fossa.

As the artery crosses over the optic nerve, it gives off branches of short posterior ciliary arteries to the globe and the large supraorbital branch. Numerous small muscular branches arise in this area as well. This branch passes anteriorly and superiorly along the superior rectus and levator palpebrae superioris to the supraorbital foramen or notch. It supplies the muscles associated with its course.

The posterior and anterior ethmoid arteries are the next branches of the ophthalmic artery as it continues on the medial superior aspect of the orbit. These arteries give blood to the ethmoid air cells and the frontal sinus and finally terminate as they enter the cranium as small meningeal branches to the dura mater. The medial palpebral arteries arise slightly anterior and inferior to the pulley of the superior oblique muscle. They leave the orbit and supply the eyelids from the medial aspect.

The terminal branches are the supratrochlear and the dorsal arteries. The former leaves the orbit at the medial angle and supplies the skin of the forehead in this area. The latter exits the orbit above the medial palpebral ligament and supplies the dorsum and root of the nose and skin in this area.

Orbital Nerves [7,8,11,47] (Figs. 12–32 to 12–34)

The complex structure and function of the orbit necessitate an intricate neural system. From a surgical anatomic view, the sympathetic and parasympathetic nerve functions are interworked with the larger, more readily identified cranial nerves. For this reason, only the cranial nerves and their position and anatomic considerations will be discussed here.

SENSORY NERVES

Cranial nerve II, the optic nerve, enters the orbit through the optic canal or foramen in the sphenoid bone and takes a direct route to the posterior aspect of the globe. As this nerve enters the orbit, it is immediately enclosed in the muscular cone of the extraocular muscles and is afforded some protection by these structures. There is also some protection given by the laxity of the nerve. It is approximately 5 mm longer than the distance from the orbital canal to the posterior aspect of the globe (2.0 to 2.5 cm).

The general sensory nerves of the orbit are all branches of the ophthalmic nerve, the first division of the trigeminal nerve (cranial nerve V). This nerve branches just prior to entering the orbit via the superior orbital fissure. Two branches enter the orbit superior and lateral to the ophthalmic foramen, while the third enters through the ophthalmic foramen.

The lacrimal nerve is the smallest branch and courses along the upper border of the lateral rectus muscle to the lacrimal gland and then down to the conjunctivae and skin of the upper eyelid. The frontal nerve is the largest and runs above the levator palpebrae muscle and divides into a supraorbital branch, which leaves through the supraorbital notch and supplies the upper eyelid, forehead, and scalp in this area, and a supratrochlear nerve, which passes over the trochlea of the superior oblique muscle to the conjunctivae of the upper eyelid and the forehead.

The third branch of the ophthalmic nerve is the nasociliary, which passes through the ophthalmic foramen, over the optic nerve, and below the superior rectus muscle to the medial wall of the orbit, where it distributes its many branches. These include communications to the ciliary ganglion; a long ciliary to the globe; an infratrochlear branch, which supplies the medial angle of the conjunctiva, lacrimal sac, and the skin of the nose and eyelid in this area; and finally the anterior and posterior ethmoidals, which pass through the associated foramen to supply the ethmoid, frontal, and sphenoid sinuses and the nasal cavity.

Surgical Note: The optic nerve is protected in the orbit by the extraocular muscular cone and the fact that it is approximately 5 mm longer than the distance from the back of the globe to the optic canal, approximately 20 to 25 mm. Surgically, this allows for a fair degree of forward displacement of the globe in retrobulbar surgery and manipulation; however, the nerve is very tightly bound at the optic foramen, where the meninges blend with the periorbita. Careful attention to the position of retractors when exploring the medial wall will avoid trauma to the nerve, which exits the canal approximately 2.5 to 3.0 cm deep to the anterior lacrimal crest.

MOTOR NERVES

The remaining nerves of the orbit all enter the orbit through the superior orbital fissure (Fig. 12–34). The abducens (cranial nerve VI) and the oculomotor (cranial nerve III) pass through the oculomotor foramen, which is created by the tendinous ring of the recti muscles crossing the superior orbital fissure, and, thus, are contained within the muscular cone; the trochlear nerve (cranial nerve IV) passes above the ring and stays outside the muscular cone throughout its course. The trochlear nerve then rises to the roof of the orbit and passes medial to the superior oblique muscle, which it supplies.

The abducens supplies the lateral rectus muscle. It enters the orbit between the heads of the lateral rectus muscle and below the inferior division of the oculomotor nerve, and it passes along the inner surface of the lateral rectus. As stated previously, the trochlear nerve supplies the superior oblique muscle, while the oculomotor nerve supplies all the other extraocular muscles.

As the oculomotor nerve enters the superior orbital fissure, it separates into two divisions, a small superior and a larger inferior division. They both pass between the heads of the lateral rectus muscle. The superior division passes above the optic nerve and innervates the superior rectus and the levator palpebrae muscle, while the inferior division passes below the optic nerve and innervates the inferior and medial recti and the inferior oblique muscle.

Surgical Note: Direct or indirect trauma, either accidental or surgical in nature, to the area of the confluence of anatomy at the posterior aspect of the orbit may cause the rarely seen complications of superior orbital fissure syndrome and orbital apex syndrome. The presenting symptoms will depend on the structures involved and will localize the lesion anatomically. The advisability of surgical intervention in the presence of pretreatment complications such as these is discussed in Chapter 20.

NASAL ANATOMY

External Nasal Anatomy[1,2,4,7,16,17]

The prominence of the nose makes it a frequent target in interpersonal conflict and an often traumatized structure in other forms of facial injury. Injuries result in cosmetic and, if untreated, functional problems. Thus, an in-depth understanding of the anatomy of this area is very important.

The substructure of the external nose is composed of the cartilaginous lower half and the nasal bones superiorly (Fig. 12–43). The inferior cartilaginous structure derives some of its support from the alveolar process of the maxilla in the piriform apertures. The area of union of the maxillae in the midline forms an anterior projection, the anterior nasal spine, which lends support to the nasal tip. The bony opening of the nose is composed of two paired bones, the maxilla inferiorly and the nasal bones superiorly.

The cartilaginous portion of the external nose consists of the septal cartilage and the lateral and alar cartilages. The paired upper lateral cartilages are attached to the septal cartilage in the midline and to the undersurface of the nasal bones superiorly. They are often continuous with each other at the superior margin and, along with the septal cartilage, are considered the nasoseptal cartilage.

The lateral cartilages are triangle shaped. The base of the triangle is superior and articulates with the nasal bones. The lateral border thins to connective tissue, which separates it from the superior aspect of the alar cartilage. The medial border is thicker and blends into the septal cartilage superiorly and inferiorly has a free edge just lateral to the nasal midline.

The alar cartilages are paired, curved cartilages that support the nasal openings. These cartilages have a medial and a lateral crus. The crura are formed by a bending of the cartilage upon itself, with the medial crus of one side loosely connected with the opposite medial crus (Fig. 12–44). The part that forms the lateral crus curves gently to form the alae of the nose. Laterally and inferiorly, there is a fibrofatty tissue that makes up the remainder of the alar base.

The nasal septal cartilage articulates with the perpendicular plate of the ethmoid, vomer, maxilla, and nasal bones and the upper and lower nasal cartilages. This midline structure forms the support for much of the external nasal structure.

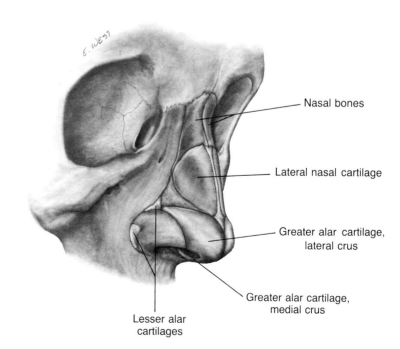

FIGURE 12–43. Substructure of external nose.

Nasal bones

Lateral nasal cartilage

Greater alar cartilage, lateral crus

Greater alar cartilage, medial crus

Lesser alar cartilages

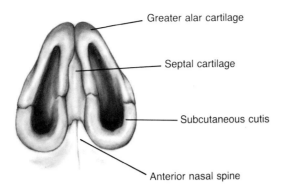

Greater alar cartilage

Septal cartilage

Subcutaneous cutis

Anterior nasal spine

FIGURE 12–44.   Inferior view of nasal septum and alar cartilages.

The arterial supply to the external nose is largely via the external carotid system by the branches of the facial and maxillary arteries and is supplemented by a small portion from the internal carotid system via the ophthalmic artery as its terminal branches perforate the orbital septum and pass downward on the lateral aspect of the nose (Fig. 12–27).

The external nasal neural innervation is complex, being derived from the supratrochlear and infratrochlear branches of the ophthalmic nerve superiorly, the infraorbital branch of the maxillary nerve laterally and inferiorly, and the external nasal branch of the nasociliary from the ophthalmic nerve to the nasal tip and skin over the dorsum inferiorly (Fig. 12–45).

Nasal Cavity Anatomy[7,16,17]

Internally, the nasal septum (Fig. 12–8) divides this paired cavity. The nasal cavity is roughly teardrop shaped in the frontal section, with the narrow area above. The walls of the internal nose are formed medially by the nasal septum; laterally by the maxilla, ethmoid, and nasal cartilages; inferiorly by the maxilla and palatine bones; and superiorly by the cribriform plate of the ethmoid bone.

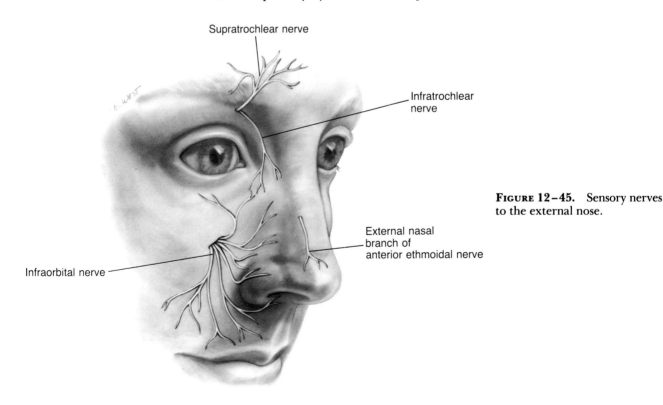

Supratrochlear nerve

Infratrochlear nerve

External nasal branch of anterior ethmoidal nerve

Infraorbital nerve

FIGURE 12–45.   Sensory nerves to the external nose.

The nasal cavity is lined by mucous membranes that are tightly attached to the underlying periosteum or perichondrium, except in the vestibule, where facial skin rolls into the nasal aperture. This mucous membrane is highly vascular.

The nasal septum is the common medial wall of the two nasal cavities (Fig. 12–8). It is formed by the perpendicular plate of the ethmoid posterosuperiorly, by the vomer posteroinferiorly, and by the septal cartilage and medial crus of the alar cartilages anteriorly and inferiorly. Below, the nasal crests of the maxilla and palatine bones complete the septum. The septum rests in the groove formed by these bones and, if displaced by trauma, will require replacement in the groove to prevent functional and aesthetic problems.

The lateral wall of the nose is formed inferiorly by the lateral wall of the maxilla and the inferior nasal concha, which is an independent bone. Below the concha is the inferior meatus. This meatus contains the opening of the nasolacrimal duct. Superiorly, the lateral wall is formed by the segments of the ethmoid bone, which form the middle and superior conchae. Beneath the middle concha is the middle meatus, which receives the opening of the frontal sinus, the anterior ethmoid air cells, and the maxillary sinus. Posterior to the middle concha on the lateral wall is the sphenopalatine foramen. Superior and posterior to the middle concha is the superior concha. It is much shorter and smaller than the others. Below it, in the superior meatus, is the opening to the posterior ethmoid air cells. The supreme nasal concha, with its associated meatus, is not generally identifiable, but in this area above and behind the superior concha is the opening of the sphenoid sinus and sometimes the posterior ethmoid air cells.

The blood supply to the nasal septum is via branches of the sphenopalatine artery, the anterior and posterior ethmoid arteries, and the facial artery. Thus, the supply is from both the internal and the external carotid systems.

The innervation of the internal nose is both general sensory and special sensory. The special sensory is via the olfactory nerve, cranial nerve II, and passes into the skull through the foramina of the cribriform plate of the ethmoid bone.

The general sensory innervation of the internal nose is via the nasociliary branch of the ophthalmic nerve, filaments from the anterior alveolar branch of the maxillary nerve, the nerve of the pterygoid canal, the nasopalatine nerve, the anterior palatine nerve, and nasal branches of the pterygopalatine nerve.

The nasociliary branch of the ophthalmic division of the trigeminal nerve gives filaments to the anterior part of the septum and lateral nasal wall (Figs. 12–46 and 12–47). The anterior alveolar nerve supplies the inferior meatus and concha, while the nerve of the pterygoid canal supplies the superior and posterior septa and the

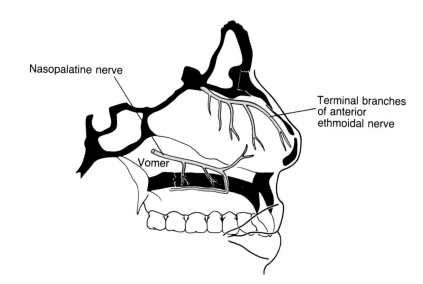

FIGURE 12–46. Innervation to the nasal septum.

Nasopalatine nerve

Terminal branches of anterior ethmoidal nerve

Vomer

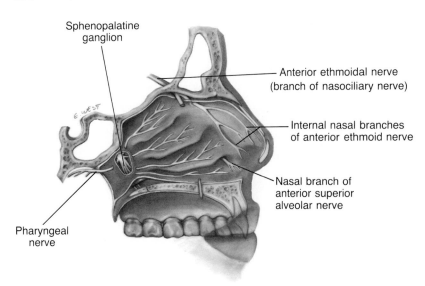

Sphenopalatine
ganglion

Anterior ethmoidal nerve
(branch of nasociliary nerve)

Internal nasal branches
of anterior ethmoid nerve

Nasal branch of
anterior superior
alveolar nerve

Pharyngeal
nerve

FIGURE 12–47.   Lateral nasal wall innervation.

superior concha. The superior branches from the pterygopalatine nerve have a distribution similar to that of the nerve of the pterygoid canal. The nasopalatine nerve supplies the middle of the septum, while the anterior palatine nerve supplies the lower nasal branches to the middle and inferior conchae.[1,4,7]

PAROTID REGION (Fig. 12–48)

The parotid gland is the largest of the salivary glands and occupies the parotid facial space. This space generally extends from the ramus of the mandible anteriorly, from the tympanic bone and the mastoid process posteriorly, and superiorly by the zygomatic arch. The inferior extent reaches to the angle of the mandible, and a

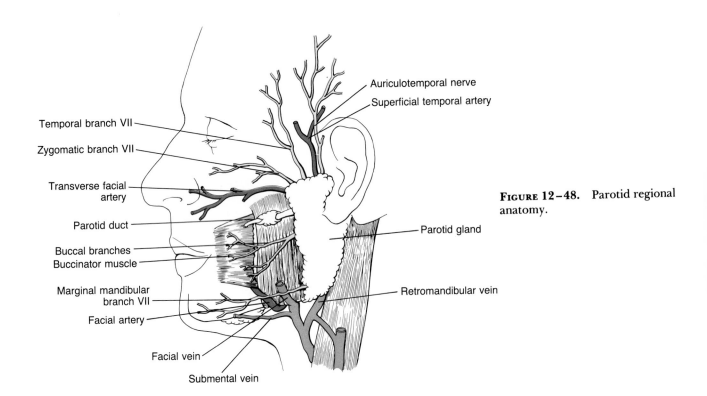

Auriculotemporal nerve

Superficial temporal artery

Temporal branch VII

Zygomatic branch VII

Transverse facial
artery

Parotid duct

Buccal branches

Buccinator muscle

Marginal mandibular
branch VII

Facial artery

Facial vein

Submental vein

Parotid gland

Retromandibular vein

FIGURE 12–48.   Parotid regional anatomy.

cervical portion reaches below, along the sternocleidomastoid muscle. There is a connective tissue investment that sends septa inward among the lobules of the gland.

The parotid gland is composed of a large superficial portion and is in the shape of an inverted triangle lying on the ramus of the mandible. This portion may have an accessory glandular mass extending beyond the limits of the masseter muscle anteriorly. The smaller, deeper portion of the gland is connected by a broad isthmus around the posterior border of the mandible. This deep portion may extend as far as the pharyngeal wall.

The parotid duct, or Stensen's duct, usually leaves from the apical portion of the superficial lobe and then runs forward on the masseter muscle to its anterior margin. The duct then turns medially, piercing the buccinator muscle obliquely to reach the mucous membrane of the cheek. At approximately the second molar, the duct opens into the mouth. The course of the duct approximates a line drawn from the concha of the ear to the commissure of the lips. Its length is normally around 5 cm.

The most important structure entering and leaving the gland are the facial nerve and its branches, the posterior facial vein, the external carotid artery with its branches, the superficial temporal artery, and the internal maxillary artery. The auriculotemporal nerve traverses the upper portion of the parotid gland.

Incisions to deep soft tissue and hard tissue should be horizontal rather than vertical, when possible, to avoid potential damage to the parotid duct and terminal branches of the facial nerve. Soft tissue trauma to the duct could lead to extraoral fistula formation.

SUBMANDIBULAR GLAND[3,6,18] (Fig. 12–49)

The submandibular gland occupies a space on the medial aspect of the mandible in the submandibular fossa. Its lower pole extends inferiorly, covering the intermediate tendon of the digastric muscle. The gland is closely related medially to the stylohyoid, digastric, and styloglossus muscles and to the hyoglossus and posterior border of the mylohyoid anteriorly. The submandibular duct, or Wharton's duct, arises from the upper inner aspect of the gland and is often accompanied by the extension of the gland itself. The duct courses around the posterior border or free margin of the mylohyoid muscle and then runs anteriorly along the inner surface of the sublingual gland after crossing the lingual nerve superiorly. The duct ends at the base of the tongue near its tip.

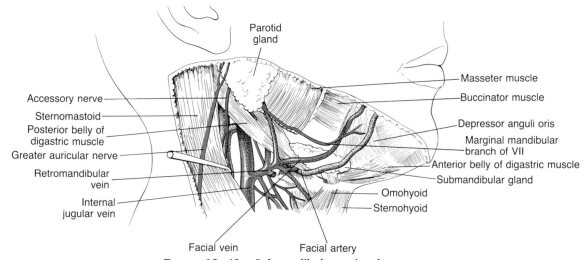

FIGURE 12–49. Submandibular regional anatomy.

Like the parotid gland, the submandibular gland is enclosed in a facial capsule, a derivative of the investing layer of the deep cervical fascia.

Structures closely related to the gland include the facial artery, which may be embedded but is at least closely related to its inner surface and upper border. During extraoral open reduction of the body or angle of the mandible, the fascia and gland may come into view. In a case in which the fragments may be significantly displaced, the fascia may be disrupted and may require repair.

FLOOR OF THE MOUTH[3,6,18] (Figs. 12–50 and 12–51)

Key to the surgeon in repairing soft tissue trauma to the floor of the mouth is an understanding of the anatomic position of various important structures, such as Wharton's duct, the lingual nerve, the sublingual artery, the sublingual gland, the hypoglossal nerve, and the submandibular gland proper. Each of these structures has been described by itself, but at this point it is important to visualize the relationship of these structures to one another (Fig. 12–50).

The submandibular or Wharton's duct exits the superior aspect of the gland, coursing above the posterior free edge of the mylohyoid muscle between the inner surface of the mandible and the lateral surfaces of the hyoglossus and genioglossus muscles. The duct lies lateral to the hypoglossal nerve, and it begins below the lingual nerve. The lingual nerve descends lateral to the duct. At this point, both the duct and the lingual nerve pass around the lower border of the sublingual gland and then are positioned medially. The lingual nerve continues to run below the duct and curls medially on the genioglossus muscle. This arrangement forms almost a complete loop. The Wharton's duct, as it passes on the medial side of the sublingual gland, may receive the major sublingual duct, or Bartholin's duct. The last few millimeters of the anterior portion of the submandibular duct lie immediately below the oral mucosa, where the duct terminates by emptying from the sublingual papilla.

The sublingual artery passes along the side of the genioglossus muscle between the muscle and the sublingual gland, where it supplies both the gland and the muscles of the tongue. The deep lingual artery runs more medially below the mucous membrane on the inferior surface of the tongue. Bleeding from either of these vessels may be brisk in superficial lacerations of the mouth floor, or the vessels may be inadvertently transected during exploration, requiring ligation.

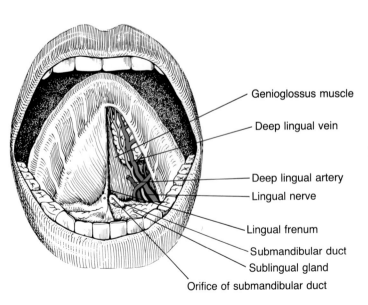

Genioglossus muscle

Deep lingual vein

Deep lingual artery
Lingual nerve

Lingual frenum

Submandibular duct
Sublingual gland

Orifice of submandibular duct

FIGURE 12–50.   Floor of mouth.

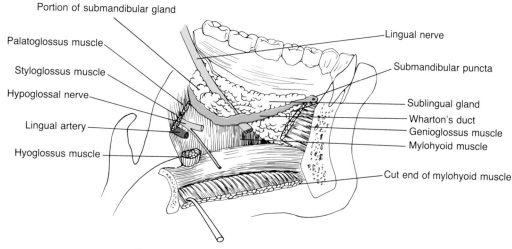

FIGURE 12–51. Sublingual anatomy.

Acknowledgment. Artwork was provided by GERYGRAPHICS, 2020 W. Main St., Durham, NC. The artist is Elizabeth West.

REFERENCES

1. Dingman RO, Moorman WC: Meniscectomy in treatment of lesions of temporomandibular joint. J Oral Surg 9:214, 1951.
2. Fried LA: Anatomy of the Head, Neck, Face, and Jaws. 2nd ed. Philadelphia, Lea and Febiger, 1980.
3. Gregg JM: Surgical anatomy. *In* Laskin DM (ed): Oral and Maxillofacial Surgery. Vol I. St Louis, CV Mosby, 1980, pp 3–49.
4. Hollinshead WH: Anatomy for Surgeons: The Head and Neck. Vol I. 2nd ed. New York, Harper and Row, 1968.
5. Jackson IT, Schiele UU, Adham M: The conjunctival approach to the orbital floor and maxilla—advantages and disadvantages. Plast Reconstr Surg 19:46, 1987.
6. McVay CB: Surgical Anatomy. 6th ed. Philadelphia, WB Saunders Company, 1984.
7. Pansky B, House EL: Review of Gross Anatomy. London, Macmillan, 1969.
8. Rehman I, Hiatt N: Descriptive Atlas of Surgical Anatomy. New York, McGraw-Hill Book Company, 1965.
9. Sarnat BG: The Temporomandibular Joint. 2nd ed. Springfield, IL, Charles C Thomas, 1964.
10. Sicher H, DuBrul EL: Oral Anatomy. 6th ed. St Louis, CV Mosby, 1975.
11. Wolff E: Anatomy for the Eye and Orbit. Philadelphia, WB Saunders Company, 1968.
12. Converse JM, Firmin F, Wood-Smith D, et al: The conjunctival approach in orbital fractures. Plast Reconstr Surg 52:656, 1973.
13. Goss CM: Gray's Anatomy of the Human Body. 28th ed. Philadelphia, Lea and Febiger, 1970.
14. Jackson IT, Munro I, Salyer K, Whitaker L: Atlas of Craniomaxillofacial Surgery. St Louis, CV Mosby, 1982.
15. Holt JE, Holt GR: Ocular and Orbital Trauma. St Louis, American Academy of Otolaryngology, 1983.
16. Lee KJ: Comprehensive Surgical Atlas in Otolaryngology and Head and Neck Surgery. New York, Grune and Stratton, 1983.
17. Rowe NL, Williams J: Maxillofacial Injuries. Vol I. London, Churchill-Livingstone, 1985, pp 1–42.
18. Schultz RC: Facial Injuries. 2nd ed. Chicago, Year Book Medical Publishers, 1977.
19. Ritter FN: The Paranasal Sinuses: Anatomy and Surgical Technique. 2nd ed. St Louis, CV Mosby, 1978.
20. Matsunaga RS, Simpson W, Toffel PH: Simplified protocol for the treatment of malar fractures. Arch Otolaryngol 103:535, 1977.
21. Briggs PC, Heckler FR: Lacrimal gland involvement in zygomaticofrontal fracture sites. Plast Reconstr Surg 80:682, 1987.
22. Gillies HD, Kilner P, Stone D: Fractures of the malar-zygomatic compound: With a description of a new x-ray position. Br J Surg 14:651, 1927.
23. Karlan MS, Cassisi NJ: Fractures of the zygoma: A geometric biomechanical and surgical analysis. Arch Otolaryngol 105:320, 1979.
24. Pozatek ZW, Kaban LB, Gurainick WC: Fractures of the zygomatic complex: An evaluation of surgical management with special emphasis on the eyebrow approach. J Oral Surg 31:141, 1973.
25. Crewe TC: Significance of the orbital floor in zygomatic injuries. Int J Oral Surg 7:235, 1978.
26. Converse JM, Hogan VM: Open sky approach for reduction of naso-orbital fractures. Plast Reconstr Surg 46:396, 1970.

27. Peri G, Chabannes J, Menes R, et al: Fractures of the frontal sinus. J Maxillofac Surg 9:73, 1981.

28. Dingman RO, Natvig P: The mandible. Part I. General characteristics. *In* Dingman RO, Natvig P (eds): Surgery of Facial Fractures. Philadelphia, WB Saunders Company, 1964.

29. Halazonetis JA: The "weak" regions of the mandible. Br J Oral Surg 6:37, 1968.

30. Huelke DF: Association between mandibular fractures related to teeth and edentulous regions. J Oral Surg 22:396, 1964.

31. Kazanjian VH, Converse JM: The Surgical Treatment of Facial Fractures. Baltimore, The Williams and Wilkins Company, 1949.

32. Dingman RO, Converse JM: The clinical management of facial injuries and fractures of the facial bones. *In* Converse JM: Reconstructive Plastic Surgery. Vol II. 2nd ed. Philadelphia, WB Saunders Company, 1977.

33. Tebo HG, Telford IR: An analysis of the relative positions of the mental foramina. Anat Rec 106:254, 1950.

34. Rajchel J, Ellis E, Fonseca RJ: The anatomical location of the mandibular canal: Its relationship to the sagittal split osteotomy. Int J Adult Ortho Orthogn Surg 1:37, 1986.

35. Mathog RH: Maxillofacial Trauma. Baltimore, The Williams and Wilkins Company, 1984.

36. Nahum AM: The biomechanics of maxillofacial trauma. Clin Plast Surg 2:59, 1975.

37. Dingman RO, Natvig P: Surgery of Facial Fractures. Philadelphia, WB Saunders Company, 1964.

38. Wakely CPG: Surgery of temporomandibular joint. Surgery 5:697, 1939.

39. Blair VP: Consideration of contour as well as function in operations for organic ankylosis of lower jaw. Surg Gynecol Obstet 46:167, 1928.

40. Hendrix JH: Open reduction of mandibular condyle: A clinical and experimental study. Plast Reconstr Surg 23:283, 1959.

41. Hoopes JE: Operative treatment of fractures of the mandibular condyle in children using the post-auricular approach. Plast Reconstr Surg 46:357, 1970.

42. Killey HC: Fractures of the Mandible. 2nd ed. Bristol, England, Rev. Rep. Wright, 1974.

43. Thurow RC: Muscular control of the mandible. *In* Atlas of Orthodontic Principles. 2nd ed. St Louis, CV Mosby, 1977.

44. Olson RA, Fonseca RJ, Zeitler DL, Osbon DBF: Fractures of the mandible: A review of 580 cases. J Maxillofac Surg 40:23, 1982.

45. Georgiade NG: Plastic and Maxillofacial Trauma Symposium. St Louis, CV Mosby, 1969.

46. Lempert J: Improvement of hearing in cases of otosclerosis. New one stage surgical technic. Arch Otolaryngol 60:566, 1938.

47. Jones LT: Orbital anatomy. *In* Proceedings of the Second International Symposium on Plastic and Reconstructive Surgery. St Louis, CV Mosby, 1967.

CHAPTER 13

EARLY ASSESSMENT AND TREATMENT PLANNING OF THE MAXILLOFACIAL TRAUMA PATIENT

JOHN F. HELFRICK, D.D.S., M.S.

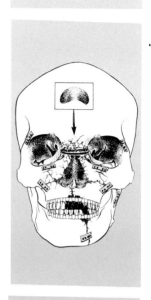

RESUSCITATION AND STABILIZATION

The quality of the primary evaluation and management frequently determines whether or not the trauma patient survives his or her injuries. When a severely traumatized patient is initially assessed, it is critical for the surgeon to approach this phase of management in an orderly and systematic manner. Injuries to the head and neck frequently involve the airway and major vessels; therefore, the ABCs of resuscitation must be strictly adhered to in the primary phase of assessment and management of the patient with maxillofacial trauma.

Airway and Ventilatory Management

The surgeon's first concern should be for the patient's airway. Debris should be removed from the upper airway, and an oral or nasal airway should be inserted. These airways are tolerated by both the unconscious and the conscious patient. In the event of severe multisystem trauma that has resulted in an unstable airway, it is frequently advisable to perform an oral or nasotracheal intubation. This intubation must be done with caution, and when there is the potential for a cervical spine injury, the head must be stabilized by taping it to the table or by supporting it with sandbags.

A nasotracheal approach may be preferable and may result in less head and neck manipulation than an oral intubation. Although severe midface and nasal injuries may be present, nasal intubation can still be done by a skilled clinician. In those uncommon situations in which oral or nasal intubation cannot be accomplished, cricothyroidotomy is the procedure of choice. Rarely is a tracheostomy performed as an emergency procedure. Oral or nasal intubation is performed, and if prolonged airway management or pulmonary toilet procedures or both are necessary, a tracheostomy can then be done as an elective procedure in a more controlled environment.

Oral or nasotracheal intubation should generally be performed in the presence of severe head injury with loss of consciousness, maxillary fractures in which the

279

maxilla has been posteriorly and inferiorly displaced, unstable mandibular fractures usually involving the parasymphyseal region, and in those cases in which there has been significant chest trauma resulting in rib fractures. Patients with rib fractures who have been intubated and who are going to have a general anesthetic are usually candidates for prophylactic chest tube insertion. This practice limits the potential for the development of a tension pneumothorax during administration of the anesthetic. Patients in hypovolemic shock or those with severe abdominal injuries that will require a laparotomy are also candidates for intubation. It must once again be stressed that the head and neck must not be manipulated during intubation in those patients in whom a cervical spine injury has not been ruled out.

At the time of initial airway management, the clinician must be aware of the potential for an injury to the tracheobronchial tree. Injuries can occur to the trachea and to either the right or the left mainstem bronchus. Clinical signs such as cyanosis, wheezing, hoarseness, and subcutaneous emphysema may indicate that the patient has a significant tracheobronchial injury. Of these findings, probably the most common are wheezing and, if the patient is able to talk, a hoarseness in the voice. These findings should alert the clinician to the potential for tracheobronchial injury, and care must be taken to assure that a transected but splinted trachea is not displaced during the intubation procedure. If these injuries are suspected, an individual skilled in bronchoscopy should be immediately consulted.

Once the airway has been established, it is important to ascertain whether or not the patient is ventilating. The most common way of ventilating the nonexchanging patient in the early phases of management is by the attachment of an Ambu bag to the endotracheal tube. A ventilator may ultimately be necessary for respiratory support.

Cardiovascular and Fluid Management

Once the airway has been managed and the patient is being properly ventilated, the clinician must then control any external bleeding and stabilize the patient's cardiovascular system. External hemorrhage is best controlled by direct digital pressure, which will not result in damage to any major vessels or nerves. This is particularly true in the head and neck region, where blind clamping with a hemostat may result in injuries to important anatomic structures.

While the bleeding is being controlled, lost fluid must be replaced. Ideally, whole blood that has been properly typed and cross-matched should be given to the patient. However, typed and cross-matched whole blood may not always be immediately available. Initially, fluid therapy with a balanced electrolyte solution, such as lactated Ringer's (normal saline is a second choice), is initiated in two or more sites with a large-caliber catheter. The most preferable sites for the initiation of fluid therapy are in the upper extremities, assuming that there are no apparent injuries to the arms or shoulders. Fluids administered through sites in the lower extremity may never reach the central circulation in cases of long bone or abdominal vascular injuries.

During the initial fluid management, the vital signs are assessed by monitoring the blood pressure, pulse, urinary output, and central venous pressure (CVP). The insertion of a Swan-Ganz catheter to measure the pulmonary wedge pressure is generally indicated only in those patients with a history of severe cardiovascular disease. Its routine use in trauma patients is not indicated. Of critical importance is the assessment of the pulse pressure (systolic pressure minus diastolic pressure), which narrows in cases of severe hypovolemia. It is urinary output, however, that gives the clinician the most reliable information concerning the patient's current volume status and consequently the quality of organ perfusion. An output of at least 50 ml/hr should be expected from the Foley catheter.

Once the fluids have been started, it is important to establish the patient's normal blood volume. This volume is generally determined by recognizing that the blood volume is 7 per cent of the body weight in kilograms in a normal adult and 8 to 9 per cent of the body weight in the pediatric patient. In the management of an obese patient, the ideal body weight of that individual is utilized in the determination of the normal blood volume. Proper fluid replacement therapy may be critical to the patient's survival. As previously mentioned, properly cross-matched, type-specific blood is the preferred fluid for the management of hypovolemic shock. If fully cross-matched blood is not available, type-specific or "saline cross-matched" blood, which can be obtained within 10 minutes, is the second blood of choice. Finally, type O negative blood can be given in an emergency when neither fully cross-matched nor type-specific blood is available. Vasopressors should not be used in the management of hypovolemic shock.

When the blood is being administered, it should be warmed and passed through a micropore filter. The administration of large volumes of cold blood can result in cardiac arrhythmias. To prevent a coagulopathy when large volumes (greater than 10 units) of blood are being administered, it is appropriate to transfuse a unit of platelets for every 10 units of blood administered. Fresh frozen plasma, which will replace coagulation factor VIII and fibrinogen, should be administered after every six units of blood given to the patient. The utilization of calcium is controversial, but it may be used when large amounts of blood are infused very rapidly (greater than 100 ml/min) and is generally given in 2-ml doses of 10 per cent calcium chloride solution. The total amount administered should not exceed 1 g.

Neurologic Examination

Once the airway has been established, the patient is breathing or is being ventilated, and the cardiovascular system has been stabilized, the surgeon can proceed with a general assessment of the patient. The patient should be disrobed, and the neurologic examination should begin with an evaluation of the level of consciousness.

The patient who arrives at the emergency room and is unconscious or, more important, the patient who arrives alert and becomes unconscious should receive a very rapid neurologic assessment. The patient's level of consciousness is of primary importance, and the *AVPU* mnemonic can be used to organize the evaluation:

    A: Alert
    V: Responds to vocal stimuli
    P: Responds only to painful stimuli
    U: Unresponsive

In the unconscious patient, the first step is to consider a differential diagnosis quickly. The most commonly utilized mnemonic is *AEIOU-TIPPS.*

   AEIOU:
    A: Alcohol
    E: Epilepsy
    I: Insulin
    O: Opiates
    U: Urea

   TIPPS:
    T: Trauma
    I: Infection
    P: Poison
    P: Psychiatric manifestations
    S: Shock

Determining the level of consciousness is the first and most important phase of the neurologic examination. Next, the patient is asked to move the extremities, and finally, the level of sensory function is determined with a sharp object. As previously mentioned, when identifying specific organ injuries in the multiply traumatized patient, it is extremely important to rule out cervical spine fractures and dislocations.

There are six cardinal signs of cervical cord injuries, as follows:

1.   Flaccid extremities, especially with areflexia

2. Diaphragmatic breathing
3. Ability to flex forearms but not extend them
4. Facial grimace in response to pain above the clavicles but not below
5. Hypotension without evidence of hemorrhage (spinal shock)
6. Priapism

If the fracture-dislocation occurs above C3, C4, and C5, the phrenic nerve function will be disrupted and the patient's ventilation will require mechanical control. Because of potentially life-threatening cervical cord injuries, the patient's head and neck must be stabilized until lateral cross-table films, showing all seven vertebrae, have been obtained and the cervical spine has been cleared of any significant injuries.

In addition to an evaluation of motor function, an assessment of sensation can assist the surgeon in determining the level of spinal cord injury. The sensory loss at various cord levels is as follows:

1. Two inches behind the tip of the ear: level C2
2. Top of the shoulder: level C4
3. Tip of the thumb: level C6
4. Tip of the middle finger: level C7
5. Tip of the fifth finger: level C8
6. At the nipple line: level T4
7. At the lower sternum: level T6
8. At the level of the umbilicus: level T10
9. Just below the iliac crest: level L1
10. Just above the knee cap: level L3
11. Top of the fifth toe: level S1

The various types of cord injuries include complete transection, which results in quadriplegia with bilateral sensory and motor loss and loss of autonomic control (spinal shock); central cord syndrome secondary to hemorrhage or edema, which can be manifested as weakness in the extremities; anterior cord syndrome, which results in the complete loss of motor function distal to the level of the injury; and transverse hemisection of the cord, which results in contralateral pain and temperature loss and ipsilateral motor, proprioceptive, and autonomic loss below the lesion. These are reviewed in greater depth in Chapter 7.

ORAL AND MAXILLOFACIAL EXAMINATION

Once the patient has been stabilized and cleared for cervical spinal cord injuries, the surgeon can begin an orderly evaluation of the maxillofacial region. If possible, a medical history and a history of the events surrounding the injury should be obtained.

Knowing the cause of the trauma will alert the clinician to specific types of injuries. A sharp, penetrating injury is more likely to injure nerves and major vessels than is blunt trauma, which is more likely to result in fractures of the facial skeleton. A person thrown from a car is more apt to have multisystem injuries than is a person involved in a low-speed accident in which the injured person has remained in the vehicle. The specific organ injuries expected from various types of trauma are reviewed in greater depth in the chapters devoted to those anatomic regions.

Knowing the events surrounding the injury can also assist the surgeon in the examination process. For example, a person struck in the eye with a baseball would be expected to have a pure blow-out fracture or other injuries confined to the eye and periorbital region. A low-caliber gunshot injury with small entrance and exit wounds would be less likely to cause massive internal injuries than would a high-caliber gunshot wound. This helpful information can be obtained from the patient, emergency personnel, or the patient's friends and family. The surgeon should also seek information relating to the patient's medical history. A mnemonic that is helpful in the immediate assessment of the patient is *AMPLE:*

A: Allergies
M: Medications the patient may be taking
P: Past illnesses
L: Last meal
E: Events preceding the injury

It is important to understand that the time of the last meal (or alcoholic drink) must receive special consideration in the traumatized patient. Significant trauma will decrease gut motility, and the patient who would have otherwise cleared his or her stomach of contents may, in fact, vomit these contents during the induction of anesthesia or following surgery. Therefore, nasogastric suction and techniques to prevent vomiting and aspiration during intubation and anesthesia must be employed in the traumatized patient. Caution must be taken when inserting a nasogastric tube in a patient with a Le Fort II or III injury, as the tube may penetrate the anterior cranial fossa if it is passed injudiciously.

The surgeon should perform a brief assessment of the patient's central neurologic status. An ongoing appreciation for the patient's level of consciousness during the examination is extremely important. A deterioration in the patient's alertness usually indicates increasing intracranial pressure, which, in the case of an epidural hematoma, requires immediate surgical intervention. If the level of consciousness has been altered, the surgeon must determine whether this alteration is secondary to a central problem or another cause. The *AEIOU-TIPPS* mnemonic mentioned previously can be of assistance in establishing a differential diagnosis.

The clinical evaluation of the maxillofacial region must be organized and sequential and should be performed prior to ordering radiographs and imaging scans. Obtaining maxillofacial radiographs is not an emergency and should not pre-empt the general physical and maxillofacial examinations. The head and neck evaluation must be methodical, and without the use of a strictly adhered to method, significant injuries may be missed. One approach organizes the examination from "inside out and bottom up," according to the following systems.

The oral examination proceeds in the following order:

1. Soft tissues
2. Nerves
3. Skeleton
4. Dentition

The maxillofacial examination proceeds in the following order:

1. Soft tissues
2. Nerves
3. Skeleton

EXAMINATION OF THE ORAL CAVITY

The surgeon can now turn his or her attention to injuries involving the oral cavity and maxillofacial skeleton. This portion of the patient's examination is not on an emergency basis and should only be started once the patient has been stabilized and the airway secured.

Soft Tissue Examination

The evaluation and the treatment are performed "inside out and bottom up." The surgeon must once again evaluate the oral and pharyngeal soft tissues for lacerations or penetrating injuries. The tongue is frequently lacerated. Bleeding must be

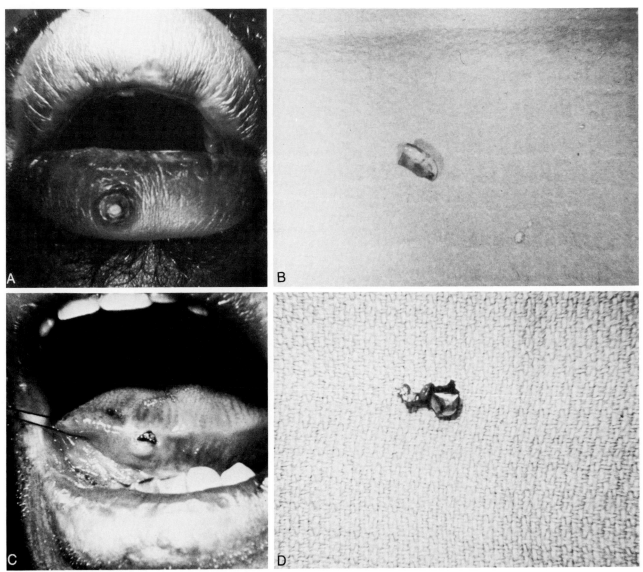

FIGURE 13–1. *A,* The presence of a foreign body in the lower lip of a patient who had previously had a lip laceration surgically repaired. *B,* Exploration of the lower lip disclosed the presence of a tooth fragment. *C,* The extrusion of a foreign body from the tongue of a patient who had a tongue laceration repaired. *D,* Exploration of the area disclosed the presence of a dental bridge.

controlled, and these soft tissue injuries must be explored for tooth fragments and other foreign bodies (Fig. 13–1*A* to *D*). The orifices of Stensen's and Wharton's ducts must be evaluated for patency and salivary flow. Areas of soft tissue swelling and ecchymosis are also identified, as they frequently reflect an underlying bone injury.

Special attention should be given to lacerations involving the attached alveolar and palatal mucous membranes. Vertical lacerations in the alveolar gingiva are frequently associated with underlying mandibular, maxillary, or alveolar arch fractures. An anterior-to-posterior laceration of the hard palate is usually associated with paramedian fractures of the palate (Fig. 13–2*A* to *F*).

Neurologic Examination

Once the soft tissues have been evaluated, the surgeon must perform a neurologic examination. Nerves commonly injured as a result of oral and perioral trauma are the following.

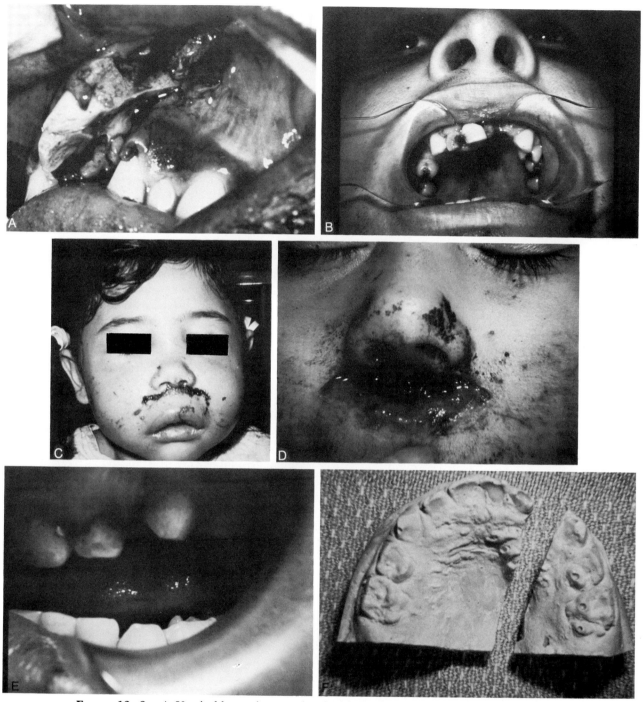

FIGURE 13–2.   *A*, Vertical laceration associated with an obvious alveolar arch fracture; however, these fractures may be more subtle, and vertical gingival laceration may indicate an underlying fracture. *B*, Evaluation of the palate in a patient who had sustained a maxillary injury may disclose a laceration indicating a paramedian fracture. *C*, Lacerations may appear to be superficial because of the early approximation of the tissues to one another secondary to the formation of a fibrin coagulum. These tissues must be pulled apart and explored carefully. *D*, Separation of the soft tissues noted in *C* disclosed a maxillary fracture with exposed dental follicles in this 2-year-old patient. *E*, Further examination disclosed a step in the patient's maxillary dental occlusion and a small vertical laceration. *F*, Further examination disclosed a hemi–Le Fort I fracture with a mobile greater segment and a stabilized lesser segment, as shown on the sectioned dental model.

Inferior Alveolar Nerve. This nerve is frequently injured as a result of mandibular fractures. A fracture involving the inferior alveolar canal may result in lip anesthesia on the affected side, which may be permanent.

Lingual Nerve. Although this nerve is less commonly traumatized, injuries will result in anesthesia or paresthesia of the anterior two thirds of the tongue. In addition, because the chorda tympani fibers are carried with the lingual nerve, injuries to this structure will result in alterations in taste (Fig. 13–3).

Skeletal Examination

Once the soft tissue, neurologic, and dental examinations have been completed, the skeletal examination is begun with the mandible. Once again, it is very helpful to know the events relating to the injury. For example, chin lacerations resulting from a blunt injury are frequently associated with subcondylar fractures. An altercation in which a right-handed person hits an individual in the left jaw—a very common scenario—frequently results in left-angle and right-parasymphysis fractures. Therefore, knowing the cause of the injury can be very helpful in establishing a diagnosis.

The mandible is evaluated by both intraoral and extraoral observation and palpation. Palpation of the oral and facial soft tissues may disclose pain, crepitation, or induration—all important clinical findings. Pain, swelling, and induration may indicate an infection associated with the mandibular fracture, especially those that are at least 48 hours old. Because mandibular fractures that involve the dentition are, by definition, compounded intraorally, they frequently become infected. Soft tissue swelling secondary to edema must be differentiated from that associated with an infected fracture site.

Mandibular excursions should be evaluated. An inability to open greater than 35 mm or deviate 6 mm to the right or left indicates either a mechanical problem or trismus secondary to a mandibular fracture or a pre-existing temporomandibular joint (TMJ) disorder. Pain in the preauricular or masseteric area on palpation may indicate an injury to the condyle or mandibular angle. Mandibular deviation upon opening to the affected side is pathognomonic of a condylar fracture.

Limited opening, preauricular pain, and an anterior open bite are indicative of bilateral subcondylar fractures; however, in the absence of maxillary or mandibular teeth or both, the primary occlusal finding in these patients may be a decrease in the posterior interarch space. A condylar injury associated with bleeding from the external auditory canal in a child is of considerable concern. Trauma of this severity in a young child may result in mandibular ankylosis and growth abnormalities.

FIGURE 13–3. Severe mandibular fracture, resulting in both inferior alveolar and lingual nerve injuries.

Fractures involving the mandibular body, symphysis, and angle can usually be detected by firm bimanual palpation and an evaluation of the patient's occlusion. Crepitation, mobility, and step abnormalities in the patient's occlusion are pathognomonic of mandibular fractures. Lip anesthesia or paresthesia is also a common finding in fractures involving the mandibular body and angle. It is important to document this finding prior to proceeding with treatment.

Dental Examination

The teeth are evaluated in terms of quantity, quality, and occlusal relationships. The presence of a full complement of teeth is of considerable assistance in the establishment of a diagnosis and treatment plan. With a knowledge of occlusion, including the ability to analyze wear facets, the surgeon can determine the presence or absence of a malocclusion based upon jaw displacement secondary to trauma. This knowledge is critical for those treating maxillofacial trauma, as the malocclusion noted in the injured patient may be either developmental or traumatic in origin. The trauma surgeon must be able to differentiate between the two, so that normal form and function can be restored (Fig. 13–4).

The dentition must be evaluated for fractures—either horizontal or vertical— and for mobility. A tooth may be mobile as a result of a root fracture, periodontal disease, or a jaw fracture that parallels the long axis of the tooth. Bleeding from the gingival crevice usually indicates that the mobility of the tooth is a result of trauma and not periodontal disease. A number of teeth that are loose and move in unison are usually associated with a fracture involving a dental-osseous segment. This fractured segment may or may not be involved with a complete fracture of the maxilla or mandible (Fig. 13–5). Missing teeth must also be accounted for. If teeth are missing, chest and abdominal radiographs must be reviewed. Although displaced teeth are usually swallowed, the mainstem bronchi and the lungs should be carefully evaluated. Because of the acute angle with which the left mainstem bronchus exits the trachea, foreign bodies that have been aspirated are most commonly found in the right lung or bronchus (Fig. 13–6A and B). Specific management of the dentition is discussed in Chapter 15.

A full complement of teeth in the patient with maxillofacial trauma is frequently

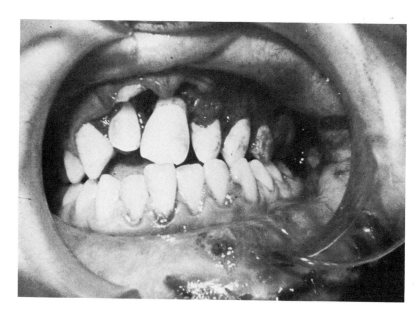

FIGURE 13–4.   The ability to evaluate a malocclusion is critical in the diagnosis and management of maxillofacial injuries. A crossbite, for example, may be the result of trauma or may be a developmental abnormality.

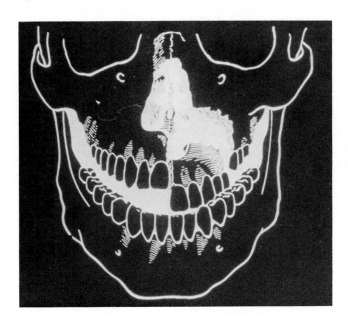

FIGURE 13–5. Maxillary and mandibular alveolar arch fractures may or may not be associated with basal bone injuries. It is difficult to treat these injuries and to obtain a routinely acceptable result. The prognosis is improved by early management.

a mixed blessing. It aids in the diagnosis and management of the fractures; however, it may contribute to a compromise of the patient's airway following definitive surgery. If the patient is to be placed into intermaxillary fixation (IMF), a determination must be made prior to extubation regarding the potential for compromise of the patient's respiration by obstruction of the nasal and oral airways. Nasal swelling or fractures and other nasal injuries requiring packing, in conjunction with a full complement of teeth, oral swelling, and arch bars, may necessitate a tracheostomy. In the partially or completely edentulous patient, this is usually not necessary. However, the lack of dentition frequently complicates the treatment plan and may dictate a more aggressive surgical approach. Therefore, an in-depth understanding of and ability to assess the dentition are critical in the evaluation and management of the patient with maxillofacial trauma.

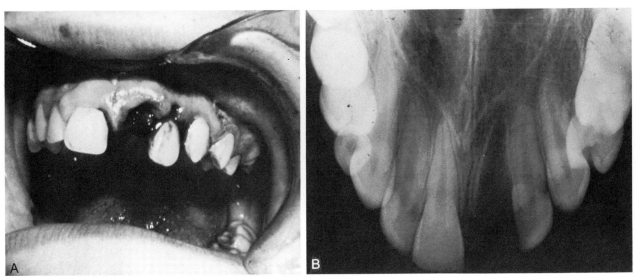

FIGURE 13–6. *A,* When teeth appear to be missing, they must be accounted for. A chest radiograph and flat plate of the abdomen must be obtained to rule out aspiration of the teeth or dental fragments. *B,* A dental radiograph must also be obtained to determine whether or not a fractured dental root fragment remains.

EXTRAORAL EXAMINATION

Soft Tissue Examination

Careful and thorough inspection of the soft tissues is a critical part of the maxillofacial evaluation. Bleeding from lacerations must be controlled. Once the bleeding has been controlled and the patient has been stabilized, the prudent surgeon should obtain photographs that will be part of the medical (and legal) record. The lacerations must be thoroughly washed and explored for foreign bodies, including tooth fragments. Occasionally, a dental periapical or occlusal film of the soft tissues will assist in this evaluation. Lacerations in hair-bearing areas should be exposed by shaving the hair adjacent to the injuries; however, since regrowth of the eyebrows is sporadic, they should not be shaved.

The clinician must never minimize the importance of a small laceration indicating a penetrating wound. It should be assumed that a penetrating wound of the upper or lower eyelid is associated with a globe injury until proved otherwise. Similarly, it should be assumed that a penetrating wound of the soft palate has extended into the middle cranial fossa. These wounds must be explored carefully. In addition, a penetrating wound that traverses the oral or maxillofacial structures and enters the neck region must be assumed to have injured major vessels and requires surgical or imaging (arteriogram) evaluation or both.

A laceration with bleeding from the external auditory canal is frequently seen with severe TMJ injuries or middle cranial fossa injuries. A basilar skull fracture may also result in cerebrospinal fluid (CSF) otorrhea. The source of the bleeding can usually be identified once the external canal has been cleaned. In the case of the condylar fracture, a laceration is generally present along the anterior wall of the canal. A perforation or bulging of the tympanic membrane (hemotympanum) usually indicates a basilar skull fracture.

The surgeon should be alert to subconjunctival hemorrhage, which may reflect an orbital or periorbital injury. Of even greater importance is the identification of blood in the anterior chamber of the eye. This condition, known as hyphema, should be evaluated by an ophthalmologist and is discussed at greater depth in Chapter 20.

Of similar importance is the evaluation of the nose—particularly the septum—for the presence of a septal hematoma. If present, the hematoma should be drained to avoid septal necrosis and, ultimately, the development of septal perforations. The nasal examination may also reveal CSF rhinorrhea. This rhinorrhea results from fractures involving the base of the skull and the escape of CSF through the ethmoid, sphenoid, or, most commonly, the frontal sinus and cribriform plate areas (Fig. 13–7A and B).

Tissue discoloration should also be noted. Ecchymosis behind the ear (Battle's sign) is indicative of a basilar skull fracture involving the middle cranial fossa; however, this is usually a late (24 hours) finding (Fig. 13–8). Bilateral periorbital ecchymosis (raccoon eyes) is commonly seen as a result of a fracture of the base of the anterior cranial fossa. Ecchymosis in the buccal fold frequently indicates a fracture of the maxilla or zygoma or an isolated fracture of the lateral wall of the maxillary sinus.

The surgeon should now carefully palpate the soft tissues. A crackling sound in the subcutaneous tissues usually indicates the presence of air within the tissues. A soft tissue radiograph will confirm this finding. Subcutaneous emphysema is not uncommon in upper airway injuries, particularly those involving the walls of the maxillary sinus.

Neurologic Examination

The maxillofacial neurologic examination should emphasize the following nerves.

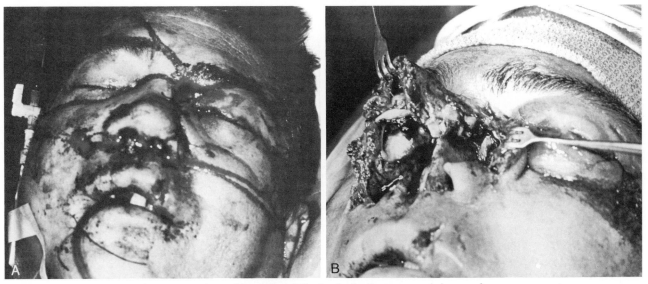

FIGURE 13–7.   *A,* A patient with midface injuries, including a severe injury to the nose, presents with a clear fluid coming from the left nostril, indicating cerebrospinal fluid (CSF) rhinorrhea. Clinical photographs were obtained prior to definitive management. *B,* Further exploration of the nose failed to disclose a septal hematoma.

Facial Nerve.   This nerve is commonly injured as a result of facial lacerations or penetrating wounds. The nerve function can be easily assessed in the conscious patient by asking the person to use the muscles of facial expression (Fig. 13–9*A* and *B*). This evaluation should be completed and noted prior to the injection of a local anesthetic or the induction of general anesthesia. A nerve stimulator to evaluate nerve function can be used in the unconscious patient (Fig. 13–10*A* to *E*).

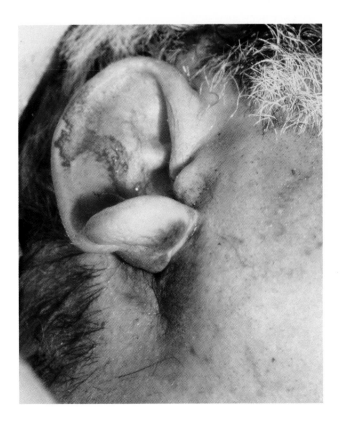

FIGURE 13–8.   Battle's sign, indicating a basal skull fracture as a result of severe head trauma.

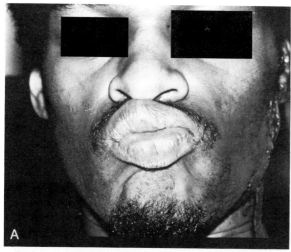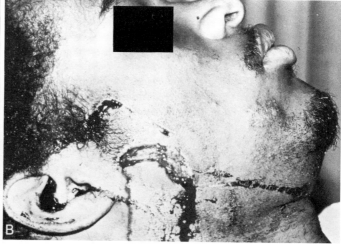

FIGURE 13–9.   *A*, Lacerations in the area of the facial nerve must be evaluated carefully. *B*, In the conscious and alert patient, the nerve can be easily assessed by asking the patient to perform maneuvers that evaluate the function of the muscles of facial expression.

Infraorbital Nerve.   This nerve is injured as a result of fractures of the infraorbital rim, including zygomaticomaxillary (ZMC) complex and Le Fort II fractures. This nerve may also be injured as a result of orbital blow-out injuries that involve the inferior orbital fissure.

Olfactory Nerve.   This nerve is most commonly injured as a result of midface fractures that involve the cribriform plate. Anosmia resulting from transection of the olfactory nerve is usually permanent.

Oculomotor Nerve.   This nerve is most frequently injured because of intracranial nerve compression resulting from increasing intracranial pressure. The presence of a dilated pupil, indicating cranial nerve III dysfunction, should be interpreted as being reflective of a central versus peripheral (orbital) abnormality and requires urgent assessment. The surgeon must also remember that anisocoria can be a normal finding; however, serious intracranial injuries and increasing intracranial pressure must be ruled out before one assumes that a dilated pupil is a normal finding in the trauma patient.

Abducens Nerve.   Because of the long, bony intracranial course of this nerve, abducens nerve palsies are not uncommon in the patient who has suffered deceleration types of injuries. The patient will exhibit lateral rectus muscle dysfunction on lateral gaze (Fig. 13–11).

Optic Nerve.   The optic nerve can be injured either centrally or within the orbit. However, it may also be injured as a result of fractures surrounding the optic foramen that result in compression of the nerve. In the unconscious patient, optic and oculomotor nerve function can be evaluated by using the consensual light reflex (see Chapter 20). Early identification of the injury and decompression of the optic nerve in cases involving optic foramen injuries may salvage the patient's vision.

Skeletal Examination

The maxilla and zygoma may now be assessed. Ecchymosis in the maxillary buccal fold and a Class III open-bite malocclusion are indicative of a maxillary fracture. The direction and force of the injury usually drive the maxilla posteriorly and inferiorly, which results in this occlusal abnormality.

Bimanual palpation of the maxilla is extremely important but must be done properly. Placing one hand on the forehead while manipulating the maxilla with the other can give the erroneous impression of maxillary mobility. The movement of the

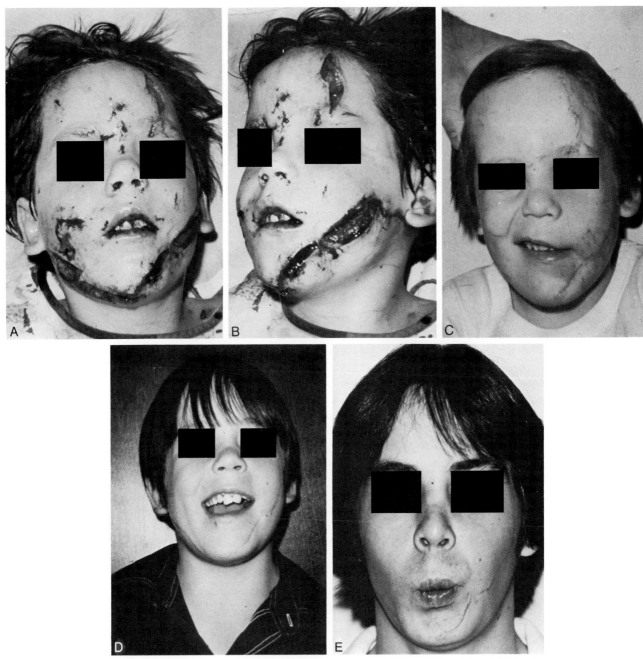

FIGURE 13–10. *A,* A 4-year-old boy presenting with severe facial lacerations. The eyebrow was not shaved, although the forehead laceration involved that structure. *B,* The left cheek laceration involved the buccal branch of cranial nerve VII. However, its involvement was distal to a vertical line from the lateral canthus of the eye, and because of the location of the lacerations and the patient's age, a decision was made not to repair this nerve. Facial nerve injuries proximal to this vertical line should be repaired. *C,* The postrepair evaluation disclosed a significant left buccal branch palsy of the facial nerve. *D,* Two years following the repair, there has been significant return of lip function. *E,* Ten years after repair, the patient has normal lip function. Note the normal configuration of the patient's left eyebrow.

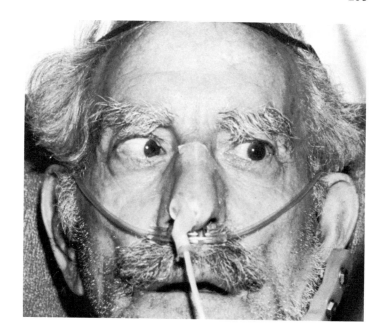

FIGURE 13–11. A patient exhibiting an inability to perform a left lateral gaze secondary to an abducens nerve palsy.

skull and maxilla within the soft tissue envelope of the face as the maxilla is pushed and pulled vertically gives the optical illusion of upper jaw movement.

The nasofrontal suture region should be palpated firmly when the maxilla is manipulated to rule out Le Fort II (pyramidal) or Le Fort III (craniofacial dysjunction) maxillary fractures. The thumb and index finger can then straddle the maxilla in the buccal fold region as the maxilla is manipulated to rule out Le Fort I (horizontal or Guérin) level fractures. Attempts should also be made to torque and rotate the maxilla. Lack of maxillary mobility, however, does not always rule out a maxillary fracture. Dependent upon the direction and force of the injury, the maxilla may be significantly impacted, and mobilization may only be possible once the patient has been anesthetized and disimpaction forceps have been used.

The infraorbital rims are now palpated and evaluated for the presence of step deformities. Anesthesia or paresthesia of the infraorbital soft tissues and the presence of a step in the infraorbital rim may indicate an isolated fracture of the zygoma or a Le Fort II level injury. The area of the frontozygomatic suture is now palpated.

Significant displacement of the lateral orbital rim may result in diplopia secondary to displacement of the lateral canthal ligament. This condition can result from grossly displaced fractures involving the zygoma or from isolated lateral orbital rim fractures. Therefore, the patient's visual acuity and extraocular movements must be re-evaluated as part of the periorbital examination.

Examination of the ZMC is completed by palpation of the zygomatic arch and buttress regions. Anesthesia or paresthesia of the soft tissues overlying the arch of the zygoma may indicate an injury to the zygomaticofacial or zygomaticotemporal nerve secondary to an arch fracture. Intraoral palpation of the buttress may disclose a step deformity—a common finding in fractures of the zygoma. Although frequently referred to as "trimalar fractures," these fractures are in fact "quadrimalar," with fractures present at the frontal suture, infraorbital rim, arch, and buttress.

The nose is then evaluated for evidence of previous hemorrhage, CSF rhinorrhea, or a septal hematoma. Although the CSF may be associated with bleeding, it is usually easy to identify. The fluid can be placed on a handkerchief, and a classic "bull's-eye" ring will develop. Some fluid can also be collected and evaluated for the presence of glucose; however, glucose is also found in blood, and this may confuse the picture. Therefore, a high index of clinical suspicion is critical in making the diagnosis of a CSF leak. The nose is palpated, and the overlying soft tissue lacerations are explored.

Finally, the nasal-orbital-ethmoid (NOE) complex is evaluated. The nose is assessed for deviations or saddle deformities. The intercanthal width (normal, 30 to 32 mm) is noted and measured. Although slight racial variations exist, measurements beyond 32 mm generally indicate the presence of traumatic telecanthus. This injury must be identified, and methods for its correction must be included in the treatment plan. Although traumatic telecanthus is not in itself associated with diplopia or other visual changes, it does result in a significant cosmetic deformity if left untreated. The triad of a flattened nasal bridge, an obtuse medial canthal angle, and an increased intercanthal distance should alert the clinician to the presence of this deformity. Palpation of the nasofrontal suture region generally reveals crepitation, and pulling the soft tissues laterally in the lateral canthal region will frequently result in a rounded or semilunar crease rather than a sharp medial canthal angle (Fig. 13–12A to C).

Traumatic telecanthus is easily differentiated from hypertelorism, in which the interpupillary distance is increased (normal, 60 to 65 mm). Hypertelorism is generally seen in congenital deformities, such as the Crouzon and Apert syndromes, and is rarely a result of trauma.

Severe injuries to the NOE region should alert the surgeon to the possibility of fractures involving the frontal bone and associated sinus. The final diagnosis of the

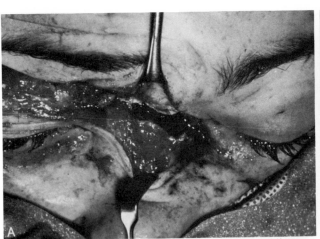

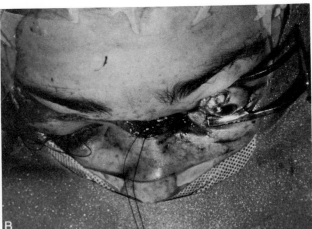

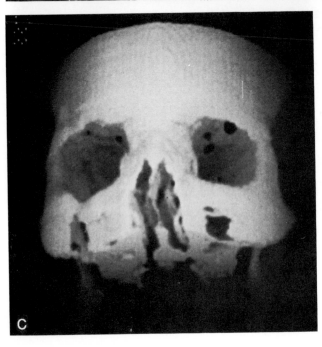

FIGURE 13–12. *A,* The nasal-orbital-ethmoid (NOE) area is explored in a patient with a severe laceration and midface injury. *B,* Examination also disclosed a laceration of the sclera of the left eye. *C,* Three-dimensional reconstruction of a computerized tomographic (CT) scan in this patient disclosed a lateral displacement of the left nasal and ethmoid bones consistent with the clinical findings of traumatic telecanthus.

extent of frontal sinus fractures is made with radiographs and computerized tomographic (CT) scans. There are two primary indications for the open management of frontal bone fractures: severe displacement, resulting in a cosmetic deformity, and fractures involving the posterior table of the frontal sinus. Posterior table fractures or injuries involving the nasofrontal duct may result in the development of a mucocele or infection that will involve the anterior cranial fossa. Therefore, frontal bone fractures must be ruled out with a thorough clinical and radiographic examination.

IMAGING EVALUATION OF MAXILLOFACIAL INJURIES

Although tremendous advances in imaging techniques have been made, the "gold standard" in maxillofacial trauma imaging is still the plain film. CT scanning and magnetic resonance (MR) imaging are of secondary importance in the initial assessment of the trauma patient.

The initial films obtained when a patient is first seen in the emergency room may not be of high diagnostic quality. This observation is particularly true in cases involving patients with severe life-threatening multisystem trauma. Since the definitive management of maxillofacial injuries is rarely an emergency, this phase of treatment is generally deferred until radiographs of diagnostic quality can be obtained and a treatment plan can be formulated.

The Panorex radiograph provides an excellent two-dimensional view of the mandible. However, to assess fracture displacement adequately in all three planes of space, a posteroanterior view of the mandible and a Towne view of the condyles are necessary. The following is an ideal "mandibular series":

1. Panoramic radiograph
2. Posteroanterior view of the mandible
3. Towne view of the mandibular condyles
4. Cephalometric radiograph

This radiograph series provides for an evaluation of the mandible in all dimensions and will supply the radiographic information necessary for prospective or retrospective case review.

When a Panorex unit is not available or when the patient's physical condition does not allow for panoramic mandibular evaluation, the posteroanterior and Towne views can be supplemented with lateral jaw and submental vertex radiographs. The Zonarc radiographic unit, although not available in all facilities, is capable of providing panoramic views while the patient is supine.

The radiograph of choice for the initial evaluation of the maxilla is the Waters sinus view. This, in combination with a submental vertex view, will provide the surgeon with valuable information concerning the maxillary, zygomatic, nasal, and periorbital regions. These views can be supplemented with a "high" panoramic view, nasal bone radiographs, and tomograms of the orbital floors in cases of blow-out–type injuries. If available, presurgical and postsurgical cephalometric radiographs will allow for a more definitive evaluation of the results of treatment. It is particularly helpful if the patient's dentist or orthodontist has a fairly recent cephalometric radiograph that can be used for presurgical planning and postoperative comparative purposes.

Three-dimensional reconstruction of CT scans can also be of assistance, particularly in cases involving severe frontal bone and NOE injuries. The surgeon must be cautious in evaluating these reconstructions in areas where the bone is thin (e.g., sinus walls), as the scans can give the appearance in these areas of a fracture when, in fact, the bone is intact. As technology advances and false-positive three-dimensional CT findings are minimized, this modality will become of greater importance (Fig. 13–13). MR imaging is currently of little benefit in the initial assessment of the traumatized patient.

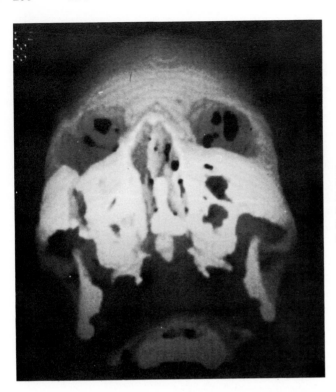

Figure 13–13. Three-dimensional reconstruction of the CT scan may be very helpful in the diagnosis of facial injuries. However, false-positive findings may be noted. Although it appeared in this three-dimensional reconstruction that there is a severe injury to the left maxilla, in fact this finding merely represented a very thin area of the antral wall.

Patients with severe bleeding that is difficult to control and those with penetrating injuries that potentially involve major vessels should be considered for arteriography. Arteriography is particularly helpful in penetrating neck wounds, lateral pharyngeal wall injuries, and cases involving excessive posterior nasopharyngeal hemorrhage, which is difficult to control (Fig. 13–14).

The specifics relating to imaging are discussed in greater detail in the chapters relating to injuries in the various anatomic regions.

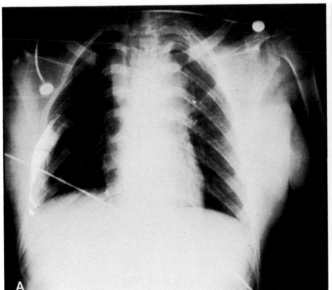
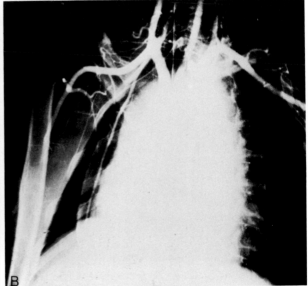

Figure 13–14. *A* and *B,* Arteriography may be indicated in the evaluation of head and neck vascular injuries. It may also be indicated to rule out other vascular injuries, such as those noted in this figure, which discloses a widened mediastinum, indicating the presence of a lacerated aorta at the ligamentum arteriosum.

TREATMENT PLANNING IN COMPLEX MAXILLOFACIAL TRAUMA

When a patient with severe maxillofacial injuries is first seen in the emergency room, the complexity of the patient's management can seem overwhelming to the surgeon (Fig. 13–15). Therefore, the clinician must be organized and systematic in both the evaluation and the management of the patient who has experienced facial trauma.

The ABCs of trauma management are followed by the orderly physical and imaging evaluation described previously. Consideration must be given to the patient's postsurgical airway. In cases involving maxillary, mandibular, and nasal injuries, particularly in those patients with a full complement of teeth, a tracheostomy must be considered. This procedure not only assures an adequate airway but also provides access for proper pulmonary toilet in those patients with chest injuries. Although nasotracheal intubation is possible even in patients with nasal bone fractures, a tracheostomy performed at the beginning of the procedure will give the surgeon direct and unobstructed access to the oral and maxillofacial region.

Once the patient has been stabilized and a diagnosis has been made, treatment begins from the "inside out and bottom up." Intraoral lacerations and minor injuries are managed. Extraoral lacerations are then closed; however, the surgeon must determine prior to closing the lacerations whether or not an open reduction of a jaw fracture should be performed through an existing laceration. Although this is a consideration, most lacerations are not ideally located, and their extension and use may result in unacceptable scarring and damage to anatomic (cranial nerve VII) structures not injured as a result of the trauma (Fig. 13–16A and B).

In cases involving multiple facial fractures, it is very helpful to chart the injuries and sequence the treatment plan on a diagram (Fig. 13–17). In the majority of cases, the reconstruction of the maxillofacial skeleton is begun with restoration of mandibular continuity. This is the base upon which the remainder of the facial skeleton will be built; therefore, the reconstruction of the mandible must be completed in all three planes of space: vertical, horizontal, and transverse. To achieve this result in severe injuries involving both the mandible and the midface, open reductions of one or both condyles may be necessary. An intact ramus, including condylar neck continuity, is necessary to ensure the vertical, horizontal, and rotational positions of the mandible.

In cases involving midface fracture displacement and fracture-dislocation of the

FIGURE 13–15. Patient with severe soft tissue and bone injuries involving the mandible and midface. When faced with such an injury, the surgeon must have a clearly defined system for the evaluation and management of the patient.

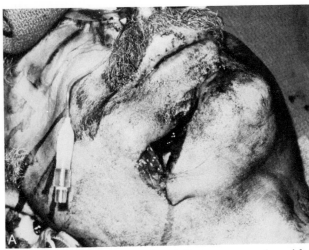 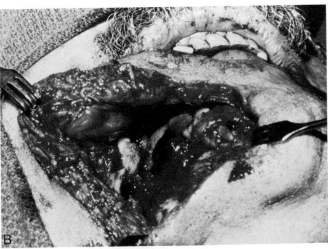

FIGURE 13–16. *A*, Patients presenting with severe facial lacerations must receive careful evaluation, and consideration must be given to using the laceration in the patient's initial management. *B*, Such a laceration provides direct access to the patient's underlying bone and dental injuries. However, in many instances the soft tissue lacerations are not ideally situated and may not be used for access to the patient's fractures.

mandibular condyles, at least one of the condyles must be anatomically reduced by an open reduction to obtain proper mandibular positioning. In those cases in which there has been minimal displacement of the condylar fragments, clinical judgment must prevail. However, the potential for further displacement of fragments during the process of fracture reduction must also be kept in mind. Fractures of the mandibular body and symphysis are then reduced.

FIGURE 13–17. *A*, A common combination of fractures in severe midface trauma includes (1) mandibular fractures—parasymphysis and bilateral subcondylar fractures; in this scenario, there is a high subcondylar fracture on the right and a low (vertical) subcondylar fracture on the left; (2) Le Fort I level fracture with a paramedian fracture of the palate; (3) bilateral zygoma fractures; (4) fracture of the left orbital floor with significant loss of continuity; and (5) nasal bone and NOE fractures. A pure Le Fort III fracture of the maxilla is rare. Combinations of Le Fort I, II, and III components are much more common.

B, The first phase of management includes re-establishment of mandibular continuity in all three planes in space—anteroposterior, transverse, and vertical. In this scenario, this re-establishment was achieved with an open reduction of the parasymphysis and left subcondylar fractures. The very high, nondisplaced right subcondylar fracture was treated in a closed manner.

C, The paramedian fracture was managed with a palatal splint, and the maxillary Le Fort I fracture was reduced by means of intermaxillary fixation.

D, The bilateral zygomaticomaxillary complex (ZMC) fractures were then reduced. With this combination of injuries, two-point stabilization of each zygoma is usually necessary. Three points may be required if continuity and stability are not satisfactory with two plates.

E, If the orbital floor fracture has resulted in enophthalmos or an abnormality in extraocular movements (usually secondary to entrapment of the inferior rectus or fat or both), reconstruction is necessary. A stabilized autograft or alloplast can be used for this purpose.

F, The final phase includes reduction of the NOE and nasal bone fractures. Frequently, an open approach to the NOE is combined with a closed (nasal packing and splint) reduction of the nasal fracture.

Although this is only one scenario, it identifies several fundamental principles in the management of complex maxillofacial injuries: (1) develop a logical treatment sequence; (2) work from the inside of the mouth out; (3) treat fractures from the bottom up—build upon the mandible; (4) restore form—in all three planes in space—*and* restore function; and (5) obtain as rigid a fixation as possible. The reader should refer to the appropriate chapters on the management of each specific injury for a more detailed explanation of surgical approaches and treatment techniques.

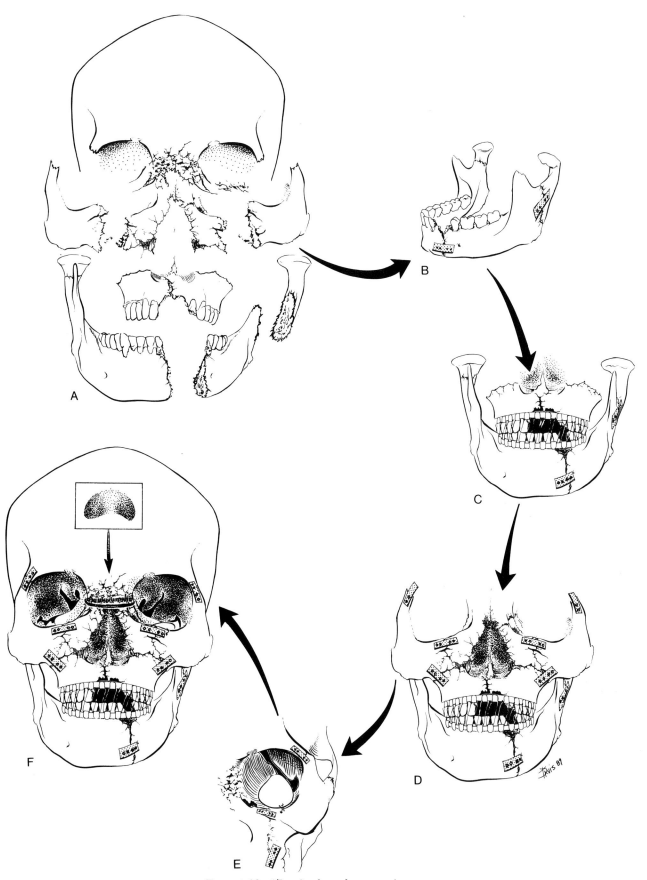

FIGURE 13-17. *See legend on opposite page*

Once the mandibular injuries have been addressed, the re-establishment of maxillary alveolar arch continuity must be accomplished. In cases of paramedian palatal fractures, arch continuity is most commonly achieved with the use of palatal splints. Le Fort level fractures are then reduced.

Isolated fractures of the zygoma, the nasal bones, and the NOE region are then managed. The zygomatic fractures are reduced, and the orbital floor injuries are repaired. The final phase of the treatment plan includes reduction of the nasal bone fractures and management of the NOE injuries.

Given the common scenario of a tongue laceration, lip laceration, bilateral subcondylar fractures, a symphysis fracture, combination Le Fort I, II, and III fractures with NOE injuries, resulting in traumatic telecanthus, an example of the treatment sequence would be as follows:

1. Tracheostomy is performed if necessary.
2. Tongue lacerations are closed.
3. Arch bars and other necessary oral appliances, such as palatal splints, are applied.
4. Open reduction of one or both condylar fractures is done. Very high subcondylar or condylar head fractures may not be amenable to open reduction. If a choice for reduction must be made, the surgeon should select the condylar fracture with the largest proximal component, such as a low (vertical osteotomy type) fracture versus a high subcondylar injury.
5. Reduction, open or closed, of the symphysis (parasymphysis) or body fractures is done.
6. The Le Fort I level injury is reduced.
7. Incisions are made in the brow, and the zygomaticofrontal fracture site is exposed. Infraorbital (subciliary) incisions can be made. These are usually necessary in cases of severe midface injuries, resulting in combination Le Fort II and III injuries. The NOE region can also be opened at this time.
8. Intraoral vestibular incisions can be used to expose the zygomatic buttress regions.
9. The midface (Le Fort II) component is reduced.
10. The zygomatic components can now be reduced. Visualization has been provided at three of the four fracture sites: buttress, infraorbital rims, and zygomaticofrontal suture. Rarely is exposure of the zygomatic arch necessary or indicated.
11. The buttress region, frontozygomatic fracture site, and, if necessary, the infraorbital rims can be either wired or, preferably, bone plated.
12. The floor of the orbit is explored and, if necessary, repaired.
13. The NOE (traumatic telecanthus) and nasal bone injuries are reduced.
14. The incisions and lip lacerations are closed.

Information on the management of specific fractures is found in the chapters relating to those injuries.

REFERENCES

1. Advanced Trauma Life Support Course: Student Manual. Chicago, IL, American College of Surgeons, 1985.
2. Alling CC, Osbon DB: Maxillofacial Trauma. Philadelphia, Lea and Febiger, 1988.
3. Rowe NC, Williams JL: Maxillofacial Injuries. New York, Churchill-Livingstone, 1985.

CHAPTER 14

RADIOGRAPHIC EVALUATION OF FACIAL INJURIES

DOUGLAS P. SINN, D.D.S.,
and NESTOR D. KARAS, D.D.S.

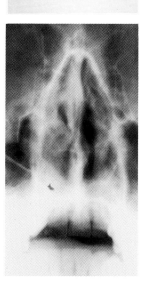

One may well imagine the difficulty of diagnosing and managing fractures of the facial skeleton prior to the advent of radiographic imaging. Now, with the availability of radiographic evaluation via modalities that include plain films, polytomography, computerized tomography (CT), and magnetic resonance imaging (MRI), the diagnostic capability through imaging is unlimited. The complete picture has turned around to such a degree that what made facial fracture management difficult in years past has now made management, through the sophistication of diagnostic methods, incredibly easier. The current state of the art is one of an enormous amount of radiographic information, which, when combined with the clinical diagnosis, makes fracture management easier than ever imagined.

The objective of this chapter is to provide the reader with information on the different imaging modalities available for specific facial skeletal injuries. Included are plain film and CT, which allow the reader to make a choice of which radiographic evaluation technique is best fitted for the injury at hand. There is no question that each of the films can be ordered for all injuries of the facial skeleton; however, the information gleaned is not always applicable to the management of each injury. Therefore, we must keep in mind that cost containment is of some consideration, and radiographic choices should be made on the basis of indication and validity in relation to the injury that is being evaluated.

The clinical examination has long been identified as one of the most important steps in diagnosing a medical disorder. The clinical evaluation must be done first, and a thorough documentation of all components of the injury is necessary. The clinical examination is then concentrated in the specific area of interest once the patient is stable and cleared for further workup. The clinical examination of the face is done in a systematic manner, the examiner being sure to identify all signs and symptoms of any significance. Once this examination is complete, the imaging alternatives are reviewed with the clinical findings to choose the correct radiographic examination. The reader can refer to Tables 14–1 and 14–2 for radiographic choices by injury.[1]

The task of correlating the clinical examination with the findings gained from the radiographs will usually result in a diagnosis that is accurate. The systematic clinical examination will direct the surgeon to the most important image findings.

TABLE 14-1. RADIOGRAPHS FOR MANDIBULAR FRACTURES

Fracture	Panorex	Towne's	Posteroanterior	Submental Vertex	Periapical	Transorbital	Occlusal
Condylar head	+	+	−	−	−	+	−
Subcondylar	+	+	0	0	0	0	0
Coronoid	+	0	+	0	0	0	0
Ramus	+	0	+	0	0	0	0
Angle	+	0	+	0	0	0	0
Body	+	0	+	0	0	0	+/−
Symphysis	+	0	0	0	0	0	+
Alveolar	+	0	0	0	+	0	0
Condylar dislocation	+	0	0	0	0	0	0

+ = needed for diagnosis; +/− = film may help in diagnosis; − = not recommended for diagnosis; 0 = not used.

Formulation of a management plan in terms of timing, operative approaches, and definitive treatment will evolve from this corroborative approach. The reader may refer to Tables 14–3 and 14–4 for major clinical findings associated with specific injuries.[1]

OVERVIEW OF MODERN DIAGNOSTIC IMAGING

A basic understanding of the technology is needed by the clinician to comprehend both applications and limitations of the various forms of diagnostic imaging. Both CT and magnetic resonance imaging (MRI) rely on reconstructive tomography and modern computing technology for the representation of anatomic cross-sections. Although neuroradiologists feel that MRI will replace CT in the years to come for imaging of the nervous system, CT has definite advantages over MRI in the diagnosis of facial fractures. The x-ray–generated CT allows for a better detailing of osseous anatomy, which is extremely helpful in the evaluation of fractures.

The CT image is a computer-generated representation of the cross-sectional area of an object generated from the mathematical manipulation of thousands of independent x-ray attenuation measurements. The reproduction of images is a result of data acquisition and processing through the CT unit. Data are acquired as a series of projections consisting of a set of individual x-ray attenuation measurements arranged along an axis. The reconstruction process produces a visual image of the plane within

TABLE 14-2. RADIOGRAPHS FOR MIDFACIAL FRACTURES

Fracture	Panorex	CT	Posteroanterior	Submental Vertex	Lateral Skull	Waters'	Lateral Nasal	Occlusal
Maxillary alveolar	+	−	−	−	−	+	−	+
Le Fort I*	+	+/−	+	+	+	+	−	−
Le Fort II*	0	+	+	+	+	+	0	0
Le Fort III*	0	+	+	+	+	+	0	0
Isolated nasal	0	0	0	0	0	+	+	0
Nasal-orbital ethmoid*	0	+	+	+	+	+	+/−	0
Orbital blow-out*	0	+	+	+	+	+	0	0
Zygomatic arch*	0	0	+	+	+	+	0	0
Zygomatic complex*	0	+/−	+	+	+	+	0	0
Basilar skull*	0	+	+	+	+	+	0	0

*Fractures that require a facial series (posteroanterior, submental vertex, lateral skull, Waters') for diagnosis or to rule out other concomitant fractures.

+ = needed for diagnosis; +/− = film may help in diagnosis; − = not recommended for diagnosis; 0 = not used.

TABLE 14-3.   CLINICAL SIGNS AND SYMPTOMS OF MANDIBULAR FACIAL FRACTURES

Fracture	Condyle	Subcondylar	Coronoid	Ramus	Angle	Body	Symphysis	Alveolar	Flail Mandible	Bilateral Edentulous Body
Airway obstruction	−	−	−	−	−	−	−	−	+	+
Asymmetry, facial	+	+	−	+	+	+	−	−	−	−
Crepitus	−	−	−	+	+	+	+	−	+	+
Deviation of mandibular opening	+	+	+	−	−	−	−	−	+/−	−
Ecchymosis, buccal vestibule	−	−	−	−	+/−	+	+/−	+/−	+/−	−
Ecchymosis, floor of mouth	−	−	−	−	−	+	+	+/−	+	+
Lengthening of face	+/−	+/−	−	−	−	+/−	−	−	+/−	+
Limitation of opening, trismus	+	+	+	+	+	+	+	−	+	+
Malocclusion	+/−	+/−	+	+/−	+/−	+/−	+/−	+	+	−
Mobility of teeth	−	−	−	−	+/−	+/−	+/−	+	+/−	−
Paresthesia, lower lip	−	−	−	+/−	+/−	+/−	−	−	−	+

+ = consistent clinical finding; +/− = possible finding; − = no clinical finding.
From Gerlock AJ Jr, Sinn DP: Clinical and Radiographic Interpretation of Facial Fractures. Boston, Little, Brown, 1981.

TABLE 14-4.   CLINICAL SIGNS AND SYMPTOMS OF MIDFACIAL FRACTURES

Fracture	Alveolar	Le Fort I	Le Fort II	Le Fort III	Zygomatico-maxillary Complex	Zygomatic Arch	Isolated Nasal	Nasal-Orbital-Ethmoid	Orbital Blow-out
Airway obstruction	−	+/−	+/−	+/−	−	−	+	+/−	−
Asymmetry, facial	−	−	−	−	+/−	+	+	+/−	−
Cerebrospinal fluid leak	−	−	+/−	+/−	−	−	+/−	+	−
Crepitus	−	+	+	+	+	+	+	+	−
Decreased extraocular muscle function	−	−	+/−	+/−	+/−	−	−	+/−	+/−
Diplopia	−	−	+/−	+/−	+/−	−	−	+/−	+/−
Ecchymosis, buccal vestibule	+	+	+	−	+	−	−	−	−
Ecchymosis, periorbital	−	−	+	+	+	−	+	+	+/−
Ecchymosis, subconjunctival	−	−	+	+	+	−	+/−	+	+/−
Enophthalmos	−	−	+/−	+/−	+/−	−	−	+	+/−
Epistaxis, bilateral	−	+	+	+	−	−	+	+	−
Epistaxis, unilateral	−	−	−	−	+/−	−	+	−	+
Infraorbital rim defect	−	−	+	−	+/−	−	−	+	−
Lateral orbital rim defect	−	−	−	+	+/−	−	−	−	−
Lengthening of face	−	+/−	+	+	−	−	−	−	−
Limitation of opening, trismus	−	−	+/−	+/−	+/−	+	−	−	−
Malocclusion	+	+	+	+	−	−	−	−	−
Medial canthal deformity	−	−	+/−	+/−	−	−	−	+	−
Mobility of teeth	+	−	−	−	−	−	−	−	−
Nasal septal deformity	−	+/−	+/−	+/−	−	−	+/−	+/−	−
Paresthesia, anterior cheek	−	+/−	+	+	+	−	−	−	+
Pupil height, unequal	−	−	+/−	+/−	+/−	−	−	−	+/−

+ = consistent clinical finding; +/− = possible finding; − = no clinical finding.
From Gerlock AJ Jr, Sinn DP: Clinical and Radiographic Interpretation of Facial Fractures. Boston, Little, Brown, 1981.

the object from which the data were obtained. A small area in the chosen matrix size of the image that represents a single attenuation value is the pixel. This area measurement is the x-ray linear attenuation coefficient of a small volume element in the object called a voxel, and it is expressed as the attenuation relative to water in Hounsfield units.[2] The result of reconstructing an image is to match an attenuation coefficient measurement with each pixel in the matrix, so that in the completed image each pixel represents the average attenuation coefficient of a voxel of tissue.

Images are generated by assigning a gray tone to a chosen range of Hounsfield unit[2] values, so that various regions of anatomy are portrayed as different shades of gray. The scanner is capable of reproducing up to 2000 tissue density levels. However, only 20 levels of gray tone can be distinguished by the human eye on a video display unit.[3] The concept of windowing allows superimposition of the limited gray scale over the range of CT numbers of interest. The range of numerical values between which the gray scale is selected to discriminate is the window width, with numbers above this range shown as white and below as black. The value chosen to represent the median tone in the gray scale is the window level. Increasing the window level widens the range of CT numbers represented by each tone, reducing contrast discrimination. Therefore, changing the window width and window level will affect the contrast between minor changes in tissue density. By electronic control of the window settings, a range of tissue densities from soft tissue to bone can be seen. Soft tissues are best seen at narrow window width and low window level, which allows greater contrast between minor changes in tissue densities, and bone is best seen at wide window width and high window level.

The scan slice thickness is determined by the collimation of the x-ray beam that passes across an axial cross-sectional slice of the patient's head. Most machines can collimate slices from 1.5 to 10 mm, which can be overlapping, touching, or separated, depending on the movement of the scanning couch.[4]

Images of soft tissue and bone can be produced in the axial, coronal, and sagittal planes, along with three-dimensional reconstructions of the skull. Coronal slices can be taken at the same time as axial slices. However, hyperextension of the neck in the scanning gantry is required for taking coronal views. Cervical injuries, a common finding in patients with facial trauma, may preclude positioning in this manner. Newer scanners require less positioning owing to the ability to change angulation of the scanning gantry. Furthermore, computer-reformated coronal and sagittal views can be produced from axial slices with a thickness between 1.5 and 5.0 mm. Three-dimensional views from a designated aspect can be produced from available packages that are added to the system. Two basic techniques are available that require many hours to process with present technology. One way to produce these images is to select a noticeable interface that occurs throughout a series of reformated slices and to assign gray scale values to it. This method produces a tonal image of the surface, reproducing the changing contours. The second way to produce the image is to simulate shadows from a hypothetical light source.[4]

RADIATION EXPOSURE

The amount of radiation exposure to the patient is always a concern with any radiographic technique. The absorbed radiation with CT will vary considerably, depending on the type of scanner, scanning technique, and exposure settings used to produce the images. The actual absorbed radiation dose delivered with CT depends on the number and energy of the photons absorbed by the patient, as well as the level of noise that can be tolerated in the image. As more photons are used to produce an image, less scatter of individual attenuation measurements or noise is produced, and the contrast discrimination of the image is enhanced. Slice thickness can also vary the amount of radiation, as thin slices require higher exposures to hold noise within acceptable limits.

The dose received from a single CT study is higher than that for plain radiography but is less than that with multiple sections produced from polytomography.[3] The skin dose can range from 0.4 to 4.7 rads, depending on the factors previously mentioned, with most machines producing in the 2.5 rad range.[5] Contiguous scans of several levels will increase the total dose, depending on the slice thickness of the images. The dose for combined axial and coronal images ranges from 3.5 to 5.0 rads.[3] The gonad dose is considerably less, ranging from 0.1 to 0.3 mrad for each complete scan.[6] This dose can be reduced even more with conventional shielding techniques. In comparison, conventional polytomography can deliver a cumulative skin dose of up to 6 rads closest to the x-ray tube.[5] The radiation levels produced by CT are well within the safe limits of radiation exposure to the patient, and when taking into account how valuable these images are in helping the clinician diagnose and treat certain facial injuries, the amount of radiation exposure should not be a dissuasive consideration in patients who could benefit from such diagnostic procedures.

CLINICAL APPLICATION OF COMPUTERIZED TOMOGRAPHY

Fractures of the facial skeleton in which CT examinations are most valuable are those associated with midface injuries (Table 14–2).[1] The region from the supraorbital rim to the maxilla is where CT imaging helps dramatically in the diagnosis of facial fractures. Furthermore, CT is able to demonstrate air or hemorrhage in the cranium, orbits, and/or soft tissues; suspected cervical spine injuries may also be examined at the same time cranial or facial views are taken. Injuries associated with the orbits and paranasal sinuses may require coronal views to establish the full extent of the injury. These images should be taken, if possible, directly at the time of the initial scan or should be reformated from axial slices. Coronal images can show the amount of mediolateral displacement of the zygoma in zygomaticomaxillary complex fractures, as well as the displacement of bone fragments and extraocular muscle position in orbital blow-out fractures of the medial and inferior walls. Fractures of the roof of the orbit and the cribriform plate are also shown better on coronal views. When ordering CT images of the patient with facial trauma, it is helpful to know that 5-mm slices are sufficient to show areas such as the frontal bone and maxilla; however, complex anatomic regions such as the orbits and nasal cavity require cuts that are 2 to 3 mm in thickness. If three-dimensional CT reconstructions or reformating of coronal views will be obtained, smaller slices (2 to 3 mm) are desired for better image resolution. At least one normal anatomic slice should be obtained both superior to and inferior to the injured region to identify the extent of the fractures.

The clinical and plain film radiographic examination is of paramount importance for the initial diagnosis of facial injuries, and the decision to obtain supplemental CT studies must be made from this information. Not every midface injury will warrant CT evaluation; however, if complex fractures of the facial skeleton are suspected, both axial and coronal CT scans will be extremely helpful in characterizing the extent of the injuries.

RADIOGRAPHIC CHOICES BY INJURY

Mandibular Fractures

It is the opinion of the authors that mandibular fractures as a group are best evaluated and diagnosed with plain films and polytomograms. The mandibular series, which includes a right and left oblique view, posteroanterior film, and lateral skull film, combined with a panogram, will provide adequate information to make the diagnosis of most mandibular fractures. In the following sections, examples of man-

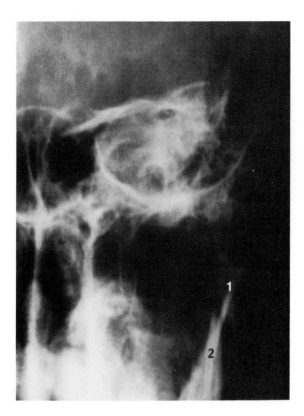

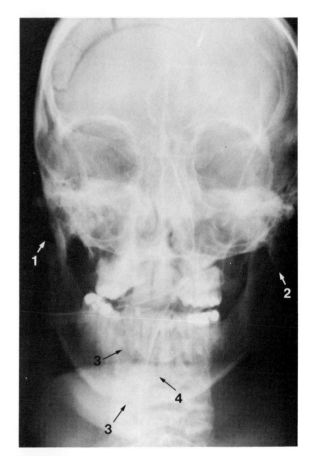

FIGURE 14–1. Towne's projection of the mandible showing a subcondylar fracture. The condylar segment (1) is displaced lateral to the ramus (2).

FIGURE 14–2. Posteroanterior (PA) radiograph of flail mandible with right (1) and left (2) subcondylar fracture and symphysis fractures (3) and (4). Note bilateral flaring of mandibular angles with malocclusion and anterior open bite.

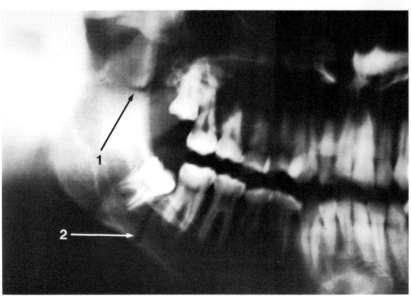

FIGURE 14–3. Panoramic radiograph showing a fractured coronoid process of the mandible (1) and fracture at the angle of the mandible (2).

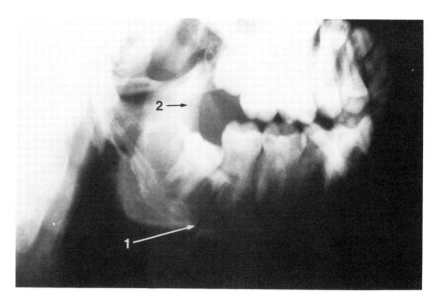

FIGURE 14–4. Oblique view of the mandible showing a complete fracture at the angle of the mandible (1) and a coronoid fracture (2).

dibular subcondylar fractures, coronoid process fractures, ramus, angle, and body fractures, as well as symphysis and alveolar fractures, are clearly described. Different films are selected for their validity and the information needed for both diagnosing and treating these fractures (Figs. 14–1 to 14–10). It would not be appropriate to discuss the diagnosis of mandibular fractures from a radiographic standpoint without including the flail mandible, which includes a symphysis and bilateral condyle fracture in combination. Though well known by the practitioner who has experience in maxillofacial trauma, in some cases even the most astute examiner can be fooled by

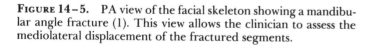

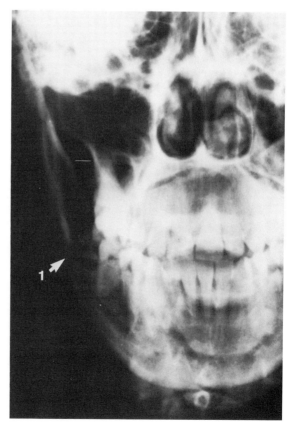

FIGURE 14–5. PA view of the facial skeleton showing a mandibular angle fracture (1). This view allows the clinician to assess the mediolateral displacement of the fractured segments.

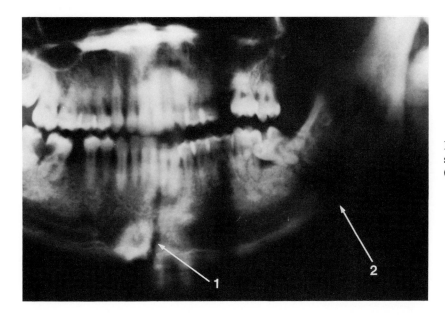

FIGURE 14-6. Panoramic radiograph showing a mandibular symphysis fracture (1) and mandibular angle fracture (2).

FIGURE 14-7. Occlusal radiograph of mandibular symphysis fracture shows amount of mediolateral displacement of the fracture.

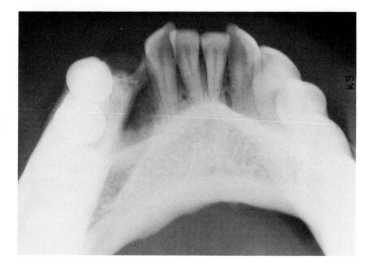

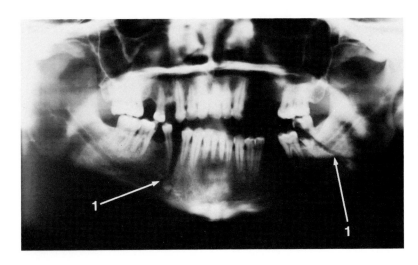

FIGURE 14-8. Panoramic radiograph showing bilateral complete mandibular body fractures (1).

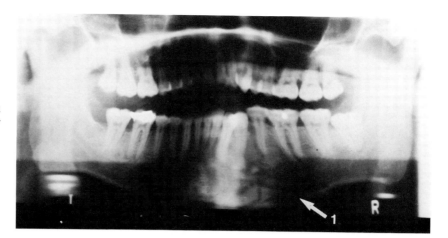

FIGURE 14–9. Panoramic radiograph showing comminution of a mandibular symphysis fracture (1).

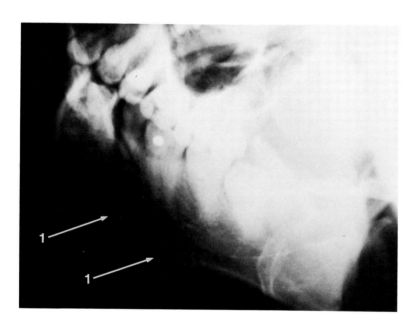

FIGURE 14–10. Oblique view showing extent of comminution reaching into body region of the mandible (1).

this life-threatening combination of mandibular fractures. The relationship of tongue attachment to the anterior mandible and the loss of anterior support, allowing the tongue to fall posteriorly and obstruct the oral airway, create a serious problem.

Edentulous Mandibular Fractures

Fractures of the edentulous mandible can include all variants discussed earlier, with few or no diagnostic problems. However, it is important to emphasize the fact that edentulous mandibular fractures most commonly occur in the body area of an atrophic jaw and, along with a threat to the airway, can be most difficult to diagnose and treat (Fig. 14–11). Postoperative sequelae and complications can occur relating to poor vascularity of the area, as well as a lack of medullary bone for healing capacity. The cortical bone present is frequently of poor enough quality that bone graft may be necessary for treatment.

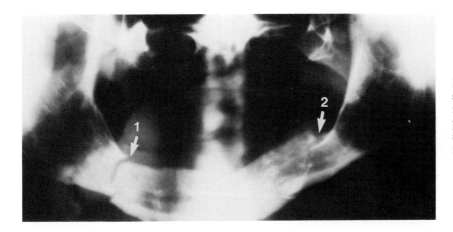

FIGURE 14–11. Panoramic radiograph showing edentulous mandibular body fractures (1) and (2). Note inferior and posterior displacement of the anterior segment due to pull of the suprahyoid muscles.

Maxillary Fractures

The maxilla is identified as a frequently fractured component of the facial skeleton. Some variant of injury to this area is included in most midface fractures. The simplest example of this injury is the maxillary alveolar fracture, which includes the portion of the maxilla that supports the dental units. This fracture is best seen on the standard panogram, occlusal film, and Waters' view radiograph (Figs. 14–12 and 14–13).

Le Fort Fractures

Le Fort fractures as a group include those fractures of the maxilla and midface as described by Rene Le Fort in 1900. These fracture classifications have been fraught with much controversy from a diagnostic and radiographic standpoint. With the advent of CT, combined with plain films and polytomograms, the diagnosis of the Le Fort fractures has been simplified (Figs. 14–14 to 14–23).

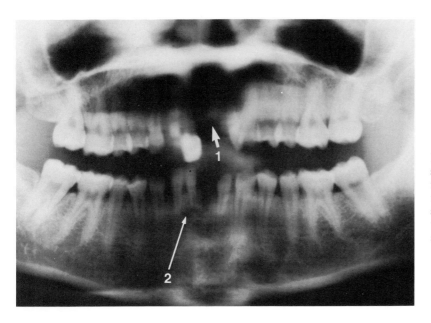

FIGURE 14–12. Panoramic radiograph showing dentoalveolar fractures. The severity of these fractures varies considerably and may include fracture of the alveolar crest, as seen here in the maxilla (1), or fracture in the apical one third of the roots of teeth, as seen in the mandible (2).

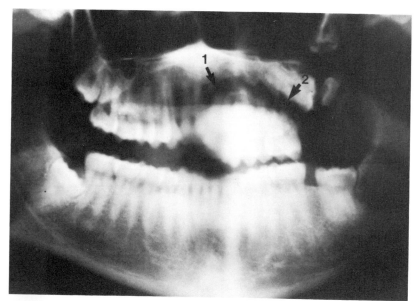

FIGURE 14–13. Panoramic radiograph showing dentoalveolar fracture that incorporates a quadrant of teeth in the maxilla. Note amount of displacement of the alveolar segment (1) and (2) resulting malocclusion.

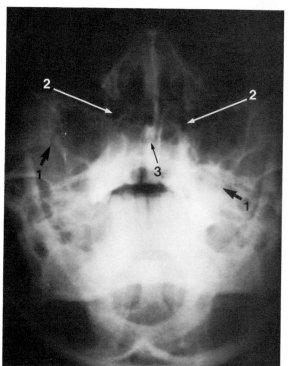

FIGURE 14–14. Waters' view of Le Fort I fracture showing fractures of the lateral walls of the maxilla (1) and medial walls of the maxillary sinus (2). Note fracture of the nasal spine of the maxilla (3) and deviation of the nasal septum.

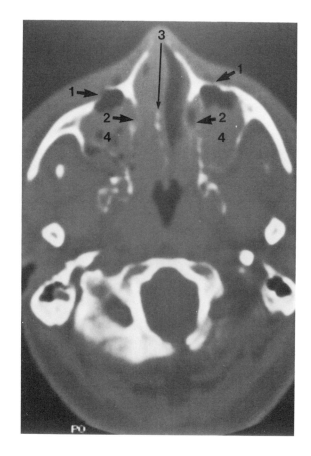

FIGURE 14–15. Axial computerized tomography (CT) of Le Fort I fracture showing bilateral fractures of the lateral maxillary walls (1) with bilateral fractures of the medial wall of the maxillary antra (2) and fracture of the vomer and ethmoid bones (3). Opacification of both antra represents hemorrhage in the maxillary sinus and nasal cavity (4).

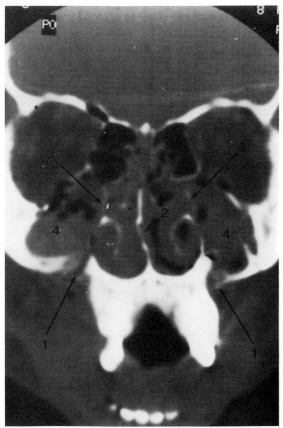

FIGURE 14–16. Coronal CT of Le Fort I fracture showing bilateral fractures of the lateral maxillary walls, with telescoping of the maxillary complex superiorly into the antra (1). Fracture of the vomer and perpendicular plate of the ethmoid bones (2), obliteration of the medial walls of the maxillary sinuses (3), and hemorrhage in both antra and nasal cavity are seen (4).

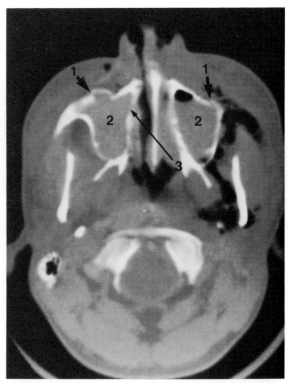

FIGURE 14–18. Axial CT of Le Fort II fracture showing fractures at the lateral walls of the maxilla (1) with hemorrhage in both antra (2). Some discontinuity of the medial walls of the maxilla can also be seen (3).

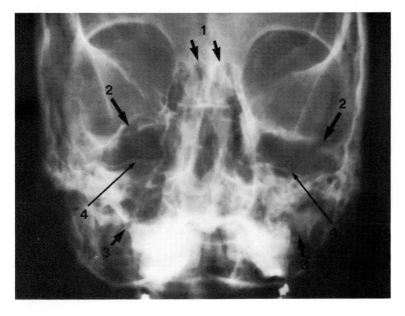

FIGURE 14–17. PA view of Le Fort II fracture showing piriform rim deviation to the left, with comminution of the nasal bones (1) and bilateral infraorbital rim fractures (2). The lateral walls of the maxilla are fractured bilaterally (3), and an air-fluid level due to hemorrhage can be seen in both maxillary sinuses (4).

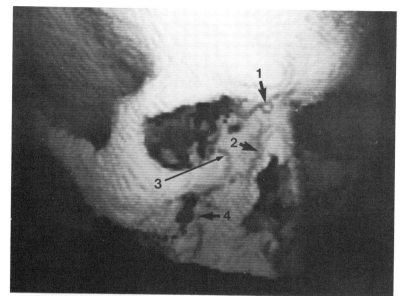

FIGURE 14–19. Three-dimensional CT reconstruction of Le Fort II fracture showing fractures of the nasal bones (1) and frontal process of the maxilla (2). Bilateral fractures of the infraorbital rims (3) with comminuted fractures of the lateral wall of the maxilla (4) are also seen.

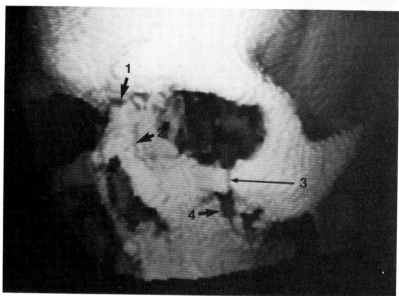

FIGURE 14–20. See legend for Figure 14–19.

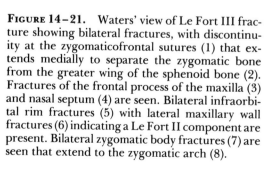

FIGURE 14–21. Waters' view of Le Fort III fracture showing bilateral fractures, with discontinuity at the zygomaticofrontal sutures (1) that extends medially to separate the zygomatic bone from the greater wing of the sphenoid bone (2). Fractures of the frontal process of the maxilla (3) and nasal septum (4) are seen. Bilateral infraorbital rim fractures (5) with lateral maxillary wall fractures (6) indicating a Le Fort II component are present. Bilateral zygomatic body fractures (7) are seen that extend to the zygomatic arch (8).

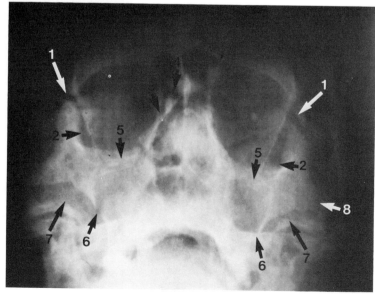

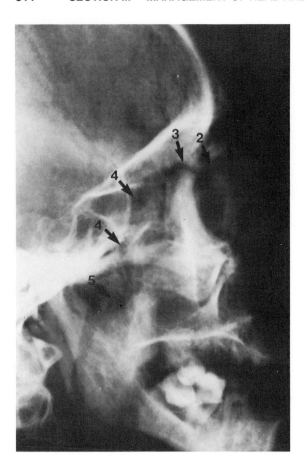

FIGURE 14–22. Lateral view of the skull showing the extent of the Le Fort III fracture from the nasal bones (1) to the medial wall of the orbit (2), traversing to the zygomaticofrontal suture (3) and extending down the cranial base (4) to the pterygoid plate (5).

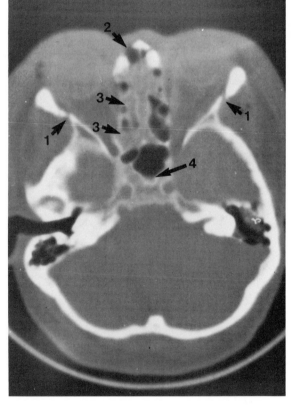

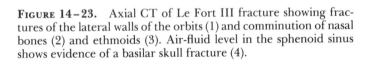

FIGURE 14–23. Axial CT of Le Fort III fracture showing fractures of the lateral walls of the orbits (1) and comminution of nasal bones (2) and ethmoids (3). Air-fluid level in the sphenoid sinus shows evidence of a basilar skull fracture (4).

Malar Fractures

The isolated zygomatic complex fracture is most frequently evaluated in Waters' and submental vertex films. It may include a zygomatic arch fracture, which can be evaluated on both plain films and CT. Careful evaluation with CT, and possibly MRI, will yield information relative to the soft tissue components of the orbit and integrity of the walls of the orbital complex (Figs. 14–24 to 14–26).

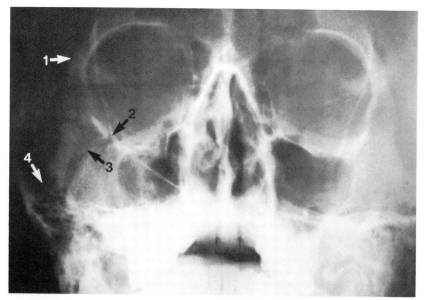

FIGURE 14-24. Waters' view of zygomaticomaxillary complex fracture showing fracture through the zygomaticofrontal suture (1), with an infraorbital rim fracture (2) extending into the body of the zygoma (3) and zygomatic arch (4).

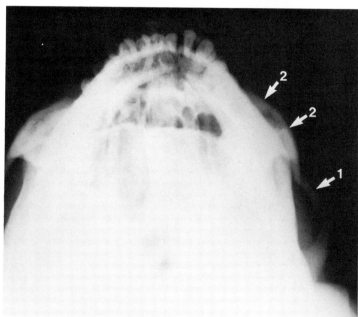

FIGURE 14-25. Submental vertex view showing depressed fractures of the zygomatic process of the temporal bone (1). Posterior displacement of the zygomatic process of the maxilla (2) compared with the opposite side represents a posteriorly displaced zygomaticomaxillary complex fracture.

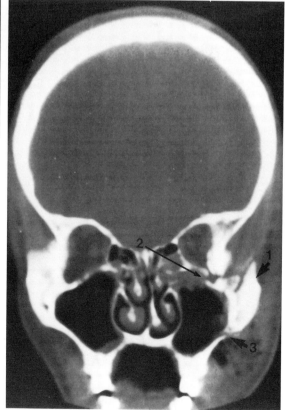

FIGURE 14-26. Coronal CT of zygomaticomaxillary complex fracture showing lateral displacement of the zygomatic body (1) caused by separation of the orbital process of the zygoma from the orbital surface of the greater wing of the sphenoid bone. Fracture of the floor of the orbit (2) and the lateral wall of the maxillary sinus (3) is also seen.

Nasal Orbital Fractures

Among the most difficult fractures of the facial skeleton to diagnose and treat are those that involve the nasal-orbital-ethmoid complex. These have been divided into three categories: isolated nasal fractures, nasal-orbital-ethmoid complex fractures, and orbital blow-out fractures of the weaker supporting walls of the orbital compartment (Figs. 14–27 to 14–40).

Text continued on page 320

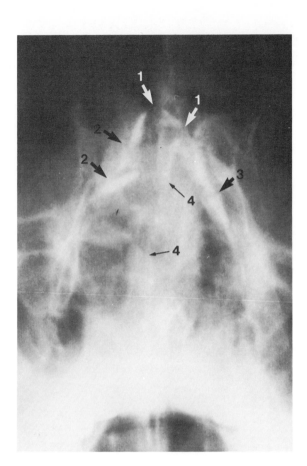

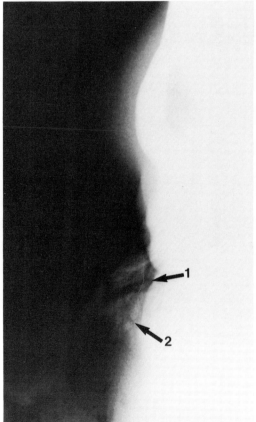

FIGURE 14–27. Waters' view of nasal fracture showing fracture with displacement of the nasal bones (1) and frontal processes of the maxilla (2) and (3). Note fractures with discontinuity of the nasal septum (4).

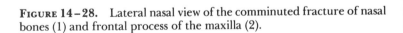

FIGURE 14–28. Lateral nasal view of the comminuted fracture of nasal bones (1) and frontal process of the maxilla (2).

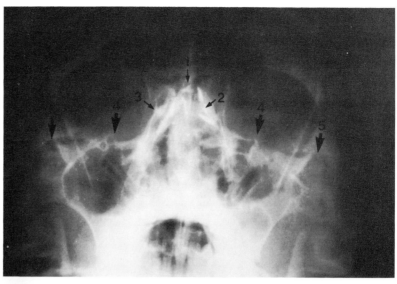

FIGURE 14-29. Waters' view of nasal-orbital-ethmoid fracture showing discontinuity of the nasal bones (1), medially displaced left frontal process of maxilla (2), and fracture with lateral displacement of right frontal process of maxilla (3). Bilateral infraorbital rim fractures (4) extending into the bodies of the zygoma (5) are also present.

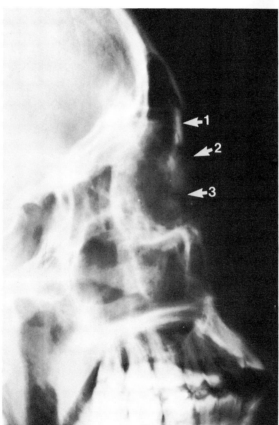

FIGURE 14-30. Lateral skull film showing fracture of the anterior table of the frontal sinus (1) with comminution of the nasal bones (2) and frontal process of the maxilla (3).

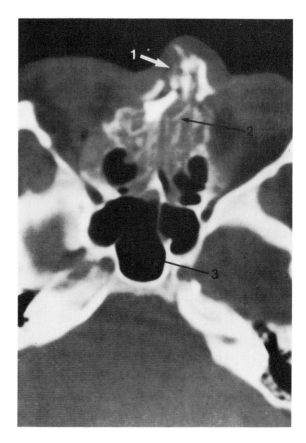

FIGURE 14-31. Axial CT of nasal-orbital-ethmoid fracture showing comminution with displacement of nasal complex (1), including fracture of vomer (2) and ethmoid bones. Note clear sphenoid sinus (3).

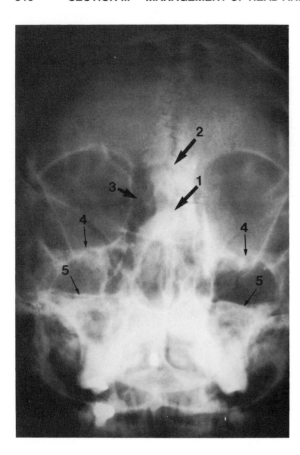

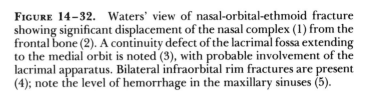

FIGURE 14–32. Waters' view of nasal-orbital-ethmoid fracture showing significant displacement of the nasal complex (1) from the frontal bone (2). A continuity defect of the lacrimal fossa extending to the medial orbit is noted (3), with probable involvement of the lacrimal apparatus. Bilateral infraorbital rim fractures are present (4); note the level of hemorrhage in the maxillary sinuses (5).

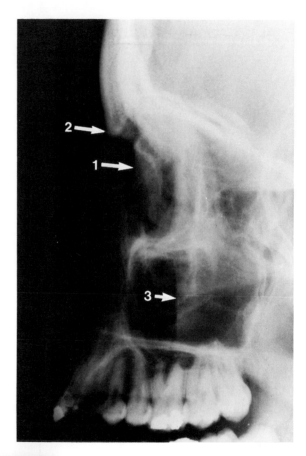

FIGURE 14–33. Lateral skull film of nasal-orbital-ethmoid fracture showing posterior and inferior displacement of the nasal complex (1) with marked separation from the frontal bone (2). Note that the air-fluid level in the antrum is shown in a vertical orientation because the patient was placed in a supine position (3). Taking a lateral head film in this position is common in trauma patients, who may be unable to ambulate.

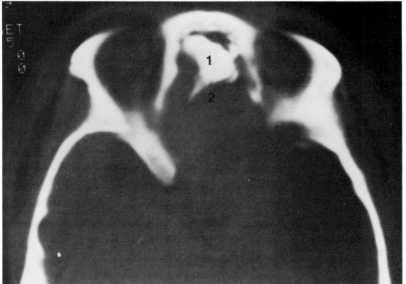

FIGURE 14–34. Axial CT of the nasal-orbital-ethmoid fracture shows that the cribriform plate, represented by this bony mass (1), has been displaced into the anterior cranial fossa (2).

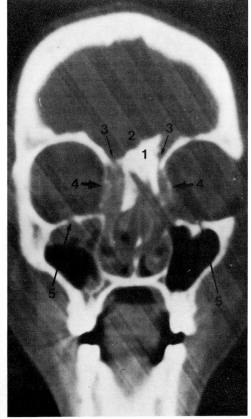

FIGURE 14–35. Coronal CT of nasal-orbital-ethmoid fracture shows the fractured cribriform plate (1) extending into the anterior cranial fossa (2). Bilateral fractures of the infraorbital rims are present (3), with comminution of the ethmoid bones (4) in the medial orbit.

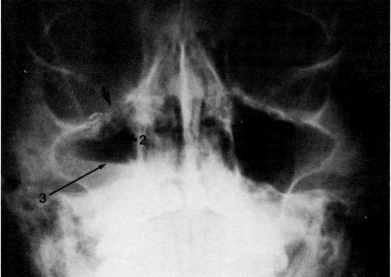

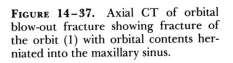

FIGURE 14–36. Waters' view showing orbital blow-out fracture with continuity defect of the orbital floor (1) and a portion of the periorbita displaced into the maxillary sinus (2). Note air-fluid level in the maxillary sinus (3).

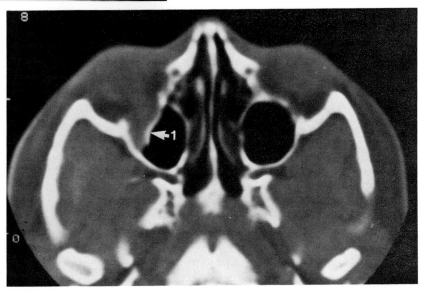

FIGURE 14–37. Axial CT of orbital blow-out fracture showing fracture of the orbit (1) with orbital contents herniated into the maxillary sinus.

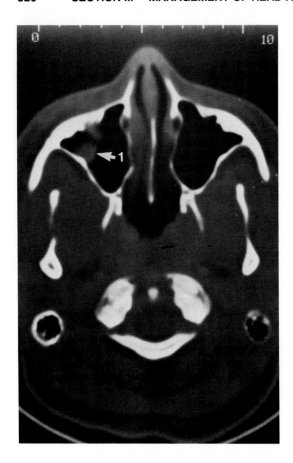

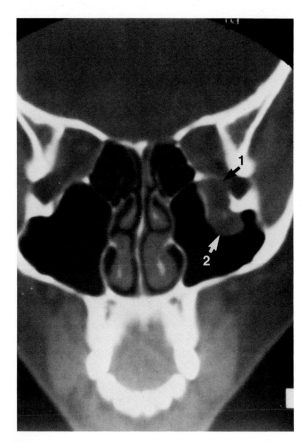

FIGURE 14–38. Axial CT of orbital blow-out fracture showing herniated periorbital contents in the maxillary sinus (1).

FIGURE 14–39. Coronal CT of orbital blow-out fracture showing discontinuity at floor of the orbit (1) with displacement of periorbita into the maxillary sinus (2).

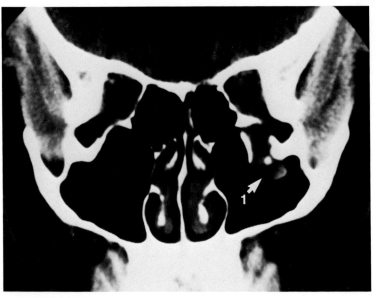

FIGURE 14–40. Soft tissue window of coronal CT helps to establish the extent of entrapment of the periorbital tissue in the maxillary sinus (1).

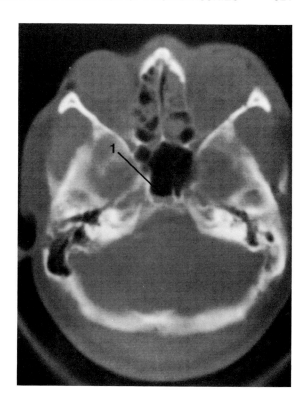

FIGURE 14–41. Axial CT showing air-fluid level in the sphenoid sinus (1), indicating a basilar skull fracture along with other injuries.

Basilar Skull Fractures Associated with Midface Injuries

Included here for completeness are films illustrating fractures of the basilar skull components (Figs. 14–41 and 14–42).

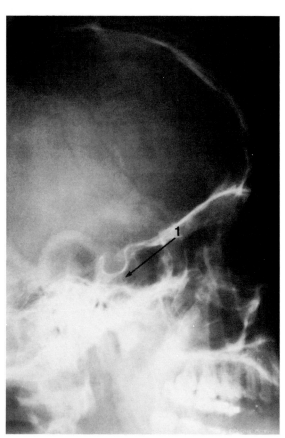

FIGURE 14–42. Lateral skull radiograph can also be used to assess a patient for a base of skull fracture. Although many times it is difficult to see the sphenoid sinus owing to superimposition of the zygomatic arch, articular fossa, and/or external auditory canal, by looking for air-fluid levels in the sphenoid sinus, this injury can be ruled out. As explained in Figure 14–33, the air-fluid level many times will have a vertical orientation because of the supine position of trauma patients at the time the film is exposed (1).

CONCLUSION

The preceding imaging examples are not meant to represent every radiographic possibility for each facial fracture. It is hoped that the reader will use Tables 14-1 and 14-2 to correlate the clinical examination and potential fractures with imaging choices.[1] The progress made in radiographic evaluation has been extensive. The practitioner must carefully examine the patient and make appropriate choices for the most useful radiographs. Then the correct diagnosis can be made and a treatment plan finalized.

REFERENCES

1. Gerlock AJ, Sinn DP, McBride KL: Clinical and Radiographic Interpretation of Facial Fractures. Boston, Little, Brown, and Company, 1981.
2. Hounsfield GN: Computerized transverse axial scanning (tomography). Part 1. Description of system. J Radiol 46:1016, 1973.
3. Rowe NL, Williams JL: Maxillofacial Injuries. London, Churchill-Livingstone, 1985.
4. Stevens JM, Valentine AR, Kendall BE: Computed Cranial and Spinal Imaging. Baltimore, The Williams and Wilkins Company, 1988.
5. North AF, Rice J: Computed tomography in oral and maxillofacial surgery. J Oral Surg 39:199, 1981.
6. Perry BJ, Bridges C: Computerized transverse axial scanning (tomography). Part 3. Radiation dose considerations. Br J Radiol 46:1048, 1973.

CHAPTER 15

DIAGNOSIS AND MANAGEMENT OF DENTOALVEOLAR INJURIES

MICHAEL P. POWERS, D.D.S., M.S.

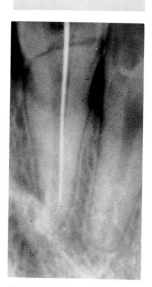

Traumatic injuries to the teeth and supporting structures are commonly seen in the injured patient. These injuries can be isolated, as can occur in childhood falls, or can be in association with multisystem injuries, as seen in automobile accident victims. Dentoalveolar trauma ordinarily occurs from falls, playground accidents, abuse, bicycle accidents, motor vehicle accidents, assaults, altercations, and athletic injuries. Injuries to the dentoalveolar structures can result from direct trauma to the teeth or from indirect trauma, usually from forced occlusion, as the mandibular dentition is forcibly closed against the maxillary dentition.[1-3]

Direct trauma usually causes injury to the maxillary central incisors because of their relatively exposed position.[1-6] Protruding incisors with incompetent lip coverage (Fig. 15–1), as seen in individuals with Class II Division I type of malocclusions or as a result of oral habits such as thumb sucking, are predisposing factors to maxillary incisor trauma. Dental injuries are approximately twice as frequent among children with protruding incisors than among children with normal occlusions.[1-5,7,8] Indirect trauma to the teeth and supporting structures usually results from a blow to the chin, and if the teeth are out of occlusion or not protected by a mouthguard, they are forced into occlusion, resulting in damage to the posterior teeth or anterior soft tissues[3] (Figs. 15–2 and 15–3).

Injuries to the dentoalveolar structures increase in frequency substantially as a toddler begins to attempt to walk and run, around 1 year of age.[3,6,9,10] The incidence of injury to the dentoalveolar structures in school-age children has been reported to be approximately 5 per cent, usually resulting from falls on playgrounds and from bicycle accidents.[11] Lacerations to the chin and vermilion border of the lip, as well as crown fractures, are commonly seen in this age group.[12] Participation in contact sports, such as hockey, soccer, football, basketball, boxing, and wrestling, can result in oral trauma. The use of an intraoral mouthguard during both athletic practice and competition has been found to reduce intraoral injuries significantly in both contact and noncontact sports.[13]

Mucosal or gingival lacerations and mobile incisors are seen in oral injuries as a result of child abuse. More than two million cases of child abuse were reported in the

FIGURE 15-1. Exposed maxillary incisors with incompetent upper lip coverage are frequently involved in trauma associated with falls and facial injury. Teeth may be fractured or avulsed, and associated injury to the lower lip is commonly encountered.

United States in 1986.[14] Abuse should always be considered if the child's injuries show a marked discrepancy between the clinical evaluation and the history reported by the supervising adult or if there appears to be a considerable period between the time of injury and when treatment is sought[2] (Fig. 15-4).

A significant number of dentoalveolar injuries are associated with the management of the comatose patient[15] or the patient undergoing general anesthesia.[16-18] Lockhart and colleagues[19] surveyed 133 directors of training programs in anesthesiology and found that an average of 1 in every 1000 tracheal intubations resulted in

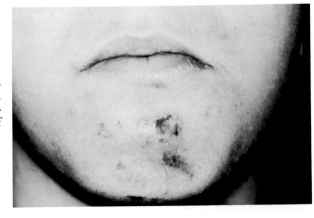

FIGURE 15-2. Indirect trauma to the dentoalveolar structure is usually the result of falls and blows to the chin. Abrasions and lacerations of the soft tissues of the chin should be further investigated for damage to the posterior teeth or anterior vestibule of the mandible (see Fig. 15-3).

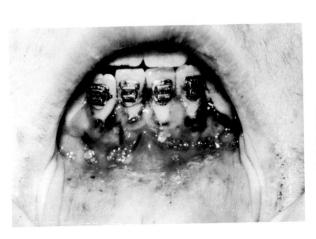

FIGURE 15-3. Indirect trauma from traumatic occlusion can result in crown fractures of the posterior teeth, lacerations to the anterior vestibule and gingiva of the mandible, and alveolar fractures or displacement of the anterior teeth of the maxillary or mandibular arch.

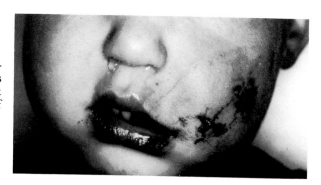

FIGURE 15-4. The clinical presentation of injury should correlate with the history reported by supervising individuals. Falls commonly result in lacerations to the chin rather than to the left side of the cheek, more commonly seen with blows. (Courtesy of Dr. J. Berg, Houston, TX.)

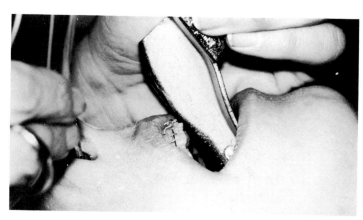

FIGURE 15-5. Trauma to the maxillary central incisors may be associated with endotracheal intubations from a fulcrum effect on the teeth with elevation of the tongue. Preanesthesia dental examinations and the use of protective guards may be helpful in the prevention of dentoalveolar injury during intubation for general anesthesia.

dental trauma (Fig. 15-5). They also reported that 90 per cent of the dental complications may have been prevented with a screening dental examination of the patient and the use of mouth protectors. Dental professionals are often asked to evaluate these injuries; good documentation of the injury is essential, as these cases may become involved in litigation. An analysis of 541 closed claims during a 36-month period from 1978 to 1980 by the National Association of Insurance Commissioners in the United States disclosed the finding that broken teeth and cardiac arrest with brain damage were the complications of delivery of general anesthesia most often resulting in litigation. Furthermore, the Risk Management Foundation found that the most frequent anesthesia-related claim from 1976 to 1983 involved damage to the teeth[19, 20] (Fig. 15-6).

FIGURE 15-6. Damage to the teeth was the most frequent general anesthesia-related claim found by the Risk Management Foundation[20] between 1976 and 1983. Lockhart[19] reported that 90 per cent of the dental complications associated with general anesthesia in their study were preventable. (From Risk Management Foundation: Anesthesia claims analysis show frequently low, losses high. Risk Mgmt Found 4:1-2, 1983; with permission.)

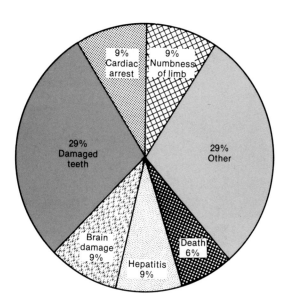

EXAMINATION AND DIAGNOSIS

Injuries to the teeth and supporting structures should be considered an emergency situation, as successful management of the injury requires proper diagnosis and treatment within a limited time. The patient should be relieved of pain and displaced teeth and alveolar fractures should be reduced as quickly as possible to improve the prognosis for survival of these structures. A complete history of the mechanism and events of the injury should be taken and a thorough clinical and radiographic examination done quickly to ensure proper diagnosis and treatment (Fig. 15 – 7).

A history can provide valuable information regarding the nature of the injury and any alterations in the normal occlusion, such as open bites or crossbites that were present before the injury. The nature of the accident can give insight into the type of injury to be suspected, such as injuries to the maxillary anterior teeth with falls or associated jaw fractures with blows to the chin. If the history of the injury does not correspond to the clinical presentation of the injury, abuse should be considered.[21] The time interval between the injury and presentation to the clinic is critical, as the success of treating luxated teeth, avulsed teeth, crown fractures with and without pulp exposure, as well as alveolar fractures, may be influenced by delayed treatment. The sooner the injury is treated, the more favorable the prognosis.[3] Alterations in normal occlusion reported by the patient may indicate displaced teeth, dentoalveolar fractures, and/or jaw fractures.

It is important that all teeth be accounted for at the time of examination. Missing teeth or pieces of teeth that have not been left at the scene of the accident must be considered to have been aspirated, swallowed, or displaced into soft tissues of the lip, cheek, floor of the mouth, neck, nasal cavity, or maxillary sinus. A radiographic examination of the head and neck, chest, and abdomen must be done to rule out the presence of teeth or fragments within these tissues or organs (Figs. 15 – 8 to 15 – 12).

A thorough clinical examination should include an inspection of soft tissues for embedded fragments of tooth or debris. Lacerations, abrasions, and contusions should be examined and evaluated for damage to vital structures, such as the parotid duct, submandibular duct, nerves, or blood vessels. Abnormalities in occlusion can indicate fractures of the jaws or dentoalveolar structures or displacement of teeth. The direction of displacement of teeth should be noted. In the primary dentition, the dislocation of the apex of the displaced primary tooth can possibly damage the succedaneous tooth. Fracture of the alveolar socket is common in displaced teeth. All teeth should be tested for abnormal mobility that would suggest displacement of teeth or alveolar or jaw fractures. Disruption of the vascular supply to the pulp should be expected in the case of axial mobility.[3]

All crowns of the teeth should be cleansed of blood and debris before examination for fractures of the crown and exposure of the pulp (Fig. 15 – 13). The color of

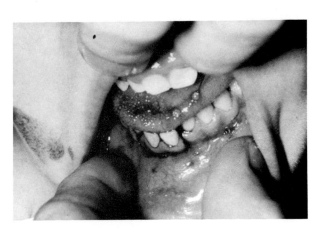

FIGURE 15 – 7. A thorough clinical evaluation may be difficult in the pediatric trauma victim. Alterations in occlusion, lacerations of the gingiva, and mobility of teeth are suggestive of additional dentoalveolar injury. General anesthesia or intravenous sedation may be required for complete examination and treatment. (Courtesy of Dr. J. Berg, Houston, TX.)

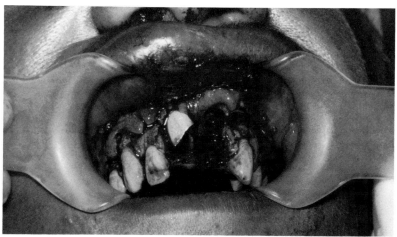

FIGURE 15–8. All teeth must be accounted for at the time of examination. Trauma to the maxillary anterior teeth in an automobile accident resulted in apparent avulsing of the maxillary central and lateral incisors (Nos. 9 and 10), along with displacement of tooth No. 8 and gingival lacerations.

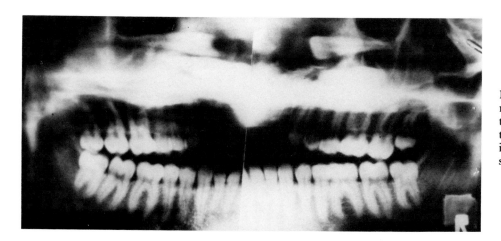

FIGURE 15–9. A panoramic radiograph reveals that the teeth had been intruded into the soft tissues and the nasal cavity. (Courtesy of Dr. G. Pedersen, Cleveland, OH.)

FIGURE 15–10. A young man involved in a motor vehicle accident suffered multiple avulsive injuries when he was hit by a piece of wood. A thorough clinical and radiographic examination recovered all of the segments, but reimplantation was not possible. Two large segments were found at the scene.

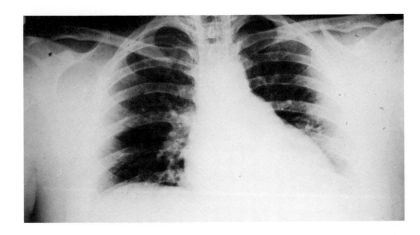

FIGURE 15–11.   An anteroposterior head and neck radiograph located a canine tooth that was pushed across the oral cavity and into the soft tissue of the lateral neck.

FIGURE 15–12.   The bicuspid was located on a chest radiograph in the right mainstem bronchus. Teeth are frequently aspirated during the traumatic episode and are usually located in this position. The tooth was removed by bronchoscopy prior to repair of the facial injury. (Courtesy of Mr. D. Patton, Swansea, Wales.)

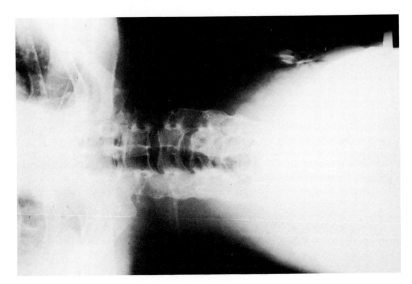

the traumatized tooth should be noted, as color changes may occur over time, indicating alterations in tooth vitality. The involved teeth should be tapped or percussed with the handle of a mouth mirror to evaluate damage to the periodontal ligament. Pain elicited with percussion is suggestive of injury to the periodontal ligament.

Pulp vitality testing in acutely traumatized teeth is of questionable value, as these procedures require the cooperation of a relaxed patient to avoid false-negative reactions. Mechanical stimulation and electric vitalometers have been advocated for test-

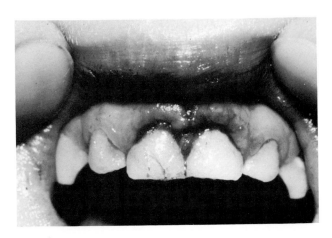

FIGURE 15–13.   The crowns of the teeth should be cleansed of blood and debris for evaluation of crown fractures and possible pulpal exposures.

ing the vitality and sensory perception of the dental pulp. Thermal tests—such as heated gutta-percha, ice, ethyl chloride, carbon dioxide, and dichlor-difluormethane—are usually of little value for several months. Although the functional repair of pulp nerve fibers has been shown to be re-established approximately 35 days following reimplantation, the electric pulp tester is of little or no value in teeth with incompletely formed apices.[22] The interpretation of vitality tests performed immediately after traumatic injuries is complicated by the fact that sensitivity responses are temporarily decreased, especially after luxation injuries. Repeated vitality tests show that normal reactions can return after a few weeks or months.[3]

Radiographic evaluation of dentoalveolar injuries should include a panoramic radiograph and periapical radiograph of the involved teeth. Multiple periapical radiographs taken at differing angulations are useful to demonstrate root fractures that are minimally displaced. The radiographic examination should provide information concerning the following[23]:

1. Presence of root fractures
2. Degree of extrusion or intrusion
3. Presence of pre-existing periodontal disease
4. Extent of root development
5. Size of the pulp chamber and root canal
6. Presence of jaw fractures
7. Tooth fragments and foreign bodies lodged in soft tissues

Teeth that have been displaced laterally or extruded radiographically exhibit a widening of the periodontal ligament space or displacement of the lamina dura, whereas intruded teeth often demonstrate an absence of the periodontal ligament space. Fracture of the alveolar process may appear radiographically as a small radiolucent line, in some instances blurred on the panoramic radiograph but detectable on periapical radiographs (Fig. 15–14).

Foreign bodies within the soft tissues of the floor of the mouth, lips, or cheeks can be viewed radiographically by placing the film between the soft tissues and alveolus. The floor of the mouth can best be visualized by an occlusal film with the beam directed from a submental approach. The exposure time for radiographs of soft tissues should be reduced by approximately one third.

CLASSIFICATION

Many systems have been developed to classify various traumatic injuries to the teeth and supporting structures.[11, 24-28] The World Health Organization System,[12]

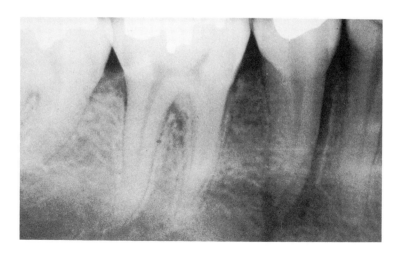

FIGURE 15–14. A fracture of the mandible noted on a periapical radiograph through the second bicuspid. Note the widened periodontal ligament associated with the second bicuspid.

modified by Andreasen,[3] includes injuries to the teeth, supporting structures, gingiva, and oral mucosa based on anatomic, therapeutic, and prognostic considerations.

Injuries to Hard Dental Tissues and Pulp (Fig. 15–15)

CROWN INFRACTION (FIG. 15–15A)

A crown infraction is an incomplete fracture or crack of the enamel without loss of tooth substance.

UNCOMPLICATED CROWN FRACTURE (FIG. 15–15B and C)

An uncomplicated crown fracture is a fracture confined to the enamel or involving the enamel and dentin without exposing the pulp.

COMPLICATED CROWN FRACTURE (FIG. 15–15D)

A complicated crown fracture involves enamel and dentin with exposure of the pulp.

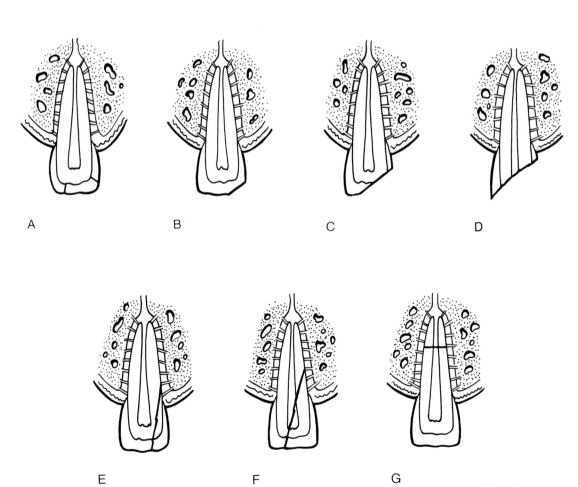

FIGURE 15–15. Injuries to the hard dental tissues and pulpal tissues. *A*, Crown infraction. *B* and *C*, Uncomplicated crown fracture. *D*, Complicated crown fracture. *E*, Uncomplicated crown-root fracture. *F*, Complicated crown-root fracture. *G*, Root facture.

UNCOMPLICATED CROWN-ROOT FRACTURE (FIG. 15–15E)

An uncomplicated crown-root fracture involves enamel, dentin, and cementum without exposure of the pulp.

COMPLICATED CROWN-ROOT FRACTURE (FIG. 15–15F)

A complicated crown-root fracture is a fracture involving enamel, dentin, and cementum with exposure of the pulp.

ROOT FRACTURE (FIG. 15–15G)

A root fracture involves dentin, cementum, and the pulp.

Injuries to the Periodontal Tissues (Fig. 15–16)

CONCUSSION (FIG. 15–16A)

A concussion is an injury to the tooth-supporting structures without abnormal loosening or displacement of the tooth, but with marked reaction to percussion.

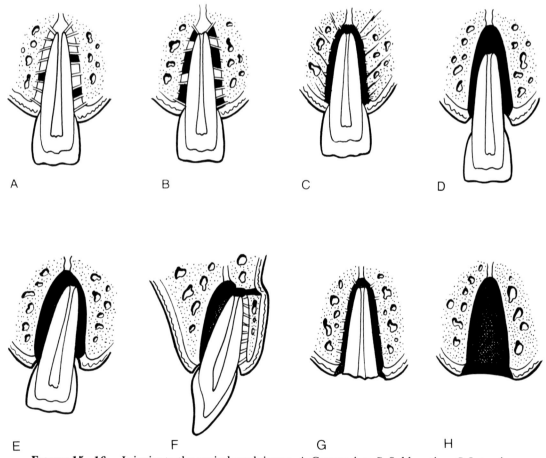

FIGURE 15–16.   Injuries to the periodontal tissues. *A,* Concussion. *B,* Subluxation. *C,* Intrusive luxation. *D,* Extrusive luxation. *E* and *F,* Lateral luxation. *G,* Retained root-crown fracture. *H,* Exarticulation.

SUBLUXATION (LOOSENING) (FIG. 15–16B)

A subluxation is an injury to the tooth-supporting structures with abnormal loosening, but without displacement of the tooth.

INTRUSIVE LUXATION (CENTRAL DISLOCATION) (FIG. 15–16C)

Intrusive luxation is displacement of the tooth into the alveolar bone with comminution or fracture of the alveolar socket.

EXTRUSIVE LUXATION (PERIPHERAL DISLOCATION, PARTIAL AVULSION) (FIG. 15–16D)

An extrusive luxation is partial displacement of the tooth out of the alveolar socket.

LATERAL LUXATION (FIG. 15–16E and F)

A lateral luxation is displacement of the tooth in a direction other than axially, accompanied by a comminution or fracture of the alveolar socket.

RETAINED ROOT FRACTURE (FIG. 15–16G)

A retained root fracture is a fracture with retention of the root segment, but loss of the crown segment out of the socket.

EXARTICULATION (COMPLETE AVULSION) (FIG. 15–16H)

An exarticulation is a complete displacement of a tooth out of the alveolar socket.

Injuries to the Supporting Bone (Fig. 15–17)

COMMINUTION OF THE ALVEOLAR SOCKET (FIG. 15–17A)

Crushing and comminution of the alveolar socket occur, together with intrusive and lateral luxation.

FRACTURE OF THE ALVEOLAR SOCKET WALL (FIG. 15–17B and C)

A fracture of the alveolar socket is confined to the facial or lingual socket wall.

FRACTURE OF THE ALVEOLAR PROCESS (FIG. 15–17D and E)

A fracture of the alveolar process may or may not involve the alveolar socket.

FRACTURES OF THE MANDIBLE OR MAXILLA (FIG. 15–17F and G)

A fracture involving the base of the mandible or maxilla and often the alveolar process may or may not involve the alveolar socket.

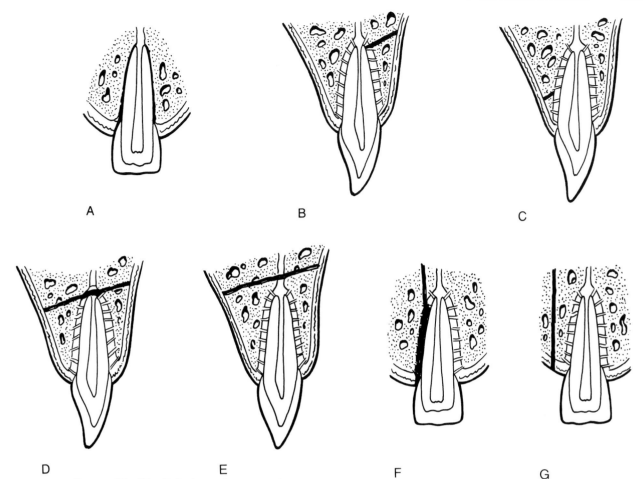

FIGURE 15–17. Injuries to the supporting bone. *A*, Comminution of the alveolar socket. *B* and *C*, Fracture of the alveolar socket wall. *D* and *E*, Fracture of the alveolar process. *F* and *G*, Fracture of the mandible and maxilla.

Injuries to the Gingiva or Oral Mucosa

LACERATION OF GINGIVA OR ORAL MUCOSA

A shallow or deep wound in the mucosa results from a tear and is usually produced by a sharp object.

CONTUSION OF GINGIVA OR MUCOSA

A bruise is usually produced by impact from a blunt object and results in submucosal hemorrhage without a break in the mucosa.

ABRASION OF GINGIVA OR ORAL MUCOSA

A superficial wound produced by rubbing or scraping of the mucosa, leaving a raw, bleeding surface.

TREATMENT

After obtaining a thorough history and performing a clinical and radiographic examination, several factors should be considered in the definitive treatment of the dentoalveolar injury. Consideration with regard to the age of the patient, cooperation of the patient, injury to the primary or permanent dentition, location and extent of the injury, residual bone support, periodontal health of the remaining teeth, fracture of supporting bone, vitality of teeth, whether apical foramina are wide or narrow, injury to soft tissues, and extent of any concomitant head, chest, or abdominal injuries may affect the treatment of the dentoalveolar injury. Lack of cooperation on the part of the patient, especially young children and the mentally retarded, may require the use of general anesthesia or intravenous sedation.

The periodontal health of the involved and adjoining teeth must be evaluated for osseous support of the traumatized teeth and to determine if the adjoining teeth can be used for splinting if indicated. The prognosis of traumatized teeth is generally better in younger patients and those having vital teeth with wide apical foramen, teeth with intact soft tissues, teeth with no root fractures, and maximal bone support.[29] Any blow to a tooth, even in the absence of obvious dental injury, can endanger pulpal vitality either by severing the apical vessels or through secondary pulpal hyperemia and congestion, resulting in ischemia and possibly leading to necrosis. Therefore, long-term dental follow-up is required. The patient should be informed that future endodontic therapy may be necessary, regardless of the severity of injury to the teeth and supporting structure[3, 30-34] (Fig. 15–18).

The treatment of traumatized primary incisors is complicated by the size of the pulp cavity, susceptibility of the developing permanent tooth, and cooperation of the child. Heroic methods designed to maintain the primary incisors after trauma should be discouraged. The loss of primary incisors does not require space maintenance as growth occurs, regardless of which primary incisors are involved, but loss of primary molars may require space maintenance to prevent mesial drift of the permanent first molar.[3,5,30,35] If the primary incisor is lost before the roots begin to be absorbed (between the ages of 3 and 4), eruption of the succedaneous permanent tooth is often delayed. However, this delay usually does not create additional orthodontic problems. If the primary tooth is lost after 25 per cent of the permanent incisor root has formed (between the ages of 4 and 5), then eruption of the permanent successor is often accelerated.[5]

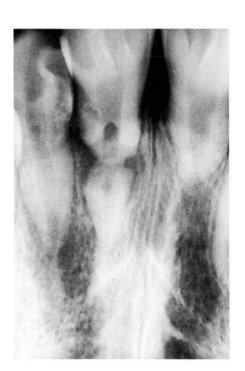

FIGURE 15–18. Root resorption is a major complication associated with dentoalveolar trauma. Resorption due to toxic by-products and bacteria from the necrotic pulpal tissue may be seen months to years following trauma to the tooth. Note the various degrees of resorption associated with the maxillary incisors—early external resorption of the lateral incisor, resorption about a middle third root fracture of the central incisor, and total resorption of the apical root in the other central incisor. (Courtesy of Dr. J.A. Wallace, Fox Chapel, PA.)

Injuries to Hard Dental Tissues and Pulp (Fig. 15–15)

CROWN INFRACTION

No treatment is indicated for crown infraction or cracks in the enamel layer (see Fig. 15–15A). The vitality of the traumatized tooth should be evaluated in periodic follow-up to monitor the pulpal health of the involved tooth.

CROWN FRACTURES

For crown fractures that involve the enamel only (see Fig. 15–15B), treatment is limited to smoothing of sharp edges or restoration with an acid-etch composite restoration (Fig. 15–19). If there is a significant amount of dentin exposed, measures should be taken to promote secondary dentin deposition by the pulpal tissue. A calcium hydroxide liner is placed over the exposed dentin, and the tooth form restored with a composite restoration. The tooth should be evaluated periodically for alterations in pulpal health.

If the pulpal tissue is exposed (see Fig. 15–15C), measures must be quickly taken to attempt to preserve the vitality of the neurovascular tissue. If the tooth is relatively sound, a pulp-capping procedure with calcium hydroxide liner and composite restoration should be done. The pulp-capping procedure should be performed within 24 hours after injury and is limited to small exposures in the pulpal cavity (Fig. 15–20). A cervical pulpotomy involves removing 2 to 4 mm of pulpal tissue subadjacent to the exposure, placing a calcium hydroxide base, and restoring with an acid-etch composite restoration.

A cervical pulpotomy is indicated in cases in which the injury is more than 24 hours but less than 96 hours old and in cases involving immature teeth with incomplete apex closure. Calcium hydroxide paste has been demonstrated to promote closure of the apex of the immature tooth.[3] Completion of root canal therapy is usually indicated by closure of the apex. Closure of the apex can be confirmed by serial radiographs, usually within 3 to 6 months.

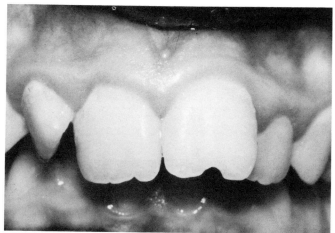

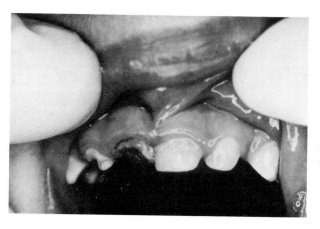

FIGURE 15–19. Crown fractures that involve only the enamel layer require only smoothing of the sharp edge of build-up with an acid-etch composite restoration.

FIGURE 15–20. Crown fractures with significant pulpal tissue involvement in the primary dentition should be extracted. (Courtesy of Dr. J. Berg, Houston, TX.)

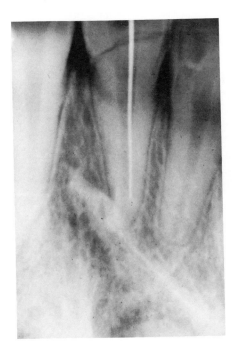

FIGURE 15–21. Mature, fully formed teeth with crown fractures that have significant pulpal tissue exposure should have endodontic treatment, and the canals should be filled with gutta-percha to avoid post-traumatic complications associated with pulpal necrosis. (Courtesy of Dr. J.A. Wallace, Fox Chapel, PA.)

If the teeth are mature and fully formed with significant exposure of the pulpal tissue, total pulp removal is indicated (Fig. 15–21). The canals should be completely endodontically treated and filled with gutta-percha to avoid post-traumatic complications associated with pulpal necrosis. Follow-up examinations are required to evaluate all traumatized teeth (with pulpal exposures treated conservatively for degenerative pulpal necrosis) and to determine if definitive root canal therapy is needed.

CROWN-ROOT FRACTURE (FIG. 15–15E and F)

Primary teeth with any type of crown-root fracture should be extracted.[3, 30] In the permanent dentition, fractures of the enamel, dentin, and cementum (uncomplicated) depend on the location of the fractured segment. If the fracture line is above or slightly below the cervical margin, the tooth can be restored, as with a crown fracture. Occasionally, crown-lengthening procedures are required to allow for restoration of the margin. If the fracture continues too apically to allow for adequate restoration, extraction of the tooth may be indicated. If the pulp is involved (complicated), the level of the fracture determines the treatment. Extraction of the apical segment is indicated when the coronal fragment compromises more than one third of the clinical root and in cases of vertical root fracture. Surgical exposure of the fracture surface is indicated when the coronal fragment compromises one third or less of the clinical root to provide access for a restorative margin. Orthodontic elevation of the fracture surface has been recommended when the coronal fragment involves one third or less of the clinical root.[3] If the tooth is mature and restorable, endodontic treatment is indicated. If the apex is open, a pulpotomy should be performed with a calcium hydroxide base and should be followed radiographically for closure of the apex, after which definitive root canal therapy and permanent restoration can be initiated.

ROOT FRACTURES (FIG. 15–15G)

Root fractures in primary teeth without mobility can be preserved and should exfoliate normally. If there is mobility or dislocation of the coronal segment, the tooth should be removed without attempts to remove the apical fragments, which could possibly damage the permanent tooth.

With root fractures in the permanent dentition, the prognosis of the involved

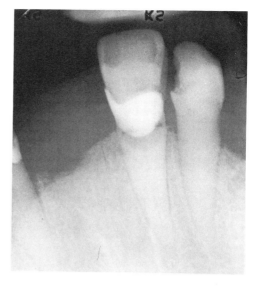

FIGURE 15–22. Teeth with large cervical restorations or decay are suscep- tible to root fractures at the cervical margin. Restoration options include removal of the retained root or endodontic treatment of the retained root and build-up with a crown, post, and core system.

tooth and the indicated treatment are dictated by the level of the fracture along the horizontal aspect of the root. If the fracture is in the apical third of the root, the prognosis is good and minimal treatment is indicated. The coronal fragment of the tooth generally remains vital, and endodontic treatment is usually not necessary. If the fracture occurs near the cervical margin (Fig. 15–22), either both the coronal and apical fragments are extracted or only the coronal portion is removed, complete endodontic treatment is done on the retained apical portion, and restoration is com- pleted with a crown over a post and core. Fractures in the middle third of the root have a good prognosis, especially if there has been minimal displacement of the coronal portion of the tooth (Figs. 15–23 to 15–28). The segments will usually heal

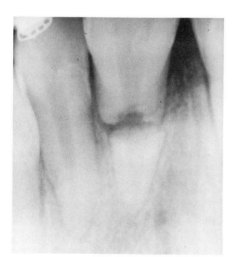

FIGURE 15–23. Fractures in the middle third of the root have a good prog- nosis if there has been minimal displacement of the coronal portion of the tooth. In this case, there has been significant displacement of the coronal portion, and resorption about the fragmented segments is noted.

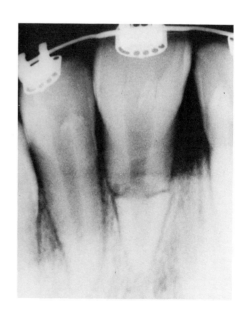

FIGURE 15–24. Orthodontically, the coronal segment was slowly reposi- tioned so that alignment could be obtained.

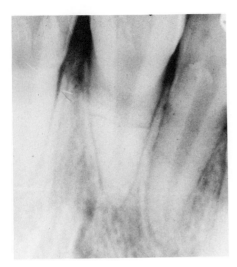

FIGURE 15–25.   Good alignment of the coronal and apical segments was obtained.

FIGURE 15–26.   Endodontic therapy was done first with a calcium hydroxide paste in the canal.

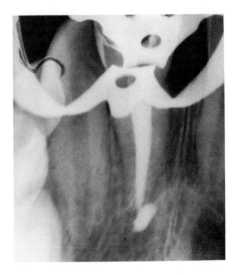

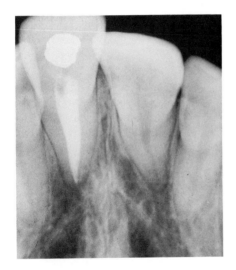

FIGURE 15–27.   Endodontic treatment was completed with a gutta-percha filling material.

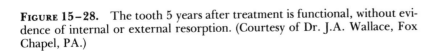

FIGURE 15–28.   The tooth 5 years after treatment is functional, without evidence of internal or external resorption. (Courtesy of Dr. J.A. Wallace, Fox Chapel, PA.)

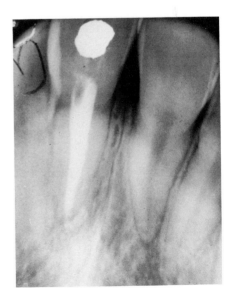

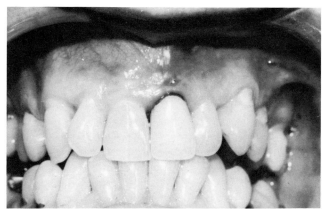

FIGURE 15–29. A traumatized central incisor with full crown coverage continued to be painful for a prolonged period. There was occasional purulent material that drained from a fistula in the facial mucosa. The infection was controlled by antibiotics but returned after cessation of antibiotics.

without the need for endodontic therapy. The stable fixation of teeth with fractured roots is essential for good healing and successful treatment. Fixation is usually accomplished by rigid splinting for at least 2 to 3 months. Extraction is indicated for both permanent and primary teeth with vertical root fractures[3] (Figs. 15–29 and 15–30).

Injuries to the Periodontal Tissues (Fig. 15–16)

CONCUSSION (FIG. 15–16A)

No treatment is indicated for concussion other than palliative therapy. Again, with traumatic injury to the teeth, periodic follow-up evaluation of pulpal health is necessary. Pulpal necrosis may develop several weeks or months after injury.[3]

SUBLUXATION (FIG. 15–16B)

A subluxated tooth is both sensitive to percussion and mobile. Symptomatic treatment such as a soft diet and, if necessary, occlusal adjustments to remove the involved tooth from any traumatic effects of occlusion will allow the tooth to stabilize.

FIGURE 15–30. Extraction of the involved tooth revealed a vertical root fracture. (Courtesy of Dr. J.A. Wallace, Fox Chapel, PA.)

Occasionally, nonrigid splinting to adjacent teeth is required. Concussed and subluxated teeth have a reported farily high incidence of pulpal complications;[36] therefore, teeth with concussion or subluxation injuries require periodic follow-up evaluations.

INTRUSIVE LUXATION (FIG. 15–16C)

Intrusive luxation of a tooth involves compression of the tooth into the alveolar socket and occurs typically when a child falls and impacts the maxillary incisors.[1, 3, 26] Intrusion of the tooth can range from minimal impaction to complete disappearance within the alveolus and supporting jaw. A percussion test on the intrusive luxated tooth produces a dull metallic sound similar to that of an ankylosed tooth, which is useful in differentiating the intruded tooth from a tooth that is partially erupted.[3] Treatment of intrusive luxated teeth is controversial, and no optimal treatment has been determined.[3, 36, 37] Recommended treatments include allowing the tooth to re-erupt if the tooth is immature, immediate surgical repositioning of the tooth into its proper place in the arch, splinting to adjacent teeth, and low force orthodontic repositioning of both immature and mature intrusive luxated teeth over a period of 3 to 4 weeks, with endodontic therapy done within 2 to 3 weeks to arrest external root resorption.[3]

In the primary dentition, the permanent successor develops lingually to the primary incisor.[5] If the intruded tooth impinges on the permanent tooth, the primary tooth should be extracted immediately, as atraumatically as possible, to avoid injury to the permanent tooth bud. If the intruded tooth is facially displaced and appears not to have involved the permanent successor, the tooth should be allowed to re-erupt spontaneously. If, during the eruption phase the gingiva becomes infected, the tooth should be removed and the patient should be placed on antibiotics such as penicillin to avoid damage to the permanent tooth germ[3] (Fig. 15–31).

EXTRUSIVE LUXATION (FIG. 15–16D)

The tooth that is partially displaced out of the alveolar socket should be digitally manipulated into proper position as soon as possible. The tooth should be splinted with a nonrigid material, such as monofilament nylon or thin (28 gauge) wire, to allow some physiologic movement of the involved tooth so that ankylosis of the tooth may be prevented (Fig. 15–32). There is a high probability that the tooth will require endodontic therapy.[1, 36] Follow-up examinations with radiographic and vitality evaluations must be done periodically to avoid loss of the tooth. The extruded primary tooth should be removed to prevent damage to the succedaneous tooth.[3]

LATERAL LUXATION (FIG. 15–16E and F)

Lateral luxation of the tooth is usually accompanied by comminution or fracture of the alveolar socket. In lacerations of the gingiva, the tooth can be forced through

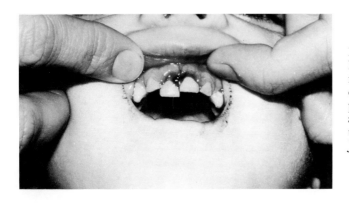

FIGURE 15–31.   Intrusive and extrusive luxations of maxillary incisors are seen commonly in the pediatric patient who falls. The succedaneous tooth develops at the palatal aspect of the primary tooth. If the root of the tooth impinges on the permanent tooth, the primary tooth should be removed as atraumatically as possible to avoid further damage. The extruded primary tooth should be extracted. (Courtesy of Dr. J. Berg, Houston, TX.)

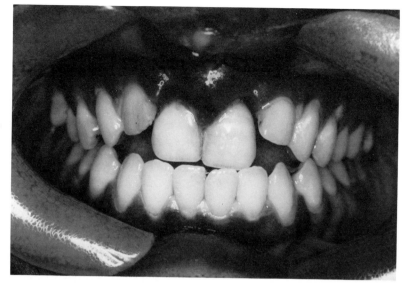

FIGURE 15–32. The maxillary central incisors have been extrusively luxated during an altercation. The area is irrigated clean of debris, and with the patient under local anesthesia, the teeth are digitally manipulated into proper position in the alveolar sockets.

the alveolar plate. The tooth and alveolar bone can usually be digitally manipulated into proper position and splinted to adjacent stable teeth. Any large gingival laceration, which is common with this type of injury, should be sutured. The tooth should be stabilized for 2 to 8 weeks, depending on the extent of the displacement.[3, 36] Endodontic therapy may be required, and follow-up examinations are necessary.

AVULSION (EXARTICULATION) (FIG. 15–16*H*)

A true dental emergency exists with complete avulsion of the tooth from the alveolar socket. The prognosis of the pulp and periodontal tissue is directly related to the proper diagnosis and to the action taken at the scene of the accident — usually not by individuals trained in dental techniques.[1, 3–5, 23, 26, 31, 36, 38] The most frequently involved teeth are the maxillary central incisors; avulsion of these teeth usually occurs between the ages of 7 and 10 years, when the permanent incisors are erupting. According to Andreasen, the loosely structured periodontal ligaments and resilient alveolar bone surrounding erupting teeth favor avulsion over other injuries.[3]

The goal of reimplanting teeth after traumatic avulsion is to maintain the viability of the cells of the pulp and periodontal ligament, which would assist reattachment and avoid post-traumatic complications of root resorption.[3, 22, 36, 39–41] The success of reimplantation is inversely related to the length of time the tooth is out of the socket. The sooner the tooth is reimplanted, the better the prognosis. Andreasen and Hjørting-Hansen[41] observed that after a period of 2 or more years 90 per cent of the teeth reimplanted in less than 30 minutes following avulsion exhibited no discernible resorption of roots. In contrast, root resorption was seen in 95 per cent of the teeth reimplanted after an extraoral period of greater than 2 hours.

Because time is critical, reimplantation at the site of injury has the best prognosis.[3, 22, 23, 36, 39–41] Telephone instructions to the patient, parent, or supervising personnel should be to inspect the tooth for debris, to cleanse with saline or milk or by simply sucking or spitting on the tooth, and to place the tooth back into the socket immediately. After reimplantation, the tooth should be held in place with light pressure en route to the office or clinic. If the tooth cannot be replaced, it should be stored in the buccal vestibule or under the tongue of the patient unless, because of the extent of injury or the age and cooperation level of a child, there is a concern that the tooth may be aspirated or swallowed. The tooth can then be stored in the mouth of the parent or supervising adult for transportation without adverse consequences. If neither option is available, the tooth can be stored in milk, saline (1 teaspoon of salt added to 8 ounces of water), or a saliva-soaked towel. Storage in tap water has been documented to have adverse effects on periodontal healing and is not recommended for cleansing or transportation of avulsed teeth.[3, 42] The tooth should never be allowed to dry. Even short drying periods of the avulsed tooth can do irreversible damage to the periodontal ligament and can cause rapid loss of the tooth through resorption.[3, 36]

Upon arrival at the dental office, the teeth and traumatized tissue should be inspected and evaluated. If the patient does not have the tooth, careful clinical examination must be performed to rule out aspiration, swallowing of the tooth, intrusive luxation, or displacement of the tooth in surrounding soft tissues of the head and neck (Figs. 15–11 and 15–12). Chest, abdominal, panoramic, and facial films should be obtained to rule out adverse possibilities. If the tooth has been left at the scene of the accident, every attempt should be made to retrieve it.

The tooth should be evaluated to determine whether it is of the primary dentition. The root of the tooth should be inspected for evidence of resorption, or a radiograph should be taken of the alveolar bone to locate a succedaneous tooth. Avulsed primary teeth should not be reimplanted[3, 4, 22, 36] (Fig. 15–33).

Andreasen[3] proposed that the following conditions should be considered before reimplanting a permanent tooth:

1.   The avulsed tooth should be without advanced periodontal disease.
2.   The alveolar socket should be reasonably intact to provide a seat for the avulsed tooth.
3.   There should be no orthodontic considerations, such as significant crowding of the teeth.
4.   The extra-alveolar period should be considered. If the tooth is reimplanted within 30 minutes of avulsion, there is a good chance of successful reimplantation. For extra-alveolar periods greater than 2 hours, complications associated with marked root resorption increase significantly.
5.   The stage of root development should be assessed. Survival of the pulp is possible in teeth with incomplete root formation if reimplantation is accomplished within 2 hours after injury.

If the tooth has been successfully reimplanted prior to evaluation by the dentist, a radiograph should be obtained to verify the position within the alveolar socket and to assess the extent of damage to surrounding structures (i.e., root fractures, intrusive luxations). The involved tooth should be splinted with a semirigid splint for 7 to 10 days. If there has been a concomitant alveolar fracture, a rigid splint should be used for 3 to 4 weeks. If the tooth is transported to the office or requires repositioning, the tooth should be gently cleansed of debris with a saline-soaked gauze. To avoid damage to vital periodontal tissues and cementum, no effort should be made to scrape the tooth surface or sterilize it with solutions before reimplantation. The tooth should

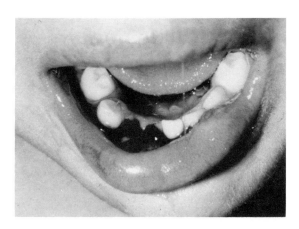

FIGURE 15–33.   Avulsed primary teeth should not be reimplanted. Radiographs should be obtained to evaluate the primary teeth, the adjacent primary teeth, and the supporting bone. The socket site should be inspected, debris and fragments should be removed, and the area should be irrigated, with appropriate sutures placed for reapproximation of soft tissues. (Courtesy of Dr. J. Berg, Houston, TX.)

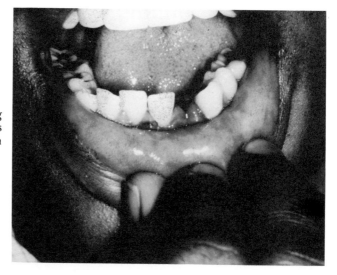

FIGURE 15-34. A lateral incisor completely avulsed during an altercation. The tooth was located, and the patient was informed over the telephone to place the tooth in his mouth and to get to the dental clinic as quickly as possible.

then be gently manipulated into proper position using digital pressure. It is not necessary to suction the blood clot from the socket before reimplantation.

The tooth should be splinted, and gingival lacerations sutured as indicated. The traumatized teeth should be removed from the occlusion, and the patient maintained on a soft diet for 2 to 3 weeks. Care should be taken with removal of the splint after 7 to 10 days, as the involved tooth will still be mobile. Splinting longer than 7 to 10 days may promote root resorption[3] (Figs. 15–34 to 15–38).

Andreasen[3] has categorized periodontal healing of avulsed teeth into three groups based on histologic evaluation, as follows.

Healing with a Normal Periodontal Ligament. The periodontal ligament of the avulsed tooth completely repairs. Small areas of resorption on the root surface are repaired by new cementum deposits. A normal periodontal space can be seen radiographically, and a normal percussion sound can be elicited.

Healing with Ankylosis (Replacement Resorption). The blood clot in the damaged periodontal ligament of the avulsed tooth is organized into granulation tissue that is replaced by bone. The tooth becomes ankylosed, and the root is gradually replaced by bone. Radiographically, the normal periodontal space is not evident. The areas of root resorption can be detected within 2 months of injury, beginning in the apical third of the root, and most cases are evident 1 year after reimplantation.

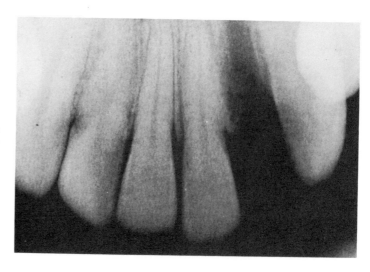

FIGURE 15-35. Upon arrival at the dental clinic, a radiograph revealed no obvious damage to the supporting bone or surrounding teeth.

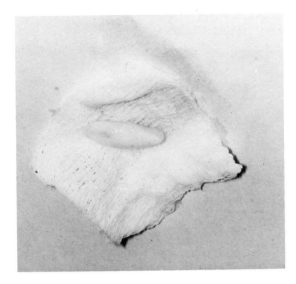

FIGURE 15–36.   The tooth is gently cleansed of debris with a saline-soaked gauze without scraping or the use of sterilization solutions to avoid damage to the periodontal tissues and cementum. The tooth is then gently manipulated into the alveolar socket and splinted for 1 week.

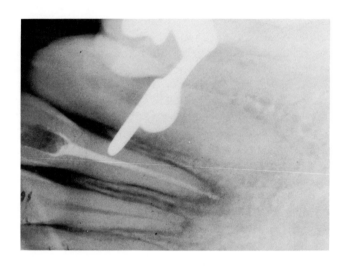

FIGURE 15–37.   Endodontic therapy should be initiated 2 weeks after reimplantation of the tooth. The canal is first filled with calcium hydroxide paste, and treatment is eventually completed with a gutta-percha filling material.

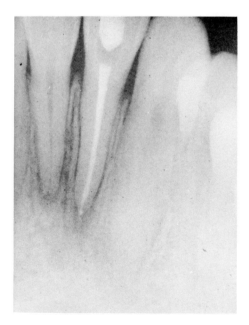

FIGURE 15–38.   The tooth remains functional without evidence of root resorption 5 years after implantation. (Courtesy of Dr. J.A. Wallace, Fox Chapel, PA.)

In the fully developed jaw, ankylosis of teeth presents no difficulty. The teeth may be maintained until root replacement leads to loosening and exfoliation. However, in younger patients in whom maturation of the alveolar structures has not occurred, ankylosis may interfere with normal growth of the alveolar process. When infraocclusion is diagnosed in these individuals, the tooth should be extracted to prevent malocclusion.[22]

Inflammatory Resorption.   The etiology of inflammatory resorption is a communication between surface resorption and pulp via the dental tubules. Toxic by-products and bacteria from the necrotic pulpal tissue seep into the periodontal tissues and cause an inflammatory reaction.[43] Resorption is accelerated, and within a few months the root may be completely resorbed. Inflammatory resorption is common after reimplantation of the permanent incisors in the 6- to 7-year-old child.

Root resorption is the major complication associated with traumatically avulsed teeth. The loss of vitality of the periodontal ligament influences the progression of resorption of the root surface. Even short drying periods of the avulsed tooth can have an adverse effect on the periodontal ligament. Unless treated, inflammatory resorption can result in rapid loss of the reimplanted tooth as early as 3 months after reimplantation.

Appropriate endodontic therapy can arrest the resorptive process. All reimplanted teeth with complete root formation should be treated endodontically.[3, 41, 44] Andreasen has demonstrated that extraoral root canal procedures, as well as root canal filling materials, injure the periodontal ligament, resulting in increased ankylosis when compared with nonendodontically treated avulsed teeth. He recommends that endodontic treatment should be initiated 1 to 2 weeks after reimplantation to halt development of inflammatory resorption as well as to allow reformation of periodontal fibers.[3]

If more than 2 hours have elapsed before reimplantation can be achieved, extraoral endodontic therapy should be accomplished,[41] and the canal should be filled with calcium hydroxide, which has been shown to be effective in arresting inflammatory resorption.[3] In teeth with prolonged extra-alveolar time, application of 2 per cent phosphate-acidulated sodium fluoride for 20 minutes has been experimentally shown in animal models to slow replacement resorption.[45, 46] Studies have yet to confirm similar results in human teeth.[3, 41]

Immature teeth with wide open foramen reimplanted before 2 hours after avulsion should be reimplanted and splinted without endodontic therapy for possible revascularization of the pulp. Radiographic examination should be done after 2 or 3 weeks, and if root resorption is noted, endodontic therapy should be initiated immediately and calcium hydroxide paste should be packed into the root canal to eliminate inflammatory resorption.[3] After arresting the resorption and closure of the apex, a final endodontic restoration should be completed.

Tetanus prophylaxis or booster injection should be administered after injury if the last injection was given more than 5 to 10 years previously. Human tetanus antitoxin, 250 units given intramuscularly, is recommended for dirty wounds untreated for more than 25 hours.[47] Antibiotic coverage with penicillin or erythromycin is indicated to minimize bacterial activity in the periodontal and pulpal tissues as well as the twice daily use of a 0.12 per cent chlorhexidine (Peridex) rinse for 7 to 10 days.

The prognosis of reimplanted permanent teeth is guarded, as many teeth are destroyed by root resorption. Successful reimplantation requires expedient treatment at the time of the accident and close follow-up (Fig. 15–39).

Injury to the Supporting Bone (Fig. 15–17)

COMMINUTION OF THE ALVEOLAR BONE (FIG. 15–17A)

Comminution of the alveolar socket is usually associated with lateral or intrusive luxation injuries. The fractures are generally reduced with digital manipulation, and

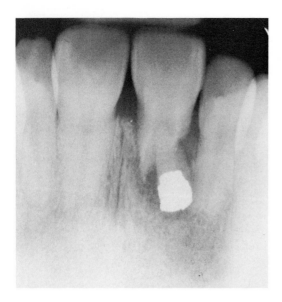

FIGURE 15–39. If more than 2 hours have elapsed since avulsion of the tooth or the periodontal ligament has not been kept moist, there should still be an attempt to reimplant the tooth, with the patient and parents being made aware of the poor prognosis. This central incisor was avulsed in a playground accident when the patient was 8 years old. The patient reported that she put the tooth in her pocket and got to her family dentist after approximately 3 hours, with the tooth still in her pocket. After informing the family of the poor prognosis, her dentist apparently retrogradely filled the canal with amalgam and replaced the tooth. The tooth functioned for nearly 20 years without difficulty except discoloration. Mobility of the tooth due to resorption of the root eventually required extraction of the tooth.

the luxation injury is treated. Follow-up for evidence of root resorption of the involved teeth is indicated.

FRACTURE OF THE ALVEOLAR SOCKET WALL (FIG. 15–17*B* and *C*)

Alveolar socket wall fractures are usually associated with luxation injuries. There usually is mobility of the buccal osseous plate with the involved teeth and evidence of contusion of the gingiva or mucosa. Reduction of the fracture involves simultaneous digital pressure of the coronal aspect of the crown and apex along the fracture site. After reduction of the fracture, the occlusion should be checked and the involved teeth removed from the forces of traumatic occlusion. Soft tissue lacerations should be sutured, and the involved teeth should be splinted rigidly for 4 weeks to allow for osseous healing. Alveolar process fractures with primary teeth that are not significantly displaced or easily manipulated back into proper position may not require splinting, as the bone heals quickly in children. The child should be maintained on a soft diet for 2 weeks.[3] Periodic follow-up examinations are required to monitor pulpal health.

FRACTURES OF THE ALVEOLAR PROCESS (FIG. 15–17*D* and *E*)

Fractures of the alveolar process are predominantly found in the anterior teeth and premolar region of children in older age groups.[3] These injuries may be isolated or may be seen in conjunction with other dental and/or facial injuries. The patient frequently reports that the occlusion has been changed, as the involved segment has shifted from the original position (Fig. 15–40).

Treatment involves reduction of the involved segment and stabilization for 4 weeks to allow for osseous healing. Closed reduction of the alveolar fracture may be accomplished with digital manipulation of the alveolar and dental segment. Stabilization can be satisfactorily accomplished with rigid splinting techniques or the use of a lingual splint (Fig. 15–41). An open reduction of the alveolar fracture may be required if the alveolar segment is significantly displaced or the involved teeth are displaced so that the roots are "locked" over the osseous plate. A vestibular incision is made below the fracture line, and a subperiosteal flap is elevated to expose the fracture site. A No. 1 or No. 9 periosteal elevator can be used in the fracture line to elevate the segment and place the alveolus into proper position. Frequently, no

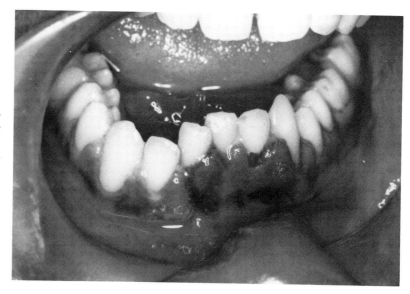

FIGURE 15–40. Alveolar process fracture associated with anterior mandibular teeth. The segment moves as one unit with teeth and bone. Note the contusion of the gingival and mucosal tissues.

osseous fixation is required, but if indicated, the segment can be wired or a bone plate placed after re-establishment of the proper occlusion is verified. Rigid splinting of the involved teeth or use of an Erich arch bar for 4 weeks provides adequate stabilization for osseous healing (Fig. 15–42).

Careful follow-up is mandatory to evaluate pulpal necrosis and periapical inflammation. Such complications are rather frequent and apparently related to the time interval between injury and fixation. Teeth splinted within 1 hour after injury de-

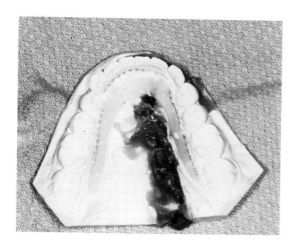

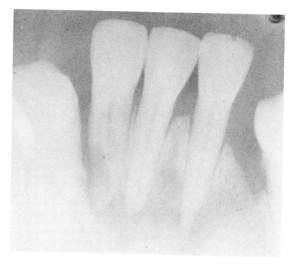

FIGURE 15–41. The segment was digitally manipulated into proper occlusion and position. A lingual splint was fabricated to fixate the involved segment rigidly.

FIGURE 15–42. Adequate stabilization and immobilization are required for osseous healing of a dentoalveolar fracture. This patient was involved in an accident 5 years prior to this radiograph and lingually displaced the mandibular incisors and alveolar bone. The teeth were repositioned digitally without splinting or removal from traumatic occlusion. The segment healed to a fibrous nonunion, with root resorption of the lateral incisors that required removal of the entire segment.

velop pulpal necrosis less frequently than teeth splinted after longer periods.[3] Tetanus booster is usually not indicated unless the wound has been contaminated with road debris, dirt, and so on. Coverage with penicillin or erythromycin and the use of chlorhexidine oral rinse are recommended.

FRACTURE OF THE MAXILLA AND MANDIBLE
(FIG. 15–17F and G)

The management of maxillary and mandibular fractures is discussed in Chapters 13 and 16.

Splinting Techniques

Splinting provides stabilization of traumatized teeth and prevents further damage to the pulp and periodontal tissues during the healing period. The maintenance of oral hygiene and the prevention of infection are important in promoting periodontal healing during stabilization. No portion of the acrylic composite or wire of the stabilization device should impinge on the gingival margins of the teeth. Splints that irritate the gingiva and cause gingival inflammation prevent the resolution of the inflammatory response in the marginal gingiva. The patient must be able to keep the gingival tissues as clean as possible, which is difficult with cap splints, foil splints, and cold-curing acrylic splints.

Erich arch bars or lingual splints or both can be used for stabilization of alveolar process fractures if the teeth within the segment are stable. If the teeth are mobile, the supporting wires—if positioned apically to the cervical prominence—may have a tendency to elevate the tooth slowly.

Interdental wiring techniques, such as figure-of-eight wiring and loop wiring,[23, 47] can be used but are technically difficult and troublesome. The patient may have difficulty cleaning about the wires, and the wires may slip apically below the cervical prominence of the tooth and elevate the tooth or damage the cemental surface.

The requirements for an acceptable splint are as follows[3]:

1. It is easy to fabricate directly in the mouth without lengthy laboratory procedures.
2. It can be placed passively without causing forces on the teeth.
3. It does not contact the gingival tissues and thus cause gingival irritation.
4. It does not interfere with normal occlusion.
5. It is easily cleaned and allows for proper oral hygiene.
6. It should not traumatize the teeth or gingiva during application.
7. It allows an approach for endodontic therapy.
8. It is easily removed.
9. It provides good aesthetic results.

ACID-ETCH RESIN SPLINT

Acid-etch resin fixation techniques provide a relatively easy, versatile method for stabilization of teeth with effective, aesthetic composite resin materials.[3] The labial surfaces are cleaned as best as possible of blood and debris. The use of a cotton roll or gauze in the vestibule and over gingival lacerations will assist in keeping the surface as clean and dry as possible. The teeth are air dried, and a 50 per cent phosphoric acid gel is applied to the incisal third of the traumatized and adjacent teeth as indicated. After the gel has been on the surface for approximately 60 seconds, it is removed with a water spray. The teeth are then air dried to reveal a frosty white surface, signifying a successful etch. Depending on the composite resin system used, the teeth are stabi-

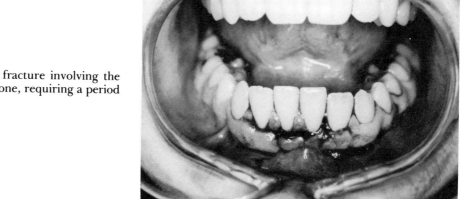

FIGURE 15–43. A dentoalveolar fracture involving the mandibular incisors and alveolar bone, requiring a period of rigid fixation for 4 weeks.

lized with a band of the material along the etch surfaces. The composite resin material is then allowed to cure or is cured with an ultraviolet light with the light-activated systems. Light-activated systems provide longer working time and better control of the material. The occlusion should be checked, and the splint should be altered if it interferes with proper occlusion. The splint should be smoothed and polished for improved hygiene and comfort to the patient.

This method provides excellent stabilization and allows the patient to keep the teeth and gingiva clear, as the splint is away from the periodontal tissues. The material is then removed after the indicated stabilization period, and the teeth are pumiced smooth. Care must be taken during removal of the acrylic material from the involved teeth as they will still be fairly mobile after the stabilization period and may accidentally be extracted.

A modification of this technique involves the use of a wire to splint the traumatized teeth instead of a composite bridge (Figs. 15–43 to 15–46). The wire should be of proper stiffness to provide either rigid fixation (24 gauge) or semirigid fixation (28 gauge), as indicated by the injury. This technique is useful in cases of missing teeth or in a mixed dentition in which teeth are not fully erupted and the edentulous area needs to be spanned.[3]

The wire is cut and modified to lie passively along the facial aspect of the teeth that are to be splinted. The facial surfaces are prepared by the acid-etching method previously described, and the wire is bonded to the teeth with a composite resin restorative material. Light-activated composite resin systems allow for flexibility and control of the involved segments. The wire can first be secured to the anchor teeth

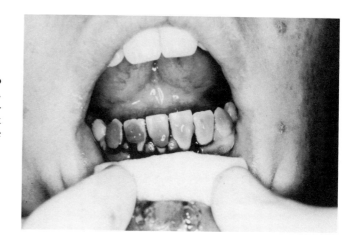

FIGURE 15–44. The labial incisors of the involved teeth to be used as an abutment are cleaned of blood and debris. The cotton roll is placed in the vestibule and over the gingival lacerations. The teeth are air dried, and a 50 per cent phosphoric acid gel is applied to the facial surfaces of the teeth for approximately 60 seconds.

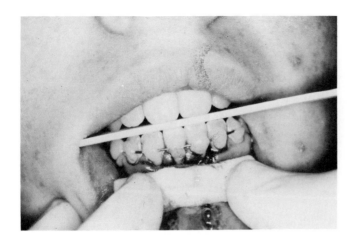

FIGURE 15–45. Following the removal of the phosphoric acid gel with water, the teeth are air dried. A rigid wire (24 gauge) is fashioned to follow the contour of the arch passively and is secured to the teeth with a composite resin restoration material.

with composite resin and activated with the UV light. The involved teeth then can be individually repositioned correctly and bonded to the wire. The occlusion is checked for interferences, and the composite material is smoothed. A wire splint can also be fixated to the teeth with orthodontic brackets. The wire provides excellent stabilization as well as clear gingival margins and interproximal areas to allow for hygiene of these areas. A radiograph should be obtained following reduction and stabilization to verify proper alignment of the teeth and alveolar segments.

SEMIRIGID SPLINT

If there are no associated alveolar fractures, a semirigid splint that allows physiologic movement of the traumatized tooth is indicated.[3, 36] Andreasen[3, 43] has shown that rigid splinting of reimplanted mature and autotransplanted immature teeth increases the incidence of root resorption. The acid-etch composite resin technique with materials such as waxed dental floss, suture[22], flexible braided orthodontic wire,[23] or monofilament nylon line[36] provides stabilization of the traumatized tooth and allows for physiologic movement of the tooth under function to minimize ankylosis and root resorption.

The involved tooth and two stable adjacent teeth to provide support are acid etched as previously described. A single strand of 20- to 30-pound test monofilament nylon line is cut to size and secured to the first abutment tooth with a composite resin system. The remaining abutment and traumatized teeth are secured to the nylon line in order with the composite resin system as tension is maintained on the free end of

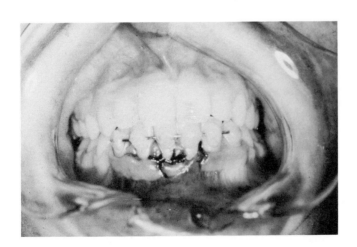

FIGURE 15–46. After the resin has been cured, any excess material is removed and polished. The occlusion is checked, and the involved teeth are removed from the traumatic occlusion. (Courtesy of Dr. S. Reynolds, Des Moines, IA.)

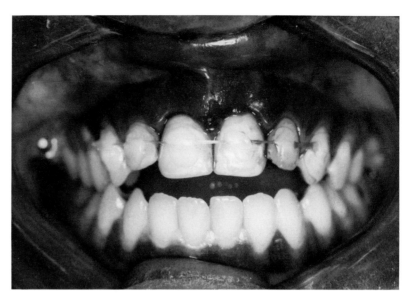

FIGURE 15–47. To allow for physiologic movement of the involved maxillary central incisors, the teeth are fixated semirigidly with dental floss to the stable abutment teeth. The teeth are all prepared in the usual fashion with an acid-etch technique, and the dental floss is secured to the teeth in order from canine to canine. The involved teeth are usually removed from traumatic occlusion (not required in this case owing to the existing skeletal anterior open bite), and the patient is maintained on a soft diet.

the nylon line with hemostats. The resin is then smoothed and polished after all teeth are secured and the occlusion is verified[48] (Fig. 15–47; also see Fig. 15–32). A radiograph should be obtained to check for proper root position after splinting.

Restoration

Following dentoalveolar trauma, normal form and function of the masticatory system should be restored by the restorative dentist. Restorations for crown injuries include composite acid-etch build-ups and full-crown coverage.

Crown-root fractures after endodontic therapy are usually restored with a customized cast core cemented into the retained root and coverage with a full crown.[3] With the loss of the dentition or supporting alveolar bone or both, various dental implant systems can be used to support a bridge and restore function. If large amounts of alveolar bone have been lost, especially if the facial osseous plate has been avulsed, bone grafts may be required to provide adequate osseous support for the implants (Figs. 15–48 and 15–49).

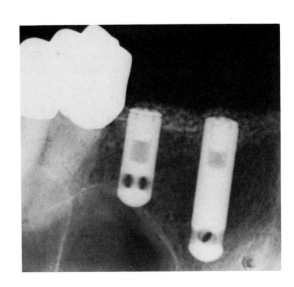

FIGURE 15–48. Restoration of function following dentoalveolar trauma and loss of teeth can be accomplished with various implants or implanted materials, such as hydroxyapatite granules.

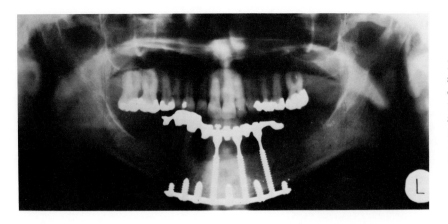

FIGURE 15–49. Following partial avulsion of the teeth and alveolus in the mandible in an automobile accident, a modified transmandibular implant supporting a fixed appliance was used to restore mandibular function. (Courtesy of Dr. H. Bosker, Groningen, The Netherlands.)

PREVENTION

Mouth Protectors

The use of mouth protectors in patients undergoing tracheal intubations for general anesthesia has been shown to reduce the incidence of dental trauma.[19] The use of seat belts and shoulder harnesses in automobiles has been advocated to reduce injury in automobile accidents, including facial and dental trauma as the victim hits the steering wheel, dashboard, or windshield during impact. Preventive orthodontics should be considered for children with increased maxillary overjet as a precaution against traumatic injury to the exposed teeth.[3]

The use of intraoral mouthguards has been demonstrated to be an effective means of reducing the degree and incidence of dentoalveolar trauma associated with contact sports.[48a,49–57] In 1960, a joint commission of the Bureau of Dental Health Education and the American Association for Health, Physical Education, and Recreation reviewed the literature on football injuries and found that when high school football players did not wear face masks or mouth protectors, 50 per cent of all their injuries occurred around the mouth. The committee concluded that most of these injuries could be prevented by a properly fitted mouthguard.[57] In 1962, the National Alliance Football Rules Committee required high school football players to use mouthguards and face guards.[54] In 1967 alone, it was estimated that 25,000 to 50,000 injuries were prevented by the use of intraoral mouth protectors.[58] Studies done with the Notre Dame football program, when face guards were mandatory but mouth protectors were seldom worn or accepted on a team basis, indicated that more than one of five injuries to football players were to the hard and soft tissues of the oral cavity.[49,59] The National Collegiate Athletic Association (NCAA) Football Rules Committee recommended the mandatory use of mouthguards in 1970, and the mouthguard rule went into effect with the 1973 football season. In the 1970 season, 280 cases of oral injury requiring treatment were reported. With a mandatory rule for mouthguard protection in the 1973 season, the reported number of cases fell to 55.[55]

Currently, organized football programs at some elementary and junior high school levels, as well as backyard and sandlot football, are the only levels of the sport not covered by mandatory mouthguard rules. If well-accepted injury figures are conservatively projected, more than 200,000 injuries are being prevented annually. The incidence of mouth injuries among football players in 1981 was between 0.35 per cent and 0.45 per cent.[54]

Enforcement of the mandatory mouthguard rules is difficult, as many officials report that they cannot determine whether a player has a mouthguard if the material is transparent.[52] Athletes occasionally are reluctant to use a mouthguard because they believe the guards are troublesome and prevent adequate breathing. The NCAA has modified the mouthguard rule for the 1990 football season to require that all mouthguards be yellow to facilitate their visualization by the officials on the playing field.[55a] Research at the University of Michigan revealed that yellow mouth protectors were easier to detect at various distances than were clear mouth protectors or none at all.[60] Enforcing the use of mouthguards should be the responsibility of coaches and trainers and not officials or referees during game time. Compliance should be enforced at all times during practice when the chance of dental injury is equal to or greater than that found during the actual game.[52]

Currently, mouth protectors are required only in organized football, hockey, and boxing matches.[61] Mouth protectors are recommended for most sports, such as wrestling, rugby, soccer, basketball, gymnastics, racquetball, lacrosse, field hockey, martial arts, skiing, and weight lifting, to minimize injury of teeth and supporting structures through direct or indirect trauma from falls, collisions, and clenching of the teeth.[62] The participation of girls and women in competitive athletics has increased dramatically in recent years. The injury of female athletes has been found to be similar to that of male athletes involved in the same sporting activity.[63] Female athletes should be educated and encouraged by coaches and officials to use mouth protectors to prevent dental injury.[54]

Mouthguards may be divided into three types: (1) ready-made or stock protectors, (2) mouth-formed protectors, and (3) custom-made protectors.[49, 54, 57, 61, 64, 65-67]

The most desirable qualities of a mouthguard are retention, comfort, allowance for ease of speech and breathing, resilient material, and provision of protection for the teeth, gingiva, and lips.[54] Mouthguards that are not stock varieties are usually fabricated for the maxillary arch. For the athlete with a Class III malocclusion, the mouthguard should be manufactured to cover and protect the prominent mandibular teeth.[53]

For maximal protection, the mouthguard should be designed and constructed according to the following specifications.[61]:

1.   The occlusal surface of all teeth is covered for protection and to prevent possible overeruption of teeth.

2.   The flanges cover the alveolus and are trimmed $\frac{1}{8}$ inch short of the depth of the buccal vestibule for maximal retention and to give protection to the lip and gingiva.

3.   The material extends distally to include the second molars and is relieved for clearance of the frena.

4.   The material extends lingually no more than $\frac{1}{4}$ inch onto the palatal mucosa, tapering at the margins to avoid lingual bulk, which may interfere with speech and breathing or trigger a gag reflex.

STOCK MOUTH PROTECTORS

The stock mouth protector is the simplest and cheapest mouthguard. It is purchased over the counter and does not require fitting. These mouthguards are constructed of latex or silicone material and provide minimal protection, as they are loose fitting and can be held in place only by keeping the teeth together and the jaws closed. The stock type of protector is uncomfortable to the participant, as it is difficult to breathe around the mouthguard and tends to irritate the gingiva and buccal vestibule.[49, 54, 61, 64, 65-67]

MOUTH-FORMED PROTECTORS

The mouth-formed protector is probably the most popular and universally used mouthguard.[49] There are two major types of mouth-formed protectors: the shell-liner type and the thermoplastic type.[56, 61, 66] The shell-liner mouthguard consists of a preformed outer shell of latex rubber or plastic that fits loosely about the maxillary teeth. The tray tends to be bulky but can be trimmed for comfort and improved fit in the vestibule. The shell is then relined with a polymer-monomer soft curing material similar to that used for soft relining of dentures. The materials are mixed, placed in the outer shell, and carried to the mouth to set in 5 to 7 minutes.[49, 54, 61, 66, 67] The disadvantages of this type of protector limit the usefulness of this mouthguard. Repeated biting on the reline material causes it to spread and lose retention of the teeth. The liner can gradually become hard as it is continually exposed to the oral fluids. The protector tends to be bulky and open the bite if not properly fitted. This type of protector is not recommended for athletes with orthodontic braces or other appliances.[66]

The thermoplastic type of mouth-formed protector is the most widely used mouthguard, as it is cheap and durable and can be resoftened and refitted if it loses retention. The mouthguard is a thermoplastic shell of polyvinyl acetate ethylene that is immersed in boiling water for 30 seconds, dipped quickly in cold water, and placed in the mouth over the maxillary teeth. The material is then adapted to the teeth with the fingers. The vestibule extension can be trimmed and molded for comfortable coverage of the alveolus and soft tissues. The teeth can be occluded into the material while it is warm to provide minimal opening of the closed bite.[49, 54, 66]

CUSTOM-MADE MOUTH PROTECTORS

Custom-made mouthguards are fabricated over stone models made from alginate impressions of the athlete's maxillary teeth. A thin sheet of thermoplastic material, commonly polyvinyl-polyethylene with a thickness of $\frac{1}{16}$ to $\frac{1}{8}$ inch,[66] is adapted to the model to provide comfortable, individualized mouth protection. There is no excessive bulk, so the athlete can breathe, speak, and be understood while not having to hold the mouthguard continually in position with the teeth or cheeks. The interocclusal thickness remains thin and uniform to allow for even occlusion when the athlete bites into the protector. Excellent retentive properties add to the comfort and do not cause the wearer to take the guard out of his or her mouth continually, which would increase the chances of soiling or misplacing the mouth protector.[49]

After the stone model has been made from an alginate impression, a thin sheet of thermoplastic material is heated and is vacuum formed over the model to cover all of the teeth. The vacuum method of adapting the material produces a guard of uniform

FIGURE 15–50. The mouthguard should extend to $\frac{1}{8}$ inch short of the depth of the buccal vestibule, with clearance of the frena. (Courtesy of Mr. A.J. Duffy, Ann Arbor, MI.)

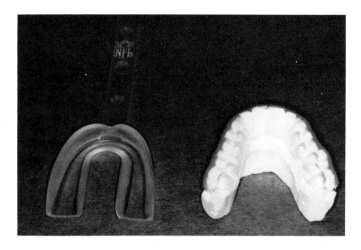

FIGURE 15–51. The thermoplastic type of mouth-formed protector *(left)* is immersed in boiling water for 30 seconds, dipped for 1 second in cool water, and contoured over the maxillary teeth. The material is adapted to the teeth with the fingers and is trimmed to ⅛ inch short of the vestibular depth. Construction of custom-made protectors *(right)* of similar thermoplastic material is adapted in the laboratory to a stone model made from an alginate impression of the athlete's maxillary dentition.

thickness and maximal retention about the natural contours of the teeth.[66] The material is allowed to cool completely on the model to avoid distortion.

The mouthguard is then trimmed from the palate and ⅛ inch short of the buccal vestibule, with clearance for the buccal and lingual frenum (Fig. 15–50). The edges are smoothed and rounded with a stone wheel or placed on the model and flamed with an alcohol torch and adapted with fingers.[51,66] The athlete's name should be secured to the mouthguard for identification. The stone models are kept by the coaches, trainers, or dentists, so that a replacement mouthguard can be made if needed. The disadvantage of the custom-fitted mouthguard is the time and expense involved with management, construction, and delivery of the protector (Fig. 15–51).

A mouthguard must be easy to fabricate (Fig. 15–52), comfortable, able to accommodate the needs of an individual's dentition, durable, easily held in place, and able to provide adequate protection to the teeth, jaws, and cranial structures. No matter which mouthguard is used, the athlete should be instructed to rinse the protector under cold tap water after each use. It should then be stored in a rigid container.[66] Unfortunately, some school officials believe that dentists are willing to assist with oral protection only if custom-fitted mouthguards are used. Regardless of the type of protector used, players will benefit if a dentist is available to offer advice on

FIGURE 15–52. The thermoplastic material is heated and then vacuum formed to the stone model. This method produces a mouthguard of uniform thickness and maximal retention about the natural contours of the teeth. The material is then removed from the model, trimmed to the appropriate dimensions, and smoothed; if desired, a strap can be added.

FIGURE 15–53.   A thermoplastic mouth-formed or custom-made mouthguard may have a strap attached to the helmet. The strap secures the mouthguard to the face mask and allows the athlete to remove the mouthguard during breaks in competition without misplacing the mouthguard or soiling the mouthguard on the ground.

FIGURE 15–54.   Enforcement of a mandatory mouthguard rule is difficult if the mouthguard material is transparent or without a strap to the helmet. The National Collegiate Athletic Association (NCAA) has modified the rule, beginning with the 1990 football season, to require that all mouthguards be yellow to facilitate their visualization by officials on the field.[55a] Compliance should also be stressed by coaches and supervising adults during practice and sandlot activities.

its fit and form and on the health of the player's mouth. The thermoplastic variety of mouthguard is recommended if it is to be placed or formed by the athlete; however, supervision of the fitting procedure by a dentist is recommended. The most desirable protector is the custom-made mouthguard, fabricated by a dentist from a thermoplastic material[54] (Figs. 15–53 and 15–54).

REFERENCES

1. Berkowitz R, Ludwig S, Johnson R: Dental trauma in children and adolescents. Clin Pediatr 19:166, 1980.
2. Dodds RN, Holcomb JR, England MC: The avulsed tooth. Va Dent J 61:8, 1984.
3. Andreasen JO: Traumatic Injuries to the Teeth. 2nd ed. Copenhagen, Munksgaard, 1981.
4. Medford HM: Acute care of avulsed teeth. Ann Emerg Med 11:559, 1982.
5. Moss SJ, Maccaro H: Examination, evaluation and behavioral management following injury to primary incisors. NYS Dent J, February 1985, pp 87–92.
6. Johnson JE: Causes of accidental injuries to the teeth and jaws. J Public Health Dent 35:123, 1975.
7. Lewis TE: Incidence of fractured anterior teeth as related to their protrusion. Angle Ortho 29:128, 1959.
8. McEwen JD, McHugh WD, Hitchin AD: Fractured maxillary central incisors and incisal relationships. J Dent Res 46:1290, 1967.
9. Andreasen JO: Etiology and pathogenesis of traumatic dental injuries. A clinical study of 1,298 cases. Scand J Dent Res 78:339, 1970.
10. Levine N, Paedo D: Injury to the primary dentition. Dent Clin North Am 26:461, 1982.
11. Ellis RG, Daury KW: The Classification and Treatment of Injuries to the Teeth of Chil-

dren. 5th ed. Chicago, Year Book Medical Publishers, 1970.

12. Application of the International Classification of Diseases and Stomatology, IDC-DA. 2nd ed. Geneva, WHO Organization, 1978.

13. Heintz WD: Mouth protection for athletics today. *In* Godwin WD, Long BR, Cartwright CB (eds): The Relationship of Internal Protection Devices to Athletic Injuries and Athletic Performance. Ann Arbor, MI, University of Michigan, 1982.

14. Laskin DM: The recognition of child abuse. J Oral Surg 36:349, 1978.

15. Piercell MP, White DE, Nelson R: Prevention of self-inflicted trauma in semicomatose patients. J Oral Surg 32:903, 1974.

16. Wasmuth C: Legal pitfalls in the practice of anesthesiology. Complications to endotracheal anesthesia. Anesth Analg 39:138, 1960.

17. Star EG: Damage to teeth by oral airways. Pract Anesth 11:347, 1976.

18. Wright RB, Mansfield FF: Damage to teeth during the administration of general anesthesia. Anesth Analg 53:405, 1974.

19. Lockhart PB, Feldbau EV, Gabel RA, et al: Dental complications during and after tracheal intubation. J Am Dent Assoc. 112:480, 1986.

20. Risk Management Foundation: Anesthesia claims analysis show frequently low, losses high. Risk Mgmt Found 4:1, 1983.

21. Tate RJ: Facial injuries associated with the battered child syndrome. Br J Oral Surg 9:41, 1971.

22. Camp JH: Replantation of teeth following trauma. *In* Current Therapy in Dentistry, Vol. VII. McDonald RE et al (eds): St. Louis, CV Mosby, 1980.

23. Assael LA, Ellis EE: Soft tissue and dentoalveolar injuries. *In* Peterson LJ et al (eds): Contemporary Oral and Maxillofacial Surgery. St. Louis, CV Mosby, 1988.

24. Sanders B, Brady FA, Johnson R: Injuries. *In* Pediatric Oral and Maxillofacial Surgery. St Louis, CV Mosby, 1979.

25. Basrani E: Fractures of the Teeth. Philadelphia, Lea and Febriger, 1985.

26. Sweet CA: A classification and treatment for traumatized anterior teeth. J Dent Child 22:144, 1955.

27. Ulfohn R: Casos insólitos de fracturas coronaries con curación espontánae. Rev Assoc Odontal Argent 62:11, 1974.

28. Ingle JI, Frank AC, Natkin E, Nutting EE: Diagnosis and treatment of traumatic injuries and their sequelae. *In* Ingle JJ, Beveridge EE (eds): Endodontics, 2nd ed. Philadelphia, Lea and Febiger, 1976.

29. Narang R: Management of traumatized teeth and alveolus. *In* Goldman H, Gilmore H, Irby W, McDonald R (eds): Current Therapy in Dentistry. St Louis, CV Mosby, 1977.

30. Josell SD, Abrams RG: Traumatic injuries to the dentition and its supporting structure. Pediatr Clin North Am 29:717, 1982.

31. McDonald RE, Avery DR: Dentistry for the Child and Adolescent. St Louis, CV Mosby, 1977.

32. Amsterdam JT, Hendler BH, Rose LF: Emergency dental procedures. *In* Roberts JR, Hedges HJ (eds): Clinical Procedures in Emergency Medicine. Philadelphia, WB Saunders Company, 1985, pp 946–977.

33. Hildebrandt R Jr: Dental and maxillofacial injuries. Clin Sports Med 1:449, 1982.

34. Medford HM, Curtis JW: Acute care of severe tooth fractures. Ann Emerg Med 12:364, 1983.

35. Smith RJ, Rapp R: A cephalometric study of the development relationship between primary and permanent maxillary central incisor teeth. J Am Soc Dent Child 26:36, 1980.

36. Antrim DD, Bakland LK, Parker MW: Treatment of endodontic urgent care cases. Dent Clin North Am 30:559, 1986.

37. Turley PK, Joiner MW, Hellstrom S: The effect of orthodontic extrusion on traumatically intruded teeth. Am J Orthod 85:47, 1984.

38. Castaldi CR, Brass GA: Dentistry for the Adolescent. Philadelphia, WB Saunders Company, 1980.

39. McDonald RE, Avery DR: Dentistry for the Child and Adolescent. St Louis, CV Mosby, 1978.

40. Grossman LI, Ship II: Survival rate of reimplanted teeth. Oral Surg 29:899, 1970.

41. Andreasen JO, Hjørting-Hansen E: Replantation of teeth. I. Radiographic and clinical study of 110 human teeth replaced after accidental loss. Acta Odontol Scand 24:263, 1966.

42. Andreason JO: The effect of the extra-alveolar period and storage media upon periodontal and pulpal healing after reimplantation of mature permanent incisors in monkeys. Int J Oral Surg 10:43, 1981.

43. Andreasen JO: Effect of pulpal necrosis upon periodontal healing after surgical injury in rats. Int J Oral Surg 2:62, 1973.

44. Barbakow FH, Austin JC, Cleaton-Jones PE: Experimental reimplantation of root-canal filled and untreated teeth in the vervet monkey. J Endodont 3:89, 1977.

45. Shulman LB, Gedalia I, Feingold RM: Fluoride concentration in root surfaces and alveolar bone of fluoride-immersed monkey incisors three weeks after reimplantation. J Dent Res 52:1314, 1973.

46. Shulman LB: Allogeneic tooth transplantation. J Oral Surg 30:395, 1972.

47. Levison ME: Clostridial infection. *In* Rose LF, Kaye D (eds): Internal Medicine for Dentistry. St Louis, CV Mosby, 1983.

48. Antrim DD, Ostrowski JS: A functional splint for traumatized teeth. J Endodont 8:328, 1982.

48a. Peterson D.: Personal Communication, 1988.

49. Mollenkopf JP: The mouth protector for the young athlete. *In* McDonald RE, Hurt WC, Gilmore HW, Middleton RA (eds): Current Therapy in Dentistry. Vol 7. St Louis, CV Mosby, 1980, pp 521–525.

50. Castaldi GR: First aid for sports-related dental injuries. Phys Sportsmed 15:81, 1987.

51. Shaull KL: Fabrication of personalized custom mouthguards for athletes in contact sports. National Association of Dental Laboratories, Trends and Techniques, October 1985, pp 10–13.

52. Duda M: Which athletes should wear mouth guards? Phys Sportsmed 15:179, 1987.

53. Godwin WC, Craig RG, Koran AK, et al: Mouth protectors in junior football players. Phys Sportsmed 10:41, 1982.

54. Bureau of Health, Education and Audiovisual Services and Council on Dental Materials, Instruments and Equipment: Mouth protectors

and sports team dentists. J Am Dent Assoc 109:84, 1984.

55. National Collegiate Athletic Association Rules Committee Minutes: National Total Operative Football Injuries, 1970–1986.

55a. Nelson D: Personal Communication, 1988.

56. Nei SH: Prevention of injuries to anterior teeth. Int Dent J 24:30, 1974.

57. Report of the Joint Commission on Mouth Protectors of the American Association for Health, Physical Education and Recreation and the American Dental Association. Chicago, American Dental Association, 1960.

58. Heintz WD: Mouth protectors: A progress report. J Am Dent Assoc 77:632, 1968.

59. Moon DG: Football mouth protectors. J Indianapolis Dist Dent Soc 15:10, 1961.

60. Wilkinson EE: An Evaluation of Mouth Protectors. Masters Thesis, University of Michigan, Horace H. Rackham School of Graduate Studies, 1984.

61. Stevens OO: Prevention of traumatic dental and oral injuries. In Andreasen JO (ed): Traumatic Injuries of the Teeth. Philadelphia, WB Saunders Company, 1982.

62. Heintz WD: Mouth protectors for athletes today. In Godwin WC, Lang BR, Cartwright DC (eds): The Relationship of Intraoral Protective Devices to Athletic Injuries and Athletic Performance. Ann Arbor, MI, University of Michigan, 1982.

63. Albohm M: Implication for the female athlete. In Godwin WC, Lang BR, Cartwright DC (eds): The Relationship of Intraoral Protective Devices to Athletic Injuries and Athletic Performance. Ann Arbor, MI, University of Michigan, 1982.

64. Heintz WD: Mouth Protection in Physical Athletics. Seattle, National Athletic Trainers Association, 1982.

65. Wilkinson EE, Powers JM: Properties of custom-made mouth protector materials. Phys Sportsmed 14:77, 1986.

66. Powers JM: Materials, fabrication and properties of mouth protectors. In Godwin WC, Lang BR, Cartwright DC (eds): The Relationship of Intraoral Protective Devices to Athletic Injuries and Athletic Performance. Ann Arbor, MI, University of Michigan, 1982.

67. Bureau of Dental Health Education and Bureau of Economic Research and Statistics: Evaluation of mouth protectors used by high school players. J Am Dent Assoc 68:430, 1964.

CHAPTER 16

MANDIBULAR FRACTURES

ROBERT BRUCE, D.D.S., M.S., and
RAYMOND J. FONSECA, D.M.D.

HISTORY OF MANDIBULAR FRACTURES

Any discourse on the management of mandibular fractures would be deficient without a historical perspective, for much of the knowledge relating to jaw fractures has been known for centuries. It is apparent, when reviewing the literature, that statements attributing a technique or device to a specific surgeon are difficult to document, since treatment methods developed in an evolutionary manner, with bursts of surgical creativity occurring during periods of war.

The earliest known written record describing mandibular fractures is found in the Edwin Smith Papyrus,[1,2] a unique Egyptian treatise written in hieroglyphics about 1650 BC. Smith was an American Egyptologist who purchased the document in Thebes from a native in 1862. Although Smith recognized the value of the document, he was unable to translate it. This task fell to Dr. James Henry Breasted in 1930.[3] The Papyrus is probably a copy of an original written about 3000 BC by a physician associated with the pyramid builders. It is unique because it is the first to describe surgical conditions. Other older medical papyruses generally are lists of prescriptions and describe diseases as demoniacal intrusions. The Smith Papyrus consists of 48 surgical cases, systematically organized, beginning with the head and proceeding downward through the thorax, where the incomplete document ends. Each case is organized as follows: (1) title, (2) examination, (3) diagnosis, (4) treatment, and (5) glosses. The diagnosis directs the physicians to choose one of three verdicts: (1) "an ailment that I will treat," (2) "an ailment with which I will contend," and (3) "an ailment not to be treated."

Case 24 in the Papyrus describes a fracture of the mandible. The surgeon writes that it is less serious than a compound comminuted fracture of a long bone but describes it as fatal nonetheless. The case states

If thou examinest a man having a fracture in his mandible, thou shouldst place thy hand upon it. Shouldst thou find that fracture crepitating under thy fingers, thou shouldst say concerning him: One having a fracture in his mandible, over which a wound has been inflicted, and he has a fever from it. An ailment not to be treated.

The cause of death in this case probably was sepsis.

Case 25 describes a dislocation of the mandible and its reduction:

> If thou examinest a man having a dislocation in his mandible, shouldst thou find his mouth open and his mouth cannot close for him, thou shouldst put thy thumbs upon the ends of the two rami of the mandible in the inside of his mouth, and thy two claws (fingers) under his chin and thou shouldst cause them to fall back so that they rest in their places.

This was considered a treatable ailment.

Case 26 states

> If thou examinest a man having a wound in his lip, piercing through to the inside of his mouth, thou shouldst draw together that wound with stitching.

The Egyptian surgeon considered this "an ailment that I could treat."

Case 27 describes a chin wound. The text states

> If thou examinest a man having a gaping wound in his chin, penetrating to the bone, thou shouldst palpate his wound. If thou shouldst find his bone uninjured, not having a split, or a perforation in it . . . an ailment I will treat. Thou shouldst apply for him two strips on that gash. Thou shouldst bind it with fresh meat the first day, and thou shouldst treat it afterward with grease, honey, and lint every day until he recovers.

The literature relating to medicine and mandibular fractures is scarce until the glorious age of Greece, when Hippocrates, the "Father of Medicine," wrote his famous medical manuscripts.[4] Prior to Hippocrates, medicine was controlled by religious cults loyal to Asclepius, son of Apollo, the Sun God. Priest-physicians were in charge of medical sites, and treatment combined therapeutics with religion. Hippocrates, the son of a physician-priest, was born in 460 BC on the Island of Cos, the home of a famous medical temple. Hippocrates based his practice on scientific observation rather than mysticism. Gahhos and Ariyan evaluated the voluminous *Hippocratic Collection (Corpus Hippocraticum)* and presented those sections dealing with facial fractures and teeth, an excerpt of which follows:[5]

Fractures of the Mandible

XXXII.   Displaced but incomplete fractures of the mandible where continuity of the bone is preserved should be reduced by pressing the lingual surface with the fingers while at the same time counterpressure is applied from the outside. Following the reduction, displaced or loosened teeth adjacent to the fracture are fastened to one another—not only the two adjacent but several—using gold wire or, lacking that, linen thread until the bone has consolidated. Following the wiring, compresses soaked in cerate and a light loose bandage are applied. One should keep in mind that bandaging a fractured jaw properly may do little good, while done badly will do great harm. The lingual surface of the mandible should be palpated periodically and if displaced it should be manually reduced again. Holding the mandible throughout the healing period would be the ideal management, but this is not possible.

XXXIII.   Complete mandibular fractures, which are rarely seen, are reduced in the manner just described. Following the reduction, the teeth should be fastened together. This will greatly contribute to immobilization especially if the two bony ends are well approximated and the wires tightly fastened. Describing the rest of the procedure in writing is not a simple task. The mandible is splinted using Carthaginian leather as a thin outer layer in children and full thickness in adults. Strips of leather three finger breadths wide or as wide as necessary are prepared. One end is fastened to the mandible using gum—which by the way is better than glue—about a finger breadth or so from the fracture site. A slit is made on the strap to allow for the protrusion of the chin. This constitutes the lower part of the splint. Another strap of the same width or a little wider is fastened to the upper part (proxima) of the jaw, equidistant from the fracture site. This is similarly slit to allow passage around the ear. The straps are tapered off at their junction, where the ends meet and are tied together. The fleshy surface of the leather is placed toward the skin, because it adheres better. Carefully, so as not to displace the mandible, traction is applied on the straps especially the one going around the chin, and they are tied to each other on the top of the head. Afterwards a bandage is placed around the forehead and another over the straps to keep them from moving. . . . This type of immobilization with fastened straps is convenient, easy to manage and allows for many readjustments. Unintelligent physicians who are good with their hands prove themselves in the management of fractures of the mandible above all other injuries.

XXXIV.   Anyone can treat separations of the symphysis at the chin. With the two ends of the bone forcefully separated, the protruding part is pushed inwards while the collapsed end is forced outwards. This method of reduction is easier than trying to force the over-riding bones into position. With completion of the reduction, the teeth are wired to each other as previously described. Subsequently cerate, a few compresses and a bandage are applied. Recovery is rapid and the teeth come out healthy with a well done bandage and the patient at rest. Otherwise the teeth remain displaced and become damaged and useless.

After Hippocrates, there were few new ideas on the treatment of jaw injuries for centuries. Subsequent authors have modified the Hippocratic method.

Brophy, in his *Textbook of Oral Surgery*,[6] describes the work of Aulus Cornelius Celsus (about 30 BC – AD 50), a Roman writing the first medical treatise in Latin — *De Medicina*.[7] In Chapter 7 of his eighth book of medicine, Celsus writes

In fractures of the other bones we frequently find one fragment detached from the other; in the mandible the fragments, although thrown out of place, always adhere one to another. Consequently, in this fracture we must, first of all, replace the fragments to their normal position, pressing from the inside of the mouth and from the outside with the forefinger and thumb of both hands. Then in the case of a transverse fracture (in which case an unevenness in the level of the teeth is produced) it is necessary, after having set the fragments in place, to tie together the two teeth nearest to the fracture with a silk thread (bristle, horsehair) or else, if these are loose, the next ones. After this one should apply externally, to the part corresponding to the lesion, a thick compress dipped in wine and oil and sprinkled with flour and powdered alibanum. This compress is to be fixed in place by means of a bandage on a strip of soft leather with a longitudinal slit in the middle to embrace the chin, the two ends being tied together above the head. . . . Fractures of the lower jaw and of the maxilla commonly heal from the fourteenth to the twentieth day.

The use of a chin bandage mentioned by Celsus was a perfection of the Hippocratic method, and Brophy felt that Celsus should be credited with the bandage rather than Galen (AD 131)[8] or Soranus of Ephesus Junior (AD 97), who wrote two treatises on bandages and fractures.[9] In his text, Soranus mentions the chin bandage *"capistrum simplex ant duplex"* (single or double rope) and coined the term *"frunda"* (sling).

With the fall of the Roman Empire, the center of learning shifted to the Arabic school of medicine. The Islamic authors of the ninth and tenth centuries — Rhazes (841–926), Ali Abbas (died 994), Serapion (tenth century), Avicenna (Ibn-Sena) (980–1037), and Albucasis (Abre 1-Qasim) (1050–1122) — essentially followed the Hippocratic methods as taught by Celsus and Galen. Avicenna's textbook *The Canon*[10] contains a chapter on mandibular fractures. The author inserts numerous *inquit sapiens* (says the erudite, referring to Hippocrates) throughout the chapter. Avicenna states that after first aid has been given, the operator should be called to re-establish the level of the maxillary arches. His bandage is described in detail:

Put the two ends from the two sides over the head to the end of the mandible, then from here again to the nape of the neck; then to the place below the chin and over the two maxillary bones to the crown; from here again to the place below the nape of the neck; and put another ligament over the forehead and across the back of the head and fasten everything; and put over all a soft cloth.

The first European medical school was established in the eleventh century in Salerno, Italy. A classic textbook of surgery called *Maestro Ruggero from Parma* was written in Salerno in 1180.[6] The treatment of mandibular fractures was described under the section of poultices and ointments:

Take olibanum, mastic, colophene, glue, dragon blood; all this must be mixed with liquified resin and becomes ointment which is placed over till the complete consolidation, and everything must be fixed with the little lances, in order that the portions be prevented from moving out of place.

The author mentions the importance of establishing proper occlusion:

In the fractures of the mandibula, the lower teeth are not in contact with the upper ones and the patient cannot masticate. The patient must be taken by the lower maxilla and this must be moved here and there until the lower teeth will touch the upper ones.

In 1275, the Italian Guglielmo Salicetti (William of Saliceto) wrote about mandibular fractures in his book *Cyrurgia*.[11] The treatment methods described were essentially those of Hippocrates, but in a later edition printed at Lyons in 1492,[12] the reader was advised first to wire the teeth adjacent to the fracture together and "this done tie the teeth of the uninjured jaw to the teeth of the injured jaw in this way." Thus is found the first mention of intermaxillary fixation as we know it today.

The celebrated French surgeon Ambroix Paré wrote *Cinq Livres de Cherurgie*, published in Paris in 1572.[13] In this text, he describes treatment of mandibular fractures with a modification of the so-called sling of Galen:

> There will be applied a leather ferule, such as from which the soles of a boot are made, which has been divided in the middle at the level of the chin, long and wide as the mandible: and there will be made a ligature with a band two fingers wide and as long as necessary, cut at the two ends, leaving only one inch, and at the level of the chin it will be parallelly cut for the purpose of embracing and pressing better over the chin: and at the four extremities, the shorter will be sewed at the top of the head to a night cap or calotte and the other two longer ends will be kept transversely and sewed behind the same cap, everything done as skillfully as possible in order to hold well the fracture.

Leake, in his "History of oral surgery",[14] states there were approximately 20 treatises published in the sixteenth century that dealt with dental and oral problems. These included the German text of Walther Ryff (1500–1570), published in the 1540s, which contained an illustration of a fractured mandible treated by gold wires intertwined among all of the teeth.[15]

The famous French dental surgeon Pierre Fauchard (1678–1761) was particularly proficient in his writings on dentistry. His *Le Chirurgien Dentiste* consisted of dissertations on orthodontics, anatomy, surgery, prosthetic dentistry, and pathology.[16] His contemporary, Robert Bunon (1702–1748), authored four dental treatises and related two cases of fractures of the mandible treated by binding the teeth.[17] One case involved a fracture through the body in which the bicuspids were lost and the adjacent teeth loosened. He filled the edentulous space with a block of walrus bone containing two holes. He then ligated threads to the block and mandibular teeth to consolidate the teeth and heal the fracture.

The effects of the elevator and depressor muscles on fragments of mandibular fractures were described by Frenchmen F. Chopart and P.J. Desault in 1795, in their *Traité des Maladies Chirurgicales*.[18] They also described an extraoral appliance for use on mandibular fractures (Fig. 16–1). The splint was made of a brace of metal covering the mandibular teeth and was held in position by counter-pressure from a plate of sheet iron under the chin. The two pieces were joined by screws, which tightened the two pieces of metal against the mandibular teeth, immobilizing the fracture. Historically, Chopart's device is important because it was the beginning of the use of various dental prosthetic devices in an effort to immobilize mandibular fracture fragments.

From a review of the literature through the eighteenth century, it is apparent

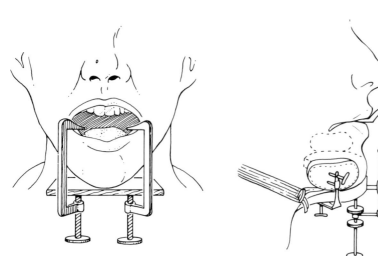

FIGURE 16–1. Chopart and Desault (1795) used viselike devices to treat mandibular fractures.

that the accepted method of treating mandibular fractures was the application of some type of bandage in an attempt to achieve immobilization of the mandibular fracture after reduction. This approach was sometimes combined with ligation, using thread or gold wire, of the teeth adjacent to the fracture. Experienced surgeons of today can appreciate the difficulties our predecessors must have had in maintaining reduction and immobilization with a bandage, no matter how cleverly applied. Apparently, these problems were noticeable early, as Brophy states in a discussion of the historical use of bandages[6]:

> Fabricius from Aquapendente (1600) limits himself with supplying the inefficiency of the sling of the chin with tow when already Teoderico Borgognoni of Bolona (midthirteenth century) had thought to supply it with a small cushion.

In the 1800s, hundreds of articles appeared in the English and American literature as scientific writing and publishing were facilitated. New and improved intraoral and extraoral devices were developed as the profession of dentistry grew and flourished. The number of adequately trained dental practitioners in the United States was small in the 1700s, with most dental surgery being carried out by barber-surgeons and operative dentistry done by silversmiths and jewelers. In 1820, there were about 100 dentists in the United States for a population of 9.6 million people, for a ratio of 1 : 100,000. By 1860, the ratio had increased to 18 : 100,000. Table 16–1 shows the type of treatment used for mandibular fractures and the results of treatment used in Bellevue Hospital in New York City, published in 1857.[19]

The following case, as documented by Physick[20] in 1822, is representative of the difficulties patients must have encountered in the treatment of a fractured mandible:

> On the 29th day of March, 1820, I unfortunately had my under jaw broken in two places, on the right side transversely, and on the left obliquely. I sent, immediately on receiving the injury, for three physicians, who proceeded to reduce the jaw in its proper place, and to keep it so by means of bandages — but, on applying the bandages, the jaw invariably slipped out of place. Several fruitless attempts to secure it were made, on the same, and on the following day.
>
> The physicians continued both days endeavouring to replace it, every fifteen or twenty minutes, when, at length, being nearly exhausted with pain, I was so fortunate as to set it myself — and by tying a handkerchief around my jaws, it remained in place nearly twenty-four hours. But, once more thrown out of place, I set it again — and did the same the following day.
>
> After suppuration took place, and during its continuance, it was discovered by the physicians, that the broken part of the jaw on the left side, extending back, was considerably out of place, inclining outwards — to remedy which, a compress was applied, and suffered to remain so long, that the jaw was pressed in further than its natural position.
>
> In three months from the time that the accident occurred, suppuration ceased, and, on

TABLE 16–1.   ELEVEN CASES OF FRACTURE OF THE INFERIOR MAXILLA*

No.	Sex	Age	Cause	Point of Fracture	Dressings	Treated	Union
1.	M	45	Thrown from carriage	Shaft of right side and ramus of left side	Gutta-percha	137 d	None
2.	M	40	Blow	Symphysis	Four-tailed bandage, cork between teeth	37 d	Firm
3.	M	35	Blast of rock	Entire body of jaw comminuted	None	Death on 11th d	Firm
4.	M	54	Blow under the jaw	Shaft near angle	Barton's	27 d	Firm
5.	M	45	Fall from a ladder	Ramus of both sides	None	29 d	Firm
6.	M	30	Direct blow	Shaft of left side	Barton's	12 d	Firm
7.	M	55	Indirect blow	Ramus of left side	Gibson's	—	Firm
8.	M	35	Direct blow	Shaft of left side	Gutta-percha	34 d	Firm
9.	M	46	Direct blow	Ramus of right side	Barton's	23 d	Firm
10.	M	36	Direct blow	Symphysis	Gutta-percha	19 d	None
11.	M	19	Direct blow	Shaft of left side	Gutta-percha	5 d	None

* Taken from Bellevue Hospital Study, New York, 1857.

examination, it appeared that the transverse fracture had united, and the other remained without any disposition to unite. The teeth, on this side, were turned from their upright position considerably into the mouth—forming a horizontal shelf over the side of the tongue.

In the month of November, 1820, I came to Philadelphia, and applied to Dr. Physick, who removed the teeth contained in that part of the jaw which was pressed into the mouth. This afforded me considerable relief. But still I experienced great inconvenience from the pain occasioned by the motion of the fractured parts in the broken jaw, whenever I attempted to bite any substance as hard as a crust of bread. My bodily strength gradually decreased, as I had a very sickly appetite, and was rendered incapable of receiving proper nourishment. My frame being debilitated in this manner, I seriously felt the effects of changes in the weather—and every time I contracted a cold, it settled in my jaw; afterwards, I was unable to eat anything except spoon victuals, and from the slight hopes I entertained of ever recovering from this misfortune, I was rendered truly unhappy, and felt retched, when compelled to enter into any of my usual avocations.

I returned to Huntingdon in December, 1820, where I remained until the 27th of April, 1822, when I again went to Philadelphia to receive assistance from the skill of Dr. Physick, who introduced a seton from the inside of the mouth, nearly through the centre of the bone—in consequence of which, a discharge of matter took place immediately, and in six weeks afterwards small pieces of bone came out.

At the expiration of six weeks, the outside of the bone became very much inflamed, and continued so for three or four days, accompanied with very acute pain—after which, the pain subsided, and the inflammation decreased. In the course of the eleventh week, the change for the better was so great, that there was no motion in the jaw, as before, which had united, and has daily gained a considerable share of strength since that time.

On the 26th day of July, 1822, Dr. Physick removed the seton, and from appearances, I have every reason to believe, that in the course of a short time, I shall cease to feel the slightest inconvenience from this dangerous and unfortunate occurrence.

Through the 1800s and early 1900s, several methods were used to reduce and immobilize mandibular fractures. Although hundreds of techniques were advocated in the literature of the 1800s, most are variations of bandages and external appliances; extra-intraoral appliances; monomaxillary wiring, including bars, monomaxillary splints, intermaxillary wiring, and splints; guides or glides; and internal fixation, including wires, plates, and screws.

Bandages and External Appliances

Hippocrates was the first to mention bandages as a method to immobilize fractures of the mandible.[4] Although the bandages and dressings used by the ancients were modified with time, it was not until 1816, when John Rhea Barton first described the Barton bandage, that any one type of bandage became standard in treating fractures of the mandible (Fig. 16–2).[21] The Barton and later the Gibson (1838) bandages had anteroposterior chin neck turns, which tended to drive the mandible posteriorly, probably resulting in many deformities and malunions.[22] Garretson published the first textbook devoted solely to oral surgery in 1862, in which he wrote of a double roller bandage tying in front of the chin.[23] Roldon used a double roller bandage of plaster of paris, which he described in 1903.[24] It was essentially a Barton bandage with the same disadvantages. Even in World War I, the same type of bandage was used, as described by Pickerill in 1918.[25] Several authors described variations on the Barton bandage in the 1900s, and finally Rosenthal, in 1936, wrote about a "bird face" deformity that he ascribed to the continued use of a bandage that exerted backward pressure on the chin.[24]

Hippocrates used Carthaginian leather straps in conjunction with wiring of the teeth in the treatment of mandibular fractures.[4] During the early Christian era, physicians depended more on external appliances and less on wiring of the teeth. The materials used were leather, starched cloth, and waxed cloth, frequently reinforced by metal strips. Chin pieces were added, made up of cardboard, steel, gutta-percha, plaster of paris, and modeling compound. The advantages of extraoral appliances over bandages were that they could be adjusted without being completely removed

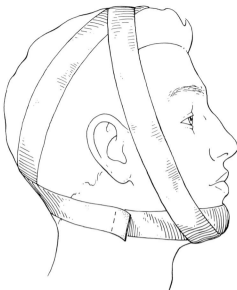

Figure 16–2.   The Barton bandage, named for John Rhea Barton.

and that they often gave a more firm and even distribution of pressure. The disadvantages were that the appliances were unable to immobilize the fracture fragments and that the added chin cups tended to force the mandible back, resulting in malunion.

Although the literature of the 1800s is replete with the mention of various types of external appliances, the following are representative. The Bouisson apparatus (1843) is illustrative of the typical features of the extraoral appliance.[26] The headpiece was made of canvas or of lamb's leather padded with chamois skin. The leather chinpiece was in the shape of a four-tailed bandage. Elastic inserts connected the headpiece with the chinpiece, producing an undesirable posterior traction on the chin.

Von Szymanowski, in the mid 1800s, popularized the use of plaster of paris for surgical splints and also used the material for chin cups and head caps.[27] Bean, an officer in the Army of the Confederate States of America, used an external appliance in conjunction with an intraoral splint, but there was no connection between the appliances.[28-30] The extraoral appliance consisted of a small (3 to 4 cm) wooden chinpiece that hung in the center of a larger (10 cm), long chinpiece. Metal sideplates were attached to the chinpiece and were kept in place by head straps.

Erichsen, in 1869, described a bandage of gutta-percha bound to the chin by a four-tailed bandage.[31] In 1894, Parkhill described an elaborate harness (Fig. 16–3).[32] The purpose was to hold the mandible forward and upward without resorting to internal splints. External appliances were used even into the 1900s. Kazanjian's apparatus (circa 1916) combined a gutta-percha chinpiece connected with a headpiece by elastic bands.[33] He eliminated the posterior strapping, thus avoiding posterior pressure on the chin.

Extra-Intraoral Appliances

In 1795, Chopart and Desault described the use of a clamplike device to splint a fractured mandible.[18] Cord or lead covered the teeth, and a piece of wood was placed beneath the chin. This viselike arrangement, with a multitude of variations, was used well into the twentieth century. Dorrance and Bransfield listed the disadvantages of these splints: (1) It is impossible to gain proper occlusion; (2) they are not applicable to fractures extending posterior to the teeth; (3) they are useless in bilateral fractures; (4) drooling is encouraged around the connecting rods as they leave the mouth; and (5) the extraoral parts rarely distribute pressure evenly along the mandible, resulting in dental movement, skin necrosis, and decreased stability.[34]

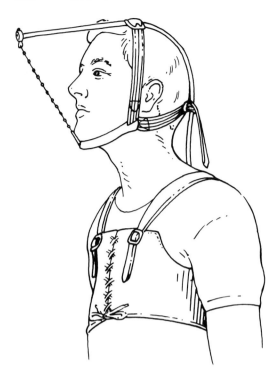

FIGURE 16–3. Parkhill (1894) described a harness to hold the mandible forward and upward without resorting to internal splints.

They stated that

> The power of example is so great, however, that in 1936, more than 150 years after its introduction we find the extra-intraoral splint continuing to be used. Refinements in materials, in models, and in details of application are numerous and frequent. The principle itself remains unchanged, an erroneous conception perpetuated by tradition.

Examples of extra-intraoral appliances follow. Chopart and Desault[18] were the first to conceive the idea of using a vise type of apparatus to hold a fractured mandible. Rütenick (1799) added steel connecting clamps attached to a wooden chinpiece by spikes.[35,36] Variously shaped silver pieces were made to fit the teeth, and fabric bands ran from the chinpiece to a light head cap. Similar viselike apparatuses were described by Bush (1822),[37,38] Hauselet (1827),[24] Hartig (1830),[39] and Lonsdale (1840).[40] Sawyer, in 1856, was one of the first to describe a mouthpiece made from a wax model of the teeth.[41] Hayward, in 1860, was the first to use a splint consisting of swedged metal covering the teeth connected with metal bars that extended out from the angle of the mouth and back to the side of the cheek. These bars were then connected with a bandage under the chin.[42] This type of splint, with variations, became known as the Kingsley splint (Fig. 16–4).

Variations of this splint were used during the American Civil War (1861–1865). Thomas Brian Gunning (1840–1889), an Irish-born, apprentice-taught dentist from New York, was the first American to use reverse arms from an interdental splint.[43–45] He also used double arms extraorally for anchorage to a head cap and soft rubber chin support (Fig. 16–5). Gunning was one of the first to use vulcanite in a custom-fitted splint to immobilize fractured mandibular fragments, and if the fracture was difficult to maintain, he constructed a single vulcanite splint for both jaws, to provide intermaxillary fixation. This splint contained a space to allow access for food and liquids. Gunning was able to test his splint firsthand when, in 1862, he was thrown from his horse and fractured his mandible. He reduced his own fracture, securing it with silk thread around the teeth on either side of the fracture. A vulcanite splint was constructed and inserted the following day. According to Gunning, he was able to resume seeing his patients that afternoon.

Gunning was also to play a role in U.S. history. In 1864, he was called to treat William H. Seward, Secretary of State under President Abraham Lincoln. Seward

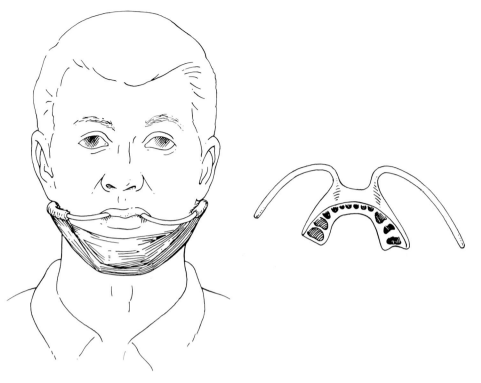

FIGURE 16–4. The Kingsley splint (1861): an interdental splint with two reverse arms extending extraorally, supporting a sling under the chin that stabilized the splint.

sustained bilateral body fractures of his mandible while jumping from his carriage. The surgeons who attended Seward were unable to reduce the fractures with bandages and ligatures, and treatment was further complicated when an attempted assassin lacerated Seward's cheek and parotid duct, thus compounding the fractures. Gunning was called to Washington, and after belittling the surgeon's treatment, recommended that a vulcanite splint be made to incorporate the edentulous maxilla and the partially edentulous mandible. Seward, along with his physicians and friends,

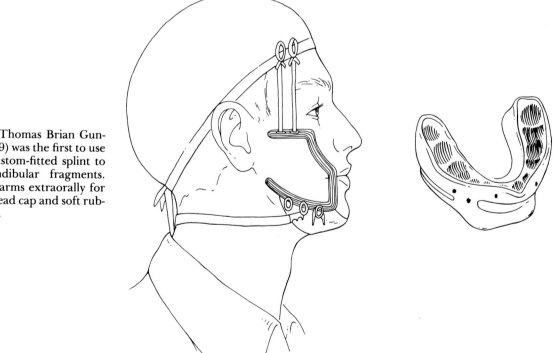

FIGURE 16–5. Thomas Brian Gunning (1840–1889) was the first to use vulcanite in a custom-fitted splint to immobilize mandibular fragments. He used double arms extraorally for anchorage to a head cap and soft rubber chin support.

rejected the treatment, and Gunning returned to New York. Two weeks later, he was summoned back to Washington to resume Seward's treatment. The one-piece vulcanized splint containing a space for eating was secured by screws driven into the remaining mandibular teeth. Sixty-eight days later, the splint was removed, but the fracture on one side had not healed. Gunning removed necrotic bone from the site and reapplied a new splint, which Seward wore for 4 more months. When it was removed, Gunning declared the fracture healed. Controversy raged when, in 1879, W. St. G. Elliot, writing in the *New York Medical Journal,* claimed that he had interviewed a Japanese dentist who, after examining Seward, found that the mandible was useless and no union had occurred.[46] Gunning waged war with the *Journal's* publisher and editor, insisting on a retraction, which never came. Apparently, Gunning let it be known that the Surgeon General, as well as the medical directors of the Army and Navy, were incompetent. Gunning's treatment methods were slowly recognized in the years to come, but Gunning and his family felt that his achievements were never fully appreciated.

At about the same time (1864), J. B. Bean, a civilian dentist in Atlanta, Georgia, developed a custom-made vulcanite splint that was held in place by bandages.[28-30] Bean had treated some 100 cases of fractured jaws in Atlanta, "giving his services gratuitously." In 1864, he was asked by Dr. E.N. Covey, Medical Inspector of the Confederate Army, to care for jaw fractures in the Confederate wounded in a specialized ward in the Blind School Hospital in Macon, Georgia. Covey detailed several of the cases treated by Bean, one involving a major general[29]:

> Case 50—Major General J. P. A., army of Tennessee. Vul. sclop.; compound fracture of inferior maxilla. Wounded August 31, 1864, at Jonesboro, Georgia. Minie ball entered left cheek one-half inch from angle of jaw, one inch from the bone and alveoli containing the two bicuspids of the left side, and all of the incisors and cuspids and first bicuspid of right side. The ball, after leaving the body of the bone, near the apex of the fang of the second left bicuspid, passed upward through the side of the tongue; wounding the left ranal [ranine] artery, and cutting the centre of the dorsum of the tongue (the mouth of the patient being open at the time), it passed out at the right angle of the mouth; fracturing and carrying away the crown of the superior right lateral incisor. Fragments of bone & c. were removed on the field, and when the patient reached private quarters in Macon, Georgia, on September 3, the wound was in good condition, hemorrhage having subsided.

> The patient was perfectly quiet; and being unable to articulate, he communicated his wishes by writing. The fragment of bone, containing the front teeth, was very much displaced, being projected forward until there was a quarter of an inch of space between the bicuspids of the right side and the lower incisors; these last closed inside of the upper teeth before the injury, but now projected beyond them for more than a quarter of an inch; it was not possible, under the circumstances of the case, to reduce this displacement, and much less to retain it in place by any means ordinarily adopted.

> September 3—Tongue much swollen, and parts quite sensitive to any kind of disturbance. In consultation with Surgeons Bemiss, Gamble, Green and others, it was determined, on account of the wounding of the ranal artery, to leave the case undisturbed for a day or two longer, but in the meantime to construct the necessary apparatus for the treatment.

> September 4—Tongue much swollen, patient still unable to articulate; communicates his wishes entirely by writing.

> September 5—Swelling somewhat subsided; no signs of hemorrhage; patient able to swallow milk and other liquid food with comparative ease; made wax impressions of upper teeth, and of each fragment separately of lower jaw.

> September 6—Patient still improving, yet no disposition to self-adjustment of the fragment; made proper measurements, and proceeded with the manufacture of the splint.

> September 8—Some small spicule of bone removed, and the position and condition of the fragment carefully examined. The surgical treatment being entrusted to Surgeons Bemiss and Lundy, but little notice was taken of the symptoms.

> September 10—Applied interdental splint, and found the displacement of the lower fragment so great, that the teeth could not be made to occupy their places in the splint. The fragment being quite movable, it was lifted and forced somewhat outwardly, and the tube of a syringe introduced between the bicuspids of the right side and the fracture. The wound

was then carefully but freely syringed with tepid water, in order to remove the debris that was supposed to be interposed between the apices of the fangs of the teeth and their respective positions in the lower fragment. By carefully introducing a curved instrument (an aneurism [sic] needle) between the bicuspids on the right, and another beyond the bicuspids on the left, the fragment was then lifted upward, pressed backward, and forced into position. The splint was then applied, the teeth forced into their places and the whole confined, by means of the mental compress and the occipito-frontal bandage. This operation caused some pain to the patient, but it was by no means severe.

September 11—Teeth are well adjusted in the splint and are in perfect position; patient quite easy, and able to imbibe liquid food with facility.

September 15—Swelling very much subsided; external wound healing.

September 20—Fragments in perfect position and not at all displaced, on the removal of the splint.

September 28—Patient left Macon.

November 1—The General called, and I find the fragment perfectly united and the patient able to use the teeth, these being quite firm; no deformity exists, and speech is but little impaired; external wound scarcely noticeable; artificial substitutes, for the lost teeth, will doubtless entirely restore the speech.

Monomaxillary Wiring, Bars, and Arches

There is some archeologic evidence that wiring teeth adjacent to the fracture site was used by Phoenicians, Egyptians, and Etruscans. The first written reference to monomaxillary wiring was by Hippocrates, who used both gold wire and thread.[4] After the Greeks, numerous authors advocated using wire ligatures to treat mandibular fractures, including Celsus,[7] Haly Abbas,[47] Bruno of Longbourg,[24] William of Saliceto,[11] Hieronymus Brunschwig,[48] Giovanni Vigo,[49] and Guy deChauliac.[50] Paré, in the seventeenth century, referred to the use of wires and ligatures in the treatment of mandibular fractures.[51] In the eighteenth and nineteenth centuries, little was added regarding wiring techniques, because it became apparent that monomaxillary wiring without supplemental fixation was unsatisfactory.

The first written record of the use of a monomaxillary wire splint was that of Hammond in 1873.[52] The splint was either constructed directly on the patient or adapted to a model and then wired to the teeth. The original Hammond splint was modified by Sauer (1881),[53] Kolmar (1886),[24] Martin (1887),[54] Crombie (1904),[55] Wassmund (1927),[24] and others. Various materials and tube fixtures were used, but the disadvantages remained the same, that is, mobility of fracture segments and lack of proper control of the occlusion.

Monomaxillary Splints

As dentistry became more sophisticated in the mid 1800s, dentists used more and more ingenuity in designing various types of splints to treat mandibular fractures. Muetter, in 1855, designed a silver clamp that fit over teeth adjacent to the fracture site.[24] White, in 1864, constructed a cast-silver splint on a model made after reduction of the fragments.[56] Moon, in 1874, was the first to wire a metal splint to the mandibular teeth.[57] Gilmer, in 1881, suggested the use of an open band splint made on a reconstructed model.[58] The occlusal surfaces of the teeth were not covered by metal. Martindale, in 1894, made a swedged-metal splint that was cemented on the teeth.[59] Thomas' splint (1893) consisted of two pieces of metal that fit on the lingual and buccal surfaces of the mandible, held in place by spikes that were driven into the mucosa and bone.[60] In general, over time, splints were usually cast of gold and clamps became more sophisticated, tying lingual and buccal components together.

The obvious fault with monomaxillary splints, of course, is that they function only in fractures in which teeth are present on either side of the fracture site. Edentulous patients or fractures proximal to the teeth cannot be readily treated by these splints.

Intermaxillary Wiring

Several authors give credit to William of Saliceto[12] as the first to use intermaxillary fixation, but others credit Gilmer (1887), an American, as the first to use the technique.[61] Gilmer passed wires around the individual maxillary and mandibular teeth and then joined the wires from the opposing arch. Gilmer's technique was modified by many authors, the most notable being Oliver,[62] Baker,[63] and Ivy.[64]

These techniques became popular in the late 1800s and early 1900s, but they tended to lack universal application. In cases involving loose, fractured, or missing teeth, the arches used by orthodontists offered advantages. The famous American orthodontist Angle described many methods of intermaxillary fixation using bands and other orthodontic techniques.[65]

Sauer, in 1889, adapted an iron wire to the teeth and attached it with fine ligature wires.[66] In 1901, Gilmer was apparently the first to use full arch wires on both the maxilla and the mandible.[67]

Rubbrecht (1916) placed orthodontic bands on two or more teeth on each side of the fracture, and an arch wire was soldered to the bands after reduction of the fracture.[68]

Ivy and Curtis (1926) discussed the use of half-round German silver arch bars attached to the maxillary and mandibular teeth and connected by the wires.[69] Prefabricated arch wires of 18-karat gold or nickel silver were introduced by Jelenko in 1927.[24]

Open Reduction and Internal Fixation Sutures

Early reports describing open reduction of mandibular fractures with wire internal fixation were presented by Buck in 1846[70] and Kinlock in 1859.[24] Buck used a simple loop of iron wire and Kinlock used a silver wire loop in the reduction of mandibular fractures. In 1869, Thomas presented two cases in which he used his method for open reduction of mandibular fractures.[71] The following excerpt is the second case, reprinted here to show the "state of the art" for open reduction in the mid 1800s. In regard to the last paragraph, we can presume Mr. Thomas was not trained in dentistry.

Thomas B————, a ship-carpenter, was struck by a piece of timber on the face, which threw him from the stage on which he worked, and he fell a depth of seventeen feet. On examining him an hour after the accident, there was found a fracture of the lower jaw on the right side, at the situation of the first and second molar teeth, which had been knocked out by the force of the blow. There was great mobility of the fractured part, more than I recollect seeing before in fractures in that situation. The remaining teeth were firmly in situ. Having had the inside of the mouth well exposed by drawing aside the cheek, my assistant kept the third molar tooth steady with a piece of wood directed across the mouth from the left side whilst a hole was drilled across the tooth from its front to its inner surface, this tooth holding firm in the posterior portion of the fracture. A strong silver wire was then passed through the hole and brought forward, passing it between the bicuspid and canine teeth; the ends were then drawn tight and twisted, making the fracture firm. The site was tightened every four days, and in three weeks there was moderate union; in four weeks it was sufficiently secure to allow the wire to be removed and the jaw used. This was the only treatment in the shape of mechanical appliance. An opiate was given every other night. This patient was also with difficulty restrained from using his jaw for masticating . . .

The passage of a fine drill in the situation described in the above cases does not appear to have endangered the teeth, care being taken to strike, if possible, the interspaces of their roots. The body of the tooth which was drilled in the second case was attended with but little discomfort to the patient, and which the skill of the dentist will probably make good again.

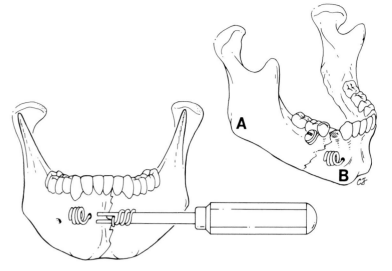

Figure 16–6. The Thomas principle (1869) presented a technique of intraoral open reduction with silver wire osteosynthesis. The spiral spring–like termination was tightened intermittently "until union was secured." *A*, proximal segment; *B*, distal segment.

The "Thomas principle," employing a wire through drill holes with a spiral spring–like termination that was tightened periodically, was used through the nineteenth century (Fig. 16–6). Other case reports of wire sutures were presented by Wheelhouse (1867),[24] Davis (1894),[72] Carter (1898),[73] and Cale (1892).[74] The general disregard for dentition is exemplified by Brophy's method of placing wire sutures.[6]

The incidence of infection and bone necrosis with wire sutures was high in the days before antibiotics, as demonstrated by this quote from Dorrance and Bransfield in 1941[34]:

> While at the present time some oral surgeons advocate the use of this method, the vast majority are in accord that infection invariably follows its use. When infection does occur the wire has to be removed and not infrequently a large part of the bone is lost through osteomyelitis. If wire suturing is attempted or if no other method appears available in a given case, it should be done in such a way that the mouth is not open.

Bone Plates

Gilmer (1881) described a method of mandibular fracture fixation using two heavy rods placed on either side of the fracture and wired together.[58] The rods were pushed through skin, bone, and mucous membrane and were wired on both the mouth and the skin sides. Dorrance and Bransfield state that the earliest reference to the use of true bone plates was that of Schede, who, around 1888, used a solid steel plate held by four screws.[34] During World War I, Kazanjian used wire sutures through bone fragments and tied the wire to an arch bar for fixation.[75]

Mahé (1900) used multiple plates to secure multiple mandibular fragments after applying a monomaxillary splint.[76] A similarity to the plating systems used at present can be noted.

Ivy (1915) illustrated the use of Sherman's steel plates but abandoned the method because of infection and necrosis.[77] Cole (1917) used silver plates and screws on each side of the fracture and then silver wires to the plates, to immobilize the fracture.[78] Vorschütz (1934) introduced two long screws through skin into bone, reduced the fracture, and held the screws in position by the use of a plaster of paris bandage (similar to the Joe Hall Morris appliance of today).[79]

Edentulous Mandibular Fractures

The history of treating fractures of edentulous jaws began with a report by Baudens (1844), who used circumferential wiring to reduce and fix the bone.[80]

Gunning used splints, as described previously.[43-45] Robert (1851) used silver wire passed circumferentially around the mandible with a needle and tied the wire around a piece of lead that had been molded to the edentulous mandible.[81] Gilmer (1881) describes a gutta-percha or vulcanite splint used by G.V. Black that was maintained by circumferential wires of silver or platinum.[58] Pickerill (1913) passed screws into the bone on either side of the fracture and maintained them with a connecting steel bar.[25] Circum-mandibular wiring to maintain a denture splint was described often by Ivy and Curtis in the early 1900s.[69,82,83]

STATISTICS ASSOCIATED WITH MANDIBULAR FRACTURES

Demographic data relating to mandibular fractures are difficult to evaluate because of the many variables associated with the studies. Statistics relating to mandibular fractures are available from countries throughout the world. However, most are retrospective. The studies discuss maxillofacial injuries generally, but some present data specifically relating to mandibular fractures. The information is as diverse as the countries and the people who inhabit them. Although much of the demographic information on maxillofacial injuries that appears in English-language journals comes from the United States,[84-95] England,[96,97] Germany,[98,99] the Netherlands,[100-101] and the Scandinavian countries.[102-106] Many of the other countries throughout the world are well represented. Examples are India,[107-109] Nigeria,[110,111] Kuwait,[112] France,[113,114] Libya,[115,116] Greece,[117,118] Turkey,[119] Jordan,[120] New Guinea,[121] South Africa,[122,123] New Zealand,[124] Greenland,[125] Korea,[126] Finland,[127] and Scotland.[128]

Data from industrialized nations with large numbers of vehicles tend to show multiple mandibular fractures occurring with severe concomitant facial fractures and associated nonmaxillofacial injuries, situations that require extensive treatment. Statistics from smaller Third World countries tend to show that mandibular fractures are usually isolated, single, nondisplaced fractures caused by assaults and treated only by intermaxillary fixation. A striking example relates to etiology; Thorn and colleagues[125] reported that 156 jaw fractures in Greenland (90 per cent) were due to interpersonal violence, whereas Adekeye,[111] in a study of facial fractures in Nigeria, reported that 76 per cent were related to vehicular accidents. Olson and associates[95] demonstrated vehicular accidents to be the cause of fractures in 48 per cent, whereas in the study of Ellis and coworkers,[128] vehicular accidents accounted for only 15 per cent of the fractures. Conversely, the study of Ellis and coworkers[128] showed the incidence of assaults to be 55 per cent, compared with 34 per cent in the study of Olson and associates.[95] The difference may be explained by the environmental and social characteristics of the locality under study. The study of Olson and associates[95] took place at the University of Iowa in a small, American, university-dominated city near a busy interstate highway. The surrounding area is primarily rural. Ellis and coworkers[128] derived their sample of patients from Canniesburn Hospital in Glasgow, Scotland. The city is an old, highly industrialized area with high unemployment and relatively high alcohol intake, where personal usage of automobiles is less common than in the United States.

Classification is also not standardized. Schuchardt and colleagues[99] placed 18 per cent of their fractures in the miscellaneous category. Bernstein and McClurg's study[84] included only two categories, vehicular and assault. Hagan and Huelke,[85] Rowe and Killey,[96] and Salem and coworkers[86] did not list work-related mandibular fractures. The definition of the assault category seems apparent, but in most studies vehicular accidents include those involving automobiles, bicycles, motorcycles, motor-assisted bicycles, passengers, and pedestrians.

Similar discrepancies exist with studies describing the location of mandibular fractures. Most authors refer to "regions." [96,99,102,113] Others define specific anatomic sites. Hagan and Huelke[85] limited the mandibular body to that area between the mental foramen and the second molar and were one of the few investigators to describe midline fractures. Schuchardt and colleagues[99] did not describe symphyseal fractures; instead, they defined all fractures anterior to the angle as body fractures. Kelly and Harrigan[87] limited the symphysis to the area of the incisors and included the canine area in the region of the body. Rowe and Killey,[96] Nordenram,[102] and Hedin, Ridell, and Söremark[103] regarded the canine area as an independent region. Chuong and associates[88] defined the angle as the distal aspect of the second molar to the "lowest point on the ramus," while Dingman and Natvig[89] defined the angle as bounded by the anterior border of the masseter muscle and by an oblique line extending from the third molar area to the posterosuperior attachment of the masseter muscle. The ramus, coronoid process, and alveolar process regions are often only partly discussed or completely omitted. Some authors do not anatomically define fracture areas or sites,[95,128] whereas Mallett[90] listed each fracture according to the individual teeth it involved or whether it was between teeth.

In spite of the many limitations associated with an analysis of data on mandibular fractures, it is interesting generally to compare and contrast studies presented in the English-speaking journals. Specific data related to mandibular fractures are presented in Tables 16–2 to 16–7. In studies of all types of facial fractures, data relating specifically to mandibular fractures were collected and included in the tables, where applicable. In an effort to make some generalizations regarding mandibular fractures, similar data from studies within industrialized countries were tabulated and means were established. The authors recognize the scientific limitations associated with such efforts.

TABLE 16–2. AGE AND SEX OF PATIENTS WITH MANDIBULAR FRACTURES

AUTHOR	APPROXIMATE AGE (%)								SEX (%)	
	0–10	11–20	21–30	31–40	41–50	51–60	61–70	71–80	M	F
Hagan, Huelke[85] (316 patients)	6	29	29	17	8	7	3	1	73	27
Melmed, Koonin[123] (889 patients)	6	17	35	22	13	4	3	—	80	20
Schuchardt et al[99] (1174 patients)	6	17	32	18	16	8	3	—	88	12
Olson et al[95] (580 patients)	3	26	42	14	7	5	3	—	78	22
Ellis et al[128] (2137 patients)	2	15	31	22	16	9	3	1	76	24
James et al[92] (253 patients)	6	25	43	12	12	—	3	—	70	30
Bernstein, McClurg[84] (156 patients)	3	28	36	11	14	6	2	—	75	25
Goldberg, Williams[91] (202 patients)	—	8	34	29	16	9	3	—	72	28
Larsen, Nielsen[106] (286 patients)	10	26	32	15	7	6	3	<1	73	27
Donaldson[124] (355 patients)	—	—	—	—	—	—	—	—	82	12
Nair, Paul[107] (313 patients)	2	18	36	22	11	8	2	>1	93	7
Taher[112] (526 patients)	3	2	53	25	13	4	—	—	95	5
Khan[122] (234 patients)	>1	3	48	20	11	14	—	—	81	19
Abiose[110] (104 patients)	4	18	47	20	12	2	1	—	85	15
Malden[121] (16 patients)	—	—	—	—	—	—	—	—	75	25

TABLE 16-3. ETIOLOGY OF MANDIBULAR FRACTURES (%)

AUTHOR	VEHICULAR	ASSAULTS	WORK	SPORTS	FALLS	MISCELLANEOUS
Freidel, Achard[114]	64	5	19	8	—	4
Hagan, Huelke[85]	56	17	—	3	10	14
Nordenram[102]	59	12	9	6	12	2
Rowe, Killey[96]	35	27	—	9	15	14
Schuchardt et al[99]	32	37	10	3	—	18
VanHoof et al[101]	66	8	13	9	—	4
Müller[101a]	28	33	28	8	—	3
Olson et al[95]	48	34	1	2	8	7
Ellis et al[128]	15	55	3	4	21	2
Salem et al[86]	26	44	—	6	12	12
James et al[92]	25	53	10	—	—	12
Larsen, Nielsen[106]	50	20	7	4	17	2
Bernstein, McClurg[84]	65	73	—	—	—	18
Adekeye[111]	76	13	8	1	—	2
Heimdahl, Nordenram[105]	18	63	2	3	13	1
Donaldson[124]	40	16	10	17	11	6
Nair, Paul[107]	40	25	1	—	24	11
Khan[122]	15	82	2	2	—	—
Abiose[110]	81	14	1	2	2	—
Thorn et al[125]	3	89	1	—	—	8
Spengos et al[118]	65	8	7	4	15	1
Zachariades et al[117]	57	8	8	4	—	23
Voss (1982)[104]	15	54	5	9	5	12

Sex

Unequivocally, most mandibular fractures occur in male subjects, in a ratio of approximately 3 : 1. Studies vary with a high of about 9 : 1 and a low of about 2 : 1. Although few authors address this problem, the reasons probably relate to the higher number of male drivers in the world and the higher number of assaults involving boys and men.

Age

The largest percentage (35 per cent) of mandibular fractures occur in individuals between the ages of 20 and 30. The age groups of 10 to 20 and 30 to 40 are next in frequency and are about equally divided, with percentages of approximately 20. After the age of 40, the incidence begins to decline, with 15 per cent of mandibular fractures occurring in those in the 40 to 50 age group and 3 per cent occurring after age 60. In the literature, only about 3 per cent of mandibular fractures occur in those under age 10. Women tend to sustain fractures between the ages of 30 and 40, whereas fractures in men occur between the ages of 20 and 30 years. It is interesting that in a study from Jordan, Karyouti[120] reported that the individuals most susceptible to facial fractures were those in the 0 to 5 age group. He believed this finding to be a reflection of a young society in which 51 per cent of the population is under age 14.

Etiology

In spite of the many variables associated with the etiology of mandibular fractures, there is no doubt that vehicular accidents and assaults are the primary causes of mandibular fractures throughout the world. The literature showed that 43 per cent

TABLE 16-4. LOCATION OF MANDIBULAR FRACTURES (%)

AUTHOR	SYMPHYSIS	BODY	ANGLE	RAMUS	CONDYLAR PROCESS	CORONOID PROCESS	ALVEOLAR PROCESS
Freidel, Achard[114]	29	12	18	4	26	2	9
Hagan, Huelke[85]	15	21	21	2	36	2	3
(319 patients, 576 fractures)							
Hedin et al[103]	17	21	20	1	41	—	—
(1517 fractures)							
Kelly, Harrigan[87]	7	36	35	<1	21	1	—
(3338 fractures)							
Melmed, Koonin[123]	7	40	31	3	17	2	—
(909 patients)							
Nakamura, Gross[94]	21	27	24	5	20	1	2
Nordenram[102]	34	15	13	—	38	—	—
Rowe, Killey[96]	20	25	18	—	37	—	—
(973 patients, 1447 fractures)							
VanHoof et al[101]	13	24	14	2	47	<1	—
(797 patients, 1256 fractures)							
Müller[101a]	—	41	26	3	28	—	2
(2582 fractures)							
Schuchardt et al[99]	—	52	20	4	24	—	—
(922 fractures)							
Olson et al[95]	22	16	25	2	29	1	3
(580 patients, 936 fractures)							
Ellis et al[128]	9	33	23	3	29	2	1
(2137 patients, 3124 fractures)							
Kapoor, Srivastava[109]	8	26	34	1	30	1	—
(299 patients, 495 fractures)							
Salem et al[86]	17	45	31	6	28	1	8
(523 patients, 803 fractures)							
James et al[92]	14	27	31	6	20	3	—
(253 patients, 422 fractures)							
Mallett[90]	24	22	31	9	13	1	—
(885 patients, 1194 fractures)							
Moore et al[93]	19	24	27	13	16	1	—
(56 patients, 100 fractures)							
Larsen, Nielsen[106]	23	14	17	2	37	1	6
(286 patients, 487 fractures)							
Bernstein, McClurg[84]	15	30	25	9	17	—	4
(156 patients, 234 fractures)							
Goldberg, Williams[91]	11	48	27	2	12	—	—
(202 patients, 305 fractures)							
Adekeye[111]	26	48	15	1	11	<1	—
(1106 patients, 1615 fractures)							
Heimdahl, Nordenram[105]	9	29	26	3	23	2	—
(91 patients, 136 fractures)							
Park et al[126]	43	6	22	4	18	<1	<1
(424 fractures)							
Donaldson[124]	3	45	11	3	33	—	5
(355 patients)							
Nair, Paul[107]	14	30	25 (angle + ramus)		17	—	14
(313 patients)							
Khan[122]	5	49	39	2	5	—	—
(234 patients)							
Abiose[110]	17	49	7 (angle + ramus)	—	8	—	2
(104 patients)							
Khalil, Shaladi[115]	15	30	21	3	21	—	10
(187 patients, 327 fractures)							
Sawhney, Ahuja[108]	33	20	24	1	22	—	—
(123 patients)							
Spengos et al[118]	12	28	10	6	30	1	3
(243 patients, 375 fractures)							
Güven[119]	20	34	25	1	10	—	—
(215 patients)							

TABLE 16-5. FACIAL FRACTURES ASSOCIATED
WITH MANDIBULAR FRACTURES (%)

Author	Mandible Alone	Mandible and Other Facial Fracture
Larsen, Nielsen[106]	77.6	22.3
Hedin et al[103]	84	6
VanHoof et al[101]	45	11
Müller[101a]	75	9
Rowe, Killey[96]	56	10
Schuchardt et al[99]	58	6
Adekeye[111]	62	14
Kelly, Harrigan[87]	39.8	37.6
Ellis et al[128]	82.8	17.2
Kapoor, Srivastava[109]	80.6	13
Salem et al[86]	83.2	16.8
Bernstein, McClurg[84]	82	18
Heimdahl, Nordenram[105]	86	72
Taher[112]	78	22
Khalil, Shaladi[115]	85	15
Karyouti[120]	66	44
Thorn et al[125]	99	1
Spengos et al[118]	77	23
Park et al[126]	84	16

of mandibular fractures were caused by vehicular accidents, 34 per cent were caused by assaults, 7 per cent were work related, 7 per cent occurred as a result of a fall, 4 per cent occurred in sporting accidents, and the remainder had miscellaneous causes. Dental and facial injuries incurred in sporting accidents were specially evaluated by Hill and colleagues[97]; of 130 patients, 31 per cent sustained a fractured mandible, and 26 per cent had dental and alveolar fractures. Sane and Ylipaavalniemi[127] studied 8640 accidents occurring in Finnish soccer players. They found that 6.4 per cent of the injuries occurred in the maxillofacial and dental regions. Of these, 81 per cent

TABLE 16-6. NUMBER OF FRACTURES PER MANDIBLE (%)

Author	Single Fracture	Multiple Fractures
Nakamura, Gross[94]	56.3	43.7
Moore et al[93]	39	61
Hagan, Huelke[85] (1.8 fractures/patient)	46.4	31.9(2 fractures), 19.5(3 fractures), 2.5(4 fractures), 0.6(6 fractures)
Adekeye[111]	57.3	39.6(2 fractures), 2.8(3 fractures), 0.3(4 fractures)
VanHoof et al[101] (1.58 fractures/patient)	57	43
Rowe, Killey[96]	59	30(2 fractures), 9(3 fractures), 0.4(4 fractures), 2.6(comminuted)
Ellis et al[128]	48.5	44.4(2 fractures), 7.1(3 or more fractures)
Kapoor, Srivastava[109]	54.5	30.76(2 fractures), 11.4(3 fractures), 3.34(comminuted)
Goldberg, Williams[91] (1.5 fractures/patient)	51	49
Salem et al[86]	55	38(2 fractures), 4(3 fractures), 3(4 or more fractures)
James et al[92] (1.8 fractures/patient)	42	45(2 fractures), 8.9(3 fractures), 2(4 fractures), 0.8(5 fractures), 0.8(6 fractures)
Mallett[90]	67	32(2 fractures), 1(multiple)
Bernstein, McClurg[84]	54(unilateral)	46(bilateral)
Park et al[126]	84	16

TABLE 16-7. NONMAXILLOFACIAL TRAUMA ASSOCIATED WITH MANDIBULAR FRACTURES (%)

Author and Fracture Type	Face, Head, and Neck Trauma	Skull	Cerebrospinal Injury	Other Fracture	Thorax	Abdomen	Other
	Soft Tissue Face Laceration						
VanHoof et al[101] 1420 facial bone 1256 mandible	33	—	49	17	4	1	4
Rowe, Killey[96] 1500 facial bone 999 mandible	40	3	3	11	—	—	5
Olson et al[95] 580 mandible	30	26	4	18	8	6	—
Ellis et al[128] 4711 facial bone 2137 mandible (90% had no other injuries)	—	0.75	—	4	1.36	0.05	1.36
	Head and Neck Injuries						
Park et al[126] 910 facial bone 229 mandible	59	—	—	22	11	2	6
Kapoor, Srivastava[109] 320 facial bone 299 mandible	46	—	—	40	8	6	—
Adekeye[111] 1447 facial bone 900 mandible	19	—	16	9	1	<1	2

affected the teeth or alveolar process and 11 per cent were fractures of the mandible and the middle third of the face. Linn and associates[100] reported on 319 patients treated for sporting accidents in the Netherlands, where 15 per cent sustained a fracture of the mandible and 5.5 per cent fractured the mandibular alveolar process or luxated teeth or both.

There are few studies on mandibular fractures caused by gunshot injuries in civilians. Khalil from Libya[115] reported on 18 patients, 8 of whom had mandibular fractures and soft tissue injuries. Three cases were related to fights, the others being accidental. Vaillant and Benoist[113] (in France) evaluated 14 cases of bullet wounds of the mandible. The age of the patient ranged between 6 and 68. Two children were victims of accidents, and the adults were either suicide or assault victims.

Location of Mandibular Fractures

In the cases evaluated for fracture location, mean percentages were as follows: body (29 per cent), condyle (26 per cent), angle (25 per cent), symphyses (17 per cent), ramus (4 per cent), and coronoid process (1 per cent). As discussed, the variables are enormous, but certainly, as a generalization, fractures occurring in the body, condyle, and angle do not differ much in incidence, and ramus and coronoid process fractures are rare.

Facial Fractures Associated with Mandibular Fractures

Mandibular fractures were the only facial bone fractures in an average of 70 per cent of the patients. The literature is generally divided between patients with mandibular and midface fractures and those with mandibular and "other facial bone" fractures. Of the patients reported, 15 per cent had another facial bone fracture along with the fractured mandible.

Number of Fractures per Mandible

Studies involving the number of fractures per mandible show remarkable consistency. There was a range of 1.5 to 1.8 mandibular fractures per patient. A mean of 53 per cent of the patients had unilateral fractures, 37 per cent of the patients had two fractures, and 9 per cent had three fractures; however, many authors simply reported "single," "double," "more than two," or "single and multiple," so statistical analysis is impossible. It can be said that approximately 50 per cent of the patients with mandibular fractures had more than one fracture.

Nonmaxillofacial Trauma Associated with Mandibular Fractures

The literature dealing with concomitant nonmaxillofacial injuries associated with mandibular fractures is difficult to interpret with the wide variation in reported injuries. In the study of Ellis and colleagues,[128] 90 per cent of the patients had no other injuries, probably because the etiology was primarily assault. Olson and colleagues[95] reported associated injuries in 46.6 per cent of all patients treated, most of whom were involved in vehicular accidents. VanHoof and coworkers[101] reported cerebrospinal injuries in 49 per cent of their cases, whereas Rowe and Killey[96] noted such injuries in only 3 per cent. Kapoor and Srivastava[109] noted other (nonfacial) fractures in 40 per cent of their cases, and Adekeye[111] found other fractures in 9 per cent of his cases.

CLASSIFICATION OF MANDIBULAR FRACTURES

Mandibular fractures have been classified in several ways, using terminology that has not been standardized. For example, the term *simple fracture* is defined by Assael and Tucker as ". . . a complete transection of the bone with minimal fragmentation of the fracture site."[129] Rowe and Killey define simple fractures as ". . . linear fractures which are not in communication with the exterior."[96] Kruger states that a simple fracture ". . . is one in which the overlying integument is intact. The bone has been broken completely but it is not exposed to air. It may or may not be displaced. It may be comminuted."[130] Whitestone and Raley define it as follows: ". . . the overlying mucosa is intact with no potential sources of direct communication."[131] Thus, certain authors emphasize linear, while others state that it can be comminuted and still others primarily emphasize intact overlying tissues.

For the sake of this discussion, the following fracture terms have been adapted from *Dorland's Medical Dictionary*[132]:

1. *Simple, or closed:* A fracture that does not produce a wound open to the external environment, whether it be through the skin, mucosa, or periodontal membrane

2. *Compound, or open:* A fracture in which an external wound, involving skin, mucosa, or periodontal membrane, communicates with the break in the bone

3. *Comminuted:* A fracture in which the bone is splintered or crushed

4. *Greenstick:* A fracture in which one side of the bone is broken, the other being bent

5. *Pathologic:* A fracture occurring from mild injury because of pre-existing bone disease

6. *Multiple:* A variety in which there are two or more lines of fracture on the same bone not communicating with one another

7. *Impacted:* A fracture in which one fragment is firmly driven into the other

8. *Atrophic:* A spontaneous fracture resulting from atrophy of the bone, as in edentulous mandibles

9. *Indirect:* A fracture at a point distant from the site of injury

10. *Complicated or complex:* A fracture in which there is considerable injury to the adjacent soft tissues or adjacent parts; may be simple or compound

Classification by Anatomic Region

Mandibular fractures are also classified by the anatomic areas of involvement. These are as follows: symphysis, body, angle, ramus, condylar process, coronoid process, and alveolar process. Dingman and Natvig[89] defined these regions as follows:

1. *Midline:* Fractures between central incisors
2. *Parasymphyseal:* Fractures occurring within the area of the symphysis
3. *Symphysis:* Bounded by vertical lines distal to the canine teeth
4. *Body:* From the distal symphysis to a line coinciding with the alveolar border of the masseter muscle (usually including the third molar)
5. *Angle:* Triangular region bounded by the anterior border of the masseter muscle to the posterosuperior attachment of the masseter muscle (usually distal to the third molar)
6. *Ramus:* Bounded by the superior aspect of the angle to two lines forming an apex at the sigmoid notch
7. *Condylar Process:* Area of the condylar process superior to the ramus region
8. *Coronoid Process:* Includes the coronoid process of the mandible superior to the ramus region
9. *Alveolar Process:* The region that would normally contain teeth

Kazanjian and Converse classified mandibular fractures by the presence or absence of serviceable teeth in relation to the line of fracture.[133] They felt their classification was helpful in determining treatment. Three classes were defined:

Class I: Teeth are present on both sides of the fracture line.
Class II: Teeth are present on only one side of the fracture line.
Class III: The patient is edentulous.

They believed that Class I fractures could be treated by a variety of techniques, using the teeth for monomaxillary or intermaxillary fixation. Class II fractures, usually involving the condyle-ramus angle or partially edentulous body of the mandible, require intermaxillary fixation. Class III fractures require prosthetic techniques or open reduction methods, or both, for stabilization.

Rowe and Killey divided mandibular fractures into two classes: (1) those not involving basal bone and (2) those involving basal bone.[96] The first class primarily comprised alveolar process fractures. The second class was divided into single unilateral, double unilateral, bilateral, and multiple.

Kruger classified mandibular fractures into simple, compound, and comminuted.[130]

Krüger and Schilli took into account many of the above classifications and developed four categories of mandibular fractures[134]:

I. Relation to the external environment
   A. Simple
   B. Compound

II. Types of fractures
   A. Incomplete

    B. Greenstick
    C. Complete
    D. Comminuted

III. Dentition of the jaw with reference to the use of splints
    A. Sufficiently dentulous jaw
    B. Edentulous or insufficiently dentulous jaw
    C. Primary and mixed dentition

IV. Localization
    A. Fractures of the symphysis region between the canines
    B. Fractures of the canine region
    C. Fractures of the body of the mandible between the canine and the angle of the mandible
    D. Fractures of the angle of the mandible in the third molar region
    E. Fractures of the mandibular ramus between the angle of the mandible and the sigmoid notch
    F. Fractures of the coronoid process
    G. Fractures of the condylar process

    An important classification of mandibular angle and body fractures relates to the direction of the fracture line and the effect of muscle action on the fracture fragments. Angle fractures may be classified as (1) vertically favorable or unfavorable and (2) horizontally favorable or unfavorable. Figures 16–7 through 16–10 demonstrate the various types.

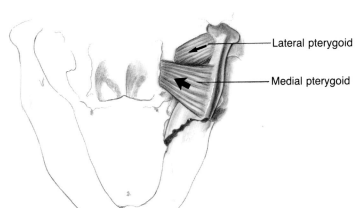

Lateral pterygoid

Medial pterygoid

FIGURE 16–7. Vertically favorable fracture.

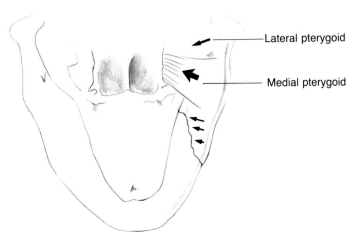

Lateral pterygoid

Medial pterygoid

FIGURE 16–8. Vertically unfavorable fracture.

FIGURE 16-9.   Horizontally favorable fracture.

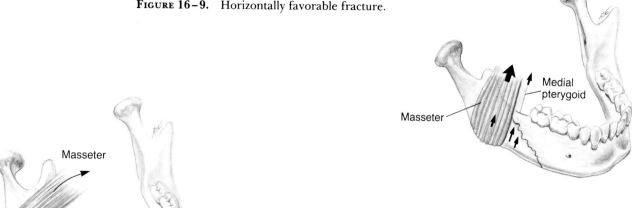

FIGURE 16-10.   Horizontally unfavorable fracture.

In fractures of the angle of the mandible, the muscles attached to the ramus (masseter, temporalis, and medial pterygoid) displace the proximal segment upward and medially when the fractures are vertically and horizontally *unfavorable* (Fig. 16-11). Conversely, these same muscles tend to impact the bone, minimizing displacement in horizontally and vertically *favorable* fractures. The farther forward the

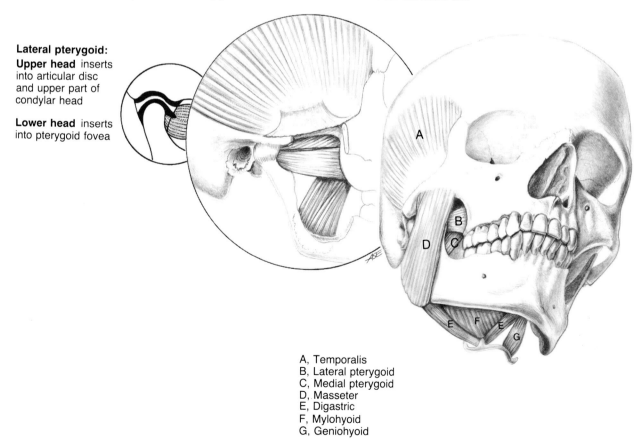

Lateral pterygoid:

Upper head inserts into articular disc and upper part of condylar head

Lower head inserts into pterygoid fovea

A, Temporalis
B, Lateral pterygoid
C, Medial pterygoid
D, Masseter
E, Digastric
F, Mylohyoid
G, Geniohyoid

FIGURE 16-11.   Muscles of mastication, which have a displacing influence on mandibular fractures.

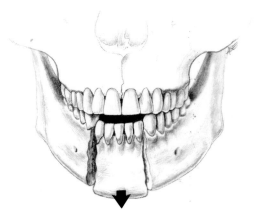

FIGURE 16-12. Inferior and posterior displacement of the symphysis of the mandible in bilateral fractures in the cuspid area.

fracture occurs in the body of the mandible, the more the upward displacement of those muscles is counteracted by the downward pull of the mylohyoid muscles. In bilateral fractures in the cuspid areas, the symphysis of the mandible is displaced inferiorly and posteriorly by the pull of the digastric, geniohyoid, and genioglossus muscles (Fig. 16-12).

Condylar fractures are generally classified as extracapsular, subcondylar, or intracapsular. Condylar fractures are influenced by location and muscle action. The external pterygoid muscle has a tendency to cause anterior and medial displacement of the condylar head, depending on the location, the severity of the fracture, and the effect of the supporting capsule (Fig. 16-13). In 1934, Wassmund described five types of condylar fractures.[24] Type I is defined as a fracture of the neck of the condyle with relatively slight displacement of the head. The angle between the head and the axis of the ramus varies from 10 to 45 degrees. He states that these fractures tend to reduce spontaneously. Type II fractures produce an angle from 45 to 90 degrees, resulting in tearing of the medial portion of the joint capsule. In type III, the fragments are not in contact, and the head is displaced mesially and forward owing to traction of the external pterygoid muscle. The fragments are generally confined

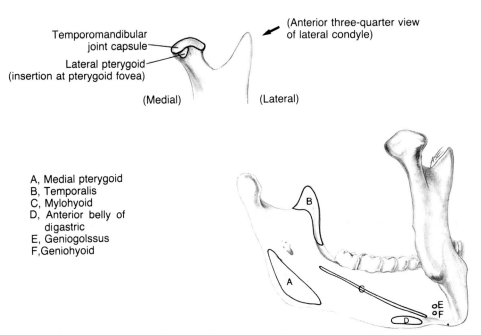

FIGURE 16-13. The external pterygoid muscle tends to cause anterior and medial displacement of the condylar head.

within the area of the glenoid fossa. The capsule is torn, and the head is outside the capsule. Wassmund recommended an open reduction for this fracture type. Type IV fractures of the condylar head articulate on or forward to the articular eminence. The type V group consisted of vertical or oblique fractures through the head of the condyle, and Wassmund suggested a bone graft to make a new condylar head of the fracture when considerable displacement of the fragments has occurred.[24]

DIAGNOSIS OF MANDIBULAR FRACTURES

History

A thorough history is imperative for the proper diagnosis of mandibular fractures. The patient's health history may reveal pre-existing systemic bone disease, neoplasia with potential metastases, arthritis and related collagen disorders, nutritional and metabolic disorders, and endocrine diseases that may cause or be directly related to the fractured jaw. The history will also reveal significant medical and psychiatric problems that will influence the management of the patient and perhaps even dictate treatment modalities.

A history of temporomandibular joint dysfunction can have significant legal and post-treatment ramifications. More than one clinician or radiologist has been led astray by not obtaining an adequate history of previous mandibular trauma or fracture.

The type and direction of traumatic force can be extremely helpful in diagnosis. Fractures sustained in vehicular accidents are usually far different from those sustained in personal altercations. Since the magnitude of the force can be much greater, automobile and motorcycle accident victims tend to have multiple, compound, comminuted mandibular fractures, whereas the patient hit by a fist may sustain single, simple, nondisplaced fractures.

The object used can also influence the type and number of fractures. A blow from a broad, blunt object (2 × 4 piece of wood) might cause several fractures (e.g., symphysis and condyle) because the impact area of force is sustained throughout the bone, whereas a smaller, well-defined object (hammer or pipe) may cause a single comminuted fracture, since the force is so concentrated.

Knowing the direction of force can help the clinician to diagnose concomitant fractures. An anterior blow directly to the chin can result in bilateral condylar fractures (Fig. 16–14), and an angled blow to the parasymphysis may cause a contralateral condylar or angle fracture. A patient with teeth clenched together at the moment of impact is more likely to have dental and alveolar process fractures than basal bone

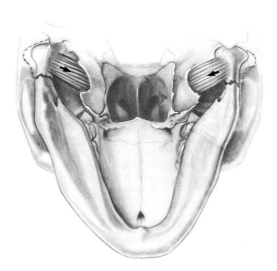

FIGURE 16–14. Trauma in the form of an anterior blow directly to the chin can cause bilateral condylar fractures.

fractures. Even knowing where the patient was sitting in an automobile may help in the diagnosis of mandibular or other injuries. Chest injuries caused by noncollapsible steering wheels, facial fractures caused by striking unpadded dashboards, and facial lacerations from nonsafety glass are only a few examples of predictable injuries that have been eliminated by the use of seat belts and by effective automotive safety engineering.[135,136]

Clinical Examination

The signs and symptoms of mandibular fractures are as follows.

CHANGE IN OCCLUSION

Any change in occlusion is highly suggestive of mandibular fracture. Patients should be asked if their bite feels different. A change in occlusion can result from fractured teeth, fractured alveolar process, fractured mandible at any location, and trauma to the temporomandibular joint and muscles of mastication. Post-traumatic premature posterior dental contact or anterior open bite may result from bilateral mandibular condylar or angle fractures (Fig. 16–15) as well as from maxillary fractures with inferior displacement of the posterior maxilla. Posterior open bite may occur with anterior alveolar process or parasymphyseal fractures. Unilateral open bite may occur owing to ipsilateral angle and parasymphyseal fractures (Fig. 16–16). Posterior crossbite can result from midline symphyseal and condylar fractures with splaying of the posterior mandibular segments.

Retrognathic occlusion is associated with condylar or angle fractures (as well as forward displaced maxillary fractures), and prognathic occlusion can occur with effusion of the temporomandibular joints, with protective forward posturing of the mandible (also retropositioning of the maxilla). These are only a few of the multiple occlusal disharmonies that can exist, but any change in occlusion has to be considered the primary diagnostic sign of mandibular fracture.

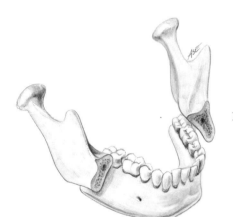

FIGURE 16–15.   Bilateral angle fractures can cause an open bite.

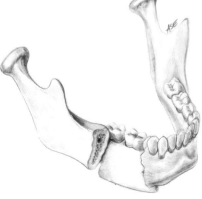

FIGURE 16–16.   Unilateral open bite may be the result of ipsilateral angle and parasymphyseal fractures.

ANESTHESIA, PARESTHESIA, OR DYSESTHESIA OF THE LOWER LIP

Although changes in sensation in the lower lip and chin may be related to chin and lip lacerations as well as blunt trauma, numbness in the distribution of the inferior alveolar nerve after trauma is almost pathognomonic of a fracture distal to the mandibular foramen. Conversely, most nondisplaced fractures of the mandibular angle, body, and symphysis will not be characterized by anesthesia, so the clinician must not use lip anesthesia as the sole feature in diagnosis.

ABNORMAL MANDIBULAR MOVEMENTS

Most patients presenting with a fractured mandible will have limited opening and trismus owing to guarding of the muscle of mastication. There are, however, certain mandibular fractures or associated facial fractures that will result in predictable abnormal mandibular movements. A classic example is deviation on opening toward the side of a mandibular condylar fracture. Because lateral pterygoid muscle function on the unaffected side is not counteracted on the opposite side by the nonfunctioning lateral pterygoid muscle, deviation results. Inability to open the mandible may be caused by the impingement of the coronoid process on the zygomatic arch either from fractures of the ramus and coronoid process or from depression of a zygomatic arch fracture. Inability to close the jaw can be the result of fractures of the alveolar process, angle, ramus, or symphysis, causing premature dental contact. Lateral mandibular movements may be inhibited by bilateral condylar fractures and fractures of the ramus with bone displacement.

CHANGE IN FACIAL CONTOUR AND MANDIBULAR ARCH FORM

Although facial contour may be masked by swelling, the clinician should examine the face and mandible for abnormal contours. A flattened appearance of the lateral aspect of the face may be the result of a fractured body angle or ramus. A deficient mandibular angle can occur with unfavorable angle fractures in which the proximal fragment rotates superiorly. A retruded chin can be caused by bilateral parasymphyseal fractures. The appearance of an elongated face may be the result of bilateral subcondylar, angle, or body fractures, allowing the anterior mandible to be displaced downward. Facial asymmetry should alert the clinician to the possibility of mandibular fracture. The same holds true for mandibular arch form. If there is a deviation from the normal U-shaped curve of the mandible, fracture should be suspected.

LACERATIONS, HEMATOMA, AND ECCHYMOSIS

Trauma significant enough to cause loss of skin or mucosal continuity or subcutaneous-submucosal bleeding certainly can result in trauma to the underlying mandible. Lacerations should be carefully inspected prior to closure. The direction and type of fracture may be visualized directly through the laceration, thus gaining diagnostic information that may be impossible to ascertain clinically or radiographically. The common practice of closing facial lacerations before treating underlying fractures should be discouraged from both a diagnostic and a treatment standpoint. The diagnostic sign of ecchymosis in the floor of the mouth indicates mandibular body or symphyseal fracture (Fig. 16–17).

LOOSE TEETH AND CREPITATION ON PALPATION

A thorough examination of the teeth and supporting bone can help to diagnose alveolar process, body, and symphyseal fractures. A force strong enough to loosen

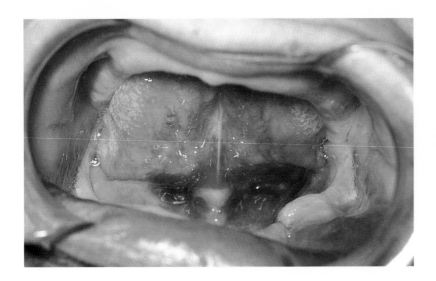

FIGURE 16–17. Ecchymosis in the floor of the mouth is a significant diagnostic sign of mandibular body or symphyseal fracture.

teeth certainly can fracture the underlying bone. Multiple fractured teeth that are firm indicate that the jaws were clenched during traumatic insult, thus lessening the effect on the supporting bone. The mandible should be palpated using both hands, with the thumb on the teeth and the fingers on the lower border of the mandible. By slowly and carefully placing pressure between the two hands, crepitation can be noted in a fracture. Too often, this simple diagnostic technique will be overlooked in favor of extensive (and expensive) radiographic diagnostic methods.

DOLOR, TUMOR, RUBOR, AND COLOR

Pain, swelling, redness, and localized heat have been noted as signs of inflammation since the time of the ancient Greeks. All of these are excellent primary signs of trauma and can greatly increase the index of suspicion for mandibular fracture.

Radiographic Examination

The following are types of radiographs that are helpful in the diagnosis of mandibular fractures:

1. Panoramic
2. Lateral oblique
3. Posteroanterior
4. Occlusal
5. Periapical
6. Reverse Townes
7. Temporomandibular joint, including tomograms
8. Computerized tomography (CT) scan

The single most informative radiograph used in diagnosing mandibular fractures is the panoramic type, showing the entire mandible, including condyles (Fig. 16–18).[137] The advantages are simplicity of technique, the ability to visualize the entire mandible in one radiograph, and the generally good detail. The disadvantages are as follows: The technique usually requires the patient to be upright (machines that allow the patient to be prone are available), which may make it impractical in the severely traumatized patient; it is difficult to appreciate buccal-lingual bone displacement or medial condylar displacement; and fine detail is lacking in the temporomandibular joint area, the symphysis region (depending on type of equipment), and the dental and

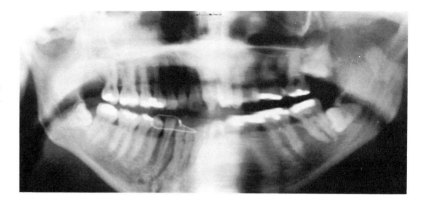

FIGURE 16–18. Panoramic radiograph, the single most informative radiograph in diagnosis of mandibular fractures.

alveolar process region. A secondary but important disadvantage is that panoramic radiographic equipment is not present in all hospital radiology facilities.

The lateral oblique view of the mandible can be of help in the diagnosis of ramus, angle, and posterior body fractures (Fig. 16–19). The technique is simple and can be done in any radiology department. The condyle region is often unclear, as is the bicuspid and symphysis region. The Caldwell posteroanterior view demonstrates any medial or lateral displacement of fractures of the ramus, angle, body, and symphysis (Fig. 16–20). The condylar region is not well demonstrated on this view, but midline or symphyseal fractures can be well visualized. The anteroposterior view is occasionally used for patients who cannot be positioned in the supine position; however, there is considerable magnification and distortion. The mandibular occlusal view demonstrates discrepancies in the medial and lateral position of body fractures and also shows anteroposterior displacement in the symphysis region (Fig. 16–21). The reverse Townes view is ideal for showing medial displacement of condyle and condylar neck fractures (Fig. 16–22). Transcranial lateral views of the temporomandibular joint are helpful in detecting condylar fractures and anterior displacement of the condylar head. Periapical dental films show the most detail and can be used for nondisplaced linear fractures of the body as well as alveolar process and dental trauma. Plain tomograms can be used in an anteroposterior and lateral direction when greater detail is necessary. The CT scan is ideal for condylar fractures that are difficult to visualize; however, greater expense and radiation exposure limit its use to those cases that cannot be diagnosed with plain films and panoramic tomography (Fig. 16–23).[138]

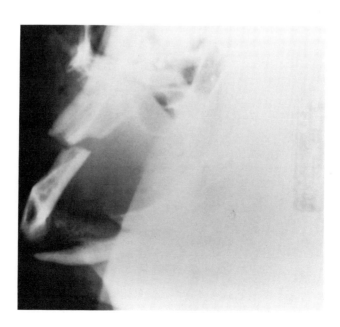

FIGURE 16–19. The lateral oblique view of the mandible is helpful in diagnosing ramus, angle, and posterior body fractures.

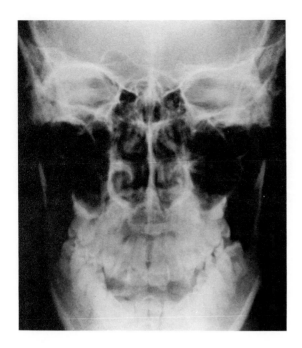

FIGURE 16–20.   The Caldwell posteroanterior view shows medial or lateral displacement of fractures of the ramus, angle, body, and symphysis.

FIGURE 16–21.   With the mandibular occlusal view, discrepancies in the medial and lateral positions of body fractures and anteroposterior displacement of the symphysis can be shown.

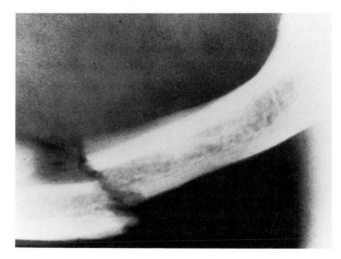

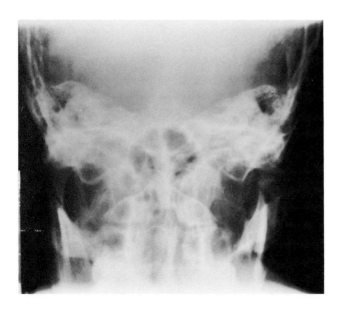

FIGURE 16–22.   The reverse Towne view is most helpful for showing medial displacement of the condyle and condylar neck fractures.

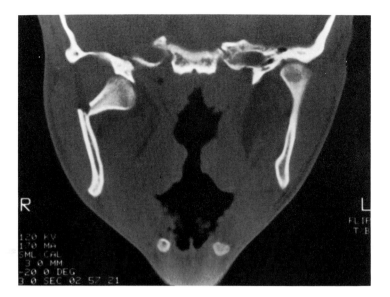

FIGURE 16–23. Computerized tomographic (CT) scan is ideal for condylar fractures.

In summary, as with most other imaging procedures, it is usually optimal to have views of the mandible in two planes oriented at 90 degrees to each another. Ideal imaging includes sections in axial and coronal planes; however, practical considerations of time, the patient's condition, and cost mandate selectivity. Thus, the history, the physical examination, and an understanding of what structures will be best shown by certain images dictate the proper radiographic techniques.[139,140]

GENERAL PRINCIPLES IN THE TREATMENT OF MANDIBULAR FRACTURES

Throughout this book, specific chapters have been devoted to preoperative, operative, and postoperative treatment of facial fractures. The purpose of this section is to present *general* principles used in the management of mandibular fractures.

1. *The patient's general physical status should be carefully evaluated and monitored prior to any consideration of treating mandibular fractures.*

It must be emphasized that any force great enough to cause a fractured mandible is capable of injuring any other organ system in the body. This is obvious when dealing with massive "crush" injuries of the face with concomitant multiple organ system involvement. However, it is all too easy for the clinician to focus on an obvious isolated mandibular fracture without noting a fractured cervical spine, subdural hematoma, pneumothorax, cardiac tamponade, or ruptured spleen. The downward spiral to disaster can begin by not following this principle.

The literature is replete with case reports of isolated fractures of the mandible in which life-threatening medical conditions become apparent after treatment was instituted. Post-traumatic thrombotic occlusion of the internal carotid artery associated with mandibular fractures (and no other apparent injuries) was diagnosed 24 hours after the injury in one case and 9 hours after in another.[141] Banna also reported a case and reviewed the literature on post-traumatic thrombotic occlusion of the internal carotid artery after minimal neck trauma.[142] Basal skull fracture associated with an undisplaced body fracture of the mandible became apparent 48 hours after the injury.[143] Gordon and colleagues described a patient with a unilateral body fracture of the mandible who developed symptoms of a ruptured spleen 5 days after the injury and 3 days after arch bars had been placed.[144] Bertolami and Kaban reported on a case of a 20-year-old woman involved in an automobile accident who sustained a 3-cm chin laceration without malocclusion or limitation of mandibular movement.[145] After 8 hours, radiographs were reviewed and showed a nondisplaced fracture of the angle of the mandible and a fracture of the second cervical vertebra. Minton and Tu noted a case of bilateral cervical subcutaneous emphysema, pneumothorax, and pneumomediastinum secondary to a bilateral fractured mandible without other apparent injuries.[146]

2. *Diagnosis and treatment of mandibular fractures should be approached methodically, not with an "emergency-type" mentality.*

Patients rarely die of mandibular fractures, so there is time to evaluate carefully and thoroughly the nature and extent of mandibular injuries. Diagnosis on the basis of history and local physical and radiographic examination should be expedited in an orderly, efficient manner, and treatment should be instituted in a controlled environment and fashion. This is not, however, to condone prolonged, unnecessary delay, which can increase the potential for infection and nonunion.

3. *Dental injuries should be evaluated and treated concurrently with treatment of mandibular fractures.*

Teeth are often injured with mandibular fractures, and although the teeth might not have to be restored immediately, dental knowledge is vitally important in determining which teeth can and should be maintained. (a) Fractured teeth can become infected and jeopardize bone union; however, an intact tooth in the line of fracture that is maintaining bone fragments can be protected with antibiotic coverage (Fig. 16–24A and B). (b) A second molar on an otherwise edentulous posterior fracture segment should be maintained to prevent superior displacement of the fragment in intermaxillary fixation. (c) Mandibular cuspids are the cornerstone of occlusion and

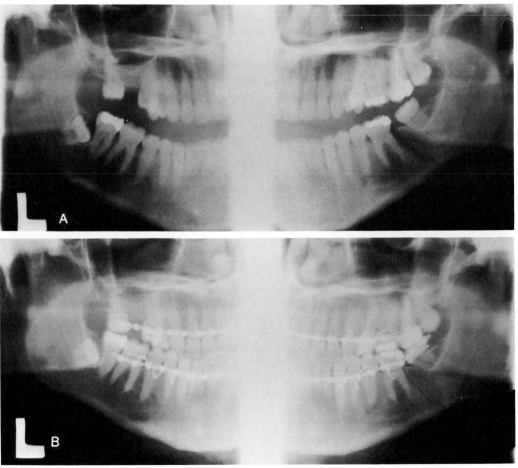

FIGURE 16–24. *A* and *B*, An intact tooth in the line of fracture can be maintained to prevent displacement of the segment.

should be maintained at all costs. (d) Some teeth are not critical to restoration and can be removed when their prognosis is doubtful and when maintenance might adversely affect fracture treatment. For example, a lone mandibular incisor adds little to future bridge or partial denture construction; however, a single molar tooth in an otherwise edentulous posterior quadrant can be critical to dental rehabilitation. (e) Some fractured teeth cannot be salvaged no matter how critical they might be. For example, a molar tooth might be split mesially and distally, so that reconstruction would be impossible. Maintenance of this tooth during intermaxillary fixation may result in severe discomfort and perhaps infection.

4. *Re-establishment of occlusion is the primary goal in the treatment of mandibular fractures.*

Probably because of an excellent blood supply, nonunion of the mandible is rare, so it is apparent that bone fragments do not have to be in tight approximation to heal. In addition, facial aesthetics in most cases will not be adversely affected by slight fragment displacement. However, function can be seriously compromised when improper treatment results in malocclusion. Impressive-appearing radiographic bone adaptation should not be the primary treatment goal.

5. *With multiple facial fractures, mandibular fractures should be treated first.*

The old adage "inside out and from bottom to top" applies to the proper sequence to follow when treating facial fractures. To build a foundation upon which the facial bones can be laid, it is proper that the mandible be reconstructed first, although with the use of rigid fixation, deviation from this principle can be allowed. All intraoral surgery should be done prior to any extraoral open reductions or suturing of facial lacerations. Too often, lip and skin wounds that have been meticulously closed in an emergency room are inadvertently, or even necessarily, reopened during the treatment of mandibular fractures. Gross debridement and control of hemorrhage should be combined with temporary measures to reapproximate extraoral wounds, thus allowing definitive treatment to be carried out after the intraoral procedures are completed.

6. *Intermaxillary fixation time should vary according to the type, location, number, and severity of the mandibular fractures as well as the patient's age and health and the method used for reduction and immobilization.*

Historically, a period of 6 weeks of intermaxillary fixation has been used to allow healing to occur. However, this time is only empiric and should vary with the patient and clinical situation.[147] A simple, nondisplaced greenstick mandibular fracture occurring in a healthy child would certainly require less intermaxillary fixation time than multiple, grossly comminuted, compound mandibular fractures occurring in an elderly, unhealthy patient.[148] With the advent of rigid fixation techniques, intermaxillary fixation might be eliminated or maintained with light elastics for short periods.

7. *Prophylactic antibiotics should be used for compound fractures.*

There are ample studies in the literature that demonstrate the advantages of antibiotics in the management of compound mandibular fractures, and in spite of the number of new antibiotics, penicillin still remains the agent of choice.[106,149,150]

8. *Nutritional needs should be closely monitored postoperatively.*

Excellent reduction and fixation techniques may fail in a patient with significant weight loss and a catabolic nutritional status.

9. *Most mandibular fractures can be treated by closed reduction.*

With the current enthusiasm for open reduction and rigid fixation in the treatment of mandibular fractures, it is important to remember that closed reduction techniques have a long history of success.[151] Although open techniques have advantages, such as more exacting bone fragment reapproximation and earlier return to function by the patient, there are significant disadvantages as well. They may subject the patient to prolonged anesthesia, may increase the risk of infection and metal rejection, may cause damage to adjacent teeth and nerves, may result in intraoral or extraoral scarring, and may increase hospitalization time and cost. The following sections present relative indications for open or closed techniques.

Indications for Closed Reduction

NONDISPLACED FAVORABLE FRACTURES (FIG. 16–25)

The simplest means possible should be used to reduce and fixate mandibular fractures. For the reasons specified previously, open reduction can carry an increased risk of morbidity, so, if possible, closed techniques should be used for treatment.

GROSSLY COMMINUTED FRACTURES (FIG. 16–26A and B)

Because of the excellent blood supply to the face, small fragments of bones will coalesce and heal if the associated periosteum is not disturbed. Comminuted fractures should be managed as a "bag of bones," utilizing closed techniques to establish normal occlusion without violating the integrity of the vascular supply to the bone fragments.

FRACTURES EXPOSED BY SIGNIFICANT LOSS OF OVERLYING SOFT TISSUES

Fracture repair is somewhat dependent upon soft tissue coverage and vascular supply. Soft tissue coverage should be established by rotational flaps, microvascular grafts, or (if the area is small) secondary granulation. Wires, screws, and plates may decrease the chance of successful bone union by further disrupting the covering soft tissue.

EDENTULOUS MANDIBULAR FRACTURES (FIG. 16–27A to C)

These fractures present a special challenge because the inferior alveolar vascular supply to the bone is severely compromised, there is little cancellous bone (with associated osteoblastic endosteum) for repair, and the fractures usually occur in the elderly, in whom the normal healing potential can be retarded. Open reduction requires stripping of the covering periosteum, further inhibiting osteogenesis. Closed reduction using a mandibular prosthesis held in place by circum-mandibular wires offers a more conservative approach. If delayed healing or nonunion occurs and open reduction is necessary, a supplemental bone graft across the fracture site should be considered. In severely atrophic edentulous ridges, open reduction with primary bone grafting may be indicated, since proper alignment of the fractured ends of bone may be impossible because of the small cross-sectional diameter of the mandibular body.

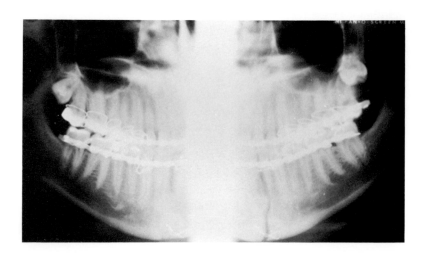

FIGURE 16–25. A nondisplaced favorable fracture.

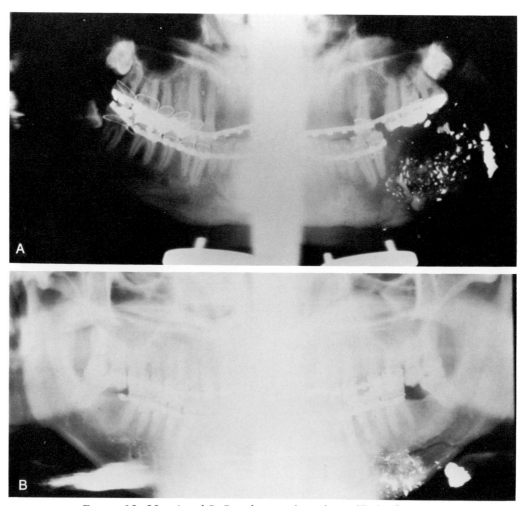

FIGURE 16–26. *A* and *B*, Grossly comminuted mandibular fractures.

MANDIBULAR FRACTURES IN CHILDREN WITH DEVELOPING DENTITIONS (FIG. 16–28*A* and *B*)

Open reduction with wires or plates carries a risk of damage to the developing tooth buds, which occupy a major portion of the mandible in children. If open reduction is necessary because of gross displacement of the fragments, fine wires should be placed at the most inferior border of the mandible, engaging only the cortex. Closed reduction is indicated with special wiring techniques (continuous loop) or fabricated acrylic splints maintained by circum-mandibular wiring. A special concern in children is fractures of the mandibular condyle. Damage to the condylar growth center can result in retarded growth of the mandible and facial asymmetry. Intracapsular condylar fractures in children can also lead to ankylosis of the joint, so early mobilization (after 7 to 10 days of intermaxillary fixation) is indicated.

CORONOID PROCESS FRACTURES

Fractures of the coronoid process are rarely isolated and are usually simple and linear with little displacement, although with extreme trauma the bone may be displaced into the temporal fossa. Isolated fractures of the coronoid process will cause trismus and swelling in the region of the zygomatic arch. There may be swelling in the retromolar area and a lateral crossbite. Treatment is usually instituted only if the occlusion is compromised or if the fractured coronoid process impinges on the zygomatic arch, inhibiting mandibular movement.[152]

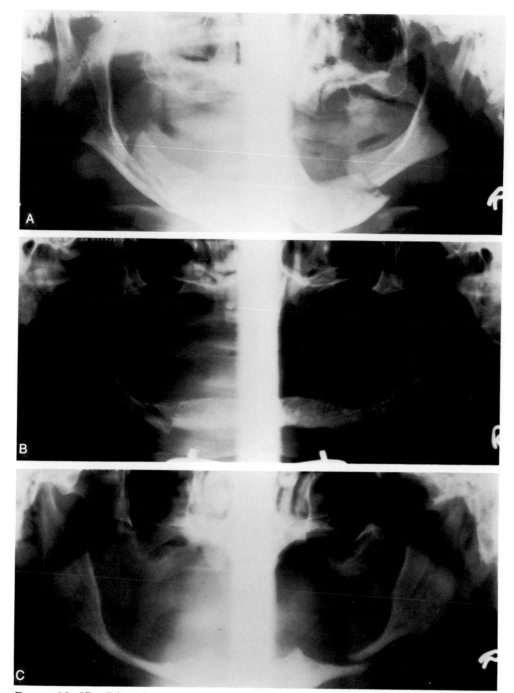

FIGURE 16–27. Edentulous mandibular fractures.   *A*, Minimal atrophy. *B*, Moderate atrophy. *C*, Severe atrophy.

CONDYLAR FRACTURES (FIG. 16–29)

Most condylar fractures can and should be treated via closed techniques if the occlusion is compromised. Early jaw mobilization and physical therapy are indicated to prevent ankylosis or limited jaw movements. This subject is covered in detail in Chapter 17.

FIGURE 16–28. *A*, A mandibular fracture in a child with a developing dentition. *B*, Treatment with closed reduction and lingual splint.

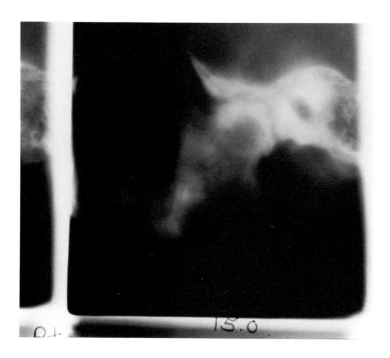

FIGURE 16–29. Condylar fractures can result in ankylosis if improperly treated or untreated.

Indications for Open Reduction

DISPLACED UNFAVORABLE FRACTURES THROUGH THE ANGLE OF THE MANDIBLE

Open reduction is indicated for this fracture when the proximal fragment is displaced superiorly or medially and reduction cannot be maintained without intraosseous wires, screws, or plating (Fig. 16–30A and B).

DISPLACED UNFAVORABLE FRACTURES OF THE BODY OR THE PARASYMPHYSEAL REGION OF THE MANDIBLE (FIG. 16–31A and B)

The mylohyoid, digastric, geniohyoid, and genioglossus muscles may further displace the fragments. When treated by a closed reduction, parasymphyseal fractures tend to open at the inferior border, with the superior aspects of the mandibular segments rotating medially at the point of fixation. With medial rotation of the body of the mandible, the lingual cusps of all premolars and molars move out of occlusal contact. If the constriction is not corrected, masticatory inefficiency and negative periodontal changes occur.[153]

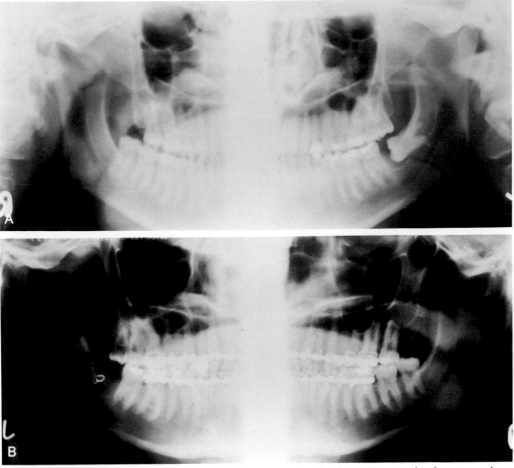

FIGURE 16–30. *A* and *B*, An indication for an open reduction. The proximal segment is minimally displaced superiorly, a third molar is in the proximal segment, and reduction cannot be maintained without intraosseous wires, screws, or plating.

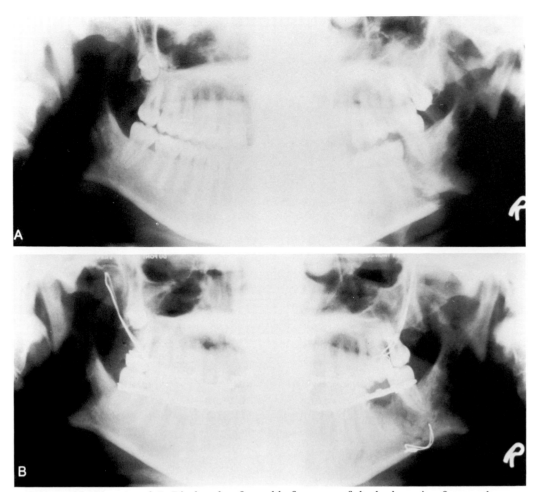

FIGURE 16-31. *A* and *B*, Displaced unfavorable fractures of the body region frequently require open reduction.

MULTIPLE FRACTURES OF THE FACIAL BONES

In multiple fractures of the facial bones, open fixation of the mandibular segments provides a stable base for restoration.

MIDFACE FRACTURES AND DISPLACED BILATERAL CONDYLAR FRACTURES

With midface fractures and displaced bilateral condylar fractures, one of the condylar fractures should be opened to establish the vertical dimension of the face. If this is not done, any type of suspension wiring, such as that from the frontozygomatic suture area to the mandible, would tend to collapse and telescope the fractures of the midface and condyles, resulting in a foreshortened facial appearance.

FRACTURES OF AN EDENTULOUS MANDIBLE WITH SEVERE DISPLACEMENT OF THE FRACTURE FRAGMENTS

In fractures of an edentulous mandible with severe displacement of the fracture fragments, open reduction should be considered to re-establish continuity of the mandible (Fig. 16-32). The technique is especially helpful with a nonatrophic mandible when there are *no dentures,* so that the occlusion is not an immediate concern. In this situation, plating of the mandible without intermaxillary fixation should be a

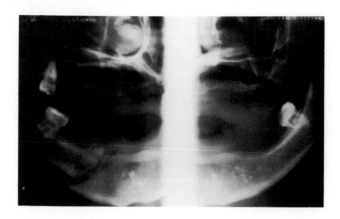

FIGURE 16–32. Edentulous or partially edentulous mandibles that are not atrophic but are severely displaced should be opened.

strong possibility. As the mandible becomes extremely atrophic, consideration must be given to the amount of blood supply to the bone and the effect of an open surgical procedure on the compromised vascularity. Supplemental bone grafts have to be considered in extremely atrophic mandibular fractures.

EDENTULOUS MAXILLA OPPOSING A MANDIBULAR FRACTURE

When a maxilla opposing a mandibular fracture is edentulous or contains insufficient teeth to allow intermaxillary fixation, open reduction should be considered. Open reduction with rigid fixation of the mandibular fractures would eliminate the need for intermaxillary fixation. However, if the patient's condition warrants closed reduction, a prosthesis could be constructed for the maxilla, it could be stabilized with palatal screws or circumzygomatic wires, and routine intermaxillary fixation could be utilized to treat the fractured mandible.

DELAY OF TREATMENT AND INTERPOSITION OF SOFT TISSUE BETWEEN NONCONTACTING DISPLACED FRACTURE FRAGMENTS

When treatment has been delayed and soft tissue becomes interposed between noncontacting displaced fracture fragments, open reduction should be utilized. There are instances in which the treatment of mandibular fractures is delayed because of head injury or other serious medical problems, so that with time connective tissue grows between the bone fragments, inhibiting osteogenesis. When treatment is finally instituted, scar tissue must be removed and treatment completed via an open approach.

MALUNION

When a poor result is obtained after mandibular fracture treatment, various types of osteotomies will have to be done via open surgical approaches to correct the deficiencies.

SPECIAL SYSTEMIC CONDITIONS CONTRAINDICATING INTERMAXILLARY FIXATION

There are situations in which mandibular functional movement is necessary, and open rigid fixation techniques can provide that option. For example, patients with difficult-to-control seizures, psychiatric or neurologic problems, compromised pulmonary functions, and eating or gastrointestinal disorders could benefit from open rigid fixation techniques.

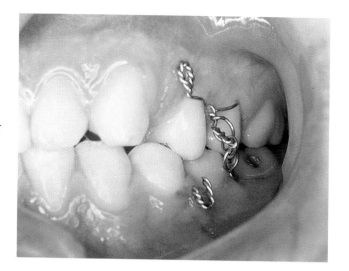

FIGURE 16–33. Ivy loops are effective for certain types of fractures.

Treatment of Mandibular Fractures

Literally hundreds of techniques are available to treat mandibular fractures, as outlined in the section on history. However, state-of-the-art treatment methods are currently limited and well defined.

TECHNIQUES FOR CLOSED REDUCTION AND FIXATION OF DENTULOUS MAXILLA AND MANDIBLE

The Erich arch bar and, occasionally, eyelet (Ivy loops) and continuous loop (Stout) wiring are used for intermaxillary fixation (Figs. 16–33 and 16–34). Advantages of the arch bar are availability, low cost, ease of adaptation and application, and applicability in a dental arch with occasional missing teeth. A disadvantage of the arch bar is that it tends to rest on the gingiva and can result in periodontal inflammation. In addition, the arch bar cannot be easily used to span long edentulous spaces without incorporation of an acrylic-type prosthesis in the edentulous space. The Ivy loop and Stout wire techniques are less damaging to the periodontium, and wire is always readily available. However, these wiring techniques are time consuming, and the wire can fatigue and break when tightened during weeks of intermaxillary fixation. Re-

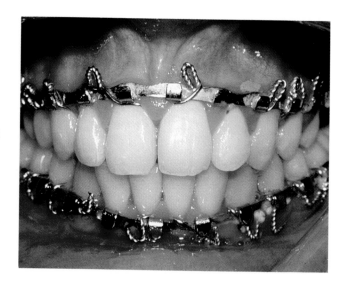

FIGURE 16–34. Arch bars are versatile and frequently used in the treatment of mandibular fractures.

placement necessitates opening the fractured mandible and reapplying the entire wire. Conversely, with an arch bar, a broken wire around one tooth can be easily removed, and interarch fixation can be maintained without replacing the wire.

Wires used for intermaxillary fixation techniques can orthodontically move teeth, so precautions have to be taken, especially when wiring the maxillary and mandibular incisors. Finer wire can be used for these teeth, or the clinician may choose not to incorporate the incisors with the arch bar wiring in totally dentulous patients. Fortunately, if the teeth are inadvertently moved, they tend to move back to their original position when the wires are removed, but this may not always occur.

TREATMENT OF PARTIALLY EDENTULOUS MANDIBLE

If the patient is partially edentulous, a pre-existing partial denture can be wired to either jaw using circum-mandibular or circumzygomatic wiring techniques. If no prosthesis is available, impressions can be taken, and acrylic blocks can be fabricated, incorporated with an arch wire, and applied to the remaining teeth. The acrylic prosthesis is wired to the mandible with circum-mandibular wires.

TREATMENT OF EDENTULOUS MANDIBLE

If the patient is completely edentulous, dentures can be wired to the jaws using circum-mandibular and circumzygomatic wires, or, in the case of a maxillary denture, a palatal screw fixation can be placed to hold the denture (Fig. 16–35). If dentures are not available, impressions are taken of the jaws, and acrylic base plates are processed and used as dentures. An arch bar can also be processed into the dentures, or holes can be placed into the flange of the denture for intermaxillary wires. Prosthetic incisor teeth can be removed for existing dentures, and space can be made in the acrylic to allow food intake (Gunning splint) (Figs. 16–36 to 16–38).

In treating concurrent fractures of the mandible and maxilla in edentulous patients, secondary wires from the circumzygomatic wire holding the upper denture in place to the circum-mandibular wires should always be used to prevent upward telescoping of the maxilla when tightening the intermaxillary fixation. If the circumzygomatic wires are inappropriately tightened, impaction of the maxilla can occur, resulting in shortening of the face and disruption of the occlusion.

A technique that should probably be considered semiclosed (or semi-open) is the Biphasic pin fixation (Roger Anderson or Joe Hall Morris appliance) technique. In this approach, pins are placed on either side of the fracture site, and after fracture

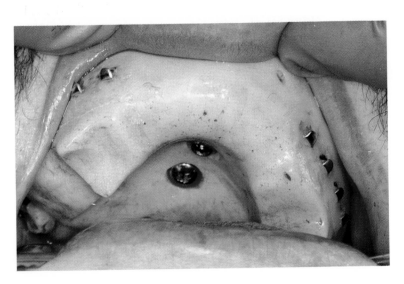

FIGURE 16–35.   A palatal screw can be used to hold the splint or denture in place.

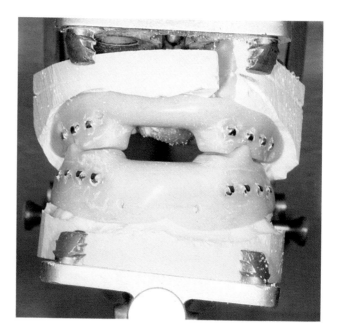

FIGURE 16-36. Gunning splint used for edentulous mandibular fractures.

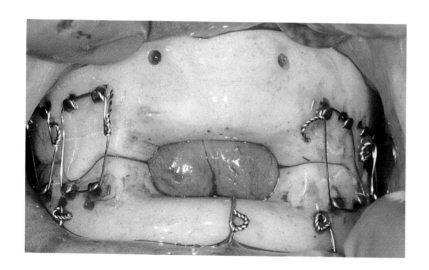

FIGURE 16-37. Gunning splint used for edentulous mandibular fractures.

FIGURE 16-38. Gunning splint used for edentulous mandibular fractures.

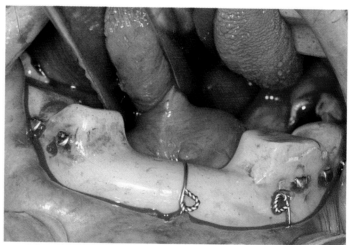

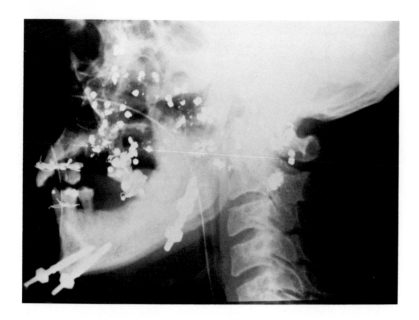

FIGURE 16–39. The biphasic pin fixation technique is very useful in fractures in which there is comminution or infection.

reduction, an external appliance, followed by an acrylic bar, is placed to maintain the bone fragments in their proper position (Figs. 16–39 and 16–40). A variation of this technique, in which a monophasic appliance is used, has been discussed by others.[154,155] Although this technique can be used in dentulous or edentulous patients, it is most valuable in the following situations: (1) in edentulous cases, to maintain space where bone is missing because of either severe trauma or resection; (2) in severely comminuted fractures; and (3) when intermaxillary or rigid fixation cannot be utilized. A more detailed discussion of managing edentulous patients with fractures is presented in Chapter 28.

Techniques for Open Reduction and Fixation

Just as there are a multitude of techniques for closed reduction and fixation, there are also many methods of open reduction and types of orthopedic hardware available to establish bone approximation. As previously discussed, open reduction

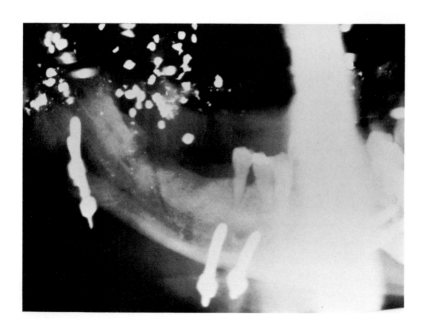

FIGURE 16–40. The biphasic pin fixation technique.

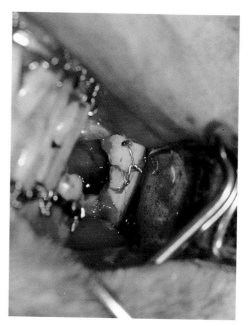

FIGURE 16–41. Technique for intraoral open reduction of mandibular fracture at third molar area.

should be used in specific situations because of the morbidity attendant on open procedures.

WIRE OSTEOSYNTHESIS

Historically, open techniques were done through a skin incision or laceration, and wires were generally used to maintain the fracture fragments. With the advent of modern orthognathic surgery, intraoral open surgical approaches have become the standard (Figs. 16–41 to 16–43), and although wire osteosynthesis is still widely used in the United States, techniques developed in Europe that use metal plates and screws for rigid fixation have become widely accepted in this country as well. Wires are often simpler to place and, in most cases, will maintain the bone fragments and prevent bone displacement by muscle pull until healing occurs. However, wires lack rigidity, directional control, and surface-to-bone-surface contact area to maintain rigidity

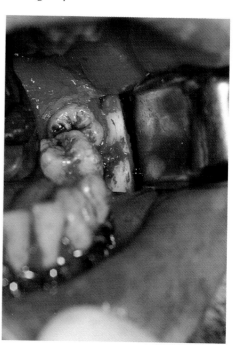

FIGURE 16–42. Technique for intraoral open reduction of mandibular fracture at third molar area.

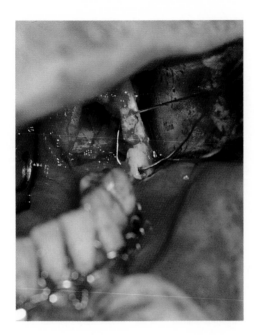

FIGURE 16–43. Technique for intraoral open reduction of mandibular fracture at third molar area.

under function, so intermaxillary fixation must be used, whereas with screw or plate rigid fixation, intermaxillary fixation is usually unnecessary.[156]

Wire osteosynthesis is most commonly used for angle fractures at the superior border of the mandible; the wire is placed via an intraoral approach. Concomitant removal of an impacted third molar allows excellent access and easy placement of the wire (Fig. 16–44). Parasymphyseal or midsymphyseal fractures are also often reduced and fixed, with wire osteosynthesis placed via an intraoral approach, and the wire is positioned beneath the teeth, inferior alveolar canal, and mental foramen. As discussed previously, fractures in this area are often oblique, causing telescoping. In this case, the wire must be placed through both segments of bone, which may be millimeters away from the buccal fracture line. If, however, the fracture is perpendicular to the buccal surface of the mandible, wire should be placed in a figure-of-eight fashion to cradle the lower border as well as to bring the two edges of the fracture together.

RIGID FIXATION

Although the subject of rigid fixation is discussed throughly in Chapter 33, a short summary of the philosophy and techniques is included here for completeness.

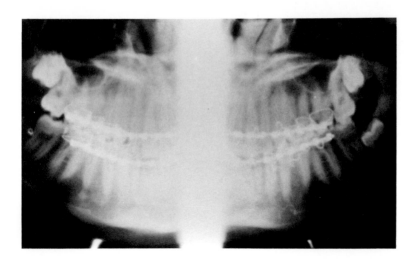

FIGURE 16–44. Removal of a third molar allows excellent access and easy placement of the wire.

Jones and VanSickels recently reported on this subject and presented a thorough literature review.[156]

The use of bone screws and compression plates for the treatment of mandibular fractures is derived from concepts developed in orthopedic surgery. Essentially, three goals are desired: (1) anatomic reduction, (2) fracture fragment compression, and (3) rigid immobilization. Anatomic reduction is thought to promote primary bone repair, resulting in direct lamellar bone formation in medullary bone without a cartilaginous phase. In cortical bone, longitudinal growth of capillaries and osteogenic cells across the fracture line occurs by way of tunnels. Compression is thought to promote healing, probably because of closer apposition of the bone fragments. Rigid immobilization theoretically allows osteogenesis to occur in an ideal environment without the negative influence of mobility at the fracture site.

Currently, a multitude of "systems" are available for rigid fixation. They consist of various plates and screws of stainless steel, cobalt-chromium alloy (Vitallium), or titanium. Bone plates with eccentrically positioned holes create compression across a fracture. The screws placed at an angle in the holes tend to converge as they are tightened, bringing the bone fragments together. Other metal plates are designed to be slightly convex, so that when they are tightened on the buccal surface of the bone, compression occurs on the lingual surface. The plates are held with monocortical screws (these present less danger to nerve vessels and tooth roots) or bicortical screws (enhanced stability). Taped screw holes allow maximal contact between the screw and the bone surface area. Self-taping screws are more easily applied.

A lag screw technique has also been developed in which a screw hole on one side of a tangential fracture is overdrilled. When the screw is tightened and engages cortical bone on the opposite side of the fracture site, compression occurs.

Of paramount importance to many of these systems is the concept of a tension band across the mandible. Because of muscle actions, different areas of the mandible are under different forces at the same time (compression, tension, or neutral). Metal plates positioned over areas of maximal tension allow equal distribution of forces over the fracture surface, eliminating displacement by muscle action.

As expected, these sophisticated techniques are not without difficulty, as discussed in the following section on complications.

Although anatomic reduction, compression, rigid fixation, tension bands, and various metal appliances are important in the treatment of difficult-to-manage long-bone fractures, it has not been shown that these same approaches are vital to the treatment of mandibular fractures. Perhaps the one overriding value of these techniques is the elimination or decreased time of intermaxillary fixation. Whether the advantages of this technology outweigh the disadvantages is yet to be proved.

COMPLICATIONS ASSOCIATED WITH MANDIBULAR FRACTURES

Complications following the treatment of mandibular fractures are rare. From a literature review and our experience, it appears that the most common complication is infection or osteomyelitis. Contributing factors seem to be preoperative oral sepsis, teeth in the line of fracture, alcoholic or metabolic disturbances, prolonged time prior to treatment, displacement of fracture fragments, poor compliance by the patient, and probably iatrogenic causes via open fixation procedures.

Infection and Teeth in the Line of Fracture

Statistics relating to mandibular fractures and complications are not universal and must be evaluated on the basis of the country and the socioeconomic conditions of the population served. This principle is certainly true regarding infections. Khan, from Harare, Zimbabwe, reported a 22.5 per cent preoperative incidence of infection associated with facial fractures and a postoperative infection rate of 18 per cent.[122]

Abiose, from Ibadom, Nigeria, reported a preoperative infection rate of 56.25 per cent, but he felt the infection "did not necessarily accompany delay nor unduly complicate definitive treatment." [110] From a historical standpoint, it is interesting to compare current results regarding infection with those reported by Chambers and Scully in an article written about mandibular fracture treatment in India during World War II.[157] Of 124 patients treated for mandibular fractures, 46 per cent had teeth extracted from the line of fracture and 44 per cent had postoperative infections and delayed union.

Kelly and Harrigan, while admitting that "a certain percentage of patients treated were lost in follow-up," reported that 66 cases (2.3 per cent) of a total of 3329 fractures (including ramus, coronoid, and condyle) required a surgical procedure — extraoral, necessitating drainage, or sequestrectomy or saucerization.[87] The most common organisms isolated were *Staphylococcus* (60 per cent), *Streptococcus* (20 per cent), and others (14 per cent), including two instances of actinomyocosis *(Actinomyces)* and one of *Klebsiella*. Cultures were apparently not done for anaerobes.

Melmed and Koonin, in a review of 909 cases of mandibular fractures from Cape Town, South Africa, found 85 cases of "sepsis" and four cases in which osteomyelitis developed.[123] Of the 85 "sepsis" cases, 4 occurred with open reduction, 5 were caused by a tooth in the line of fracture, 8 resulted from the application or removal of Gunning-type splints, 25 resulted from "very poor teeth," and 43 (50 per cent) were caused, the authors felt, by a delay of more than 48 hours in seeking treatment after injury.

Olson and colleagues, in their analysis of 580 cases of fractured mandible, found that 156 (26.9 per cent) had some type of complication, including infection, respiratory conditions, neurologic problems, delayed healing, and nonunion.[95] They felt that

> Complications are the most common in the vehicular-accident victim who has sustained multiple injuries. The patient who sustains only mandibular fracture with or without facial laceration, seldom experiences complications.

In one of the few prospective studies in the literature, James and associates evaluated 253 consecutive patients with 422 mandibular fractures and found a postoperative infection rate of 6.95 per cent (16 of 230 fractures with sufficient follow-up).[92] There were 261 teeth directly associated with mandibular fractures, 39 per cent of which were extracted at the time of treatment. The postoperative infection rate had no bearing on whether the tooth in the line of fracture was extracted or not. They used antibiotic therapy routinely for all patients with compound fractures. Of these patients, 46 did not continue taking antibiotics after hospital discharge and in 4, postoperative infection developed. Of the 177 fractures that required an open reduction, 12 (6.78 per cent) became infected. Six of the 12 infections were associated with angle fractures in which the tooth in the line of fracture was extracted at the time of surgery. In contrast to the study of Olson and colleagues,[95] most of their infected fractures were related to injuries involving interpersonal violence. The authors' data supported the concept that healthy teeth in the line of fracture do not increase the incidence of infection, and in many instances, their aid to stabilization outweighs the consideration of infection. It is interesting that both aerobic and anaerobic organisms were obtained from cultures on the 16 patients with postoperative infections, with alpha-hemolytic streptococci and *Bacteroides* organisms found most often. The majority of the organisms cultured were penicillin sensitive.

Two studies showed remarkably similar results. Amaratunga (191 patients, 226 fractures) found an infection rate of about 5 per cent, with or without teeth in the line of fracture.[148] Schneider and Stern (157 patients, 199 fractures) found complications, including delayed union, infection, and odontalgia, in 5 per cent of the patients who had teeth in the line of fracture.[158] Bernstein and McClurg studied 156 consecutive patients with fractures of the mandible and found that in 20 patients (12.82 per cent) infections developed; four of the infections were related to teeth in the line of fracture.[84] Prophylactic antibiotics did not seem to affect the incidence of infection.

Chuong and Donoff found little difference in the incidence of infection when comparing the retention of teeth in the line of fracture with the extraction of teeth in the fracture site (14 per cent versus 11 per cent, respectively).[159] However, they were careful to point out that teeth in the line of injury that are significantly mobile, have root exposure in markedly distracted fractures, or interfere with either reduction or fixation of the fracture were extracted. These selection criteria are perhaps more stringent than most clinicians would subscribe to. Roed-Petersen and Andreasen also found that there was much less pulp necrosis in teeth involved in the fracture site when the fracture was treated within 48 hours (15 per cent versus 37 per cent for those treated later).[160]

In a study of 26 mandibular fractures, Chan and colleagues reported that 8 developed complications including soft tissue infections, osteomyelitis, malunion, and nonunion.[161] A common feature in all was infection of teeth in the line of fracture and poor compliance or noncompliance with the treatment plan. The results of their literature review and retrospective study are presented in Table 16–8.

The Effect of Closed Reduction Versus Open Reduction on the Incidence of Infection

In a retrospective review of 100 fractures in 56 patients, Moore found a postoperative infection rate of 9.8 per cent in those managed with open reduction compared with a rate of 8.9 per cent in those who were treated by closed reduction.[93] There were too few cases to generalize on the effect of teeth in the line of fracture. Surprisingly, nine patients (16.1 per cent) had soft tissue infection.

The Effect of Antibiotics on Complication Rate

Larsen and Nielsen cite studies showing infection in 36 of 104 patients with mandibular fractures prior to the use of antibiotics, a 19 per cent incidence of infection in a partially preantibiotic period (1943 to 1953), and a current infection rate of 0 per cent.[106] Their own study of 229 patients showed a 0.4 per cent incidence of infection. They attribute their low infection rate to early treatment, thorough wound cleaning before treatment of compound fractures, and prophylactic antibiotics.

Zallen and Curry, in a prospective randomized study (64 patients) of antibiotic usage in the treatment of fractures with teeth in the line of fracture, found a complication rate of 6.25 per cent in those patients who received antibiotic coverage compared with a complication rate of 50.33 per cent in those who did not.[150]

TABLE 16–8. STUDIES OF MANDIBULAR FRACTURES INVOLVING TEETH

AUTHOR	NO. OF PATIENTS	TEETH IN FRACTURE LINE	INFECTION, DELAYED, NONUNION	INCIDENCE OF COMPLICATIONS (%)
Neal and Wagner	519	260	87	32
Kahnberg	—	185	14*	13
Wilkie	250	190	—	8
Zallen and Curry	64	64	36*	50 (without antibiotics) 6 (with antibiotics)
Ridell	84	—	20*	4.2
Roed-Peterson	1	110	27*	25
Kromer	113*	60	32	53
Chan et al	26	26	8	30

* Data modified from statistics presented in cited references.
From Chan DM, Demuth RJ, Miller SH, Jastak JT: Management of mandibular fracture in unreliable patient populations. Ann Plast Surg 13:298, 1984; with permission.

Limchayseng studied 158 mandibular angle fractures and found infections, in spite of postoperative antibiotics, in 25 per cent of the cases in which third molars were retained in the line of fracture.[149] In his study, however, 86 per cent of the third molars were removed prior to fracture reduction and fixation. He also reported a higher infection rate when fractures were moderately or grossly displaced. Fractures treated by rigid fixation showed a higher incidence of infection (28 per cent) than did those managed with open reduction with superior border wire fixation (6 per cent); however, fractures with more displacement tended to be treated with rigid fixation.

The Effect of Extraoral Versus Intraoral Surgery on Complication Rate

Wagner and colleagues studied the morbidity associated with extraoral open reduction (82 patients, 100 fractures) and found a complication rate of 13 per cent, including a wound or bone infection rate of 10 per cent (Figs. 16–45 to 16–49).[162] Sixty-seven fractures were associated with teeth, and in 32 instances the teeth were removed before reduction. The group with teeth in the line of fracture had 9 of the total of 13 postoperative complications, including 3 wound infections and 6 infected fractures that required sequestrectomies.

Kerr analyzed 755 facial fractures and noted post-treatment infections in 3 middle third fractures and 13 mandibular fractures.[163] Nine of the 13 involved extraoral open reduction and lower border wiring. In 7 of the 9 cases, the offending organism was *Staphylococcus pyogenes,* and the onset was within 4 to 10 days after treatment. The cases were treated by incision and drainage, without removal of the wire. Kerr felt this indicated that the infection had not involved the fracture itself but was a superficial wound infection introduced at the time of operation.

Chuong and Donoff evaluated their mandibular fracture cases treated via an intraoral approach.[159] Of 372 fractures, 161 were treated by open reduction, 31 via an intraoral approach, and 23 involved removal of an impacted or partially erupted third molar and placement of an intraoral upper border wire. Three body fractures in

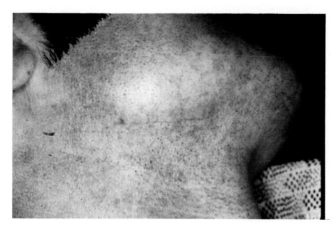

FIGURE 16–45. Preoperative view of mandibular fracture treated by open reduction as shown in Figures 16–46 through 16–49.

FIGURE 16–46. Technique for extraoral open reduction of mandibular fracture (Risdon): Skin and subcutaneous incision.

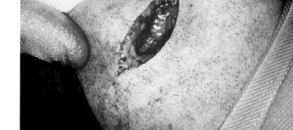

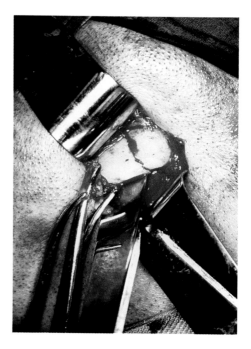

FIGURE 16–47. Technique for extraoral open reduction of mandibular fracture (Risdon): Exposure of fracture site.

FIGURE 16–48. Technique for extraoral open reduction of mandibular fracture (Risdon): Holes placed in proximal and distal segments.

FIGURE 16–49. Technique for extraoral open reduction of mandibular fracture (Risdon): Wires placed in holes in segments.

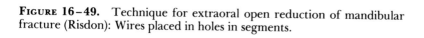

edentulous portions of the mandible, as well as five symphyseal fractures, were treated by intraoral wire fixation. Four complications were seen in the 31 fractures (12.9 per cent) treated by the intraoral approach. Two cases of dehiscence of the angle, one case of infection of the symphysis, and one case of inadequate reduction and fixation of the angle were noted. In all cases, union progressed in 4 to 5 weeks.

Freihofer and Sailer found a complication rate of 7 per cent in 148 patients with 178 wiring sites approached intraorally, combined with 4 weeks of intermaxillary fixation. Complications included occlusal abnormalities (3 per cent), delayed bone union (3 per cent), pseudoarthroses (0.5 per cent), and osteomyelitis of the fracture site (0.5 per cent).[164]

The Effect of Wire Osteosynthesis Versus Rigid Fixation on Complication Rate

In an extensive review, Theriot and associates found the reported infection rate to be variable when comparing wire osteosynthesis with bone plate osteosynthesis in the treatment of mandibular fractures.[165] The range was between 0.5 and 14.7 per cent for wire osteosynthesis, with European studies having the lowest rate of infection (1.1 per cent via an extraoral approach and 0.5 per cent via an intraoral approach). U.S. authors reported infection rates from 6.6 per cent to a high of 14.7 per cent when wire osteosynthesis was used in a limited number of patients.

The data derived from the literature review of Theriot and associates shows an initial high rate of infection associated with bone plate osteosynthesis, decreasing as authors became more proficient with the technique.[165] Theriot and associates cite studies on the incidence of infection with bone plates by Kahnberg and Ridell—3 of 11 patients infected (27 per cent); Strelgow and Friedman—5 of 26 (19.2 per cent); and Sourgis and colleagues—25 infections in 171 patients (14.6 per cent). They also reported on the results of Champy and coworkers—a 3.8 per cent infection rate in a series of 183 patients—and Luhr—a 3.5 per cent infection rate using compression plate osteosynthesis. In their own prospective study of 75 patients with 126 mandibular fractures, Theriot and associates reported infection in 4 of 34 patients with 52 fractures treated by bone plate osteosynthesis and 2 infections in 41 patients with 74 fractures treated by wire osteosynthesis.

Tu and Tenhulzen, using AO/ASIF and Osteosystems, reported removing the plates in 11.4 per cent of their patients because of complications in using the Champy system for mandibular fractures (183 cases).[166] Becher reported infection (3.8 per cent), malunion (0.5 per cent), nonunion (0.5 per cent), and the need for occlusal equilibration (4.8 per cent) while using the Champy system.[156] In 50 cases, Cawood found infection in 6 per cent and malocclusion in 8 per cent.[167]

Souyris and colleagues published results of a 12-year study using cobalt-chromium alloy (Vitallium) plates with bicortical self-taping screws placed along the inferior border of the mandible.[156] Postoperative infections occurred in 14.5 per cent of their patients (25 of 171 patients), 20 additional patients required removal of the plates because of a late (months to years) developing inflammatory reaction, and 15 per cent of the patients had occlusal discrepancies that were managed by occlusal equilibration.

Luhr, using Vitallium cobalt-chromium plates with bicortical self-taping screws, reported an infection rate of 5.7 per cent (105 cases) for extraoral placement and 3.2 per cent (255 cases) for intraoral placement.[156]

Delayed Healing and Nonunion of Mandibular Fractures

Delayed healing and nonunion of the mandible are rare and occur as a result of violating the treatment goals outlined in the previous section. Infection is certainly the greatest factor, but severity of the injury, inadequate reduction, lack of fracture stability, uncooperative patients, alcoholism, and metabolic and nutritional deficiencies all play a major role in prolonged healing.

Kelly and Harrigan reported 34 nonunions of the mandible out of 3338 mandibular fractures (1 per cent).[87] Infection accounted for the greatest number of nonunions, and lack of cooperation by the patient (i.e., removal of intermaxillary fixation) was second. The most common site of a nonunion was in the body of the mandible. Melmed and Koonin had 20 cases of nonunion resulting from 909 fractures of the mandible (2.2 per cent).[123] They believed that alcoholism, delay in seeking treatment, and carious teeth contributed to the problems of management and complications. The prospective study of James and colleagues showed delayed union (no clinically evident union after 8 weeks) in 9 of 253 patients (3.5 per cent) and nonunion in 3 patients (1 per cent).[92] Of the delayed unions, four were in the angle, four were in the body, and one was in the symphysis. Seven patients had open reduction, and four had preoperative or postoperative infection. Two nonunions occurred in the angle, and one occurred in the body. Moore and colleagues found a nonunion rate of 1.8 per cent in 56 patients with 100 mandibular fractures.[93] The nonunion occurred in a 74-year-old person with bilateral fractures of an atrophic, edentulous mandible. Bernstein and McClurg reported delayed union in 5 of 156 patients with mandibular fractures.[84] The diagnosis was made by eliciting pain when the fracture site was torqued, and treatment consisted of additional intermaxillary fixation time. In a study from Sweden, Heimdahl and Nordenram found 2 patients with osteitis and osteomyelitis, causing severe bone loss and pseudoarthrosis, from among 100 patients.[105] They believed that abuse of alcohol or narcotics or both resulted in uncooperativeness on the part of patients (23 per cent) and contributed to the nonunion. Chuong and Donoff defined delayed union as mobility of the fracture site after 5 weeks of treatment with maxillomandibular fixation.[159] Using this rather strict criterion, they found that delayed union occurred in 12 (3.1 per cent) of 372 mandibular fractures. No cases of nonunion were reported.

Delayed Healing and Nonunion Related to Fixation Techniques

Bochlogyros reviewed the German literature and cases from the University of Münster, West Germany.[168] He compiled the nonunion cases and categorized them by treatment method: (1) closed reduction and intermaxillary fixation, (2) interosseous wiring, and (3) stable compression plate fixation. The results are shown in Tables 16–9 to 16–11. He found that the factors predisposing to nonunion are delay in treatment, inadequate immobilization, and osteomyelitis of the fracture site prior to and after surgery.

TABLE 16–9.   INCIDENCE OF NONUNION OF FRACTURES OF THE MANDIBLE AFTER CLOSED REDUCTION AND INTERMAXILLARY FIXATION, REPORTED BY VARIOUS AUTHORS

AUTHORS	YEAR	NO. OF PATIENTS	NONUNION
Wassmund	1943	1500	2 (0.1%)
Köle	1956	665	(0.6%)
Herrmann et al	1960	556	8 (1.4%)
Paschke and Berz	1961	385	5 (1.3%)
Müller	1967	2258	17 (0.8%)
Trauner	1973	530	4 (0.8%)
Claudi and Spiessl	1975	68	1 (1.5%)
Mathog and Boies	1976	577	14 (2.4%)
Krüger	1982	104	1 (0.96%)
Bochlogyros	1985	529	3 (0.6%)

From Bochlogyros PN: Non-union of fractures of the mandible. J Maxillofac Surg 13:189, 1985; with permission.

TABLE 16–10.   INCIDENCE OF NONUNION OF THE MANDIBLE AFTER INTEROSSEOUS WIRING, REPORTED BY VARIOUS AUTHORS

AUTHORS	YEAR	NO. OF PATIENTS	NONUNION
Edgerton and Hill	1952	434	18 (4.5%)
Plumpton and Crawford	1955	30	1 (3%)
Freihofer and Sailer	1975	148 (178 fr.)	1 (0.5%)
Schegg et al	1975	450	2 (0.5%)
Bochlogyros	1985	139	1 (0.7%)

From Bochlogyros PN: Non-union of fractures of the mandible. J Maxillofac Surg 13:189, 1985; with permission.

Alcoholism and Delayed Healing

Alcohol abuse and mandibular fractures are closely interrelated both in etiology and in the increased incidence of complications.[123,125,169] Citing an extensive literature review on alcohol and its relation to mandibular fractures, Adele and colleagues did a retrospective study on 401 patients with fractures of the body of the mandible.[170] The most significant variable relating to delayed healing was the frequency of alcohol abuse. They state that ". . . the frequency of patients with alcohol problems and psycho-social handicaps is reported high in most studies on jaw fractures." The patients in the delayed healing group were more frequently intoxicated by alcohol at the time of trauma and at the first visit. As a group, they were much less likely to keep appointments and were more apt to remove their own maxillomandibular fixations. Eid and associates found that complications were more likely to occur in the presence of an alcoholic state, poor oral hygiene, and uncooperativeness.[171] Recognizing the delayed healing problem in alcoholics, Cannell and Boyd set up a specific treatment protocol especially for the vagrant alcoholic patient.[172] These patients were kept in the hospital for a month or longer. Open reduction was avoided if possible, and additional fixation was used (metal cap splints when possible). When open reduction was necessary, a minimal amount of periosteum was reflected, and heavy antibiotic coverage was instituted.

In spite of all their precautions, infection of fractures or wounds occurred in 12 of the 16 cases in the series. In eight of these cases, rigid fixation was used after thorough cleansing of open fracture sites, removal of teeth in fracture lines, and strict attention to aftercare. The authors quote Selberman and coworkers, who postulate that the accumulation of hepatic fat might lead to diffusion of fatty emboli capable of impairing local blood supply. Cannell and Boyd believed that the quality of the mandibular bone was poor and that movement of the fracture sites because of noncompliance was the most likely precursor of infection.[172] The authors also speculated on secondary osteoporosis, osteomalacia, and vitamin deficiency in the undernourished alcoholic. Perhaps the subject is best summed up by the statement of Heimdahl and Nordenram, who concluded that the "treatment of these patients is . . . not only surgical but very much social."[105]

TABLE 16–11.   INCIDENCE OF NONUNION OF THE MANDIBLE AFTER STABLE COMPRESSION PLATE FIXATION, REPORTED BY VARIOUS AUTHORS

AUTHORS	YEAR	NO. OF PATIENTS	NONUNION
Slchmitz et al	1975	220	2 (0.9%)
Scharf and Reuter	1975	82	1 (1.2%)
Bochlogyros	1985	78	3 (3.9%)

From Bochlogyros PN: Non-union of fractures of the mandible. J Maxillofac Surg 13:189, 1985; with permission.

Nerve Disorders

The most commonly injured nerve associated with mandibular fractures is the inferior alveolar nerve and its branches—the mylohyoid, the dental branches, the incisive branch, and, most particularly, the mental nerve. Rarely, other branches of the mandibular nerve may be injured—masseteric nerve (condylar fractures), buccal nerve (intraoral lacerations associated with angle or body fractures), auriculotemporal nerve (condylar fractures), and lingual nerve (intraoral lacerations). The prominent sign of inferior alveolar nerve deficit, of course, is numbness or other sensory changes in the lower lip and chin.

A rare but impressive nerve deficit is that associated with the mandibular branch of the facial nerve. The tell-tale motor dysfunction of the musculature of the face or lips can result from trauma in the region of the condyle, ramus, and angle of the mandible, as well as from lacerations affecting the facial nerve, particularly the distribution of the marginal mandibular branch.

Most of the sensory and motor functions of these nerves will improve and return to normal with time; however, lacerations or nerve tissue loss produced by grossly displaced fracture fragments, soft tissue loss, or gunshot wounds can result in permanent deficits.

There are few studies of sensory nerve deficit associated with mandibular fractures. Moore and colleagues (56 patients, 100 fractures) reported an incidence of mental nerve paresthesia of 1.89 per cent and facial nerve damage of 1.8 per cent.[93] It is not known if the deficit was permanent. Larsen and Nielsen reported permanent sensory disturbances in the area of the mental nerve following mandibular fracture in 19 patients, corresponding to 8 per cent of the 229 patients evaluated.[106]

Milford and Loizeaux reviewed the literature and cited cases of Taylor, Kennedy, and Kent, who had reported on false aneurysm and partial facial paralysis secondary to mandibular fractures.[173] They also noted one case of facial paralysis following a fracture of the mandibular condyle, coronoid process, and symphysis. Paralysis was due to edema in the fallopian canal, and function returned with time.

Rapids and Brock also reported a case of a 5-year-old patient with hemiparalysis of the face after a minimally displaced fracture of the condyle on the same side.[174] Recovery was complete 2 months after surgery.

Schmidseder and Scheunemann reported on nerve injury following condylar neck fractures.[175] They found post-traumatic neurologic complications in 8 of 237 fractures. One case involved the chorda tympani, with unilateral loss of taste in the tongue. One case involved the facial nerve, resulting in total paresis. Five cases involved the auriculotemporal nerve, in two of which Frey's syndrome developed. One case involved the buccal branch of cranial nerve V_3 and occurred 7 days after a condyle was grossly medially displaced. Most of these cases improved with time.

Conclusion

From this review, it is apparent that infection is the most common type of complication arising from the treatment of mandibular fractures. Although the incidence varies, it would seem that between 5 and 10 per cent is average. Preoperative oral sepsis, with grossly carious and periodontally involved teeth, contributes to the problem, and unless diseased teeth are important for reduction and fixation of the fracture, they should be removed. Prolonged delay in treatment contributes to infection as well.

Although it would be expected that open reduction would contribute to infection, this is not evident in a review of the literature. In addition, there appears to be little difference between the infection rates of intraoral and extraoral open reduction procedures.

Rigid fixation techniques are initially seen to result in a higher complication rate, but as surgeons become more proficient with the methods, complication rates fall.

Delayed union results from infection, lack of fracture stability, uncooperativeness on the part of patients, and alcoholism. Nonunion is extremely rare.

It is evident that alcohol abuse plays a major role in the etiology of mandibular fractures and results in a higher rate of complications following treatment. Whether this higher complication rate is simply due to noncompliance or is a result of metabolic dysfunction is unclear.

There are too few studies on the incidence of permanent nerve damage associated with mandibular fractures to allow any conclusions.

Finally, more controlled prospective studies on the various methods of reduction and fixation of mandibular fractures are necessary to establish clinical protocols.

REFERENCES

1. Smith E: Papyrus. Translated by Breasted JH (1930).[3]
2. Lipton JS: Oral surgery in ancient Egypt as reflected in the Edwin Smith Papyrus. Bull Hist Dent 30:108, 1982.
3. Breasted JH: The Edwin Smith Surgical Papyrus. Chicago, University of Chicago Press, 1930.
4. Hippocrates: Oeuvres Complètes. English translation by ET Withington. Cambridge, MA, 1928.
5. Gahhos F, Ariyan S: Facial fractures. Hippocratic management. Head Neck Surg 6:1007, 1984.
6. Brophy TW: Oral Surgery. A Treatise on the Diseases, Injuries and Malformations of the Mouth and Associated Parts. York, PA, The Maple Press, 1915.
7. Celsus AC: De Medicine. Florence, Nicolaus Laurentii, 1478.
8. Galen: Claudii Galeni Opera Omnia. Kühn CG (Ed). Hipp. Art. comment. Tomus XVIII:1, Leipzig, Germany, 1829.
9. Soranus of Ephesos: De Fascilis. Liberg J (ed). Corp. Med. Graec. IV. Leipzig, Germany, 1924.
10. Avicenna: Canonis Medicinae, libri V. Strassburg, France, before 1473.
11. Salicetti G (William of Saliceto): Cyrurgia, 1275.
12. Prévost N: Translation of Salicetti's Cyrurgia into French. Lyons, France, 1492.
13. Paré A: Cinq Livres de Cherurgie. Paris, 1572.
14. Leake D: History of oral surgery. *In* Guralnick WC (ed): Textbook of Oral Surgery. Boston, Little, Brown, and Company, 1968.
15. Ryff (Rivius) WH: Die gross Chirurgei, oder vollkommene Wundartzeney. Franckfurt, Germany, 1545.
16. Fauchard P: Le Chirurgien Dentiste. Paris, 1728.
17. Bunon R: Expériences et Démonstrations Faites à l'Hôpital de la Salpêtrière. Paris, 1746.
18. Chopart F, Desault PJ: Traité des Maladies Chirurgicales. Vol I. Paris, 1795.
19. Bellevue Hospital: Mandibular Fractures. New York, 1857.
20. Physick PS: A case of fracture of the bone of the under jaw, successfully treated with a seton. Philadelphia, J Med Phys Sci, 1822, pp 116–118.
21. Barton JR: A systematic bandage for fractures of the lower jaw. Am Med Recorder Phila 2:153, 1819.
22. Gibson W: The Institutes and Practice of Surgery. 5th ed. Philadelphia, Carey, Lea and Blanchard, 1838.
23. Garretson JE: A System of Oral Surgery: Being a Treatise on the Diseases and Surgery of the Mouth, Jaws, Face, Teeth and Associate Parts. Philadelphia, JB Lippincott, 1862.
24. Roldon, Hauselet, Bruno of Longbourg, et al: Cited in Dorrance GM, Bransfield JW: The History of Treatment of Fractured Jaws. Vols 1 and 2. Washington, DC, 1941.
25. Pickerill HP: The "screw-lever" splint. Odont Sec Roy Soc Med 11:90, 1917–1918.
26. Bouisson EF: Recherches et observations sur quelques variétés rares de luxations. J Soc Med Prat de Montpel, 1843.
27. Von Szymanowski J: Der Gypsverband, mit besonderer Berücksichtigung der Militair—Chirurgie. St Petersburg, Russia, Eggers and Company, 1857.
28. Bean JB: Quoted by Covey EM (1866)[29] and Schwartz (1944).[30]
29. Covey EM: The interdental splint. Richmond Med J 1:81, 1866.
30. Schwartz L: The development of the treatment of jaw fractures. J Oral Surg 2:193, 1944.
31. Erichsen JE: The Science and Art of Surgery. Being a Treatise on Surgical Injuries, Diseases, and Operations. 5th ed. London, J Walton, 1869.
32. Parkhill C: A new apparatus for the treatment of fractures of the inferior maxilla. JAMA 23:467, 1894.
33. Kazanjian VH: Immediate treatment of gunshot fractures of the jaws. Br Dent J 37:297, 1916.
34. Dorrance GM, Bransfield JW: The History of Treatment of Fractured Jaws. Washington, DC, 1941.
35. Rütenick: Quoted by Branco FG (1825).[36]
36. Branco FG: Über die fraktur des Unterkiefers nebst Beschreibung und Abbildung der Rütenickschen Maschine. (Rust's) Magazin ges Heilk 18:3, 1825.
37. Bush F: Quoted by Malgaigne, JF (1847).[38]
38. Malgaigne JF: Traité des Fractures et des Luxations. Vol 1. Paris, 1847.
39. Hartig F: Beschreibung eines neuen Appar-

ates zur Retention des Unterkiefers. J Chir Augenhk (Berlin) 14:496, 1830.

40. Lonsdale EF: A Description of Three Instruments for the Treatment of Fractures of the Lower Jaw, Fractures of the Patella, and for Tying Uterine Polypi. London, J Churchill, 1940.

41. Sawyer AF: Fracture of the hyoid and inferior maxillary bones with fracture and dislocation of the thyroid cartilages and other injuries. Am J Dent Sci 6:250, 1856.

42. Hayward HH: Fracture of the lower jaw. Cosmos 2:183, 1860–1861.

43. Gunning TB: Treatment of fractures of the lower jaw by interdental splints. Br J Dent Sci 9:481, 1866.

44. Fraser-Moodie W: Mr. Gunning and his splint. Br J Oral Surg 7:112, 1869.

45. Romm S: Thomas Brian Gunning and his splint. Plast Reconstr Surg 78:252, 1986.

46. Elliott WG: Gunshot wounds of the mouth. New York Med J 29:267, 1879.

47. Haly Abbas filius: Libertotius Medicine Necessaria Continens Quem Saprentissimus Haly filius Abbas discipulus. Lugduni, typ. J. Myteructe, 1523.

48. Brunschwig H: The Noble Experyence of the Vertuous Handy Warke of Surgeri. London, P Treverus, 1525.

49. Vigo G: Opera Domini Joannis de Vigo in Chyrurgia. Lugduni, 1521.

50. DeChauliac G: Chirurgia parva et Cyurgia Albucasis. Venice, 1500–1501.

51. Paré A: The Works of the Famous Chirurgion, Ambrose Parey, translated out of Latin and compared with the French by T Johnson, T Cotes, and R Young. London, 1634.

52. Hammond GE: New treatment of fractured maxillae. Mth Rev Dent Surg 1:547, 1872–1873.

53. Sauer C: Herstellung eines neuen Verbandes bei Unterkieferbrüchen. Dtsch Vjschr Zahnhk 21:362, 1881.

54. Martin C: Du Traitement des Fractures du Maxillaire Inférieur par un Nouvel Appareil. Rev Chir (Par.), 1887, vii, 881–903. Paris, 1887.

55. Crombie J: A modification of Hammond's splint for the treatment of certain fractures of the mandible. Br Med J 2:67, 1904.

56. White HM: Fractures of the lower jaw. Cosmos 6:197, 1864–1865.

57. Moon H: Mechanical appliances for treatment of fracture of the jaws. Br J Dent Sci 17:303, 1874.

58. Gilmer TL: Fractures of the inferior maxilla. Ohio State J Dent Sci 1:309; 2:14, 57, 112, 1881–1882.

59. Martindale JH: Points of common interest, both to dental and naso-laryngeal surgeons. Dent Rev 8:473, 1894.

60. Thomas JD: A case of fracture of the jaw. Dent Rev 8:530, 1894.

61. Gilmer TL: A case of fracture of the lower jaw with remarks on the treatment. Arch Dent 4:388, 1887.

62. Oliver RT: Management of fractured lower jaw. Indiana Dent J 1:83, 1898.

63. Baker HA: Treatment of protruding and receding jaws by use of intermaxillary elastics. New York, New York Institute of Stomatology. Transactions. pp 5–17, 1903.

64. Ivy R: Prosthesis of the anterior portion of the lower jaw. Penn Dent J 3:93, 1899–1900.

65. Angle EH: The Angle System of treating fractures of maxillary bones. Br J Dent Sci 33:484, 1890.

66. Sauer C: Nothverband bei kieferbrüchen aus Eisendraht. Dtsch Mschr Zahnhk 7:381, 1889.

67. Gilmer TL: Multiple fracture of the lower jaw complicated by double fracture of the upper jaw. Am Med Assoc J 43:8, 1904.

68. Rubbrecht O: The treatment of fractures of the jaws by a new method. Br Dent J 37:337, 1916.

69. Ivy R, Curtis L: Fractures of the mandible. Dent Cosmos 68:439, 1926.

70. Buck G: Fracture of the lower jaw with replacement and interlocking of the fragments. Annalist NY 1:245, 1846.

71. Thomas HO: Cases in surgery illustrative of a new method of applying the wire ligature in compound fractures of the lower jaw. Br J Dent Sci 12:113, 1869.

72. Davis GG: The Principles and Practice of Bandaging. Detroit, GS Davis, 1891.

73. Carter TS: Fractures of the inferior maxilla treated by a modified method of wire suture. J Br Dent Assoc 19:260, 1898.

74. Cale GW: Clinical Report of Six Surgical Cases. St Louis, Clinique V, 1892.

75. Kazanjian VH: Immobilization of wartime, compound comminuted fractures of the mandible. Am J Orthodont Oral Surg 28:551, 1942.

76. Mahé G: Essai Critique sur le Traitement de la Fracture du Maxillaire Inférieur. Paris, No 517, 1900.

77. Ivy RH: Fracture of condyloid process of the mandible. Ann Surg 61:502, 1915.

78. Cole PP: Dental surgery and injuries of the jaw. Br J Dent Sci 60:77, 1917.

79. Vorschütz J: Bemerkung zur Dauer der Behandlung der Wirbelfrakturen. Zentralbl Chir 61:548, 1934.

80. Baudens JBL: Communications verbales. Bull Acad Méd (Paris), 1844, pp 230 ff., 341 ff.

81. Robert A: Nouveau procédé de traitement des fractures de la portion alvéolaire de la machoire inférieure. Bull Gén Thérap (Paris) 42:22, 1852.

82. Ivy RH, Curtis L: Fractures of the Jaws. Philadelphia, Lea and Febiger, 1931.

83. Ivy RH, Curtis L: Fractures of the Jaws. 2nd ed. Philadelphia, Lea and Febiger, 1938.

84. Bernstein AL, McClurg SR: Mandibular fractures: A review of 156 consecutive cases. Laryngoscope 87:957, 1977.

85. Hagan EH, Huelke DF: Analyses of 319 case reports of mandibular fractures. J Oral Surg 19:93, 1961.

86. Salem JE, Lilly GE, Cutcher JR, Steiner M: Analysis of 523 mandibular fractures. Oral Surg Oral Med Oral Pathol 26:390, 1968.

87. Kelly DE, Harrigan WF: A survey of facial fractures: Bellevue Hospital, 1948–1974. J Oral Surg 33:146, 1975.

88. Chuong R, Donoff RB, Guralnick WC: A retrospective analysis of 327 mandibular fractures. J Oral Maxillofac Surg 41:305, 1983.

89. Dingman RO, Natvig P: Surgery of Facial Fractures. Philadelphia, WB Saunders Company, 1964.

90. Mallett SP: Fractures of the jaw: A survey of 2,124 cases. J Am Dent Assoc 14:657, 1950.

91. Goldberg MG, Williams AC: The location and occurrence of mandibular fractures: An analysis of 202 cases. Oral Surg Oral Med Oral Pathol 28:336, 1969.

92. James RB, Fredrickson C, Kent JN: Prospective study of mandibular fractures. J Oral Surg 39:275, 1981.

93. Moore GF, Olson TS, Yonkers AJ: Complications of mandibular fractures: A retrospective review of 100 fractures in 56 patients. Nebr Med J 70:120, 1985.

94. Nakamura T, Gross CW: Facial fractures: Analysis of five years of experience. Arch Otolaryngol 97:288, 1973.

95. Olson RA, Fonseca RJ, Zeitler DR, Osborn DB: Fractures of the mandible: A review of 580 cases. J Oral Maxillofac Surg 40:23, 1982.

96. Rowe NR, Killey HC: Fractures of the Facial Skeleton. Baltimore, The Williams and Wilkins Company, 1968.

97. Hill CM, Crosher RF, Mason DA: Dental and facial injuries following sports accidents: A study of 130 patients. Br J Oral Maxillofac Surg 23:268, 1985.

98. Bochlogyros PN: A retrospective study of 1,521 mandibular fractures. J Oral Maxillofac Surg 43:597, 1985.

99. Schuchardt K, Schwenzer N, Rottke R, Lentrodt J: Ursachen häufigkeit und Localisation der Frakturen des Gesichtsschädels. Fortschr Kiefer Gesichtschir 11:1, 1966.

100. Linn EW, Vrijoef MMA, deWijn JR, et al: Facial injuries sustained during sports and games. J Maxillofac Surg 14:83, 1986.

101. VanHoof RF, Merkx CA, Stekelenburg EC: The different patterns of fractures of the facial skeleton in four European countries. Int J Oral Surg 6:3, 1977.

101a. Müller W: Häufigkeit, Sitz und Ursachen der Gesichtsschädelfrakturen. *In* Reichenbach E (ed): Traumatologie in Kiefer-und Gesichtsbereich. Leipzig, Barth, 1969, pp 47–58.

102. Nordenram A: Fractura mandibulae: En oversikt med redovisning av 207 frakturer. Odont Foren T 31:23, 1967.

103. Hedin M, Ridell A, Söremark R: Käkfrakturer i Sverige 1966–1967. Swed Dent J 64:49, 1971.

104. Voss R: The aetiology of jaw fractures in Norwegian patients. J Maxillofac Surg 10:146, 1982.

105. Heimdahl A, Nordenram A: The first 100 patients with jaw fractures at the Department of Oral Surgery, Dental School, Huddinge. Swed Dent J 1:177, 1977.

106. Larsen OD, Nielsen A: Mandibular fractures. 1. An analysis of their etiology and location in 286 patients. Scand J Plast Reconstr Surg 10:213, 1976.

107. Nair KB, Paul G: Incidence and aetiology of fractures of the facio-maxillary skeleton in Trivandrum: A retrospective study. Br J Oral Maxillofac Surg 24:40, 1986.

108. Sawhney CP, Ahuja RB: Faciomaxillary fractures in North India. A statistical analysis and review of management. Br J Oral Maxillofac Surg 26:430, 1988.

109. Kapoor AK, Srivastava AB: Maxillofacial fracture: An analysis of 320 cases. *In* Jacobs JR (ed): Maxillofacial Trauma: An International Perspective. New York, Praeger Publishers, 1983.

110. Abiose BO: Maxillofacial skeleton injuries in the Western States of Nigeria. Br J Oral Maxillofac Surg 24:31, 1986.

111. Adekeye EO: The pattern of fractures of the facial skeleton in Kaduna, Nigeria: A survey of 1447 cases. Oral Surg Oral Med Oral Pathol 49:491, 1980.

112. Taher AAY: Maxillofacial injuries due to road traffic accidents in Kuwait. Br J Oral Maxillofac Surg 24:44, 1986.

113. Vaillant JM, Benoist M: Bullet wounds of the mandible in civil practice. Int J Oral Surg 10:255, 1981.

114. Freidel C, Achard R: Considerations sur le traitement des fractures de la mandibule. Sur une expérience de près de 2,000 cas. Rev Stomatol Chir Maxillofac 72:687, 1971.

115. Khalil AF, Shaladi OA: Fractures of the facial bones in the eastern region of Libya. Br J Oral Surg 19:300, 1981.

116. Khalil AF: Civilian gunshot injuries to the face and jaws. Br J Oral Surg 18:205, 1980.

117. Zachariades N, Papavassiliou D, Popaemetriou I, Koundouris I: Fractures of the facial skeleton in Greece. J Maxillofac Surg 11:142, 1983.

118. Spengos MN, Zotales N, Demetroglou D: A pattern of facial fractures in Greece. Int J Oral Surg 10:248, 1981.

119. Güven O: A comparative study on maxillofacial fractures in central and eastern Anatolia. J Cranio-Max-Fac Surg 16:126, 1988.

120. Karyouti SM: Maxillofacial injuries at Jordan University Hospital. Int J Oral Maxillofac Surg 16:262, 1987.

121. Malden NJ: Management of mandibular fractures in the highlands of Papua New Guinea. Int J Oral Maxillofac Surg 16:160, 1987.

122. Khan AA: A retrospective study of injuries to the maxillofacial skeleton in Harare, Zimbabwe. Br J Oral Maxillofac Surg 26:435, 1988.

123. Melmed EP, Koonin AJ: Fractures of the mandible: A review of 999 cases. J Plast Reconstr Surg 56:323, 1975.

124. Donaldson KI: Fractures in the facial skeleton. A survey of 335 patients. NZ Dent J 57:55, 1961.

125. Thorn J, Mogeltaft M, Hansen PK: Incidence and aetiological pattern of jaw fractures in Greenland. Int J Oral Maxillofac Surg 15:372, 1986.

126. Park HS: A study of facial bone fractures of Koreans. J Korean Acad Maxillofac Plast Surg 11:206, 1989.

127. Sane J, Ylipaavalniemi P: Maxillofacial and dental soccer injuries in Finland. Br J Oral Maxillofac Surg 25:383, 1987.

128. Ellis E, Moos KF, El-Attar A: Ten years of mandibular fractures: An analysis of 2,137 cases. Oral Surg Oral Med Oral Pathol 59:120, 1985.

129. Assael LA, Tucker MR: Management of facial fractures. *In* Peterson LJ, Ellis E, Hupp JR, Tucker MR (eds): Contemporary Oral and Maxillofacial Surgery. St Louis, CV Mosby, 1988.

130. Kruger GO (ed): Textbook of Oral Surgery. 4th ed. St Louis, CV Mosby, 1974.

131. Whitestone B, Raley L: Diagnosis and management of mandibular fractures. Ontario Dentist 62:68, 1985.

132. Dorland's Illustrated Medical Dictionary.

27th ed. Philadelphia, WB Saunders Company, 1988.

133. Kazanjian VH, Converse JM: Surgical Treatment of Facial Injuries. 3rd ed. Baltimore, The Williams and Wilkins Company, 1974.

134. Krüger E, Schilli W (eds): Oral and Maxillofacial Traumatology. Vol 1. Chicago, Quintessence Publishing Company, 1982.

135. Arajärvi E, Lindqvist C, Santavirta S, et al: Maxillofacial trauma in fatally injured victims of motor vehicle accidents. Br J Oral Maxillofac Surg 24:251, 1986.

136. Perkins CS, Layton SA: The aetiology of maxillofacial injuries and the seat belt law. Br J Oral Maxillofac Surg 26:353, 1988.

137. Chayra GA, Meador LR, Laskin DM: Comparison of panoramic and standard radiographs for the diagnosis of mandibular fractures. J Oral Maxillofac Surg 44:677, 1985.

138. Horowitz I, Abrahami E, Mintz SS: Demonstration of condylar fractures of the mandible by computed tomography. Oral Surg 54:263, 1982.

139. Dolan K, Jacoby C, Smoker W: The radiology of facial fractures. Radiographies (Monograph 9) 4:577, 1984.

140. Johnson DH: CT of maxillofacial trauma. Radiol Clin North Am 22:131, 1984.

141. Fieldhouse J: Post traumatic thrombotic occlusion of the internal carotid artery: Report of two cases. J Oral Surg 36:539, 1978.

142. Banna M: Hemiplegia following mandibular fracture. Br J Oral Surg 18:17, 1980.

143. Curran JB, Vogt P: Diplopia as a sign of basal skull fracture accompanying a fractured mandible: Report of a case. J Oral Surg 30:845, 1972.

144. Gordon NC, Swann N, Khosla VM, Lim RC: Delayed rupture of the spleen in a patient with mandibular fracture. J Oral Surg 35:597, 1979.

145. Bertolami CN, Kaban LB: Chin trauma: A clue to associated mandibular and cervical spine injury. Oral Surg 53:122, 1982.

146. Minton G, Tu KF: Pneumomediastinum, pneumothorax and cervical emphysema following mandibular fractures. Oral Surg 57:490, 1984.

147. Maw RB: A new look at maxillo-mandibular fixation of mandibular fractures. J Oral Surg 39:189, 1981.

148. Amaratunga NA: The relation of age to the immobilization period required for healing of mandibular fractures. J Oral Maxillofac Surg 45:111, 1987.

149. Limchayseng LRG: Evaluation of treatment outcome of mandibular angle fractures. Review: 1988 Annual Scientific Sessions Abstracts. J Oral Maxillofac Surg 48:12, 1988.

150. Zallen RD, Curry JT: A study of antibiotic usage in compound mandibular fractures. J Oral Surg 33:431, 1975.

151. Winstanley RP: The management of fractures of the mandible. Br J Oral Maxillofac Surg 22:170, 1984.

152. Rapidis AD, Papavassiliou D, Popadimitrious J, et al: Fractures of the coronoid process of the mandible. Int J Oral Surg 14:126, 1985.

153. Messer EJ, Keller JJ: A rational approach to the mandibular parasymphyseal fracture. J Oral Surg 34:808, 1976.

154. Schaefer SD, Wessberg GA, Heaton SL: Monophasic extraskeletal mandibular fixation in head and neck surgery. Ann Otol Rhinol Laryngol 91:292, 1982.

155. Wessberg GA, Wolford LM: Monophase extraskeletal fixation principle for use in severe mandibular trauma. Int J Oral Surg 11:1, 1982.

156. Jones JK, VanSickels JE: Rigid fixation: A review of concepts and treatment of fractures. Oral Surg 65:13, 1988.

157. Chambers IG, Scully C: Mandibular fractures in India during the Second World War (1944 and 1945): Analysis of the Anawdon Series. Br J Oral Maxillofac Surg 25:357, 1987.

158. Schneider SS, Stern M: Teeth in the line of mandibular fractures. J Oral Surg 29:107, 1971.

159. Chuong R, Donoff RB: Intraoral open reduction of mandibular fractures. Int J Oral Surg 14:22, 1985.

160. Roed-Peterson B, Andreasen JO: Prognosis of permanent teeth involved in jaw fractures. Scand J Dent Res 78:343, 1970.

161. Chan DM, Demuth RJ, Miller SH, Jastak JT: Management of mandibular fractures in unreliable patient populations. Ann Plast Surg 13:298, 1984.

162. Wagner WF, Neal DC, Alpert B: Morbidity associated with extraoral open reduction of mandibular fractures. J Oral Surg 37:97, 1979.

163. Kerr NW: Some observations on infection in maxillofacial fractures. Br J Oral Surg 4:132, 1966.

164. Freihofer HPM, Sailer HF: Experiences with intraoral transosseous wiring of mandibular fractures. J Maxillofac Surg 1:248, 1973.

165. Theriot BA, VanSickels JE, Triplett RG, Nishioka GJ: Intraosseous wire fixation vs. rigid osseous fixation of mandibular fractures. J Oral Maxillofac Surg 45:577, 1987.

166. Tu HK, Tenhulzen D: Compression osteosynthesis of mandibular fractures. J Oral Maxillofac Surg 43:585, 1985.

167. Cawood JI: Small plate osteosynthesis of mandibular fractures. Br J Oral Maxillofac Surg 23:77, 1985.

168. Bochlogyros PN: Non-union of fractures of the mandible. J Maxillofac Surg 13:189, 1985.

169. McDade AM, McNicol RD, Ward-Booth P, et al: The aetiology of maxillofacial injuries with special reference to the abuse of alcohol. Int J Oral Surg 11:152, 1982.

170. Adele R, Eriksson B, Nylin O, Ridell A: Delayed healing of fractures of the mandibular body. Int J Oral Maxillofac Surg 16:15, 1987.

171. Eid K, Lynch DJ, Whitaker LA: Mandibular fractures—the problem patient. J Trauma 16:658, 1976.

172. Cannell H, Boyd R: The management of maxillofacial injuries in vagrant alcoholics. J Maxillofac Surg 13:121, 1985.

173. Milford ML, Loizeaux AD: Facial paralysis secondary to mandibular fracture: Report of case. J Oral Surg 30:605, 1972.

174. Rapids AD, Brock DO: Delayed facial paralysis after a condylar fracture. Br J Oral Surg 14:220, 1977.

175. Schmidseder R, Scheunemann H: Nerve injury in fractures of the condylar neck. J Maxillofac Surg 5:186, 1977.

CHAPTER 17

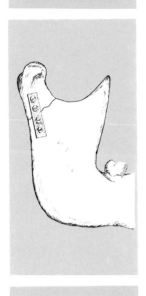

MANAGEMENT OF INJURIES TO THE TEMPOROMANDIBULAR JOINT REGION

L. GEORGE UPTON, D.D.S., M.S.

Injuries to the temporomandibular joint (TMJ) and associated structures are of clinical significance owing to the frequency of injuries seen, as well as the potential for residual altered form and function. This chapter addresses the management of injuries to the TMJ as well as fractures of the condylar neck and base. Trauma to these structures may produce alterations in maxillomandibular position in addition to producing varying degrees of pain and dysfunction.

ANATOMIC CONSIDERATIONS

As a prerequisite to managing injuries in this region, one should have a clear understanding of the anatomy involved. The TMJs represent a bilateral articulation of the mandible to the cranium, and they accommodate the movements of the lower jaw. Functionally, the condyles of the mandible move in different ways; these movements can generally be divided into rotational and translational movements (Fig. 17–1). Early interincisal opening up to about 26 mm can be achieved by pure rotation of the head of the condyle in the glenoid fossa. Opening beyond that point requires the condyle to translate down the articular eminence, sliding forward to achieve more mouth opening. Thus, with certain types of internal joint derangements, approximately 25 to 26 mm of interincisal opening can be achieved, even though the condylar head in fact moves very little owing to disc-condyle interference. Normally, these movements exist in combination during speaking and chewing patterns.

The articular disc, or meniscus, is an important component of the TMJ. It absorbs some of the functional stresses and facilitates smooth gliding of the condyle down the articular eminence. The disc is a biconcave structure that is positioned from the superiormost aspect of the mandibular condyle to the anteriormost aspect in the closed position of the jaw. The meniscus consists primarily of dense collagen with little vascularity. The posterior attachment of the disc is highly vascular and is richly innervated by the auriculotemporal branch of the trigeminal nerve. Along the anterior attachment is the superior head of the lateral pterygoid muscle. The articular disc

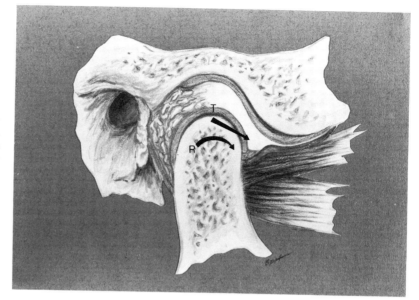

FIGURE 17–1. Drawing of the temporomandibular joint (TMJ) in the closed-mouth position. Arrows illustrate the rotation (R) and translation (T) movements of the condyle when the mouth opens.

divides the lower and upper joint spaces. The posterior bar of the disc is normally about 3 mm thick, the thinner central area is about 1 mm thick, and the anterior bar is normally about 2 mm thick. In the open position, as the condylar head moves forward, the disc rolls to a posterior position on the head of the condyle. The meniscus should always maintain a position of maximal interface between the contact points of bone of the two structures, the condyle and the temporal bone (Fig. 17–2).

There are important muscle attachments associated with the joint itself. The superior head of the lateral pterygoid attaches to the anterior medial aspect of the articular disc, or meniscus, and to the anteromedial condylar neck. It is thought to stabilize the disc during closure. The inferior head of the lateral pterygoid muscle functions to open the mouth through its insertion on the anteromedial neck of the condyle. When activated, it pulls the condyles down the eminence into an open-mouth position.

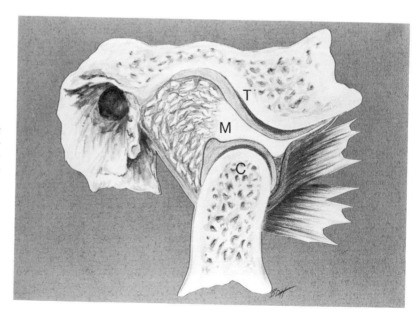

FIGURE 17–2. Drawing of the TMJ in the open-mouth position. Note the forward position of the meniscus (M) relative to the temporal bone (T) and the posterior position relative to the condyle (C).

INCIDENCE AND CLASSIFICATION OF TEMPOROMANDIBULAR JOINT FRACTURES

The published incidence of mandibular fractures involving the condyle varies widely. Early reports cite this frequency to be 8 per cent,[1] whereas more recent reports note the incidence to be as high as 30 to 40 per cent.[2] This discrepancy may be related to the difference in evaluators as well as to the development of more sophisticated radiographic techniques. Of 120 condylar fractures reported by the C.J. Lyons study,[1] 30 were noted bilaterally. The incidence of multiple mandibular fractures may be as high as 58 per cent.[3] The strongest correlation of condylar fractures in that study was noted with fractures of the symphysis and the contralateral condyle. Thompson[4] found a high correlation between bilateral condylar fractures and fractures of the symphysis or parasymphyseal region. This was not found to be the case by others.[5]

The primary cause of condylar fractures is trauma to the mandible. The origin of trauma varies significantly from one culture to another. In the United States, the primary sources are motor vehicle accidents and personal violence.[2,3,6] The origin of fractures in the pediatric group shifts to other sources, primarily falls.[5,7]

Numerous authors have proposed classification systems for condylar fractures.[8-17] A recent classification system set forth by Wood[18] is an anatomic system that describes the level of fracture, the position of the condylar head relative to the articular fossa, and the relationship of fractured segments. Displacement of the condylar segment most frequently occurs anteriorly and medially, reflecting the influence of the lateral pterygoid muscle pull[19] (Fig. 17–3). However, in some instances, the displacement of the condyle is noted to occur laterally[6] and posteriorly,[1] and in other instances, the condyle may be displaced into the external auditory canal or intracranial fossa.[20-22]

DIAGNOSTIC FINDINGS

When the patient with condylar fractures is examined shortly after the traumatic event, a number of classic findings can be noted. These include the following:

1. Evidence of facial trauma, especially in the area of the mandible and symphysis

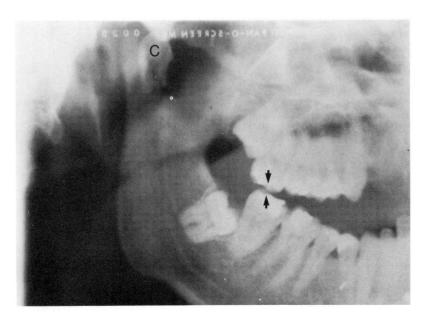

FIGURE 17–3. Radiograph illustrating anterior and medial displacement of condyle (C), reflecting the direction of pull of the attached medial pterygoid muscle. Note hyperocclusion of the posterior dentition (arrows).

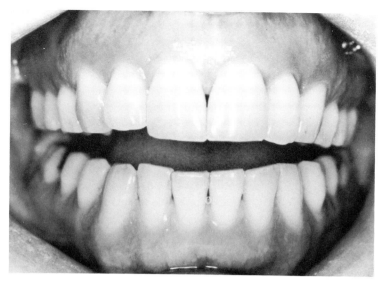

FIGURE 17–4. Clinical picture of an anterior open bite secondary to bilateral condylar fractures and resultant loss of posterior vertical dimension.

2. Localized pain and swelling in the region of the TMJ
3. Limitation in opening
4. Deviation, upon opening, toward the involved side
5. Posterior dental open bite on the contralateral side
6. Shift of dental occlusion toward the ipsilateral side with possible crossbite
7. Blood in the external auditory canal
8. Pain upon palpation over the fracture site
9. Lack of condylar movement upon palpation done either transmeatally or laterally over the condyle
10. Upon protrusion, deviation of the mandible toward the involved side
11. Inability of the patient to go into mandibular excursion away from the involved side
12. Difficulty in lateral excursions as well as protrusion
13. Generally, the occurrence of anterior open bite with bilateral subcondylar fractures (Fig. 17–4).

The radiographic evaluation may include a variety of films. The film obtained with the Orthopantomograph is the most useful screening film[23]; however, this equipment is not always available. Other radiographs that have been shown to be useful over the years include the low Towne view, right and left lateral oblique views of the mandible, posteroanterior mandibular view, and various TMJ views. Special studies would include tomography of the TMJ regions, both coronally and sagittally. These same views can be well represented by computerized tomography (CT).[24] Most recently, evaluation of the TMJ with magnetic resonance imaging (MRI) has been described.[25]

It is not uncommon to see patients with subcondylar fractures that have not been diagnosed initially. In these instances, the patient may present at a later date, describing a gradual opening of the bite[26] as well as persistent pain and dysfunction.[27,28]

TREATMENT OF CONDYLAR FRACTURES

The management of condylar fractures can be divided into nonsurgical and surgical treatments. Within the area of fracture management, there is much controversy and varied opinion related to the specific treatment modalities. The variety of opinions is related to the complexity of the functional anatomy of this region as well as to the impact of the age of the patient, the type of fracture, concomitant injuries, and associated anatomic findings.

The general consensus in the literature is that in most cases management of condylar fractures is best achieved through nonsurgical means. The obvious advantage is the avoidance of morbidity and complications associated with surgery. Numerous reviews of patient series indicate a high percentage of success with nonsurgical management.[1,6,29-31]

Nonsurgical Management of Condylar Fractures

Approaches to managing condylar fractures nonsurgically vary from doing nothing to employing sophisticated mechanical devices. In general, condylar fractures that do not require active treatment are those in patients in whom the functional range of motion and occlusion are essentially normal and there is no significant pain associated with the injury. This situation is most commonly seen in nondisplaced or minimally displaced fractures. As with any other area of biology, a wide range of anatomic and functional findings may be noted. If the patient's pain and dysfunction are significant, temporary immobilization of the maxillomandibular complex is indicated. Similarly, if significant deviation of the mandible occurs upon opening or if varying degrees of malocclusion are noted, active treatment is required. For patients who are able to establish an occlusal relationship but who have deviation upon opening, simple muscle training in front of a mirror may be adequate. The addition of Class II elastic forces on the involved side and vertical elastic forces on the noninvolved side may be beneficial in other cases.

In instances in which the degree of condylar displacement has resulted in an alteration in the ramus height, producing malocclusion, establishment of a normal maxillomandibular relationship is indicated through intermaxillary fixation.[31] The length of intermaxillary fixation is determined by the age of the patient as well as by the location and severity of fracture displacement.[32] In general, extracapsular condylar fractures in an adult, without major displacement, may be managed with intermaxillary fixation for 2 to 4 weeks, depending upon the degree of displacement. After this, Class II elastic forces on the involved side, combined with exercises, may be indicated to facilitate functional rehabilitation of the range of mandibular movement. In cases of intracapsular fractures with possible intracapsular hematoma, the concern for ankylosis is much greater.[33,34] This concern is especially true for children. Under these circumstances, the likelihood of major disruption in occlusion is not as great owing to eruptive and adaptive processes, and conversely, the need for early mobilization is of greater importance. Consequently, immobilization is avoided or kept to a minimum if possible. Early return to function and active physical therapy are appropriate in patients who require intermaxillary fixation.[35]

Some authors advocate the use of other devices to allow re-establishment of normal form and function with the avoidance of intermaxillary fixation. These include special extracranial fixation devices,[36,37] functional devices,[38,39] and intraoral orthodontic appliances.[40] These are recommended primarily for children who are continuing to experience active mandibular growth.

Pediatric Considerations in the Treatment of Condylar Fractures

Condylar fractures in the child represent a special problem, primarily because of varying degrees of active growth within the condyle and ramus. Since one of the primary growth centers is in the area of the condyle itself, disturbance in this region is felt by many to create potentially significant mandibular deformity as a child reaches adulthood.[41,42] It also appears that children are more susceptible to ankylosis in instances of intracapsular fracture and hematoma.[34]

There is no consensus regarding what happens to the condylar head after fracture-dislocation in children. Some believe that the condylar head will reposition itself, provided space is established through intermaxillary fixation.[43,44] Others believe that the condylar head is resorbed and a new condylar head grows from the condylar stump.[45,46] In some patients, it appears that the previous condyle does not reposition itself and that a new condyle may grow and, in some instances, be later identified as a "double condyle."[47]

Because of legitimate concerns for ankylosis associated with intracapsular condylar fractures, and potential subcondylar fractures that produce hematoma within the joint space itself in young children, there is an attempt either to avoid or to abbreviate the period of intermaxillary fixation. Consequently, in children it is even more important to avoid intermaxillary fixation when pain is minimal and occlusion is satisfactory.[32] When intermaxillary fixation is indicated because of pain or malocclusion, fixation lasting from 1 to 3 weeks is appropriate, depending upon the age of the patient and degree of displacement of the condylar fracture.[32] As in adults, postoperative functional rehabilitation is appropriate through the use of Class II elastics or functional exercise therapy or both.[2] A more detailed discussion of the management of fractures in children is presented in Chapter 27.

Surgical Correction of Condylar Fractures

Although the majority of condylar fractures appear to be successfully treated with nonsurgical techniques, a certain percentage of patients will have an unsatisfactory result. Ankylosis, malocclusion, continued pain, and dysfunction are examples of residual difficulties associated with condylar fractures.[1,26,48,49] Therefore, surgical intervention has been advocated for various types of condylar fractures.[50-52] These indications will vary from surgeon to surgeon.

It would be most appropriate prior to considering surgical intervention to evaluate a patient carefully through clinical and radiographic means to determine if nonsurgical management would likely lead to unsatisfactory results. An example of such potentially troublesome conditions is severe condylar displacement with and even without significant malocclusion. The potential morbidity with such major condylar displacements includes the predisposition for subsequent malocclusion, and even in instances when this is not the result, patients may experience pain and dysfunction from the pseudoarthrosis that subsequently occurs. Clearly, fracture-dislocations into the auditory canal or intracranial fossa[53,54] and an anterior position that prevents reasonable mandibular movement are indications for open reduction. An exception in the latter case may be if the surgeon can manually manipulate the condylar segment into a more functional position.[19] Another situation indicating open reduction is bilateral condylar fractures associated with a comminuted Le Fort-type craniofacial disjunction.[50] Such a procedure to re-establish craniomandibular relations should be considered an alternative to extracranial stabilization or plate fixation.

Surgical Considerations in Condylar Fractures

Traditionally, the vast majority of condylar fractures have been treated with nonsurgical techniques. As previously indicated, this is partially because of the good results achieved. In addition, however, nonsurgical techniques have been used because of the fear of complications associated with surgery. These concerns are justified because of the difficulties encountered with surgical approaches to the TMJ. Until recently, the traditional approach to this region was associated with altered function of the temporofrontal branches of the facial nerve, with a postoperative incidence as high as 25 to 30 per cent.[55] In most of these cases, the alteration was temporary. Less commonly, hyperhidrosis can be a complication of this approach.

SURGICAL APPROACHES TO THE TEMPOROMANDIBULAR JOINT

The three most commonly described approaches to fractures involving the condyle include the preauricular approach, the submandibular approach, and the intraoral approach. Access through each of these three approaches varies significantly, and each combination of operations is dictated by the specific type of problem and the surgical treatment plan decided upon.

Advantages of the preauricular approach, which may involve preauricular, endaural, or postauricular incisions, include the following:

1. Maximal access to intracapsular injuries, including disc injury
2. Direct access for condylar head and high condylar neck fractures for various means of fixation
3. The ability to confirm directly proper condyle-disc-fossa relationships after reduction.

The disadvantages of this approach include the following:

1. Risk to upper branches of the facial nerve
2. Gustatory hyperhidrosis
3. Potential surgical scar of the joint apparatus itself
4. Scar on face, though normally not cosmetically unpleasing
5. Limited access to low condylar neck fractures

Advantages of the submandibular approach include the following:

1. Good access to the mandibular ramus and condylar neck region
2. A surgical dissection, which, to most oral and maxillofacial surgeons, traditionally has been more familiar than the preauricular approach
3. Avoidance of risking damage to the upper branches of the facial nerve

The disadvantages of this approach include the following:

1. Risk of damage to the marginal mandibular branch of the facial nerve.
2. Limited access to high condylar neck and condylar fractures.
3. Poor direct access to high condylar fractures for application of certain fixation techniques.
4. Inability to inspect the TMJ proper.

Advantages of the intraoral approach include the following:

1. No external scar
2. Ease of access
3. No risk to the facial nerves

The disadvantages of this approach include the following:

1. Limitation in the access to condylar or high condylar neck fractures
2. Difficulty in having access to place fixation devices
3. Inability to inspect the TMJ directly

SURGICAL APPROACHES TO THE CONDYLE

Technique

A detailed description of the Risdon and preauricular approaches is presented in Chapter 12. The preauricular approach historically has had a relatively high incidence of facial nerve involvement.[55] Consequently, variations have evolved that have dramatically reduced the incidence of facial nerve complications. Modifications of the earlier approaches include elimination of the hockey stick forward extension on the superior pole, elimination of the subcutaneous flap dissection, and an approach to the joint region through a subtemporal fascial-periosteal envelope. Such an approach allows avoidance of the facial nerve branches by staying first posterior and then deep to the nerve.[56] Skin incisions include preauricular, endaural, and posterior auricular.[57]

Methods of Fixation of Condylar Fractures

Transosseous wiring is the most common means of transosseous stabilization of the bone segments associated with condylar fractures[48,57] (Fig. 17–5A). This technique relies on the availability of equipment and a familiarity with transosseous wiring techniques involving other traumatic and surgical fractures of the facial bones. This technique is easiest to use in low condyle–ramus fractures owing to the density of bone and ease of access. If possible, two transosseous wires are utilized for stabilization. The higher the fracture occurs along the condylar process, the more difficult it is to use transosseous wiring, because of both the smaller size of the bone structure and the decreased bone density. Classically, this technique is associated with difficulty in passing wire from a medial to lateral surface of the bone segment in an area that is poorly accessible. This procedure normally requires a wire-passing drill bit or a fine secondary wire to pull the transosseous wire through the drill hole from a medial to lateral direction. Messer[58] describes a technique of essentially creating a lariat around the condylar neck segment and passing two transosseous wires through the distal segment, achieving osseous stabilization (Fig. 17–5B).

Rigid fixation using small bone plates is another alternative (Fig. 17–5C). Whether it be compression plates, as described in the European literature,[59,60] or the fixation plates currently being used in orthognathic surgery,[50] this can be an effective means of transosseous fixation. In high fractures, the plate may be placed directly through the preauricular approach, while in those fractures for which the submandibular approach is used, drill holes are placed using a percutaneous cannula.[51]

Various techniques using threaded pins have also been described. One of the simplest involves the use of a Kirschner wire that is threaded from the inferior aspect of the condylar neck upward into the condylar head. The wire is then cut approximately 3 cm inferior to the fracture site. A groove in the lateral ramus region is made to correspond to the exposed portion of the wire. The wire is inlaid into this groove, and the bone segments are aligned. With the use of two transosseous wires, the Kirschner wire is then secured to the ramus segment[60] (Fig. 17–6A).

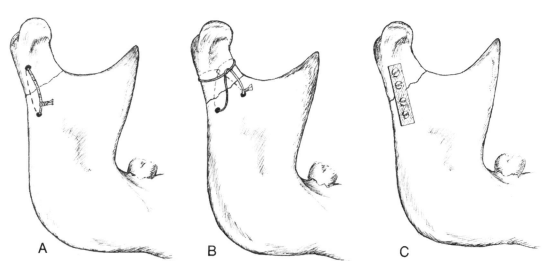

FIGURE 17–5. *A*, Drawing illustrating transosseous wiring technique. *B*, Variation of transosseous technique described by Messer.[58] *C*, Metal plate for fracture fixation.

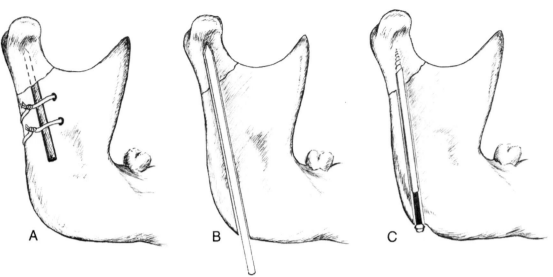

FIGURE 17-6. *A*, Drawing illustrating use of the Steinmann pin, which is cut and inlaid into ramus segment and secured by wire. *B*, Long pin technique with threading through ramus into condylar segment. *C*, Technique to reduce fracture under compression using nut at lower ramus area, as described by Petzel.[62,63]

A technically more difficult technique involves threading the Steinmann pin from the inferior aspect of the ramus upward through the condylar neck and into the condylar head segment, which has been positioned into the normal anatomic relationship to the ramus segment[61] (Fig. 17-6*B*). This technique can produce good anatomic reduction and fixation, provided the pin does not perforate the buccal or lingual cortical plates prior to emerging from the stump of the distal segment in the fractured area.

A sophisticated modification of the previous technique is described by Petzel.[62,63] He creates a flat surface on the inferior border of the ramus and, using special instrumentation, drills a hole up through the ramus and then inserts a pin into the condylar head segment. Once the condylar head has been reduced and fixed, the pin is cut and a nut is placed at the end of the threaded pin. As it is tightened, it tends to create a compression effect on the fracture site (Fig. 17-6*C*). With this technique, the patient is able to function immediately. The pin is removed at a later date.

It is evident from the techniques previously described that the surgeon has a variety of procedures from which to choose when considering open reduction of condylar and subcondylar fractures. He or she must first, however, weigh the advantages and disadvantages of open reduction versus the risks and outcome of a closed procedure.

Late Management of Condylar Fractures

A long-term sequela of condylar fractures is pain in the TMJ region as well as in the associated masticatory muscles. Limitation in opening and lateral excursions may be noted, as well as deviation on opening. In instances of fracture malunion, significant malocclusions may be seen.

EVALUATION OF CHRONIC TEMPOROMANDIBULAR JOINT INJURIES

In patients presenting with complaints months to years after condylar fractures, the clinician should be alert to certain problems. These include adhesions, disc derangements, disc perforations, osteoarthritis, ankylosis, and various maxillomandibular discrepancies secondary to malunions of the condylar head.[48,64] Other abnormalities noted in association with condylar fractures include chronic pain of the masticatory muscles and malocclusions.[52]

Depending upon the type of injury sustained within the joint, different diagnostic procedures are indicated. These include history and clinical examination as well as a variety of imaging techniques. Evidence of lateral or endaural TMJ pain upon palpation and clicking or crepitation are important signs of underlying pathology. Palpation of the symptomatic masticatory muscles is beneficial for the evidence it can provide of pain in the joint versus the muscle upon forced opening. The occlusal relationship of the patient and the range of motion should also be evaluated. Panographic radiographs are beneficial in providing a view of the condyle-ramus relationship, and transcranial views may yield additional information on the anatomy of the condyle and glenoid fossa. Tomography is useful for better details on the anatomy of the condyle and glenoid fossa and their inter-relationship. For evaluation of possible ankylosis, tomography and CT provide the greatest amount of information. For suspected disc derangements, arthrography is the most useful, with MRI also supplying pertinent data. For condylar malunions that create an abnormal maxillomandibular relationship, additional studies consistent with standard orthognathic case workups are appropriate.

LATE MANAGEMENT OF DYSFUNCTION

Alteration in the functional range of mandibular movements secondary to condylar fractures may be related to significant change in joint anatomy. Patients may also have residual dysfunction acquired secondary to a less severe initial injury without major anatomic alteration. These patients are most amenable to physical therapy, with the goal being to retrain the masticatory muscles in patterns that allow a more normal mandibular range of movement.[31] Classically, the physical therapy is directed toward increasing condylar translation on the traumatized side, thus reducing deviation on opening and enabling the mandible to shift away from the site of the previous injury. It will also allow reduction of compensatory movements of the uninvolved joint. Physical therapy involves applying moist heat to the masticatory muscles to facilitate increased extensibility and decrease tenseness. Active and passive stretching of the involved side may also be appropriate. Exercises in front of a mirror are beneficial. Range-of-motion exercises should be done at least four times a day, preceded by the application of moist heat to the associated muscles. If the muscles are symptomatic, anti-inflammatory medications and soft diet are also appropriate. In instances of masticatory muscle hyperactivity, such as bruxism, the addition of an occlusal bite splint may be efficacious.

LATE MANAGEMENT OF INTRA-ARTICULAR INJURIES

Some long-term sequelae of intra-articular injuries include adhesions, disc derangements, and perforations.[48,65] Generally, if the symptoms from such associated injuries are not managed successfully through nonsurgical means, including a joint rest regimen, moist heat, anti-inflammatory medications, occlusal splint therapy, and physical therapy, then surgical intervention may be considered. For significant adhesions, lysing through an open procedure is the most common technique utilized. Recently, the use of arthroscopy to release adhesions in the TMJ has been introduced.[66]

Disc derangements may be managed through a variety of surgical procedures, with each procedure having advocates. Procedures described include meniscus repair,[67,68] meniscorrhaphy,[69-71] meniscectomy with implant,[72-74] meniscectomy without implant,[75-77] and condylotomy.[78] If the articular disc is of fairly normal configuration and perforation only is noted, an attempt to repair the perforation can be carried out, as suggested in laboratory studies.[79] The use of dermal grafts to repair the perforation has also been described.[80]

MANAGEMENT OF TEMPOROMANDIBULAR JOINT INJURIES

Condylar fractures with resultant intra-articular hematoma may lead to ankylosis of the TMJ,[81] which occurs commonly before the age of 10.[82] If ankylosis occurs unilaterally or bilaterally during the developmental period of the patient, significant alteration in mandibular development may occur. In the adult, while the form of the mandible may not be altered, an inability to open the mouth adequately may lead to significant compromise in the maintenance of good dental hygiene as well as in the proper mechanical preparation of food for digestion. Increased risks with anesthesia morbidity are also noted because of the difficulties associated with direct laryngoscopy during endotracheal intubation.

A variety of approaches have been described for managing ankylosis of the TMJ.[83-86] If bone fusion is localized, as determined by tomography or CT scans, an approach to the joint proper is indicated, with removal of the bridge of bone in the associated area (Fig. 17-7). Placement of a temporary Dacron-reinforced Silastic sheet for approximately 1 to 2 months should be considered. If major bone fusion occurs, attempts to redefine the joint space with bone-cutting instruments may be appropriate. Normally, in this instance the articular disc is either no longer present or unrepairable. Consequently, the use of an intrapositional material, such as temporal fascia,[87] dermal grafts,[88] muscle,[89] cartilage,[90] silicone,[91,92] and other alloplasts,[93] has been described. These procedures, of course, usually require a preauricular approach to the TMJ. In instances of major bone fusion of the joint region, a gap arthroplasty involving the superior portion of the ramus may also be considered via a Risdon approach. In this instance, again an alloplast is generally interposed to prevent reankylosis, although some feel it is not necessary.[94,95] Total joint replacement has also been described[96,97] and is discussed in Chapter 31.

Frequently, a coronoid section is carried out as an adjunctive procedure in treating ankylosis to facilitate postsurgical rehabilitation. In addition, stripping of the masseter attachments on the ramus may be considered. On a long-term basis, however, this may not prove to be beneficial owing to the ultimate need to restretch the foreshortened muscles to a more functional length. Active opening exercises and physical therapy are also appropriate in all of these instances in an attempt to return the foreshortened muscles to a normal functional length and to prevent reankylosis.[98]

MANAGEMENT OF MALOCCLUSIONS

Various degrees of malocclusion may be seen secondary to injuries of the TMJ and condylar regions. The degree of malocclusion may be related to both severity and timing of injury. In instances of unilateral condylar fracture malunions, the loss in ramus height may be expressed in various degrees of midline deviation toward the affected side and development of ipsilateral hyperocclusion. An open bite may develop on the opposite side. In bilateral fracture malunions, classically an anterior open bite is noted.

Children who sustain injuries in this area may have disturbances in the growth potential of the mandible. This disturbance may be seen in ankylosis or in joint damage with resultant degenerative arthritic changes. In unilateral cases, deviation of the mandibular occlusion toward the affected side may occur, as well as an upward

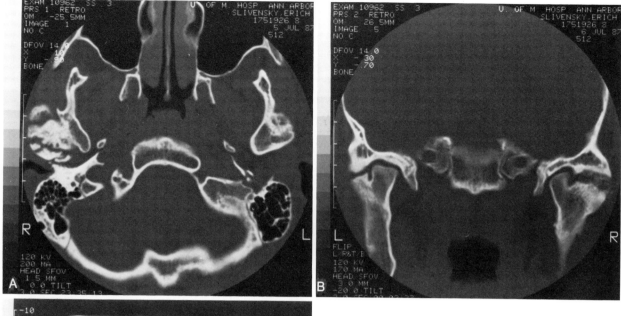

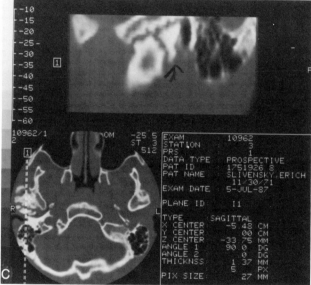

FIGURE 17-7. Computerized tomographic (CT) scan of bilateral ankylosis of TMJ secondary to bilateral condylar fractures. *A*, Transverse view. *B*, Coronal view. *C*, Sagittal view.

cant to the occlusal plane secondary to disturbance of the downward growth of the mandibulomaxillary complex on the involved side. Bilateral involvement may produce significant Class II dental-skeletal malrelationships.

In treating malocclusion secondary to ankylosis, the initial phase is to manage the joint ankylosis through intervention, as previously described. Pediatric malocclusions secondary to joint injury may be favorably modified over time, utilizing functional appliances to enhance normal form through stimulating a more normal function.[41] In addition, functional appliances may reduce the tendency for abnormal maxillary compensatory changes. In some instances, these appliances may provide adequate management of the malocclusion. In other cases, however, the appliance is an adjunct to surgical intervention in acquiring the degree of correction that may ultimately be achieved. Such appliances may obviate a maxillary component to the surgery.

The surgical management of traumatically produced malocclusions differs from that of the standard developmental malocclusions in various ways. In many patients with traumatic malocclusion, the dentition is normal, thus obviating presurgical orthodontic preparation. In addition, in many patients the problem is unilateral, a feature that is much less commonly seen in those patients with developmental deformity.

Finally, these patients usually have normal overlying muscle and soft tissue anatomy, which will more easily accommodate the repositioning of the skeleton without the tendency for relapse. Treatment planning for these patients requires essentially the same protocol as that used for standard orthognathic surgical corrections.

A variety of surgical procedures may be utilized in the management of a spectrum of traumatically induced malocclusions. For instance, in patients with a unilateral fracture malunion resulting in deviation of the mandible and opposite arch crossbite without significant joint complaints, a sagittal osteotomy may bring about a satisfactory return of function. On the other hand, if the patient is experiencing joint pain along with pseudoarthrosis secondary to the condylar malunion, intervention within the joint region may be appropriate. Intervention must certainly be considered if the patient has failed to respond to therapy directed at controlling myofascial pain components. Repositioning malunited condylar segments in the late post-traumatic period is technically difficult to accomplish because of remodeling and deformity of the condyle-ramus segments. In instances of minor malrelationships, a procedure similar to a vertical ramus osteotomy to reposition the proximal segment superiorly in the glenoid fossa may be considered.[52,99] In most severe condylar malunions, condylectomy has been advocated.[100] Reconstruction with costochondral rib grafts or alloplastic joint prosthesis[96,101] may be a possible solution. These procedures apply to both unilateral and bilateral cases.

For bilateral fracture malunions with resultant severe anterior open bite, the ramus segments should be approached with caution in any attempt to correct the malocclusion through lengthening the shortened ramus. It may be difficult to re-establish condyle-ramus height owing to prolonged muscle foreshortening. As a result, the anteroposterior dimension may be adequately achieved through either mandibular sagittal osteotomies or condyle replacements, as previously described. The open bite component, however, while treated with mandibular sagittal osteotomies, may be more reliably managed with a posterior maxillary intrusion osteotomy.

DISLOCATION OF THE TEMPOROMANDIBULAR JOINT

Dislocation of the TMJ may be defined as a forward movement of the condyle in front of the articular eminence that requires some form of manipulation to achieve reduction. Dislocation is in contrast to subluxation, in which the patient can reduce the condyle back into the fossa normally. Dislocations of the condyle occur rarely and may be preceded by a history of trauma as well as prolonged dental work or extraction of molars. The most frequent event preceding dislocation is yawning. The common denominator in this condition is the stretching of capsule ligaments, thus causing a loss of condylar stability. It is believed that this condition is aggravated by a pain–muscle spasm complex that causes the masticatory muscles to contract, thus locking the condyle in front of the articular eminence. Another aggravating condition may be phenothiazine medication, which is shown to produce muscle spasm, thus enhancing the potential for dislocation.[102] The longer the dislocation remains unreduced, the more difficult it is to reposition the condyle.

Acute TMJ dislocation is generally managed with manual reduction. This technique involves the slow development of forces in a direction that forces the condylar head downward and then behind the articular eminence to return it to the glenoid fossa. Care is taken not to apply immediate force and thus irritate the already tight muscles, producing more pain and muscle spasm. Appreciation for the muscular component is underscored by the observation that spontaneous reduction has been seen to occur following the intravenous administration of diazepam. Injection of a local anesthetic in the periarticular area has also been successful.[103] As previously mentioned, the longer the interval of dislocation, the less likely that these measures will achieve reduction. In these instances, a general anesthetic may be required. In rarer circumstances, a difficult reduction may be assisted by placement of traction wires at the angles of the mandible.[104]

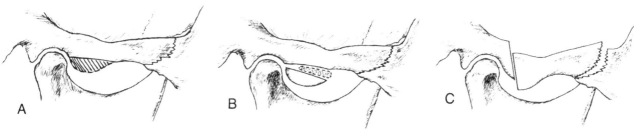

Figure 17–8.   *A*, Drawing illustrating removal of articular eminence to facilitate spontaneous reduction of condylar dislocation. *B*, Augmentation of articular eminence through interposition of Proplast. *C*, Augmentation of articular eminence through downfracture osteotomy.

After reduction of the dislocation, the mandible is restrained in its ability to open by some form of skeletal control, through either arch bars or Barton bandage–type devices. The purpose is to prevent immediate redislocation through continued lateral pterygoid and suprahyoid muscle spasm. The restriction of opening, however, is not seen to allow tightening of the loosened capsular ligaments in most cases. Consequently, with chronic dislocation, the use of sclerosing solutions injected into the joint spaces has been advocated.[105,106] This practice has risks of hypomobility within the joint as well as possible threat to the facial nerve. The technique has not been uniformly successful.

A variety of surgical approaches have been advocated to manage the problem of recurrent dislocation. Methods include tightening of the capsular ligaments of the TMJ,[107–109] scarification of the oral mucosa,[110] scarification of the temporal tendon,[111] various implants associated with the articular eminence,[112–114] osteotomies with inferior positioning of the anterior portion of the eminence[115–117] (Fig. 17–8), deepening of the glenoid fossa by resection of the articular disc,[118] lateral pterygoid myotomy,[119–121] bone onlay grafts of the articular eminence,[122,123] condylotomy,[124] condylectomy,[125] ligation of the condyle to the zygomatic arch using mersilene strips,[126,127] and attachment of Vitallium mesh to the zygoma to prevent forward condylar movement.[128] Additional methods include augmentation of the eminence through interpositional grafting with Proplast[129] (Fig. 17–8) or simply removing the barrier to spontaneous reduction through eminectomy[130,131] (Fig. 17–8).

As in other clinical problems, reversible treatment should first be employed prior to surgical intervention. In the selection of irreversible intervention, potential risks and complications must be balanced against the expected outcome. In general, the less the internal joint structures are altered, the more desirable the procedure. It is apparent from the wide variety of approaches described that there is no ideal solution to this clinical problem.

It is evident that trauma to the TMJ region may result in significant long-term disability. Successful management of these injuries requires careful evaluation and comprehensive treatment planning in regard to both skeletal and soft tissue components. Because of the complexity of structures in this region, it may be very difficult to achieve a complete return to normal function after injury in spite of the best efforts made on the patient's behalf.

REFERENCES

1. Lyons JC: Fractures involving the mandibular condyle: A post treatment survey of 120 cases. J Oral Surg 5:45, 1947.
2. Olson RA, Fonseca RJ, Zeitler DL, Osborn DB: Fractures of the mandible: A review of 580 cases. J Oral Maxillofac Surg 40:1, 1982.
3. James BR, Frederickson C, Kent JN: Prospective study of mandibular fractures. J Oral Surg 39:275, 1981.
4. Thompson HG, Farmer AW, Lindsay WK: Condylar neck fractures of the mandible in children. Plast Reconstr Surg 34:452, 1964.
5. Leake D, Doykos III J, Habal MB, Murray

JE: Long-term follow-up of fractures of the mandibular condyle in children. Plast Reconstr Surg 47:127, 1971.

6. Blevins C, Gores RJ: Fractures of the mandibular condyloid process. Results of conservative treatment in 140 patients. J Oral Surg 19:392, 1961.

7. Fortunato MA, Fielding AF, Guernsey LH: Facial bone fractures in children. Oral Surg Oral Med Oral Pathol 53:225, 1982.

8. Ruedi G: Zur Klink der Gelenkkopffracturen des Unterkiefers. Schweiz Monatsschr Zahnhik 38:727, 1928.

9. DuFourmental L: Chirurgie de l'Articulation Temporomaxillaire. Paris, Masson and Company, 1929.

10. Thoma KH: Traumatic injury of the condyloid process of the mandible. N Engl J Med 218:63, 1938.

11. James WW, Fickling BW: Injuries of the Jaws and Face. London, John Bale and Staples, 1940.

12. Walker DG: Original communications. Br Dent J 72:265, 1942.

13. Thoma KH: Fractures and fracture dislocations of the mandibular condyle: A method for open reduction and internal wiring and one for skeletal fixation, with a report of 32 cases. J Oral Surg 3:3, 1945.

14. Goodsell JO: Tantalum in temporomandibular arthroplasty: Report of a case. J Oral Surg 5:41, 1947.

15. Rowe NL, Killey HC: Fractures of the Facial Skeleton. 2nd ed. London, E and S Livingstone, 1968.

16. Gilhuus-Moe O: Fractures of the Mandibular Condyle in the Growth Period. Part II. Experimental Subcondylar Fractures in Young Guinea Pigs. Thesis, Universitetsforlaget, Oslo, 1969, pp 145–210.

17. Lindahl L: Condylar fractures of the mandible. Int J Oral Surg 6:12, 1977.

18. Wood GD: The fractured condyle. Dental Update 8:219, 1981.

19. Leonard JR, Mancoll W, Duncan DG: Condylectomy. Role in treatment of jaw fractures. Arch Otolaryngol 87:117, 1968.

20. Pirok DJ, Merrill RG: Dislocation of the mandibular condyle into the middle cranial fossa. Oral Surg 29:13, 1970.

21. Zecha JJ: Mandibular condyle dislocation into the cranial fossa. Int J Oral Surg 6:141, 1977.

22. Copenhover RH, Dennis MJ, Kloppedal E, et al: Fracture of the glenoid fossa and dislocation of the mandibular condyle into the middle cranial fossa. J Oral Maxillofac Surg 43:974, 1985.

23. Chayra GA, Meador LR, Laskin DM: Comparison of panoramic and standard radiographs for the diagnosis of mandibular fractures. J Oral Maxillofac Surg 44:677, 1986.

24. Horowitz I, Abrahami E, Mintz SS: Demonstration of condylar fractures of the mandible by computed tomography. Oral Surg 54:263, 1982.

25. Chiles DG, Wilk RW, Harms SE: Magnetic resonance imaging in the diagnosis of temporomandibular disorders with a report of two cases. J Craniomand Pract 4:306, 1986.

26. Rees M, Weinberg S: Fractures of the mandibular condyle: Review of the literature and presentation of five cases with late complications. Oral Surg 73:37, 1983.

27. Gilhuus-Moe O: Fractures of the Mandibular Condyle in the Growth Period. Thesis, Universitetsforlaget, Oslo, 1969.

28. Helkimo M: Epidemiological surveys of dysfunction of the masticatory system. Oral Sci Rev 7:54, 1976.

29. Kromer H: Closed and open reduction of condylar fractures. Dent Rec 73:569, 1953.

30. MacLennan WD: Consideration of 180 cases of typical fractures of the mandibular condylar process. Br J Plast Surg 5:122, 1952.

31. Beekler DM, Walker RV: Condyle fractures. J Oral Surg 27:563, 1969.

32. Amaratunga NA: The relation of age to the immobilization period required for healing of mandibular fractures. J Oral Maxillofac Surg 45:111, 1987.

33. El-Mofty S: Cephalometric studies of patients with ankylosis of the temporomandibular joint. Oral Surg 44:153, 1977.

34. Topazian RG: Etiology of ankylosis of the temporomandibular joint: Analysis of 44 cases. J Oral Surg 22:227, 1964.

35. Walker RV: The consultant. J Oral Surg 24:366, 1966.

36. Vazirani S: Medial dislocated condyle fracture: Intraoral reduction with new devices. Dent Dig 74:422, 1968.

37. MaClennan W: Treatment of fractured mandibular condylar process: A useful bandage. Br J Oral Surg 14:226, 1977.

38. Hotz R: Functional jaw orthopedics in the treatment of condylar fractures. Am J Orthod 73:365, 1978.

39. Spitzer WJ, Zschiesche S, Steinhauser EW: Treatment of condylar fractures in children with functional orthodontic appliances. In Hjorting-Hansen E (ed): Proceedings from 8th International Conference on Oral and Maxillofacial Surgery (I.A.O.M.S.). Chicago, Quintessence Publishing Company, 1985, p 192.

40. Schettler D, Rehrmann A: Long-term results of functional treatment of condylar fractures with long bridle according to A. Rehrmann. J Maxillofac Surg 3:14, 1975.

41. Coccaro PJ: Restitution of mandibular form after condylar injury in infancy (a 7-year study of a child). Am J Orthod 55:32, 1969.

42. Engel MB, Brodie AG: Condylar growth and mandibular deformities. Surgery 22:976, 1947.

43. Walker DG: The mandibular condyle: 50 cases demonstrating arrest in development. Dent Pract 7:160, 1957.

44. Boyne PJ: Osseous repair and mandibular growth after subcondylar fractures. J Oral Surg 25:300, 1967.

45. Walker RV: Traumatic mandibular condylar fracture dislocations: Effect on growth in the macaca rhesus monkey. Am J Surg 100:850, 1960.

46. Anderson MF, Alling CC: Subcondylar fractures in young dogs. Oral Surg 19:263, 1965.

47. Stein LD, Steed DL, Ryan DE, Wampler HW: Removal of a medially attached, fractured condyle via an intraoral approach: Report of a case. J Oral Surg 37:357, 1979.

48. Curphey JE: The fracture dislocation of the temporomandibular joint. In Hjørting-Hansen E (ed): Proceedings from 8th International Conference on Oral and Maxillofacial Surgery (I.A.O.M.S.). Chicago, Quintessence Publishing Company, 1985, p 187.

49. MacLennan WD: Consideration of 180 cases

of typical fractures of the mandibular condylar process. Br J Plast Surg 5:122, 1952.

50. Zide MF, Kent JN: Indications for open reduction of mandibular condyle fractures. J Oral Maxillofac Surg 41:89, 1983.

51. Peters RA, Caldwell JB, Olsen TW: A technique for open reduction of subcondylar fractures. Oral Surg 41:273, 1976.

52. Harper RH, Weinberg SW: Treatment of malunited, unusually displaced bilateral condylar fractures: Report of a case. J Oral Surg 36:716, 1978.

53. Copenhaver RH, Dennis MJ, Kloppedal E, et al: Fracture of the glenoid fossa and dislocation of the mandibular condyle into the middle cranial fossa. J Oral Maxillofac Surg 43:974, 1985.

54. Zecha JJ: Mandibular condyle dislocation into the cranial fossa. Int J Oral Surg 6:141, 1977.

55. Dolwock MF, Kretzschmar DP: Morbidity associated with the preauricular and perimeatal approaches to the temporomandibular joint. J Oral Surg 40:699, 1982.

56. Popowich L, Crane RM Jr: Modified preauricular access to the temporomandibular apparatus. Oral Surg 54:257, 1982.

57. Kreutziger K: Surgery of the temporomandibular joint. I. Surgical anatomy and surgical incisions. Oral Surg 58:637, 1984.

58. Messer EJ: A simplified method of fixation of the fractured mandibular condyle. J Oral Surg 30:442, 1972.

59. Koberg WR, Momma WG: Treatment of fractures of the articular process by functional stable osteosynthesis using miniaturized dynamic compression plates. Int J Oral Surg 7:256, 1978.

60. Brown AE, Obeid G: A simplified method for the internal fixation of fractures of the mandibular condyle. Br J Oral Maxillofac Surg 22:145, 1984.

61. Stephenson KL, Graham WC: The use of the Kirschner pen in fractures of the condyle. Plast Reconstr Surg 10:14, 1952.

62. Petzel JR: Instrumentation and technique for screw-pin osteosynthesis of condylar fractures. J Maxillofac Surg 10:8, 1982.

63. Petzel JR: Functionally stable traction-screw osteosynthesis of condylar fractures. J Oral Maxillofac Surg 40:108, 1982.

64. Schwipper V, Holtje WJ, Keutken K: Conservative or surgical treatment of fractures of the condyle in adults. In Hjorting-Hansen E (ed): Proceedings from 8th International Conference on Oral and Maxillofacial Surgery (I.A.O.M.S.). Chicago, Quintessence Publishing Company, 1985, p 179.

65. Mercuri LG, Campbell RL, Shamaskih RG: Intra-articular meniscus dysfunction surgery. Oral Surg 54:613, 1982.

66. Sanders B: Arthroscope surgery of the temporomandibular joint: Treatment of internal derangement with persistent closed lock. Oral Surg 62:361, 1986.

67. Armandale T: Displacement of the interarticular cartilage of the lower jaw and its treatment by operation. Lancet 1:411, 1987.

68. McCarty WL Jr, Farrar WB: Surgery for internal derangements of the temporomandibular joint. Oral Surg 42:191, 1979.

69. Weinberg S: Eminectomy and meniscorrhaphy for internal derangements of the temporomandibular joint. Oral Surg 7:241, 1984.

70. Weinberg S, Cousens G: Meniscocondylar plication: A modified operation for surgical repositioning of the ectopic temporomandibular joint meniscus. Oral Surg 63:393, 1987.

71. Nespeca JA, Merrill RG: Sliding capsular discopexy. Oral Surg 63:9, 1987.

72. Ryan DE: Meniscectomy with Silastic implants. In 1984 Clinical Congress on Reconstruction with Biomaterials. Current Assessment and Temporomandibular Joint Surgical Update, San Diego, CA, January 20–22, 1984.

73. Kiersch TA: The use of Proplast Teflon implants for meniscectomy and disk repair in the temporomandibular joint. In 1984 Clinical Congress on Reconstruction with Biomaterials. Current Assessment and Temporomandibular Joint Surgical Update, San Diego, CA, January 20–22, 1984.

74. Bessette RW, Katzberg RW, Natiella JR, Rose MJ: Diagnosis and reconstruction of the human temporomandibular joint after trauma or internal derangement. Plast Reconstr Surg 75:192, 1985.

75. Kiehn CL: Meniscectomy for internal derangement of temporomandibular joint. Am J Surg 83:364, 1952.

76. Silver CM: Long term results of meniscectomy of the temporomandibular joint. J Craniomand Pract 3:46, 1985.

77. Westesson P, Eriksson L, Lindstrom C: Destructive lesions of the mandibular condyle following diskectomy with temporary silicone implant. Oral Surg 63:143, 1987.

78. Ward TG, Smith DC, Sommar M: Condylotomy for mandibular joint arthrosis. Br Dent J 103:147, 1947.

79. Stewart HM, Hann JR, DeTomasi DC, et al: Histologic fate of dermal grafts following implantation for temporomandibular joint meniscal perforation. A preliminary study. Oral Surg 62:481, 1986.

80. Letz M, Irby W: Repair of the adult temporomandibular joint meniscus with an autogenous dermal graft. J Oral Maxillofac Surg 42:167, 1984.

81. Topazian RG: Etiology of ankylosis of the temporomandibular joint: Analysis of 44 cases. J Oral Surg 22:227, 1964.

82. Shafer BS, Hine MK, Levy BM (eds): The Textbook of Oral Pathology. 3rd ed. Philadelphia, WB Saunders Company, 1974, p 652.

83. Dingman RO: Ankylosis of the temporomandibular joint. Am J Orthod Oral Surg 32:120, 1946.

84. Rowe NL: Surgery of the temporomandibular joint. Proc R Soc Med 65:383, 1972.

85. Ward TG: Surgery of the temporomandibular joint. Ann R Coll Surg 28:139, 1961.

86. Topazian RC: Comparison of gap and interposition arthroplasty in the treatment of temporomandibular joint ankylosis. J Oral Surg 24:205, 1966.

87. Blair VP: Operative treatment of ankylosis of the mandible. Surg Gynecol Obstet 19:436, 1914.

88. Georgaide N, Altany F, Pickrell K: An experimental and clinical evaluation of autogenous dermal grafts used in the treatment

of temporomandibular joint ankylosis. Plast Reconstr Surg 19:321, 1957.

89. Risdon F: Ankylosis of the temporomandibular joint. J Am Dent Assoc 21:1933, 1934.

90. Stuteville OH, LanFranchi RP: Surgical reconstruction of the temporomandibular joint. Am J Surg 90:931, 1955.

91. Bromberg BE, Song IC, Radlaver CB: Surgical treatment of massive bony ankylosis of the temporomandibular joint. Plast Reconstr Surg 45:66, 1969.

92. Silag JL, Schow CE: Temporomandibular joint arthroplasty: Review of the literature and report of a case. J Oral Surg 28:920, 1970.

93. Lindsay JS, Fulcher CL, Jazima HJ: Surgical management of ankylosis of the temporomandibular joint: Report of two cases. J Oral Surg 24:264, May 1966.

94. Doorance GM, Webster D, McWilliams H: Arthroplasty upon temporomandibular joint. Ann Surg 79:485, 1924.

95. Joo YJ, Kinnman J: Ankylosis of the temporomandibular joint. Laryngoscope 17:2008, 1967.

96. Kent JM, Lavelle WF, Dolan KD: Condylar reconstruction: Treatment planning. Oral Surg 37:489, 1979.

97. Kummonna R: Functional rehabilitation of ankylosed temporomandibular joints. Oral Surg 46:495, 1987.

98. El-Mofty S: Surgical treatment of ankylosis of the temporomandibular joint. J Oral Surg 32:202, 1974.

99. Kwapis BW, Dyer MH, Knox JE: Surgical correction of a malunited condylar fracture in a child. J Oral Surg 31:465, 1973.

100. Rowe NL: Surgery of the temporomandibular joint. Proc R Soc Med 65:383, 1972.

101. Hahn GW, Corgill DA: Surgical implant replacement of the fractured displaced mandibular condyle. Report of three cases. J Oral Surg 28:898, 1970.

102. Hiatt WR, Schwartz RA: Spontaneous dislocation of the mandible during prochlorperazine therapy: Report of a case. J Oral Surg 24:255, 1966.

103. Dingman RO, Natvig P: Surgery of Facial Fractures. Philadelphia, WB Saunders Company, 1964, p 186.

104. Hayward JR: Prolonged dislocation of the mandible. J Oral Surg 23:285, 1965.

105. Schultz LW: Report of ten years experience in treating hypermobility of the temporomandibular joints. J Oral Surg 5:202, 1947.

106. McKelvey LE: Sclerosing solution in the treatment of chronic subluxation of the temporomandibular joint. J Oral Surg 10:28, 1952.

107. Hudson HNG: Operation for recurrent subluxation of temporomandibular joint. Br Med J 2:254, 1945.

108. Boudreaux R, Spire E: Plication of the capsular ligament of the temporomandibular joint. J Oral Surg 26:330, 1968.

109. McFarlane WJ: Recurrent dislocation of the mandible: Treatment of seven cases by a simple surgical method. Br J Oral Surg 14:227, 1977.

110. Herrmann M: Die Luxation im Kiefergelenk unter Berücksichtigung einer neuen Behandlungsmethode der habituellen Luxation. Zahnaerztl Ref 55:67, 1955.

111. Maw RB, McKean TW: Scarification of the temporal tendon for treatment of chronic

112. Patton DW: Recurrent subluxation of the temporomandibular joint in psychiatric illness. Br Dent J 153:141, 1982.

113. Findlay JA: Operation for arrest of excessive condylar movement. J Oral Surg 22:101, 1964.

114. Schade GJ: Surgical treatment of habitual luxation of the temporomandibular joint. J Maxillofac Surg 5:146, 1977.

115. LeClerc GL, Girard C. Un nouveau procédé de butée dans le tractement chirurgical de la luxation récidivante de la michoire inférieure. Mem Acad Chir 69:457, 1943.

116. Gosserez M, Dautrey J: Osteoplastic bearing for treatment of temporomandibular luxations. *In* Transactions of Second Congress of Oral Surgery. Copenhagen, Munksgaard, 1961.

117. Chausse JM, Richter M, Bettex A: Deliberate, fixed extraarticular obstruction: Treatment of choice for subluxation and true recurrent dislocation of the temporomandibular joint. J Craniomaxillofac Surg 15:137, 1987.

118. Dingman RO, Moorman WC: Meniscectomy in treatment of the lesions of the temporomandibular joint. J Oral Surg 9:214, 1951.

119. Bowman K: New operation for luxation in the temporomandibular joint. Acta Chir Scand 99:96, 1949.

120. Laskin DM: Myotomy for management of recurrent and protracted mandibular dislocations. Congr Int Assoc Oral Surg 4:264, 1973.

121. Miller GA, Murphy EJ: External pterygoid myotomy for recurrent mandibular dislocation: Review of the literature and report of a case. Oral Surg 42:705, 1976.

122. Myrhaug H: New method of operation for habitual dislocation of the mandible: Review of former methods of treatment. Acta Odont Scand 9:246, 1951.

123. Rehrmann A: Beseitigung der Unterkieferluxation durch osteoplastische Verriegelung. Fortschr Kieferorthop 17:21, 1956.

124. Ward TG: Surgery of the mandibular joint. Ann R Coll Surg 28:139, 1961.

125. Litzow TJ, Royer RQ: Treatment of longstanding dislocation of the mandible: Report of one case. Mayo Clin Proc 37:399, 1962.

126. Georgaide N: Ligation of the condyle to the zygomatic arch. Surgical correction of chronic luxation of mandibular condyle. Plast Reconstr Surg 36:339, 1965.

127. Merril RG: Habitual subluxation and recurrent dislocation in a patient with Parkinson's disease. J Oral Surg 26:473, 1968.

128. Howe AG, Kent JN: Implant of articular eminence for recurrent dislocation of temporomandibular joint. J Oral Surg 36:523, 1978.

129. Randzio J, Fischer-Brandies E: Augmentation of the articular tubercle in treatment of chronic recurrent temporomandibular joint luxations. Oral Surg 61:19, 1986.

130. Irby WB: Surgical correction of chronic dislocation of the temporomandibular joint not responsive to conservative therapy. J Oral Surg 15:307, 1957.

131. Blankestijn J, Boering G: Myrhaug's operation for treating recurrent dislocation of the temporomandibular joint. J Craniomand Proc 3:245, 1985.

CHAPTER 18

FRACTURES OF THE ZYGOMATIC COMPLEX AND ARCH

EDWARD ELLIS III, D.D.S., M.S.

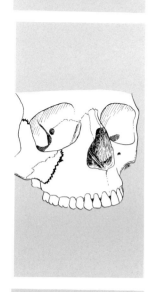

If excuses are needed for the writing of the present paper, they are to be found in the comparatively common occurrence of the fracture discussed, in the extreme scarcity of mention of it or its treatment in surgical literature, and in the fact that even well-known pathological museums do not contain a single example. Modern text-books of surgery and fractures deal with fractures of the malar-zygomatic compound so sparingly that one must be content with a few stray references or a paragraph on maxillary fractures, or be guided by a terse sentence or two covering this subject.

H.D. Gillies, T.P. Kilner, and D. Stone, 1927[1]

Zygomatic fractures are common facial injuries, representing either the most common facial fracture[2-14] or the second in frequency after nasal fractures.[3,15-17] The high incidence probably relates to the zygoma's prominent position within the facial skeleton, frequently exposing it to traumatic forces. The incidence, etiology, and age and sex predilection of zygomatic injuries vary, depending largely upon the social, economic, political, and educational status of the population studied. Most studies indicate a male predilection, with a ratio of approximately 4:1 over female subjects.[15,16,18-27] Most authors also agree that the peak incidence of such injuries occurs around the second and third decades of life.[8,19,20,23-26,28,29] The cause of zygomatic injury in some studies is predominantly altercations,[8,16,18,20,21,26,27] whereas in others, motor vehicle accidents account for a more substantial number.[4,6,15,22-25,28,30,31] The etiology of injuries sustained is greatly affected by the nature of the population in these studies; in the former studies, the populations were from industrialized areas with high rates of unemployment, where the rate of interpersonal violence is very high.

In those zygomatic fractures caused by altercations, the left zygoma is most commonly affected,[12,18,20,21,24-26,31] presumably because of the greater number of right-handed individuals. This predilection disappears in those unilateral fractures caused by motor vehicle accidents. Bilateral fractures of the zygoma are uncommon, accounting for approximately 4 per cent of 2067 cases of zygomatic fracture in a 10-year review by Ellis and coworkers.[26] Bilateral fractures in that study were more commonly the result of motor vehicle accidents than altercations, indicating more severe trauma than that inflicted in altercations.

Since the gross shape of the face is largely influenced by the underlying osseous structure, the zygoma plays an important role in facial contour. Disruption of zygomatic position also has great functional significance, causing impairment of ocular and mandibular function. Therefore, for both cosmetic and functional reasons, it is imperative that zygomatic injuries be properly and fully diagnosed and adequately treated.

ANATOMY

The zygoma is a major buttress of the facial skeleton and is one of the principal structures through which occlusal forces are transmitted and distributed to the base of the skull. It is a thick, strong bone, roughly quadrilateral in shape with an outer convex (cheek) and inner concave (temporal) surface. The convexity on the outer surface of the zygomatic body forms the point of greatest prominence of the cheek. Therefore, the zygoma plays a major role in facial contour.

The zygoma is roughly the equivalent of a four-sided pyramid (Fig. 18–1). It has temporal, orbital, maxillary, and frontal processes and articulates with four bones — the frontal, sphenoid, maxillary, and temporal (Fig. 18–2). The body of the zygoma extensively articulates with the maxilla along the anterior maxilla and along the orbital floor (Fig. 18–2B). The suture between these two bones lies just lateral to the infraorbital foramen and runs laterally from the infraorbital rim to the undersurface of the zygomaticomaxillary buttress. It forms the superolateral aspect and part of the superoanterior aspect of the maxillary sinus. The zygoma also has a narrow, weak articulation with the zygomatic crest of the greater wing of the sphenoid bone at the lateral aspect of the inferior orbital fissure (Fig. 18–3A). It forms a major portion of the lateral aspect and floor of the orbit. The frontal process is thick and triangular in cross-section, with a facial, orbital, and temporal surface. Because of its thickness, it is a frequent site for wire or bone plate fixation following fracture. The temporal process is flat and projects posteriorly to articulate with the zygomatic process of the temporal bone; the combination of the two makes up the zygomatic arch. The zygomaticotemporal articulation is a very thin and delicate connection that fractures frequently and with minimal force.

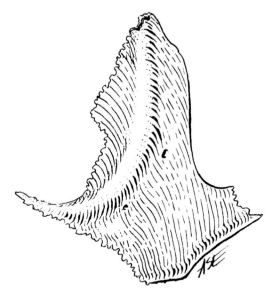

FIGURE 18–1. Illustration of the disarticulated zygoma. It has four processes: the frontal, temporal, orbital, and maxillary. It constitutes the lateral portion of the orbit.

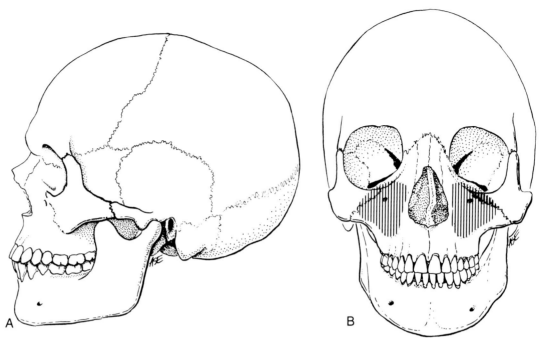

FIGURE 18-2.   **Illustration showing the anatomic position of the zygoma.**   *A*, Lateral view of skull demonstrating its articulation with the temporal, frontal, and maxillary bones. *B*, Frontal view of skull demonstrating its articulation with the maxillary, frontal, and sphenoid bones. The "hash marks" demonstrate the extent of the maxillary sinus. Note that the zygoma forms the superolateral aspect of the sinus.

The zygoma provides origin to a major portion of the masseter muscle along the body and temporal process. The temporal fascia also attaches along the arch and posterolateral edge of the temporal process. The zygoma also provides attachments for the temporal and zygomaticus muscles. The strong infraorbital and lateral orbital rims protect the orbital contents.

TERMINOLOGY AND FRACTURE PATTERNS

> The malar bone represents a strong bone on fragile supports, and it is for this reason that, though the body of the bone is rarely broken, the four processes— frontal, orbital, maxillary, and zygomatic—are frequent sites of fracture.
>
> *H.D. Gillies, T.P. Kilner, and D. Stone, 1927[1]*

The fracture pattern of any bone will depend upon several factors, including the direction and magnitude of the force. Fracture lines thus created pass through the areas of greatest weakness of a bone or between bones. Owing to the strong buttressing nature of the zygoma and the thin bones surrounding it, most injuries involving the zygoma are accompanied by disruption of adjacent articulating bones. This disruption occurs because when a force is applied to the body of the zygoma, it is distributed through its four processes to the adjacent articulating bones, many of which are weaker than the zygoma. Although the zygomatic bone is involved, it is rare to have an isolated fracture of the zygoma in which the fracture lines are completely within this bone or through only the sutures surrounding it.

Zygomatic or malar fracture is the term commonly used to describe those fractures involving the lateral one third of the middle face. Because of the impure nature

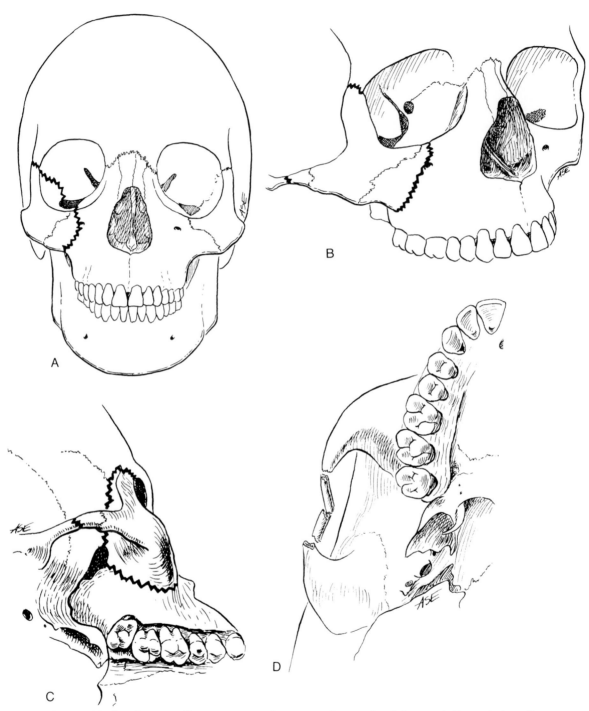

FIGURE 18–3.   Common fracture pattern in zygomatic complex injury.   *A*, Frontal view of skull showing fracture medial to zygomaticomaxillary suture and along zygomaticosphenoid suture within orbit. *B*, Oblique frontal view of skull showing fractures through frontozygomatic suture and posterior to zygomaticotemporal suture. *C*, Temporal view of skull showing fractures extending from the inferior orbital fissure both superiorly through the zygomaticosphenoid suture and inferiorly through the zygomatic buttress of the maxilla. *D*, Inferior view of skull showing triple fracture through zygomatic arch.

of zygomatic fractures, other terms have been adopted in describing such fractures. Zygomaticomaxillary, zygomaticomaxillary compound,[32] zygomatico-orbital,[26] zygomatic complex,[33,34] malar, trimalar, and tripod fractures have all been used to describe the clinical entity of fractures involving the zygoma and adjacent bones. The last two terms are misnomers, since the zygoma has not three but four processes, and their use should be condemned. The terms zygomatic and zygomatic complex are perhaps the most common and are used throughout this chapter, since the zygoma is the major bone involved in such fractures, and for the sake of simplicity. The term zygomatic *complex* helps distinguish those fractures that involve the zygoma and adjacent bones from isolated zygomatic *arch* fractures and is used when the distinction is necessary.

The inferior orbital fissure is the key to remembering the usual lines of zygomatic complex fractures. Three lines of fracture extend from the inferior orbital fissure in an anteromedial, superolateral, and inferior direction (Fig. 18–3). One fracture extends from the inferior orbital fissure anteromedially along the orbital floor, predominantly through the orbital process of the maxilla, toward the infraorbital rim. In its course, the infraorbital canal is usually crossed, as the fracture frequently extends through the infraorbital rim to the facial surface of the maxilla above or even slightly medial to the infraorbital foramen. The fracture extends from the infraorbital rim in the maxilla laterally and inferiorly under the zygomatic buttress of the maxilla. Comminution of the infraorbital rim and bone along the anterior and lateral maxilla is common, with frequent involvement of the infraorbital foramen. The fracture therefore rarely involves the zygomatic bone along the orbital floor and the anterior and lateral aspects of the face; the fracture lines are predominantly within the maxilla.

A second line of fracture from the inferior orbital fissure runs inferiorly through the posterior (infratemporal) aspect of the maxilla and joins the fracture from the anterior aspect of the maxilla under the zygomaticomaxillary buttress (Fig. 18–3C).

The third line of fracture extends superiorly from the inferior orbital fissure along the lateral orbital wall posterior to the rim, usually separating the zygomaticosphenoid suture (Fig. 18–3A and C). Extending superiorly, laterally, and anteriorly toward the lateral orbital rim, the fracture frequently separates the frontozygomatic suture at the lateral orbital rim. However, the fracture through the lateral orbital rim is occasionally superior or inferior to the frontozygomatic suture.

A zygomatic complex fracture that follows this pattern will usually have one additional fracture line—that through the zygomatic arch. Since the point of least resistance to fracture is not at the zygomaticotemporal suture but approximately 1.5 cm more posteriorly, the point of fracture *when single* is usually in the approximate middle of the zygomatic arch, in the zygomatic process of the temporal bone. Frequently, however, there will be three fracture lines through the arch, producing two free segments when the fractures are complete (Fig. 18–3D). These can be displaced by associated muscle pull or may be pushed medially into the infratemporal fossa. Often, the fractures will be incomplete, or "greenstick," fractures, producing a medial or lateral warping of the zygomatic arch without significant upward or downward displacement.

The preceding description is for the "common" or "usual" zygomatic (complex) fracture. However, the variability of these fractures is great, owing to the differences in magnitude and direction of force, the amount of soft tissue covering the zygoma, and the density of the adjacent bones. Frequently, the lines of fracture will be in different locations from those described previously. Meyer and coworkers,[11] using radiographs to summarize the course of fracture lines in 100 isolated zygomatic injuries, found fractures in the body of the zygoma in almost 40 per cent of cases, as opposed to the more common medial location along the anterior maxillary surface. There may be single or multiple lines of fracture (i.e., comminution). There may be gross displacement or none at all. Because of the infinite number of possible variations, one must assess each zygomatic fracture independently and determine the extent and location of the fractures present.

CLASSIFICATION OF ZYGOMATIC FRACTURES

It is probably fair to say that the classification of zygomatic fractures varies with the pen of each author who tries to describe them. The result has been a confusing array of classification systems, which either try to describe the anatomic position of the displaced bone or classify them using position as well as criteria for postreduction stability.

Schjelderup[35] was one of the first to classify zygomatic fractures. His classification divided zygomatic fractures into five types: Type I occurred when the displaced zygomatic bone hinged on the maxillary and frontal attachments; type II occurred when the displaced zygoma hinged on the maxillary attachment; and type III occurred when the zygoma hinged on the frontal attachment. Furthermore, if the zygoma was detached en bloc, it was given the classification of type IV and, when grossly comminuted, type V.

Knight and North's classification,[36] which is the most quoted and most often used, resulted from their examination of the types of fracture patterns seen on a Waters radiograph in 120 clinical cases. Comparing operative findings with preoperative classification, they determined the postreduction stability for each class of fracture. Their classification divides zygomatic fractures into six groups and four subdivisions. Group 1 contains undisplaced fractures (6 per cent of cases) and group 2 contains isolated, displaced arch fractures (10 per cent). Displaced body fractures might be unrotated (group 3, 33 per cent) or medially rotated (11 per cent), either outward at the malar buttress (group 4A) or inward at the frontozygomatic suture (group 4B). Laterally rotated fractures (22 per cent) might be displaced either upward at the infraorbital margin (group 5A) or outward at the frontozygomatic suture (group 5B). Group 6 (18 per cent) included cases with additional fracture lines across the main fragment.

Rowe and Killey[6] recognized that displacement of the zygomatic bone might be a consequence of axial rotation around a vertical (or longitudinal) axis or of en bloc displacement. Their fracture classification contains eight types of fracture and seven subdivisions. Fractures showing no significant displacement are type 1, and isolated fractures of the zygomatic arch are type 2. Type 3 fractures are rotated around a vertical axis internally (type 3a) or externally (type 3b). Type 4 fractures are rotated around a longitudinal axis medially (type 4a) or laterally (type 4b). Type 5 includes fracture-displacement of the complex en bloc medially (type 5a), inferiorly (type 5b), or laterally (type 5c). Type 6 comprises displacement of the orbital floor either inferiorly (type 6a) or superiorly (type 6b), and type 7 is the displacement of the orbital rim segments. Finally, type 8 fractures are complex comminuted fractures. Rowe and Killey[6] claimed that types 4a and b, 5a to c, and comminuted fractures were unstable fractures that frequently required fixation.

Yanagisawa[37] reviewed 200 cases of zygomatic fracture using three radiographic views—the oblique posteroanterior (Waters), the posteroanterior (Caldwell), and the submental vertex projections—and modified the Rowe and Killey classification by adding the posterior en bloc displacement to type 5. Furthermore, his classification omitted the type 6 fracture of Rowe and Killey (displacement of the orbital floor), as he considered these associated conditions rather than primary zygomatic fractures. Thus, the Yanagisawa classification contains seven types of fracture with eight subdivisions, with prediction of postreduction stability and, furthermore, with proposals for treatment of each group.

Spiessl and Schroll[38] classified zygomatic fractures based on treatment considerations. Their classification involved seven types: Type 1 were isolated zygomatic arch fractures; type 2 were fractures with no significant displacement; type 3 were partially displaced medially; type 4 were totally displaced medially; type 5 were those with dorsal displacement; type 6 were those with inferior displacement; and type 7 were comminuted fractures.

Henderson[39] classified zygomatico-orbital fractures into seven divisions: (1) nondisplaced fractures, (2) isolated zygomatic arch fractures, (3) zygomatic complex fractures in which there is displacement but the frontozygomatic fracture is nondistracted, (4) zygomatic complex fractures in which there is displacement and distraction of the frontozygomatic suture, (5) pure blow-out fractures, (6) fractures of the orbital rim only, and (7) comminuted or multiple fractures. Separation at the frontozygomatic suture was used in this classification, since it was considered a key to determining the need for fixation following reduction.

Larsen and Thomsen[22] felt that the previously described classification systems led to a better understanding of the nature of zygomatic fractures but were impractical for common usage. They created a very simple yet practical classification for zygomatic fractures, which grouped them into stable and unstable types. Their classification included three groups. Group A comprised fractures showing minimal or no displacement and hence requiring no intervention. Group B included fractures with great displacement and disruption at the frontozygomatic suture and comminuted fractures. These fractures usually required reduction as well as fixation. Group C comprised fractures of all other kinds, which usually required reduction but no fixation.

In 1985[34] Rowe changed his 1968 classification and, like Larsen and Thomsen,[22] gave it more clinical significance by dividing zygomatic fractures into stable and unstable varieties.

All of the preceding classifications were based upon findings from plain radiographs. It was only natural that Fujii and Yamashiro in 1983 reclassified zygomatic fractures, using cross-sectional computerized tomography (CT), by the post-traumatic position of the zygoma.[40] They classified fractures into four types. Type 1 fractures consisted of those in which there was no evidence of displacement. Type 2 fractures were isolated fractures of the zygomatic arch. Type 3 fractures included those in which the body of the zygomatic complex was fractured without rotation in an anteroposterior direction (Z-axis). In these cases, the zygoma was fractured in one piece, and the body component was either dissociated or depressed into the sinus. Type 4 fractures included cases in which the body of the malar complex was rotated along with the Z-axis; usually, the fractured segment was displaced distinctly in a posteromedial (inward) direction. These cases were subdivided into three subgroups, depending on the location or site of the rotational axis at the infraorbital rim. Type 4a fractures had the axis of rotation at the bases of the arch, and type 4b, at the zygomaticomaxillary suture. Type 4c fractures were those involving the zygoma, the main body of the maxilla, and the palate.

The main purpose of classifying zygomatic fractures should be improved treatment based upon greater knowledge of the anatomy of the fracture, as proposed by the authors who have established these classifications. However, it is often difficult to place patients in one of 10[36] or 15[37] groups to determine the appropriate treatment. A further complicating factor is that fractures rarely fit neatly into one category. Yanagisawa[37] pointed out that the zygoma is frequently displaced in more than two directions, but for ease of classification, the fracture is usually classified according to its principal direction of displacement.

With the preceding review, one can gain an appreciation for the confusion and disparities present in the literature concerning classification of zygomatic fractures. Whether a patient receives better treatment from being classified into one system or another is doubtful, and one should not dwell upon the many classification systems available. Like so many other aspects of surgery, it is extremely rare to find two patients who have exactly the same condition. It therefore behooves the clinician to evaluate each case individually and to use whichever classification system makes him or her feel most comfortable. Whether the clinician chooses to prescribe treatment based upon the experience of others for a given case of fracture rests with him or her; however, with proper surgical management, the nature of the treatment should depend more upon the surgical findings than upon statistical prescription.

DIAGNOSIS OF ZYGOMATIC FRACTURES

> In a typical case diagnosis may be made at sight once the characteristic appearance has been fully recognized. A peculiar facies is present, due chiefly to a certain flatness of contour and an absence of expression on the affected side.
>
> *H.D. Gillies, T.P. Kilner, and D. Stone, 1927[1]*

The diagnosis of zygomatic fractures is primarily based upon the clinical and radiologic examinations, although the history frequently strongly suggests the possibility that one may exist and gives an indication of the nature, direction, and force of the blow. It should be stressed that the clinical examination is frequently difficult to perform adequately owing to the nature of the patient's mental state and the amount of facial edema and pain. The swelling may conceal facial deformity, which appears only when the swelling has subsided. If the examination can be performed immediately after injury, prior to the onset of edema, more information can be obtained from the clinical examination. Since there are no sensitive indicators of zygomatic fractures (such as the teeth provide in maxillary or mandibular fractures) and because the concomitant soft tissue edema and contusion that frequently accompany zygomatic injuries can obscure clinical findings, the use of *both* imaging and clinical features is very important when diagnosing zygomatic fractures.

Clinical Examination

The first priority after ascertaining the neurologic status of a patient with suspected zygomatic fracture is assessing the visual status of the involved eye. A thorough ocular and funduscopic examination should be performed, with complete documentation of the findings. Ocular injuries, such as vitreous hemorrhage, hyphema, globe laceration, severance of the optic nerve, corneal abrasions, and so on, were found in 4 per cent of patients with midfacial trauma by Turvey[12] and in 5 per cent of patients with zygomatico-orbital fractures by Livingston and colleagues.[41] Ophthalmologic consultation was deemed necessary in approximately 5 per cent of 2067 cases of zygomatico-orbital injuries reported by Ellis and colleagues.[26] Therefore, if there are any significant or *questionable* findings, ophthalmologic consultation should be obtained.

Examination of the zygoma involves inspection and palpation. Inspection is performed from the frontal, lateral, superior, and inferior vantages. One should note symmetry, pupillary levels, the presence of orbital edema and subconjunctival ecchymosis, and anterior and lateral projections of the zygomatic bodies. The most useful method of evaluating the position of the body of the zygoma is from the superior view. The patient can be placed in a recumbent position or can recline in a chair. The surgeon inspects from a superior vantage, evaluating how the zygomatic bodies project anterior and lateral to the supraorbital rims, comparing one side with the other. When performing this examination, it helps to place the index finger below the infraorbital margins, along the zygomatic bodies, pressing into the edematous tissues to palpate and reduce the visual effect of edema simultaneously (Fig. 18–4).[42] The superior view is also helpful in evaluating possible depression of the zygomatic arches. One should not forget to perform an intraoral examination, since zygomatic fractures are often accompanied by ecchymosis in the superior buccal sulcus and by maxillary dentoalveolar fractures.

Palpation should be systematic and thorough, comparing one side with the other. The orbital rims are palpated first. The infraorbital rims are palpated with the index finger, moving the finger rhythmically from side to side along the rim. The lateral orbital rims are palpated with the index finger and thumb. One should also use the index finger along the inner aspect of the lateral orbital rim, as one may frequently

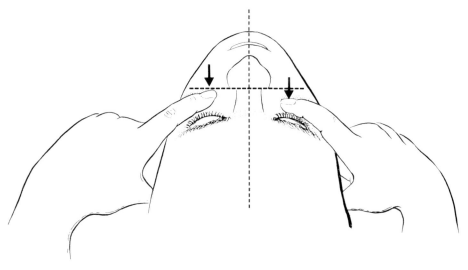

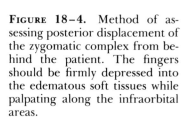

FIGURE 18-4. Method of assessing posterior displacement of the zygomatic complex from behind the patient. The fingers should be firmly depressed into the edematous soft tissues while palpating along the infraorbital areas.

detect fractures by palpating inside the orbital rim as opposed to along the lateral aspect. When fractures are present, palpation will frequently be accompanied by exquisite tenderness. The body of the zygoma and the zygomatic arch are best palpated with two or three fingers moving in a circular motion, comparing with the opposite side. The zygomatic buttress of the maxilla is palpated intraorally with one finger, checking for hematoma or irregularities.

Signs and Symptoms

Several signs and symptoms accompany zygomatic fractures. The presence and severity of these greatly depend upon the extent and type of the zygomatic injury. For instance, facial flattening will be more pronounced in those injuries in which the zygomatic body has been greatly displaced as opposed to those in which the fracture is nondisplaced. Similarly, zygomatic arch fractures might be expected to produce less ocular disruption than zygomatic complex fractures. The following signs and symptoms can accompany zygomatic fractures and therefore should be evaluated.

Periorbital Ecchymosis and Edema.   Edema and bleeding into the loose connective tissues of the eyelids and periorbital areas are the most common signs following fracture of the orbital rim.[43,44] Swelling, often massive, may be present and is most dramatic in the periorbital tissues, where the eyelids may be swollen closed. The ecchymosis may be in the inferior lid and infraorbital area only or around the entire orbital rim.

Flattening of the Malar Prominence.   A characteristic sign and striking feature of zygomatic injury is a flattening of the normal prominence in the malar area. This is an especially common finding in zygomatic complex injuries, reported in 70 to 86 per cent of cases,[22,26,29] especially when there has been distraction of the frontozygomatic suture and medial rotation and/or comminution.[26] Flattening may be difficult to discern soon after injury if edema is present; however, one can usually gain an appreciation for this sign by depressing the index fingers into the soft tissues of the zygomatic areas and comparing one side with the other from above the patient (Figs. 18-4 and 18-41A and B).

Flattening over the Zygomatic Arch.   A characteristic indentation or loss of the normal convex curvature in the temporal area accompanies fractures of the zygomatic arch. Visual and digital comparison with the opposite side is extremely helpful for detecting depressions of the zygomatic arch (see Fig. 18-41A and B).

Pain.   Unless there is mobility of the fractured segment, severe pain is not normally a feature of zygomatic injuries, though the patient will complain of discomfort associated with the attendant bruising. Palpation of the fracture sites will also elicit a painful response.

Ecchymosis of Maxillary Buccal Sulcus.   An important sign of zygomatic or maxillary fracture is ecchymosis in the maxillary buccal sulcus. This ecchymosis may occur even with a small disruption of the anterior or lateral maxilla and should be sought with suspected zygomatic fractures.

Deformity at Zygomatic Buttress of Maxilla.   Intraoral palpation of the anterior and lateral aspects of the maxilla will frequently reveal irregularities of the normal smooth contour, especially in the area of the zygomatic buttress of the maxilla. Comminuted fragments of bone are also frequently palpable, with resulting crepitation. If no tenderness is experienced during this maneuver, the chances are that no fracture exists. The absence of pain makes a zygomatic fracture unlikely, but its presence does not establish one, since pain can be due to soft tissue injury or maxillary fracture.

Deformity of Orbital Margin.   Fractures running through the orbital rim will often result in a gap or step deformity if displacement has occurred. This deformity is a frequent finding at the infraorbital and lateral orbital rims when zygomatic fractures are present.[43,44] These areas may also be tender to the touch.

Trismus.   Limitation of mouth opening frequently accompanies zygomatic injuries, being present in approximately one third of cases,[26,44,45] and has an even higher incidence in isolated fractures of the zygomatic arch (45 per cent).[26] The reason often cited for postfracture trismus is impingement of the translating coronoid process of the mandible on the displaced zygomatic fragments. Whether this impingement actually occurs in the majority of cases is doubtful, since the amount of displacement to produce actual mechanical interference is great. A more likely explanation is muscle spasm secondary to impingement by the displaced fragments, especially on the temporalis muscle (Fig. 18–5). An associated finding is deviation toward the fractured side when the mouth is opened.

Abnormal Nerve Sensibility.   An important symptom, present in approximately 50 to 90 per cent of zygomatic complex injuries, is an impaired sensation of the infraorbital nerve.[22,26,43–48] Infraorbital nerve paresthesia is more common in fractures that are displaced than in those that are not.[48] Although it is difficult to differentiate true anesthesia from the altered sensation of swollen, edematous tissue, as the swelling decreases, infraorbital nerve anesthesia will become apparent. Infraorbital anesthesia occurs when the fracture through the orbital floor or the anterior maxilla

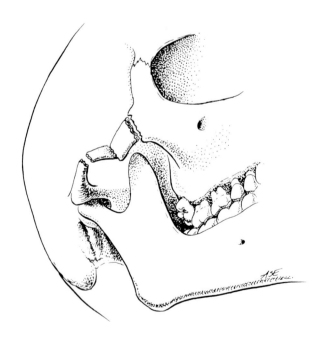

FIGURE 18–5. Illustration of depressed zygomatic arch impinging upon the temporalis muscle or coronoid process or both, limiting mandibular excursions.

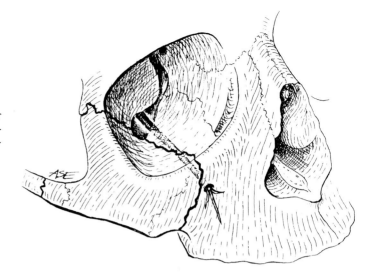

FIGURE 18-6. Typical fracture extends along or through the infraorbital groove or canal along the orbital floor and frequently across the infraorbital foramen on the facial surface of the maxilla.

causes tearing, shearing, or compression of the infraorbital nerve along its canal or foramen (Fig. 18-6). When the line of fracture is lateral to the infraorbital groove and foramen (less common), the infraorbital nerve will be spared. Disruption of the infraorbital nerve will cause anesthesia of the lower eyelid, upper lip, and lateral aspect of the nose. Most commonly, sensation returns in 2 to 5 months[49]; however, some neurosensory deficit can be noted in up to 42 per cent of patients on follow-up examination,[48] and as many as 25 per cent of patients may show permanent total loss of sensibility.[45,47,48]

A related symptom may be altered sensitivity of the maxillary teeth and gingiva. When altered sensitivity is present, the clinician should suspect a disruption of the intraorbital nerve within its canal where the middle and anterior superior alveolar nerves take origin.

Epistaxis. Whenever the sinus mucosa is disrupted, hemorrhage into the sinus is possible. Most fractures through the sinus wall that have had even a minor amount of displacement will tear the lining mucosa, producing internal bleeding. Because the maxillary sinus drains into the nose via the middle meatus, unilateral hemorrhage from the nose is possible and occurs in approximately 30 to 50 per cent of zygomatic complex injuries.[26,44]

Subconjunctival Ecchymosis. Subconjunctival hemorrhage is a frequent finding in zygomatic fractures, present in 50 to 70 per cent of cases.[26,44] It may accompany even a hairline crack through the orbital rim *if the periosteum has been torn*. Its absence does not rule out an orbital rim fracture, since if there has been no disruption of the periosteum, bleeding that might occur can accumulate in a subperiosteal location and not become visible under the conjunctiva. When present, subconjunctival ecchymosis usually will have no posterior limit and will be bright red owing to the ability of oxygen to diffuse through the conjunctiva to the collection of blood.

Crepitation from Air Emphysema. Fracture through a sinus wall, with tearing of the lining mucosa, allows air to escape into the facial soft tissues if the pressure within the sinus is greater than that within the tissues. The soft tissues of the periorbital area, especially the eyelids, are prone to inflation with air because of their loose areolar nature. When this inflation occurs, one can palpate and produce crepitation, indicating subcutaneous emphysema. This is most easily accomplished by alternatively rolling two fingers gently over the tissue, which will produce a characteristic "crackling" sensation. It is an uncommon finding after zygomatic fractures, but the potential for air emphysema is constant. When present, however, it can be alarming to the patient. The emphysema will disappear spontaneously in 2 to 4 days without treatment. The significance of emphysema is its potential for infection through the communication between the sinus and the soft tissues.

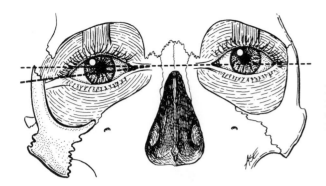

FIGURE 18–7. Illustration demonstrating how inferior displacement of the zygoma results in depression of the lateral canthus and pupil because of depression of the suspensory ligaments that attach to the lateral orbital (Whitnall's) tubercle.

Displacement of the Palpebral Fissure. The lateral palpebral ligament is attached to the zygomatic portion of the orbital rim. Displacement of the zygoma carries the palpebral attachment with it, producing a dramatic visual deformity. When the zygoma is displaced in an inferior direction, the lateral palpebral ligament is also depressed, causing a downward slope to the fissure (antimongoloid slant) (Fig. 18–7).

Because the orbital septum is attached to the infraorbital rim, inferior or posterior displacement of the inferior orbital rim causes depression of the lower eyelid, giving it a shortened appearance.[50] This condition may cause more sclera to be exposed below the iris and an apparent ectropion.

Unequal Pupillary Level. With disruption of the orbital floor and lateral aspect of the orbit, which frequently accompanies zygomatic fractures, loss of osseous support for the orbital contents and displacement of Tenon's capsule and the suspensory ligaments of the globe permit depression of the globe (see Fig. 18–36).[51] This condition is manifested clinically as an unequal pupillary level, with the involved pupil at a lower level than the normal side (Fig. 18–7).

Diplopia. Diplopia is the name given to the symptom of "blurred vision." It is important to distinguish between two varieties of diplopia. Monocular diplopia, or blurring of the vision through one eye, with the other closed, requires the immediate attention of an ophthalmologist, since it usually indicates a detached lens, hyphema, or other traumatic injury to the globe. Binocular diplopia, in which the blurring of vision occurs only when looking through both eyes simultaneously, is common and occurs in approximately 10 to 40 per cent of zygomatic injuries.[15,22,26,35,36,43,44,52–60] Binocular diplopia that develops following trauma can be the result of soft tissue (muscle or periorbital) entrapment; neuromuscular injury; intraorbital or intramuscular hematoma or edema; or a change in orbital shape, with displacement of the globe causing a muscle imbalance. Enophthalmos and globe ptosis associated with marked displacement of the globe can also cause diplopia.

A useful point in differentiating the cause of diplopia is the finding that general edema of the orbit usually causes diplopia in the extremes of upward and downward gaze. Almost complete lack of eye movement in one direction is present with mechanical interference or neuromuscular injury, most commonly muscle entrapment. The diagnosis of diplopia can be very difficult in the early stages when severe edema of the orbit and eyelids is present. Diplopia of edema or hemorrhage origin should resolve in a few days, whereas entrapment of orbital tissues will not.

One can determine whether the fracture has orbital contents through the orbital floor by a forced duction test. Small forceps are used to grasp the tendon of the inferior rectus through the conjunctiva of the inferior fornix, and the globe is manipulated through its entire range of motion (Fig. 18–8). An inability to rotate the globe superiorly signifies entrapment of the muscles in the orbital floor. This test should differentiate between entrapment of orbital contents and paralysis due to neuromuscular injury or edema. It should be performed routinely in those individuals who cannot rotate the globe into an upward gaze.

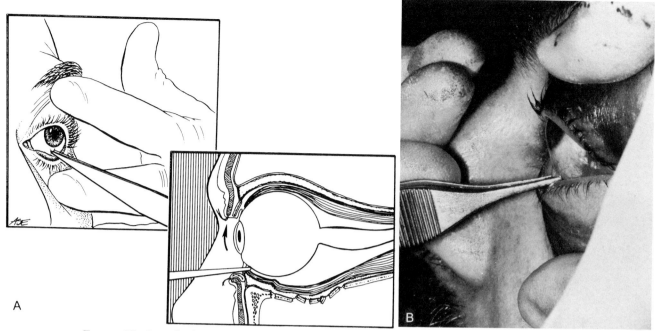

FIGURE 18-8.   The forced duction test to determine if there is a physical impediment to ocular motility. *A*, Illustration showing the grasping of the inferior rectus muscle. *B*, Clinical photograph of same.

Enophthalmos.   If the zygomatic injury has produced an increase in the orbital volume, most commonly by lateral and inferior displacement of the zygoma or disruption of the inferior and lateral orbital walls, or both, or has resulted in a decrease in the volume of orbital contents by herniation of orbital soft tissues, enophthalmos can result. This is a difficult diagnosis to make on an acute basis unless the condition is severe, as adjacent soft tissue edema always produces a relative enophthalmos. Once the swelling has dissipated, enophthalmos becomes more obvious and is frequently associated with ptosis of the globe. The clinical manifestations of enophthalmos are accentuation of the upper lid sulcus and narrowing of the palpebral fissure, causing pseudoptosis of the upper lid. The anterior projection of the globe, as viewed from above, will be reduced on the side of injury. Zygomatic fractures are associated with enophthalmos in approximately 5 per cent of cases prior to treatment.[22,26,44]

Radiographic Evaluation

Nothing is more valuable to the surgeon in determining the extent of injury and the position of the fragments—both before and after operation—than a good skiagram.

H.D. Gillies, T.P. Kilner, and D. Stone, 1927[1]

Many radiographic techniques and views are available for examining fractures of the zygoma. Plain films and CT have their place in determining the type, location, magnitude, and direction of displacement of zygomatic fractures. The importance of the radiographic examination of the zygoma can be inferred by the numerous classification systems for zygomatic fractures that rely upon such findings.[6,35-38,40,61-65] In fact, nearly every classification system for zygomatic fractures is based upon radiographic findings.

The use of CT for the diagnosis of zygomatic fractures has become more common in recent years.[66] Fujii and Yamashiro[40,67] and Finkle and coworkers[66] have demonstrated the versatility and usefulness of CT for this purpose. There is no arguing with the fact that the amount of information that can be obtained from CT is greater than that obtained from one or two plain films. This does not mean that plain radiographs have no place in the diagnosis and treatment planning of zygomatic injuries. The vast majority of zygomatic fractures can be identified using plain films. This is especially true for those fractures that are minimally displaced and that are accompanied by normal eye signs. However, additional radiographs with better definition, such as CT, are often necessary following acquisition of plain films. CT is especially helpful when the orbital floor appears to be comminuted, when the posterior extent of the fracture within the orbit is not clear, when there are associated orbital soft tissue injuries and/or marked enophthalmos,[68–71] or when there are associated craniofacial injuries.[72] For these injuries, it is optimal to obtain *both* axial and coronal high-resolution scans. The axial scan is extremely helpful in evaluating the medial and lateral orbital walls, while the coronal scan defines the extent of orbital floor injury. Reformatted coronal views (from axial scans) are not as helpful but may be necessary if the patient cannot be properly positioned owing to injury. Three-dimensional CT scans, while glamorous, offer no additional information beyond that which is already present in the two-dimensional scans.

It is beyond the scope of this chapter to describe the details of CT. However, a description of the plain radiographs useful in the diagnosis of zygomatic fractures will be presented, as these are helpful in determining the nature of the fracture patterns. The standard radiographic views for plain films that are used to establish the presence or absence of zygomatic fractures are the posteroanterior oblique and submental vertex views. Although other plain films, such as orbital views, posteroanterior skull views (Caldwell's view), and lateral skull radiographs, as well as panoramic tomograms, are occasionally helpful, they will not be described here, as they can be considered optional for diagnosing zygomatic fractures. It should be noted, however, that usually two views, the posteroanterior oblique and the submental vertex, are necessary for the reliable diagnosis of zygomatic fractures.[73]

POSTEROANTERIOR OBLIQUE VIEW

The posteroanterior oblique view, which is a modified posteroanterior view of the skull specific for structures in the middle third of the face, has also been known as the Waters,[74] occipital mental, and paranasal sinus views. It can be performed with the patient upright (Fig. 18–9A and B) or supine (Fig. 18–9C) (anteroposterior oblique or a reverse Waters view), with only slight variation in technique. The diagnostic quality of the film taken with the patient in a supine position is poorer owing to the enlargement and distortion of the facial structures; however, the supine position is helpful in patients who cannot stand or be turned facedown for any reason (e.g., suspected cervical spine injuries).

The posteroanterior oblique radiograph is taken with the patient's head or the central ray, or both, positioned to distort and enlarge the middle third structures and to free the sinuses from superimposition of denser structures by projecting the petrous ridge of the temporal bone inferiorly, below the maxillary sinuses. This view provides excellent assessment of both maxillary sinuses and their walls, the zygoma and its processes, and the anterior rim of the orbits (Fig. 18–10A). The zygomatic arch, although foreshortened, can also be assessed. Occasionally, it will be helpful to obtain both the normal view and a more oblique projection, or an "exaggerated" Waters view, each view highlighting different aspects of the anatomy (Fig. 18–10B).[15,73,75]

A fracture of the zygoma will usually appear on the posteroanterior oblique view as a separation in the area of the frontozygomatic suture, a separation along the infraorbital rim, a break in the normally smooth curvature of the zygomaticomaxil-

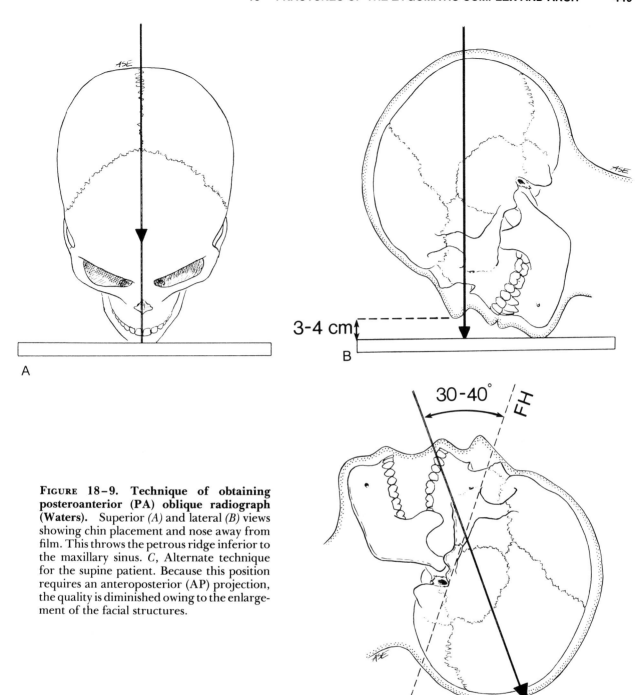

FIGURE 18–9. Technique of obtaining posteroanterior (PA) oblique radiograph (Waters). Superior *(A)* and lateral *(B)* views showing chin placement and nose away from film. This throws the petrous ridge inferior to the maxillary sinus. *C,* Alternate technique for the supine patient. Because this position requires an anteroposterior (AP) projection, the quality is diminished owing to the enlargement of the facial structures.

lary (buttress) area, and perhaps a separation or buckling of the zygomatic arch (Fig. 18–11). One must be cognizant of the normal radiolucent line at the frontozygomatic and zygomaticomaxillary suture areas, which may be confused with a fracture.[73] It is imperative for at least two fractures to be visualized radiographically before one can be firm in establishing the diagnosis of zygomatic fracture.[34]

Comparing the shape of the anterior rim of the orbit of one side with that of the other will often give a clue to the presence and severity of a zygomatic fracture. Most commonly, the involved orbit will appear greater in circumference owing to the downward and outward displacement of the zygoma. The involved maxillary sinus may appear smaller than the contralateral one if the zygoma is depressed. If there are

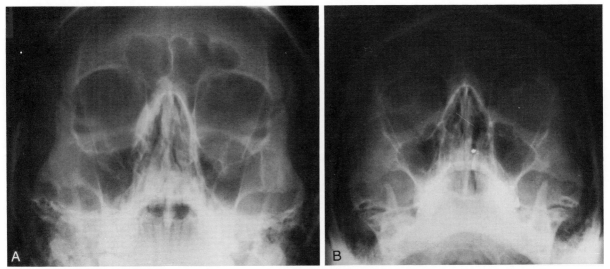

FIGURE 18–10. *A,* Normal PA oblique radiograph. Note the radiolucent frontozygomatic suture, which is a normal finding. The zygomatic arch can be followed posteriorly, with no irregularities observed. Similarly, there is continuity of the lateral maxillary wall. The sinuses are not cloudy and are bilaterally symmetric, as are the orbits. *B,* "Exaggerated" PA oblique view in a normal patient. This view allows comparison of the distance between the zygomatic body and the coronoid processes. When a zygomatic fracture is present, this distance may be diminished on the side of the fracture. The zygomatic arches are easily observed in this view.

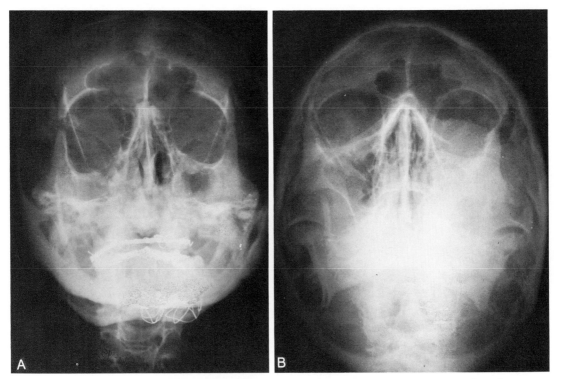

FIGURE 18–11. PA oblique radiographs in two patients with zygomatic complex fractures. *A,* Right-sided fracture showing great separation at the frontozygomatic suture, enlargement and distortion of the right orbit, and a cloudy right maxillary sinus. *B,* Left-sided fracture showing alteration in the shape and size of the left orbit, clouding of the left maxillary sinus, discontinuity of the left lateral maxillary wall, and disruption of the left zygomatic arch.

no mandibular fractures, a helpful measure is the distance between the tip of the coronoid process and the body of the zygoma. This distance will be decreased from the normal side when the body of the zygoma has been displaced inferiorly. The bleeding into the maxillary sinus frequently associated with zygomatic fractures will appear as a radiopaque clouding of the antrum. Comparison of the antral density of one side with that of the other is helpful. Because of the disruption of the orbital floor that accompanies zygomatic injuries, one may see orbital contents herniating into the involved maxillary sinus if the sinus has not been completely filled with blood.

SUBMENTAL VERTEX VIEW

The submental vertex view is also known as the skull axial, jug-handle, or infero-superior skull view. It can also be performed with slight variation in technique in patients who cannot adequately dorsiflex the head, although it may have to be omitted in those patients with possible cervical spine injuries (Fig. 18–12). This view is excellent for visualizing the contour of the body of the zygomas bilaterally, as well as the outline of the maxillary sinus. The zygomatic arches are comparably seen in this view, especially if the radiation dosage is reduced, since the arches may be "burned out" when a full exposure is made.

A zygomatic fracture will usually be seen as a loss of the normal anterolateral projection of one zygomatic body when compared with the other and as an overriding or "buckling" fracture of the zygomatic arch (Fig. 18–13). One must be constantly aware of the quality of the radiographic technique, since a slight head tilt to one side or the other will produce asymmetries of an artifactual nature.

INTRAORAL TANGENTIAL ZYGOMATIC RADIOGRAPH

A simple radiograph that can be taken in the office with dental radiographic equipment is the intraoral tangential zygomatic radiograph. This view is uncomplicated and extremely useful for zygomatic arch fractures that can be managed in the office. The technique involves placing an occlusal radiograph film between the maxillary and mandibular teeth, with its long axis from front to back, positioned as far laterally and posteriorly as the cheek will allow (Fig. 18–14). The machine is posi-

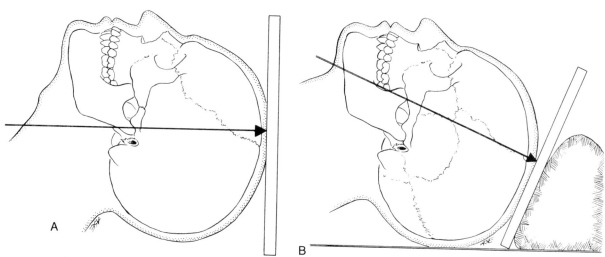

FIGURE 18–12. Technique for obtaining submental vertex radiograph. *A,* Lateral view showing projection of x-ray and position of patient. *B,* Lateral view showing projection of x-ray and position of patient who cannot dorsiflex the neck.

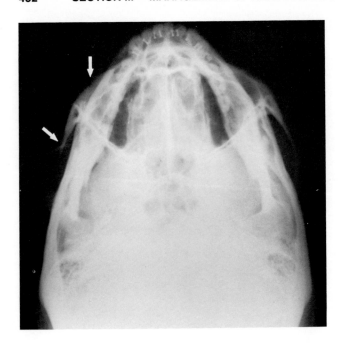

FIGURE 18–13. Submental vertex radiograph demonstrating posterior displacement of the zygomatic body and a "buckling" of the arch.

tioned so that the central ray passes downward and slightly forward along the side of the cranium and into the temporal fossa. The angle toward the midsagittal plane to project the zygomatic arch onto the film is between 5 and 10 degrees. The zygomatic arch and coronoid process are easily projected onto the film with this technique (see Fig. 18–41C through E).

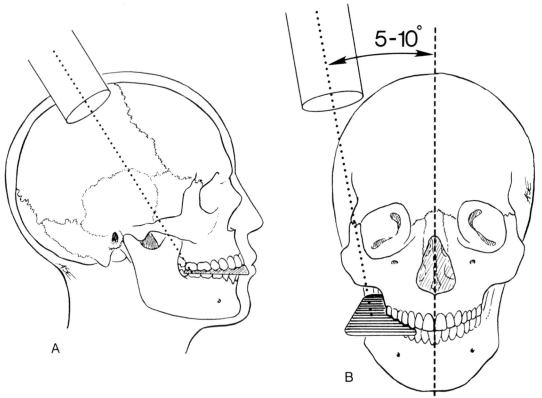

FIGURE 18–14. Technique of intraoral tangential radiograph. Lateral (A) and frontal (B) views showing the placement of the occlusal x-ray film and the direction of the x-ray beam.

TREATMENT OF ZYGOMATIC FRACTURES

> The methods of treating a fractured malar bone recommended by the various writers who have reported cases include simple digital manipulation under general anesthesia, external manipulation by means of a cow-horn dental forceps grasping the edges of the bone, traction and elevation by means of wire or heavy bone elevators passed through small local external incisions, and elevation via incision in the mucosa of the gingival sulcus at the canine fossa.
>
> Our technique, which has now been used successfully in a number of cases, differs from those mentioned.
>
> *H.D. Gillies, T.P. Kilner, and D. Stone, 1927[1]*

Since Duverney[76] first described the zygomatic fracture, numerous methods have been suggested to treat it. These treatments range from nonintervention and observation to open reduction and internal fixation. Since many fractures are either nondisplaced or minimally displaced, intervention is not always necessary. In fact, investigations reveal that between 9 and 50 per cent of zygomatic fractures do not require operative treatment (Table 18–1).

The decision to intervene should be based upon signs, symptoms, and functional impairment. The decision need not be made hastily, as zygomatic fractures are not emergencies and treatment can be delayed if necessary. However, during the first week following trauma, the soft tissues will undergo changes consistent with the usual sequence of wound healing. The form they will ultimately take will depend upon the underlying bony architecture. If a comminuted fracture of the zygoma is not treated for several days after injury, an excellent reduction may be compromised by the soft tissue scarring and change in morphology that occur between the time of injury and fracture repair. Optimally, fractures are treated prior to the onset of edema from the traumatic incident. In practice, however, this is rarely possible. Once edema has become moderate to severe, postponement of surgery for several days makes both thorough examination and surgical treatment much easier and more reliable. Postponement, therefore, of the decision whether or not to operate until facial edema resolves is recommended when there is question about the *necessity* for intervention. Radiographic findings, in the usual instance, should not be the only reason for surgical treatment but should be used in conjunction with clinical signs and symptoms. However, if the radiographic findings are so dramatic that intervention will definitely

TABLE 18–1. REPORTED INCIDENCE OF ZYGOMATIC FRACTURES NOT REQUIRING SURGICAL TREATMENT

STUDY	SAMPLE SIZE	PERCENTAGE *NOT* REQUIRING SURGERY
Carlson and Mårtensson, 1969[43]	144	16
Wiesenbaugh, 1970[44]	71	21
Lund, 1971[28]	62	42
Melmed, 1972[19]	270	43
Pozatek et al, 1973[99]	85	9
Haidar, 1977[18]	108	43
Larsen and Thomsen, 1978[22]	137	16
Afzelius and Rosén, 1980[13]	214	16
Adekeye, 1980[23]	337	47
Balle et al, 1982[29]	105	25
Pospisil and Fernando, 1984[116]	117	37
Fischer-Brandies and Dielert, 1984[25]	97	12
Foo, 1984[24]	77	30
Ellis et al, 1985[26]	2067	23
Kristensen and Tveterås, 1986[27]	74	49

be necessary, it may be advantageous to perform the surgery irrespective of the facial edema present, as the final soft tissue contour may be superior to that attained when surgery has been postponed. If the decision not to intervene is made, the patient should be observed for 2 to 3 weeks, and a regimen of soft diet and prophylactic antibiotics should be implemented.

One should always remember that if a force is sufficient to produce a fracture of the zygoma, it is also sufficient to produce intracranial injuries. Zygomatic fractures are not life-threatening injuries and should not be given priority over more acute problems. There is also no need to hasten treatment if the neurologic state of the patient is in question, as zygomatic fractures can be satisfactorily treated in several days, once the facial edema has resolved.

Another important consideration when deciding whether or not to intervene is the status of the opposite eye. If the patient has diminished vision in the eye on the side opposite the fracture for any reason, one may decide not to treat the displaced zygoma associated with the only normally functioning eye. Although the risk to vision is minimal when treating zygomatic fractures, loss of sight in the only functioning eye would be a catastrophe. The patient can more easily endure a cosmetic defect than blindness.

If intervention is deemed necessary, proper treatment, as in any displaced fracture, will require reduction and, if necessary, fixation. Since closed reduction using external manipulation is impossible, all reduction techniques are operative procedures (i.e., open) in the sense that the skin or mucosal surfaces are violated.

The fact that there are so many methods available for both the reduction and the fixation of zygomatic fractures indicates that there is no technique that is always superior to the others. There are few, if any, techniques that are always satisfactory for every type of zygomatic fracture, so the surgeon's judgment and ability to apply satisfactory techniques to a given fracture will be the deciding factors in whether the patient receives appropriate treatment. It should be stressed that satisfactory results can be achieved using a number of techniques. It is not so much the actual technique that is important, but the proper application of principles that will produce satisfactory results.

One must be aware that zygomatic complex fractures can result from both high- and low-energy injuries. Those resulting from altercations seem to be more linear in character and displaced en bloc. These can frequently be treated with limited exposure, simple reduction, and simple methods of fixation, if necessary. Conversely, high-energy injuries, such as those sustained in motor vehicle accidents, produce more comminution and are much less amenable to simple methods of treatment. These fractures usually require extended open reduction and rigid fixation techniques. The surgeon must therefore be aware of the nature and extent of the injury while planning treatment. *Most of this chapter is devoted to the more common type of zygomatic compound fracture—that resulting from low-energy injuries.* Other chapters discuss the management of high-energy panfacial fractures. Fortunately, the principles presented are the same for both high- and low-energy injuries; the only difference between the manners in which they are managed is the extent of intervention, which is much greater in high-energy injuries.

The fractured zygoma is perhaps the least understood and most frequently mistreated facial fracture. Much of the difficulty in treating this stems from the complex and multiple anatomic relationships the zygoma maintains within the facial skeleton. The most common mistake made in clinical practice is to assume that if the infraorbital and lateral orbital rims have been reduced, the zygoma will be in its proper position. One must remember that the zygoma has four major processes that articulate with adjacent bones. It is only when three are properly positioned that one can be sure of an accurate reduction. It may be more helpful to think of the zygoma as a four-legged chair. If three of the four legs are on the floor, the other must also be. On the other hand, if two legs are on the floor, two may also be off the floor. Therefore, reducing the orbital rim fractures (two legs of the chair) does not in any way guarantee that the entire complex has been properly reduced, since the zygoma can rotate inferiorly and medially. In this instance, the fractures through the zygomatic buttress of the maxilla and zygomatic arch are left improperly aligned,[77] producing a flattened appearance to the face in the area where the body of the zygoma normally gives soft tissue support.

Because of the complex anatomic details and because there are no sensitive clues to accurate and stable reduction, some surgeons have suggested that each zygomatic fracture should be treated aggressively, with open reduction and internal fixation of *at least* two of its four major processes.[17,77–82] Dingman and Natvig,[78] for instance, state the following: "While closed reduction techniques are popular and attractive in the management of fractures in this region, the experienced surgeon will be quick to see, in many cases, the limitations that closed methods impose." The main controversies in the treatment of zygomatic fractures, therefore, are twofold: (1) whether surgical exposure of the zygoma in two or three locations is necessary to determine if the reduction has been adequate; and (2) whether fixation devices are *routinely* necessary.

Determining if the Zygoma Has Been Properly Reduced. There should be no doubt that observation of the fracture in three of its four processes will allow the surgeon to determine the postreduction position accurately. Karlan and Cassisi[77] have shown this to be true in a clinical review of their patients. The question therefore becomes, *is this always necessary?* Incisions used to expose the lateral orbital, infraorbital, and zygomaticomaxillary areas (intraorally) not only take time but also have the potential to produce complications of their own, irrespective of the zygomatic fracture for which they are being employed. The orbital rims can usually be readily palpated, so the improvement of fracture alignment gained by opening these areas is frequently minimal.

There are several instances, however, when surgical exposure becomes helpful.

1. When preoperative signs and symptoms and/or radiographs indicate the need for orbital floor exploration, gaining access to the orbital floor and infraorbital rim prior to elevation of the zygoma is prudent.

2. If one must operate while excessive facial edema is present, surgical exposure to determine zygomatic position is helpful.

3. If one cannot determine during the surgery whether the reduction has been adequate, exposure will provide the necessary verification.

4. Exposure is required if fixation devices are deemed necessary from the pre- or intraoperative assessment of the fracture.

Thus, surgical exposure will depend upon the circumstances and the experience of the surgeon; however, given the above, it will be frequently performed. *If there is any doubt about the postreduction position, one should verify postreduction zygomatic position with exposure,* remembering that even though the orbital rims are reduced, the body of the zygoma can be rotated medially. Exposure and exploration of other areas help to determine when the zygoma has been properly reduced. Fractures at the zygomatic arch and the internal orbit along the greater wing of the sphenoid are sensitive indicators of zygomatic complex position; however, exposure of the zygomatic buttress of the zygoma provides one of the most valuable clues to adequacy of zygomatic position, if it is not severely comminuted. With this exposure, one will also have excellent exposure of the infraorbital rim.

The Need for Fixation. Several surgeons feel that reduction, by itself, does not produce adequate stability of the fractured zygoma, claiming that the downward pull of the masseter muscle will cause a medial rotation of the zygomatic body prior to healing (Fig. 18–15).[9,77,78,81,83–85] Albright and McFarland[83] went so far as to recommend intermaxillary immobilization following fracture reduction to help decrease the pull of the masseter muscle on the repositioned zygoma. Evidence for the possibility that masseter muscle pull can distract a repositioned zygoma is suggested by Karlan and Cassisi's work,[77] in which zygomatic fractures were created in fresh cadavers and

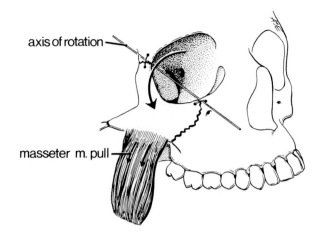

axis of rotation

masseter m. pull

FIGURE 18–15. Illustration showing how the zygomatic complex can rotate inferiorly and medially even when wired at the frontozygomatic and infraorbital areas. The masseter muscle may contribute to this distraction.

a static force was applied to the zygoma in the line of anticipated masseter muscle tension. They noted that the zygoma was easily displaced by the application of little force. Whether this experiment, which used osteotomies, accurately reproduces the clinical fracture situation, however, is unknown.

A majority of surgeons disagree with the concept that fixation should be *routinely* applied following reduction of zygomatic fractures.[8,13,15,23–29,34,57,65,75,86–94] These surgeons apply fixation to zygomatic fractures only *where indicated.* The indications for when to apply fixation seem to vary with the surgeon and the type of fracture, so the incidence of fixation application varies widely (13 to 100 per cent; see Table 18–2).

Many surgeons use radiographic classifications to determine whether fixation will be necessary, their past experience with each class of fracture indicating the usual stability of the fracture after reduction. For instance, besides comminuted fractures,

**TABLE 18–2.   REPORTED INCIDENCE OF THE NEED FOR FIXATION
IN ADDITION TO REDUCTION**

STUDY	SAMPLE SIZE*	PERCENTAGE REQUIRING FIXATION
Mansfield, 1948[53]	149	38
Nysingh, 1960[15]	200	60
Knight and North, 1961[36]	120	40
Fryer et al, 1969[88]	196	40
Wiesenbaugh, 1970[44]	75	13
Lund, 1971[28]	26	17
Melmed, 1972[19]	131	21
Pozatek et al, 1973[99]	77	58
Matsunaga et al, 1976[231]	147	100
Haidar, 1977[18]	84	77
Larsen and Thomsen, 1978[22]	137	24
Hoyt, 1979[91]	11	27
Laufer et al, 1976[248]	70	18
Adekeye, 1980[23]	179	23
Balle et al, 1982[29]	79	29
Foo, 1984[24]	43	25
Pospisil and Fernando, 1984[116]	74	39
Fischer-Brandies and Dielert, 1984[25]	81	51
Ellis et al, 1985[26]	1521	30
Champy et al, 1985[92]	1030	79
Kristensen and Tveterås, 1986[27]	37	30

* Only those cases that were surgically treated in the above studies are included in this figure.

Rowe and Killey[6] mentioned unstable fractures as those showing wide separation of, or displacement at, the frontozygomatic suture (types 4a and b and 5a, b, and c of their 1968 classification). Rowe's 1985 classification[34] indicates that those fractures that have rotated around the horizontal axis (either medially or laterally), those that have been dislocated en bloc, and comminuted fractures are unstable. Others also recommend fixation based upon radiographic separation of the frontozygomatic suture.[15,22,35,36]

The efficacy of using simple elevation (without fixation) when indicated has been demonstrated by Larsen and Thomsen.[65] They re-examined 87 patients several months to years after elevation of their fractures by the Gillies temporal approach and found only 2 patients with residual deformity. In contrast, one third of those patients in whom fracture instability necessitated some sort of fixation had malunited fractures. The results of their study may indicate that the severity of the injury is more important than whether or not fixation is applied in producing residual defects. Similarly, Fischer-Brandies and Dielert[25] re-examined 41 cases of zygomatic fracture treated with elevation using a hook and found no postsurgical displacement. Taken together, these studies indicate that the pull of the masseter muscle does not seem to effect postreduction stability with any regularity.

An important point regarding the stability of zygomatic complex fracture reduction is the state of the fracture ends. When there is no comminution of the osseous processes, the fracture will be more likely to remain stable without fixation devices. However, when comminution of the fragments occurs, instability will usually result and fixation devices become necessary. Thus, comminuted fractures behave totally differently from linear fractures. *If there is any question regarding the stability of a reduced zygomatic fracture, it is prudent to apply fixation!*

Principles in the Treatment of Zygomatic Fractures

In the treatment of any zygomatic (complex) fracture that requires surgical intervention, consideration should be given to each of several steps in a sequential and orderly manner (Table 18–3):

1. *Prophylactic antibiotics.* The incidence of infection following either zygomatic fracture or fracture reduction is extremely low; however, it is difficult to discern, since many surgeons use prophylactic antibiotics as a matter of routine. This practice also makes it difficult to determine the effectiveness of antibiotics in preventing infection of these fractures. Because the maxillary sinus is involved, zygomatic fractures can be considered to be compound, and prophylactic antibiotics are proba-

TABLE 18–3. STEPS IN SURGICALLY TREATING A ZYGOMATIC COMPLEX FRACTURE

1. Prophylactic antibiotics
2. Anesthesia
3. Clinical examination and forced duction test
4. Protection of the globe
5. Antiseptic preparation
6. Reduction of the fracture
7. Assessment of reduction
8. Orbital floor exploration and reconstruction
9. Determination of necessity for fixation
10. Application of fixation device
11. Assessment of ocular motility
12. Protection of fracture
13. Postsurgical ocular examinations
14. Postsurgical radiographs

bly appropriate, especially given the fact that the orbital contents are also frequently violated. The antibiotics chosen should cover routine sinus bacteria (i.e., ampicillin, clindamycin, or a cephalosporin).

2. *Anesthesia.* For zygomatic complex fractures, general anesthesia with oral intubation is helpful. The anesthesiologist or anesthetist should be positioned so that the surgeon has access to the side of the fracture *and* the head of the table. It is very important to have complete access to the top of the patient's head for visual comparison of one side with the other. (Isolated zygomatic arch fractures can be treated with the patient under local anesthesia, with or without sedation, when the patient is cooperative and an intraoral or percutaneous approach is used.)

3. *Clinical examination and forced duction test.* After induction of general anesthesia, the surgeon should take the opportunity to examine the patient more carefully. An examination with the patient under anesthesia allows the surgeon much more freedom and the use of more digital force than can be allowed while the patient is awake. This examination will help confirm previous diagnoses and may reveal new information. It is very important to look at the patient from the superior view and visualize both zygomas simultaneously. Unless the swelling is marked, one should be able to determine an asymmetry. Placing the forefinger across the infraorbital area or on the malar prominence should help one discern the asymmetry. A forced duction test should also be performed at this time.

4. *Protection of the globe.* The cornea must be protected from inadvertent trauma. There are several ways to provide this protection; perhaps the simplest is by placement of a scleral shell (corneal shield) after application of an ophthalmic ointment. Temporary tarsorrhaphy can also be used by suturing the dermal surfaces of the upper and lower eyelids together with a 6-0 nylon suture.

5. *Antiseptic preparation.* The type of preparation necessary will depend largely upon the types of approaches one anticipates. It is good practice, however, to prepare the forehead and *both* periorbital areas and cheeks to the level of the mouth and laterally on both sides to the preauricular area. This practice allows comparison with the opposite side during surgery. Another useful suggestion is *always* to prepare the mouth with throat pack and antiseptic rinse, since an oral approach to the sinus and zygoma is frequently useful.

6. *Reduction of the fracture.* The fractures should be reduced by whatever means the surgeon feels appropriate (techniques described further on).

7. *Assessment of reduction.* The most important step in the management of zygomatic fractures is to determine *at the table* whether the fracture has been properly reduced. This will be obvious for those who have opened the fracture at three sites. If exposure of three sites has not been performed, the areas that should be palpated first to determine reduction are the orbital margins. These should be smooth and continuous if reduction has been satisfactory. This finding by itself, however, is inadequate verification that the zygoma is properly positioned. Although the zygomaticofrontal suture area provides the strongest pillar of the zygoma, it is one of the worst indicators of proper reduction of the entire complex, even when surgically exposed and examined directly. One should also palpate in the maxillary vestibule. If there is any flatness still visible, the zygoma has not been properly elevated. *If there is any doubt about proper reduction, exposure is mandatory!* In this instance, an incision in the maxillary vestibule offers an excellent exposure of the zygomaticomaxillary buttress and the infraorbital rim.

8. *Orbital floor exploration and reconstruction.* By definition, the orbital floor is fractured in zygomatic complex fractures. However, the magnitude and extent of orbital floor disruption varies from a linear crack to fragmentation of the entire floor. In many, perhaps the majority, of simple zygomatic fractures, there is no herniation of periorbital contents into the sinus with entrapment of ocular muscles or enophthalmos. However, these problems do occur in a certain percentage of cases. Davies[95] noted significant orbital floor disruption in 47 per cent of patients with zygomatic fractures; Sacks and Friedland[96] noted this in two thirds of zygomatic complex frac-

tures; Crewe[97] noted significant disruption in a majority of zygomatic fractures; and Crumley and Leibsohn[60] noted that in 39 per cent of zygomatic fractures comminuted fractures of the orbital floor were present. Of interest, however, is the fact that many clinical reviews found intervention necessary in a much smaller percentage of cases. For instance, Andersen and colleagues[98] found it necessary to reconstruct the orbital floor in 6 of 32 zygomatic fractures. Pozatek and colleagues[99] explored the orbital floor in 20 per cent of their patients with zygomatic fractures; Ellis and associates[26] explored it in approximately 15 per cent of zygomatic fractures. These reviews, taken in concert with the information provided by Davies,[95] Sacks and Friedland,[96] and Crewe,[97] might indicate that significant orbital floor disruption is left untreated by many surgeons.

Although some surgeons believe that exploration of the orbital floor should be performed routinely when operating on a zygomatic fracture,[17,81,83,89,95–97,100,101] most do not. These surgeons would argue that exploration of the orbital floor should depend upon preoperative and intraoperative findings. Since binocular diplopia can be due to many factors, this finding *alone*, especially early after trauma, should not be used to decide whether or not to explore the orbital floor.[25,50] Several series of patients have shown that most cases of post-traumatic diplopia resolve without intervention.[15,54,55,57,102] However, if diplopia has not resolved within 7 days, orbital floor exploration and possible reconstruction should be considered. Complicating the decision of whether or not to explore the orbital floor is the finding that *early* intervention seems to produce more consistent and complete resolution of diplopia than when surgery is delayed.[50,59,96,103–105] However, in these series of patients, "early" surgery was surgery undertaken within 2 weeks of fracture. Therefore, if one delays fracture repair for 7 days and the patient still has diplopia, orbital floor exploration may be indicated without fear of missing a chance for satisfactory results.

Other factors to be considered in deciding whether or not to explore the orbital floor include the following: (1) clinical signs of a large defect, such as depressed globe, enophthalmos, limitation of eye movement, and positive forced duction test; (2) imaging signs of a large defect (> 5 mm) or when there is herniation of orbital contents into the maxillary sinus (Fig. 18–16); and (3) when surgical access to the fracture places one at the orbital rim. When there is a question about the necessity to intervene and plain radiographs are equivocal, CT can be extremely helpful in delineating the fractures and the position of periorbital soft tissues. *If comminution of the orbital floor or prolapse of orbital soft tissues into the antrum is noted, exploration and possible reconstruction should be performed.*[106,107] Given these considerations, exploration of the orbital floor will therefore be necessary in many cases.

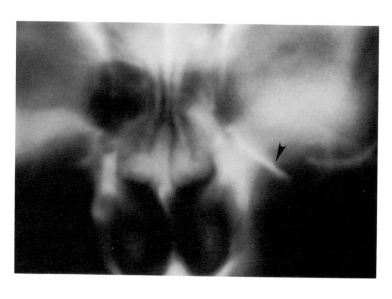

FIGURE 18–16. Tomogram showing large fracture of orbital floor. This finding suggests a large defect of the orbital floor. CT would be extremely useful in evaluating the osseous defect.

When indicated, exploration should be carried out concomitantly with reduction of the zygomatic fracture. In these instances, the orbital floor should be exposed prior to elevation, so that the open rim also serves as a guide to reduction. It is unwise at this point, however, to try to free any trapped tissue, since elevation of the zygoma may separate bone fragments and make this much easier following reduction. Assessment of the need for orbital floor reconstruction is made after reduction (and fixation if necessary), since the actual defect will then be revealed (techniques described below).

In those cases of minimally displaced fractures in which no ocular signs of entrapment or enophthalmos are noted preoperatively and the patient is treated by simple reduction, orbital floor exploration is unnecessary unless a postreduction forced duction test produces positive findings (rare). In most of these cases, reduction of the zygoma will bring about an adequate alignment of the orbital floor.[34] *However, one should never avoid exploring the orbital floor for fear of causing harm to orbital tissues — this occurrence is extremely rare!*

9. *Determination of necessity for fixation.* The second most important step in surgically treating zygomatic fractures (following determination of whether the reduction has been satisfactory) is ascertaining whether the reduction will be stable by itself or whether it needs some form of fixation. If constant reduction force is necessary to maintain position, the zygoma should be stabilized with some form of fixation device. If the zygomatic position is deemed appropriate and does not require constant application of reduction force, one should press on the malar eminence with the fingers, using considerable pressure, and see if displacement results. If it does not, then fixation devices may be unnecessary. Many minimally displaced fractures are stable once reduced. *However, the only way one can ensure that postsurgical displacement will not occur is by the application of fixation devices!*

10. *Application of fixation device.* The methods used to stabilize the fractured zygoma vary with the imagination of the surgeon. There are general principles involved, however, and these are discussed further on.

11. *Assessment of ocular motility.* Another forced duction test should be performed at the end of all active treatment, with the possible exception of suturing, to verify that the treatment did not create entrapment of orbital contents.

12. *Protection of fracture.* In those cases in which fixation devices have not been applied, the side of the fracture should be protected from application of external force — even the weight of the head against a pillow. This factor is most important in the immediate postsurgical period (i.e., recovery) while the patient is still sedated.

13. *Postsurgical ocular examinations.* The pupillary reflexes should be monitored postoperatively, and the fundus should be examined periodically. Visual acuity must also be checked. Because of surgically induced edema, binocular diplopia will probably be present, depending upon the surgical procedure.

14. *Postsurgical radiographs.* The posteroanterior oblique and submental vertex radiographs (as a minimum) should be ordered the day after surgery to assess the reduction radiographically.

Many techniques are advocated for reducing and stabilizing zygomatic fractures. These will be described by the surgical approach used after a presentation of the incisions employed to gain access to the periorbital areas. Techniques of orbital floor exploration and reconstruction will then be discussed.

Periorbital Incisions

A standard series of incisions have been used extensively for approaching the orbital rim and zygoma. It should be stated that whenever possible, existing lacerations are used for this purpose. In the absence of lacerations, however, properly placed incisions offer excellent access with minimal morbidity and scarring.

Protection of the cornea is mandatory during all operations about the orbit. If one is operating on the dermal side of the eyelids to approach the orbital rim or orbital

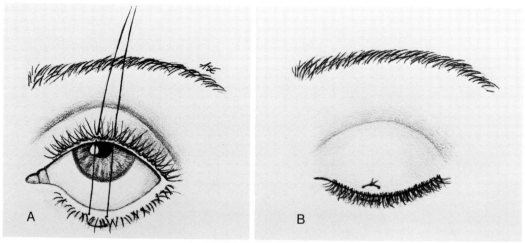

FIGURE 18-17. *A* and *B*, Technique of temporary tarsorrhaphy.

floor or both, a temporary tarsorrhaphy (Fig. 18–17) or scleral shell (Fig. 18–18) may be used after application of a bland eye ointment.[108] These are simply removed at the completion of the operation.

The use of dilute epinephrine solutions prior to incision is of benefit for two reasons. The first is the hemostasis that they provide. The second purpose of the solutions is to separate the tissues intentionally prior to incision. This latter use becomes very important when operating on the thin eyelids. The solutions can be used to "balloon out" the tissue, facilitating incision. One must remember, however, to mark the line of incision prior to injecting the solution, since the tissues will distort and a perceptible crease may disappear after injection.

Approaches to the Lateral Orbital Rim

SUPRAORBITAL EYEBROW INCISION

A popular incision that is used to gain access to the lateral orbital rim is the eyebrow incision (Fig. 18–19). There are no neurovascular structures of any signifi-

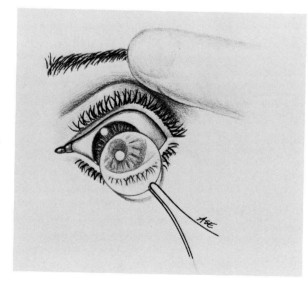

FIGURE 18-18. Scleral shell used for ocular protection.

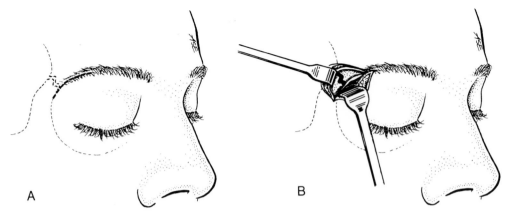

FIGURE 18–19.   Supraorbital eyebrow approach to frontozygomatic suture.   *A,* Most of the incision is within the confines of the eyebrow. *B,* Exposure of the fracture.

cance to be watched for while using this approach, and it gives simple and rapid access to the frontozygomatic area. Since the incision is made almost entirely within the confines of the eyebrow, the scar is usually imperceptible. However, it will not be hidden if used in individuals who have no eyebrows extending laterally along the orbital margin. In this instance, another incision may be indicated.

Technique.   Prior to incising the skin, the lateral orbital rim should be palpated to reveal the location of the fracture site. It is usually located at the frontozygomatic suture area, which is at the inferolateral aspect of the eyebrow. However, the fracture may be more inferiorly positioned, and the incision may then need to be placed below the eyebrow a given amount. Wide undermining of tissues above and below the incision usually makes it unnecessary to extend the incision far below the hair-bearing skin.

The skin is supported over the orbital rim using two fingers, and a 2-cm incision is made. It should be stressed that there is no reason to shave the eyebrow prior to incision, as the hair may not grow back. The incision should be parallel to the hair of the eyebrow to avoid cutting hair shafts, which might also retard growth of the eyebrow hair. The incision is made to the depth of the periosteum in one stroke, and after minimal undermining, another incision through the periosteum completes the sharp dissection.

Two sharp periosteal elevators are used to expose the lateral orbital rim on the lateral, medial (intraorbital), and posterior (temporal) surfaces. The fracture will usually be located at the inferior extent of the wound, requiring wide undermining of the periosteum to allow the tissues to be retracted inferiorly to provide better access to the fracture (Fig. 18–19*B*). It should be mentioned that if one stays in the subperiosteal space, there is virtually no chance of damaging vital structures. The incision is closed in two layers, the periosteum and the skin.

LOWER LID OR BLEPHAROPLASTY INCISIONS

The subciliary or lower lid incisions used to expose the infraorbital rim and orbital floor (described further on) can also be used to expose the lateral orbital rim. When these incisions are to be used for this purpose, lateral extension of the incisions for 0.5 to 1.0 cm and wide subperiosteal dissection will allow the necessary access to the lateral aspect of the orbit up to and including the frontozygomatic suture.[109] In the process of subperiosteal dissection, the lateral palpebral ligament and suspensory ligaments are stripped from the orbital tubercle of the zygoma. This procedure presents no apparent problem if the injury is acute and the periosteal tissues are securely sutured at the completion of the operation.

This technique is not recommended for the inexperienced surgeon, since it can be fraught with difficulties in access and postoperative swelling. Properly performed, however, it is an excellent method for simultaneously exposing the infraorbital and frontozygomatic areas, resulting in an imperceptible scar.[109]

Incisions to Expose the Infraorbital Rim

Several incisions made through the lower eyelid to gain access to the infraorbital rim and orbital floor have been described. The major difference between them is whether the incision is placed in the skin or conjunctiva. When placed on the dermal side of the eyelid, they differ in both the position of the skin incision (Fig. 18–20) and the level at which the muscle is transected to expose the orbital septum and periosteum. There are advantages and disadvantages to each incision, and indications are based upon the particular needs of the operative procedure.

INFRAORBITAL INCISION

The infraorbital incision[110-112] has been used extensively for several years and has long been the "standard" incision for approaching the infraorbital rim and orbital floor. It is still used by many surgeons; however, it has recently fallen into disfavor. The major disadvantage is that since it lies just over the infraorbital rim, there may be a noticeable scar after healing.[113] This scar is particularly troublesome in young individuals, in whom it increases in size with growth. There are several stated advantages to this incision, however, which include the following: (1) The incision is simple, since there is a short and direct path to the infraorbital margin; (2) the avoidance of the orbital septum and periorbital fat is usually assured in this location; (3) there is an almost nonexistent incidence of postsurgical ectropion[114]; and (4) the incision can be extended both medially and laterally, if necessary, to provide improved access. It is still an acceptable standard by which other incisions are compared and, for an inexperienced surgeon, perhaps the technique of choice.

Technique. The location of the infraorbital incision is just over the infraorbital rim. The incision should be placed within the eyelid tissue, at the inferior extent, not the tissue of the cheek (Fig. 18–20). The fracture should be palpated to identify its position, and an incision over the fracture is made. One must be mindful of the position of the lacrimal sac in incising toward the medial end of the rim. Superior cosmetic results are achieved when the incision is kept along the medial side of the orbit, extending laterally not farther than the pupil. The incision can be extended laterally beyond the pupil and orbital confines if necessary, but the incision should not turn superiorly to follow the lateral aspect of the rim. It should instead curve inferi-

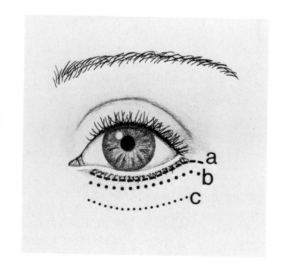

FIGURE 18–20. Incisions used to expose the infraorbital rim and orbital floor: a, subciliary or blepharoplasty incision; b, lower eyelid incision; and c, infraorbital incision.

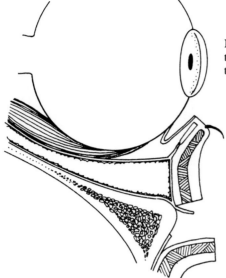

FIGURE 18–21. Illustration showing the cross-sectional anatomy of the infraorbital incision. Note that the incision was stepped at the periosteal level prior to incising the bone. The periosteum is incised slightly below the infraorbital rim.

orly and laterally to maintain an adequate margin of skin on the lower eyelid to help provide for lymphatic drainage. In its simplest form, an incision is made through skin, subcutaneous tissue, orbicularis oculi muscle, and periosteum. However, in practice, the incision should always be stepped—incising through skin and orbicularis muscle and undermining inferiorly prior to making an incision through periosteum (Fig. 18–21). Stepping the incision provides ease of closure and helps prevent direct healing between skin and periosteum, which produces a noticeable depression. Prior to incision through periosteum, one should palpate the orbital rim. The incision to bone should be slightly (approximately 3 mm) inferior to the orbital rim, below the attachment of the orbital septum, so that periorbital fat is avoided and a tight closure is facilitated. One must not make this incision too far inferior to the orbital rim, or the infraorbital neurovascular bundle will be transected. Subperiosteal elevation of the tissues over the infraorbital rim and orbital floor provides excellent access to the orbital rim and floor. This incision is always closed in at least two layers, the periosteum and the skin (Fig. 18–22).

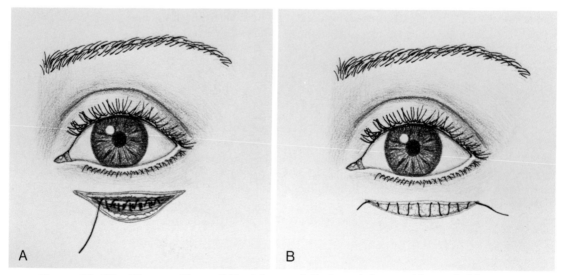

FIGURE 18–22. Closure of lower lid incisions. *A*, Periosteal closure with resorbable suture. *B*, Running subcuticular suture in dermis. It is unnecessary to suture the orbicularis oculi muscle.

LOWER EYELID INCISION

The lower eyelid incision, also known as the subtarsal incision, is one of the more frequently employed incisions for access to the infraorbital rim and orbital floor. Its main advantages are that (1) it is relatively easy, (2) the incision is placed in a natural skin crease so that the scar is imperceptible, and (3) it is associated with minimal complications. It has few disadvantages.

Technique.   The lower eyelid incision is made in a natural skin crease approximately half the distance between the lash margin and the orbital rim (see Fig. 18–20). The length of the incision can be from the lacrimal punctum medially to a point up to 1.0 to 1.5 cm lateral to the lateral canthus, if needed. The lateral aspect of the incision should continue in the skin crease, trailing off inferiorly, leaving a wide margin of intact skin above the incision to promote lymphatic drainage.

Once the skin is incised, one has three options. The first is to dissect between the skin and the muscle until the orbital rim is reached, at which point another incision through muscle and periosteum is made to bone (Fig. 18–23A). The second option is to incise through muscle at the same level as the skin incision and dissect down just anterior to the orbital septum to the orbital rim (Fig. 18–23*B*). The third option is a combination of these, in which subcutaneous dissection toward the rim proceeds for a few millimeters, followed by incision through the muscle at a lower level, producing a step incision, and then following the orbital septum to the rim (Fig. 18–23*C*).[115] Blunt scissors are useful during the dissection to the infraorbital rim, no matter which option is chosen, using a spreading motion.

Although advocated by several surgeons, each has advantages and disadvantages. The first option, in which a subcutaneous dissection that produces a skin flap to the level of the rim is made, leaves one with an extremely thin skin flap. It is a technically difficult flap to elevate, and accidental "button-hole" dehiscence can occur. A further problem that may occasionally be seen is a slight darkening of the skin in this area after healing. Presumably, the thin skin flap becomes avascular and acts essentially like a skin graft. An increase in the incidence of ectropion has also been noted, as opposed to which the dissection is made deep to the orbicularis oculi.[116] Entropion, lash problems, and occasional skin necrosis have sometimes been experienced after the "skin only" flap.[116,117] The second option, in which the dissection is made between muscle and orbital septum, is technically less difficult. Care must be taken, however, since the thin orbital septum can be easily violated, resulting in the herniation of periorbital fat into the wound. The skin and muscle flap, however, presumably maintain a better blood supply, and pigmentation of the lower lid has not been a finding.[118] The third technique, in which a layered dissection is used, is probably the simplest of the three and avoids the disadvantages of the others. One difficulty that can be encountered, however, is that the later repositioning of the

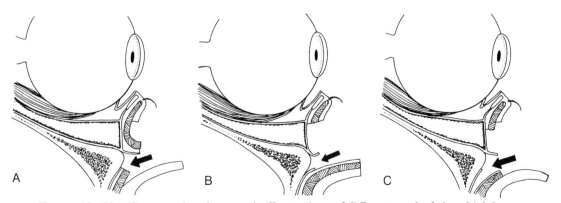

FIGURE 18–23.   Cross-sectional anatomic illustrations of different methods by which lower lid incisions can be made.   *A*, Subcutaneous dissection. *B*, Submuscular dissection. *C*, Layered dissection.

orbicularis oculi muscle during closure may not always be ideal, and distortions of the lower lid may arise.[113,119]

In any of these techniques, the incision through the periosteum should be placed just below the orbital rim to avoid the insertion of the orbital septum along the orbital margin. Closure should be in at least two layers, the periosteum and the skin. It is difficult and of little value to attempt to suture the orbicularis oculi. The running subcuticular suture is an excellent suture for the thin skin of the eyelid.

SUBCILIARY INCISION

The subciliary incision, also called the infraciliary or blepharoplasty incision, has gained favor with several surgeons in the United States over the past 10 to 15 years. However, recent studies have shown postsurgical complications that have caused many to abandon this approach to the infraorbital rim and orbital floor for management of fractures.[83,113,114,117,120,121] The problems encountered with this incision, however, are probably more related to the level of dissection (between skin and muscle) than to the location on the eyelid where the incision was placed (see previous discussion). This incision is merely a lower lid incision done at a higher level than in the lower lid, just below the eyelashes (see Fig. 18–20). The main advantage to this incision is the imperceptible scar it creates. The disadvantages are as follows: (1) The procedure is technically more difficult than the lower lid incision; (2) there is a higher risk of postoperative ectropion[114,117,122–124]; and (3) if a subcutaneous dissection is used, adaptation of the skin to the muscle may not be smooth. This incision is still popular, and when dissection is performed between the muscle and orbital septum, results have been excellent.[118]

Technique. The skin incision is made approximately 2 mm inferior to the gray line of the lower eyelid along the entire length of the lid. The incision may be extended laterally approximately 1.0 to 1.5 cm in a natural crease inferior to the lateral canthal ligament. The depth of the incision is down to the tarsal plate, at which point the dissection turns inferiorly along it and the orbital septum until the infraorbital rim is reached. (Alternatively, the dissection can be made anterior to the orbicularis oculi muscle, as described earlier; however, this is not recommended because of the postsurgical complications described previously.) Closure is also as described previously.

TRANSCONJUNCTIVAL INCISION

The transconjunctival incision, also called the inferior fornix incision, was originally described by Bourguet in 1928.[125] Two basic transconjunctival incisions have since been described—the preseptal and retroseptal approaches—which vary in the relation of the orbital septum to the path of dissection. Tenzel and Miller[126] developed the transconjunctival retroseptal incision, while Tessier[127] elaborated on the transconjunctival preseptal incision. The retroseptal approach is more direct than the preseptal approach and is easier to perform; however, the periorbital fat is encountered. This is a particularly frustrating problem when one is attempting to maintain as much fat as possible to prevent enophthalmos. Converse and colleagues[128] added a lateral canthotomy to the transconjunctival retroseptal incision for improved lateral exposure. The advantage to the transconjunctival approaches is that they produce superior cosmetic results when compared with any other commonly used incision, as the scar is hidden behind the lower lid. Other advantages are that (1) these techniques are rapid and (2) no skin or muscle dissection is necessary. Their main disadvantage is the limitation of access to the infraorbital rim and orbital floor that they provide. The access can be greatly improved by extending the incision across the lateral canthus and onto the skin surface (lateral canthotomy); however, the main advantage of this incision is then compromised. In a study by Wray and colleagues,[117] in which the transconjunctival incision was used for orbital floor and rim fractures, lateral canthotomy was necessary in 56 per cent of incisions to improve access. Other disadvantages of the transconjunctival incision are that the lower lid seems to shorten vertically slightly and it is an unnecessarily complicated approach.[123]

Because of the limited access, this incision has generally been reserved for fractures of the orbital rim and floor in which there is no need for extensive wiring procedures, such as pure blow-out fractures. Since it is often difficult to know how much disruption of the orbital rim and floor might accompany a given zygomatic fracture, this incision is not recommended for routine use in zygomatic fractures unless lateral canthotomy is used. This incision then becomes very useful.[106]

Technique for Retroseptal Transconjunctival Incision. In any transconjunctival incision, the cornea must be protected. As a tarsorrhaphy is precluded, a corneal shell should be placed to protect the globe. The lower eyelid is everted by two traction sutures placed through the tarsal plate, and the lower border of the tarsal plate is identified. (A Desmarres retractor is an excellent instrument to retract the lower lid.) Another traction suture is placed through the conjunctiva at the inferior fornix to assist while undermining the conjunctiva. An incision through the conjunctiva is made immediately above the lower border of the tarsal plate, extending medially from the lacrimal punctum and laterally to the canthus (Fig. 18–24A). If the incision is placed farther inferiorly, near the inferior fornix, the periorbital fat will herniate into the field. The conjunctiva is undermined toward the fornix, traction sutures through the ocular conjunctiva assisting in retraction. Once the periosteum is reached, another incision through it is made. Some surgeons prefer to make only one incision through both conjunctiva and periorbita, exposing the orbital rim in one stroke (Fig. 18–24B).[126] A sharp periosteal elevator is inserted, and the periorbita is dissected from the orbital floor (Fig. 18–24C). A broad, malleable retractor should be placed as soon as feasible to protect the orbit and to confine the periorbital fat. The orbital rim can also be exposed by dissecting anteroinferiorly (Fig. 18–24F). The incision is closed in two layers if possible, using resorbable sutures through the periosteum and running 6-0 plain gut suture through the conjunctiva (Fig. 18–24G). The periosteum may be difficult to close; some surgeons do not attempt closure of this layer.[129]

Technique for Preseptal Transconjunctival Incision. The lower eyelid is everted, and the tarsal plate is identified. Traction sutures are applied as described previously. An incision from the lacrimal punctum to the lateral canthus is made 2 to 3 mm inferior to the tarsal plate, through the conjunctiva and orbital septum. It may be easier to use sharp-pointed scissors than a scalpel in making this incision. Dissection to the orbital rim is carried out *anterior* to the orbital septum using blunt scissors (Fig. 18–24D). The periosteum should be exposed to a point approximately 3 mm inferior to the infraorbital rim prior to incising it. Once assured that the periosteum at the anterior portion of the infraorbital rim is properly identified, an incision through it should be made with a scalpel (Fig. 18–24E). This approach tends to confine the periorbital fat but is technically more difficult than the retroseptal approach. The periosteal and the conjunctival incisions should be closed following the operation.

Technique for Lateral Canthotomy. If exposure is found to be too limited using one of the techniques just described, a lateral canthotomy can be included in the incision. This is simply performed by inserting one end of sharp iris scissors into the lateral palpebral fissure and cutting through in a horizontal (lateral) direction (Fig. 18–25A). The transconjunctival incision is then connected with the canthotomy by isolating the inferior arm of the lateral canthal tendon and dividing it (Fig. 18–25B and C). The added exposure the lateral canthotomy provides should allow access along the lateral orbital rim. The inferior limb of the lateral canthal tendon is sutured to the lateral orbital rim using 4–0 Prolene. The incision in the conjunctiva is closed with running 6–0 plain gut suture (Fig. 18–25D). The small skin incision at the lateral canthus is closed with 6–0 silk or nylon suture.

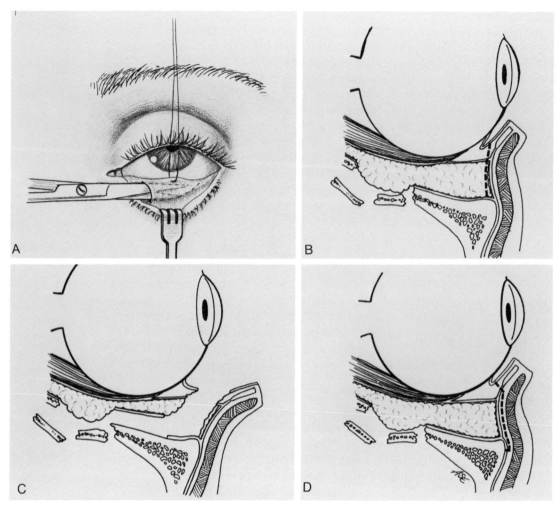

FIGURE 18–24.   **Transconjunctival incisions.**   *A,* Initial incision through conjunctiva. *B* and *C,* Cross-sectional illustrations of retroseptal approach. *D* and *E,* Cross-sectional illustrations of preseptal approach. *F,* Exposure of orbital rim and floor. *G,* Closure.

Complications of Orbital Floor Incisions

Several complications can result from the incisions described for approaching the infraorbital rim and orbital floor. Minor complications, such as dehiscence, hematoma or seroma, and lymphedema, are more bothersome than difficult to handle. When large, hematomas and seromas can be decompressed with a needle and syringe. Lymphedema will subside with time, especially if the lower lid is supported in its proper position. Dehiscence of a wound may require nothing more than observation, unless it is large, at which point wound care and resuturing may be necessary.

One problem that may accompany any incision to gain access to the infraorbital rim and orbital floor is a vertical shortening of the lower lid after healing. This condition probably occurs as a result of scarring between the tarsal plate and the periosteum, which shortens the orbital septum. To help prevent this problem, superior support of the lower lid for several days (or until gross edema has resolved) following surgery is beneficial. The most direct method to achieve this is through the use of a Frost suture, in which a suture is placed through the dermal surface of the lower lid just inferior to the gray line and is taped to the forehead (Fig. 18–26). This method closes the eye, supports the lower lid, helps in the dissipation of lid edema, and allows one to examine the globe and vision by simply removing the tape from the forehead and opening the eyelids.

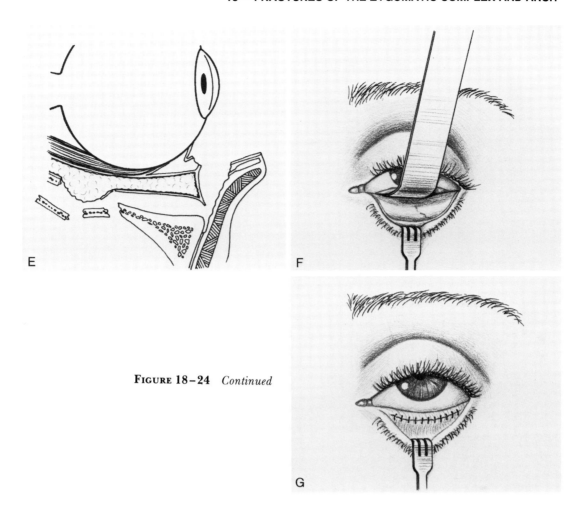

FIGURE 18–24   *Continued*

Postsurgical ectropion is a distressing problem, although most cases are self-limiting. Ectropion, or an outward curl to the lower eyelid, is classified as mild when there is only slight lifting of the lid from the globe. Moderate ectropion occurs when there is shortening in the vertical height of the lower eyelid that is associated with lifting of the lid from the globe. Severe ectropion is a combination of shortening of the eyelid and true eversion of the eyelid, not just a lifting away. Mild and moderate ectropion usually resolve with the passage of time and with gentle massage of the lid. Severe ectropion may require surgical correction.

Postsurgical ectropion occurs in 37 to 42 per cent of subciliary incisions.[114,116,117] It appears that the subciliary incision produces more ectropion than the lower lid or infraorbital incision.[123] Pospisil and Fernando[116] claim that a major factor in the development of ectropion is the plane of dissection within the lower lid. If the dissection is made in the subcutaneous plane, anterior to the orbicularis oculi muscle, ectropion is more common than when the dissection is made posterior to the muscle. They also noticed more ectropion in cases in which edema of the lid was present *prior* to operation. They recommend delaying surgery until the initial edema has resolved.

Other Incisions for Zygomatic Surgery

MODIFIED PREAURICULAR INCISION FOR EXPOSURE OF THE ZYGOMATIC ARCH

An extremely useful incision was described by Al-Kayat and Bramley[130] for access to the temporomandibular joint and zygomatic arch. It is essentially an ex-

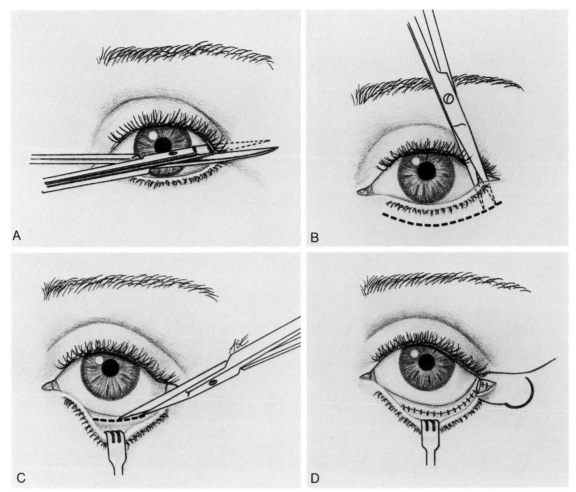

FIGURE 18–25.   Lateral canthotomy combined with transconjunctival approach to orbital floor. *A,* Initial full-thickness incision through lateral canthus. *B,* Canthotomy incision connected with incision in conjunctiva. *C,* Usual conjunctival incision. *D,* Canthotomy closure in two layers.

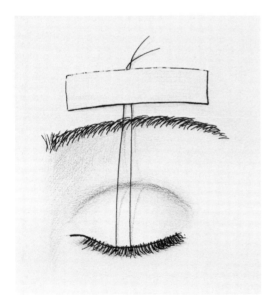

FIGURE 18–26.   Frost suture placed through the skin of the lower lid and taped to the forehead to provide support to the lower lid.

tended preauricular incision that takes into account the course of the temporal branches of the facial nerve and avoids them. In a series of cadaver dissections, they found that the temporal branches cross the zygomatic arch within a dense fusion of the periosteum of the zygomatic arch, the outer layer of temporal fascia, and the superficial fascia (subcutaneous tissue) from 8 to 35 mm anterior to the external auditory meatus. Their incision and dissection are designed to avoid these branches while providing excellent exposure of the zygomatic arch.

Technique. The skin incision is shaped like a large question mark and begins 4 to 6 cm above and anterior to the top of the helix (Fig. 18–27A). The superior extent of the incision is completely within the hairline and is therefore cosmetically acceptable. The lower part of the incision can be made as in any preauricular approach,

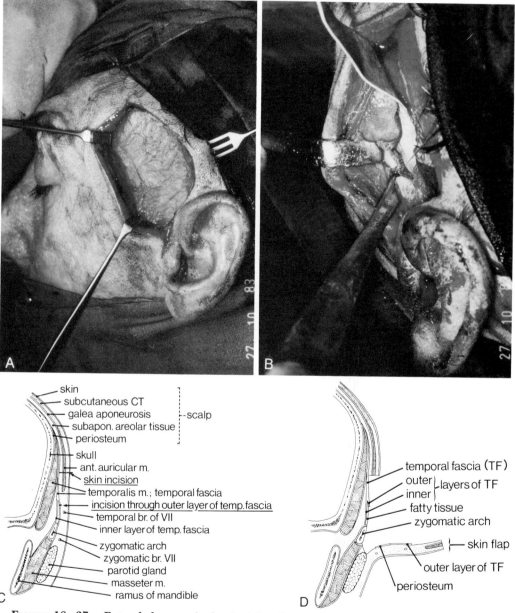

FIGURE 18–27. Extended preauricular incision for exposure of the zygomatic arch. *A,* Initial incision to the depth of the temporal fascia, followed by a second incision through the outer layer of the temporal fascia. The fractured zygomatic arch is exposed *(B). C* and *D,* Cross-sectional anatomy of the lateral aspect of the head, showing the two incisions used to expose the zygomatic arch.

either anterior to the tragus or endaurally. The depth of the superior aspect of the incision is to the temporal fascia (Fig. 18–27A). Dissection of the skin flap at the level of the temporal fascia can then proceed, reflecting the flap forward and downward. At a point approximately 2 cm above the zygomatic arch, the temporal fascia bifurcates, one layer extending lateral and one layer extending medial to the arch. Between these two layers, areolar tissue containing some fat can usually be visualized. No further dissection inferior to this bifurcation should proceed superficial to the temporal fascia, or the temporal branches of the facial nerve may be encountered.

To avoid these branches, a 45-degree incision is made through the *outer layer* of temporal fascia, beginning at the root of the zygomatic arch (near the articular tubercle) and upward and forward toward the posterior aspect of the lateral orbital rim (Fig. 18–27C and D). Once inside this pocket, dissection inferior to the arch is made without fear of encountering the temporal branches of the facial nerve. The dissection can be continued as far anteriorly as the frontal process of the zygoma, and posteriorly the incision can be joined to the preauricular dissection, which follows the external auditory canal. Subperiosteal dissection of the zygomatic arch is readily provided by incision along the superomedial aspect from within the dissected pocket (Fig. 18–27B). Closure is performed in layers.

CORONAL INCISION

The coronal, or bifrontal, flap, modified to include some of the advantages of the modified preauricular flap of Al-Kayat and Bramley,[130] is an extremely useful incision for surgery of the zygoma and arch. Although it may initially appear as a radical approach to the management of zygomatic fractures, it provides excellent access to the orbits, zygomatic bodies, and zygomatic arches with virtually no complications.[131] It is an extremely useful incision when there is comminution of the supraorbital and lateral orbital rims and of the zygomatic body and arch. The scar produced is hidden within the hairline and is therefore invisible.

Technique. In contrast to the earlier practice of extensive shaving of the head prior to incision, shaving the hair from the operative field need not be extensive. A 2-cm strip of hair can be removed in the immediate area of the incision, and the adjacent hair can be prepared. If the hair is long, it can be accumulated into clumps with sterile elastics (once prepared) to minimize the annoyance of loose hair in the operative field during the procedure. The drapes can be sutured or stapled to the scalp, covering the posterior scalp and confining this hair. If a unilateral procedure is planned, the incision may be hemicoronal, in which the superior aspect of the incision extends just across the midline and slightly anteriorly, ending at least 2 cm posterior to the hairline. For bilateral procedures, a strip across the superior aspect of the head is shaved.

In placing the incision, two factors should be borne in mind. The first is the hairline of the patient—not just the present but the anticipated future hairline. In male patients, minor recession of the hairline with age might make the scar visible if the incision is placed just behind the hairline. Therefore, the incision should be placed along a line extending from one preauricular area to the other, several centimeters behind the hairline (Fig. 18–28A). The incision can even be made farther posteriorly, if necessary, without a significant reduction in access to the operative field. The second factor that should be considered is the amount of inferior access required for the procedure. In the usual instance, the coronal incision may extend inferiorly to the level of the anterior border of the helix. If necessary, the coronal incision can be extended inferiorly to the level of the lobe of the ear, providing improved access at the inferior portion of the wound for zygomatic arch and infraorbital exposure.

The incision is made with a No. 10 blade through skin, subcutaneous tissue, and galea. This incision will bring one into a plane of loose areolar connective tissue overlying the pericranium. The flap margin can be rapidly and easily lifted and dissected from the pericranium within this plane. Upon incision, the anterior and

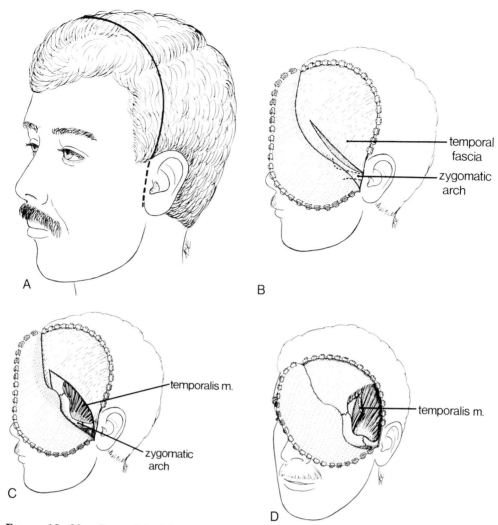

FIGURE 18–28.   Coronal incision.   *A*, Location of incision. Placement of incision should be well behind the hairline. *B*, Dissection of the flap done anteriorly above the pericranium and temporal fascia. A second incision is made through the temporal fascia and pericranium above the supraorbital rim. *C*, Dissection of the temporal fascia with the scalp flap and incision through the periosteum along the orbital and zygomatic margins exposes the osseous structures. *D*, Temporal muscle can be reflected if needed.

posterior wound margins are elevated for 1 to 2 cm to allow application of hemostatic clips (Raney clips). This practice will prevent continuous bleeding from the vascular scalp throughout the procedure. There should be little hemorrhage encountered throughout the remainder of the procedure, although small vessels running through the pericranium from the skull may require cauterization. The anterior flap is elevated from the pericranium with finger dissection or the use of a blunt periosteal elevator. Along the lateral aspect of the skull, the temporal fascia will become visible where it inserts into the pericranium, the plane of dissection superficial to it. Once the flap has been elevated to within approximately 2 cm of the body of the zygoma and zygomatic arch, these bones can usually be seen through the covering fascia. The *superficial layer of temporal fascia* is incised approximately 2 cm superior to the zygomatic arch, beginning at the root of the zygomatic arch and continuing anteriorly and superiorly (Fig. 18–28*B*). On incision of the superficial layer of temporal fascia, a layer of fat and areolar tissue are encountered. If one has difficulty discerning layers due to edema and/or hematoma, incision through both layers of temporal fascia, exposing the temporal muscle, will provide safe visualization of the zygomatic body and arch. Further dissection made inferiorly at this level provides safe access to the zygomatic arch. From the root of the zygomatic arch, a periosteal incision is then made along the superior aspect of the arch, and it is exposed subperiosteally (Fig. 18–28C). The pericranium is now incised across the forehead and down along the lateral orbital rim. The periosteal incision at the lateral rim is connected with that over the zygomatic arch. Periosteal elevation then exposes the frontozygomatic fracture line and is continued around the lateral orbital rim and into the orbit. Periosteum is elevated along the posterior aspect of the zygoma and into the temporal fossa to the buttress region (Fig. 18–28D). The infraorbital rim can also be visualized to some extent with wide undermining. If access to the infraorbital area is necessary, the zygomatic arch and body should be thoroughly dissected prior to exposing the infraorbital areas, to relax the tissues. Occasionally, depending upon the degree of exposure needed and the location of the fracture over the infraorbital rim, a separate incision to expose the infraorbital rim is required (see preceding discussion).

Once the fracture reduction and fixation have been accomplished, the wound is closed in layers. The periosteum over the arch should be closed, followed by closure of the temporal fascia and periosteum. A lateral canthopexy is performed by drilling a hole through the lateral orbital rim just below the frontozygomatic suture for passing of the suture. The suture can be secured to the temporal fascia or tied to the bone plate or wire in the zygoma at the frontozygomatic suture area. The scalp incision is closed in two layers using 2-0 chromic catgut through the galea and either sutures or staples on the skin surface. The use of a flat suction drain is optional. The skin sutures or staples are removed in 7 to 10 days.

Reduction Techniques

TEMPORAL APPROACH

An approach that has been popular through the years for reduction of both zygomatic complex and zygomatic arch fractures is the temporal approach. First described by Gillies and coworkers in 1927[1] for use in zygomatic arch fractures, this approach has proven versatility for both zygomatic arch and zygomatic complex fractures. One of its greatest advantages is that it allows the application of great amounts of controlled force to disimpact even the most difficult zygomatic fractures. It is therefore especially useful when treating a fracture late, when partial consolidation has occurred. The Gillies temporal approach is also a very quick and simple method, rarely requiring more than 15 to 20 minutes, unless fixation techniques are necessary.[91] The temporal approach is associated with few complications, and although the middle temporal veins may be encountered during instrumentation,[132] the hemorrhage encountered is rarely of any consequence.

Several surgeons think that this technique should be reserved for zygomatic arch fractures only, being ineffective for displaced or rotated zygomatic body fractures.[37,99] An overwhelming majority of surgeons, however, disagree with this presumption and use it as the main method for reducing zygomatic fractures.[13,15,18,19,24,26,28,29,34,36,65,75,86,90,133,134]

Technique. A 3-cm × 3-cm area of hair is shaved approximately 2.5 cm above and 2.5 cm anterior to the helix of the ear. It is unnecessary to isolate the area completely from adjacent hair. A cotton pellet is placed within the external auditory canal to prevent blood from entering during surgery. Frequently, the bifurcation of the superficial temporal artery is visible once the hair is shaved and serves as an excellent landmark for incision. A 2.5-cm incision is made through skin and subcutaneous tissue at an angle running from anterosuperior to posteroinferior in the area previously shaved. This incision can usually be placed superior to the bifurcation of the superficial temporal artery, between and thereby avoiding both branches. The incision is carried down through skin and subcutaneous tissue until the white, glistening surface of the temporal fascia is visualized (Fig. 18–29A). This incision can usually be made with one stroke of the scalpel. At this level, one should be above the point

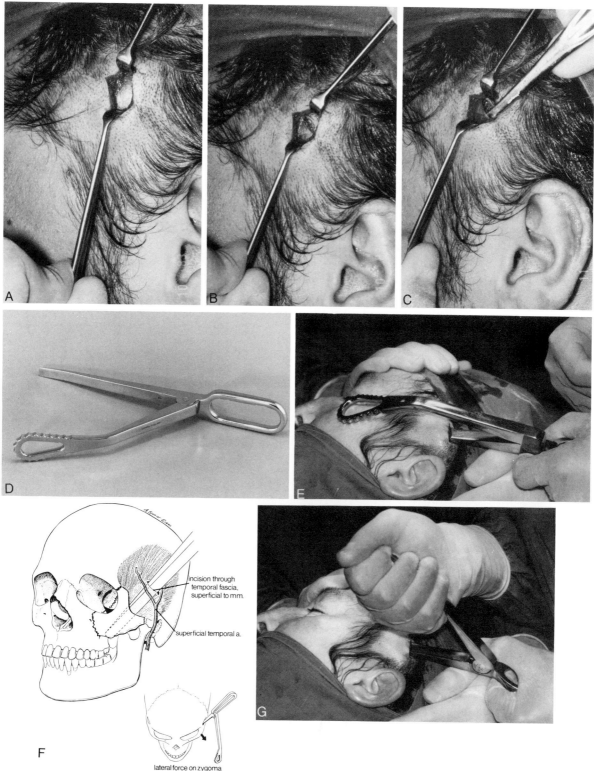

FIGURE 18–29. The Gillies temporal approach to elevation of the zygoma. *A,* Initial incision to the level of the temporal fascia. *B,* Second incision through the temporal fascia to the underlying muscle. Note the muscle, which will usually bulge out slightly through the incision. *C,* A flat periosteal elevator is inserted deep to the temporal fascia (between the fascia and the muscle) and is swept anteriorly and posteriorly as it is advanced inferiorly. In this manner, the deep surface of the temporal fascia is freed from the temporalis muscle. The periosteal elevator is advanced inferiorly until the medial surface of the zygomatic arch and temporal surface of the zygomatic body are identified. It is then withdrawn, and the Rowe zygomatic elevator *(D)* is inserted in this same plane *(E).* When the handle of the Rowe elevator is allowed to contact the skin, the depth of the blade beneath the zygoma can be determined. *F,* Two hands are used to elevate the zygoma. The working end of the elevator should be on the temporal surface of the zygomatic body for initial elevation. *G,* Illustration of Gillies approach.

where the temporal fascia splits into two layers, one attaching lateral and one medial to the zygomatic arch. It is important that the incision be above this point of bifurcation so that the elevator can be easily placed medial to the zygomatic arch. If the incision is below the layer of the temporal fascia bifurcation, the elevator will be placed within the space above the arch, and medial placement will be difficult.

Once exposure of the temporal fascia is complete, a second, deeper incision is carefully made for the full length of the skin incision through the fascia (Fig. 18–29B). At this point, one should see the underlying temporalis muscle bulge through the incision. If this is not seen, the incision may have possibly been placed too low, and into the space above the arch. In this case, the incision should be deepened until temporalis muscle is visible. It must be remembered *that the temporalis muscle is the key structure in this dissection.* A flat instrument, such as a large Freer elevator or the broad end of a No. 9 periosteal elevator, is then inserted between the temporalis muscle and the temporal fascia (Fig. 18–29C). The instrument is swept back and forth while the tip is moved inferiorly, until the medial aspect of the zygomatic arch and the infratemporal surface of the body of the zygoma are felt. The instrument should glide quite freely in this plane, as there is no dense attachment between the temporalis muscle and temporal fascia. It may be difficult, however, to pass the instrument medial to the zygomatic arch if there has been medial displacement, especially in those areas of fracture. In this instance, the tip of the instrument must be pressed medially until the medial aspect of the zygomatic arch is reached. The entire extent of the arch and zygomatic body should be palpated with the instrument to determine the location and extent of fractures. Bimanual palpation, with one hand placed externally over the soft tissue of the side of the face, is frequently helpful. The periosteal elevator is removed, and a flat instrument of sufficient rigidity is inserted into this same plane to reduce the fracture. Originally, a Bristow elevator was used, and it was necessary to use the superior margin of the wound and adjacent skull as a fulcrum to obtain the required leverage to reduce the fracture. It was necessary to place gauze under the instrument at the point of fulcrum to avoid bruising the scalp. Although this instrument can still be used, it should be used with care, as damage to the cranium has occurred.[135] An ingenious instrument that has since been designed for zygomatic elevation and allows one to exert large amounts of controlled force without using the skull as a fulcrum is the Rowe zygomatic elevator (Fig. 18–29D). It has a flat blade on its working end for insertion medial to the zygomatic arch and body. It has two handles for grasping during use. The first is one in direct line with the working end and is used primarily for stabilization. The second handle is on the external lifting lever, which is, in turn, attached to the area of the stabilizing handle. When the stabilizing handle is kept in one position and the lifting handle is activated, the working blade can generate large amounts of force beneath a zygoma. The instrument was designed so that the two arms are approximately the same length. This design allows constant knowledge of the depth of insertion of the working blade by collapsing the hinge between the two arms and seeing where the external handle lies in relation to the zygoma (Fig. 18–29E).

Once the Rowe zygomatic elevator is in position at the proper depth, the external handle is elevated while the other handle stabilizes the working blade position. Firm anterior, superior, and lateral elevation is applied to the body of the zygoma in cases of zygomatic complex fractures or to the arch in cases of arch fractures (Fig. 18–29F and G). During elevation, an assistant must palpate the frontozygomatic and infraorbital areas while steadying the head against the elevator's pull. An audible crunch or crack usually accompanies the elevation. If strong resistance is felt, one must consider that the zygoma is greatly impacted, in which case more force may be necessary, or that the tip of the elevator may have been placed too far medially, through the temporalis muscle. In the latter case, one might be applying elevation to the coronoid process or medial aspect of the ramus of the mandible. Once the body of the zygoma has been elevated, the instrument's working blade should be swept posteriorly and laterally, reducing or "ironing out" any zygomatic arch fractures. The surgeon must then verify that any steps at the osseous zygomatic processes have been eliminated. Once adequate reduction and resistance to displacement have been verified, the elevator is withdrawn and the incision is closed in one or two layers.

BUCCAL SULCUS APPROACH

Another popular technique for the reduction of zygomatic fractures is the approach through the maxillary buccal sulcus. Keen published an article on this technique in 1909,[136] and it is used with favor by many surgeons today.[37,137] The major advantage, as in most intraoral approaches, is the avoidance of any external scar. It can be used for both zygomatic complex and zygomatic arch fractures. Although the use of this approach for elevation has several laudable attributes, unstable fractures may require external incisions for application of stable methods of fixation.

Keen Technique. A small incision (approximately 1 cm) is made in the mucobuccal fold just beneath the zygomatic buttress of the maxilla. The incision can be made from anterior to posterior or from medial to lateral and should extend through mucosa, submucosa, and any buccinator muscle fibers. The sharp end of a No. 9 periosteal elevator or curved Freer elevator is inserted into the incision, and with a side-to-side sweeping motion, the infratemporal surfaces of the maxilla, zygoma, and zygomatic arch are contacted and the soft tissue is dissected in a *supra*periosteal manner. A heavier instrument can then be inserted behind the infratemporal surface of the zygoma, and with superior, lateral, and anterior force, the bone can be reduced (Fig. 18–30A). The use of one hand over the side of the face to assist in the reduction procedure is extremely helpful. One should take care to avoid using the anterior maxilla as a point of fulcrum.

Several different instruments can be used to accomplish this maneuver, including those designed specifically for this purpose, such as the Monks or Cushing (joker) elevator. However, any suitable instrument of sufficient rigidity with a bend on the end to engage the infratemporal surface of the zygoma will do. A right-angle retractor, a bone hook, a large Kelly hemostat, and a urethral sound are satisfactory instruments for this purpose. Another instrument that can be used very successfully through the buccal sulcus approach is a simple dental extraction forceps. It is used in a

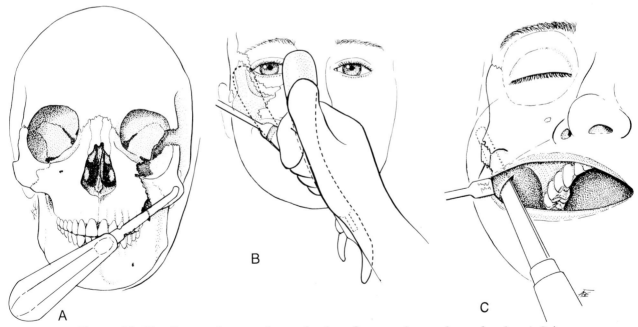

FIGURE 18–30. Intraoral approach to reduction of zygomatic complex and arch. *A,* Suitable elevator inserted on the temporal surface of the zygomatic body for elevation. *B,* Dental extraction forceps used in a manner similar to the Rowe zygomatic elevator. *C,* Flat instrument used to reduce a depressed zygomatic arch.

manner similar to that of a Rowe zygomatic elevator in that the hinge portion of the forceps is the stabilizing handle and one of the forceps handles is the elevating handle. The other forceps handle becomes the working end and engages the posterior aspect of the zygoma. Controlled force can very easily be applied in this manner.

A flat instrument such as a Seldin retractor can then be used to follow the medial surface of the zygomatic arch and elevate it laterally if necessary. This same approach is used on isolated zygomatic arch fractures. It must be stressed that when the temporal surface of the zygomatic body is followed laterally, one must stay close to bone, or the instrument may become placed on the medial side of the coronoid process. Although some clinicians do not feel that the intraoral approach can be used effectively for zygomatic arch fractures,[78,111] this has not been the experience of all. The incision in the mucobuccal fold need not be sutured.

Technique of Lateral Coronoid Approach. In 1977, Quinn described a lateral coronoid approach for zygomatic arch fracture reduction.[138] This approach is not useful for fractures of the zygomatic complex but is a simple method for isolated fractures of the arch. A 3- to 4-cm intraoral incision is made along the anterior border of the ramus through mucosa and submucosa. The incision is not made to bone but to the depth where the temporalis muscle inserts on the ramus. The wound is deepened superiorly, following the lateral aspect of the temporalis muscle with blunt dissection. This maneuver will bring the instrument (or finger) between the temporalis muscle and zygomatic arch, which should be readily palpable. The buccal fat pad will probably be encountered but is of no concern. A flat-bladed, heavy elevator is inserted into this pocket, taking care to ensure its proper placement lateral to the coronoid process, and the arch is elevated while the clinician palpates extraorally along the arch (Fig. 18–30C). The wound is closed in one layer.

ELEVATION FROM EYEBROW APPROACH

A popular technique in the United States for the elevation of zygomatic fractures is through the eyebrow incision (described previously).[17,78,99,139] The advantages of this technique are that the fracture at the orbital rim is visualized directly and that fixation of the fracture at this point can be undertaken through the same incision when necessary. The disadvantage is that it is difficult to generate large amounts of force, especially in the superior direction.[9,37,86]

Technique. Once exposure of the fracture at the frontozygomatic area of the lateral orbital rim has been accomplished, a heavy instrument is inserted posterior to the zygoma, along its temporal surface. The instrument is then used to lift the zygoma anteriorly, laterally, and superiorly while one hand palpates along the infraorbital rim and body of the zygoma (Fig. 18–31A). Instruments that are useful for this purpose are the Dingman zygomatic elevator, a urethral sound, or even a large Kelly hemostat. The arch can also be approached from this exposure and reduced (Fig. 18–31B).

PERCUTANEOUS APPROACH

A very direct route to elevation of the depressed zygoma is through the skin surface of the face overlying the zygoma. This approach has been used extensively in many countries throughout the world. The advantage of the technique is that one can produce forces anteriorly, laterally, and superiorly in a very direct manner, without having to negotiate adjacent structures with the instruments. The major disadvantage is a scar on the face in a very noticeable location. However, in practice, this is more a theoretical than real disadvantage, as the incision sites are rarely visible 2 to 3 weeks following surgery.

Technique. This is probably the most simple of all techniques, as no soft tissue dissection is necessary. Several instruments can be used to elevate the zygoma. The bone hook, introduced by Strohmeyer in 1844,[140] has probably been the most widely used instrument and is advocated by many (Fig. 18–32A).[25,87,88,93,94,101,141–144] Very

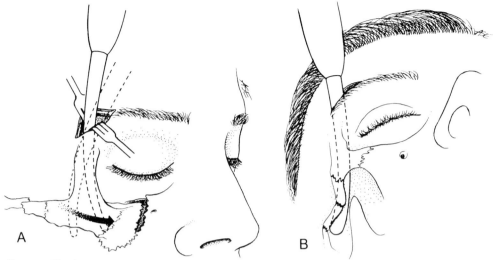

FIGURE 18–31.   Elevation of zygomatic compound from eyebrow approach.   *A*, Dingman zygomatic elevator placed along temporal surface of zygoma for anterior, lateral, and superior elevation. *B*, Elevator used to reduce zygomatic arch fracture.

simply, the point of the hook is inserted through the soft tissues of the malar area at a point just inferior and posterior to the prominence of the zygoma, so that it engages the infratemporal aspect (Fig. 18–32*B*). Poswillo[143] draws two intersecting lines on the face to determine the proper location for application of the bone hook. The first is a vertical line dropped from the lateral canthus of the eye. The second is a horizontal line drawn laterally from the ala of the nose. A small stab incision is made at the point of intersection of these lines, and the hook is inserted. The hook is then rotated to engage the temporal surface of the zygoma. One must be cognizant of the area of application of the point of the hook on the back of the zygoma, assuring that the hook has not slipped into the inferior orbital fissure, which can cause venous hemorrhage, subsequently resulting in ocular injury. Strong traction in any direction can then be applied to reduce a displaced zygoma (Fig. 18–32*C*).

FIGURE 18–32.   Elevation of zygomatic compound using a bone hook.   *A*, Bone hook. *B*, Illustration demonstrating anterior and lateral traction using percutaneous bone hook. *C*, Clinical photograph of the use of a bone hook. The dotted lines on the face represent those discussed in the text. Note finger placement at infraorbital rim during elevation to detect reduction.

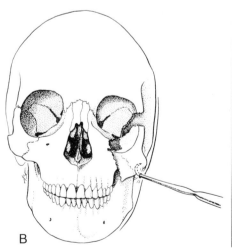

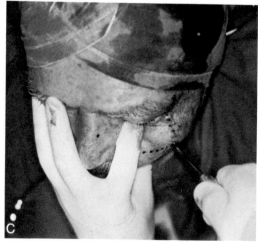

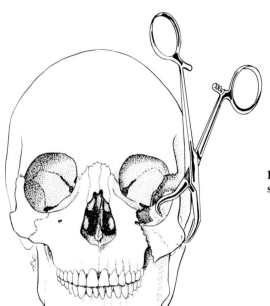

FIGURE 18–33. Elevation of zygomatic compound using a towel clip inserted percutaneously.

Another instrument that has been used, especially in emergency rooms while the patient is under local anesthetic, is a large, heavy towel clip.[86] The points of the towel clip are inserted through the soft tissues of the inferior eyelid and malar area, one entering the orbit along the lateral infraorbital margin and the other inserted underneath and behind the zygomatic body (Fig. 18–33). In this manner, the zygoma can be elevated with considerable force.

A large bone screw, such as the Carroll-Girard screw, is another instrument that has been used with some frequency for elevating zygomas (Fig. 18–34A). It resembles an elongated corkscrew with a T-bar handle and contains threads on its working end. This screw can be threaded into the body of the zygoma following placement of a hole and can then be used as a handle to reduce the displaced zygoma (Fig. 18–34B).

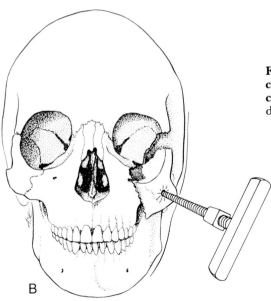

FIGURE 18–34. Elevation of zygomatic compound using a bone screw inserted percutaneously. *A*, Bone screw. *B*, Illustration demonstrating use of bone screw.

Any of these instruments (and probably others) are useful in the transcutaneous approach to the zygoma. The possible application of one or two monofilament sutures is all that is necessary to care for the wounds created by their use.

INTRASINUS APPROACH

One approach to the reduction of zygomatic fractures that is not extensively used is by way of the maxillary sinus. It has been claimed a useful approach when comminution of the body of the zygoma is diagnosed and one would like to use an antral pack to produce acceptable facial contour. Since the advent of internal fixation, however, there has been little need for packing of the sinus and, therefore, for this approach to reduction.

Although the original approach, as described by Lothrop in 1906,[145] involved an intranasal approach through the inferior meatus, the more acceptable approach is through a Caldwell-Luc procedure. Advantages claimed for this procedure[99] are that (1) the orbital floor can be concomitantly visualized and (2) this approach allows stabilization of the zygomatic and orbital floor fractures with an antral pack.

Technique.   A horizontal incision is made a few millimeters above the mucogingival junction from the canine region to the second molar region. This incision will allow closure over sound bone at the commencement of the procedure. A subperiosteal dissection exposes the lateral maxillary wall and zygoma. Frequently, gross comminution will be present, providing access to the interior of the sinus. If there is only a linear fracture, a Caldwell-Luc type of opening should be made above the tooth roots, saving the bone in saline for possible use, if needed, on the orbital floor. The sinus is cleansed of blood and osseous debris. The sinus, the sinus walls, and the orbital floor are evaluated using a fiberoptic light source and direct vision. If the zygoma is not grossly comminuted, a large, curved instrument, such as a Kelly hemostat or bone hook, is placed within the sinus, engaging the inner aspect of the zygomatic eminence, and is used to elevate the fracture. The opposite hand should palpate the orbital margins as this is performed.

If the zygomatic eminence is comminuted, elevation of the bone fragments with finger pressure should be possible, followed by packing the sinus with iodoform gauze or other packing material (see "Technique of Sinus Packing," further on).

Orbital Floor Exploration

In the treatment of zygomatic complex fractures, orbital floor exploration is a supplementary procedure that is frequently, but not always, indicated. However, when there is a question about the status of the orbital floor and periorbital tissues, exploration should be performed.

Intrasinus Approach to the Orbital Floor.   The orbital floor has been approached directly through skin incisions and indirectly through the maxillary sinus. Some surgeons use both approaches simultaneously. The antral approach to the orbital floor has historically been predicated on the ability to realign the orbital floor without making external incisions when the orbital floor has been depressed but there is no herniation of soft tissues through the periorbita. Packing the sinus with either gauze or a balloon to provide support to the orbital floor for 2 weeks was thought to allow healing to take place.[43,146-150] In practice, however, this is rarely possible and should not be used as the routine approach to the orbital floor.

Combined Intrasinus and External Approach to the Orbital Floor.   The intrasinus approach has met with considerable success by those who employ it; however, it is "blind" in that one does not directly see the periorbital tissues. A combined approach, in which one has direct access to the orbital floor and access to the sinus, is advocated by other surgeons.[41,55,106,151] Once the orbital floor is exposed and the periorbital tissues have been repositioned, a sinus pack or balloon is placed under

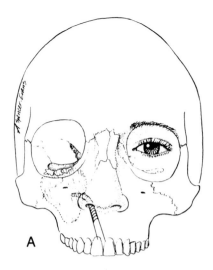

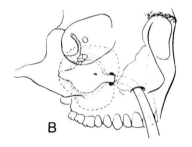

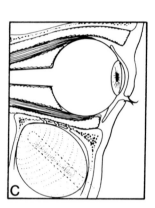

FIGURE 18–35. **Illustrations demonstrating the use of an antral balloon to support orbital floor fracture.** *A*, Nasal antrostomy performed with a curved nasal rasp. *B*, Antral balloon inserted and inflated. *C*, Balloon shown supporting orbital floor.

direct vision and used for support until healing occurs (Fig. 18–35). In this latter case, the packing can be performed under direct visualization to ensure that there is no excessive encroachment of the pack on the orbital contents. However, it is still necessary to have a significant osseous scaffold along the orbital floor for healing to take place. This is rarely the situation; fragmentation or loss of bone (or both) is the rule, necessitating placement of an implant or transplant.

Orbital floor implants or transplants have also been placed using this dual approach, with the sinus pack as supplemental support for the implant or transplant.[55,106] However, recent evidence suggests that the concomitant use of antral packs and orbital floor implants increases the chance of infection.[152,153] The combined use of antral packs and lyophilized dura, however, has met with good success.[106]

External Approach to the Orbital Floor. The most common and recommended method of orbital exploration and reconstruction is performed through a skin incision. With use of any of the aforementioned approaches to the infraorbital rim and orbital floor, the periorbita is gently elevated along the floor of the orbit. It must be remembered that the orbital floor is inferior to the level of the rim, so that when the periorbita is elevated, one must be careful to follow the contour of the rim, or perforation of the periorbita will occur. The subperiorbital dissection should extend beyond the full length of the access incision. Comminution of the infraorbital rim is commonly present, and the larger osseous pieces should be preserved, if possible. It is always easier to dissect the periorbita from sound bone toward the fractured areas. Protection of the periorbita and globe is facilitated after dissection by placement of a malleable retractor. The area of disrupted floor may be a very narrow crack, usually along the infraorbital groove, or may be severely comminuted. When it is comminuted, it becomes difficult to dissect the periorbita from the thin bone spicules. One must continue dissection posteriorly along the floor until sound bone is found. This practice usually requires dissection posterior to the globe. Areas of periorbital fat dishiscence through the periorbita into the maxillary sinus must be gently freed. Small bone spicules from the orbital floor can be removed if they are free of soft tissue attachments.

For those fractures in which the defect is a narrow linear groove, no reconstruction is usually necessary. When a larger defect is noted and the periorbita has been disrupted, reconstruction of the orbital floor is necessary to prevent enophthalmos and ptosis of the globe (Fig. 18–36A). The need for placement of an orbital floor implant to support the periorbital tissues was necessary in two of three cases of orbital floor exploration by Pozatek and colleagues[99] and Wiesenbaugh.[44] Ellis and colleagues[26] found it necessary to place implants in one of three cases when the floor of the orbit was explored.

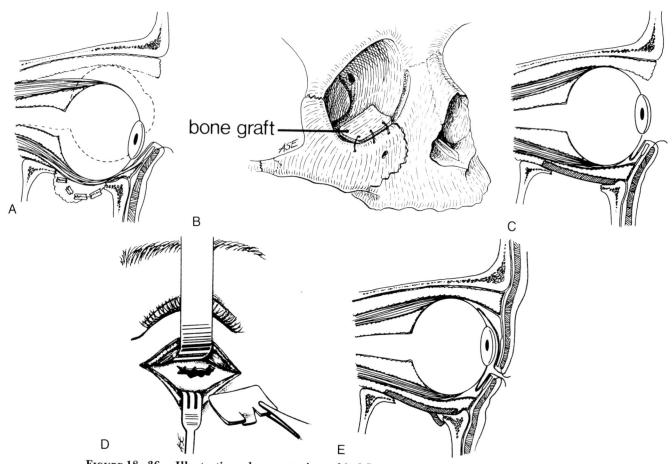

FIGURE 18–36. **Illustrations demonstrating orbital floor reconstruction.** *A,* Fractured orbital floor. Note inferior displacement of globe. Enophthalmos and displacement at the globe occur more often when the defect is large and posterior to the globe or when associated with medial and lateral wall fractures. The fracture shown here is small and is drawn as an example. *B,* Bone graft secured to orbital rim to reconstruct orbital floor defect. Bone screws are useful in securing implants or transplants also. The implant or transplant must cover the entire defect. *C,* Implant used to bridge orbital floor defect. Note that it is placed posterior to orbital rim, which assists in stabilizing the implant and helps prevent anterior migration. *D,* Tongue flap cut into implant to prevent anterior displacement once it is placed *(E).*

Materials in Orbital Floor Reconstruction. A host of materials have been used to reconstruct the orbital floor, including autogenous bone,[4,34,65,86,98,144,154-160] autogenous cartilage,[4,44,161,162] allogeneic bone and cartilage,[157,163-166] methyl methacrylate,[167-172] silicone polymer,[8,19,26,44,56,81,95,96,99,151,168,170,173-179] Dacron-urethane,[180] aluminum oxide ceramic,[181,182] Teflon (tetrafluoroethylene polymer),[8,146,147,152,170,173,176,183-187] gelatin film (Gelfilm),[44,86,177,188-190] Supramid,[170,191,192] polyethylene,[168,170,193] polyvinyl sponge,[39] lyophilized dura,[25,38,100,106,158,194-203] and metal sheets or mesh.[159,204-206]

Some surgeons do not believe that bone should be used because of the theoretical necessity of soft tissue coverage on both sides, which cannot usually be assured.[8] Melmed[19] also believes that adhesions develop between bone grafts and herniated muscle or fat and therefore does not use bone for reconstruction of the orbital floor. However, bone has been used extensively for many years with excellent results and is always the material of choice when the orbital defect is large.[4,34,65,86,98,144,154-159] Autogenous bone can be obtained from a number of donor sites. Most commonly, the iliac crest has been used.[34,65,98,154,155] However split ribs,[156] the calvarium, the anterior surface of the opposite maxilla,[144,157,158] and the buccal cortex of the mandible all serve as excellent donor sites. When bone is used, it should be borne in mind that some resorption will eventually take place, so adequate volume should be transplanted to offset this eventuality when one is attempting to decrease the volume of the orbit. The use of allogeneic bone and cartilage is less common but may have merit. The possibility of infection from the open sinus, which does not seem to be a problem with autogenous bone tissues, may preclude the widespread use of allogeneic tissues, although European surgeons have noted good results.[157,163-166]

Although autogenous grafts are the preferred material in principle, there is associated donor site morbidity and increased operative time involved in graft harvesting and carving. These factors led to the development and acceptance of alloplastic substitutes for use in orbital floor reconstruction. Criticism directed at the use of alloplastic materials cites complications of infection, extrusion, and implant displacement.[207-211] However, with careful technique, good results have been reported using alloplastic implants (see "Complications," further on). The most commonly used alloplastic implants are silicone polymers and Teflon sheets. The silicone polymers come in various thicknesses — the 1-mm thickness usually suffices for most small defects. A useful form of silicone polymer sheet is that which is reinforced with a Dacron mesh. This mesh helps provide resistance to tearing when wires are inserted to secure the implant. Teflon implants have had excellent results and are more stiff than silicone implants. This makes them slightly more difficult to handle and shape; however, either implant suffices. The choice of implant usually depends upon availability and the preference of the surgeon.

A major advantage of lyophilized dura, bone, cartilage, and bioresorbable products such as gelatin film, when compared with alloplastic implants, is that they are not only able to provide necessary support to the orbital tissues but also are incorporated or replaced within the body, minimizing the chance of late reactions. Gelfilm has been shown to undergo slow degradation over a 10-week period, with bone bridging occurring simultaneously in orbital floor defects created in adult rhesus monkeys.[188] Similarly, lyophilized dura has been shown to become organized with endogenous connective tissues within a few weeks following transplantation.[212,213] The use of lyophilized dura has been widespread in Europe, with less use in the United States.

Principles in Orbital Floor Implant or Transplant Placement. Since the objective of orbital floor reconstruction is to support the periorbital soft tissues and partition the antrum from the orbit, any of the aforementioned materials will suffice. The decision is usually based upon the availability of the products, the preference of the surgeon, and, most important, the size of the defect. When the defect is large, autogenous bone is the material of choice, since using an alloplast in this circumstance necessitates a very large implant, which will be difficult to stabilize along the minimal osseous margins. Alloplastic implants should be reserved for smaller defects. No matter what material is used, however, certain principles should be kept in mind.

1. *The size of the implant or transplant.* As small an implant or transplant as possible should be used. If too long an implant or transplant is used, it will contact the posterior margin of the inferior orbital fissure and tend to migrate anteriorly.[34] The implant or transplant must be of sufficient size to be supported along *all* margins by sound bone. Prior to placement of any implant or graft, one must be certain that its *posterior* edge is resting on sound bone. Perhaps the most common error in the placement of an implant or transplant is leaving the posterior edge unsupported. To ensure proper placement, dissection back toward the orbital apex is necessary to establish the posterior extent of the defect. If it is impossible to establish a sound posterior margin, the posterior edge of the material must be well supported, both laterally and medially. The implant or transplant must be stabilized so that it cannot migrate posteriorly, toward the orbital apex.

2. *The thickness of the implant or transplant.* The implant or transplant thickness is usually determined by the flexibility of the material. If the material is flexible, a thicker piece is necessary to reconstruct a large defect without allowing sagging of the periorbital soft tissues into the sinus. The use of lyophilized dura in large orbital floor defects is prohibited unless supplementary measures are used (such as antral pack) because of the lack of rigidity and the great flexibility of dura.

3. *The volume of the implant or transplant.* For management of orbital floor fractures associated with zygomatic fractures, it is probably only necessary to restore the original volume to the orbit. More bulk can be implanted if there is significant preoperative enophthalmos present. However, this may be unnecessary.

4. *Tension-free placement of the implant or transplant.* The implant or transplant must be passive when inserted into the wound. In other words, there should be no tendency for an implant to "buckle," for its edges to curl up or down, or for the implant to migrate when placed. If any such condition occurs, the pocket is too small or the implant is too large.

5. *Stabilization of the implant or transplant.* The implant or transplant either must be fashioned so that it cannot be displaced or must be secured with sutures, wires, or bone screws (Fig. 18–36B). Most commonly, orbital floor implants migrate anteriorly. This migration probably occurs because the implant has been improperly sized and placed under tension. The implant should not extend over the infraorbital rim. It can usually be placed so that its anterior end is behind the rim, with the rim acting as a physical impediment to anterior migration (Fig. 18–36C). Stabilization with wires will help prevent migration. Another proven method to stabilize orbital floor implants is by the fashioning of a "tongue" or "flap" on the implant that tucks under the anterior edge of the osseous defect in the orbital floor (Fig. 18–36D and E).[214] The implant must also be secured so that it cannot move posteriorly, toward the orbital apex. Optic nerve injury from implant migration has been reported (see "Complications," further on). The use of cyanoacrylate tissue adhesive to secure alloplastic implants or allogeneic or autogenous transplants to the orbital floor has recently been reported by Tse.[192] This may become a popular method in the future.

6. *Careful closure of the wound.* The periorbita must be carefully closed with resorbable sutures. This practice is extremely important, as it ensures the proper positioning of the orbital septum and helps to adapt the tissues over the implant or transplant.

Fixation Techniques

The recent application of rigid internal fixation techniques to zygomatic complex fractures has dated all of the older techniques of fixation. There is no better method of providing stable fixation to an unstable zygomatic fracture than to rigidly secure it internally. The obvious advantage to bone plates is that stabilization in three planes of space can be provided. Champy and colleagues,[92] using a single bone plate in the frontozygomatic region of 595 patients, noted only 13 (2.1 per cent) malpositions months to years following surgery. Similarly, Wangerin and colleagues[93] found that only 1 of 40 patients treated with a bone plate at the frontozygomatic suture had malposition on follow-up. They, as well as several other surgeons,[52,101,215-217] believe that a single bone plate in this area provides adequate three-dimensional stability of the unstable zygoma and is much superior to the use of a wire. For the details of internal fixation using bone plate osteosynthesis, the reader is referred to Chapter 33.

The following section presents the details and operative techniques for applying the common types of nonrigid or semirigid fixation to zygomatic fractures. The surgeon should use those techniques with which he or she is most familiar, since a satisfactory result will depend more on attention to specific details and objectives than on the type of fixation applied.

INTERNAL FIXATION BY WIRE OSTEOSYNTHESIS

Transosseous wire fixation of the frontozygomatic, infraorbital, zygomaticomaxillary, and zygomaticotemporal areas has been advocated at one time or another, either singly or in combination, for fixation of zygomatic complex fractures.[6,17,22,38,45,52,58,77-82,110,146,155,218-223] When internal wire stabilization of the fractured zygoma is deemed appropriate, the surgeon has a number of options available when selecting the location of wire application. Pozatek and colleagues[99] found that 20 of 45 fractures could be made stable by a single wire at the frontozygomatic suture. The others required additional fixation by infraorbital wiring or antral packs or both. The study by Karlan and Cassisi[77] offers important information relative to the efficacy of various forms of wire fixation techniques. A static force was exerted along the line of masseter muscle pull to zygomatic fractures that were created in fresh cadavers. A single wire placed across the fracture line at the frontozygomatic suture did not prevent medial and posterior rotation of the zygoma when as little as 2.25 kg of force was applied. Wiring the fracture at the frontozygomatic and infraorbital areas produced good stabilization even with large forces. If the infraorbital area was comminuted, however, the zygoma rotated downward. A wire at the zygomatic buttress of the maxilla inhibited this rotation. Combining the results of this study with clinical experience, these authors concluded that since the infraorbital rim is so frequently comminuted (60 per cent of cases), opening and applying a wire to this area produced little benefit in most cases. They believe that a more appropriate combination of fixation techniques is to place wires at the frontozygomatic and zygomaticomaxillary (buttress) areas. Others have also recommended the zygomatic buttress of the maxilla as a point of application of fixation wires[22,58,155,221-223] or, when the fracture is comminuted, bone plates.

The use of wiring at both the frontozygomatic and the infraorbital areas, advocated by many surgeons,[17,77-80] was found to be only partially effective in a follow-up of 27 patients by Larsen and Thomsen.[65] They found that nine of these patients had residual deformity, thus corroborating the findings of Karlan and Cassisi.[77] Similarly, Düker and Olivier[52] and Altonen and associates[20] noted a 30 per cent and 13 per cent incidence of flattening over the malar prominence, respectively, on follow-up when internal fixation with wires was used. Wavak and Zook,[81] using cadavers, determined that two-point stabilization is inadequate and that wiring at the orbital rims should be supplemented with an antral pack.

The limitation of using wire to stabilize a fracture is that it produces a one-dimensional force of apposition. Direct apposition of bone is necessary for a wire to provide needed support. This requirement cannot always be met at the infraorbital rim or zygomatic buttress of the maxilla owing to comminution. Rotation about a point of bony apposition is also possible with wire fixation. However, because of its availability and ease of use, it is still employed by many surgeons.

Technique for Frontozygomatic Wire Fixation.   The soft tissue incision and dissection for approaching the frontozygomatic area were described previously. Once exposure and reduction of the fracture have been accomplished, wiring across the fracture can be done.[218] One should carefully determine the obliquity of the fracture prior to drilling the holes, since the fracture is often irregular and it is easy to drill a hole into the fracture if one is not careful. The hole should be located at least 5 mm away from the fracture to prevent the wire from pulling through the bone and into the fracture line.

The holes and wires can be placed in one of two ways. The holes can be drilled from the lateral aspect of the orbital rim into the orbit after retraction and protection of the orbital tissues (Figs. 18–37A and B). Next, 24- or 25-gauge wires are placed in these holes and twisted on the lateral surface of the orbital rim. In the second technique, the holes can be drilled from the lateral aspect of the orbital rim through to the temporal side of the rim (Fig. 18–37C and D).[78] The wire is then passed so that the twist is in the temporal fossa. This latter technique is technically more difficult and offers no significant mechanical advantage. The fact that the twist is behind the orbital rim instead of on the lateral aspect is a theoretical advantage; however, it is rare for a patient to complain of a palpable wire twisted on the lateral aspect of the orbit. In either case, the wire is cut short and adapted well to the bone surfaces, followed by soft tissue closure in layers.

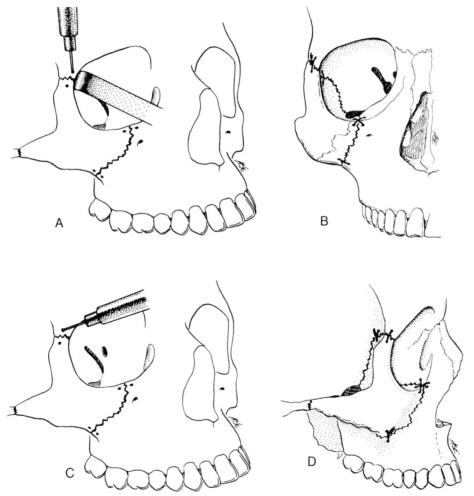

FIGURE 18–37. Wire fixation of unstable zygomatic fracture. *A,* Holes at frontozygomatic area drilled into orbit. *B,* Wires inserted. The twist of the frontozygomatic wire is on the lateral aspect of the orbital rim. Note a figure-of-eight wire at the infraorbital rim. A simple horizontal mattress wire is more commonly placed in this location; however, either suffices. The wire at the zygomatic buttress of the maxilla offers the great mechanical advantage of stabilizing the fractured zygoma; however, comminution in this area usually necessitates placement of a bone plate instead of a wire. *C,* Holes at frontozygomatic area drilled into the temporal fossa. *D,* Wires twisted in the temporal fossa. This latter wire placement is more difficult and offers no mechanical advantage.

Technique for Infraorbital Wire Fixation.   Because the bone at the infraorbital rim is thin and frequently comminuted, one must place the drill holes in a very careful manner. If one pulls the wire through the bone and into the fracture, it may be extremely difficult for another hole to be made. Therefore, one must use lighter gauge wire (26 to 28 gauge), place the holes at least 5 mm away from the fracture, and be extremely careful when tightening. When drilling the holes, the direction should be from approximately 5 mm below the rim on the anterior surface, obliquely into the orbit, ending approximately 5 mm behind the orbital rim. The drill will thus pass through the anterior surface of the maxilla, the maxillary sinus, and the floor of the orbit. A retractor must protect the orbital contents at all times when one is working in this area. A direct (horizontal mattress) wire or figure-of-eight wire (or both) can be used for wiring the infraorbital area (Fig. 18–37).

The infraorbital rim is frequently comminuted with zygomatic fractures, leaving several small pieces of bone, some of which may not be found. Several surgeons have pieced these fragments together with fine wire to establish continuity. This procedure is a very difficult undertaking and offers no stability to the fractured zygoma. Therefore, when comminution is noted, one should consider spanning the defect with a thin bone plate or using a bone graft or both. One should take care not to tighten a wire in this area if bone is missing, as this will move the zygoma medially, into an abnormal position.

FIXATION BY INTERNAL PINS

The use of a Kirschner wire (K-wire) or a Steinmann pin for stabilizing facial fractures was first introduced by Brown and McDowell in 1942.[224] They used it for mandibular fractures. In 1950, Fryer first reported its use in stabilizing the fractured zygoma.[225] In 1952, Brown, Fryer, and McDowell[226] reported the use of K-wires for stabilizing midfacial fractures, and a subsequent 20-year review[227] showed this method to be reliable, safe, and stable. Vero,[228] Larsen and Thomsen,[22] Silverton and colleagues,[229] and Larrabee and associates[230] concurred with this statement and used the transfacial approach for stabilizing zygomatic fractures, in which the pin is inserted through the stable zygoma and nasal cavity and into the fractured zygoma.

In 1983, Brown and Barnard described an alternative technique of K-wire fixation whereby the pin is inserted from the lateral aspect of the nose on the side opposite the fracture.[134] Matsunaga and colleagues,[9,231] Cleland and Morrison,[232] and Pospisil and Miotti[14] use another variation in which the K-wire is first inserted through the fractured zygoma and downward through the nasal cavity and into the maxilla at various locations.

The advantages claimed by proponents for the use of internal K-wire fixation include the following: (1) A minimal amount of specialized equipment is necessary; (2) most operating rooms have the necessary equipment; (3) the technique is very fast and easy; (4) there is minimal scar; (5) the fixation is sufficiently rigid in three planes of space; (6) one pin can be used to stabilize bilateral zygomatic fractures when the transfacial approach is used; and (7) complications such as infections are rare.

Potential disadvantages include the following: (1) The zygoma must be properly reduced prior to insertion, since, once placed, there is no "adjustability"; (2) a second procedure is necessary to remove the pin; (3) the orbital contents may be impaled on a nasoendotracheal tube; and (4) these techniques are ineffective if there is comminution of the body of the zygoma.

In any technique for inserting K-wires to stabilize fractured zygomas, there are certain principles that must be adhered to. First, oral intubation is preferable to nasal intubation to minimize the risk of impaling the tube during K-wire insertion. Second, proper reduction of the zygoma must be achieved *prior* to K-wire placement. Unfortunately, this is not always possible when the fractures are unstable. In the transfacial or transnasal approaches, one should insert the K-wire to the point of engaging the fractured bone, and then the assistant must reduce the fracture prior to and during the time when the wire engages the zygomatic body. Similarly, in those techniques that first engage the fractured zygoma, the fracture should be reduced prior to the pin's engaging stable osseous tissue. Following K-wire insertion and before cutting the pin, one must carefully determine if the zygoma is positioned as desired. If not, the wire can be backed out and advanced again after a more suitable reduction. Occasionally, distraction at the frontozygomatic or infraorbital area or both occurs. If this cannot be controlled by digital force, the application of a wire or plate at the fronto-zygomatic area may be necessary. One can use either threaded (a Steinmann pin) or unthreaded pins (K-wire) for this method of fixation, depending upon personal preference.

Technique for Transfacial K-wire.   The most inferior part of the body of the zygoma on the nonfractured side is palpated. A wire of sufficient rigidity (at least .062 inch) is drilled through the skin 5 mm above the edge of the inferior border of the zygomatic body on the nonfractured side. A skin incision is unnecessary. With an assistant steadying the head, the K-wire is drilled directly through the intact zygoma in a horizontal direction, aiming for the same point on the opposite (fractured) zygoma. The K-wire will pass through the intact zygoma, the lateral nasal wall, the nasal septum, the lateral nasal wall on the other side, and then into the fractured (but completely reduced) zygomatic body (Fig. 18–38A). If a hand drill is used, one can readily feel the pin pass through these structures. When the assistant feels the pin exiting the fractured zygomatic body, advancement of the pin should stop. In this manner, there will be no external scar on the fractured side. The pin either can be left protruding slightly from its point of entrance or can be cut off just below the surface of the skin. Retrieval after 4 weeks is simply performed with a wire twister while the patient is under local anesthetic.

Prior to engaging the fractured zygoma, the K-wire may simply push the inferior aspect of the zygomatic body laterally. If the fractures through the infraorbital and lateral orbital rims have been stabilized with transosseous wire fixation, it is unnecessary actually to engage the fractured zygomatic body. In this case, the K-wire will serve to support the zygomatic buttress of the maxilla in a lateral position, and adjustment of the amount of zygomatic prominence can be achieved by advancing the K-wire.

When bilateral zygomatic fractures are stabilized in this manner, the procedure is performed similarly; however, one must ensure complete reduction of both zygomas prior to beginning K-wire insertion.

Technique for Inserting Transnasal K-wire.   The K-wire is inserted and secured in either a hand drill or a power drill through the skin of the side of the nose opposite the fracture. The point of entry should be approximately midway between the ala of the nose and the medial canthus and should be started as far posteriorly as possible and sufficiently inferior to the eye to ensure that the chuck of the drill does not traumatize the globe in the final stages of drilling. The K-wire should be directed toward the inner aspect of the fractured zygomatic body, aiming inferiorly and posteriorly (Fig. 18–38B and C). The K-wire will sequentially pass through the frontal process of the maxilla on the intact side (lateral nasal wall), the nasal septum, and the lateral nasal wall on the fracture side and finally will contact the inner aspect of the fractured zygoma. At this point, one must carefully evaluate the position of the fractured zygoma. The K-wire can be adjusted, if necessary, to provide optimal malar position.

As with any internal K-wire fixation method, one must be sure that the zygoma has not been displaced too far laterally, separating the frontozygomatic and infraorbital margins. If this separation occurs, one may try to hold these in position while the tip of the K-wire actually engages the fractured zygoma or one may place transosseous wires in the frontozygomatic or infraorbital area or both. The K-wire is cut just above the skin surface and can be removed easily at a later time, with the patient under local anesthetic (Fig. 18–38D and E).

Although a possible hazard in placement is damage to the nasolacrimal duct, this complication has not been reported. The probable reason why this is not a usual

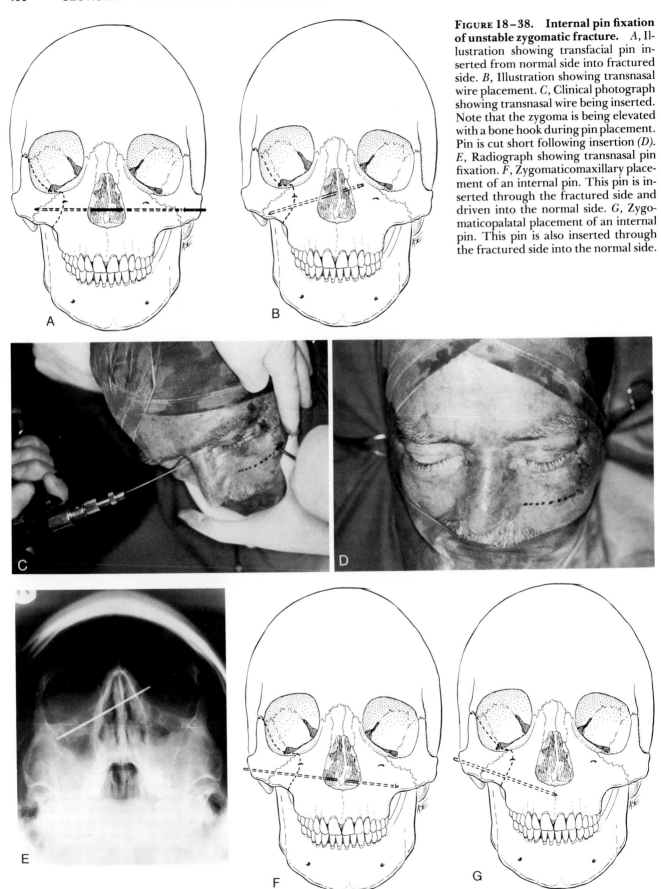

FIGURE 18–38. **Internal pin fixation of unstable zygomatic fracture.** *A,* Illustration showing transfacial pin inserted from normal side into fractured side. *B,* Illustration showing transnasal wire placement. *C,* Clinical photograph showing transnasal wire being inserted. Note that the zygoma is being elevated with a bone hook during pin placement. Pin is cut short following insertion (*D*). *E,* Radiograph showing transnasal pin fixation. *F,* Zygomaticomaxillary placement of an internal pin. This pin is inserted through the fractured side and driven into the normal side. *G,* Zygomaticopalatal placement of an internal pin. This pin is also inserted through the fractured side into the normal side.

complication is that the K-wire is placed anterior to the nasolacrimal duct when it passes through the frontal process of the maxilla.

Alternative Techniques. The oblique K-wire technique of Pospisil and Miotti[14] (zygomaticomaxillary) is a simple and versatile technique that may seem easier to the novice than the other techniques just described. In this technique, the K-wire is inserted first through the fractured zygoma (after proper reduction) and is directed inferiorly and anteriorly toward the opposite zygomatic buttress of the maxilla. The K-wire sequentially passes through the fractured zygomatic body, the lateral nasal wall on the fractured side, the nasal septum, the lateral nasal wall on the intact side, and the anterior wall of the maxilla near the zygomatic buttress (Fig. 18-38F). The wire should be stopped before it penetrates the oral mucosa on the opposite side. The wire is then cut off and removed at a later time.

This method can also be used for bilateral fractures, but one must insert two wires and be sure that the K-wires insert into the zygomatic buttress area of the maxilla inferior to the lines of fracture.

The technique described by Matsunaga and colleagues[9,231] (zygomaticopalatal) is similar to that just described, with the exception that the K-wire is driven more anteriorly and inferiorly, aiming for the palate at a point 2 cm posterior to the anterior nasal spine (Fig. 18-38G).

These methods are extremely versatile and pose less risk to orbital contents than the transfacial approach. With either method, one must be careful about the location of the teeth within the maxilla, or devitalization can occur.

EXTERNAL FIXATION

External fixation of zygomatic fractures either by wires suspended from plaster or metal head frames[133,144,146,233-235] or by pins connected to one another with universal joints or cold-curing plastic[2,26,36,236-238] has been used for years. Kazanjian[146] used an infraorbital approach and placed a wire through the infraorbital rim. With the use of rubber band traction between the wire and an outrigger on a head frame, the fracture was stabilized. Since then, others have suspended other points along the fractured zygoma to outriggers of head frames. The most common variety of external fixation in use today is one in which a pin placed in the supraorbital rim is connected with a pin in the body of the zygoma.

The advantages of this technique include the following: (1) There is three-dimensional stabilization of the zygoma; (2) the method has adjustability; (3) the technique is independent of the other bones of the midface, which may be unstable; and (4) there is minimal scarring. Disadvantages include the following: (1) There are difficulties as well as an unaesthetic appearance associated with wearing an external apparatus for several weeks; (2) it is necessary to have specific hardware available; and (3) the technique is not useful when the zygomatic body is comminuted.

In a study of 54 patients who had zygomatic fractures stabilized with external pins, Findlay and colleagues[239] reported a good position of the zygoma on follow-up in all but approximately 10 per cent of their patients. They noted, however, that 35 per cent of their patients also required frontozygomatic wire osteosynthesis to achieve satisfactory fixation. Scars from the pin were noted in 13 per cent of their patients, one requiring revision. When Findlay and colleagues compared these patients with those who underwent sinus packing for fixation, they found that external pins were a far superior form of fixation in all ways.

Technique for External Pin Fixation. Following reduction of the fracture, two holes are placed, one in the supraorbital rim and one in the body of the fractured zygoma. The supraorbital rim is first approached. The point of entry of the hole should be at the junction of the lateral and middle one third of the supraorbital rim of the frontal bone and approximately 5 mm superior to the orbital rim. It is imperative that 5 mm of bone be left inferior to the pin, or the hole may weaken this area, with resultant fracture of the supraorbital rim. A small stab incision is made at the appropriate site within the eyebrow. A hand drill is used with a proper-sized bit to drill the hole. The direction of the drill is 45 degrees to the Frankfort horizontal plane and approximately 30 to 45 degrees to the sagittal plane, aiming inferiorly, posteriorly, and medially toward the posteromedial aspect of the orbital floor. This orientation will be approximately perpendicular to the surface of the bone of the supraorbital rim. The hand drill is slowly advanced while an assistant's finger is placed deeply within the superior aspect of the orbit, between the globe and the roof of the orbit and beneath the area of drilling (lacrimal fossa). The assistant will palpate the drill when it penetrates the roof of the orbit, and the drilling should cease.

The self-threading pin is then inserted by using a hand wrench, until the assistant feels the point of the pin pierce the roof of the orbit or until resistance is felt upon finishing the threaded portion of the pin. The pin should now be firmly seated in the bone to the point where the patient's head can easily be lifted off the table, using the pin as a handle.

Surgeons who have never placed a supraorbital pin may be reluctant to do so because of the potential anatomic hazards of this location. However, one should not fear placing the supraorbital pin, for upon examining the anatomy of the orbit relative to the skull, one will find that the orbit enlarges greatly just inside the rim. The roof of the orbit in the lateral third is thus at a much higher location than the supraorbital rim, with dense cortical bone intervening. Occasionally, the frontal sinus will extend this far laterally and be entered. Entering of the sinus by the pin is not associated with problems.

A second pin is then placed within the body of the zygoma. A small stab incision is made over the greatest point of convexity of the reduced zygoma, and the hole is drilled perpendicular to the osseous surface. This practice will usually result in the pin's extending from the skin surface in an anterior and lateral direction.

The operator should check the fracture for proper reduction, paying particular attention to fractures through the lateral and infraorbital rims, and the two pins should be connected with another pin and two universal joints (Fig. 18–39A and B). It is usually necessary in unstable fractures to elevate the zygoma at the same time that the fixation device is tightened. An elevator can provide this support, as can the

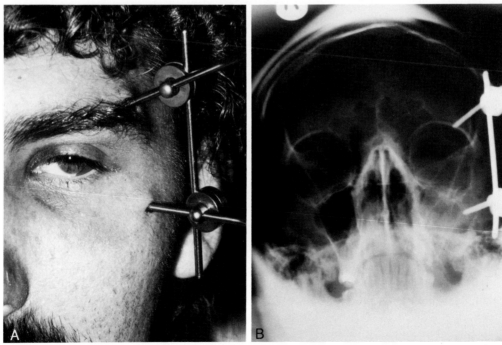

FIGURE 18–39.   Clinical photograph (A) and radiograph (B) of external pin fixation of unstable zygomatic fracture.

zygomatic pin. Once the fixation device is tightened, the position of the zygoma should be verified and, if necessary, adjusted. One can also adjust the position of the zygoma later, if needed, once the edema has resolved. The pins can be simply removed without anesthetic in 3 to 4 weeks after surgery.

There are a number of threaded pins that can be used for this type of fixation. Moule, Toller, and Morris pins, among others, serve this purpose well. One should be sure to use the appropriate-size drill bit for the type of pin used. The shortest pins available should be used to avoid excessive protrusion beyond the face. The Morris pin system allows removal of the universal joints after application of cold-cured acrylic. This feature prevents the possibility of loosening of the fixation device.

One must give specific instructions to patients who receive external pin fixation, especially in the upper, lateral part of the face. There have been unfortunate accidents in which the pins of the supraorbital rim have been sheared off when they have been caught on a stationary object by a quick turn of the head. There have also been reports of others being injured, especially children, by the forgetfulness of those people wearing external fixation appliances.

INTRASINUS SUPPORT FOR ZYGOMATIC FRACTURES

Rowe[34] lists three instances in which one may consider using intrasinus materials for fractures of the zygoma: (1) when the zygomatic complex is unstable following reduction; (2) when there is gross comminution of the zygomatic complex; and (3) when there is comminution of the orbital floor *without* bone loss. Historically, these indications were virtually absolute. Today, however, with advances in internal fixation and primary bone grafting techniques, the use of intrasinus materials for supporting either the orbital floor or unstable zygomatic fractures is much reduced.

For intrasinus materials even to have a chance of being effective in supporting zygomatic fractures, there must be total stability of the remainder of the maxillary sinus and processes of the zygoma. Therefore, with concomitant fractures of the maxilla, these first have to be stabilized and suspended prior to placing supporting material within the maxillary sinus; otherwise, the maxilla will simply be displaced inferiorly. Similarly, if the frontozygomatic and infraorbital fractures of a zygomatic complex fracture have not been stabilized, packing the maxillary sinus may cause displacement in these areas. This is why wiring of the infraorbital and lateral orbital rims has usually been advocated by those surgeons who routinely use antral packs for supplemental fixation.[81] If the orbital floor is comminuted, one must be cognizant that the packing material should not exert undue pressure on this area. Considering these limitations, one can see that the indications for sinus packs become very limited. However, one indication for sinus packing that is as absolute today as it has ever been is the grossly comminuted fracture of the zygomatic body. Other forms of fixation usually require an intact zygomatic body or at least large pieces of bone to be effective. Packing the sinus can support and shape even small fragments of bone into some semblance of normal contour.

There has been great debate over the effectiveness of placing materials within the maxillary sinus to support a fractured zygomatic complex. Several studies indicate that this is an unsatisfactory method of stabilizing zygomatic fractures, especially when comparison is made with alternate forms of fixation.[20,77,239,240] Other surgeons feel that antral packing alone,[19] or in combination with wiring of the orbital margins,[15,79,81] is a completely satisfactory method for stabilizing zygomatic fractures. Because of the difficulty in determining the amount of pack necessary to produce acceptable reduction, overpacking of the sinus has been advocated.[81]

A number of materials have been placed within the maxillary sinus for internal fixation of zygomatic fractures. Balloons, Penrose drain material, plastic tubing,[2] Penrose drain material stuffed with gauze,[81,111] and, perhaps most commonly, strip gauze have all been used for this purpose. Gauze has probably been used most extensively owing to its ready availability. Different types of solutions have been used to impregnate the gauze prior to placement. These include iodoform, antibiotic ointments, and Whitehead's varnish. The use of these solutions is predicated on the belief that they will help prevent a malodorous infection from developing within the sinus while the pack is in place. Further, the solutions create less compressibility and impart a more rigid consistency to the strip of gauze, making packing a more effective fixation technique. One should avoid the excessive use of these solutions. This is especially true of the antibiotic *ointments,* which have a petroleum jelly base. Excess ointment should be "squeezed out" of the strip gauze to prevent residual petroleum jelly base from being extruded at the time of pack removal. This material has the potential of causing a granulomatous reaction within the tissues.

The use of an antral balloon instead of a packing material has been advocated for both reduction and fixation of midfacial fractures.[85,93,241-248] The balloons have been inserted either transantrally or transnasally, and reported results have been mixed. Wangerin and colleagues,[93] using a Foley balloon catheter, found this technique to be ineffective in obtaining satisfactory reduction of the fracture and found the fracture to be unstable once reduced. Further, infraorbital nerve dysfunction and sinus health were found to be worse when this technique was used, in comparison with other techniques in which nothing was placed within the sinus. Fain and colleagues[85] and Laufer and colleagues[248] used a sinus balloon in addition to a wire or plate at the frontozygomatic suture and noted good results. Some surgeons reject the use of balloons because they are unable to exert pressure selectively against the fractured bone, instead exerting pressure in all directions.[25,83,249]

Several complications have been associated with the use of antral packing or balloons. McCoy and colleagues[4] reported a case in which packing of the maxillary sinus caused fragments of bone to be forced against the optic nerve, producing blindness. They condemned this method as dangerous, archaic, and ineffective. Finlay and colleagues[250] found that patients treated with gauze packing of the sinus soaked in Whitehead's varnish showed significantly more infraorbital nerve dysesthesias (52 per cent of patients) and antral infections (30 per cent of patients) than did patients treated with external pin fixation. Oroantral fistulae were also recorded in 13 per cent of these patients. Similarly, Altonen and colleagues[20] found a higher incidence of infraorbital nerve dysesthesias (57 per cent) in their patients who underwent antral packing as opposed to other methods of fixation.

Technique of Sinus Packing (Fig. 18–40).   If the pack is used for lateral support of the zygomatic buttress of the maxilla, one should pack from a lateral to medial direction, along the floor of the sinus, in a methodical manner that will facilitate pack removal. It is unnecessary to fill the sinus completely with packing material, and the orbital floor should not be packed against unless there is concomitant orbital floor injury with depression of the orbital contents. Once packing is complete, the position and shape of the malar prominence must be evaluated, and if it is depressed, more material may need to be inserted. One must also verify that the orbital rim fractures have not been distracted. If this occurs, open reduction with internal fixation at the orbital rims may be necessary.

If comminution of the zygomatic body is present, the pack must be larger, filling the sinus. If there is concomitant comminution of the floor of the orbit, one must be careful to make sure there has been no gross increase in intraorbital pressure by evaluating the fundus for spontaneous venous pulsations following pack placement.[55] If these are absent, the pack should be removed immediately and the fundus again checked for spontaneous venous pulsations. Once their presence is verified, the procedure can be repeated.

There are a number of possibilities for securing the end of the packing material. The pack can be left within the sinus, and oral closure follows, with retrieval accomplished through reopening through the same incision. The end of the pack can also be brought out through the end of the original incision farthest away from the osseous void of the sinus wall and can be retrieved later by simply pulling the end. A more sound method is to bring the end out through a stab incision slightly away from the

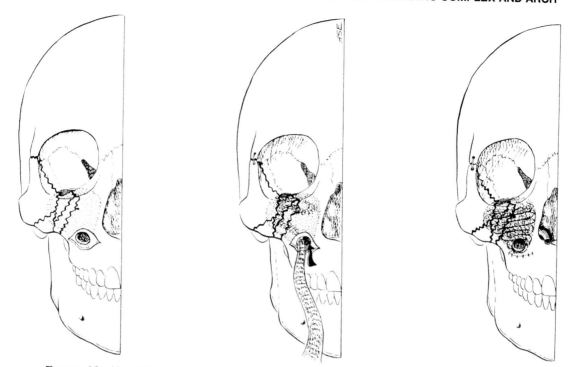

FIGURE 18–40. Illustration of technique for packing maxillary sinus to stabilize comminuted zygomatic fracture. Caldwell-Luc incision and approach to sinus is followed by inserting a pack, which is brought out through a nasal antrostomy.

original incision. It is unnecessary to suture the opening in the mucosa after pack removal, as it will heal by secondary intention. Another popular technique is for the end of the pack to be brought out through a nasal antrostomy made at the time of surgery (Fig. 18–40). The antrostomy should be placed within the inferior meatus along the nasal floor. A curved rasp or hemostat can be used to create the opening with ease. Smoothing of the bony margins around the antrostomy is necessary so that pack removal can be facilitated.

When used for comminuted fractures, the packing material should be retained for approximately 14 days. The pack can then be removed in increments, a portion every other day, or the entire pack can be removed all at once. Local anesthesia is not usually necessary for this procedure if the pack is removed via the nose; however, it may be needed for intraoral removal.

ZYGOMATIC ARCH FRACTURES

Fractures of the zygomatic arch most frequently are the result of fractures of the entire zygomatic complex. However, isolated fractures of the arch without other injuries do occur when a force is applied directly from the lateral aspect of the head. The incidence of these varies, but usually isolated zygomatic arch fractures constitute fewer than 10 per cent of zygomatic injuries.[8,13,20,24,26,28,29,36] However, others have noted higher incidences, possibly related to the nature of the population.[12,37,99] Conceivably, many isolated zygomatic arch fractures either may be unnoticed by the patient or are deemed of insufficient significance to seek treatment.

Isolated zygomatic arch fractures will characteristically result in a V-shaped indentation of the lateral aspect of the face, with the apex deep toward the sigmoid notch (Fig. 18–41B). There may be only one definite line of fracture, with bending or greenstick fractures in two other areas to produce a W-type configuration to the arch and a V-shaped cosmetic deformity (Fig. 18–41C). Occasionally, three definite lines

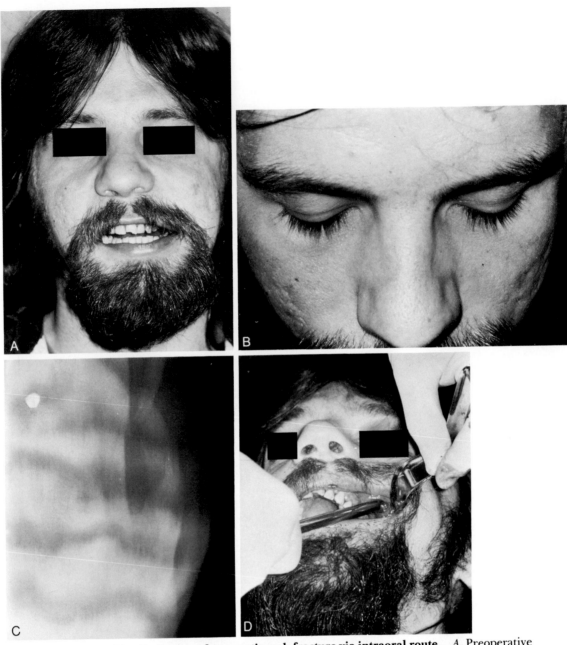

FIGURE 18–41.   Reduction of zygomatic arch fracture via intraoral route.   *A*, Preoperative photographs of patient showing limited mandibular opening and a flattening over left zygomatic arch (*B*). *C*, Preoperative intraoral tangential radiograph showing medial displacement of zygomatic arch fragments. *D*, Urethral sound inserted via a small incision in the maxillary vestibule. The instrument is placed medial to the zygomatic arch, and elevation in the area of the displaced fracture is performed while the other hand palpates along the arch (*E*). *F*, Postoperative radiograph showing reduction. *G*, Immediately postoperatively, patient has regained mobility of the mandible. *H*, Metal and gauze eye patches, which can be used to protect the reduced arch for several days (*I*).

of fracture, producing two free segments, will occur. In this case, the normal convexity of the temporal area will be gone. Flattening of the side of the face was noted in 57 per cent of isolated zygomatic arch fractures in a study by Ellis and colleagues.[26]

Trismus may accompany zygomatic arch fractures owing to impingement of the fractured segment on the temporalis muscle (Fig. 18–41*A*). Trismus was noted in 45 per cent of 166 isolated zygomatic arch fractures by Ellis and colleagues[26] and in 67

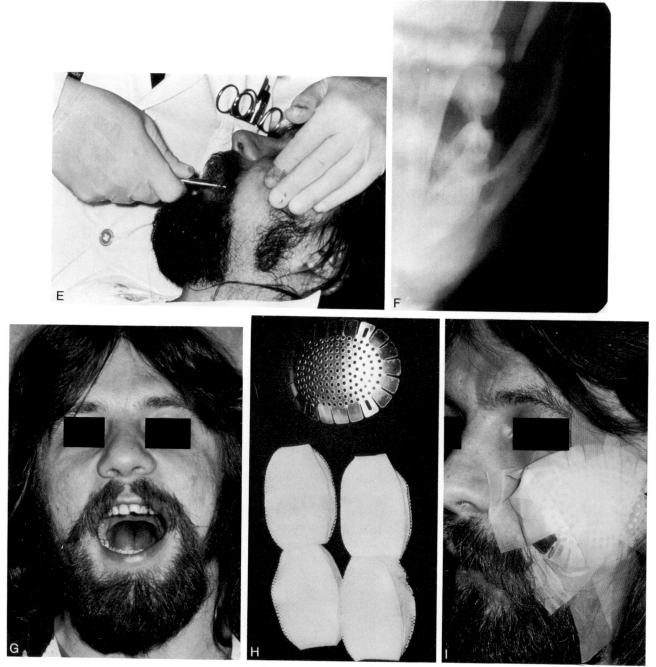

FIGURE 18–41. *Continued*

per cent of cases in Knight and North's series.[36] The patient may have difficulty shifting the mandible toward the injured side. An occasional yet interesting finding has been that of some visual disturbance, such as diplopia occurring early after injury[8,26] and subconjunctival ecchymosis.[26,83]

The necessity for treatment of these injuries is based upon the clinical detection of cosmetic or functional disturbances. In the study by Ellis and colleagues,[26] 20 per cent of zygomatic arch fractures were not treated. However, other studies show a variable ratio of treated versus nontreated zygomatic arch fractures.[20]

Reduction of these fractures can be simply accomplished by any of the techniques already described for zygomatic complex fractures. The use of a percutaneous bone hook, the Gillies temporal approach, and an intraoral approach are all acceptable techniques. Another technique that has been described is the insertion of a Foley balloon catheter under the temporal fascia, medial to the arch.[251] Once in place, the balloon is filled with radiopaque contrast dye until the zygomatic arch has acceptable form. The catheter is stabilized in position by suturing it to the scalp and is removed in 2 to 3 weeks.

The need to stabilize zygomatic arch fractures will vary with the location of the injury, the number of fractures, and the displacement of the segments. Ellis and colleagues[26] found that 10 of 126 (7.3 per cent) isolated zygomatic arch fractures treated in their study required fixation. Other surgeons have reported that almost every zygomatic arch fracture is stable once elevated.[26,36,37,99]

Stabilization of depressed zygomatic arch fractures has been achieved in a number of ingenious ways. Most commonly, the use of percutaneous circumferential wires or heavy suture passed around the arch with an aneurysm needle or Mayo trocar and tied to an external object has served this purpose well (Fig. 18–42). Plastic oral airways,[252] metal eye shields,[253] short pieces of endotracheal tubing,[254] and orthopedic finger splints[255,256] have all been used as the external devices. The passing of an awl and tightening of wires in this region of the face might be expected to damage branches of the facial nerve; however, this complication has not been reported. Some surgeons have placed materials such as gauze and balloons between the zygomatic arch and the lateral aspect of the mandible through an intraoral approach[78]; however, this approach is usually unnecessary.

Occasionally, the zygomatic arch will require open reduction and fixation. Those fractures that are in several segments or that are grossly displaced are candidates for this form of treatment. The zygomatic arch can be safely approached from either a hemicoronal or an extended preauricular incision. The temporal fascia is the guide to the depth of the initial scalp incision. Unlike with the Gillies approach, however, one does not incise through the fascia but instead dissects superficially to it. Once the dissection is just superior to the arch, one must then incise through the superficial layer of the temporal fascia, entering the small space delineated by a splitting of this fascia 1 to 2 cm above the arch. In this manner, the temporal branches of the facial nerve will be avoided. Once the arch has been identified by subperiosteal dissection, it can be manually repositioned and stabilized. Although wires have been used for this purpose, long, thin bone plates allow better maintenance of the normal arch morphology and should be used when possible. When they are used, one should be cognizant of the normal flat configuration of the zygomatic arch. Bone plate fixation that provides too much curvature to the arch will result in a noticeable cosmetic defor-

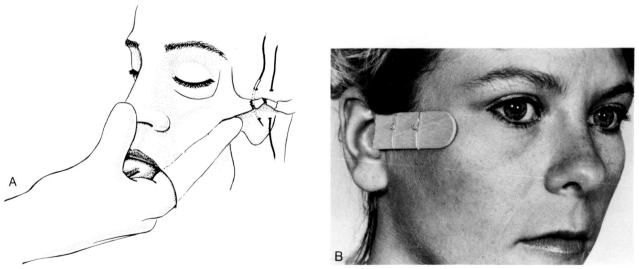

FIGURE 18–42.   One method of stabilizing a reduced zygomatic arch fracture.   *A*, A large, curved needle or awl is used to pass heavy suture or fine wires around the zygomatic arch. *B*, The wires are then secured to a stable object, such as a tongue blade or aluminum finger splints, until healing has occurred.

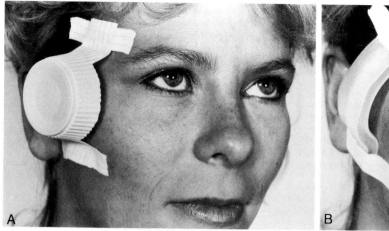
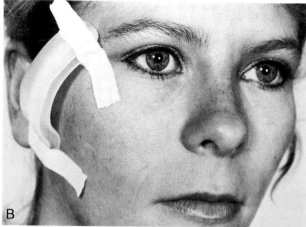
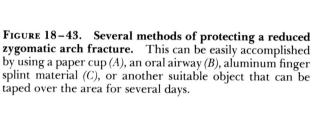
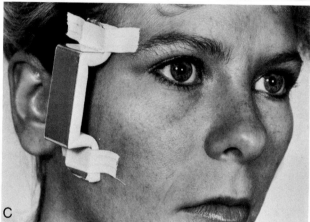

FIGURE 18–43. **Several methods of protecting a reduced zygomatic arch fracture.** This can be easily accomplished by using a paper cup (A), an oral airway (B), aluminum finger splint material (C), or another suitable object that can be taped over the area for several days.

mity. Although the zygomatic arch is called an "arch," in reality it is not all that curved.

After the reduction of zygomatic arch fractures, one must protect the side of the head from injury. The force of the weight of the head resting on a pillow is sufficient to displace even a properly reduced fracture. There are many materials available that can be taped to the side of the head for protecting the zygomatic arch following reduction. Commonly used and readily available materials that can be formed and applied for this purpose are paper cups, metal eye patches, aluminum finger splints bent in a staple configuration,[257] and a host of others (Fig. 18–43). Ideally, they should be left in place for 2 to 3 weeks.

COMPLICATIONS

Nerve Disorders

Occasionally, a patient who has had treatment of a zygomatic fracture will complain that the upper teeth, especially the anteriors, feel numb or "different," and even painful to heat, cold, or light touch. In most cases, a return of normal sensation to the upper teeth occurs in 4 to 12 weeks.[49] However, in some cases, the altered sensation persists, and anesthesia of the superior alveolar nerves by local infiltration may not alleviate these complaints. When confronted with this scenario, the clinician should suspect a disruption of the infraorbital nerve within its canal where the middle and anterior superior alveolar nerves take origin, with possible neuroma formation. Surgical exploration may be necessary when the altered sensation is bothersome to the patient.

Implant Extrusion, Displacement, and Infection

Possible risks that always exist when an alloplastic material is used include infection, displacement, and extrusion of the implant. Infection usually occurs early and may result in the need for implant removal. These complications are uncommon but do occur on occasion. Aaronowitz and colleagues[152] reported a 3.9 per cent *early* complication rate (within 1 month of surgery) when Teflon implants were used to reconstruct the orbital floor. These complications consisted of infections and the improper placement of the implant, necessitating removal in all cases. They also found a 2.8 per cent *late* complication rate, which included one patient with a cutaneous-antral fistula. Their data were subsected to statistical analysis to determine if any preoperative or intraoperative findings correlated with the complication rate. The only positive correlation was that between the concomitant use of antral packs and implants. They therefore recommended that this practice be avoided. The association between antral packs and implants has also been noted by Spira.[153]

Polley and Ringler[184] reviewed 230 Teflon implants used on the orbital floor over a 20-year period and found only one postoperative infection that necessitated implant removal. There were no other complications. In their series, the implants were not routinely sutured to the orbital floor.

Particularly distressing are the occasional occurrences of severe, acute foreign body reactions to silicone[258] and Teflon[259] orbital floor implants many years after implantation. It may be that slight trauma to the implant precipitates this reaction, as one of the patients reported was subjected to a blow to the orbit, which preceded the acute reaction. In these subjects, implant removal and at least partial removal of the inflammatory tissue allowed resolution of the process. Other series have shown complication rates ranging from 3 to 15 per cent when alloplasts other than Teflon were used.[96,147,170,172,174–177,185,260–262]

When the implants become displaced or extruded, they should be removed (Fig. 18–44). It is not usually necessary to place another at the time of surgery; however, if enophthalmos or ptosis occurs, reconstruction of the orbital floor can be undertaken secondarily.

Persistent Diplopia

Binocular diplopia present initially after zygomatic fracture is, in most cases, due to edema or hematoma of one or more extraocular muscles or their nerves and to

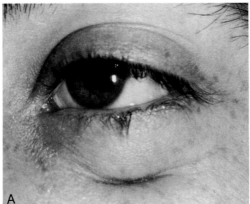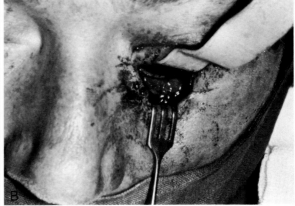

FIGURE 18–44. Photographs of a patient who had a silicone implant used to reconstruct his orbital floor 13 months previously. For the past several months, he had intermittent swelling and drainage from this sinus tract *(A)*. At surgery, the implant was found to be surrounded by chronic inflammatory tissue and was removed *(B)*. The sinus tract was excised to gain access to the orbital floor. He had no further problems following implant removal.

intraorbital edema or hematoma. In these cases, resolution of diplopia following fracture treatment (if necessary) usually occurs spontaneously within 5 to 7 days.[262,263] Occasionally, muscle entrapment is the cause of diplopia; however, this should be apparent upon the performance of a forced duction test.

Persistent diplopia occurs in a small percentage of patients after what appears to be appropriate treatment. The percentage ranges from 3 to 15 per cent in reported series.[8,13,15,29,47,52,54–57,59,60,102,263–265] The cause of persistent diplopia is not known, but the condition has been thought to result from scar contracture and adhesions either within ocular muscles or between them and other structures. Neural injuries from the trauma or operation may also produce persistent diplopia. It should be pointed out that few of these patients complain of their diplopia, and blurring of vision may be found only in upward and lateral gaze. If the condition is bothersome, the patient should be referred to an ophthalmologist for evaluation and possible treatment with exercises or surgery or both.

Enophthalmos

Enophthalmos may be present even after what appeared to be proper treatment at the time of operation. Few patients are aware of it, and it therefore seldom presents a clinical problem unless severe. The incidence of enophthalmos varies considerably from one report to the next, depending upon how much orbital retrusion is considered to represent enophthalmos. The usual figure is low, reported between 5 and 12 per cent.[27,29,60] However, Altonen and colleagues[20] noted enophthalmos in 41 per cent of their patients! The reason for this high incidence probably stems from the 26 per cent incidence of "slight" enophthalmos in their series. If one takes away the 26 per cent who had "slight" enophthalmos, the figure becomes a more understandable 15 per cent.

Enophthalmos has been thought to be caused by a loss of the volume of orbital contents, an increase in the volume of the bony orbit, a loss of ligament support, scar contracture, or a combination of these. The most popular theories of the mechanism of enophthalmos have been bony orbit enlargement and fat atrophy. A study by Manson and colleagues,[71] in which patients demonstrating post-traumatic enophthalmos were evaluated with quantitative CT, found that an increase in bony orbital volume was indeed present in these cases. Others have demonstrated similar findings.[69,266] The study by Manson and colleagues, however, did not find a loss of soft tissue volume within the orbit, which might signify fat atrophy. It is probably unusual to have great losses of orbital soft tissue volume unless infection has occurred, producing post-traumatic fibrosis and atrophy of the periorbital fat.[104,115,124,173,262,267–272] Most commonly, post-traumatic enophthalmos is thus due to an increase in bony orbital volume. Even after restoration of the orbital rims and floor at the time of surgery, defects occurring posteriorly along the medial or lateral wall or both areas are common and frequently overlooked and are probably the main reason for postoperative enophthalmos.[71,273–275]

Enophthalmos is difficult to correct secondarily; however, improvement is possible. The goal of surgery is to reduce the orbital volume by placing a space-occupying material behind the globe, thus displacing the globe anteriorly. A space-occupying material placed in front of the globe will worsen the enophthalmos, and that placed along the axis of the globe will only shift the globe to the opposite side.

Several materials have been used to decrease orbital volume: glass beads,[276–278] silicone sheets or sponges,[279–282] Teflon beads,[283] cartilage grafts,[284] and hydroxylapatite.[285] The advantage to the use of nonresorbing materials is that they maintain their bulk within the orbit; however, there is always the chance of extrusion, migration, and infection. When large osseous defects are present, the use of bone or cartilage is more appropriate, since it not only reconstructs the osseous defects but also can be "bulked" to reduce intraorbital volume further.[71,115,271,286] The implant or bone must usually be placed in several locations within the orbit to affect the anterior projection of the globe, and therefore, access to almost the entire circumference of the orbit is often necessary. Most commonly, the orbital floor, the medial wall, and the posterolateral wall of the orbit require implants or grafts, posterior to the axis of the globe.

Blindness

Reduced vision and blindness have occasionally been noted after the treatment of zygomatic fractures. Ord[287] reports that the incidence of postoperative retrobulbar hemorrhage and blindness following treatment of zygomatic fractures is 0.3 per cent. Blindness has also been reported in patients after orbital floor reconstruction.[209,288-292] These are extremely rare occurrences but have devastating consequences.

There are several causes of reduced vision following trauma or fracture repair. Direct damage to the optic nerve from displacement of a fracture segment or from a fractured optic canal is rare, but possible.[4,267,293-295] Postmortem investigations, however, have demonstrated that injury to the optic nerve resulting from optic canal fractures is rarely the result of osseous compression, laceration of the nerve, or hemorrhage into the nerve itself. More often, hemorrhage into the optic sheath or contusion of the nerve results in edema and compression.[293,296,297] The injury may lead to secondary compression of the vascular supply to the nerve where the nerve sheath is fixed to its bony surroundings. Another cause of blindness following zygomatic fracture or fracture repair is retrobulbar hemorrhage.

When blindness follows fracture repair, a major question is, *what caused the blindness, the trauma or the surgery?* The answer to this question is very important from a surgical standpoint and is obviously of interest from a medicolegal standpoint. Unfortunately, one cannot always know the answer. If the patient was blind before surgery, the answer is obvious. But most instances of blindness associated with zygomatic fractures have followed surgical intervention. One may therefore think it obvious that blindness occurring after surgical intervention, when not present before, is due to the surgery. However, there have been reports in which blindness occurred days after injury, even when no surgery has been performed.[298,299] Spontaneous retrobulbar hemorrhage has also been noted following fracture but prior to fracture repair.[300,301] Thus, if the fracture had been treated, the treatment might have been thought responsible for the blindness. Unfortunately, there is no ideal way to sort out these problems.

Retrobulbar or Intraorbital Hemorrhage.   Intraorbital and retrobulbar hemorrhage can occur from either the traumatic event or the surgery to repair the fractured zygoma. Reduced vision and blindness resulting from orbital hemorrhage have been reported in several cases of zygomatic fracture and fracture repair.[6,287,295,300,302-307] The cause of reduced vision and blindness in these cases is not clear but has been thought by many to be retinal artery occlusion. The occlusion of the retinal artery may be secondary to either direct compression of the artery or may result from sufficient stretching until it goes into spasm. Stretching of the retinal artery may be made possible by hemorrhage into or around the muscle cone, which causes protrusion of the eye. Because the muscles are fixed posteriorly to the tendinous ring, they are stretched along with the nerves and vessels of the globe. Another explanation for the reduced vision has been offered by Hayreh,[308] who postulated that increased intraocular pressure reduces the perfusion of the anterior head of the optic nerve in a progressive manner. Whatever the mechanism, the increase in intraorbital pressure from hemorrhage causes changes that can lead to blindness if not halted.

The signs and symptoms of retrobulbar hematoma include a tense proptosis; periorbital swelling, which may be in the process of increasing in size; retro-orbital pain; dilatation of the pupil; and ophthalmoplegia. Hueston and Heinze[309] state that "retrobulbar hemorrhage is not an emergency, total blindness is." If the process becomes static at this point, and vision and retinal circulation are maintained, observation is indicated.[287,309,310] Fortunately, the vast majority of retrobulbar or intraorbital hemorrhages do not progress to produce visual impairment,[311,312] and when they do, most produce only transient or partial loss of vision.[310-313] Most ophthalmologists either do not treat retrobulbar hemorrhages or treat them conservatively with the application of ice, sedatives, bed rest, and/or diuretics such as intravenous mannitol.[310,311] Observation for signs of visual impairment is warranted, though. Gradual absorption of the hemorrhage occurs, and full range of motion usually returns in several weeks; however, there have been cases reported in which blindness occurred days after surgery and the development of the hematoma.[209,287]

When the point is reached that the optic nerve and retinal artery become involved, the pupil becomes fixed and nonreactive to light. Funduscopic examination may reveal a pale, edematous fundus with blurring of the disc margins. The classic sign of arterial occlusion or spasm—the macula's appearing as a bright ("cherry") red spot—is infrequently observed in reported cases.[314] These findings associated with vision loss constitute and should be considered a medical emergency, as permanent loss of vision will occur in several minutes if the orbit is not immediately decompressed. Hueston and Heinze[309] claim that survival of the optic nerve head is at stake in this situation, and 60 minutes of ischemia appears to be the limit of survival and recovery, although Rowe claims that 15 to 20 minutes is a more likely figure.[34]

An ophthalmologist should be summoned immediately while orbital decompression is instituted. If one has placed an antral pack, this should be immediately removed. Orbital decompression can then be performed by a variety of approaches. If one has already used a transantral approach to reduce or fix the fractured zygoma, this approach can be used to decompress the orbit. The orbital floor should be carefully but quickly removed, and the periorbita should be incised, if not already disrupted. This procedure should provide an avenue for the escape of accumulated blood and create an immediate increase in orbital volume. Careful and gentle suctioning into the periorbital tissues, using thin polyethylene tubing, may also detect pockets of hemorrhage.

If one has made an incision at the infraorbital rim for fracture reduction, it should immediately be reopened. If no blood is encountered below the periorbita, the periorbita should be incised, if not already lacerated from the injury, and blood should be evacuated. Careful blunt dissection through the periorbital tissues and dissection through the muscular septum between the lateral and inferior rectus muscles allows one to drain the intramuscular cone. Aspiration with a short piece of polyethylene tubing may help find areas of sequestered blood.[34]

If there were no periorbital incisions made during fracture reduction or fixation, a 2-cm inferior lid incision should immediately be made. In contrast to the usual approach to the infraorbital rim, however, incision *through* the orbital septum is desired when surgically decompressing the orbit. Blunt scissors should be inserted within the wound along the inferior aspect of the orbital floor and should be spread to evacuate accumulated blood. Dissection into the muscular cone, as just described, may also be necessary.

If any of these measures do not meet with success, as indicated by the expulsion of fresh hemorrhage and the beginning of relief of proptosis, access to the superolateral aspect of the orbit should be provided. This access can be achieved rapidly and safely by an eyebrow approach with dissection through the periorbita.[315,316] Decompression via a lateral canthotomy, as well as small, curvilinear incisions above and below the lateral canthus, has also been advocated.[209,317]

Decompression of the globe by perforating the anterior chamber of the eye has been said to be an effective treatment of retrobulbar hemorrhage[309,318]; however, many surgeons doubt its effectiveness.[310,311] In any event, it is not recommended as an emergency measure by those who are not ophthalmologists.

Other measures that should be used in conjunction with those previously described are control of the systemic blood pressure, if high; bed rest; and possibly diuretics (intravenous mannitol, 200 ml of a 20 per cent solution; 500 mg of acetazolamide [Diamox] given intravenously) and high doses of systemic steroids (3 mg/kg of dexamethasone initially, 2 mg/kg every 6 hours). Ophthalmologic follow-up is mandatory.

Maxillary Sinusitis

Post-traumatic maxillary sinusitis is an uncommon complication, occurring in fewer than 5 per cent of cases.[45,319] The cause is probably inflammation of the sinus membrane, causing occlusion of the ostium. Post-traumatic maxillary sinusitis usually responds to antibiotic and decongestant therapy within a day or two.

Ankylosis of Zygoma to Coronoid Process

Extracapsular ankylosis of the mandible to the zygoma following zygomatic fracture is a very rare complication, reported on few occasions.[239,320-322] It has also been observed after facial infections,[323] fractures or osteotomy of the mandible,[324-327] and tumor surgery in the pterygoid fossa.[328] When noted, it is usually a fibrous connection between the coronoid process and the arch of the zygoma. However, in the case reported by Ostrofsky and Lownie,[322] bony ankylosis was found in a patient who had not sought treatment for a zygomatic fracture. Similarly, the patient reported by Findlay[239] had primarily fibrocartilaginous fusion, with histologic evidence of bone formation within the resected tissue. The amount of limitation of mandibular motion varies considerably, depending upon the type and amount of tissue connecting the mandible and the zygoma. The patient will not usually complain of pain when the point of maximal opening is reached. He or she may also have difficulty going into lateral excursions toward the side of the prior zygomatic fracture.

The cause of extracapsular ankylosis may be improper reduction of the zygoma, leaving the arch in close proximity to the coronoid process. However, the case reported by Kellner and colleagues[321] showed a well-reduced zygoma postsurgically. Their patient developed a postoperative infection that may have induced sufficient cicatrization to prevent normal mandibular motion. Another cause for extracapsular ankylosis may be untreated zygomatic fractures, as noted in the cases reported by Findlay[239] and Ostrofsky and Lownie.[322]

When limited mandibular motion develops following a fracture of the zygoma, one must consider the possibility of extracapsular ankylosis between the mandible and the zygoma. However, all conditions that can produce limited mandibular mobility, such as myositis ossificans, intracapsular temporomandibular joint derangement or ankylosis, muscular spasm or fibrosis, and tetanus, must also be considered. The differentiation is not usually extremely difficult. If there is associated joint pain, one would be more likely to consider internal derangement as a possible cause. Manipulation while the patient is under general anesthesia is an excellent diagnostic measure that will frequently help to determine the cause of hypomobility. If the hypomobility resolves once the patient is paralyzed, the origin can be considered to be muscular or possibly due to an internal derangement (closed lock) over which the condyle is being forced under anesthesia. If opening is still restricted once the patient is paralyzed, intracapsular or extracapsular ankylosis of either bony or fibrous origin may be the cause. Temporomandibular joint and facial radiographs (plain films, tomograms, and CT) will help to rule out bony ankylosis.

If the diagnosis of ankylosis between the coronoid process and zygomatic arch is made, surgery will be necessary. The decision of where to operate will depend upon cosmetic and functional considerations. If the patient's zygoma is in an acceptable position cosmetically, and if there are no ocular problems that might suggest that malar osteotomy and orbital reconstruction would be more appropriate treatment, then coronoidectomy by either an external or an intraoral approach should alleviate the mechanical obstruction. However, the patient will require vigorous physical therapy to prevent postsurgical hypomobility secondary to scar formation.

Malunion of the Zygoma

Malunion of the zygoma can be the result of improper reduction, improper fixation, or nonintervention when operation was indicated. The last-named situation happens on occasion when the patient's medical condition precludes early operative intervention, when treatment is not sought by the patient, or when the patient declines surgery until later. The signs and symptoms are the same as those in a patient with a fresh zygomatic fracture, including flattening of the malar prominence, enophthalmos, altered pupillary level, and limitation of mandibular motion, among others.

When confronted with this problem, one has two treatment alternatives—camouflaging the defect with implants or transplants or repositioning the malposed bone. The advantages and disadvantages of malar implant or transplant and osteotomy should be understood. In cases of malunion when minor deformity is present and limited to flattening of the malar eminence with little orbital involvement, subperiosteal implants or transplants can be inserted to restore normal facial form. Implants and transplants are also useful when the zygoma is so comminuted that it cannot be mobilized and repositioned in one piece. A host of implant-transplant techniques and materials are available for this purpose. There are advantages and disadvantages to the use of any material, and several materials have been used for malar augmentation. Bone has been used less frequently than alloplastics owing to the difficulty in contouring bone and the unpredictable amounts of resorption that may occur. Most surgeons have used silicone or Proplast implants in a subperiosteal manner. The implant techniques described are beyond the scope of this chapter, and the reader is referred to Chapter 29 for details. If necessary, a coronoidectomy can be performed along with implantation to improve the range of mandibular motion.

When functional deficits occur along with cosmetic deformity, zygomatic osteotomy should be considered, as it will correct both concomitantly. If zygomatic refracture or osteotomy is selected as the appropriate treatment modality, preoperative CT is warranted. The areas of fracture, the position of the globe, the orbital volume and shape, and the defects in the orbital floor and lateral aspect should be thoroughly investigated. Restoring a severely malposed zygoma to its proper position after malunion while simultaneously correcting existing orbital defects is a very difficult and challenging undertaking. The zygomatic complex must usually be refractured or, more appropriately, osteotomized to allow repositioning. Fixation is always necessary, and restoration of normal globe position may require bone grafts to the bony orbit. There are several techniques of zygomatic osteotomy that have been used in the past.[80,329-334] All can produce good results with proper attention to detail.

Various soft tissue access incisions allow visualization of the osseous anatomy for osteotomy. Some surgeons refracture using standard incisions, such as the eyebrow, inferior lid, and intraoral.[80,330-334] Another approach that greatly facilitates zygomatic osteotomy is the hemicoronal flap used in conjunction with an infraorbital incision (see "Coronal Incision," previously).[220,329] The zygoma can be totally freed of all external soft tissue attachments from this approach, facilitating osteotomy and repositioning. Although one might fear the zygoma will resorb or become infected after extensive stripping of soft tissues, this is a rare occurrence in craniofacial surgery, in which large segments of osseous tissue are completely stripped from their soft tissue attachments and replanted.[335] If the old fracture site is visible, it can be used as the line of osteotomy. However, the fracture along the orbital floor should be used

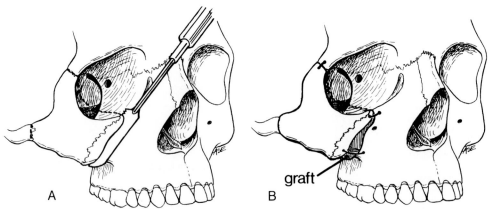

FIGURE 18–45. *A,* Illustration demonstrating the areas of osteotomy to reposition the mal-aligned zygomatic compound. In most instances, the old fracture site will be visible and may serve as the osteotomy site. *B,* Following repositioning, it may be necessary to bone graft the area of the zygomatic buttress of the maxilla to rotate the body of the zygoma outward and upward. Bone plates stabilize the repositioned zygoma much better than wires and should be used if possible.

only if it does not extend too far posteriorly, toward the orbital apex. A sharp osteotome, thin bur, or saw can be used to make the necessary bone incisions (Fig. 18–45*A*). Care is taken to protect the infraorbital neurovascular bundle within its groove along the orbital floor as well as at its exit from the infraorbital foramen on the anterior surface of the maxilla. The orbital contents must be protected as well.

The most difficult osteotomy to make is that extending from the inferior orbital fissure along the temporal surface of the maxilla to the zygomatic buttress area of the maxilla. This procedure is greatly facilitated by the use of the hemicoronal flap, which permits access to this difficult area. A sharp osteotome can be easily inserted from the temporal approach into the inferior orbital fissure and can be used to create a fracture down the infratemporal aspect of the maxilla. The osteotomy along the anterior maxillary wall can be extended inferolaterally until it meets the posterior osteotomy at the zygomatic buttress of the maxilla. Some surgeons also use an intraoral approach in the maxillary vestibule to help complete this osteotomy.[336] This is a helpful optional incision, since it may be necessary to place bone grafts into the zygomatic buttress area, especially if nonrigid forms of fixation are applied along the orbital rims. Prior to mobilization, the zygomatic osteotomies should be carefully checked to verify that all osseous incisions have been completed. If mobilization is attempted while some bony areas are still intact, aberrant fractures may occur.

Once the zygoma is mobilized, it is repositioned. If the malunion is longstanding, it may be necessary to excise bone in some areas where callus and new bone have formed, to permit proper reduction. The lateral orbital rim may need to have some bone subtracted for proper repositioning; however, this is not always the case. The zygoma is best stabilized with bone plates at the frontozygomatic and possibly infraorbital areas. If necessary, bone grafts are inserted into bony voids (Fig. 18–45*B*). The floor of the orbit is reconstructed as previously described, with care being taken to correct defects in the lateral wall of the orbit. When the zygoma is comminuted by trauma, it may be necessary to onlay graft or implant over the malar prominence to re-establish normal contour. The zygomatic arch can be reconstructed with a strip of cranial bone or rib.

REFERENCES

1. Gillies HD, Kilner TP, Stone D: Fractures of the malar-zygomatic compound, with a description of a new X-ray position. Br J Surg 14:651, 1927.

2. Dawson RLG, Fordyce GL: Complex fractures of the middle third of the face: Their early treatment. Br J Surg 41:254, 1953.

3. Middleton DS: Management of injuries of

the nose and upper jaw. Proc R Coll Med 46:476, 1953.

4. McCoy FJ, Chandler RA, Magnan CG Jr, et al: Fracture of the zygoma. Plast Reconstr Surg 29:381, 1962.

5. Schuchardt K, Schwenzer N, Rottke B, Lentrodt J: Fortschr Kiefer Gesichtschir 11:1, 1966.

6. Rowe NL, Killey HC: Fractures of the Facial Skeleton. Edinburgh, Livingstone, 1968.

7. Morgan BDG, Madan DK, Bergerot JPC: Fractures of the middle third of the face—a review of 300 cases. Br J Plast Surg 25:147, 1972.

8. MacLennan WD: Fractures of the malar (zygomatic) bone. Edinburgh R Coll Surg 22:187, 1977.

9. Matsunaga RS, Simpson W, Toffel PH: Simplified protocol for treatment of malar fractures. Based on a 1,220-case eight-year experience. Arch Otolaryngol 103:535, 1977.

10. Deutschländer-Wolff J, Riediger D, Veigel W: Ursachen, Häufigkeit und Auftreten periorbitaler Frakturen. Fortschr Kiefer Gesichtschir 22:10, 1977.

11. Meyer H, Reuter E, Schilli W: Ursachen und Verlauf der Frakturen der lateralen Orbita. Fortschr Kiefer Gesichtschir 22:23, 1977.

12. Turvey TA: Midfacial fractures: A retrospective analysis of 593 cases. J Oral Surg 35:887, 1977.

13. Afzelius L, Rosén C: Facial fractures. A review of 368 cases. Int J Oral Surg 9:25, 1980.

14. Pospisil OA, Miotti A: Oblique zygomatic maxillary Kirschner wire in the treatment of malar fractures. Injury 17:135, 1986.

15. Nysingh JG: Zygomatico-maxillary fractures with a report of 200 consecutive cases. Arch Chir Neerl 12:157, 1960.

16. Lundin K, Ridell A, Sandberg N, et al: One thousand maxillo-facial and related fractures at the ENT-Clinic in Gothenburg. A two-year prospective study. Acta Otolaryngol 75:359, 1973.

17. Schultz RC: Facial Injuries. Chicago, Year Book Medical Publishers, 1977.

18. Haidar Z: Fractures of the zygomatic complex in the south-east region of Scotland. Br J Oral Surg 15:265, 1977.

19. Melmed EP: Fractures of the zygomatic-malar complex. Afr Med J 46:569, 1972.

20. Altonen M, Kohonen A, Dickhoff K: Treatment of zygomatic fractures: Internal wiring-antral-pack-repositioning without fixation. A comparative follow-up study. J Maxillofac Surg 4:107, 1976.

21. Muller EJ, Schoeman HS: Zygomatic-maxillary fractures: A statistical analysis of 1,233 cases. J Dent Assoc S Afr 32:585, 1977.

22. Larsen OD, Thomsen M: Zygomatic fractures. II. A follow-up study of 137 patients. Scand J Plast Reconstr Surg 12:59, 1978.

23. Adekeye EO: Fracture of the zygomatic complex in Nigerian patients. J Oral Surg 38:596, 1980.

24. Foo GC: Fractures of the zygomatic-malar complex: A retrospective analysis of 76 cases. Sing Dent J 9:1, 1984.

25. Fischer-Brandies E, Dielert E: Treatment of isolated lateral midface fractures. J Maxillofac Surg 12:103, 1984.

26. Ellis E, El-Attar A, Moos KF: An analysis of 2,067 cases of zygomatico-orbital fracture. J Oral Maxillofac Surg 43:428, 1985.

27. Kristensen S, Tveterås K: Zygomatic fractures: Classification and complications. Clin Otolaryngol 11:123, 1986.

28. Lund K: Fractures of the zygoma: A follow-up study on 62 patients. J Oral Surg 29:557, 1971.

29. Balle V, Christensen PH, Greisen O, Jörgensen PS: Treatment of zygomatic fractures: A follow-up study of 105 patients. Clin Otolaryngol 7:411, 1982.

30. Martin BC, Trabue JC, Leech TR: An analysis of the etiology, treatment and complications of fractures of the malar compound and zygomatic arch. Am J Surg 92:90, 1956.

31. Hitchin AD, Shuker ST: Some observations on zygomatic fractures in the eastern region of Scotland. Br J Oral Surg 2:114, 1973.

32. Gerrie JW, Lindsay WK: Fracture of maxillary-zygomatic compound with atypical involvement of orbit. Plast Reconstr Surg 11:341, 1953.

33. Banks P: Killey's Fractures of the Middle Third of the Facial Skeleton. Bristol, England, John Wright and Sons, 1981.

34. Rowe NL: Fractures of the zygomatic complex and orbit. In Rowe NL, Williams JL (eds): Maxillofacial Injuries. Vol 1. London, Churchill-Livingstone, 1985, pp 435–537.

35. Schjelderup H: Fractures of the upper and middle thirds of the facial skeleton. Acta Chir Scand 99:447, 1950.

36. Knight JS, North JF: The classification of malar fractures: An analysis of displacement as a guide to treatment. Br J Plast Surg 13:325, 1961.

37. Yanagisawa E: Pitfalls in the management of zygomatic fractures. Laryngoscope 83:527, 1973.

38. Spiessl B, Schroll K: Gesichtsschaödel. In Nigst H (ed): Spezielle Frakturen und Luxationslehre. Vol 1. Stuttgart, Georg Thieme Verlag, 1972.

39. Henderson JW: Orbital implants of polyvinyl sponge. Proc Mayo Clin 38:553, 1963.

40. Fujii N, Yamashiro M: Classification of malar complex fractures using computed tomography. J Oral Maxillofac Surg 41:562, 1983.

41. Livingston RJ, White NS, Catone GA, Thomas RF: Treatment of orbital fractures by an infraorbital-transantral approach. J Oral Surg 33:586, 1975.

42. Rich JD, Zbylski JR, LaRossa DD, Cullington JR: A simple method for rapid assessment of malar depression. Ann Plast Surg 3:151, 1979.

43. Carlson O, Mårtensson G: Fractures of the zygomatic bone. Svensk Tandläk T 62:167, 1969.

44. Wiesenbaugh JM: Diagnostic evaluation of zygomatic complex fractures. J Oral Surg 28:204, 1970.

45. Schmoker R, Spiessl B, Holtgrave E, Schotland C: Ergebnisse der operativen Versorgung von Jochbeinfrakturen. Fortschr Kiefer Gesichtschir 19:154, 1975.

46. Reuther J, Hausamen JE, Esswein W: Neurologische Störungen nach Frakturen im Kiefer und Gesichtsbereich. Fortschr Kiefer Gesichtschir 21:290, 1976.

47. Waldhart E: Ergebnisse einer Kontrolluntersuchung von Patienten mit Jochbeinfrakturen. Fortschr Kiefer Gesichtschir 19:166, 1875.

48. Jungell P, Lindqvist C: Paresthesia of the in-

fraorbital nerve following fracture of the zygomatic complex. Int J Oral Maxillofac Surg 16:363, 1987.

49. Tajima S: Malar bone fractures: Experimental fractures on the dried skull and clinical sensory disturbances. J Maxillofac Surg 5:150, 1977.

50. Converse JM, Smith B, Wood-Smith O: Malunited fractures of the orbit. In Converse JM (ed): Reconstructive Plastic Surgery. Vol 2. Philadelphia, WB Saunders Company, 1977, pp 989–1033.

51. Mustarde JC: The role of Lockwood's suspensory ligament in preventing downward displacement of the eye. Br J Plast Surg 21:73, 1968.

52. Düker J, Olivier D: Drahtosteosynthese der Jochbeinfrakturen. Fortschr Kiefer Gesichtschir 19:156, 1975.

53. Mansfield OT: Fracture of the malar-zygomatic compound. Br J Plast Surg 1:123, 1948.

54. Barclay TL: Diplopia in association with fractures involving the zygomatic bone. Br J Plast Surg 11:147, 1958.

55. Hötte HH: Orbital Fractures. London, Heinemann Medical Books, 1970.

56. Reny A, Strickler M: Fractures de l'orbite: Indications Ophthalmologiques dans les Techniques Opératoires. Paris, Masson & Cie, 1969.

57. Neyt L: Zygomafracturen. Proefschrift ter verkrijging van het Doctoraat in der Geneeskunde aan der Rijksuniversiteit te Groningen. N.V. Boekdrukkerji Dijkstra Niemeyer, Groningen, 1972.

58. Tajima S, Sugimoto C, Tanino R, et al: Surgical treatment of malunited fractures of zygoma with diplopia and with comments on blow-out fractures. J Maxillofac Surg 2:201, 1974.

59. Hakelius L, Pontén B: Results of immediate and delayed surgical treatment of facial fractures with diplopia. J Maxillofac Surg 1:150, 1973.

60. Crumley RL, Leibsohn J: Enophthalmos and diplopia in orbital floor fractures. Pac Coast Otolaryngol Ophthalmol Soc 57:105, 1976.

61. McIndoe AH: Diagnosis and treatment of injuries of the middle third of the face. Br Dent J 71:235, 1941.

62. Moore FT, Ward TG: Complications and sequelae of untreated fractures of the facial bones and their treatment. Br J Plast Surg 1:257, 1949.

63. Rowe NL: Fracture de l'os de la pommette. Rev Stomatol Chir Maxillofac 61:534, 1960.

64. Himmelfarb R: Classification and treatment of malar fractures. Oral Surg 26:753, 1968.

65. Larsen OD, Thomsen M: Zygomatic fractures. II. A simplified classification for practical use. Scand J Plast Reconstr Surg 12:55, 1978.

66. Finkle DR, Ringler SL, Luttenton CR, et al: Comparison of the diagnostic methods in maxillofacial trauma. Plast Reconstr Surg 75:32, 1985.

67. Fujii N, Yamashiro M: Computed tomography for the diagnosis of facial fractures. J Oral Surg 39:735, 1981.

68. Marsh JL, Gado M: The longitudinal orbital CT projection: A versatile image for orbital assessment. J Plast Reconstr Surg 75:308, 1983.

69. Bite U, Jackson IT, Forbes GS, Gehring DG: Orbital volume measurements using three-dimensional CT imaging. J Plast Reconstr Surg 75:503, 1985.

70. Manson PN, Clifford CM, Su CT, et al: Mechanisms of global support and posttraumatic enophthalmos. I. The anatomy of the ligament sling and its relation to intramuscular cone orbital fat. Plast Reconstr Surg 77:193, 1986.

71. Manson PN, Grivas A, Rosenbaum A, et al: Studies on enophthalmos. II. The measurement of orbital injuries and their treatment by quantitative computed tomography. Plast Reconstr Surg 77:203, 1986.

72. Neumann PR, Zilkha A: Use of the CAT scan for diagnosis in the complicated facial fracture patient. J Plast Reconstr Surg 70:683, 1982.

73. Srinivasan B, Sundararajan CR: Fallacies in the diagnosis of zygomatic fractures. Int J Oral Surg 7:246, 1978.

74. Waters JW, Waldron CW: Roentgenology of accessory nasal sinuses describing modification of occipito-frontal position. Am J Radiol 2:633, 1915.

75. Hopkins R: Fractures of the zygomatic complex. Ann R Coll Surg Engl 49:403, 1971.

76. Duverney JG: De la fracture de l'apophyse zygomatique. Traité Maladies Os 1:182, 1751.

77. Karlan MS, Cassisi NJ: Fractures of the zygoma. A geometric, biomechanical and surgical analysis. Arch Otolaryngol 105:320, 1979.

78. Dingman RO, Natvig P: Surgery of Facial Fractures. Philadelphia, WB Saunders Company, 1964.

79. Kwapis BW: Treatment of malar bone fractures. J Oral Surg 27:538, 1969.

80. Bernstein L: Delayed management of facial fractures. Laryngoscope 80:1323, 1970.

81. Wavak P, Zook EG: Immobilization of fractures of the zygomatic bone with an antral pack. Surg Gynecol Obstet 149:587, 1979.

82. Mathog RH: Reconstruction of the orbit following trauma. Otolaryngol Clin North Am 16:585, 1983.

83. Albright CR, McFarland PH: Management of midfacial fractures. Oral Surg 34:858, 1972.

84. Elsahy NI, Vistnes M: An alternate method in the treatment of zygomatic fractures. Acta Chir Plast (Praha) 15:51, 1973.

85. Fain J, Peri G, Thevonen VD: The use of a single frontozygomatic osteosynthesis plate and a sinus balloon in the repair of the lateral middle third of the face. J Maxillofac Surg 9:188, 1981.

86. Banovetz JD, Duvall AJ: Zygomatic fractures. Otol Clin North Am 9:2, 1976.

87. Hovinga J: Some aspects of zygomaticomaxillary fractures. Arch Chir Neerl 28:197, 1976.

88. Fryer MP, Brown JB, Davis G: Internal wire-pin fixation for fracture dislocation of the zygoma. Plast Reconstr Surg 44:576, 1969.

89. Hofmann WB: Injuries of zygomatic and maxillary bones. Otolaryngol Clin North Am 303, 1969.

90. Mayer DM: Fractures of the body and arch of the zygoma. In Georgiade NG (ed): Plastic and Maxillofacial Trauma Symposium. Vol 1. St Louis, CV Mosby, 1969.

91. Hoyt CJ: The simple treatment of zygomatic

fractures: The Gillies approach after fifty years. Br J Plast Surg 32:329, 1979.

92. Champy M, Gerlach KL, Kahn JL, Pape HD: Treatment of zygomatic bone fractures. *In* Hjørting-Hansen E (ed): Oral and Maxillofacial Surgery: Proceedings from the 8th International Conference on Oral and Maxillofacial Surgery. Chicago, Quintessence Publishing Company, 1985, pp 226–228.

93. Wangerin, K, Busch HP, Conrad HG: Complication incidence of zygomatic bone fractures using different operation methods. *In* Hjørting-Hansen E (ed): Oral and Maxillofacial Surgery: Proceedings from the 8th International Conference on Oral and Maxillofacial Surgery. Chicago, Quintessence Publishing Company, 1985, pp 236–238.

94. Krüger E: Treatment of lateral midfacial fractures. *In* Krüger E, Schilli W, Worthington P (eds): Oral and Maxillofacial Surgery. Vol 2. Chicago, Quintessence Publishing Company, 1986, p 169.

95. Davies AS: Traumatic defects of the orbital floor. Br J Oral Surg 10:133, 1972.

96. Sacks AC, Friedland JA: Orbital floor fractures—should they be explored early? Plast Reconstr Surg 64:190, 1979.

97. Crewe TC: Significance of the orbital floor in zygomatic injuries. Int J Oral Surg 7:235, 1978.

98. Andersen M, Vibe P, Nielsen IM, Hall KV: Unilateral orbital floor fractures. Scand J Plast Reconstr Surg 19:193, 1985.

99. Pozatek ZW, Kaban LB, Guralnick WC: Fractures of the zygomatic complex: An evaluation of surgical management with special emphasis on the eyebrow approach. J Oral Surg 31:141, 1973.

100. Bütow KW, Eggert JH: The versatility of modern therapy in mid-facial trauma. Br J Oral Maxillofac Surg 22:448, 1984.

101. Götzfried HF: Combination of miniplate osteosynthesis and transconjunctival approach for reduction of zygomatic fractures. *In* Hjørting-Hansen E (ed): Oral and Maxillofacial Surgery: Proceedings from the 8th International Conference on Oral and Maxillofacial Surgery. Chicago, Quintessence Publishing Company, 1985, pp 229–231.

102. Barclay TL: Some aspects of treatment of traumatic diplopia. Br J Plast Surg 16:214, 1963.

103. Bartkowski SB, Krzystkowa KM: Blow-out fracture of the orbit. Diagnostic and therapeutic considerations and results in 90 patients treated. J Maxillofac Surg 10:155, 1982.

104. Hawes MJ, Dortzbach RK: Surgery on orbital floor fractures. Influence of time of repair and fracture size. Ophthalmology 90:1066, 1983.

105. Westphal D, Koblin J, Loewen U: Orbitabodenfrakturen. Fortschr Kiefer Gesichtschir 22:12, 1977.

106. Luhr HG: Midface fractures involving the orbit and blow-out fractures. *In* Krüger E, Schilli W, Worthington P (eds): Oral and Maxillofacial Traumatology. Vol 2. Chicago, Quintessence Publishing Company, 1986, pp 197–222.

107. Deutschberger O, Kirschner H: Intraorbital fractures: New concepts in diagnosis and surgical indications. Ann Ophthalmol 3:380, 1971.

108. Constable JD, Carroll JM: Emergency treatment of the exposed cornea in thermal burns. Plast Reconstr Surg 46:309, 1970.

109. Manson PN, Ruas E, Iliff N, Yaremchuk M: Single eyelid incision for exposure of the zygomatic bone and orbital reconstruction. Plast Reconstr Surg 79:120, 1987.

110. Thoma KH: Oral Surgery. St Louis, CV Mosby Company, 1958.

111. Kazanjian VH, Converse JM: Fractures of the zygoma. *In* The Surgical Treatment of Facial Injuries. 2nd ed. Baltimore, The Williams and Wilkins Company, 1959.

112. Natvig P, Dortzbach RK: Facial bone fractures. *In* Grabb WC, Smith JW (eds): Plastic Surgery. 3rd ed. Boston, Little, Brown, and Company, 1979, p 255.

113. Becker R, Austermann KH: Zur Wahl des bei operativer Versorgung von Orbita-frakturen. Fortschr Kiefer Gesichtschir 22:33, 1977.

114. Holtmann B, Wray RC, Little AG: A randomized comparison of four incisions for orbital fractures. Plast Reconstr Surg 67:731, 1981.

115. Converse JM, Cole G, Smith B: Late treatment of blow-out fracture of the floor of the orbit. Plast Reconstr Surg 28:183, 1961.

116. Pospisil OA, Fernando TD: Review of the lower blepharoplasty incision as a surgical approach to zygomatico-orbital fractures. Br J Oral Maxillofac Surg 22:261, 1984.

117. Wray RC, Holtmann B, Ribaudo JM, et al: A comparison of conjunctival and subciliary incisions for orbital fractures. Br J Plast Surg 30:142, 1977.

118. Heckler FR, Songcharoen S, Sultani FA: Subciliary incision and skin-muscle eyelid flap for orbital fractures. Ann Plast Surg 10:309, 1983.

119. Georgiade NG: The management of acute midfacial-orbital injuries. Clin Neurosurg 19:301, 1972.

120. Luhr HG; Die primäre Rekonstruktion von Orbitabodendefekten nach Trauma und Tumoroperationen. Dtsch Z Mund Kieferheilk 57:1, 1971.

121. Habal MB, Chaset RB: Infraciliary transconjunctival approach to the orbital floor for correction of traumatic lesions. Surg Gynecol Obstet 139:420, 1974.

122. Converse JM, McCarthy JG, Wood-Smith D, Coccaro PJ: Principles of Craniofacial Surgery. *In* Converse JM (ed): Reconstructive Plastic Surgery. Vol 4. Philadelphia, WB Saunders Company, 1977, p 2446.

123. Converse JM: Discussion of "a randomized comparison of four incisions for orbital fractures." Plast Reconstr Surg 67:736, 1981.

124. Converse JM: Orbital fractures. *In* English FM (ed): Otolaryngology. Vol 4. New York, Harper and Row, 1981, pp 1–22.

125. Bourguet J: Notre traitement chirurgical de poches sous les yeux sans cicatrice. Arch Prov Chir Arch Fr Belg Chir 31:133, 1928.

126. Tenzel RR, Miller GR: Orbital blow-out fracture repair, conjunctival approach. Am J Ophthalmol 71:1141, 1971.

127. Tessier P: The conjunctival approach to the orbital floor and maxilla in congenital malformation and trauma. J Maxillofac Surg 1:43, 1973.

128. Converse JM, Firmin F, Wood-Smith D, Friedland JA: The conjunctival approach in orbital fractures. Plast Reconstr Surg 52:656, 1973.

129. Shemen LJ, Meltzer M: Inferior fornix incision for orbital rim and floor fractures. Laryngoscope 96:1164, 1986.

130. Al-Kayat A, Bramley P: A modified pre-auricular approach to the temporomandibular joint and malar arch. Br J Oral Surg 17:91, 1979–80.

131. Shepherd DE, Ward-Booth RP, Moos KF: The morbidity of bicoronal flaps in maxillofacial surgery. Br J Oral Maxillofac Surg 23:1, 1985.

132. Longmore RB, McRae DA: Middle temporal veins—a potential hazard in the Gillies' operation. Br J Oral Surg 19:129, 1981.

133. Bingham CB: The fractured malar. Oral Surg 8:13, 1955.

134. Brown J, Barnard D: The trans-nasal Kirschner wire as a method of fixation of the unstable fracture of the zygomatic complex. Br J Oral Surg 21:208, 1983.

135. Zachariades N, Papavassiliou D: Iatrogenic epidural hematoma complicating reduction of a zygomaticomaxillary complex fracture. J Oral Maxillofac Surg 45:524, 1987.

136. Keen WW: Surgery: Its Principles and Practice. Philadelphia, WB Saunders Company, 1909.

137. Pennisi BR, Capozzi A: An elevator for reducing fractures of the zygomatic arch. Plast Reconstr Surg 45:403, 1970.

138. Quinn JH: Lateral coronoid approach for intraoral reduction of fractures of the zygomatic arch. J Oral Surg 35:321, 1977.

139. Shumrick DA: Malar and zygomatic fractures. In Mathog RH (ed): Maxillofacial Trauma. Baltimore, The Williams and Wilkins Company, 1977, pp 340–349.

140. Strohmeyer L: Handbuch der Chirurgie. Vol. 1. Freiburg, Switzerland, 1844.

141. Brown JB, Fryer MP: Fracture-dislocation of zygoma and orbit. Postgrad Med 6:400, 1949.

142. Ginestet G, Dupuis A: Les fractures de l'os malaire et du plancher de l'orbite et leur traitement. Gaz Med France 73:479, 1966.

143. Poswillo D: Reduction of the fractured malar by a traction hook. Br J Oral Surg 14:76, 1976.

144. Rončević R, Malinger B: Experience with various procedures in the treatment of orbital floor fractures. J Maxillofac Surg 9:81, 1981.

145. Lothrop HA: Fractures of the superior maxillary bone caused by direct blows over the malar bone. Boston Med Surg J 154:8, 1906.

146. Kazanjian VH: Fracture of the zygoma. Suspension method (1933). In Kazanjian VH, Converse JM: Surgical Treatment of Facial Injuries. Baltimore, The Williams and Wilkins Company, 1974.

147. Freeman BS: The direct approach to acute fractures of the zygomatico-maxillary complex and immediate prosthetic replacement of the orbital floor. Plast Reconstr Surg 29:587, 1962.

148. Tovi F, Pitchazade N, Sidi J, Winer T: Healing of experimentally induced orbital floor defects. J Oral Maxillofac Surg 41:385, 1983.

149. Van Herk W, Hovinga J: Choice of treatment of orbital floor fractures as part of facial fractures. J Oral Surg 31:600, 1973.

150. Rosenberg L, Tovi F, Gatot A: Alternative surgical method for repair of the fractured orbital floor. Laryngoscope 95:1004, 1985.

151. Kirkegaard J, Greisen O, Højslet PE: Orbital floor fractures: Early repair and results. Clin Otolaryngol 11:69, 1986.

152. Aaronowitz JA, Freeman BS, Spira M: Long-term stability of Teflon orbital implants. Plast Reconstr Surg 78:166, 1986.

153. Spira M: Commentary on orbital floor fractures—should they be explored early? Plast Reconstr Surg 64:400, 1979.

154. Converse JM: Two plastic operations for repair of orbit following severe trauma and extensive comminuted fracture. Arch Ophthalmol 31:323, 1944.

155. Manson PN, Crawley WA, Yaremchuk MJ, et al: Midface fractures: Advantages of immediate extended open reduction and bone grafting. Plast Reconstr Surg 76:1, 1985.

156. Gruss JS, MacKinnon SE, Kassel EE, Cooper PW: The role of primary bone grafting in complex craniomaxillofacial trauma. Plast Reconstr Surg 75:17, 1985.

157. Obwegeser HL, Chaussee GM: Verschiedene Knochenmaterialien zur Rekonstruktion von Orbitabodendefekten. 9th ed. Stuttgart, Georg Thieme Verlag, 1975, p 191.

158. Schüle H, Weimar J: Untersuchungen zur Therapieplanung bei Orbitafrakturen. Fortschr Kiefer Gesichtschir 19:188, 1975.

159. Callahan A: Bony depressions, particularly depressions of the floor of the orbit. Trans Am Acad Ophthalmol Otolaryngol 875, 1953.

160. Bagatin M: Reconstruction of orbital defects with autogenous bone from mandibular symphysis. J Craniomaxillofac Surg 15:103, 1987.

161. Constantian MB: Use of auricular cartilage in orbital floor reconstruction. Plast Reconstr Surg 69:951, 1982.

162. Stark RB, Frilech SP: Conchal cartilage grafts in augmentation rhinoplasty and orbital floor fracture. Plast Reconstr Surg 43:591, 1969.

163. Freihofer HP Jr: Die Rekonstruktion von Orbitadefekten. In Fortschritte der Kiefer- und Gesichts-Chirurgie. Bd. XXII, hersg., von K. Schuchardt. Stuttgart, Georg Thieme Verlag, 1977.

164. Sailer HF: Clinical experiences with lyophilized bank cartilage for contour rebuilding of the face. Presentation, 2nd Congress of European Association of Maxillofacial Surgeons, Zurich, 1974.

165. Sailer HF: Experiences with the use of lyophilized bank cartilage for facial contour correction. J Maxillofac Surg 4:149, 1976.

166. Sailer HF: Gefriergetrockneter Knorpel in der rekonstruktiven Gesichtschirurgie. Fortschr Kiefer Gesichtschir 24:56, 1979.

167. Jones DE, Evans JN: "Blow-out" fractures of the orbit: An investigation into their anatomical basis. J Laryngol 81:1109, 1967.

168. Lipshutz H, Ardizone RA: Further observations on the use of silicones in the management of orbital fractures. J Trauma 5:617, 1965.

169. Abrahams W: Repair of orbital floor defects with premolded plastic implant. Arch Ophthalmol 75:510, 1966.

170. Browning CW, Walker RV: The use of alloplastics in 45 cases of orbital floor reconstruction. Am J Ophthalmol 60:684, 1965.

171. Bennett JE, Armstrong JR: Repair of defects

of bony orbit with methyl methacrylate. Am J Ophthalmol 53:285, 1962.

172. Gamble JE: Orbital floor implants. Arch Otolaryngol 89:596, 1969.

173. Converse JM, Smith B, Obear MF, Wood-Smith D: Orbital blow-out fractures: A ten year survey. Plast Reconstr Surg 39:20, 1967.

174. Daieff CY, Flageul G, Benharoun C, et al: A propos de le reconstruction de 56 planchers de l'orbite par lame de Silastic. Conclusions actuelles de notre experience. Ann Chir Plast 22:279, 1977.

175. Goldman RJ, Hessburg PC: Appraisal of surgical correction in 130 cases of orbital floor fracture. Am J Ophthalmol 76:152, 1973.

176. Greenwald HS, Keeney AH, Shannon GM: A review of 128 patients with orbital fractures. Am J Ophthalmol 78:655, 1974.

177. Burres SA, Cohn AM, Mathog RH: Repair of orbital blow out fractures with Marlex mesh and Gelfilm. Laryngoscope 91:1881, 1981.

178. Erich JB: Treatment of fractures of the zygoma and floor of the orbit. Am J Surg 112:432, 1966.

179. Lermann S, Cramer LM: Blowout fractures of the orbit. Am J Ophthalmol 57:264, 1964.

180. Leake P, Michielli S, Pizzoferrato A, Freeman S: Histologische Untersuchungen der Weichgewebsreaktion auf Implantate mit elastischem Überzug. Zahn Prax 31:291, 1980.

181. Niederdellmann H, Schilli W, Düker J, et al: Osteosynthesis of mandibular fractures using lag screws. Int J Oral Surg 5:117, 1976.

182. Frenkel G, Reuther J, Dörre E: Reconstruction of defects of the orbital floor with plates of dense aluminum-oxide-ceramic. Dtsch Z Mund-Kiefer-Gesichts-Chir 4:253, 1980.

183. Lindorf HH, Steinhäuser EW: Spätrekonstruktion von orbitaboden und Jochbeinprominenz mit einem vascularisierbaren Kunstoff. Dtsch Zahn Z 32:318, 1977.

184. Polley JW, Ringler SL: The use of Teflon in orbital floor reconstruction following blunt facial trauma: A 20-year experience. Plast Reconstr Surg 79:39, 1987.

185. Hardin JC: Blow-out fractures of the orbit. Schumpert Med Q 3:125, 1984.

186. Quereau JVD, Souders BF: Teflon implant to elevate the eye in depressed fracture of the orbit. Arch Ophthalmol 55:685, 1956.

187. Keen RR: Orbital fractures treated with Teflon implants. Oral Surgery: Transactions of the IVth International Conference on Oral Surgery. Copenhagen, Munksgaard, 1973.

188. Levinson SR, Canalis RF: Experimental repair of orbital floor fractures. Arch Otolaryngol 103:188, 1977.

189. Keeney AH, Greenwald HS, Shennon GM: Orbital fractures: Blowout and rim. In Symposium of the Orbit and Adnexa. St Louis, CV Mosby, 1974, pp 24–33.

190. Gozum E: Blowout fractures of the orbit. Otol Clin North Am 9:477, 1976.

191. Emery JM, Noorden GK, Sclernitzauer DA: Orbital floor fractures: Long term follow-up of cases with and without surgical repair. Trans Am Acad Ophthalmol Otolaryngol 75:802, 1971.

192. Tse DT: Cyanoacrylate tissue adhesive in se-

curing orbital implants. Ophthalmol Surg 17:577, 1986.

193. Rubin LR: Polyethylene—three year study. Plast Reconstr Surg 7:131, 1951.

194. Lentrodt J: Zur Diagnostik und Therapie der Orbitabodenfrakturen. Dtsch Zahn Mund Kieferheilk 60:232, 1973.

195. Schwenzer N, Steinhilber W: Therapie mit Orbitabeteiligung. In Banaschewski E (ed): Traumatologie des Gesichtsschädels. Munich, Werk-Verlag, 1974.

196. Rolffs J: Ergebnisse der primären Orbitarekonstruktion bei Mittelgesichtsfrakturen. Fortschr Kiefer Gesichtschir 19:184, 1975.

197. Schlote HH, Cordes V: Technik und Ergebnisse der Versorgung von Orbitabodendefektfrakturen mit lyophilisierter Dura. Fortschr Kiefer Gesichtschir 19:174, 1975.

198. Frietag V, Flick H, Reichenbach W: Augenmotilität nach Mittelgesichtsfrakturen mit Orbitabeteiligung. Fortschr Kiefer Gesichtschir 22:117, 1977.

199. Faupel H, Linnert D, Schröder F, Schargus G: Ophthalmologische Nachuntersuchung von Mittelgesichtsfrakturen. Fortschr Kiefer Gesichtschir 22:113, 1977.

200. Schilli W, Niederdellmann H: Verletzungen des gesichtsschädels. In Burri C, Herfarth C, Jäger M (eds): Aktuelle Probleme in Chirurgie und Orthopädie. Vol 8. Bern, Switzerland, Hans Huber, 1980, p 66.

201. Luhr HG: Lyophilisierte Dura zum Defektersatz des Orbitabodens nach Trauma und Tumorresektion. Med Mitt (Melsungen) 43:233, 1969.

202. Luhr HG: Die primäre Rekonstruktion von Orbitabodendefekten nach Trauma und Tumoroperationen. Dtsch Zahn Mund Kieferheilk 57:1, 1971.

203. Luhr HG, Maerker R: Transplantation of homologous dura in reconstruction of the orbital floor. A five-year experience. Oral Surgery: Transactions of the 4th International Conference on Oral Surgery. Copenhagen, Munksgaard, 1973, p 340.

204. Prowler H: Immediate reconstruction of the orbital rim and floor. J Oral Surg 23:5, 1965.

205. Kummoona R: Chrome cobalt and gold implant for the reconstruction of a traumatized orbital floor. Oral Surg 41:293, 1976.

206. Kummoona R, Fattam SN: Reconstruction of the orbital floor with chrome cobalt mesh. J Oral Surg 33:542, 1975.

207. Wolfe SA: Correction of a lower eyelid deformity caused by multiple extrusions of alloplastic orbital floor implants. Plast Reconstr Surg 68:429, 1981.

208. Kohn R, Romano PE, Puklin JE: Lacrimal obstruction after migration of orbital floor implant. Am J Ophthalmol 82:934, 1976.

209. Nicholson DH, Guzak SV: Visual loss complicating repair of orbital floor fractures. Arch Ophthalmol 86:369, 1971.

210. Alpar JJ: Unusual complication of orbital floor blow-out fracture repair. Ann Ophthalmol 9:1173, 1977.

211. Wolfe SA: Correction of a persistent lower eyelid deformity caused by a displaced orbital floor implant. Ann Plast Surg 2:448, 1979.

212. Lentrodt J, Luhr HG, Metz HJ: Tierexperimentelle Untersuchungen zur Frage der primären Deckung von traumatischen De-

fekten des Orbitabodens. Dtsch Zahn Z 23:1418, 1968.

213. Iannetti G, D'Arco F: The use of lyophilized dura in reconstruction of the orbital floor. J Maxillofac Surg 5:58, 1977.

214. Smith B, Putterman AM: Fixation of orbital floor implants. Arch Ophthalmol 83:598, 1970.

215. Schilli W, Niederdellmann H, Härle F: Schrauben und Platten am Mittelgesicht und Orbitaring. Fortschr Kiefer Gesichtschir 22:47, 1977.

216. Schilli W, Ewers R, Niederdellmann H: Bone fixation with screws and plates in the maxillofacial region. Int J Oral Surg 10:329, 1981.

217. Düker J, Härle F, Olivier D: Drahtnaht oder Miniplatte—Nachuntersuchungen dislozieter Jochbeinfrakturen. In Fortschritte der Kiefer u Gesichtschirurg. Bd. XXII, hersg., von K. Schuchardt, R. Becker. Stuttgart, Georg Thieme Verlag, 1977.

218. Gill WD: Fractures of the facial bones with special reference to involvement of the paranasal sinuses and orbits. South Med J 27:197, 1934.

219. Adams WM: Internal wiring fixation of facial fractures. Surgery 12:523, 1942.

220. Krüger E: Indikation und Technik der operativen Kieferbruchbehandlung. Dtsch Zahn Z 19:1057, 1964.

221. Gorman JM: Malar fractures: Silicone wedge stabilization. Br J Oral Surg 17:244, 1979–80.

222. Rowe LD: Spatial analysis of midfacial fractures with directional and computed tomography: Clinicopathologic correlates in 44 cases. Otolaryngol Head Neck Surg 90:651, 1982.

223. Perino KE, Zide MF, Kinnebrew MC: Late treatment of malunited malar fractures. J Oral Maxillofac Surg 42:20, 1984.

224. Brown JB, McDowell F: Internal wire fixation for fractures of jaw. Surg Gynecol Obstet 74:227, 1942.

225. Fryer MP: A simple, direct method of reducing a fracture-dislocation of the zygoma. Surg Clin North Am 30:1361, 1950.

226. Brown JB, Fryer MP, McDowell F: Internal wire fixation for fracture of upper jaw, orbit, zygoma and severe facial crushes. Plast Reconstr Surg 9:276, 1952.

227. Fryer MP, Brown JB, Davis G: Internal wire-pin fixation for fracture-dislocation of the zygoma. Twenty year review. Plast Reconstr Surg 44:576, 1969.

228. Vero D: Jaw injuries: The use of Kirschner wires to supplement fixation. Br J Oral Surg 6:18, 1968.

229. Silverton JS, Bostwick J, Jurkiewicz MJ: The transmaxillary K-wire. Ann R Coll Surg Engl 60:329, 1978.

230. Larrabee WR, Irwin TM, et al: Use of transverse Kirschner wires in comminuted facial fractures. South Med J 72:1265, 1979.

231. Matsunaga RS, Simpson W, Toffel PH: Simplified protocol for management of malar fractures. Otorhinolaryngology 84:818, 1976.

232. Cleland H, Morrison WA: A simple rapid method of fixation of unstable zygomatic fractures. Aust N Z J Surg 55:607, 1985.

233. Kazanjian VH: Tumors of mouth and jaws. N Engl J Med 201:1200, 1929.

234. Crawford JM: Appliances and attachments for treatment of upper jaw fractures. Naval Med Bull 41:1151, 1943.

235. Le Quang C, Dufourmentel C: Technique de contention des fractures craniofaciales: Le cerclage de l'orbite. Ann Chir Plast 22:331, 1977.

236. Grignon JL: Technique opératoire. In Chirurgie Maxillo-faciale. Paris, Prelat, 1962.

237. Delaire J, Billet J, Le Roux JC, et al: La contention dans les fractures de l'os malaire. Rev Stomat Chir Max Fac 72:623, 1971.

238. Duckert LG, Boies LR: Stabilization of comminuted zygomatic fractures with external suspension apparatus. Arch Otolaryngol 103:381, 1977.

239. Findlay IA: Ankylosis of the coronoid to the zygomatic bone. Br J Oral Surg 10:30, 1972.

240. Kirivanta U: Silmakuopan pohjan painemurtuma. Duodecim 82:665, 1966.

241. Shea JJ: A new technique for stabilizing zygomatic fractures. JAMA 96:418, 1931.

242. Jarabak JP: Use of Foley catheter in supporting zygomatic fractures. J Oral Surg 17:39, 1959.

243. Anthony DH: Diagnosis and surgical treatment of fractures of the orbit. Am Acad Ophthalmol 56:580, 1952.

244. Jackson VR, Abbey JA, Glanz S: Balloon technic for treatment of fractures of the zygomatic bone. J Oral Surg 14:14, 1956.

245. Mark HI: Reduction of a zygomaticomaxillary complex fracture by the antral balloon technique. Oral Surg 14:753, 1961.

246. Gutman D, Laufer D, Neder A: The use of the Foley catheter in the treatment of zygomatic bone fractures. Br J Oral Surg 2:153, 1965.

247. Maran AGD, Gover WG: The use of the Foley balloon catheter in the tripod fracture. J Laryngol Otol 85:897, 1971.

248. Laufer D, Goldberg P, Gutman D, Selektar M: Treatment of fractures of the zygomatic bone. J Oral Surg 34:445, 1976.

249. Rowe NL: Fractures of the orbital floor. Oral Surgery: Transactions of the IVth International Conference on Oral Surgery. Copenhagen, Munksgaard, 1973, p 302.

250. Finlay PM, Ward-Booth RP, Moos KF: Morbidity association with the use of antral packs and external pins in the treatment of the unstable fracture of the zygomatic complex. Br J Oral Maxillofac Surg 22:18, 1984.

251. Podoshin L, Fradis M: The use of the Foley balloon catheter in zygomatic-arch fractures. Br J Oral Surg 12:246, 1974.

252. Van der Wal KGH, de Visscher JGAM: Fixation of the unstable zygomatic arch fracture. J Oral Surg 39:783, 1981.

253. Blevins C, Gross RD: A method of fixation of the unstable zygomatic arch fracture. J Oral Surg 37:602, 1979.

254. Jones GM, Speculand B: A splint for the unstable zygomatic arch fracture. Br J Oral Maxillofac Surg 24:269, 1986.

255. Ash DC, Mercuri LG: External fixation of the unstable zygomatic arch fracture. J Oral Maxillofac Surg 42:621, 1984.

256. Goldsmith MM, Fry TL: Simple technique for stabilizing depressed zygomatic arch fractures. Laryngoscope 96:325, 1986.

257. Dunley RE: A simple device for postreduction protection of the fractured zygoma. J Oral Surg 36:648, 1978.

258. Sewall SR, Pernoud FG, Pernoud MJ: Later

reaction to silicone following reconstruction of an orbital floor fracture. J Oral Maxillofac Surg 44:821, 1986.

259. Mauriello JA, Flanagan JC, Peyster RG: An unusual late complication of orbital floor fracture repair. Ophthalmology 91:102, 1984.

260. Bromberg BE, Rubin LR, Walden RH: Implant reconstruction of the orbit. Am J Surg 100:818, 1960.

261. Browning CW: Alloplastic materials in orbital repair. Am J Ophthalmol 63:955, 1967.

262. Emery JM, von Noorden GK, Schlernitzauer DA: Orbital floor fractures: Long-term follow-up cases with and without surgical repair. Trans Am Acad Ophthalmol Otolaryngol 75:802, 1971.

263. Noordgard JO: Persistent sensory disturbances and diplopia following fractures of the zygoma. Arch Otolaryngol 102:80, 1976.

264. Tempest MN: Management of displaced fractures of the malar bone and zygomatic arch. A review of 275 consecutive cases. Transactions of the Meeting of the 2nd International Society of Plastic Surgery, 1960, pp 251–258.

265. Dickoff KJ: Unilateral Orbital Trauma: A Clinical and Follow-up Study of 146 Cases. Thesis, Helsinki, 1975.

266. Stahlnecker M, Whitaker L, Herman G, Katowitz J: Evaluation and secondary treatment of posttraumatic enophthalmos. Presented at the American Association of Plastic and Reconstructive Surgery Meeting, Coronado Beach, CA, April 29, 1985.

267. Rankow RM, Mignogna FV: Surgical treatment of orbital floor fractures. Arch Otolaryngol 101:19, 1975.

268. Converse JM, Smith B: Reconstruction of the floor of the orbit by bone grafts. Arch Ophthalmol 44:1, 1950.

269. Converse JM, Smith B: Blowout fracture of the floor of the orbit. Transactions of the 2nd Congress of the International Society of Plastic Surgeons, 1959, pp 280–289.

270. Converse JM, Smith B: Enophthalmos and diplopia in fractures of the orbital floor. Br J Plast Surg 9:265, 1975.

271. Smith B, Regan WF Jr: Blowout fractures of the orbit. Mechanism and correction of inferior orbital fracture. Am J Ophthalmol 44:733, 1957.

272. Stanley RB, Mathog RH: Evaluation and correction of combined orbital trauma syndrome. Laryngoscope 93:856, 1983.

273. Pearl RM, Vistnes LM: Orbital blowout fractures: An approach to management. Ann Plast Surg 1:267, 1978.

274. Dulley B, Fells P: Orbital blowout fractures. Br Orthop J 31:47, 1974.

275. Moos KF, Le May M, Ord RA: Investigation and management of orbital trauma. Int J Oral Surg [Suppl]10:229, 1981.

276. Obear M: Posttraumatic ocular muscle imbalance and enophthalmos, diagnosis and treatment. In Corneo-Plastic Surgery. London, Pergamon Press, 1969.

277. Smith B, Obear M, Leone CR: The correction of enophthalmos associated with anophthalmos by glass bead implantation. Am J Ophthalmol 64:1088, 1967.

278. Taiara C, Smith B: Correction of enophthalmos and deep sulci by posterior subperios-teal glass bead implantation. Br J Ophthalmol 75:741, 1973.

279. Stallings JO, Pakiam AI, Cory CC: A late treatment of enophthalmos: A case report. Br J Plast Surg 26:57, 1973.

280. Burghouts JM, Otto AJ: Silicone sheet and bead implants to correct the deformity of inadequately healed orbital fractures. Br J Plast Surg 31:254, 1978.

281. Spira M, Gerow FJ, Hardy BS: Correction of post-traumatic enophthalmos. Acta Chir Plast 16:107, 1974.

282. Sergott TJ, Vistnes LM: Correction of enophthalmos and superior sulcus depression in the anophthalmic orbit: A long-term follow-up. Plast Reconstr Surg 79:331, 1987.

283. Fries R: Some problems in therapy of traumatic enophthalmos. Proceedings of the 2nd International Symposium on Orbital Disorders. In Modern Problems in Ophthalmology. Vol 14. Basel, Switzerland, S Karger, 1975, pp 637–740.

284. Coster DJ, Galbraith JEK: Diced cartilage grafts to correct enophthalmos. Br J Ophthalmol 64:135, 1980.

285. Zide MF: Late posttraumatic enophthalmos corrected by dense hydroxylapatite blocks. J Oral Maxillofac Surg 44:804, 1986.

286. Mathog RH, Archer KF, Nesi FA: Posttraumatic enophthalmos and diplopia. Otolaryngol Head Neck Surg 94:69, 1986.

287. Ord RA: Post-operative retrobulbar haemorrhage and blindness complicating trauma surgery. Br J Oral Surg 19:202, 1981.

288. Slack WJ: Blindness: A complication of the repair of a fracture of the floor of the orbit. Minn Med 57:958, 1974.

289. Emery JM, Huff JD, Justice J: Central retinal artery occlusion after blowout fracture repair. Am J Ophthalmol 78:538, 1974.

290. Gillissen JPA, Oei TH: Follow-up of orbital fractures treated surgically. Mod Prob Ophthalmol 14:471, 1975.

291. Cullen GCR, Luce CM, Shannon GM: Blindness following blowout orbital fractures. Ophthalmol Surg 8:60, 1977.

292. Bleeker GM: Miscellanea. In Bleeker GM, Lyle TK (eds): Fractures of the Orbit. Amsterdam, Excerpta Medica, 1970, p 230.

293. Manfredi SJ, Raji MR, Sprinkle PM, et al: Computerized tomographic scan findings in facial fractures associated with blindness. Plast Reconstr Surg 68:479, 1981.

294. Lipkin AF, Woodson GE, Miller RH: Visual loss due to orbital fracture. Arch Otolaryngol Head Neck Surg 113:81, 1987.

295. Wood GD: Blindness following fracture of the zygomatic bone. Br J Oral Maxillofac Surg 24:12, 1986.

296. Hughes B: Indirect injury to the optic nerves and chiasma. Bull Johns Hopkins Hosp 111:98, 1962.

297. Walsh FB, Foyt WF: Clinical Neuro-Ophthalmology. Vol 3. 3rd ed. Baltimore, The Williams and Wilkins Company, 1969, p 2362.

298. Miller GR: Blindness developing a few days after midfacial fracture. Plast Reconstr Surg 42:384, 1968.

299. Bernard A, Sadowsky D: Monocular blindness secondary to a nondisplaced malar fracture. Int J Oral Maxillofac Surg 15:206, 1986.

300. Magoon RC: Orbital fracture and retrobul-

bar haemorrhage. Am J Ophthalmol 55:370, 1963.

301. Morris RA, Ward-Booth P: Delayed spontaneous retrobulbar haemorrhage. J Maxillofac Surg 13:129, 1985.

302. Gordon S, McCrae H: Monocular blindness as a complication of the treatment of a malar fracture. Plast Reconstr Surg 6:228, 1950.

303. Butt WD: Sudden blindness following reduction of a malar fracture. Ann Plast Surg 2:522, 1979.

304. Penn J, Epstein E: Complication following late manipulation of impacted fracture of the malar bone. Br J Plast Surg 6:65, 1953.

305. Gordon S: Malar fracture. Intra-orbital haemorrhage during open reduction. Plast Reconstr Surg 20:65, 1957.

306. Ord RA, Awty MD, Pour S: Bilateral retrobulbar haemorrhage: A short case report. Br J Oral Maxillofac Surg 24:1, 1986.

307. Varley EWB, Holt-Wilson AD, Watson PG: Acute retinal artery occlusion following reduction of a fractured zygoma and its successful treatment. Br J Oral Surg 6:31, 1968.

308. Hayreh SS: Anterior Ischaemic Optic Neuropathy. New York, Springer-Verlag, 1975, pp 21–23, 31–71.

309. Hueston JT, Heinze JB: Second case of relief of blindness following blepharoplasty. Plast Reconstr Surg 59:430, 1977.

310. Huang T, Horowitz T, Lewis SR: Retrobulbar haemorrhage. Plast Reconstr Surg 59:39, 1977.

311. DeMere M, Wood R, Austin W: Eye complications with blepharoplasty or other eyelid surgery. Plast Reconstr Surg 53:634, 1974.

312. Duke-Elder S: System of Ophthalmology. Vol XIV. St Louis, CV Mosby, 1972, p 285.

313. Lemoine AN Jr: Discussion of "acute retrobulbar hemorrhage during elective blepharoplasty," by Hartley et al. Plast Reconstr Surg 52:12, 1973.

314. Heinze JB, Hueston JT: Blindness after blepharoplasty: Mechanism and early reversal. Plast Reconstr Surg 61:347, 1978.

315. Fry HJH: Orbital decompression after facial fractures. Med J Aust 1:264, 1976.

316. Ord RA, El-Attar A: Acute retrobulbar hemorrhage complicating a malar fracture. J Oral Maxillofac Surg 40:234, 1982.

317. Kraushar MF, Seelenfreund MH, Freilich DB: Central retinal artery closure during orbital hemorrhage from retrobulbar injection. Trans Am Acad Ophthalmol 78:66, 1974.

318. Hartley JH, Lester JC, Schatten WE: Acute retrobulbar hemorrhage during elective blepharoplasty. Plast Reconstr Surg 52:8, 1973. (Discussions by Lemoine, Rees, and Newell, 52:12, 1973.)

319. Schwenzer N: Befunde an der Kieferhöhle nach Mittelgesichtsfrakturen. Fortschr Kiefer Gesichtschir 19:167, 1975.

320. Warson RW: Pseudoankylosis of the mandible after a fracture of the zygomaticomaxillary complex: Report of case. J Oral Surg 29:223, 1971.

321. Kellner MJ, Sher M, Stoopack JC: Extracapsular fibrous ankylosis of the mandible after open reduction of a zygomatic arch fractures: Report of case. J Oral Surg 37:665, 1979.

322. Ostrofsky MK, Lownie JF: Zygomatico-coronoid ankylosis. J Oral Surg 35:752, 1977.

323. Gridly MS: Abnormal bony connections between the skull and mandibles. Oral Surg 7:954, 1959.

324. Williams AC, Rothman B, Matzkin M: Ankylosis of the coronoid process to the zygomatic arch and maxilla: Report of case. J Oral Surg 26:804, 1968.

325. Brown JB, Peterson LW: Ankylosis and trismus resulting from war wounds involving the coronoid region of the mandible: Report of three cases. J Oral Surg 4:258, 1946.

326. Allison ML, Wallace WR, Van Wyl H: Coronoid abnormalities causing limitation of mandibular movement. J Oral Surg 27:299, 1969.

327. Troyer SH: Ankylosis of the coronoid process of the mandible to the zygomatic arch subsequent to the surgical correction of prognathism: Case report. J Hosp Dent Pract 5:19, 1971.

328. Lindsay JS, Fulcher CL, Sazima HJ: Surgical management of ankylosis of the temporomandibular joint: Report of two cases. J Oral Surg 24:264, 1966.

329. Kawamoto HK: Late posttraumatic enophthalmos: A correctable deformity? Plast Reconstr Surg 69:423, 1982.

330. Hooley JR, Freedman G: Delayed treatment of a fracture of the zygomatic complex. Oral Surg 24:585, 1967.

331. Rabuzzi DD: Revision surgery for maligned midfacial fractures. Otolaryngol Clin North Am 7:107, 1974.

332. Dingman RO, Harding RL: Treatment of malunion fractures of facial bones. Plast Reconstr Surg 7:505, 1951.

333. De Vylder J, Rapuano R, Straigos GT: Correction of neurologic and cosmetic deficits secondary to untreated zygoma fracture. J Oral Surg 5:559, 1976.

334. Braun TW, Sotereanos GC: Orbital tripod osteotomy for facial asymmetry. J Oral Surg 36:20, 1978.

335. Tessier P, Callahan A, Mustarde JC, et al: Symposium on Plastic Surgery in the Orbital Region. Vol 12. St Louis, CV Mosby, 1976.

336. Karlan MS, Skobel BS: Reconstruction for malar asymmetry. Arch Otolaryngol 106:20, 1980.

CHAPTER 19

DIAGNOSIS AND TREATMENT OF MIDFACE FRACTURES

DANIEL LEW, D.D.S., and DOUGLAS P. SINN, D.D.S.

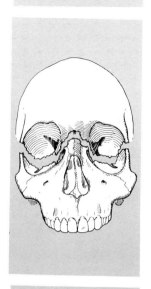

The reconstruction of the midface following trauma demands uncompromising care. The face is intimately bound up with our self-image. It is a region that is responsible for our senses of smell and vision and for providing our voice its resonance through the presence of the air sinuses.

Three buttresses allow the face to absorb inferosuperiorly directed forces admirably. These are the canine, the zygomatic, and the pterygoid pillars. The superior support of these pillars is the arc formed by the inferior and superior orbital rims and the zygomatic arches. Fractures of the midface often defy classification owing to the severity of the force and the multidirectional source of the trauma. The Le Fort classifications define the weakest areas of the midface complex when it is assaulted from a frontal direction at different levels.[1] The Le Fort type I fracture results from a force delivered above the level of the teeth. The fracture courses from the lateral border of the pyriform sinus across the lateral antral wall, behind the maxillary tuberosity, and across the pterygoid junction. The nasal septum may be fractured, and the nasal cartilage may be derailed (Fig. 19–1).

Because of the pull of both the external and the internal pterygoids, the maxilla may assume a posterior and inferior position. A classic open bite may be noted in this fracture.

The Le Fort type II fracture results from a force delivered at the level of the nasal bones. The fracture line occurs along the nasofrontal suture, through the lacrimal bones, and across the infraorbital rim in the region of the zygomaticomaxillary suture. The fracture then courses inferiorly and distally, following a parallel through a somewhat higher path than the Le Fort type I fracture. It completes its course along the lateral antral wall at the junction of the pterygoid plates. The nasal septum may be derailed, and the nasal bones may be displaced (Fig. 19–2).

The Le Fort type III fracture is caused by a force at the orbital level; the resulting fracture is a craniofacial dysjunction. The fracture line courses through the zygomaticotemporal and zygomaticofrontal sutures, along the lateral orbital wall, through the inferior orbital fissure, and medially to the nasofrontal suture. The fracture ends at the pterygomaxillary fissure (Fig. 19–3).

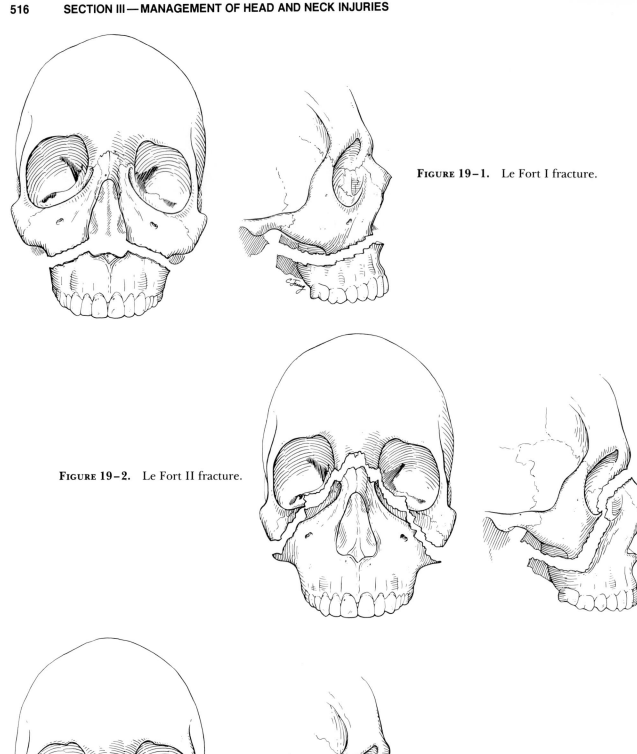

FIGURE 19–1. Le Fort I fracture.

FIGURE 19–2. Le Fort II fracture.

FIGURE 19–3. Le Fort III fracture.

EMERGENCY CARE

The emergency care delivered to a patient with a fractured midface follows a disciplined course. The airway is immediately evaluated for the existence and the location of an obstruction. A supraglottic obstruction can be caused by the accumulation of oral secretions and debris. The areas are manually cleared of fractured teeth, dentures, and blood clots. The patient should be placed in a lateral decubitus and mild Trendelenburg position. If oral or nasal bleeding is obstructing the airway, intraoral wounds should be managed locally for control. If the bleeding cannot be controlled, the oral cavity should be packed with gauze following the placement of either a nasopharyngeal or an endotracheal tube. An endotracheal intubation should not be attempted unless possible cervical fractures have been ruled out or stabilized. This injury is found in 8.7 per cent of cases of trauma from automobile accidents.[2]

Rotation or flexion-extension of the head can be lethal; bone fragments can impinge upon or lacerate the spinal cord. Care must be taken to obtain a good view of the entire length of the cervical spine, since fractures frequently occur at the C6–7 level. To prevent movement, a cervical collar should be fitted, or sandbags should be placed on either side of the neck. In a conscious patient, the cervical spine fracture is diagnosed by the presence of pain in the cervical region, paresis, and/or loss of sensation in the upper or lower limbs. When an upper airway obstruction is present in association with a fractured cervical vertebra, a tracheostomy or cricothyroidotomy should be performed to avoid manipulation during intubation. A cricothyroidotomy is generally easier to perform in patients with concomitant cervical spine injuries.[3] The procedure is contraindicated in patients with an injured, infected, or tumorous larynx; in children under the age of 18[4]; in patients who have previously undergone prolonged endotracheal intubation; and, finally, in patients who have endured endotracheal intubation for longer than 7 days.[5,6] If intubation is done prior to tracheostomy, it is best accomplished via fiberoptic visualization.

A lower airway obstruction, such as a laryngeal or a tracheal fracture or injury, is a clear indication for a tracheostomy. A tracheostomy is also indicated when frequent pulmonary toilet will be performed, when anesthetics have to be given repeatedly, and if the patient's dead space has to be diminished, as in concomitant chronic obstructive pulmonary disease (COPD). A patient with increased intracranial pressure levels has to be maintained at low carbon dioxide levels and should undergo a tracheostomy. Finally, if, in the clinician's judgment, the reconstructive procedures will be hampered by the presence of an endotracheal tube, a tracheostomy is indicated.

After the airway is controlled, the patient's blood volume must be ascertained. Vital sign monitors and a central subclavian catheter will quickly indicate whether the patient is hypovolemic. Two intravenous lines, one in the upper and one in the lower extremity, should be established. Normal saline or lactated Ringer's solution should be infused until blood is typed and cross-matched. In the absence of hypovolemia, no more than 50 ml/hr of glucose-saline solution should be given to minimize cerebral edema.

Although it is not common for blood loss from facial trauma to plunge a patient into hypovolemia, the extensive vascularity of the region lends itself, on occasion, to massive blood loss. This is true if one of the numerous major blood vessels is violated or if continuous oozing takes place. Wounds that have penetrated the platysma should be explored, and an arteriogram and esophagram should be performed.

Midface bleeding usually manifests as epistaxis. Control of epistaxis demands an understanding of the vascular supply to the region. One should first determine the site of the bleeding. Good visualization is mandatory; the mucous membranes should be shrunken and anesthetized with phenylephrine hydrochloride (Neo-Synephrine) or 10 per cent cocaine solution or both. Once the area is anesthetized, one can look at the bleeding site. If the bleeding is from the septal wall, the anterior or posterior ethmoidal artery is commonly the source. The posterior aspect of the septum is supplied by the nasopalatine, the greater palatine, and the superior labial arteries.

Bleeding from the superior lateral nasal wall emanates from the anterior and posterior ethmoidal arteries. From the posterior aspect, the source is the sphenopalatine artery. Bleeding from the anterior aspect commonly comes from the nasal branch of the facial artery.

If a vasoconstrictor-soaked pledget of cotton does not control the bleeding, one can attempt cauterization with silver nitrate solution. Persistent bleeding may be controlled by introducing an anterior nasal pack. Failure to control the bleeding may then require a posterior nasal pack or a pressure balloon.

It is mandatory to maintain the patient's head in a forward position. This practice prevents blood from draining freely into the pharynx and causing airway embarrassment.

If the bleeding still has not ceased, an arteriogram is best performed to determine the source of the bleeding. Either embolization or ligation may be required to control the bleed from the ethmoidal or the internal maxillary artery. To ligate the ethmoidal arteries, a curvilinear 3-cm incision is made above the attachment of the medial canthal ligament and below the trochlear ligament. A subperiosteal dissection is carried out, exposing the confluence of the frontolacrimal and frontoethmoid sutures. The frontoethmoid suture is followed posteriorly, care being taken not to puncture the thin lamina papyracea. The anterior ethmoidal artery is identified and ligated with a silver hemoclip. The involved posterior ethmoidal artery is similarly ligated as one dissects farther laterally. Care must be taken not to injure the optic nerve.

Ligation of the maxillary artery, when indicated, is carried out via a Caldwell-Luc approach. The mucoperiosteum is retracted from the posterior wall, and a window is made in the wall with a bur. The window is enlarged, and the posterior periosteum is cut, exposing adipose tissue. This tissue is removed, exposing the small branches of the internal maxillary artery. An operating microscope is utilized to expose the bleeding site, and silver hemoclips are used to ligate the bleeders. The superior periosteum is replaced, and the incision is closed. An alternate approach is to ligate the ipsilateral external carotid artery in the usual manner.

After stabilization of the patient's condition, a complete facial examination is done. A radiographic examination is necessary but can be delayed until the patient's condition is fully stabilized and he or she can undergo an often prolonged procedure. The face is evaluated for any lacerations and any obvious depressions in the skull. Asymmetry of the facial areas is noted, and any discharge from either the nose or the ear is assumed to be cerebrospinal fluid until proved otherwise. Neither the nose nor the ear should be packed if a cerebrospinal fluid leak is suspected. This practice will help in the prevention of a retrograde infection resulting in meningitis.

The facial skeleton is palpated so that any bone discontinuity may be noted. Examination should be performed bimanually in a disciplined manner. The supraorbital rim is examined first, and the examiner progresses downward to include the lateral and infraorbital rims, where extensive edema may quickly make an examination difficult (Fig. 19–4). The zygomatic arches are palpated as well as the nasal bones, and the examination ends with assessment of the maxilla and mandible.

The mandibular opening is evaluated for either a fractured zygomatic arch or a laterally displaced zygoma, which can obstruct the forward movement of the coronoid process. The buccal vestibule is palpated with the index finger (Fig. 19–5). Crepitation and displacement of the lateral antral wall and the zygoma can be easily appreciated by this maneuver. The occlusion is evaluated, and the absence and quality of dentition are noted, for these factors may greatly influence the method of treatment.

Ecchymotic areas, especially in the palate, are common findings in fractures of the maxilla. The pharynx is examined for lacerations or retropharyngeal bleeding. The patient should be questioned about a salty, metallic-tasting discharge, which is an

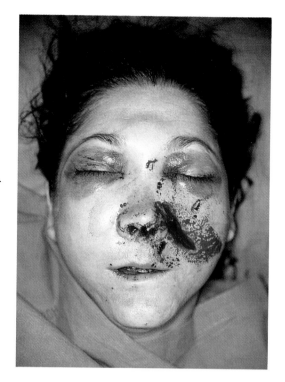

FIGURE 19–4. Extensive facial edema makes the examination very difficult.

indication of cerebrospinal fluid drainage. If that diagnosis is made, the patient should be placed in a head-elevated position to reduce cerebrospinal fluid pressure. Nose blowing should be discouraged.

The orbits are now evaluated. Periorbital edema and ecchymosis are often the initial signs of orbital trauma. The globe may essentially be protrusive owing to gross edema and may make a full examination difficult. Gross visual acuity is determined in both eyes. The existence of binocular diplopia is noted, pupillary size and shape are recorded, and the extent of strabismus, if present, is similarly noted. The location and extent of a subconjunctival hemorrhage are delineated (Fig. 19–6). A funduscopic examination is utilized to determine the existence of intraocular hemorrhage. Note is taken of any lid lacerations; these must be quickly repaired to prevent contracture. A through-and-through lid laceration requires a three-layer closure. A 6–0 nylon pull-

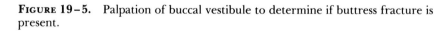

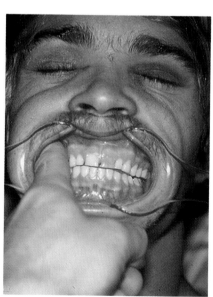

FIGURE 19–5. Palpation of buccal vestibule to determine if buttress fracture is present.

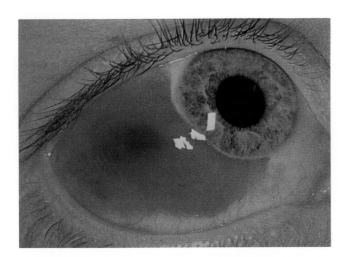

FIGURE 19–6. Subconjunctival ecchymosis with no lateral limit should instill in one a high index of suspicion of osseous orbital fractures.

out suture may be used on the conjunctiva; included in this suture is a small portion of the tarsus. This measure splints the edges of the tarsus in a satisfactory fashion.

The orbicularis oculi muscle is sutured next with 5–0 gut sutures, and the skin is closed with 6–0 silk sutures. Extreme care must be exercised in preventing any protruding knots, as these may injure the cornea. Exact approximation of the lid margins is obtained with 6–0 silk suture placed in the gray line. Crepitation perceived on palpation is indicative of orbital emphysema; this is caused by communication with the ethmoid sinus and, secondarily, with the maxillary sinus. The attachment of the medial canthal ligament is evaluated by feeling for tautness in the region after pressing on the lateral aspect of the globe (Fig. 19–4). Further indication of disruption of the medial canthal ligament is a rounding of the lacrimal lake, epiphora, and an increased intercanthal distance.

Ocular injuries are common in midface trauma. Holt and colleagues,[7] in studies of 1436 cases of maxillofacial injuries, found that 60 per cent of patients sustained midface trauma, of which 76 per cent suffered eye injuries. Seventy-nine per cent of these injuries were minor, but 12 per cent of victims suffered serious injury that resulted in either loss of vision or the need for reconstructive measures. Cruse and associates[8] reported findings in 33 patients who sustained nasal-orbital-ethmoid fractures. Severe ocular injury with initial or subsequent loss of vision occurred in 30 per cent of the patients. It is, therefore, clear that all facial fractures that involve the orbit should prompt consultation with an ophthalmologist.

Once the patient's condition is fully stabilized, a radiologic evaluation may be undertaken. At the minimum, a lateral skull view, a Waters view, and a reverse Waters view, together with a posteroanterior and anteroposterior view of the skull, should be taken. The most preferred modality, however, is a computerized tomographic (CT) scan taken in the coronal plane and, when indicated, in the sagittal plane. A lateral skull view is useful in demonstrating the presence of fluid in the paranasal sinuses and of intracranial air. The orbits and the sinuses are best shown by taking the angled posteroanterior view. The Towne view is useful in demonstrating the zygomatic arches as well as the vertical rami of the mandible. The zygomatic arches are best visualized on the classic submental vertex view. The Waters view shows the antra most clearly (Fig. 19–7). If the patient is unable to lie on the back, a reverse Waters (fronto-occipital) view can be used. The disadvantage of this view is the increased distance from the facial bones to the film.

The preferred radiologic modality in midfacial injuries is a CT scan (Fig. 19–8). Indeed, a scan taken in the appropriate view or views can stand alone as a diagnostic radiologic tool, without the need for tomography or plain views.

CT scans in the axial and coronal views will most clearly demonstrate damage to the orbital structures and will delineate the nature and extent of damage to the

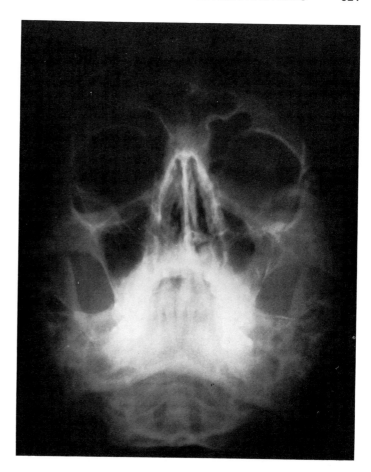

Figure 19–7. The Waters view showing midface fracture.

nasoethmoid region. The location of a cerebrospinal fluid leak will often be noted with the aid of a scan. The CT scan will also demonstrate the extent of edema internally and externally, as well as the presence of foreign bodies often missed on conventional films. The CT scan is superior to magnetic resonance imaging (MRI) when attempting to evaluate the bone disruption of the region. For soft tissue damage, MRI is the preferred modality.

Once the patient's condition is stabilized, there is little need to hurry the patient to surgery. There is a grace period of approximately 10 days. This grace period is fortuitous, since in many cases the rapidly developing edema saturates the midface. There is also a need for the surgeon to be able to formulate a reasonable treatment plan. This formulation cannot always be immediately achieved, since time is often needed for the full extent of the disruption to be diagnosed.

FRACTURES OF THE MAXILLA

The maxilla and the palatine and nasal bones form the bulk of the midface. The maxillary bones help in the formation of the three major cavities of the face: the upper part of the oral cavity and the nasal and orbital fossae. The maxillary sinus, which is small at birth, assumes a larger and more inferior position in the maxilla with maturity, until it forms the major bulk of the midface. This factor adds to the distinct weakness of the region. Because of the many articulations that the maxilla forms with the surrounding bone, it is difficult at times to categorize fractures in that region. Two common maxillary fractures, however, will be discussed — the Le Fort type I, or Guérin's, fracture (see Fig. 19–1) and the Le Fort type II, or pyramidal, fracture (see Fig. 19–2).

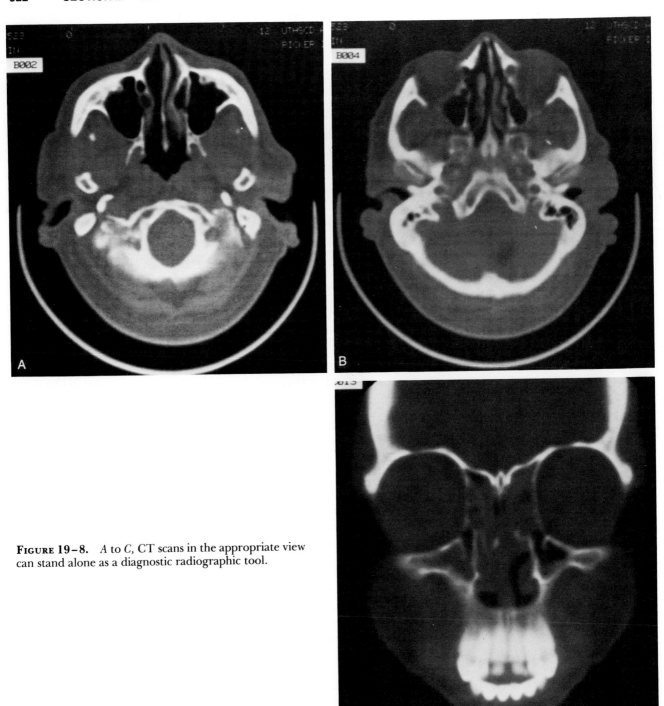

FIGURE 19–8. *A to C,* CT scans in the appropriate view can stand alone as a diagnostic radiographic tool.

The internal and external pterygoid muscles together are responsible for the posterior and inferior pull seen in fractures of the maxilla. This is true whether they are Le Fort type I or II.

The blood supply to the maxilla is via the major palatine arteries. Together with the superior and posterior alveolar arteries, they supply the hard and soft palate. In the anterior region, the terminal branch of the nasopalatine artery reaches the incisive foramen and there supplies the mucoperiosteum of the anterior part of the palate. The sensory nerve supply is via the second division of the trigeminal nerve.

This nerve emerges from the infraorbital foramen and thence courses to supply the lateral nasal, the superior labial, and the inferior palpebral regions. It also supplies the labial mucosa and the anterior teeth.

Le Fort type I fractures are caused by a force delivered above the apices of the teeth. The entity is usually posteriorly and inferiorly displaced, creating the classic open bite. This fracture can be present as an impacted, immovable, or a free-floating segment.

Hypoesthesia of the infraorbital nerve may be present owing to the edema that occurs. A unilateral fracture can occur, with the fracture coursing through the palatal suture line or adjacent to it. A palatal ecchymotic area is usually noted, together with either a malocclusion or a displacement of the fractured fragment.

Treatment of Unilateral Maxillary Fractures

If the fracture fragment is mobile, digital pressure may be utilized to reduce the fracture. The teeth in the fractured segment are loosely wired to the maxillary arch bar. The teeth in the unfractured segment are securely ligated. Intermaxillary fixation is now carried out on the unfractured side and completed on the fractured side after reduction and tightening of the interdental wires of that fragment. Intermaxillary wiring is removed after 4 weeks, by which time satisfactory stabilization will have occurred.

Occlusal splints can also be utilized for the reduction of this fracture. First, an alginate impression of both maxillary and mandibular arches is taken. The correct occlusion is created on the cast, and an intermaxillary splint is constructed. Arch bars are placed on both maxillary arches. The maxillary bar is cut at the fracture line. The interdental splint is wired first to the stable fragment, and the fractured portion of the arch is manually reduced into the splint and secured with 24-gauge wire. The mandible is then passively guided into the splint, and intermaxillary wiring is completed. Reduction is usually attained with minimal difficulty, especially if it is undertaken soon after the injury has occurred. On occasion, impacted fractures are encountered, and these may not be responsive to digital manipulation. Rowe disimpaction forceps is an excellent tool for achieving reduction.

An open reduction may be utilized if the fracture fragment appears to be unstable following attempted reduction. In this case, application of arch bars and an occlusal splint is necessary prior to the placement of interosseous wiring or bone plates. Interosseous wiring can be accomplished by the use of 24- or 26-gauge wire in two locations along the fracture site. Reconstruction miniplates can be used most effectively in both the buttress and the canine pillar areas or where adequate bone exists. Rigid plating is unforgiving in not providing one with the ability to compensate once the fragments are secured. With rigid fixation, there is no need for the patient to endure intermaxillary fixation. Teeth in the line of fracture are left in place unless there is excessive mobility or unless the fracture has occurred through the coronal two thirds of the tooth.

An edentulous, minimally fractured hemimaxilla demands only digital reduction of the fragments. However, when the fractured fragment contains teeth and the unfractured one is edentulous, therapy comprises an open reduction and the use of interosseous wiring or semirigid plate fixation. The technique for these procedures is described in detail in the following section.

TREATMENT OF A LE FORT TYPE I FRACTURE

An early reduction of this fracture as a rule presents minimal difficulty. Beyond 7 to 10 days, increasing force has to be applied to complete a reduction.

A minimally displaced fracture is reduced and immobilized by intermaxillary

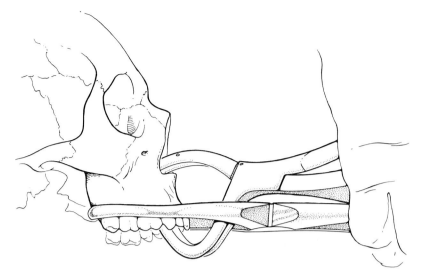

FIGURE 19–9. Disimpaction forceps in place.

wire fixation. One month of immobilization is usually sufficient for healing to occur. In the case of severe comminution, it may be necessary to extend the period to 6 weeks. An impacted fracture or one not easily reduced because of early fibrous union should be treated by the use of either a Rowe or a Hayton-Williams disimpaction forceps. The beaks of the Rowe forceps are placed along the nasal floor and against the palate. They are used as a pair or singly. To protect the nasal mucosa and the palatal mucoperiosteum, it is wise to place rubber tips on the beaks. By means of a rocking and rotating motion, the maxilla is pulled forward and downward (Fig. 19–9). The presence of a nasal endotracheal tube does not preclude the use of these forceps. The Hayton-Williams forceps are braced against the maxillary tuberosities. An anterior rocking motion will usually disimpact a recalcitrant maxilla. An open reduction has to be used when a delayed reduction or severe impaction resists closed reduction methods. In this case, a bilateral incision is made in the buccal vestibule, extending from the cuspid eminence to the region of the first molar. The lateral antral wall and the zygomatic buttress areas are exposed, and the fracture line is followed with a large chisel to the pterygoid plate region. Use of a Rowe or a Hayton-Williams forceps can now complete the task of reduction.

The fixation methods available are varied. Internal fixation is useful in the absence of comminution of the lateral antral wall and zygomatic buttress area. This method is precise and is usually performed without suspension wiring. After the correct reduction and the placement of the maxilla in correct intermaxillary fixation, the buccal fold incision previously described is utilized to determine which areas contain sufficiently sturdy bone to withstand the placement of either interosseous wiring or plates. Usually, intrabony holes are made in the canine eminence and in the buttress region. These are made approximately 0.5 cm superior and inferior to the fracture lines. Twenty-four-gauge wires are used for interosseous fixation, four-point fixation is a minimal requirement for stability, and intermaxillary fixation is optional. Removal of interosseous wiring is usually unnecessary unless it interferes with subsequent denture construction. Rigid fixation utilizing miniplates is the most desirable method of fixation. It eliminates, as does interosseous wiring, the need for intermaxillary fixation. The method offers stability, minimal likelihood of relapse, and the opportunity to resume normal daily activities at a faster rate. The drawback is the need for a perfect reduction, for the rigidity of the plates makes this an unforgiving technique. The plates must be perfectly adapted so that no torque is present in the plate. It is essential that the plates lie passively along the bone and not cause a change in the occlusion. Care should also be taken to position the maxillomandibular complex passively prior to plating. This positioning will ensure that the condyles are properly seated in the fossa and will prevent the subsequent development of an open bite. After the completion of fixation, the intermaxillary fixation should be removed and the occlusion should be checked by using the passive movements of the mandible.

Extraskeletal fixation is effective, if imprecise. It is useful in patients who have sustained a severely comminuted fracture and in patients who cannot endure intermaxillary fixation for medical or psychologic reasons. The halo head frame is a most useful device. It uses four-point fixation. Bone screws are used to secure the frame against the skull and are inserted into the outer table only. The use of the frame allows one greater versatility than provided by the plaster head cap. Traction and fixation points are more variable, and the superior stability results in greater comfort for the patient. The frame can be used for rigid or semirigid suspension, as well as for traction.

Suspension wires can be used instead of skeletal fixation or to supplement interosseous wiring. In the case of a midpalatal fracture, the use of suspension wires is possible. A rigid arch bar or splint is used for reduction and for attachment of the suspension wires. The rigidity of the splint prevents lateral displacement.

In the case of an edentulous maxilla, two approaches are available. If minimal comminution exists, a bilateral open reduction with direct interosseous wiring or plating will give a most satisfactory result. A maxillary acrylic splint constructed after taking an alginate impression of the corrected position of the maxilla can be used to articulate against the mandibular teeth. In the absence of mandibular teeth, the patient's dentures or a mandibular splint can be used, placed in a proper relationship and then attached to the respective bones by means of circum-mandibular wires for the mandible and circumzygomatic and nasal spine wiring for the maxilla.

It is important to remember that at least three-point fixation is essential for the stability of a maxillary splint; otherwise, the constant downward pull of the mandible will result in the displacement of the splint and subsequently of the maxilla. A maxillary splint can also be immobilized by placing small-diameter Steinmann's pins through the flanges of the splint and into the canine eminence. This measure provides a most stable and secure splint. Palatal screws are an alternate method of splint fixation. They are, however, not as stable as the Steinmann pin fixation previously described.

The use of maxillary and mandibular splints, as well as dentures, is seldom required and not preferred. These splints can cause significant airway, feeding, and oral hygiene problems.

Skeletal suspension, as stated, depends on the location of the fracture line. The basic requirements are that the suspension exist superior to the fracture line and that the bone complex be intact. The surgeon's preference is usually the deciding factor. The points ordinarily used are the pyriform, the zygomatic arch, the zygomatic buttress, and the infraorbital, the lateral orbital, and the superior orbital rims. The pyriform fossa is used only in very low Le Fort type I fractures. In this case, the suspension wiring is carried out through a horizontal high buccal fold incision in the region of the lateral and cuspid teeth. A mucoperiosteal flap is developed to expose the lateral inferior bony borders of the nasal cavity. The nasal mucosa is gently reflected from the medial aspect, and a tissue retractor is interposed to protect the nasal mucosa. A bone drill is utilized to make a hole in the bone approximately 0.5 cm from the superior bony border. A 24-gauge wire is passed through the hole and over the superior boundary of the pyriform fossa and is attached to the maxillary bar.

Circumzygomatic wiring is carried out by means of an awl. This instrument is introduced medially to the zygomatic arch and exited intraorally in the buccal fold at about the second bicuspid region. A 24-gauge stainless steel wire is secured to the awl, and the instrument is withdrawn, hugging the medial border of the zygomatic arch. It is carefully elevated superior and lateral to the arch and is again inserted into the oral cavity at approximately the point of the initial oral perforation. The wires are passed bilaterally and are attached to the previously placed arch bar. Although there is a degree of posterior angulation to this suspension wire, it is of minimal importance as long as the wires are basically passive in a superior direction. The sole function of suspension wires should be to prevent the fractured entity from being pulled downward by the mandible. The anteroposterior position of the fractured complex is determined by the intermaxillary occlusion.

Zygomatic buttress wiring is done through an intraoral high buccal fold incision. The incision extends anteroposteriorly approximately 3 cm. Following the development of a mucoperiosteal flap superior to and into the fracture line, the sturdy zygoma is exposed. An anteroposterior hole is drilled superior to the fracture line, and a 24-gauge stainless steel wire is passed through this most dense and supportive bone. Suturing of the incision is carried out in routine fashion. This method provides vertical suspension.

Infraorbital rim wiring is a popular method of suspension, for it also has no posterior angulation and, therefore, can be easily used to provide superior traction on the fractured maxilla. The infraorbital rim is exposed laterally to the infraorbital foramen. The rim is dissected free from its periosteal attachments. A J retractor is introduced to tent the soft tissue over the rim. The straight handpiece attached to a bone drill is again utilized to pierce the bone in a superior and medial direction. Twenty-four-gauge wire is introduced through the rim opening and is reintroduced into the oral cavity. Care must be taken to protect the globe contents with a retractor prior to piercing the bone and passing the wire.

Zygomaticofrontal wiring takes advantage of the strong zygomaticofrontal suture area. The incision site is in the lateral aspect of the orbital rim; the thumb and forefinger are placed on the medial and lateral aspects of the rim, respectively; with the tissue taut, the incision over the rim is made. The initial sharp dissection is carried out to reach the periosteum, which is then incised, exposing the underlying rim. A periosteal elevator is utilized to reflect the periosteum laterally, and a hole is drilled lateromedially above the zygomaticofrontal suture line. A 24-gauge stainless steel wire is attached to an awl and passed under the zygomatic arch and into the oral cavity, where bilateral attachments to the arch bar or splint are made. A pull-out wire is usually attached to the suspension wire at its apex to facilitate its removal at the completion of the suspension. Closure is done in layers, and the skin is closed with 6–0 suture.

In the absence of comminution of the lateral wall, direct interosseous wiring or plating is the technique of choice (Fig. 19–10). As already stated, a four-point fixation is mandatory. This method of immobilization is precise and elegant, but unforgiving.

It is possible to combine rigid plating and interosseous wiring when an insufficient bulk of bone exists for secure plating. After the completion of plating, the intermaxillary fixation should be removed and the mandible allowed its normal excursion. This practice ensures that the condyles are in their proper anatomic position. Intermaxillary fixation is unnecessary with this technique; however, an occlusal splint is often used when the occlusion is uncertain.

LE FORT TYPE II OR PYRAMIDAL FRACTURES

The Le Fort type II fracture is often referred to as a pyramidal fracture, with the apex of the pyramid being the nasofrontal suture. The classic manifestation of this fracture is bilateral periorbital edema, at times accompanied by ecchymosis, giving rise to the "raccoon sign." Hypoesthesia of the infraorbital nerve is also a common finding. This condition occurs either because of direct trauma or because of the rapid development of edema. A malocclusion may be noted and is often associated with an open bite. A step deformity may be palpated in the infraorbital rim area. This deformity can be accentuated by grasping the anterior maxillary teeth and moving the fractured complex anteroposteriorly. A step deformity might also be noted in a nasofrontal suture area and, again, is accentuated by moving the entire complex. Cerebrospinal fluid rhinorrhea is possible owing to a dural tear, usually in the region

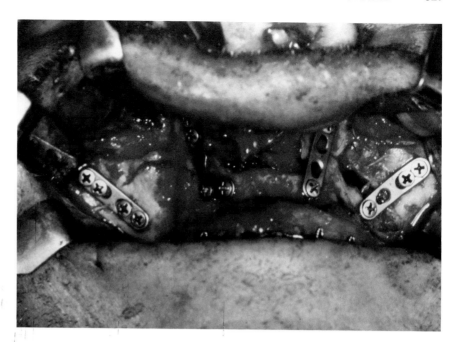

FIGURE 19–10. Rigid bone plates to stabilize the Le Fort I level fracture.

lateral to the cribriform plate. However, disruption of the sphenoid, ethmoid, and frontal sinuses can also take place, producing a dural tear and communication with a subarachnoid space (see Fig. 19–2).

Cerebrospinal fluid was first described by Willis in 1676. Cerebrospinal fluid otorrhea occurs in 7 per cent of basilar skull fractures and can be seen emanating from the external auditory canal.[9] As a rule, leakage is noted immediately following trauma. Infrequently, a week or two will pass before the phenomenon is apparent. A blood clot or brain tissue may obstruct the passage of the fluid. After lysis of the clot or an increase in intracranial pressure, leakage will be seen.

The diagnosis of cerebrospinal fluid rhinorrhea is straightforward if the fluid is not mixed with blood, nasal secretions, and/or lacrimal secretions. Clear cerebrospinal fluid should be collected in a vial, and a glucose level of 45 mg/dl confirms its existence, as well as the absence of sediment. Cerebrospinal fluid will not stiffen a handkerchief, while nasal secretions will do so. Cerebrospinal fluid will also form characteristic concentric rings when poured on linen. It is really impossible to determine the extent of cerebrospinal fluid leakage in the presence of blood; one should assume its existence until proved otherwise. The patient should be questioned about whether he or she has experienced the characteristic salty taste of cerebrospinal fluid. When a tentative diagnosis is made, the patient should be placed in a semirecumbent position and instructed not to strain, sneeze, or blow the nose. These measures are designed to minimize an increase in intracranial pressure. Meningitis is the inherent risk in a basal skull fracture with a concomitant dural tear. It should be noted that the absence of leakage does not imply the absence of a tear. Malec[10] reported a case of cerebrospinal fluid rhinorrhea 12 years following injury.

The use of antibiotics to counter the development of meningitis secondary to a dural tear is controversial. Meningitis can develop in spite of antibiotic therapy. The resulting infection can occur because of either opportunistic or resistant organisms, as well as the presence of an unusual concentration of resident flora (E. Benzel, personal communication).[11] Others have found that patients having fractures of the midface with cerebrospinal fluid rhinorrhea did not develop meningitis if antibiotic therapy was instituted.[12-14]

There is also some controversy regarding which antibiotic regimen is the most efficacious. The literature is conflicting on whether it is best to use antibiotics that permeate the blood-brain barrier and are truly prophylactic or ones that will traverse the barrier only when the latter is inflamed. We use a combination of chloramphenicol and nafcillin, since coverage of the most common organisms implicated in traumatic meningitis is obtained (E. Benzel, personal communication). The danger of meningitis secondary to a conservatively treated dural tear is lifelong. Patients must be adequately followed.[15]

The presence of a basilar skull fracture with a dural tear is not a contraindication to the reduction of midface fractures. On the contrary, a mobile midface often creates a pumping action that results in increased cerebrospinal fluid leakage. Early reduction and immobilization are, therefore, indicated. If cerebrospinal fluid leakage has not ceased 3 to 4 weeks following reduction, surgical correction of the leak is indicated.[16]

Treatment of Le Fort Type II Fractures

Reduction of fractures either digitally or by means of a Rowe disimpaction forceps is usually sufficient. Intermaxillary fixation, at times augmented with suspension from either the zygomatic arches laterally or the superior rims, will provide adequate stability. The minimal period of immobilization is 4 weeks.

On occasion, the superior aspect of the complex is unstable owing to a comminution of the adjacent nasal bones. The orbital floor and the medial orbital wall may also be comminuted. The signs of entrapment of the orbital contents are noted, and the appropriate walls should be explored to free the entrapment. The zygomaticomaxillary suture and the floor of the orbit can be approached through a standard blepharoplasty or transconjunctival incision. These approaches allow direct interosseous wiring or the use of miniplates in the infraorbital rim area.

The standard blepharoplasty incision is commenced by suturing the lids to prevent corneal damage. The approach to the rim is approximately 2 to 3 mm below the palpebral margin, usually in an existing skin crease (Fig. 19–11). The initial incision is through skin, followed by a sharp dissection of the skin to the level superior to the rim. At this point, the muscle is sharply incised, exposing the periosteal layer. Dissection is carried out about 2 cm inferior to the rim, and the periosteum is incised and reflected superiorly, exposing the rim. This step also allows easy access into the floor. At this point, any entrapped orbital tissue is freed.

When interosseous wiring is used, holes are drilled 0.25 cm lateral or medial to the fracture line in a superior direction through the rim. Wiring is carried out using 26- or 24-gauge wire. Similarly, rigid fixation is the recommended procedure, espe-

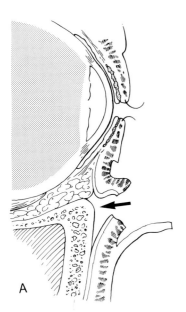
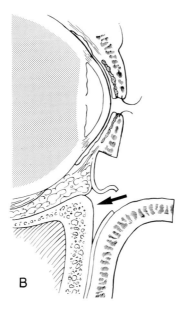

FIGURE 19–11.   *A* and *B,* Step incision for subciliary approach.

A   B

cially if one wishes to avoid intermaxillary fixation. It should be noted that intermaxillary fixation should be carried out prior to the fixation of the infraorbital rims. Intermaxillary fixation may be removed if the fracture appears to be stable and the occlusion reproducible. Rim fixation can be performed through the transconjunctival approach to the infraorbital rim recommended by Tessier.[17] The technique offers the advantage of not leaving a scar and the disadvantage of limited access.[18] Alternately, the standard blepharoplasty incision can be used.

The presence of a laceration in the nasal bridge area may be utilized to place a rigid plate across the nasofrontal suture, thus providing stability to the superior aspect of the fractured complex. This measure could be augmented with intermaxillary fixation to provide satisfactory reduction and immobilization of the fracture. Alternately, rigid fixation utilizing miniplates can be obtained by reducing and fixating the nasofrontal suture, as well as both zygomaticomaxillary sutures. Intermaxillary fixation in that case will again not be necessary, since the rigid three-point fixation of the fracture will provide adequate stability.

Le Fort type II fractures often manifest with fractures of the medial orbital wall. Diagnosis of a medial wall fracture is made most consistently by the limitation in abduction of the globe. This finding is often seen in conjunction with globe retraction. The extent of the disruption is best illustrated by taking a coronal CT scan. Indeed, the best method of evaluating damage to the region is by the use of a CT scan or, alternately, by means of tomograms taken in a coronal section. Medial wall fractures accompany 20 per cent of floor fractures.[19] The clinical symptom indicative of the fracture, besides abduction, is, on occasion, limitation in adduction.[20] The damage may or may not involve the attachment of the medial canthal ligament. A forced duction test can confirm the presence of medial rectus muscle paresis.

The surgical approach to the region is the classic medial canthal incision, in case of an intact attachment of the medial canthal ligament. The periosteum, together with the incised medial canthal ligament, is raised off the nasal bone. The lacrimal sac is elevated from the fossa, and fat or muscle tissue (or both) is freed and repositioned in the orbit. A sheet of silicone or Marlex mesh is placed against the wall if it is deemed that further herniation will occur. Closure is carried out in layers, with the medial canthal ligament carefully and securely resutured.

FRACTURES OF THE NASAL-ORBITAL-ETHMOID REGION

The nasal-orbital-ethmoid area is bounded laterally by the two orbital cavities. Anteriorly, the space is demarcated by the frontal process of the maxilla, the nasal bones, and the nasal process of the frontal bone (Fig. 19–12). The posterior boundary is the anterior portion of the sphenoid. The roof of the space is formed in the central portion of the cribriform plate of the ethmoid.

The nasal-orbital-ethmoid region has low resistance to a direct frontal force.[21] The result is a posterior impaction and comminution of the ethmoids. The region is marked by a sturdy external nasal component and medial orbital rim and the extremely fragile ethmoid complex and medial antral wall. The fragile perpendicular plate of the ethmoid component of the nasal septum, together with the ethmoid air cells, is easily crushed. The posterior displacement removes the dorsal support of the nose. As a result, the classic dorsum depression and the elevation of the nasal tip are noted. The lacrimal apparatus, the medial canthal ligament, and the anterior ethmoidal artery are all contained in this region. Cruse and associates[8] evaluated 182 major facial fractures. Approximately 18 per cent sustained nasal-orbital-ethmoid fractures. The average age was 31 years. Motor vehicle accidents were responsible for 70 per cent of the cases, and 63 per cent had associated severe nonfacial injuries. Central nervous system injuries were noted in 51 per cent of the patients, with 42 per cent presenting with cerebrospinal fluid drainage. Stranc,[22] in his survey of 100 midface fracture cases, reported a 12 per cent incidence of telecanthus.

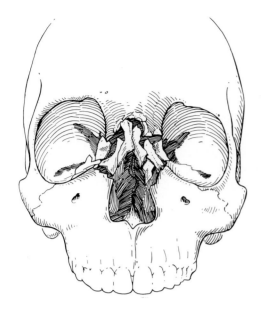

FIGURE 19–12. Nasal-orbital-ethmoid fracture.

The diagnosis of fractures in this region is usually made by physical findings aided by a CT scan. Routine films often fail to demonstrate the degree and location of the disruption. This failure is due to the overlapping of the bony architecture. CT scanning has become the definitive imaging modality for this region. Axial scanning is routinely performed, supplemented by coronal cuts if no cervical spine fractures exist.

The symptoms of a nasal-orbital-ethmoid injury do vary. In its most complete form, it is demonstrated by a fractured nose, often comminuted and posteriorly displaced; a widened nasal bridge; and a splaying of the nasal complex. Epistaxis is a common finding. Severe periorbital edema accompanies injury in most cases. Disruption of the medial canthal ligament can occur, resulting in traumatic telecanthus. The average intercanthal distance is between 33 and 34 mm for white men and between 32 and 33 mm for white women.[23] If it is difficult to measure the intercanthal distance because of edema, measuring the interpupillary distance and dividing it by half will give a fair approximation of the intercanthal distance. Finally, damage to the lacrimal apparatus can take place, usually in its distal part. Epiphora, occurring shortly after the traumatic incident or as a late development, indicates an obstruction of the lacrimal apparatus. Once the edema has subsided, the palpebral fissure will become narrowed, there will be an obliteration of the carbuncle, and finally there will be a flattening of the base of the naso-orbital valley.

Treatment of nasal-orbital-ethmoid injuries must be directed toward the proper reduction of nasal fractures, the correction of medial canthal ligament disruption, and the correction of traumatically induced lacrimal system abnormalities.

Nasal fractures are treated either immediately before edema manifests itself or after its disappearance. The grace period is usually 7 to 10 days. The symptoms of nasal fractures include an obstructed airway, deviation of the nasal bones and the septum, epistaxis, and crepitation. Confirmation should be obtained by either coronal axis CT scan or lateral and occipital mental views. The absence of external bone disruption should not exclude the possibility of derangement of the nasal infrastructure.

The nose must be carefully examined. A good light is essential. Blood clots are removed with the aid of a fine suction tube. The nasal mucosa is anesthetized with topical anesthesia, and a vasoconstrictor is used as well. The nasal cavities are sprayed. A few minutes later, a cotton applicator soaked in 5 per cent cocaine solution is placed beneath the nasal dorsum. A second applicator is next introduced into the depth of the middle meatus. By this means, the branches of the pterygopalatine ganglion are anesthetized. Local anesthesia is now obtained by injecting the incisive foramen and infiltrating the membranous parts of the septum, as well as the inferior, lateral, and basal areas of the nose.

Simple nasal fractures are usually treated by means of a closed reduction. A simple displacement can be reduced manually. One thumb is laid atop another, and pressure is applied against the nose. A reduction is often accompanied by a crackling noise. A unilateral depressed fracture requires the insertion of a reduction blade beneath the entrapped fragment to elevate it gently.

A comminuted fracture is reduced with the aid of Walsham's forceps. Once these fragments are moved into anatomic position, the fragments can be supported. This measure can be carried out by gingerly packing the nose with ½-inch iodoform gauze dipped in antibiotic solution. Both nares are packed to provide support for the septum as well as the nasal bones. It is important not to overpack the nose, so as not to displace the fractured fragments, or to leave the packing in for too long a time, since infection can occur. If the septum is displaced, it should be noted that nasal packing in itself cannot always provide adequate support. If the nasal septum is derailed, it should be reduced, and if lacerated, it should be sutured with 4–0 suture.

Widely displaced and comminuted nasal fractures are treated in three ways. Lead plates are utilized to maintain comminuted fractures in position following a closed reduction. An open reduction can be done with direct interosseous fixation. This method can use either a rigid plate or stainless steel wires. A combination of the two previous techniques is occasionally necessary. Lead plates or aluminum splints backed by foam are custom-cut to the size of the lateral nasal walls. Two 26-gauge wires are passed transnasally, one above the nasofrontal suture and one through the septum (Fig. 19–13). The nasal fractures are reduced in the usual manner, and the wires are passed through the plates. To prevent tissue pressure necrosis, these wires are not secured too tightly. When necessary, ½-inch iodoform gauze dipped in antibiotic solution can be placed in both nares to provide lateral pressure on the nasal bones against the plates. The plates should be left on for a period of 10 to 20 days. This technique has the disadvantage of applying imprecise pressure to the lateral nasal walls and may create a pinched nose appearance.

Severely displaced fractures should be treated by an open reduction. There are a number of approaches to the region. If a laceration exists in the area, it should be utilized; otherwise, a 2- to 3-cm midline incision bridging the nasofrontal suture can be used; a lateral nasal incision coursing medial to the medial canthal ligament attachment may be used unilaterally or bilaterally or may be joined transversely either at the apex or at the midportion of the incision. Through these approaches, one can perform plate fixation, wire osteosynthesis, medial canthal ligament repair, or, if necessary, a dacryocystorhinostomy. Miniplate osteosynthesis is one preferred modality for treatment, since there is less tendency for relapse. A more extensive dissection is often necessary, and the plates should be placed adjacent to the thickest skin.

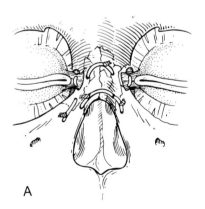
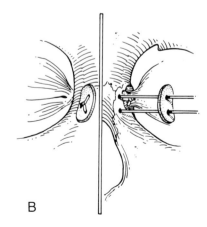

FIGURE 19–13. *A* and *B*, Nasal plates and wire fixation.

A

B

The open reduction offers the most precise method of treating comminuted nasal fractures. Bone attached to periosteum should not be discarded or removed. The jigsaw puzzle that one often encounters can be put together using 28- or 30-gauge wires where necessary. If large segments exist, miniplates are useful for maintaining the fragments in position and preventing subsequent relapse. Anatomic reconstruction of the external nose does not ensure an aesthetic appearance. A distorted septum is usually responsible for a nose that is not straight; merely forcing the septum into the midline will not guarantee its assuming a straight and supportive position, nor will nasal packing ensure a maintained position once the fracture has been reduced. Two methods are available and should be utilized: (1) provision of internal splinting and (2) performance of a submucous resection or a septoplasty.

Once the nose has been anatomically reconstructed, traumatic telecanthus, if it exists, can be addressed. The medial canthal ligament acts like a tendon of insertion for the orbicularis oculi muscle. Laterally, the ligament attaches to the margins of the tarsal plates. This attachment takes place lateral to the carbuncle and establishes the limits of the inner canthus. The medial canthal ligament consists of a sturdy superficial anterior limb and a relatively smaller, deeper posterior one.[24]

ANATOMY OF THE MEDIAL CANTHAL LIGAMENT

The anterior limb, because of its size and location, is clinically palpable. It inserts into a thickened portion of the frontonasal process of the maxilla along the anterior lacrimal crest. The superior aspect of the limb provides a lateral cover of the lacrimal sac, with the exception of the superior part of the dome. The smaller posterior limb consists of an extension of the orbicularis oculi muscle known as Horner's muscle, as well as the lacrimal fascia. The limb inserts into the thin posterior lacrimal crest. Palpating the medial canthal tendon while pressing on the lateral canthal area will help determine the integrity of the ligament. The eyelashes can also be grasped and pulled laterally, resulting in a taut lid if the tendon is intact. This procedure should be carried out on both lids.

An MRI scan or a CT scan is often diagnostic of the damage to the region; plain films offer little help. Traumatic telecanthus can occur, with a lateral splaying of the nasal bones carrying the canthal ligaments laterally with them. Owing to their lateral excursion, the nasal bones can override the lacrimal crest and sever the medial canthal ligament. Severe comminution of the region can cause a displacement of the ligament together with a small bony attachment.

To correct a laterally displaced canthal ligament attached to a large portion of bone, anatomic reduction and immobilization of the comminuted fractures are undertaken. A 2-cm incision is made approximately 10 mm medial to the insertion of the medial canthus. By following the anterior lacrimal crest in a superoinferior direction and by careful dissection, the bone bearing the attached canthal ligament is exposed. If possible, 26-gauge wire is utilized to wire the fragment to the adjacent bones. If it is found that the fracture is somewhat unstable and there is a lateral pull on it, transnasal wiring should be done. This is accomplished by making an incision that is 1 cm in length on the opposite side. A hole is made through the unstable bone fragment as well as through bone on the contralateral side just medial to the lacrimal crest. A double 30-gauge wire is then threaded through the two holes transnasally by means of a curved needle or an awl. The wire is now tightened over a small portion of a fractured stainless steel bur. The metallic bur is most useful, since the bone in the area of the lacrimal crest will often allow the thin wire to cut through it. Twisting the wire will reduce the fracture most satisfactorily.

A similar procedure is used when the canthal ligament has been disrupted but is still attached to a small piece of bone.[25] A completely detached medial canthal ligament is treated by threading, in mattress fashion, a 28-gauge wire through its stump and then passing it transnasally by means of a curved Keith or spinal needle. The wires

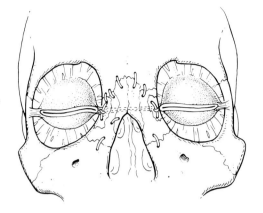

FIGURE 19–14. Wiring technique for nasal-orbital-ethmoid fracture.

are then threaded through; a hole is made in the contralateral side in the lacrimal crest region, and the wires are tightened under direct vision. Again, it is important that the wires be tightened over a broken-off fissure bur placed both at the tendon and at the bone sites. After being tightened, the wires are buried (Fig. 19–14).

If one has to perform a bilateral canthoplasty, a separate mattress wire is sutured through one tendon, and the wire is passed transnasally to be sutured to the opposite stump. Again, the wires are tightened under direct vision over a broken-off fissure bur, and the ends are buried. In case the ligaments cannot be identified, the tissue in the area of the tendon should be utilized in the canthoplasty.

In cases in which a blow-out fracture occurs in either the medial or the inferior orbital wall, the blow-out should be repaired prior to the performance of a canthoplasty. Late reconstruction of traumatic telecanthus is rarely fully satisfactory. The combination of an open reduction and treatment of medial canthal ligament disruption is considered the procedure of choice today.[8,25,26] The results obtained are superior to those obtained with external plates. The use of external plates for the reconstruction of medial canthal disruption is rarely satisfactory unless displacement is minimal. When late reconstruction is necessary, an osteotomy can be successfully performed when the medial canthal ligament has remained attached to a displaced lacrimal crest. Overcorrection is desirable in all canthal repair procedures.

The lacrimal system has the potential for disruption in a nasal-orbital-ethmoid fracture. The system consists of a lacrimal gland situated in the superior lateral anterior portion of the orbit and of two lacrimal canaliculi, which drain the eye via puncta that are situated in the medial aspect of each eyelid. From the puncta, the ducts (measuring usually 1 cm in length) pass vertically and then medially to join, either together or independently, the lacrimal sac. The sac sits in the lacrimal fossa (measuring about 12 mm by 3 mm) and is protected laterally and inferiorly by the lateral limb of the medial canthal ligament and medially by the weaker medial limb of the ligament. The sac drains into the inferior meatus via the nasolacrimal duct. The duct is about 20 mm in length, half of which is bony.

Eighty per cent of lacrimal secretions are carried by the inferior canaliculi; therefore, a nonfunctional superior canaliculus does not have to result in epiphora.

The incidence of injury to the system appears to be less than originally proposed. Gruss and colleagues, in evaluating 46 patients with nasal-orbital-ethmoid injuries, reported that postoperative epiphora was primarily due to lid malposition and not to nasolacrimal obstruction.[27] Of this group, 17.4 per cent eventually required a dacryocystorhinostomy. Harris and associates[28] recommended primary silicone intubation of the disrupted distal lacrimal pathway. The tube is left in place for 4 to 6 months. They concluded that if probing is unimpeded and the pathway is intact, intubation is not necessary. However, intubation of a lacerated nasolacrimal duct may prevent future cicatricial obstruction. Intubation that bypasses a disrupted distal nasolacrimal pathway was also recommended by Harris and coworkers.[28] This procedure, in reality, is akin to a dacryocystorhinostomy.

We prefer the immediate intubation of the nasolacrimal system, since the morbidity is minimal and the possibility of avoiding a dacryocystorhinostomy is greatly increased. It should be noted that disruption of the nasolacrimal system is not the sole cause of epiphora. Aging, with the resultant pulling away of the puncta, is a common cause of epiphora. Paralysis of cranial nerve VII and disruption of the medial canthal ligament are also causes of epiphora, along with obstruction of the valve of Hasner, the distal opening of the nasolacrimal duct.

The portion of the nasolacrimal system that is most prone to damage is the nasolacrimal duct.[29] Approximately 20 per cent of traumatic nasolacrimal injuries require a dacryocystorhinostomy.[27,29] A proper and detailed workup is mandatory before one can correctly undertake the reconstruction of the nasolacrimal system. A detailed history is mandatory. Epiphora may be secondary to trauma to the region or may be a coincidental finding. A history of iritis, dacryocystitis, allergies, previous nasal surgery, or a tumor resection can indicate an etiology that is unrelated to the trauma sustained.

The physical examination should include an assessment of the puncta for any discharge and an evaluation of the sac for enlargement, redness, or a fistula. One should check the patient for lagophthalmos, ectropion, and patency of the puncta.

The patency of the nasolacrimal system can be ascertained by the Jones 1 and Jones 2 tests.[30] The Jones 1 test is carried out by injecting 2 per cent fluorescein dye into the conjunctival sac and, after 5 minutes, noting if the dye emerges in the nose. A cotton applicator is placed under the inferior turbinate, following shrinkage of this region with 5 per cent cocaine. If no dye is noted on the applicator, the patient should be instructed to blow the nose. Alternately, the head should be placed in a forward position to allow drainage to occur more freely, and not into the pharynx. A contraindication to the performance of a dye test is the presence of a dacryocystitis.

If no dye is retrieved from the nose, the Jones 2 test should be carried out to determine the location of the obstruction in the system. The dye is flushed out of the sac, and a cannula is inserted into the inferior canaliculus via an anesthetized punctum. The patient's head is bowed forward, and saline is injected into the system. The appearance of fluid in the nose containing the dye indicates a partial blockage that was overcome by the injection. That problem is amenable to surgical correction via a dacryocystorhinostomy. Similarly, a dacryocystorhinostomy should be performed if there is reflux of fluid occurring from the opposite punctum, indicating that the obstruction exists at or below the level of the nasolacrimal sac.

Intubation macrodacryocystography is a useful means of determining the exact location of an obstructed system and is an alternate method to the Jones 1 and 2 diagnostic tests.[31] It demonstrates the location of the disruption and the location and size of the sac. The technique of a dacryocystorhinostomy has undergone many variations, a testament to the problems that have not always been solved.

A dacryocystorhinostomy is designed to bypass the nasolacrimal duct by anastomosing the lacrimal sac with the nasal mucosa. The procedure is usually performed with the patient under general anesthesia. The nose is packed with gauze impregnated with a mixture of 5 per cent cocaine and 1 per cent phenylephrine hydrochloride.

An incision is made in the skin overlying the medial canthal ligament, approximately 1 cm medial to the inner canthus and extending inferiorly about 2 cm and commencing approximately 0.5 cm above the level of the attachment of the medial canthal ligament. A Bowman probe is passed through the lower punctum and canaliculus to enter the sac. This probe demarcates the position of the sac, as well as the location for the formation of the nasal opening. The incision is carried medially, and the orbicularis oculi muscle and fascia are incised to reveal the medial canthal ligament. The ligament is exposed and resected, the lacrimal fascia is opened, and the incision is continued inferiorly to expose the lateral and medial aspects of the sac. The sac is dissected free from its bony moorings, and the bony ostium is made opposite the lower part of the sac with a 10-mm trephine bur. The lacrimal bone and part of the anterior lacrimal crest are removed. The opening is enlarged with Kerrison forceps to measure at least 15 mm in length and 10 mm in width. The sac and the nasal mucosa are incised longitudinally opposite the ostium. Releasing transverse incisions are made superiorly and inferiorly. The posterior nasal and sac flaps are sutured, as are the corresponding anterior ones. Sutures (4–0 Vicryl) are used in the closure. The overlying tissue is closed in layers.

Hollwich[32] modified the classic technique by suturing the posterior flaps of both the nasal mucosa and the sac. The anterior mucosal flap of the sac is sutured to the overlying subcuticular skin. Busse reported a success rate of 84.9 per cent using this technique.[33]

There are a few important factors to keep in mind when performing this procedure. The nasal opening must be large enough, its borders must be smooth so that granulomas do not form, and daily lavage with Ringer's solution should be commenced on the second postoperative day and continued for about 4 weeks. In the case of an obstruction of the nasolacrimal system that was not diagnosed during the initial facial reconstruction, a dacryocystorhinostomy can be safely performed 3 to 4 months after the initial reconstruction.

DIAGNOSIS AND TREATMENT OF LE FORT TYPE III FRACTURES

Craniofacial dysjunction occurs in Le Fort type III injuries (Fig. 19–15). The symptoms are the classic dish face, and the fact that mobility of the zygomaticomaxillary complex is often accompanied by cerebrospinal fluid leakage, edema, and periorbital ecchymosis. Traumatic telecanthus can be perceived as well as epiphora. After the clinical diagnosis, the findings can be confirmed by a CT scan or MRI or both. These are the most useful imaging aids in determining the extent of the injuries. Hard and soft tissue damage can then be fully evaluated. Plain films, previously discussed for Le Fort type II and nasal-orbital-ethmoid injuries, are necessary only if the other imaging modalities are unavailable.

The edema should be allowed to subside, and a treatment plan should be developed. A tracheostomy or a cricothyroidotomy should be considered if a fractured mandible also exists.

The general principles in the treatment of a mangled midface are to establish a stable outer framework and proceed medially to reconstruct the central portion of the face. The inferior boundary that should be established is the correct occlusal plane over an intact mandible. If there is a fracture of the maxilla that is separate from the upper midface, it should be reduced initially into satisfactory occlusion with an intact mandible, and the upper midface should be reconstructed on it. If there is a fracture of the mandible, it should be rigidly immobilized following reduction.

Once a correct occlusion is established, the anteroposterior and lateral position of the complex is then obtained. The superior and lateral boundaries of the upper midface now have to be established. The approach to these areas can be through either a bicoronal flap or the standard incisions, exposing the zygomaticofrontal, zygomaticomaxillary, and nasofrontal sutures.

Whitenburg and Meyer[34] compared the bicoronal flap and the infraorbital, lateral, orbital, and nasofrontal incisions in terms of their effect on local blood flow. The study, carried out on *Macaca* monkeys, demonstrated that the "multiple incision approach" is more biologically sound than the bicoronal incision approach in the Le Fort III osteotomy. The bicoronal approach has much to commend it. The exposure of the nasoethmoid complex, the lateral rims, and the zygomatic arch is excellent. It is cosmetically acceptable because the incisions are hidden in the preauricular

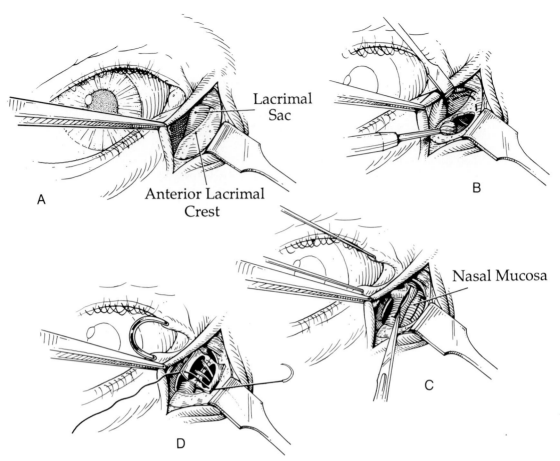

FIGURE 19–15.   *A–D,* Technique for dacryocystorhinostomy.

areas as well as behind the hairline. In patients with a receding hairline or the probability of baldness, this approach should be reconsidered.

The standard high preauricular incisions are extended superiorly and bilaterally (Fig. 19–16), drawn across the scalp and the hairline. The flap is extended anteriorly in a plane superficial to the pericranium. The periosteum is incised superior to the supraorbital ridges, and the dissection is continued subperiosteally. The zygomatico-frontal suture is exposed, as well as the medial canthal ligament attachments. The supraorbital and lateral orbital rims are easily exposed, as well as the zygomatic arches. The supraorbital nerve should be carefully dissected, and the frontalis branch of the facial nerve should be avoided by dissecting just under the temporalis fascia when exposing the zygomatic arches. The floor of the orbit has to be exposed via an infraorbital rim incision.

After completion of the procedure, the flap is replaced; the periosteal incision must be closed to ensure that the eyebrows assume their preoperative position. Alternately, the classic lateral brow infraorbital and nasoethmoid sutures can be exposed via the standard incisions. Rigid fixation is the preferred way to guarantee a stable entity following reduction. Semirigid plate fixation is the modality of choice, and placement of plates in the nasofrontal and the zygomaticofrontal suture areas ensures the vertical and anteroposterior position of the upper midface.

The infraorbital rim is exposed via a standard blepharoplasty incision, and the floor of the orbits is examined for a possible blow-out. If this injury is noted, it is corrected in the appropriate manner. Small defects are corrected by placement of a homologous graft. Large defects are treated by an autogenous hip bone graft. If the defect is so large that the bone graft has no shelf on which to set, a Steinmann pin driven through the infraorbital rim and into the medial and lateral walls forms a base

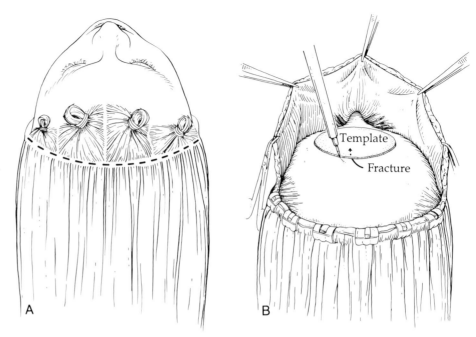

FIGURE 19–16. *A* and *B*, Bicoronal flap.

on which to set the graft. On frequent occasions, the zygoma is fractured in conjunction with a craniofacial dysjunction. The bicoronal flap can be utilized to correct this deformity, together with the classic blepharoplasty approach.

The zygomatic fracture is reduced via the classic Gillies procedure. A 2-cm incision is made in the temporal region parallel to the temporal vessels when the bicoronal flap is not used. It is carried through the skin to the superficial temporal fascia; the fascia is then incised, and the deep fascia is approached. A urethral sound or a Rowe zygoma elevator is introduced between the muscle and fascia so that the instrument slides medial to the zygomatic arch. When a urethral sound is used, a gauze pad placed over the temporal bone acts like a fulcrum point. The limitation to the use of the zygoma elevator, be it applied through an inferior or a superior approach, is noted when treating a floating zygoma. In this case, one has to reduce the fracture in three different planes. An eye or a Carroll-Girard screw inserted into the most prominent point of the zygomatic arch is a most useful device and can manipulate the fracture into an acceptable anatomic position. Semirigid fixation and rigid fixation are the standard treatment methods for unstable zygomatic fractures.

Antral packing done via a Caldwell-Luc approach provides a useful method for the treatment of a comminuted body rim or orbital floor. The standard Caldwell-Luc approach is utilized. A ½-inch iodoform gauze, preferably run through an antibiotic ointment, is packed into the antrum. The end of the gauze is exited through a nasal antrostomy or into the buccal vestibule anterior to the lateral wall opening. The front end of the iodoform gauze is placed along the floor of the maxillary sinus, and then packing is continued in a to-and-fro manner until the roof of the sinus is almost reached. At that point, the zygoma is reduced into its final position, and the packing is continued until the very top of the sinus. One should place a thin ribbon retractor along the floor of the orbit, raise the retractor somewhat if the floor is fractured, and then pack gently under it to obtain the desired pressure against the rim and the floor of the orbit. It is wise to overpack, which is one of the drawbacks to this technique. This method is somewhat imprecise, and the settling of the packing allows the zygoma at times to assume an inferior and medial position. Second, if bleeding emanates from the orbit owing to the packing of the sinus, there is now an obstruction to the evacuation of the blood from the orbital cavity. This obstruction can lead to compression of the optic nerve and, subsequently, to blindness. Packing is left in place for 3 weeks and then removed. The sinus is irrigated copiously for another week.

Semirigid and rigid fixation methods are precise and offer maximal stability. If semirigid fixation is employed, at least two-point fixation is necessary to avoid the medial and inferior relapse tendency. Lund[35] has reported a 40 per cent relapse rate with this technique. Only one-point fixation is required in the case of a greenstick fracture in either the zygomaticofrontal suture or, less commonly, the zygomaticomaxillary suture. To obtain two-point fixation, the lateral and infraorbital rims are usually exposed.

The three basic approaches to the infraorbital rim are the subconjunctival approach, the infraciliary approach, and the lower lid skin crease approach. The subconjunctival approach has the advantage of not leaving a facial scar and the disadvantage of limited access, along with compression of the canaliculi when lateral traction is applied. It makes little difference whether one uses a high subciliary or a low crease incision. Some have maintained that the low crease results in a lower incidence of ectropion and is faster to perform.[36] We use the former for floor exploration and the latter more frequently with rim disruption. Once the rim is exposed, the floor is explored and the contents, if trapped, are freed.

After determining the damage to the floor, osteosynthesis can be performed. Either horizontal or figure-of-eight wiring can be done. The holes are made far enough from the fracture line to allow a secure fixation of the fragments without the wire cutting through the bone. Fixation is not accomplished until the floor has been freed. Osteosynthesis is then completed. If support for the orbital floor contents is needed, it is provided at that time. The zygomaticofrontal suture is approached via the classic lateral brow incision. The eyebrow must not be shaved when this incision is performed.

To lash together the ruptured suture, 24-gauge wire is commonly used. The dissection and passing of the wires are usually performed on the lateroinferior aspect of the rim in preference to the medial dissection, which leads one into the orbit and may occasionally disrupt the lateral canthal ligament. The wiring is carried out under direct vision, and the final wiring is done simultaneously with the tightening of the infraorbital rim. This practice allows one the opportunity to evaluate the continuity of both suture lines, as well as the position of the floor.

A further guide in assessing the position of the fractured zygoma is the position of the floor of the orbit. If no disruption has occurred, a smooth continuity of the floor is one more indication that the fractured zygoma is now in an acceptable anatomic position.

Although it is common to obtain two-point fixation at the zygomaticofrontal and zygomaticomaxillary sutures, one may choose to proceed intraorally and wire the zygomaticomaxillary suture in the buttress area. This practice is useful and provides further assurance that the medial migration of the fracture will not take place. As already noted, the bone in this area is usually thick, and if no comminution is encountered, it is a useful method to ensure an aesthetically acceptable result.

In the case of a comminuted zygoma, interosseous wiring can be used to reconstruct the rim, and antral packing can be employed to hold out the fragmented zygoma. External fixation is clearly recommended in this type of fracture, especially if the lateral antral wall and the medial or posterior wall of the sinus are comminuted. We prefer the Joe Hall Morris pin fixation into the major portion of the zygoma, joined to a pin placed in the supraorbital rim.

The most appealing approach in the treatment of a fractured zygoma is the use of compression miniplating. A number of factors commend this method. The fragments are rigidly fixed and less liable to undergo a rotation. If proper reduction can be obtained, a single plate at either the lateral or the infraorbital rim fracture site will produce proper immobilization. One can also span a comminuted defect with a plate and wire the intermediate segments to the plate. When treating a fractured zygoma with rigid fixation of the zygomaticofrontal suture, one must be sure that any disruption of the floor is small and has not caused entrapment.

Other methods have been recommended. Sailor[37] used a staple to span a fracture site, and Matsunaga and colleagues[38] used a ⅛ Steinmann pin introduced through the body of the zygoma and lodged in the hard palate as a method of obtaining rigid fixation.

BLOW-OUT FRACTURES

The classic blow-out fracture, by definition, implies an intact orbital rim and a disruption of one of the walls or the floor of the orbit (Fig. 19–17). It may be caused by a blow to the orbit by an object larger than the outer structure of the orbit, producing a momentary increase in intraorbital pressure. This increased pressure in turn causes the weakest portion of the orbit to give way, usually the orbital wall of the ethmoid or the roof of the maxillary antrum or both. By this mechanism, the fractured walls act like a safety valve and spare the globe.

Pfeiffer[39] was the first to report a case of a blow-out orbital injury. Emery and colleagues[40] reported that 24 of 159 blow-out fractures had concomitant ocular injuries. The critical clinical symptoms vary but may include circumorbital edema and/or ecchymosis, proptosis, and ophthalmoplegia, as well as diplopia in the upper and lateral gaze. Enophthalmos may be a late finding.

The forced duction test is mandatory to assess for entrapment of the infraorbital tissue. A CT or MRI scan will most convincingly demonstrate the presence of the blow-out. Coronal scanning is preferred for connective tissue, floor, and medial wall disruptions. The transverse sections are excellent for medial wall evaluation.[41]

A Waters view is a standard radiograph in the absence of other diagnostic modalities. For an evaluation of the orbital floor, the modified Waters view is preferred. The patient should be upright so that antral fluid will not clog the sinus, a condition seen when the patient is horizontal. The classic teardrop shadow extending below the level of the orbital rim must have embedded in it calcified deposits of bone, or else it may merely represent a submucosal hematoma. Tomograms of the orbit taken in a reverse Waters position, as well as anteroposteriorly, will complete the retinologic examination.

The treatment of blow-out fractures has engendered much controversy. The problem is determining which injuries are likely to lead to the development of enophthalmos or diplopia or both without surgical intervention.

Surgical intervention should be undertaken if both the radiographic findings and the forced duction test indicate a blow-out fracture with entrapment. In cases in which either radiographic findings or clinical findings are negative, it is wise to weigh

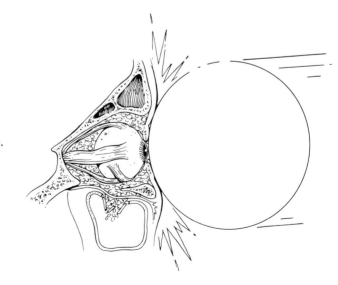

FIGURE 19–17.   Blow-out fracture.

the alternatives. A positive forced duction test in the absence of edema is an indication for exploration. If enophthalmos is visible in spite of a negative forced duction test, surgery should be undertaken. In this case, a CT scan or an MRI scan is invaluable in demonstrating the disruption. A negative forced duction test and an abnormal CT scan for tissue prolapse are indications for exploratory surgery, if only because the degree of damage is unknown and a large disruption of the floor can eventually lead to enophthalmos.

Repair of the orbital floor should take place within 2 weeks or sooner if possible. Failure to free entrapped tissue and correct bone disruption can result in unsatisfactory corrective surgery. The surgical approaches for exploration of the orbital floor are the same as those described for exposing the infraorbital rim. The classic Caldwell-Luc approach to the antrum can be used as well to push the infraorbital contents carefully into the orbit and support the contents with antral packing.

The reason for repairing a floor defect is to support the orbital contents and to create a smooth base. In cases in which Lockwood's ligament is not intact, significant herniation of the orbital contents can take place through the walls of the orbit. In these cases, the orbital contents have to be recovered. Once that has been accomplished, the defect has to be closed to prevent reherniation of these tissues. This closure can be accomplished via the use of autogenous, homogeneous, or alloplastic grafts. Autogenous grafts have the advantage of high acceptability and the disadvantage of requiring a second surgical procedure. Donor sites have been the iliac crest, the ipsilateral or contralateral antral wall, the outer table of the calvarium, the lateral wall of the mandibular body, the mastoid bone,[42] and the nasal septum cartilage.[43] Homogeneous bone[44] and cartilage[45] have also been used with success, as well as freeze-dried dura.[46]

Alloplasts are frequently used to reconstruct the orbital wall. Among them have been methyl methacrylate,[47] Teflon, Silastic,[48] and Marlex mesh. Alloplasts have the advantages of negating a second operative site, ready availability, and lack of resorption. The disadvantages are the risks of extrusion and infection.[49] The extrusion can be minimized if the graft is placed subperiosteally and sutured to the rim. The graft should be shaved in a pyramidal fashion, with the apex pointing toward the depth of the orbit. That shape approximates the contour of the floor. Care must be taken not to push the graft too far posteriorly, for there is always a danger of applying pressure on the optic nerve. That situation is unlikely, for the nerve is surrounded by a muscle cone and enters the posterior aspect of the orbital cavity above the floor level.

Autogenous bone grafts should be used in cases of complex floor disruption, especially in the absence of lateral and medial floor support, which would act like struts for an alloplastic graft. Traditionally, the bone graft has been wired to the rim or supported by antral packing. The latter course has given rise to complications ranging all the way from lack of constant support caused by settling of the packing to infection to nonunion. As previously stated, we utilize 0.62 threaded Steinmann's pins inserted through the inferior aspect of the rim and into the lateral and medial orbital walls or through the rim and into the graft.

The external nasal architecture is now reconstructed; the internal nasal anatomy is corrected in the manner previously described. A medial wall blow-out, if present, is corrected by the placement of a Marlex or Silastic graft. The lacrimal system is next evaluated with a Jones 1 and 2 test or a dacryocystogram. If a dacryocystorhinostomy has to be performed, a cannulation of the nasolacrimal system is carried out at this point. Finally, a medial canthal ligament repair is completed. Immediate bone grafting should be considered if sufficient soft tissue is present. Grafting not only avoids a second invasion into the area but also increases the chances of a good cosmetic result by decreasing fibrosis and contracture of the soft tissue. Comminuted nasal fractures can now be supported by external plating if that is deemed necessary. After the passing of transnasal wires, nasal packing is introduced, if required. Although rigid fixation via the use of miniplates is the technique of choice, occasionally that is not possible.

External support is necessary if intermaxillary fixation cannot be endured, especially in patients with abdominal injuries or contaminated wounds or in psychotic patients. Patients who have sustained muscle injuries and who have fragmentations and loss of soft tissue are excellent candidates for this technique.

In cases of a grossly comminuted mandible, external fixation may have to be applied to the mandible and to the midface when large segments of the skeletal framework are absent. Absent bone segments should be replaced with autogenous bone. Alloplastic materials should be used with caution, since they increase the risk of infection and have the potential for extrusion. The most popular donor sites for these bone grafts have been the rib, the ilium, and the cranial bones. Cranial bone has the following advantages: It has a low rate of bone resorption, as well as proximity to the operative site, and its harvesting produces an inconspicuous scar and minimal morbidity. Its use is not advantageous when a patient has the propensity to male pattern baldness and when large amounts of bone are necessary. The complication rate in late reconstruction of facial fractures by Tholler and colleagues was 15 per cent. Malunited fractures are treated by appropriate osteotomies.[50]

We place our patients on an antibiotic regimen for about a week following surgery. Early ambulation and participation in daily life are encouraged. Proper nutrition and emotional support, together with close follow-up care, are essential ingredients in the patient's re-entry into normal life.

REFERENCES

1. Le Fort R: Etude Expérimentale sur les Fractures de le Menchoire Supérieure Revue Chirurgicale 20.08, 1901.
2. Cornell University Automotive Crash Injury Research: The Injury Producing Accident: A Primer of Facts and Figures. Ithaca, NY, 1961.
3. Feinberg S, Peterson L: The use of cricothyroidotomy in oral and maxillofacial surgery. J Oral Maxillofac Surg 45:873, 1987.
4. Gleeson MJ: Cricothyroidotomy, a satisfactory alternative to tracheostomy. Clin Otolaryngol 1:2, 1984.
5. Sise MJ, Shackform SR, Cruickshank JC, et al: Cricothyroidotomy for long term tracheal access. A prospective analysis of morbidity and mortality in 76 patients. Ann Surg 200:13, 1984.
6. Greis ZH, Quanstrom O, Willen R: Elective cricothyroidotomy: A clinical and histopathological study. Crit Care Med 10:387, 1982.
7. Holt JE, Holt GR, Blodgett JM: Ocular injuries sustained during blunt facial trauma. In Proceedings of the American Academy of Ophthalmology, San Francisco, CA, November 1982.
8. Cruse CW, Blevins PK, Luce EA, et al: Nasoethmoid-orbital fractures. J Trauma 20:551, 1980.
9. Robinson RG: Cerebrospinal fluid rhinorrhea meningitis and pneumoencephalos due to nonmissile injuries. Aust N Z J Surg 39:328, 1970.
10. Malec R, Relac O, et al: Late results of surgical treatment of cerebrospinal fluid fistulas in the anterior fossa. Spornick Vadeckych Praci Lekaroke Fakulty KuV Hradci Kralove 15:393, 1972.
11. Miles JP, Garretson HD, Shields CB, et al: Prophylactic antibiotics in basilar skull fractures. In Meeting Abstracts, 33rd Annual Meeting of the Southern Neurosurgical Society, Dallas Neurosurgery 8:495, 1981.
12. Leech PT, Paterson A: Conservative and operative management for cerebrospinal fluid leakage after closed head injury. Lancet 1:1013, 1973.
13. MaGee EE, Cauthen JC, Brackett CE, et al: Meningitis following acute traumatic cerebrospinal fistula. J Neurosurg 33:312, 1970.
14. Dawson RL, Fordyce GL: Complex fractures of the middle third of the face and their early treatment. Br J Surg 43:254, 1953.
15. Jennett B, Teasdale G: Management of Head Injuries. Philadelphia, FA Davis, 1981, p 205.
16. Loew F, Pertuiset B, Chaumer EE, et al: Traumatic spontaneous and postoperative cerebrospinal fluid rhinorrhea. Adv Tech Stand Neurosurg 11:169, 1984.
17. Tessier P: The conjunctival approach to the orbital floor and maxilla in congenital malformations and trauma. J Maxillofac Surg 1:3, 1973.
18. Wray RC, Holtmann B, Ribaudo JM, et al: A comparison of conjunctival and subciliary incisions for orbital fractures. Br J Plast Surg 30:142, 1977.
19. Thering HR, Bogart JN: Blowout fractures of the medial orbital wall with entrapment of the medial rectus muscle. Plast Reconstr Surg 63:848, 1979.
20. Leone CR, Lloyd WC III, Rylander G, et al: Surgical repair of medial wall fractures. Am J Ophthalmol 97:349, 1984.
21. Swearingen J: Tolerance of the Human Face to Crush Impact. Oklahoma City, OK, Office of Aviation Medicine, FAA Civil Aeromedical Research Institute, 1965.
22. Stranc MF: Primary treatment of nasoethmoid injuries with increased intercanthal distance. Br J Plast Surg 23:8, 1970.
23. Waardenburg PJ: A new syndrome combining developmental anomalies of the eyelid, eyebrows and nose root with pigmentary defects of the iris and head hair and with congenital deafness. Am J Hum Genet 3:195, 1951.

24. Robinson TJ, Stranc MF: The anatomy of the medial canthal ligament. Br J Plast Surg 23:1, 1970.

25. Mustgrade JC: Repair and Reconstruction in the Orbital Region. 2nd ed. Edinburgh, Churchill-Livingstone, 1980, pp 168, 263.

26. Epker BN: Open surgical management of naso-orbital-ethmoid fractures. *In* Transactions of the IVth International Conference on Oral Surgery, Amsterdam, May 1971.

27. Gruss JJ, Hurwitz JJ, Nik NA, et al: The pattern and incidence of nasolacrimal injury in naso-orbital-ethmoid fractures. The role of delayed assessment and dacryocystorhinostomy. Br J Plast Surg 38:116, 1985.

28. Harris GJ, Fuerste FH, et al: Lacrimal intubation in the primary repair of midfacial fractures. Ophthalmology 94:242, 1987.

29. Stranc MF: The pattern of lacrimal injuries in nasoethmoid fractures. Br J Plast Surg 23:339, 1970.

30. Jones CT, Loobig JC: Surgery of the Eyelids and Lacrimal System. Birmingham, AL, Aesculapius Publishing Company, 1976.

31. Hurwitz TJ, Welham RN, Malsey MD: Intubation macrodacryocystography and quantitative scintillography: The complete lacrimal assessment. Trans Am Acad Ophthalmol Otolaryngol 81:575, 1976.

32. Hollwich F: Ubereine Modifikation de totischen operation. Klin Mbl Augenheilk 170:631, 1977.

33. Busse H: The Kaleff-Hollwich technique and results of external dacryocystorhinostomy operation. J Maxillofac Surg 7:135, 1979.

34. Whitenburg GJ, Meyer MW: Flap design and the LeFort III osteotomy blood flow investigation. J Maxillofac Surg 41:314, 1983.

35. Lund K: Fractures of the zygoma. A follow-up study of 62 patients. J Oral Surg 29:556, 1971.

36. Holtman B, Wray RC, Little AG: A randomized comparison of four incisions for orbital fractures. Plast Reconstr Surg 67:731, 1981.

37. Sailor HF: Osteosynthesis of orbital margin fractures via the transconjunctival approach using staples. J Maxillofac Surg 5:184, 1977.

38. Matsunaga, Simpson W, Toffel PH: Simplified protocol for treatment of malar fractures. Arch Otolaryngol 103:535, 1977.

39. Pfeiffer RL: Traumatic enophthalmos. Arch Ophthalmol 30:718, 1943.

40. Emery SM, Noorden GK, Sckernitzaur DA: Orbital floor fractures, long term follow-up of cases with and without surgical repair. Trans Am Acad Ophthalmol Otolaryngol 75:802, 1971.

41. Koorneef L, Zonneveld FW: Orbital anatomy, the direct scanning of the orbit in three planes and their bearing on the treatment of motility disturbances of the eye after orbital "blowout" fractures. Acta Morphol Neerl Scand 23:229, 1985.

42. Hotte H: Orbital fractures. Tijdschr Ziekenverpl 24:991, 1971.

43. Weisenbaugh JM, Beic MC: Orbital floor repair with nasal cartilage. *In* Transactions of the International Conference of Oral Surgery, Madrid, 1973.

44. Hyatt GW: The bone homograft, experiments and clinical applications. Symposium on Bone Graft Surgery. Am Acad Orthodont 17:133, 1960.

45. Fox SA: Use of preserved cartilage in plastic surgery of the eye. Arch Ophthalmol 18:182, 1947.

46. Luhr HG: Lophilistierte dura zum Defects Ersatz des Orbitabodens nach Trauma and Tumorresection en Medizinische Mitteil (Melsungen) 43:233, 1969.

47. Bennett JE, Armstrong JR Jr: Repair of defects of bony orbit with methyl methacrylate. Am J Ophthalmol 57:285, 1962.

48. Cramer LM, Tooze JM, Lerman S: Blowout fractures of the orbit. Br J Plast Surg 12:171, 1965.

49. Browning CW: Alloplast materials in orbital repair. Am J Ophthalmol 63:955, 1967.

50. Tholler SR, Zarem HA, Kawamoto HK, et al: Surgical correction of late sequelae from facial bone fractures. Am J Surg 154:149, 1987.

CHAPTER 20

OPHTHALMIC CONSEQUENCES OF MAXILLOFACIAL INJURIES

GORDON N. DUTTON, M.D., F.R.C.S., and
ISAM AL-QURAINY, M.B., Ch.B., M.C.OPHTH., D.O.

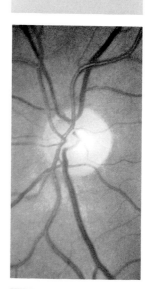

A number of factors protect the globe from injury. These include the prominence of the bones of the orbit and the natural reflexes of self-protection, namely, blinking, averting the head, and protecting the eye with the hand or forearm. Despite these factors, the eye may sustain injury, but the resilient structure of the globe allows it to withstand blows of considerable force without rupture.

Retrospective studies of patients who have sustained midfacial fractures indicate that up to 20 per cent may sustain serious ocular injury warranting ophthalmologic referral.[1-6] Orbital floor fractures have been associated with a 40 per cent incidence of ophthalmic complications.[7]

Some ophthalmic injuries may be clearly apparent. However, there are other potentially blinding complications that can easily be missed unless they are actively sought. Inadequate care can result in blindness, with its attendant social and medicolegal implications. Examination of the eyes is mandatory for every patient who has sustained midfacial trauma severe enough to cause a fracture.

This chapter reviews methods of ophthalmic examination and the ophthalmic consequences of injury and provides guidelines with regard to which patients warrant ophthalmologic referral.

OPHTHALMIC ASSESSMENT

The assessment comprises, in this order, the history, the evaluation of visual function, and the examination for structural disorders.

History

The following data are recorded:

1. The time, place, and circumstances of the injury.
2. The exact nature of the injury.

3.   The nature of the object that caused the injury (a kick is more likely to damage the eye than a head butt).

4.   The velocity and vector of the traumatic force.

5.   Were glasses worn? These may either have protected the eye or have given rise to a glass foreign body.

6.   The antecedent visual status. How good was the vision before the injury? This information may be very important, especially if legal claims are involved. If the patient was in the armed forces, he or she would have had good vision in each eye. If he or she had visited an optometrist or ophthalmologist in the past, there may be a record of the visual acuity.

Clinical Examination

ASSESSMENT OF VISUAL FUNCTION

At the time of initial assessment, the visual acuity, which is a measure of the resolving power of the eye, is determined in *every* case of fracture of the midface, if at all practicable. The distance acuity is assessed with the patient at 6 m (20 feet) from a Snellen chart. The test letters are constructed so that each portion of the letter is separated by 1 minute of arc; thus, the complete test letter subtends a total angle of 5 minutes of arc at the eye, for an eye with 6/6 (20/20) vision.

The visual acuity is recorded using two numbers. The upper number records the distance of the patient from the chart, while the lower number provides an index of the size of the letter and represents the distance at which that letter subtends 5 minutes of arc; that is, when placed at 60 m, the top letter subtends 5 seconds of arc at the eye. If the patient can read only the top letter of the chart, the visual acuity is 6/60 (20/200).

One eye must be fully covered while the acuity is determined. If the patient cannot read at 6/6 (20/20) and yet does not have glasses for distance, the acuity is measured with the patient looking through a pinhole (this can easily be improvised with a card and a pin). If the acuity improves, then the most likely cause for poor acuity is a refractive error. Occasionally, the acuity improves in patients with cataracts or opacities in the vitreous.

When the visual acuity is less than 6/60 (20/200), the distance at which the top letter can be read is recorded (e.g., 3/60 or 10/200). When the chart cannot be read, the patient is asked to count fingers (CF), and the distance at which this is achieved is documented (e.g., CF, 0.5 m). If the acuity is less than this, the perception of hand movements is recorded as HM or the perception of light only as PL.

In some patients with multiple injuries, it may be possible to assess only the visual acuity for near. The reduced Snellen letters subtend the same angle at the eye at 0.33 m as the full Snellen letters at 6 m.

For convenience, the clinician can carry a means of assessing visual acuity for near in his or her pocket. For older patients, the near acuity must be determined with the use of reading glasses or a pinhole (Fig. 20–1) because the ability to accommodate declines with age.

If a formal means of visual acuity assessment is not available, then an estimation of visual acuity is made using a newspaper or paper currency.

VISUAL ACUITY IN CHILDREN

It is equally important to assess the visual acuity in a child following facial injury. The most practical method for a child who is unable to read letters is the Sheridan-Gardiner test. Single Snellen letters are shown to the child from a distance of 6 m (20 feet), and the child points to the identical letter on a chart held by either a second examiner or a parent who is sitting with the child.

Figure 20-1. Pinhole occluder and portable visual acuity device for practical assessment of visual acuity in the injured patient. When presented at 0.33 m, each line of letters approximates to the near equivalent of 6/60, 6/36, 6/24, 6/18, 6/12, 6/9, and 6/6, respectively. (Courtesy of Clement Clarke International, London.)

VISUAL FIELDS

The visual fields are assessed in patients who have sustained severe head trauma, in those who are aware of a defect in their vision, and in those whose behavior indicates that a visual field defect may be present. Confrontation methods of visual assessment are most commonly used to screen for a visual field defect. However, more sensitive methods must be used if a minor defect is to be detected. The authors recommend the following strategy.

Testing Central Visual Function. The patient is instructed to look at a red object with each eye in turn, and he or she is asked to compare the color for each eye. A patient with traumatic optic neuropathy will be aware of color desaturation, that is, the red will look duller with the affected eye. Next, the patient is told to look at the examiner's nose with each eye in turn and is asked whether any part of the examiner's face appears either missing or blurred. This is an accurate method of detecting a paracentral scotoma, which may, for example, be caused by a choroidal tear.

Binocular Visual Field Testing by Quadrants. This method is used to test for homonymous visual field defects. The examiner sits opposite the patient. The patient is asked to look at the examiner's eyes. Both hands are placed in the lower outer quadrants and then in the upper outer quadrants. The patient is asked to identify a small movement of the extended forefinger of each hand. The examiner moves each finger in turn and then moves both together. The patient is asked to point at the moving finger (or fingers). A patient with a left homonymous hemianopia, in which the left field of vision in each eye is deficient, will not point to the moving fingers on the left. A patient with a visual inattention defect in that area will not perceive movement when the finger is moved in the other half of the visual field at the same time. Inattention hemianopia is indicative of unilateral diffuse occipital pathology.

Assessment of the Central Visual Field to Confrontation. Traumatic damage to the visual pathways is more likely to cause impairment of the central 30 degrees of visual field than the periphery. Therefore, a small target, such as a small red pin, should be used to screen for such defects. The examiner sits opposite the patient and closes one eye. The examiner asks the patient to cover one eye with the palm of the hand and to fixate on the examiner's eye. The red target is introduced from the periphery to the center along a coronal plane halfway between the examiner and patient. The patient is instructed to say "now" as soon as he or she becomes aware of the head of the pin. The examiner is specifically looking for a quadrantic field loss; therefore, the pin is introduced into the fields along the oblique meridians (if the examiner tests only in the horizontal and vertical meridians, he or she may well miss the field defect).

To determine the sensitivity of the technique, the examiner checks the position and dimensions of the blind spot by placing the target in his or her own blind spot. The examiner's blind spot should correspond approximately to that of the patient.

Testing Peripheral Visual Field.   This is accomplished using a large white pin. The patient is asked to cover one eye. Sitting opposite the patient, the examiner introduces the target from behind the patient and moves it in an arc of an approximate radius of 0.33 m, centered on the patient's eye. The target should be identified as soon as it comes into the extreme peripheral field of vision. This technique can be modified for use in children. One eye of the child is patched. The child is given a toy to play with. The examiner stands behind the child and introduces the target into the periphery. As soon as it is seen, the child turns his or her head to look at the target.

Subjective Visual Field Assessment.   Occasionally, all the previously described tests may be normal but the patient still complains of impaired vision. The examiner sits opposite the patient. The examiner closes one eye and covers one eye of the patient. The patient is asked to fixate on the examiner's pupil, and the examiner places the red pin close to his or her face in each quadrant of the patient's visual field adjacent to the examiner's eye. The patient is asked to compare the colors in each position. In particular, in cases with traumatic chiasmal damage, the patient is aware of color desaturation in the upper temporal fields, but there may be no other detectable visual field defect with any of the other methods used.

When a visual field defect is detected, more accurate charting of the defect by perimetry may be required to determine the pattern and extent of the defect.

THE PUPILS

If the visual acuity is reduced, with no improvement upon use of the pinhole, the pupils are tested to seek evidence of an afferent pupillary defect, which indicates severe ocular injury, retinal detachment, or traumatic optic neuropathy.

Direct and Consensual Pupillary Reflexes.   These reflexes are tested first. The background illumination is diminished by switching off the lights or drawing the curtains. The patient is asked to fixate into the distance to relax his or her accommodation. A penlight source is used to illuminate the eyes from below, but not from the front, as this could cause an accommodative reflex. The light is shone twice into one eye, and the direct and consensual reflexes are observed. The procedure is repeated for the other eye. An obvious afferent pupillary defect, in which the pupil reacts poorly to direct stimulation but briskly to consensual stimulation, can be detected by this method.

Swinging Flashlight Test.   This test is used to detect a subtle defect caused, for example, by incomplete optic nerve damage. The pupils are illuminated in the same manner, but on this occasion the light is shone into each eye for about 2 seconds and then swung rapidly to illuminate the other eye. For an incomplete right afferent pupillary defect, when the light is shone in the right eye, both pupils constrict. When the light is swung to the left eye, both pupils constrict further. When the light reilluminates the right eye, the pupils return to their previous resting position and dilate slightly. This technique can be used even in the presence of a unilateral third nerve palsy in which one pupil is poorly reactive or nonreactive. The swinging flashlight test is performed, and the size of the contralateral pupil is determined for both its direct and its consensual reflexes. Any difference in size indicates a relative afferent pupillary defect. (For example, a fracture at the right orbital apex may damage the right oculomotor and optic nerves. The right pupil would, therefore, not react either directly or consensually owing to the oculomotor nerve damage. However, the left pupillary diameter will be smaller for its direct response than for the consensual response in the right eye.)

The Photo-Stress Test.   This simple and useful clinical test detects macular dysfunction and helps to distinguish between traumatic optic neuropathy and traumatic damage to the retina in a patient with blurred vision in one eye. The visual acuity is determined for each eye. The photo-stress test is carried out on each eye in turn. A bright flashlight is shone into one eye for 30 seconds. The patient immediately looks at the visual acuity chart again, and the time taken for him or her to read the line above the previously recorded acuity is documented. The procedure is repeated for the other eye. The normal recovery time is between 10 and 30 seconds. A prolonged recovery time indicates retinal injury. A difference in recovery time of more than 10 seconds between the two eyes is suggestive of unilateral retinal injury. If there is no difference between the eyes, the cause of reduction in visual acuity is more likely to be impaired optic nerve function.

Examination for Structural Disorders

EXAMINATION OF THE ANTERIOR SEGMENT

Careful examination of the anterior segment of the eye is essential if clinical signs of ocular trauma are to be detected. Ideally, a slit-lamp should be used. Operating loupes with focal illumination provide a useful alternative. The anterior segment of the eye is examined carefully for any of the pathology described in the next section.

OPHTHALMOSCOPY

Ophthalmoscopy Through Dilated Pupils. This is indicated in all patients with a reduced visual acuity. Tropicamide 1 per cent produces rapid pupillary dilation (in Caucasian eyes) with little effect on accommodation and with a return to normal within a few hours. The addition of phenylephrine 10 per cent may be required for eyes of people of black lineage (the examiner must check first for any history of cardiac dysrhythmia). The contraindications to pupillary dilation are as follows:

1. An iris-supported intraocular lens, which could be dislodged if the pupil was dilated

2. A history of intermittent blurring of vision and pain in the eye, suggestive of angle-closure glaucoma

3. A shallow anterior chamber

Although the optic disc can be assessed without dilating the pupil, the central and surrounding retina cannot be adequately examined.

The reader will no doubt be conversant with the appearance of the retina (Fig. 20–2) and the use of the direct ophthalmoscope. The following hints may, however, be of value:

1. The examiner looks through the ophthalmoscope from a distance, examin-

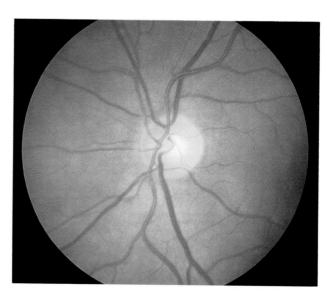

FIGURE 20–2. Photograph of the normal optic disc and retina.

ing the red reflex initially. By this means, the examiner will identify any opacities in the media—for example, vitreous hemorrhage or traumatic cataract.

2.   The patient is asked to fixate into the distance with the other eye. (If he or she focuses for near, the examiner will have difficulty focusing the ophthalmoscope.)

3.   If a bright light reflex gets in the way, it is reflecting from the cornea. The ophthalmoscope is rotated very slightly, and the light reflex will diminish or disappear, as it will no longer be reflected back along the examiner's visual pathway.

4.   To observe a scene through a keyhole, the eye needs to be placed close to the keyhole. The same principle applies to ophthalmoscopy—the closer to the patient's eye the examiner is, the wider the angle of view.

5.   To examine the fovea, the patient is asked to look at the light.

6.   To examine the peripheral retina, the patient is asked to move his or her eye in sequence in different directions. When the patient looks up, the examiner is looking at the upper retina as it is brought down into view, and the same principle applies to the other positions of gaze.

EXAMINATION OF EYE MOVEMENTS

Eye movements are commonly impaired following facial and head injury. It must be remembered, however, that an antecedent squint is not uncommon. Moreover, ptosis, blurred vision due to the eye injury, amblyopia, and a history of patching the eye in childhood may all prevent the patient from experiencing double vision. Eye movements are, therefore, objectively assessed in all patients sustaining an injury likely to be complicated by a motility disorder (e.g., a blow-out fracture). Figure 20–3 indicates the primary positions of action of each of the extraocular muscles. The eye movements into each of these positions of gaze are examined.

The assessment of eye movements is a skilled procedure. The following strategy is suggested as a means of identifying those patients warranting referral.

The examiner sits directly opposite the patient and uses a penlight to examine the eye movements. The penlight is moved in a manner similar to that for peripheral visual field testing. The light is held at approximately 0.33 m from the patient. The examiner observes the exact position of the light reflexes on the cornea with respect to the pupil. The patient is asked to follow the light. The light is moved in an arc directly upward, with the light constantly directed at the eyes, and the symmetry of the light reflexes and the symmetry of the positions of gaze are closely examined (Fig. 20–3). The skilled observer is able to detect most motility disorders.

The cover/uncover test is performed while the patient fixates on the light in the primary position of gaze and in the positions of gaze in which double vision is experienced and a motility disorder has been detected. An eye occluder or piece of card is used. The examiner watches one eye and covers the other one. The eye the examiner is watching should not move. If the eye does move to look at the light, it is a "squinting" or deviated eye. The procedure is repeated for the other eye. This method provides an objective means of validating and quantifying the patient's subjective double vision.

The Forced Duction Test.   This test is performed on a patient with a motility

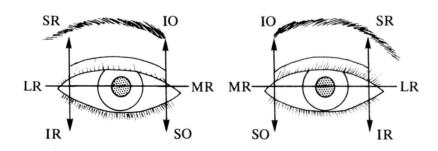

FIGURE 20–3. Diagram illustrating the actions of the extraocular muscles. SR = superior rectus; IR = inferior rectus; LR = lateral rectus; MR = medial rectus; SO = superior oblique; IO = inferior oblique.

disorder in whom the differential diagnosis between entrapment and muscle weakness is in doubt. Topical local anesthetic (e.g., benoxinate) is instilled into both eyes. The conjunctiva in line with the muscle in question is grasped just adjacent to the corneoscleral junction (the limbus) with a pair of fine-toothed forceps, and the globe is gently rotated. The procedure is repeated for the other eye to allow a comparison between eyes to be made. The force required to rotate the globe is estimated in relation to the normal contralateral eye. Tethering of the globe is indicative of entrapment.

An alternative means of rotating the globe is to use a cotton-wool bud soaked in local anesthetic and to rotate the globe by pressing the bud onto the eye and applying a tangential force. With practice, this method can be equally sensitive and is less likely to cause subconjunctival hemorrhage.

THE POSITION OF THE GLOBE

In every case of facial fracture, the position of the eye should be carefully examined. The eyes may be displaced in any one of three dimensions.

Horizontal Displacement. This displacement is measured by comparing the distance from the center of the bridge of the nose to the center of the pupil on each side.

Vertical Displacement. This displacement is most easily assessed using a short clear plastic ruler, which is held horizontally with reference to symmetric landmarks, such as the eyebrows. Any vertical displacement of one eye with respect to the other is then measured with a second ruler. (A vertical displacement of the globe may be misinterpreted as a squint; however, the light reflexes are symmetric and there is no diplopia.)

Anteroposterior Displacement (Enophthalmos or Exophthalmos). This displacement is most accurately measured using an exophthalmometer. Such instruments, however, use the lateral orbital margin as the reference point, which precludes their use in cases in which there is bone displacement or asymmetric swelling of the soft tissues of the orbital margin. An alternative means of assessment in such cases is to examine the patient from above, comparing the positions of the corneas with respect to the supraorbital margins. With experience, a fairly accurate assessment can be obtained with this method.

MINOR EYE INJURIES

Subconjunctival Hemorrhage and Bruised Eyelids

Subconjunctival hemorrhage with bruised eyelids commonly follows midfacial injury. Blood may track forward from an orbital injury, or bleeding may take place locally. A clear demarcation line to the bruising of the eyelid suggests orbital hemorrhage. Such bruising is usually benign, but it may be related to severe ophthalmic injury. Careful examination of the eye is required in every case.

Corneal Abrasion or Corneal Foreign Body

This injury causes severe pain, blurring of vision, photophobia, and lacrimation (except in the presence of corneal anesthesia). Loss of the corneal epithelium may be caused by direct injury to the eye or inadequate eyelid closure due to facial palsy, eyelid laceration, or injury during surgery. Alcohol-based skin preparations, incomplete eyelid closure, and accidental injury to the cornea during surgery must all be carefully avoided. When such a lesion is suspected, fluorescein stain allows a diagnosis to be made.

Treatment

After the administration of one drop of topical local anesthetic (which allows clinical examination and gives temporary pain relief), a short-acting cycloplegic agent, such as cyclopentolate (which alleviates pain due to ciliary spasm), and a topical antibiotic are instilled. An oral analgesic may also be required. If a foreign body is present, it is removed. A corneal foreign body is removed with great care, preferably using binocular magnification. A foreign body on the surface of the cornea can usually be lifted off by using a hypodermic needle held tangential to the corneal surface, ensuring throughout the procedure that the patient is unable to move forward toward the needle. A pad and bandage are applied, and the patient is examined 24 hours later.

NONPERFORATING EYE INJURIES

A blunt injury severe enough to cause an orbital fracture may also damage the eye. Depending on the nature, direction, and force of the injury, any anatomic component of the globe may be disrupted. The effects of blunt injury can be divided into those resulting from distortion and those due to concussion. Both types of injury are commonly seen in the same eye.

A high-speed anteroposterior force results in marked distortion of the globe[8] (Fig. 20–4). The eye is transiently deformed, with marked distention in the coronal plane and shortening of the anteroposterior dimension. The sclera is inelastic, and the aqueous and vitreous cannot be compressed. The iris, ciliary body, zonule of the lens, and peripheral retina may be torn from their insertions, and in severe cases the sclera may rupture. Distortion of the posterior segment of the eye can result in a tear of the choroid associated with subretinal hemorrhage and, in the most severe case, avulsion of the optic nerve from the globe.

The concussional component of the injury results from a coup-contrecoup effect. The cells of the cornea, lens, retina, and choroid are all susceptible to such injury and may transiently or permanently cease to function.

In this section, the results of injury to each component of the eye are discussed separately. However, almost any combination of injuries can occur.

Conjunctiva and Cornea

Swelling of the conjunctiva (chemosis) is common in association with subconjunctival hemorrhage and resolves spontaneously. A tear of the conjunctiva is suggestive of a more severe blunt injury. In every case, internal injury to the globe must be sought.

Loss of the corneal epithelium (Fig. 20–5) is fairly common and causes the same signs and symptoms as a corneal erosion.

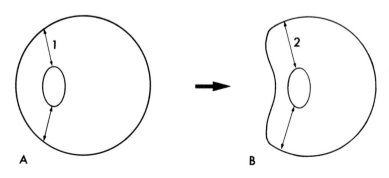

A   B

FIGURE 20–4. *A* and *B*, Diagram illustrating distortion of the eye produced by anteroposterior injury to the globe. During the brief period of distortion, the coronal diameter is elongated, and the zonule, iris, ciliary body, and vitreous adhesions to the peripheral retina are stretched (arrows 1 and 2), thus resulting in lens subluxation, angle recession or iridodialysis, cyclodialysis (rare), and retinal dialysis, respectively.

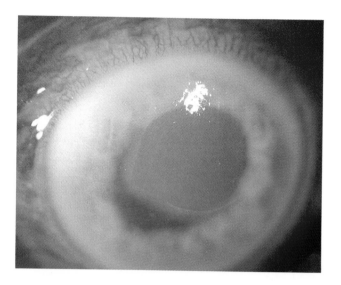

FIGURE 20–5. Photograph of a corneal erosion stained with fluorescein dye. There is also a diffuse subconjunctival hematoma due to the injury.

The corneal endothelium comprises a monolayer of cells that probably do not replicate following injury. Their function is to maintain the clarity of the cornea by pumping water out of the cornea and into the anterior chamber. Damage to the corneal endothelium results from a combination of contusion, reactive inflammation, and raised intraocular pressure.[9] This condition may culminate in permanent edema if the endothelial cell population is reduced below a critical level. Recovery of corneal clarity can take place in some patients after a number of months. However, if corneal edema is persistent, a penetrating corneal graft is required to restore visual function.

Anterior Chamber

The anterior chamber comprises the space between the cornea and the iris and is occupied by aqueous fluid secreted from the ciliary processes. Blunt trauma can result in bleeding into the anterior chamber (hyphema) (Fig. 20–6) and inflammation.

HYPHEMA

Hyphema, or bleeding in the anterior chamber, probably results in most cases from tearing of blood vessels at the root of the iris.[10] When the patient is vertical, the blood settles at a fluid level, the height of which should be measured daily. The amount of bleeding is related to the long-term prognosis.[11] A history of blurring of vision after the patient lies down, which gradually clears spontaneously when the patient is erect, indicates that a small hyphema may have been missed. The majority of

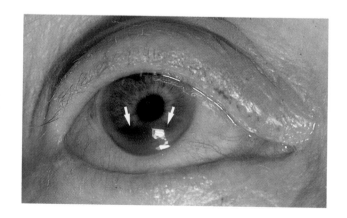

FIGURE 20–6. Horizontal fluid level of blood in the anterior chamber (hyphema; *arrows*) secondary to blunt eye injury.

patients with hyphema are admitted to the hospital and observed. In most cases, spontaneous resorption of hemorrhage takes place, but in a small portion rebleeding can occur. Severe hemorrhage may be associated with impairment in the drainage of aqueous, which leads to a raised intraocular pressure. Under these circumstances, blood staining of the cornea may take place. Oral intake of aspirin increases the incidence of rebleeding and is absolutely contraindicated.

TRAUMATIC IRITIS

Traumatic iritis is common. Injury to the iris results in the release of protein and inflammatory cells into the anterior chamber, which can be observed by means of a slit-lamp microscope. Traumatic iritis is treated by using topical steroids (e.g., dexamethasone or betamethasone) and a drug such as atropine to dilate the pupil. This treatment prevents the iris from sticking down to the lens behind (posterior synechiae).

Abnormal Depth of the Anterior Chamber

On macroscopic examination, the anterior chambers are compared by viewing each eye obliquely from the side, to provide an approximate estimate of depth. The slit-lamp is used to obtain a more accurate assessment. Shallowness of the anterior chamber may suggest hemorrhage into the choroid, a choroidal detachment, swelling of the lens, or leakage of aqueous through a penetrating wound.

Deepening of the anterior chamber suggests that the lens may have been subluxated or dislocated.

Iris and Pupil

An iridodialysis (Fig. 20–7) results when the iris is ripped from its root. This condition is clearly apparent on direct ophthalmoscopy because a red reflex is seen through the tear as well as through the pupil.

Traumatic mydriasis (Fig. 20–8) is common following blunt eye injury. In this case, the pupil fails to react both directly and consensually. Pupil sphincter rupture can be seen with the slit-lamp. It produces a widely dilated pupil and is permanent. On the other hand, a mid-dilated pupil without a pupil sphincter rupture ordinarily recovers its function during the ensuing weeks.

A spastic miosis (small pupil) is common after less severe blunt injury to the globe.

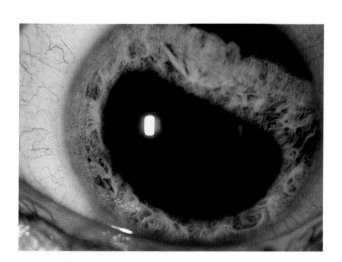

FIGURE 20–7. Iridodialysis. The superior iris has been ripped from its insertion by a blunt compressive eye injury.

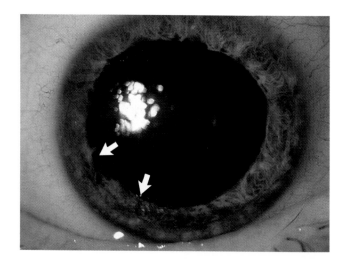

FIGURE 20–8. **Traumatic mydriasis.** The arrows indicate the points at which the pupil sphincter has been torn.

In such cases, the miosis may be accompanied by a transient spasm of accommodation brought about by axonal reflexes. This spasm may be followed within minutes or hours by a paralytic mydriasis.

Care should be taken to exclude other causes of pupillary dilation, such as an antecedent Adie's pupil and, in the unconscious patient, a cranial nerve III palsy resulting from intracranial injury with tentorial herniation of the cerebrum.

Angle Recession

In some cases, the iris may be partially stripped from its root without being torn completely. In severe injury, this may take place for the 360-degree circumference of the eye. Lesser degrees of angle recession are more common.

This injury results in damage to the cells that line the surface of the trabecular meshwork. As the name implies, this structure is like a fine three-dimensional web or sponge through which the aqueous passes into the canal of Schlemm and then returns to the blood stream. Subsequent fibrosis and scarring in the region of the angle can diminish the outflow of aqueous and thereby result in a raised intraocular pressure. This can occur either acutely or many years later. In one long-term prospective study, the total incidence of glaucoma at 10-year follow-up was found to be 10 per cent, with 6 per cent of cases having late onset.[12]

Angle recession occurs at the time of injury and may be seen by gonioscopic examination (slit-lamp examination using a prism system to see into the angle) permanently thereafter. It can, however, be easily missed if this examination is not done. The medicolegal implications are obvious.

Lens

Subluxation of the lens (Fig. 20–9) is most easily diagnosed following full dilation of the pupil. The margin of the subluxated lens can then be seen. Additional clinical signs include a reduction in visual acuity, deepening of the anterior chamber, and wobbling of the iris, which is seen as a fine shimmer as the patient moves the eye (iridodonesis).

In severe cases, the lens may be dislocated. In this situation, it lies freely in the vitreous, and an aphakic correction is required to allow the patient to see. Rarely, the lens may dislocate into the anterior chamber. This dislocation is an ophthalmic emergency, as it may interfere with the flow of aqueous and cause an unusual form of acute glaucoma.

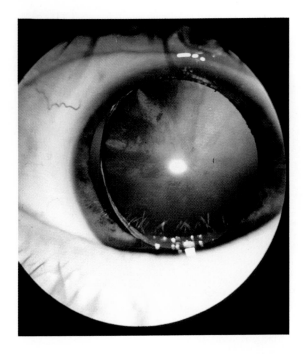

FIGURE 20–9. **Subluxation of the lens.**   The edge of the lens is seen to be distinct from the dilated pupil margin.

Both subluxation and dislocation of the lens result in a change in the patient's refraction. However, in such cases, the injury is likely to have been severe enough to give rise to other reasons for visual impairment. In addition, the lens is likely to develop opacities (cataract) with time.

Small, discrete subepithelial and subcapsular lens opacities or a rosette-shaped posterior subcapsular cataract (Fig. 20–10) may develop shortly after severe concussive injury. In serious cases, the pupillary margin is impacted upon the anterior surface of the lens to leave a pigmented ring (Vossius' ring) deposited on the anterior lens capsule. The presence of such a ring indicates that the injury has been very severe and that the eye should be thoroughly examined for other pathology.

Rupture of the lens capsule may also take place. This rupture allows aqueous humor into the lens, which then becomes opalescent. Release of soft lens matter into the eye can result in severe inflammation. Lens protein is sequestered from the immune system during embryonic development and is thus perceived by the immune system as "foreign." This situation can result in a severe inflammatory reaction within the eye. Surgical removal of the lens is indicated in such cases.

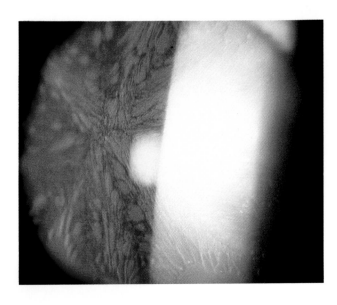

FIGURE 20–10. **Traumatic posterior subcapsular cataract.** This red reflex photograph illustrates the "sunflower" appearance that characterizes such cataracts.

Ciliary Body

The functions of the ciliary body are to produce aqueous humor, which provides nutriment for the eye and maintains the intraocular pressure, and to bring about accommodation of the lens. When the ciliary muscle contracts, the zonule relaxes and the lens adopts a more biconvex shape, which causes the eye to focus for near.

Damage to the ciliary body can, therefore, result in impairment in the formation of aqueous and a consequent reduction in intraocular pressure. Moreover, injury to the ciliary muscle gives rise to impairment in accommodation, which is a fairly common short-term sequela of eye injury. The patient complains that he or she has difficulty in focusing, and clinical examination reveals that the near point of accommodation (the nearest point at which he or she can focus clearly) is farther away than prior to the injury. There is no specific treatment for either of these conditions. The intraocular pressure is normally restored during the few days following injury, and accommodation similarly recovers spontaneously in most cases.

Traumatic cyclodialysis refers to the tearing of the ciliary body from its root. This condition is unusual and results from severe blunt eye injury. A persistent very low intraocular pressure may indicate that a cyclodialysis has taken place.

CHANGES IN INTRAOCULAR PRESSURE

Reduced Intraocular Pressure. The intraocular pressure is commonly reduced after blunt trauma to the eye. The normal range of intraocular pressure is 12 to 20 mm Hg. A pressure between 5 and 10 mm Hg may follow blunt injury, presumably because of damage to the ciliary body. However, the intraocular pressure may be reduced to 0 to 2 mm Hg when the differential diagnosis includes cyclodialysis, scleral rupture, and severe diffuse injury to the ciliary body. A persistently low intraocular pressure may be associated with choroidal effusions.

Raised Intraocular Pressure. Glaucoma can be defined as a condition in which the intraocular pressure is sufficiently raised to cause damage to ocular structures, whether it be transient or permanent. Ocular hypertension, on the other hand, is a condition in which the intraocular pressure is raised without detectable damage to the eye.

The causes of raised intraocular pressure include angle recession, traumatic iritis, hyphema, blockage of the trabecular meshwork by lens debris, and ghost cell glaucoma, which is a condition that occasionally follows hemorrhage into the vitreous. Multiple ghost cells, which are erythrocytes without hemoglobin, are seen histologically to occlude the trabecular meshwork.

Treatment comprises reduction in intraocular pressure with a topical beta-blocker, such as timolol; oral or parenteral acetazolamide or dichlorphenamide may also be required. Traumatic iritis is treated as described previously. If the lens has been damaged and is causing glaucoma, surgical removal of the lens is indicated. When a hyphema is severe enough to cause significantly raised intraocular pressure, surgical removal of the blood is considered to prevent the complications of staining of the cornea and ocular damage caused by the high pressure.

When the intraocular pressure is very low or very high, this can be detected by gentle palpation of the globe using the forefingers through the closed eyelid. A comparison is made between the two eyes. A markedly raised pressure gives rise to the ophthalmoscopic sign of spontaneous arterial pulsation at the optic nerve head. This sign occurs when the intraocular pressure is sufficiently elevated to be above the diastolic perfusion pressure of the central retinal artery. During diastole, the central retinal artery collapses but becomes patent during systole. This phenomenon may be seen when the intraocular pressure is above 40 mm Hg.

A marked, acute rise in intraocular pressure may rarely occur following eye injury. It causes severe pain, photophobia, and a sensation of seeing halos around lights. Clinical examination reveals a mid-dilated, nonreacting pupil; circumlimbal infection (i.e., a red eye, particularly the area of the sclera close to the cornea); and hardness of the eye upon palpation. Corneal edema prevents examination of the posterior segment by direct ophthalmoscopy. On the other hand, a gradual rise in intraocular pressure may cause no symptoms or a mild, aching pain around the eye. In the chronic case, gradual cupping of the optic nerve head ensues, with progressive loss of visual field.

In cases in which the intraocular pressure is not controlled by using drugs, surgical treatment by trabeculectomy is considered. In this operation, a fistula is created between the anterior chamber and the subconjunctival space.

Retinal Injury and Choroidal Injury

RETINAL DETACHMENT

The distortional effects of concussive injury may cause retinal detachment (Fig. 20–11). The vitreous gel is firmly adherent to the peripheral retina, and the acute coronal distention that accompanies anteroposterior blunt eye injury can result in the retina being torn. This condition causes a retinal dialysis (Fig. 20–12) or the formation of a retinal hole because the distortional forces produce vitreous traction at the retinal periphery. Laboratory experiments indicate that the majority of retinal breaks caused by contusion are formed at the time of injury.[8,13]

It has been suggested that virtually all cases of retinal dialysis are secondary to trauma.[14] Approximately 10 per cent of traumatic retinal detachments occur immediately, 70 per cent within 2 years, and 20 per cent more than 2 years after injury.[15] Retinal dialysis is most common in the superonasal quadrant. Retinal hole formation is probably caused by local retinal hemorrhage and necrosis. In these cases, the holes are most commonly found in the inferonasal quadrant, which is the most frequent site of impact.

Injuries to the globe may also cause changes in the vitreous (syneresis) in which the vitreous gel collapses and tearing of the peripheral retina results. The patient may complain of the sudden development of floaters (due to the condensation of the vitreous and vitreous hemorrhage) accompanied by a sensation of flashing lights in the periphery of the vision. Any patient presenting with such symptoms should be carefully examined by a surgeon who specializes in retinal detachment.

The embryologic derivation of the eye is such that the retina is not firmly adherent to the underlying pigment epithelium. If a hole or tear develops, fluid derived from the vitreous may pass through the hole and gradually lift the retina off. As soon as the retina is detached, the part that is detached does not function.

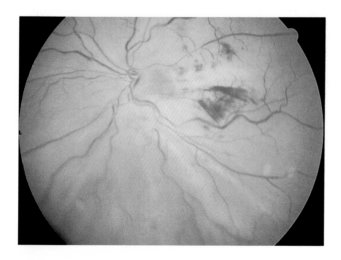

FIGURE 20–11.   Retinal detachment. A severe blunt injury has resulted in intraretinal hematoma and retinal detachment.

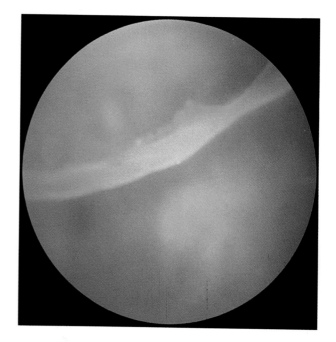

FIGURE 20–12. **Retinal dialysis**. This peripheral retinal photograph shows the torn edge of the retina, which is curled over.

Treatment of a retinal detachment is complex and not always successful in restoring normal vision. It is, therefore, important to prevent retinal detachment by sealing the retinal holes by means of photocoagulation or cryotherapy. All patients who have sustained significant blunt ocular injury sufficient to cause any of the internal anatomic disturbances described previously should be seen by a surgeon specializing in retinal detachment to screen for and treat peripheral retinal breaks and tears.

Exudative retinal detachment is a rare sequel to blunt eye injury. Extensive blunt injury to the retina can result in the accumulation of subretinal fluid, presumably because the pigment epithelium is damaged to such an extent that it is unable to pump the water through, into the choroid. In these cases, the retina may flatten spontaneously, but the prognosis for the recovery of vision is poor.

TRAUMATIC RETINAL EDEMA

Traumatic retinal edema is also known as commotio retinae or Berlin's edema (Fig. 20–13). If the injury involves the retina of the posterior pole, the patient complains of rapid loss of vision following the injury. If, however, the injury is more peripheral, the patient may be asymptomatic, as only the peripheral visual field is

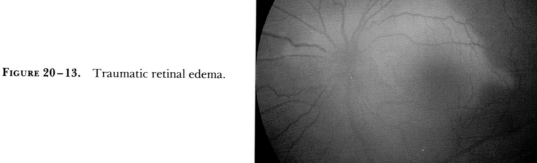

FIGURE 20–13. Traumatic retinal edema.

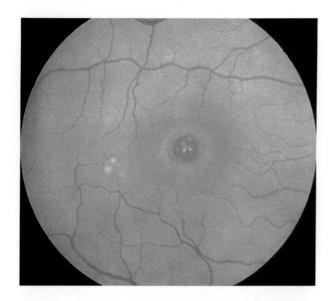

FIGURE 20-14.   Macular hole. There is a central retinal hole resulting from necrosis after eye injury.

affected. The majority of patients report a rapid improvement in vision during the first 40 minutes or so after injury.[16] In some cases, however, severe injury may not be accompanied by such rapid improvement, and fluorescein angiography demonstrates that there is breakdown in the function of the pigment epithelium of the retina.[16,17] Experimental studies have shown that following severe injury, fragmentation of the photoreceptor outer segments and damage to the retinal pigment epithelium occur at the site of impact and gradual regeneration of the photoreceptor segments subsequently takes place.[18]

In some cases, after central retinal edema, a hole (Fig. 20-14) or cyst may develop at the macula and central vision does not return.

TRAUMATIC PIGMENTARY RETINOPATHY

Following a very severe blunt injury to the retina, photoreceptor disruption and damage to the pigment epithelial cells occur to such an extent that post-traumatic replication and migration of pigment epithelial cells give rise to a clinical pattern indistinguishable from that of retinitis pigmentosa. This condition is accompanied by little recovery of function.[19,20]

RETINAL AND VITREOUS HEMORRHAGE

Rupture of the blood vessels may be accompanied by hemorrhage into the retina and into the vitreous, with loss of vision. Spontaneous recovery of vision accompanies resolution of the vitreous hemorrhage. Occasionally, fibrosis in the vitreous can result in a tractional retinal detachment.

CHOROIDAL TEAR

Tears of the choroid (Fig. 20-15) characteristically occur circumferential to the optic disc and follow concussional injury in which the eye is severely compressed and distorted. The patient is aware of loss of central vision. This vision loss is attributable initially to extensive subretinal hemorrhage. The tear of the choroid cannot at this stage be seen. Over the ensuing weeks, as the hemorrhage resolves, the choroidal tear becomes apparent, and a line of underlying white sclera, usually concentric with the optic disc, can be seen on ophthalmoscopy. If the tear does not pass through the fovea, the prognosis for spontaneous recovery of vision is good. However, a lesion beneath the fovea results in loss of central vision. A choroidal tear can be complicated by the

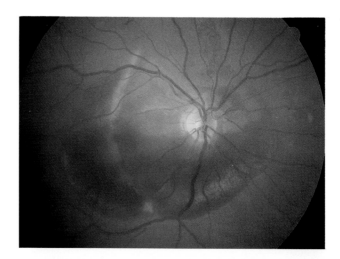

FIGURE 20-15. *A traumatic choroidal tear* has resulted in subretinal hematoma, which is clearing to reveal the tear passing through the macula.

development of abnormal new blood vessels beneath the retina, which may themselves bleed. In some cases, such a lesion may warrant laser photocoagulation. All patients with a choroidal tear should, therefore, be evaluated and followed up by an ophthalmologist.

CHOROIDAL EFFUSION

In cases of ocular hypotonia (see previous discussion), the choroid may detach from the underlying sclera owing to the accumulation of underlying plasma-like fluid. Treatment for the hypotonia (e.g., by closing a scleral rupture surgically) usually results in spontaneous reapposition of the choroid.

SCLERAL RUPTURE

It is important to recognize that a rupture of sclera may be "silent" and that the only clinical sign is ocular hypotonia. The most common site of indirect rupture of the sclera is the superonasal quadrant close to the limbus.[21] In one series of 34 cases of scleral rupture, 18 per cent were associated with orbital fracture.[21] If a scleral rupture is not repaired, persistent hypotonia or the ingrowth of fibrous tissue into the eye may develop. In addition, sympathetic ophthalmia, in which inflammation of the other eye occurs, may rarely complicate scleral rupture.

Surgical exploration is indicated in the majority of cases of persistent hypotonia for which there is no alternative explanation, as repair of the scleral rupture is usually accompanied by restoration of intraocular pressure and prevents the complication of fibrous ingrowth.

AVULSION OF THE OPTIC NERVE

In very severe injuries, the optic nerve may be avulsed from the eye, with accompanying permanent loss of vision (Fig. 20-16).

PERFORATING EYE INJURIES

It is important to recognize that perforation of the globe may accompany orbital fractures, particularly in patients who have been involved in road traffic accidents.

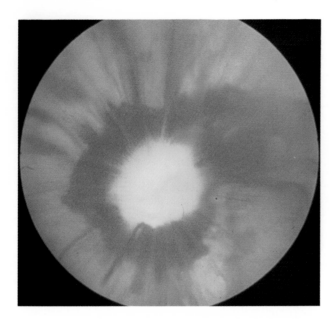

FIGURE 20–16.   Optic nerve avulsion.   Severe trauma has resulted in the optic nerve's being avulsed from the eye.

Any patient who has sustained multiple facial lacerations must be suspected of having a corneoscleral laceration until proved otherwise.

A detailed history of the nature of the circumstances surrounding the injury is required. Penetrating injuries still continue to be missed and are a major source of litigation. Perforation may be caused by a small fast-flying missile, resulting in a retained intraocular foreign body, or by a sharp implement.

The visual acuity is ascertained (when possible). The eye is inspected with great care, with the examiner taking every precaution to preclude pressure on the globe, which could result in the herniation of ocular contents. The eyelids are, therefore, retracted without direct pressure on the ball of the eye. The eye and adnexa are examined for the following:

1. Laceration or perforation of the eyelids
2. Evidence of a foreign body
3. Perforation of the globe
4. Asymmetry of the pupil, which could be due to prolapse of the iris
5. Opacification of the ocular media caused by intraocular hemorrhage
6. A shallow anterior chamber
7. Prolapse of the iris, ciliary body, or vitreous.

Radiologic examination is mandatory for all cases of suspected retained intraocular foreign bodies. All patients with confirmed or suspected perforating eye injuries should be transferred immediately to the care of an ophthalmologist. No food or drink is given in preparation for emergency surgery. A light pad is applied to the eye, but to avoid undue pressure, no bandages are applied. Perforating injuries are managed by the ophthalmologist by direct repair of the perforation using 10–0 nylon for the cornea and 5–0 or 7–0 sutures for the sclera. If there has been iris incarceration for more than 24 hours, this is excised. When the lens has been damaged, this is commonly removed at the time of surgery, and if there is lens debris or hemorrhage within the vitreous, this is removed by means of vitrectomy either as a primary or as a secondary procedure. Donor corneal material may be required if there has been loss of corneal tissue.

An ophthalmologist's opinion must be immediately sought because endophthalmitis is a major complication of such injuries and appropriate prophylactic antibiotic treatment must be instituted as soon as possible. Intravenous broad-spectrum antibiotics are indicated if perforation is obvious and surgical repair is delayed.

PERFORATING INJURIES OF THE ORBIT

Nonorganic intraorbital foreign bodies, such as airgun pellets, are usually inert, and it is commonly considered safer to leave such a foreign body in the orbit than to remove it. However, if an airgun pellet is immediately accessible, surgical removal is indicated. An airgun pellet may ricochet off the sclera as it enters the orbit. Therefore, full clinical examination of the peripheral retina is indicated in every case because necrosis of the choroid and retina occurs at the impact site (Fig. 20–17) and a subsequent retinal detachment may ensue. Such a detachment can be prevented by appropriate and timely surgery.

A high index of clinical suspicion is required if there is a small perforating wound of the eyelid. A detailed history may provide useful information. A foreign body retained in the orbit may be radiopaque, but organic material, such as a thorn or a piece of wood, may be radiolucent and may require computerized tomography (CT) for optimal imaging.[22] Detailed scrutiny of the radiographs is required to exclude perforation of the orbital roof, which may lead to the development of a brain abscess.[23] Perforation of the globe should also be considered in the presence of such an injury.[24]

RETROBULBAR HEMORRHAGE

Intraorbital hemorrhage is a common sequel to midfacial fracture. In the majority of cases, this problem resolves spontaneously, with no adverse sequelae. Venous hemorrhage probably causes no problem, but arterial hemorrhage can lead to compromise of optic nerve function and central retinal artery obstruction. This complication is most likely in young individuals, in whom the orbital septum is inelastic and impermeable, thus preventing spontaneous decompression by anterior displacement of the globe and leakage of blood into subcutaneous tissues. Arterial bleeding may occur as a direct result of the injury, perhaps from rupture of the infraorbital artery or the anterior or posterior ethmoidal arteries, or it may occur as a postoperative complication of surgical exploration of the orbit.

Clinical Features

The patient complains of a severe aching pain accompanied by progressive loss of vision. Proptosis occurs and is accompanied by raised intraocular pressure, marked subconjunctival hemorrhage, and gross eyelid swelling. As vision is lost, the pupil becomes fixed and dilated.

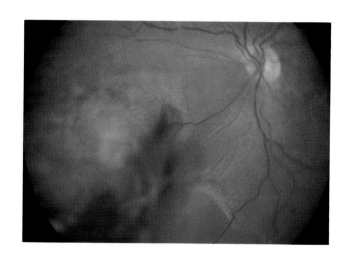

FIGURE 20–17. Chorioretinal necrosis and hematoma due to an airgun pellet injury to the sclera.

Management

Arterial bleeding within the orbit is an ophthalmic emergency. The visual acuity, pupillary reaction, and intraocular pressure are recorded initially at 5-minute intervals. (In the unconscious patient, reliance is placed on the pupillary reaction and intraocular pressure alone.) In some cases, spontaneous decompression takes place and surgical intervention is not required. In this situation, progressive loss of vision, proptosis, and elevation of intraocular pressure are documented for the first 10 to 20 minutes, but the vision spontaneously recovers thereafter. No treatment may be required.

If, after 20 minutes, spontaneous recovery does not occur, the loss of vision is progressive, the intraocular pressure becomes markedly elevated (*e.g., 30 to 40 mm Hg, with a normal range of 12 to 20 mm Hg*), and the pupil reaction becomes sluggish, immediate therapeutic intervention is required. In the postsurgical case, the surgical wound is opened and blood may escape under pressure. The patient may be aware of an immediate spontaneous improvement in vision, and the normal pupillary reaction returns. The source of bleeding is arrested.

In other cases, the source of bleeding may not be known. The patient may be treated medically with a slow intravenous injection of acetazolamide (500 mg), which reduces intraocular pressure. When the site of the hemorrhage is not known, surgical treatment comprises lateral canthotomy, in which the palpebral aperture is widened, and lateral cantholysis, in which a pair of sharp-pointed scissors is used to divide the lateral canthal ligament. This procedure allows the globe to move forward and is usually accompanied by a temporary and sometimes permanent improvement in vision. If imaging facilities are available, an immediate orbital CT scan is performed, and any loculus of blood is drained. When a CT scan is not available and visual function deteriorates further, division of the orbital septum superiorly and inferiorly, with insertion of drains, is carried out. Only rarely is this procedure accompanied by release of hemorrhage; however, it does allow for prolapse of orbital fat and thereby gives rise to orbital decompression, which may be accompanied by improvement in visual function.

TRAUMATIC OPTIC NEUROPATHY

Rowbotham[25] has classified traumatic optic neuropathy on the basis of a review of 3.6 per cent (66 cases) of 1800 patients with facial injury.

Anterior Marginal Tear (12 per cent).   This tear is diagnosed on the basis of the following signs. The development of a nerve fiber bundle visual field defect associated with early optic nerve pallor in one sector is suggestive of anterior optic nerve injury. This problem may be accompanied by spasm of the retinal vessels and, in some cases, hemorrhage at the optic disc margin that is associated with subsequent pigmentation. The disturbance of visual acuity and visual field depends upon the site and severity of the injury. Loss of vision is incomplete, but only little recovery takes place. The mechanism of damage is probably torsion of the globe with respect to the optic nerve.

Damage to the Anterior Optic Nerve (13 per cent).   This condition follows frontal head injury and is usually accompanied by a local skull fracture. There is evidence of injury to the optic nerve behind the level of the optic disc but anterior to the entry of the central retinal artery.

Clinical examination of the posterior pole reveals the appearance of a central retinal artery occlusion with retinal edema in which the retina is pale and the retinal arteries are attenuated. Severe and complete loss of vision was seen in the majority of Rowbotham's cases.

Canalicular Optic Nerve Damage (65 per cent).   In most cases (70 per cent), this damage follows frontal injury. The patient is subject to immediate loss of vision.

The prognosis for vision is poor, with fewer than 20 per cent of patients developing useful recovery of vision. Pallor of the optic disc ensues with an average time of onset of 23 days. In Rowbotham's series, visual field loss occurred primarily in the lower visual field in 70 per cent of cases, which lent support to a vascular etiology for this injury, as it mirrored the clinical features of presumed hypertensive and arteritic posterior ischemic optic neuropathy.[25] Such injury is probably due to stretching, thrombosis, or tearing of the small vessels supplying the optic nerve, and surgical decompression is probably not indicated. The indication for surgical exploration is that of initial recovery of vision with late deterioration, in which case the deterioration may occasionally be reversed by dividing the traumatic arachnoid adhesions that may develop.

Heinze[26] carried out a study of the pathology of the optic nerve in patients who sustained traumatic optic neuropathy and subsequently died. In the majority of cases, hemorrhage into the optic nerve sheath was seen. In only 1 of 21 cases was laceration of the nerve observed, and partial division of the optic chiasm occurred in one other case.

Comparison of groups of patients treated with or without operative decompression of the optic nerve reveals that the overall prognosis for visual recovery is the same in both groups, with improvement in vision in 25 to 40 per cent and no recovery in the remainder.[27] Recovery of vision has, however, been reported following removal of a hematoma in the optic nerve sheath.[28] The role of decompression procedures remains controversial, and the indications are not clear. It has been suggested that a narrowed or dislocated optic foramen, accompanied by slowly progressive loss of vision, provides a relative indication for surgical exploration.[28]

Unlike with rapid loss of vision, for which there is probably no effective treatment, high-dose steroids may be of benefit if there is gradual, progressive loss of vision.

Chiasmal Injury

Frontal injury close to the midline is most likely to give rise to chiasmal injury. Although occasional cases of chiasmal tears have been reported,[26] in the majority of instances, no microscopic injuries are seen. The result is immediate bitemporal hemianopia, which may be explained by occlusion of the central chiasmal artery. In some cases, optochiasmal injuries may occur in which the eye on one side is blind and the eye on the other side has temporal hemianopic field loss. Patients complaining of subtle impairment in visual function following head injury should undergo a detailed examination of the visual field, as subtle upper quadrantic bitemporal field defects may occur that would otherwise be missed.

Surgical exploration has been advocated in those cases in which late deterioration of vision has occurred owing to presumed optochiasmal arachnoiditis. In such cases, a neurosurgical opinion should be sought.

DISORDERS OF OCULAR MOTILITY

Disturbances in ocular motility may arise from (1) disorders of the central control of eye movement; (2) injury to cranial nerves III, IV, or VI; or (3) orbital injury with associated muscle injury or entrapment.

Disorders of Central Control of Eye Movement

IMPAIRMENT OR FAILURE OF CONVERGENCE

This impairment may follow closed-head injury. The exact pathogenesis is uncertain but may be related to upper midbrain injury. When convergence is impaired, the patient complains of difficulty in reading and looking at near objects. Complete paralysis of convergence causes symptoms of double vision whenever the patient attempts to focus for near. In the majority of cases, spontaneous recovery takes place. Diplopia resulting from failure of the convergence has also been reported after whiplash injuries to the cervical spine.[29] In some cases, it may be difficult to determine whether failure of convergence results from organic pathology or is functional in origin.

LOSS OF FUSION

Loss of fusion of the images from both eyes may result in double vision. In this condition, the patient is unable to maintain single fused images when synoptophore, prism, or stereoscopic tests are employed.[30,31] Trauma is also a well-recognized cause of the breakdown of a pre-existing latent squint that has received orthoptic treatment by patching in the past.[32] The patient complains of constant diplopia. Both cerebral contusion with or without skull fracture and whiplash injury may cause this problem. Spontaneous recovery may or may not occur. As all tests of fusion require a subjective assessment by the patient, the results may on occasion be difficult to interpret, especially when compensation is involved.

LATERAL GAZE PALSY

Lateral gaze palsy is a condition in which there is impairment of the deviation of both eyes in a horizontal direction. Lesions of either the frontal cortex or the pons may cause this condition, with or without persistent conjugate deviation of the eyes. In cerebral contusion, the eyes are deviated toward the damaged side, and spontaneous recovery of function usually occurs within 1 to 4 weeks.[32] Pontine lesions, on the other hand, manifest a range of other clinical signs and tend not to improve. Caloric tests and the doll's eye phenomenon provide methods of distinguishing between the two pathologies. With cerebral lesions these tests are normal, whereas with pontine dysfunction they are abnormal.

SKEW DEVIATION

Skew deviation is a condition in which there is a vertical disparity in the position of the eyes on eccentric gaze. This condition may result from a closed-head injury. However, the sign is not of localizing value.[32]

PARINAUD'S SYNDROME

Parinaud's syndrome results from midbrain trauma. The pupils are mid-dilated and fixed, and there is impairment in convergence and paresis of upward gaze.[32]

POST-TRAUMATIC NYSTAGMUS

Post-traumatic nystagmus may occur as a result of trauma to the petrous part of the temporal bone, with associated damage to the labyrinthine system, or may be due to brainstem trauma.[32]

Cranial Nerve Injury

In a series of 1000 cases of ocular nerve palsies,[33] 16.8 per cent were found to be traumatic in origin (30 per cent, cranial nerve III; 14.5 per cent, cranial nerve IV; 34 per cent, cranial nerve VI; and 21.5 per cent, combinations). In a detailed neuropathologic assessment of patients in whom cranial nerve palsies developed after road traffic accidents but who failed to survive, cranial nerve III injuries comprised avulsion from the brainstem or contusion necrosis and intraneural-perineural hemorrhage in the region of the superior orbital fissure in equal proportion. There were six cases of abducens nerve injury. In five cases the nerve had been avulsed, and in only one was damage found at the point where the abducens nerve passes over the tip of the petrous temporal bone. Hemorrhage into the extraocular muscles close to the globe was found in 12 cases. This hemorrhage was commonly, but not invariably, associated with orbital fracture.[26]

CRANIAL NERVE III PALSY

Cranial nerve III palsy typically occurs following a frontal blow to the head, such as in a motorcycle accident. The condition is usually unilateral. There is ptosis, fixed dilation of the pupil (caused by the unopposed action of the sympathetic supply), and abduction with slight depression of the globe (caused by the unopposed actions of the lateral rectus and superior oblique muscles). Three outcomes are possible: (1) no recovery, (2) recovery because of regeneration, and (3) aberrant regeneration. Recovery may take between 6 and 9 months to occur. When aberrant regeneration occurs, paradoxical eye movements are observed. Typically, eyelid elevation occurs on attempted adduction or downward gaze. Pupil constriction and accommodation may accompany downward gaze, with pupil dilation on abduction. Co-contraction of the vertical recti may result in the restriction of upward gaze.

CRANIAL NERVE IV PALSY

Cranial nerve IV palsy may be unilateral or bilateral. The superior oblique muscle is responsible for depression of the globe in adduction and also produces intorsion. Vertical diplopia, which may be accompanied by torsional double vision (in which the two images appear to be rotated with respect to each other), occurs. Torsion is especially problematic with bilateral cases. Frontal anteroposterior trauma is the most common cause.[34] The presumed site of injury is the origin of the trochlear nerve from the posterior brainstem, perhaps following contrecoup injury upon the tentorium cerebelli. Spontaneous recovery may occur 3 to 6 months after injury. Surgery for the squint is deferred to allow recovery to take place.

CRANIAL NERVE VI PALSY

Cranial nerve VI palsy results in failure of abduction. The nerve may be damaged at its exit from the brainstem or within the cavernous sinus. Abducens palsy may also result from a traumatic caroticocavernous sinus fistula. Surgery for the squint is again deferred to allow spontaneous recovery to take place.[32]

Referral to an ophthalmologist is indicated for all cases of such cranial nerve injury. Sequential assessment is carried out to determine whether recovery is taking place prior to considering whether extraocular muscle surgery is indicated.

Ocular Motility Disorders Due to Orbital Injury

Diplopia is a common sequel to orbital injury. Causes include entrapment of an extraocular muscle or its adjacent fascia, intramuscular hemorrhage and edema, orbital hematoma, disinsertion of an extraocular muscle, and injury to the trochlea, through which passes the superior oblique tendon.[35]

ANATOMY OF THE ORBIT

The anatomy of the orbit is described in Chapter 12. The orbital walls are thin and are protected anteriorly by the thick orbital rim. The weak areas constitute the floor anterior to the inferior orbital fissure, which continues medially as the lamina papyracea of the ethmoid. The medial half of the orbital floor is weakened further by the infraorbital canal or groove. Fine connective tissue septa surround the globe and invest the muscles and other intraorbital contents. They connect with the periorbita of the orbit. In the case of an orbital fracture, entrapment of the septa may result in motility disturbance. The extensive interconnections of these septa probably contribute to the wide range of motility disorders that may follow an orbital wall fracture with little radiologic evidence of entrapment of soft tissue.[36]

Blow-out Fracture

Pfeiffer (1943)[37] was the first to review a series of cases with traumatic enophthalmos and proposed a possible mechanism of orbital floor fracture. In 1957, Smith and Regan[38] reproduced blow-out fractures experimentally in cadavers. They demonstrated that posterior impaction of the globe may cause a "blow-out" of the thin orbital floor by transmission of sudden pressure.

Similar fractures can, however, also be produced by blunt injury to the inferior orbital rim of a skull without orbital contents.[39] When a small missile (e.g., a squash ball) strikes the eye, a blow-out fracture is unlikely to occur, whereas a large, compressive object is more likely to cause such an injury. These data suggest that a compressive bone injury contributes significantly to the development of a pure blow-out fracture. Thus, both hydraulic forces and buckling of the inferior orbital floor probably contribute to the orbital floor blow-out fracture.[40] Converse and Smith[41] introduced the concepts of the pure blow-out fracture, in which only the orbital floor is involved, and the impure lesion, in which the compression produced in an orbital rim fracture causes a similar pathology.

CLINICAL SIGNS

The clinical signs of blow-out fracture are as follows:

1. *Enophthalmos* may initially be masked by tissue swelling. It may result from the combined effects of prolapse of orbital fat, enlargement of the size of the orbital cavity, fat necrosis due to trauma or infection, and fibrotic shortening of extraocular muscles.

2. *Impairment of eye movement*, which may cause diplopia,[42] may be due to muscle entrapment, fascial entrapment, injury to extraocular muscles, intraorbital or intramuscular hemorrhage, nerve damage, or the breakdown of a previously latent squint that becomes manifest.

Double vision may not occur for a number of reasons. One eye may have poor vision because of, for example, amblyopia. The authors have seen a number of cases in which there had been either previous eye injury or intrinsic eye pathology (e.g., retinal detachment) that perhaps contributed to the failure of the patient to take evasive action. Some patients who have received successful patching for amblyopia when they were children are unaware of double vision despite normal acuity in each eye. This situation is because of alternating fixation, in which the patient chooses to use one eye or the other but never both simultaneously. In such cases, the motility disorder does not per se provide an indication for surgery.

Typically, there is restriction of up and down gaze. Elevation of intraocular pressure on attempted upward gaze is suggestive of entrapment. Occasionally, retraction of the globe on upward gaze may be seen, owing to inferior rectus muscle entrapment. This is a subtle clinical sign in which the eye retracts back from the lower eyelid by about 0.5 to 1.0 mm. The eye movements are examined as described previously. It is important to differentiate between entrapment and muscle bruising. Retraction of the globe, elevation of intraocular pressure on upward gaze, and a positive forced duction test can be helpful in this regard. Fast up and down eye movements (saccades) are also examined. The examiner holds an extended forefinger of each hand in the upper and lower visual fields and instructs the patient to look up and down at them in turn. Typically, with muscle bruising, a slower eye movement is observed, whereas with entrapment a rapid eye movement occurs but is of incomplete amplitude. Such eye movements can be measured by electronystagmography. In specialized units, electromyography may be helpful. Patients with entrapment often grimace owing to the sudden onset of pain engendered by eye movement.

3. *Pseudoptosis and deepening of the supratarsal fold* accompany the enophthalmos. If the eyelid covers the pupil, the patient will attempt to elevate both eyelids, and lid retraction will be seen on the opposite side.

4. *Orbital emphysema* may be seen shortly after injury but absorbs spontaneously.

5. *Infraorbital nerve anesthesia* may occur. This clinical sign probably is not an indication for surgical exploration. In 55 per cent of cases, the symptoms resolve within 1 year,[43] and many patients are symptom free in 2 years. However, persistent pain and dysesthesia may be a sequel, especially to an orbital rim fracture.

6. *Serious injury to the eye* can occur in up to 40 per cent of cases.[5,7,44-46] Visual function is therefore assessed in all cases, and a detailed slit-lamp and ophthalmoscopic examination of the globe should be done in every case to check for treatable pathology that might otherwise be missed.

INVESTIGATIONS FOR BLOW-OUT FRACTURE

Imaging studies for blow-out fractures include plain radiographs, tomography, and CT. Positive-contrast orbitography has also been described[47] but is now rarely used. The occipitomental and lateral radiographs provide images of the orbital floor. A fracture may be seen, and the hanging drop sign may signify herniation of orbital contents but must be distinguished from a submucosal hematoma and chronic polypoid sinus disease (which is likely to be bilateral). The exaggerated Waters view may demonstrate an orbital floor fracture not shown by the standard view.[48] Both linear tomography[49] and hypocycloidal tomography[50] provide a sensitive means of detecting a blow-out fracture.

Computerized tomography in oblique planes (half-axial and semisagittal) has been employed to demonstrate inferior entrapment and lateral delineation of the orbit, respectively.[51]

MEDIAL WALL BLOW-OUT FRACTURE

These fractures are reported to accompany orbital floor blow-out fractures in between 21 per cent[52] and 70 per cent[53,54] of cases. It is important to recognize this condition because of the potential sequelae of enophthalmos or, more rarely, entrapment, resulting in restriction of lateral gaze, for which the results of late surgery are poor. The clinical signs of restriction of abduction and retraction of the globe on horizontal gaze should be sought in all cases.[55,56] Subcutaneous emphysema and epistaxis should increase the index of suspicion for this diagnosis. Plain radiographs and CT may reveal an opaque ethmoid sinus. Hypocycloidal tomography has been advocated to show displacement of bone.[57] Ultrasonography has also proved effective in demonstrating such pathology.[58]

BLOW-IN FRACTURE

Blow-in fractures of the orbital floor and medial wall have also been described.[59,60] Fragments of bone not only may interfere with motility but may also threaten optic nerve function.

TREATMENT AIMS

The aims of treatment are to preserve normal binocular vision by restoring normal ocular motility and to prevent cosmetically unacceptable enophthalmos. The field of binocular single vision (BSV) is the area within which the patient has single vision. The aim with regard to ocular motility is to obtain as large a field of BSV as possible, centered upon the primary position of gaze and downward gaze. It may not be possible to abolish double vision entirely.

Whether surgical repair of the orbital floor should be carried out—and if so, when—is a subject of controversy. On the one hand, on the basis of their findings of 57 patients, Putterman and colleagues[61] concluded that no patient with a pure blow-out fracture should be operated on immediately but that patients should be kept under observation for 4 to 6 months or longer. On the other hand, early surgical treatment of orbital fractures has been advocated for the majority of cases, whether or not diplopia is present.[62] The results of the majority of studies show that repair of the orbital floor is indicated when symptomatic diplopia or cosmetically unsatisfactory enophthalmos is present 14 days after the injury.[42,44,52,63] Late surgery may mean that orbital fibrosis takes place, with irreparable impairment of extraocular muscle function. Very early surgery results in a lot of unnecessary operations.

Marked enophthalmos with an extensive orbital floor defect at the time of the initial examination will not resolve spontaneously, and surgical repair of the orbital floor can be carried out at any time. A motility disorder is common following surgery. Gradual recovery of eye movement subsequently takes place in the majority of cases. Those patients who remain symptomatic may require glass prisms or surgery for the squint.

There is anecdotal evidence suggesting that orthoptic exercises may expand the field of BSV.[64] There have been no clinical trials of this treatment, but it is logical to teach the patient to develop as wide a range of eye movement as possible. In theory, this therapy may have the combined benefits of diminishing the scarring (fibroblasts cannot grow across moving tissue planes), increasing the range over which the patient can fuse images, and sustaining the power of the extraocular muscles after injury.

Fractures of the Orbital Roof

The incidence of orbital roof fractures in patients suffering facial bone fractures is approximately 5 per cent.[65,66] Undisplaced, blow-in, and blow-out fractures have all been described.[67,68] In addition, penetrating injuries may perforate the orbital roof and enter brain tissue. Careful neurologic assessment and comprehensive radiologic evaluation are required if such an injury is suspected. A range of clinical sequelae have been described. Bone fragments can interfere with superior rectus muscle function and cause impairment of elevation and ptosis of the upper eyelid.

The orbital roof is particularly weak at its posterior aspect and in the region of the superior orbital fissure and optic canal. Thus, the optic nerve and nerves passing through the superior orbital fissure may all be injured in various combinations. Epidural hematoma, depressed fracture of the superior orbital rim, persistent pneumocephalus with cerebrospinal fluid rhinorrhea, and tension pneumocephalus have all been reported.[69,70] Prolapse of orbital tissue into the frontal air sinus may also occur.[67]

A forced duction test may be positive, particularly in the upward direction, because the bones may impinge on the muscle and mechanically restrict upward gaze. This finding can cause diagnostic confusion with an inferior blow-out fracture.[71] The surgical repair of such fractures has been described in Chapter 18.

Trauma to the Trochlea

The superior oblique muscle passes through the trochlea close to the medial superior orbital margin. If the muscle is injured, subsequent fibrosis can result in tethering, which in turn leads to restriction of elevation of the eye in adduction. Entrapment of the superior oblique tendon in an orbital roof fracture has also been described.[72] Many patients recover spontaneously, but injection of steroids or ophthalmic surgical intervention may be required.

DISPLACEMENT OF THE GLOBE

The eye may be displaced in any dimension following orbital injuries, namely, anteroposteriorly, horizontally, or vertically.

Proptosis

Proptosis is common initially, owing to hematoma and swelling of orbital tissues. In the majority of cases, this condition resolves spontaneously. Subperiosteal hematoma, notably of the orbital roof,[73] may give rise to persistent proptosis associated with downward displacement of the globe. Persistent proptosis may also result from inward displacement of orbital bone fragments.

Enophthalmos

Enophthalmos is a common late sequel that may initially be masked by intraorbital tissue swelling and hematoma. Expansion of the orbit, prolapse of soft tissue through a blow-out fracture, necrosis of soft tissue, and fibrosis all contribute to the clinical picture.[74] A sunken upper eyelid may be a factor in the poor cosmetic appearance. Impaired ocular motility may or may not be present.

Vertical Displacement

Vertical displacement commonly accompanies orbital fracture. In the acute phase, the eye may be displaced upward by hematoma. In the late phase, downward displacement of the globe is more common.

Horizontal Displacement

Horizontal displacement occurs laterally when the medial ligament has been severed or the orbital bones have been laterally displaced.

Traumatic Herniation of the Globe into the Maxillary Sinus

This disorder has been reported[75,76] to have good recovery of visual function following surgical restoration of the normal anatomy.

Clinical evaluation is described in the ophthalmic assessment section of this chapter. Surgical treatment is indicated for those patients having an unsatisfactory cosmetic appearance. Deep recession of the upper eyelid may accompany enophthalmos. In such cases, packing of the orbital floor beneath the periosteum may give good cosmetic results.

In cases in which enophthalmos is accompanied by a blind eye, a good cosmetic result may be obtained by using a positive (magnifying) lens in spectacles.

INJURIES TO THE EYELIDS

Eyelid Swelling and Hematoma

Eyelid swelling and hematoma are common following orbital injury. These injuries are usually innocuous but may indicate major underlying ocular injury. Spontaneous resolution takes place during the ensuing weeks.

Widening of the Medial Canthus

Widening of the medial canthus due to disruption of the nasoethmoid complex must be recognized and treated by transnasal wiring at the time of primary surgery.[41,77] Traumatic detachment of the lateral canthus should also be treated at the time of primary surgery.[76]

Eyelid Lacerations

Eyelid lacerations should be treated within 72 hours. It is better to wait for good operating room facilities and to carry out formal surgery than to perform an unsatisfactory repair in the middle of the night. The eye and orbit are examined for evidence of injury, and a high index of clinical suspicion is maintained for retained foreign bodies. Radiographic examination, including CT, is performed if retained organic material is suspected. Appropriate antitetanus treatment is provided, and the wound is immediately debrided. Corneal exposure is an indication for immediate treatment.

SURGICAL REPAIR

Surgical repair requires accurate repositioning in layers and not just superficial skin closure. When the eyelid margin has been severed, the integrity is restored with a nonabsorbable suture passing through the gray line. This step is carried out first and allows subsequent accurate suture placement. The tarsal plate is sutured with an absorbable stitch, with care being taken that this passes through only a partial thickness of the plate to prevent corneal damage. Tissue should not be disposed of, as even free material may take. Local skin grafts and flaps may be required if there has been gross loss of tissue.

Repair of the upper eyelid requires great care to avoid ptosis. The wound is explored to ensure the integrity of the levator and superior rectus muscles and of the globe. The levator complex is then carefully isolated, and any lacerations are sutured. The integrity of the orbital septum is restored. The eyelid is then repaired. Failure to recognize damage to the levator may result in unsightly ptosis, which is difficult to repair by secondary surgery.[78]

Eyelid Avulsion

Avulsion of the eyelids requires immediate surgery to protect the cornea. In the interim, eye ointment or 1.5 per cent methyl-cellulose is instilled to prevent corneal ulceration. At surgery, the remaining conjunctiva is mobilized and sutured across the cornea.[79] An appropriate skin flap is then chosen, depending upon the remaining tissue available, and is drawn across the conjunctiva. Subsequent division of the skin flap and reconstruction are carried out at a later date.

Progressive Shortening of the Lower Eyelid

This condition, caused by fibrosis, may occasionally complicate any approach to the inferior orbital floor. The insertion of a scleral graft as an "extension" to the lower border of the tarsal plate provides a satisfactory cosmetic result.[78]

NASOLACRIMAL INJURIES

Damage to the lacrimal drainage system has been reported in only 0.5 per cent of 337 midface fractures.[80] The infrequent occurrence of epiphora following nasal fractures is probably due to the protective influence of the medial canthal ligament, which may prevent tearing of the upper lacrimal pathways.[81]

Postoperative epiphora is frequently due to malposition of the lower eyelid.[82] In severe nasal-orbital-ethmoid fracture, open reduction is usually preferable to avoid malpositioning of the bone fragments, which can lead to nasolacrimal apparatus obstruction.[82] In most cases of nasolacrimal injury, it is the bony canal that is obstructed.

Dacryocystorhinostomy is indicated no sooner than 3 months following injury, as spontaneous recovery of function may take place. In addition, some individuals do not develop epiphora in the long term and, therefore, do not warrant surgery. Nasolacrimal obstruction can occasionally be complicated by bacterial dacryocystitis and abscess formation. This condition is treated by drainage of the abscess and appropriate systemic antibiotics. Irrigation of the abscess cavity using an antibiotic such as gentamicin, administered via a lacrimal cannula through the canaliculus, may expedite recovery of the condition. Dacryocystorhinostomy is indicated when the infective episode has resolved.

Canalicular Lacerations

Lacerations of the canaliculi are repaired at the time of primary surgery, ideally with the use of an operating microscope. Detailed descriptions of this surgery are available in standard ophthalmic surgical texts. Direct suture of the canalicular walls over an appropriate stent probably gives the best results. However, the results of surgery are often disappointing, and secondary intervention may be required.

INDIRECT OPHTHALMIC CONSEQUENCES OF INJURY

Traumatic Retinal Angiopathy (Purtscher's Retinopathy)

Multiple discrete, superficial infarcts of the retina manifesting as loss of central vision, accompanied by the development of multiple cotton-wool spots adjacent to the optic nerve head (Fig. 20–18), may appear as a result of severe skull fracture, chest compression, and long-bone fractures. Although the pathogenesis is unknown, a sudden increase in pressure within the retinal venules has been incriminated[83], as have fat emboli. The patient complains of loss of vision in one or both eyes 24 to 48 hours after injury. There is no specific treatment, but the prognosis is good, with spontaneous, gradual recovery of vision taking place during the ensuing 2 to 3 months in most cases.

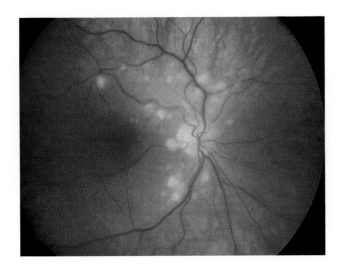

Figure 20–18. Traumatic retinal angiopathy (Purtscher's retinopathy). Multiple cotton-wool spots are present in the retina of this patient, who sustained a severe head injury.

Caroticocavernous Sinus Fistula and Arteriovenous Anastomosis

Fistula formation between the arterial and venous systems may occur within the week following a severe skull injury. The condition is usually painful. The clinical signs comprise gradually increasing ophthalmoplegia, chemosis, proptosis, and dilated blood vessels (both of the conjunctiva and of the eyelids), which may be accompanied by pulsating exophthalmos. In some cases, an intracranial bruit may be heard. The intraocular pressure is usually raised, and loss of vision may ensue if the condition becomes more severe. Neurosurgical referral is indicated.

Facial Palsy

All patients who develop facial palsy as a result of injury should be assessed for the presence of Bell's phenomenon. The patient is asked to close the eyes, and the degree of cover of the cornea is determined. The cornea is examined in detail for the development of ulceration. Tarsorrhaphy is indicated in cases in which there is corneal ulceration, and ointment is instilled at night in those cases in which corneal coverage is incomplete.

Papilledema

Examination of the optic nerve heads for the development of papilledema is essential in all patients suspected of having raised intracranial pressure, resulting, for example, from a chronic subdural hematoma.

THE RELATIONSHIP BETWEEN MAXILLOFACIAL AND EYE INJURIES

In a recent prospective study in which we carried out full ophthalmic assessment of 363 patients with midfacial fractures caused by blunt facial trauma, 56 patients were found to have suffered transient or permanent vision loss. Causes of impaired vision varied from minor, self-healing corneal injuries to optic nerve avulsion. Permanent loss of vision ensued in eight cases and was due to traumatic optic neuropathy in each case.

Road traffic accidents caused the highest proportion of impaired vision (29 per cent), while simple falls caused the lowest proportion (6 per cent). Other causes of facial trauma, such as assaults and sports and industrial accidents, were associated with intermediate frequencies of reduced vision (15 per cent).

The type of facial fracture was found to be an important factor in relation to visual deterioration. Comminuted malar fractures were associated with a 41 per cent incidence of visual impairment, in contrast to 15 per cent for the whole series. It is perhaps not surprising that in our series the most important predictor of underlying ocular injury was a reduced visual acuity.

In conclusion, all patients who sustain midfacial trauma resulting in fracture should have their visual acuities determined at the time of examination. The findings of our study indicate that all patients with reduced visual acuity and those with comminuted malar fractures are likely to have sustained ocular injury that warrants referral to an ophthalmologist. The index of suspicion for ocular injury should also be high in patients with midfacial fractures caused by road traffic accidents. Considerable care should be taken to ensure that all patients who may have sustained eye injuries in association with midfacial fracture are managed appropriately to prevent such blinding complications as angle-recession glaucoma and retinal detachment. The medicolegal implications are obvious.

REFERENCES

1. Holt GR, Holt JE: Incidence of eye injuries in facial fractures: An analysis of 727 cases. Otolaryngol Head Neck Surg 91:276–279, 1983.
2. Holt JE, Holt GR, Blodgett JM: Ocular injuries sustained during blunt facial trauma. Ophthalmology 90:14–18, 1983.
3. Jabaley ME, Lerman M, Sanders HJ: Ocular injuries in orbital fractures. A review of 119 cases. Plast Reconstr Surg 56:410–417, 1975.
4. Miller GR, Tenzel RR: Ocular complications of midfacial fractures. Plast Reconstr Surg 39:37–42, 1967.
5. Milauskas AT, Fueger GF: Serious ocular complications associated with blowout fractures of the orbit. Am J Ophthalmol 62:670–672, 1966.
6. Petro J, Tooze FM, Bales CR, Baker G: Ocular injuries associated with periorbital fractures. J Trauma 19:730–733, 1979.
7. Fradkin AH: Orbital floor fractures and ocular complications. Am J Ophthalmol 72:699–700, 1971.
8. Delori F, Pomerantzeff O, Cox MS: Deformation of the globe under high speed impact: Its relation to contusion injuries. Invest Ophthalmol 8:290–301, 1969.
9. Slingsby JG, Forstot SL: Effect of blunt trauma on the corneal endothelium. Arch Ophthalmol 99:1041–1043, 1981.
10. Tonjum AM: Gonioscopy in traumatic hyphema. Acta Ophthalmol 44:650–664, 1966.
11. Runyan TE: Concussive and Penetrating Injuries of the Globe and Optic Nerve. St Louis, CV Mosby, 1975.
12. Kaufman JH, Tolpin DW: Glaucoma after traumatic angle recession. A ten-year prospective study. Am J Ophthalmol 78:648–654, 1974.
13. Weidenthal DT, Schepens CL: Peripheral fundus changes associated with ocular contusion. Am J Ophthalmol 62:465–477, 1966.
14. Ross WH: Traumatic retinal dialyses. Arch Ophthalmol 99:1371–1374, 1981.
15. Cox MS, Mackenzie-Freeman H: Traumatic retinal detachment. In Mackenzie-Freeman H (ed): Ocular Trauma. New York, Appleton-Century-Crofts, 1979, pp 285–293.
16. Hart JCD, Frank HJ: Retinal opacification after blunt nonperforating concussional injuries to the globe. A clinical and retinal fluorescein angiographic study. Trans Ophthalmol Soc UK 95:94–100, 1975.
17. Friberg TR: Traumatic retinal pigment epithelial edema. Am J Ophthalmol 88:18–21, 1979.
18. Blight R, Hart JCD: Structural changes in the outer retinal layers following blunt mechanical nonperforating trauma to the globe: An experimental study. Br J Ophthalmol 61:573–587, 1977.
19. Cogan DG: Pseudoretinitis pigmentosa. Report of two traumatic cases of recent origin. Arch Ophthalmol 81:45–53, 1969.
20. Crouch ER Jr, Apple DJ: Post-traumatic migration of retinal pigment epithelial melanin. Am J Ophthalmol 78:251–254, 1974.
21. Cherry PMH: Rupture of the globe. Arch Ophthalmol 88:498–507, 1972.
22. Brock L, Tanenbaum HL: Retention of wooden foreign bodies in the orbit. Can J Ophthalmol 15:70–72, 1980.
23. Mono J, Hollenberg RD, Harvey JT: Occult transorbital intracranial penetrating injuries. Ann Emerg Med 15:589–591, 1986.
24. Goldberg MF, Tessler HH: Occult intraocular perforations from brow and lid lacerations. Arch Ophthalmol 86:145–149, 1971.
25. Rowbotham GF: Acute Injuries of the Head: Their Diagnosis, Treatment, Complications and Sequels. Edinburgh, E & S Livingstone, 1964, pp 408–433.
26. Heinze J: Cranial nerve avulsion and other neural injuries in road accidents. Med J Aust 2:1246–1269, 1969.
27. Walsh FB, Hoyt WF: Clinical Neuro-Ophthal-

mology. Vol 3. 3rd ed. Baltimore, The Williams and Wilkins Company, 1969.

28. Gjerris F: Traumatic lesions of the visual pathways. *In* Vinken PJ, Bruyn GW (eds): Handbook of Clinical Neurology. Vol 24. Amsterdam, North Holland Publishing Company, 1976, pp 27–57.

29. Anderson M: Loss of accommodation and convergence following whiplash injury to the cervical spine. Br Orthop J 18:117, 1961.

30. Hart CT: Disturbances of fusion following head injury. Proc R Soc Med 62:704–706, 1969.

31. Stanworth A: Defects of ocular movement and fusion after head injury. Br J Ophthalmol 58:266–271, 1974.

32. Lee J: Ocular motility consequences of trauma and their management. Br Orthop J 40:26–33, 1983.

33. Rucker CW: Paralysis of the third, fourth and sixth cranial nerves. Am J Ophthalmol 46:787–794, 1958.

34. Burger LJ, Kalvin NH, Lawton Smith J: Acquired lesions of the fourth cranial nerve. Brain 93:567–574, 1970.

35. Von Noorden GK: Management of trauma of the muscles and optic pathways. *In* Mackenzie-Freeman H (ed): Ocular Trauma. New York, Appleton-Century-Crofts, 1979, p 323.

36. Koorneef L: Sectional Anatomy of the Orbit. Amsterdam, Aeolus Press, 1981.

37. Pfeiffer RL: Traumatic enophthalmos. Arch Ophthalmol 30:718–726, 1943.

38. Smith B, Regan WF: Blow-out fracture of the orbit. Mechanism and correction of internal orbital fracture. Am J Ophthalmol 44:733–739, 1957.

39. Fujino T, Makino K: Entrapment mechanism and ocular injury in orbital blowout fracture. Plast Reconstr Surg 65:571–576, 1980.

40. Tajima S, Sugimoto C, Tanino R, et al: Surgical treatment of malunited fracture of zygoma with diplopia and with comments on blowout fracture. J Maxillofac Surg 2:201–210, 1974.

41. Converse JM, Smith B: Naso-orbital fractures. Trans Am Acad Ophthalmol Otolaryngol 67:622–634, 1963.

42. Crumley RL, Leibsohn J, Krause CJ, Burton TC: Fractures of the orbital floor. Laryngoscope 87:934–947, 1977.

43. Gillison TPA, Oei TH: Follow-up of orbital fractures treated surgically. *In* Bleeker GM, (ed): Modern Problems in Ophthalmology: Orbital Disorders. Basel, Karger, 1975, pp 471–473.

44. Emery JM, von Noorden GK, Schlernitzauer DA: Orbital floor fractures: Long-term follow-up of cases with and without surgical repair. Trans Am Acad Ophthalmol Otolaryngol 75:802–812, 1971.

45. Dodick JM, Berrett A, Galin MA: Hypocycloidal tomography and orbital blow-out fracture. Am J Ophthalmol 68:483–486, 1969.

46. Liebsohn J, Burton TC, Scott WE: Orbital floor fractures: A retrospective study. Ann Ophthalmol 8:1057–1062, 1976.

47. Milauskas AT, Fueger GF, Schulze RR: Clinical experiences with orbitography in the diagnosis of orbital floor fractures. Trans Am Acad Ophthalmol Otolaryngol 70:25–39, 1966.

48. Keene J, Doris PE: A simple radiographic diagnosis of occult blow-out fractures. Ann Emerg Med 14:335–338, 1985.

49. Gould HR, Titus CO: Internal orbital fractures: The value of laminagraphy in diagnosis. Am J Roentgenol Radium Ther Nucl Med 97:618–623, 1966.

50. Dodick JM, Galin MA, Kwitko ML: Concomitant blowout fracture of the orbit and rupture of the globe. Arch Ophthalmol 84:707–709, 1970.

51. Yamamoto Y, Sakurai M, Asari S: Towne (half-axial) and semi-sagittal computed tomography in the evaluation of blowout fractures of the orbit. J Comput Assist Tomogr 7:306–309, 1983.

52. Dulley B, Fells P: Orbital blow-out fractures: To operate or not to operate, that is the question. Br Orthop J 31:47–53, 1974.

53. Jones DEP, Evans JNG: "Blow-out" fractures of the orbit: An investigation into their anatomical basis. J Laryngol Otol 81:1109–1120, 1967.

54. Pearl RM, Vistnes LM: Orbital blowout fractures: An approach to management. Ann Plast Surg 1:267–270, 1978.

55. Miller GR, Glaser JS: The retraction syndrome and trauma. Arch Ophthalmol 76:662–663, 1966.

56. Rauch SD: Medial wall blow-out fracture with entrapment. Arch Otolaryngol 111:53–55, 1985.

57. Thering HR, Bogart JN: Blowout fracture of the medial orbital wall, with entrapment of the medial rectus muscle. Plast Reconstr Surg 63:848–852, 1979.

58. Ord RA, LeMay M, Duncan JG, Moos KF: Computerized tomography and B-scan ultrasonography in the diagnosis of fractures of the medial orbital wall. Plast Reconstr Surg 67:281–288, 1981.

59. Dingman RO, Natvig P: Surgery of Facial Fractures. Philadelphia, WB Saunders Company, 1964.

60. Zizmor J, Noyek AM: Orbital trauma. *In* Potts DG, Newton TH (eds): Radiology of the Skull and Brain. St Louis, CV Mosby, 1971.

61. Putterman AM, Stevens T, Urist MJ: Nonsurgical management of blow-out fractures of the orbital floor. Am J Ophthalmol 77:232–239, 1974.

62. Smith B, Converse JM: Early treatment of orbital floor fractures. Trans Am Acad Ophthalmol Otolaryngol 61:602–608, 1957.

63. Soll DB, Poley BJ: Trapdoor variety of blowout fracture of the orbital floor. Am J Ophthalmol 60:269–272, 1965.

64. King EF, Samuel E: Diseases of the orbit and sphenoidal sinus. 1. Fractures of the orbit. Trans Ophthalmol Soc UK 64:135–153, 1945.

65. McLachlan DL, Flanagan JC, Shannon GM: Complications of orbital roof fractures. Ophthalmology 89:1274–1278, 1982.

66. Schultz RC: Supraorbital and glabellar fractures. Plast Reconstr Surg 45:227–233, 1970.

67. Curtin HD, Wolfe P, Schramm V: Orbital roof blow-out fractures. AJR 139:969–972, 1982.

68. Sato O, Kamitani H, Kokunai T: Blow in fracture of both orbital roofs caused by sheer strain to the skull. J Neurosurg 49:734–738, 1978.

69. Flanagan JC, McLachlan DL, Shannon GM: Orbital roof fractures—neurologic and neu-

rosurgical considerations. Ophthalmology 87:325–329, 1980.

70. Wesley RE, McCord CD: Tension pneumocephalus from orbital roof fracture. Ann Ophthalmol 14:184–190, 1982.

71. McLurg FL, Swanson PJ: An orbital roof fracture causing diplopia. Arch Otolaryngol 102:497–498, 1976.

72. Al-Qurainy IA, Dutton GN, Moos KF, et al: Orbital injury complicated by entrapment of the superior oblique tendon: A case report. Br J Oral Maxillofac Surg 26:336–340, 1988.

73. Wolter JR: Subperiosteal haematomas of the orbit in young males: A serious complication of trauma or surgery in the eye region. J Pediatr Ophthalmol Strabismus 16:291–296, 1979.

74. Converse JM, Cole G, Smith B: Late treatment of blow-out fracture of the floor of the orbit. A case report. Plast Reconstr Surg 28:183–191, 1961.

75. Berkowitz RA, Putterman AM, Patel DB: Prolapse of the globe into the maxillary sinus after orbital floor fracture. Am J Ophthalmol 91:253–257, 1981.

76. Beirne OR, Schwartz HC, Leake DL: Unusual ocular complications in fractures involv-ing the orbit. Int J Oral Surg 10:12–16, 1981.

77. Steidler NE, Cook RM, Reade PC: Residual complications in patients with major middle third facial fractures. Int J Oral Surg 9:259–266, 1980.

78. Collin JRO: Immediate management of lid lacerations. Trans Ophthalmol Soc UK 102:214–215, 1982.

79. Achauer BM, Menick FJ: Salvage of seeing eyes after avulsion of upper and lower lids. Plast Reconstr Surg 75:11–15, 1985.

80. McCoy FJ, Chandler RA, Magnan CG, et al: An analysis of facial fractures and their complications. Plast Reconstr Surg 29:381–391, 1962.

81. Stranc MF: The pattern of lacrimal injuries in nasoethmoid fractures. Br J Plast Surg 23:339–346, 1970.

82. Gruss JS, Hurwitz JJ, Nik NA, Kassel EE: The pattern and incidence of nasolacrimal injury in naso-orbital-ethmoid fractures: The role of delayed assessment and dacryocystorhinostomy. Br J Plast Surg 38:116–121, 1985.

83. Archer DB: Traumatic retinal vasculopathy. Trans Ophthalmol Soc UK 105:361–384, 1986.

CHAPTER 21

TRAUMATIC INJURIES TO THE FRONTAL SINUS

HENRY T. HOFFMAN, M.D.,
and CHARLES J. KRAUSE, M.D.

Injury to the frontal sinus most often results from blunt trauma, although penetrating injuries also occur (Fig. 21–1). The frontal sinus is most frequently damaged as a result of a motor vehicle accident in which the patient strikes the dashboard or steering wheel with his face.[1,2] From a large series of facial injuries, Schultz found that 70 per cent of frontal sinus fractures were due to automobile accidents, 20 per cent resulted from assault, and the bulk of the remainder were caused by falls, industrial accidents, and athletic injuries.[3] Trauma from pool cues, baseball bats, axes, and a variety of projectiles, including a flying typewriter, has been reported to cause frontal sinus fractures.[4,5] Frontal sinus fractures are relatively uncommon when compared with other facial injuries, representing from 5 per cent to 15 per cent of all facial fractures.[6,7]

Currently, the most common indication for surgery on the frontal sinus is trauma.[8] Although restoration of the normal contour of the forehead is an important indication for repair of a fractured sinus, a more compelling reason to operate is to prevent potential infectious complications. The proximity of the frontal sinus to the brain makes untreated disease in this area potentially fatal (Fig. 21–2). Meningitis and brain abscess are feared sequelae of frontal sinus infection occurring with frontal sinus trauma.

Complications from frontal sinus fractures may not appear for years following injury and may result from obstruction of sinus drainage or from mucosa trapped in a fracture line. Mucocele formation may occur in this situation. Bacterial contamination of the mucocele may then result in a mucopyocele, with spread of infection to the orbit and brain. Incomplete obstruction of sinus drainage may produce acute or chronic infections of the frontal sinus.

Timely and correct treatment of injury to the frontal sinuses can turn a potentially lethal process into one handled with minimal morbidity and no functional deficit.

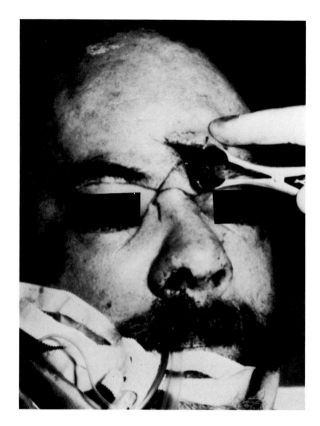

FIGURE 21 – 1. An open fracture through the anterior table, allowing preoperative inspection of the interior of the frontal sinus. (Courtesy of Dr. J. Weingarten.)

ANATOMY

Adult Anatomy

The frontal sinus is an air-filled cavity lined by ciliated respiratory epithelium encased in bone (Fig. 21 – 3). A posterior table of thin bone separates the sinus from

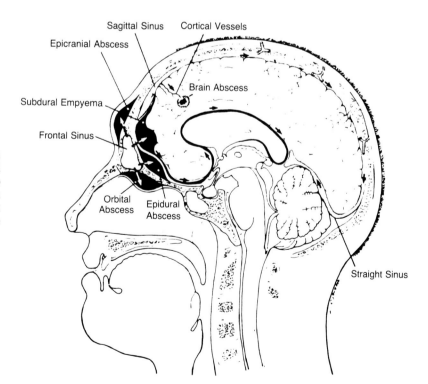

FIGURE 21 – 2. The spread of infection from an injured frontal sinus to adjacent orbit and brain may occur acutely or may develop months to years following injury. (From Mohr RM, Nelson LR: Frontal sinus ablation for frontal osteomyelitis. Laryngoscope 92:1006 – 1015, 1982; with permission.)

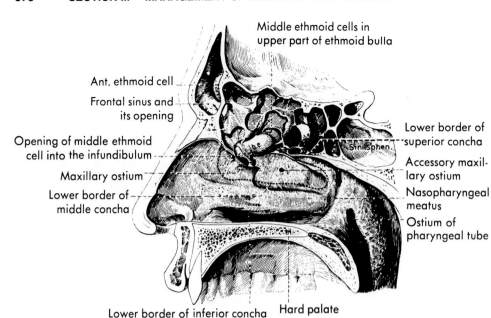

Middle ethmoid cells in
upper part of ethmoid bulla

Ant. ethmoid cell

Frontal sinus and
its opening

Opening of middle ethmoid
cell into the infundibulum

Maxillary ostium

Lower border of
middle concha

Lower border of
superior concha

Accessory maxil-
lary ostium

Nasopharyngeal
meatus

Ostium of
pharyngeal tube

Lower border of inferior concha   Hard palate

FIGURE 21–3. Anatomy of the frontal sinus and its drainage in relation to the ethmoid sinuses and anterior cranial fossa. (From Corning HK: Lehrbuch der topographischen Anatomie für Studierende und Ärtze. Munich, JF Bergmann, 1923.)

the dura of the frontal lobe. The anterior table of the sinus is covered by a soft tissue layer of frontalis muscle, orbicularis oculi muscles, supraorbital nerves, supratrochlear nerves, blood vessels, and skin. The eyebrows and buttress of the supraorbital rims demarcate the lower anterior border of the frontal sinus. Posteriorly, the floor of the frontal sinus consists of the orbital part of the frontal bone, which, in extensively pneumatized sinuses, may overlie the optic nerve.[9] Anteriorly, the floor of the sinus overlies the anterior ethmoid sinuses and nasal cavity.[10] The nasofrontal duct draining the sinus originates from the posteromedial part of the sinus floor.

The drainage of the frontal sinus is variable. Kasper, from a study of 100 frontal sinuses, found that 34 per cent of the sinuses drain through the ethmoid infundibulum. Sixty-two per cent of the sinuses drained into the frontal recess, distinct from the ethmoid drainage system. In the remaining 4 per cent, the nasofrontal duct was in direct anatomic continuity with the ethmoid infundibulum.[11]

The frontal sinus may drain into the nose via the nasofrontal duct or may empty directly into the middle meatus.[9] Only 15 per cent of frontal sinuses actually drain through a true duct; the remainder open directly into the nose through an ostium.[12, 13]

The size and shape of the frontal sinuses vary among patients and between the two frontal sinuses in individual patients (Fig. 21–4). Ritter noted complete agenesis of one of the frontal sinuses in 4 per cent of the specimens he examined.[14] The two frontal sinuses are separated by an intersinus septum, which is frequently located to one side of the midline. Additional incomplete intrasinus septa are frequently seen.

Embryology

Each of the sinuses begins as an outgrowth from the nasal chamber. Although the maxillary sinuses and ethmoid sinuses begin their development in utero, the frontal sinus exists only as small cephalic evagination of the middle meatus until after birth.[14, 15] Between the ages of 1 and 2 years, this evagination begins to invade the frontal bone, so that by age 3 it extends several millimeters above the frontonasal suture.

The frontal sinuses continue to grow to the point that they become recognizable radiographically by age 6 or 7. A growth spurt during puberty brings their size to nearly that of an adult. Although most frontal sinuses have reached their maximal size by age 20, growth may continue to age 40.[10]

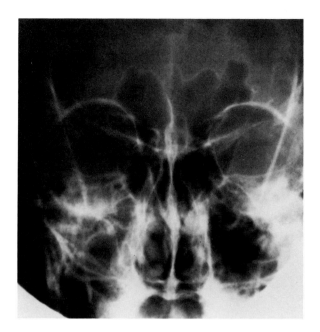

Figure 21–4. Normal asymmetric frontal sinuses, as depicted on a Caldwell view, with eccentric location of intersinus septum.

The initial cephalic evagination from the middle meatus that develops into a frontal sinus may arise from the frontal recess or from the ethmoid infundibulum.[9] In the latter case, the frontal sinus may be considered an anterior ethmoid air cell that is distinguished from the other ethmoid air cells only by its pneumatization of the frontal bone.[10] Multiple accessory frontal sinuses may exist if more than one ethmoid sinus invades the frontal bone.[10]

FUNCTION AND PHYSIOLOGY

A large number of functions have been attributed to the paranasal sinuses in a generally unsuccessful effort to attach physiologic importance to them.[14] The fact that neither surgical ablation nor developmental agenesis of the frontal sinus leaves the patient with a perceivable deficit argues against their functional importance. The sinuses are silent structures that become apparent only when their physiology is altered by disease processes.

Jahn, who describes the sinuses as phylogenic remnants, lists functions that have been ascribed to the sinuses: production of mucus, storage of mucus, resonator for the voice, humidification and warming of inhaled air, accessory area of olfaction, conservation of heat from the nasal fossae, definition of facial contours, and a "surge tank" to dampen the pressure differential that develops during inspiration.[16] Negus argues that lightening of the skull, the function commonly ascribed to the sinuses, does not apply to the frontal sinuses. A single plate would serve the same purpose.[17]

The primary purpose of the frontal sinuses may be to serve as mechanical barriers to protect the brain from trauma. As air-filled, compressible cavities, the paranasal sinuses appear to function by absorbing energy that would otherwise by imparted to more vital structures.[18] Schultz notes that the sinuses function well in this regard, as documented by those extensive crush injuries to the upper midface that are received with little damage to the brain or eyes.[3]

A normally functioning frontal sinus contains respiratory epithelium that secretes mucus that drains through the nasofrontal ostium. A patent ostium and intact ciliary action of the mucosa are necessary to keep the sinus air filled and free of disease.[14] Interference with these mechanisms leads to the accumulation of secreted mucus. If the mucus builds up behind an obstructed duct, a mucocele develops that may act as an expanding tumor, eroding bone and exerting a mass effect on adjacent brain and orbit.[19, 20] Infection may occur in this situation, resulting in a mucopyocele, with the potential danger of life-threatening intracranial infection.

Partial obstruction of the nasofrontal duct or the presence of diseased mucosa lining the sinus may also interfere with the drainage of the sinus and predispose to chronic sinusitis or recurrent episodes of acute sinusitis. Every episode of frontal sinus infection requires prompt attention because of the danger of extension to the adjacent brain and eyes.

DIAGNOSIS

Initial Evaluation

Although some fractures of the frontal sinus may be obvious to the examiner from across a room, many are characterized by a paucity of signs and symptoms. A high index of suspicion and low threshold for ordering radiographic studies are necessary to diagnose frontal sinus fractures in these cases. Patients with trauma to the glabella and frontal bone should have sinus radiographs as a part of their early evaluation.

Standard trauma management should accompany the initial evaluation of a patient with a suspected frontal sinus injury. Once the airway is secured and adequate circulation ensured, attention is then directed to those injuries, as ordered by a hierarchy of descending importance.

As with any patient sustaining significant maxillofacial injury, the cervical spine should be stabilized until a roentgenogram is obtained and demonstrates that all seven cervical vertebrae are normal.

History and Physical Examination

A history should be obtained whenever possible and should include information about the events surrounding the accident. The awake patient should be questioned about visual difficulties, numbness, pain, and sense of smell. It is helpful to elicit a previous history of nasal or sinus disease.[18]

Sequelae from untreated frontal sinus fractures frequently do not become apparent until months, years, or even decades after the injury. A history of previous head trauma should be sought from patients with recurrent frontal sinusitis. A thorough radiographic evaluation in these patients may demonstrate a fracture impairing frontal sinus drainage.

Often, the acutely injured patient is unconscious, requiring that the initial information come from the physical examination alone.

The extent of soft tissue injury overlying the sinus can be misleading and may not reflect the degree of injury to the sinus below.[21] Noyek and Zizmor write that posterior table frontal sinuses are actually more common in the presence of an intact anterior table "when the elastic anterior wall resists the stress of impact."[22] Other authors have not found this to be the case and have actually reported that posterior table fractures rarely occur without an associated anterior wall fracture.[12]

Soft tissue swelling is often seen over the frontal region, even in cases in which the anterior table is depressed. Swelling of the supraorbital region may not allow for the diagnosis of a depressed fracture on palpation.[23]

A careful neurologic examination is mandatory and should be repeated at intervals to evaluate for the development or progression of a neurologic deficit. Cranial nerve assessment as an integral part of this examination is especially important. Cerebrospinal fluid (CSF) leakage should be searched for either through an open wound or as drainage from the nose.

Although injury to the frontal sinus does not usually require immediate treatment in the emergency room, a delay in diagnosis can complicate a treatment course that would have been uneventful with timely intervention. A study of 80 patients with frontal sinus fractures reported by Frenckner and Richtner in 1960 related that in fewer than half were the fractures diagnosed in the emergency room.[1] In 20 per cent of the patients with posterior wall fractures evaluated in this study, the fracture was diagnosed only after an intracranial infection developed.[1] Bordley and Farrior found that 50 per cent of patients with posterior table fractures develop clinical evidence of their injury only with the development of late signs and complications.[18]

Radiographic Evaluation

As new developments in the field of radiology have occurred, radiographic evaluation of the frontal sinus has improved. Failure to diagnose frontal sinus fractures has become less common with the current range of radiographic techniques available to the clinician.

Plain film roentgenography has served as the keystone for evaluating sinus disease ever since Caldwell reported on the radiographic examination of the paranasal sinuses in 1918.[24] With the advent of tomography, computerized tomography (CT), and magnetic resonance imaging (MRI), plain film evaluation of the sinuses has come to be used more often for screening and follow-up than for definitive evaluation.

The frontal sinuses may be evaluated with each of the traditional plain film views obtained in a standard series, including the Caldwell, Waters, lateral, and submental vertex views.

The Caldwell view, considered best overall for evaluation of the frontal sinuses, demonstrates the septa and the margins of the lamina dura (Fig. 21–4). The Waters view adds little other than occasionally helping to visualize the periphery of the frontal sinus. Both the submental vertex and the lateral views allow for imaging of the anterior and posterior tables.[24] Dentition may obscure imaging of the frontal sinus on the submental vertex view, in which case an extended submental vertex view, or "European view," may be used to inspect the posterior wall of the frontal sinus.[23]

Plain sinus films are relatively crude tools to evaluate posterior wall frontal sinuses. Prior to the common use of tomography, posterior wall fractures were diagnosed with precision only by direct operative inspection. Frenckner and Richtner reported a series accrued during the period from 1947 to 1958, during which time they visualized roentgenographically only 18 of the 64 posterior wall fractures they verified at surgery. This finding led them to conclude that even in the absence of evidence of posterior wall fracture, all anterior wall fractures should be explored to rule out the possibility of an associated posterior wall fracture.[1]

Despite suffering from a lack of sensitivity, plain films of the paranasal sinuses may demonstrate findings that indicate significant injury to the posterior wall. Calvert listed plain film radiographic features suggestive of posterior table fractures with dural disruption:

1. A displacement identified in the posterior table
2. A gap in the posterior table
3. A vertical fracture line wider below than above
4. A fracture line crossing from one anterior cranial fossa floor to the other
5. A medial displacement of the zygomatic process of the frontal bone and a tilt of the crista galli
6. An intracranial pneumatocele[25]

Tomography, developed in 1926 and refined in the 1970s, greatly enhanced the preoperative evaluation of frontal sinus fractures.[26] Several studies from the early 1980s found that fine bone detail was better imaged by complex motion tomography than by CT scanning.[23, 26, 27] However, the newer CT scans allow for improved bone detail and have generally supplanted polytomography as the definitive radiographic examination for injury to the frontal sinus (Fig. 21–5).[28]

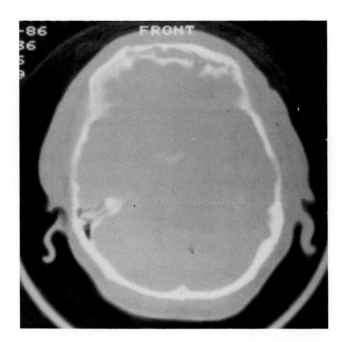

FIGURE 21–5. Computerized tomographic (CT) scan demonstrating a displaced posterior table fracture of the frontal sinus. (Courtesy of Dr. J. Weingarten.)

In a series of 50 consecutive frontal sinus fractures evaluated by Stanley and Becker, 48 were treated with surgical exploration, allowing for the correlation of preoperative radiographic impressions with direct surgical observation. All frontal sinus fractures were demonstrated preoperatively on CT scans, whereas only 88 per cent of the plain film series showed fracture lines. Plain film evaluation of posterior wall fractures was even less sensitive, demonstrating only 9 fractures of the 28 present, all of which were imaged with CT.[12]

Despite this improved imaging of frontal sinus injuries, radiographic evaluation of the frontal sinus drainage system is still poor.[5, 12, 23, 29] From their observations, Stanley and Becker conclude that the status of the frontal sinus drainage system can be only indirectly determined radiographically through correlation with associated fractures. Isolated fractures of the anterior table of the frontal sinus and transverse linear fractures through both the anterior and the posterior tables above the floor of the sinus are not associated with damage to the nasofrontal duct or ostia. CT evidence for fractures of the floor of the sinus, the nasoethmoid complex, and inferiorly located fractures of the posterior wall should be considered indirect evidence of injury to the frontal sinus drainage system. Depressed fractures of the posterior table are also linked with damage to the nasofrontal duct.[12]

The exquisite bone imaging provided by CT scanning makes it the best imaging technique for the evaluation of facial trauma. MRI may be used to supplement CT scanning in selected situations. Mucocele and brain are isodense on CT imaging but on MRI they have different characteristics that allow them to be distinguished (Fig. 21–6A and B).[30]

Associated Injuries

NEUROLOGIC

Significant intracranial injury occurs more commonly with injury to the frontal sinus than with injury to the mandible or midface, owing to both the proximity of the frontal sinus to the brain and the great forces required to cause a frontal sinus fracture. Nahum has measured the force necessary to fracture the frontal sinus to be two to three times greater than that required to fracture the zygoma, maxilla, or mandible (Fig. 21–7).[31] Consultation with a neurosurgeon is appropriate in cases

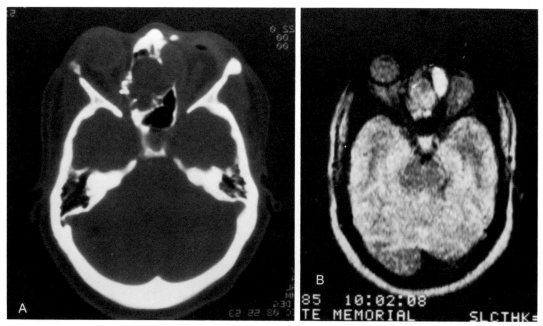

FIGURE 21–6. *A,* CT scan of paranasal sinuses of a patient who sustained a gunshot wound to the face, requiring left orbital exenteration and fascia lata repair of a large anterior fossa dura tear. A mass located along the left medial orbital wall could represent mucocele or herniated brain. *B,* The different characteristics of brain and mucocele on magnetic resonance imaging (MRI) identify this medial orbital mass as a mucocele, clearly distinguished from brain.

when CSF leak is present or when dural or brain injury is suspected. Some authors propose that neurosurgical consultation be obtained in all cases of frontal sinus fractures.[32]

OCULAR

Even before the operation the patient with a frontal sinus fracture should be examined by an eye specialist, as the possible existence of unobserved blindness before the operation may lead to a shock for the surgeon when the patient several days after the operation reports that he is blind of one eye.[1]

Although one would like to avoid shocking a surgeon today just as Frenckner advocated 40 years ago, there are reasons other than documenting blindness for enlisting the help of an ophthalmologist early in the evaluation of a patient with a frontal sinus fracture. Holt and Holt, in a study of 727 patients with facial fractures

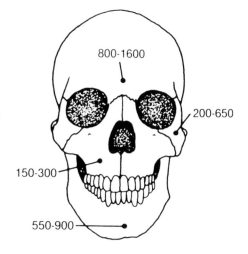
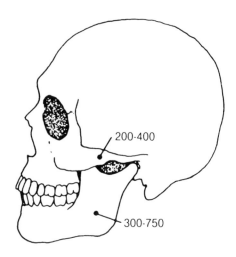

FIGURE 21–7. The forces, measured in pounds, that are necessary to fracture the frontal sinus are two to three times greater than those needed to fracture the zygoma, maxilla, or mandible. (From Nahum AM: The biomechanics of maxillofacial trauma. Clin Plast Surg 2:59, 1975; with permission.)

receiving formal ophthalmologic consultation, found that 89 per cent of those with frontal sinus fractures had associated eye injuries.[33]

Elevated intraocular pressure secondary to trauma, with bleeding in the anterior chamber, is a serious condition that requires urgent care. Lens dislocation, retinal separation, penetrating wound of the globe, and optic nerve compression also require acute management by an ophthalmologist.[33] Orbital entrapment may occur with injuries to the frontal sinus that involve the roof of the orbit.[23]

Early consultation with an ophthalmologist in the emergency room should be considered in every case of frontal sinus fracture.

CEREBROSPINAL FLUID LEAK

Head injury is the most common cause of CSF leakage. In 1954, Lewin described a 2 per cent incidence of CSF leakage in association with significant head injuries.[34] The incidence of CSF leak occurring with frontal sinus fractures has been reported to be higher.

The presence of a CSF leak in association with a frontal sinus fracture should be considered evidence for dural disruption coupled with a posterior table fracture.[6] Colorless fluid seen through an open fracture of the sinus is an indication of such an injury.

A CSF fistula should also be suspected in cases in which colorless rhinorrhea is present in a patient who has suffered head trauma. CSF rhinorrhea may arise from areas other than the frontal sinus, including the cribriform area, the fovea ethmoidalis, the sphenoid sinus, and even the temporal bone, with CSF finding its way to the nose by way of the eustachian tube. There may, however, be no outward signs of a frontal sinus CSF fistula if the nasofrontal duct is obstructed and if the overlying skin and anterior table are intact.

A traumatic CSF fistula of the frontal sinus is a life-threatening process deserving urgent attention. Prior to the routine use of an aggressive approach to this lesion, meningitis was a common sequela. Frenckner described 7 cases of meningitis resulting from 35 frontal sinus fractures referred to the otolaryngology department that had been observed for an average of 6 days on another service.[1]

The early diagnosis of a CSF leak resulting from a frontal sinus fracture generally hinges on the demonstration of fluid coming from the wound or nose. Although it is not recommended as part of the evaluation of the acutely injured patient, the diagnosis of CSF rhinorrhea may be made by positioning the patient with the head in a dependent position and collecting the draining fluids for analysis.

A variety of tests have been devised to differentiate CSF from normal nasal secretions. A glucose level greater than 30 mg/dl is commonly held to indicate that the nasal drainage is CSF.[6] Other indicators used to identify nasal drainage as originating from the CSF include low protein and potassium concentrations and a CSF-specific band of transferrin seen on serum protein electrophoresis (Table 21–1).[35]

When the source of post-traumatic CSF rhinorrhea is not readily apparent, identification of the site of dural injury is important. CT demonstration of an isolated fracture at a site consistent with the clinical presentation is often sufficient to localize the fistula and allow for formulation of a treatment plan. A variety of techniques used to identify the site of a CSF leak share the strategy of injecting a measurable material intrathecally and assaying for its appearance in selected areas. Fluorescein and radioactive tracers (indium) have been injected by lumbar puncture and searched for by placing individually labeled intranasal pledgets in the middle meatus, cribriform area, and posterior inferior meatus. Leakage from the frontal sinus or anterior ethmoid sinus, the cribriform or sphenoid sinus, and the eustachian tube will cause a corresponding fluorescence or elevation of radioactive counts in the pledget located in the appropriate region. Intrathecal metronidazole may allow visualization of the CSF leak on CT scan when the flow volume of CSF is substantial.[6]

Persistent opacification of a traumatized frontal sinus may indicate a CSF leak

TABLE 21-1. REFERENCE VALUES FOR CEREBROSPINAL FLUID (CSF),
NASAL SECRETIONS, AND SERUM*

	CSF	NASAL SECRETIONS	SERUM
Glucose (nmole/L)	2.5–3.9	0.6–1.4	3.5–5.2
Protein (grams/L)	<0.5	>2	60–80
Potassium (nmole/L)	2.5–3.5	12–26	3.3–4.8

* From Meurman O, et al: A new method for the identification of cerebrospinal fluid leakage. Acta Otolaryngol 87:366–369, 1979; with permission.

into the frontal sinus with obstruction of the frontonasal duct. Although this persistent opacification is more commonly due to retained blood or mucus, a CSF leak should be considered a possible cause and diagnosed at the time of frontal sinus exploration.

FACIAL FRACTURES

Frontal sinus fractures are often accompanied by fractures of other facial bones. Levine and colleagues described associated facial fractures in 14 of 21 patients with frontal sinus fractures. Le Fort and nasoethmoid complex fractures were commonly seen in association with anterior table fractures. Orbital blow-out fractures and malar fractures were less common.[27]

Schultz reported associated nasal fractures in 64 per cent of patients with fracture of the supraorbital and glabellar regions. Fractures of the maxilla and zygoma were present in 25 per cent of these patients, and mandibular fractures were present in 11 per cent.[36]

SURGICAL APPROACHES TO THE FRONTAL SINUS

Nasofrontal Duct Cannulation

The frontal sinus is accessible to operative treatment primarily through external approaches. A skin incision is required for all approaches except intranasal cannulation of the nasofrontal duct. This procedure is difficult because of the variable anatomy of the nasofrontal duct and may cause additional trauma and scarring.[37] Therefore, cannulation of the duct has no place in the contemporary treatment of frontal sinus injuries.

Frontal Sinus Trephination

Although trephination of the frontal sinus is most commonly used in the treatment of acute frontal sinusitis, it is a useful approach, both diagnostically and therapeutically, for selected frontal sinus fractures.

Access to the frontal sinus is gained through an incision under or through the medial aspect of the eyebrow and is carried down through periosteum. A drill or chisel is then used to enter the anterior floor of the frontal sinus (Fig. 21–8). A depressed anterior wall fracture may be reduced using an elevator inserted through the trephination. The ipsilateral posterior table may be inspected through this approach, although the exposure is limited. Patency of the nasofrontal duct may be assured by demonstrating the drainage of dye into the nose when it is administered through the trephination.[32]

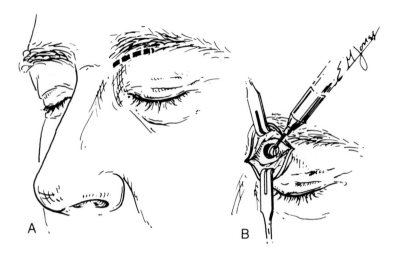

FIGURE 21–8. Limited access to the frontal sinus is provided by frontal sinus trephination. (From Lawson W: Frontal sinus. *In* Blitzer A, Lawson W, Friedman WH (eds): Surgery of the Paranasal Sinuses. Philadelphia, WB Saunders Company, 1985, p 123; with permission.)

Frontoethmoidectomy

The frontal sinus may be approached through an incision extending from below the medial border of the eyebrow inferiorly midway between the medial canthus and the dorsum of the nose. The frontoethmoidectomy approach, variably called the Lynch or Knapp procedure, allows for combined access to the ipsilateral ethmoid and frontal sinuses (Fig. 21–9).

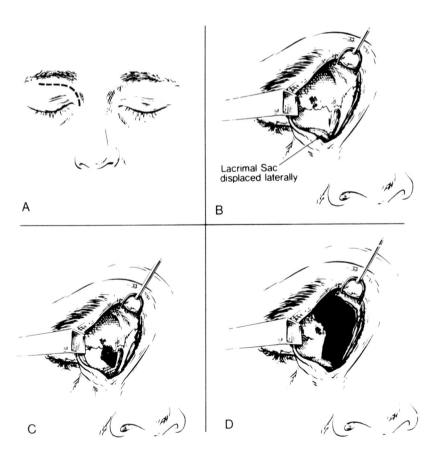

Lacrimal Sac
displaced laterally

FIGURE 21–9. Greater exposure to the frontal sinus than can be obtained by trephination is provided by the Lynch procedure, or frontoethmoidectomy. Reconstruction of the drainage system is an integral part of this procedure. *A,* Incision. *B,* Exposure of lateral wall of ethmoid with lacrimal sac displaced out of its fossa. *C,* Entry into the ethmoid sinus through the lamina papyracea at the posterior aspect of the lacrimal fossa. *D,* Exposure through the floor of the frontal sinus, employing the Lynch procedure. (From Lawson W: Frontal sinus. *In* Blitzer A, Lawson W, Friedman WH (eds): Surgery of the Paranasal Sinuses. Philadelphia, WB Saunders Company, 1985, p 130; with permission.)

Osteoplastic Flap

The osteoplastic flap allows a direct approach through the anterior wall of the frontal sinus but preserves the anterior wall by hinging it inferiorly on the blood supply coming through periosteum and soft tissue. The forehead contour is preserved with replacement of the bone-periosteal flap over the frontal sinus (Fig. 21–10).

This approach is commonly used to treat traumatic injuries because of the wide exposure of both frontal sinuses that it affords (Fig. 21–11). A number of procedures may be performed through this approach, including exploration of both frontal sinuses, repair with wiring of anterior table fractures, fat obliteration, and removal of the posterior wall with "cranialization" (see further on).

The osteoplastic flap procedure may be performed through an overlying laceration, a brow incision, or a coronal flap. The coronal incision is generally preferred because it not only provides the best exposure to the sinus but also allows the neurosurgeon access to perform an anterior craniotomy if the findings at the time of frontal sinus exploration warrant it (Fig. 21–12). This flap also offers the advantage of camouflaging the scar in hair-bearing skin (Fig. 21–13). An exception exists in men who either are bald or have a predilection to progressive hair loss (Fig. 21–14). In these patients, a brow incision heals with a more acceptable scar than is seen with an exposed coronal incision. Numbness of the forehead is expected when using the brow incision, as a result of transecting the supraorbital nerves.

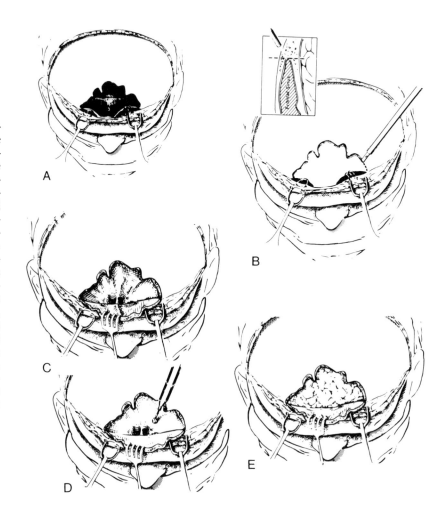

FIGURE 21–10. The osteoplastic flap sinusotomy offers excellent exposure to the frontal sinuses, here shown through a coronal incision with fat obliteration of the sinus. *A,* Template fashioned from a Caldwell view radiograph obtained preoperatively is positioned above the supraorbital rims to locate the frontal sinuses. *B,* A beveled cut (see insert) is made with an oscillating saw through bone into the sinus. *C,* A curved chisel is used to transect the intersinus septum, and the osteoplastic flap is fractured inferiorly, hinged on periosteum and overlying soft tissue. *D,* Mucosa is meticulously removed from the sinus. *E,* Remaining mucosa of the nasofrontal duct is everted inferiorly, and the sinuses are obliterated with fat. (From Lawson W: Frontal sinus. *In* Blitzer A, Lawson W, Friedman WH (eds): Surgery of the Paranasal Sinuses. Philadelphia, WB Saunders Company, 1985, p 141; with permission.)

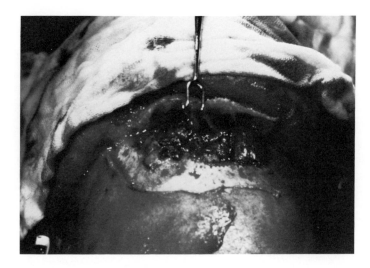

FIGURE 21–11. Exposure to the frontal sinuses with elevation of an osteoplastic flap. Note that periosteum is incised and elevated in an area larger than the bone flap so that it will overlie the bone cuts upon replacement of the flap. Also note the mucocele filling the frontal sinus.

FIGURE 21–12. Wide exposure to frontal sinuses and frontal bone through a coronal incision. The anterior cranial fossa is readily accessible to the neurosurgeon employing this approach.

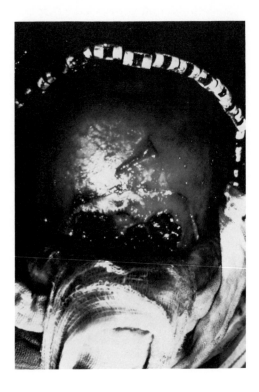

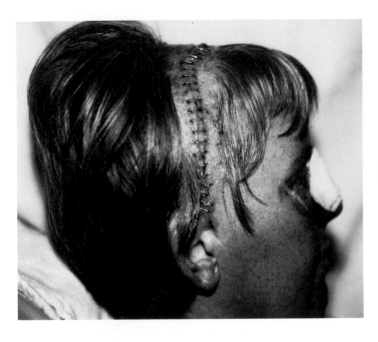

FIGURE 21–13. Coronal incision.

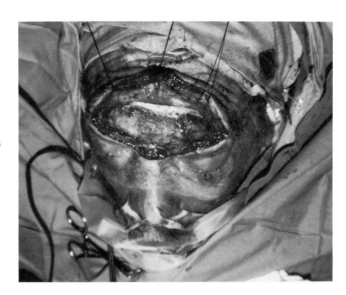

FIGURE 21–14. Exposure to the frontal sinuses through a brow incision. (Courtesy of Dr. J. Weingarten.)

Frontal Sinus Ablation

A variety of procedures have been described that sacrifice the anterior wall to obtain adequate exposure so that all diseased tissue may be removed and the sinus may be ablated. The frontal sinus "collapse," or the Reidel procedure, allows the overlying soft tissue to obliterate the sinus by collapsing inward to meet the posterior table after meticulous removal of all sinus mucosa. A brow or coronal incision may be used for access.

Reconstruction of the forehead and brow contour is most commonly performed 6 to 12 months later, at which time the healing is complete and assessment for persistence of disease is more definitive. Metallic plates and alloplastic materials such as methyl methacrylate have been used as implants to provide contour to the depressed area.[38, 39] Other materials, such as Proplast, have also been used by surgeons to reconstruct the forehead defect.[8]

The frontal sinuses may also be ablated through a procedure termed "cranialization," without deforming the forehead contour. Cranialization is performed through an osteoplastic sinusotomy. The posterior table is removed to allow the brain to expand forward to fill the frontal sinus cavity. Care must be taken to remove all mucosa from the sinus walls and to plug the frontonasal ducts with fat or fascia to prevent mucocele formation (Fig. 21–15A and B). In cases of severe head trauma involving the frontal sinus and brain, this procedure allows the brain to decompress acutely into the frontal sinus defect (Fig. 21–16).[40-43]

CLASSIFICATION OF FRACTURES

The management of trauma to the frontal sinuses varies according to the fracture type present. There are several different classification schemes that share the common features of segregating the fracture type by involvement of the anterior table, posterior table, or both, and by categorizing the fracture as either linear or displaced. Fractures through the nasofrontal duct commonly occur in association with other fracture types. Isolated fractures through the nasofrontal duct may be considered in a separate category. Other features, such as the degree of contamination, the presence of a CSF leak, and exposure of the brain, are also used by some authors to categorize these fractures.[2, 40] We present a simplified classification scheme to allow for a comparison between reported series of frontal sinus fractures (Table 21–2).

Unfortunately, most studies of frontal sinus fractures are retrospective examina-

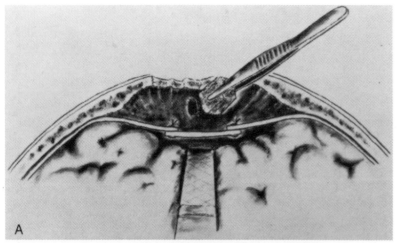

FIGURE 21–15. *A,* Cranialization involves removal of the posterior table to allow the brain to expand anteriorly into the frontal sinus. Defects in the dura are closed primarily or with a fascia graft. Fascia or muscle plugs are used to occlude the nasofrontal ducts after meticulous removal of mucosa. *B,* Brain fully expanded into frontal sinus defect. Segments of anterior table are positioned and wired. (From Donald PJ, Bernstein L: Compound frontal sinus injuries with intracranial penetration. Laryngoscope 88:225–232, 1978; with permission.)

tions of treatments that have been individualized without adherence to a protocol. Owing to the relative infrequency of this type of injury, such studies report only small numbers of patients and rarely demonstrate a clearly superior method of management for an individual fracture type. As a result, controversy persists regarding the best methods of management.

Published series of treatment results for frontal sinus fractures frequently suffer from inadequate follow-up. The feared long-term sequela of frontal sinus fracture—mucocele and mucopyocele formation—may take many years to manifest. Because the patient is generally asymptomatic during this period, it is difficult to maintain adequate follow-up. As a result, treatment failures may not be registered. The large

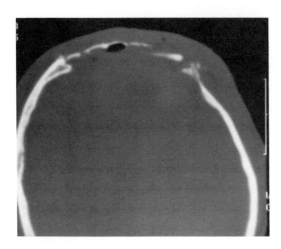

FIGURE 21–16. Early postoperative CT scan following cranialization procedure for a frontal sinus fracture with extensive comminution of the anterior and posterior tables. The anterior table was reconstructed with segments of the posterior table that were denuded of mucosa and wired into place. Note resolving pneumatocele. (Courtesy of Dr. J. Weingarten.)

TABLE 21-2. CLASSIFICATION OF FRONTAL SINUS FRACTURES
Anterior table fracture
Linear
Displaced
Posterior table fracture
Linear
Displaced
Nasofrontal duct injury

subset of patients injured through altercations (members of the local "knife and gun club") have been noted to be less likely to pursue follow-up care after an injury.[4]

Comparisons among studies are difficult in part because of differences in the populations of patients studied. A study of patients with isolated anterior wall fractures managed by observation in New Orleans from 1967 to 1977 demonstrated a significant infection rate, prompting the conclusion that surgical exploration "should be strongly considered in every case of frontal sinus fracture, even in apparently isolated anterior table injuries."[44] Subsets of anterior table fractures were not identified as open or closed or as displaced or linear in this study. In contrast, a study done in Cincinnati during the same period found no suppurative sequelae in 30 patients with closed, nondisplaced fractures of the anterior wall treated nonsurgically.[45]

Despite conflicting reports regarding the best way to treat frontal sinus injuries, general principles have been identified that have yielded consistently favorable results through many years.

TREATMENT OF FRONTAL SINUS FRACTURES

The status of the anterior wall, the posterior wall, and the nasofrontal duct determines the need for operative intervention of frontal sinus fractures. If an indication for frontal sinus surgery is found with reference to any one of these three areas, the sinus should be explored. Although a treatment plan may be formed on the basis of the preoperative evaluation, the surgeon must be ready to modify this plan based on the findings at the time of exploration. As is true in any surgical problem, a risk-benefit evaluation must be made to determine the least operative intervention that will achieve the optimal result.

Anterior Table Fractures

LINEAR (NONDISPLACED) ANTERIOR TABLE FRACTURES

The capacity of CT scanning to provide detailed images of the frontal sinuses has directed most modern authors to advocate observation of nondisplaced anterior table fractures of the frontal sinus (Table 21-3). However, the frontal sinus drainage system continues to be difficult to assess even with the sophisticated CT scans currently available.[12] As a result, patients with frontal sinus fractures treated nonoperatively require follow-up evaluations to ensure that the sinuses remain clear and air-containing.[46]

DISPLACED ANTERIOR TABLE FRACTURES

There is general agreement that significantly displaced fractures of the anterior wall should be treated surgically, although "minimally displaced" fractures are placed in the nonoperative treatment category.[4, 27]

Controversy exists, however, regarding the best surgical approach to be used

TABLE 21-3.   TREATMENT OF LINEAR ANTERIOR TABLE FRACTURES

STUDY	NUMBER	PAST TREATMENT	RESULTS	SUGGESTED PROTOCOL
Shreveport, LA, 1977–1986, Shockley et al[4]	28	Observe	Not stated	Observe
Cincinnati, 1970–1977, Whited[45]	30	Observe*	No complications	Observe
Philadelphia/ San Francisco, 1978–1983, Levine et al[27]	4	Observe	No complications	Observe
Minneapolis, 1969–1984, Duvall et al[46]	48	Observe (trephination required in 3 for acute sinusitis)	No complications	Observe

* Variable antibiotics and decongestants were used. Most other studies mention the use of antibiotics parenthetically and do not administer them per protocol.

(Table 21–4). The approach to the depressed anterior wall fracture may be made through an associated laceration, a brow or "butterfly" incision, a bicoronal flap, a Lynch incision, or a frontal sinus trephination.

A frontal sinus trephination approach may be used in most fractures that do not require wiring. The posterior wall of the ipsilateral sinus may be evaluated through the trephine if the frontal sinus is not large. The status of the nasofrontal duct may be assessed as well by searching for nasal drainage of methylene blue instilled into the sinus. Anterior table fractures can be stabilized by using an inflated balloon catheter brought out through the trephination.[47] This technique is considered less than optimal by some surgeons because of potential damage to the mucosa surrounding the frontonasal duct. The use of an absorbable substance such as Gelfoam to provide

TABLE 21-4.   TREATMENT OF DISPLACED ANTERIOR TABLE FRACTURES

STUDY	No.	TREATMENT	RESULTS	SUGGESTED PROTOCOL
Shreveport, LA, 1977–1986, Shockley et al[4]	17	Explore and elevate fragments	Not stated	Explore and elevate depressed fragments
Philadelphia/San Francisco, 1978–1983, Levine et al[27]	4	Obliterate*	No complications	Explore all—either obliterate or ensure adequate drainage
	2	Explore and elevate fragments		
New Orleans,† 1967–1977, Larrabee et al[44]	5	Observe	3 Complications	Explore all
	13	Explore and elevate fragments	No complications	
	6	Obliterate	1 Complication	
	1	Ablate	No complications	
Minneapolis, 1969–1984, Duvall et al[46]	7	Observe	1 Case of sinusitis, treated medically	Open reduction when necessary
	12	Open reduction, wire fragments		
	3	Reduction without wiring	‡	
	3	Obliteration		

* Three of the four with depressed anterior wall fractures were found to have nasofrontal duct injury at the time of exploration and were obliterated.

† Although linear and depressed anterior table fractures were not separated, the authors conclude from their data that "exploration with reduction should be strongly considered in every case of frontal sinus fracture, even in apparently isolated anterior table injuries."

‡ Complications in the 18 patients treated surgically were, as a group, "chronic pain, decreased forehead sensation, and cosmetic deformity."

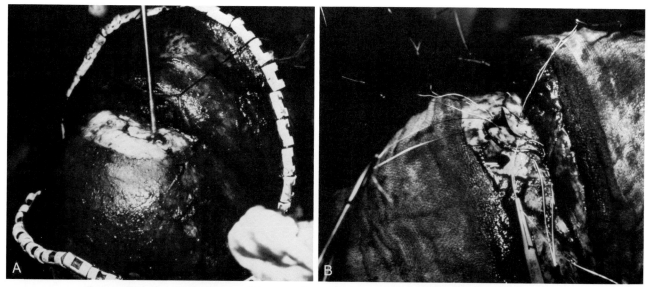

FIGURE 21–17. *A,* Exposure of depressed anterior wall fracture, employing a coronal incision. An associated depressed posterior table fracture was treated with fat obliteration of the sinus through an osteoplastic sinusotomy. *B,* Wiring the comminuted segments of the anterior table.

temporary support to a depressed anterior wall has been advocated by Duvall.[46] Others suggest that those anterior wall fractures that require support should be treated with obliteration, using the underlying fat to stabilize the anterior wall.[5]

Depressed anterior wall fractures that are mobile or comminuted should be reduced and stabilized through a direct approach via a preexisting laceration, a brow incision, or a coronal incision (Fig. 21–17*A* to Fig. 21–18*D*). Although the frontal sinus is most commonly explored through an osteoplastic flap, sufficient evaluation of the sinus may sometimes be possible through a large fracture of the anterior wall.

Posterior Table Fractures

LINEAR (NONDISPLACED) POSTERIOR TABLE FRACTURES

Controversy currently exists regarding the preferred treatment of frontal sinus fractures of this type. Donald writes that all posterior wall fractures should be explored because of the difficulty in assessing the degree of posterior wall displacement without direct inspection. As support for exploring all such fractures, he cites the two infectious complications that Newman and Travis reported from a series of five nondisplaced posterior wall fractures treated nonoperatively (Table 21–5).[23] Yet in the same study, Newman and Travis suggest that nondisplaced posterior table fractures may simply be observed unless an associated CSF leak or nasofrontal duct injury is demonstrated.[48]

Without citing data to support their approach, Levine and colleagues and Shockley and coworkers propose that all nondisplaced fractures of the posterior table be explored and treated with either sinus obliteration or ablation.[4, 27]

Experiments performed on laboratory animals support a conservative approach to nondisplaced fractures of the posterior table. Hybels and Newman evaluated the natural history of posterior table fractures using a cat model. As expected, they demonstrated that mucocele formation occurred in the presence of nasofrontal duct obstruction and when mucosa was inadequately removed in obliterated sinuses. They were able to demonstrate that with adequate drainage of the sinus, mucosa did not grow into fracture lines. From this finding, they conclude that the fibroblastic healing response proceeds more rapidly than mucosal growth.[49] Hybels and Newman also

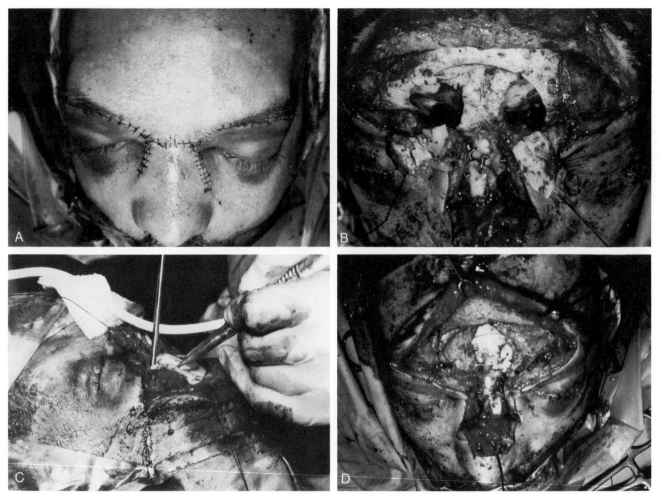

FIGURE 21–18. The treatment of a closed fracture of the frontal sinus with marked comminution of the anterior table associated with a linear fracture of the posterior table. Treated by fat obliteration of the sinus through an osteoplastic flap sinusotomy. *A*, Brow incision with inferior extensions for access to the nasal dorsum. *B*, Comminuted segments of the anterior table are hinged inferiorly on periosteum, demonstrating the interior of the frontal sinuses and nasofrontal ducts. *C*, Mucosa lining the sinus is removed with a drill. *D*, Fragments are wired into place after obliteration of the sinus with fat. (Courtesy of Dr. J. Weingarten.)

showed that healing of the posterior wall occurred with new bone formation if the fracture line was depressed less than the width of the posterior table. Fractures associated with either loss of bone or with a separation between fragments greater than the width of the posterior table healed with fibrous tissue filling the defect.[49]

As a result of those experiments and a review of clinical data, Hybels concludes that nondisplaced or minimally displaced fractures of the posterior table may be dealt with nonoperatively if there is no evidence of associated CSF leak or injury to the nasofrontal duct area.[21]

Donald states that nondisplaced posterior wall fractures may not heal by bony union. He relates that dural tears often exist adjacent to these posterior wall defects which may predispose the patient to meningitis, should an episode of frontal sinusitis develop. He therefore supports the practice of fat obliteration of the frontal sinus in all cases in which nondisplaced fractures of the posterior wall exist.[23]

Other studies support a conservative approach to nondisplaced fractures of the posterior wall. Of 9 nondisplaced fractures that involved both the anterior and the posterior walls and that were treated nonoperatively, Duvall and colleagues found no

TABLE 21-5.   TREATMENT OF NONDISPLACED POSTERIOR TABLE FRACTURES

STUDY	No.	TREATMENT	RESULTS	SUGGESTED PROTOCOL
Shreveport, LA, 1977–1986, Shockley et al[4]	2	Explore and obliterate	No complications	Explore all and obliterate
Philadelphia/San Francisco, 1978–1983, Levine et al[27]	3 1	Explore (1 obliterate) Observe	No complications	Explore all and obliterate
Ann Arbor, MI, 1961–1971, Newman et al[48]	5	Observe	2 Complications*	Observe unless associated CSF leak
New Orleans,† 1967–1977, Larrabee et al[44]	2 2 6 1	Observe Explore Obliterate Ablate	2 Complications‡ No complications No complications No complications	Explore all, reduce fracture, obliterate only if reduction alone is not sufficient Reduction
Minneapolis, 1969–1984, Duvall et al[46]	9 2	Observe "Limited frontoethmoidec-tomy"	No complications No complications	Observe

* (1) Large epidural abscess developed within 3 weeks of injury in association with acute frontal sinusitis; (2) meningitis complicating mucopyocele was treated 10 years after injury, with previously undetected fracture through frontonasal duct seen in association with posterior table fracture.

† Differentiation between displaced and nondisplaced fractures not made.

‡ Complications not identified with frontal sinus type. One with postoperative CSF leak that resolved with sequela of "chronic sinus pain."

complications. These 9 fractures constituted a subset of a series of 112 frontal sinus fractures followed for an average of 6 years.[46]

DISPLACED POSTERIOR TABLE FRACTURES

In several articles in the general plastic surgery literature, it is argued that concern about long-term complications of frontal sinus fractures is overstated and that elevation of depressed anterior wall fractures to restore forehead contour is all that is needed regardless of the status of the posterior wall.[3, 36, 50] However, most physicians who deal with frontal sinus infections recognize the life-threatening consequences of an inadequately treated frontal sinus fracture. Most authors today agree that operative intervention is required in all cases of significantly displaced posterior table fractures. Controversy remains regarding the optimal surgical treatment (Table 21–6).

TABLE 21-6.   TREATMENT OF DISPLACED POSTERIOR TABLE FRACTURES

STUDY	No.	TREATMENT	RESULTS	SUGGESTED PROTOCOL
Shreveport, LA, 1977–1986, Shockley et al[4]	12	Obliterate	Not stated	Obliterate or cranialize
Philadelphia/San Francisco, 1978–1983, Levine et al[27]	8	Obliterate or cranialize	1 Complication	Obliterate usually, cranialize with severe comminution
New Orleans,* 1967–1977, Larrabee et al[44]	2 2 6 1	Observe Explore Obliterate Ablate	2 Complications No complications No complications No complications	Explore all, reduce fracture, obliterate only if reduction alone is not sufficient
Minneapolis,† 1969–1984, Duvall et al[46]	13 7	Obliterate Cranialize	2 Complications 5 Complications	Obliterate, avoid cranialization if possible

* Differentiation between displaced and nondisplaced fractures is not made. Complications are not identified with frontal sinus type.

† Obliteration complications: seroma (1), mucopyocele (1). Cranialization complications: CSF leak (2), meningitis (1), cosmetic deformity (2).

Minimally displaced posterior table fractures are defined as those in which the fragments are separated by less than the width of the cortical thickness of the bone. These fractures are generally treated in the same fashion as nondisplaced fractures.

Those fractures with greater displacement may trap mucosa in the frontal sinus line. This problem requires surgical attention, since continued growth of mucosa may result in meningitis, cerebritis, or brain abscess.[32] Damage to the frontonasal duct is frequently associated with displaced fractures of the posterior table and should also be evaluated at the time of exploration.[12]

Larrabee and associates advocate open reduction of posterior table fractures when the nasofrontal duct is intact. Their experience with a high postoperative infection rate when sinus obliteration was done prompted them to suggest that reduction be done in favor of obliteration. The high postoperative infection rate they noted may have been related to the large number of open fractures they treated as well as to the use of methyl methacrylate rather than fat to obliterate the majority of the sinuses.[44] As a result of several animal studies and numerous clinical reports, fat is currently thought to represent the optimal material for use in frontal sinus obliteration.[21,51,52]

Most authors advocate obliteration for frontal sinus fractures with displacement of the posterior table. Donald concurs, except in cases involving extensively comminuted posterior wall fractures. For these cases, he suggests that cranialization of the sinus be done. He believes that the extensive bone debridement and dural grafting necessary in these cases decrease the vascular bed needed to support a fat graft.[23,43]

Although Donald reported no cases of meningitis, mucocele, or CSF leak related to the use of cranialization in 21 cases of posterior wall fracture, Duvall and associates reported a high complication rate when employing this procedure.[46] Three of the seven patients they treated with cranialization developed either postoperative meningitis or a CSF leak. A cosmetic deformity resulted from the procedure in two others. In contrast, from a group of 13 posterior table fractures of comparable severity treated with fat obliteration, only two complications arose—a mucopyocele and a seroma. As a result, Duvall and associates advocate sinus obliteration with fat, even in the most severe posterior table fractures.[46]

Nasofrontal Duct Fractures

A major difficulty in treating nasofrontal duct fractures is making the diagnosis. The advances in radiographic imaging that have improved the evaluation of fractures involving the anterior and posterior walls have not yet allowed for a definitive appraisal of the status of the nasofrontal duct.[4,48] The variable anatomy of the frontal sinus drainage system and its association with the ethmoidal labyrinth make it difficult to assess radiographically.

In a series of 21 frontal sinus fractures surgically treated by May and associates, 20 were found to have a damaged nasofrontal duct at the time of operation.[29] From this study, May concludes that all fractures of the frontal sinus should be explored to evaluate and treat occult nasofrontal duct injury.[29]

Other studies have shown a lower, yet significant, incidence of nasofrontal duct injury associated with frontal sinus fractures. Newman and Travis reported that one third of the 63 frontal sinus fractures they studied had an associated injury to the nasofrontal duct. Despite this finding, they state that exploration of the nasofrontal duct is not indicated unless its involvement is suspected on clinical grounds.[48]

Stanley and Becker were able to predict with accuracy involvement of the nasofrontal drainage on the basis of the CT appearance of associated fractures. Fractures isolated to the anterior table or involving both tables in a transverse fashion above the floor of the sinus were not associated with damage to the nasofrontal duct. They conclude that the frontal sinus need not be explored in these cases if the only indication for exploration is to assess the status of the drainage system.[12]

The surgical treatment of fractures impairing drainage of the frontal sinus requires either reconstruction of the sinus drainage system or obliteration of the sinus. Unilateral obstruction of the nasofrontal duct has been treated by removing the intersinus septum to allow drainage down the contralateral duct.[23, 32] Concern about the reliability of this drainage route has made this procedure less popular in cases of frontal sinus trauma. Hybels and Newman, using a cat model, demonstrated mucocele formation in a frontal sinus they attempted to drain by removing the intersinus septum after plugging the ipsilateral nasofrontal duct. Fibrous tissue had replaced the previous intersinus septum, interfering with drainage from the injured sinus.[49]

Catheter placement through the nasofrontal duct without enlarging the duct has been used by surgeons in the past to improve drainage from the frontal sinus. This technique should be avoided owing to the great possibility of duct stenosis secondary to circumferential trauma to the mucosa.[32, 53]

Nasofrontal duct reconstruction may be used for frontal sinus fractures when preoperative assessment has shown that the posterior wall does not require surgical attention. This procedure is done through a frontoethmoidectomy approach and may be accomplished with or without stenting of the duct. Advocates of this approach argue that it is a lesser procedure with fewer complications than the osteoplastic flap and allows direct access to the ethmoid air cells.[54] The procedure can be done bilaterally if both nasofrontal ducts are injured.

The osteoplastic flap approach to the frontal sinus may be used for exposure to enlarge the frontonasal duct, to obliterate the frontal sinus, or to cranialize the frontal sinus. The versatility of this flap, coupled with the excellent exposure it provides to all parts of both frontal sinuses, has made this approach the most popular one in dealing with frontal sinus fractures.

Surgical Considerations

TIMING OF PROCEDURE

Frontal sinus fractures do not require immediate surgical attention unless they are associated with a neurosurgical or opthalmologic emergency. Patients not requiring operative treatment for associated injuries should be observed for head trauma for 48 hours prior to frontal sinus exploration.[48] Many frontal sinus fractures actually receive their initial operative treatment years after the injury, when complications related to impaired sinus drainage or mucocele develop.

Although traumatic CSF leaks from other areas are often observed for a period of up to 3 months because of the high rate of spontaneous resolution, it is usually best to repair the CSF leak and treat the fractures as soon as the patient is stabilized.[55]

TREATMENT OF OPEN AND CONTAMINATED WOUNDS

A frontal sinus fracture in a patient with chronic sinusitis is an indication for urgent surgical treatment to ensure that the contaminated sinus cavity does not spread infection to the brain and eye.

Open fractures of the frontal sinus may be contaminated with the introduction of bacteria and foreign matter into the sinus. A subset of frontal sinus fractures termed "through and through" defects by Donald are open fractures extending through dura and exposing brain.[23, 40] Traditional treatment of these injuries involved debridement of contaminated bone to prevent the development of osteomyelitis.[41, 56] A collapse procedure was then done, with the depressed forehead defect repaired at a second stage as a cranioplasty.

Donald reports success in treating these injuries with cranialization and conservation of the forehead contour. He preserves the comminuted anterior wall fragments and sterilizes them with meticulous cleansing and soaking in providone-iodine

(Betadine). He then replaces the anterior wall fragments and wires them into place. Systemic coverage with a broad-spectrum antibiotic has helped prevent infectious complications.[23, 40, 41]

Medical Management

Most authors support the practice of treating patients who have acutely traumatized frontal sinuses with broad-spectrum antibiotics.[46] Systemic vasoconstrictors are also sometimes used but are of questionable value.[18, 48] Dependent drainage is advocated by some to aid in the clearing of a blood-filled frontal sinus.[18] Patients should also be warned against blowing their nose to prevent the accumulation of intracranial air in the event they have a posterior table frontal sinus fracture.[48]

The most important aspect of the nonoperative management of frontal sinus fractures is observation, both clinically and radiographically, for signs indicating the need for operative intervention. A Caldwell view obtained immediately after the injury will commonly show an opacified frontal sinus, usually as a result of blood in the sinus. A repeat Caldwell view should be obtained 3 to 5 days later. Persistent opacification should be taken as evidence for impaired drainage of the frontal sinus. The sinus should then be explored, and either frontal sinus obliteration or reconstruction of the nasofrontal duct should be considered.[18, 48]

REFERENCES

1. Frenckner P, Richtner NG: Operative treatment of skull fractures through the frontal sinus. Acta Otolaryngol 51:63–72, 1960.
2. Pollak K, Payne EE: Fractures of the frontal sinus. Otolaryngol Clin North Am 9:517–522, 1976.
3. Schultz RC: Frontal sinus and supraorbital fractures from vehicle accidents. Clin Plast Surg 2:93–106, 1975.
4. Shockley WW, Stucker FJ, Jr, Gage-White L, et al: Frontal sinus fractures: Some problems and some solutions. Laryngoscope 98:18–22, 1988.
5. May M: Nasofrontal-ethmoidal injuries. Laryngoscope 87:948–953, 1977.
6. Jacobs JR: Cerebrospinal fluid fistula. In Mathog RH (ed): Maxillofacial Trauma. Baltimore, The Williams and Wilkins Company, 1984, pp 297–302.
7. Smith HW, Yanagisawa E: Paranasal sinus trauma. In Blitzer A, Lawson W, Friedman WH (eds): Surgery of the Paranasal Sinuses. Philadelphia, WB Saunders Company, 1985, pp 299–315.
8. Schenck N, Tomlinson MJ: Frontal sinus trauma: Experimental reconstruction with Proplast. Laryngoscope 87:398–407, 1977.
9. Hollinshead WH: Anatomy for Surgeons. Vol I: The Head and Neck. 2nd ed. Hagerstown, MD, Harper and Row, 1968, pp 784–785.
10. Moss-Salentijn L: Anatomy and embryology. In Blitzer A, Lawson W, Friedman WH (eds): Surgery of the Paranasal Sinuses. Philadelphia, WB Saunders Company, 1985, pp 1–22.
11. Kasper KA: Nasofrontal connections: A study based on 100 consecutive dissections. Arch Otolaryngol 23:322–343, 1936.
12. Stanley RB, Becker TS: Injuries of the nasofrontal orifices in frontal sinus fractures. Laryngoscope 97:728–731, 1987.
13. Gross C: Pathophysiology and evaluation of frontoethmoid fractures. In Mathog RH (ed): Maxillofacial Trauma. Baltimore, The Williams and Wilkins Company, 1984, pp 280–287.
14. Ritter F: Anatomy of the paranasal sinuses. In English G (ed): Otolaryngology. Vol 2. Philadelphia, Harper and Row, 1985.
15. Meyer DB: Prenatal development of facial skeleton. In Mathog RH (ed): Maxillofacial Trauma. Baltimore, The Williams and Wilkins Company, 1984, pp 1–20.
16. Jahn AF: General principles. In Blitzer A, Lawson W, Friedman WH (eds): Surgery of the Paranasal Sinuses. Philadelphia, WB Saunders Company, 1985, pp 114–119.
17. Negus V: The Comparative Anatomy and Physiology of the Nose and Paranasal Sinuses. Edinburgh, Churchill-Livingstone, 1958.
18. Bordley JE, Farrior JB: Frontal sinus fractures and complications. In English G (ed): Otolaryngology. Vol 4. Philadelphia, Harper and Row, 1985.
19. Price HI, Danziger A: Computerized tomographic findings in mucoceles of the frontal and ethmoid sinuses. Clin Radiol 31:169–174, 1980.
20. Hesselink JR, Weber AL, New PFJ, et al: Evaluation of mucoceles of the paranasal sinuses with computed tomography. Radiology 133:397–400, 1979.
21. Hybels RL: Posterior table fractures of the frontal sinus. II. Clinical aspects. Laryngoscope 87:1740–1745, 1977.
22. Noyek AM, Zizmor J: Radiology of the nose and paranasal sinuses. In English G (ed): Otolaryngology. Vol 2. Philadelphia, Harper and Row, 1985.
23. Donald PJ: Frontal Sinus and Nasofrontoethmoidal Complex Fractures: A Self Instructional Package. AAO-HNS Committee on Continuing Education, 1980, pp 11–42.
24. Dolan KD: Paranasal sinus radiology. Part

1A. Introduction and the frontal sinuses. Head Neck Surg 4:301–311, 1982.

25. Calvert CA: Discussion on injuries of the frontal and ethmoidal sinuses. Proc R Soc Med 35:805–810, 1942.

26. Rowe LD, Miller E, Brandt-Zawadski M: Computed tomography in maxillofacial trauma. Laryngoscope 91:745–757, 1981.

27. Levine SB, Rowe LD, Keane WM, et al: Evaluation and treatment of frontal sinus fractures. Otolaryngol Head Neck Surg 95:19–22, 1986.

28. Noyek AM, Kassell EE: Computed tomography in frontal sinus fractures. Arch Otolaryngol 108:378–379, 1982.

29. May M, Ogura JH, Schramm V: Nasofrontal duct in frontal sinus fractures. Arch Otolaryngol 92:534–538, 1970.

30. Hoffman HT, et al: Magnetic resonance imaging in the evaluation of mucoceles of the ethmoid sinus. (in preparation).

31. Nahum AM: The biomechanics of maxillofacial trauma. Clin Plast Surg 2:59, 1975.

32. Holt GR, Blaugrund SM, Shugar JM, et al: Fractures of the paranasal sinuses. In Goldman JL (ed): The Principles and Practice of Rhinology. New York, John Wiley and Sons, 1987, p 533.

33. Holt GR, Holt JE: Incidence of eye injuries in facial fractures: An analysis of 727 cases. Otolaryngol Head Neck Surg 91:276–279, 1983.

34. Lewin W: Cerebrospinal fluid rhinorrhea in closed head injuries. Br J Surg 42:1–18, 1954.

35. Meurman O, Irjala K, Suonpää J, Laurent B: A new method for the identification of cerebrospinal fluid leakage. Acta Otolaryngol 87:366–369, 1979.

36. Schultz RC: Supraorbital and glabellar fractures. Plast Reconstr Surg 45:227–233, 1970.

37. Naumann HH: Surgery of the paranasal sinuses. In Naumann HH (ed): Head and Neck Surgery. Vol 2. Stuttgart, West Germany, George Thieme Verlag, 1980, pp 403–423.

38. Failla A: Operative management of injuries involving the frontal sinuses. Laryngoscope 78:1833–1852, 1968.

39. Olson NR, Newman MH: Acrylic frontal cranioplasty. Arch Otolaryngol 89:116–119, 1969.

40. Donald PJ: Frontal sinus fractures. In Cummings CW, Fredrickson JM, Harker LA, (eds): Otolaryngology Head and Neck Surgery. Vol 1. St Louis, CV Mosby, 1986, pp 901–921.

41. Donald PJ, Bernstein L: Compound frontal sinus injuries with intracranial penetration. Laryngoscope 88:225–232, 1978.

42. Donald PJ: Frontal sinus ablation by cranialization. Arch Otolaryngol 108:142–146, 1982.

43. Donald PJ, Ettin M: The safety of frontal sinus fat obliteration when sinus walls are missing. Laryngoscope 96:190–193, 1986.

44. Larrabee WF Jr, Travis LW, Tabb HG: Frontal sinus fractures—their suppurative complications and surgical management. Laryngoscope 90:1810–1813, 1980.

45. Whited RE: Anterior table frontal sinus fractures. Laryngoscope 89:1951–1955, 1979.

46. Duvall AJ, Porto DP, Lyons Dean, Boies CR, Jr: Frontal sinus fractures: Analysis of treatment results. Arch Otolaryngol Head Neck Surg 113:933–935, 1987.

47. Lawson W: Frontal sinus. In Blitzer A, Lawson W, Friedman WH (eds): Surgery of the Paranasal Sinuses. Philadelphia, WB Saunders Company, 1985, pp 120–145.

48. Newman MH, Travis LW: Frontal sinus fractures. Laryngoscope 83:1281–1292, 1973.

49. Hybels RL, Newman MH: Posterior table fractures of the frontal sinus. I. An experimental study. Laryngoscope 87:171–179, 1977.

50. Dingman RO: Commentary. In Schultz RC: Supraorbital and glabellar fractures. Plast Reconstr Surg 45:233, 1970.

51. Donald PJ: The tenacity of the frontal sinus mucosa. Otolaryngol Head Neck Surg 87:557–566, 1979.

52. Denneny JC: Frontal sinus obliteration using liposuction. Otolaryngol Head Neck Surg 95:15–19, 1986.

53. Cullom MM: External operations on the frontal sinus. Arch Otolaryngol 11:304–321, March 1930.

54. Porto DP, Duvall AJ: Long-term results with nasofrontal duct reconstruction. Laryngoscope 96:858–862, 1986.

55. Carmel PW, Komisar A: Cerebrospinal fluid rhinorrhea. In Blitzer A, Lawson W, Friedman WH (eds): Surgery of the Paranasal Sinuses. Philadelphia, WB Saunders Company, 1985, pp 260–269.

56. Nadell J, Kline DG: Primary reconstruction of depressed frontal skull fractures including those involving the sinus, orbit and cribriform plate. J Neurosurg 41:200–207, 1974.

CHAPTER 22

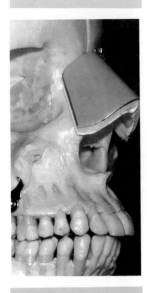

NASAL FRACTURES

JAMES K. PITCOCK, M.D.,
AND ROBERT M. BUMSTED, M.D., F.A.C.S.

The treatment of fractures of the nose has been the subject of medical writing since the Egyptians.[1] Through the ensuing centuries, the basic treatment philosophy (reduction of the fracture with return of normal form and function) has remained essentially unchanged, with a few additions in the past century because of the development of intranasal surgical techniques.[2-7] In this chapter, we attempt to review a "gray scale" of treatment options available to the practitioner managing nasal trauma. By understanding the cause-and-effect relationships between the severity of injury and the degree of deformity, the rhinologist can decide what treatment options are available and, more important, which option is best for the patient with this particular injury. We will not describe a single "black and white" flow-sheet type of classification that is so common in today's medical training. Moreover, we hope that by understanding the forces of injury in combination with the options for repair and good surgical judgment, the surgeon will be able to make the correct diagnosis and select an appropriate treatment plan for the patient.

ANATOMY

The nose is a midline central facial structure that fulfills both cosmetic and functional purposes. Cosmetically, it helps construct the central frame of the face, and its symmetry is very important in defining facial symmetry. Alone, the nose is not an object of beauty. Its function on a face aesthetically is to give the face balance and allow the eyes, cheeks, and mouth to define the beauty that each face possesses. Functionally, the nose is the entry point for nasal respiration, which is the normal state for humans. Oral breathing is regarded as a sign of some form of upper airway pathology; therefore, nasal obstruction is considered a disease entity that has stimulated a great amount of research into the role of the nose and nasal cavity in both physiologic and psychologic disorders.

Anatomically, the nose is formed by the union of rigid and flexible struts, that is, bone and cartilage, respectively (Fig. 22–1). The bony nose is the top half, and the

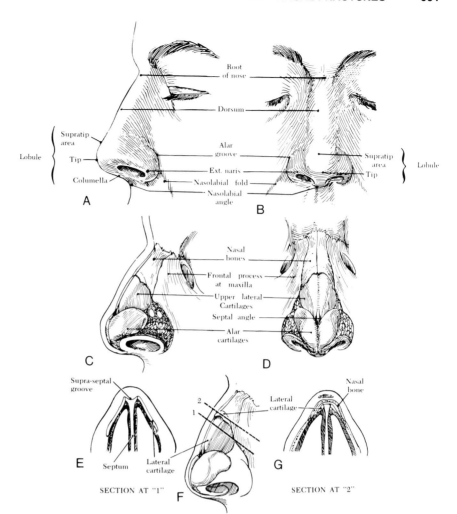

FIGURE 22-1. *A-G*, The surface and structural anatomy of the nose. (From Rees TD: *In* Aesthetic Plastic Surgery. Vol. 1. Philadelphia, WB Saunders Company, 1980, p 54; with permission.)

cartilaginous nose is the lower half. The nasal bones themselves are flat, rectangle-shaped sheets of bone that are thick superiorly where they interdigitate with the frontal bone and thin inferiorly where they attach to the upper lateral cartilages of the nose. The nasal processes of the frontal bone and the maxilla provide superior and lateral support, respectively, for the nasal bones, and these supporting structures are thicker and significantly stronger than the nasal bones themselves. In the midline, the nasal bones fuse to form a "pup tent"–like arrangement, with the perpendicular plate of the ethmoid supporting the midline like a tent pole. The bony anastomosis along this suture line between the three bones is rigid, so the bony nose must be functionally considered a tripod rather than a bipod.

The cartilaginous nose is formed from the combination of two paired upper lateral cartilages (ULCs), two paired lower lateral cartilages (LLCs), a single midline septal cartilage, and a few sesamoid cartilages found at various areas within the soft tissues. The ULCs are paired, flat, triangular sections of hyaline cartilage that are tightly attached superiorly to the inferior edge of the nasal bone by strong fibrous connective tissue. This junction is not end to end but is actually overlapping, with the nasal bone lying over the ULCs. In the midline, the two ULCs are firmly attached to each other and to the quadrangular cartilage of the anterior nasal septum. Although this union is not continuous, the fibrous attachment is very strong, so this portion of the nose must also be considered a tripod. Laterally, the ULC has soft tissue attachments to the fibrofatty tissues of the nasal alae and the lateral nose. The paired LLCs have a medial crus that lies lateral to the caudal septal cartilage, defining the columella of the nose. The lateral crus of the LLC can be divided into its more medial dome area, where it defines the size and conformation of the nasal tip, and the lateral segment, which supports the nasal alae and functions to prevent the nose from collapsing during inspiration. The sesamoid cartilages lie along the lateral inferior margins of the LLC. In the midline, there are fibrous attachments between structures that help define nasal tip projection; however, these are not as strong or as consistent as those seen with the ULC-septal attachment. The inferior caudal end of the nasal-septal cartilage is attached by a decussating fibrous band to the anterior nasal spine of the maxilla, which helps prevent posterior rotation of the septum and loss of nasal tip support. Covering this bony and cartilaginous skeleton are soft tissue and mucosa internally and soft tissue, muscle, and skin externally. The nasal musculature—the nasalis, the depressor septi, and the procerus—contributes to the soft tissue bulk of the nose and has only slight function in facial motion or respiration. The skin and subcutaneous tissues over the bony nose are thin and mobile, whereas those over the cartilaginous nose are thicker and more adherent to the underlying structures. The nasal skin is highly variable in its thickness, and its content of sweat glands seems to increase with increasing skin thickness. Just inside the anterior nares, the skin covering of the nose transforms to mucous membrane, forming the consistent mucocutaneous junction. This line demarcates the beginning of the vibrissae, or nasal hairs, that act as a filter for the upper airway. Internally, the mucous membrane is firmly adherent to the perichondrium, and this plane is maintained as the mucoperichondrium becomes mucoperiosteum as the bony nasal cavity is entered.

The details of the anatomy of the remainder of the face—the maxilla, the orbits, and the floor of the anterior cranial fossa—are covered in Chapter 12. However, an understanding of the inter-relations between these structures and the nose is essential if nasal trauma is to be adequately evaluated and treated.

CLASSIFICATION OF INJURIES

Many different and often excessively complex methods of classifying nasal-septal injuries have been proposed.[8-12] Several of these have been correlated with cadaveric studies in which the nose was struck either directly with a hammer or indirectly utilizing a heavy object to strike a connecting rod applied at various angles to different nasal structures. The ingenuity with which these studies were done is admirable; however, our clinical experience tells us that the injuries we treat frequently do not fall into any of the classic patterns described. Thus, the Le Fort classification, although universally known by surgeons, is insufficient to diagnose and treat facial injuries because the mechanism of injury (heavy, low-velocity objects versus high-velocity objects) is not always relevant in today's high-speed, mechanical environment.

To understand the variations in the degree of injury that a clinician encounters, one must review basic physics and the concept of the transfer of energy. When an object (e.g., a ball) is thrown, it carries a specific amount of energy that dissipates slowly through friction and gravity until it falls to earth or strikes another object. At the point where the ball hits the object, the amount of energy transferred is dependent on the following:

1. The energy of the ball at the time of impact
2. Whether or not the ball hits and transfers all of its energy to the target or bounces off, retaining a portion of its energy

The distribution of the energy in the target (i.e., a human face) is then also dependent upon a number of factors:

1. Surface area of the ball's striking surface
2. Surface area of the target site

3. If the face is able to recoil, that is, transfer some of the energy into motion, thereby decreasing its local effect

4. The structural composition of the target tissues

To make these points relevant, we will use an example. If a baseball is thrown at a person and strikes that person in the face, the amount of energy could be roughly estimated from an analysis of whether or not the person was allowed to recoil or whether his or her head was up against an immovable object. The area of the face hit by the ball is also important. If the ball struck the stronger malar eminence, it might or might not have sufficient force to break the bone or its attachments. If it struck the weaker nose, it is more likely the nose would be fractured owing to its thin frame and lack of significant deep supporting structures.

To extrapolate on this thought and bring in the momentum theory, $\frac{1}{2}MV^2 =$ kinetic energy (KE), we find that the contact energy of a ball thrown by an old, out-of-shape surgeon at 50 miles per hour is one fourth of what it would be if the ball was thrown at 100 miles per hour by a professional baseball pitcher.

$$50 \text{ miles per hour} \times 1\text{-lb baseball} = 2,689 \text{ ft/lb}$$

$$100 \text{ miles per hour} \times 1\text{-lb baseball} = 10,756 \text{ ft/lb}$$

This result is due to the velocity's being squared. That is why, when a person is thrown against a windshield at 10 miles per hour, the effects are much less devastating than at 30 or 60 miles per hour. For example, for a 150-pound man in a car,

$$150 \text{ lb} \times 10 \text{ miles per hour} = 16,141 \text{ ft/lb of KE}$$

$$150 \text{ lb} \times 30 \text{ miles per hour} = 145,200 \text{ ft/lb of KE}$$

$$150 \text{ lb} \times 60 \text{ miles per hour} = 580,800 \text{ ft/lb of KE}$$

Another point to be discussed is surface area. Just as it is easier to penetrate something solid with a pointed rather than a blunt object, a smaller striking surface area makes the energy distribution per square centimeter higher, resulting in a greater chance of causing damage. In other words, a light tap from a hammer on the face causes only mild soft tissue trauma and no bone trauma; however, if that tap is applied to an osteotome with its narrow tip, a surgeon can easily cut through the facial bones.

Now that we understand basic energy transfer, we can try to classify nasal and facial injuries into a fairly workable system, that is, the energy of injury.

Low-energy injuries are best described as simple injuries caused by low-velocity trauma. "Simple" here refers to the pattern of bone injury with noncomminuted bone fragments and not to the ease of surgical repair. A surgeon would expect to see simple, low-energy injuries in the following situations:

1. Injuries created during hand-to-hand social altercations (specifically excluding hand-held weapons, such as sticks, pool cues, and pipes)
2. Most sports injuries
3. Uncomplicated falls, such as tripping
4. Low-velocity motor vehicle accidents

With these patients, greenstick or incomplete fractures can be seen in addition to the simple displacement or floating-fragment injury that typifies this degree of nasal trauma (Fig. 22–2A and B).

High-energy injuries are those in which there is a higher amount of energy absorbed by the nasal-facial skeleton, with comminution of bone fragments and associated injuries to the nasal soft tissue and orbital-facial skeleton (Fig. 22–3A and

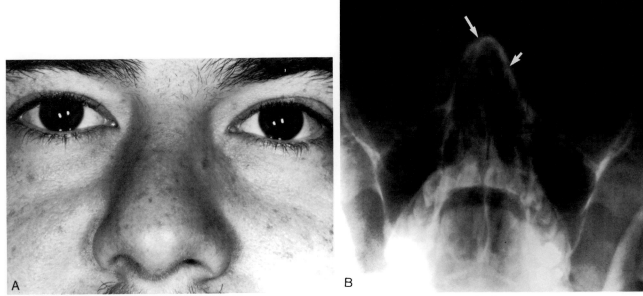

FIGURE 22–2. *A*, Photograph of patient after a blow to the left side of the nose during a basketball game. Note angulation of the nasal pyramid to the right and infracture of the left nasal bone. *B*, A Waters view of face demonstrating the left nasal fracture *(short arrow)* and rotation of the pyramid to the right *(long arrow)*.

B). The types of accidents in which these more severe injuries can occur include the following:

    1.   Injuries sustained from the application of leveraged force to the nose, such as blows with sticks, pool cues, pipes, and so on

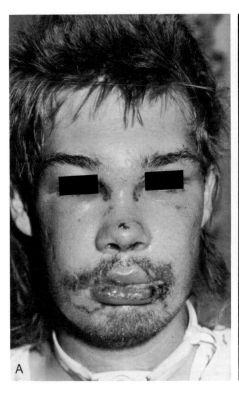
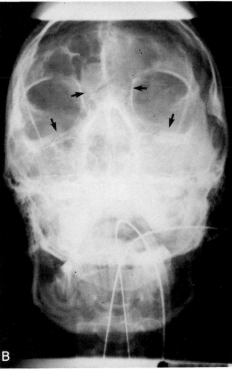

FIGURE 22–3. *A*, Photograph of patient involved in a high-speed motor vehicle accident; he struck his nose on the steering wheel. Note flattening and shortening of the nose. *B*, Radiograph of facial bones demonstrating multiple facial fractures *(arrows)*.

2. Falls from heights
3. Sports injuries with a fast-moving projectile, such as a ball or puck
4. High-velocity motor vehicle accidents

The difference between these two levels of injuries is not rigid. Moreover, the injuries are quite variable, with the surgeon using the patient's history in addition to the findings on examination to gauge the index of suspicion for potential associated injuries to the central nervous system, cervical spine, or orbital-facial skeleton.

Every patient who presents with a facial injury must receive an adequate initial workup, no matter how trivial the injury appears. A complete history of the details of the injury, in association with a past history of nasal-septal trauma or deformity, epistaxis, or nasal breathing problems, is essential if an adequate evaluation is to be performed. A complete head and neck examination, although at times difficult on a traumatized patient, is also required. Care should be taken to prevent causing any unnecessary pain or restarting a hemorrhage. If possible, initial photographs should be taken for documentation. External and internal nasal symmetry should be inspected after adequate vasoconstriction and topical anesthesia. Gentle suctioning or mechanical cleansing with Lathary probes is frequently required for adequate evaluation of the nasal cavity and septum. In addition, a surgeon must never forget, although he or she was consulted for nasal trauma, to look for associated head and neck injuries within the central nervous system, temporal bones, cervical spine, or orbital-facial skeleton. At this point, the surgeon must believe that the degree of injury he or she finds matches the history of the injury elicited from the patient. If they do not match, a mental re-evaluation is necessary to ensure against missed injuries.

Radiologic evaluation should, at a minimum, include facial bone and nasal radiographs for low-energy injuries.[13] With higher energy injuries, a computerized tomographic (CT) scan of the brain and midface should be done, with radiographic clearance of the cervical spine and mandible and any other survey films deemed necessary in a search for associated skeletal or soft tissue injuries. If the trauma has been high energy, then blood studies should be obtained, including a complete blood count (CBC)—which may not reflect the actual degree of blood loss until rehydration has occurred—and a clot should be saved for possible type and cross-match if the bleeding has been heavy or there are associated injuries that may require immediate surgical intervention. We do not routinely recommend a blood transfusion for a low hematocrit (i.e., packed cell volume [PCV] = 25) unless there is a medical necessity, such as ischemic cardiac disease, because of the risk and fear of blood-borne infections. Instead, the patient is told about the anemia, treated with iron and vitamins, and allowed to replace his or her own red blood cell volume. With patients who have a poor ability to replace red blood cells, such as those with liver disease, a transfusion may eventually be necessary if surgical intervention is contemplated. If surgery is to be delayed and it is believed that a transfusion may be necessary, a directed donor may be obtained and processed (at least 24 hours) to lessen the patient's anxiety, if not the actual risk of transfusion-related disease.

PATTERNS OF INJURY

The nose can be struck from three basic directions:

1. From the side (lateral injury)
2. From the front (sagittal injury)
3. From below (inferior injury)

Lateral injuries are the most common and can vary in severity from an isolated simple infracture of the nasal bone to complete disruption of the nasal skeleton with intranasal and extranasal soft tissue injuries. Anterior blows of low energy usually disrupt the

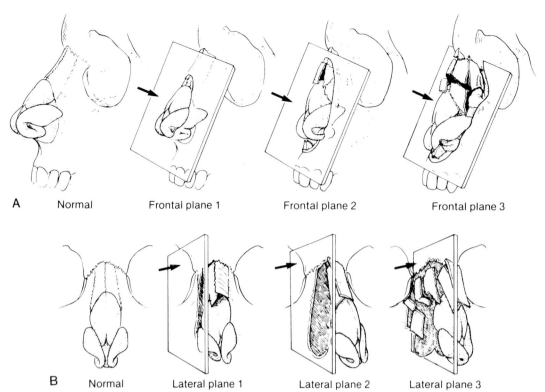

A   Normal   Frontal plane 1   Frontal plane 2   Frontal plane 3

B   Normal   Lateral plane 1   Lateral plane 2   Lateral plane 3

FIGURE 22–4.   *A* and *B*, Demonstration of the increasing degree of injury with increasing force to the nose. (From Mathog RH: *In* Cummings CW [ed]: Otolaryngology. Vol. 1. Head and Neck Surgery. St Louis, CV Mosby, 1986, p 626; with permission.)

septum before actually causing nasal pyramid injuries. With increasing energy, these injuries can cause a significant separation and communication of the nasal bones in addition to nasal-orbital-ethmoid fractures or other midface injuries (Fig. 22–4*A* and *B*). Inferior blows often fracture or disrupt the premaxillary spine–septum complex, fracturing the septum where it is pedicled at the spine. Bony nasal injuries are rare except when there is such high energy that avulsion occurs, with significant associated soft tissue disruption. All low-energy injuries can usually be repaired via a closed reduction. Early or late repair is possible; however, we prefer a delayed reduction (5 to 10 days after injury) and repair performed at an outpatient surgical facility. We prefer a delayed repair in this setting for the following reasons.

Time.   A delay in treatment allows resolution of soft tissue edema and gives the surgeon time to study old photographs, if available, and to plan an appropriate repair. This delay also permits a careful second look for any missed injuries in the head and neck or elsewhere. In addition, a delay gives the surgeon time to develop a patient-physician relationship based on trust and preoperative counseling and not just on the "luck" of the call schedule or emergency room referrals.

Outpatient Surgery.   In our experience, repairs performed in the emergency room or office (specifically an office not prepared for outpatient surgery) have a higher incidence of incomplete reduction that requires additional surgery for correction in the future. An outpatient surgery setting, although more expensive, allows improved local anesthesia with sedation and adequate monitoring, gives the patient the option of a general anesthesia, and provides the surgeon with complete instrumentation and supplies so that a change from a closed to an open technique may be made if it becomes necessary. Finally, an outpatient setting takes the burden of speed off the surgeon, who can ensure stable reduction and internally splint the fractures if the initial reduction is not stable.

TREATMENT

Low-Energy Injuries

Local anesthesia with sedation is our preferred approach for these types of injuries. We begin with a gentle spray of either 4 per cent cocaine or 4 per cent lidocaine (Xylocaine) in combination with 1 per cent phenylephrine hydrochloride (Neo-Synephrine) (Fig. 22–5). A transoral block of the sphenopalatine ganglion is performed via injection of the greater palatine foramen with 1.5 ml of 1 per cent lidocaine with 1:100,000 epinephrine given bilaterally if septal work is to be done. This maneuver markedly reduces posterior nasal cavity bleeding and greatly improves posterior nasal anesthesia. If the septum is not markedly deviated, cocaine paste or flakes can be applied with a Lathary probe transnasally, posterior to the middle turbinate to block the sphenopalatine ganglion at the sphenopalatine foramen. In addition, the anterior ethmoid artery and nerve can be blocked transnasally with cocaine to improve anterior nasal anesthesia. It is prudent to leave the Lathary probes in place for approximately 5 minutes to ensure that a block has been established. If not, the probe is adjusted, and another 5 minutes is allowed to pass. Following this step, the nose gets a vasoconstrictive field block with 1 per cent lidocaine (Xylocaine), with 1:100,000 epinephrine slowly injected to protect against tachycardia and hypertension. This step should include sublabial injections along the nasal spine, the septum, and the inferior and middle turbinates, as well as the standard soft tissue injections used in rhinoplasty. With local anesthesia, effect relies more on accuracy of placement than on volume, a fact that can be difficult to transmit to junior residents. If additional vasoconstriction of the nasal mucosa is desirable and if it can be tolerated by the patient, 4 per cent cocaine spray, 0.5 per cent phenylephrine hydrochloride (Neo-Synephrine), or oxymetazoline can be used as either a spray or a pack. Once the blocks have been placed, an adequate amount of time should pass to allow for the vasoconstrictive properties to take effect. The surgeon must not fall into the trap of immediately manipulating the nose after injection. The anesthetic properties take effect almost immediately, and although it may be painless for the patient, the surgeon will produce excessive bleeding that persists throughout the remainder of the procedure. We even place our anesthetic vasoconstrictive blocks with a general

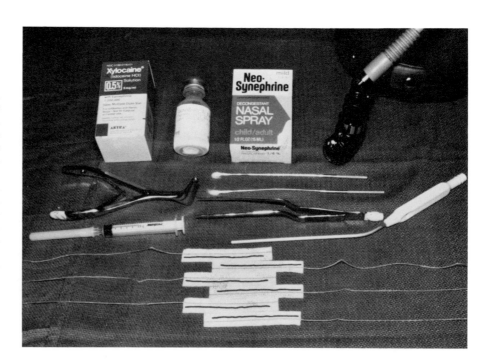

FIGURE 22–5. Medication and instrumentation used to provide local vasoconstrictive anesthesia to the nose and nasal cavity. Instruments include nasal speculum, bayonet forceps, Frazier-type suction, Lathary probes, headlight, 3-ml syringe with a 1½-inch 27-gauge needle and ½-inch × 3-inch cottonoids. Medications include 4 per cent cocaine, phenylephrine hydrochloride (Neo-Synephrine), and lidocaine (Xylocaine) with epinephrine.

anesthetic and then slowly prepare the patient, scrub, and allow the medication time to do its job.

After adequate anesthesia, the face is again visualized and palpated for symmetry and fracture lines, and the intranasal structures are carefully examined for mucosal lacerations, bone spurs, and so on. The area of the middle meatus should be examined to ensure that infracture of the middle turbinate has not occurred, impairing the function of the osteomeatal complex. If the status of this complex is in doubt, nasal sinus endoscopes are excellent for evaluating this complex and, if necessary, repairing it (Fig. 22–6). Nasal fractures are then reduced as necessary. If there is a simple noncomminuted displacement injury, then an Asch forceps or Goldman septal displacer can be used to distract the fracture and return it to its original position. Once in place, it should be evaluated for stability. If the fragment is not stable initially, then the surgeon must consider internal splinting or, if necessary, open reduction and fixation. Internal splinting can be accomplished with nasal packing, Silastic blocks that are carved to shape, or Silastic sheets that are stacked and stitched together as needed.[14-16] If Silastic is to be used, then a through-and-through nasal stitch to a button, lead plate, or another piece of Silastic may be necessary to guarantee proper retention. A key factor is to be sure that the stitch is not too tight, causing skin or mucosal pressure necrosis.

Adequate bone reduction, stabilization of fragments, and complete mucosal coverage are the essentials of therapy for nasal fractures. The last is often the most important consideration when it comes to the prevention of late sequelae. If the septum is involved in the injury, thin Silastic sheeting is trimmed to fit and is sewn on either side of the septum with a 3–0 nylon trans-septal suture. This procedure allows support of mucosal flaps and prevents synechiae from forming between the turbinates and septum, a complication that can lead to narrowing of the nasal airway, deviation of the septum, and twisting of the nasal-septal complex, with subsequent nasal deformities.

If there has been a history of prior trauma with septal deformation, then, as an adjunct to simple repair, an elective septoplasty can be performed to improve breathing and mobilize the nasal-septal tripod for easier manipulation and repositioning. Once the area is open, evaluation and repair of septal fractures, twists, or dislocations are facilitated. With anterior or inferior injuries, an open septal technique allows suture fixation of the caudal septum to the nasal spine or premaxilla, maintaining nasal tip projection, a problem that is commonly seen with these types of injuries.

At the completion of the procedure, the nose and face should be inspected and palpated for symmetry and stability of reduction. Gentle packing with antibiotic-impregnated gauze or Telfa helps to control any hemorrhage and internally supports the nasal-septal pyramid. The skin should be cleaned and degreased, and $\frac{1}{2}$-inch Steri-strips or $\frac{1}{2}$-inch paper tape is placed on the nose to maintain symmetry and act as a base for the placement of a nasal splint. We feel that tincture of benzoin should not be placed on the nasal skin prior to placement of the tape. If this is done, the thin nasal skin can inadvertently be removed with the tape. Adequate preparation with degreasers is important to allow adequate tape adhesion to the nose. It should, however,

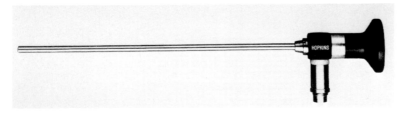

FIGURE 22–6. A zero-degree nasal sinus endoscope for accurate intranasal examination. (Courtesy of the Karl Storz Endoscopy America, Inc.)

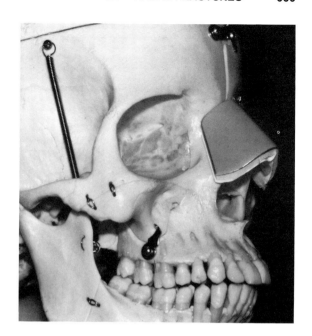

FIGURE 22-7. Note placement of prepackaged adhesive nasal splint. It should be placed only over the nasal bones and should not cover the cartilaginous lower nose.

be noted that this is a personal preference and that many noted nasal surgeons use benzoin or Mastisol on the nose for its increased adhesive properties. The choice of a nasal splint is truly individualized, and many surgeons swear by a certain material or design. Our choice is one of the many prepackaged splints simply because they are convenient and can be found in nearly every operating room (Fig. 22-7).

When using a splint, the surgeon must be sure to mold it and, if necessary, trim it prior to removing the adhesive backing. Once placed, it should not be removed and replaced. The splint should cushion the nose, maintain an already adequately reduced and stabilized nasal fracture, and remind the patient that he or she needs to be careful not to allow anything to contact the nose until the surgeon gives clearance. The splint is not to be used as an attempt to maintain an unstable reduction in the hope that it will heal properly.

After reduction, antibiotics and analgesics should be given to the patient with a typed list of postoperative instructions and follow-up appointments. If the septal injury is minimal and internal splinting with packing is not necessary, Telfa nasal packs can be removed on the third postoperative day. If packing for support is necessary, we usually wait until the fifth to seventh postoperative day to remove the packing. The external splint is gently removed routinely on the seventh postoperative day by gentle dissection with a blunt probe between the tape and nasal skin. Once removed, gentle cleansing with adhesive remover and degreaser is done, and the nasal cavity is decongested and anesthetized with topical spray. A thorough visual examination for maintenance of reduction and symmetry is done externally as well as intranasally. Gentle palpation should confirm adequate reduction without fragment rocking or motion. If motion is still present, the nose is retaped, and a new splint is placed for another 7 days, possibly with a new partial nasal pack. After full evaluation of the external nose and satisfaction with the repair, topical anterior ethmoid nerve blocks are placed as described previously, and septal splints are removed. Anterior ethmoid nerve anesthesia gently improves the patient's tolerance of the procedure. In addition, if a smaller superior pack needs to be replaced, the anterior ethmoid nerve block facilitates placement.

If all is well, the patient is given back the original external splint after it has all the previous tape removed and is told to wear the splint at night for another week. This instruction is to remind the patient to be gentle with the nose and to keep the head elevated. Limitations in activity include no strenuous lifting or activity for 4 additional weeks and no contact sports for at least 6 weeks and only then after clearance by the physician. The patient must be made to understand that his or her nose is still not healed and that minor trauma could easily displace it again, negating all of the surgeon's efforts and renewing the patient's discomfort. Postoperative visits at 7 days, 14 days, and 6 weeks are routine in our practice. Of course, these are just guidelines, and judgment must be used in regard to seeing the patient frequently enough to ensure proper healing as well as acceptable psychologic status and satisfaction on the patient's part. If, after removal of the splint and packing, the nose is found to be inadequately or incompletely healed, there are four options open to the surgeon and the patient:

1. Repack and splint the nose in the office to offer additional healing time after attempting to re-reduce the fracture with the patient under local anesthesia.

2. Immediately (within the next 2 to 3 days) return to the outpatient surgery suite to attempt to reduce the nose again and replace the splint and packing for another 7 days.

3. Immediately return to the outpatient surgery suite for a planned open reduction in an attempt to realign the fractures and fix them internally.

4. Discuss the options with the patient and, if he or she desires, wait and watch. If, in 3 to 6 months, the patient is dissatisfied with appearance or function, then return to the outpatient surgery suite for an open revision procedure.

Complex Injuries

The repair of complex nasal injuries with comminution of bone fragments, associated soft tissue trauma, or other injuries from high-energy trauma is a great challenge to the surgeon. This type of repair is not for the novice, and whoever accepts the case must be well versed in the evaluation and treatment of injuries involving the entire nasal-facial-orbital complex.

The key to success with these types of injuries is an initial complete physical assessment with recognition of all injuries, not just those that are immediately life threatening. This is especially true for the central nervous system and the cervical spine. Once the patient is found to be free from associated immediate life-threatening injuries, the head and neck can be more thoroughly evaluated. As always, the evaluation should begin with a thorough head and neck history and physical examination. Immediate treatment is aimed at preservation of tissue, prevention of infection, and identification of all facial injuries. Multiple consultations with specialists in neurosurgery, otolaryngology/head and neck surgery, general (trauma) surgery, ophthalmology, oral and maxillofacial surgery, and neuroradiology are common.

Once a baseline of information has been gathered, a priority list for treatment is established, and a plan is initiated. Immediate treatment of high-energy nasal-septal injuries should include the following:

1. A complete extranasal and intranasal examination with adequate anesthesia and vasoconstriction
2. Identification of external nasal and intranasal lacerations
3. Identification and control of sites of hemorrhage

Once the injury has been evaluated, the surgeon again has the option of immediate or delayed repair. Immediate repair is indicated for soft tissue trauma with lacerations of the external nose or through-and-through nasal tears. These lacerations should be cleaned, copiously irrigated with normal saline to remove debris, and closed in layers if necessary. Superficial external nasal lacerations may require only a Steri-Strip closure or epidermal sutures, whereas a through-and-through tear of the alae will require closure of the mucosa, cartilage, subcutaneous tissue, and skin. Our choice of sutures for this procedure is chromic (4–0) for the mucosal layer, clear nylon (5–0) for the cartilage, chromic or Vicryl for the subcutaneous layer (5–0), and nylon for the skin (6–0, 7–0). Every effort should be made to preserve tissue, and we believe that it is foolish to contemplate a more complex local flap or tissue transfer in the acute situation. Our reason is that in the acute setting the risk of infection with subsequent flap failure is higher and the surgeon has no knowledge of how the patient will heal, what size the final defect will be, and what additional procedures will ultimately be necessary. It is prudent always to inform the patient at the beginning of treatment that revision or staged operations are often needed. In these higher energy nasal injuries, it is unusual for the surgeon to be able simply to reduce a fracture and stabilize it with a closed procedure. Often, open septal procedures allowing a septo-plasty with mobilization and subsequent repair of the quadrangular cartilage are needed.[17,18] Depending on the degree of injury, additional exposure via open nasal procedures can be used to facilitate repair. With open procedures, care should be taken not to devitalize bone and cartilage because of the unpredictability of free fragment resorption and the increased risk of infection. A standard rhinoplasty expo-sure with intercartilaginous incisions and mobilization of the nasal skin over the bridge region can allow the surgeon access to improve the reduction of free bone fragments or fragments that are difficult to distract.[19] If small comminuted fragments of bone can be palpated over the bridge, this technique allows for their removal or an improved chance of reduction. Open rhinoplasty, with its improved exposure of the nasal tip, anterior septum, and upper lateral cartilages, is a great help in repairing unstable injuries or those involving disruption of the upper lateral cartilage to the nasal bone (Fig. 22–8). If unrecognized and not repaired, this injury can lead to a persistent depression on the nose, with movement of the upper lateral cartilage inward on inspiration, leading to collapse of the nasal valve area and to nasal airway obstruction. The main advantage of an open rhinoplasty technique is that it allows the surgeon direct access to the lower or cartilaginous nose, ensuring identification and direct repair of all injuries.

The third type of open exposure for nasal injuries is the "H" or open-sky tech-nique originally described by Converse[20] (Fig. 22–9). This technique combines bilat-eral medial canthal incisions with a transverse nasal bridge incision, giving access to the bony nasal skeleton and its attachments superiorly to the frontal bone, laterally to the maxilla, and deep to the ethmoids. Direct wiring of multiple fragments is possible via this approach; however, we have recently begun to use a miniplate fixation system to allow secure anchoring to a more stable structure (i.e., frontal bone or maxilla), with subsequent improved support to the entire bridge. Careful realignment of the incisions, with meticulous repair, is essential to minimize the scar in such a cosmeti-cally conspicuous area. In addition, one should never close a deep nasal laceration

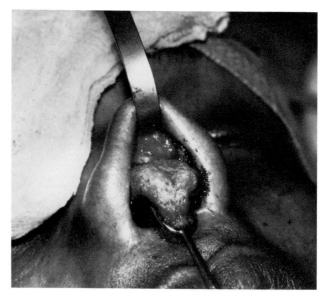

FIGURE 22–8. Exposure provided during an open rhino-plasty of the nasal tip structures.

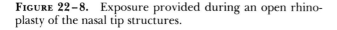

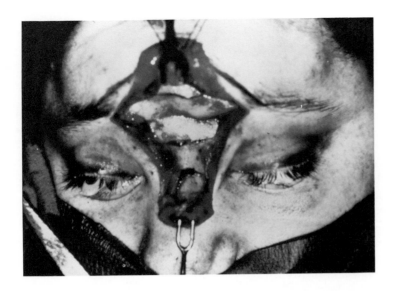

FIGURE 22–9. "Open sky" approach demonstrating multiple fractures of the nasal bones that can be repaired under direct vision.

without gentle exploration for other possible injuries. It is often far easier to identify and reapproximate a transected cartilage strip through a laceration primarily than to attempt to identify, mobilize, and repair scarred cartilage fragments at a later date.

The choice of setting for nasal repair is frequently more dependent on the patient and his or her medical condition than on the surgeon's preference. If there are other injuries that require simultaneous repair, an inpatient hospital setting is necessary. If additional surgeons are planning to treat the patient while he or she is under the same anesthetic, it is the head and neck surgeon's responsibility to ensure that no transnasal tubes or monitors are placed and that the oral endotracheal tube is placed in the midline with no distortion of the face or nose. If given a choice, it is our preference to treat the patient last, after the other services have completed their work. This practice allows the surgeon not to be rushed and also guarantees adequate protection of the nose and face during transport of the patient, a subject that is often not of primary importance to the general or orthopedic surgeon.

The reconstructive surgeon should master three special techniques if he or she hopes to treat high-energy, complex nasal injuries effectively. The first is intranasal wiring for the treatment of traumatic telecanthus.[21,22] With injuries that involve the medial canthal ligaments bilaterally, the medial canthus is displaced laterally, making the nose appear much broader without actually increasing the interpupillary distance (Fig. 22–10). This injury is approached through bilateral medial canthal incisions. These can be connected across the midline if more exposure of the nasal bridge is necessary. Fine 26-gauge wire is threaded through the fibrous region of the medial canthal ligament, and if no fracture lines are available, a hole is drilled at an appropriate point in the nasal bones bilaterally. A 19-gauge spinal needle is bent with the trocar still in place to prevent obliteration of the canal and is carefully passed through the perforations intranasally, making sure not to perforate the globe. The trocar is removed, and the wires are then passed retrogradely through the needle so that the wire loop is closed on one side. The loop is then twisted until the slack is reduced and the medial canthi are at a normal distance. The excess wire is trimmed, and the twist is tucked into a fracture line or along the lamina papyracea. If needed, external buttons or lead plates can also be used to stabilize the nasal bridge (Fig. 22–11).

The second special technique is used to suspend the nasal-orbital-ethmoid complex anteriorly after an infracture injury.[23] A halo device is attached to the skull, and the nasal bridge is repaired with direct wiring or plating. The nose is internally splinted with carved silicone blocks and is secured transnasally to lead plates or silicone sheets. A pair of transnasal wires are passed through the internal splints and secured into a loop. A second intermediate loop is then attached to the frame and

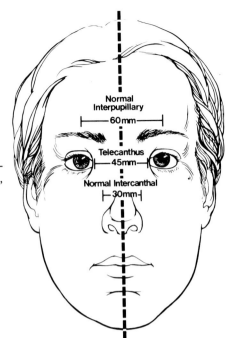

FIGURE 22–10. The normal and pathologic distances of the naso-orbital complex in traumatic telecanthus. (From Holt GR: Otolaryngol Clin North Am 18:90, 1985; with permission.)

tightened until the nasal-orbital-ethmoid complex is returned to its proper position and angle. This wire is left in place for 6 weeks to 3 months, or until the fracture is stabilized, and is then removed. This prolonged suspension requires meticulous observation and treatment of the wound to prevent pressure necrosis of the nose.

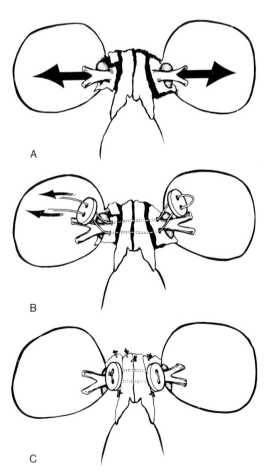

FIGURE 22–11. Demonstration of the technique used to repair traumatic telecanthus. *A,* Bilateral nasoethmoid complex fractures. *B,* Transnasal wire insertion through Silastic button. *C,* Closure over Silastic button, maintaining reduction. (From Holt GR: Otolaryngol Clin North Am 18:90, 1985; with permission.)

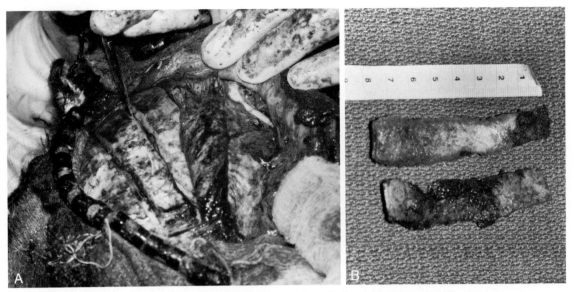

FIGURE 22–12. *A,* Demonstration of final harvesting of calvarial bone graft with an osteotome after outlining graft with a drill. *B,* Inner and outer tables after splitting. Inner table will be returned to the skull for protection of the brain, and outer table will be used to graft bone defect.

A third technique that should be familiar to the reconstructive surgeon is the use of split calvarial free bone grafts for the replacement of missing or nonsalvageable bone fragments[12] (Fig. 22–12). Again, we do not recommend this technique in the acute situation, for reasons previously stated. This technique can be used to replace bony defects of the nose, frontal bone, and medial orbital walls. The defect size is first measured, and a template is made to fit. This template is then transferred to the skull, where diploic bone covers most areas except for the squamous portion of the temporal bone. Care must be taken to avoid the sagittal sinus and the areas of the cranial emissary veins. The contour of the bone defect can often be approximated, depending on the location on the skull chosen for harvesting. Small segments of bone can be harvested by outlining a slightly larger piece of skull with a drill to cut through the outer cortex. A small, curved osteotome is then used to divide the diploë. A slightly larger piece is outlined because it is easier to trim to fit than make up for a graft that is too small. Larger sections (strips greater than 2.5 cm wide) will often require complete inner and outer table removal, with subsequent division by osteotome of the plates through the diploë and with return of the inner table to the skull. The outer table can then be shaped and wired or plated to restore bony nasal-frontal-orbital continuity.

These three special techniques are infrequently used; however, familiarity with them will allow the reconstructive surgeon to care for the most severely damaged noses with the greatest chances of success. A more detailed discussion of nasal-orbital-ethmoid injuries is presented in Chapter 19.

CONCLUSION

The nasal fracture is often an overlooked and underestimated facial injury. Nasal symmetry and function are of great importance to the patient, and inadequate or inappropriate treatment is unacceptable in view of the current litiginous climate. If the surgeon approaches this acute injury with the same forethought as he or she would an elective cosmetic septorhinoplasty, the surgeon will be rewarded with better results and, therefore, more satisfied patients.

REFERENCES

1. Breasted JH: Edwin Smith surgical papyrus. *In* Facsimile and Hieroglyphic Transliteration with Translation and Commentary. Chicago, University of Chicago Press, 1930.
2. Gilles HD, and Kilner TP: The treatment of the broken nose. Lancet 1:147–149, 1928.
3. Woodward FD: The management of recent fractures of the nose and sinuses. Ann Otol Rhinol Laryngol 44:264–273, 1935.
4. Metzenbaum MF: Recent fracture of the nasal base lines of both outer nasal walls, with divergent displacement. Arch Otolaryngol 34:723–735, 1941.
5. Belker DJ: Nasal fractures. Arch Otolaryngol 48:344–361, 1948.
6. Fomon S, Schattner A, Bell JW, et al: Management of recent nasal fractures. Arch Otolaryngol 55:321–342, 1952.
7. Lowenthal G: Diagnosis and early treatment of lesser facial fractures. Ann Otol Rhinol Laryngol 62:995–1034, 1953.
8. Clark GM, Wallace CS: Analysis of nasal support. Arch Otolaryngol 92:118–123, 1970.
9. Stranc MF, Robertson GA: A classification of injuries of the nasal skeleton. Ann Plast Surg 2:468–474, 1979.
10. Harrison DH: Nasal injuries: Their pathogenesis and treatment. Br J Plast Surg 32:575–584, 1979.
11. Murphy JAM, Busuttil A, Vaughan G: A pathological classification of nasal fractures. Injury 17:338–344, 1986.
12. Gruss JS: Naso-ethmoid orbital fractures: Classification and role of primary bone grafting. Plast Reconstr Surg 75:303–315, 1985.
13. Clayton MI, Lesser THJ: The role of radiography in the management of nasal fractures. J Laryngol Otol 100:797–801, 1986.
14. Sear AJ: A method of internal splinting for unitable nasal fractures. Br J Ear Surg 14:203–209, 1977.
15. Wadley JK: Correction of unstable nasal fractures by intranasal support. Laryngoscope 89:327–331, 1978.
16. Colclasure JB, Graham SS: Support of unstable nasal fractures with silicone rubber wedge splints. Arch Otolaryngol 111:443–445, 1985.
17. Jordan LW: The management of acute injuries of the nasal septum. Laryngoscope 77:1121–1129, 1967.
18. Holt GR: Immediate open reduction of nasal septal injuries. Ear, Nose Throat J 57:345–354, 1978.
19. Goldman IB: When is rhinoplasty indicated for correction of recent nasal fractures? Laryngoscope 55:689–700, 1964.
20. Converse JM, Hogan VM: Open sky approach for reduction of naso-orbital fractures. Plast Reconstr Surg 46:396–398, 1970.
21. Stranc MF: Primary treatment of naso-ethmoid injuries with increased intercanthal distance. Br J Plast Surg 23:8–25, 1970.
22. Holt GR, Holt JE: Nasoethmoid complex injuries. Otolaryngol Clin North Am 18:87–98, 1985.
23. Wurman LH, Salk JG, Flannery JV: Halo external fixation of nasal fractures. Laryngoscope 93:1212–1216, 1983.

CHAPTER 23

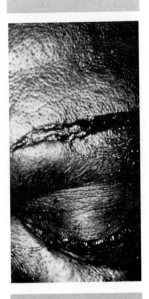

MANAGEMENT OF SOFT TISSUE INJURIES

MICHAEL P. POWERS, D.D.S., M.S.,
JAMES BERTZ, D.D.S., M.D., and
RAYMOND J. FONSECA, D.M.D.

Soft tissue injuries to the facial structures are commonly encountered in the treatment of the traumatized patient. Soft tissue wounds may be limited to the superficial structures, but more serious injuries may extend to involve anatomic structures such as the facial bones; the sensory and motor nerves of the face; the parotid, submandibular, or nasolacrimal glands or ducts; or the dentoalveolar structures. Soft tissue injuries include abrasions, contusions, "clean-cut" lacerations, contused lacerations, bites, burns of various degrees, and avulsive wounds.

INITIAL EXAMINATION

The initial management of the injured individual must include establishment of the airway, control of hemorrhage, and stabilization of injuries to other major systems prior to evaluation of facial soft tissue wounds. Fractures of supporting facial bones then must be ruled out by careful clinical and radiographic examination. Fractures should be reduced and stabilized before final soft tissue repair. Because of the excellent blood supply to the facial region, facial lacerations do not require immediate treatment. During the assessment period or during treatment of other injuries, the wounds should be kept moist with gauze soaked in an antibiotic solution until final management.

Hemorrhage associated with most head and neck wounds can be substantial but can usually be controlled with local measures of pressure and clamping, ligation, and/or electrocautery of visibly bleeding vessels. Scalp wounds or disruption of major vessels may result in blood loss to the point of hypovolemic shock. According to Lynch,[1] if a patient exhibits shock with facial trauma, one of three conditions is usually present: (1) The trauma is very extensive and complex, with underlying facial fractures or oropharyngeal wounds, or both, and possible intracranial injury; (2) treatment has been inordinately delayed, and an extended period of controlled hemorrhage or repeated episodes of bleeding have occurred; or (3) the head and neck wounds are associated with other, unrecognized injuries, such as long-bone fractures or chest or abdominal trauma.

Persistent bleeding should be evaluated by direct inspection to avoid damage to other vital structures. The wound may bleed after cleansing and debridement. Copious irrigation with saline or balanced salt solutions will assist with removal of blood clots and granulation tissue that may slowly ooze. Direct pressure will assist in the control of bleeding from the wound surface and will limit hematoma formation. Hematoma formation is a major cause of infection and wound breakdown. If hemostasis cannot be achieved, drains should be considered.[2]

It is recommended that before final treatment of the wounds and after cleaning of the skin, photographic records be obtained for insurance and legal purposes. Lawsuits are initiated more and more on the basis of results, not negligence, and lay people often expect nearly perfect results, whether these are realistic or not.[3]

Follow-up photographs will aid in the assessment of healing and scar maturation as well as the need for future scar revision.[3]

Wounds can be divided into two groups—clean and contaminated. Prophylactic antibiotics are usually not indicated in clean, fresh lacerations of the skin. The probability of contamination increases rapidly and is directly related to the length of time that has elapsed since the initial injury. The contamination of the clean wound is usually via *Streptococcus* and *Staphylococcus* on the skin of the face and multiple bacteria if the mucosal layers are violated. Wounds that involve the mucosal linings of the oral cavity and pharynx, especially through-and-through lacerations from skin through the mucosal layers, should be considered contaminated. Saliva may carry normal oral flora to deeper structures, and wound infections may develop.

Wounds that have been contaminated by foreign materials, such as dirty gravel, metal, tooth fragments, grass, wood, glass, and organic materials, must be thoroughly examined in the initial phase, and the material must be removed to prevent wound infections. The wounds should be thoroughly irrigated with a balanced salt solution as well as cleansed with detergent soaps and thoroughly irrigated with Ringer's lactate or normal saline. Animal bites should be cleansed with detergents and water to remove the animal's saliva and other contaminants from the wound before closing primarily. Tetanus prophylaxis should be instituted with contaminated wounds. With a previously immunized patient, if a course of active immunization has not been given within 10 years of the injury, a booster dose of 0.5 ml of tetanus toxoid is recommended. In unimmunized patients, passive immunization with hyperimmune (human) tetanus globulin, followed by a course of active tetanus immunization, should be instituted.[1,4,5] Antibiotics such as penicillin, cephalosporin, and other drugs active against gram-positive organisms are the drugs of choice in soft tissue injuries.

After the patient's condition has been stabilized or if there are minimal associated injuries, definitive treatment of the soft tissue wounds should be done. Clean wounds may be closed primarily up to 48 hours following injury. This delay in the primary closure of soft tissue wounds may be indicated if the supporting facial bones have been fractured. Treatment of the fracture should be completed before final soft tissue closure, as the wound may provide access to the fracture site and the closure may be damaged during fracture reduction.

Delayed primary wound closure is also indicated in patients with extensive facial edema or subcutaneous hematoma and when the wound margins are badly contused and tissues are devitalized. Primary repair in such damaged tissues is difficult, and the possibility of bacterial infestation with wound breakdown is increased. Limited debridement to remove devitalized tissue, moist dressings, and antibiotic therapy until resolution of the edema and control of infection are indicated until definitive treatment of the wounds can be accomplished.

Open wound treatment, formerly universally accepted for contaminated wounds and bite injuries, is no longer practiced for facial wounds, except abrasive wounds.[6] Immediate definitive treatment of maxillofacial injuries was employed in the Vietnam Conflict. Wounds of the face and anterior cervical region were repaired with primary closure when possible. Minimal, careful debridement was performed, and the anatomy was restored to as normal a position as possible. Except when very destructive wounds with loss of important parts were present, most of these patients could expect no major impairment of function.[7]

Open wounds allowed to heal with granulation tissue leave large, unsightly wounds on the face. The wounds should be mechanically debrided and closed primarily or, in the case of defects, closed primarily by local flaps or skin grafts. If the wound is to be treated by delayed primary closure because of contamination, edema, fractures, or other clinical findings, the patient should be treated with systemic antibiotics, the wound should be cleansed and debrided, and a sterile dressing should be placed until final treatment can be given.[8]

Repair of the soft tissue wounds may be done with the patient under local or general anesthesia, depending on a variety of circumstances. If injuries are extensive, general anesthesia is indicated. If no jaw fractures exist, it is best to intubate orally for injuries above the occlusal plane and nasally for those below. It may be necessary to change the route of intubation during the procedures. With fractures of the maxilla, mandible, and/or dentoalveolar structures, as well as soft tissue injuries, nasoendotracheal intubation is required to allow for placement of intermaxillary fixation, if only temporarily, if rigid fixation is used. A tracheotomy may be required if airway management dictates so for presurgical, surgical, or postsurgical care.

Local anesthesia with or without premedication may be used in cases of less severe wounds, such as small lacerations, contusions, or abrasions. A 1 per cent lidocaine with 1:100,000 epinephrine solution may be injected into the wound margin. If possible, nerve blocks are helpful to minimize the amount of solution required for this field block in large wounds and to avoid distortion of the tissues by the anesthetic solution.

No matter whether treatment is provided in the emergency room or in the outpatient clinic, with the patient under local anesthesia, the same care and diligence should be observed in treating the soft tissue wounds as in the operating room when the patient is under general anesthesia. The cleansing of the clean wound involves washing the skin and removing foreign bodies from the wound. Soaps do not harm the skin surface, as the thick, cornified layer of epidermis protects the underlying tissue surface, but soaps may enter the wound and cause cellular damage and necrosis. Toxic materials, such as alcohol, hydrogen peroxide, and benzalkonium chloride, and strong soaps, such as hexachlorophene and povidone-iodine, should not have direct contact with the open wound, as these materials kill cells on contact.[9,10] If these materials are used around the wound, the wound should be thoroughly irrigated with balanced salt solutions (Ringer's lactated solution or normal saline). A rule regarding the application of antiseptic is never to put anything in a wound that could not be comfortably tolerated in the conjunctival sac.[10,11]

If the laceration extends into the scalp, moustache, or beard, the area should be shaved to provide good access for debridement and repair.[8] Areas such as the eyebrows or the hairline should never be shaved but, rather, clipped closely with scissors to provide a landmark for accurate positioning of the soft tissues during the closure.[12] It is important that the alignment of the eyebrow or hairline not be altered, as improper orientation is very unaesthetic and the hair can be used as a guide for reconstruction.

The wound must again be inspected for the presence of foreign materials. A pulsive-type irrigating device is useful to remove debris, necrotic tissue, and loose material. An abrasive wound that may have ground dirt, glass, or other debris into the wound should be scrubbed with a scrub brush or toothbrush and detergent soap to remove the foreign material. A No. 15 blade may be used to scrape material that cannot be brushed clean or to remove deeply embedded particles, frequently seen with blast injuries. All material should be removed, and time should be taken to clean the wound as completely as possible. If allowed to remain within the tissue, the contaminant may become a source of infection or may heal as a permanent "tattoo" that is difficult to treat with future procedures. Polymyxin B sulfate ointment may be used on the wound to remove residual grease or tar that cannot be removed with routine scrubbing techniques. The wound should then be copiously irrigated with a balanced salt solution. Time spent meticulously debriding traumatic wounds in the primary repair period will prevent unfavorable or unaesthetic results from infection, hypertrophic scars, and foreign body granulomas.[8,13]

Rapid and complete invasion of the wound space by fibroblasts is a critical step in normal healing. Dead tissue fragments, hematomas, and foreign bodies act as physical barriers to fibroblast penetration.[10] Debridement of facial wounds should be limited to obviously devitalized and necrotic tissue. Radical excision of soft tissues in the facial region should be avoided. Because of the rich blood supply to the region, excessive debridement is unnecessary, and tissue will survive with a very small pedicle. It is better to err on the side of retaining tissues that may not eventually survive rather than remove tissues that are needed for a satisfactory repair of the injury. If the wound margin is extremely irregular and reapproximation is difficult, the irregular edges should be excised to produce clean wound margins and minimize scar formation. Occasionally, additional small incisions are helpful to reapproximate tissues and break up straight-line scars.

During the final examination, it is extremely important to evaluate whether vital tissues have been damaged. Deep lacerations across the course of the branches of the facial nerve, hypoglossal nerve, and sensory branch of the trigeminal nerve should be evaluated for possible transection. A nerve stimulator may be helpful to stimulate the appropriate muscle groups in the nonparalyzed patient under general anesthesia. If a nerve has been damaged, appropriate microsurgical techniques should be used to attempt to restore function of the nerve. In some avulsive injuries, secondary nerve graft procedures may be indicated. During the examination phase and initial treatment, the severed nerve trunks should be identified and marked by colored tags so that they can be easily located in future reconstruction procedures.

ANATOMY OF THE SKIN

The skin covers the body in various degrees of thickness, elasticity, texture, and mobility, and it makes transitions into mucosal membranes about the oral cavity, nostrils, and eyelids. The thickness of the skin on the facial region ranges from 0.013 inch over the upper eyelid, 0.030 to 0.040 inch over most of the face, approximately 0.065 inch over the eyebrows, and 0.080 to 0.090 inch over the neck.[14]

The skin is an extensive sensory organ with numerous nerve endings to provide feedback to touch, pressure, temperature, and painful stimuli. It serves as protection from loss of body fluids to dehydration, invasion of pathogenic organisms, and excessive ultraviolet radiation. The skin is also responsible in temperature regulation for heat loss through evaporation.[15] Subcutaneous voluntary muscles in the face and neck allow for movement of the skin and for facial expression.

The skin is composed of the surface layer epidermis and the underlying dermal layer (Fig. 23–1). The epidermis is stratified squamous epithelium with five layers (in order from the surface to the dermal layer): the stratum corneum, stratum lucidum, stratum granulosum, stratum spinosum, and stratum germinativum. The epidermis sends projections into the dermis, and irregularities of the dermis interlock with the epidermis; these are called epidermal pegs and dermal papillae, respectively.[15]

The stratum germinativum, or basal layer, is usually one or two cells thick and has much mitotic activity.[14] The basal layer is responsible for regeneration of the cells in the epidermis in the repair process and for normal turnover of cells in the epidermis. On the face, regeneration is both from the germinal layer and from the epidermal pegs. Because of the large number of epidermal pegs on the face, a significant portion of the epidermal layer can be removed without significant scarring.[16] The stratum spinosum, or prickle cell layer, consists of polyhedral cells with ovoid nuclei. The granular layer is named for its histidine-rich cytoplasmic granules of keratohyalin,

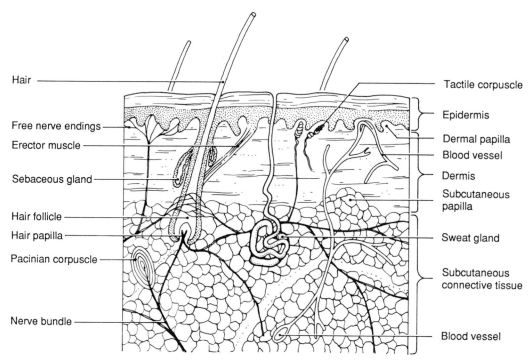

FIGURE 23–1. Cross-section of the skin, which consists of three layers—the epidermis, dermis, and subcutaneous connective tissue.

thought to be important in keratin formation.[17] Changes in granular cell layer formation are seen in the development of the healing wound.[16] The stratum lucidum is found only on the palms and soles. The stratum corneum is the outermost layer of the epidermis and is formed of keratinized, flattened cells that are usually without nuclei. The corneum layer is responsible for the variable thicknesses of skin found on the body.[17]

The dermis is divided into two layers—a superficial papillary layer and a deeper reticular layer. The papillary zone is a thin, finely textured zone immediately beneath the epidermal rete ridges. The papillary layer gives rise to the dermal papilla with fine fibrils of collagen and provides a blood supply to the avascular epidermal layer.[15] The papillary dermis and epidermis together form a functional unit that provides an important metabolic area for retaining the normal integrity of the skin.[16,17]

The reticular layer of the dermis is a thick, dense mass of collagenous and elastic connective tissue fibers. Reticular fibers, which give the layer its name, are young, finely formed collagen fibers with a narrower diameter than that of mature collagen.[17] Elastic and other collagen fibers in the papillary dermal layer tend to be perpendicularly orientated to the overlying epidermal layer, while the fibers within the reticular layer are mainly orientated tangentially to the epidermal layer.[15] Collagen fibers provide the skin with tensile strength, whereas the elastic fibers give the skin its elastic properties.

The orientation of the fibers in the reticular layer and their relation to the epidermal layer create lines of tension in the skin that are greater in a plane perpendicular to the reticular layer fibers than in a plane parallel to these fibers. The predominant orientation of the fiber bundles in relation to the surface differs in different regions of the body; these patterns were described by Langer in 1861.[18] He punched holes in the skin of cadavers and noted the direction of the gape of the wound, indicating the line of tension. The Langer lines run parallel to the principal fiber bundles of the reticular layer and thus produce less tension on the wound margins.

The Langer lines usually indicate the most favorable direction for surgical inci-

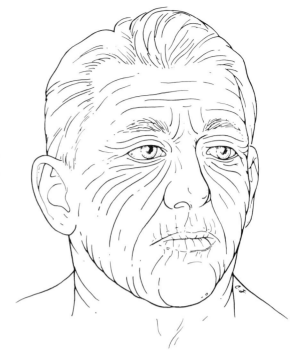

FIGURE 23–2.   The Langer lines run parallel to the principal fiber bundles of the reticular layer and produce less tension on the wound margins.

sions on the skin, except in some areas of the facial region because of the close relationship between the muscles of facial expression and the skin. The most inconspicuous scars are those that fall within natural creases or wrinkle lines in the skin.[3] When the facial muscles contract, they produce tension on the skin in a direction perpendicular to that of the muscle group. Thus, favorable crease lines for surgical incisions on the face run parallel to the muscles of facial expression; they may not coincide with Langer's lines and in some areas, such as the upper lip, may run perpendicular to them[12] (Fig. 23–2).

The dermis also contains a small amount of fat, numerous blood vessels, lymphatics, nerves and sensory nerve endings, hair follicles, sweat and sebaceous glands, and smooth muscle. The dermis is supported by subcutaneous connective tissue that is thinner in the facial region than in most of the body and is nonexistent in the eyelids. The muscles of facial expression are within the subcutaneous layer and insert into the reticular layer of the dermis.[15]

SUTURE MATERIAL

The selection of suture material is based on the condition of the wound, the tissues to be repaired, the strength and knot-holding characteristics of the suture material, and the reaction of the surrounding tissues to the suture material.[3,10] Suture material can be classified as absorbable or nonabsorbable, natural or synthetic, and braided or monofilament. Synthetic, nonabsorbable sutures include Dacron (Mersilene, Polydek, Tuedek, Ethibond, and Tycron), nylon (Ethilon and Dermalon), and polypropylene (Prolene and Surgilene). Natural, nonabsorbable sutures include silk, cotton, and metals such as stainless steel, tantalum, and titanium. Natural, absorbable sutures are made of catgut, plain, and chromic collagen. Synthetic, absorbable sutures include polyglycolic acid (Dexon), polyglactic acid (Vicryl), and polydioxanone (PDS).[19] Table 23–1 summarizes the grading of various suture materials.

Braided suture may allow bacteria to travel between the braids and has a high risk of suture abscess. For this reason, braided sutures should not be used in the head and neck region, especially on the face.

Catgut collagen is from sheep or cattle intestine. To minimize tissue reaction,

TABLE 23-1. GRADING OF VARIOUS SUTURE MATERIALS

Suture	Tensile Strength	Wick Action	Infec- tion	Reac- tivity	Comments
Nylon	+++	0	0-+	+	Minimal transient acute inflamma- tory reaction; very strong; least infectivity; poor knot-holding ability, requires 6 knots.
Polypro- pylene	+++	+	0-+	+	Minimal transient acute tissue reactivity; very strong; nonab- sorbable; easier to tie and holds knot better than nylon, requires only 3 knots; no tissue ingrowth; excellent for skin and for a pull-out suture.
Silk	+++	++++	++++	++++	Knots very well; easy to sew; more tissue reaction to this suture material than to others.
Mersilene Dacron	+++	++	+	++	Slight erythema and induration at suture site has been reported in 2% of cases; a good overall suture; easy to tie and holds knot well.
PGA (Dexon) Vicryl	+	++	+	++	Very low infectivity rate; should not be used where tensile strength is needed for prolonged periods (in rats 2 weeks after implantation of Vicryl approxi- mately 55% of its tensile strength was lost).
Chromic gut	++	+	++	+++	Causes more tissue reactivity than do other absorbable sutures commonly used; absorbed faster, but tends to retain its tensile strength better; not preferred except in mucosa or muscle closure because of its tissue reac- tivity.

From Simon RR and Brenner BB: Emergency Procedures and Techniques, 2nd Ed. Williams and Wilkins, Baltimore 1987.

increase tensile strength, and slow the absorption rate by macrophage activity, catgut can be coated with a thin layer of chromic compound. The material is absorbed within tissues by macrophage proteolytic and hydrolytic breakdown. The chromic catgut suture will lose its tensile strength within 7 to 10 days and tends to break down more quickly in the presence of infection. This suture material is generally used for sub-epithelial wounds that are not infected or under tension.[3] The advantages of chromic catgut materials include absorbability, tensile strength, and knotting qualities. The disadvantages include the wide range of biologic variability in loss of tensile strength over time as well as a broad range of reactions to these materials by individual patients.[19]

A thin chromic catgut suture has been used recently for closure of the epidermal layer in facial wounds. The 6-0 catgut material (Davis and Beck 6-0 mild chromic or Ethicon 6-0 rapidly absorbing gut) is absorbed within 3 to 5 days and does not have to be removed. The material may be used with sterile strips to relieve surface wound tension.[3,20]

Polyglycolic acid (Dexon) and polyglactic acid (Vicryl) are synthetic, absorbable materials that are polymers of hydroacetic and lactic acid, respectively. The sutures are made of braided strands, and use in the epidermal layer is discouraged. Less inflammatory reaction is found with synthetic, absorbable suture materials, as they are broken down by enzymatic digestion, while the natural, absorbable materials, such as catgut suture, are absorbed by foreign body inflammatory response. The absorbable, synthetic materials are absorbed by water hydrolysis rather than macrophage activity and maintain tensile strength for 30 to 45 days. This material has been reported to have less tissue reaction, better handling ability, and more tensile strength than catgut suture.[19] These suture materials are recommended in the tongue and other areas of the face that are subject to active animation or tension.[3] The undyed material should be used below the skin of the face.

Polydioxanone (PDS) suture material has the advantage of being a monofilament, absorbable suture with a long absorption period and high tensile strength.[19] Tissue reaction to the material is minimal, but there is a tendency for the PDS suture to extrude through the wound over time. Because of this, it is recommended that this suture material be used only in tissue layers deeper than the subcuticular layer[3] or be used, in a 6 – 0 size, in the closure of the epidermal layer in the face.[4]

Silk is a nonresorbable material that is dyed, braided, and treated with a resin or wax. Because silk is a natural protein, it will absorb over time within the wound. The material has extremely good handling characteristics and is some surgeons' choice for intraoral wounds and those near the margin of the eyelid.[3,19] Because the material is braided, there may be more of an incidence of tissue reaction and formation of suture marks or tracks.

Nylon and polypropylene (Prolene) are synthetic, monofilament materials that are excellent for skin closure in the facial region. The tissue reactivity is minimal, and they have good tensile strength. The handling and knot-tying properties are not favorable, and knots tend to slip with time.[3,19] These materials are best used for subcuticular pull-out sutures or epidermal sutures that are removed in 5 to 7 days.[4] Skin sutures should be removed as soon as practical because of the development of inflammatory reactions, epithelium-lined tracks about the suture, or small stitch abscesses that will leave suture scars.[10]

Microporous tape for wound closure is useful alone or in conjunction with subcutaneous or skin sutures to decrease tension at the wound margin. Skin tape comes in 1/8-, 1/4-, and 1/2-inch wide strips that may be reinforced with rayon filaments to increase the tensile strength of the strips. The skin margin is prepared with tincture of benzoin to provide better adhesiveness for the tape. The tape should be placed perpendicular to the wound on one skin side first; the wound margins are then pulled together with the fingers or by an assistant, and the tape is secured to the skin on the other side of the wound. Thus, tension over the wound is diminished. Prior to placement of the tape, a thin coat of antibiotic ointment may be placed along the wound margin to protect the wound from skin oils and bacteria. To remove the adhesive tape and not separate the epithelial margins, the ends should be lifted equally toward the wound margin and then lifted evenly from the wound.[3] There are basically two varieties of needles: cuticular and plastic. Cuticular needles are sharpened 12 times whereas plastic needles are sharpened an additional 24 times and designed to produce less trauma during penetration of tissues for cosmetic closures. Cuticular needles may be designated as C (cuticular) and FS (for skin). Plastic type needles may be labeled as P (for premium or plastic) and PS (plastic surgery). A number is used to indicate the size of the needle within the various manufacturer's series. The larger the number, the smaller is the needle size within that specific series.[61]

CLASSIFICATION AND MANAGEMENT OF SOFT TISSUE WOUNDS

Contusions

Contusions are usually produced by blunt trauma that results in edema and hematoma formation in the subcutaneous tissues. The hematoma will usually resolve without incident or need of treatment unless the hematoma is large or becomes infected. Usually, the overlying skin and mucosa are intact, but if the contusion is associated with a laceration, the contused margins should be excised before closure.[1,4,13] The margins should be undermined at the subcutaneous level to allow for closure of the mucosal or skin layer without tension. If the contused laceration involves vital structures, such as the eyelid or nose, that would not tolerate tissue removal, debridement and primary closure should be delayed until the contusion resolves.[13]

Abrasions

Abrasions result from deflecting-type trauma, such as sliding along pavement, dirt, or glass, that removes the epithelial layer and papillary layer of the dermis and leaves the raw, bleeding reticular layer of the dermis exposed. This type of wound may be painful owing to exposed nerve endings in the reticular dermal layer. Care should be taken to clean small particles and dirt from the dermal layer as soon as possible to avoid fixation within the tissues and formation of a traumatic tattoo. Local anesthesia should be used, and the wound should be scrubbed clean with a mild soapy solution, followed by copious irrigation with saline. The abrasion should be covered with a thin layer of antibiotic ointment, such as bacitracin, and dressed with cotton gauze or covered with an antibiotic-coated cellulose acetate gauze.[4,5,13,21]

Epithelialization is completed 7 to 10 days after injury without significant scarring if the epidermal pegs have not been completely removed.[5,12] After 3 days, the epidermal cells begin to migrate onto the abraded dermis. At 14 days, fibroblast and capillary formation in the dermis increases, and new elastic fibers develop by 3 months. Regeneration is not complete for 6 to 12 months.[12]

If the wound extends deeply into the dermal layer, significant scarring from granulation tissue formation will result. Excision of the remaining dermal tissue or excision of secondary scar tissue, with primary closure of the skin wound with 4–0 chromic sutures in the dermal layer and 6–0 nylon sutures at the surface, is indicated.[2,9,12]

Lacerations

Lacerations may be sharp, with little jaggedness or contusion of the wound margins; they may have contused, ragged, or stellate margins, as seen in a crushing type of injury; or they may involve partial avulsion of tissues that remain pedicled to surrounding structures. After examination, debridement, and irrigation, the wound should be repaired in layers.

SIMPLE LACERATIONS

Simple lacerations may be clean, contaminated, or contused. Clean lacerations may be repaired with little debridement or preparation required. Contaminated wounds should be cleaned and closed primarily, even if a delay of up to 5 or 7 days after trauma is necessary. Contused wounds should be evaluated, and contused tissue should be removed about the margins of the wound if enough tissue is available or should be delayed until the contused tissue stabilizes enough to allow for primary closure of the wound. If the laceration is beveled and ragged, the beveled portion of the wound should be excised with supporting dermal tissue to provide perpendicular skin edges and to permit closure with some wound margin eversion to prevent excessive scar formation.[1,13] Undermining of soft tissue wound margins is helpful in the suturing of tissues without extensive tension at the wound margin. Excessive undermining should be avoided, as natural wound contraction may lead to tissue elevation at the margins of the wound and to excessive scarring. Displaced tissue should be returned to the original anatomic position and orientation. Only occasionally is there an indication for changing the direction of the wound margins by Z-plasty or for making tissue allowance for scar contracture at the time of primary wound repair.[4] These procedures should be done at a secondary revision procedure if indicated.

WOUND CLOSURE

With the closure of facial wounds, minimal tissue trauma during repair is important to avoid excessive scarring of the wound margins. Meticulous attention to detail is necessary to minimize tissue injury and to prevent further scarring from poor suturing techniques. Skin hooks should be used for retraction and stabilization of tissues during debridement and repair, and when tissue forceps must be used, only those with multiple fine teeth, such as Adson-Brown forceps, should be employed. Wound edges should be grasped only at the level of the subcutaneous tissue to avoid puncture marks on the skin surface.[14] The wound margins should be undermined slightly to prevent undue tension on the wound margins and to permit closure of the wound in layers with subcutaneous tissues and eversion of the wound margin.[13] Unless required to elevate rotational flaps, excessive undermining of the facial tissues should be avoided to prevent unnecessary scarring and distortion of adjacent features, such as the ala of the nose, commissure of the mouth, eyelid, and so forth. Only

TABLE 23-2. BASIC CLOSURES AND THEIR ADVANTAGES AND DISADVANTAGES

SUTURE	ADVANTAGES	DISADVANTAGES
Simple interrupted	Permits good eversion of the wound edges. Is commonly used and can be applied rapidly.	Proper technique to provide eversion of edges requires practice to master. Eversion is not as good in difficult wounds as with other techniques. Does not relieve extrinsic tension from the wound edges.
Continuous over and over	Can be applied rapidly to close multiple lacerations and large wounds.	Apposition of the wound edges and eversion are more difficult to achieve. Inclusion cysts may form.
Continuous single-lock stitch	Can be applied rapidly. Apposition of the wound edges is more complete than with the continuous over and over stitch. Less epithelialization of the tracts.	Apposition of the wound edges is not as perfect as with the simple interrupted unless the procedure is mastered well.
Vertical mattress stitch	Unsurpassed in its ability to provide eversion of the wound edges and perfect apposition. Relieves tension from the skin edges.	Takes time to apply. Produces more cross-marks.
Horizontal mattress stitch	Reinforces the subcutaneous tissue. Relieves extrinsic tension from the wound edges more effectively than does the vertical mattress.	Does not provide as good apposition of the wound edges as does the vertical mattress.
Half-buried horizontal mattress	Relieves intrinsic tension and vascular compromise when approximating the tip of a flap.	Takes skill to master proper technique in order to provide perfect apposition of the wound edges.
Continuous mattress	Can be rapidly placed in order to approximate large lacerations in cosmetically unimportant areas.	Does not provide good apposition of the wound edges or eversion.

From Simon RR and Brenner BB: Emergency Procedures and Techniques, 2nd Ed. Williams and Wilkins, Baltimore 1987.

sharp blades and scissors should be used for debridement and preparation of wound margins. Appropriate suture material on an atraumatic cutting needle is desirable for facial wounds. The sutures should be placed to allow slight elevation of the wound margin, and with the tying of surgical knots, it is important to remember to "approximate, not strangulate."[8,14] Table 23–2 lists basic closures and their advantages and disadvantages.

Wound closure should follow examination, debridement, and preparation of the wound margins, if indicated, to allow meticulous alignment of the tissues. Key landmarks, such as the eyebrows, mucosal margins of the lip and nose, eyelids, and other anatomic structures, must be aligned and repaired properly. Key sutures placed to approximate these landmarks prior to closure of the remaining wound margins will assist in proper orientation. Irregularities in the wound should be noted and approximated. Straight-line portions of the laceration may then be closed, with the first suture placed to bisect the wound into equal sections and subsequent sutures placed in a similar fashion to provide even closure and avoid creation of "dog-ears" at the end of the wound. Should dog-ears develop, then the sutures should be removed and closure should be attempted again; or a skin hook can be inserted in the end of the wound, the tissue can be elevated, and redundant tissue can be incised around the base on one side of the wound margin.[22] Every attempt should be made to accomplish closure without the need for removing tissue because of dog-ears (Figs. 23–3A to C and 23–4A to E).

Wounds in the facial region should be repaired in layers to provide anatomic alignment and avoid dead space. Deep layers should be approximated with 3–0 or 4–0 absorbable sutures, and the skin should be repaired with 5–0 or 6–0 suture. If the muscular layer is involved, the tissues should be approximated with absorbable sutures tied lightly to avoid crushing of the muscle.[5] Subcutaneous sutures placed in the subcutaneous layer and reticular dermal layer are useful to close dead space, minimize wound tension at the skin level, and assist with eversion of the wound margins. Slight eversion of the wound margin is desirable to produce a scar that will be level with the adjacent skin after scar contraction is completed.[13,14] It is important that the knot on the subcutaneous suture be inverted, or "buried," so that the knot does not lie between the skin margin and cause inflammation or infection. To bury the knot, the first pass of the needle should be from within the wound and through the lower portion of the dermal layer. The needle should then be passed through the dermal layer at approximately the same level in the opposite wound margin and

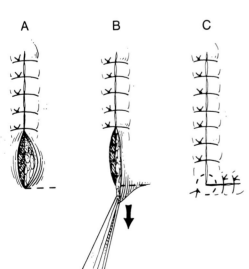

FIGURE 23–3. *A–C,* When wound margins are closed unevenly, there is a potential for "dog-ear" development. The surgical technique of removing a "dog-ear" by a right-angle extension of the incision is demonstrated.

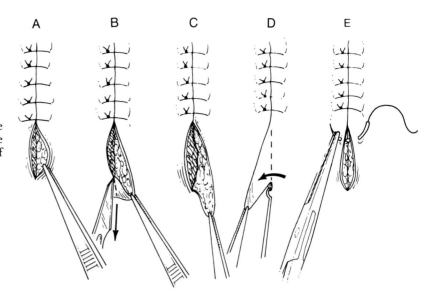

FIGURE 23-4. *A-E,* Another technique for removal of a "dog-ear" is a straight-line extension of the incision, with excision of the excess tissue and straight-line closure.

should emerge through the subcutaneous tissue again at a level similar to that of the subcutaneous suture of the opposing wound margin. If the sutures are placed at different levels, the wound margins may be unlevel at the skin and may produce an unacceptable scar. Unlevel suturing in the subcutaneous layers may be indicated to level off an oblique wound through the tissues. The suture should be tied, and the skin wound margins should be approximated under minimal tension (Figs. 23-5A to C, 23-6, and 23-7A and B).

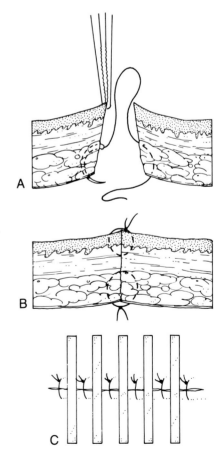

FIGURE 23-5. Closure of skin in layers with *(A)* buried dermal suture, *(B)* skin suture with eversion of the wound margin, and *(C)* adhesive strip application.

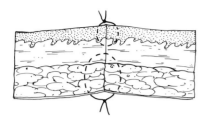

FIGURE 23–6.   Proper closure of skin laceration in layers.

Skin sutures are placed in an interrupted fashion or as a continuous subcuticular pull-out suture. Interrupted sutures should be of 5–0 or 6–0 strength, and nylon, polypropylene (Prolene), and polydioxanone (PDS) suture materials are indicated, but occasionally 6–0 chromic gut suture may be used. Sutures should be placed close to the wound margin and close enough to each other to relieve all wound margin tension.[13] Excessive numbers of sutures are unnecessary. The needle should enter the tissue at a 90-degree angle to the skin surface, approximately 2 mm from the wound margin. The needle should then be passed into the wound by rotation of the wrist along the arc of the needle. The needle should pass through the dermal layer to assist in eversion of the wound margin. The needle should then be passed through the tissue of the opposite wound margin at the same level in the dermal layer and should exit the skin at the same distance from the wound margin as that of the insertion.[8,14] The suture should be tied without undue tension to prevent suture marks (Figs. 23–8A to F and 23–9A to D).

In lacerations without extensive tissue loss, meticulous attention should be paid to hair and eyebrow alignment, wrinkle continuity, and orientation of muscle movements to produce unobtrusive scars and restore normal anatomic function.[23]

Blanching of the skin indicates that the knot is too tight. Uneven wound margins with closure indicate that too deep a bite of subcutaneous tissue was enclosed in the suture. Scalloped edges with open wound margins between sutures are the result of bites of tissue that are too small.[14] A thin line of antibiotic ointment may be placed over the wound and adhesive strips placed over the sutures to minimize tension around the wound margins. One technique involves placement of adhesive strips between sutures to allow for taking out the sutures without the need for removing the plastic strips.[6]

Skin sutures in the face should be removed 4 to 6 days after placement. Sutures in thin-skinned areas, such as the eyelid, should be removed 3 to 5 days following placement.[4] Alternate sutures can be removed beginning at 4 days, and the wound should be supported by adhesive strips. The remaining sutures may be removed 2 days later. Suture marks are usually caused by three factors: skin sutures left in place longer than 7 days, resulting in the epithelialization of the suture track; tissue necrosis

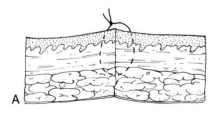

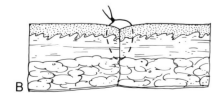

FIGURE 23–7.   *A,* Improper wound closure, with excessive tissue taken with suture. *B,* Improper wound closure, with inversion of wound edge.

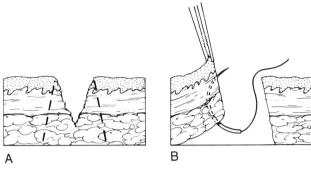

FIGURE 23–8. *A–F,* Laceration margins "freshened" to allow parallel edges; deep inverted dermal suture and "running," or continuous, subcuticular suture.

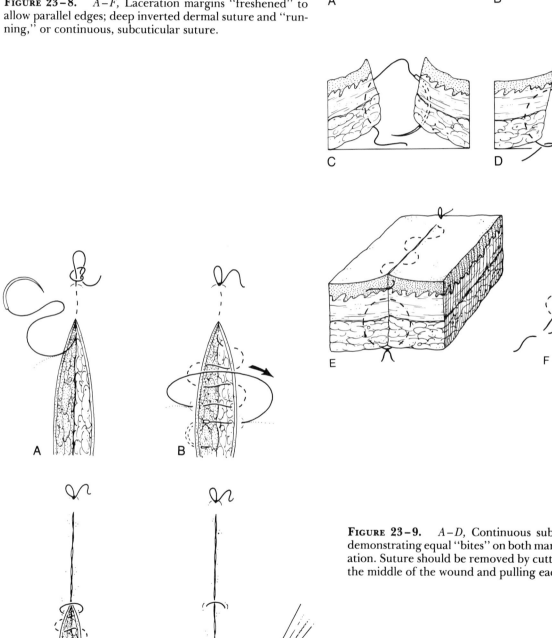

FIGURE 23–9. *A–D,* Continuous subcuticular suture demonstrating equal "bites" on both margins of the laceration. Suture should be removed by cutting the suture in the middle of the wound and pulling each knotted end.

from sutures that were tied too tightly or became tight from tissue edema; or the use of reactive sutures in the skin.[5] Interrupted skin sutures should not be used in patients who are subject to hypertrophic scars.[24]

The continuous subcuticular suture is a good suture for approximation of the skin margins and can be left in place for 3 to 4 weeks without the formation of suture tracks.[13] Polypropylene or nylon synthetic monofilament materials of 4–0 strength are used for the subcutaneous suture. After absorbable sutures are placed to close deep tissues, the needle is passed through the skin 5 to 10 mm from the wound edge into the wound at the dermal layer. A small hemostat should be placed on the free end of the suture. The needle is passed back and forth through the dermal layer at the same level in the dermis on opposite margins of the wound and parallel to the epithelial layer. Skin hooks are useful to manipulate the wound margin during placement of the needle and to orient the tissues for proper placement of the suture, which is critical for level approximation of the wound margins. It is also helpful to have an assistant "follow," or keep a slight amount of tension on, the suture material already placed in the wound to facilitate proper orientation of the suture in the dermal layers. It will make removal of the suture in long wounds easier if the suture is brought out through the epithelium near the wound margin and is reinserted at the same level through the epithelium. The suture is continued through the dermal layer to the end of the wound. At the end of the wound, the needle is passed out through the skin 5 to 10 mm from the margin. The ends of the suture can be tied in a knot above the skin or secured to the skin with adhesive strips. A thin line of antibiotic ointment should be placed at the wound margin and adhesive strips used to relieve tension at the margin. If areas in proximity to the wound margin are not level upon closure of the wound with continuous subcuticular sutures, interrupted sutures or adhesive strips can be placed to level the margin. The suture is removed by cutting one free end of the suture at the skin level or by cutting the epithelial loop and pulling the suture out the free end. As the suture is removed, support should be given to the wound margin to avoid pulling the wound open. The wound should then be supported with adhesive strips.

STELLATE LACERATIONS

Ragged lacerations usually have a contused portion because of the blunt, crushing trauma that is usually responsible for this type of injury. To facilitate closure, ragged edges should be trimmed with a scapel blade to make beveled wound margins perpendicular.[13] Interrupted sutures should be used to close the wound as far as the stellate portion of the wound margin, when multiple lacerations meet (Fig. 23–10A and B). Strangulation of the flap tip is commonly encountered with placement of interrupted skin sutures through such small portions of tissue. A partially intradermal horizontal mattress suture placed through the dermal layer of the tissue flap and exiting the skin on the larger portion of the wound is useful to close the triangular

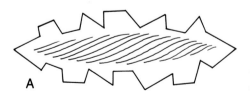

A

B

FIGURE 23–10. *A* and *B,* Interrupted sutures should be used to close the wound as far as the stellate portion of the wound margin, when multiple lacerations meet. The zigzag-plasty uses multiple squares, rectangles, and triangles to break up the wound line with excision of a large skin lesion.

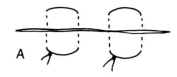

FIGURE 23–11. *A* and *B*, A partially intradermal horizontal mattress suture placed through the dermal layer of the tissue flap and exiting the skin.

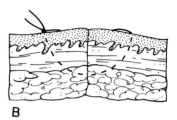

wound without impairing the blood supply in the tip of the flap[25] (Fig. 23–11*A* and *B*). Adhesive strips will assist in relieving tension on the wound margin.

FLAPLIKE LACERATIONS

Flaplike lacerations involve significant undermining of the soft tissue, usually at the subcutaneous tissue or supraperiosteal level, without loss of tissue. The techniques of wound debridement and preparation already discussed must be meticulously followed. It is not uncommon to find debris in deep tissues under the flapped tissues. Preparation should include minimal debridement of involved tissues and removal of beveled wound margins for perpendicular closure. The excellent blood supply to facial structures will support tissues on very small pedicles.[4,13,15]

In flap wounds, pressure dressings play an important role in minimizing dead space and limiting hematoma and fluid formation within the deep tissues. Hematoma and lymph pooling may become infected or may promote fibrin deposition and excess scar formation beneath the flap.[4]

Avulsion Injuries

The actual loss of tissue with facial wounds is fairly rare. Even if the initial evaluation suggests a loss of tissue, meticulous examination reveals that the tissue margins have been retracted or rolled under the wound margin. If small areas of tissue are missing, simple local undermining of the skin may provide for primary closure without tension on the wound margins. If there has been a significant loss of tissue and the wound cannot be closed free of tension with local undermining, the raw surface should be covered by a skin graft, local flaps, or apposition of the skin margin to the mucous membrane.[8,13,14] Under no circumstance should a wound on the face be allowed to heal by secondary granulation tissue because of excessive scar formation.

SKIN GRAFTS

Free skin grafts are classified according to the thickness of the graft. Split-thickness skin grafts consist of the epidermis and a portion of the dermis and can be further classified as thin (0.008 to 0.012 inch), medium (0.013 to 0.018 inch), and thick (0.018 to 0.028 inch). Full-thickness skin grafts include both the epidermis and the dermis.[26] Thinner grafts rapidly vascularize and will survive under less than optimal conditions. Split-thickness grafts can be expanded if required and have multiple donor sites that heal with minimal scarring at the donor site. Thin split-thickness grafts should be used on the face as a tissue dressing to prevent infection until repair with flap procedures can be used to reconstruct the defect.[14]

The thicker a split-thickness graft, the more closely it will resemble the qualities of color match, texture, and limited contraction of a full-thickness skin graft. Thick split-thickness grafts are ideal and often provide a definitive repair for large, clean defects. The anterolateral area of the neck can serve as a donor site for skin grafts to the face, since the skin is similar in color and texture.[4]

Full-thickness skin grafts provide tissue of good color and texture match but are limited by their devascularization at the defect site. Optimal wound conditions are required, and the donor must be able to be closed primarily. Full-thickness skin grafts are usually used to repair small defects in the lip, nose, eyelid, or eyebrow. In general, donor sites that are as close as possible to the defect should be selected to achieve the best possible color match and a texture approximating that of the surrounding skin. Such donor sites include the postauricular area, upper eyelid, supraauricular area, and antecubital fossa.[4] Free composite grafts can be obtained from the ear to reconstruct primarily avulsions of the nasal alar base. These grafts will survive if no part of the graft is more than 1.0 to 1.5 cm away from the nutrient bed.[13]

With free skin grafts, pressure dressings should be left in place for 7 to 10 days to prevent hematoma or fluid accumulation and to facilitate profusion of the graft. The grafted skin should be kept well lubricated with oil-based lotion to prevent excessive drying, and prolonged exposure to the sun should be avoided.[26]

FLAPS

Local or regional flaps provide one-stage repair of avulsion defects with similar tissue that has its own vascular supply and is not reliant on the perfusion of damaged tissues, as with free skin grafts. The disadvantages include additional incisions and elevation of tissues on the face and increased scarring. In the design of all flaps, the blood supply and venous drainage are of prime concern. The method of closing the secondary defect must be planned before the procedure. Facial flaps do best when based laterally or inferiorly, with the incisions following normal skinfolds and lines of expression.[4] The basic skin flaps used with the face are advancement, rotational, transpositional, and microvascular anastomosis.

Advancement flaps involve making two parallel incisions from the defect and undermining the tissue until the flap can be advanced into the defect under minimal tension. Dog-ears created at the base of the flap should be carefully excised. Rotational or rotation-advancement flaps use a semicircular flap to rotate tissue into a defect and primary closure of the secondary defect. This flap requires careful planning to keep the incision from crossing too many natural skinfolds. The circumference of the circle should be eight times the size of the defect and at least twice the diameter.[8,14]

Transpositional flaps involve swinging flaps into areas of defect over healthy tissue, with a secondary defect at the donor site that is closed primarily by undermining adjacent tissues or by coverage with a free skin graft. The donor site is usually in the neck or scalp region, and closure is within the natural creases or in the hair. With large defects, a flap may have to be swung up from the chest region.[14]

Microvascular anastomotic flaps are not usually indicated in defects of the face, although some favorable results have been reported with reconstruction of scalp wounds.[27] With facial avulsive defects, adequate arteries or veins may not be close enough to the defect for successful anastomosis. When successful, these flaps provide excellent coverage but are often bulky on the face and may require multiple revisions to thin. Conventional coverage with a free skin graft or local skin flaps may provide a superior result with a much simpler operative procedure.[4]

APPOSITION OF THE SKIN MARGIN TO MUCOSAL MEMBRANES

With full-thickness defects in the cheek, nose, or lip—such as commonly seen with gunshot wounds—that cannot be treated by skin grafting or flap procedures primarily, the mucous membrane and skin margin should be undermined and closed primarily; with primary closure of the wounds, infection, delayed healing, and scar contracture will be avoided.[8,13] There will be no distortion of local tissues around the defect, which will allow for secondary reconstruction of the defect, with stable anatomic landmarks.

INJURIES TO STRUCTURES REQUIRING SPECIAL TREATMENT

The Lip

The lip provides special challenges to repair following trauma because of the anatomy of the region of the vermilion border, which involves the transition of mucosal tissue to skin; the associated edema of the tissues after trauma to the area; and the unaesthetic and difficult to correct "puckering" defect that results from an irregular vermilion margin. Scars or defects that affect the sphincter activity of the orbicularis oris muscle produce drooling, functional difficulties with eating, and alterations in speech. After examination, a single 5–0 nylon suture should be placed at the mucocutaneous line, or "gray or white" line, to reorient this important junction (Fig. 23–12). The wound should be debrided, hemostasis achieved, and local anesthesia placed in the surrounding tissues or via mandibular or mental nerve blocks. Blocks are preferred to prevent unnecessary edema in tissues to be approximated. The wound should then be closed in layers. The muscular layer is reapproximated with 3–0 or 4–0 chromic sutures, the dermis and subcutaneous tissues are closed with 4–0 or 5–0 chromic sutures, the skin should be carefully approximated with 6–0 nylon sutures placed evenly, and the mucosal layer is loosely reapproximated with 4–0 chromic suture.

In avulsive injuries to the lips, one fourth of the upper lip and up to one fourth of the lower lip can be lost without resultant functional or aesthetic defects.[28] The tissue margins should be straightened, with removal of a full-thickness wedge of lip tissue to facilitate closure. If there has been an extensive avulsive injury, an Abbé-Estlander flap between the affected lip and the opposite lip can be used to rotate tissue into the avulsed area. Another type of rotational flap is the Karapandzic flap, which utilizes full-thickness perioral tissue about the oral stoma. The lips are advanced along with the orbicularis oris, neurovascular bundle, and underlying mucosa to close the defect. The major complication is the reduced size of the oral stoma.[3]

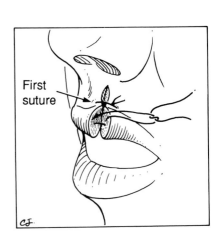

FIGURE 23–12. The "white" or "gray" line of the vermilion border of the lip should be sutured first to ensure an anatomic match.

The Ear

The external ear consists of the pinna, the external auditory meatus, and the tympanic membrane. The pinna consists of a thin central area of relatively avascular cartilage that depends on the thin overlying layer of skin for blood supply.[15] The ear has a very good blood supply and can maintain large portions on very small pedicles. Conservative debridement and manipulation should be used to maintain as much tissue as possible. Sutures should be first used to reapproximate known landmarks and then should be placed to reapproximate adjoining tissues. The skin should be approximated with 6–0 or 7–0 nylon sutures or other fine suture material. Suturing of the cartilage is usually unnecessary and may lead to devitalization of the region of cartilage or may provide a pathway for infection. If sutures in the cartilage are required, fine chromic sutures are recommended[29] (Figs. 23–13A to C and 23–14A and B).

In avulsive injuries involving segmented portions of the external ear that are missing or attached only with a small pedicle flap, the tissue should be returned to proper anatomic position and secured with sutures to the skin. The skin from the dorsum of the ear should be dermabraded and attached to a skin flap elevated from the mastoid region for a vascular bed.[30] Postoperative treatment should include bed rest, use of a supportive bandage, application of ice to cool the replanted part and to decrease the metabolic rate within the segment, heparin anticoagulant treatment, and antibiotics to cover gram-positive bacteria.

Total amputation of the external ear is a difficult repair and reconstructive problem. Plastic surgical grafting procedures to reconstruct the external ear with rib cartilage, skin flaps, Silastic, or silicone implants have variable results[31,32] and are rarely satisfactory. Some success has been reported with microvascular techniques. The superficial temporal artery or posterior auricular arteries are used, but there are difficulties with artery size and poor venous drainage that currently make salvage difficult.[30]

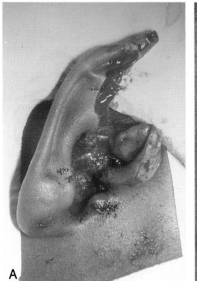 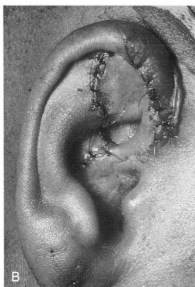 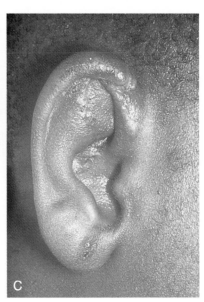

FIGURE 23–13. The excellent blood supply to the ear can support large portions of tissue on very small pedicles. The first sutures should reapproximate known landmarks and secondary sutures should reapproximate adjoining tissues. Conservative debridement should be used to maintain as much tissue as possible.

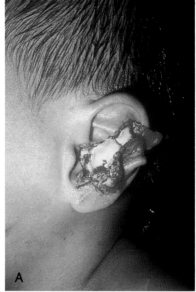
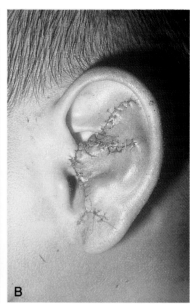

FIGURE 23–14. *A* and *B*, A stellate ear laceration with exposure of cartilage is reapproximated and sutured primarily.

Prosthetic rehabilitation of the external ear and other specialized facial structures has been greatly improved with the development of silicone and plastic materials for more reliable and stable color match, comfort, and durability.[18,33] Attachment of the prosthesis to glasses is the most common method used, although some prostheses are held with glue to the skin margins.[24] The disadvantages with gluing are that the glue may not tolerate sweat or oils and that allergic skin reactions are possible. Retention and good fit with an eyeglass-supported prosthesis are also difficult to achieve. With the development of osseointegrated implants and techniques for placement of the implants in the mastoid region, zygomatic buttress, and other supporting bone, prosthetic devices can be anchored to replace missing external ears, orbits, and noses.[31]

Sometimes the skin of the external ear is lost, but the cartilage is preserved. If only a small defect exists or the perichondrium still covers the cartilage, a skin graft should be used to cover the defect.[34] A good donor site is the retroauricular skin of the contralateral ear. When the perichondrium is missing, the best treatment is coverage with a retroauricular skin flap.[30]

Hematomas of the ear should be aspirated with a fine needle or small incisions in dependent drainage areas. A hematoma that is not removed may become fibrosed and cause a thickened ear, known as a "cauliflower ear" (Fig. 23–15). Dressings are

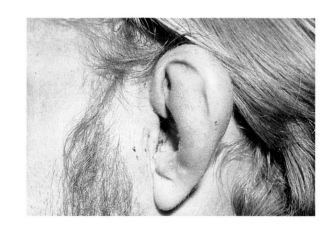

FIGURE 23–15. A hematoma that is not removed may become fibrosed and cause a thickened ear known as a "cauliflower ear."

extremely important and should be molded to the shape of the ear, both to support the ear and to provide gentle pressure to prevent recurrence of the hematoma.[34] One technique is to place cotton balls soaked in antibiotic solution along the area involved. A mixture of rubber base or silicone impression material is pressed into the ear, with a cotton ball in place to protect the external auditory meatus. The material is allowed to set and acts as an excellent compressive bandage. The dressing should be left in place for 5 to 7 days.

The Nose

The nose is the most prominent structure on the face and is commonly traumatized. Many injuries result in fractures to the bony structure with or without soft tissue involvement. As in the treatment of any bone fractures, the underlying bones must be repaired before soft tissue wounds are closed. The bone and cartilage substructure of the external nose is covered by muscle, subcutaneous tissue, and skin and has an internal lining of mucous membrane and glandular structures. The entire nose has an excellent blood supply like other structures on the face, and most lacerations, wounds, and incisions of the skin of the nose heal readily and rapidly.[35] Examination of the internal nose requires a nasal speculum, excellent lighting, and suction. Anesthesia with a 5 per cent cocaine solution and lidocaine with epinephrine may be required for an adequate examination. The mucosa is inspected for evidence of lacerations, and exposure of the cartilage is noted. The septal cartilage should be evaluated for displacement, buckling, and possible fracture. The septum must be assessed for the presence of hematoma, which would appear as a boggy, blue elevation of the mucosa.[36] Once diagnosed, a septal hematoma should be evacuated through small mucosal incisions or by needle aspiration. A running 4–0 chromic suture is placed through and through the septum to prevent recurrence.[30] If untreated, the septal hematoma may become infected, and septic necrosis of the cartilage is possible. With destruction and collapse of the septum, the nose loses its supporting framework, and retraction of the columella and saddling of the middle third of the nose result. The septum may also become quite thick secondary to subperichondrial fibrosis.[4,30,35]

Mucosal tears may be associated with bone fractures or penetrating objects. Suturing should be attempted with thin, absorbable sutures. Exposed septal cartilage does not pose any difficulty as long as the mucosa is intact on the other side of the septum. If the cartilage is divided, a mucosal flap should be designed to cover the area at least on one side.[35]

Lacerations of the skin of the nose should be closed after inspection and debridement with 6–0 nylon or other nonabsorbable suture. Partial avulsions and through-and-through lacerations should be closed by suturing the mucosal layer with fine absorbable sutures, placing the knots so that they are in the nasal cavity. Key sutures should be used to align landmarks to ensure proper orientation, especially about the nasal rim. Repair should then continue with approximation of the cartilage with 5–0 chromic suture and closure of the skin with 6–0 nylon suture (Fig. 23–16A and B). Because of the thick sebaceous skin over the nasal tip and the high content of bacteria, suture abscesses are common and the skin is prone to develop scars.[5,35] Sutures should be removed after 4 days and reinforced with adhesive strips.

Avulsive wounds of the nose may require skin grafts. Skin grafts are ideally done with full-thickness postauricular grafts, which give the best possible match of color and texture. Split-thickness skin grafts can be used if required and are best obtained from exposed body areas, such as from the neck or forearm.[4] Davis and Shaheen[8] report that nearly 50 per cent of composite grafts will fail even in ideal conditions and are only used if the following conditions apply:

1. The wound edges are cleanly cut and viable.
2. There is no prospect of infection.

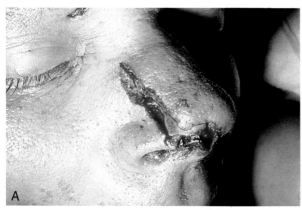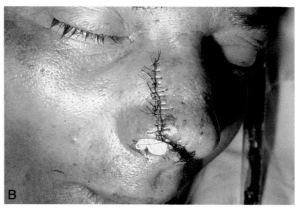

FIGURE 23–16. *A* and *B,* Fracture of the nasal bones with concomitant laceration. The nasal fractures were reduced, the nose was packed, and the laceration was closed in layers.

3. Primary repair is not delayed.
4. No part of the graft is more than 0.5 cm from the cut edge of the wound.
5. All bleeding is controlled.

The Eyebrow

Reconstruction of the eyebrow is extremely difficult, and transplants to the eyebrows are not always cosmetically satisfying.[6] Therefore, efforts to repair eyebrows without resultant distortion or defects are important. The eyebrow should not be shaved but, rather, lightly clipped if necessary to assist the surgeon in proper alignment of the eyebrow. The wound should be inspected and underlying fractures of the frontal sinus or supraorbital rim repaired before closure. As little tissue as possible should be removed and sutured into place. If nonvital tissue must be removed, then incisions should be made parallel to the hair follicles to injure as few as possible. Special care should also be taken to avoid tight, constricting sutures in the area, since hair follicles are very sensitive to decreases in blood flow[5,36] (Figs. 23–17*A* and *B* and 18*A* to *C*).

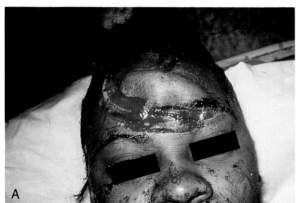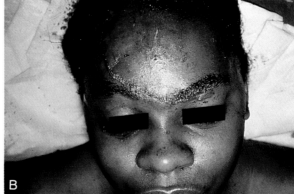

FIGURE 23–17. *A* and *B,* Severe forehead laceration with involvement of the eyebrows. Eyebrows are reapproximated first to ensure anatomic alignment.

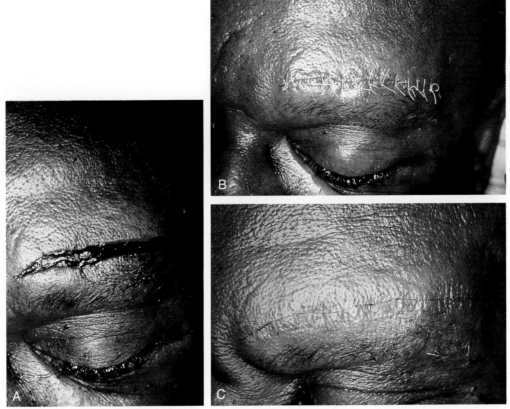

FIGURE 23–18. *A–C,* The eyebrow is maintained, and the laceration is closed in an interrupted fashion, with good cosmetic result.

The muscular layer should be closed with fine, absorbable suture to avoid spreading of the tissue and scar formation. The skin should be approximated with 6–0 nylon suture. Vertical displacements that may develop can usually be corrected by a Z-plasty procedure, while horizontal displacements can be corrected by scar revision and realignment of the parts. These procedures should be performed 6 to 12 months following the accident, after the scar tissue has softened[37] (Fig. 23–19*A* to *C*).

The Eyelid

The treatment of injuries to the eyelid is important to restore not only the appearance of the individual but also, and more important, the vital function of the structure. The major function of the eyelid is to protect the globe and prevent drying of the cornea and adjacent tissue. The eyelids aid in removal of tears through the canalicular system. With any type of injury to the orbit, eyelids, and globe, an ophthal-

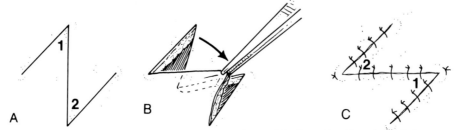

FIGURE 23–19. *A–C,* The Z-plasty technique is useful when the direction of the scar needs to be changed or the scar line must be broken.

mology consultation is mandatory to assess for global injury and defects in vision. Even if no defects are initially apparent, early baseline records are required.

As in any surgical procedure, a detailed understanding of the anatomy of the region is required to assist in the proper repair of traumatic injuries to the eyelids.

The eyelids are composed (in order from the skin to the conjunctival layer) of the skin, alveolar tissue, orbicularis oculi muscle, tarsus, septum orbitale, tarsal (meibomian) glands, and conjunctiva.[38] The lid margin is formed by the junction of the skin and mucous membrane and is delineated by a gray line. The superior tarsus is of a semilunar shape to conform to the configuration of the globe, and it assists in keeping the conjunctival mucosa intact with the cornea. The tarsal plates are long, thin plates of connective tissue that also aid with the form and support of the eyelid.[39]

The levator muscle inserts into the skin of the upper lid and the upper margin of the tarsus and is responsible for elevation of the upper lid. The muscular layer over the tarsus is also anchored to the medial and lateral aspects of the orbit by the medial and lateral canthal ligaments. The orbital septum is peripheral to the tarsus and forms a fibrous sheet attached to the periosteum about the circumference of the orbital rim. The septum maintains the orbital contents in the proper position.[38,39]

Lacerations of the eyelids can be divided into two categories: wounds that involve the lid margin and those that do not. Simple lacerations that do not involve the margin should be closed primarily. Following evaluation for possible injury to the orbit, globe, and punctal and canalicular systems, debridement with minimal tissue removal should be accomplished. Lacerations should be closed in layers, restoring the integrity and orientation of the skin, muscle, tarsal, and conjunctival layers. Deep sutures are not recommended in the lower eyelid, as the orbital septum may be inadvertently sutured, creating a cicatricial ectropion as the wound heals.[30] Lacerations of the upper eyelid must be explored to identify damage to the levator muscle. At the point where the levator attaches to the superior portion of the tarsus, an upper lid fold is normally created. If the fold is violated, it should be restored by repair of the muscle-tarsus junction and suture of the subcutaneous layer to the deep structures.[30] Sutures should be removed in 48 to 72 hours to avoid suture tracks of epithelium.[38]

Marginal lacerations must be repaired carefully and accurately to avoid functional and cosmetic defects. The most common identifiable structures are the lash line, the meibomian gland orifices, and the gray line (junction between the conjunctival mucosa and skin.)[30] Three 6–0 nylon sutures should be placed at the marginal rim to align and properly orient these structures on either side of the laceration. The sutures should not be tied. Fine, absorbable sutures are placed to close the fascial border, but no other deep sutures are placed because of the risk of ectropion in the lower lid. A slight eversion of the lid margin must be obtained with the marginal sutures to allow for wound contraction of the lid margin. The transmarginal sutures at the gray line and lash line are left long and are secured to the skin surface to prevent corneal abrasion[30,38] (Figs. 23–20A to C and 23–21A to C).

Avulsive injuries to the eyelids are treated with full-thickness skin grafts from the postauricular region or the other upper eyelid.[39] With avulsive injuries of the lid margins, careful placement of all pedicled tissues will usually be maintained owing to the excellent blood supply in the region. Full-thickness eyelid avulsions of less than 25 per cent of the lid length can be approximated primarily as a simple laceration.[5] Lateral canthotomy to dissect the skin and conjunctiva free from the lateral canthal tendon, to free all structures between the conjunctiva and skin, and to allow for release of horizontal tension can be used. Ordinarily, 5 to 10 mm may be gained in lid length in the horizontal direction.[38] Larger defects require grafts or flaps, such as an Abbé-type rotational flap from the unaffected eyelid.[30]

The Oral Mucosa and Tongue

Lacerations of the oral mucosa and tongue should be inspected, especially for pieces of teeth or restorations, and debrided like other wounds. The wounds should

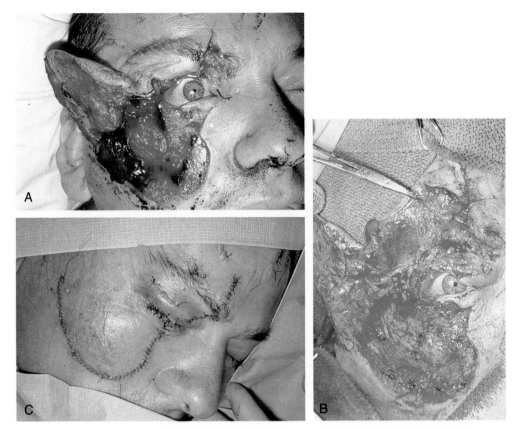

FIGURE 23–20.   *A–C,* Significant laceration to eyelid and cheek region. Careful debridement and examination must be done to identify important structures such as the parotid duct and facial nerve. Structures must be repaired primarily and the wound closed in layers.

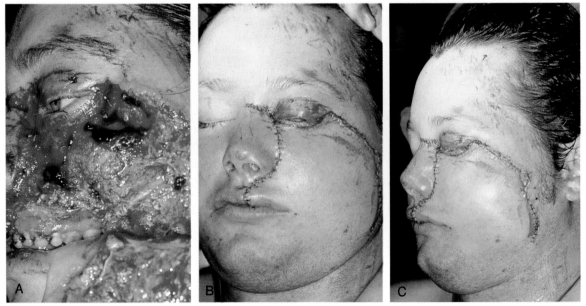

FIGURE 23–21.   *A–C,* Laceration involving the eyelid, cheek, and intraoral structures. The laceration is sutured from the inside out. Intraoral closure should take place prior to extraoral facial closure. The lacrimal apparatus is identified and repaired about a Silastic catheter.

be thoroughly irrigated with normal saline and sutured loosely. Mucosal wounds should be sutured with 3–0 or 4–0 chromic gut suture. Deep lacerations should be closed in layers, with chromic gut sutures in the muscle layers to prevent formation of a hematoma. The tongue should be closed in layers as well, with 4–0 Vicryl (dyed) suture in the superficial layers.

The tongue has a rich blood supply, and injuries to the tongue or floor of the mouth may cause serious hemorrhage that potentially threatens the airway. The airway may become compromised some time after trauma to the tongue or lacerations of the floor of the mouth if veins are damaged, resulting in swelling of the tongue into the oropharynx.[7,21]

The Salivary Glands or Ducts

Injuries to the parotid or submandibular gland should be evaluated and repaired if possible. Injuries to the parotid or submandibular ducts must also be assessed. If the duct has been transected, repair around a thin polyethylene tube is required. From the anterior border of the gland, the parotid duct extends forward approximately 1 cm below the zygoma. The location of the duct on the face may be visualized as the middle third of a line from the tragus of the ear to the middle of the upper lip. The duct is approximately 4 to 6 cm in length and 5 mm in diameter. The parotid or Stensen's duct runs transversely through the buccinator muscle to empty into the oral cavity at the buccal mucosa, directly across from the maxillary second molar. Lacerations involving the parotid duct frequently damage the buccal branch of the facial nerve owing to close approximation of the two structures (Fig. 23–22).

When the parotid duct has been lacerated, both ends of the duct must be located and sutured together. The distal portion of the severed duct is usually located first by placing a lacrimal duct probe or polyethylene cannula through the Stensen's duct orifice in the mucosal wall of the oral cavity just lateral to the second maxillary molar and passing the probe through the laceration site. The proximal segment can then be located by expressing saliva from the parotid gland. A Silastic catheter should be placed through the severed segments, and repair should be made over the catheter. The repair should be done with 6–0 nylon interrupted sutures. Approximately 2 cm of stent should extend from the orifice, and the stent should be secured to the oral mucosa with one or two nonabsorbable sutures (Fig. 23–23A to D). The Silastic stent should remain in place for 5 to 7 days, and the patient should be given sialogogues, such as lemon drops, to prevent scar formation at the anastomosis site.[8,30]

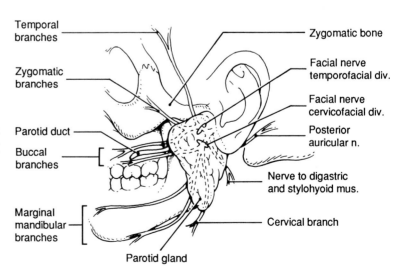

FIGURE 23–22. Lacerations of the parotid duct frequently damage the buccal branch of the facial nerve because of the close approximation of the two structures.

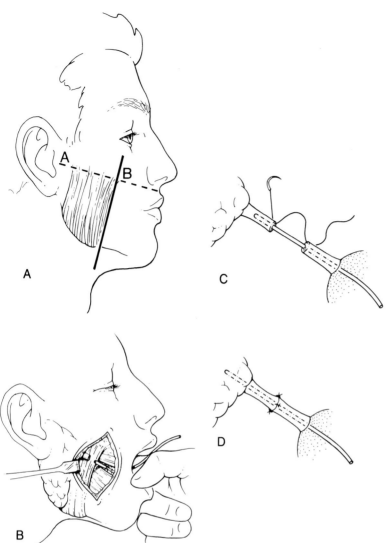

FIGURE 23–23. *A,* The parotid duct typically is found along the plane from the tragus of the ear to the middle of the upper lip. Point A at the posterior border of the masseter muscle is usually where the hilus of the parotid gland is located and the duct begins. The duct runs with the buccal branch of the facial nerve for a small distance and traverses the buccinator muscle to open into the oral cavity across from the maxillary second molar at Point B. *B,* Lacerations across this region should be investigated thoroughly for possible damage to the facial nerve or parotid duct. Injuries to these structures should be primarily repaired. A small Silastic tube should be inserted through Stensen's duct from the mouth, canulated through the proximal stump, and passed along into the hilus of the gland. *C* and *D,* The duct should be reapproximated with 6–0 nylon interrupted sutures over the Silastic tube. The tube should be left in place for approximately one week.

After repair of the duct, the overlying soft tissues are closed in layers to prevent formation of a fistulous tract and a sialocele. If a sialocele does form, it should be treated by aspiration and a pressure dressing over the area to eliminate collection.

A swelling over the course of the duct that slowly increases in size after trauma to the area may be suggestive of an injury to the duct that was not detected during the initial examination. If the diagnosis is made within 48 hours of the injury, an exploratory operation with repair is indicated.[8] With injury to the salivary ductal system, prophylactic antibiotics, such as penicillin or cephalothin, should be used.[30]

The submandibular duct runs laterally and superiorly from the gland to its orifice in the oral cavity behind the mandibular incisors. The mandibular duct is approximately 5 cm long and courses near the lingual nerve before the nerve enters the tongue. A small polyethylene catheter is placed in the orifice and through the distal segment. The proximal segment is located by massage of the gland, so that saliva from the transected duct is found. The catheter is then advanced into the proximal segment. Several 4–0 chromic sutures should be placed to secure the transected ends of the duct about the catheter. The catheter should then be cut in the oral cavity and secured to the mucosal tissues by sutures. The catheter should remain in place for 5 to 7 days and should be removed only after assurance that the duct will remain patent without the catheter.

The Lacrimal Apparatus

Tears produced by the lacrimal gland drain across the surface of the cornea to the medial portion of the eye, where they enter the puncta of the upper and lower lid margins and proceed to the canaliculi in the nasolacrimal apparatus. The tears then drain into the inferior meatus of the nose. More than half of the tear drainage volume is normally evacuated through the inferior canaliculus, and when this pathway is traumatically interrupted, it is important that it be repaired when possible.

Any lacerations of the medial third of the lower lid should immediately raise suspicion of injury to the inferior canaliculus. Establishing hemostasis of the laceration is mandatory for finding the injury. The canaliculus is a fairly large, white-walled tube near the cut end of the canaliculus and may be located by placing a lacrimal duct probe through the punctum and into the wound. The canaliculus begins at the punctum and proceeds perpendicular to the eyelid margin for approximately 2 mm and then turns medially and proceeds to the nasolacrimal apparatus. Magnifying loops of 2X or 3X power should be available to help locate the lacerated ends of the canaliculus. Another method of locating the lacerated canaliculus is to infiltrate the upper canaliculus with air and to instill sterile water or saline into the laceration line, allowing the liquid to pool. Air will pass through the canalicular apparatus and will bubble through the saline or water, demonstrating the site of the laceration.

When lacerated ends of the canaliculus have been located, they can be repaired using a Vier stainless steel rod wedged onto black silk. The rod is passed through the punctum into the laceration site and then into the medial portion of the canaliculus to align the cut ends. The laceration is stabilized with small chromic gut sutures, and the rod is left in place for 4 to 6 weeks. The free end of the silk material of the Vier rod is tied into place to help stabilize the rod and, of course, is used to retrieve it at the time of removal.

Through-and-through margin injuries to the eyelid must be repaired in at least three layers to prevent notching as healing progresses. The deep layer contains the conjunctiva and tarsus and should be closed with 4-0 or 5-0 chromic gut interrupted sutures, and the knots should be tied into the wound so that they do not irritate the cornea. The middle layer is the orbicularis oculi muscle, which is closed with interrupted 5-0 chromic gut sutures, and then the skin is finally closed. Great care should be taken to approximate the tarsus and ciliary margin accurately. Once these structures have been sutured, the remainder of the eyelid can generally be properly repaired without difficulty.

The Scalp

The scalp and forehead are portions of the same highly vascularized anatomic unit responsible for protection of the skull. They consist of five layers, which can best be remembered by the mnemonic SCALP. In order from the skin to the cranial bone, the layers are skin (S), subcutaneous tissue (C), aponeurosis layer (A), loose subepicranial space (L), and pericranial layer (P)[15] (Fig. 23-24).

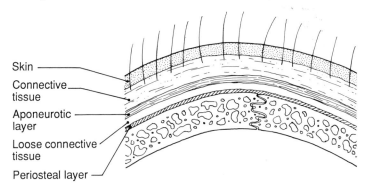

FIGURE 23-24.   The layers of the scalp can be remembered by the mnemonic SCALP—skin, connective tissue, aponeurotic layer, loose connective tissue, and periosteal or pericranial layer.

Skin
Connective tissue
Aponeurotic layer
Loose connective tissue
Periosteal layer

The thickness of the epidermis and dermis of the scalp varies from 4 to 8 mm, so the scalp is one of the thicker regions of the body; only the back, soles, and palms are thicker.[15] The subcutaneous layer has many large vessels that anastomose freely. Because this layer is so inelastic, the blood vessels minimally contract when severed and tend to bleed easily; thus, large amounts of blood loss are seen in a very short period.[23]

The aponeurosis layer consists of the galea aponeurosis, which connects the paired occipital muscles and paired frontal muscles. The galea is a tough, inelastic tissue that is attached firmly to the skin and subcutaneous layers and moves freely over the subepicranial space below.[8] The subepicranial space lies between the galea aponeurosis and the pericranium. It is traversed by small arteries and emissary veins connecting the scalp veins with the venous sinuses of the skull. Infections and thrombosis in this layer may be passed to the cranium or sinuses via these vessels.[15]

The pericranium is very vascular and can be easily stripped from the cranium. The pericranium will accept a free graft readily because of its excellent vascularity. The outer table of the skull will not accept a free graft, and the pericranium is therefore extremely important in any avulsive injury to the scalp.[8] Avulsed scalp flaps are replaced if the tissue is not badly damaged, and most survive. Free graft survival depends on the presence of pericranium over the skull.

Injuries to the scalp should be evaluated for possible accompanying skull fractures and intracranial trauma. A simple laceration should be treated like other lacerations on the face, with evaluation, hemostasis, debridement, and primary closure (Fig. 23–25A and B). It is unnecessary to shave the hair from the region, but scissors should be used to trim the hair in the area around the laceration. Closure is easy if the scalp defect is less than 2.5 cm wide. If larger defects are encountered, flaps should be used.[27]

With avulsion of the skin of the scalp, the examiner must not only carefully ascertain the status of the pericranium but also look for evidence of fractures of the cranium. As with other avulsive defects of the face, healing by secondary granulation must be avoided owing to the cosmetic and functional defects that result from excess scar formation and contracture. The scalp offers unique challenges, as the cranial bones depend on the pericranial tissues for their blood supply.[15] The scalp has an excellent blood supply in the subcutaneous tissue and pericranial layers that support avulsed tissue, skin grafts, and various flaps.

If the pericranial tissues are intact and the cranium has not been fractured, defects in the scalp that cannot be closed primarily should be covered with a split-thickness skin graft (Fig. 23–26A to E). After stabilization and healing of the defect, the area can be reconstructed by various advancement or rotational flaps to bring similar tissue into the defect, with or without atraumatic tissue expansion (Fig.

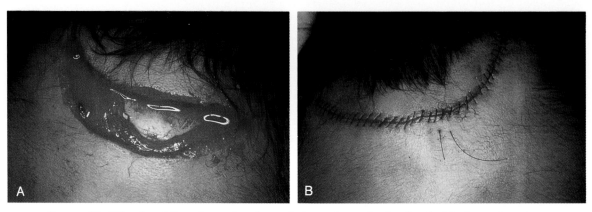

FIGURE 23–25. An oblique laceration through the scalp on the forehead with the pericranium intact. The laceration is closed primarily in layers.

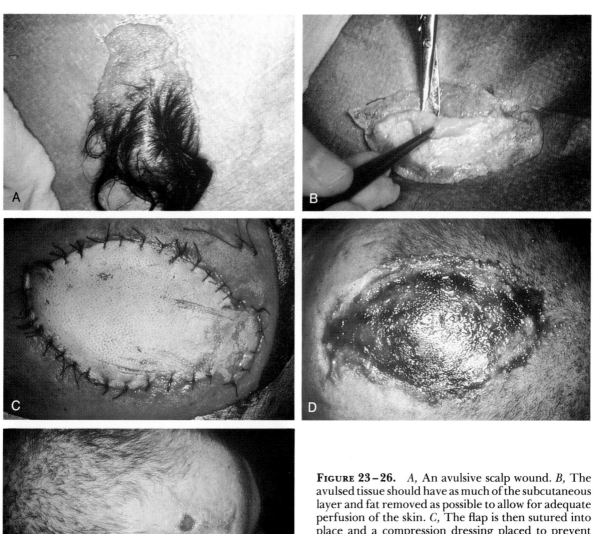

FIGURE 23–26. *A,* An avulsive scalp wound. *B,* The avulsed tissue should have as much of the subcutaneous layer and fat removed as possible to allow for adequate perfusion of the skin. *C,* The flap is then sutured into place and a compression dressing placed to prevent hematoma formation below the flap. *D,* The flap becomes revascularized and *E,* eventually heals with hair-bearing tissue except for a small defect that will heal by secondary epithelialization.

23–27*A* to *C*). Tissue expansion is an alternative in the closure of wound defects because it provides donor tissue of the same color, texture, and thickness with minimal scar formation and minor donor site morbidity.[22] Tissue expansion involves developing donor tissue without depriving the donor site of tissue.

If the pericranium has been lost, the exposed cortical cranial bone will not support a skin graft. When bone is exposed in large avulsive injuries of the scalp, primary closure with flap procedures is indicated.[8] The flap procedures used with scalp defects include advancement flaps, transpositional flaps, rotation-advancement flaps, and microvascular free scalp flaps.[4,8,23]

ADVANCEMENT FLAPS

Advancement of the scalp into defect wounds is difficult because the galea aponeurosis is thick and not very elastic and does not stretch under traction. The flap

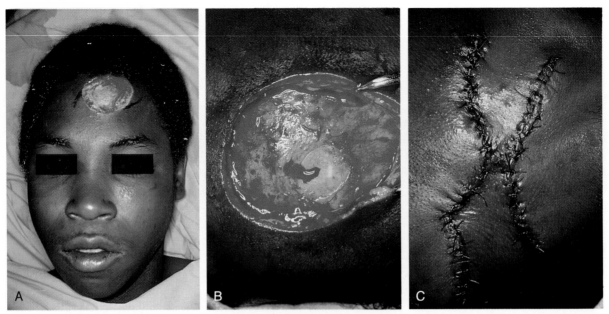

FIGURE 23–27. A large avulsive forehead wound with loss of the pericranium tissue and exposed bone. The wound is closed primarily with rotational advancement flaps.

must be widely undermined in the subepicranial space, and multiple longitudinal incisions are made in the galea parallel to the skin margin to facilitate closure of the defect. Split-thickness skin grafts should then be placed over the exposed pericranium.

TRANSPOSITIONAL FLAPS

Transpositional flaps involve the transfer of tissue from one section to the defect, accepting that a secondary defect will be left in the donor area.[8] The donor area is usually in a less aesthetic region, such as the occipital area of the head, and is covered with a skin graft.

ROTATION-ADVANCEMENT FLAPS

A rotation-advancement of local flaps to cover defects is the treatment of choice when the pericranium has been destroyed.[13] To assist with stretching of the tissue, the galea should be released with multiple incisions parallel to the longer axis of the flaps. Orticochea[23,27] devised a technique for closing cutaneous defects of the scalp with a three-flap procedure that mobilizes large flaps based on the superficial temporal, occipital, posterior auricular, and supraorbital arteries, which supply blood to the scalp. Orticochea described the cutaneous covering of the skull and used five different applications of the three-flap rotation-advancement technique in reconstruction of the forehead, right temporal region, left temporal region, central region of the skull, and nape of the neck.

MICROVASCULAR FLAPS

McLean and Buncke (1972) described a microsurgical reconstruction of a bare cranial defect with a free omental transplant anastomosed to the superficial temporal artery and vein and covered with a free split-thickness skin graft.[13]

Ohmori has described the use of microsurgical free scalp transfer, which permits the grafted scalp to have a natural hair direction at the recipient site. Four types of free flaps based on the superficial temporal, posterior auricular, and occipital vessels have been described. Reconstruction with microvascular free flaps is seldom indicated in emergency situations.

If the pericranium has been destroyed and small scalp defects cannot be covered by local flaps, bur holes should be made through the outer table until pinpoint bleeding is found in the bone. A split-thickness skin graft can be placed over the bleeding bone. If the grafted skin is lost or the outer table of cranial bone undergoes necrosis, an osteotome or bur should be used to expose the diploë, and a split-thickness skin graft should be reapplied.[13]

Scar Formation

Hypertrophic, contracted scars are produced when inflammation is present within healing wounds. The main factors responsible for inflammation within wound surfaces are contamination, foreign bodies, hematoma formation, crush injury, devitalized necrotic tissue, dead space, and operative trauma.[23] Keloids are the result of an overactive production of fibrous tissue during wound healing, perhaps caused by increased tension around the wound margins. Keloids are defined as scars within the skin that grow beyond the confines of the original wound and tend to be darker than the normal skin, whereas hypertrophic scars are raised scars which remain within the boundaries of the wound.[40] Certain individuals are predisposed to keloid formation, and the patient usually can report a history of keloid formation. Keloids occur more frequently in younger age groups of dark skinned races and in areas of thick skin rather than in areas where the skin is thin.[40] Patients who tend to form keloids usually produce reactions at other sites such as vaccination sites. Keloids will generally form in areas of increased skin tension in individuals.

Approximately 12 hours following injury, epithelial migration begins. In primary closed wounds, complete epithelialization can be complete within 48 hours. If wound margins are open, secondary repair begins with migration of epithelial cells from the margin. Epithelial cells will not cover necrotic tissue or highly inflamed tissue. Epithelial cells can migrate from 1 to 3 cm, but closure occurs after 5 to 7 days by the process of contracture of the wound margins.[41]

The contracture of facial wounds should be avoided, as the resultant scar usually leaves a considerable functional and cosmetic defect. Wound contracture is due to fibroblasts that migrate to the wound margin from surrounding tissues and rapid collagen synthesis at the wound margin by the fibroblasts. Rapid collagen synthesis lasts 2 to 4 weeks. The immature scar tissue is usually irregular, raised, and purplish in color due to increased capillaries, collagen, and fibroblasts. The final phase of wound repair, the maturation phase, involves resorption of excess collagen, decreased number of fibroblasts, and decrease in number or size of capillaries. This phase may last for 6 months to 2 years, and it is in this phase that the scar contracts and widens and may hypertrophy or form a keloid.[3,42,43,44]

Hypertrophic scars are usually self-limiting and over time will soften, fade, and flatten. Scars should be revised secondarily only after they have undergone maximum maturation for as long as 12 months.[3,45] If a scar crosses the favorable lines of tension —lines that follow underlying muscle contraction on the face—the tension on the skin wound margins will tend to pull the wound margins apart. Poor operative technique is commonly the cause of hypertrophic scars. Wounds that are not closed evenly, failure to close in layers and relieve tension at the wound margin, and improper debridement and preparation of the wound before closure all result in excessive scar formation.[3,5,45]

In general, wounds that are within favorable lines on the face heal without incident. If the scar is noticable and less than 2 cm in length, the scar tissue can usually be totally excised and simply closed primarily. If the scar is longer than 2 cm and is easily visible, the scar line should be "broken up" from a straight line into multiple small segments to break the scar line visually and alter the forces of tension on the wound margin to limit contracture.[44] Broken-line closure techniques include the w-plasty, the zigzag-plasty, and the z-plasty.[3,13,23,44]

The w-plasty involves excision of the scar tissue with multiple small triangles with as many incisions made within the favorable lines of tension as possible. The base and apex of the triangles should be perpendicular to the scar line. The incisions should also be made perpendicular to the skin to allow for even closure. The wound margins should be undermined and meticulously closed in layers.[23,44]

The zigzag-plasty gives better results for breaking up of linear scars due to the more random nature of the scar line. The zigzag-plasty consists of a series of rectangles and squares between the triangles of the w-plasty. The procedure requires more operative time and technique but tends to better camouflage the scar line.[44] The wound margins should be undermined and closed meticulously in layers.

The z-plasty was first described by Horner (1837) and further developed by Denonvilliers (1854) for correction and alteration of scars to a more favorable position.[23] The z-plasty can alter the direction of scars across the lines of tension, to fall more closely within the favorable lines. The z-plasty is a local transpositional flap consisting of a central limb with limbs extending from each end in opposite directions at an angle between 40 and 60 degrees. The change in direction of the central limb depends on the size of the angles of the z-plasty. If both angles of the z-plasty are 60 degrees, the central limb will rotate 90 degrees when the flaps are transposed. Smaller angles will cause less transposition. The z-plasty will also increase the scar length by up to 200 percent.[44]

The z-plasty should be used for scars that are over 40 degrees from the line of tension because the technique can change the axis of the scar, relieve the tension in the tissues of the area, and prevent linear scar contracture.[23] The w-plasty and zigzag-plasty procedures along with simple excision of small wounds are indicated for scar revision of most facial wounds.[44]

With the development of a hypertrophic or keloid scar, the patient should be instructed to massage the scar at least three to four times daily with a corticosteroid cream. If the scar develops into a keloid, then steroid injections should be initiated. Farrior[3] recommends a preoperative regimen of Kenalog 40, 40 mg/ml (triamcinolone acetonide) and lidocaine 2 per cent, 1:100,000 epinephrine times one dose followed by interlesional injections of Kenalog 40 mixed with lidocaine 1 per cent, 1:100,000 epinephrine at a 1:4 dilution at a 3-week interval for three injections. The injections should be made evenly throughout the lesion and improvement may be seen within this period with steroid therapy alone.

After 3 months without acceptable improvement, the lesion should be excised. The excision should be made just within the margin of the keloid to avoid creating a new tissue reaction. An intralesional injection of the triamcinolone solution should be placed before excision of the lesion to also inhibit tissue reaction. The wound margins are slightly undermined to limit wound surface tension. The wound is closed in layers with a deep synthetic absorbable suture, subcutaneous suture of polypropylene, and multiple adhesive skin tapes to minimize wound tension. The suture and skin tapes should remain for 3 to 4 weeks and triamcinolone injections begun 2 weeks postoperatively. If hyperplastic changes occur following removal, steroid injections should continue on a biweekly basis for 2 months. If no hyperplastic changes are noted, the steroid injections should be tapered off over six months.[3,44]

In patients with a tendency to form hypertrophic scars, the application of a pressure dressing and splinting may be preventive. A firm pressure dressing may disrupt the synthesis of collagen by decreasing circulation to the area. It may take months of splinting and pressure to aid in the prevention of hypertrophic scars.[46]

REFERENCES

1. Lynch J: Trauma to the facial skin. *In* Stark RB (ed): Plastic Surgery of the Head and Neck. New York, Churchill-Livingstone, 1987.
2. Hughes NC: Basic techniques of excision and wound closure. *In* Operative Surgery: Plastic Surgery. 4th ed. London, Butterworths, 1986.
3. Thomas JR, Holt GR: Facial Scars: Incision, Revision and Camouflage. St Louis, CV Mosby, 1989.
4. Schultz RC: Facial Injuries. 3rd ed. Chicago, Year Book Medical Publishers, 1988.
5. Zook EG: The Primary Care of Facial Injuries. Littleton, MA, PSG Publishing Company, 1980.
6. Schuchardt K, Kruger E, Lentrodt J, et al: Injuries to the soft tissues. *In* Kruger E, Schilli W (eds): Oral and Maxillofacial Traumatology. Vol 2. Chicago, Quintessence Books, 1986.
7. Osbon DB: Early treatment of soft tissue injuries of the face. J Oral Surg 27:480, 1969.
8. Davis PKB, Shaheen OH: Soft tissue injuries of the face. *In* Rowe NC, Williams JL (eds): Maxillofacial Injuries. Edinburgh, Churchill-Livingstone, 1985.
9. Goslen JB: Physiology of wound healing and scar formation. *In* Epstein E, Epstein E Jr (eds): Skin Surgery. 5th ed. Springfield, IL, Charles C Thomas, 1982.
10. Madden JW, Aken AJ: Wound healing: Biologic and Clinical features. *In* Sabiston DC Jr (ed): Textbook of Surgery: The Biologic Basis of Modern Surgical Practice. Philadelphia, WB Saunders Company, 1986.
11. Jones RC, Shires GT: Principles in the management of wounds. *In* Schwartz SI (ed): Principles of Surgery. 5th ed. New York, McGraw-Hill Book Company, 1989.
12. Donald PC, Bernstein L: Soft tissue trauma to the face and neck. *In* Paparella MM, Shumrick DA (eds): Otolaryngology. 2nd ed. Philadelphia, WB Saunders Company, 1980.
13. Dingman RO, Converse JM: The clinical management of facial injuries and fractures of the facial bones. *In* Converse JM (ed): Reconstructive Plastic Surgery. 2nd ed. Vol 2. Philadelphia, WB Saunders Company, 1977.
14. Bailey BJ: Basic principles of plastic surgery in the head and neck. *In* Paparella MM, Shumrick DA (eds): Otolaryngology. 2nd ed. Philadelphia, WB Saunders Company, 1980.
15. Woodburne RT: Essentials of Human Anatomy. New York, Oxford University Press, 1983.
16. Milikan LE: Surgical anatomy of the facial skin. *In* Thomas JR, Holt GR (eds): Facial Scars: Incision, Revision and Camouflage. St Louis, CV Mosby, 1989.
17. Stal S, Spira M: Anatomy and physiology of the skin. *In* Stark RB (ed): Plastic Surgery of the Head and Neck. New York, Churchill-Livingstone, 1987.
18. Bulbulian AH: Facial Prosthetics. Springfield, IL, Charles C Thomas, 1973.
19. Postlethwait RW: Operative surgery: Antisepsis, techniques, sutures and drains. *In* Sabiston DC Jr (ed): Textbook of Surgery: The Biological Basis of Modern Surgical Practice. Philadelphia, WB Saunders Company, 1986.
20. Webster RC, McCollough EG, Giandello PR, Smith RC: Skin wound approximation with new absorbable suture material. Arch Otolaryngol 3:517, 1985.
21. Alling CC, Osbon DB: Maxillofacial Trauma. Philadelphia, Lea and Febiger, 1988.
22. Radovan C: Tissue expansion in soft tissue reconstruction. Plast Reconstr Surg 74:482, 1984.
23. Serrano RA, Rosado CR, Orticochea M, Ohmori K: Scalp, skull and eyebrow. *In* Stark RB (ed): Plastic Surgery of the Head and Neck. New York, Churchill-Livingstone, 1987.
24. Maxillofacial prosthetics. *In* Robinson JE (ed): Proceedings of an interprofessional conference sponsored by The American Academy of Maxillofacial Prosthetics. Public Health Service Publication No. 1950, September 1966.
25. Mathog RH: Maxillofacial Trauma. Baltimore, The Williams and Wilkins Company, 1984.
26. Bartlett SP, Swann KW: Management of soft tissue injuries. *In* Burke JF, Boyd RJ, McCabe CJ (eds): Trauma Management: Early Management of Visceral, Nervous System and Musculoskeletal Injuries. Chicago, Year Book Medical Publishers, 1988.
27. Orticochea M: New three-flap reconstruction technique. Br J Plast Surg 24:184, 1971.
28. MacIntosh R: Sliding block resection and reconstruction in cases of carcinoma of the lower lip. J Oral Surg 38:417, 1980.
29. Humber PR, Kaplan IB, Horton CE: Trauma to the Ear: Hematoma, laceration, amputation, atresia, and burns. *In* Stark RB (ed): Plastic Surgery of the Head and Neck. New York, Churchill-Livingstone, 1987.
30. Foster CA, Sherman JE: Surgery of Facial Bone Fractures. New York, Churchill-Livingstone, 1987.
31. Bränemark RI, Zarb GI, Albrektsson T: Tissue-integrated prosthesis. *In* Osseointegration in Clinical Dentistry. Chicago, Quintessence Publishing Company, 1985.
32. Furnas DW (ed): Symposium on deformities of the external ear. Clin Plast Surg 5:315, 1978.
33. Rahn AO, Boucher LJ: Maxillofacial Prosthetics: Principles and Concepts. Philadelphia, WB Saunders Company, 1970.
34. Barwick WJ, Klein HW: Soft tissue injuries of the face. *In* Serafin D, Georgiade NG (eds): Pediatric Plastic Surgery. St Louis, CV Mosby, 1984.
35. Beekhuis GJ: Nasal fractures. *In* Paparella MM, Shumrick DA (eds): Otolaryngology. 2nd ed. Philadelphia, WB Saunders Company, 1980.
36. Humber PR, Horton CE: Trauma to the nose. *In* Stark RB (ed): Plastic Surgery of the Head and Neck. New York, Churchill-Livingstone, 1987.
37. Wang MKH, Macomber WB, Elliott RA: Deformities of the eyebrow. *In* Converse JM (ed): Reconstructive Plastic Surgery. 2nd ed. Philadelphia, WB Saunders Company, 1977.
38. Converse JM: Reconstructive Plastic Surgery. Philadelphia, WB Saunders Company, 1977.
39. Kraissl CJ: The selection of appropriate lines

for elective surgical incisions. Plast Reconst Surg 8:1, 1951.

40. Ketchum CD, Cohen IK, Masters FW: Hypertrophic Scars and Keloids: A Collective Review. Plast Reconstr Surg 53:140, 1974.

41. Bromberg BE: Trauma to the orbit. *In* Stark RB (ed): Plastic Surgery of the Head and Neck. New York, Churchill Livingstone, 1987.

42. Epstein E Jr: Wound healing. *In* Epstein E, Epstein E, Jr. (eds): Skin Surgery. Springfield, IL, Charles C Thomas, 1982.

43. Alvarez, OM: Biology of the dermis: wound healing. *In* Fitzpatrick TB, Freedberg IM: Dermatology in General Medicine. New York, McGraw-Hill, 1987.

44. Gunter, JP: Scar Revision. *In* Paparella MM and Shumrick DA (eds): Otolaryngology, 2nd ed. Philadelphia, WB Saunders Co., 1980.

45. Schultz RC: Facial Injuries, 3rd ed. Chicago, Year Book Medical Publishers, Inc., 1988.

46. Simon RR, Brenner BE: Emergency Procedures and Techniques, 2nd ed. Baltimore, Williams and Wilkins, 1987.

INDEX

Note: Page numbers in *italics* refer to illustrations; page numbers followed by t refer to tables.